NORDDEUTSCHER LLOYD BREMEN

1857 - 1970

History — Fleet — Ship Mails

Volume Two

Edwin Drechsel

Foreword: The Rt. Hon. the Earl Jellicoe

Cordillera Publishing Company
Vancouver, B.C.

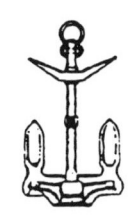

Copyright 1995 © Edwin Drechsel

Canadian Cataloguing in Publication Data

Drechsel, Edwin,
    Norddeutscher Lloyd, Bremen, 1857-1970

    Includes index
    ISBN 1-895590-08-6 (v.1).   ISBN 1-895590-14-0 (v.2)

    1. Norddeutscher Lloyd. 2. Merchant Marine — Germany —
History. 3. Mail Steamers — History. I. Title
HE945.N66D73 1994   623.8'24'0943   C94-910327-6

Cover Artwork by Wendy C. Mars
Typesetting by Gunderson Typesetting, 263-210th Street, Langley, B.C., Canada
V3A 7R2

Printed and bound by
    Friesen Printers
    P.O. Box 720, Altona, Manitoba
    Canada R0G 0B0

Published by
    Cordillera Publishing Company
    8415 Granville Street, Box 46
    Vancouver, B.C.
    Canada V6P 4Z9

All rights reserved. No part of this publication may be reproduced, or transmitted in any form or by any means, electronic or mechanical, including photocopy, recording or any information storage and retrieval system, without the prior written permission of the author or his agent.

The cover picture is from the painting of Columbus *done by commission of the Norddeutscher Lloyd Bremen in 1924, by Harry Hudson Rodmell, courtesy of Arthur G. Credland, Keeper of Maritime History, Hull City Council Museums and Art Galleries, Hull, Yorkshire. The painting now is there.*

Table of Contents

Foreword by The Rt. Hon. the Earl Jellicoe . . . . *v*

Introduction. . . . . *vi*

1. A New Start *1*

    Fleet List: 1920 - 1970 . . . . *18*

    Ships #279 — 308. . . . . *19*

2. Mergers - Risks and Challenges *51*

    Ships #309 — 384x: Freighters and New Trades. *58*

3. Bremen and Hamburg: Hapag and Lloyd. *117*

    Ships #385 — 416. . . . . *127*

4. Again Mail Handling at Sea *157*

    Ships #417 — 425. . . . . *170*

5. Again Blue Ribbon *191*

6. The Lloyd Flies. *201*

7. Passengers: The Heart of the Lloyd's Business. *229*

8. Masters Next to God *257*

    Ships #426 — 431. . . . . *273*

9. 1930s - Chaos and Confusion. *283*

10. Ad Astra per Aspera *291*

    Ships #432 — 443. . . . . *308*

11. Fun and Games at Sea. *323*

12. The Lloyd Sails and Rows *341*

Color Album *353*

    Ships #444 — 455a. *371*

13. North Atlantic Community: Merger on Trial *385*

14. Countdown to — and Again War	415
Ships #456 — 471x	*444*
15. A Second New Beginning	455
Ships #472 — 489	*471*
16. From Crossing to Cruising with Ship Posts	497
Ships #490 — 506	*515*
17. A Young Again Centenarian - 1957	535
18. From Little Boxes to Big Boxes	543
Ships #507 — 531	*558*
19. Marriage at Age 123 and 113 - 1970 - 1994	585
20. Bremen, the Weser: The Lloyd's Port, River and Coastal Operations	605
Register of Port, River and Coastal Seas Vessels	615
Epilogue	665
Addendum	667
Sources	672
Bibliography	673
Glossary	677
Index of Small Craft Names	678

    Emblem of the City of Bremen.   Houseflag of the Norddeutscher Lloyd.

These flags of the City-State of Bremen and the Norddeutscher Lloyd were inadvertently reversed in Volume I.

Foreword

Having read through, with ever growing interest and enjoyment, the first volume of Edwin Drechsel's splendid and comprehensive history of that great German shipping line, The Norddeutscher Lloyd Bremen, I count it a real honour to have been invited by the author to write this short introduction to his equally splendid and comprehensive Volume II.

Like the author, I have quite a lot of salt water in my genes — on both sides of my family. My maternal grandfather, Charles Cayzer, the son of a poor schoolmaster in East London, went to sea aged 15, as did Edwin Drechsel's father, as a Master's Clerk in a sailing ship. Later, after much struggle and many vicissitudes, he founded the Clan Line, in its day one of the largest cargo carrying companies in the United Kingdom, indeed in the world.

My paternal grandfather, John Henry Jellicoe, for his part also had the sea in his blood, rising to become Marine Superintendent of the Royal Mail Line. It was perhaps natural that his son having spent his childhood near the docks of Southhampton, should have made the Royal Navy his career.

For my father, the Admiral, the Merchant Navy always meant a great deal. He also held the German Navy — and the German High Seas Fleet was his adversary in the First World War — in the highest esteem. It was therefore natural, having learned that the *Bremen* was docking in Southampton in November 1934 on the start of her 100th round trip, that my father should have visited her together with my mother. As we read in this volume it was only my father's death the following year that prevented the author's parents from accepting my parents' invitation to stay with us in the Isle of Wight.

Following my father's funeral at St. Paul's Cathedral, my mother received a rather striking letter from the ex-Kaiser. In it he wrote "I am glad that my dear Grandson was able to represent me at Lord Jellicoe's funeral in my name as Chief of my old Imperial Navy and of the Officers and men still living who once belonged to it, and to present our last respects to the illustrious Admiral, whose stirling qualities as gallant leader, splendid sailor, and chivalrous antagonist... will forever be treasured in our hearts".

That "dear Grandson" was Prince Friedrich, the youngest son of the Crown Prince— Fritzi, and friend of my youngest sister. There is a charming picture of him, together with my mother and sister — also on the *Bremen* at Southampton.

Fritzi, came to stay with us in the summer of 1936 and I travelled back with him in the *Bremen* in August to stay with his parents in Potsdam for the Olympic Games. I remember the trip very well — that fine ship, the two attractive American ladies whom we met on board and a most enjoyable lunch in Bremen on our way to Potsdam. Curiously and coincidentally, six years later behind the German lines in the North African Desert my Special Air Service contingent captured a nice young German Medical Officer who turned out to be the son of our Bremen host and hostess. I am glad to relate that he later escaped!

But enough of that. Since my family's brief visit on board in 1934, and my short voyage in 1936, the *Bremen* and the Norddeutscher Lloyd have always had a rather special place in my mind's eye. It is good that Edwin Drechsel has done full justice in these two memorable volumes to this very great shipping enterprise.

Jellicoe

Introduction

It is early 1995 and all the Lloyd people I knew and write about are gone. The Lloyd itself lives on in name only: half of Hapag-Lloyd A.G., Germany's largest shipping, transport and travel activity. It was formed in 1970 from the merger of the Lloyd and the Hamburg-Amerika Linie. It is largely managed from Hamburg, although the passenger operation and little else is centered in Bremen. There are still a *Bremen* and *Europa*, traditional Lloyd names, the only passenger ships now in service, both chartered.

This work is the last NDL watch. It follows a distinguished succession of earlier recorders of Lloyd activities: from Dr. Moritz Lindemann in 1892, the Lloyd-commissioned works by Dr. Neubaur in 1907, an interim history in 1927, and Dr. George Bessel's Centennial history in 1957; Hans-Jürgen Witthöft's "NDL" of 1973 and of "Hapag-Lloyd" in 1974; Also the writings of Arnold Kludas: his five-volume "History of German Passenger Shipping", two of NDL vessel histories, his "Bremen and Europa", and his "Hapag-Lloyd" postscript to the life of the Lloyd.

The number of people who traveled on or knew some one who came over on the Lloyd is declining each year. I guesstimate the overall figure at some twenty-five millions based on the 1990 Census stating that forty percent of the then 250 million American had some one who immigrated via Ellis Island. NDL was the largest-ever trans-Atlantic passenger carrier and of these immigrants.

I believe that the Lloyd will live on in history and be of interest to more than those mainly ships-oriented. As Kamill Sandorfy, a Hungarian-born Canadian put it: "The Lloyd was one of the great things people spoke about when I was a youngster." That was in 1930. Hungarian emigrants were a significant element for the Lloyd. Volume I shows a Hungarian as the ten millionth passenger in 1912.

The Lloyd had an independent life of 113 years, interrupted by two world wars after which it had to start again almost from scratch. This time span encompasses the era of Atlantic liner shipping and the historic emigration from Europe to the Americas. Today's immigrants come by air. But Bremen and Bremerhaven remain busy with container and some cruise shipping. There are still Lloyd Strassen in Bremen and Bremerhaven, and a Lloyd Street in Baltimore. From 1868, Baltimore was the second U.S. destination after New York.

Readers of Volume I have told me "it is a book to browse; open almost any page and there is something interesting or new." I credit this to the personalization of NDL in these two volumes. The history of any enterprise is largely the story of people making things happen. As Historian David McCullough put it: "The dead past is full of nothing but life. Stir around in the past and that's what you always find: Human Beings."

It is the thread of people-involvement that puts flesh on the otherwise dry and statistical bones of history. I had intimate knowledge of and/or contacts with many Lloyd people or those involved with the Lloyd. I quote or mention some whom I did not know directly because they had experiences that help to tell the story, and fill in details that otherwise would be missing.

Arnold Kludas told me "You are the last one" who can do the Lloyd story. That lets me set the record straight where that record is distorted or blurred. In some cases I may be making history where facts are uncertain or inconclusive. I draw and state conclusions, although some questions never will be answered. The reward is that readers will find things that bring memories or new dimensions to something they know, experienced, or wondered about. I realize that not every one remembers correctly, even about something that happened in their lives, including this writer. Any errors are mine alone.

There is still a maritime tradition that touches people's lives. We use many sea-related terms without thinking of the shipping actuality on which they are based: - All ship-shape and Bristol Fashion. - Has your ship come in? - To jump ship. - To make waves. - The tide's running out (on this idea). - To take a new tack. - To learn the ropes (something sail ship sailors did in their spare time). - Don't let it sink your hopes. - Pull up the (Jacob's) ladder. - To stick in or rest on your oar. - Its a sea-change event. These are implanted in our culture and literature.

The number of people who own or go out in boats, sail or powered, is in the millions; it grows generation after generation. Although no longer do boys run away to sea at fifteen. There are still a few who just sail away, across the oceans, around the world. They make headlines because many of us, I believe, wish "I could do that." Modern technology helps. An ocean sailor can have a Weatherfax that tells him what's ahead. The Global Satellite Positioning System makes it possible to find vessels in trouble, if they are so equipped, with pinpoint accuracy. A French round-the-world sailor in difficulty was found that way in the South Atlantic. This 1995 year the Americas Cup will play to millions who will watch and read about the challenge of far-out technologies and highly-trained crews, including the first all-women America^3.

Maritime Museums offer exhibits to attract and remind the public of its maritime culture and tradition, such as the new museum in Astoria, Oregon and the Customs House Maritime Museum in Newburyport, Massachusetts. The Smithsonian Institution in 1994 opened its Postal Museum, showing on the promotional pamphlet a U.S.S. Oklahoma Registry postmark of 1941 and "Some of our most popular Exhibits have been canceled." I have added to maritime history recording this postal dimension, the Ship Post cancellations and marks of NDL vessels. The Lloyd's fleet had more sea and ship postal-route markings, including the U.S.-German Sea Post service 1891-1914 and 1925-1939, than any other line. The Ship Postal cancels shown in these two volumes are largely from my "1886-1986, A Century of German Ship Post," published in 1987 in London by Christie's Robson Lowe affiliate.

There are other expressions of a continued interest in things maritime:

- There is an active Apostleship of the Sea, part of the U.S. Roman Catholic Conference. Its staff supports seamen's centers in various ports, and issues a Catholic Maritime News. Seamen's Churches and Missions exist in many ports around the world.

- The new Center for the Arts at San Francisco's Yerba Buena complex resembles an ocean liner with porthole-like windows, a flagpole like a ships mast, and ship-style metal stairways. The Sydney Opera Houses roofs are soaring sails. As are those, tall as a square rigger, of San Francisco's St. Marys Cathedral. And the two sets of five sails above Vancouver's passenger-ship terminal.

- A new video Ships Ahoy is aimed at children but probably is attractive to adults as well: "Ride the Tugboats as they maneuver the big ships; Hop aboard a fishing boat and go to sea; Load and unload a giant container vessel; Watch the fireboats as they quench a fire or welcome a ship, as happened with the Liberty Ship *Jeremy OBrien* returning to San Francisco from the D-Day ceremonies; Tour the giant aircraft carriers ...." All of it exciting, and related to the sea.

Nostalgia tends to adorn history with fancier clothing than it actually had. It can assume aspects of fact and fiction and weave them into a myth. It, in turn, is limited only by the reader's imagination. This is being written as the Myth of California: Orange groves and eternal sunshine, is proving to be quite different from the reality: earthquakes, floods, slides, fires and drought every year.

The past does put its hand on the shoulders of today, whether we know the past or not. One example: Germany's Deutsche Bank, and the U.S. Federal Reserve Bank assertively use interest rates to try to control inflation, this because of what Germany went through in the early 1920s. In January, 1995 the Deutsche Bank alerted holders of depression-devalued gold and dollar bonds from 1924-1930 to their rights to unpaid interest, sixty-one years after the Lloyd asked its bondholders to accept reduced interest and repayments in 1933 so that the enterprise could survive. See "1930s ..."

If there is much Drechsel in this work it is because my Father in many ways was near the center or the direction of activity and change during the forty years he served the Lloyd, and beyond as an example, under leaders who shaped him. There is also much about the Hamburg-Amerika Linie. In the 1930s depression there was need for cooperation by Lloyd and Hamburg. In 1970, the outcome: Hapag-Lloyd A.G. The history of each has a large and continuing thread of the other throughout its existence. My Father from all I know was the only one who ever commanded a Lloyd ship and a Hapag ship. In 1939, on his last visit to Germany, Hapag honored him as "Unser Kapitän," Our Captain.

The Lloyd is remembered in literature. Mark Twain was the earliest. Travelling on Havel #81 in the 1890s he wrote "In (her) one can in several respects be more comfortable than in the best hotels on the Continent." C.S. Forester used up German royalties from his Hornblower series by travelling frequently and in the best cabins on *Bremen* and *Europa*. "They were exceedingly comfortable ships" he wrote.

Irwin Shaw in his "Sailor off the Bremen" in the New Yorker wrote about the 1936 pier demonstrations in New York, and how one Nazi crew member got his come-uppance. Herman Wouk in "The Winds of War" has his main character Captain Pug Henry travel on *Bremen* in 1939 "to brush up on my German," and meeting his future wife Pamela on board. And many others. Books about life at sea are on best-seller lists because of a continuing interest in history or nostalgia for other times for which there are no current challenges.

Most of the old family and familiar names of shipowners, and the ship-names they used over decades, are gone: Ellerman, Blue Funnel, Hansa. I can understand that some captains might be reluctant to serve on vessels named *Alligator Triumph* or *Golden Bond Trailblazer*. Just as some captains of old refused transfer to new ships where they could not command from an open bridge. (Volume I).

Today, the huge cruise and container ships are such costly investments to build and operate that ownerships change and consortia run joint schedules. It is difficult to establish close relationships. On passenger vessels the crews are multi-national. They owe little loyalty to owners. As the Lloyd's then senior captain still from prewar, Otto Prehn, wrote as far back as 1950, "today's crews are workers, not seamen." On container ships, fourteen has become the standard-size. The unions have had to down-size. They no longer speak to the public or the authorities with the clout they had into the 1950s.

The flight to flags of convenience to allow reduction of crewing and safety adherence has made even tiny Belize a maritime power in terms of tonnages registered. The development of national lines to carry their own cargoes has further weakened the former maritime superpowers: Britain, Norway, Japan, and their traditional shipping enterprises. The U.S. shipping industry, too, is on the skids. There is a move to eliminate the U.S. Maritime Commission or put it into an umbrella bureau. The maritime industry's functions and needs are hardly understood or listened to.

The shipper and buyer of goods now is interested only in the conveyor belt from manufacturer to distant consumer. The individual segments are on the computer, but not otherwise of much concern. The end-buyer does not connect the imported item with how it reached him. Only if there is suddenly no supply for some unknown (shipping strike?) reason.

Nowadays only aficionados travel by ship to get somewhere. Those who go cruising number in the millions and are increasing rapidly. They travel on two levels: the mass market with ships able to carry two thousand or more voyagers, and the small, intimate vessels, including some under sail, with capacities for fifty to one hundred and fifty, in very luxurious surroundings at very high prices.

There are persons further to Volume I whom I want to thank for their help in important ways. Among them are:

Relatives in Germany: - the Heinz Kunert Family in Dresden, the Arthur Meyer family in Wedel.

- Reinhold Thiel and his "Argo," a key segment of the Lloyd's expansion into freight shipping from the mid-1920s.

- William Schell, marine surveyor, for information and photographs and for his technical comments.

- Robert Parkinson of the Steamship Historical Society of America and Andrew Kilk of the World Ship Society for fostering continuing interest in shipping.

- Arnold Kludas for his extensive research and writings which have been of invaluable help to me, and for our personal relationship beginning with the Belgian Nautical Research Association, from 1985 with my visits to the Schiffahrts Museum in Bremerhaven where he was Librarian, and since in his retirement. Between us, I believe, we have done justice to the record of the Lloyd.

My special thanks to Arthur Credland, Keeper of Maritime History at the Hull City Museums and Art Galleries, Yorkshire, for sending me the City of Kingston upon Hull Museums and Art Gallaries booklet on Marine Artist Harry Hudson Rodmell, and a color print of *Columbus* which he painted for the Lloyd in 1924. That initiative led to its use on the dust jacket of this volume.

I am grateful for Lord Jellicoe's kind foreword. Our Fathers met in a brief encounter on *Bremen* in November, 1934. It sparked an immediate rapport based on mutual friendships and a shared love for and experiences of the sea. Lord Jellicoe, in turn, continued the Admiral's ties to the sea as First Lord of the Admiralty, the post once held by Winston Churchill. He is now President of the Royal Geographic Society.

My abiding thanks to Johan and Pat Gunderson for their professional job of layout and typesetting, and to my publisher, S.C. Heal of Cordillera Publishing Company, for his oversight and guidance.

Also to our daughter Ildi Varga and husband Roger Holdstock for bringing us their friends Dennis and Linny Stovall who, as Blue Heron Publishing Company, organized and set the pattern with Volume I.

And always my gratitude to my wife, Ilona Bolya Drechsel, for sharing the burden, for her patience, and for giving up many things we normally would have done together during my immersion in research and writing. Inadvertently, she was not credited for my photo on the Volume I dust jacket.

Nothing that is remembered dies. This work is dedicated to keeping alive the Norddeutscher Lloyd Bremen, the people who made its name synonymous with service and dedication, those who travelled on the Lloyd, for many of them the experience of a lifetime, and those who recorded its activities over the years. May it also prove to be rewarding reading.

March, 1995

170 Hillcrest Road
Berkeley, California
U.S.A. 94705

CHAPTER 1

A New Start

Into 1916 there was still some belief that Germany would come out of the war with much of her former standing. Ships under construction in August, 1914 were completed and laid up. In 1916 and 1917, massive orders were placed by the Lloyd (some 360,000 gross tons) and other lines to offset their war losses. Steel plating was hoarded at some shipyards, even workers taken on, against the time when peace would return. But not one of these orders actually was begun by war's end.

During the war there had been a very occasional word from crew members of the thirty-two NDL ships interned in U.S. or U.S.-controlled waters; they became prisoners when the U.S. entered the war in April, 1917. On 2 May, 1918, Carl Gastmeyer, 2. Officer on *Kronprinzessin Cecilie* in 1914, sent from Prisoner-of-War Camp at Hot Springs, N.C., a Y.M.C.A. Aid for Interned Aliens card to Willy Drechsel in Bremen. They had been friends since sailship days (p.214, Vol.1) "I send to you and (wife) Stella and your dear children all good wishes and hearty greetings from your physically well friend." The card was also signed by Charles Polack, Captain of *Kronprinzessin Cecilie* (p.416 ff, Vol.I), "To you and your dear family I send from scenically beautiful Hot Springs heartiest greetings." And from R. Wurpts, Captain during the 1920s, "True greetings to all the Wurpts family." Messages to be passed on, but that all was well.

Revolution and mutinies broke out in Germany in November, 1918: refusals by soldiers against further fighting, by sailors, especially firemen, the worst job on any coal-fired vessel, against the fleet making one more desperate "last battle", and attacks against their officers. Drechsel, Commander of the Submarine School's mother ship *Meteor* was rescued by his own men from sailors who had seized him to put him "against the wall." Lt. Commander Count Felix (a happy name for this man) von Luckner, of sailship raider fame, the "Sea Devil" in Lowell Thomas' book, told Drechsel that while walking along the Duesterbrook Allee at the Kiel Waterfront three sailors tried to tear off his epaulettes. (this most likely actually happened during later uprisings after von Luckner returned from New Zealand P.O.W. camp in July, 1919) Luckner was a massively strong man; he could bend a silver Thaler piece out of shape between his thumb and forefinger. In the U.S. on lecture tours after the war he would tear telephone books apart when asked to show his strength. The three ended up in hospital.

After the Armistice of 11 November, 1918, the German Navy was surrendered to the British at Scapa Flow in the Orkneys, the land-encircled anchorage where the Royal Navy had its main wartime base and security. In December, 1918 the Lloyd's *Bremen* #99, *Hannover* #114, *Scharnhorst* #204, *Schleswig* #181 and *Sierra Ventana* #256 brought home the crews of these warships, most soon scuttled by order from Berlin. (Most were eventually raised and scrapped by the British; some never will be.) *Sierra Ventana* on 18 December lay off Helgoland to escort the first twenty submarines to be delivered to the British at Harwich and bring back their crews. She then

1

Prisoner-of-War Postcard from Carl Gastmeyer, in 1914 I. Officer on Kronprinzessin Cecilie, *also signed by that ship's Captain Charles Polack, and R. Wurpts, in the 1920s Lloyd captain, and Th. Schröder. "Dear Willy! to you and Stella and your dear children we all wish you well, hearty greetings from us all physically well ... Carl." Also: Heartiest Greetings - Charles Polack, and Sincere Greetings - R. Wurpts. They returned in late 1919. Captain Polack became Kurmaster for the Lloyd at Norderney Spa. See Volume 1, p. 322, 330, 269 etc.*

twenty submarines to be delivered to the British at Harwich and bring back their crews. She then made two voyages from Copenhagen with French prisoners of war, at once was seized by France at Brest, along with *Scharnhorst*, before any specific division of German ships had been decided by the Allies.

In February, 1919 four transports reached Germany with the first crew members from ships stranded overseas by the war. *Roon #187* reached

Felix Graf von Luckner was a hero during the War, for his daring raider experience with a sailing ship and not one life lost. And he was respected by the enemy. This explains the acceptance and success of his overseas trips, and later around the world, in the 1920s. See "Passengers." Here from his home his thanks to a woman who made a cushion for him. It was timely as the cold was coming. Sent via the Field Post on his ship SMS Panther, a very small light cruiser. He, like my father, was born in Dresden. They knew each other before again meeting in Kiel.

Prinz Heinrich ate on Meteor *one more time on 18 October, 1918. He evidently took the menu with him, came across it, and sent it to my Father, on 25.5.1921 from Hemelingen, his estate near Eckernförde, some 40 miles due NW of Kiel. He wrote on the back of the menu "I did not elude your outstanding ship's band: playing with warmth, intensity and ... some false notes." He added: "I appreciate your detailed letter. By coincidence, on my return from Holland (where he visited the Kaiser) I travelled with Chief Inspector Oeding to Bremen and was told in strictest confidence the rebuilding plans of our Lloyd (sic). I am astonished at the building plans, but pleased at the enterprise being shown in these dark times." He signed "with Greetings and a Handshake my Dear Drechsel, your devoted Heinrich Prinz & Prinzessin." The Prince wrote again on 22 June, 1923. "With all my heart I thank you for your letter and attachments. (description of the Battle of Jutland memorial from* München *on its delivery voyage from Stettin to Bremerhaven.) It is moving for me that this honor to our former Naval comrades occurred on a ship of the Lloyd, which is so close to my heart (see p.31). I am reminded (the idealist philosopher) Johann Gottlieb Fichee's words: "Du sollst an Deutschlands Zukunft glauben, an Deines Volkes Auferstehen. Lass diesen Glauben Dir nicht rauben, trotz Allem - Allem was gescheh'n!"*
"You must believe in Germany's future; That it will rise again. Don't let this Belief be shaken, Despite anything - anything that may happen." Fichte, 1762-1814, wrote after the overruning of the German states by Napoleon. Co-Director, from 1942, Dr. Kulenkampff in 1922 was berth neighbor at the Kiel Yacht Club to Prinz Heinrich's Ayesha, *named for the sailship on which the landing unit escaped after SMS Emden's destruction. Vol. 1 p. 358.*

A New Start   3

This item was found after completion of Volume I but is part of the continuing story. On 25 September, 1918 the Kaiser for the last time ate aboard one of his naval ships at Kiel: Meteor, *prewar one of Hapag's two white cruising yachts, then Mother and Home Port ship of the submarine school and fleet. Prinz Heinrich was with the Kaiser. The menu indicates that the Kaiserliche Marine lived best during the war under difficult times, worst the shortage of food and fuel. "Kaiseressen" in Commander Drechsel's hand: Imperial Meal.*

```
           Crabs in Butter, Toast
           Boullion with Marrow
     Sea Tongue Filet with Holl. Sauce
                Potatoes
       Lamb ribs surrounded by fresh
               Vegetables
            Preserved Fruits
    Chocolate Pudding with Vanilla Sauce
             Fruit - Coffee
```

Bremerhaven on 23.12.1919 with more than one thousand crew members from the 45 German ships interned in the Netherlands East Indies. Some 4,270 Lloyd people did not return from the war, people who lived on in NDL records until these were almost entirely destroyed in World War II.

At the end of the War, NDL had left, including ships still with the now no longer "Imperial" Navy, 27 ships, plus smaller, harbor and resort craft, of 221,893 gross tons compared with 494 high-seas ships and smaller craft of 982,952 tons in 1914.

The Treaty of Versailles brought a further loss of some 318,000 tons. Included were all wartime completions, all German ships of more than 1600 tons and one-half those between 1000 and 1600 tons. Left for the Lloyd were the 1914 tender *Grüssgott* of 781 tons, the new tug *Spica*, 12 lighters finished during the war, and the prewar fleet of tugs, barges and resort vessels, a total of 57,671 tons.

On 21 March, 1919, the first ship left Germany for Britain for delivery to the Allies. By the 24th, thirty-five ships had left Hamburg. In Bremen, crews at first refused to man vessels. The first Lloyd ships, *Zeppelin* #269, *Prinz Friedrich Wilhelm* #243, and freighter *Waldeck* #263 left on the 27th; on the 28th *Prinz Ludwig* #217, *Giessen* #240, *Frankfurt* #113, and *Altenburg* #269. Then *Bremen* #99, *Königin Luise* #98, *Chemnitz* #176, *Meiningen* #268, *Dessau* #265, *Remscheid* #272, *Gera* #275, *Erfurt* #276, these six were war-completed freighters, *Lippe* #271 and *Heilbronn* #273. *Berlin*, interned in Norway after minelaying in 1914, did not return until June, 1919. The formal Allied peace with Germany was signed on 28.6.1919, that between the U.S. and Germany and the other Central Powers not until August, 1921.

The Treaty of Versailles also mandated delivery of Germany's best railroad rolling stock to the Allies. This made Germany's rivers and canals, and the North and Baltic seas, the basic routes for transporting goods and people. Fortunately, what the Lloyd had left exactly fitted these needs: resort steamers, tenders, tugs and barges. These went into round-the-clock operation to the extent that the dire shortage of coal permitted.

1919 was a day-by-day struggle for every one in Germany. The Allied blockade nearly to mid-1919. Then German ships were allowed to pick up foodstuffs in controlled quantities.

What kept the Lloyd going during these difficult times was the strong loyalty of its personnel, their determination to rebuild their enterprise, and the many supporters overseas, largely first and second-generation Germans who had emigrated or travelled on the Lloyd. And had got into the habit of returning by the thousands. This was why the Lloyd in the winter of 1913-14 rebuilt its oldest four-stack express steamer #100 *Kaiser Wilhelm Der Grosse* to improve emigrants' facilities at sea, and to let the new Americans return in style, to prove to family, friends and their country of origin that they had made it in America.

Besides these emigrants from all over Europe, there were pre-war passengers and freight shippers by the many thousands all over the world who remembered the Lloyd nostalgically, its captains and personnel, the service rendered to them: "life above the normal" on the ships. This was an unmeasurable resource that sometimes shows on balance sheets as "good will."

On 14 July, 1919 the U.S. resumed trading with Germany; the Kerr Line with freight and a few passengers served Hamburg, with HAPAG as port-agent. John Maxtone-Graham in *"The Only Way To Cross,"* Collier Books, New York, 1978, wrote "Hamburg and Bremen were cities of unemployment, ... and political unrest. Herbert Hartley, who ultimately commanded the *Leviathan*, arrived in ... 1919 carrying a cargo of lard. The crossing had been rough and several hogsheads had been fractured. Yet so critical were local food supplies that ... stevedores brought crusts of bread to the piers and soaked up the stuff from the bilges." On 8 October, 1919 the first German arrived in the U.S. since war broke in April, 1917.

The resort (sidewheeler!) steamers that had run from the Weser River to the North Sea islands came back into service. At Whitsuntide 1919, *Lachs* made the first trip from Wilhelmshaven to the Friesian island of Wangerooge, then on to Norderney. There in the Spring of 1920 the Lloyd leased the Kurhaus to provide work for its former shipboard hotel personnel. Captain Charles Polack, back from POW camp in the U.S., became

„Ach, schicken Sie ihn mir doch einmal auf Urlaub!"

Lovely color postcard sent in June, 1918 "Ah, Please send him to me on leave!" request by a young lady, addressed to "Your Wellborn Highness", Captain of SMS Meteor *Cdr. W. Drechsel, apologizing for bothering to request that the Sailor Heinr. Flügge, U-Boots-Schule, Kiel, be granted an 8-14 days leave in middle July to Hamburg: Purpose: "Engagement." Most Respectfully, Marta Holz.*

> **Hemmelmark, Kr. Eckernförde.**
> **Den 27. April 1929.**
>
> Die übergroße Zahl von Beweisen herzlicher Teilnahme, die mir anläßlich des Heimganges meines lieben Vaters zugegangen ist, bewegt mich tief. Sie macht es mir gleichzeitig unmöglich jedem einzelnen ein persönliches Wort des Dankes zu schreiben, was ich so gern getan hätte.
>
> Ich kann daher meinen bleibenden Herzensdank nur dadurch sagen, indem ich jedem im Geiste die Hand drücke, der in diesen schweren Tagen mit mir fühlte und zugleich meines Vaters in Verehrung gedachte.
>
> *Waldemar,*
> *Prinz von Preussen*

The son of Prinz Heinrich and Prinzess Irene, all three had Lloyd ships named after them, sent word of the Admiral's death on 27 April, 1929.
Thanking the untold number who had shown their sympathy and grief. "I can only express my everlasting heartfelt thanks in that in my thoughts I press the hand of each one...."
Waldemar, Prinz von Preussen.

The future Captain Drechsel evidently was the only one to command both a Hapag ship, its former 3,600 tons cruising yacht, *Meteor* built in 1904, and a Lloyd vessel, *Bremen 3*. *Meteor* in the war was the Mother Ship of the Kiel Submarine School, and for submarines there between patrols. It was in Kiel at the end of the war. This Artist Card, how did the writer still find this near the end of the war? shows a lovely young woman asking her Sweethearts commanding officer "Ah, why don't you send him to me on leave?" The message to Commander W. Drechsel is exactly that, in flowery terms, "Your High Wellborness. if I burden you with these lines. Please permit me to ask for the Sailor Heinr. Flugge (SMS Meteor, now at Kiel, U-Boat School) a leave of 8 - 14 days for mid-July to Hamburg: Purpose: Engagement." "Most respectfully," signed Marta Holz, in Wiesbaden. The author assumes his Father granted the leave, remembering his own difficulties of becoming engaged to Estelle Smith in far-away Adelaide, South Australia while he continued months at sea as Fourth Office on various Lloyd ships, this in 1902.

Some time in September, 1918, *Meteor* was the last naval ship that the Kaiser visited at Eckernförde, some 25 kms. N.W. of Kiel, with his staff and Brother Prinz Heinrich, Admiral of the Baltic Fleet. The author was visiting there, with his Mother, his eight-years old sister Evelyn, he was then four. They were told that on this day they were not to come on board to visit their Father. They did go to the gangway, barefooted. The guard obviously knowing who they were let them on board. Going down the empty promenade deck they came to the front, turned left and there ... was a group massively with gold braid. The Kaiser must have asked: "Whose children are these, Drechsel?" And: "Mine, Your Majesty ..." So they met the Kaiser and, more importantly for the author, Prinz Heinrich who in December wrote a long letter from which the author quoted in the Epilogue of Volume I, and again in 1921, 1922 and 1923. Had he been Kaiser there would have been no World War I, nor II. The Kaiser abdicated in November and fled to Holland. Our Pension was right above the beach. Naval aviators would come afternoons for tea with guests, driving their float planes onto the gently sloping sands. When they returned to leave the author and other little boys playing would push them out and turn them around, and off they went.

"The exception in the postwar restrictions on or reductions in transportation was towing. It was expanded to the North and Baltic Seas" as the most efficient in transporting goods. Here one of the NDL tugs is towing two lighters. These have set sails to help reduce the consumption of coal by the tug. This highlights how small the new beginning was. Photo from Hans Jürgen Witthöft's Norddeutscher Lloyd, Koehler, 1973.

Kurmeister. During July, 1919 service was restricted, even temporarily stopped, because of the lack of coal. In November, 1919, trains stopped running for ten days to accumulate enough coal for the winter. When in June, 1920 the resort steamer *Glückauf* of 1900 was rebuilt as a combination freighter-tug to open a new service between the Baltic and Scandinavia, the Lloyd yearbook reported this as "a noteworthy enrichment of our capacity." In addition, a lighter service was opened to carry wood from Finland and Sweden to Holland.

The Treaty of Versailles had given Poland access to the Baltic with the "Polish Corridor." This cut off East Prussia from the rest of Germany. In mid-1920, NDL with its resort steamers and tender *Grüssgott* opened a Swinemünde-Zoppot-Danzig connection, and an emigrant feeder service between Libau and Stettin with two purchased and rebuilt former minesweepers. It all helped to keep Lloyd people busy and Germany rebuilding. But it took years for the former seagoing staff to be reabsorbed one by one as ships were built, or bought back.

In January, 1920 the Treaty of Versailles went into effect. February brought NDL its first freight agency business when Holt's Blue Funnel Line and Ellerman & Bucknall S.S.Co. began calling at

Seydlitz on NDL's first postwar passenger voyage, at Buenos Aires, from Bremerhaven on 12 November, 1921. In the center, in front, Captain F. Rehm, ex- NDL Yearbook 1925.

Hamburg and Bremen on their first-ever service from Germany to the Far East. NDL became the Central European agent, and handled port operations. In March, Nippon Yusen Kaisha opened its similar route, with the Lloyd as agent and port representative. Now there were two sailings a month to the Far East. Not until December, 1921 could Hapag, and in January, 1922 the Lloyd put their own first ships on this run. The joint sched-

Heinz Schuengel, who had been in China for the Lloyd when war broke, in early 1921 became deputy for the Director of the Bremerhaven Agency, second only to Bremen in the Lloyd organization. In 1922, he became in the U.S. General Manager for the Lloyd. In 1933, with the splitting off of the money-draining Lloyd and Hapag north Atlantic passenger services from these two companies, he returned to Bremen as Director of the new NORDA. He died in 1939 just before the war broke.

ule with the British ships meant that the Germans were handled by the same port agents as Holt and E & B.

Understandable there was worldwide hostility to anything German.

Bernard Huldermann, biographer of Hapag's General Director Albert Baliin, states p. 208 in the English version (Cassell & Co., London, 1922) that "it is alleged that, at the close of the war, the British Government approached some of the country's leading shipping firms with the suggestion that they should buy up the Hamburg-American Line or the North German Lloyd," this to prevent re-emergence to their 1914 positions of No. 1 and No. 2 in world rank.

On 12 November, 1921 at *Seydlitz's* departure as the Lloyd's first postwar passenger sailing, General Director Carl Stimming told Captain Friedrich Rehm "We cannot impress (the world) with the amount of our material, only with the spirit with which it is imbued."

When the first German passengers in a German ship, Hapag's *Havelland*, reached Port Said at yearend 1921, they were refused landing permission. The Holt-Ellerman agents intervened, got approval for landing but with an early curfew.

In February, 1922, the French refused to let Hamburg South American Line's *Cap Polonio* on its war-aborted maiden voyage call at Boulogne. Nor would they let German ships call at their former colonies of Togo and Kamerun. When in early 1923 Hapag's New York representative, Carl Lederer was proposed as sole arbiter for the Atlantic (Passenger) Conference, there was major opposition. He was reluctantly confirmed as of 1 July as the individual best suited for this job.

In March, 1924 5¼ years after warend, when *Elberfeld* #298 was en route to Australia with the author, Mother and sister, at Antwerp it was first in line to enter the inner harbor, but was locked through last. Arriving at Adelaide on April 26th, ANZAC Day, commemorating Australian and New Zealand losses at Gallipoli in WWI, the authorities were less than welcoming despite South Australia having been in large numbers settled by Germans. Import restrictions against former enemies remained in effect. Canada outright forbade any German immigration into 1927.

In contrast to the reception for German ships elsewhere, when *Seydlitz* arrived in November, 1921 at Spanish ports en route to the La Plata, local officials boarded the ship to the sounds of the "Marcha Real," and the ship's band played the popular "Cancion del Soldado," Song of the Soldier. Similar celebrations welcomed the ship in South America. In January, 1922, NDL rejoined the Atlantic (Passenger) Conference.

At *Seydlitz's* departure on 12 February, Lincoln's Birthday, on the first NDL ship to North America, Herr Stimming pointed out that prewar from 1858 into 1895 the Lloyd had taken three million passengers to North America and that a multiple of that figure among Americans had some relationship with NDL. The 1990 Census reported that some forty percent, or near one hundred million Americans, had some one who entered this country via Ellis Island. This author's estimate is that given the passenger numbers and percentages carried trans-Atlantic by the Lloyd, about one-fourth of these or some twentyfive millions had some one who came over on the Lloyd. When on February 27, 1922 *Seydlitz* arrived in Hoboken, New York the pier was jammed with welcomers. Hundreds were turned away from the 2600 seats-filled Lexington Theater in Manhattan for the welcome celebration. By the end of 1922, NDL again had a weekly service to Hoboken.

As the Bremen-New York run had been the

THE FLEET

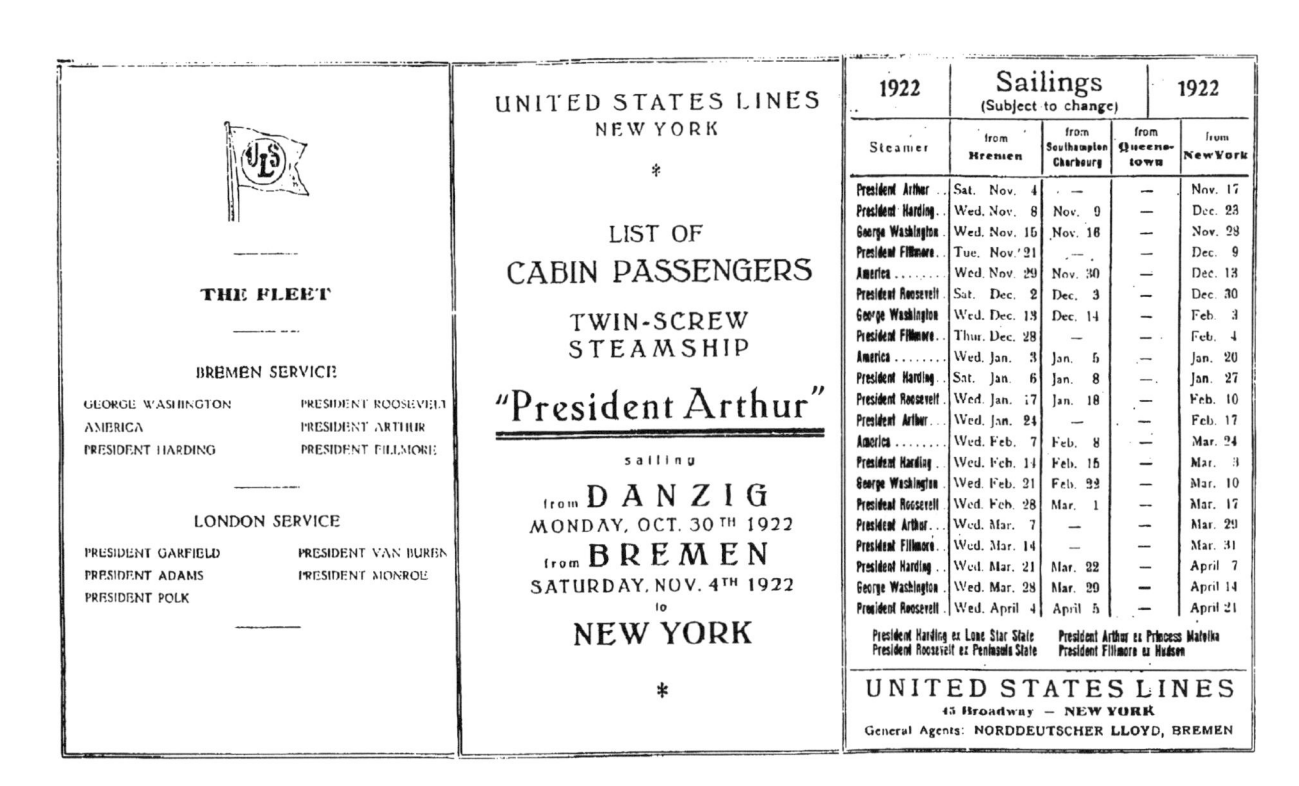

BREMEN SERVICE

GEORGE WASHINGTON	PRESIDENT ROOSEVELT
AMERICA	PRESIDENT ARTHUR
PRESIDENT HARDING	PRESIDENT FILLMORE

LONDON SERVICE

PRESIDENT GARFIELD	PRESIDENT VAN BUREN
PRESIDENT ADAMS	PRESIDENT MONROE
PRESIDENT POLK	

UNITED STATES LINES
NEW YORK

✻

LIST OF
CABIN PASSENGERS

TWIN-SCREW
STEAMSHIP

"President Arthur"

sailing

from **DANZIG**
MONDAY, OCT. 30TH 1922

from **BREMEN**
SATURDAY, NOV. 4TH 1922

to

NEW YORK

✻

1922	Sailings (Subject to change)			1922
Steamer	from Bremen	from Southampton Cherbourg	from Queenstown	from New York
President Arthur	Sat. Nov. 4	—	—	Nov. 17
President Harding	Wed. Nov. 8	Nov. 9	—	Dec. 23
George Washington	Wed. Nov. 15	Nov. 16	—	Nov. 28
President Fillmore	Tue. Nov. 21	—	—	Dec. 9
America	Wed. Nov. 29	Nov. 30	—	Dec. 13
President Roosevelt	Sat. Dec. 2	Dec. 3	—	Dec. 30
George Washington	Wed. Dec. 13	Dec. 14	—	Feb. 3
President Fillmore	Thur. Dec. 28	—	—	Feb. 4
America	Wed. Jan. 3	Jan. 5	—	Jan. 20
President Harding	Sat. Jan. 6	Jan. 8	—	Jan. 27
President Roosevelt	Wed. Jan. 17	Jan. 18	—	Feb. 10
President Arthur	Wed. Jan. 24	—	—	Feb. 17
America	Wed. Feb. 7	Feb. 8	—	Mar. 24
President Harding	Wed. Feb. 14	Feb. 15	—	Mar. 3
George Washington	Wed. Feb. 21	Feb. 22	—	Mar. 10
President Roosevelt	Wed. Feb. 28	Mar. 1	—	Mar. 17
President Arthur	Wed. Mar. 7	—	—	Mar. 29
President Fillmore	Wed. Mar. 14	—	—	Mar. 31
President Harding	Wed. Mar. 21	Mar. 22	—	April 7
George Washington	Wed. Mar. 28	Mar. 29	—	April 14
President Roosevelt	Wed. April 4	April 5	—	April 21

President Harding ex Lone Star State   President Arthur ex Princess Matoika
President Roosevelt ex Peninsula State   President Fillmore ex Hudson

UNITED STATES LINES
45 Broadway — NEW YORK
General Agents: NORDDEUTSCHER LLOYD, BREMEN

Danzig had become the new emigration port for Eastern Europe, and American and other lines extended their routes that far. NDL were General Agents in Germany and Danzig. The PRESIDENT ships were all-new U.S. vessels ordered during the war but completed after, George Washington *the former NDL liner,* America *ex-Hapag. United States Lines was the successor to the U.S. Mail S.S. Co. with which NDL had made the agency agreement in 1921. The opening wedge for NDL itself to return to the North Atlantic. Below:* George Washington *in Bremerhaven.*

A New Start

reason for the founding of the Norddeutscher Lloyd in 1857, so now postwar in the 1920s it was central to the effort to rebuild. A Lloyd official in New York commented later. "Our ships contributed to help reverse the mistrust and negative feelings about Germany in America." Captain Nicholas Johnsen of NDL's flagship *Columbus* had a deep sense for instilling friendship for the Lloyd and therefore for Germany in the travelling public. In his circle of influence the Mayor of New York, Jimmie Walker, became an intimate member. He had always been friendly to Germans: the Steuben Society was an important political element, and public figures led its annual Steuben Day Parade down Broadway. Walker often was Captain Johnsen's guest on *Columbus* with, probably, the U.S. Customs Service (this was Prohibition time!) deliberately staying away.

The war had made the U.S. a major maritime power, a role it had held in the mid-19th century with its clipper ships. But it lacked the operating expertise, the contacts abroad to operate worldwide new services. It therefore needed representation and agency such as the Lloyd and Hapag could provide in Europe.

In 1920, the U.S. Shipping Board owned the bulk of the war-seized foreign shipping. On 20 May, 1920 it contracted with the new U.S. Mail S.S.Co. to open routes from New York:-to Queenstown and Cherbourg, returning via Southampton;- to Dover, Boulogne and Danzig; - Boston to Queenstown, Cherbourg and Bremerhaven, returning via Southampton - Cherbourg, with eight former NDL vessels: *George Washington* #246, *Kronprinzessin Cecilie* #234, *Kaiser Wilhelm II* #186, *Princess Alice* #191, *Rhein* #116, *Neckar* #161, and *Köln* #112, and three ex-Hapag steamers, *America, President Grant* and *König Wilhelm II*, "all oil burners." Not quite true. *George Washington* was not converted to oil-burning until 1942.

In June, 1920, a Lloyd team of President Philipp Heineken, Directors Max Walter and Carl Stapelfeldt, Prokurist (empowered to sign) Seyde, and Inspector (Port Operations chief) Oeding, travelled to New York to work out an agency/representation agreement with U.S. Mail. It was signed on 27 August, but the Lloyd operated under it before then. The first sailing from New York was *Susquehanna* on 4 August, formerly NDL's *Rhein*, the ship on which in September, 1901 the author's future parents first met. It reached Bremerhaven with 170 passengers on the 18th, then continued on to Danzig. It had been made a City-State by Versailles, now was the new emigration port for Eastern Europe, with Bremen and Hamburg inoperative. The Hoover Commission had an agency there; its prime task to provide one hot meal daily for some 1.3 million Polish children, many in areas that had been German until 1919. Canada had an Emigration Office in Danzig. *Rhein* left Bremerhaven on 4 September for New York with 2100 passengers, mail and cargo. In February, 1921 the *New Rochelle,* ex Hapag's *Hamburg*, joined this service, in March the *Antigone*. ex NDL's *Neckar*.

Also in February, 1921 U.S. Mail opened its New York-Naples-Genoa service with *Pocahontas*, Ex-NDL's *Prinzess Irene*; two weeks later it was joined by the *Princess Matoika*, ex NDL's *Princess Alice*. Only five round-trips were made by the latter, then it was transferred to the Danzig route. *Pocahontas* was laid up in Gibraltar on her third voyage with engine problems. She lay there for more than a year; then the Lloyd bought her back, reportedly with enough copper ballast in her bottom to repay the purchase price.

In August, 1921, the ex-NDL *George Washington* #246, it kept its name, joined the New York-Bremen service for one voyage only before U.S. Mail collapsed. It had insufficient capital and no maritime operating experience.

The ships remained in service under the new United States Lines. It continued to Bremerhaven with its larger vessels into 1929, then switched to Hamburg as its turnaround port, except for *Leviathan*, which turned at Southampton, until the War. After that war, the U.S. Lines, with the 1940 U.S.-built *America* and then the *United States,* returned to Bremerhaven as its continental port.

In September, 1920 NDL had re-opened a Bremen-Brazil service with *Vegesack*, followed in November by sister *Bremerhaven,* the first newbuildings following the war, only 1620 tons, ships that prewar never would have been used on highseas routes.

Rapot, the first of seven vessels chartered from the NDL-befriended Roland Line, sailed in October. In 1922, several newly-completed Lloyd freighters, then the first new passenger vessels entered this service. On 7 October, 1922 *Göttingen* was the first post-war sailing to Australia in a joint schedule with Holt's Blue Funnel Line and the prewar Deutsch-Australische Dampfschiffs Gesellschaft, D.A.D.G.

Late 1920 brought a change of command at the Lloyd. General Director Philipp Heineken and President Carl Stimming exchanged jobs: Heineken became President, Stimming the new General Director, the operating authority.

Many German sailing ships were caught abroad by the war, twelve of them in the Gulf of

California, eventually bought by Captain Robert Dollar, others in Chile, including NDL's School Ship *Herzogin Cecilie* #143, see "The Lloyd Sails."

In December, 1919 the Segelschiff Kontor GmbH. (Sailship Agency) was founded in Hamburg to care for the ships and crews and try to get them home. The Reichsmarine tug *Arbeit* was sent out to tow home any ships unable to make it on their own, as many had been purposefully damaged to keep them from being used by the U.S. or its Allies. Four of six NDL vessels had to be towed; all were loaded with needed cargoes. All had to be repaired for turnover to the Allies.

The fact that Danzig had become independent of Germany by the Versailles Treaty gave the Lloyd the opportunity to hold onto some prewar ships. *Columbus* and an unnamed sister were building at the Schichau Yard in Danzig when war broke. Danzig's new status automatically exempted the two ships from forced turnover to the Allies. The Lloyd in 1920-21-22 could not use a 32,500 tons passenger ship. There was no route it could serve under the German flag. NDL did need many smaller passenger vessels and freighters. Britain, in contrast, needed large passenger ships to replace wartime losses and give both Cunard and White Star Lines three vessels each for their Southampton-Cherbourg-New York route. Hapag's *Imperator* became *Berengaria* as Cunard's third ship; *Columbus* became White Star's *Homeric* to round out its trio. In return for NDL giving up *Columbus* it was allowed to retain the above six returned vessels: *Göttingen* #237, *Gotha* #239, *Holstein* #251, *Seydlitz* #188, *Yorck* #221, and *Westfalen* #218, an exchange of 39,505 tons for *Columbus'* 34,351 tons. This exchange became known as The Columbus Agreement, signed on 5 August, 1921. These and several other prewar Lloyd vessels repurchased: *Prinzess Irene* #149, *Hannover* #144, *Derfflinger* #242, *Lützow* #241, freighter *Lippe* #271 let NDL re-open routes sooner than it could have done had it needed to await new-buildings at a time of material shortages and labor unrest.

Some improvements were made to these old vessels to make them acceptable for Middle Class passengers: some windowing in of Promenade Decks, more baths and running water. The Lloyd's first new-buildings were basically prewar designs: *Köln*, *Crefeld*, *Sierra Nevada*, *München* #293 almost, so that the competition outmoded

Mail from Bremen to their representative at the Vulcan A.G. Shipyard in Stettin, 1921-1924.

them. But they survived in Lloyd service into the depression.

On 21 February, 1921 an elaborate NDL new-building program was announced: 47 vessels of some 420,000 tons. This Fleet Reconstruction Act was the result of a shipping lines-Government agreement largely worked out by the then-NDL Director General Heineken. Ship acquisition costs were divided: 80.5% Government funding, 19.5% Shipping Firms. Ten percent of Government funds could be used to purchase vessels rather than building them, this to enable an earlier resumption of prewar routes. The exchange rate at the time was M60.70 to the Dollar. Prewar it had been M4.23.

Little-known historical incidents occurred in March-April, 1921, at various shipyards. The Blohm & Voss yard in Hamburg was occupied on 23 March by largely Communist-controlled labor unions. A similar stoppage occurred at the A.G. Vulcan shipyard in Stettin. There Captain W. Drechsel headed a staff, two captains and four engineers, representing NDL during the construction of eight new ships 1920-1924. Here is his report of what happened:

"It is March, 1921. There is intense activity everywhere. A tremendous undertaking: renewal of the Norddeutscher Lloyd's fleet. Everywhere the burning forges from where red-hot rivets are thrown to the men at millions of bored holes in steel plates. Hundreds of pressed-air hammers drive in these rivets with a numbing staccato: the song of work, but ear-splitting. With difficulty even mouth-to-ear can one make oneself understood. The goal is to get the ships into the water at scheduled times, despite endless delays in material procurement, to make room on the ways for the next hull.

"For the first time in the history of German shipbuilding were workers from the supply industries of South Germany involved: Bavarians, Swabians and other Southern Dialects are heard among the usual Plattdeutsch, Low German. Workers, shipyard management and the Lloyd team are pulling together: Engineers Lampe, Wirthmann, Lamsbach and Haake; Captains Carl Mundt and Drechsel. For the shipyard: Dr. Wertbrecht, Manager, Dr. Linder, Shipbuilder.

"Suddenly came a day when all this productive work and energy was brought to a standstill by a Communist flareup: 6000 workers laid down their jobs for who knows what reasons. All exhortations by the Works Management to discuss problems with the foremen was blocked by the Communist leaders. It was evident many of the workers felt forced to follow commands to lay down work.

"A group of radical workers occupied the office building. Management escaped being caught or imprisoned there by escaping in a motor boat; office personnel also had left. However, we Lloyd representatives were not bothered in our second-story offices.

"The entire worker group had laid down tools at Noon, but none left the shipyard. The non-participating foremen and supervisors who tried to leave were beaten, put into pushcarts and dumped into the roadway outside the gate. Later in the afternoon some hundreds of police cleared the areas and closed the gates of the shipyard. After that, it needed only a handfull to keep traffic moving, the area cleared. Everywhere throughout Stettin there was unrest. No one knew what would happen next. The Communist leaders, — they kept warning everybody that 'if you don't go willingly we will use force' — organized several days after the stoppage a parade of many thousands through the main streets of the city. The mayor was forced to walk at the head of the march hat in hand.

"At the shipyard we from the Lloyd were not alone. Members of the Allied Control Commission, mostly officers in uniform, were inspecting everywhere and took inventory of everything. Most noticeable were the young French officers, Kepis jauntily at an angle, cigarettes in their lips, even in areas with combustible materials. At the yard were still many items originally ordered and made during the war for the German Navy, including some 150 search-light mirrors. These were all broken by the French officers with evident glee with small hammers. British and American officers, some with pipes, stood by and watched stoically. Nothing more than these activities of the Allied officers could emphasize our impotence to prevent such deliberate destruction.

"Five days passed and still the Communists controlled the surface life of Stettin. The iron gates remained closed. Into this atmosphere suddenly appeared on the fifth day an old friend, Captain Nicholas Johnsen, now commander of the Lloyd's largest vessel *Grüssgott* running in the East Prussia service. He had come from Swinemünde to see the rebuilding of the Lloyd's fleet. He was distressed to see before his eyes what was happening. There lay the Lloyd and Roland Linie ships in different stages of construction, but no workers. I told him 'the day will come when these and other ships again will carry our flags across the seas.' Johnsen replied gruffly: 'Neither of us will experience what you are saying. These new-buildings will rust on their slipways.' With that he bade us Goodbye and left.

"Two days later around 10 AM the watchman at the main entry telephoned that a large number of women with children had massed on the street outside and demanded to talk to the shipyard management. Indeed. Where were these gentlemen at this time? Out of curiosity, sympathy and duty I went to the gate, standing inside, opposite the nearest woman, as representative of the construction contractor. What I now saw touched the heart: crying women, screaming children; all traffic blocked. When I was able to make vocal contact with one of the women leaders, obviously a worker's wife, she begged me in the name of thousands of families of the locked-out workers to convince the managers to get in immediate touch with these women with regard to reopening the Vulcan Yard. She and those with her in simple but moving words described the suffering of these families since the closing of the yard. One has to remember the dire shortages of food and other necessities right after the war to understand today what these women were telling. 'Our men leave the house in the morning in order to escape the suffering and leave to us women the task of trying to find food for the children. We haven't been given credits for some time now. We mothers often go hungry to bed so that the children have something.' Some of the other women also told of need, suffering, even of suicide because of these events. And the shipyard (women) leader at the end: 'Gentlemen (others from the Lloyd must have come down): We are at the end. Either you give our men a chance to work again or we shall cut our own throats and those of our children.'

"I promised to do my utmost, knowing that

the Vulcan management obviously also wanted to return to full activity. Then followed a tiring telephone war. It took me four hours to reach the directors: Dr. Weitbrecht for the ship construction, Director E. Linder for the machine division, and the business director Karl Trappen, and bring them to reality. It was agreed that management would meet the next morning, Tuesday, with a group of not more than twenty women representative of the workers, in the board room of the main building. This understanding became public knowledge that very evening to the thousands of worker families in the entire area.

"On the Tuesday morning we saw the same situation: in the street between the upper and lower Hof (yard area). Thousands of women with their children. The police allowed the delegation of twenty women to enter via a small gate. I led the group to the Directors' boardroom where they were greeted in a friendly manner by the three directors and besought to seat themselves. The opponents eyed each other. What was shattering then and I today still think back with sorrow to that meeting, was to heard what the women had to say. The three directors evinced full understanding for the situation. Director Trappen said "If we reopen the yard, what assurances do we have that our past proficiency and hard work will return? We are a business enterprise and we cannot and will not be held subject to the moods of the workers." The group leader: "Open these portals tomorrow, Wednesday at 1 o'clock and we women shall see to it that our men on time and in full numbers will appear." But since work resumption required considerable advance preparation, the re-opening could not take place until Friday, the third morning.

"On Friday, between 7 and 8 a.m. immense numbers of women and children, some very serious, others in happier mood, led the men, fathers, brothers, sons to work. It did not take long that the Vulcan Yard hummed with renewed vigor and productivity.

"But the picture as an observer would have seen it that morning as the crowds of workers passed into the gates was a far different one from that we had witnessed before. The shipyard seemed more a barracks training ground than a ship construction site. Thousands of the workers

Field Marshall von Mackensen with Staff Captain W. Daehne, Captain of Columbus *from 1936. Field Marshall von Mackensen's visit to the Vulcan Shipyard was unexpected, but it set the end to the unrest and sealed a new spirit of all-out building of ships. Field Marshall August von Mackensen World War I hero to German forces, last in the Balkans, here visiting the* Bremen *in Bremerhaven, in 1929 or 1930, when Staff Captain W. Daehne still wore 3½ stripes rather than later when the Staff Captains on* Bremen *and* Europa *wore four stripes, under the Commodore. Photo R. Fleischhut,* Bremen's *ship photographer. Also in Collection of Dr. Hückstädt.*

wore in a spirit of festivity with any old soldier's cap, old uniform jacket or both, whatever they could find. Many wore the ribbons of the decorations they had earned during the war. What an about-face from the Communist-inspired revolt. And with this full resumption of activity at the Vulcan it seemed the rest of the people in Stettin went about their tasks with renewed vigor. One again saw expressions of hope rather than tragedy.

"One day without notice there showed up His Excellency Field Marshall von Mackensen (he headed Germany's war activities in the East), whose ancestral home was in Fallenwalde, a suburb of Stettin. The yard management was greatly concerned. There were still opposition-minded men among the workers. But his gray Excellency insisted he was going to inspect the shipyard. He came, he saw, and he conquered! In his beribboned uniform he met and received greetings and exchanged these with workers (some of whom must have served under him), many standing at attention, and expressing good wishes. The members of the Allied Control commission were not to be seen. It was a moving occasion. And from that day it was again: fullout to work. And, without further interruptions the Lloyd construction program concluded at the end of December, 1923. *Stuttgart* was the last one to leave, in January, 1924." Captain Drechsel ended his account with this verse, source unknown:

Der Gott, der Eisen wachsen liess,
Der hat' es gern gesehen,
Dass daraus nicht nur Schwert und Spiess,
Nein, Schiffe auch entstehen!

The God who fashioned worlds of iron,
Assuredly will smile on seeing
That more than swords and spears for war
Ships for commerce come into being."

Germany was in dire need of so much food and materials to replace what had been used up or lost by war, that Herr Stimming at the 21 December, 1921 general meeting told stockholders that despite the world surplus shipping tonnage and resulting low freight rates "for us the conditions are that we are able to meet only the most urgent shipper demands, so that the capacity available to us can be operated relatively satisfactorily."

Almost as soon as the rebuilding program worked out by the shipping lines and government was going full-out, inflation began to erode available funding. New capital-raisings had to be made: on March, 1921 by NDL from 250 to 475 million Marks, on 21 December to 600 million Marks, and at the 15 May, 1923 annual meeting to one Milliard Marks. This is the European term, in U.S. terms One Billion Marks. All this proved inadequate to meet runaway costs.

This catastrophic German inflation experience is the reason its Bundesbank still today is reluctant to make money too easy. NDL's gross earnings for 1923 were 1,011,064,593,072,959,905.63 Marks. A prewar bond issue of 49 millions was paid off at par, less than $1 in 1923 terms. Many businesses, including NDL and Bremer Vulkan shipyard issued *Notgeld*, emergency monies, for which they held specific deposits in banks so that salaries and supplies could be paid "in house."

Under this impact, the need to lay up newly-completed passenger ships for lack of passengers, forced the cutback of NDL's 420,000 tons building program to 256,000 tons. At the Stettiner Vulcan six 13,300 tons passenger vessels were ordered; two only were built. Three *Sierra Nevada* types of 8,700 tons were ordered; only it was built. Five 4,200 tons and three 6,200 tons freighters were cancelled. In late 1923, Germany's Mark was stabilized at the prewar M4.23 to the Dollar. This was confirmed in 1924 by the Dawes Plan covering its international obligations. In May, 1924, when Captain Drechsel was transferred to Hoboken as Inspector in charge of shore operations, the Lloyd directors gave him an "extraordinary" grant of one thousand Gold Marks to help defray moving

Inflation currency went into the high Milliarden, in Europe the equivalent of U.S. billions. One (U.S.) Billon Marks surcharged on One Thousand Marks.
Emergency notes issued by various businesses for paying their employees who would then spend it locally with merchants, etc. who would be paid from that firm's account in the bank stated.

5,000,000,000 Mark note from the Lloyd, and Fifty Marks from the Bremer Vulkan shipyard.

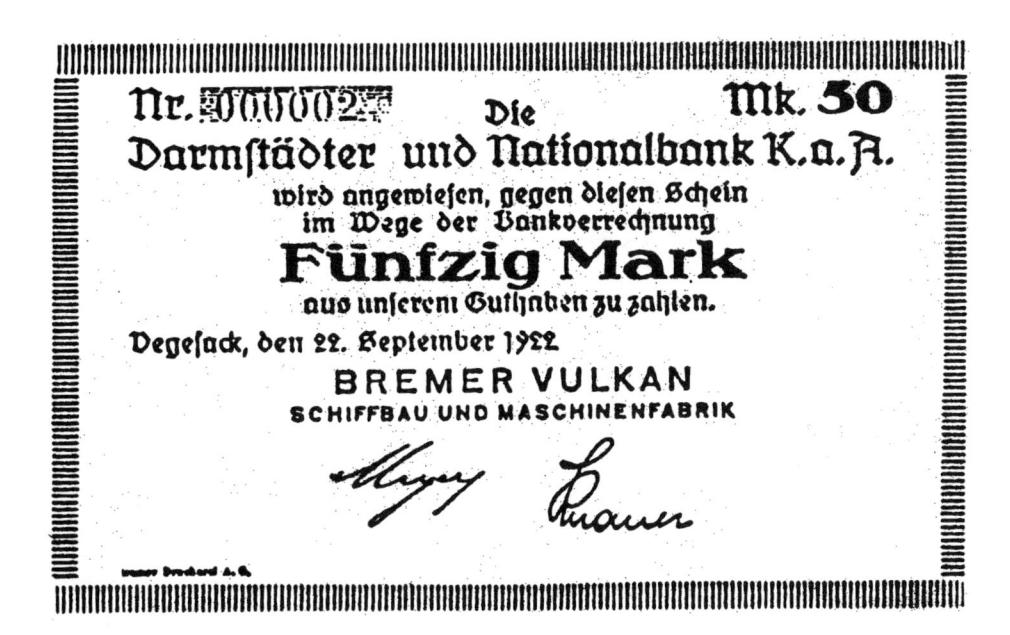

expenses from Stettin to New Jersey.

During the year, passenger ships *Coblenz* #301 and sisters *Trier* #304 and *Fulda* #307 (NDL's first passenger motor ship), the *Sierras Cordoba* #302 and *Morena* #306, *Stuttgart* #303 (oil-fired sister of *München* of 1923), and *Columbus* entered service. In 1925, with completion of *Berlin* #308 as the last in the rebuilding program and resumption of cruising NDL was operating basically as it had prewar, though with no express sailings.

Passenger totals on the North Atlantic run had gradually increased for the Lloyd: 31,858 in 1924, helped by *Columbus* entering service, and 54,649 in 1925, 6.29% of all travellers on the route. Bremen could be satisfied that the Lloyd again was an acknowledged entity in world shipping seven years after the end of the war.

But an objective look at the entire ship park showed that there was a mishmash of disparate types, ages, sizes, speeds, and route suitabilities:
- *Köln* #285 and *Crefeld* #286 were prewar freighter designs completed in passenger

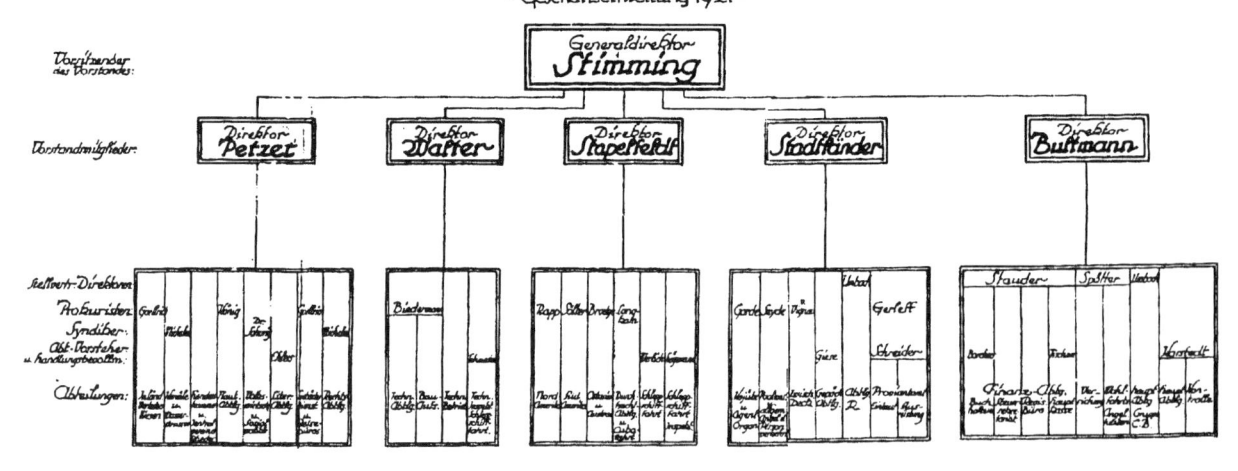

The Operating Management of the Lloyd, Yearbook 1920/21, and Philipp Heineken, President of NDL and Chairman of the Board of Directors. In 1925, Herr Stapelfeld is sans t.

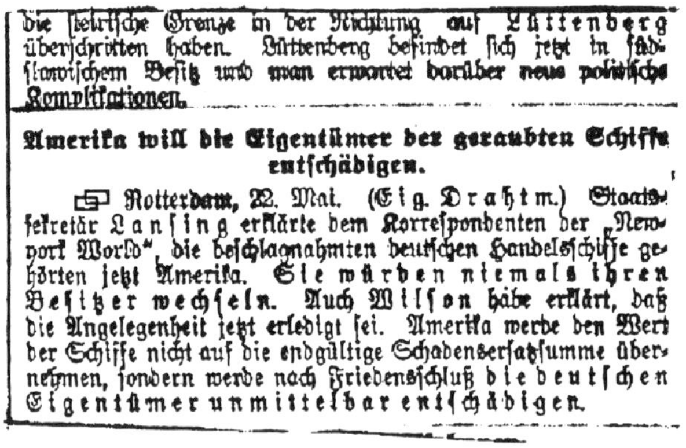

There was one hopeful but long-range gleam amid the gloom. Six months after the Armistice, the Kiel Newspaper carried this 22 May, 1919 report from Rotterdam: The U.S. Secretary of State Lansing told the New York World reporter that the seized German vessels (more than 100 of them) now belonged to the U.S. They would never change their owner. President Wilson had declared the matter closed. The U.S. would not include their value in the final Reparations Settlement but after the Peace Treaty "the German owners would be compensated." The headline to the item "America will recompense the owners of the Robbed Ships."

Right: Meteor, the Hapag prewar cruising yacht that in the war served the Kiel Submarine School as Mother ship and as dormitory ship for submarine crews between their forays. Artist's name unknown.

16 *Norddeutscher Lloyd Bremen*

versions. Both were designed as emigrant ships to the U.S. But the immigration quota restrictions forced a shift to the South America run, still heavily emigrant and seasonal worker movements.

- The six vessels of the WESER class were outdated when built; they required sponsons to stabilize them. As combination passenger-freighter vessels they were too slow, at 12½ knots (the same slow "speed" as *Köln* and *Crefeld*) for the long voyages to the Far East.
- The same problem of stability for an outdated design forced the building of sponsons on the three SIERRA steamers. Unlike their three prewar name-sisters which had tastily-designed public rooms and mahogany lacquered lifeboats, these three failed to give the Lloyd a strong position in the South America trade. This was a major reason why NDL bought up millions of competitor Hamburg-South American Line shares: to control the competition. The smaller *Sierra Nevada* #289 had a second blind stack to try to disguise her out-of-datedness.

It was obvious that a complete overhaul of NDL's organization, fleet and services was needed if it were not again, as was happening in 1914, be at the end of an era instead of the start of a new and better one. This is what led NDL in November-December 1925 to make a move long-considered: the absorption of separately-operating shipping lines NDL had largely or wholly owned for some years:

The Roland Linie A.G. with its wholly-owned subsidiary "Argo", and in turn its wholly-owned subsidiaries of Rhederei A.G. von 1896, and Hanseatische Dampfschiffahrts Gesellschaft.

The Dampfschiffs Reederei "Horn". The one-ship "Seefahrt" Dampschiffs Reederei; and Hamburg-Bremer Afrika-Linie.

The rationale was to reduce overhead by eliminating multiple separate management staffs, to allocate from a wide variety of ship types vessels to services that best utilized their type, size and speed. And thus to provide tonnage for new services and/or more frequent services. The next six years were years of further acquisitions, the Lloyd peaking in size in 1931, caught up in a momentum that in that year was overwhelmed by outside events that forced a complete reversal of

By January, 1926 the Lloyd again was at the wheel; the postwar building program had been completed with Berlin *in September, 1925. That December, a large fleet of freighters was absorbed by taking over old Lloyd-backed, partly owned shipping enterprises. Expansion was on the way.*

1925-1931: to achieve the very benefits of applying managements and ship types best suited to individual services. The wild card in the above fusions was Roland's Director General Ernst Glässel. He it was who largely pushed through the next years' growth, then was blamed and ousted when the house of cards threatened to collapse. That is a following story.

A New Start   17

Fleet of the Norddeutscher Lloyd 1920-1970

Bremer Vulkan sold the first postwar vessels not delivered as reparations to the Lloyd (#279 and 280) and Hapag (sisters of #279). They were built for the yard's account. The price was paid at delivery on specially favorable terms. On their side, the two lines committed themselves in the years 1925-1930 to give Bremer Vulkan yearly the first 16,000 gross tons of new orders. Hapag's orders more than met this commitment, NDL's did not. The B.V. Chronology gives the four sisters Order Nos. 664-667; many preceding numbers were either scratched or given to other ships built later, but then bearing earlier numbers. An example of how "official" data, also tonnages, dimensions (always metric) speeds, horsepower, etc., vary by source and during ships' lives. The ship numbers are from the original Belgian Nautical Research Association NDL fleet list of 515 vessels by the author in 1961. Dates are always Day: Month: Year.

Pattern for basic ship details

BNRA No. **Ship Name**   Years in NDL service
Builders   Year of build   Tonnage   Length x Width. See #48
Type of Engine   Horsepower   Speed   Number of screws

   All vessels are single screw unless **, ***only *Ravenstein* #495, *Reifenstein* #496 and *Rothenstein* #497, or **** only *Bremen* #417, *Europa* #424 and *Bremen* #511

Passengers per Class   Crew Size (numbers vary by season)

Where the passenger capacity is not known or none were carried the Crew size is shown on the third (engines) line.

> The ship biography from Launch to scrapping is given. Information included varies according to the activities or importance of the ship. If some basic information is lacking this is indicated with FFW, further facts wanted. Occasionally, numbers are out of sequence due to new information since the original 1961 listing.

NDL Fleet:
Ships 279 — 308

Westfalen #218 returned in June, 1920 under tow from Chile around Cape Horn. Badly damaged, it needed major repairs. It made one 1921 voyage. In January, 1922, it was NDL's first ship in the joint Far East service with Hapag and Blue Funnel Line.

Vegesack was the Lloyd's first new vessel after the war. Its island and superstructure were built out to make room for crew and passengers amidships. It soon passed on to a subsidiary as too small for further use by NDL. Theodor Siersdorfer collection.

VEGESACK. Nach Umbau. Theodor Siersdorfer Foto.

279. *Vegesack*		1920-1922/1925-1933	
Bremer Vulkan, Vegesack #664	1920	1566	75.41x10.95
Triple Expansion		720	9
7		25	

Launched 30.8.1920, Del.25.9.1920. First new ship for NDL. MV "beginning of September", followed in October by chartered *Rapot,* in November by *Bremerhaven,* to North Brazil. In 1922, when NDL needed larger vessels, sold with #280 to Dampfschiffs, Reederei "Horn," Lübeck, midships enlarged, higher masts. 12/1925 back to NDL in its fusion with Roland Linie; it had acquired "Horn" in late 1922. 8/12/1933 to Sovtorgflot, Vladivostock, ren. *Ola.* In war under Allied control. 1945 returned to USSR. 1960 RLR.

Bremerhaven, *sister of* Vegesack, *here in Hong Kong with NDL's express liner* Scharnhorst, *late 1930s when the ship ran through the Pacific islands to New Guinea and the Solomons.*

280. ***Bremerhaven***	1920-1922/1925-1937/1938-1941	
Bremer Vulkan,		
Vegesack #667	1920	1566/1615 75.41x10.95
Triple Expansion	720 9	
7	25	

Launched 9/11/1920. MV 11/1920 to N.Brazil. 29/7/1922 to D.S.R. "Horn," Lübeck. 12/1925 back under NDL with merger. 20/2/1929 left Hong Kong in renewed NDL service to New Guinea. 7/3/1929 arr. Rabaul. Carrying freight at cut-rates, ship could not cope with cargo offered, so *Friderun* #325 was added in 10/1932, line extended to the Solomons. From 12/1936 foreign vessels were allowed only in major New Guinea ports. 8/12/1936 to Colyer, Watson & Co., Rabaul, a new Inter-Island Shipping Co. founded in Hong Kong, as operator. 1937 ren. *Island Trader*. The former Chinese crew was replaced by Melanesians under white officers; it ran only among British islands. 3/6/1937 brought water to Kokopo for evacuees from Rabaul because of the volcano eruption. 29/1/1938 left Rabaul for overhaul in H.K. 26/4/1938 back to NDL, ren. *Bremerhaven*, ran along China coast. 6/9/1939 took refuge in Dairen with *Fulda* #307 and *Augsburg* #399. 6/8/1940 "sold" to Japan, ren. *Heiun (Teiun) Maru*, Teikoko K.K., Tokyo. 1/1/1942 ran onto Japanese mine in 16.05N, 120.20E in Lingayen Gulf, sank.

Hameln *was built prewar by and for the Rickmers interests of Bremerhaven, during the war went to H.C. Horn, in 1921 was bought from the British who got it as war booty.* William Schell Photo.

281. **Hameln**	1921-1929		
Rickmerswerft,			
Bremerhaven #150	1907	4173	111.89x14.53
Triple Expansion	1600	10.5	34

Launched 16/3/1907 as *Andree Rickmers,* Rickmers Rhederei, Bremen. 8/1914 caught at Antwerp by war. 10/10/1914 recaptured by Germany. 2/6/1917 to H.C. Horn, Schleswig, ren. *Hilda Horn*. 24/12/1918 *Hilda* for J. Pedersen, Hadersleben. 25/6/1919 del. to Britain, mngd. by R. Gordon & Co., London. 26/11/1921 bought by NDL, renamed, M.V. to Brazil. 11/1929 to Cie. Fluviale et Maritime Ouest Africain, Le Havre, ren. *Indenie*. 9/9/1931-2/1937 LU in Rotterdam. 2/1937 to Nordseewerke, Emden for BU, arr. 10/3/1937. In October, 1919 Captain W. Drechsel was assigned to the Vulcan A.G. Shipyard in Stettin-Bredow as construction supervisor-representative for NDL during the building of #282, 287-289, 291, 293, 296, and 303 (and 372 for Roland Linie?). During this time, the author attended all launchings.

282. **Minden**	1921-1929		
Vulcan A.G., Stettin #648	1921	4165	115.13x15.55
Triple Expansion	1800	10.5	
12	42 (1936-48: 39-Chinese)		

Launched 7/10/1921. 12/1921 MV to Brazil. 1938-1939 rebuilt by Deutsche Werft, Hamburg, Lengthened to 124.20 meters with new bow and cruiser stern, 4200 HP turbines, 14.5 knots, 8 passengers, 4318 Ts., put into South Africa-South America service, a new route for NDL. 6/9/1939 left Rio de Janeira to get home. 24/9/1939 scuttled 125 miles off the Faroes in 62.06N, 15.34W when *HMS Calypso* caught her. The five ships of this class never attained the 11+ knots expected of them.

Minden *was the first of eight freighters and passenger ships built at the Vulcan of Stettin 1921-1924. Most units of this class were rebuilt in the late 1930s as too slow.*

283. *Schlesien 2*	1921-1935		
J.C. Tecklenborg,			
Geestemünde #245	1912	7044	149.20x18.60
Triple Expansion	3700	12	
12	52-59		

Launched 30/4/1912 as *Karnak* for Kosmos Linie, Hamburg. 8/1914 took refuge in Iquique, served Graf Spee Squadron as supply vessel. 28/10/1914 took refuge in Antofagasta. 26/9/1917 seized by Chile after the crew damaged the engines. 1920 towed to Germany for repair and delivery to Allies. 29/7/1921 assigned to Shipping Controller, London, but remained in Germany. 13/1/1922 bought by NDL, ren., 21/1/1922 entered Far East service. 4/8/1935 to Köhlbrandwerft, Hamburg for BU.

Schlesien *was built prewar for the Kosmos Line for West Coast South America service. Assigned to the Allies, it stayed in Germany as surplus to Allied needs. It was bought by NDL in 1921.* Copyright Wolfgang Fuchs.

22 *Norddeutscher Lloyd Bremen*

Pfalz 284. *Sister of* Schlesien. *It too remained in Germany after the war, in 1922 was bought by the Lloyd.* Copyright Wolfgang Fuchs.

284. Pfalz 3   1921-1932
Flensburger S.B.Ges. #324   1912   7121   149.35x18.54
Triple Expansion   3700   12
12   48-60 (so 1926)

Sister of #283. Launched 31/8/1912 as *Ramses* for Kosmos Linie, Hamburg. MV.10/1/1912 to South America, West Coast. 8/1914 at Valparaiso, attached to Spee Squadron. 26/10/1914 at Battle of Coronel. 11/1914 interned in Chile. 9/1917 engine damaged by crew. 1920 towed to Hamburg. 29/7/1921 assigned to Shipping Controller, London, remained in Germany as unneeded. 2/1922 bought by NDL, ren., put into Far East service. 11/1932 one of several ships sold to USSR, Sovtogflot, Odessa, ren. *Tiflis*. 1937 *Tbilisti*. 7/9/1943 sunk off mouth of Yenisei River by mine laid 28/8/1943 by U-636. On 5 August, 1921 the "Columbus Agreement" was signed with Britain confirming that NDL could retain *Göttingen* #237, *Hannover* #114, *Holstein* #251, *Seydlitz* #188, *Westfalen* #218 and *Yorck* #221 in exchange for *Columbus 1* #267.

Köln *and sister* Crefeld 286 *were built on prewar freighter-designed hulls for the North America emigrant traffic. When the U.S. reduced allowable inflow, they were diverted to South America.* Köln *at Bremerhaven shortly before its maiden voyage to Buenos Aires. The original double-mountings are in this departure scene.*

Köln *after removal of the emigrant facilities and the extra lifeboats.*

285. **Köln 3** 1922-1940
Bremer Vulkan, Vegesack #591   1922   9265   150.36 x 18.51
Triple Expansion   4400   12.5
Middle Class-350, II-364, Dormitories-370 164-183

Launched 12/11/1921, same hull as last prewar freighters, now a combiship for emigrants. 3/1922 MV to South America, due to enactment of U.S. immigration limits. 7/1928 ran to Canada when immigration prohibition lifted. 12/1930 made a freighter voyage to U.S. East Coast. 1934 converted by Bremer Vulkan to freighter, 7881 tons, 53 crew. 27/6/1940 stranded on the Argosgrund S. of Gefle en route Lulea-Hamburg with iron ore, total loss. *Köln* and #286 had engines begun prewar. B.V. lists them as 4000 HP, NDL as 4400.

286. **Crefeld 2** 1922-1941
Flensburger S.B.Ges.#360   1922   9573   150.87x18.51
Triple Expansion   4400   12.5
Middle-350, III-364 in cabins, 370 in Dormitory Deck 164 (1926-192)

Launched 23/12/1921. 6/1922 MV to South America. 6/1928 re-opened (from 1914) Canada Route with lifting of prohibition on German immigration, now II-35, III-212. 1934 rebuilt by Seebeck Werft as freighter, 8045 Ts., 57 crew. 26/8/1939 at Massawa. 4/4/1944 scuttled but failed to block entry into harbor. 4/6/1943 raised to clear harbor.

287. **T.S. Porta 2** 1922-1946
Vulcan A.G., Stettin #649   1922   4162   115.13x15.50
Turbine   1660   10.5
12, certificate for 18   42

Launched 1/12/1921. Evidently still during construction the 1800 triple expansion engine was replaced by the 1660 HP turbine, NDL's first such freighter. 4/1922 MV to Brazil. 1939-1940 rebuilt at Danziger Werft, cruiser bow & stern, 124.20 meters, 4200 HP turbines, 14.5 knots, 4417 Ts., intended for South Africa-South America route, work completed during war. 2/8/1946 assigned to

Porta 287 was the Lloyd's first turbine-powered ship. One of four rebuilt in the 1930s for higher speeds. In 1955, it again was under the Lloyd flag as Trierstein.

Holland at Bremerhaven, ren. *Walcheren* by N.V. Reederei "Amsterdam", 4401 Ts., but LU sans so being used. 2/1950 sold to F. & A. Vinnen & Co., Bremen, overhauled by NDL's Technical Service, Bremerhaven, engines retuned to 2850 HP to save fuel, 13 knts. 5/1950 ren. *Adolf Vinnen*, 8 passengers, 12/4/1955 bought for NDL's Roland Linie service, ren. *Trierstein*. Late 1960 LU. 2/6/1961 to Teh Hu S.S. Co., Hong Kong, Panama principal. 9/1961 ren. *Amonea*, Cia. de Nav. Victoria Neptuno S.A., Panama. 28/1/1964 arr. Hong Kong for BU by Peninsula Shipbreaking Co., work began 29/4/1964.

288. **Nienburg 2**	1922-1946		
Vulcan A.G., Stettin #651	1922	4154	115.18x15.50
Triple Expansion	1800	10	
13, certificate for 18	50 (1937-37)		

Nienburg *288 as built.*
Robert Potts Collection.

Nienburg *288, sister of* Porta, *as rebuilt in 1963 and named* Giuseppe, *registered in Buenos Aires.* William Schell Collection.

Launched 25/3/1922. MV 6/1922 to Brazil, Captain Adolf Winter. 11/1934 to Hamburg-Bremer Afrika-Linie, mgd. by Woermann Line, Hamburg but with Bremen key on stack. 1938 rebuilt by Deutsche Werft, Hamburg, cruiser bow & stern, 123.50 meters, 4200 HP turbines. 14.5 knots, 4318 tons for South Africa-South America route. 1939 Chinese crew mutinied off Buenos Aires with wheat cargo for South Africa. 8/9/1939 arr. at Buenos Aires, LU. 10/19/1940 "sold" to Lloyd Argentino, a paper concern. In service as *Belgrano*. 1943 to Flota Mercante del Estado, ren. *Rio Juramento*. 18/3/1961 arr. Buenos Aires from Antwerp with engine damage, LU. 1962 to Empresas Lineas Maritimas Argentinas, S.A. 1963 to Finmare, S.A., ren. *Giuseppe*. 1965 BU at Buenos Aires.

289. **Sierra Nevada 2**	1922-1932		
Vulcan A.G., Stettin #666	1922	8741	133.50x17.25
2x Triple Expansion	4400	13.5	* *
I-112 II-82 III-1115	250-210		

Launched 2/5/1922, intended first of three sisters, others cancelled. MV.16/9/1922 to New York. 7/1925 reformed as Middle Class vessel, Cabin-221, III-416 in dormitories ren. *Madrid*. Later reconfigured to C-249, III-274 in cabins, 301-Dormitories. 1934 chartered, 16/5/1935 sold to Hamburg-Süd, remained reg. in Bremen. 9/1939 at Las Palmas. 30/11/1940 ordered home. Steel hawser found wrapped around one screw (Dinklage). Second blind stack removed. 11/12/1940 left Las Palmas, 28th arr. at Penhoet. 15/2/1941 auxiliary/dormitory ship for submarine crews. 9/12/1941 sunk by air attack off Den Helder, 12 dead.

Sierra Nevada *being launched on 2 May, 1922 at the Vulcan Yard in Stettin.*

Sierra Nevada *was built for the South America passenger trade, a grade higher than* Köln *and* Crefeld. *The second stack is blind, intended to make the ship seem larger.*

Weser *was the first of six sisters built for the Far East service, second most important route for the Lloyd. The ships were too slow and had sponsons for stability. They were sold off when a buyer could be found in the 1930s. Nautical Photo Agency.*

290. *Weser 3*	1922-1932		
A.G. "Weser", Bremen #323	1922	9444	146.00x17.56
2x Triple Expansion	4200	12.5	* *
I-74, II-90 1	42		

Launched 7/6/1922. Delivery 28/10/1922. MV. to South America. 8/10/1931 LU in Bremen. 2/1933 sold to A.G. "Weser" for BU.

291. *Eisenach 2*	1922-1935		
Vulcan A.G., Stettin #562	1922	4177	115.13x15.50
Triple Expansion	1800	10.5	
12	49		

Launched 20/7/1922. MV.10/1922 to South America. 1935 badly damaged in collision with *HMS Ramillies*. Forward crew quarters were crushed, several men killed. This led to pressure to relocate

Eisenach #291 during her trials and delivery in October, 1922. At left, 2.Officer Edmund von Reeken. Director Max Walter, head of Technical activities at the Lloyd. The lady probably represents the city of Eisenach. The ship's captain has his hands on Captain Drechsel's shoulders.

Eisenach *291 (where Martin Luther was imprisoned at the Wartburg), a standard-design freighter whose hull dimensions were matched by NDL's first post World War II vessels. A delegation from the city attended the launch and trial trip.*

freighter crew quarters to aft; such work was done on subsequent overhauls. Sold to Soc. Commerciale Bulgare de Nav., Varna, repaired, ren. *Rodina*. 19/9/1941 mined and sank 25 miles from Burgas.

Turpin Ex-*Freiburg* #152 was repurchased and put into service in 1922. *Prinzess Irene* #99 was repurchased in July, 1922, towed from Gibraltar to Bremerhaven, was rebuilt, returned to service as *Bremen 3* on 7/4/1923.

The *Ship of Fools* by Katherine Anne Porter, 1945, Little, Brown & Co., New York, describes a voyage of the *S.S. Vera* from 22.8. to 17.9. 1931 from Vera Cruz via Havana, Santa Cruz, Vigo, Gijon, Boulogne and Southampton to Bremerhaven. The ship, route and some of the happenings are based on *Werra*. The story tells "They had come from South America the long way and were en-route to Bremerhaven. There were worrying reports of hurricanes. It was advised in Vera Cruz that *Vera* would sail with several days delay because it sat fast on a sandbank at Tampico as a result of a hurricane." This incident actually occurred in 1931. Captain Drechsel, NDL Inspector in Hoboken, flew to Tampico to free the vessel. As he reached the port, *Werra* had just got loose and was still in sight heading for Vera Cruz, Havana and home.

Vera was a combi Passenger-Freight vessel, "very steady and broad-bottomed in her style, (it had sponsons as did the entire class) walloping from one remote port to another, year in year out, reliable and homely as a German housewife."

Arrived in Havana on the third day; late evening again out to sea. In Gijon, *Vera* anchored in the harbor, stopped off Boulogne to unship passengers; students there jumped into the tender. "In Southampton, no tender came out, only a cutter with fiscal-control officers. Nobody left the ship." Later, a film was made from the book, with Oskar Werner, Simone Signoret and Mel Ferrer. A painting of the ship for the harbor scene was made by Whitlock.

Whitlock painted a Las Palmas, Canaries port scene with Vera, *shown as two stacked. The ship carried the Bremen-La Plata Seapost with Registry service, a cover from 12.5.1928.*

ERNESTO TRAULSEN

Agencia Comecial y Maritima Tampico, Tamps.
Meyren, Eversbusch y Cia. Apartado 42

Ernesto Traulsen, the NDL Agent in Tampico.

Werra 292. *Second of six sisters for the Far East. They also in season ran to North, Central and South America.* Werra *was the model for* Vera *in "The Ship of Fools" by Katherine Anne Porter, a 1931 voyage from Tampico via islands and wayports to Bremerhaven. The opening of the story with the ship stuck in Tampico by a hurricane actually happened. Inspector Drechsel flew from New York to Brownsville, crossed the border (where the author also crossed in February, 1945 en route to the Chapultepec Conference in Mexico City) on 16 August, 1931. Just as he reached the port,* Werra *was leaving, having just been freed. Made into a film later.*

```
292. Werra 2              1923-1935
A.G. "Weser", Bremen #324   1923    9476    146.00x17.58
2x Triple Expansion         4200    12.5          * *
I-74 II-90                  145
```

Launched 21/9/1922. 24/1/1923 MV to East Asia, then ran to LaPlata, 1933 Bremen-Havana-Galveston. 12/8/1935 sold to "Italia" SpA, Genoa for Genoa-South America service. ren. *Calabria*, 9515 Ts. 1936 to Lloyd Triestino. 10/6/1940 seized in Calcutta, British Flag, British India S.N.Co., managers. 8/12/1940 sunk by U-103, 380 miles W. of Glaway in 4 52.43N, 18.07W. en route Freetown-Glasgow.

Norddeutscher Lloyd
BREMEN

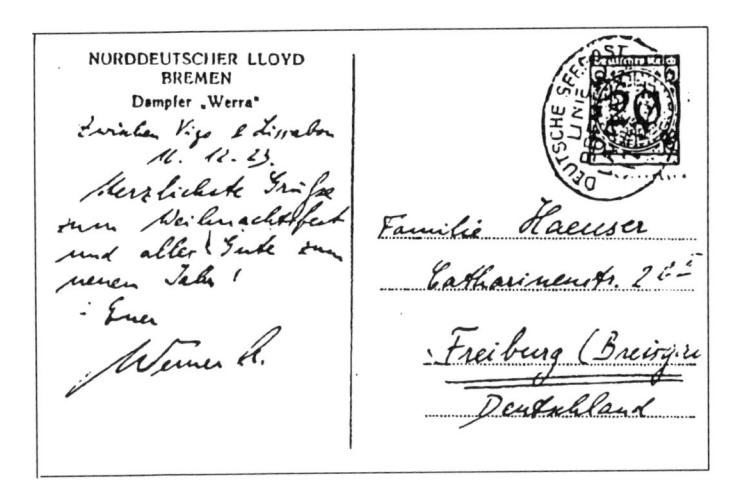

293. *München 3*	1923-1945		
Vulcan A.G., Stettin #669	1923	13325	166.58x19.81
2x Triple Expansion	8500	15	* *
I-170 II-350 III-558-602	356 (263.2.1930)		

Keel laid 1920. Launched 25/11/1922. MV. 21/6/1923 to Hoboken, coal-fired. Winter 1925-1926 reformed to: Cabin-494, T-266, III-251. Summer 1925 with *Lützow* resumed cruising. 11/2/1930 extensively burned through explosions and fire in New York. Partly repaired in Newport News, rebuilt by Deschimag, Bremen to oil firing, exhaust turbines, Promenade Deck glassed in, extended aft, 10,560 HP, 16.3 knots, 14690 Ts., now: Cabin-214, Tourist-358, III-221. FV.20.1.1931 as *General Von Steuben*. From 1935 did only Strength through Joy cruises. Painted white. See #434*: 496 one-

München on her delivery voyage from Stettin around Denmark to Bremerhaven passed the scene of the Battle of Jutland, Battle of the Skagerrak in German. The Lloyd's President Philipp Heineken gave an address. Here the wreath in memory of those fallen on both sides is dropped into the sea, 6 June, 1923.

München *leaving Bremerhaven on 10 January, 1928, with ice floes in the Weser.* Herbert Gastmeyer Photo.

class. 1936 further modified by Deschimag, forward king posts removed, given tiled pool. 1938 ren. *Steuben*. 3/6/1940 dormitory ship in Danzig. 8/1944 hospital evacuation transport in the Baltic for wounded and refugees from the East. 22/12/1944 staff ship for Commodore, Submarines, Baltic, painted gray and armed. 9-10/2/1945 sunk by Soviet submarine S-13 off Stolpmünde, in 54.41N, 16.51E. Some 2700 dead out of the nearly 4000 on board.

294. *Sierra Ventana 2*	1923-1935		
Bremer Vulkan, Vegesack #610	1923	11,392	155.70x18.83
2x Triple Expansion	6200	14	* *
I-222, II-179, III-712	275-300		

Launched 16/5/1923. MV. 8/9/1923 to Hoboken, then to South America, also to Cuba-Mexico in early 1930s in NDL's new "Ozean Linie". 13/8/1935 to "Italia" for its Genoa-South America service, then 1936 transport in Ethiopian campaign. 1937 to Lloyd Triestino, the old Lloyd Austriaco during Austrian ownership of Trieste. 29/12/1940 torpedoed by Greek submarine *Proteus* of Saseno Island, Albania in 40.31N, 19.02E. Sunk in turn by Italian torpedo boat *Antares*.

On 20/9/1923 *Derfflinger* #242 repurchased by NDL, re-entered service, sailing to Hoboken.

Morton Allan's arrival directory shows 1923 *Porta* and *Eisenach* in Bremen-Baltimore service, and *Werra* arriving Galveston, via Havana, on 17 October, *Hannover* on 15 December, and *Canopic* (White Star!) arriving New York from Bremen on 18 November and 22 December. It is an example of how British lines entered the trade with Germany starting in 1920-1921 when Lloyd and Hapag had no ships. The British lines gradually relinquished German services.

Sierra Ventana was the first of three sisters built for upgrading NDL's South America service. The ships also made occasional voyages to the U.S., and in the 1930s to Cuba and Mexico. Sold off to Italy, it was lost in the Mediterranean in the war. The log is from an October, 1923 voyage to New York, 13.59 knots average. The sisters were intended for 14.5 knots service speed. Originally the promenade decks forward were not glassed in.

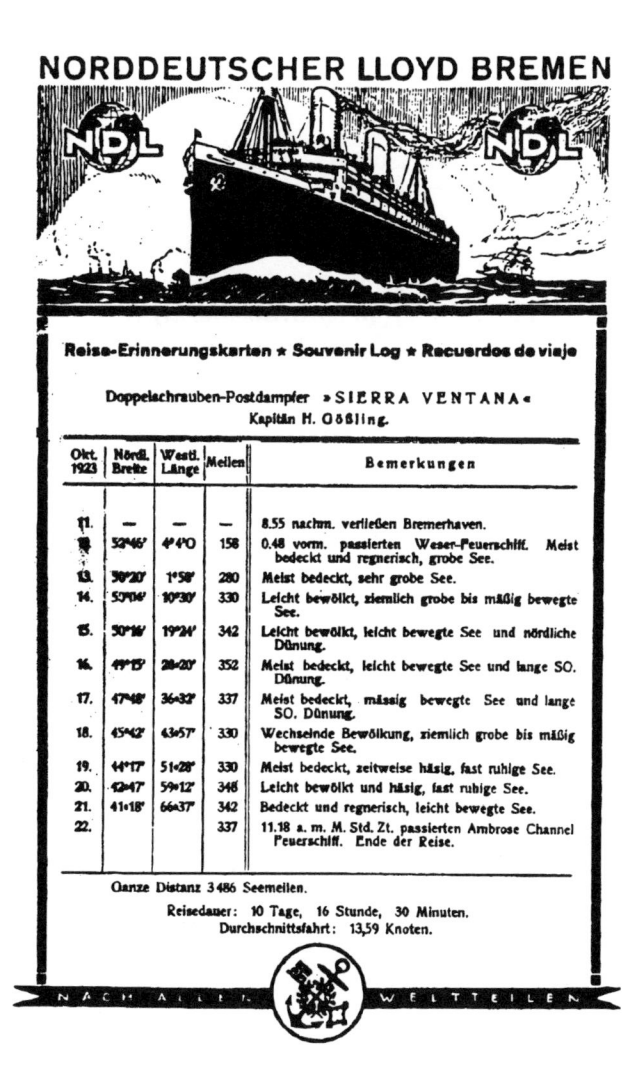

A slow voyage log en route to New York by Sierra Ventana *in 1923. The ships were built to average 14.5 knots, but rarely managed this.*

NORDDEUTSCHER LLOYD BREMEN

Reise-Erinnerungskarten ★ Souvenir Log ★ Recuerdos de viaje

Doppelschrauben-Postdampfer »SIERRA VENTANA«
Kapitän H. Ößling.

Okt. 1923	Nördl. Breite	Westl. Länge	Meilen	Bemerkungen
11.	—	—	—	8.55 nachm. verließen Bremerhaven.
12.	52°46′	4°4′O	158	0.48 vorm. passierten Weser-Feuerschiff. Meist bedeckt und regnerisch, grobe See.
13.	50°20′	1°58′	280	Meist bedeckt, sehr grobe See.
14.	53°04′	10°30′	330	Leicht bewölkt, ziemlich grobe bis mäßig bewegte See.
15.	50°19′	19°24′	342	Leicht bewölkt, leicht bewegte See und nördliche Dünung.
16.	49°15′	28°20′	352	Meist bedeckt, leicht bewegte See und lange SO. Dünung.
17.	47°48′	36°32′	337	Meist bedeckt, mässig bewegte See und lange SO. Dünung.
18.	45°42′	43°57′	330	Wechselnde Bewölkung, ziemlich grobe bis mäßig bewegte See.
19.	44°17′	51°28′	330	Meist bedeckt, zeitweise häsig, fast ruhige See.
20.	42°47′	59°12′	348	Leicht bewölkt und häsig, fast ruhige See.
21.	41°18′	66°37′	342	Bedeckt und regnerisch, leicht bewegte See.
22.			337	11.18 a. m. M. Std. Zt. passierten Ambrose Channel Feuerschiff. Ende der Reise.

Ganze Distanz 3486 Seemeilen.
Reisedauer: 10 Tage, 16 Stunden, 30 Minuten.
Durchschnittsfahrt: 13,59 Knoten.

NACH ALLEN WELTTEILEN

295. *Aachen 2*	1923-1940		
J.C. Tecklenborg,			
Geestemünde #312	1923	6274	137.44x17.21
Triple Expansion	3200	12	
12	53-59		

Launched 20/3/1923. MV. 5/1923 to East Asia. 1938 engine upgraded to 4000 HP with Bauer-Wach exhaust turbine, new bow, 140.14m.B.P., 6388 Ts., 14kns. 20/8/1939 left Progreso for Bremen. 11/9. arr. Tromsö, took from *Wiegand* #381 250 tons coal. 29/9. arr. Holtenau, Kiel Canal, with cotton, copper, woods and piece goods. 14/4/1940 sunk in Narvik Fjord by British destroyers during the invasion of Norway. 10/1951 refloated by Norsk Bergningskompagni, assigned to Holmen & Vaboe, Kritiansand for rebuilding and renaming to *Oakhill*. 30/11/1951 under tow from Narvik to Bergen struck rocks near Bessaker, broke in two. 1/12/1951 sold for BU "as lies."

295 Aachen and sister Elberfeld were intended for the Australia service, important to the Lloyd pre-War as a subsidized Imperial Mail Route (Volume I), operated with passenger liners. These two, typical freighters, could take up to twelve passengers. More required a doctor. In 1924, the author and his family's voyage to Australia on Elberfeld, stokers were hired in Antwerp, "ruffians" in the notes I have. Sometimes in the heat they fainted, were brought onto deck, force-fed coffee and as soon as they were able to stand, went back to work. They did not get much to eat. My Mother's purse with an ivory chain, money and keys was stolen one day, the purse later found on deck with the keys still inside. Captain Bolte did not dare come near these Black Gang men. He had a Doberman Pinscher for protection.
Nautical Photo Agency.

296 **M.S. *Erfurt 2***	1923-1944		
Vulcan A.G., Stettin #653	1923	4201	115.13 x 15.56
MAN Diesel	1800	10.5	
12, certificate for 18	36		

Launched 3/1923. Last of 9 "Roland" class ships for Roland, NDL and Kosmos. The 10th was cancelled. Five were rebuilt. Reg. 6/1923. First NDL motor ship, no stack, only a smoke vent. MV to Brazil 27/11/1926 en route San Francisco-Bremen, after passing Panama Canal had a major fire in No.3 Tweendeck, ret. 17/12 to Colon for temporary repairs. 1939-40 rebuilt at Danziger Werft (International S.B.Co.) to 4200 HP, 14 kns, 124.20m, cruiser stern, 4325 Ts., intended for South Africa-South America service. 30/3/1944 off Fehmarn Island hit mine, sank. Her old Diesel from the rebuild in 1939, along with a new M.A.N., put into *Tannstein* #498.

296 Erfurt *was the Lloyd's first motor ship, as sister* Porta *was the first turbine-powered vessel: Attempts to operate exact sister ships with different engines as a guide for future construction. The silhouette is from Armin Wulle's "Stettiner Vulcan," Koehler, 1989 shows the early habit of no smokestacks for Diesel-powered vessels.*

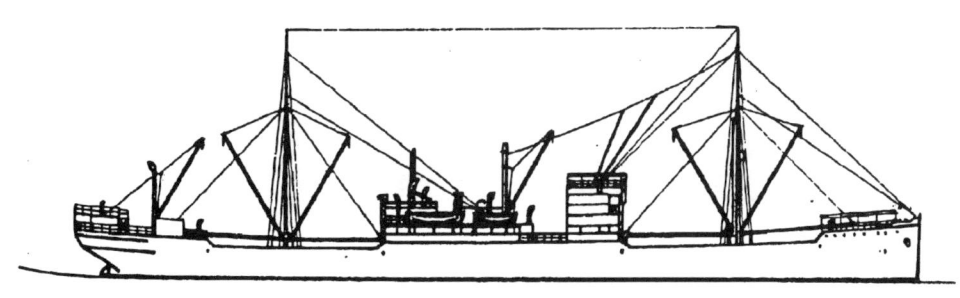

297. *Ludwigshafen*   1923-1925
Krupp Germaniawerft, Kiel #415 1923   5918   119.94x16.55
Triple Expansion, oil firing   11
12   59

Launched 13/4/1923. MV. 5/1923 to East Asia. With *Königsberg* #305 and *Ilmar* #360, the only Lloyd ships with goalpost masts. 11/1930 off Panama the nitrate cargo burned. Crew abandoned ship, returned and put out the fire. 1934 chartered, 1935 sold to Hamburg-Süd in reorganization of services still reg. in Bremen. 1936 stranded off French coast, was pulled off. 3/12/1937 ren. *Tijuca*. 4/8/1940 Transporter H(avre) 43, intended for Operation Seelöwe, the invasion of Britain. 6/3/1945 mined off Anholt, towed to Aarhus, burned out. 5/1945 seized there as prize by Britain. 16/1/1946 assigned to Denmark. 1947-1948 rebuilt at Kiel, ren. *Marie Skou*, Ove Skou, Copenhagan. 1/1956 VIVA II, Viva Cia. Maritima, Panama. 7/1959 sold to Rotterdam, resold to East Germany, arr. 7/1959 at Rostock for BU. 8/1960 towed to Hamburg for scrapping by Eisen & Metall Ges.

297. Ludwigshafen *with* Königsberg *were the only Lloyd ships built with goal post masts.* Ilmar *#360 also had them, but was bought from Holland.* Ophelia, *acquired with the "von 1896" Rhederei, had two sets of goal post king posts.*

298. Elberfeld *in 1926 was the first NDL vessel to be given an exhaust turbine, using spent but lower temperature steam than the reciprocating engine could use. This upped speed by one-half knot and saved fuel.*

298. *Elberfeld* J.C.Tecklenborg,	1923-1927		
Geestemünde #313	1923	6272	137.44x17.21
Triple Expansion	3200	12	
12	60		

Launched 3/6/1923. MV to East Asia. 3/3/1924 left for Australia under Captain Gerhart Bolte who, in retirement reached age 100. The author, Mother and sister made that voyage, arrived in Adelaide on 26 April, Gallipoli Day. 1926 by Technical Service given Bauer-Wach exhaust turbine, 4000 HP, 12.75 kns. 21/11/1927 stranded at Bajo Aceitero, between Cape Trafalgar and Zahana en route Continent-Vladivostock, allegedly because a light was moved sans "Notice to Mariners."

299 Saarbrücken *"Our Steamer and my cabin while leaving Hoek van Holland for the open sea."* The card was mailed on board with the East Asiatic Line Sea Post in 9.1926.

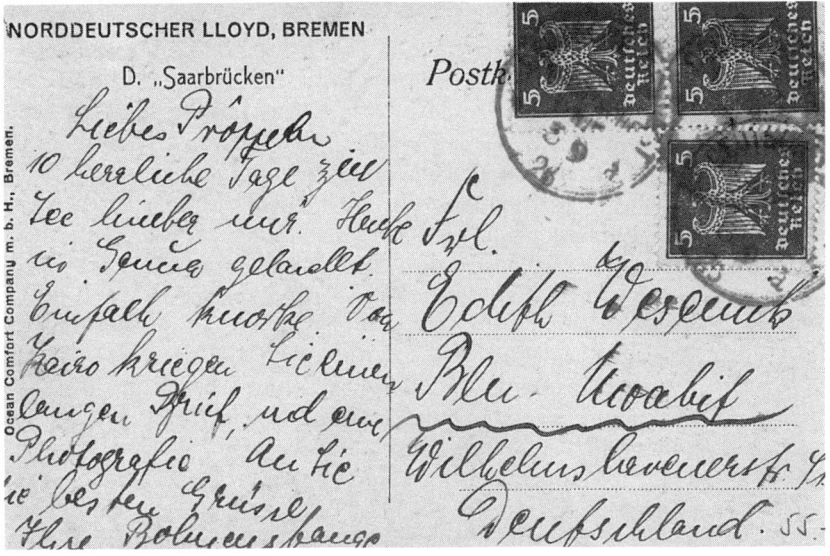

299 Saarbrücken, *built for the Far East run was sold to Italy in 1935 when the three express steamers entered service. Here as* Toscana *with double boat mountings compared with the single ones when built, and a bigger smokestack. The sponsons gave stability.*

299. *Saarbrücken* 1923-1935
A.G. "Weser", Bremen #325   1923   9429   145.97x17.57
2x Triple Expansion   4200   12.5   * *
I-98, II-142   176

Launched 28/6/1923. MV. 10/11/1923 to East Asia. 8/1935 to "Italia," SpA, Genoa, ren. *Toscana*. 1936 to Lloyd Triestino, 9584 tons. 1940-1945 hospital ship. 1943 in Allied service with Italy's switch of sides in the war. 1945 to Lloyd Triestino, emigrant ship to Australia. 12/1960 LU at Trieste. 21/2/1962 arr. Genoa for BU by ARDEM SpA. Work began 3/1962, BU completed at Vado Ligure.

300. *Columbus 2*   1923-1939
F. Schichau, Danzig #929   1923   32,364   236.20 x 25.30
2x Triple Expansion   28 000   19   * *
I-478 II-644 III-602

Ordered 1913 sans name. By start of war in 8/1914 only double bottom completed. During the war assigned name *Hindenburg*. 17/6/1922 launch attempted, stuck on ways. 12/8/1922 launch as *Columbus* successful. 22/11/1923 completed, last major vessel with piston engines. Interior furnishings installed by NDL's Technical Service in Bremerhaven. LU as Immigration Quota for Germany used up. A 1 July, 1923 schedule had shown the M.V. for 11/10/1923, then 12 December, 23 January, 1924 and 23 February listed as "at Bremerhaven." MV. 22/4/1924. On board were: President Philipp Heineken, Retiring Technical Director Max Walter, Passenger Director Adolf Stadtländer, Captain Paul König, chief of the Nautical Division (D.O.R.-I) Evening 30 April lay "off Pier 4, Brooklyn." 1 May passengers landed. 22/2/1927 first cruise for Raymond & Whitcomb. to the West Indies. 2/8/1927 ship hit a submerged object; one shaft and engine broke up. Returned home sans passengers but with freight. 10/1927 engine from *Schwaben* #386 built in as temporary replacement, 5500HP, now 17.knots. 3-4/1928 configuration changed, replacing II and II classes with Tourist-228, III-500. 4.1932 again changed for greater interchange ability of First and Tourist for cruises, always "One Class." 1929 rebuilt at Blohm & Voss, Hamburg with turbines, three new boilers, new smokestacks, to resemble *Bremen* and *Europa* now 15 vs 17 lifeboats per side, alleged 23 knots top speed, operated at maximum 21.5kns, 49 000 HP. 6/12/1929 trials, now I-349 II-649 III-679, 32,581 tons. Average speeds on North Atlantic: 1934- 21.1kns, 1935-20. 49kns, 1936-20.77kns. 11-12/1937 Lido Deck with pool installed at Atlantic Basin Iron Works, Brooklyn. 19/8/1939 left New York with 725 passengers on West Indies cruise. They were landed in Havana with war threat; ship took refuge below Vera Cruz. *Hameln* #372 brought oil and water (See "War"). 14/12/1939 under orders from Berlin left to get home, around Florida into the Atlantic, followed by U.S. naval vessels. 19th caught by *HMS Hyperion* 320 miles off Cape Hatteras. Ship set afire and scuttled. 576 crew taken to New York by *USS Tuscaloosa*, housed on Ellis Island immigration station. 14/1/1940 in two special trains 512 men sent to California, 4.30 AM 18th arr. Oakland, taken to Angel Island, former Quarantine Station in San Francisco Bay. With U.S. entry into the war in 12/1942, to POW camps in New Mexico.

Columbus *as originally built, with tall thin stacks, and well deck forward. This as seen in July, 1927 from* Stuttgart *#303.*

"THE WORLD'S LARGEST WORKING MODEL OF AN OCEAN LINER VISITS THIS PORT"
20 December, 1929. This 12-meter working model of Columbus *was built at Engineer Max Bartsch's Ship Model school in Dresden. In 1929 it was brought to New York on* Bremen *and voyaged around the harbor as promotion for the rebuilt* Columbus, *now faster and with stacks like* Bremen *and* Europa's. *The author and his friend Gustav Uhlig spent some hours on board during the cruise on the Hudson River and Upper Bay.*

The Columbus *model against the New York skyline at W. 42nd Street Ferry, and the Hudson River Day Line steamers at right. December, 1929.*

Greetings from the model's builder, Max Bartsch: "In remembrance of our submarine days, which gave me the idea ... I greet you, my Dear Comrade Drechsel." Your devoted.

The Lido Deck with Dance Floor and Pool built onto Columbus *in late 1937 where the skylights and King Posts were on the Boat Deck. Where would the orchestra have been placed? Surprisingly, the double-mounting of several lifeboats was never changed. Note Boat 17 and 18. This would indicate twenty boats total. But photos show more. The ship behind is the French Line's* Champlain.

During all of its fifteen years of service for NDL Columbus *carried Sea and Ship Posts, trans-Atlantic the oval and double-ring* **Deutsch-Amerikanische Seepost** *and the* **U.S.-German Sea Post**, *these staffed by German and U.S. postal personnel. A Spain cruise still had the Sea Post; later cruises were labelled Ship Posts, instigated by the Lloyd itself as a service to passengers and crews, and as promotion. Its last cruises in 1939, were around Africa and to the West Indies. While in the West Indies in late August, 1939 war threatened and the passengers were landed in Havana; the ship took refuge in, then near Vera Cruz. Trying to get home from there in December it was caught up by* HMS Hyperion *and scuttled. See "Countdown to War...."*

Columbus *did not have the Sea Post printed Registry label, as did* Bremen *and* Europa. *This one was hand-provided on board. Below:* Columbus.

301.*Coblenz 2*	1924-1935		
A. G. "Weser", Bremen #326	1924	9449	145.97x17.57
2 Turbines	3900 (4600?) 12.5		* *
I-98	II-138 169		

Launched 17/8/1923. MV. 2/2/1924 to East Asia. 8/1935 to Italian Government, mngd. by "Italia," Genoa, ren. *Sicilia*. 1936 to Lloyd Triestino after Ethiopian war service. 11/2/1941 Hospital Ship. 5/4/1943 sunk in Naples Harbor by British air attack. Postwar raised and BU.

Coblenz *in Hong Kong with sampans alongside with or for cargo. The ship was given turbines to compare with four of her sisters fitted with reciprocating engines and* Fulda *with Diesel drive.*

Sierra Cordoba, one of three South America line Sierras, in the 1930s painted white for cruising. Repeat passengers called her Sierra Reimers *after her well-liked Captain.*

302. **Sierra Cordoba 2**	1924-1936		
Bremer Vulkan, Vegesack #611	1924	11,492	155.70x18.84
2x Triple Expansion	6200	14	* *
I-160 III-1143, later Cabin-522, Dormitories-414			235 - 298

Launched 26/9/1923. MV. 26/1/1924 to La Plata ports. From 7/1927 also did cruising. 6/1928 configuration Cabin-220, Tourist-179, III-710. 1932 did some North Atlantic voyages. 1935 sold to Deutsche Arbeitsfront for Strength through Joy cruising, managed by NDL, 1000 One Class. 29/3/1940 Kriegsmarine dormitory ship at Kiel. From 5/1945 housed British forces at Hamburg. 13/1/1946 burned out. 18/1/1948 under tow to Britain for BU, line broke, drifted for days until stranding off Fanö island near Esbjerg. Crew rescued by Fishcutter *Astrid* of Blankenese. 1957 blown up, sections salvaged, and BU by Eisen & Metall Ges., Hamburg, rest sank in 55.50N, 7.30E. 1930-1931 made Polar, North Cape cruises. 1932 was hotel ship for Eucharistic Congress at Dublin. 1939 carried 1200 Baltic Germans from Riga to Germany in exchange of population.

303. **Stuttgart 2**	1924-1938		
Vulcan A.G., Stettin #670	1924	13,367	166.80x19.80
2x Triple Expansion, oil fired.	8500	15.5	* *
I-171 II-338 III-594			

Keel laid 1921. Launched 31/7/1923. Trial-delivery trip 4/1/1924. Captain G. Grahn had only arrived on 17 December at Stettin. The crew left Bremen on the 28th. Many were transfers from sister *München*. MV. 15/1/1924 to Hoboken. 1928 - Cabin-297, Tourist-324, III-395. 1933-1934 served as unemployed seamen's training ship in Bremerhaven. Into 1937 made some Far East voyages. 1938 reconfigured for Strength through Joy, single-class, worker cruising, 990 berths, managed by NDL. In war was hospital ship. 9/10/1943 set afire by air attack at Gdynia, burned out. Wreck towed out and sunk in Danzig Bay with uncounted dead.

Stuttgart *almost ready to sail, 1920s. People are leaving on the forward gangway, the last one up. Third Class passengers topside aft; a few crew members below them.* Frank Pichardo Collection.

How a different paint scheme can ruin the looks of a ship. Stuttgart *in the late 1930s as a Strength through Joy cruise ship in Hamburg.* Von Seggern photo.

Lützow #241, repurchased, FV 14/6/1924 to Hoboken
Anhalt 1 #262, 1914-1919, repurchased, served NDL 1924-1932
Dessau 2, #265, 1915-1919, repurchased, served 1924-1935.

---

304. Trier *in Genoa, laid up between Far East voyages? Her open Promenade Deck is canvassed in. Later she ran to Canada. An August 25, 1930 postcard says: "This boat is very pretty, steadfast against waves and winds (the sponsons help), the trip from Montreal, along the coast of Canada, Newfoundland and Labrador was very interesting, and icebergs...."*

304. **Trier 2**	1924-1936		
A.G. "Weser", Bremen #327	1924	9415	145.97x17.57
2x Triple Expansion	4200	12.5	**
I-98 III-138	183		

Launched 11/1923. Delivery 12/7/1924. MV. 3/1/1925 to East Asia. 1930 ran Bremen-Canada. 1936 ran onto Spanish coast in fog, sold off as unsuitable for further service. 7/1936 bought by Turkey (from underwriters?), rebuilt as Submarine Depot Ship *Erkin*. 1956 sold to M.K.E. Seyman for BU in Turkey.

305. Motor Ship Königsberg, *the third such for NDL trying out different forms of power; the Lloyd was both hyper-cautious and in advance of technology, at different times.*

305. **M.S. Königsberg**   1924-1940
A.G. "Weser," Bremen #333   1924   6465   137.25x17.15
2x M.A.N. Diesels   3200   12   * *
7   41-44

Ordered as *Bonn*. Launched 13/6/1924 as *Königsberg*, with streamlined Flettner rudder, eliminating the normal rudder machine. 7/1924 del. although builder lists as 11/1924. M.V. to Australia. 28/8/1939 left Quebec, 13/9 arr. Belem unable to get through the blockade to Germany. Left Belem 28/5/1940 to get home with copper, rubber after 600 tons of oil transloaded to raider *Widder* on 6/6/1940. 16/6/1940 scuttled ca.100 miles off Vigo when a French auxiliary cruiser came up, in 41.16N, 10.37W.

306. Sierra Morena, third of the South America sisters. Here in 1929 at the Blohm & Voss Shipyard in Hamburg, where Columbus, right, #300 *is being rebuilt. At left in floating dock the Hamburg-South American Line's* Cap Polonio.

306. **Sierra Morena**   1924-1935
Bremer Vulkan, Vegesack #612 1924   11 430   155.70x18.84
2x Triple Expansion   6200   14   * *
I-150 II-270 III-890   210-298

Launched 3/6/1924. MV. 25/10/1924 to La Plata. 1931 in Cuba-Mexico service. 1932 LU. 1934 chartd. to Deutsche Arbeitsfront, 20/7/1934 ren. *Der Deutsche* for Strength through Joy cruising; 1935 sold to D.A.F., managed by NDL, now 875 one-class. 1940 transport, then accommodation ship at Gdynia. 7/1944 troop transport. 3/5/1945 damaged in air attack off Fehmarn Island, beached, later towed to Kiel, used for University housing. 18/3/1946 assigned to USSR, 1947 towed to and rebuilt by Warnowwerft, Warnemünde for Pacific Coast service, ren. *Asia*. 9/6/1950 del. to Sovtorgflot Vladivostock. 1963 BU there.

307. M.S. Fulda in Hong Kong in May, 1939 after her conversion to freighter. Directly behind her NDL's Marburg #411 and another Lloyd freighter. Don E. Gammon Photo.

307. **M.S. Fulda**	1924-1940		
A.G. "Weser," Bremen #328	1924	9492	145.97x19.05
2x Sulzer Diesels	4200	12.5	* *
I-89 III-159	152		

Launched 8/1924. MV. 14/12/1924 to East Asia. 7/1927 at Shanghai Chinese revolutionaries tried to seize *Fulda, Münsterland* (Hapag), *Bertram* and *Deike Rickmers*; they were released after a week. 1935 convt. to freighter, 24 passengers, 7744 Ts., her sisters sold off when the new *Scharnhorst* #438, *Gneisenau* #440 and *Potsdam* #439 came into service. 7/1937 briefly seized by Chinese while resisting the Japanese invasion at Shanghai. 9/1939 took refuge in Dairen with *Augsburg* #399 and *Bremerhaven* #280. 28/9/1940 "sold" to Japan, ren. *Teikoko* (later *Teikei* or *Teikai*) *Maru* for Teikoku Sempaku K.K., Tokyo. 30/12/1944 sunk SW of Cape Bolinao, Luzon in 17.18N, 119.25E by U.S. air attack.

307. President Paul von Hindenburg in October, 1926 visiting the Motor Ship Fulda in Bremen with Bürgermeister Dr. Donandt. Photo Staatsarchiv Bremen.

308. Berlin *at Pier 42, North River, Manhattan in the 1920s. She was called "The Little Columbus." After the war, the Soviets got the ship, renamed it* Admiral Nakhimov, *serving in the Black Sea. The ship in 1962-1963 shuttled Soviet military into and out of Cuba. In 1986, it collided with a freighter at night. Hundreds were lost. For the Lloyd,* Berlin *carried the U.S.-German Sea Post with U.S. and German postal clerks, two styles of Deutsch-Amerikanische Seepost, also with postal clerks, and Linie New York Seepost, only German personnel and a West Indies cruise Ship Post handled by the Purser's office. In Soviet ownership,* Admiral Nakhimov *had two different Ship Posts 1960s-1980s.*

308. **Berlin 3**	1925-1945		
Bremer Vulkan, Bremen #614	1925	15 286	174.30 x 20.98
2x Triple Expansion	12 000	16.5	* *
I-301 II-284 III-515, 1487 if Tweendeck used.			326-363

Launched 24/3/1925. MV. 26/9/1925 to Hoboken. Called the "Small Columbus." Given the same superheated engines as *Stuttgart* #303 and turbo-centrifuged boiler fueling. This gave 3500 more HP, presumably one knot more speed to the 1900 tons larger ship. But *Berlin* never averaged over the years even 16 knots in North Atlantic service. 11/1928 rescued 23 from the sunken *Vestris*. Fall 1929 Cabin-403, Tourist-287, III-357. 1932 to Cabin-257, Tourist-261, III-361. 13/9/1938 last dep. from New York. 17/10/1938 LU. 19/12/1938 voyage to Australia to carry emigrant Jews. 5/1939 made two Kraft durch Freude cruises. LU. 17/7/1939 under Kriegsmarine charter dmgd. off Swinemünde by boiler explosion, 17 dead, repaired by Blohm & Voss, Hamburg. 23/8/1939 became Hospital Ship "A". 12/11/1939 LU. at Danzig. 14/4/1940 at Copenhagen during invasion of Denmark and Norway. 1944 dormitory ship in Gdynia. 31/1/1945 mined off Swinemünde. During towing off again hit a mine, sank, one dead. 27/2/1946 assigned to USSR. 1948 refloated, towed to and rebuilt by Warnow Werft, Rostock. King posts before bridge removed. 17 053 Ts., 870 passengers. 2/5/1947 del., ren. *Admiral Nakhimov* for Black Sea Shipping Co. During the Soviet buildup in Cuba and the withdrawals after the missile crisis, *Admiral Nakhimov* was the largest ship ferrying personnel. On 31/8/1986 it sank in 15 minutes after late-evening sailing from Novorossiysk in collision with inbound grain freighter *Pyotr Vasev*. Of 1234 on board, 423 lost. First major calamity admitted under Gorbachov glasnost policy. Both captains were jailed for negligence.

The various Sea and Ship Posts, and On Board markings, used by Berlin *1925-1939.*

Russ Drag Feet In Withdrawing Men From Cuba

S.F. News Call Bulletin, Fri., March 15, 1963

WASHINGTON (AP) —The Soviet Union appears to have fallen behind in fulfillment of its promise to get several thousand troops out of Cuba by mid-March.

Indications are a large group will be leaving Havana this weekend.

For the last several days U. S. officials have declined to discuss numbers of troops that have left Cuba.

ACCORDING to official quarters here, the situation presently is this:

Since the removal promise was made to the United States Feb. 18, about 1800 or 1900 have left Cuba on four Soviet ships. The latest of those vessels to sail, the Gruzia, left Havana Sunday. It was reported by the Russian Communist Party newspaper Pravda to be carrying aviation mechanics, artillery experts, engineering troops and tank soldiers.

Another Soviet ship, the 15,286-ton Admiral Najimov, is in Havana harbor and there are reports in the Cuban capital it will depart this weekend with about 2000 Russian military specialists.

SO FAR as U. S. authorities are concerned the number who have sailed on Soviet ships during the last four weeks is considered fairly definite but the identification of those departing is by no means certain. For example, it is assumed here that many undoubtedly were Russians, but some could have been Cubans going to the Soviet Union. Some could also have been Soviet civilian advisers to the Castro government.

2000 Russians Sail From Cuba

17 March, 1963

Washington

Although the Administration refused to make any statement on the withdrawal of "several thousand" Russian troops by yesterday's Moscow - proposed deadline, it appeared that the Soviet promise was kept.

U. S. press service reports from Havana said that a Russian ship, the passenger liner Admiral Najimov, left Havana with about 2000 Russians aboard.

Havana dispatches indicated that the Admiral Najimov pulled out after the tightly guarded dock area had been crowded all day long with Russians boarding the ship.

Reporters in Havana said that the 13,286-ton Russian liner took on about 2000 homeward bound Russians in various dress, including military uniforms, before she sailed.

ORDERS

Almost a month ago Premier Khrushchev notified President Kennedy that the Soviets would pull several thousand troops out of Cuba by yesterday, March 15.

Despite the reported troop movement from Havana, U.S. officials maintained a tight-lipped secrecy about the operation.

As reports reached Washington during the day that the Admiral Najimov was loading in Havana, the Administration refused to comment or speculate whether the Soviet government would keep its promise.

No executive branch spokesman would comment on the Soviet troop movements. The orders reportedly came from President Kennedy.

State Department Press Of-

*Admiral Nakhimov, ex-*Berlin, *shuttled between Cuba and the USSR, in the process filling in some details on the Cuban Missile Crisis.*

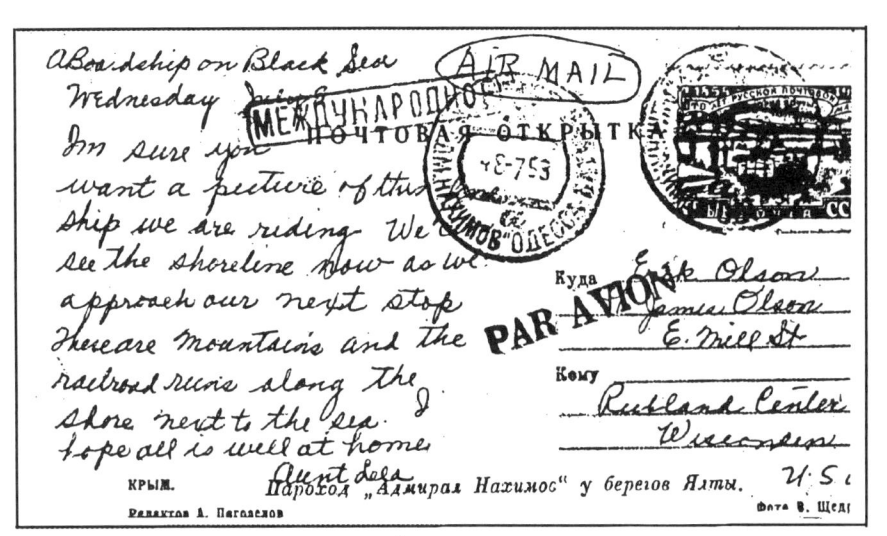

"On Board in the Black Sea, 8.7.1963 ... We can see the coast as we approach our next harbor. There are mountains, and the railroad runs along the sea...." *Russian Ship Post from* Admiral Nakhimov, ex-Berlin.

In 1984, a different style of Ship Post marking from Admiral Nakhimov.

In 1938, Berlin *made one voyage to Australia carrying Jewish emigrants.*

50   Norddeutscher Lloyd Bremen

CHAPTER 2

Mergers — Risks and Challenges

Among the several shipping companies merged into the Lloyd in late 1925 the Roland Linie, Hamburg-Bremer Afrika-Linie and the Dampfschiffs-Rhederei Horn, Lübeck operated under their own flags. Later, when they ran under their old names, as did Roland Linie and Hamburg-Bremer Afrika Linie, they carried the Lloyd flag. The Horn ships were mostly renamed, put into different trades or sold off, so that a separate Horn operation no longer existed. A New Horn Linie, from the same old-shipping-family interests, was reborn after the Second War. It operated reefer cargo services. For a while, the firm was owned fifty-fifty by Hapag-Lloyd and the C.G.T., French Line. It then bought out the Hapag-Lloyd share.

The Lloyd came into existence in 1857 through the merger of three Weser River towing and shipping firms and an insurance company. With the right leaders: H.H. Meier and Edward Cruesemann, to forge the pieces into an operating whole. The first ten years after the opening of the New York Line in 1858 proved the dangers of going it alone: In 1860 only one of the four ships ordered remained in service: one burned out; one suffered major storm damage, so that both were sold off as not further usable; the third's broken shaft took six months to replace. That left one ship in service the first half of 1860. Not until 1863 were four ships available to give the operation promised in 1858.

In the century and a third since then, as the Lloyd gained expertise and financial strength, usually alone, sometimes with partners, it added lines; it bought into other firms or bought them out to control or eliminate competition. All to maintain its independence and strength, free even of government support. Until, in 1970, the Lloyd did lose its independence, as did Hapag, its Hamburg counterpart, in their merger under the pressures of the container revolution. As Benjamin Franklin put it: Together we stand; divided we fall.

After New York, Baltimore was the next-largest trade potential for a German shipping enterprise. In 1868, NDL found the local partner that made a new service feasible: the Baltimore & Ohio Rail Road. It wanted to expand its import-export cargoes. The two formed a 50-50 shipping line partnership that survived until the Lloyd was strong enough ten years later to buy out the B & O.

In 1890, the Dampfschiffs Gesellschaft Hansa of Bremen wanted to buy the Lloyd's British services: lines to London, Hull and Leith opened in 1857 as bread and butter for the New York line. The Lloyd was not yet adjusted to its larger mission overseas. It did begin sharing in that year with the Hansa its South America freight schedule, their ships alternating.

In 1897, with four new large ships in service to Australia and alternately to New York, and what would prove to be the NDL's Blue Ribbon holder to come: *Kaiser Wilhelm Der Grosse*, nearly ready for the New York line, there was new thinking in Bremen. It ceded its seven Birds (ships all named for birds) serving the British Isles, along with its docks, storehouses, the entire organization, to the Dampfschiffs Gesellschaft Argo, formed in 1896 with Lloyd help. Operations continued unbroken.

In 1899, during a months-long world tour, General Director Wiegand decided that the Lloyd needed distributor and feeder lines in the Far East to expand the service area of the East Asiatic network, just that year expanded from a monthly to a fortnightly frequency and extended to Japan direct, ending a one-ship branch connection from Hong Kong. NDL bought from Alfred Holt its East Indian Ocean S.S.Co. and its thirteen ships, and the Scottish Oriental S.S. Co. with fourteen vessels. This led to NDL buying one sailship and ordering another to use as training vessels for officers to replace the British ones on this new fleet of coastal ships.

In 1901, the Lloyd bought the four MEI-named steamers ordered and operated by its China agents, Melchers & Co., from Shanghai up the Yangtse River, expanding the coastal routes served by the ex-British vessels. It chartered, then bought six ships built by Rickmers to open its own China-coastal network, the first oil-burner fleet.

These new services by the Lloyd and Hapag were too much for the Chinesische Küstenfahrt Gesellschaft of Hamburg, Chinese Coastal Shipping Co. It was liquidated; the Menzell Group taking over its vessels. Some it transferred in 1906 to a new service to German Kamerun and German Southwest Africa, encouraged by the increased traffic demand caused by the 1904-1907 Herero Uprising in GSWA. The new lines ran from Hamburg in competition with the Woermann Line and Hapag, as Hamburg-Bremer Afrika-Linie. To strengthen this new connection to Africa via Bremen, NDL bought HBAL's majority shares and in June, 1907 moved its seat to Bremen. The Hamburg vs Bremen competition and antagonism now had a new dimension. This so weakened the Africa-trades leader, Woermann, that Hapag took over eight of its vessels to give it a share in the West Africa trades. A year later, wisdom and losses brought Lloyd and Hapag to their senses with an understanding to share the traffic. In 1916, when the Woermann Trading Co. gave up ownership of the Woermann Line and its East Africa sister, Deutsch Ost-Afrika Linie, the shares were sold to Hapag, the Lloyd and the Stinnes interests. In 1921, Stinnes sold its shares to Hapag and the Lloyd. NDL sold off at a profit shares it held in the United Austrian Shipping Co. and the Holland-America Line to pay for its expanded Woermann holdings.

The meshing of services to West Africa resumed in 1920 out of necessity to get back into a trade completely lost in 1914 to the war. HBAL's new *Winfried* in November, 1920 was the first newly-built German ship to again show the Black, White and Red flag along Africa's coast. Soon a small red and gold-striped corner piece was inserted into this flag as a reminder that there now was a new Germany after the Kaiser Reich. Subsequent accommodation with the British and Dutch competition helped to meet problems of the German inflation, low freight volumes and escalating costs. On 28 November, 1925 came the absorption of HBAL into NDL and its reforming as a 100%-owned entity, but continuing the cooperation with the Hamburg-based lines. Occasionally, Lloyd and ex-Roland Line freighters ran under the HBAL flag. In the 1930s, as part of a general German shipping reorganization forced by the depression and the National Socialist government, Woermann again took over HBAL management. The ships remained registered in Bremen with the Bremen key on the stacks.

A somewhat parallel history developed with the Roland Linie. It was founded in 1905 to give Bremen its rightful place in traffic to the west coast of South America, a trade dominated by Hamburg's Kosmos Linie. Without direct participation, the Lloyd nevertheless stood behind the Roland Linie in its struggle against Hamburg interests. In 1907, as with HBAL, came an agreement to share the traffic rather than fight for it with cutthroat unprofitability. The entire Roland

Linie fleet was lost in the war and to the peace settlement.

Fortunately Roland Linie had two large freighters of NDL's *Gera* #275 type under construction at the Bremer Vulkan. In 1920, it and the other German lines trying to re-establish themselves needed many smaller vessels to reopen services rather than a few large vessels. Roland Linie made an exchange with the Dutch Van Nievelt, Goudriaan & Co. for ten small ships of an almost equal tonnage to its two big ones. This enabled the Roland Linie to open different lines, as before in consort with Kosmos of Hamburg. In 1924, Hapag joined the agreement, providing tonnage for a "German West Coast Service" via the Panama Canal and the Strait of Magellan, a line to the West Coast of Central America via the West Indies and, with the United American (Harriman) lines for which Hapag had the agency in Germany, to the U.S.-Canada West Coast. When in December, 1925 NDL absorbed the Roland Linie and seven other separately registered firms already owned or controlled, a total of 81 vessels of 196,769 gross tons, Roland Linie's General Director, Ernst Glässel, who had been responsible for the rapid postwar buildup, became deputy to the Lloyd's General Director Carl Stimming. And remained General Director of the Roland Linie, kept as a separate entity. A direct conflict of authority with Herr Stimming.

With Roland came the "Seefahrt" Dampfschiffs Reederei, a one-ship company almost 100% owned. Herr Glässel was Director General.

In 1922, Roland Linie had acquired the "Argo" of Bremen with its predominantly small ships serving Britain (the old Lloyd routes into 1897), the Baltic, and with the Deutsche Levante Linie, owned by Hapag, to the Near East. Argo, however, for a time remained a separate operation. But its Manager, Richard Adler, soon became head of NDL's European trades as these expanded with further absorptions and takeovers.

Along with Argo in 1922 had come its ownership of Hanseatische Dampfschiffahrts Gesellschaft with five vessels, bought in 1902 but operated separately. And Argo's ownership of Dampfschiffs Rhederei von 1896, also kept separate with its "O" ship names, first of sail ships, then powered vessels. "Von 1896" subsequently got some of the small Roland Linie vessels acquired by the 1920 exchange with the Dutch. Total control of "Von 1896" was acquired by NDL

Five Roland Linie ships while already owned by the Lloyd but still with their old ochre-black topped stacks, in Port of Bremen in the late 1920s. The Roland Ships changed to the yellow/golden Lloyd stack in 1933.

in 1926, along with Argo's and Roland Linie's share-holdings. The "O" names appeared in 1928 NDL fleet listings; later they came under "Hanseatische" and eventually went to Argo in its 1933 refounding as an independent.

The Roland Linie continued visibly, with its black-topped ochre stacks, into 1932; some Lloyd freighters were similarly painted. Then all NDL ships bore the traditional yellow funnel. The name Roland Linie Schiffahrts Gesellschaft, and a companion Orlanda Reederei (this was the Roland Linie telegraph code) reappeared after the war as the registered owners of NDL's postwar ships out of fear unresolved claims might lead to their seizure overseas. Until this residual liability was taken over by NDL's bankers in 1955, and the Crossed Anchor and Key flag with an Oak Wreath was again raised on all the ships.

In June, 1970, the preserved legal entity was reformed with 50% participation by the old Bremen firm of Unterweser Reederei, URAG, to enter the bulk cargoes business. Ships ordered for NDL's half were given the names *Roland Bremen*, etc. Eventually, this ended when the bulk business was dropped as too competitive and unprofitable after the 1970 merger of Hapag and Lloyd.

Also taken over at the end of 1925 was the D.S.R. Horn with its 12 ships. As Lloyd vessels they were mostly given "Argo" Bird names after the merger, transferred to other NDL managements, or sold off.

In 1927, NDL acquired the *Globus Reederei*, all the ships with GER.... names, some already in fleet lists and a few in 1927-1928 schedules. The firm was founded in 1915 by Roland Linie Director General Ernst Glässel and his Prokurist (empowered to sign) Heinrich Hemsoth to import ores from Scandinavia. Hemsoth became a Vorstand (Management) member in 1922 when it was converted into a limited-liability company. The Globus ships were sold off in the depression. 1934 registers do not mention the company.

On 1.4.1928, NDL acquired the *Weidtmann Linie*, managed by Henry Stahl & Co., with three ships, one immediately sold off. The company eventually went to the "Hanseatische" along with its captain, later inspector, until his death in 1957.

Baltische Reederei became NDL-controlled in February, 1928, reorganized into a separate corporation. It took over two small NDL vessels. In 1934, they all were absorbed by the Mathies Reederei of Hamburg. It was the 1928 reorganization of an old Hamburg family shipping concern. The vessels were carried by the Lloyd as "Fleet of the Mathies Reederei" in 1928-1932 NDL reportings. In June, 1934 it was spun off in the overall reorganization of German shipping. Dampfschiffahrts Gesellschaft "Neptun," Bremen was 98% NDL-acquired, but never folded into its fleet lists or schedules. It, too, was sold off in 1933. NDL and the D.S.Ges.Hansa exchanged shares to assure friendly relations. With this, control of Neptun and others, the Lloyd owned, controlled or could influence practically all of Bremen's high-seas shipping.

NDL had acquired majority share control of *Stettiner Dampfer Co*. In the December, 1930 decision to split up this company, the Lloyd acquired eight vessels, and maintained ownership but they were sold off to befriended companies or for breaking up.

In 1930, Deputy Director Ernst Glässel made an agreement "behind Hapag's back" (this was right after a March, 1930 Hapag-Lloyd joint-operations agreement) with H. Schuldt including its affiliate Ozean Dampfer Co. of Flensburg to acquire four of its ships in exchange for some cash and four Lloyd ships. NDL then chartered two large Hamburg-Süd passenger liners to replace its

LEVANTE DEUTSCHE					NORDDEUTSCHER LLOYD / HAMBURG-AMERIKA LINIE LEVANTE-LINIE	
Dampfer	Hamburg ab	Bremen ab	Antwerpen ab	Route	Dampfer	
**Smyrna	29. 1.	30. 1.	7. 7	—	Süd	Smyrna
Tinos	9. 2.	10. 2.	8. 8	18. 2.	Süd	Tinos
Derindje	9. 2.	11. 2.	9. 9	19. 2.	Nord	Derindje
*Galilea	13. 2.	15. 2.	10. 10	—	Nord.	Galilea
Amantea	23. 2.	25. 2.	11. 11	2. 3.	Süd	Amantea
ein Dampfer	23. 2.	25. 2.	12. 12	4. .3	Nord	ein Dampfer

Ships owned by NDL, acquired with the Stettiner Dampfer Co., operated under the flag and management of the Deutsche Levante Linie, as did some vessels owned by Hamburg-Amerika Linie. Here Amantea, *direct to Malta, Alexandria, Syria and Cyprus on the Southern Line. 1932.*

The largest Lloyd-founded but separate management firm began in 1902 as the German Machine and Armature Factory, from that broaded into everything needed on a ship including the building of tugs, small vessels and eventually two Lloyd freighters in 1958 and 1960. It no longer exists, overwhelmed by changing needs and technologies.

own South America *Sierra* ships put into this same trade.

It was NDL's large ownership of Hamburg-Süd shares that made these liners available, to the chagrin of Hamburg-Süd itself and of Hapag, which until then had maintained extensive Caribbean services with magnificent vessels, all modern motor ships. NDL had begun accumulating H-S shares in the 1920s as a protection against being pushed out of the South America trade in which it had never really matched the other German competition. In 1930, NDL raised its holdings to 60%, against Hah Süd (German nickname) disapproval. This, see below, practically destroyed, along with the H. Schuldt deal, the Hapag-Lloyd 30-years operating union signed on 22 March, 1930. Hah-Süd got its revenge. In 1934, it got back its two ships chartered to the Lloyd, and all NDL South America routes except to North Brazil.

Over the years, as its interests broadened, NDL or NDL people helped organize firms of tangential interest. Some of these were:

- Deutsche Südsee Phosphat Ges., Bremen to exploit such deposits in the German colonies in the Pacific Ocean, spread over an area the size of the Continental U.S. From World War I most of these became Japanese, then in and from WWII U.S. Trust Territories, some since with a loosened relationship. Director Wiegand was instrumental in getting the firm organized; it named its small inter-island vessel for him.

Ships alongside the Atlas Werke being completed or having equipment installed. Port of Bremen, 1967.

Mergers - Risks and Challenges 55

Ocean Comfort Company m.b.h.
SCHIFFSAUSRUSTUNG
IMPORT — EXPORT

Bremerhaven-Mitte   Bremen-Übersee
verl. Schleusenstraße   Schuppen 14/III
Ruf: 2668   Ruf: 83297

The Ocean Comfort Company still exists as a supplier of some shipyard services to Lloyd vessels, mostly to passengers.

- The Lloyd in 1902 founded the Norddeutsche Maschinen & Armaturen Fabrik, on the former terrain of the old A.G. "Weser" shipyard which it had outgrown. The firm gradually expanded into almost all the equipment needed inside ships, and then into shipbuilding itself, under the name of Atlas Werke. It built a tug for the Lloyd and *Greif* for the then "Argo" in the 20s, and *Amisia*, later folded into the Lloyd in the 1925 mergers. Almost the entire terrain of Atlas was destroyed during the war. In 1945, the first new work was pouring a replacement propeller for the *Europa*, being taken over by the U.S. Navy. The first pour did not work, and had to be repeated. In 1958 and 1960 Atlas completed the freighters *Lechstein* #508 and *Nabstein* #515, the only high-seas vessels it

The Technischer Betrieb, Technical Service, was the major in-house services facility: keeping the Lloyd fleet in proper operating shape, making components for repairs and replacements, and in time handling major conversions (Q.E.2, Cunard Adventurer, etc.); and building some tugs for the Lloyd. In fact, a Ship Yard. Here from the 1977 annual report, hence newer facilities than prewar. The job shown: building and inserting a 20.5 meters mid-section into the chemical tanker Silverosprey. *Hapag-Lloyd A.G.*

ever built for the Lloyd. The firm no longer exists, a victim of the world ship-shipbuilding crisis of the 1960s and 1970s.
- "Ocean Comfort Company" appears on many Lloyd postcards over the years, a small services company to handle also renting of deck chairs, shops on ships both Lloyd and other lines, things requiring special personnel. The firm has spread into ship furnishings and some import and export to expand its connections.
- There was also a Lloyd Dynamo Werke, A.G. in Bremen, with a branch called Süddeutsche Lloyd Dynamowerke, Erlangen, so a South German Lloyd, with Lloyd interests involved.
- Norddeutsche Hütte A.G. which smelted foreign and domestic ores. Co-founded by Dr. Wiegand in the early century. It later became independent, then closed down as did so many smaller German firms.
- Hansa-Lloyd, also organized with Dr. Wiegand's participation, to build passenger and commercial vehicles. It went out of business as worldwide automobile competition favored the giant concerns, Borgward was another Bremen automobile firm that had to close down, losing the port much of its car exports.
- The Lloyd also formed a ship-model testing facility to supplement those of ship-yards and naval architects. In time, this was sold off.
- Right after the war, in 1919 NDL became involved in flying. See "The Lloyd Flies."
- The major "in-house" interest was the Technischer Betrieb, Technical Service, founded on the west side of Bremerhaven's old harbor in 1863 as a repair facility, the making of ship equipment and components that were sent overseas, as to Singapore, Hong Kong, etc. for needed repairs there. In the 1930s it was sold to the Kriegsmarine, but after the postwar reshuffles again became part of the Lloyd, then of Hapag-Lloyd, and now is called the Hapag-Lloyd Werft. Probably its best-known project was the year-long conversion and rebuilding of *QE2* from a steam to a Diesel-electric-driven vessel, adding a complete super-deck of large suites, as was done also on the *France* and other vessels as a way to expand capacity, especially for those able to pay the highest fares. In 1945, and until the Lloyd could again begin operating and building ships, the T.B., along with tugs, barges and a small resort business, provided cash flow at the most difficult period in NDL's existence.
- There were also smaller ownerships, such as the Lloyd Hotel in Bremen prewar, some interest in the Hotel Columbus, whose maitre'd became that in *Bremen's* sun-deck restaurant. I recall the snapping of his fingers when personnel did not notice passenger needs, or act quickly enough.

These mergers, acquisitions and involvements over the century expressed NDL's spreading global outlook. This took on a larger scale in the 1890s when the reliance on passenger shipping at times seemed threatened by depressions, changes in origins of emigrants to the U.S., and nationalistic competition. The new interest was to expand the carriage of cargoes at a time when NDL was the largest ocean passenger carrier in the world. In the 1930s this meant forming the "Lloyd Colombiano" to give a local presence to the new Balboa to Guyaquil line to feed into and distribute from its expanding west coast South America service.

On *Trier* in the 1920s passenger Joachim Wiese commented "On Board a Lloyd ship the cargo is given first-class treatment, and one is equally considerate of the passengers." He must have been watching the cargo handling en route to the Far East. A German shipper put it: "Sie sind gut betreut Beim Norddeutschen Lloyd." Betreut and Lloyd rhyme. "You are cared for well, At the N.D.L."

Today, as Hapag-Lloyd, the business is entirely freight except for the cruise ship *Europa 5*, built in 1982, and the 1994-chartered small *Bremen*, again a *Bremen* and *Europa*.

In the nearly 140 years since the Lloyd was founded, it had its up and downs, became what today would be called a conglomerate. It remains in Hapag-Lloyd, working to live up to what that name implies from the record of history.

NDL Fleet:
Ships 309 — 384x
Freighters ... and New Trades

On 25/11/1925 NDL announced its intention of proposing fusion contracts to Roland Line A.G., Hamburg-Bremer Afrika-Linie A.G., and Dampfschiffs-Reederei "Horn." These absorptions were ratified on 19 and 21 December, and the merger documents completed by year end. Involved were:

- **Roland Linie** with 53 high-seas vessels of 143,749 tons. The Roland Linie was founded in 1905 with NDL moral, later major support, to provide for Bremen a direct connection to the West Coast of South America instead of being subject to Hamburg-based lines. Roland Linie included Dampfschiffs Gesellschaft Argo formed in 1896 (in 1897 taking over NDL's ships and services with Britain) and on 16/12/1922 acquired by Roland. Also, Hanseatische Dampfschiffahrts Gesellschaft, bought in 1902 by "Argo" but operating separately. And including Roland's and Argo's holdings in Rhederei A.G. von 1896, also kept separate.

- **Hamburg-Bremer Afrika-Linie** with nine high-seas vessels, 26,459 tons. The line was founded 27/10/1906 in Hamburg to provide Bremen-based service to West and German Southwest Africa, separate from those of the Woermann and Deutsch Ost-Afrika Lines. On 29/6/1907 it was decided to move the seat to Bremen after NDL had acquired the fleet of H. Menzell & Co., also known until bankruptcy as Chinesische Küstenfahrt, serving the Chinese coast. This it had transferred to West Africa routes to flee the cut-rate competition.

- **Dampfschiffs-Reederei "Horn"** with twelve ships, 19,329 tons.

- **Hanseatische Dampfschiffahrts Gesellschaft** with five ships, 4,927 tons.

Including ships under construction at the end of 1925 this gave the Lloyd a total of 117 absorbed and under-construction ships of 553,166 tons, plus controlled, resort, towing and diverse craft for a total of 418 bottoms of 613,056 tons, almost two-thirds the size prewar. This made the Lloyd briefly Germany's largest shipping enterprise until Hapag, too, went on an acquisition spree in 1926. That year began with depressed freight rates due to overtonnaging. In May, the coalminers and supporting general strike forced Britain to import coal. This strengthened freight rates, making 1926 overall, with the Lloyd's growing passenger numbers, a good recovery year.

A 1927 Directory of German Shipowners lists separate Boards (Aufsichtsrat) of Directors for the Lloyd, Roland Linie and Hamburg-Bremer Afrika-Linie. Earnst Glässel, who almost parallelled Albert Ballin's coming to Hapag with the Carr Linie and becoming the guiding genius of the Hamburg firm, was the "Reederei-direktor ... berechtigt die (Roland Linie) allein zu vertreten." The Enterprise Director alone empowered to represent the Roland Line. He is listed as Director of all three: NDL, RL, and HBAL. NDL's 1925 yearbook states "All services for the time being will be continued under the old names and flags." The fiction of independence was thus preserved. Roland Linie kept its black-topped ochre stacks. In fact, NDL freighters were similarly painted into the 1930s when most mergers and acquisitions were rescinded. The synergy of togetherness had backfired under the impact of Black Friday, world depression and collapsing economic structures.

The following five ships were taken over with the Hanseatische Dampfachiffahrts Gesellschaft, Lübeck. It had been acquired by "Argo" in 1902 but operated separately into 1927 when Rhederei A.G. von 1896, Hamburg, by then wholly-NDL owned, was folded into "Hanseatische." (see 401x)

#309 Brun Von Warendorp. *One of five ships taken over in 1925 with the Hanseatische Dampfschiffahrts Gesellschaft, along with several other companies in a merger mania. Sister Bussard #349.* Photo Deutsches Schiffahrtsmuseum, Bremerhaven.

309. **Brun von Warendorp**	1925-1932		
Atlas Werke, Bremen #128	1915	999	65.99 x 10.02
Triple Expansion	700	10	18

Launched 1 4/11/1914, reg. 6/1915. 3/7/1915 trials and delivery to Hanseatische D.S.Ges., Lübeck. 4/1927 ren. *Hecht,* reg. in Hamburg, included in NDL fleet lists. 1932 in re-incorporated Hanseatische D.S.Ges., Hamburg with most other small NDL vessels. 1/1/1933 under "Argo," Bremen. 20/10/1946 to Greek Govt., ren. *Parga.* 1949 C.Scrivanos & G.Pappas, Mediterranean Shipping Agency, Piraeus, managers. 1956 Pappas & Eleifteriades. 1958 G.Scrivanos & Eleifteriades, Praeus. 1959 BU in Greece.

#310 Castorp, *and sisterships* Fredenhagen *and* Pleskow *were taken over by merger in late 1925. They pushed the Lloyd into operating smaller ships in local trades. These it gave up again in the 1930s. Ex-Arnold Kludas Collection.*

310. ***Castorp***	1925-1932		
Atlas Werke, Bremen #143	1920	1005	69.50 x 10.03
Triple Expansion	700	10	
10	18		

Launched 30/7/1920 for Hanseatische. 5/1927 ren. *Forelle,* class repairs at Bremen, reg. in Hamburg. 1932 tfd to "Argo.," but listed as "Hanseatische." At times chrtd. by Marine Observatory, including during the Spanish Civil War. In 1938 to Kriegsmarine. Not listed in 1939 Weyer's, nor Gröner/Jung/Maas. 1940 at Aalborg for conversion to survey ship. 1942 cmplt., ren. *Triton.* 6/10/1944 sunk by air attack at Stralsund.

#311. Estland *was absorbed in the late 1925 mergers, later renamed* Luleälf, *among various owners. It survived for 40 years before being sunk in a collision.*

311. *Estland* 1925-1926
Schiffs Werft von Henry Koch, Lübeck #78
                    1896   877   61.17 x 9.05
Triple Expansion   415.450   9
9   16

Launched 4/1896 for Hanseatische, Lübeck as *Zar*. 1/8/1914 seized by Russia in Gulf of Finland, ren. *Nas*, Russian Navy. 5/1915 ren. *No.9 Koksher*. 25/2/1928 back in German control at Reval. 27/5/1919 again *Estland* for Hanseatische. 20/8/1926 to Baltische Reederei, Hamburg, ren. *Luleälf*.

In February, 1929 in the coldest winter in long memories, the Baltic was so thickly iced in that even icebreakers could not clear harbor entrances. The pre-1914 battleships *Schleswig Holstein* and *Elsass* were used to clear passages for ice-bound ships. On the 9th, *Schleswig Holstein* was off the Darsserort Light House with *Luleälf*, *Götaälf* and *Lisa* in its wake. It wirelessed: "Shall try to tow *Luleälf* and *Götaälf* to Warnemünde." But it itself got stuck. *Götaälf* sank through ice-compression of her hull, among several ships damaged or lost. (Finnish icebreaker finally cleared the Kiel Canal.) 17/8/1933 to Mathies Reederei, Hamburg, then still owned by NDL. 6/1936 to Madame Sofia Dimitriu fu Costantino, Catania, ren. *Umbertas*. 9/1/1937 sank en route Venice-Catania near Isola Grossa after collision with Italian steamer *Morea*.

#312 - Cali, ex Fredenhagen. *Absorbed by merger in 1925, it connected ports on the Colombian and Ecuadorian coasts to Lloyd ships serving the South America West Coast at the Panama Canal, along with* Manizales *#313. In 1937-1938 new ships were built for this connection.* Hapag-Lloyd A.G.

312. *Fredenhagen* 1925-1938
S.W. von Henry Koch, Lübeck #232
                    1915   1023   69.50 x 10.02
Triple Expansion   700   9.5
10 + 14 on deck   18

Launched 5/1915 for Hanseatische, Lübeck. Delivery 22/3/1917, 999 Ts. 3/1921 reclassified, 1023 ts. 12/1925 fusion with NDL. 9/8/1926 ren. Cali to the new (Roland Linie) feeder service on west coast, South America. 1932 back to "Argo," control, reg. for Hanseatische in Hamburg. 4/8/1933 back to NDL, again on west coast, South America with Manizales #313. 2/1937 both sold for M225,000 to Fontbona y Cordero Ltda., Valparaiso. 1/7/1938 wrecked off Caldera en route Valparaiso-Iquique with general cargo.

#313 Pleskow *ran as* Manizales *from the Panama Canal to smaller Colombian and Ecuadorian ports not called at by NDL's South America West Coast service.* Hapag-Lloyd Photo.

313. ***Pleskow***　　　　　　　　1925-1938
S.W. von Henry Koch, Lübeck #233
　　　　　　　　　　1915　　　1023　　　69.50 x 10.02
Triple Expansion　　　700　　　9.5
17 + 20 deck　　　　17- 26

Launched 7/1915 for Hanseatische. 12/3/1918 trials and delivery, 999 Ts. 12/1925 to NDL with merger of Roland group. 3/1926 reclassified, 1023 Ts. 4/1926 ren. *Manizales* for NDL's new West Coast South America (Roland Linie) feeder service. The two ships were replaced 1938-1939 by *Bogota* #447 and *Quito* #449. 1932 back under Hanseatische, Hamburg. 1/1/1933 back under Argo control, reg. in Bremen. 4/8/1933 back to NDL for West Coast feeder service. 11/1938 to Fontbona y Cordero Ltda., Valparaiso with #312, ren. *Junin*. 1941 to Martinez, Pereira y Cia., Valparaiso. 1956 to Guillermo Prochelle, Valdivia. 5/1959 LU in Valdivia River awaiting conversion to a lighter.

The following twelve vessels were acquired by NDL through merger from and with the Dampfschiffs-Reederei Horn, Lübeck. In 1922, Franz Horn had sold his majority share to NDL, which at that time transferred *Vegesack* #279 and *Bremerhaven* #280 to Horn as being too small for further NDL use. The Flensburger Dampfschiffs Gesellschaft von 1869 in 1924 was absorbed by Horn.

The shipping name "Horn" goes back to 1882 when Heinrich C. Horn founded the H.C. Horn firm in Schleswig. The ships mostly bore names of members of the family. After the death of the founder, his sons Henry and Franz jointly led the firm from Schleswig. They then had some disagreements and Henry in 1900 transferred to Lübeck, 1921 to Flensburg and later to Hamburg. The postwar Horn Line with "Horn" and a geographic feature like *Horncap* is a direct successor to the firm H.C. Horn. It became owned by Erich Müller-Stinnes. At the same time, there was a new H.C. Horn firm which continued the use of family names. From these changes going back to 1900 stems the confusion about family, names and ships, including in the several registers: Germanischer Lloyd, Bureau Veritas and Lloyd's.

The Dampfschiffs-Reederei Horn was founded in 1901 in Lübeck by Franz Horn, but vessels with the Horn name do not appear until 1906. After that ships with Horn names were listed in registers as belonging to H.C. Horn, not to the Reederei Horn. In 1909, Germanischer Lloyd indicated the same telegraphic address "Horn" for H.C. Horn, D.S. Reederei Horn, and Fruchtdampfer (Fruit steamer) A.G. Compounding the confusion: in 1913 H.C. Horn and D.S. Reederei Horn had the same British agents.

The son who was to be the successor of Franz Horn as head of the firm fell in the First World War. As a result, the Father more and more lost interest in the business. In 1920, he withdrew as Chairman and Managing Director, but held onto his majority interest into 1922 when he sold it to the Lloyd. Franz Horn's successor with all his authority and power was his Prokurist Richard Adler, with power to sign and commit the firm. Separately, Herr Adler took over ownership of the Argo-Reederei after in 1932 it had been released by NDL in the backtracking from the many mergers and acquisitions of the 1920s, and continued it as Argo-Reederei A.G. in Bremen. The firm still is active in Continental and Mediterranean shipping with only three vessels, against a one-time peak of more than forty.

#314 Hornbach, taken over in 1925, later named Fasan, a bird name typical of the small-ships local services.
Copyright Schiffsfotos Jansen.

314. ***Hornbach***	1925-1931		
Flensburger S.B.Ges. #392	1923	1543	80.01 x 12.01
Triple Expansion	800	10	
	20		

Launched 15/9/1923 as *Quarta* for Flensburger D.S.Ges. von 1869. 13/8/1924 to D.S.R. Horn, Lübeck, ren. *Hornbach*. 12/1925 through fusion to NDL who since 1922 had held the majority shares. 7/1926 ren. *Fasan,* an Argo bird name, to run in the North and Baltic Seas. 8/12/1930 included in an exchange of vessels with Ocean D.Co., Flensburg (H. Schuldt), 1931. ren. *Heinrich Schuldt*, Hamburg. 25/9/1931 Flensburger D.Co. as operator. 12/10/1931 ren. *Lenita* by A/B Lerberget, Joel Fänge, manager, Lerberget. 1936 Fänge & Pahlssons Reederiet, mgr. 6/1939 *Kontum*, Cie. Cotiere de L'Annam, Saigon. 10/3/1945 scuttled in the Bassac, Mekong Delta, refloated by Japanese. 10.1945 again in French ownership. 20/3/1946 hit a mine and sank in Cape St. Jaques anchorage (Vung Tau) off Saigon in 10.40N, 107.30E. 5/1951 wreck sectioned and removed for BU.

#315 Hornburg, *later given the bird name* Fink *in local services, one of five sisterships among the twelve "Horn" fleet taken over in 1925. Courtesy Reinhold Thiel's "Argo".*

315. **Hornburg**	1925-1934		
F. Schichau, Elbing #1147	1924	1004	70.07 x 10.21
Triple Expansion	600	9	18

Launched 5/6/1924 for D.R. Horn, Lübeck. 3/8/1924 delivery 12/1925 through fusion to NDL. 7/1926 ren. *Fink*. 1/1/1933 under Argo. 12/8/1945 in Lübeck. 11/6/1946 assigned to USSR, ren. *Mazdok*. 1952 a new *Mazdok* in registers. 1960 RLR.

#316 Horncap *was acquired by merger in 1925, after the war went to Poland as* Kolobrzeg. *It remained in service into 1957. ex-Merchant Ships 1963, Journal of Commerce. See #323 for Photo.*

316. **Horncap**	1925-1931		
S.W. von Henry Koch, Lübeck #286			
	1921	2369	90.10 x 12.98
Triple Expansion	1000	9.5	25

Launched 20/12/1920. 4/1921 trials, delivery to D.S.R. Horn, 12/1925 to NDL in merger. 1926 ren. *Yalta*, Deutsche Levante Linie, Hamburg, mgrs. Included in an 8.12.1930 exchange between NDL and Flensburger D.Co. (H. Schuldt). 2/1931 ren. *Hansburg*. 24/5/1938 *Schleswig-Holstein*, Lübeck Linie. 7/1940 requisitioned for conversion to hospital ship, work not done. 1941 began conversion to Navigation Training Ship, ren. *Herkules*. IS.1/1943. From 15/1/ to 10/5/1945 brought 21,500 refugees from East Prussia to West Germany. 9.4.1945 damaged at Hela in air attack. 5/1945 at Kiel. 15/3/1946 assigned to USSR, ren. *Ochakov*. 20/8/1947 to Zegluga Polska, Gdynia, Gdynia-America Shipping Lines, mgrs. 1948 ren. *Kolobrzeg*. 2878 Ts. 1951 firm merged into Polskie Linie Oceanicsne, Gdansk. 12/7/1954 engine damaged while clearing Weymouth for the Mediterranean. Took eight weeks to repair. 15/12/1957 arr. Stettin for BU.

Horneck #317 was renamed Drossel by the Lloyd for Argo's short routes in Northern Europe. It survived the war. Courtesy Reinhold Thiel's "Argo" H.M. Hauschild Verlag.

317. **Horneck**	1925-1934		
F. Schichau, Elbing #1148	1924	999	70.04 x 10.20
Triple Expansion	600	9	18

Launched 2/8/1924 for "Horn." 9/1924 trials and delivery. 12/1925 to NDL in merger. 7/1926 ren. *Drossel*. 1/1/1933 to "Argo." 3/1955 to Erich Drescher, ren. *Sottorf*, Hamburg, mgrs. Leonhardt & Blumberg. 12/1956 to Captain Settimo Scampinato, Catania, later Syracuse, ren. *Galas*. 1965 BU in Italy but remained in Lloyd's Register into 1982. Sister of #309.

318 **Hornfels**	1925-1934		
S.W. von Henry Koch, Lübeck #239			
	1921	3970	121.92 x 16.06
Triple Expansion	1800	10.5	
4	30		

Launched 10/1921 for Horn, Lübeck. 21/12/1921 delivery 12/1925 to NDL in merger. 7/1926 ren. ULM. 1/8/1935 to Bock, Godeffroy & Co., Hamburg, DLL managers. 10/1935 ren. *Manissa*. 5/12/1937 en route Alexandria-Antalya stranded in heavy weather two miles SW of Adalia Light House.

#318 Hornfels as renamed Ulm, city-name typical of NDL's high-seas freighters. 1937 lost in the eastern Mediterranean by stranding.

319. *Hornhöh*	1925 - 1927		
F. Schichau, Elbing #1123	1922	969	70.07 x 10.24
Triple Expansion	700	9	18

Launched 29/4/1922 as *Secunda* for Flensburger D.S.Ges. von 1869. 8/1922 delivery 8/1924 sold to "Horn," ren. *Hornhöh*. 12/1925 to NDL in merger. 9/1926 ren. *Möwe* 4, typical Argo name. 4/11/1927 en route Mäntyluoto-Pernau sunk by explosion in foreship (mine?), west of Ösel Island. Two engineers and steward drowned. Rest of crew landed near Zerel Lighthouse. The Latvian Coast Guard took them to Reval. For photo see sister #320.

#320 Hornland was acquired by merger in 1925. Here in Belgian ownership in the 1950s Jean Marie *with a cargo of logs before her loss in a storm en route Kotka-Ostende. Sister of* Horneck *#317,* Hornhöh *#319,* Hornsee *#321,* Hornland *#320. William Schell Collection.*

320. *Hornland*	1925-1934		
F. Schichau, Elbing #1124	1922	750	69.98 x 10.24
Triple Expansion	750	9	18

Launched 5/8/1922, 9/1922 trials as *Tertia* for Flensburger D.S.G. von 1869. 24/7/1924 to "Horn," ren. *Hornland*. 12/1925 to NDL in merger. 7/1926 ren. *Taube*. 1/1/1933 under "Argo." control. 1/1937 with deck load iced over captain ran onto Prerow Bank off Rügen Island to prevent capsizing. Pulled off by *Heinrich Grammerstorf*. Given up by insurers as Constructive Total Loss. Argo had vessel salvaged and repaired for M250,000. 1/7/1945 to Britain at Methil, ren. *Empire Contour*, W. Coombs & Son, Llanelly, mgrs, 938 Ts. 18/2/1947 to Soc. Commerciale Antoine A. Vloebergh, Antwerp. 5/1947 ren. *Jean Marie*. 12/12/1951 foundered in 58.40N, 20.30E off Stockholm in cargo shift during storm en route Kotka-Ostende.

321. Hornsee after being absorbed by NDL was assigned to "Argo" routes, renamed Rabe, Raven. Sister of Hornland #320. Courtesy Reinhold Thiel's "Argo" H.M. Hauschild Verlag.

321. **Hornsee**	1925-1934		
F. Schichau, Elbing #1136	1923	994	70.10 x 10.21
Triple Expansion	600	9	18

Launched 29/9/1923. 12/1923 reg. 26/12/1937 grounded in Kieler Fjord, got off with the help of *Strauss* #398x. 12/1925 to NDL in merger. 7/1926 ren. *Rabe*. 1/1/1933 to Argo. 6/3/1944 mined and sank off Stavanger.

322. **Hornsriff**	1925-1933		
F. Schichau, Elbing #1137	1924	992	69.95 x 10.24
Triple Expansion	600	9	18

Launched 15/12/1923. 4/1924 trials & delivery. 12/1925 to NDL in fusion. 7/1926 ren. *Wachtel* for traditional Argo North & Baltic sea services. 1/1/1933 to the new independent Argo. 20/10/1944 sunk by aircraft in Nieuwe Waterweg by Portershaven en route Hoek van Holland - Rotterdam.

322. Hornsriff, sister of Hornland #320. This from Friedrich Christians Blaas collection.

323. Hornsund, sister of Horncap #316. 1927 renamed Pera 2 and assigned to Deutsche Levante Linie services.

323. Hornsund   1925-1931
S.W. von Henry Koch, Lübeck #241
                           1924   2392   90.10 x 12.98
Triple Expansion   1100   9.5   27

Launched 28/1922, delivery 17/10/1922. 12/1925 to NDL in merger. 1/1927 ren. *Pera 2*, mgnd by Deutsche Levante Linie. 27/3/1931 ren. *Norburg* by Flensburger D.Co. (H.Schuldt). 9/1939 LU in Burgas. 1941 Kriegsmarine transport. 12.9.1941 damaged by Greek submarine *Glaukos*, put ashore off Heraklion. 1943 towed to Trieste. 5/4/1945 found abandoned there ashore. Later BU.

Vegesack #279 and *Bremerhaven* #280 back to NDL as a result of the "Horn" merger.

The following nine vessels were acquired by NDL in the December, 1925 absorption of the Hamburg-Bremer Afrika-Linie, plus *Ingo* #387 then under construction. HBAL's entire fleet of fourteen vessels in 1914 plus smaller Africa-based coastal craft, were lost through confiscation in enemy ports, on war service or through surrender under the Treaty of Versailles. The ships NDL acquired were all new construction except for *Henner* #326, a prewar unit assigned to Britain but not taken over. Most of the ships remained in West Africa trades. Some, carrying passengers, were given DEUTSCHE SEEPOST Hamburg-Westafrika cancellers.

324. Arnfried *was one of five sisterships taken over in 1925 with the Hamburg-Bremer Afrika Linie. They were all turbine driven. It stayed in the West Africa service under the Lloyd.*

324. T. S. Arnfried 1925-1932
J. Frerichs & Co.,
Einswarden #315   1922   2332   95.10 x 13.05
Turbine Drive   1150   10
8   39

Launched 1/10/1921, delivery 2/1922 to H.B.A.L. 12/1925 to NDL in merger. Remained as NDL's share in a joint German West Africa service 12/1932 to Sovtorgflot, Leiningrad, ren. *Ladoga*. 1960 RLR.

325. T. S. Friderun   1925-1942
J. Frerichs & Co.,
Einswarden #317   1922   2464   95.07 x 13.10
Turbine Drive   1150   10
8   39

Launched 6/1922; delivery 10/9/1922. To NDL in 1925 merger. 8/1932 rebuilt by A. G. "Weser", Bremen for New Guinea-Solomons-Hong Kong service, now: Cabin-20, III-29 plus Deck passengers; given triple expansion engine, 1200 HP, 10 knots. A 5/11/1932 schedule mentions "40 Asiatics aft." Ran with *Bremerhaven* every 4-6 weeks. 21/11/1932 first arrival in Rabaul, extension to Sydney-Melbourne planned. 15/8/1939 left Hong Kong, due at Rabaul 5/9 via Manila-Saigon-Madang-Salamaua. With war sought shelter at Menado, Celebes. 10/5/1940 was seized with Germany's invasion of Holland, ren. *Meroendoeng*, N.E. Indies Government, Batavia. 3/2/1942 sunk in Tandjong Priok to block harbor. See #280, 428, 429.

325. Friderun *was absorbed with the Hamburg-Bremer Afrika Linie in 1925, a line formed and supported by NDL before 1914. In the 1930s it ran between Hong Kong and New Guinea and the Solomons with Bremerhaven #280.*

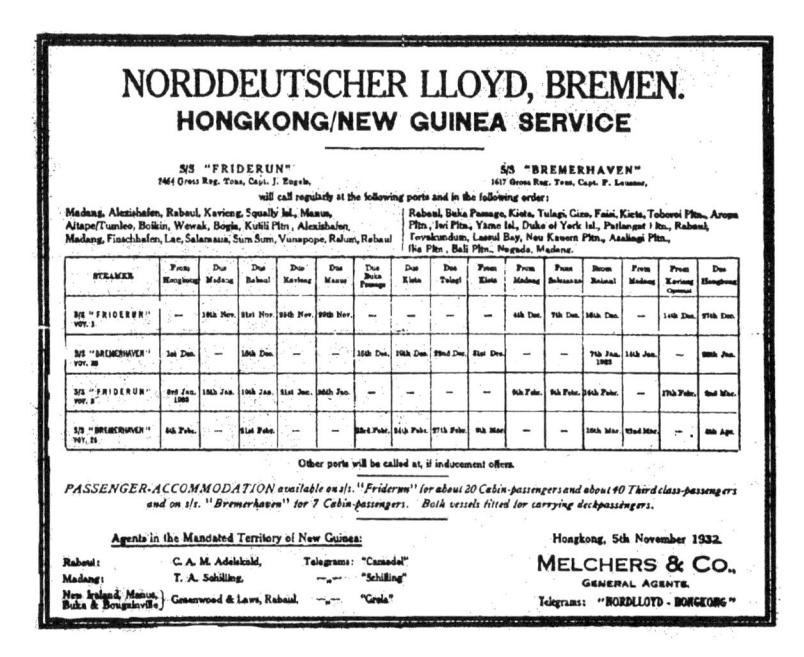

Mail from either Friderun *or* Bremerhaven. *Written at Rabaul, capital of TNG, former GNG, "Tomorrow we continue to Manila and on to Hong Kong." The Rabaul-picture p.c. instead of being landed at Manila was put ashore uncancelled in Hong Kong as providing quicker onward dispatch to Europe. Without shipboard postal attention, the card received the Hong Kong* Paquebot *(ship mail arrival) marking as per U.P.U. requirements.*

For the "Lloyd in the South Seas" see volume I.

70   *Norddeutscher Lloyd Bremen*

326. Henner, built pre World War I for Hamburg-Bremer Afrika Linie, but Laid Up by Allied Shipping Controller in Germany, then resold to NDL's affiliate. In 1925, merged into the Lloyd, and renamed Henner, here in the floating dock at Hamburg.

326. *Henner*	1925-1931		
J. Frerichs & Co.,			
Einswarden #251	1912	3367	104.49 x 14.66
Triple Expansion	1900	11	
12	44-35		

Launched 21/2/1912 as *Wigbert*, delivery 25/4/1912 to HBAL. 12/3/1917-30/9/1918 served as mine barrage clearer. 8/1919-1921 under Shipping Controller but LU in Germany. 1921 bought by R. M. Sloman, Hamburg. 28/11/1921 resold to HBAL, ren. *Walburg*. 11/2/1922 ren. *Henner*. 1922-1932 in Hamburg-West Africa service. 12/1925 to NDL in merger. 1932 to Sovtorgflot, Odessa but reg. in Vladivostock as *Okhotsk*. Also traded as *Ussuri*? FFW. 1960 RLR.

#327 Immo, one of nine vessels acquired by NDL in 1925 with the Hamburg-Bremer Afrika Linie. Among several Lloyd ships sold to the USSR in the depression. Most were lost without a record during the war. Copyright Schiffsfotos Jansen.

327. *T. S. Immo* 1925-1931
J. Frerichs & Co.,
Einswarden #319 1923 2329 95.10 x 13.10
Turbine Drive 1150 10
8 39

Launched 2/1923, delivery 10/4/1923 to HBAL. 12/1925 to NDL with fusion. 11/1932 to Sovtorgflot, Leningrad, ren. *Volkhov.* 1952 a new *Volkhov.* 1960 RLR. Wartime histories of Soviet-owned ships largely remain a mystery.

328. Turbine Freighter Irmgard. *It also went to the USSR in the 1930s; in 1941 hit a mine in the Gulf of Finland and sank.* Arnold Kludas Collection.

328. *T. S. Irmgard* 1925-1932
J. Frerichs & Co.,
Einswarden #316 1922 2328 95.10 x 13.05
Turbine Drive 1150 10
8 43

Launched 15/11/1922, delivery 21/12/1922 to HBAL. 12/1925 to NDL in fusion. 1922-1932 in West Africa service. 11/1932 to Sovtorgflot, Leningrad, ren. *Luga.* 29/8/1941 en route Reval-Kronstadt hit a mine and sank.

329. Ivo *was a sister of* Irmgard, *went to the Soviet Union in 1932, and disappeared from final records.* Wolfgang Fuchs Copyright.

329. *T. S. Ivo*	1925-1932		
J. Frerichs & Co.,			
Einswarden #318	1922	2329	95.10 x 13.10
Turbine Drive	1150	10	
8	42		

Launched 15/11/1922. Delivery 21/12/1922 to HBAL. 12/1925 to NDL in fusion. Continued in West Africa trades. 11/1932 to Sovtorgflot, Leningrad, ren. *Svir.* 1960 RLR.

330. *Wigbert*	1925-1934		
J. Frerichs & Co.,			
Einswarden #301	3648		110.54 x 15.30
Triple Expansion	2100	11	
11	40-45		

Launched 29/12/1920, delivery 23/4/1921 to HBAL. Into 1939 ran to West Africa. 12/1925 to NDL in fusion. 11/1934 to Deutsche Afrika Linie, the merged schedule of NDL, Hapag, Woermann Linie and Deutsch Ost-Afrika Linie. Kept Bremen registry and Bremen key on stack. 10/1935 under Woermann mngmt. 3751 Ts. 10/4/1940 sunk by HMS submarine *Triton* in the Kattegat en route to Oslo in the Invasion of Norway.

330. Wigbert *was used as a training ship for future officers, hence carried eight lifeboats when cadets and teachers were on board, as here in Bremen. It's name-mark says P.D.,* Passenger Steamer.

331. Winfried, built 1920 for the Hamburg-Bremer Afrika Linie, and merged into NDL in 1925, shown in colors of the Deutsche Levante Linie in the 1930s.

331. **P. D. Winfried**	1925-1934		
J. Frerichs & Co.,			
Einswarden #300	1920	3751	110.34 x 15.33
Triple Expansion	2100	11	
11	40		

Launched 6/1920, MV. 30/10/1920, first new German-built ship to West Africa since prewar. 12/19/5 to NDL in fusion. Also used for crew training: 1926 - 5 teachers, 31 cadets. 1/8/1935 to Bock, Godeffroy & Co., Hamburg. 10/1935 ren. *Yalova* by Deutsche Levante Linie, Hamburg. 1/9/1939 LU in Varna. 1940 Kriegsmarine transport. 28/9/1941 torpedoed by submarine *HMS Tetrarch* off Aghios Georgios Island, Gulf of Salamis, in 37.04N, 24.02E. Again struck 29th, beached on south side. 3/10/1941 sank.

332. **Wolfram**	1925-1934		
J. Frerichs & Co.,			
Einswarden #302	1921	3648	110.55 x 15.30
Triple Expansion	2100	11	
11	43-36		

Launched 6/1921, delivery 20/8/1921 to HBAL. In West Africa trades into 1939. 12/1925 to NDL in fusion. 11/1934 to Deutsche Afrika Linie, depression-merged service of NDL, Hapag, Woermann Line and Deutsch Ost-Afrika Linie. Reg. in Bremen with Bremen key on stack. Mngd. by Woermann, Hamburg. 6/3/1940 to Sea Transport Group, part of planning for Operation Seelöwe, the invasion of Britain. 10/11/1942 off Vlieland ran onto a mine and sank.

332. Wolfram, went to NDL with the mergers of 1925, in the 1930s was part of the German Africa Lines joint services. It is shown with ten lifeboats? Were (deck) passengers carried along the African coast? Or were they used lying off coasts for unloading and loading. H.M.I. Photo.

Sea Posts of the Hamburg-Bremer Afrika-Linie and the German Africa Service: With the absorption of the Hamburg-Bremer Afrika-Linie in 1925, NDL for the first time became directly involved in year-round Africa trading. Into 1914, there had been only occasional calls made at Mediterranean African ports by Far East or Australia Mail liners, and by the few NDL cruises and Mediterranean services. The HBAL vessels had used the normal **Hamburg-Westafrika** Sea Posts since resumption of this service in 1920; in fact *Winfried #331* was the first newly-built German ship to West Africa after the war, in November, 1920. The oval **Hamburg-Westafrika** Seapost had been in use since 1894, and was very extensively used, the numbers running to LXIII. The African countries, including European colonies, used the German Sea Posts as a quicker postal system than their own, including as a coastal service. Proof that the Sea Post concept of 1886 was a useful idea and service.

From 1924, new **Hamburg-Westafrika and Hamburg-Ostafrika** Sea Posts with capital letters were introduced. Some of the H.B.A.L. ships used an *Ostafrika* Sea Post, although seemingly they served only to West Africa. In the 1930s new saddle-type Sea Posts to East and West Africa came into use, and then a standard double-ring design with small letters, almost entirely on freighters.

A July, 1928 schedule for the joint German Africa Service. Gerrat of the 1927-acquired Globus Reederei was in H.B.A.L. service until Laid Up in 1932.

From Wigbert *in 1936.*
The oval **Hamburg-Westafrika**
Sea Posts is known from:
Arnfried - *LIX* - *4.8.1925*
Atto - *LII* - *13.6.1931*
Henner - *XXXXXI* - *9.9.1928*
Ivo - *XXXIV* - *10.10.1917*
Wigbert - *LVII* - *24.7.1936*
Winfried - *XXVIII* - *14.10.1922*
Wolfram - *XXI* - *1.6.1928*

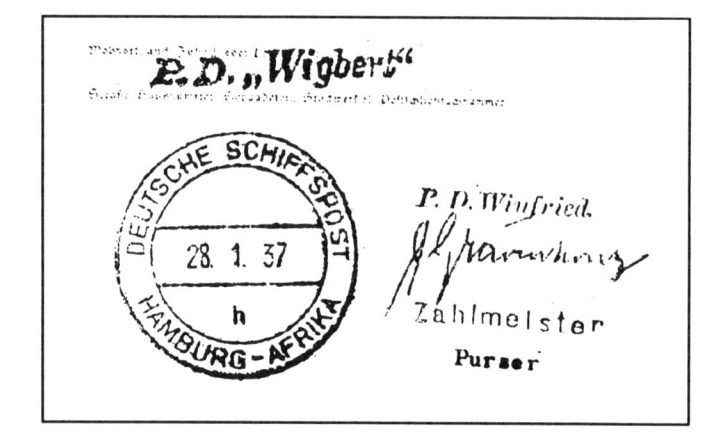

The round **Hamburg-Oastafrika** *is known only from* Ilmar #395. *The double-ring* Hamburg-Afrika *is known:*
h - *from* Wigbert *in 1937*
k - *from* Tübingen *in 1937*
x - *from* Wolfram *in 1937.*

The marks from Wigbert *and* Winfried *used a name-stamp P.D. "Wigbert", Passenger Steamer. It was the crew-training ship so could have some 80 persons on board to use this Travelling Sea Post Office.*

The new **Hamburg-Westafrica** *Sea Post in the 1920s from P.D. (Passenger Steamer) Ingo.*

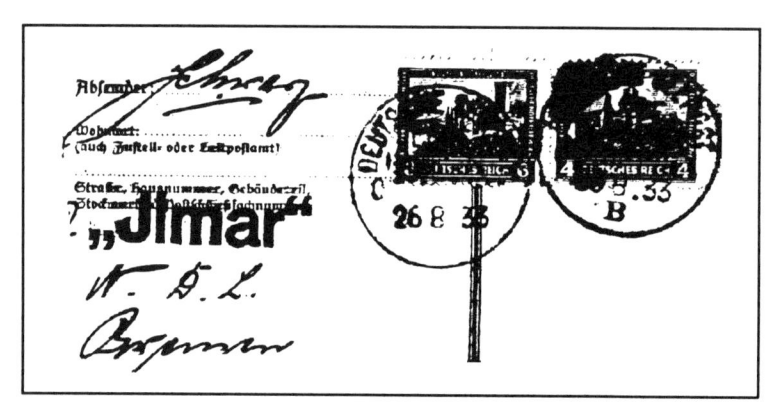

The new **Hamburg-Ostafrika**, *although P.D. (Passenger Steamer)* Ilmar *evidently ran only to West Africa. Did B fall out of the left date-stamp?*

The following 53 ships were merged into NDL with the absorption of the Roland Line in December, 1925. It in turn had acquired twenty vessels with takeover of the D. S. Reederei Argo on 16/12/1922. Many of its end NDL vessels on Argo routes went back to it when Argo was spun off on 1/1/1933. The "Roland Linie" designation for services to the west coast of South America continued into 1932, as did the black and ochre stacks. Three of the ships which Roland had acquired in its 1920 exchange for *Rapot* and *Wido* remained in the fleet and went to NDL. The Roland Linie was founded in 1905 with seat in Bremen to provide a service from that city to the South America west coast and break Hamburg's monopoly on that route. Eventually, Bremen and Hamburg came to an agreement to end rate-cutting competition, and provide a roughly overall joint schedule. After WWII, when the Lloyd feared seizure of its ships abroad over actual or claimed prewar indebtednesses, the new ships ran under the name and colors of Roland Linie Schiffahrts Ges. or Orlanda Reederei's, until 1955 when NDL again emerged as owner and operator with its old colors and flag. Then, in 1970 before the Lloyd and Hapag merger, the Roland Linie again appeared briefly as a joint NDL-URAG (Unterweser Reederei, Bremen) operation of bulk-cargo vessels.

333. *Achaia*   1925-1931
J. Frerichs & Co.,
Einswarden #333   1923   2288   90.28 x 13.05
Triple Expansion   1000   9   29

Launched 26/7/1923 as *Hanna Kimme*, delivery 8/9/1923 to H. Kimme, Bremen. 27/11/1925 bought by Roland Linie, ren. *Achaia*. 12/1925 to NDL. 1926-1931 mngd. by Deutsche Levante Linie. 27/3/1931 to Flensburger D. Co. (H. Schuldt) in an exchange of vessels, ren. *Troyburg*. 21/8/1941 stranded on voyage Petsamo-Stettin off Farsund, sank the 25th.

333. Achaia. *One of 53 ships absorbed with the Roland Linie in 1925. It served the West Coast of South America. Sisters:* Angora *#342 and* Athena *#345 also were taken over.* P.A. Kleinschmidt, Ship Photos.

334. Adler 3, built in 1900 for the "Argo," gave good service for fifty years until broken up in 1950 in Italy. Frank Pichardo Collection.

334. *Adler 3*	1925-1933		
Bremer Vulkan, Vegesack #437	1900	1170	71.54 x 9.45
Triple Expansion	900	11	
8	18		

Launched 31/3/1900, 2/5/1900 I.S. for Argo. Listed in B.V.'s Chronology as 1304 Ts, 126 passengers. 6/1920 to Shipping Controller; not put into service. 10/1921 repurchased by Argo. 12/1922 Argo into Roland Linie. 12/1925 both into NDL. 4/1933 tfd to new Argo when NDL gave up intra-European lines. 25/8/1938 ren. *Aar*, resold to F. Italo Croce, Genoa, ren. *Ezilda Croce*. 6/5/1950 arr. Savona for BU.

In 1922, Argo opened a new Near East service for which it ordered four vessels: *Arkadia, Anatolia, Arta* and *Attika* at A. G. "Weser." After Argo's fusion of 16/12/1922, Roland Linie continued this route. From 5/1926 this service was managed by Deutsche Levante Linie. From 1/8/1935 there again was a Bremen-Levant service, under the newly constituted Atlas Levante Linie, founded and owned by Richard Adler, Argo chief. Germanischer Lloyd confuses *Arkadia* #335 and *Arta* #344. Both supposedly were built named *Aegina* for Argo. Lloyd's Register later got it right: *Aegina* built as *Arkadia, Arta* as *Naimes*, both by A. G. "Weser."

335. *Aegina*	1925-1941		
A. G. "Weser", Bremen #356	1922	2447	100,80 x 14.05
Triple Expansion	1400	10	30

Launched 6/1922 as *Arkadia* for Argo. Delivery 19/8/1922. 12/1922 Argo fused into Roland Linie. 2/1923 ren. *Aegina* to avoid confusion with Hapag's *Arcadia*. 12/1925 fusion with NDL. 1925-1935 mngd. by Deutsche Levante Linie. 9/1939 on voyage Rosario-Trieste arr. Venice for LU. 16/4/1941 sunk by Force "K", *HMS Janus* and other British destroyers, off Libya with *Adana* of DLL, *Arta* #344, and Hapag's *Iserlohn*. The British had deciphered the German Code with "Ultra" and knew from German wireless traffic with the Afrika Korps what, when and where ships would be at sea.

335. Aegina, with Anatolia and Attika built for "Argo" in 1922 for the routes to the Levant. Built as Arkadia, but renamed to avoid confusion with Hapag's ship of the same name, in the same service. Copyright A. Duncan, Gravesend.

336. Albatross was completed for Argo in World War I, survived the second war, one of five Lloyd-Argo ships to do so. It ran mostly in the North Sea area. Near-sister Greif *#356.* Copyright Wolfgang Fuchs.

336. **Albatross**	1925-1932		
Stettiner Oderwerke, ex-Möller & Holberg, #658			
	1915	985	71.81 x 10.24
Triple Expansion	1250	11.5	
16	21		

Launched 6/1915, trials 19/11/1917 for Argo. 12/1922 merged into Roland Linie, 12/1925 into NDL. From 1/1/1933 again Argo, Bremen. 30/4/1954 arr. at Eisen & Metall, Hamburg for BU, one of five NDL-Argo ships to survive the war. The others: *Drossel* #317, *Ibis* #359, *Pinguin* #374 and *Specht* #355.

337. **Alda**	1925-1939/1951-1960		
Vulcan Werke, Stettin #647	1921	4177	115.83 x 15.60
Triple Expansion	1800	10.5	
12	40		

Launched 23/8/1921 for Roland Linie. IS 10/1921. 12/1925 to NDL. 27/5/1936 ren. *Eisenach 3*. 27/4/1939 rebuild completed by A.G. "Weser", Bremen: 2 turbines geared to one shaft, 4800 HP, 14 kns, 4364 tons, lengthened to 124.20, with cruiser bow, stern, crew 37. 1/9/1939 arr. Puntarenas, Costa Rica, LU.

When on 31/3/1941, a Monday, President Roosevelt ordered 65 German, Italian and Danish ships in U.S. waters into protective custody, those in other waters had orders from Germany to destroy themselves to prevent U.S.-friendly nations from doing the same. At Puntarenas, *Eisenach* and the Italian *Fella* were set afire by their crews when local militia were coming out to the ships. *Eisenach* on the 29th had asked for 2500 gallons of Diesel oil, was refused. Both ships had partly opened their vents so the ships would burn out before sinking. The captains were unaware they sat over a sandbank, onto which both settled. *Fella's* captain put down a Jacob's ladder to let the military aboard. *Eisenach's* captain refused. The two crews came off in ship boats and landed at the

Muella, breakwater quay. *Eisenach's* captain and four officers in the motorboat tied up to a buoy, expecting the ship to burn and sink. Plates buckled. When the military came alongside to take Captain and officers ashore, the captain refused to let the lines be undone. So the military climbed in, untied and took the five to shore. Both crews were taken to San Jose in an express train and lodged in the penitentiary. They were held incommunicado. *Weser* #434, *Eisenach* and Hapag's *Havelland* had entered Puntarenas in early September, 1939. *Havelland* was moved to Manzanillo on 8/10/1939. *Weser* left 20/6/1940 under orders to head for Japan. It was caught of Manzanillo by *HMCS Prince Robert*. *Fella* had arrived 5/6/1940 when Italy joined the war on Germany's side. 11/1941 refloated. 1942 ren. *Oceanica*, Cia. Oceanica Ltda. LU at Salina Cruz, Mexico still damaged. 1942 to Julio Ribeiro Campos, Oporto, ren. *Ultramarino*. Put into service? 1948 towed to by NDL's Kurefjord #128 small craft from Lisbon to Bremerhaven, LU. 10/7/1951 bought by NDL, repaired. 9/1951 ren. *Traunstein*, 3/1956 fire in hold in New Orleans. Late 1959 LU in Bremerhaven. 29/9/1960 towed to Eisen & Metall, Wilhelmshaven for BU.

Alda #337 as built in 1921 for the Roland Linie but sister of NDL's Minden *#282 and her four sisters. Unusual for a freighter to have windows in forward part of superstructure. The Lloyd sisters did not have this. Renamed* Eisenach *in 1936.*

Lloyd and Hapag jointly served both coasts of Central America. This business mail is from the Agent in Puntarenas to the one in Puerto Limon, on the Caribbean Coast. Collection of William Lyons.

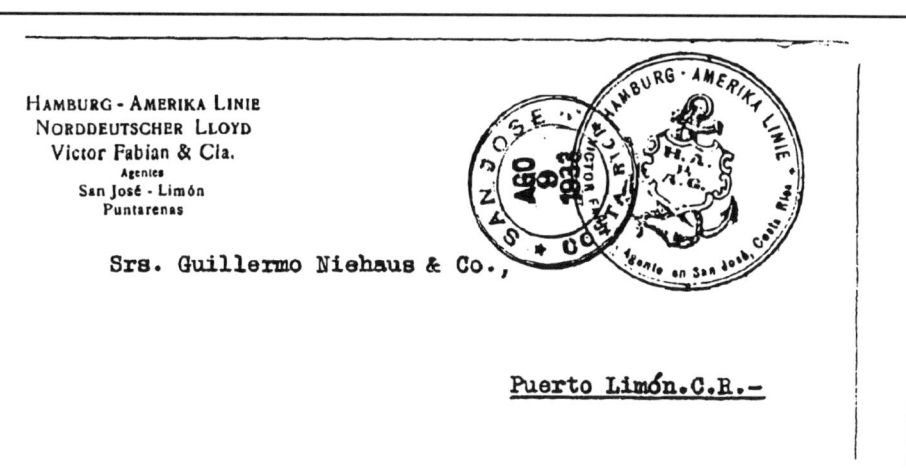

Ship Mail from Eisenach while in service the West Coast of South America, to Punta Arenas, Chili.

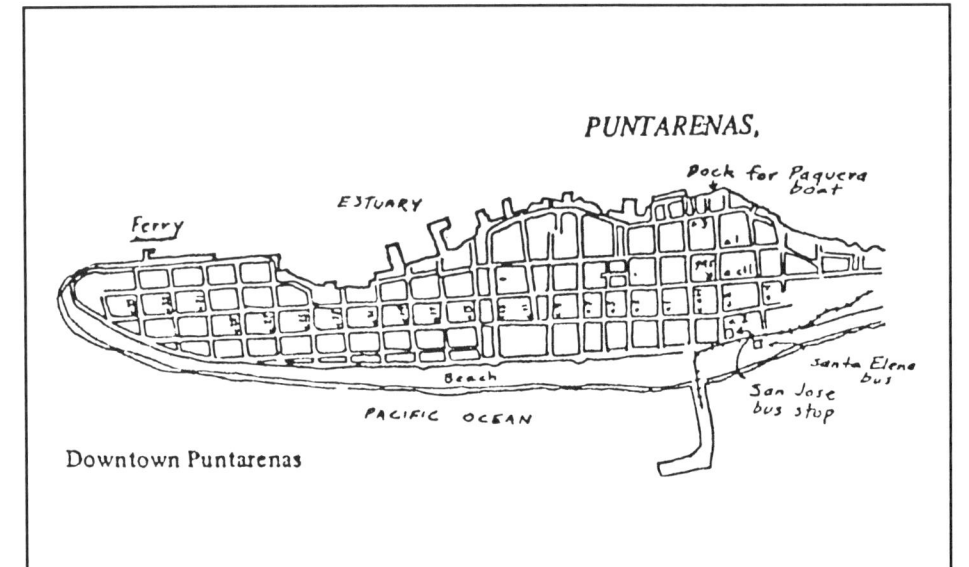

The Puntarenas downtown peninsula. The ferry runs across the Gulf of Nicoya to Playa Naranjo. The muella, hooked pier, is where the Eisenach a n d Fella crews were landed. The railroad line to San Jose extends to the muella; there the crews were put onto special expresses to the Capital.

Alda, then Eisenach as Ultramarino being repaired in NDL's Technical Service in Bremerhaven in 1951. Photo by Raul Maya, courtesy of William Schell.

82   Norddeutscher Lloyd Bremen

FROM LETTERS &
PICTURES TO THE EDITOR
LIFE MAGAZINE, January
16, 1942.

The letter from J.A. Weston in San Jose, Costa Rica, reads: These pictures show the salvaging of a German steamer burned and scuttled by its crew here last March (1941). Resting on a clay bank with only its bridge, funnel and masts revealed, the ship was so full of holes and so many of its plates cracked from end to end by dynamites, the job took six months and cost $175,000. Coffer dams and a retriever vessel were used. Inside the holds were found hundreds of octopuses.

EXPERTS FIRST THOUGHT SALVAGE OF SCUTTLED SHIP WAS IMPOSSIBLE

AFTER DIVERS PATCHED HOLES SHIP SLOWLY ROSE AS MACHINES PUMPED

LAST TASK WAS SCRAPING 6 IN. OF BARNACLES FROM HULL AND DECKS

#338. Alk came to the Lloyd in 1925 with the Roland Linie merger. After the war it was assigned to the USSR, and disappeared from the records. Sister Geier #354. Copyright Wolfgang Fuchs.

338. *Alk*	1925-1934		
Neptun Werft, Rostock #398	1924	1175	67.48 x 10.64
Triple Expansion	800	10	
3	16		

Launched 10/1924 for Roland Linie. Strengthened for ice. 12/1925 merged with NDL. From 1/1/1933 at Argo. 26/9/1945 assigned to Britain, ren. *Empire Contest*, mngd. by W.A. Wilson, 1946 *Vereshyagen*, Sovtorgflot, Archangelsk. 161 RLR. Sister: Geier #354.

339 *Alrich*	1925-1934		
F. Schichau, Danzig #1107	1922	4977	110.25 x 15.67
Two turbines on one shaft	1300	9	
10	39		

#339. Alrich was built as Glücksburg for H. Schuldt's lines to the West Indies and U.S. Gulf ports. It was mined and sunk during the invasion of Norway. Message from a passenger in January, 1923; "we've left Houston and are just entering Galveston en route to Mexico."

Launched 14/12/1921 for H. Schuldt (Flensburger D.Co.) as *Glücksburg,* delivery 10/5/1922. 7/1923 to Roland Linie, ren. *Alrich.* 11/1925 turbines replaced by triple expansion engine at Blohm & Voss, Hamburg, 2100 HP, 10kns. 12/1925. 12/1925 merged into NDL. 1934 to Hamburg Süd in rationalization of German shipping. 12/1937 ren. *Sao Paulo,* still reg. in Bremen. 9.1939 took shelter at Cabedello. 8/1/1940 left. 3/3/1940 arr. Hamburg through the British blockade. 10/4/1940 mined and sunk off Bratholm in the invasion of Norway, "Weserübung", in 60.30N, 5.10E.

#340 Amsel *had six different owners during its forty years of service, last home-ported in Bombay where it was broken up in 1960. Here as the Norwegian-owned* Le Norvegien II, *for service to France.* Copyright A. Duncan, Gravesend.

340. **Amsel 1** 1925-1927
Schiffswerft & Maschinenfabrik
(ex-Janssen & Schmilinsky), Hamburg #576
                           1921   1065   65.84 x 10.42
Triple Expansion   760   10   20

Launched 5/11/1920 as *Minna* for Flensburger D. Co. (H. Schuldt). Not to be confused with a *Minna* also ordered by Schuldt completed earlier in 1920 but sold before completion to Vöge & Däcker, Flensburg. IS as *Argus,* 964 Ts. (Schell). 19/2/1923 to Roland Linie. 22/2/1923 reg. as *Amsel.* 12/1925 fusion with NDL. 3.1927 ren. *Proteus* by K.N.S.M., Amsterdam. 5/1934 *Le Norvegien II* for Norske Amerika Linie, Oslo. 1952 *Mahakhursheed,* South East Asia Shipping Co., Bombay. 5/1960 BU at Bombay.

#341. Anatolia *in the 1930s ran on a new Lloyd route between South Africa and the La Plata ports, grains for South Africa. It ended up under the Argentine flag.*
Nautical Photo Agency.

341. *Anatolia*	1925-1941		
A.G. "Weser", Bremen #359	1923	2446	100.80 x 14.05
Triple Expansion	1400	10	33 (mostly Chinese)

Ordered by Argo. Launched 4/1923 for Roland Linie. 6/1923 trials. 10/1923 in Black Sea hit two mines. Crew repaired ship, got it to Rotterdam. (R. Thiel). 12/1925 to NDL. From 5/1926 to 1/8/1935 mngd. by Deutsche Levante Linie. Sometime in the 1930s the Chinese mutinied while en route Buenos Aires-South Africa with wheat. 25/8/1939 left Durban for Argentina. 4/1940 "sold" to Lloyd Argentina (Cia.Argentina de Nav. "Lloyd"), Buenos Aires, a blind. 1942 ren. *Santa Fe*, evidently not put into service. 12/9/1942 to Flota Mercante del Estado, ren. *Rio Carcaraña*. 1956- *Anamar*, Cia. de Nav. Maritima, B.A. 1963 to Cia. de Nav. Comercial, B. A. 1969 BU in Brazil.

342. *Angora*	1925-1935		
J. Frerichs & Co.,			
Einswarden #332	1923	2289	90.28 x 13.05
Triple Expansion	1000	9	
6	29		

#342. Angora *came to the Lloyd in 1925 with merger of the Roland Linie, but was managed by the Deutsche Levante Linie.* William Schell Collection.

86 Norddeutscher Lloyd Bremen

Launched 5/1923 as *Elsbeth Kimme,* delivery 14/7/1923 to Hermann Kimme, Bremen. 4/11/1925 bought by Roland Line, ren. *Angora.* 12/1925 to NDL in merger. 5/1926-1/8/1935 mngd. by Deutsche Levante Linie. 1/8/1935 to new Atlas Levante Linie, Bremen, DLL still as manager. 15/2/1937 ren. *Konya.* 1/1939 ren. *Elisabeth Bornhofen*, R.L. Bornhofen, Hamburg. 9/1939 arr. Hamburg from Canada. 4/10/1944 sunk in air attack off Bergen.

#343. Ansgir of 1923 was part of a renaming program in 1936. Here in U.S. waters with a large craft loaded onto the after well-deck.

343. *Ansgir*	1925-1941		
F. Krupp, Kiel #366	1922	4621	124.40 x 16.55
Triple Expansion	2600	10	
14	45		

Launched 11/1921 for Rhederei A.G. von 1896, Hamburg as *Octavia*. 2/1922 delivery to Roland Linie. 12/1925 to NDL in merger. 1936 ren. *Anhalt 2*, 4 passengers. 27/12/1941 attacked by British destroyers off Husevangsö, run ashore, later broken up in situ. German wrecks in Norwegian waters postwar were sold "en bloc" to Hovding Skippsopphungings who worked on them for nearly 15 years (Schell).

344. *Arta*	1925-1935		
A.G. "Weser", Bremen #357	1922	2452	100.80 x 14.05
Triple Expansion	1450	11	
10	31		

Ordered as *Aegina* by Argo. Launched 10/1922, delivery 11/12/1922. 16/12/1922 Argo absorbed by Roland Linie. 3/1923 ren. *Naimes.* 13/5/1925 ren. *Arta.* 12/1925 fusion with NDL. 5/1926-8. 1935 under Deutsche Levante Linie management in its services. 1/8/1935 transferred to newly founded Atlas Levante Linie, Bremen. 9/1939 en route Constanza-Rotterdam sought refuge in Bari, then in Trieste. 16/4/1941 in convoy to Libya with *Adana* (ex-*Atto* #347), *Arkadia* (not Argo-NDL *Aegina* ex *Arkadia* #335), and Hapag's *Iserlohn* sunk by mines and gunnery of British destroyers. See #335.

#344. Arta was built with sister Attika *in 1922 for Argo's Levant routes. These continued after the merger with NDL in 1925. Sunk during the war supplying General Rommel's Afrika Korps.* Arnold Kludas Collection.

345. ***Athena***	1925-1933		
J. Frerichs & Co.,			
Einswarden #334	1923	2286	90.28 x 13.05
Triple Expansion	1000	9	
6	29		

Launched 29/9/1923, el. 11/1923 as *Irma Kimme*, Hermann Kimme Kommandiet Ges. auf Aktien (Limited Partnership). 27/11/1925 to Roland Linie, ren. *Athena* for Argo's Near East services. 12/1925 fusion with NDL. From 5/1926 under Deutsche Levante Linie management. 2/1933 to Sovtorgflot, Leningrad, ren. *Ilmen*. 17/2/1943 evidently in error sunk by U.S. submarine *Sawfish* in Van Diemen Strait on voyage Vladivostock - Portland in ballast. See #342 Photo.

346. ***Attika***	1925-1938		
A.G. "Weser," Bremen #358	1923	3447	100.80 x 14.05
Triple Expansion	1450	11	31

Ordered by Argo for its Near East service. Launched 3/1923 for Roland Linie, trials 5/1923. 12/1925 to NDL. 5/1926 to 8/1935 mngd. by Deutsche Levante Linie. 8/1935 to the new Atlas Levante Linie, Bremen. 9/1938 *Anghyra*, Hellenic Lines, Piraeus. 27/9/1943 on fire off Mexican coast with ore cargo en route Callao-U.S. 17/10/1943 towed into San Francisco. 1944 sold as Constructive Total Loss to Cia. de Reseguros, Colon, ren. *Spartan*. After 5/1945 rebuilt. 23/5/1947 NORDIC, Rederei A/B Nordfc (E.H. Andersson), Stockholm. 25/1/1950 to Reederei Richard Schröder, Hamburg, ren. *Hubert Schröder*. 19/12/1955 while anchored in ballast off Klaipeda en route from Gdynia driven against breakwater. Sank on 20th.

#346. Attika was ordered by the Argo for its Near East service. In 1950, it was one of a number of ex-German ships owned overseas that were bought back, rebuilt and put into service at a time when Germany was not yet able to build competitive new ships. Sister of Arta #344. Hapag-Lloyd Archive.

347. *Atto*	1925-1935		
Vulcan Werke, Stettin #656	1922	4176	115.13 x 15.60
Triple Expansion	1800	11	
12	45		

Launched 2/1922, delivery 5/5/1922 to Roland Linie. 12/1925 to NDL in merger. 1/1934 to Hamburg-Bremer Afrika-Linie, mngd. by Woermann Line in German Africa Service. 10.1935 to Deutsche Levante Linie, Hamburg. 2/1936 ren. *Adana*. 9/1939 took refuge in Cagliari, LU. 16/4/1941 in Convoy with *Arta #344*, *Arkadia* and *Iserlohn* torpedoed and gunned by British destroyers east of the Kerkenna Islands, Tunisia, en route to Libya to resupply the Afrika Korps.

#347. Atto was built for Roland Linie, came to the Lloyd in merger, then ran in the joint German African Lines, but with the Bremen key on the stack.

#348. One of ten vessels acquired by Roland Linie in 1920 for two of its unneeded large freighters, renamed Adara, *then renamed* Billung *and later the bird name* Meise. Courtesy Reinhold Thiel's "Argo" H.M. Hauschild Verlag, Bremen.

348. **Billung** 1925-1934
N.V. Haarlemsche Scheepsbouw Maatj. #863
                                          1918   868   61.42 x 9.20
Triple Expansion   660   9   18

Launched 9/1918 as *Industrie* for Stoombootredeij J. & A. van de Schuyt, Amsterdam. On completion as *Adara* for Van Nievelt, Goudriaan & Co., Rotterdam. Machinery aft. 1920 one of ten Van Nievelt ships exchanged for two of Roland Linie's seven of which were sold off by the 12/1925 fusion with NDL. 7/1926 ren. *Meise*. 7/1934 to Argo. 2/9/1944 sunk by aerial bomb in Brest. 1946 raised, BU?

#349. Bussard, *one of the several under-1000 tonners that Argo operated coastally. They did not fit into NDL's operations, eventually went back to Argo when it again became independent in 1933.* Courtesy Reinhold Thiel's "Argo" H.M. Hauschild Verlag, Bremen.

349. **Bussard** 1925-1934
S.B.Ges. Unterweser,
Wesermünde #149   1921   986   65.68 x 10.52
Triple Expansion   725   10   18

Launched 7/1921 as *Siegen* for Argo, delivery 9/1921. 16/12/1922 Argo into Roland Linie. 3/1923 ren. *Bussard*. 12/1925 fusion with NDL. 16/7/1934 back to Argo. 5/3/1942 stranded and sank off of Kristiansand - S. See #309 Photo.

#350. Cavalla and its sister Smyrna *were built in 1912 for Argo. It had nine owners over a span of 37 years. In 1925 when it was absorbed by NDL, Captain Edmund von Reeken stayed on board. Here it is at Santa Cruz de Tenerife with Captain Heinrich Röhr.*
ex-Kapitäne Berichten - F. Schmidt.

350. *Cavalla*		1925-1935	
Bremer Vulkan, Vegesack #547	1912	1570	83.05 x 11.33
Triple Expansion		1500	12
2		21	

Launched 14/2/1912 as *Frankfurt* for Argo. Trials-Delivery 15/3/1912. 12/9/1919 to Deutsche Levante Linie, Hamburg, ren. *Cavalla*. 8/1/1920 to Hapag when it acquired DLL. 1921 "Atlas" Bremer Dampfer Linie, mgr. 15/6/1923 to Roland Linie. 12/1925 fusion with NDL, Captain E. von Reeken stayed on board. From 5/1926 under DLL mngmt, but in NDL fleet lists. 7/9/1935 to Atlas Levante Linie, Bremen. 8/1939 *Falkenberg*, August Bolten, Hamburg. 21/9/1945 found damaged at Bergen. 24/7/1947 to Holland, repaired. 1947 *Juri*, Cia. Maritime Hapsalo, S.A., Panama. 26/9/1949 sunk 20 miles off Vinga Lightship, probably by mine, en route Seaham-Malmö with coal.

#351 Condor *and sisters* Schwalbe *and* Sperber *were built for Argo's United Kingdom routes in 1920-1922, NDL's first overseas services already in 1857.* P.A. Kleinschmidt Photo.

351. *Condor 3.*   1925-1934
Atlas Werke, Bremen #167   1922   889   66.14 x 10.02
Triple Expansion   700   10   18

Launched 8/7/1922 as *Koblenz* for Argo. Delivery 16/11/1922. 12/12/1922 Argo absorbed by Roland Linie. 2/1923 ren. *Condor*. 12/1925 to NDL in merger. 16/7/1934 to Argo. 1939 as Kriegsmarine auxiliary. 20/4/1944 torpedoed by British aircraft as *Sperrbrecher 102* (mine-clearer), sank in 53.35N, 6.11E.

352. *Elster*   1925-1934
S.B.Ges. Unterweser, Lehe #184 1922   1136   70.29 x 10.52
Triple Expansion   50   9   19

Launched 23/5/1922 as *Freiburg* for Argo. Trials-delivery 11/9/1922. 16/12/1922 Argo to Roland Linie. 2/1923 ren. *Elster*. 12/1925 fusion with NDL. 1932 back to Argo as Hanseatische D.S.Ges., Hamburg. 16/7/1934 to Argo ownership. 16/8/1942 hit mine as *Sperrbrecher* 160 off Hoofden, put ashore, eventually sank in 52.41N, 4.37E.

#352 Elster *came to the Lloyd via Argo's merger into the Roland Linie and it, in turn into NDL in 1925. It ran on northern European routes.* William Schell collection.

353. *Falke 4*   1925-1933
Bremer Vulkan, Vegesack #527 1909   997   72.54 x 10.14
Triple Expansion   770   10   19

Launched 31/7/1909 as *Toreador* for J.D.Stürcken, Bremen. 12.1916 to Argo. ren. *Düsseldorf*. 3/10-19/11/1917 transport for Oesel Expedition, Eastern Baltic. 22/2/1918 seized at sea by British armed boarding Vessels *Ta* and *Tyne* off Grundone Rock, Norway, 64.27N, 18.28E en route Narvik-Germany with ore, Christian Salveson & Co., London, mgrs, ren *Poldorf*. Admiralty Court found the ship to have been improperly seized in Norwegian waters. 7/1919 returned to Norwegian Government. 12/1919 bought by Argo. Ren. *Falke*. 16/12/1922 Argo into Roland Linie. 12/1925 merger with NDL. 18/10/1933 to Argo. 1/10/1939 V(orpostenboot) 104 (forward warning ring). 1940 *Sperrbrecher 34* (mine-clearer). 8/8/1944 mined, sank off L'Orient as *Sperrbrecher 104*; raised after war and BU.

#353. Falke 4 was seized by the British in Norwegian waters in World War I, but returned when this was rejected by a Prize Court. It served in the next war, was sunk in shallow waters off France, later raised and broken up.
Copyright Wolfgang Fuchs.

354. *Geier 1*	1925-1934		
A.G.Neptun, Rostock #397	1924	1174	67.51 x 10.64
Triple Expansion	800	10	
3	16		

Launched 9/1924. 11/1924 trials and delivery. Strengthened for ice in Baltic. 12/1925 merger with NDL. 16/7/1934 to Argo. 8/12/1945 *Slettnes*, Norwegian Govt., K.Olsen, Stavanger, Mgr. 146 *Eletz*, Sovtorgflot, 1124 Ts. 5/1959 stricken from Soviet Register.

#354. Geier was built in 1924 for Baltic Sea service with bow-strengthening. So was her sister Alk #338.
Copyright Wolfgang Fuchs.

#355. Grandon 1 was built in Holland in 1918. It was one of ten small vessels traded to the Roland Linie for two of its large vessels in 1920. Roland needed many small ships to reopen different routes. The Dutch needed to replace large wartime losses.

355. ***Grandon 1*** 1925-1934
W.C. Boele & Zonen, Slikkerveer #564
                        1918   761   55.25 x 8.57
Triple Expansion   600   9   18

Launched 8/7/1918 as *Talita* for Stoomboot Redereij v.h. J. & A. van de Schuyt. 1920 bought by Van Nievelt, Goudriaan & Co., Rotterdam, one of ten vessels exchanged with Roland Linie for two of its vessels. 12/1920 ren. *Grandon*. 12/1925 to NDL in merger. 7/1926 ren. *Specht*. 1932 to Argo, re-founded as Hanseatische D.S. Ges., Hamburg. From 1/1/1933 back as Argo Reederei A.G., Bremen. 1939 naval auxiliary. 9/7/1945 back to Argo. 11/1953 *Willy Joerk*, W.Jörk, Jr., Hamburg. Was to be rebuilt as motorship, but work not done. 31/1/1955 arr. Hamburg for BU by W. Ritscher.

#356 Greif. Built in 1922 for the Argo. One wonders why so many only slightly-different ship sizes were built at the same time when the postwar pressure was to standardize and build quickly and cheaply. 1925 merged into NDL Arnold Kludas Collection.

356. ***Greif***   1925-1934
Atlas Werke, Bremen #171   1923   996   71.57 x 10.24
Triple Expansion   1200   11.5   21

Building for Argo when 12/16/1922 it was absorbed by Roland Linie. Launched 18/2/1923. 26/4/1923 trials and delivery. 12/1925 into NDL. 16/7/1934 to Argo. 12/11/1944 sunk by British destroyers S.E. of Egersund.

#357 Haimon 1. *was built as a passenger carrier for Hamburg-South's Genoa-La Plata route in 1898. One of many older German ships not taken over by the Allies at the end of World War I. Bought by the Roland Linie, it went in 1925 to the Lloyd but was soon sold off as too old.*

357. **Haimon 1**	1925-1928		
Blohm & Voss, Hamburg #128	1898	3810	110.13 x 13.14
Triple Expansion	2000	11.5	
18	47		

Launched 18/6/1898 as *Antonina* for Hamburg Süd, delivery 26/7/1898, 3045 Ts. MV 25/8/1898 to Brazil. 24/3/1904 bought by Hapag for its Genoa-South America route. 1912 converted to 690 Tweendeckers, 4010Ts. 8/1914 took refuge in Tampico. 1917 engines damaged by crew to prevent Allied use. 1920 towed to Hamburg for repairs. 26/6/1921 assigned to Shipping Controller; the ship remained in Germany. 11/9/1922 bought by Roland Linie, ren. *Haimon*. 12/1925 to NDL. 1926-1928 under Deutsche Levante Linie control. 2/1927 re. *Ancona* because NDL bought *Quebec City* which it renamed *Haimon 2* #389, LU. 1927 to Pereira, Carneiro & Co., Rio de Janeiro, ren. *Pirangy*. 1935 to Cia. Comercio e Navegaçao, Rio de Janeiro. 1960 to Cia. Metalurgica Austin. 9/1961 BU in Rio.

#358. Holger *was built for the new Roland Linie in 1906 for service to the West Coast, South America. Allied booty, it was bought back, in 1932 was got rid of to the USSR as too inefficient for a depression.* Robert Potts Collection.

358. *Holger* 1925-1932
Swan Hunter & Wigham Richardson, Wallsend #759
1906	5555	129.08 x 16.22

Triple Expansion 3200 12 45

Launched 22/2/1906 for Roland Linie. 4/5/1906 delivery 1914 landed prisoners from *Kronprinz Wilhelm* (See "War" - I) sinking in Buenos Aires. 20/12/1915 interned. 1920 returned to Germany. Assigned to Shipping Controller; remained in Germany, not needed. 1921 bought back, delivery 28/1/1922. 12/1925 to NDL in merger. 1932 *Tashkent*, Sovtorgflot, Odessa. 30/12/1941 sunk by German air attack at Feodosia, Black Sea.

#359 Ibis *was built for Baltic and North Sea routes in 1920, eventually ran on Argo-managed lines. It survived the war.* William Schell Collection.

359. *Ibis* 1925-1934
Howaldtswerke, Kiel #617 1920 593 57.00 x 8.90
Triple Expansion 450 9 16

Launched 4/1920 as *Lotte* for A.Fahrenheim Hamburg. 28/6/1920 delivery to Rob. M. Sloman, Hamburg. 29/12/1920 *Albert Sauber*, Reederei, Gebrüder Sauber, Hamburg. 4/1923 to Roland Linie, ren. IBIS. 12/1925 to NDL in fusion. 1/1/1933 to Argo. 15/10/1938 grounded on rocky bottom off Flamborough Head, Yorkshire. Not entered in log or reported. Discovered later. (R. Thiel). 21/2/1945 LU in Halden. 1952 back to Argo. 4/9/1939 Kriegsmarine auxiliary. 17/6/1944 ret. to Argo. 16/5/1954 arr. Bremerhaven for BU.

360. *Ilmar 1* 1925-1934
Wilton's Eng & Slipway Co.,
Rotterdam #284 1918 1128 70.16 x 10.36
Triple Expansion 750 9.5 23

Complt. 3/1918 as *Eigen Hulp IV* for Stoomboot Rederelj v.h. J. & A. van de Schuyt. Goal Post masts. Sold 1920 to Van Nievelt, Goudriaan & Co., Rotterdam, ren. *Menkar*. 1920 in exchange with Roland Linie, ren. *Ilmar*. 12/1925 to NDL in merger. 9/1926 ren.

Lerche. 7/1934 to Argo. 1/1936 *Franciska Hendrik Fisser*, Fisser & Van Doornum, Emden. 2/9/1946 to Danish Govt., P.F.Cleeman, mgr., reg. in Apenrade as *Vejnaes*. 1948 *Olivia*, A/S Vestjydsk D.S. Nordby, Erik Winther, mgr. 27/1/1951 to Pargas Kalkberg A/S. Pargas. 1955 O/Y Semtram A/B, Abö. 1963 BU there.

#360. Ilmar *was one of ten Dutch-built small vessels traded in 1920 to the Roland Linie for two of its large freighters ordered during the war when it seemed Germany might come out of it almost whole.* Copyright A. Duncan, Gravesend.

361. Ingram	1925-1939		
Nordseewerke, Emden #117	1922	3670	116.50 x 15.54
Triple Expansion	1700	10	
3	33		

Launched 5/1922 as Antares for Argo. 8/1922 trials and delivery. 16/12/1922 Argo into Roland Linie. 2.1923 ren. *Ingram*. 12/1925 to NDL in fusion. 27.5.1936 ren. *Borkum* 2/9/1939 en route New Orleans-Rosario. 9/10/1939 left Montevideo. 18/11/1939 intercepted by Auxiliary cruiser *California* off the Orkneys. 23/11/1939 entering Pentland Firth below the Orkneys torpedoed by *U-33*, gunned into flames, put ashore. Hulk refloated 18/8/1940, towed to Rosyth for BU by Metal Industries, Ltd. (Schell).

#361. Ingram *was ordered by Argo but delivered to the Roland Linie, which in 1922 had absorbed Argo. Both went into NDL in 1925. In 1939, trying to get home from Montevideo, it was caught off the Orkneys, and torpedoed while the British were trying to get her inshore. Four large hatches, the small one for cargo or bunkers. At ten knots, the ship burned 24 tons a day.* Hapag-Lloyd A.G. Photo Archive.

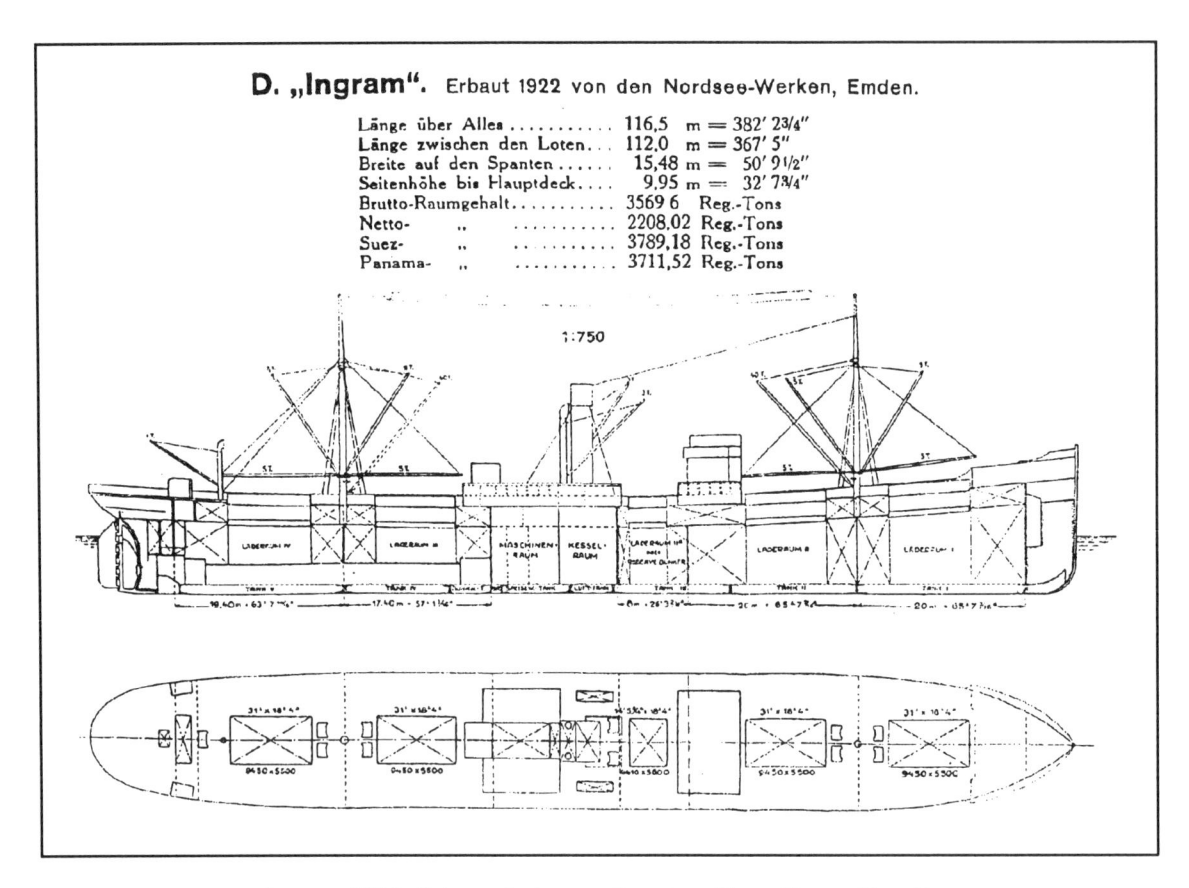

D. „Ingram". Erbaut 1922 von den Nordsee-Werken, Emden.

Länge über Alles	116,5 m = 382' 2¾"
Länge zwischen den Loten	112,0 m = 367' 5"
Breite auf den Spanten	15,48 m = 50' 9½"
Seitenhöhe bis Hauptdeck	9,95 m = 32' 7¾"
Brutto-Raumgehalt	3569,6 Reg.-Tons
Netto- „	2208,02 Reg.-Tons
Suez- „	3789,18 Reg.-Tons
Panama- „	3711,52 Reg.-Tons

Ingram #361. Schematic layout. Courtesy Hans-Jürgen Capell.

362. *Justin*   1925-1935
Flensburger S.B.Ges #323   1912   6053   136.92 x 17.74
Triple Expansion   4000   12.5
15   50

Launched 4/7/1912 as *Hobart* of Deutsch-Australische D.S.Ges., delivery 24/8/1912, Hamburg. 11/8/1914 on entering the Port Phillip Heads for Melbourne sans wireless, not knowing war existed. Ren. *Barambah*, Transport A371. 23/5/1918 to Commonwealth Government Line of Steamers, London. 29/9/1925 bought by Roland Linie. 12/1925 to NDL in fusion. 7/5/1935 arr. Bremen, BU by NDL's Technischer Betrieb, Bremerhaven.

Nach der Westküste Nordamerikas
Colon (Panamakanal)—Los Angeles—San Francisco—Portland
Seattle—Tacoma—Vancouver

Dampfer	Von Bremen	Von Antwerpen
Justin	29. September	4. Oktober
M.-S. Havel	20. Oktober	25. Oktober
M.-S. Saale	10. November	25. November 1928

Fahrtdauer Bremen—San Francisco ungefähr 35—37 Tage

In the 1920s NDL added this route to the U.S.-Canada west coasts.

Justin ran to Australia into 1914 for the Deutsch-Australische D.S. Ges. It was seized at Melbourne, renamed Barambah, here is loaded with troops and supplies. It was bought by the Lloyd in 1925 for expansion of its freight services. Ian Farquhar photo.

363. **Möwe 3**	1925-1926		
G. Seebeck A.G.,			
Geestemünde #328	1913	978	73.58 x 10.97
Triple Expansion	1350	12	
40	21		

Launched 22/12/1912, for Argo, delivery 3/1913. 16/12/1922 Argo into Roland Linie. 12/1925 merged with NDL. 26/8/1926 to Messageries Maritimes along with *Pera* #365 and *Yalta* #384 for Madagascar coastal service, ren. *Marechal Gallieni*. 25/9/1942 captured by *HMS Nyzam* in Madagascar waters, ran under French flag in Allied control. 9/1945 sold to and BU from 12/1954 by Esmailji Andulhusein & Co. at Darukhana, Bombay.

363. Möwe 3 was built pre-1914 for the Argo, was absorbed by NDL in 1925, then sold off to the Messageries Maritimes for Madagascar coastal service along with #365 - Pera, and #384 - Yalta. Courtesy Reinhold Thiel's "Argo" H.M. Hauschild Verlag, Bremen.

#364. Murla *like* Justin *was in D.A.D.G.'s Australia service into 1914. It was bought back from the British by Roland Linie in 1924, in 1932 went to the USSR as* Minsk, *this photo -* Collection Ian Farquhar.

364. ***Murla***	1925-1932		
Flensburger S.B.Ges. #349	1919	5949	136.67 x 17.14
Quadruple Expansion	4000	13	
12	51		

Near-sister of *Justin* #362. Launched 5/2/1918 as *Forst* for D.A.D.G. 5850 Ts. 27/7/1919 to Shipping Controller, G. Dodd, London, managers. 30/4/1921 Hogarth Shipping Co., Ardrossan, managers, as *Baron Ogilby*. 14/11/1924 back to Roland Linie, ren. 12/1925 to NDL with merger. 9/11/1932 *Minsk*, Sovtorgflot, Odessa. 1960 RLR.

365. ***Pera 2***	1925-1926		
Nüske & Co., Stettin #245	1918	1467	81.17 x 12.12
Triple Expansion	1450	10	25

#365. Pera *was completed in World War I, did not have to be ceded to the Allies as it was under 1600 tons. It came to the Lloyd in 1925 with the Roland merger, then was sold to Messageries Maritimes, as* Laos. *It served with an affiliate on the Indo-Chinese coast. Here being overhauled at the Taikoo Dockyard in Hong Kong.*

1914 ordered by Argo. Launched 8/1918, delivery to D.S.Ges. Hansa, Bremen as *Trostburg*. 2/1923 sold to Roland Linie, ren. for the Near East service. 12/1925 to NDL in merger. 10/1926 with *Möwe* #363 and *Yalta* #384 to Messageries Maritimes for its Madagascar coastal service, ren., *Le Myre De Villers*, Diego Suarez 1928. Ren. *Gouverneur General Paul Doumer*, Cie. Maritime Indo-Chinoise, Saigon. 1935 again M.M. 1938 Union Maritime Mediteranee (M.M.-owned), ren. *Laos*. 1939 Cie. Asiatique de Navigation, Haiphong. In night 11-12/10/1942 sank in a typhoon in the Gulf of Tonkin in 20.23N, 106.50E en route Halong Bay - Saigon with coal.

366. Phönix at 999 tons was an artificial rating to fit within a formula. Below 1000 tons ships draw lower port, lock and other fees. It ran on Argo European routes. William Schell collection.

366. **Phönix**	1925-1933		
Stettiner Oderwerke #639	1913	999	71.93 x 9.91
Triple Expansion	1250	12.5	21

Launched 28/1/1913. Trials-Delivery 12/4/1913. 16/12/1922 Argo merger with Roland Linie. 12/1925 merged into NDL. 1/1/1933 back to Argo control. 1/10/1939 V(orpostenboot) 106, outer warning line. 25/9/1941 *Sperrbrecher* (mine-clearer) 36. 25/8/1944 scuttled at St. Nazaire.

367. **Prutan**	1925-1926		
C. Lühring, Hammelwarden #12	11912	333	46.21 x 7.54
Triple Expansion	300	9.5	13

Launched 10/1912 as *Adler* for O. Normann, Oldenburg, 371 Ts. 12/10/1916 to Roland Linie, ren. *Prutan*. 12/1925 to NDL in merger. Was to have been renamed *Kranich*, 1926, but sold 9/1926 to Baltische Reederei, Hamburg as *Piteålf*. 1933 Baltische Reederei folded into Mathies Reederei A.G. Hamburg, both 1928-1934 largely owned by NDL. 4/12/1949 in hurricane-like storm sank en route Rügenwald-Emden with 500 tons rye near mouth of Weser River in 12 meters. Crew of 21 lost "Recovery Impossible" - Seeamt (Nautical Court). The wreck was found 12/12/1949 stranded sans crew.

#367. Prutan *at 333 tons was the smallest of the nearly 100 freighters NDL absorbed in late 1925. It went to affiliates, postwar was under the Mathies Reederei. It sank in a storm in December, 1949 off the Weser River with loss of the entire crew of 21. The Maritime Court found "recovery impossible." No one to blame. Here the front of the Court's findings.* Photo Copyright Wolfgang Fuchs.

Seeamt Hamburg.

Akt.Z.: 221/49.
Verkündet
in öffentlicher Sitzung
am 5.Januar 1950
gez.: Brade
Schriftführer

In
seeamtlichen Untersuchungssachen
betreffend
Untergang des Dampfers
"P I T E Å L F"
auf der Reise von der Elbe nach Emden
auf 53° 53' 51" N, 8° 03' 17" O
am 4.Dezember 1949

hat das Seeamt in seiner am 5.Januar 1950 abgehaltenen
öffentlichen Sitzung, an welcher teilgenommen haben

1. als Vorsitzender: Direktor des Seeamts Gieser
2. als Beisitzer:
   a) Kapitän Drewes
   b) Studienrat Dr.Hebecker
   c) Kapitän Woldmann
   d) Kapitän Zopff
3. als Schriftführer: Reg.Inspektor Brade
4. als Staatskommissar: Ancker

nach mündlicher Verhandlung der Sache folgenden Spruch
abgegeben:

102 *Norddeutscher Lloyd Bremen*

368. Raimund, 1936 renamed Norderney. Here still with Roland Linie stack, she is loading cotton and tobacco the old-fashioned way in a U.S. Gulf port

368. **Raimund**	1925-1941		
Nordssewerke, Emden #116	1921	3667	116.70 x 15.52
Triple Expansion	1700	9.5	
2			35 (inc. Chinese)

Launched 12/1921 as *Altair* for Argo. Trials 4/1922. 16/12/1922 Argo folded into Roland Linie. 2/1923 ren. *Raimund*. 12/1925 to NDL in merger. 27/5/1936 ren. *Norderney 2*. 2/9/1939 en route Rosario-Philadelphia LU in Para. 17/8/1941, trying to get home, scuttled 870 miles North of Maranhao on approach of auxiliary cruiser *Pretoria Castle*. Crew taken to Trinidad.

369. Rapot and two sisters came to the Lloyd in 1925 in the Roland merger. Here it is on the coast of Chile, typically loaded-unloaded off-shore.

369. **Rapot**   1925-1934
Fried. Krupp Germania Werft, Kiel #368
                                1923   5943   124.40 x 16.55
Triple Expansion   2600   10
18   52

Ordered by Rhederei A.G. von 1896. Launched 2/1923, delivery 21/3/1923 to Roland. 12/1925 to NDL in merger. 1935 to Hamburg-Süd in rationalization of German shipping. 8.1937 ren. *Santos*, reg. in Bremen. 9/1939 took refuge in Rio de Janeiro. 16/3/1940 arr. in Hamburg through the blockade. 1/12/1941 settled to bottom of Scheldt in aerial bomb attack. Raised. 11/8/1944 sunk between Helgoland and Emden by British air attack.

#370. Reiher was built for the Argo, came to the Lloyd, then again to Argo when it in 1933 was sloughed off. Renamed Flamingo *for Northern European services. Courtesy Reinhold Thiel's "Argo" H.M. Hauschild Verlag, Bremen.*

370. **Reiher 2**   1925-1933 (BV-1045)
Bremer Vulkan, Vegesack #531   1909   975   67.10 x 9.86
Triple Expansion   1000   11
52 (B.V)   18

Launched 5/10/1909 for Argo, trials-delivery 4/11/1909. 16/12/1922 Argo merged into Roland Linie. 12/1925 both to NDL. 18/10/1933 back to Argo. 3/8/1938 ren. *Flamingo*. 1/10/1939 V(or-postenboot) 109, outer warning screen. 1/10/1940 *Sperrbrecher 39*, mine-clearer. 18/2/1945 mined off Lindesnaes in 57.58N, 7.02E.

371. **Riol**   1925-1942
Nordseewerke, Emden #118   1922   3664   116.50 x 15.52
Triple Expansion   1700   9.5
2   34

Launched 9/1922 as *Arcturus* for Argo, delivery 17/11/1922. 16/12/1922 to Roland Linie in merger. 3/923 ren. *Riol*. 12/1925 merged into NDL. 7/5/1936 ren. *Helgoland 2*, new U.S. Gulf-East Coast South America service. 25/4-14/5/1938 reclassification work done at Fletcher's Shipyard, Hoboken, and crew exchange. 2/9/1939 arr. Puerto Colombia, LU. Attempt to sell ship to Colombians unsuccessful. 28/10/1940 left. 30/11/1940 arr. St. Nazaire. 31/1/1942 sank in Gulf of Finland by Bogskar after ice damage.

371. Riol, in 1936 renamed Helgoland, *here is at the Boca (mouth of the La Plata) docks in Buenos Aires, loading logs.* Luis Marden Photo for National Geographic Magazine.

372. **Roland 3**	1925-1941		
Vulcan A.G., Stettin #646	1921	4174	115.13 x 15.50
Triple Expansion	2000	10	
12	41		

Launched 7/1921, delivery 10/1921. 12/1925 to NDL in merger. 20/5/1936 ren. *Hameln 2* while in New York; also a new captain. 6-7/1939 rebuilt with cruiser bow and stern, by DESCHIMAG Weserwerft, 5000 HP, turbines, 14kns, 4351 Ts. 9/1939 sheltered at Vera Cruz. From 21/11/1939 transferred 4443 Ts. of freight to Hapag's *Arauca* for its intended attempt to get home (See "War" - *Columbus*), brought food and water to *Columbus* at its anchorage. 1/4/1941 seized by Mexico, ren. *Oaxaca*. Cia. Mexicana de Navegacion, Vera Cruz. 8.1941 first voyage New Orleans- New York. 26/7/1942 sunk by U-171 en route New Orleans - Tampico in 28.23N, 96.08W off Matagorda Bay.

372 Roland 3 was one of eight sisters built for the Roland Linie and the Lloyd in Stettin 1921-1922. All but one in the late 1930s were rebuilt with larger engines, and a longer bow, to give 14 knots. Here as renamed Hameln *after the rebuilding with cruiser stern.* Copyright Wolfgang Fuchs.

Ships 309-384x 105

#373. Schwalbe was one of three sisters that came to the Lloyd with the Argo Dampfschiffs Reederei. They served in the North and Baltic Seas in non-winter icing. Later, bigger ships were ice-strengthened.
Courtesy Gert Uwe Detlefsen and Schiffahrt International.

373. *Schwalbe 3*	1925-1934		
Atlas Werke, Bremen #148	1920	842	69.40 x 10.02
Triple Expansion	700	10.5	18

Launched 9/1920 for Argo. Trials 12/1920. 16/12/1922 Argo merged into Roland Linie. 12/1925 both merged into NDL. 16/7/1934 back to Argo. On 20/10/1037 off Ymuiden collided with *Westfalia*, Kölner Reederei, in sudden fog bank. Eight of fifteen *Westfalia* crew were lost. (R. Thiel). 13/12/1940 stranded off Utö with general cargo Germany-Abö, 17/12. slipped into deep water and sank.

374. *Schwan 3*	1925-1934		
A.G. "Neptun," Rostock #271	1907	983	76.20 x 10.36
Triple Expansion	1060	12.5	
16	21		

Launched 11/9/1907 for Argo, delivery 11/11/1907. 1919 delivery to Britain. 1921 repurchased by Argo. 16/12/1922 Argo folded into

#374. Schwan was built for Argo in 1907, and was in Argo service when sold as over-age in 1954, one of five Argo-NDL ships to survive World War II. William Schell collection.

374. Schwan before her passenger accommodations were removed. There was a steady traffic between the British Isles and Germany in these almost-overnight Argo vessels. Some could carry up to 50 persons. Here the ship as combi-vessel. From Schiffahrt International.

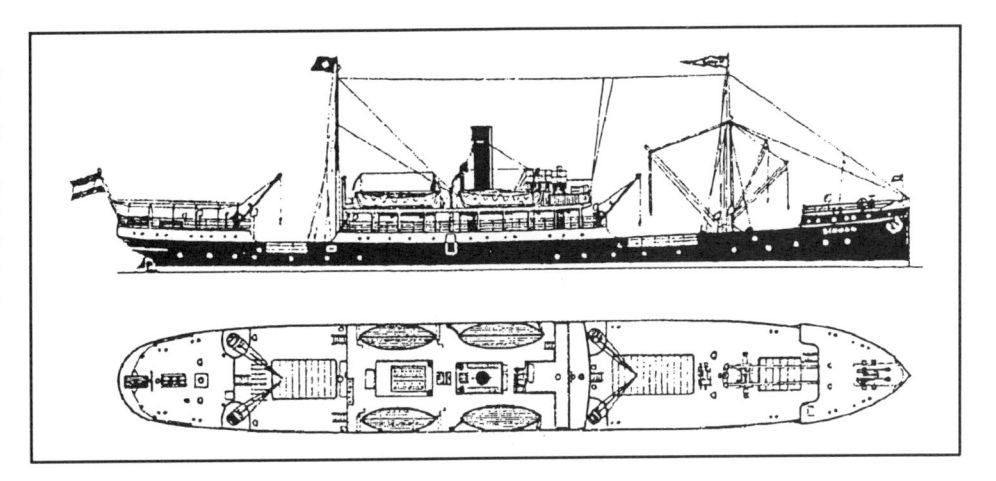

Roland Linie. 12/1925 both to NDL. 10/1933 again Argo. 26/7/1938 ren. *Pinguin*. 1939-1945 pilotage vessel. 1948-1949 modernized, passenger space removed. 25/4/1949 arr. in Hull with resumption of Argo's service to Britain one of five ex-Argo, ex-NDL ships to survive the war. 30/4/1954 arr. Hamburg for BU by W. Ritscher.

375. *Smyrna*	1925-1934		
Bremer Vulkan, Vegesack #548	1912	1660	83.35 x 11.28
Triple Expansion	1500	12	
2	24		

Launched 5/3/1912 as *Heidelberg* for Argo. Trials-delivery 29/3/1912. 1/8/1914 at St. Petersburg seized by Russia, Naval Transport *Ije*. 1918, after Brest-Litovsk Treaty back to Germany, again *Heidelberg*. 1919 sans owner in register. 12/19/1919 to Deutsche Levante Linie, ren. *Smyrna*. 8/1/1920 Hapag acquired DLL. 15/6/1923 sold to Roland Linie, remained in Near East service. 12/1925 fusion with NDL. 5.1926 under DLL management. 8/9/1935 to new Atlas Levante Linie, Bremen. 7/1939 *Süllberg*, August Bolten, Hamburg. 9/12/1942 torpedoed by *Hms Umbra* two miles south of Hammamet en route Trapani-Tunis as supply vessel for Afrika Korps in 36.14N, 10.32E.

375. Smyrna. Built as Heidelberg *for Argo, it was renamed when put into Mediterranean service and kept there by various owners. Here with DLL, Deutsche Levante Linie stack.*

#376. Sperber. One of three sisters built for the Argo. After the war, it ran under the French flag in the Mediterranean and in South-East Asia. William Schell Collection.

376. **Sperber 2**	1925-1934		
Atlas Werke, Bremen #168	1922	889	66.20 x 10.66
Triple Expansion	700	10	19

Launched 6/10/1922 for Argo as *Bonn*, delivery 21/12/1922. 16/12/1922 Argo was merged into Roland Linie. 2/1923 ren. *Sperber 2*. 12/1925 both merged into NDL. 1932 back to Argo as Hanseatische D.S.Ges., Hamburg. From 1/1/1933 again Argo Reederei A.G., Bremen. On 12/7/1937 maneuvering in Bremen Port cut in front of Hapag's *Rheinland* and was sunk. (R. Thiel). 1940 Kriegsmarine supply vessel. 11/1945 delivery to France at Kiel. 1946 *Etel*, Marine Francaise. 1948 *Commandant G. Guena*, Louis Dreyfus & Cie., Dunquerque. 10/1949 *Oued Noun*, Cie. de Nav. Paquet, Marseille. 1954 ren. *Huon Khanh*, Viet Nam Hang Hai, Saigon. Not in Coastal Recognition Book put out by the U.S. Navy ca. 1967. (Schell). 1986 Socialist Republic of Viet Nam, Hoh Chi Minh City. Still in Register 1993.

377. **Star 1**	1925-1927		
Janssen & Schmilinsky, Hamburg #587			
	1922	775	65.84 x 9.78
Triple Expansion	775	10	20

Launched 19/1/1922 as *Rudolf* for Flensburger D.Co. (H.Schuldt). Trials 22/4/1922. 2/1923 *Star* for Roland Linie. 12/1925 to NDL in merger. 3/1927 *Odysseus*, Koningljike Nederlandsch Soomboot Mij., Amsterdam. 2/12/1943 heavily damaged at Bari in ammunition explosion of nearby ship. Later hit in German air attack. 1946 back to KNSM. 10/1952 *Aias*, Cia. de Nav. y Comercio Aias, Puerto Limon, 1057 Ts. 1955 *Aeolus*, Cia.de Nav. y Comercio Degedo, S.A., Puerto Limon. 1957 *Maria Teresa*, Fernando Jimenez M., Puerto Limon. 1961 *Madrid*, Cia. Mar. Panamena del Caribe, Panama. 9/5/1963 sank off Alta Vela, Dominican Republic due to leaks, abandoned en route Puerto Cortez-Ponce with lumber in 17.29N, 71.21W.

377. Star as Odysseus *of the K.N.S.M. in the West Indies. Here painted up early in the war, before the invasion of Holland in May, 1940.* Ex Talbot Booth, Merchant Ships 1942.

377. Star 1. was acquired by the Roland Linie in 1923, after merger into NDL was sold for inter-island service in the West Indies, and survived until sunk there in a storm in 1963, named Madrid. William Schell collection.

378. **Strauss 2**	1925-1927		
Bremer Vulkan, Vegesack #438	1900	986	70.71 x 10.09
Triple Expansion	480	9	14

Launched 21/4/1900 as *Dortmund* for Argo. Trials-delivery 2/6/1900. 16/12/1922 Argo absorbed by Roland Linie. 2/1923 ren. *Strauss*. 12/1925 fusion with NDL. 30, January - 26, April/1926 caught in ice and grounded in eastern Baltic Sea. (R. Thiel). 8/1927 *Ilse Reichel*, Fried. Schmitz Rhein & Seeschiffe Reederei, Duisburg. 6/1931 Wilhelm Luers, Hamburg, Ernst Komrowski, manager. Ren. *Egeran*. 9/1/1938 left Hamburg for Duisburg, "missing since 2 10/3/1938" after passing Elbe Light Ship, per Lloyd's. Presumably sank in storm off Borkum Island.

#378. Strauss was built in 1900 for the Argo. It went missing in March, 1938 after passing the Elbe Light Ship. No trace ever was found. Arnold Kludas Collection.

379. *Targis*	1925-1930		
J.Frerichs & Co.,			
Einswarden #268	1915	5952	130.97 x 16.80
Quadruple Expansion	3200	11.5	
12	53		

Launched 15/3/1915 as *Wolfram* for Hamburg-Bremer Afrika-Linie, delivery 1/1917, LU. 3/4/1919 to Shipping Controller, F. Henderson & Co., London, managers. 1921 *Netley Abbey*, David S.S.Co., London. 1921 *Rijperkerk*, Vereenigde Nederlandsche Scheepvaart, Maat., S'Gravenshage. 17/11/1923 burned in Mediterranean en route East Africa-Amsterdam, towed to Bastia, sunk by destroyers to extinguish the fire, abandoned. 3/3/1924 salvaged, towed to and rebuilt by J.C.Tecklenborg, Geestemünde, IS. 4/9/1925 for Roland Linie, ren. *Targis*. 1/2/1925 fusion with NDL. 18/7/1930 burned en route Valparaiso-Hamburg, sank in 33.56N, 50.11W. Communist arson?

#379. Targis was delivered to Hamburg-Bremer Afrika Linie in World War I. It was British, then Dutch after the war. After a fire in the Mediterranean and sinking to put it out, the ship was bought by Roland Linie and rebuilt in Germany. Only to burn again at sea and sink, in 1930. P.A. Kleinschmidt Ship Photos.

Wido was one of four sisters built for the Roland Linie in the early 1920s. It was one of several dozens German ships sunk after the war with gas and other munitions. It had six lifeboats in this 1920s view for some sixty crew and passengers.

380. *Wido*   1925-1947
Fried. Krupp A.G., Germaniawerft, Kiel #371
                          1923   5933   124.40 x 16.55
Triple Expansion   2600   11
12   53 - 42

Launched 5/1923, delivery 27/6/1925 fusion with NDL. 27/5/1936 ren. *Dessau 2*. 1939 Mine clearer and transport. 6.8.1944 heavily damaged in air attack in Tanafjord. At war's end lay in Stavanger. 17/5/1947 sunk in the North Sea with gas munitions.

381. *Wiegand*   1925-1946
Fried. Krupp Germaniawerft, Kiel #368
                          1922   5869   124.40 x 16.55
Triple Expansion   2600   11
14   51

Launched 8/1/1922, delivery 3/1922 to Roland Linie. 12/1925 merger with NDL. 11/5/1937 35 miles south of Miami ran onto Elbow Reef. Captain committed suicide after failing to get ship off. Later was got off with minimal damage. 26/2/1939 rammed Bull S.S. Co. freighter *Lillian* eight miles south of Barnegat Light, New Jersey. *Lillian* stayed afloat 18 hours before sinking. *Wiegand* with crumpled bow and *Lillian's* crew steamed to New York, was repaired at Robbins Drydock, Brooklyn. 12/2/1939 pulling away from Pier C collided with Pacific-Atlantic S.S.Co.'s *San Rafael*. 26/2/1939 left with 7500 tons of scrap for Germany. 26.8.1939 left Philadelphia, 17.9. arr. Tromsö, transloaded 750 tons of coal into *Aachen* #295, with 750 tons ore arr. Bremen 15.10.1939. 13/4/1945 off Pillau damaged by Soviet artillery. 14/3/1946 to USSR at Kiel, ren *Mikhail Frunze*, 6799 ts. 21/10/1968 arr. Split for BU.

German Skipper Shoots Self When His Freighter Runs Aground on Florida Reef

Despondent Because His Ship, Wiegand, Comes to Grief, Captain Takes Own Life

Herald May 14, 1937

MIAMI, Fla., May 13 (/P)—Captain Otto Liedert, 45, master of the German freighter Wiegand, which ran aground in clear weather on a coral reef marked by a lighthouse, put a pistol bullet through his head today after 36 hours of vain attempts to refloat his ship.

The Coast Guard, after investigating whether any crime had been committed in territorial waters, brought the captain's body to port here pending instructions from the German Consulate at New Orleans.

The scene of the suicide, the 325-foot Wiegand of the North German Lloyd Line, is considered German territory.

Captain Liedert's body was found slumped over the desk in his cabin, a bullet wound in his right temple and a 25 caliber pistol in his right hand.

MIAMI HERALD, May 14, 1937

On the desk were letters and a suicide note in German ordering Chief Officer Hans Festesen to take command.

The Wiegand, which sailed from Philadelphia last week for Gulf ports with a general cargo, still was fast tonight on Elbow reef, near Carysfort light, 55 miles south of here.

It grounded there at high tide Tuesday evening and was stuck for its entire length.

Lieutenant R. L. Horne, commander of the Coast Guard cutter Pandora, said members of the crew reported the master "had been very depressed" by his vessel's plight.

The Pandora snapped one hawser in an attempt to pull the freighter free, others held, but the Coast Guard boat was not equal to the towing task.

The home of the Wiegand is Bremen.

Wiegand *381 was an unlucky ship. In 1937, her captain committed suicide when he ran aground and could not get off again. In 1939, the ship rammed the Bull S.S. Company's* Lillian *off the New Jersey Coast; she sank eighteen hours later; all were saved. Also in 1939, leaving her Brooklyn pier, she collided with another freighter. She did survive the war.*

> 22 ★★★★ NEW YORK DAILY NEWS, TUESDAY 28, 1939
>
> # SEA SAGA
> The News Cameraman Takes Dramatic Air Fotos As Freighter Lillian Sinks
> (NEWS Plane Airfotos by Costa; Krantz, pilot)
>
> 1—German freighter Wiegand limps into New York, her bow battered. She rammed freighter Lillian eight miles off Barnegat Light. Aboard Wiegand is Lillian's crew. Lillian kept afloat 19 hours after being struck.

382. *Witell*	1925-1936		
Flensburger S.B.Ges. #328	1913	6079	137.16 x 17.74
Triple Expansion	4000	13	
12	53		

Launched 10/10/1913 as *Canstatt* for Deutsch-Australische D.S.Ges. Hamburg, delivery 27/11/1913. 4.8.1914 seized in Brisbane, ren. *Bakara*, Transport A41. 1918 to Australian Commonwealth Line of Steamers, London. 29/9/1925 to Roland Line, ren. *Witell*. 12/1925 merged into NDL. 1926 rebuilt by J.C. Tecklenborg, Geestemünde. 1936 to Hamburg-Süd in rationalization of shipping. 1/1937 ren. *Rosario*, reg. in Bremen. 10/4/1940 sunk by Norwegian naval units in Skagerrak en route to invasion of Norway. Raised, taken to Hamburg, repaired. 9/4/1945 hit by air attacks there. 23/5/1946 assigned to Britain, then Denmark; not taken over. Repaired. 1948 *Albertina*, Pargas Rederei, Helsinki. 1950 *Kotka*. A/B Helsingfors S.S.Co., Henry Nielsen, mgr. 1956 to Ministry of Transport. 23/7/1956 sunk in Atlantic with munitions.

#382 Witell *as the Australian* Bakara. *She was seized in Brisbane when World War I broke. One of many ex-German ships repurchased during the 1920s, a quicker and cheaper way to get tonnage than to build anew.*
Ian Farquhar Collection.

#383 Witram *as the Australian* Boonah, *built 1911 as* Melbourne *for the Australian trade. 1925 bought by the Roland Linie, renamed and rebuilt.* Photo: Ian Farquhar collection.

383. *Witram*	1925-1936		
Flensburger S.B.Ges. #315	1911	6097	137.16 x 17.74
Triple Expansion	4000	13	
12	49-53		

Launched 21/11/1911 as *Melbourne* for D.A.D.G., Hamburg, delivery 29/12., 5926 Ts. 4/8/1914 seized in Sydney, ren. *Boonah*, Transport A36. Attacked by submarines: 10/1915 in Mediterranean, escaped by its own speed; 10/3/1917, off west coast of Ireland, saved by its own gun, drove under (and sank?) the attacking submarine; 23/7/1918 south of Tuskar Lighthouse, Wexford. The torpedo missed the ship. 28/3/1918 to Commonwealth Government Line of Steamers, London. 29/9/1925 bought by Roland Linie, ren. *Witram*. 12/1925 fusion with NDL. 1927 ran to U.S.-Canada west coast. 1.1933 lost rudder, towed by *Roland* #372, then turned over to Dutch salvage tug. Towing and repairs cost $400,000. 1936 to Hamburg-Süd in reshuffle of shipping. 1.1937 ren. *Buenos Aires*, reg. in Bremen. 8/3/1940 in Kriegsmarine service. 1/5/1940 S.E. of The Skaw, Norwegian coast, torpedoed by *HMS Narwhal* in 57.05N, 11.35E.

384. *Yalta*	1925-1926		
G.Seebeck A.G., Geestemünde #332			
	1914	1495	80.10 x 11.80
Triple Expansion	1500	11.5	24

Launched 24/3/1914 as *Cöln* for Argo. Trials-delivery 5/4/1914. 2/8/1914 seized in St. Petersburg, served as transport *Kotlin*. 1916 minelayer *Lena*. 19/6/1919 assigned to Shipping Controller, not delivered. 6/1922 back to Argo. 16/12/1922 Argo merged into Roland Linie. 2/1923 ren. *Yalta*. 12/1925 merged with NDL. 10/1926 with *Möwe* #363 and *Pera* #365 to Messageries Maritimes for Madagascar services, reg. in Diego Suarez, ren. *Etienne De Flacourt*. 1928 *Gouverneur General Piquet*, Soc. Maritime Indo-Chinoise, Saigon. 1934 *Sargasse*, Union Maritime Mediteranee,

Marseille. 1938 *La Marsa*, Cattarropoulos & P. Camallas, Marseille. 18/12/1942 seized there, taken over by Italy. 2/1/1943 renamed *Tivoli*. 7/1943 sunk in Naples by British air attack. 1947 raised, after repairs *Carlotta*, G. & O. Jacomino, Torre del Greco. 1955 *Anna Rosa*, Piroscafo S.r.l., Genoa (Sergio Scahsi). 1958 *Andalu*, "Arnavi" Arm. e Tspti. Marittimi, Genoa. 16/12/1959 arr. Viareggio for BU. A record twelve names!

***384 "Seefahrt" Dampfschiffs Reederei A.G.**, Emden. Formed in 1903, in 1909 it began service from Bremen, despite its Emden location, with one vessel. In 1924, it became almost 100% owned by Roland Linie. *Amisia* was its only vessel. "Seefahrt" retained its name and was not incorporated into NDL, although controlled by it. Its address was c/o NDL. Ernst Glässel was listed as Director and Manager, as he was of the Roland Linie. *Visurgis* and *Strauss* built in 1926 and 1927 were registered as "Seefahrt." But an NDL fleet list of September, 1928 includes *Amisia* and *Visurgis*, but not new buildings *Strauss* and *Lumme*, already in service. Also included were the otherwise "independent" Globus Reederei, acquired in 1927, and the ships of the Hanseatische D.S. Gesellschaft. The ships belonging to "Seefahrt" during NDL's ownership, the above three and *Lumme* #409, were in 1932 and 1933 transferred to the again-independent Argo.

Amisia	1926-1934		
Atlas Werke, Bremen #159	1921	999	68.28 x 9.75
Triple Expansion	800	10	16

Launched 11/16/1921 for "Seefahrt." 8/9/1921 trials. 12/1925 to NDL as part of Roland Linie. 1926 still listed as "Seefahrt." Also 1928, but c/o NDL in Germanischer Lloyd register. 28/7/1934 to Argo Reederei. 26/10/1945 to Norwegian Government, Ingval Björneboe, Kristiansand, manager, ren. *Oddernes*. 1946 *Mogilev*, Sovtorgflot, Archangelsk, 1175 Ts. 27/1/1969 arrived Hamburg for BU.

#384x Amisia, *a one-ship shipping company controlled by NDL through the Roland Linie.* Visurgis, *and* Strauss, *built in 1927, were registered for the same "Seefahrt" company, as were several later vessels. Part of the 1920s corporate juggling.* P.A. Kleinschmidt Photo.

#384x Visurgis, *built for "Seefahrt" in 1926, an early engine-aft design that made room for three hatches: one forward of the superstructure, and two straddling the main mast.*

Visurgis		1926-1934	
G. Seebeck A.G., Wesermünde #456			
	1926	1306	70.47 x 11.52
Triple Expansion	800	9	18

Launched 1/1926 for yard account, LU on completion. 23/11/1927 to NDL, for "Seefahrt" operation, in 1928 in NDL fleet lists. 1932 under Hanseatische D.S. Ges., Hamburg; (it on 1/1/1933 became Argo Reederei A.G., Bremen) with *Amisia, Strauss* #398* and *Lumme* #409. 26/5/1937 in fog sunk in collision with Italian *Siena*, 3222 Ts., off Terschelling Light Ship on voyage Antwerp-Riga with piece goods.

Strauss see after #398 and *Lumme* #409.

CHAPTER 3

Bremen and Hamburg: Hapag and Lloyd

The relationships between Hapag and Lloyd, and Bremen and Hamburg from 1860 on are business counterparts to many marriages: long acquaintanceship, going to the same affairs (secretly negotiating?), prickly about being seen together (others fear collusion against them), occasionally dancing together (joint services), arguing, accusations, spiting each other, finally getting married (the 1970 merger) because after all the years it seems the sensible thing to do rather than go on separately. Or, like British weather forecasts: "Overcast but clearing," or "Mostly

The announcement in March, 1930 in Bremen's Weser Zeitung of the merger under a joint Board of the Norddeutscher Lloyd and Hapag. "Bremen is experiencing a historic hour ... The Norddeutscher Lloyd and Hamburg-America Line will find their way to a great voyage together. The spirit of community will tie together Germany's two greatest shipping enterprises and their home ports of Bremen and Hamburg...."

117

Bierpatent für Große Fahrt

Beck's Bier gibt es an allen Küsten der Welt, in über 140 Ländern. Denn Beck's Bier hat den Geschmack, den Bierfreunde lieben: kräftig und frisch — ein gut ausgereiftes, blondes Bier.

BECK's BIER

Beck's and Bremen are synonymous, just as Lloyd and Bremen. The claim: Beck's is the Beer Patent for Great Voyaging, all seas. Just as Captains have Patents, Licenses, for small voyaging, and for All Seas. Beck's Beer satisfies men's thirsts, 1957. Beck's also advertised: "our standards go back to Bremen's purity laws of 1516."

clear, with light showers."

Then, less openly, the differences continue, with a dominant partner, the other seemingly deferred to, underneath resentful. As a woman loses her maiden name in marriage, so the Lloyd in Hapag-Lloyd was less seen: Lloyd's Daily list carries only Hapag; early containers had the Lloyd below the Hapag so it rarely showed. Today, little remains visible of the past except the Hapag-Lloyd painted on the side of the freighters.

In Germany's rise to nationhood and a major factor in world affairs, the centuries-long unity of the Hansa League (I-p.127) sometimes became open enmity between two members: Bremen and Hamburg. This carried over into the relations between the Lloyd, founded in 1857, and Hapag, founded in 1847. It was always a competitor, sometimes a collaborator, even friend, a rival whose presence could not be ignored. There was even competitive naming of ships for the same royal-family members pre-1914. Bremen ships would serve only Bremen Bier, Hamburg ships Hamburger Bier.

Fortunately, the difficult relations at the directorate and management levels did not always percolate down. Where there were similar or parallel operations, as at overseas ports, there usually was cooperation and mutual helpfulness. The outstanding example was in New York during the 1930s when the depression forced a North Atlantic community of interests that worked efficiently and with mutual good will.

Over the years, the two lines bought ships from or sold them to each other, or shared ships of acquired firms. In the Lloyd's first years when major ship losses postponed from 1858 until 1863 start of a fortnightly service to New York, Hapag occasionally took over NDL's mail obligations stemming from contracts with the U.S. and British Post Offices.

In 1861, NDL accepted Hapag's designations of First Class, Upper Salon, and Lower Salon over its own First and Second Class designations. In 1862, the two agreed to alternate sailings from Bremen and Hamburg to New York (Hoboken). The Lloyd in 1867 reciprocated Hapag's help with mails, making a Hamburg-New York sailing in fulfillment of its postal contract.

In the 1860s, NDL bought terrain in Hoboken and built piers that were used jointly by the Hapag until it bought land and developed it to its own needs.

In 1885, the Lloyd, Hapag, the Red Star Line and Holland-America Line formed a loose arrangement to avoid competitive rate-cutting for emigrants. In 1895, this became a pool agreement.

The climate between Lloyd and Hapag changed after 1886 following Albert Ballin becoming the latter's passenger manager. In 1888, he became a director and soon the Director General. Hapag was never the same after that. In 1889, it put the first of three twin-screw express liners into North Atlantic service. This while the Lloyd, restricted by the small dimensions of the old harbor locks in Bremerhaven, into 1891 built all its eleven express liners smaller, slower and with only one propeller. For a time that year if offered three sailings a week across the Atlantic. It was a turning point. Hapag in 1891 carried more immigrant and cabin passengers to Hoboken than the Lloyd.

That year, both lines opened lines from the Mediterranean to the U.S. as the source of emigrants shifted south from northern Europe. From December, 1892, the two ran a joint schedule as the "German Mediterranean Service." A similar joint "Yangtse Service" came about in China after the two separately opened China coastal and Yangtse lines.

In 1892, when Hapag's emigrant station in Hamburg was closed for $1\frac{1}{2}$ years by the cholera crisis, it contracted with Oldenburg and the Lloyd for use of their facilities. In the 1890s, the two lines agreed that Hapag would offer pleasure cruises, the Lloyd not entering that field after its pioneer cruise of 1890 showed Albert Ballin the potential. Hapag in turn left to NDL the contract-charter carrying of military personnel to and from Germany's overseas interests, principally China. By 1904, the Lloyd did offer cruises, but never matched Hapag's program with two yacht-like cruise liners.

In 1899, Hapag joined the Lloyd East Asia Imperial Mail operation. It shared the freighters Hapag had taken over with the Kingsin Line serving the Far East. And it built two passenger liners to NDL's design. In 1904, Hapag opted out of this partnership, dissatisfied with NDL's control of the route. There was a reverse swap of ships, NDL took one of the two passenger liners. And Hapag began its own limited passenger service to East Asia. It captured some of the traffic without making a profit at it.

In 1901, Hapag split its West Indies routes into Cuba and Mexico lines. NDL had set up a competitive service. In 1902, the two agreed for NDL to give up its Mexico route, and the two lines to offer a joint schedule to Cuba.

In 1902, Albert Ballin's negotiations led the two competitors into the Morgan Trust of trans-Atlantic shipping firms, the International Mercantile Marine Co. This gave Hapag and Lloyd an IMM guarantee of a six percent dividend, in return the two agreeing to pay IMM any time their own dividends exceeded that figure. This did happen, so some millions were paid out. But it was a small price to pay for the Lloyd and Hapag not being swallowed by the American merger mania.

In 1908, fifteen shipping firms from seven nations formed the Atlantic (Passenger) Conference. The aim: to relate a ship's size, age, speed, comfort to its passenger rates, and to prorate traffic. For the East-West services, the Lloyd got a 26.53% quota, Hapag 19.61%, or 46.14% for the two German lines. For West-East it was 18.79% for NDL and 12.35% for Hapag, or 31.14%. The two lines were carrying a disproportionate share of the emigrant traffic from Europe. The other lines carried more eastward and in the upper classes: more newsworthy but less profitable than the stream of emigrants in their huge numbers.

In 1910, the Lloyd, Hapag and the Holland-America Line joint-scheduled their Canada service. It had been overtonnaged and unprofitable for all. NDL's Willehad #89 was the first departure.

In 1913, the Lloyd and Hapag agreed with the Kingdom of Prussia to include Emden in their services: for passengers and cargo fortnightly to the U.S., at least every four weeks to East Asia, the NDL also a line to Australia.

Also in 1913, Hapag demanded a higher quota with its super-ship *Imperator* in service, and bigger sisters to follow in 1914 and 1916. The higher numbers would have to come from the Lloyd's share and the non-German lines.

However, in February, 1914 President Philipp Heineken for the Lloyd and Albert Ballin for Hapag signed a protocol under pressure from the Kaiser, a "Du" friend of Ballin, and his younger brother, Prinz Heinrich, closer to the Lloyd. This "Union of Interests" called for an eventual equality for the two on the North Atlantic. Actually, on the basis of shipping capital involved, Hapag by 1916 would be entitled to 58.8%, the Lloyd only 41.2%. This complete reversal of the former traffic ratios was unacceptable to Herr Heineken. He did agree to an eventual 55.8% and 44.2% quota. This was to be put before the Atlantic Conference in London in August. The war cancelled the meeting. The Atlantic Conference survived: Hapag and Lloyd rejoined in 1921 and 1922.

Despite this "peace" between them, Hapag in 1914 offered to serve the East Asia Imperial Mail service without subsidy in the next contract period. Since the Lloyd never made any profit on the Australia mail contract, losing the East Asia subsidy would have forced radical changes to preserve its solvency and ability to finance badly-needed new

The Lloyd's top management at Bremen with the German Ambassador to the U.S. von Prittwitz at the Line's head office in Bremen: Director General Carl Stimming, President Philipp Heineken and Deputy Director General, in 1932 taking the top spot, Herr Ernst Glässel. From June, 1928 "SEVEN SEAS," NDL's U.S.-Canada magazine.

tonnage. This was being worked out, with NDL to cede some ships to Hapag. But again, the war ended it all.

In 1916, Lloyd and Hapag jointly organized emigration bureaus in Warsaw and Kovno to help potential emigrants to the U.S. to get space on Dutch vessels. Also jointly, they organized the Deutsches Reisebüro, and a European Travel Bureau. This in wartime!

An action that seems to have had no effect in later preventing moves open and secret to buy other shipping companies, Hapag, the Lloyd and Hamburg Süd exchanged preference shares to impede any outside attempt to gain control of any one. Also in 1916, Hapag and Lloyd bought Hamburg Süd shares from the Stinnes family. It also sold them Woermann and Deutsch Ost-Afrika Linie shares.

In the turmoil following Germany losing the war and most of its shipping, Hapag in November, 1920 suggested a Union of Interests. But the Lloyd declined. It presumably felt that with the Columbus Agreement allowing it to keep three freighters and three passenger vessels, it had a head start on rebuilding. In 1922, a joint service by Hapag-Deutsche Levante Linie, owned by Hapag and Argo, owned by Roland Linie opened to the Levant.

In February, 1925, 1924 having been a poor year with U.S. immigration quotas fully in effect, Hapag, Lloyd and Stinnes joined their schedules to Santos and to the Far East. Hapag and Lloyd discussed what they could do-jointly and separately to economize, reduce competition and use of excessive tonnage, perhaps together taking over the near-bankrupt Stinnes shipping interests. Then, their chiefs travelled to the U.S. together to negotiate restitution payments for 29 Lloyd and 35 Hapag ships seized in April, 1917 when the U.S. entered the war, and for the seized Hoboken piers. This important working together included consideration of commitment to avoid using these funds, when paid, for destructive tonnage expansion.

When at the end of 1925, NDL suddenly moved to absorb freight lines it had long owned or controlled (See "Mergers") the Lloyd and Hapag were close to equality, with a very similar distribution of services. The time seemed right for another attempt at reasonable togetherness.

On 19 March, 1926 Hapag and Lloyd signed a thirty-years operations agreement maintaining their integrities but aiming at equal shares for both in all current or new services across the Atlantic, to the Levant, leaving out the Africa lines, with strived-for equality in tonnages. All services were to be scheduled and promoted as joint; costs and profits were to be allotted in accordance with respective tonnages. Overseas agencies were to be consolidated for major savings. Disclosure was postponed pending exploration of the U.S. anti-trust implications.

In May, the agreement was accepted by both boards to start on 1 June, but with continued secrecy. Meanwhile, preparing for the coordination of available and needed vessels began. The *Resolute* and *Reliance* were to enter the La Plata service. NDL's *Sierra Nevada* would replace Hapag's aged *Holsatia* in the Cuba-Mexico service. A second *Columbus* was to be ordered, see Blue Ribbon", the present one to be upgraded to give ten vessels for the Hamburg-Bremen-New York route: 4 Hapag *Albert Ballin* class, the fourth, *New York*, was due for launching in October; 4

```
ERNST GLÄSSEL                           BREMEN, 30. December 1933.
                                        BLUMENSTRASSE 5
                                        FERNRUF 24 Nr. 48400

Herrn Kapitän W. Drechsel
c/o North German Lloyd
Pier No.4 Ft.of 58th Street
 Brooklyn,NY.

Lieber Herr Kapitän!
            Ihr Schreiben vom 13. Dezember hat mich sehr er-
freut und danke ich Ihnen deshalb dafür sehr und erwidere Ihre guten
Wünsche zum Weihnachtsfest und neuen Jahr.
      Ihren Ausführungen bringe ich volles Verständnis entgegen und
möchte dazu meinerseits bemerken, dass jeder an seinem Platze seine
Pflicht tun und sich durch nichts darin beirren lassen soll. - Der von
Ihnen aufgeworfene Gedanke des Zusammenschweissens ist schon ganz recht,
es wäre das wenigstens eine grosse Sache, aber an sich halte ich ihn
für verkehrt. Es müssen beide Gesellschaften unabhängig von einander
bestehen bleiben. Die Zusammenschweissung mit einer in die Augen fallen-
den Verbilligung hat natürlich etwas Bestechendes, aber was bedeutet das
schliesslich gegenüber der Zugkraft verschiedener Gesellschaften, die
durch Jahrzehnte in einem gewissen Kampf zueinander standen und dabei
gross geworden sind.
      Die Union im Jahre 1930 sollte ganz anderen Zwecken dienen. Sie
sollte die Reibereien nach aussen ausschalten, nach innen aber jeder
Gesellschaft die Selbständigkeit lassen, damit jede Gesellschaft ihre
bisherige Klientel auch behalten könne. Es ist nun mal im Wirtschafts-
leben so, dass 1 + 1 nicht 2 ( in diesem Falle Hapag + Lloyd), sondern
höchstens 1,2 bis 1,5 ergeben. Selbstverständlich spielen die Unkosten
in den heutigen Zeiten eine grosse Rolle, aber es ist nach meinen Be-
griffen pennywise und poundsfoolish, die Kosten zusammen zu legen, denn
ebenso wie 2 Pferde mehr ziehen als eins, ebenso müssen 2 richtiggehende
Organisationen mehr schaffen als eine, wobei durchaus die Notwendigkeit
ist, dass sie stramm geführt werden und sich nicht aneinander aufreiben,
sondern sie sollen Konkurrenten aufreiben. Leider haben aber Lloyd und
Hapag sich gegenseitig aufgerieben.
      Statt der heutigen Halbheiten wäre selbstverständlich eine Ein-
heits-Gesellschaft vorzuziehen. Es würde aber für Bremen der sicheren
Tod bedeuten, wenn etwas Derartiges zur Durchführung käme. Es mag ja
sein, dass wir durch unsere beiden Schiffe in diesem Augenblick in der
Nordatlantik-Fahrt den Hamburgern etwas Voraus haben, auf die Dauer
müssen wir uns in Bremen aber nicht einbilden, dass wir der Platz für
eine deutsche Einheits-Gesellschaft bleiben werden, und noch viel we-
niger für alle die anderen Relationen. Ein absolutes Verschmelzen
Hapag-Lloyd auf dem Nordatlantik bedeutet in höchstens 5, vielleicht
schon in 3 Jahren das Verschwinden des Verschwinden einer bremischen
Reederei.
      Hoffen wir, dass die massgebenden Herren auch in der Regierung
sich in der nächsten Zeit eingehend mit den Fragen der Schiffahrt be-
schäftigen, damit ein Weg aus der Unsicherheit und dem Tasten gefunden
wird.
      Mit besten Grüssen und Wünschen
                                  stets Ihr
                                  E. Glässel
```

Prediction of former NDL Director General Ernst Glässel as to what would happen in a corporate merger of the Lloyd and Hapag. German text for historical record. December 1933.

Ernst Glässel, considered "The Father of *Bremen* and *Europa*," left the Lloyd in 1932 after stepping down as Director General. He remained in the shipping business, eventually forming his own concern. Here in December, 1933 he expresses his thoughts about the future of the Lloyd within any Hapag-Lloyd merger, limited to operations or completely as one corporation. This is three months after the two formed their North Atlantic Arbeitsgemeinschaft, working community. The letter is written to Captain Drechsel who, from New York, headed up shore-based operations. The entire German text is shown for historical reasons. Some excerpts:

"I consider a complete merger wrong.... Both firms needed to remain independent.... They grew great over the years combating each other.

"The 1930 Union had other purposes: to show common purpose to the outside, but inside leave each one wholly to its self.... It would be pennywise, pound foolish to look only at costs; one plus one is not always two; in many cases at best 1.5 or 1.2. Both needed to be firmly led and challenge each other. Unfortunately, Hapag and Lloyd constantly have antagonized each other.

"Instead of today's half-hearted measures, a total unity is to be preferred. But it would be certain death for Bremen if that came about. We may have the upper hand on the North Atlantic for the moment. But we must not delude ourselves that Bremen will remain the decision-maker for a merged entity.... An absolute merger Hapag-Lloyd on the North Atlantic would mean that in at most five years, possibly already in three, the Bremen enterprise would disappear....

With warmest greetings and wishes, ever your"

(signed) E. Glässel)

This forecast about Bremen and the Lloyd disappearing in any complete Hapag-Lloyd merger was never said publicly by Herr Glässel. There are many, certainly in Bremen and old Lloyd people, who feel this has happened as a result of the 1970 merger into Hapag-Lloyd A.G. After leaving the Lloyd in 1932, Gustav Ernst Glässel remained in shipping, with the Bremer Reederei Merkur, Glässel & Co. the operator. After the war he was "person grata" with the Americans. He became trustee for them at the Lloyd. (Hans Karstedt 5.1946.) He is on the zonal economic council, his concern mostly with shipping matters. He owns a fishing vessel which is getting good catches. His son Ernst Edmund Glässel works with him. The Father has special concern for Haus Seefahrt, and hopes to be able to get new living quarters built outside Bremen for the old valued captains or their widows. The son Ernst Glässel ran the shipping enterprise after his father's death in 1950 at age 72. In 1952, the former Lloyd Captain P.A. Petersen, with his wife on board, brought the Glässel MS *Gloria* to Townsville, Queensland, for bunkering en route to Cairns for a load of sugar for the UK. And kept in touch with old associates, as Captain Drechsel. In writing the son, he wrote: "He was until the end a model for me. His expert understanding for ... our, handling of our ships' port needs pushed us to the utmost performance." Commodore Adolf Agrens, last captain of the *Bremen* in 1939, commented in a letter to Captain Drechsel "Certainly one of the most capable individuals in his field. Only many did not want to admit this during his lifetime." In 1960, Glässel & Co. operated four ships. It no longer exists under that name.

Joint advertising during the 1930s emphasized the two concerns. Togetherness on the North Atlantic. This historical fact made it easier to say "yes" when the question of merger became urgent in 1970.

Shipping Journals carried this advertisement for Glässel & Co. services: Shipping Agents, Freight Forwarding, Ship Construction Contracting.

Lloyd cabin ships, and two fast *Columbuses*. Additional tonnage would be inserted from other routes when needed (NDL *Sierras* from South America, etc.)

Before much happened, this agreement unravelled over rivalries, largely the expansion of Ernst Glässel, now Deputy Director General since absorption of the Roland Linie in December, 1925. With *Sierra Nevada* not available, Hapag gave up the Cuba-Mexico route as *Holsatia* was over-age for further use. The agreement's failure was sealed when in July Hapag completed the purchase from the Harriman United American Lines interests of former Hapag-ships *Reliance, Resolute* and *Cleveland*, and the lease to Piers 84 and 86, North River, Manhattan, close to the Grand Central and Pennsylvania Railroad stations. This was a major attraction for passengers compared to NDL's piers in Hoboken and Brooklyn. When in October Hapag absorbed the Deutsch-Australische D.S. Ges., and D.S. Ges. Kosmos, including the Stinnes ships taken over by them in January, it again far out-sized NDL.

All this supported Herr Glässel's insistence to the NDL Aufsichtsrat (Board of Directors) and Vorstand (Management Board) that not one but two new ships had to be built if the Lloyd was once again to be competitive in its historic role on the North Atlantic.

The decision was made in December, 1926.

In the Annual Report issued on 28 March, 1927 the Vorstand announced that "In order to approach our earlier position in the New York service, we have decided to order two passenger liners which will meet the highest requirements in the international passenger traffic in every way." Ships of 46,000 tons.

The first word about *Bremen* and *Europa*. The decision was heavily based on the hope and expectation of U.S. restitution payments. The view was the old saying: "Only when we run express steamers is the Lloyd in its glory."

Hapag had known what was coming through its close relationship with Blohm & Voss shipyard, it to build one of the two ships. Immediately after the announcement another attempt was made to rationalize tonnages and participations on routes served by both parties. Hapag's price was

Commodore Kruse and his officers gave this photograph to the author's Father "with our admiration." in May, 1935, at the end of Resolute's *cruise around the world. From left:*
3. Officer G. Bursch, 4. Officer H. Davitz, 2. Officer O. V. Essen, 2. Officer P. Ölkers, Commodore Fritz Kruse, 1. Officer P. Thormöhlen, 2. Officer W. Vogel, 3. Officer R. Büschler.

ceding the *Europa*, to be built in Hamburg, in exchange for two of its *Albert Ballin* class ships. It was evident that ownership was more important than jointly operating or scheduling their ships. It was not until three years later, amidst the reality of the deepening world depression, that the two firms began cooperating effectively. Had they done that in 1927 they might not have made additional takeovers, overtonnagings and disruptions of old loyalties that had painfully to be reversed in the troublous 1930s.

The decision to build *Bremen* and *Europa* was made feasible by the expectation of U.S. restitution payments as no Reich subsidies were wanted or available. In 1928, $20 millions loan was raised in the U.S., the lenders in turn basing their willingness on the U.S. repayments to be made. With the two ships planned for maiden voyages in April, 1929, the Lloyd looked to early and sizable income to pay off the nearly One Hundred Million Marks cost of the two liners.

It came out otherwise. 1. A three-months shipyard strike postponed completion of the two ships; 2. In March, 1929 *Europa* burned out at the fitting-out quay in Hamburg. She had to be rebuilt, only entered service in March, 1930. That, and the fire lost the Lloyd fourteen months of expected and needed sizable boost in earnings to repay a final cost of the ships 28% above the original price. Thus, 3. when Black Friday hit the stock market on 25 October, 1929 the Lloyd was suddenly exposed financially. This was compounded by the resulting world depression with its disastrous reductions in passenger and freight volumes.

With mutual desperation in Bremen and Ham-

The two Commodores, Fritz Kruse - Hapag and Leopold Ziegenbein - Lloyd. On Bremen, *June, 1936.* R. Fleischhut Photo.

Handelsteil der Weser-Zeitung

11 Mai, 1932

Norddeutscher Lloyd

Geheimrat Albert in den Vorstand berufen

Bremen, 12. Mai 1932.

Der Norddeutsche Lloyd teilt mit, daß Herr Geheimrat Dr. **Albert**, Reichsminister a. D. in Berlin, in den Vorstand berufen ist und dessen Vorsitz übernehmen wird. Herr Albert wird am 1. Juni a. c. seine Tätigkeit aufnehmen und in der Hauptsache die Finanz-Angelegenheiten und die damit zusammenhängenden Geschäfte bearbeiten.

*

Last des Aufsichtsrats noch schwerer zu machen, als sie ohnedies ist, und wir halten es ebenso für falsch, der Arbeit des neuen Leiters des Norddeutschen Lloyd auch weiterhin mit vorgefaßter Meinung zu begegnen.

Die Gerechtigkeit gebietet zu sagen, daß Albert mit dem Eintritt in den Vorstand des Norddeutschen Lloyd ein erhebliches materielles Opfer bringt, denn er hat in Berlin zusammen mit dem ehemaligen deutschen Generalkonsul in Newyork, v. Lewinsky, ein großes Anwaltsbüro. Er gibt seine Praxis auf, weil ihn, wie man uns sagt, die Aufgabe, den Norddeut-

Report in the 11 May, 1932 Business Section of the Weser-Zeitung, *Bremen: Privy Councillor Albert is joining the Management Council and will be its Chairman. His main activity will be financial problems. The Lloyd and Hapag will now have a joint Management Council. Messrs. Glässel and Stadtländer, Lloyd, and Cuno and Böger, Hapag, will become colleagues.*

It was a year later, in May, 1936 that Commodore Kruse ended another cruise, that on sistership Reliance, *in New York. He then went home on leave on* Bremen, *sailing the 29th. The author was on board on a post-graduation trip. The frontispiece of Volume I is of the author with Commodores Kruse and Ziegenbein on the bridge. Here is a welcome-home Radiogram from Captain Kruse on the author's return from that trip, on 20 August.*

burg, as events overtook Germany's and the world's shipping and economies, in March, 1930 Lloyd and Hapag formed a Fifty-Years Union Agreement with a single operating Vorstand but continuing with separate Boards of Directors. Events overwhelmed this belated decision. How do you plan a new hospital when you are taking patients down ladders from one that's burning? In fact, Herr Glässel's acquisitions continued in 1930, meant as he felt at the time, to give the Lloyd a better base to meet circumstances, but in effect undermining the spirit of the March agreement.

1931 was the fateful year. The J. F. Schröder Bank, the one that had done the financial juggling that supported NDL's acquisitions and the building of *Bremen* and *Europa*, failed. The Austrian Kreditanstalt collapsed with domino effect. Britain went off gold. The U.S. imposed the Smoot-Hawley Tariff on the rest of the world. Finally, on 6 November, 1931 General Director Carl Stimming died at age 55, worn out physically and spiritually by what had to be done. By then the Lloyd's debts were a staggering 177 Million Marks, twenty millions more than at the larger Hapag. Herr Glässel became the new General Director. Now the task was to dismantle what he had spent six years building up: divesting other lines, sloughing off tonnage to scrappings and abroad, heavily to the USSR, layup of ships, discharging of crews, drastically reducing port and office staffs. And no new-buildings.

When in 1932 the Lloyd and Hapag boards asked Herr Glässel to step down he refused until it was proved to him that no way out of this dead-weight debt could be found until a Director acceptable to the Reich was in place. It had retracted, under the threat of a collapsing Lloyd and Hapag, its 1930 demand for repayment of the shipbuilding credits advanced in 1925 earlier than the 1935 due date.

The price: a New Director General. In May, 1932, the former Reichs Minister of Commerce, Dr. Heinrich Albert, became operating chief at the Lloyd. A man of legal, not shipping experience. In August, 1932 Herr Glässel gave up his post as a Director and left the Lloyd.

In January, 1933 Adolf Hitler was named Reich Chancellor. In March he was given dictatorial powers by the Nazi-controlled Reichstag. In the Fall, Dr. Albert was replaced by Dr. Rudolph Firle, the Lloyd Freight Director, and an experienced shipping person, one more acceptable to Berlin. The Lloyd, in greater difficulties than Hapag, became more subservient to Berlin.

In October, 1933 the Reich signed an agreement with the cities of Bremen and Hamburg to form the Hanseatische Betriebs Ges. Hanseatic Operations Co. the Reich to hold 50%, Hapag and Lloyd each 25%. Immediate aim was the building of three fast passenger ships for the Far East service. From then on, through reshuffling of lines, ships, large scrapping programs, selloffs even to the USSR, and credits for Germany's lead-

In March, 1939 after Captain Drechsel had gone over the design construction of Hapag's new building Vaterland *the line gave a Gabelfrühstück, Buffet Lunch, on* Hamburg *for "Our deserving former Commandant of* Meteor," *one of two white-painted cruising yachts in service until World War I. Captain Drechsel evidently was the only commandant of both a Hapag and a Lloyd steamer. The menu had a color rendering of* Meteor *on the cover. See p.411.*

ing shipping enterprises, their activity helping to restimulate shipbuilding, and under constant National Socialist government pressure, there was less Hamburg-Bremen, Hapag-Lloyd enmity, more cooperation.

Ships were traded with route and tonnage reorganizations; ships were built for the same trade to common design; schedules were consolidated; there was joint promotion, booking of passengers and freight. The most successful joint effort, in fact the model for the hopes in the eventual 1970 Lloyd and Hapag corporate merger into Hapag-Lloyd A.G., was the North Atlantic Arbeitsgemeinschaft, Operations Community, 1933-1939. This was run from Bremen by Heinz Schüngel, NDL's North America Manager in New York from 1922; in New York by the same-positioned for Hapag C. J. Beck, with NDL's John Schröder as Passenger Manager, and NDL's Inspector (Marine Superintendent) as Ship Operations manager, (See "The New York Inspectorate").

Until the war broke in 1939 (Herr Schüngel died just before) this quadriumvirate ran a highly effective and friendly operation, an admired and respected pace-setter for the rest of the shipping industry.

In 1994, the Bremen vs Hamburg rivalry remains very real. Dartmouth History Professor Tom Nichols was called out when he replied Bremen to a question about Hanseatic cities on the TV Program Jeopardy. He was right, of course, and so was the adjudged winner with Hamburg. From the November, 1994 Dartmouth Alumni Magazine.

Hamburg?   Bremen!

Nichols was re-Jeopardized

DOUBLE JEOPARDY!

Last spring we reported that govy prof Tom Nichols won $45,690 in a *Jeopardy!* winning streak. Nichols was sent packing in the fifth program when he answered "Bremen" in response to "The full name of this German city calls it a Free and Hanseatic port." Nichols's opponent said, "Hamburg." Turns out Nichols wasn't wrong; both Bremen and Hamburg are correct responses. The producers invited Nichols for a makeup program that aired October 10. Nichols won another $11,990 and got a shot at *Jeopardy's* championship show.

126   Norddeutscher Lloyd Bremen

NDL Fleet: Ships 385 — 416

385. *Franken 2*   1926-1940
Bremer Vulkan, Vegesack #634   1926   7789   155.82x19.48
Triple Expansion   NDL 5800, BV 5500   13.25
14, Certificate for 18   66-61

Launched 22/2/1926. Reg. 4.1926. *Franken* and *Schwaben* got the two engines ordered for the intended sister of *Berlin*. Instead, *Dresden*, ex-*Zeppelin* #269 was repurchased from Britain. 1934 Bauer-Wach exhaust turbine installed, now 14 knots. 1939 took refuge at Padang, Sumatra. 10/5/1940 seized by the Dutch when Germany invaded Holland, ren. *Wangi Wangi*, managed by Stoomvaart Maat. "Nederland," 25/5/1941 sunk by U 103 ca.90 mis off Monrovia in 5.24N, 12.00W en route Sydney-Freetown.

386. *Schwaben 2*   1926-1947
Bremer Vulkan, Vegesack #635   1926   7773   155.82x19.44
Triple Expansion   NDL 5800, BV 5500   13.25
12 + 3 Pullmans   72-62

Launched 10/7/1926 with engine ordered for intended *Dresden*. Reg. 26/8/1926. 9/1927 its engine was transferred to *Columbus* #300 after one of its engines collapsed with a shaft breakage on 27/8/1927. 1928 given new triple-expansion engine with Bauer-Wach exhaust turbine and large reefer capacity for U.S.-Canada West Coast service. 26/9/1939 left refuge of Santos, arr. Tromsö 29/10. 4/10/1944 partly sunk in British air attack on Bergen. Raised late 1945, LU. 13/8/1946 letter from John H. Kulenkampff, NDL Director to Capt. W. Drechsel, New York: "What is to happen to the badly damaged *Schwaben* lying at Hamburg we do not know." 31/5/1947 assigned to Yugoslavia, repaired, ren. *Bosna*, 7,453 tons, managed by Jugoslavenska LinijskaPlovidb. 9/1961 arrived Spalato for BU by Brodospas.

387. *Ingo*   1926-1934
J. Frerichs & Co.,
Einswarden #396   1926   3950   116.56x15.31
Triple Expansion   2100   11
12 + 2 Pullmans   50

385. and 386. Franken *and* Schwaben *were the first units of a new building program, Berlin #308 having been the last of the immediate postwar new construction. A sister for* Berlin *was cancelled. The engines were built into these two freighters designed around them, for the West Coast service.* 385 - Copyright by H.M.I. *and* 386 - Ludolf Timm Ship Photos - Hamburg.

387. Ingo. *All the Hamburg-Bremer Afrika-Linie ships carried a large number of boats, twelve in this view. This could be for loading/unloading at places where ships have to lie off-shore and "boys" handled the boats with cargo.*

Ordered by Hamburg-Bremer Afrika-Linie before absorption by NDL. Launched 2/1926. 9/3/1926 delivery. 10/1935 again reg. for HBAL, managed by Woermann Line, Hamburg but with Bremen Key on stack. 9/1939 LU in Trieste. 27/1/1941 sunk off Libya by submarine *HMS Upholder* while in transport service to the Afrika Korps.

388. Berengar ran on Roland Linie's West Coast routes. It spent WWI interned in Chile, then went to British operators, in 1927 was bought back by NDL. Here she is with Hamburg-South America Line stack, but with Bremen key, her home port.

388. *Berengar*	1926-1934		
Bremer Vulkan, Vegesack #537	1911	4845	127.40x16.29
Triple Expansion	3000	11	52-49

Launched 18/3/1911 for Roland Linie. 8/1914 LU in Viña del Mar, interned 26/9/1918 seized by Chile, engines had been damaged by crew to prevent Allied use. 7/1920 towed to Germany, repaired 29/7/1921 delivered to Shipping Controller, man. by Oakwin S.S.Co., Sir William Reardon Smith & Sons, managers, Cardiff. 1923 ren. *General Botha*. 3/1927 bought by NDL, ren. 1934 to Hamburg Süd in reshuffle of German shipping, in purchase-charter. 16/5/1935 reg. for H-Süd (Hamburg-South American Line), with Bremen key. 3/12/1937 ren. *Petropolis*, Hamburg. 28/9/1939 in naval service as *Sperrbrecher*, barrage clearer, XI. 15/4/1940 mined off Korsör, 4/8/1940 back in service for H.S. 29/4/1945 heavily damaged in Elbe during air raid, put ashore at Juelssand. 1946 B.U. began.

389. *Haimon 2.*	1927-1935		
Flensburger S.B.Ges #303	1910	4920	128.32x16.53
Triple Expansion	3000	11	51

Launched 30/12/1910 for Roland Linie, del. 21/2/1911. 8/1914 LU in Rotterdam. 1916 moved to Germany (even while Germany was sinking neutral Dutch vessels and had to replace these?) 8/9/1919 to Shipping Controller, managed by T.L. Duff & Co., Glasgow. 1920 to St. Just S.S. Co. (Sir Wm. Reardon Smith & Sons). 1921 ren. *Quebec City*. 2/1927 bought by NDL, ren. *Haimon 2*, forcing renaming of *Haimon 1* to *Ancona 1* #357. 8/1935 for BU to Nordseewerke, Emden.

Haimon #389 was so built in 1911 for Roland Linie, postwar was the British Quebec City until bought by NDL in 1927 and given back its old name. Arnold Kludas collection.

Dresden 2, ex-*Zeppelin* #269 repurchased and into NDL service to New York.

389X. Dresden *was launched as* Zeppelin #269, Volume I in June, 1914. It went to British service after the war, bought back in 1927 instead of building the planned sister for Berlin. While cruising off Norway she ran aground in June, 1934.

Dresden, *ex Zeppelin, was built for 15.5 knots but averaged only 13.25 in a stormy crossing in November, 1928, the same storm that sank* Vestris. *See Berlin #308 which rescued some of its people.*

Twin Screw Mail Steamer »DRESDEN«
Captain R. Wurpts

16th Journey — From Bremerhaven to Newyork

Nov. 1928	Lat. North	Long. West	Miles	Wind	Remarks
8.	—	—	—	NE 5	11⁰⁰ departure Bremerhaven, moderate to rough sea
9.	50°30	0°1 E	367	NW. 4	17²⁴ arrival Cherbourg – 18¹⁰ departure Cherbourg moderate sea
			79		
10.	51°85	7°28,5	259	SW 5/6	15²⁴ arrival Queenstown – 17⁰⁰ departure Queenst. cloudy, moderate to rough sea
			45		
11.	51°05	15°04	263	SW 5/7	„ rough sea and SW-swell
12.	50°19	22°39	292	SW/W 6	„ rough sea, very rough SW-swell
13.	49°06	30°11	301	WNW/SW 5/6/3	„ moderate to rough sea, very rough W-swell
14.	47°45	36°17	256	SW/WNW 5/11	„ rough to very high sea and WSW-swell
15.	46°13	41°40	239	WSW/WNW ⁸/⁸	„ very rough sea and swell
16.	43°41	48°32	329	WNW 8/3	„ very rough to light sea
17.	42°20	56°17	356	WSW/NNE 1/5	„ light to moderate sea
18.	41°17	64°15	362	NNE/S/WNW ³/⁶	„ moderate sea
19.	40°35	71°58	353	WSW 1/3	fog, light sea
			87	SW 6	18¹² end of the journey

Total miles: 3588.   Duration of the journey: 11 days, 6 hours, 54 minutes.   Average speed: 13,245 knotes.

Aller was the first of a series of twelve large fast freighters completed 1927-1929. They had four high masts, were named after German rivers. Although they varied in tonnage from 7,250 to 8,500, their lengths varied little, just over 160 meters except for the last two: *Isar* and *Donau* with Maier bows projecting above the water line, meant to reduce resistance. A 1/1/1928 fleet list also has "*Elbe* (under construction) ca.8000 Ts." No *Elbe* was built. However, *Este*, also a river name, came out in 1930, almost the same hull, with two masts, with higher horsepower and speed, natural progression in a series of similar ships. One wonders if the intended *Elbe* was cancelled before construction began to allow redesign into *Este?* The depression prevented building more of its type. *Este* was put onto the most competitive, high-prestige service to the U.S.-Canada West Coast with high-value reefer cargoes. See *Elbe #433, Weser #434.*

Aller *was the first of an eventual series of twelve River-Class freighters built 1927-1930, all four-masters except the last,* Este, *which had a cruiser stern unlike the counter stern of the first eleven.* Ian Farquar collection.

Ships 385 - 416   131

390. *Aller 2.*   1927-1943
Bremer Vulkan, Vegesack #643   1927   7627   160.57x19.22
Triple Expansion   6400   14
16, certificate for 18   70

> Launched 30/4/1927. Delivery 7/6/1927. Shorter stack than on sisters. Deck house only at after mast. Ran to Far East and Australia. 9/1939 LU in Lourenzo Marquez. 20/5/1943 sold to Portugal, ren. *Sofala*, Cia. Nacional de Nav., Lisbon, 7957 Ts. 24/11/1968 arr. Castellon for BU by I.M. Varela Davalillo.

In 1927 and 1928 new-style DEUTSCHE SEEPOST cancels were introduced on Lloyd ships:
 1. BREMEN-KANADA. The service began in 1928 after Canada lifted restrictions against German immigration. NDL put its middle-sized passenger ships onto this run to Montreal, later to Halifax, sometimes on to Galveston: *Seydlitz, Köln, Crefeld*. The route was given up in 1930 with the depression.
 2. BREMEN-KANARISCHE INSELN. This new Sea Post began with entry into service of *Arucas* and *Orotava* in the Fall of 1927. It lasted until the war.
 3. NORDKAPFAHRT. Used on *Lützow, Seydlitz* and *Sierra Cordoba* on their North Cape cruises. *Dresden* was using this cancel with NORDKAPFAHRT excised when she grounded and was lost in 1934.
 4. MITTELMEERFAHRT (Mediterranean). Used on *General von Steuben*. Other Lloyd cruises there continued to use from 1926 into 1935 the cruise cancel issued in 1913.
 5. SKANDINAVIEN-OSTSEEFAHRT. This was used 1927-1937 on *Stuttgart*, and *General Von Steuben* on Baltic-Scandinavia cruises.

391. *Orotava*   1927-1945
F. Krupp A.G., Kiel #488   1927   3337   102.07x14.29
Triple Expansion   2200   12.5
48   52.57

> Launched 5/1927 for the Canaries-Northern Brazil fruit trade. 9/1939 outfitted at NDL's Technical Service. Bremerhaven for 500 deck passengers for the service to East Prussia. 1940 ren. *Robert Möhring* for the captain lost in the 3/1940 scuttled sister *Arucas*. Intended as evacuation transport for Operation "Seelöwe", the invasion of England. 6/3/1945 off Sassnitz sunk through aerial bombing and naval artillery, 553 dead.

392. *Arucas*   1927-1940
Flensburger S.B.Ges. #406   1927   3359   101.19x14.29
Triple Expansion   2200   12.5
48   52-56

> Launched 2/6/1927, delivery 3/8/1927. M.V. to the Canaries, 27/11/1927 to North Brazil. Late 8/1939 en route to Bremen with cargo of bananas took refuge in Vigo. 10/2/1940 left to get home. 3/3/ east of Iceland found by *HMS York*, ship scuttled in 63.08N, 14.42W with loss of 13 in the stormy weather of 53 in crew, including Captain Robert Möhring.

Orotava *and sister* Arucas *were built for the fruit and vegetable import trade from the Atlantic Islands. With space for 48 passengers, the voyages were ideal for honeymooners and vacationers.* NDL Archive.

392. Arucas *took refuge in Vigo when the war broke. Like most other German ships caught abroad, it was ordered to try to reach home, the cargo of bananas by then had been landed and consumed. Sister* Orotava *when put into the East Prussia Sea Service during the War was renamed* Robert Möhring *for* Arucas's *captain. He went down with the ship.*

393. Amsel *was the first of six "birds" built for the Levant and general trading. The first Lloyd ocean vessels with cruiser stern. The passengers ate at the "Captain's table."* Photo Courtesy Gert Uwe Detlefsen.

393. *Amsel*	1927-1934		
A.G. Neptun, Rostock #409	1927	1756	84.20x12.90
Triple Expansion		1600	11
8	23		

First of six vessels built 1927-1928 with Bird names for "Argo" service. NDL gave Bird names to its England-Scotland lines, a tradition continued when the new "Argo" in 1897 took over NDL's services, also after its absorption by Roland Linie in 1922, and final absorption with that into NDL in 12/1925. Names thus indicated the ships' trade. Argo's Near East services had ships with "A" names. In 1930, six sisters (#393, 397, 398, 398+, 404 and 409) served the routes to Finland. The 10/1932 schedule indicates #397 and #398 had four two-bed cabins, "eating at the Captain's table." They all had Bauer-Wach exhaust turbines for more horsepower and speed or lower fuel consumption. The system was installed on most subsequent freighters, sometimes retrofitted, until new-building stopped with the depression. Launched 5/1927, first NDL ocean vessels with cruiser stern. Delivery 21/7/1927. 1934 back to the newly-independent "Argo." 1/8/1935 transferred to the newly-organized Atlas Levante Linie, Bremen. 15/4/1936 ren. *Arkadia*. 9/1939 LU in Haydar Pasa (Scutari). 29/3/1941 hit a mine, sank off Constanza. One 1946 report: Raised, rebuilt and put into USSR service. No confirmation.

394. *Grandon 2.*	1927-1934		
J.C. Tecklenborg,			
Geestemünde #247	1912	5883	142.80x17.43
Triple Expansion	3600	12	49-54

Launched 4/2/1912 as *Düsseldorf* for Deutsch-Australische D.Ges., Hamburg. 8/1914 LU in Barcelona. 8/5/1919 delivery to French Govt. 15/2/1921 to Shipping Controller, managed by Ellerman Lines, Glasgow. 1921 ren. *City Of Boston,* Hall Line, Liverpool. 7/1927 bought by NDL, ren. for South America service. 1934 buyer-charter to H. Süd, 16/5/1935 reg. for H. Süd in Bremen, key on stack. 3/8/1937 ren. *Patagonia*. 9/1939 took refuge in Montevideo. 19/11/1939 arr. Hamburg having got through the British naval blockade. 1942 into naval service. 15/4/1944 heavily damaged in bombing attack in Kirkenes. 4/10/1945 sunk by the British with gas munitions in the Skagerrak.

394. Grandon *was the fifth pre-war Deutsch-Australische D.S. Ges. vessel Roland Linie or the Lloyd bought back from Allied owners: obvious reliance on quality ship construction. The ship as originally built in 1912 named* Düsseldorf. Ian Farquhar collection.

Ancona renamed from ex-*Haimon 1*, 1925-1928 See #357

---

395. Ilmar 2   1927-1934
Bremer Vulkan, Vegesack #542   1911   5470   132.58x16.60
Quadruple Expansion   3000   11.5
12   47

Launched 28/1/1911 as *Emir* for Deutsch Ost-Afrika Linie, Hamburg. Delivery 4/3/1911. 5932 Ts. 5/8/1914 captured by *HMS Cormorant*, taken to Gibraltar, managed by Elder, Dempster & Co., Liverpool. 1916 ren. *Polladern*. 12/1917, J. Herron & Co., Liverpool, Managers. 9/1921 ren. *Sunheath*, Sun Shipping Co. (Mitchell Cotts & Co.), London. 12/4/1927 bought by NDL, ren., in service to West Africa. 10/1935 reg. for renewed H.B.A.L., Woermann Line, Hamburg, Managers, but with Bremen key on stack. 31/10/1939 to Hochsee Fischerei Ges. Anderson & Co., Hamburg, ren. *Hamburg*, a floating fishery mother ship/fishmeal factory, 6136 Ts. 4/3/1941 torpedoed and sunk in the Vaagsfjord, Lofoten Islands, by HMS *Offa*.

395. Ilmar *was another buy-back from the British. Here picking up logs in a West African stream with stack rings of the joint German service.*

396. ***Main 3.***	1927-1940		
Bremer Vulkan, Vegesack #644	1927	7624	160.57x19.22
Triple Expansion		6400	14
16		71	

Launched 30/6/1927. MV 4/8/1927 to Australia, also ran to East Asia. 4/1934 Bauer-Wach Exhaust Turbine installed, now 7250 HP, 14.5 kns. 9/4/1940 torpedoed and sunk by Norwegian destroyer *Draug* off Haugesund during the invasion of Norway. Photo with rotorship *Barbara* in "Sails."

Main *made its maiden voyage to Australia; the wool auctions there pull the fastest ships the liner-companies can provide. With the experimental Rotor Ship* Barbara, *tied up in Bremen.*

Norddeutscher Lloyd Bremen

397. Star 2 was second of the new class of small general-trade vessels, on the slow side, 11 and 11.5 knotters instead of 12 knots. The Lloyd always pushed for cutting fuel costs.
R. Kleyn Photo.

397. **Star 2.**	1927-1932/1934-1935		
Jr. Frerichs & Co.,			
Einswarden #499	1927	1724	84.12x12.86
Triple Expansion	1600	11.5	
	8	24	

Launched 7/1927. Delivery 30/8/1927 to "Hanseatische," 1933 to Argo. 1934 back to NDL. 7/9/1935 to Atlas Levante Linie, Bremen. 15/4/1936 ren. *Sparta*. 9/1939 en route Dubrovnik-Oran, LU at Calgiari. 1940-conversion to Sperrbrecher not completed. 12/7/1941 sunk off Tripoli in 34.29N, 35.49E in air attack. 1943 raised. 8/5/1945 sunk at Oreglia, between Cannes and Genoa, in air attack. 1947 raised, rebuilt at Genoa with new forepart, 2649 Ts., ren. *Sparta* for "La Fortuna" Cia Soarma de Nav., Genoa. 1949 Mario Rossi fu Geremia, Genoa. 1955 to Silvio Bonaso, Genoa. 14/2/1967 en route Ravenna-Alexandria crew abandoned ship after engine room explosion off Cephalonia. It stranded near Cape Capri. 21/2/1967 got off. 22/2/1967 after condemnation towed to Kynosoura, LU. Reportedly sold for scrapping, presumably locally.

398. **Ganter**	1927-1934		
G. Seebeck A.G.,			
Geestemünde #464	1927	1769	84.40x12.83
Triple Expansion	1600	11	
8	25		

Launched 15/9/1927. Trials 10/1927. Ice-strengthened for Baltic Sea service. 1/1/1933 in Argo charter management. 16/7/1934 sold to Argo, Bremen. 30/4/1945 damaged off Stettin in aerial attack. 13/6/1945 to Ministry of War Transport, London, ren. *Empire Consistence*, Ellerman's Wilson Line, Hull, Manager. 1948 Glen & Co., London, Manager. 1951 to Netherlands Govt., resold as *Dagny*, Rederi A/B Sally, A. Johansson, Manager, Mariehamn. 1959 "Class Withdrawn" in Lloyd's. Repaired. 1960 again classified. 1/4/1967 arr. Bremen for BU by Eckhardt & Co.

398. Ganter *was strengthened for Baltic winter ice. February, 1929 was the coldest and thickest ice in any one's memory. One Lloyd ship sank through ice crushing. Old battleships were used to try to open harbors as icebreakers weren't heavy enough. Here as the Finnish* Dagny. William Schell Collection.

GLOBUS REEDEREI. NDL fleet lists 1927-1933, when the last vessels were sold off or broken up, includes ships of the Globus Reederei. All had GER... names. Some had Lloyd captains. The Globus which NDL acquired outright in 1927 was founded on 22/4/1915 by Director Ernst Glässel and Prokurist Heinrich Hemsoth of the Roland Linie to import iron ores from Scandinavia. The first two ships were among the 18 that Roland Linie owned in 1914. Eventually, there were five vessels. In 1916, Globus contracted with the Kaiserliche Marine to manage the Russian vessels seized in the Black Sea as prizes. The war ended before this came about. On 19/12/1921 Globus was converted into a share company, Hemsoth becoming a Director. Control and management remained with Roland Linie. In 1920, he also joined the Roland Board and, in 1926, after Roland Linie was absorbed by the Lloyd, he joined its Board. In 1927, Roland's telegraphic address was ORLANDA. In 1930, it had the same telegraphic address and Postal Box address in Bremen as Roland Linie and Horn Reederei. On 26/6/1932 the liquidation of Globus was decided on. The liquidation ended on 22/4/1933 with disposal of the last vessels.

Germar ran in the "B" service to East Asia as far as Vladivostock. 1928 *Gerwin* was in the Lloyd schedule to Cuba. In the early 1930s Lloyd's carried the GER... ships as without owner; evidently all were up for sale while LU. A Globus appears in the 1950s as Globus Reederei Gmbh, Erste Deutsche Walfang Gesellschaft as overseer. The firm had no connection to the former Globus controlled by the Roland Linie, then by NDL.

Built in 1895 for China Mutual S.S.Co., 398X. Gerfrid *was the oldest of six vessels taken over in 1927 with the "Globus."* William Schell collection.

398* **Gerfrid**	1927		
D.&W. Henderson & Co., Glasgow #383			
	1895	4742	125.15x14.86
Triple Expansion	2100	11.5	
	ca. 45		

Launched 10/1895 as *Teenkai* for China Mutual S.S.Co., Alfred Holt & Co., Liverpool, owners-managers, 4930 Ts. 9/1922 bought by Globus. 18/1/1923 reg. at Bremen. 1927 merged into NDL. 20/8/1927 sold for BU, resold to Cia. de Comercio e de Nav. Mercantil, S.A., Rio de Janeiro, ren. *Merity.* 1927 Lloyd's has "classification withdrawn at owner's request." 1972 deleted from Brazilian register. 1973 BU at J.C. Tecklenborg works, Geestemünde.

Germar	1927-1933		
Swan Hunter & Wigham Richardson,			
Wallsend on Tyne #846	1911	4681	117.53x16.22
Triple Expansion	2350	45	

Launched 3/1911 as *Arabien* for East Asiatic Co., Copenhagen. 9/2/1916 to A.S.D.S. Orient, Copenhagen. 7/4/1927 bought by Globus. 1927-1928 in NDL Schedule and fleet lists. 30/7/1932 LU in Bremerhaven. 11/1932 expected sale to USSR fell through. 2/1933 sold for BU in Geestemunde at the former J.C. Tecklenborg yard.

Gernis		1927-1933		
Reiherstieg S.W., Hamburg #417	1905	3552	108.30x13.41	
Triple Expansion		1200	11.5	28
I-60 T-632		76		

Launched 28/6/1905, delivery 2/9/1905 as *Bavaria* for Hapag, 3898 Ts. 5/8/1914 LU in Havana, until 10/4/1915 kept ready as possibly supply ship for raiders. 7/4/1917 seized by Cuba, chartered to the USS Bd. 1917-1918 NOTS operation, Naval Overseas Transport Ship. 1919 LU in Bremerhaven. 1920 back to Cuba, ren. *Calixto Garcia* for A. Garcia y Cia, Havana. 12/1/1923 to Böning & Co., Bremen at auction, ren. *Lotte.* 1927 to Globus, ren. 3533 Ts. Passenger space removed. In 1927-1928 NDL schedules. 1931 managed by Deutsche Levante Linie, Hamburg. 1933 in Danzig sold for BU, 4/1934 by Blohm & Voss, Hamburg.

398x. Germar was built in Scotland for the East Asiatic Company, went into Lloyd schedules in 1927, shown here with Roland Linie black-topped stack. William Schell collection.

*398x. Gernis as the Cuban Calixto Garcia, originally was Hapag's passenger ship Bavaria, later it ran only as freighter. Ex-*Ricardo Siepmann collection.

Gerrat 1. 1927
S.B.Ges. Unterweser Lehe #122 1917   854   64.71x9.63
Triple Expansion   500

Launched 7/1917, compl. 11/1917 as ODA for D.S. Vesterhayet, Esbjerg J. Lauritzen, Operator, 922 Ts. Delivery embargoed by Goverman Govt. 22/10/1920 sold to Deutsche Petroleum Ges., ren. *Richard Hentsch*. 26/3/1919 *Hentsch*, Hamburg. 28/2/1923 to Globus, ren. 6/5/1927 to Carsten Rehder, Altona, ren. *Alfred Rehder*. 18/3/1930 *Bengt Sture*, Sture Red., A.G. Eruths, Trelleborg, Operator. 29/10/1942 en route Danzig-Oxelsund with coal torpedoed by Soviet submarine SC-406 15 mis. NW of Stilo.

140   Norddeutscher Lloyd Bremen

398x. Gerrat 2 also was built, in 1914, for the Danish East Asiatic Company, in 1927 went to NDL's West Africa routes subsidiary. The 1928 Africa Lines advertisement includes Gerrat *among freighters carrying "a limited number of cabin passengers." Where would they fit in this design?*

Gerrat 2.	1927-1933		
Ramage Ferguson, Leith #237	1914	4393	109.60x15.61
Triple Expansion	1650	39	
Some Passengers			

Launched 3/1914 as *Transvaal*, Ostasiatiske Ko., Kopenhagen 4317 Ts. 25/10/1915 to N.S.D.S. Orient. 10/6/1927 bought by Globus, ren. 1927-1932 in West Africa service of Hamburg-Bremer Afrika-Linie. 31/8/1932 LU in Bremerhaven. 11/1932 expected sale to USSR fell through. 7/1933 sold for BU at Bremer Vulkan, Vegesack.

Gerwin	1927-1933		
W. Dobson & Co.,			
Newcastle #186	1914	4169	109.60x15.61
Triple Expansion	1650	39	

Comp. 5/1914 as *Rhodesia* for A.S. D.S. Orient, owned by Det Ostasiatiske Co., Copenhagen. 7/7/1927 to Globus, ren. 11/1932 expected sale to USSR fell through. 1/1933 UB at Frerichswerft, Einswarden.

398xx. **Strauss**	1928-1933		
G. Seebeck A.G.,			
Wesermünde #468	1928	1756	84.37x12.83
Triple Expansion & Low-pressure Turbine	1550		11.5
	8	21	

Launched 12/1927, delivery 19/1/1928 to D.S. "Seefahrt", Bremen, sister of NDL's *Lumme* #409 and *Erpel* #404. Included in a 9/1928 NDL fleet list. 1/1/1933 in Argo charter, 28/7/1933 sold to Argo. 15/3/1945 sunk by mine contact 10 miles south of Kiel Lightship. 1948 raised, rebuilt by A.G. Weser, Bremen, new bow, stack, cruiser stern, 93.05m., 1926 Ts. 19/5/1951 again in service as ALTAIR. 8/4/1963 sold to R. Harmstorff, Lübeck for BU.

398x Strauss 3. *One of six sisters built 1927-1928, strongly reinforced for ice service, but also used elsewhere. Four passengers ate at The Captain's Table.* Courtesy Reinhold Thiel's "Argo" H.M. Hauschild Verlag, Bremen.

399. Augsburg *was one of a number of freighters bought in Britain in 1927 for intermediate runs while express freighters for the blue-ribbon services were being built.*

399. *Augsburg 2.*   1927-1940
Northumberland S.B. Co., Howden-on-Tyne #221
                               1915   6512   132.73x16.38
Triple Expansion   3000   12.5
4   48

3/1915 delivery as *Northwestern Miller* to Norfolk & North American S.S. Co. (Furness Withy & Co., London). 14/7/1927 rammed in English Channel, repaired. 2/1927 bought by NDL, ren., ran to East Asia, 1935 to Mexico. 9/1939 LU in Dairen, with *Fulda* #307 and *Bremerhaven* #280. 9/5/1940 sold to Wm. Müller & Co., Batavier Line, Rotterdam, with *Vreedenburg* as intended name. But next-day German invasion of Holland wiped out the sale. 5/12/1940 to Japanese Govt., ren. *Teiryo Maru*, Teikoku K.K Kaisha, Tokyo. 19/7/1944 sunk by U.S.S. *Guardfish* 150 m. N.W. of Cape Bojeados, Luzon, in 20.07N, 118.20E.

400. *Gieseen 2.*   1927-1929
Northumberland S.B. Co., Howden-on-Tyne #222
                               1915   6513   132.75x16.38
Triple Expansion   4   50

6/1915 del. as *Southwestern Miller* to Norfolk & North America S.S. Co., Furness, Withy & Co., owners, London. 12/1927 bought by NDL, ren., put into East Asia service. 12/3/1929 en route Rotterdam-Shanghai stranded on Saddle Island off mouth of Yangtse River.

400. Giessen and Augsburg were sisters built in Britain in 1915 for trans-Atlantic service. Both bought in December 1927 because of their speed, 12.5 knots, for the Far East service.

#401 Mosel in Bremen freeport. Ships handled cargo on the shoreside into sheds, even into railcars, and to and from lighters.
Bremen Staatsarchiv Photo.

401. *Mosel 2.*	1927-1941		
A.G. Weser, Bremen #870	1927	8428	162.33x19.42
Triple Expansion with Bauer-			
Wach exhaust turbine	6500	14	
16	72-59		

Launched 10/1927, delivery 12/1927. Ran to East Asia and Australia. 9/1939 LU in Kohsichang. 2/11/1940 chartered to Japan, ran from Japan. 1942 ren. *Teizui Maru*, Taikoku Sempaku K.K., Tokyo. 18/4/1945 after mine-contact run onto a reef in Shimonoseki Strait in 34.03N, 130.50E.

In 1922 the Bremen Banker J.C. Schröder joined the NDL Board of Directors. He was the financial juggler who organized the funding of the postwar fleet rebuilding, highlighted by *Bremen* and *Europa*. In 1926, Schröder bought the majority shares of A.G. Weser, Bremen to settle its fight with the Lloyd. He fused it, J.C. Tecklenborg, Geestemünde, and the Hamburg Yard of Vulcan A.G., Stettin into the Deutsche Schiffs-und-Maschinenbau A.G., called *Deschimag*. In 1927, the Stettiner Vulcan, A.G. Seebeck, the majority shares of Neptun Werft, Rostock and the Frerichs Werft in Einswarden were absorbed. When the Vulcan and Tecklenborg yards were shut down, part of their personnel went over to A.G. "Weser," then building *Bremen*.

In 28/3/1927, hardly 8½ years after the Armistice, the Lloyd announced following its annual meeting the decision to "contract for two passenger liners." This was the first publicity for the building of *Bremen* by A.G. Weser, and *Europa* by Blohm & Voss, Hamburg. All mention of these ships rated them as 46,000 tons. This seems to have been the initial-design size, before the major re-design to a size that would take the engines and structure to provide the needed 26.25 knots contract speed for six-day vessels. Anything less would have destroyed the entire purpose of building the two ships: to again make the Lloyd pre-eminent in passenger ship service.

402. *Lahn* 1927-1942
J.C. Tecklenborg, Geestemünde #423
               1927   8498   162.96x19.42
Triple Expansion, Exhaust Turbine 6500   14
               16   72

Launched 8/10/1927. 12/1927 M.V. to East Asia. Also served Australia. 26/8/1939 left Brisbane with cargo of wool, lead and zinc concentrates. 16/9/ arr. Talcahuano. 9/10/1939 left for Montevideo. 9/3/1940 to Buenos Aires. 9/7/1940 "sold" to Lloyd Argentino, ren. San Martin. 7/9/1942 to Flota Mercante del Estado, ren. *Rio Parana,* 8677 Ts., Buenos Aires, 28/6/1943 to Government agency Empresa Lineas Maritimas Argentinas, Buenos Aires. LU. or used as floating pilot station at Recalada in the Plate estuary? 1975 BU per 1985 report.

402. Lahn *left Brisbane with a full cargo days before the war broke 1 September, 1939, fled to Chile, then on to Buenos Aires, spent the rest of its service under the Argentine flag. Here she is in Genoa, to the right of Lloyd Sabaudo's* Conte Biancamano. *Prior to 1932, when the three major Italian lines were merged into the "Italia."*

403. Oder in September, 1937 with Gneisenau *escaped the typhoon that hit Hong Kong and sank some twenty vessels. Copyright* Wolfgang Fuchs.

```
403. Oder 3                         1928-1941
Vulcan Werke, Hamburg #210    1928      8516        162.96x19.42
Triple Expansion, Exhaust Turbine       6500   14
16                                 71
```

Launched 25/10/1927. Delivery 20/12/1927. Ran to East Asia and Australia. 1-2/Sept/1937 with *Gneisenau* #440 escaped damage in Typhoon while ten large, ten small ships were sunk. 9/1939 sought refuge in Massawa. 23/3/1941 scuttled in Strait of Perim when approached by *HMS Sloop Shoreham* during attempt to get to Germany.

```
404. Erpel                          1928-1933
A.G. "Neptun," Rostock #414   1928      1771        84.16x12.83
Reciprocating & Low Pressure Turbine    1550   11.5
8                                  21
```

Launched 12/1927. 27/2/1928 delivery to Hanseatische D.S. Ges., Hamburg. Ice-strengthened for Baltic services. 1/1/1933 chartered, then 5/1/1934 sold to "Argo." 12/12/1945 to Norwegian Government, ren. *Skognes*, managed by A.S.T. Thoreson, Oslo. 1946 ceded to USSR, ren. *Lado Ketskhoveli*.

404. Erpel *was ice-strengthened for winter service in the Baltic. One of six sisters.* Ex. Schiffahrt International.

1/1928 *Bremen 3*, ex *Prinzess Irene* #149 ren. *Karlsruhe* to make name-room for *Bremen 4*, under construction.

405. Neckar with the Blue Peter up at Kowloon Dock, Hong Kong. Behind is Coblenz #301 or a sister. Don Gammon Photo.

405. **Neckar 2.**	1928-1944		
A.G. Weser, Bremen #871	1928	8417	162.33x19.42
Triple Expansion, Exhaust Turbine		6500	14
16	69-51		

Launched 24/11/1927. Delivery 16/1/1928. Ran to East Asia and Australia in wool season. 3/10/1939 in mine-clearing duty as *Sperrbrecher Viii*. 26/8/1944 badly damaged at Brest by air attack and scuttled 28th.

406. **Trave 2**	1928-1943		
A.G. Vulcan, Stettin #635	1928	7956	154.42x18.47
M.A.N. Diesels	4600	13	
12-16	51		

Launched 23/11/1927, delivery 9/3/1928 for East Asia and Australia service. 1938 rebuilt by *Deschimag* Weserwerft, + 10ms, 10,000 HP Diesels, 16.5 kns, 8068 Ts. 4/7/1938 ren. *Regensburg*. 9/1939 in Yokohama refitted as supply ship for raiders *Komet* and *Orion* disguised as Japanese *Toyo Maru*. 1/1941 at Lamutrek Atoll, Carolines. 5/5/1941 left Dairen for France, made two voyages. 10/12/1941 in Pacific supplied Raider *Thor*. 12/2/1942 left Bordeaux. 10/12/1941 again in Pacific supplying *Thor*. 12/5/1942 took POWs from *Thor* N. of Tristan da Cunha and reefer cargo from seized *P & O Nankin*. It followed to Japan via Batavia. 30/3/1943 returning from Japan scuttled W. of Iceland when approached by *HMS Glasgow*.

406. Trave, one of three motorships in the River Class; all were in the 1930s given larger engines, longer bows for 3.5 knots more speed, necessary to meet the competition on the East Asia service. Nautical Photo Agency.

407. ***Nürnberg 3*** 1927-1932
Wm. Doxford & Sons, Sunderland #454
	1913	5135	128.02x16.49
Triple Expansion	3000	11.5	48

Launched 11/2, delivery 10/4/1913 as *Nordmark* to Hapag, 5106 Ts. 23/3/1919 delivery to Shipping Controller. 8/5/1919 assigned to France, but returned to Britain. 1919 managed by Ellerman & Bucknall S.S. Co., London; 1921 sold to it, ren. *Kosmo*. 7/1927 bought by NDL, ren. 1932 *Wellen*, Sovtorgflot, Vladivostock. 1960 RLR.

407. Nürnberg British built, was bought in 1927. But by depression 1932 it was surplus and was sold to the USSR. Hapag-Lloyd A.G.

"City of Dunedin"

NDL's prewar Porta *#278, one of a large series of standard freighters, was bought back from the British in 1928. Here as the Ellerman's* City of Dunedin *sketched by Peter Nicolson. Renamed* Lippe 2. #408

---

408 Lippe 2 ex Porta #278 repurchased.

---

409. **Lumme** 1928-1929
J. Frerichs & Co., Einswarden #500
                              1928   1730   83.97x12.86
Reciprocating L.P. Turbine   1550   11.5
8   25

Ordered by NDL. Launched 31/1/1928. 22/3/1928 on completion transferred to D.S. Reederei "Seefahrt", Bremen, controlled by NDL. 1932 to Hanseatische D.S. Ges., Hamburg. From 1/1/1933 managed by "Argo," 28/7/1933 sold to "Argo." 12/10/1944 torpedoed off Kirkenes by Soviet submarine S 104.

409. Lumme *in the Kiel Canal en route to the Baltic with what look like barrels of deck cargo. Copyright* Wolfgang Fuchs.

148 *Norddeutscher Lloyd Bremen*

410. Alster *here taken in New Zealand, ex* Ian Farquhar's collection. *The Wool Auction Express.*

410. **Alster**   1928-1940
A.G. Vulcan, Hamburg #211   1928   8514   162.96x19.42
Triple Expansion, Exhaust Turbine   6500   14
16   69-57

Launched 5/1/1928, delivery 25/2/1928. Ran to East Asia and Australia, in wool season. 10/4/1940 as supply ship under Captain O. Scharf, ex-*Europa*, during invasion of Norway, captured north of Bodö by destroyer *HMS Icarus*; after repair of demolition-bomb damage, taken to Kirkenes. Ore loaded for Harstad and on to Kirkwall, ren. *Empire Endurance*. Booth S.S. Co., Middlesbro, managers for Ministry of War Transport, 8570 Ts. 20/4/1941 torpedoed by U-73 in 53.05N, 23.14W, 450 miles off N.W. coast of Scotland, 5 survivors.

Effective 1/4/1928 NDL acquired the **Weidtmann Linie**, Henry Stahl & Co., Hamburg as managers. Of the three ships involved, *Friedrich Jürgen* was sold to France, renamed *Jeanne Schiaffino* by mid-year. *Zander*, 958 Ts., was carried by Lloyd's Register in 1928-29 as NDL but still registered in Hamburg. This is an error as by the end of 1928 Germanischer Lloyd has *Zander* under Hanseatische D.S. Ges. It had been owned since 1902 by "Argo," from the 12/1925 absorption of Roland Linie, and with it "Argo," controlled by the Lloyd. In 1946, it became *Mezen*, USSR. The third ship, *Butt*, 736 Ts., ex *Ludwig Stahl*, is in the 1928-29 additions as transferred directly to "Hanseatische" but with registration changed to Bremen. Some "Hanseatische" ships were registered in Bremen, some in Hamburg. An NDL fleet list in a 9/1928 passenger list includes *Zander*, ex-*Max Weidtmann*, ex-*Taunus*, and *Butt*. Both in 1932 are listed as Hanseatische D.S. Ges., Hamburg, in a 10/1932 schedule are on the Bremen-England run. From 1/1/1933 they are under "Argo" along with the other "Hanseatische" ships. The name Henry Stahl & Co. has survived as ship operators, and the name Weidtmann as the Hamburg shipping firm of Weidtmann & Ballin, the name of the former Director General of Hapag.

The Weidtmann Linie and Henry Stahl & Co. were founded in the early 1920s. In 1964, in a letter to the author Herr Henry Stahl wrote "The firm of Henry Stahl & Co. was founded by me in June, 1922. It was converted by the attorney Heinrich Günther for the Weidtmann heirs into Henry Stahl & Co. as shipping firm. I remained the sole Business Manager of this line with a service from Hamburg to London. In October, 1926 after this run was given up, I left the firm. Herr Günther took over all shares and renamed the firm Weidtmann-Linie G.m.b.h."

The Weidtmann-Stahl firm had close ties to "Argo." The later Captain Otto Dietrich was officer with "Argo" during 1909-1922, on 22/1/1922 became captain of *Taunus* of the Übersee (Overseas) Reederei, Geestemünde. *Taunus* soon was sold to Henry Stahl & Co. Captain Dietrich from 1/4/1924 to 1/4/1928, when NDL took over the firm, was Captain and Inspector for Weidtmann. From then until his death (2/9/1957) he was Captain and Inspector for "Argo," the early years while it still was part of NDL. In October, 1994 Henry Stahl & Co. with two vessels filed for bankruptcy, one of the many small operators unable to continue. By then Argo was down to three ships.

Rhederei A.G. Von 1896. The Lloyd controlled this concern through its own share holdings, plus those held by "Argo." The ships of "von 1896" never appeared in NDL schedules. In 1927 they were transferred to Hanseatische D.S. Ges. The Hamburg in fleet lists of September, 1928 and January, 1930 the ships are listed, later again as being in "Hanseatische D.S. Ges." #309. Both firms had FRACHT-LLOYD (Freight Lloyd) as Telegraphic address. The following ships were involved:

Oceana - Oliva - Olympia - Ophella - Optima - Orla - Orlanda - Ostara. *Oceana*, *Olympia* and *Optima* in June, 1930 went to Ozean D.Ko. (H. Schuldt), Flensburg, as *Hasselburg*, *Breitburg* and *Mildburg*. The others became part of the recreation of "Argo" in 1932, first as Hanseatische D.S. Ges., Hamburg, from 2/1933 again as Argo Reederei A.G., Bremen.

410x. Butt gave 45 years of steady service, for various owners, including the Weidtmann Linie and Argo, both part of NDL in the 1920s. Copyright Wolfgang Fuchs.

410x. Ostara, Olympia *and* Oceana *were all Dutch built, part of ten small vessels traded to the Roland Linie in 1920, then passed on to Rhederei A.G. von 1896 for coastal services.* From Talbot-Booth, Merchant Ships 1949-1950.

410x. Ophelia's *aftermast was a goalpost, unusual on German ships.* Ex Journal of Commerce, 1963.

410x. Oliva *was one of eight O-named ships of the Rhederei A.G. von 1896 which NDL owned. They appeared in some fleet lists, but not in schedules. Here entering Hamburg harbor.* P.A. Kleinschmidt Photo.

410x. Orla *and* Orlanda *were 1,289 tons sisters, built at Kiel in 1921.* Copyright Wolfgang Fuchs.

410x. Orlanda's *well-deck indicates she had limited cargo-weight acceptability forewward.* Copyright Wolfgang Fuchs.

Ships 385 - 416   151

410. *Butt*   1928-1932
W. Harkess & Sons, Middlesbro #178
                                1909   736   57.91x9.14
Triple Expansion   580   9   15

5/1909 delivery as *Webburn* 800 Ts. to Whiteway & Ball, Teignmouth. 1914 for W.Ball & Son, Teignmouth. 1918 J.F. Coonan, Teignmouth. 1920 Ensign Shipping Co., Teignmouth, R.F.H. Fletcher, manager. 4.1924 ren. *Ludwig Stahl*, H. Stahl & Co., Hamburg. 12/5/1927 to Weidtmann Linie, Hamburg, Henry Stahl & Co. Correspondent-Manager. 12/5/1928 under Hanseatische D.S. Ges., Hamburg. Ren. *Butt*. 2/1933 to Argo. 1943 sunk of Norwegian coast. 1944 raised and repaired. 28/8/1945 in Kiel. 12/1951 after repairs to Kurt Schubert & Co., Kiel, 721 Ts. L.F. Mathies & Co., Manager. 19/3/1954 auctioned off to P. Berendsohn, BU at the Köhlbrandwerft in Hamburg, arr. 23/3/1954.

410x. Optima *was one of the early engine-aft designs. It took a long time for the bridge structure also to go aft.*

410.** *Zander*   1928-1932
Schiffswerft & Maschinenfabrik A.G., Hamburg #595
                                1921   776   58.23x9.29
Triple Expansion   450   9   14

Launched 15/10/1921 as *Harriet* for Navis Reederei, Hamburg. 13/3/1922 to Nilsson Jr. & Rose, Wismar. 1926 *Erna II*, A.S. DS Erna II, Bergen (C.M. Iverson, manager). 5/1928 *Max Weidtmann*, Weidtmann-Linie GmbH, Hamburg. On NDL acquisition transferred to Hanseatische D.S. Ges., Hamburg, ren. *Zander*, 958 Ts. 2/1933 bought by Argo, Bremen. 19/2/1946 to USSR, ren. *Mezen*. 1961 RLR.

Zander *410x, under 1,000 tons, was acquired with* Butt. *Both in the 1930s went to Argo for its coastal services.*

411. M.S. Saale *and sister* Havel *in 1928 were NDL's lead ships on the prestige West Coast North America run. Later re-engined for the Far East service.* Robert Potts Collection.

411. *Saale 2*	1928-1941		
F. Schichau, Danzig #1197	1928	7262	153.60x18.61
Sulzer Brothers Diesel	4500	13.3	
16	50		

Launched 12/5/1928, reg. 26/7/1928. Built for East Asia route 4/10/1938 as *Marburg* back in service after lengthening by A.G. Weser, Bremen, 7564 Ts., new 10,000 HP Diesels, now 16.5 kns. 24/8/1939 passed Suez Canal, 27th arr. Genoa, 31st LU in Naples. 1940 moved to Venice, transport for Kriegsmarine. 21/5/1941 sank from mine contact off Cape Ducato, S.W. point of Lefkas Island.

412. *Havel 2.*	1928-1941		
F. Schichau, Danzig #1198	1928	7256	153.60 x 18.67
Sulzer Brothers Diesel	4500	13.5	
16	50		

412. Havel 2 *is loading 200,000 gallons of fish oil at Vancouver in October, 1934.* Photo by L. Frank for the Vancouver Harbor Board.

Ordered as *Spree* for East Asia service, launched 9/8/1928 as *Havel*. 10/10/1928 reg. Ran also to Australia. 4/3/1938 as *Coburg 2* in service after lengthening by A.G. Weser, Bremen, 10,000 HP Diesels, 17 kns. 9/1939 LU in Massawa. 4/3/1941 in attempt to reach France or Germany, scuttled in Indian Ocean on approach of *HMAS Canberra* in 08.42S, 61.42E.

413. Remscheid. One of five Deutsch-Australische ordered ships delivered to the Allies and bought in 1927-1928 by NDL. It liked the 13 knots capability of these ships to match its new River Class.

413. ***Remscheid 2***	1928-1932		
Flensburger S.B. Ges. #347	1919	5823	136.95x17.74
Triple Expansion	3600	13	49

Launched 16/8/1916 as *Waldenburg* for Deutsch-Australische D.S. Ges., Hamburg. Compl. 6/1917, LU. 8/4/1919 delivery to Shipping Controller, F.C. Strick, London, manager. 1921 *Maritime*, R.J. Thomas & Co., London & Holyhead. 1922 *Cambrian Queen*, William Thomas Shipping Co., London. 4/1928 bought by NDL, ren. 12/1932 to USSR, ren. *Kiev*, Sovtorgflot, Odessa. 13/4/1942 en route Murmansk-Island sunk by U-435 in 73.22N, 28.48E.

Three major technological changes were applied in an accelerating tempo during the 1920s aimed at improving the efficiency of ship propulsion:

1. Diesel engines. The Danes began this before 1914. Other nations followed, the U.S. most reluctantly because of union pressures; Diesels meant smaller crews. Farrell Line's *City of New York* of 1930 was for long the only U.S. ocean Diesel vessel.

2. Bauer-Wach Exhaust turbines. These took left-over steam from reciprocating engines and converted it into drive, adding half a knot or more speed.

3. The Maierform. This involved a sharply slanting forward bow; a different rib format allowed more cargo space, and a reformed stern. Dutch lines in the 1930s converted several of their liners. Into 1940, some 600 ships were built worldwide with the Maierform. For some years, A.G. Weser, Bremen held the rights. In the 1980s, Royal Interocean Lines had four sisters built in this design. The actual differences no longer are clearly recognizable.

Messageries Maritimes rebuilt its *Champollion* of 1924, 12,300 tons, with Bauer-Wach and the forward Maierform, found it added two plus knots and a much smoother flow of water. Eight Lloyd ships had the distinctive Maier bow: *Isar* and *Donau, Agira* and *Abana, Saar* and *Osnabrück, Scharnhorst* and *Gneisenau*.

414. *Isar*	1929-1947		
A.G. Vulcan, Hamburg #213	1929	9026	166.40x19.40
Triple Expansion, Exhaust Turbine		6500	14
12-16	73		

Launched 23/1/1929. Reg. 4/5/1929 for East Asia, Australia trades. Maier Bow to reduce friction, with sister *Donau*. During war, ore-carrier from Sweden and Norway. 5/1945 found damaged in Moss. 13/8/1946 letter from Johann Kulenkampff to Captain W. Drechsel: "Isar lies ready for delivery in Travemünde." It was towed to Britain and repaired. 1947 ren. *Stanroyal*, Stanhope S.S. Co., London, J.A. Billmeir & Co., managers, London. 1952 *Haran*, Hasim Mardin, Istanbul. 1959 *Necip Ipar*, Ipar Transport Co., Istanbul. 18/6/1965 BU began by H.Söker in Halic.

414. Isar *was NDL's first Maier-bow vessel, the design meant to ride over rather than through the waves. The largest so-built NDL ships with the curved bow were sisters* Scharnhorst *and* Gneisenau *of 1935. Card written December, 1930 at Antwerp by Oskar Scharf, then Staff Captain, later actual captain of* Europa.

415. *Donau 2*	1929-1945		
A.G. Vulcan, Hamburg #214	1929	9025	166.40x19.40
Triple Expansion, Exhaust Turbine		6500	14
12-16	72		

Launched 25/3/1929, delivery 6/6/1929. Maier Bow to reduce friction. Todd pulverized coal firing. MV to US-Canada West Coast. 17/1/1945 was to have sailed from Oslo with some 1200 troops being evacuated, sunk by limpet mines from British *Mardonius* stuck to hull near Dröbak, Oslofjord. Bow out of water, stern under. 10/4/1952 salvaged by German heavy-lift salvage ships *Ausdauer* and *Energie*, wreck to Norway, planned to rebuild as *Bergensiana* for Jansens Rederi A.S., Bergen, but resold for BU. 15/8/1952 left Oslo under tow for Bremerhaven where BU by Eisen & Metall.

415. Donau *made its maiden voyage to the U.S.-Canada West Coast.* Robert Potts Collection.

416. *Frankfurt 3*		1929-1941	
Bremer Vulkan, Vegesack #687	1929	5522	141.25x17.14
Triple Expansion, Exhaust Turbine		4200	13
4		50	

Launched 23/5/1929. On 26/6 from *Frankfurt* and sister *Chemnitz* at the Vulkan Yard, most of the Lloyd personnel watched as *Bremen* was towed from the *Deschimag* Weser Yard to Bremerhaven. The mast tops were hinged back to clear power cables. A day of celebration for the NDL. 10/7/1929 delivery. 6/9/1939 arr. Talcahuano, left 7/5/1941, arr. Rio de Janeiro 6/6, left 27/7/1941 for France or home. 4/8/1941, some 540 miles south of the Azores scuttled on order to stop and surrender by *HMS Cavina,* Ocean-Boarding vessel in 31.12N, 36.45W. One lifeboat with 20 aboard sailed to Lisbon.

416. Frankfurt *and sister* Chemnitz *were built to upgrade U.S. east coast freight service.* Hapag-Lloyd A.G.

CHAPTER 4

Again Mail Handling at Sea

Germany began providing Sea Post service on vessels in 1886 with opening of the Lloyd's subsidized Imperial Mail routes to East Asia and Australia, with three feeder-distributor lines. Their purpose: to support German commerce and travel on German ships. Passengers and crews found the shipboard postal services a handy way to dispatch their correspondence. As did Germans overseas where the vessels called; e.g. at any of the many ports in East, West and Southwest Africa, a local resident could come on board, buy Germans stamps and affix them and deposit the mail in a set-out mail box or at the Purser's office. At sea, this mail would be postmarked with "Deutsche Seepost" and put ashore at whatever port quickest onward handling was available. On the North Atlantic, from 1891 on when the U.S. and Germany opened a joint Sea Post service, that included sorting of mail at sea. It would be ready at the end ports for local delivery or immediate onward dispatch, saving a day or more. All this bypassed the problems of unreliable or infrequent local service, and saved having to wait for the next ship. All these services ended with the war in 1914. Some never re-opened, such as the New Guinea and Central Pacific lines, then German colonies, even a Yangtse Line, or Capetown-German-Southwest Africa.

Some Sea Post routes did resume soon after the war: Hamburg-West Africa on the Lloyd-controlled *Winfried* #331, the first new-building in that trade. On 12 November, 1921 when the Lloyd resumed its Bremen-La Plata service, a Sea Post was on board the *Seydlitz*. And when on 12 February 1922 it departed for New York, it had the Bremen-New York Sea Post on board. The Ost-Asiatische Linie and Ost-Asiatische Haupt(Main) linie, were worked on vessels going back into that trade. With resumption of cruising in 1925, the pre-war *Polarfahrt, Norwegenfahrt*, and *Mittelmeerfahrt* (Mediterranean) cruise sea posts again were used.

The NDL 1924 Yearbook carried a report on the Sea Post Service by H. Munnich, its Director. "To the branches of shipping activity largely ignored by the travelling public are the Sea Posts. Their existence on board for crews and travellers was a welcome opportunity to send and receive mail and wirelesses. This had importance for all business circles involved and overseas trade. During the building of *Columbus* #300 (in 1923) the

At New York Pier 86 the equivalent of the G.P.O.'s Late Fee Mail was available: a box or mailbox marked: "Per Schiffskasten" (Ship's Box), and name of ship sailing next. Company mail certainly was handled that way, stamping, cancellation and sorting being done by the Sea Post on board. For any one else in the know with German postage, evidently it could also be used. This mark from a 1936 mailing.

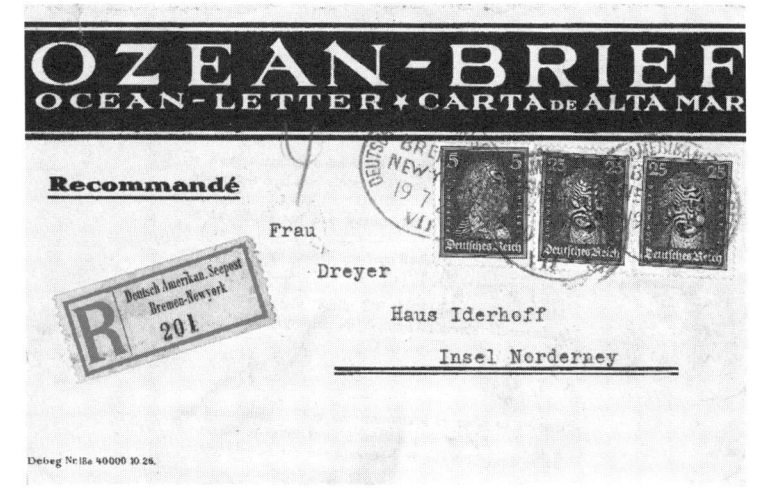

An Ocean Letter radioed from the New York-bound Columbus, *to a Lloyd ship headed for Bremerhaven, addressed to the Friesian Island of Norderney. The Sea Post and Registry were applied on this eastbound vessel.*

The former NDL George Washington, *its largest ship in 1914, was seized by the U.S. in Hoboken in 1917, became a war transport, after the war ran for the new U.S. Mail S.S. Co., which was succeeded by the United States Lines. It used both the U.S.-German Sea Post and the Deutsch-Amerikanische Seepost. Both these Sea Posts were worked by American and German clerks, the American staff in charge on eastbound voyages, the Germans westbound. The slower NDL ships had only German staff and the Bremen - New York Sea Post from 1922 into 1938.*

facilities for the mail-working room and quarters for the postal workers were built in. One held in mind that this service would help to rebuild German trade connections with abroad and strongly support them." The Deutsch-Amerikanische Seepost Bremen-New York, and the complimentary U.S.-German Sea Post, both using prewar cancellers, resumed on *Columbus* in November, 1924, in 1925 on German and U.S. vessels. At first, prewar cancellers again were used, until in 1926 new-style U.S.-German Sea Posts appeared with ship names. See Columbus #300 and Berlin #308 for the Ship Posts and Aboard-Ship markings used on these vessels. Also #324 for Ship Mails on the Hamburg-Bremen Afrika-Linie vessels, and #438 for Far East ships.

The former NDL *George Washington*, its largest ship in 1914, was seized by the U.S. in Hoboken in 1917. It became a transport, after the war ran for the new U.S. Mail S.S. Co., which was succeeded by the United States Lines. It used both the U.S.-German Sea Post and the Deutsch-Amerikanische Seepost. Both these Sea Posts were worked by American and German clerks, the American staff in charge on eastbound voyages, the Germans westbound. The slower NDL ships had only German staff on the Bremen-New York Sea Post from 1922 into 1938.

A number of new Sea Posts appeared in the 1920s as the Lloyd reopened old lines or began new ones: Bremen-Cuba was opened in 1923. It had become an important service for the Lloyd in 1901, then in conjunction with Hapag, also going on to New Orleans (in cotton-harvest time),

The Bremen-Cuba Sea Post opened in 1923; Bremen was the Continent's main tobacco-import harbor, also cotton and sugar. The Hamburg/Bremen-Mexiko route opened in 1931 also called at Cuba. The Hamburg-Mexico route, began with the H. Schuldt operations, was taken over by NDL in 1931. All three Seaposts closed in 1933-1934 with the depression, and route re-shufflings.
The Hamburg/Bremen-Mexiko Ship Posts show the Rio Panuco *and* Rio Bravo *as D., Dampfer, Steamer. Actually they were Motor Ships.*

In 1927 and 1928 a new style of **Deutsche Seepost** *cancels was introduced on Lloyd ships:*
*1. **Bremen-Kanada.** The service began after Canada in 1928 lifted restrictions against German immigration. The Lloyd put its middle-class passenger ships on this run to Montreal, later to Halifax and on to Galveston:* Seydlitz, Köln, Crefeld.
*2. **Bremen-Kanarische Inseln.** This new Seepost service was begun with entry into service of* Arucas *and* Orotava *in the Fall of 1927, and lasted until outbreak of the war in 1939.*
*3. **Nordkapfahrt.** Used on* Lützow, Sierra Nevada *and* Sierra Cordoba *on their North Cape cruises.* Dresden *was using this Seepost cancel on her June, 1934 cruise when she grounded and was lost, and had to be broken up by Stavanger salvagers.*
*4. **Mittelmeerfahrt.** Used on* General von Steuben. *Other Lloyd ships cruising the Mediterranean continued to use the earlier* **Mittelmeerfahrt** *Seepost issued in 1913 and used also and again from 1926 into 1935.*
*5. **Skandinavien-Ostseefahrt.** This was used 1927-37 on* Stuttgart, General von Steuben.

Again Mail Handling at Sea 159

Probably the rarest of the Lloyd's between-the-wars cruises was Fruit-Carrier Orotava's 1932 ***Finnlandfahrt***. *A single voyage with ship post. Other vessels before and after the war had cruised to Finland, but none with Seapost.*

Galveston and Mexico. Bremen was the Continent's major tobacco import and processing city.

Five new-design larger Sea Posts appeared only on NDL vessels 1926-1928: on two Bremen-Kanada and previously un-Sea Posted routes: Bremen-Kanarische Inseln, and three cruise marks: ***Nordkapfahrt, Mittelmeerfahrt*** and ***Skandinavien-Oststeefahrt (Baltic Sea)***.

With the expected coming into service of Bremen and Europa in the Spring of 1929, new doublering Bremen-New York Deutsch-Amerikanische Seeposts were issued in 1928 on *Stuttgart, Columbus* and *Berlin*, then on *Bremen* and *Europa*. All these had the comparable U.S.-German Sea Posts. Because of the heavy volume of mail posted on *Bremen* and *Europa*, they were given machine cancellers, with the ship name in a flag, all other mail being hand-cancelled, even the large volume of mail posted on board 1929-1935 for Catapult Dispatch from the ships at sea.

In August, 1929 the Reichspost, Berlin, in

As Bremen-New York passenger traffic expanded in the twenties in the comeback from the war, and with the prospective entry into service, in April 1929, of *Europa* and *Bremen*, a new type of **Deutsch-Amerikanische Seepost** cancels was introduced. Those for *Berlin, Columbus* and *Stuttgart* were issued in 1928. The earliest known date is 5.1.1928 from *Berlin*. The same-style cancels for *Bremen* and *Europa* went into use with their maiden voyages. That for *Bremen* has **Bremen-New York** above and below the date, no **Norddeutscher Lloyd** in the lower segment. A second type of cancel with the ship name in the flag also was used on both vessels in the machine-cancelling of mail, as thousands of pieces, many from collectors, were sent to the ships over the years. The catapult service on both ships, see "The Lloyd Flies", operated through the 1935 season. The **Deutsch-Amerikanische Seepost** operated from Bremerhaven to New York, with German postal clerks in charge. The return trip used **U.S.-German Sea Post** cancels, with U.S. postal clerks in charge. Registered mail service was available, with special labels. The double-ring Seepost cancels on *Berlin* and *Stuttgart* were used only 1928-29, are quite scarce. Those on the other three ships were used into 1939.

reply to a query by Everett Erle of San Francisco, a ship post collector and researcher, advised that 103 German Merchant Ships and two world-cruising War Ships were equipped with Ship Posts.

In 1931, NDL opened a Hamburg/Bremen-Mexiko route that also called at Cuba. This was a Ship Post, provided at the Lloyd's option and expense. The Bremen-Cuba Sea Post ended in 1933, as did the Mexiko route, victims of the depression and Hapag's competition with new ships.

From 1934 on the National Socialist Strength through Joy movement chartered, then bought, and even built ships for low-cost cruising (See "Kraft durch Freude") including some Lloyd ships, with continued management from NDL.

NDL perforated stamps were widely used in the 1920s on company mail such as to the Vulcan Shipyard in Stettin. In years when semi-postal stamps were issued these, too, were perforated. One variety: NL/B stands for Nord Lloyd Betrieb: Its Technical Service (Betrieb) in Bremerhaven. NGL perforations are also found in the 1920s as on a pair of Scott 641, 10¢ yellow, postmarked Varick St. Sta. New York, 25 July, 1929 and catapulted off Bremen for an address in Germany.

In 1932, the *Arucas* of the Canaries reefer service made a cruise to Finland with Ship Post, probably the rarest of the marks in the 1920s-1930s period: one voyage at the bottom of the depression. *Columbus* also made a cruise with a one-time **Gauturnfahrt** Ship Post, with provincial sport groups.

Cruise Ship Posts were introduced in large numbers as the Lloyd and other lines tried to keep their ships and crews occupied during the depression when liner traffic, as on the North Atlantic, declined drastically:

Westindienfahrt from *Columbus* and *Berlin*;

Englandfahrt, Madeirafahrt and **Spanienfahrt** from several ships;

Amazonas-West Indien from *General von Steuben*;

Afrikarundfahrt (around Africa) in 1939 by *Columbus*;

Südamerikarundfahrt from *Columbus* in 1937 and from *Bremen* in 1939. At its end in New York on 24 March many passengers and officers expected to meet again in 1940 on a Weltreise, cruise around the world. It was a dream.

Two new Ship Post services opened in 1935: **Seedienst Ostpreussen**, a ship service connecting Germany with East Prussia, cut off by the Polish Corridor. And a new **Bremen-Ostasien** Ship Post on three new express liners. The canceller included "Jungfernreise" on the maiden voyage.

Some cruises surprisingly had no Sea or Ship Posts: *Columbus'* 1930 Mediterranean cruise or its 1930 and 1931 round-the-world cruises, although Hapag's *Resolute* in 1929 and 1930, and *Reliance* in 1935 and 1936 had Sea Posts; *Bremen* and *Europa's* Bermuda-Nassau cruises, and *Berlin's* one-time voyage to Australia in 1938.

Registry service was available only on the main routes: Bremen-La Plata, and Bremen-New York, and then only on German ships, not on the U.S.-flag vessels even when they had D.A.S.Ps, or U.S.-German Sea Posts.

Ocean Letter service was provided on some Sea Post vessels, and some without. The procedure was to radio a "letter" to a ship, usually of the same line passing in the opposite direction on the same route. That ship would put the message into an envelope and either mail it through the on-board Sea Post or at the next port. The rate for Ocean Letters was less than wireless messages direct to shore stations.

Lloyd ships very occasionally used "buoys" to drop mail while passing close to land, usually isolated islands at sea, as did the Tin Can Mails of the South Pacific. Pre-1914 *Prinzess Irene* sometimes dropped mail while passing the Azores en route from New York to Gibraltar, items posted on board but addressed to the U.S. The casket

Card from a passenger on Robert Möhring *to Danzig, June 1941: "The night is behind us; we slept very well. Peter feels wonderful. There is a strong swell; the weather has been bad, but it is clearing." Even in wartime materials and labor were used to paint Seedienst Ostpreussen on the ship.(See page 133).*

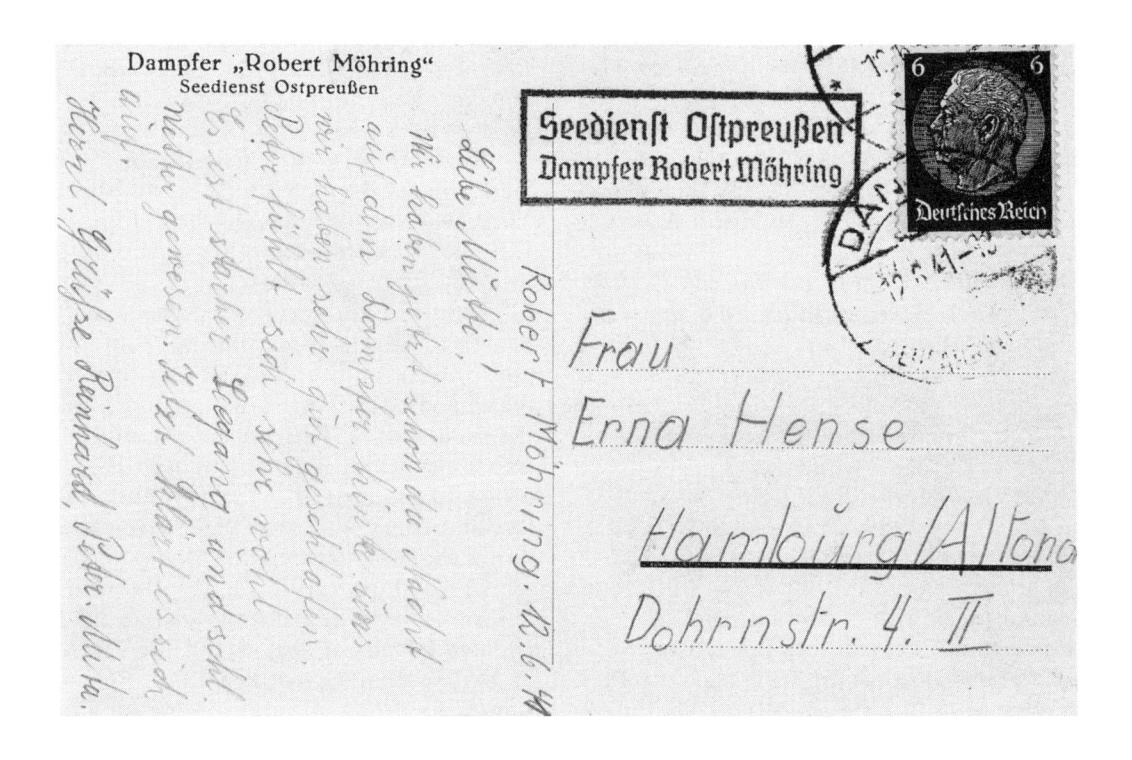

162 *Norddeutscher Lloyd Bremen*

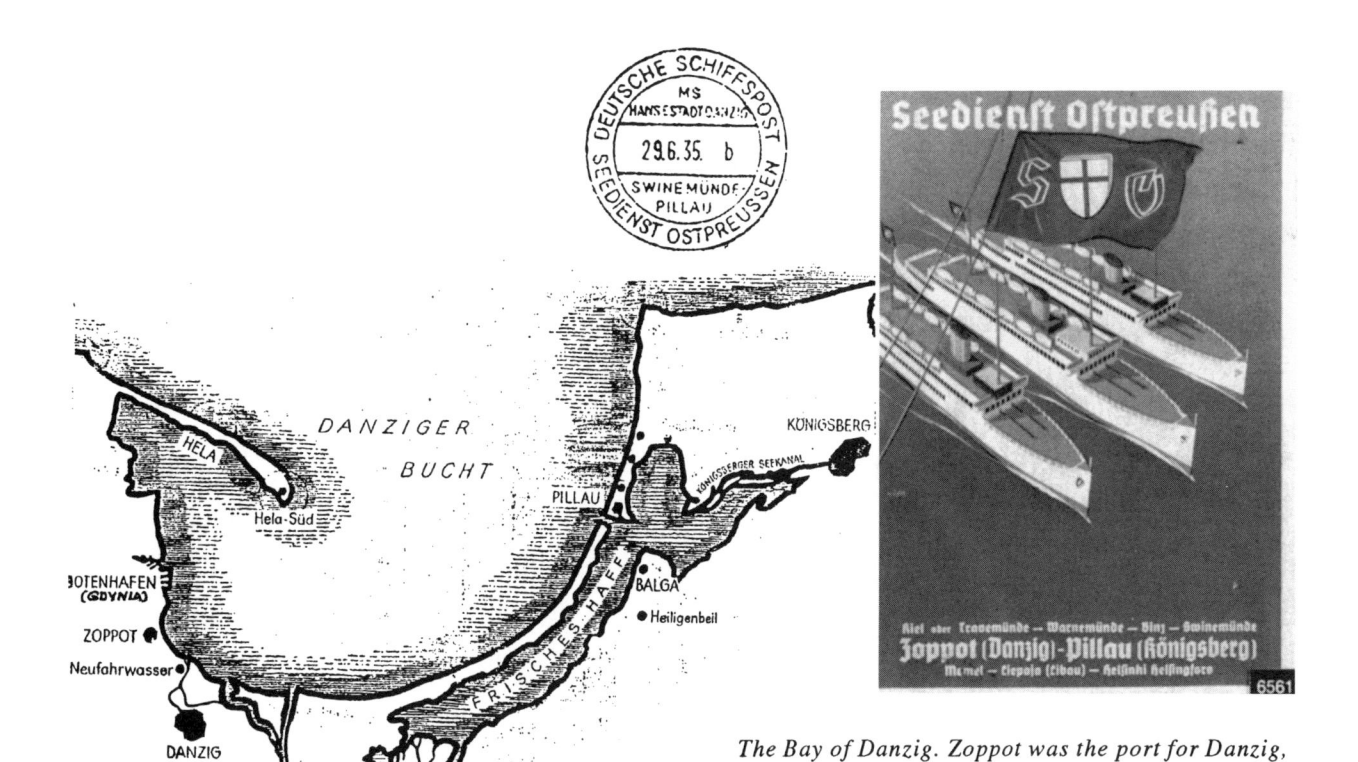

The Bay of Danzig. Zoppot was the port for Danzig, and Pillau for Königsberg. At Gotenhafen, the Polish Gdynia, Stuttgart #303 was attacked by Soviet aircraft in October, 1943 while evacuating wounded and refugees from the eastern. Some 3,000 died in the burned-out ship. It was towed out and sunk in the bay.

In opening the new National Postal Museum in 1994 the Smithsonian Institution recognized the importance of Shipboard Post Offices (the Navy has used them for nearly ninety years) and the meaningfulness of the postal cancel separate from the stamps.

The Treaty of Versailles, signed 28.6.1919, made Danzig into a Free City/State, and gave Poland broad access to the Baltic between Danzig and Germany: the Polish Corridor. In early 1919 emergency ship service with resort vessels left to Germany to East Prussia began, carrying many refugees from East Prussia to vote in the Versailles-mandated plebiscites. First service ran from Swinemünde to Zoppot for Danzig, Pillau for Königsberg, and Memel. The service was subsidized by the Reich Government. Ships for the service were built in 1926, managed by NDL and Hapag. Seapost service, *Seedienst Ostpreussen*, began May/June 1935, "a" was used on the outward trip, "b" on the return trip. The ships also had *On High Seas* marks. The three largest and newest ships in the service, including NDL-operated *Hansestadt Danzig*, ran onto mines off Öland and sank on 9.7.1941. NDL's reefer *Orotava*, renamed *Robert Möhring* for the captain who went down with *Arucas* #392, its sister ship, when scuttled to avoid capture, was serving as an additional vessel, using this ship-name mark.

Again Mail Handling at Sea 163

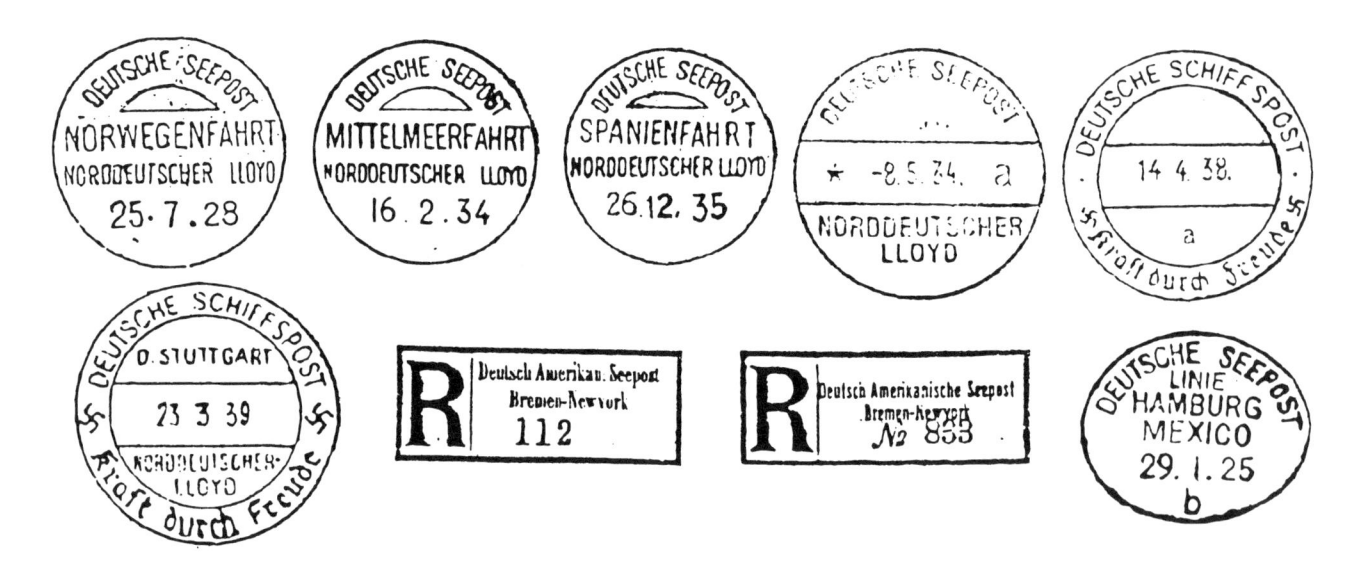

A number of Sea or Ship Posts used on Lloyd vessels are not otherwise shown. They include:
Norwegenfahrt, *used 1913-1914, again 1925-1938.*
Mittelmeerfahrt, *used 1913-1914, again 1926-1935.*
Spanienfahrt, *known 1925-1937.*
Nordkapfahrt *with that wording excised 1934-20.6.1934.*
Kraft durch Freude *- recorded only for 1936.*
Kraft durch Freude Stuttgart *1938-1939.*
Hamburg-Mexico *was used en route to Cuba and Central America by* Sierra Ventana *and other vessels not using the Hamburg/Bremen/Mexiko Ship Post.*
Registry labels are known from Bremen *and* Europa, *two types, rarely with Amerikanische spelled out. 1929-1939.*

would be picked up, money inside for local postage, and handled like ordinary mail. One has to read the messages to identify such sendings. NDL's *Tannstein* in 1959 did this headed homeward from the West Coast-Panama Canal. Mail and postage-money was put into a large coffee can painted red with a Holms light affixed, this used on lifebelts as a night light. The Ponta Delgada, Azores, mail launch was alerted with the air horn (Typhoon). Actually, U.P.U. *Paquebot* rules would have allowed using German stamps on the mail. Buoys also are located in the English Channel, and, it seems, on occasion off Barber's Point, Oahu. There in 1972 the passing German *M.S. Robert Bornhofen*, en route from Japan to the Panama Canal and Europe, dropped a five-gallon can with 16 letters and 12 postcards inside addressed to U.S.-Canada and Europe, $5 for postage, and a bottle of whisky and one of gin as "Thanks." A U.S. Air Force fishing vessel picked up the "buoy" flying a red flag, and took care of the mailing. All items reached their destinations. The Sunday Star-Bulletin & Advertiser did not report the fate of the liquids. In the 1980s, the Cocos (Keeling) Islands issued a stamp sheet depicting ten passenger vessels that from 1893 into 1973 made use of "Barrel Mail" to drop the post for the islands.

On some routes where shipboard mail-handling was a definite benefit and need an alternate method to Sea or Ship Posts was found. Instead of a postal canceller, a ship-name mark was applied, sometimes with date, on the stamp or off the stamp. If the latter, the mail would be cancelled at the next or mail-transfer port, such as Cristobal on the West Coast South America route (in the 1930s provided with a joint Lloyd and Hapag weekly service, with 28-passenger capacity freighters). The word *Paquebot* was applied under Universal Postal Union regulations for mailings at sea with postage of the ship's nationality at its domestic rates of postage. And compulsory acceptance of such mail in any port in the world without penalty for not using local postage. As elsewhere, local Germans mostly used their ships to get off late mail to Europe, sometimes even coastally. The criterion was: how best to provide a service to passengers, crews and local people along the ship's route.

Again, the war stopped all Sea/Ship Posts. The Lloyd resumed North Atlantic passenger service in 1954 with Ship Posts. With the coming of the jet-travel age, most liner routes disappeared. Ship Posts then reflected what had become primarily cruising, then fly-and-cruise, sea vacations.

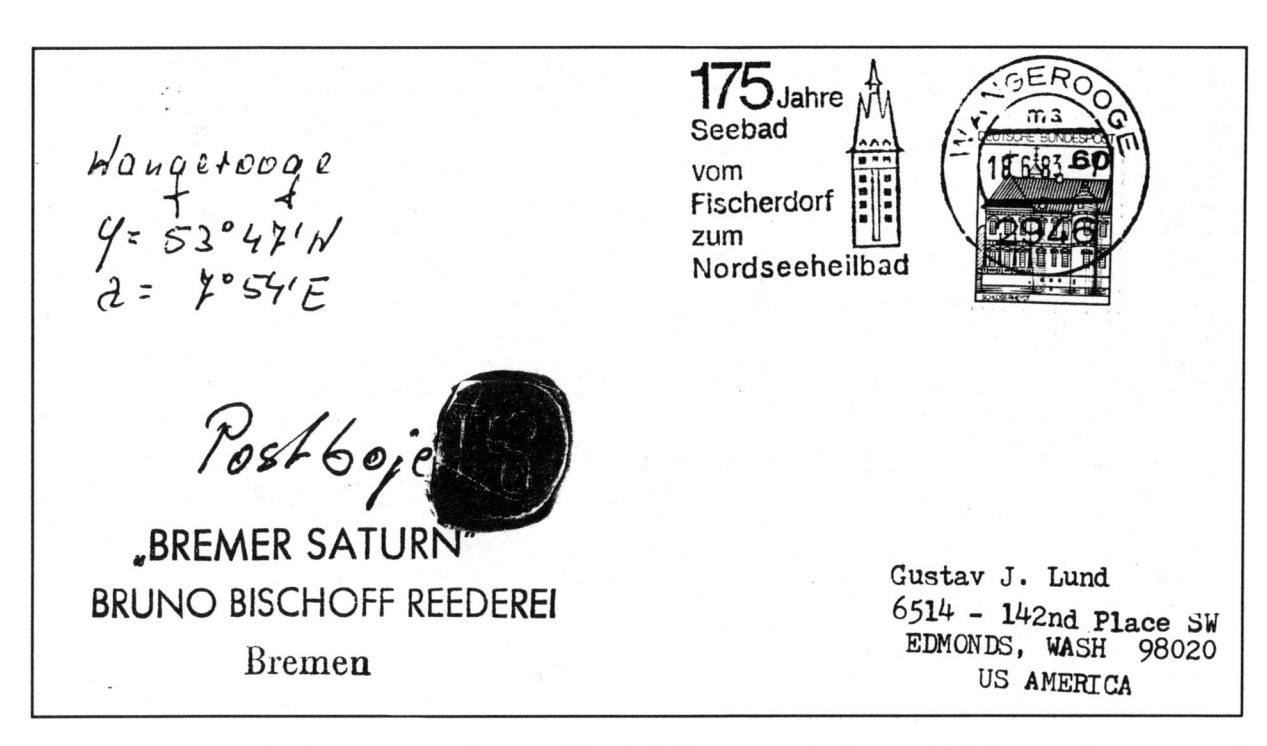

Mail dropped at the Mail Buoy off the Friesian Island of Wangerooge by Bremen M.S. Bremer Saturn *outward bound. The sender entered the coordinates. Courtesy of Gustav Lund, the author's four-decades plus collector friend.*

Color card of Prinzess Irene *sent in August 1909 by "Charlie-Lizzie" via cask thrown overboard to William J. Wolfe whose son Frank of Melbourne, Florida presented it to the author.*

Again Mail Handling at Sea   165

Ocean Letters were an extension of the Sea Post services. Senders on a ship could hand in a Wireless Letter to the radio office. They would radio it to a passing German ship headed in the opposite direction. There it was typed or written out, put into an envelope; sometimes that was Sea Posted on board, sometimes cancelled only on arrival at the next port where the radio-**Ocean Letter** was dispatched. Even Registry service was available. This example from the *Sierra Ventana*, addressed to the island of Norderney. See also the first mail item in the small-crafts list from *Telegraph* to Nordernei (sic) in 1842. The **Ocean Letter** form used on the routes via Spain to South America. "debeg" is the Deutsche Betriebs-Gesellschaft für drahtlose Telegrafie. Service Company for Wireless Telegraphy.

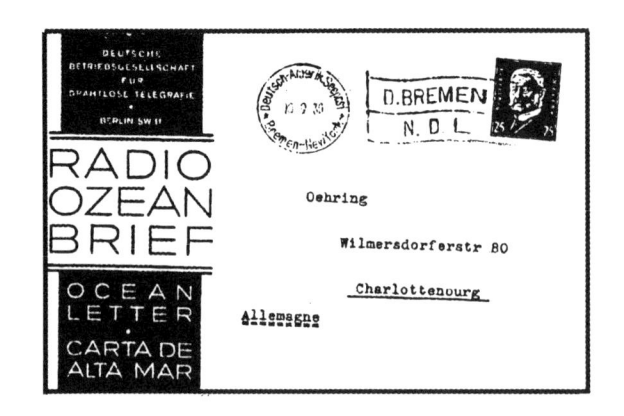

Ocean Letter sent to Bremen by a Lloyd ship heading for New York. It was mailed at the Sea Post office on board.

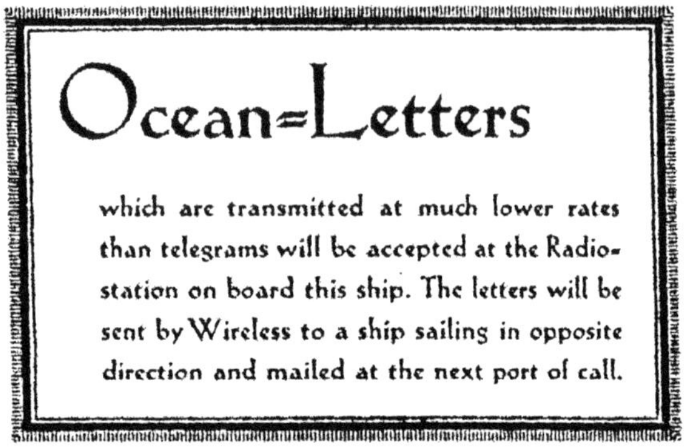

Notice in Shipboard Wireless Offices.

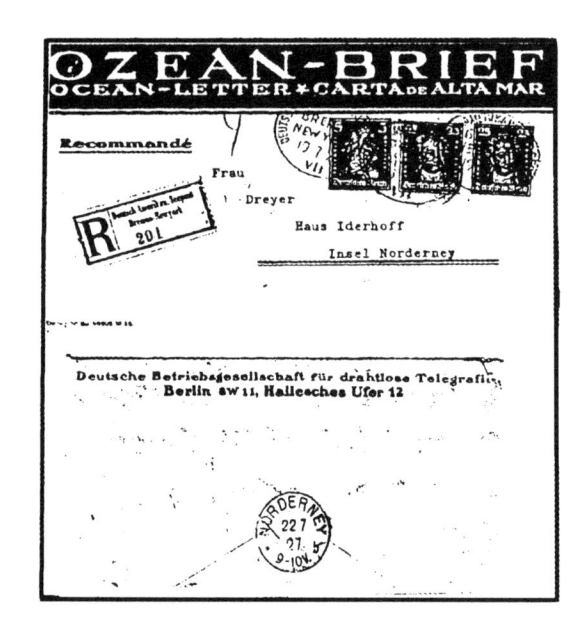

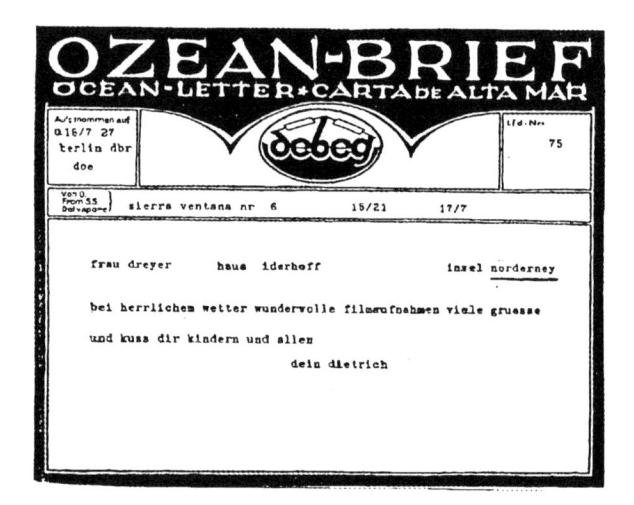

166   Norddeutscher Lloyd Bremen

Freighters and passenger vessels without Sea Post service provided an informal substitute mail service for those on board, to a lesser extent to, usually, Germans at various ports using the ship as their Post Office. This was most often so where local mail service was slow, infrequent, and uncertain. Here is a variety of freighter name-marks used for postal purposes during the 1920s and 1930s:
From *"Schwaben"*, D. *"Este,"* M.S. *"Weser"*, and her sister M.S. *"Elbe"* on the West Coast North America route. The *"Elbe"*-type mark in the 1930s was issued to many NDL vessels, including *Bremen, General von Steuben, Stuttgart,* etc. Similar versions are known from: *Minden,* one of the rebuilt freighters, one of two pairs built in 1929 for the Gulf Service, and *Erlangen,* "The Lloyd Sails," which sailed from New Zealand to Chile most of the way early in the war. *Nürnberg* and *Dresden* (see #446) were on the West Coast South America service, superb combiships, with a tile pool for 28 passengers. Also *Düsseldorf*. It, *Este* and *Weser* also have Paquebot marks with their name-stamps. This word, Portland spells it with a C, is applied as cancel or straight-line off the stamp to explain Mail Posted on the High Seas, but not postmarked there. The receiving post office must accept this under Universal Postal Union rules. The word Paquebot explains this.
Envelopes sometimes survive. One from the Reefer *Orotava,* mailed by the Las Palmas agency of the Woermann Line, West Africa specialists, in October, 1936, with Spanish stamp. No postmark, just the penned date. Acceptable as the stamp is invalidated; there is a date, the Ship's name explains where it was posted and the Spanish stamp that it was probably after leaving a Spanish port.
A similar envelope is from *Wido*, with Cristobal Paquebot cancel, the item from Buenaventura but probably dropped off in 1938 on NDL's *Bogota* #447 or sister *Quito*, acting as feeders to/distributors from the West Coast service. The D. *"Manizales"* cover is from that same service.
Plain one-line name marsk include: D. *"Eisenach,"* D.*"Roland"*, D. *"Inn,"* D.*"Nordernay"* and D. *"Aegina,"* #335, and many others. Most such mail does not survive as it usually is business, and the envelope discarded or misguided collectors tear off the stamps. Some of the stamps, as with *Eisenach*, are perforated with the business' name, to prevent private usage.

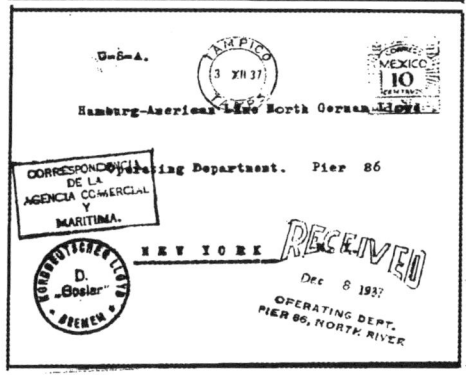

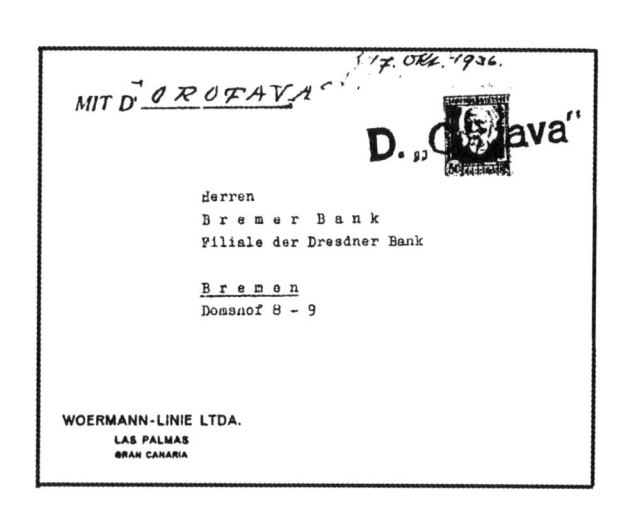

Again Mail Handling at Sea 167

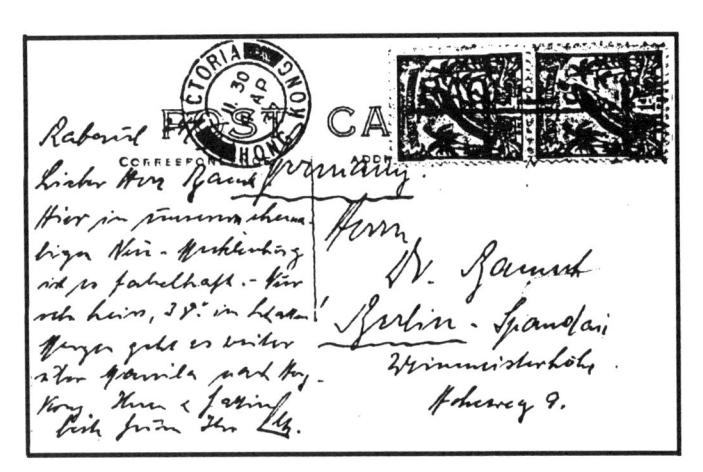

From 1893 into 1914, the Lloyd operated various New Guinea, then a German Colony, Sea Posts. In 1914, three passenger ships ran Sydney-Islands-Hong Kong-Japan. In 1932, NDL resumed this Islands-Hong Kong route with freighters Bremerhaven *and* Friderun. *Shown is mail written on board using New Guinea stamps and given Hong Kong's* **Paquebot** *(Ship Mail Arrival) mark.*

The writer, en route from the Mandated Territory of (former German) New Guinea to Hong Kong mentions "38° in the shade"- 101 degrees.

Examples of ship-name marks from freighters, most with some passenger space.

168 Norddeutscher Lloyd Bremen

Again Mail Handling at Sea

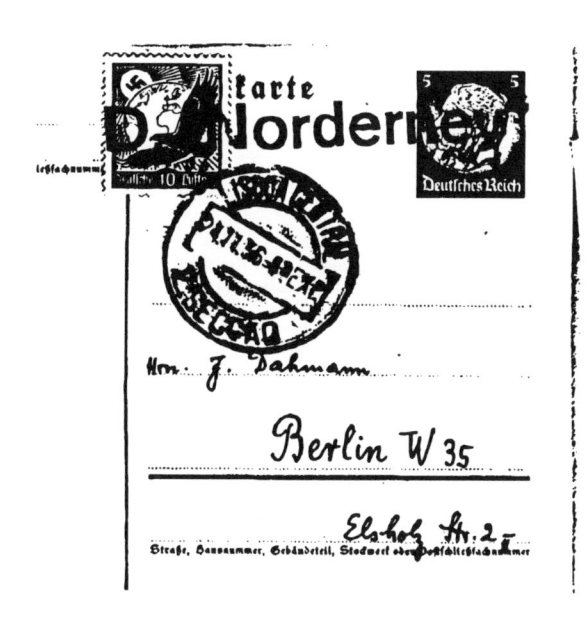

NDL Fleet:
Ships 417—425

A graceful ship steamer Bremen is
It cleaves the waves with a noisome fizz.
Alexandrine not composed by C.S. Lewis

The expectation at the time of laying of keels for *Bremen* and *Europa* was that the latter's maiden voyage would start on 3 April, 1929, leaving New York the 15th for the return voyage. *Bremen* was to depart Bremerhaven on 17 April, from New York the 29th. The ships would have met at sea on the 20th, a triumph for German shipping and shipbuilding 10½ years after the total defeat in the First War. A shipyard strike from 1/10/1928 to 4/1/1929 delayed the completion of both vessels. The rumor at the time was that the British shipbuilding industry through its unions supported the strike. This caused the loss of what would have been six months of rewarding service by both ships before the October, 1929 stock market crash, instead of only three by *Bremen*. One can speculate that circumstances might have been such under the original schedule that the March, 1929 fire on *Europa* would not have happened.

The original designs were stepups from an already-at-hand speculative "Second improved *Columbus*" design. After the ships had been contracted for on 13/12/1926 but before keels were laid in June and July, 1927 respectively, both plans were redesigned. Model tests showed that the designs would not provide the required 26.25 knots speed nor the capacity to make them the trend-setters on the North Atlantic. The 1927 redesign was heavily responsible for the final cost of the ships to be some 28% above original contract figures. A.G. Weser lost some seven Million Marks on the contract, a fact which contributed greatly to its rapid downhill slide after *Bremen's* completion, and the following depression.

Although the two were "sister ships" with overall resemblances, they were quite different.

Both had cruiser bows and sterns, but *Bremen's* thinner bow did not build up a huge "beard" of water as did *Europa*. Because of Bremen's finely cut bow, she sagged forward. But it was found she steered better when some 3' down forward, 37' against the shiplength's 34' draft. *Europa* sagged forward, despite the huge bulbous bow, and aft, despite there a broader cruiser stern than Bremen's. Despite her 1½' deeper draught than Bremen, *Europa's* bouyancy was less stable. Before entering New York her empty fuel tanks were filled with some 3500 tons of seawater so that during the frequent rudder changes from sea to bay to river to pier, the ship would remain stable. Before tying up with gangplanks on one side, tanks on the opposite side were filled with water so that the ship would not list and the bridge touch the pier. Those tanks then had to be cleaned before fuelling.

Bremen had a stream-lined Oertz rudder hung aft of the rudder post. She required some fifty seconds to make a twenty degrees change in course at sea speed. *Europa's* rudder was suspended from the bottom of the rudder post, with a large plane aft. a smaller one forward, a Balanced Rudder. The New York Times story on the record-breaking maiden voyage held that the secret of *Bremen's* speed were the bulbous bow and the rudder "shaped like an airplane wing." See "The Lloyd Sails." They had rounded superstructures, streamlined funnels, *Europa's* oval, *Bremen's* egg-shaped. Both had underwater bulbs, *Bremen's* thin, *Europa's* huge. *Bremen's* engines were less powerful than *Europa's*; she was some 3,000 tons heavier than *Bremen*.

Their plating differed, too. *Bremen's* overlapped forward, the idea being that bouncing the water rushing by over the seam would cause less friction than the suction of the plates overlapped the old way, as on *Europa*. In time, the flush welding of plates eliminated the question.

Both vessels were intended as Transports for Operation *Seelöwe*, the invasion of England. Military authorities intended to load tanks into the huge social hall, not realizing until tests were made, that *Bremen* especially had stability problems. The author travelled in a Boat Deck cabin on her in 1936. At times the ship would heel over, then stop, and then continue to heel instead of returning to upright. In high-up places on *Bremen*, such as in the elevator shafts, round sections were cut out of the steel, then were covered with wood. This added fire danger, as did the layers of paint on paint, instead of scraping off the old. The removal of the catapults took off topside weight, but the garages built there for vehicles compounded the original stability problems. Both ships were built with Martin 22mm alloy steel. This saved some 1000 tons weight. The chance for increased stability was lost by adding more topside weight even a life-sized marble bull on *Europa*. The strength of this steel became evident when in 1941 during the fire on *Bremen* attempts were made to blow a hole in her side so she would flood and settle on the bottom. But the steel was too strong. *Europa* had 4000 more effective HP than *Bremen*, but her total weight offset that, so she was always the slightly slower of the two. *Bremen* burned 870 tons of oil at 27 knots, 1040 at 28.5 knots all-out.

Soon after the ships got into operation it was evident that the low stream-lined smokestacks, effective as they looked, were too low to clear the soot, smoke and sulphur fumes off the decks. Engineers with top deck cabins developed lung and throat problems. Despite guarantees by the oil companies to supply fuel with a minimum sulphur content, the stacks had to be raised by 4.6 meters. This destroyed the graceful look without fully curing the downdraft problem. The French Line cowled *Liberte's* (ex *Europa*) funnels. This, plus more efficient burning of cleaner fuel and the 3+ knots slower running speed than *Europa* and *Bremen*, made for smog-free operation.

Propeller problems lasted during the lifetimes of the ships: vibration and cavitation at the edges from operating speeds. In 1931, propellers were being examined after each voyage. Some improvements were made with new-design propellers, as with *Normandie* shifting to three-bladed ones. But the problem of vibration stayed with the ships. On *Bremen* passengers aft in Tourist Class reported feeling the floor sway under their feet for two to three days after they got ashore, when first getting up in the morning. In the ship's lounge, drops of tea would bounce a foot or more out of cups. In *Bremen's* ballroom, pillar roof supports were added to absorb vibration. It was found that damping vibration in one spot led to it becoming noticeable elsewhere. The sturdier construction of *Europa* limited vibration. Yourkevich designed the French Line's *Normandie* with *Bremen's* December, 1929 storm experience in mind and *Europa's* in-port stability problems. He chose the finely-cut *Bremen* bow over the heavy bulbous one of *Europa*. *Normandie* got an almost Clipper bow, widely flared with a covered-over foreship, all meant to keep waves off, prevent spray from breaking against the forestructure of the Promenade Deck, and reducing vision from the bridge. The Italian *Rex* was very much a design-follower of *Bremen*, the hull and engines.

Europa readying for her March, 1930 maiden voyage. Bremen has just cast off; the crowds still outside the Columbus Quay in Bremerhaven. One can compare the two sisters: how different they are. Copyright Ocean Comfort Co., a Lloyd subsidiary.

417. **Bremen**	1929-1941		
DESCHIMAG Weser Yard,			
Bremen #872	1929 51	656	286.10x31.10
Turbines	105,000	27	****
I-723 II-600 III-908	943-967		

Launched 16/8/1928. MV to New York 16/7/1929 set new record: 4 days, 17 hours, 42 minutes, at 27.83 knots Bishop Rock-Ambrose Lightship. Return voyage also set a record, 4 days, 14 hours, 30 minutes, at 27.91 knots average. On her 7th, December, voyage, the ship went through the worst storm Captain L. Ziegenbein ever experienced; it made *Bremen* two days, six hours late, 17.6 knots average. Once, the entire foredeck to the superstructure was under water. The attempt to beat the maiden voyage record of *Rex* of 28.92 knots average made in 1932 proved impossible. In June, 1933 after engine tuning and vibration dampening, *Bremen* beat *Europa's* maiden voyage record with 28.51 knots westward. On 30/8/1939 left New York after extensive U.S. search for forbidden cargo or arms without passengers for Murmansk, doing 4065 miles in 6 days, 13 hours, 36 minutes, 25.66 knots average, one of 22 German ships that took refuge there in the weeks following outbreak of the war. Reached Germany 13/12/1939. 16-18/3/1941 burned out in Bremerhaven, fire evidently set by a disgruntled cabin boy. 1946 wrecked towed to a sandbank in the Weser at Nordenham, visible from Bremerhaven. Demolition continued into 1956.

Bremen's *launching at the Weser Werft, 16 August, 1928.*

Bremen *on her maiden voyage to New York July, 1929. The decks solid with people.*

How a ship begins, small or large; first the keel, then rib by rib the shape of the vessel takes form. Wooden framing, almost seventy years ago. One has to marvel at the architects who design the ship, the engineers who convert design into blueprints, and the constructors who put it all together, and then slide it into the water... and it floats. From Seven Seas, *August 1928.*

THE NEXT TRANSATLANTIC SENSATION

What it takes to run a 50 thousand tonner: The Officers Staff on Bremen *and* Europa*: Captain, Chief of Staff, and three each First, Second, Third and Fourth Officers, one for each watch. The same applied to the Chief Engineer's Staff. Ex-Acht Glas, Dr. Becker-Ferber, Dietrich Reimer, Berlin, 1940.*

174   *Norddeutscher Lloyd Bremen*

Special postcards and labels were prepared for the launch. The special cancel reads: STAPELLAUF LLOYDSCHNEILLDAMPFER BREMEN WESERWERFT DESCHIMAG.

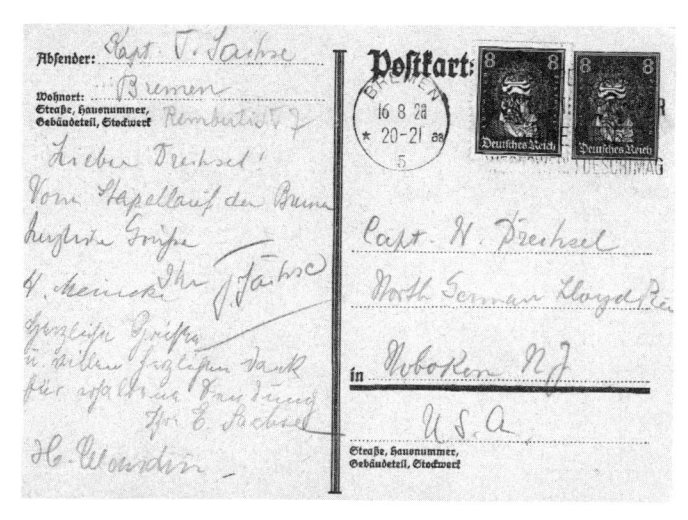

Bremen's *commemorative launching-day postmark, 16 August, 1929. Sent by old friends Captain Thilo Sachse and wife Else Sachse.*

For Bremen's *first overhaul she went to Blohm & Voss, in March, 1930. Water depth was insufficient, and she had to be lightened to get into the floating dock: two joined for her size. Prior to her maiden voyage she had gone to Southampton. With building of the new Kaiserdock in Bremerhaven* Bremen *and* Europa *could be drydocked at home.*

Die „Bremen" eingedockt

w. Hamburg, 25. März.

Der Schnelldampfer „Bremen" des Norddeutschen Lloyd, der am Montag vormittag im Hamburger Hafen eintraf, hat im Laufe des Tages infolge der Wasserverhältnisse nicht mehr ins Dock genommen werden können. Nach teilweiser Leichterung des Schiffes wurde die „Bremen" am Dienstag nachmittag gegen 13.30 Uhr in das kombinierte Dock V, VI der Werft von Blohm u. Voß genommen, wo es für die Überholungsarbeiten einige Tage verbleiben wird.

The first schedule to include Europa *and* Bremen *had the former sail on 3 April, 1929 and* Bremen *on the 17th, the 18th from Southampton and Cherbourg. With* Europa *leaving New York on the 15th, they would have met sometime on the 19th. How differently it all turned out: The Three-months shipyard strike;* Europa *burning out in March;* Bremen's *maiden voyage finally 16-22 July;* Europe *19th March, 1930.*

The Wintergarten at the front of the Promenade Deck. What a spot for afternoon tea, and in a storm. Then it could be scary, as in December, 1929.

First docking of Bremen *at Pier 4, Brooklyn Army Base, after her record-breaking voyage, 22 July, 1929. Note that much of the white stripe was scoured off at the high speed. A crew is repainting this and touching up the hull. At right a near-empty fuel-oil barge. Author's photos.*

BREMEN's 1931 Operating Statistics			
Bremerhaven - New York	Passagiere	New York - Bremerhaven	Total
I Klasse - 5607		I Klasse - 5521	11,020
II Klasse - 3808		II Klasse - 3412	7,270
Tourist - 4634		Tourist - 4710	9,341
III Klasse - 6060		III Klasse - 8464	14,524
Im Ganzen 20,109		Im Ganzen 22,107	42,216
710 Seemeilen	Höchste Tagesfahrt	648 Seemeilen	**Highest Day's Run**
27.28 Knoten	Schnellste Tagesfahrt	27.34 Knoten	Fastest Day's Run
4/18/30	Kürzeste Fahrtdauer	4/19/44	Shortest crossing time
26.51 Knoten	Jahres Durchschnittsfahrt	26.68 Knoten	Year's Average
122	Autos getragen	199	Autos Carried
75,522	Sack Post Getragen	98,379	Sacks of Mail carried
1,899 Tons	Tons Fracht Getragen	6,388	Tons of Freight Carried
Jahrensdurchschnitt - 26.40 Knoten			Year's Overall Average
			Nautical miles travelled
44 Rundreisen in Dienst	Distanz Gelaufen	314,275 Seemeilen	44 Round Voyages in Service

Over the years, some 68% of Bremen-Europa *passengers were bound for the Continent; eighty percent were non-German.*

Bremen 4's *first voyage from the A.G. Weser shipyard down the Weser to Bremerhaven, past* Frankfurt, *and* Chemnitz, *launched two days before at the Bremer Vulkan, crowded with Lloyd people and friends; mast tops folded down to pass under high tension wires, shepherded by NDL and URAG tugs. Note line to bow tug is painted out in this* Heinrich Engelke *photo. A day for pride and joy.*

First arrival of Bremen's *catapult mail plane, 22 July, 1929. The aircraft was shot off only after the finish line — Ambrose Channel Lightship — had been passed.* Author's photos.

NEW YORK TIMES
February 7, 1956

TRANSPORT NEWS OF INTEREST HERE

End Arrives for the Bremen as Parts Are Salvaged—

The final chapter in the history of the once-famous German liner Bremen, holder of the Atlantic speed record in 1929, is about to be written.

The last few sections of the double bottom of the 51,656-ton, 898-foot vessel are about to be brought to the surface by a floating crane, according to information from abroad. This will complete dismantling of North German Lloyd's former flagship.

Since March, 1941, the vessel has been lying in the lower reaches of the River Weser, after having been beached following aerial bombing during World War II in Bremerhaven. A special navigation buoy that marks the wreck is to be removed shortly.

Bremen *on the stocks at the Deschimag Yard, Bremen-Gröpelingen, during the round-the-clock rush to get ready for the 16 August, 1928 launch by President Paul von Hindenburg.*

178 *Norddeutscher Lloyd Bremen*

#418 Chemnitz's capture by a French submarine in September, 1939 while trying to get home is shown as a full-page painting in the Histoire de la Cie. General Transatlantique, the French Line. Her speed for them is given as 11.5 knots, not the 13.5 as built. Shown in a French port unloading grains. See sister Frankfurt #416.

418. *Chemnitz 2*	1929-1939		
Bremer Vulkan, Vegesack #688	1929	5522	141.25x17.14
Triple Expansion, Exhaust Turbine		4200	13.5
	4	48	

Chemnitz #418 is shown on the cover of this book published by the Naval Institute Press, by Martin Brice. *The ship was caught four weeks after war began trying to get home by the French submarine.*

Launched 22/6/1929, delivery 7/8/1929 for U.S. East Coast service. 31/8/1939 left Durban for Las Palmas, 24/9/ left there with Hapag's *Amasis* for Germany. 18/9/1939 south of Fayal captured by French submarine *Poncelet*, taken to Casablanca. 5/6/1940 ren. *Saint Bertrand*, reg. in Marseille, French Govt. With France's defeat, put under Ministry of War Transport. London managed by T.J. Brocklebank, Hull. 18/7/1940 reg. by British Govt. in Bermuda as caretaker for the French. 1945 ret. to France, managed by Cie. Generale Transatlantique, LeHavre, 6938 Ts. 1955 *Bertrande*, Hong Kong owner, reg. for Transport Maritimo Atlas S.A., Panama. 6/1957 *Senzan Maru*, Towa Sempaku K.K., Kobe, 6919 Ts. 13/9/1958 LU in Hiroshima. 11/1958 sold for BU in Osaka by Kozai K.K., work began 12/1960.

419. "The Adventurous Voyage of the Lloyd Steamer Erlangen" from New Zealand, after chopping down trees for 250 tons of firewood, to Chile in October-November, 1939, sailing part of the way. The account put out by the Hapag-Lloyd office in New York in 1940.

419. **Erlangen 2**   1929-1941
Blohm & Voss, Hamburg #484   1929   6101   143.25x17.56
Turbine   3800   13.25
6   54

Launched 31/8/1929. Reg. 10/1929. Built for Australia-New Zealand trade. 28/8/1939 left Dunedin with 2000 bales of wool, bound for Port Kembla to coal, only 250 Ts. on board. Due to radioed "war danger" warning headed for Auckland Islands south of New Zealand, put ship onto beach, cut and loaded 250 tons of wood. Sails were made to use trade winds to help reach Chile. 6/10/1939 left, sailed 1507 miles, steamed 3319 miles to Ancud. Arr. 11/11/1939. 7/1941 left for Montevideo to recoal for try to get home. 25/7/1941 scuttled to avoid capture by *HMS Canberra* south of Montevideo. Photo in "Wars".

420. **Tübingen**   1929-1934
Furness S.B. Co., Haverton Hill on Tees #21
                                1920   5453   122.38x19.51
Triple Expansion   2750   12   after rebuild
4   47

Completed 23/12/1920 as *Delaware* for A/S Norge-Mexico Gulf Lines (W. Wilhelmsen, manager), Tönsberg, 4501 Ts., 110.76 x 15.91. 9/6/1928 en route Sanda-New Orleans grounded at Argosgrund, Oeresund, ship broke, was abandoned as constructive total loss. 1929 bought by NDL, salvaged sans forepart, rebuilt, lengthened 11.6 m., given a modified cruiser stern by Howaldtswerke, Kiel, ren. *Tübingen*. I.S. 8/1929 to West Africa. To Hamburg-Bremer Afrika-Linie, as reconstituted, 2/10/1935, managed by Woermann Linie, Hamburg. 1939 returned from Teneriffe through the British blockade, 15/9/1939 arr. Murmansk, left 3/10/1939. 6/3/1940 intended as transport for Operation "Seelöwe," the invasion of England. 24/4/1945 sunk by Allied air attack in the Kattegat.

420. Tübingen was a ship on the cheap for NDL, buying a "constructive total loss" and having it rebuilt. Shown in West Africa service with the Bremen key on stack. Nautical Photo Agency.

421. *Goslar*	1929-1940		
Blohm & Voss, Hamburg #485	1929	6040	143.25x17.51
Turbine	3800	13.25	
8	53-49		

Launched 3/10/1929. MV 18/12/1929 to East Asia. 25/8/1939 was off the U.S. East Coast, headed for Paramaribo, arr. 5/9/1939. 10/5/1940 scuttled outside harbor to prevent capture by the Dutch, the day of the invasion of Holland. Crew got to Brazil.

421. Goslar was one of the many vessels scuttled to avoid capture trying to get home early in the war, or where they were interned, it at Paramaribo. The author was there in April, 1939. There is a sharp brown line where the Commewijne River meets the sea, then blue, and Goslar's grave. P.A. Kleinschmidt Photo.

422. Abana and Agira were built for Argo's Near East service, with Maier bows to ride over the waves, not through them. Both a slow 10.5 knots.

422. **Abana** 1929-1939
DESCHIMAG "Weser" Yard, Bremen #800
                                  1929   2867   93.58x14.05
Triple Expansion, Exhaust Turbine   1400   10.5
8, then   32-29

Launched 11/1929. Maier Bow, with sister *Agira*. M.V. on the "Argo" route to the Near East. Until 1/1/1935 managed by Deutsche Levante Linie. 5/5/1935 ren. *Inn*. 5/9/1939 sunk by guns of *HMS Neptune* off the Canaries in the attempt to get home from Para. (Dinklage says: 8.Sept.1939 arr. Dakar after Capture by *Neptune*.)

423. Agira survived the war, ran to the Great Lakes for the Dutch Oranje Line, was broken up in 1960, thirty years old. Copyright Wolfgang Fuchs.

423. *Agira*   1929-1939
DESCHIMAG "Weser" Yard, Bremen #881
                          1930   2867   93.58 x 14.05
Triple Expansion, Exhaust Turbine   1400   10.5
                                           8, then 12   28-31

Launched 10/12/1929. Maier Bow. MV. 23/2/1930 to Near East. To 1/8/1935 managed by Deutsche Levante Linie, Hamburg. 27/6/1936 ren. *Spree*. 3/3/1944 mined off Denmark, towed to Stavanger. 5/1945. Taken over by Allies. 25/6/1946 at Lübeck, after repairs assigned to Holland. 1947 ren. *Hedel*, managed by Veder & Co., Rotterdam. 23/4/1949 to Oranje Linje, ren. *Prins Philip Wiliem*, 2065 Ts. 2/1952 *Nilla*, Entreprises Chemiques at Electriques S.A, Vilvoorde. 1953 *Villa*, Maritime Industrial Co., Monrovia. 9/4/1960 arr. in tow at Grays, Essex for BU by T.W. Ward.

424. *Europa*   1930-1946
Blohm & Voss, Hamburg #479   1930   49,746   285.55x31.12
Turbines   90,000-26.25 contract speed
107,000-27 kns, 125,000 28 kns   ****
I-723 (143 Pullmans) II-628 III-903   965-1013

Keel laid 1/7/1927. Launched 15/8/1928. 26/3/1929 major fire while fitting out, set on bottom to prevent capsizing. 1930 ship's lifeboats towed to Bremerhaven via the Elbe-Weser Canal. MV. 19/3/1930 to New York set record: 4 days, 17 hours, 6 minutes, 27.91 knots average despite a heavy storm the last day. Unofficially, she averaged 29.7 knots. 17/2/1933 arr. in New York with $55 millions in gold bullion. Europe paying its debts. 27/6/-1/7/1933 beat record with 27.93 knots Cherbourg-Ambrose Lightship. When the catapult was removed late 1935, the space became a garage, making the ship top-heavier. Winter 1938-1939 air con-

Bremen *and* Europa. Sketched by Howard Cook. Courtesy of Douglas Duffy, executor of the estate, and William Clark. *Both fellow Dartmouth alumni. Only thirty printed of each.*

424. Europa leaving Hamburg for her trials en route to Bremerhaven.

ditioning installed in First Class social rooms. Some 40,000 kilos of paint a year were used inside and out to keep the vessel shipshape. 1940 with *Bremen* moved to Hamburg to fit out for Operation "Seelöwe," the invasion of England, never carried out. The military planned to transport tanks and armored vehicles on the promenade deck. Returned to Bremerhaven. 8/5/1945 taken over by U.S. Navy, ren. *USS Europa*, AP 117. The first postwar activity at the (former NDL) Atlas Werke, Bremen was to pour a new propeller for *Europa*. 25/8/1945 commissioned. Captain Oskar Scharf, 1. Officer J Wetzel and 6 other Germans were on board the first trip to New York. 11/9/1945-2/5/1946 transported U.S. forces home. 8/6/1946 allotted to France. The Navy wanted nothing to do with a ship whose wiring, etc., was considered defective. Also to France as part-compensation for its *Normandie*, destroyed by fire at Pier 88, Manhattan, while being converted after Pearl Harbor as a U.S. transport. 8/12/1946 at Le Havre broke loose in a storm, ripped hull in hitting the sunken *Paris*, settled to bottom. 15/4/1947 refloated. Taken to St. Nazaire for full-scale reconstruction. Basing that on U.S. ship inspection rules, passenger safety was emphasized. Water and fire bulkheading was extended to make the ship more nearly watertight. Burnable decor was replaced with metal or fire-resistant materials. New fireproof electrical wiring was installed. Steel plating was added amidships to strengthen the hull. Ballast tanks were relocated to give more stability. Passenger capacity was cut from 2,200 to 1,513. Former Third-Class quarters aft were converted to crew use. All public rooms were redecorated; First and Cabin Class dining rooms were air-conditioned. Gone (where?) was the red marble mythological *Europa* and Bull from the Promenade Deck entry hall. 10/1949 rebuilding interrupted by fire in passenger areas. Intended name *Lorraine*, but into service 17/8/1950 as *Liberté*, 51,839 Ts. vs 49,746 as *Europa,* which excluded the Promenade Deck enclosure. Now: I-569 C-562 III-382. Service speed 24.5 knots. 16/11/1961 LU in LeHavre. Intended sale for BU in Japan after plan to serve as hotel ship at the 1963 Seattle World Fair fell through because of sharp drop in world scrap prices. 30/12/1961 sold to Italy for DM63 millions for BU by Terrestre Marittima. 25/1/1962 left LeHavre in tow for La Spezia, arr. 30/1/1962. One *Europa* propeller is on display at the Krupp Villa Hügel in Essen, from a 1935 change. EUROPA's bell was returned to Germany in 1955. It had been used as alarm bell by the U.S. Navy.

#424. On Europa's *maiden voyage, March 1930. Right: Commodore Johnsen, Deputy N.D.L. General Director Ernst Glässel, Captain Paul König, head of the Nautical Dept. Ex-Sunday Section:* New Yorker Staats-Herold.

Europa *on her record-setting Maiden Voyage in March, 1930. The storm through which she plowed, and yet made it. She was driven to beat* Bremen's *record, by 36 minutes, so the new stories would center on that not, had she failed, on the fire that seriously damaged her a year earlier.*

Europa's *bulbous bow, very much larger than* Bremen's, *a major difference between the sisters. Taken in Blohm & Voss floating dock in Hamburg during the early 1930s when costs were being cut and the ships lost their white waterline. Later restored for looks.*

Europa *and* Normandie *at Quarantine taken from Bay Ridge. The Labor Day International Lifeboat races covered the area at left where now the Verrazano Bridge crosses, and to 69th Street.*

Europa's *First Docking at Pier 4, Brooklyn, March, 1930.*

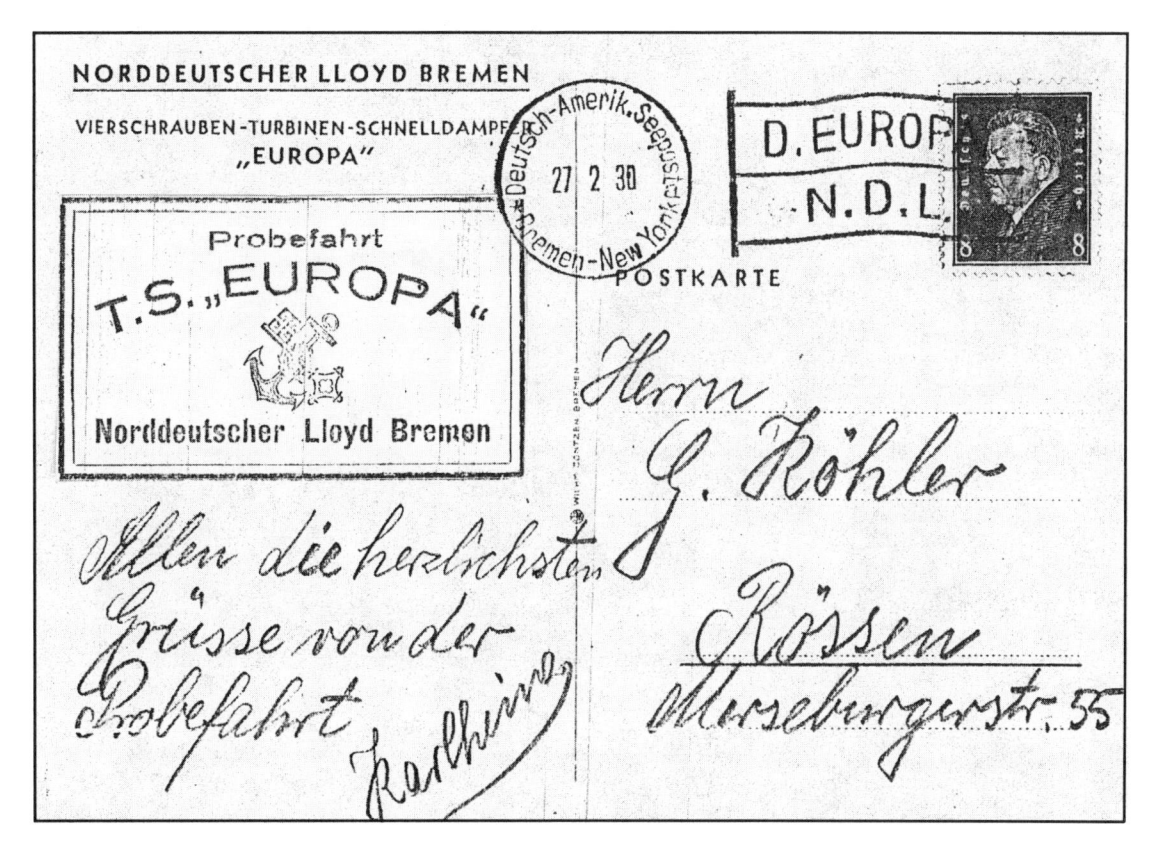

Europa *already had her German-American Sea Post on board for her trial voyage. First known date of use 27.2.1930. She also had a double-ring hand cancel. And this voyage cachet.*

Story in Bremen's Weser Zeitung *of* Europa's *record-setting Maiden Voyage, and items about the German Ambassador taking a cutter out to Quarantine; mention that General Director C.J. Stimming had a telephonic interview with the United Press Berlin Bureau, and Congratulatory telegrams to the Builders, Blohm & Voss in Hamburg and to Kommodore Johnsen, from Bremen.*

When the U.S. took Europa *in 1945, the first need was a new propeller. This is an old one displayed at the Krupps' Villa Hügel in Essen. Drawing by Pottschien.*

Long-time Lloyd Purser H.W. Müller, third generation of such.

Announcement of Europa's *Maiden Voyage on 19 March, 1930, the third unit in the Lloyd Express Service:* Bremen *and the rebuilt* Columbus *the other two. And the related meter postmark used on NDL mails.*

188   *Norddeutscher Lloyd Bremen*

Europa *late evening at Cherbourg. The ships made the calls at Southampton and Cherbourg the second day out; any delay as fog or storm made for inconvenience for passengers coming from France and delay in arrival at New York.* Bremen *lost six hours due to fog by the time she left Cherbourg on her maiden voyage. Mail sacks piled up at right.* Paul Cwojdzinski Photo.

425. Este *was the last of the twelve-units River Class series; it differed in having two not four masts, and a cruiser stern. Here shown loading down river from Bremen. Mailed by a passenger on arrival in Vancouver: "This is a very large freighter." It was the third ship to use her engine:* Schwaben *386's engine was taken out and put into* Columbus *in 1927 when one of its engines collapsed after a propeller break hitting a sunken wreck. Engine put into* Este *when* Columbus *was given turbines in 1929.*

Ships 417 - 427   189

425. *Este* 1930-1940
DESCHIMAG "Weser" Yard, Bremen #884
                                  1930   7915   158.75x19.48
Triple Expansion, Exhaust Turbine   7000   15
16   66

Launched 5/6/1930, delivery 12/8/1930. Last and fastest of the River class, built for U.S.-Canada West Coast service. *Este*, *Hannover* #452, Hapag's *Seattle* and *Mimi Horn* arr. from Cartagena in Curacao for refuge. The Dutch confiscated radio equipment and navigation instruments. 10/4/1940 seized as prize with invasion of Holland, ren. *Suriname*, managed by Koninglijke Nederlandsche Stoomboot Mij., Amsterdam. 13/9/1942 in Convoy TAG 15 en route Trinidad-New York sunk by U-558 in 20.10N, 63.33W. *Este* was the last new NDL ship built until 1934. It had been given the ex-*Schwaben* #386 engine built into *Columbus* when its collapsed after propeller-shaft breakage. *Este* also got a Bauer-Wach Exhaust Turbine.

Seven German ships took refuge in the Netherlands West Indies when war broke. Four are in this historic photo at Curacao which the author took in February, 1940: Hapag's Phrygia *in the foreground, next* Este, *then Hapag's* Vancouver *and* Alesia, *used for West Indies inter-island services. Holland took all of them.*

From the author's Summer 1936 voyages on Bremen *to Europe and return: The Bridge with Commodore Ziegenbein at left. And Lloyd tugs aiding the ship's departure from the Columbus Quay in Bremerhaven.*

CHAPTER 5

Again Blue Ribbon

In the competition for the Blue Ribbon of the North Atlantic, the practicalities were largely ignored by the Press. What pulled the public, and made for profits, was the regularity of service, even if not at the highest speed. The Cunard Line remained pre-eminent with its frequent sailings even though slower than the Guion Line. The Lloyd showed it with its eleven express liners in the 1880s-early 1890s, slower than all the main competition, but offering twice, even three-times-a-week service. The Lloyd knew it in the 1920s when it built *Bremen* and *Europa*. They won it on speed and class; they never could provide a weekly service against the slower British Cunard and White Star Lines. Eventually, it was the *Queens, Mary* and *Elizabeth*, that in peacetime could offer weekly Southampton-New York service that no other line could equal.

In 1922, the Banker Johann C. Schroeder joined the Lloyd's Board of Directors to manage the financing of its recovery programs. With entry into service of *Columbus* in April, 1924 the question of a "Second *Columbus*" began to be raised. Should there be a companion ship to improve quality and frequency of service on the Lloyd's prestige line to New York? On 8 August, 1924 Engineering Director Max Walter wrote to Inspector W. Drechsel in Hoboken "the building of such an expensive ship as a second *Columbus* undoubtedly will be a long time coming." 1924 was a bad year for NDL and trans-Atlantic shipping. Immigration into the U.S. had been sharply restricted by the new quota system. The hoped-for offset: Tourist traffic, had not yet caught on in significant numbers. But the idea of another big ship stirred Bremen.

This feeling was strengthened when the Lloyd in December, 1925 absorbed several freighter lines it had owned or controlled but which had operated on their own. (See "Mergers"). Suddenly, NDL had become a strong freighter enterprise. This put the Lloyd on a near-equal footing with the Hapag in worldwide shipping services and fleet.

In Hapag Haus in Hamburg the feeling was the opposite: suddenly the Lloyd and Bremen were pressing competitors. The two lines, it is true, had worked closely together in recent months to get from the U.S. repayments for WWI property seizures: the piers in Hoboken, and a sizeable fleet of vessels: 32 of the Lloyd's, 42 from Hapag.

In March, 1926 Lloyd and Hapag General Directors signed a twelve-paragraphs operating agreement aimed at optimal use of their tonnage and an overall equalization, both managements to remain independent without a formal merger. Arbitrary actions by both quickly undermined the intent of this agreement: in February, Hapag agreed with the Harriman interests in the U.S. to take over its United American Lines with their *Resolute, Reliance* and *Cleveland,* all ex-Hapag ships.

The Hapag absorbed the recently-merged Kosmos and D.A.D.G. fusion, which in January had taken over the Stinnes shipping interests. All this gave Hapag a passenger fleet about equal to

On fast ships such as the 20-knots White Star Majestic *pre-1900, officers would hold framed glass plates before their faces in order to look forward. On* Kaiser Wilhelm der Grosse *a Bridge wing housing met that problem.* Queen Mary *had it, but it was not repeated on* Queen Elizabeth *or liners before then or since.* Bremen *and* Europa *met the problem with this funnel wind deflector. It swept the wind over the head of any who stood on the open bridge wing, so they could train glasses forward. In 1995, similar fairings were to be added to the Golden Gate Bridge to help air flow around trusses and deck. Drawing by Robert Canfield.*

NDL's, and far-superior freighter tonnage.

At the Lloyd, there was a post-December 1925 mergers expansion attitude. With the Roland Linie had come its Director, Ernst Glässel, who now became Number Two at the Lloyd, Deputy Director General. 1926 was proving to be a good year. On the New York route the Lloyd carried 69,000 passengers, only 10,000 less than the Cunard and White Star Lines. And more than the French Line or Hapag or U.S. Lines. The first dividend, 6%, was paid for that year. This made it easier to think big under Herr Glässel's urging. The saying in Bremen was: "Only when we run express steamers is the Lloyd at its peak." It had done so 1897-1914, even for most of 1897-1907 holding the Trans-Atlantic Blue Ribbon. Could one dare think of a come-back?

In October, 1925 serious talk began, at first an "improved *Columbus*." Then talk of an express liner, 26 knots? This against grave doubts by President Philipp Heinken and Herr Walter. How can one compete with a 26-knots express steamer, a 20-knots *Columbus* and a 16.5 knots *Berlin* on the New York line? One express liner against Cunard's three on a weekly service: *Berengaria, Aquitania* and *Mauretania*. Against the White Star with its trio: *Majestic, Olympic* and *Homeric the former NDL Columbus 1*? And to be only even at best with the French Line, which was building a 43,000 tons *Ile De France*, also had the 1921 *Paris*, a better ship than *Columbus*, and the 24 knots *France*, from pre-war but refurbished and still a popular vessel.

Herr Glässel wins the arguments: it has to be two six-day ships of 46,000 tons. In December, 1926 a group from the Board of Directors and the Vorstand (Management Board) works out the details, driven by the pre-war "every Tuesday an express steamer." This confirms the decision for two six-day vessels. On 28 March, 1927, after the General Meeting for the year 1926, it is announced "in order to bring our New York service close to the former level we have decided to order two passenger vessels which will meet in every way the increased demands of international passenger traffic." The first word about *Bremen* and *Europa*. One to be built in Bremen, the other in Hamburg. Strangely nothing about upgrading *Columbus* the to fit into an express-steamer schedule. In the event, Bremen was pushed to that decision when *Columbus* on 2/8/1927 hit a submerged wreck en route to New York. This wrecked one of its reciprocating engines. It was temporarily replaced with a freighter's engine, leading to a major rebuilding with turbines for a top speed of 22½ knots after *Bremen* and *Europa* would be in service in 1929.

After taking the big jump into very cold and very deep water, it quickly was realized that the 46,000 tons could not offer the required speed nor the passenger-attracting facilities. The ships were re-designed to what became 51,000 tons vessels. The same problem occurred with *Europa 5* in 1980-1981. The design was widened after actual construction had begun. An expensive proposition for the shipyards in all three cases.

Europa's maiden voyage was set for 3 April, 1929, the return from New York on the 15th. *Bremen* was to sail the 17th, departing New York on the 30th. The ships would have met at sea on Friday, April 19th while the westbound northern track and eastbound southern track were still close enough for opposite-course ships to sight each other. With both vessels equipped with catapults for shooting off mail planes (see "The

The pilot coming on board at Ambrose Light Ship outside New York Lower Bay. It is the official end point for the trans-Atlantic speed runs. In July, 1929 Bremen's catapult airplane was not shot off until after passing Ambrose, so as not to lose minutes from the record being set. Normally, the airplane is shot off hundreds of miles at sea. See "Lloyd Flies." Photos from Columbus. Unlike this lowered gangway, pilots usually have to use the Jacob's ladder dangling over the side. It takes a bit of nerves to do this in bad weather.

Again Blue Ribbon 193

Bremen *docking at Pier 4, Brooklyn, late P.M. 22 July, 1929. Her foot-thick white stripe is scraped off from the speed of the water rushing by during the record run.* Edwin Drechsel Photo.

Lloyd Flies"), surely one of these would have been out into the air to record photographically this mid-ocean meeting of Germany's comeback in 10½ years from complete ruin at the end of World War I.

It came out otherwise. A bitter shipyard strike from 1 October, 1928 to 4 January, 1929 stopped construction for those three months. The rumor was that the British shipyard unions supported the strike as revenge for Germany being the first postwar to build express liners. Then *Europa* burned in Hamburg on 26 March, 1929 during completion of her interiors, and settled to the bottom of the fitting-out quay. *Bremen* became the sole mainstay of the New York service in July, 1929 as *Columbus* was being rebuilt to match the new ships in looks, with squat stacks, and with turbines for a higher operating speed.

Bremen's was a triumphant maiden voyage. She was examined in Southampton by British shipbuilders and competitors. Captain Leopold Ziegenbein was made an honorary member of the Master Mariners' Club, the first such case. Surely a generous gesture to a captain and a ship on the verge of ending *Mauretania's* hold on the Atlantic Blue Ribbon. But it took twenty years and modern technology, including a bulbous bow, to beat *Mauretania's* best of 26.06 average in 1909, with *Bremen's* 4 days, 17 hours, 42 minutes, and 27.83 knots average for a distance of 3,164 statute miles.

In August, 1929 *Mauretania* with her old 1907 engines retuned, and with oil instead of coal firing, proved her engineering and maintenance quality, averaging 26.85 knots to New York and 27.22 knots on the return. A magnificent performance by a 22-years old liner!

How it used to be. This posted evidently on board George Washington, *Seaposted Bremen-New York 20.8.13. Note the windbreaks on the promenade deck, patented by NDL director Helmholt. This is at Cherbourg where the Weser River pilot comes on board, this to speed getting to the quay in Bremerhaven rather than having to stop to pick him up.*

Bremen's return maiden voyage was slightly higher than outgoing: 27.91 knots. Whereas on the way to New York shooting off the mail plane only after passing Ambrose Light Ship and the record, eastward it was shot off well ahead of arrival in Cherbourg. The catapults in effect provided Blue Ribbon mail service across the Atlantic. In March, 1930, *Europa* on her maiden voyage by a bit beat *Bremen*, with 27.91 knots westward to New York in 4 days, 17 hours, six minutes. She had reached 28.91 knots on her trials with 136,000 shaft horsepower working, the author is the only one who has reported that *Europa* on her last day averaged 29.7 knots in a storm to make

Slogan meter cancel on company mail to Williams, Dimond & Co., Los Angeles, agents for the West Coast service. In German, Lloyd and Betreut rhyme: Betroit, thus: With the Lloyd means being well cared for.

Firma

Williams, Dimond & Co.

up for a 12-miles error in prior computations. An estimated 100,000 Marks of crockery, etc. were broken in the process, and the determination to beat *Bremen* to prevent, had she failed, that news reports would call her a "bad luck ship" because of the fire. During *Europa's* record voyage, with Deputy Director General Glässel on board, on 24 March in Bremen President Heineken told the annual meeting "We are not concerned with setting speed records, rather to give the international travelling public a truly improved trans-Atlantic service, and thus do our part for better relations among peoples." But how nice also to have nailed down that record for the second time!

In November, 1934 when *Bremen* on her 100th crossing bettered her own prior records, when asked "what could your ship do if pushed?" Captain Ziegenbein admitted for the first time that she had once attained the speed of 32 knots (for how long and when he did not specify), and "she made an average of thirty-one knots for twelve hours on her maiden voyage under not too favorable weather." But by that time the Italian *Rex*, designed from *Bremen's* experience, averaged 28.92 knots in 1933, with 1150 tons daily oil consumption, on a smaller displacement. *Rex's* record was made under better weather conditions than on the more northerly English Channel-New York track.

Bremen, after several attempts at a new record following fine-tuning of her engines and improved propellers reached her peak in 1933 with 4 days, 16 hours and 15 minutes and 28.51 knots average to New York. She used 1040 tons of oil a day, less than *Rex* on a smaller hull. Over a 3199 nautical miles course. And a peak day's run of 677 miles. She subsequently ran 715 miles in one day, her best ever. Her 100th birthday voyage, above, from the Cherbourg Mole to Ambrose Channel Light Ship, 3092 miles, she averaged 28.00 knots in 4 days, 14 hours, 27 minutes, a "Record in time and speed" as the voyage log claims. It was her best crossing time, given the shorter course, but not her fastest running time. Her return to Bremerhaven on 16 November was one of the few times when *Bremen* and *Europa* were together at the Columbus Quay. In June, 1936, with the author on board, *Bremen* averaged 27.26 knots from Ambrose to Cherbourg mole, and 28.70 knots on the 80 miles from the mole to Southampton. That was a race with *Leviathan*. She left Cherbourg ahead of *Bremen*. But *Bremen* beat her to Southampton by taking the inside of a channel buoy, *Leviathan* the outside. It showed that Commodore Hartley's 1923 voyage speeds were no fluke.

Ignored in the various claims to being the fastest on the North Atlantic is the account of Commodore Herbert Hartley of *Leviathan's* performance on a U.S. Shipping Board invitational for some 800 members of Congress, business people, reporters and industrialists in June, 1923 from Boston Lightship to Jupiter Lighthouse some 25 miles north of Palm Beach. Formerly *Vaterland* of 1914, *Leviathan* was one of the Hapag's threesome built to make their crossings at 23½ knots in good weather. Asked by a member of the Shipping Board whether *Leviathan* could beat *Mauretania's* records Commodore Hartley made no commitment. But heading north from Jupiter Light, Hartley "gave the order for 'valves wide open.'" Speed climbed from 22 knots, *Titanic's* speed to 23, 24, 25, 26, 27. "All's well" from the engine room. The ship reached 28.4 knots for six hours, during a 25 hours period (time-change) she covered 687 nautical miles. Average speed for the entire run back to Boston was 27.48. Thus on this demonstration cruise, *Leviathan* set three records which the record-books do not acknowledge. ("Home is the Sailor," Herbert Hartley, Vulcan Press, Birmingham, Alabama, 1955.)

The New York Times obituary at his death in May, 1957 stated "*Leviathan* for a time held the record for the Atlantic crossing with a time of five days, six hours and twenty-one minutes set in 1924." Again nothing in the international record-

Again Blue Ribbon 195

Abstract of Log

Quadruple Screw Turbine Express Steamer

„BREMEN"

51 656 Gross-Register-Tons Length: 939 feet Breadth: 103 feet

Commodore L. Ziegenbein

74th Voyage from New York to Bremerhaven

June 1933	Latitude North	Long. West	Miles	Wind	Remarks
25.	40° 11'	68° 30'	246	SE 2-3	2.25 a.m. (D.S.T.) passed Ambrose Channel Lightship. — Fair weather, slight sea.
26.	40° 22'	54° 34'	638	SSE 2 SE 2-3	Fair weather, slight sea.
27.	43° 00'	41° 03'	652	E 4 NE 3	Cloudy and clear, moderate sea.
28.	47° 25'	26° 35'	665	E 5 SE 5 WNW 3	Fair weather, slight sea and NNW-swell.
29.	49° 31'	9° 50'	677	NNW 4	Cloudy and clear, moderate sea. — 8 a.m. (G.M.T.) mailplane start.
29.	Cherbrg.	Rest	321	NNW 4	Fair weather, moderate sea. 11.40 p.m. (E.M.T.) arrival at Cherbourg, breakwater 2 miles off.
		Total	3199		

Totaldistance 3 199 seamiles
Passage: 4 days, 16 hours, 15 minutes
Average speed per hour: 28,51 knots

World's Record in speed and time

Cherbourg—Southampton . . . . 82 seamiles
Southampton—Bremerhaven . . . . 457 seamiles

Bremen logs from her 74th voyage from New York to Bremerhaven, her all-time highest average, the centennial voyage in November, 1934, Captain Ziegenbein's sixtieth birthday, and the authors voyage, the 126th to Bremerhaven. The 82 miles from Cherbourg to Southampton were done at 28.70 knots, racing the Leviathan. At the end of the record 100th crossing to New York, Commodore Ziegenbein told the ship reporters that once she had attained thirty-two knots, and, on her maiden voyage, averaged thirty-one knots for twelve hours. Despite that, she was unable to beat Rex's 28.92 knots average in a try to do that.

On the maiden voyage a number of icebergs were reported, forcing use of the southern track, 72 nautical miles longer than the northern one, a loss of some 2½ hours running time.

100

Auszug aus dem Schiffstagebuch

Vierschrauben-Turbinen-Schnelldampfer

„BREMEN"

51 656 Brutto-Register-Tons Länge: 286 Meter Breite: 31 Meter

Kommodore L. Ziegenbein

Abfahrt von Bremerhaven am 2. November 10.42 Uhr (M.E.Z.)
Distanz: 470 Seemeilen
Abfahrt von Southampton am 3. November 13.48 Uhr (M.G.Z.)
Distanz: 95 Seemeilen
Abfahrt von Cherbourg Mole am 4. November 0.30 Uhr (M.G.Z.)

100. Ausreise von Bremerhaven nach New York

Nov. 1934	Breite Nord	Länge West	Sml.	Wind	Bemerkungen
4.	49° 49'	10° 12'	335	O 6 ONO 5	0.30 (M.G.Z.) Cherbourg-Mole 1 Seemeile ab. Bewölkt und klar, ziemlich grobe See.
5.	48° 47'	27° 54'	694	NO 7 ONO 5-4	Bewölkt und klar, ziemlich grobe See und NO-Dünung.
6.	45° 13'	44° 21'	705	SSO 3 NNW 4 WSW 5	Bedeckt und klar, mäßig bewegte See.
7.	42° 18'	59° 54'	715	SSO 4-5 SO 5-6	Meist bedeckt, zeitweise regnerisch, mäßig bewegte bis ziemlich grobe See.
8.	Ambrose Feuersch.	Rest	643	WSW 6-7 W 5	Bewölkt, grobe bis ziemlich grobe See.
		Total	3092		

Passierten Ambrose-Kanal-Feuerschiff 9.57 Uhr (M. 75° W. Zt.) 8. Nov. 1934

Totaldistanz 3092 Seemeilen
Reisedauer: 4 Tage, 14 Stunden, 27 Min.
Durchschnittsfahrt pro Stunde 28,9 Knot.

Rekord in Geschwindigkeit und Zeit

Abstract of Log

Quadruple Screw Turbine Express Steamer

„BREMEN"

51 656 Gross-Register-Tons Length: 939 feet Beam: 103 feet

Commodore L. Ziegenbein

Departure from Bremerhaven November 2nd, 10.42 a.m. (E.M.T.)
Distance: 470 Miles
Departure from Southampton November 3rd, 1.48 p.m. (G.M.T.)
Distance: 95 Miles
Departure from Cherbourg breakwater November 4th, 0.30 a.m. (G.M.T.)

100th Voyage from Bremerhaven to New York

Nov. 1934	Latitude North	Long. West	Miles	Wind	Remarks
4.	49° 49'	10° 12'	335	E 6 ENE 5	0.30 a.m. (G.M.T.) Cherbourg breakwater 1 mile off. Cloudy and clear, rather rough sea.
5.	48° 47'	27° 54'	694	NE 7 ENE 5-4	Cloudy and clear, rather rough sea and NE-swell.
6.	45° 13'	44° 21'	705	SSE 3 NNW 4 WSW 5	Overcast, clear, moderate sea.
7.	42° 18'	59° 54'	715	SSE 4-5 SE 5-6	Overcast, at times rainy, moderate to rather rough sea.
8.	Ambrose Lightship	Rest	643	WSW 6-7 W 5	Cloudy, rough to rather rough sea.
		Total	3092		

Passed Ambrose Channel Lightship 9.57 a.m. (E.S.T.) November 8th, 1934

Totaldistance 3092 seamiles
Passage: 4 days, 14 hours, 27 minutes
Average speed per hour: 28,9 knots

Record in speed and time

Bremen Sets Record for Northern Crossing; Averages 28 Knots on Her 100th Voyage
New York Times, November 9, 1934

The North German Lloyd liner Bremen, arriving yesterday from Bremen and Channel ports on her 100th voyage of the Atlantic, broke her best crossing time and established a record run for the North Atlantic trade. The Bremen averaged twenty-eight knots throughout the voyage from Cherbourg to Ambrose Lightship, crossing at this sustained speed in 4 days 14 hours and 27 minutes.

On Nov. 7 she steamed 715 miles, breaking the former one-day record of the northern steamer lane by two miles.

Coincidentally with the new record Captain Ziegenbein is also making his 100th voyage of the North Atlantic and on the day of his return to Bremerhaven, the 16th, he will celebrate his sixtieth birthday.

"It's all a lot of coincidences," he said after the Bremen was tied up at her West Forty-sixth Street pier, "but it couldn't possibly have been so planned sixty years ago."

The Bremen's best previous voyage, a record run established last October, was made in 4 days 15 hours 56 minutes. Thus she took off 1 hour and 29 minutes for the westward crossing between Cherbourg Breakwater and Ambrose Light. According to the ship's log, she passed the breakwater at 3 minutes after midnight last Sunday morning. She was reported yesterday at 9:57 A. M. passing Ambrose.

Captain Ziegenbein said the ship had not enjoyed particularly propitious weather, having encountered head winds and moderate to rough seas on a part of the voyage.

The Italian liner Rex, which won the blue ribbon of the Atlantic in August, 1933, has displayed faster speed than that of the Bremen. On the Southern crossing from Gibraltar the Rex averaged 28.92 knots, made a record day's run of 736 miles and crossed in 4 days 13 hours 58 minutes.

As the Bremen came up the Hudson the Rex, tied up at West Eighteenth Street, dipped her flag in salute. Captain Francesco Tarabotto later praised the performance of the Bremen, calling it a "fine feat." The Italian captain pointed out, however, that his ship still held the record.

Captain Ziegenbein smiled when asked just how fast the Bremen could really steam, but he admitted that she had averaged more than thirty knots in an eight-hour run.

Quadruple Screw Turbine Express Steamer
„BREMEN"
51 656 Gross-Register-Tons   Length: 939 feet   Beam: 103 feet

Commodore L. ZIEGENBEIN

Abstract of Log

126th Voyage from New York to Bremerhaven

May-June 1936	Latitude North	Long. West	Miles	Wind	Remarks
30.	40°14'	69°04'	219	SW 3 West 3	3.12 a. m. (D.S.T.) passed Ambrose Channel Lightship. — Blue sky, fine and clear, slight sea.
31.	40°25'	55°18'	630	West 4-3 NW 3	Fine and clear, slight sea.
1.	42°34'	42°15'	625	East 2 South 4-8	Overcast, Southerly gale, very rough sea and rough SE-swell. Reduced speed at times.
2.	46°56'	28°38'	636	S by E 6-3 South 2	Cloudy and clear, moderate sea, decreasing swell.
3.	49°23'	12°53'	646	SW 2 NW 2-3	Fair weather, slight sea.
4.	Cherbrg.	Rest	442	NNW 3	5.30 a. m. (E. M. T.) arrival at Cherbourg breakwater.
		Total	3198		

Total Distance: 3 198 miles
Passage: 4 days, 21 hours, 18 minutes
Average speed per hour: 27.26 knots

Cherbourg—Southampton . . . . 80 seamiles
Southampton—Bremerhaven . . . . 457 seamiles

The Author's voyage in 1936. Annual average in both directions was close to 26.6 knots.

---

ing of speedy crossings. From Southampton to New York, this was eventually reduced by *Mauretania* to 5 days, 5 hours.

Evidently in 1931 when both *Queen Mary* and *Normandie* were under construction the French Line offered to stop the project if Cunard would do the same. Both became victims of the depression, but finally went ahead.

Normandie in 1935 beat *Rex* with 29.94 knots. Then came *Queen Mary*, an older design than *Normandie*, but with much stronger engines, and made a new Bishop's Rock-Ambrose record of 30.14 knots. First *Normandie* improved that, then *Queen Mary* again, to 30.99 knots. *Normandie* in time raised that to 31.20 in 1937, and *Queen Mary* to 31.69 knots in 1938. In 1952, the Navy-designed *United States* did the outward voyage in 3.10.40 minutes, the first crossing in under four days, at 35.59 knots average, returning at 34.15 knots. No warship, until the coming of the nuclear-powered aircraft carriers, could sustain that speed over trans-oceanic distances. The US's was the last legitimate, in the old sense, record crossing, winning for her the Hales Trophy. In June, 1986 a specially built speed craft 72' long made Ambrose Light-Bishop's Rock with three refuelings in 3.8.31 or 36.026 average.

In June, 1990 the Hovercraft *Great Britain* did 2922 nautical miles across the Atlantic at 39 knots average in 3 days, 7 hours, 54 minutes.

Prior to these trans-Atlantic speedsters, the fastest operating ships other than the *United States*, were the seven Sea-Land SL-7 vessels, two built in Dutch yards, five in Germany. They started in 1972, before the oil shock and boycott, to cross the Atlantic at some 33 knots. In August, 1973 *Sea Land Exchange* did Ambrose Light Ship to Bishop's Rock in 3 days, 10 hours, 2 minutes at 33.20 knots average. These 41,127 tons freighters proved invaluable as ready-lift ships for the U.S. Navy, which bought five of them. They were at Diego Suarez when Operation Desert Storm opened, ready for the purpose for which the Navy converted them, at speeds equalling those of warships.

The "New York to Frisco" records around Cape Horn were as historic in the 1800s as the Blue Ribbon in the late 19th and 20th centuries. In 1994, Isabelle Autissier of France with a crew of three made the voyage in a racing sloop in 62 days, 5 hours, 56 minutes against the 1854 record of 89 days, 21 hours by the clipper *Flying Cloud*. The challenge remains. Is the romance gone?

The Ambrose Lightship was built as No. 87 in 1908 to mark the entrance to the newly dredged Ambrose Channel into New York, due East of Sandy Hook, earlier the Blue Ribbon end point, six miles from the harbor entrance in thirteen fathoms. Prior to the new channel dug 1904-1908, the deepest-draught ships could use it only at high tide. The vessel in later paintup is at the South Street Seaport, lower Manhattan. The current platform has a helicopter landing pad. In 1970 and 1972, Ambrose at South Street Seaport was the backdrop to dory races held in connection with the National Boat Show. A British and American Crew, each two men, a woman the coxswain, rowed 15-foot Grand Banks dories, the kind shown in Homer Winslow's painting. The British coxwain, Miss Micolette Milnes-Walker, in 1971 sailed the Atlantic alone. An interesting exchange took place at Ambrose in May, 1959. A Jersey City couple booked passenger on Liberte, ex-Europa to Europe for 13 May, the husband to arrive on Constitution, where he was maitre d'hotel, six days before that date. Schedule changes cut that to four hours, the ship to arrive at 7:30. Bad weather cut that to less. The two lines were alerted. Mrs. Brigaudin sailed on Liberte at 11:30. Meanwhile, Constitution had reached Ambrose Light at 10:50; Mr. Brigaudin climbed down the Jacob's ladder, his baggage lowered by line, into the lightship's boat, on it awaited the Liberte, then reversed the maneuver, climbing up its boarding gangway at 1:40 p.m. A happy ending for everybody.

In Captain Ziegenbein's day room the symbolic Blue Ribbon hung above his desk. The Commodore's Standard flew from the masttop. (See Christmas Celebration in "Inspectorate.") The Ribbon took the place of an actual trophy. None existed until in 1935 British Member of Parliament Richard Hales donated a trophy. It went to Normandie, to Queen Mary, then in 1952 to the United States. It was kept at the American Merchant Marine Museum, Kings Point, Long Island, until British courts forced its surrender to a winner not accepted by the Shipping fraternity: an English Channel type catamaran-ferry. It did cross the Atlantic in record time. But it carried no passengers, it was not in commercial service, and had no sleeping quarters for its crew. What would be a record of an age gone, has become an artificial symbol.

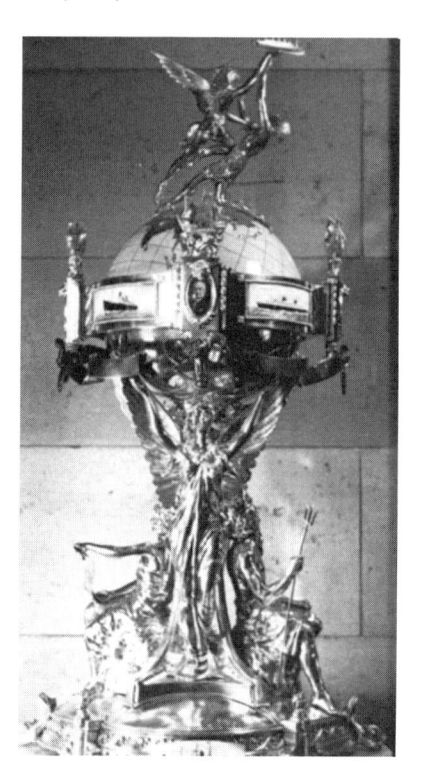

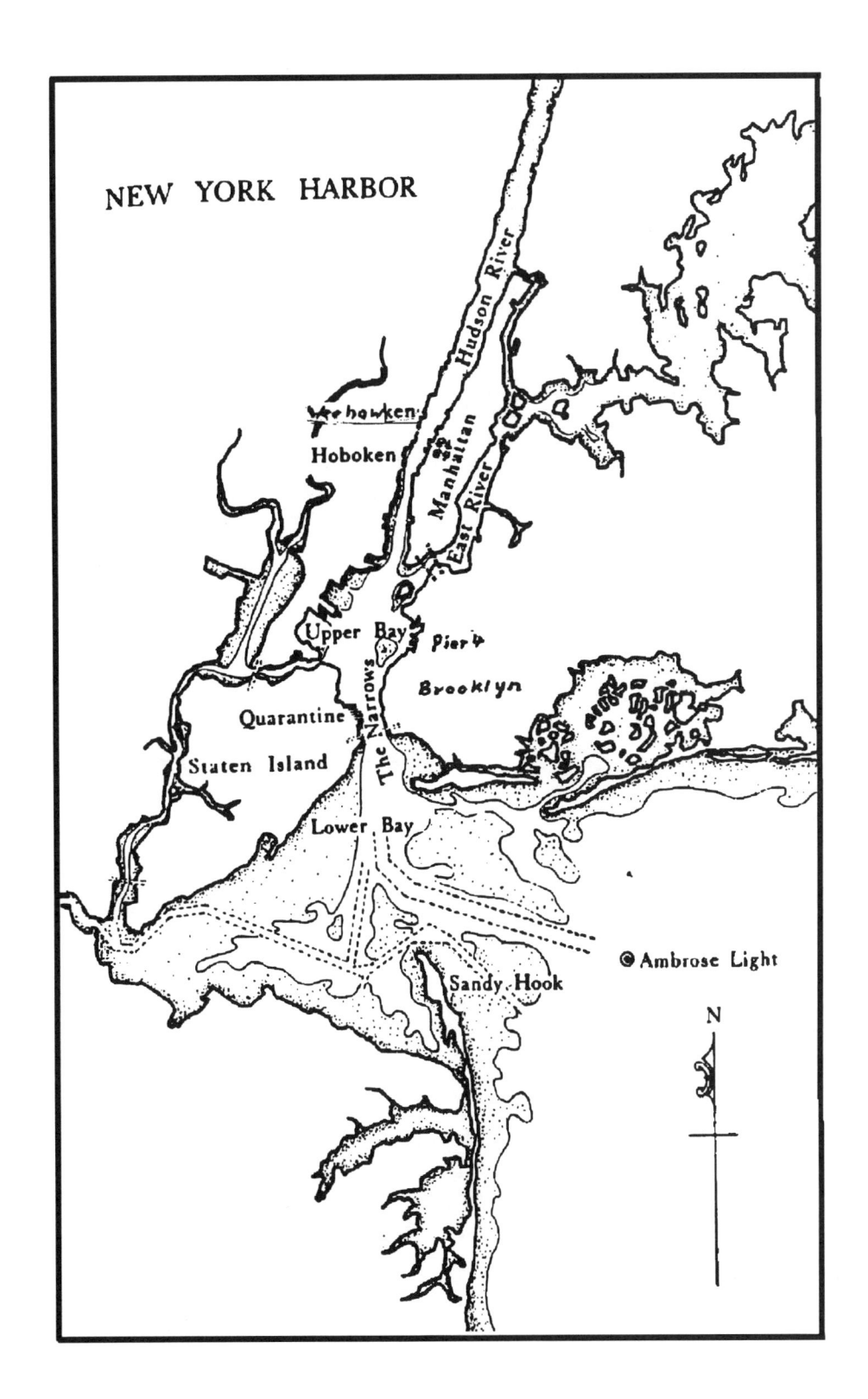

In 1929, Ambrose Channel Light Vessel marked the end of the trans-Atlantic speed runs. Map ex- The Only Way to Cross, John Maxtone - Graham Collier Books, New York 1978.

Ambrose Light today, no longer a red-painted ship bobbing on the waves. And no longer ships and speed runs to use it as the end-point. U.S. Coast Guard Photo.

CHAPTER 6

The Lloyd Flies

Ever since Daedalus, man has wanted to emulate birds' ability to fly and look down on the earth. As a child I was mystified by postcard views "Aus der Vogelschau," from the bird's view. How could man see like the birds before he could fly? There were a few pre-1900 flying pioneers: balloons, gliders, even some powered "flight." But the ability to leave the earth's surface under control is a phenomenon of the twentieth century. Graf Zeppelin's LZ 1 first flew on 2 July, 1900 over the Bodensee, Lake Constance, at Friedrichshafen. By late 1909, LZ 10, piloted by Hugo Eckener, opened inter-city passenger service. Hapag was the booking agent, as it was in the 1920s and, with the Lloyd in the 1930s.

In 1909, Count Zeppelin founded the Deutsche Luftschiffahrts A.G., Air Shipping Co., with participation from the Lloyd and Hapag. This was after he with Prinz Heinrich, the younger brother of the Kaiser, had made an Arctic exploration cruise on NDL's *Mainz* #102 to research the feasibility of trans-Polar airship flights. Also on board was Ferdinand Gluhn, 1909-1910 captain of NDL's sail training ship *Herzogin Sophie Charlotte* #143. Graf Zeppelin asked him to head up administration for the new concern. He was given indefinite leave by the Lloyd. Gluhn was killed in the crash of LZ 2 on 17, October 1913 over the Bodensee. But by outbreak of war, 42,000 persons had flown commercially in Zeppelins without further casualty.

In 1914, the Lloyd honored the pioneer of airship flying with the launch on 9 June of the 14,167 tons passenger ship *Zeppelin*. My father, then studying shipbuilding by Lloyd assignment at the Bremen Technikum, attended as guest of the Bremer Vulkan, the builder. The ship was completed during the war, and laid up. In March, 1919 it was the first NDL ship to be delivered to the Allies as war reparations.

Already in mid-1918, with the tide for Imperial German fast running out, the Lloyd had begun thinking about the potential for air traffic as a way to get back into business after the war. In the summer of 1919, the Lloyd Luftdienst Gmbh, Air Service Co., was formed with F.W. Jordan as manager. Initial research was extensive theoretical examination of international air traffic. The 1919/20 Lloyd Year Book has 40+ pages on this, plus imagined-route maps covering the world, and photos!

First a major airport at Bremen had to be developed, a Flight Harbor, completed in 1923. This would be as much a matter of economic life or stagnation for the city as was the silting up of the Weser. That cut the city off from the sea until Bremerhaven was built in 1827, and the "river correction" that has continued ever since, as ships got bigger. (See "Bremen's Thrust to the Sea.")

Early in 1920, flight arrangements were made with German and foreign aircraft-building and operating interests. NDL handled the promotion and bookings. In July, 1920 a contract was signed with the Reichspost for air mail service Berlin-Bremen-Wangerooge, one of the Friesian Islands

F. W. Jordan, director of the Lloyd Luftdienst, Lloyd Air Service, before one of the aircraft. Ex-NDL's 1919/20 Yearbook.

Sticker given out for publicity celebrating 75 years of Bremen's Airport, 1923-1988, the first three years basically a Lloyd air-service operation.

The old Bremen Airport before in 1923 the new Air Harbor was constructed. NDL Yearbook 1919/20. Passport control, out in the open!

1922 letter card with markings: Express Delivery via Aircraft of the Lloyd Ost-Flug GmbH, Lloyd-East Flight Co. Postmarked in Stettin for Munich via Nürnberg. A rare example of domestic German air operations so soon after the war.

202 Norddeutscher Lloyd Bremen

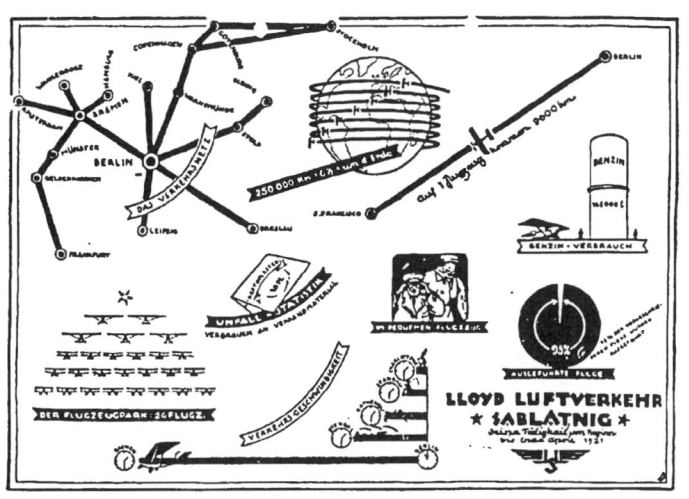

A Lloyd-Sablatnig Air Service overview from start of service in July, 1920 through April, 1921. Unusual: It even mentions that 10 meters of Pflaster (Bandaids) were used; 26 aircraft in operation, and the traffic network, from Amsterdam to Breslau, from Frankfurt to Stockholm. The daily distance flown equal from Berlin to San Francisco. Total distance flown: 6½ times around the world: 95% of scheduled flights were completed. From Hans Jürgen Witthöft's N.D.L.-Koehler, 1973.

The word Lloyd, as with shipping companies worldwide, here is used to imply capability, integrity, performance, safety ... and all these were strived for. In 1925, Aero Lloyd and other flying companies merged into Lufthansa, with Lloyd and Hapag having seats on the Board.

served by NDL resort steamers. The flying was done by Sablatnig Flugzeugbau, Aircraft Construction Co. The first daily round-trip left Berlin for Bremen on 21/7/1920. During the Frankfurt Fair flights to and from there were added. On 6 February, 1923, NDL was instrumental in merging several concerns into the Deutsche Aero Lloyd. Hapag also joined financially with its air-interests, very parallel to those of the Lloyd. In its first operating year, Aero Lloyd flew more than 300,000 miles sans accident. In 1924, some 3,600 route miles were flown daily. In 1925, night-flying was introduced.

In 1926, Aero Lloyd and the Junkers Luftverkehrs A.G., Air Traffic Co. — also the main German builder of transport aircraft — were merged into Lufthansa, still the German air carrier worldwide. Both the Lloyd and Hapag through their Aero Lloyd interests had seats on the Board of Directors.

By this time, trans-Atlantic shipping lines had become interested in flying from ships to shore with mail, even passengers someday? And from shore to ships at sea. On 25 November, 1926 Sir Alan Cobham as pilot of the DeHavilland Moth and Lady Cobham as radio officer, flew "The first air mail to arrive in New York from the East" from the White Star liner *Homeric*, launched 1913 as *Columbus* #267 for the Lloyd at Danzig. The mail was postmarked in New York 1:30 P.M. that day. It reached its destination in New Jersey the next morning.

In April, 1927 NDL's *Lützow* on a Mediterranean cruise was equipped with a Kiwull canvas apron hung from the stern to smoothen landings in a rough sea and to take onto the ship aircraft carried to give passengers a "Bird's Eye View." Interest was so great that *Columbus* the next year carried a Junkers pontoon airplane on its West Indies cruises for Raymond & Whitcomb. Flight-seeing became a regular feature on Lloyd cruises.

On 1 August, 1927 Clarence Chamberlain flew a Fokker biplane off a 100-foot ramp built over the forward deck of *Leviathan*, ex-Hapag's *Vaterland* of 1914, 86 miles off Ambrose Lightship with 916 letters. A similar ramp-type takeoff had been tried earlier from the U.S.S. *Pennsylvania*. Two days later, the U.S. Post Office Department announced that it would put aircraft on trans-Atlantic liners, including NDL's former *George Washington*, to shorten the crossing time for mails. This was never done.

On 23 August, 1928 some 400 miles off Sandy Hook, Pilot Lieutenant Louis-Marie Lermongeot was catapulted from the French Line's *Ile De France*. He landed at Quarantine Station, Staten Island, in 187 minutes. The plane was loaded with bags of mail, stamps having been specially over-printed for this flight. Today such mail brings high prices at philatelic auctions. Also, there was

The Lloyd Flies 203

In the mid-1920s shipping lines became interested in flying ship-to-shore mail service, even some day with passengers, and from shore to ships far at sea. On 25 November, 1926 Sir Alan Cobham as pilot of the DeHavilland Moth and Lady Cobham as radio officer, flew "The first air mail to arrive in New York from the East" from the White Star liner Homeric, *launched 1913 as* Columbus *for the Lloyd at Danzig. The mail was postmarked in New York 1:30 p.m. that day, arrived at its destination in New Jersey the next morning.*

room for six passengers in the 480 horsepower Loire-Olivier biplane. On another flight off the Irish coast the plane suffered some damage on take-off and had to land five miles from the ship. The crew and mail sacks were taken off by the British trawler *Children's Friend* in the setting darkness while the airplane drifted away. A French vessel found it the next day and towed it into Brest.

On 12 June, 1929 Adams Air Mail Pickup made a drop to and from *Leviathan* 65 miles from Curtiss Field, Long Island, with a hook-on cable, similar to the way the Railway Mail Service picks up wayside mail bags.

1928 was a rewarding year for Germany on the North Atlantic, less than ten years after total defeat in war. It began with a world event: on 14 April the entire Atlantic was crossed for the first time East to West by a German airplane named *Bremen*, with Captain Hermann Koehl, Major James Fitzmaurice, and E.G. Freiherr von Huenefeld. The flight was financed by the Lloyd and other Bremen concerns. This event played into the hands of New York Mayor "Jimmie" Walker, so known publicly, and his Protocol Chief Grover Whalen. The Mayor had been a valued friend of the Lloyd since the Maiden Voyage arrival of *Columbus* on 1, May 1924 under Captain Nicholas Johnsen. For the first time since the war, the City extended to Germans extraordinary attention and honors. The festive dinner for the three flyers with some 3,000 persons at the Hotel Commodore had Mayor Walker as main speaker. The 100-men Police Band alternately played American and German music and marches. As "Jimmie" was presenting the flyers to the diners he was interrupted by one: "We acknowledge the heroic deed of these gentlemen. But I must make one correction: before they left Ireland they swore a mutual oath: "Mitchell Field (the New York arrival airport on Long Island) or Heaven." But they reached neither the "Field nor Heaven." The Mayor interrupted: "Bill. When these men after hours - long flying in darkness and bad weather with fast-dropping reserves of fuel suddenly through a hole in the clouds saw land below, all three felt they were in Heaven." Warm laughter. The Mayor walked at the head of the ticker-tape parade up Broadway.

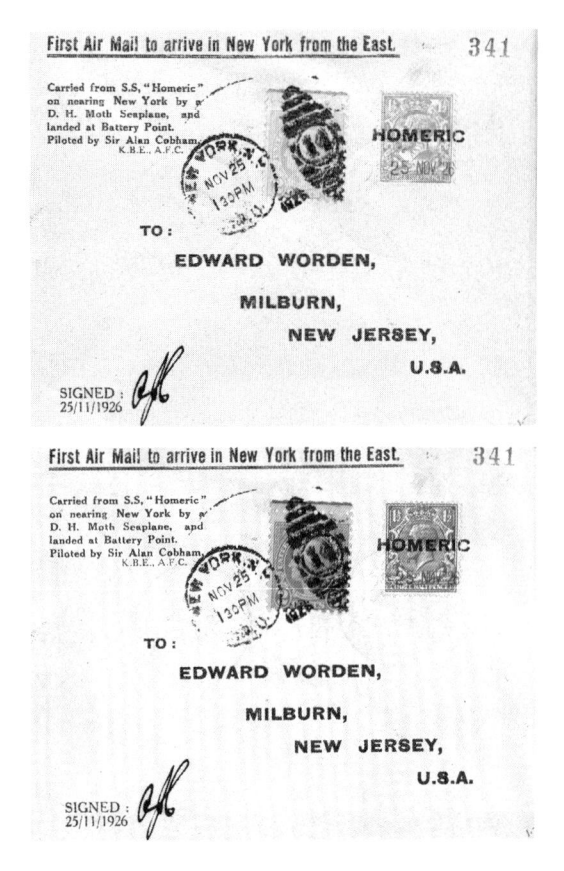

The flyers had crash-landed on Greenly Island in the mouth of the St. Lawrence. Floyd Bennet and Bernt Balchen, both from sickbeds, with Luke Schiller offered to bring in rescue supplies and personnel.

Bennett was hospitalized in Quebec with pneumonia. Colonel Charles Lingbergh flew up the serum for his medication. Herta Junkers flew north to help. The book by the three flyers of their experience is dedicated to Floyd Bennett, who died soon after, and to "those who went before and disappeared into the unknown: Nungessor

Stuttgart *in the Mediterranean, and* Sierra Ventana *and* Sierra Cordoba *on their Norway/Polar cruises carried aircraft. A wonderful way to see the Fjord and coastal country 1928 and later. The Kiwull apron can be used to flatten waves to ease the aircraft's landing, and to pull it up to the ship for lifting on board. On a* Lützow *cruise.*

On 31, July, 1927 Clarence Chamberlain flew a Fokker biplane off a 100' ramp built across the stern of Leviathan, *ex-Hapag's* Vaterland *of 1914, from 86 miles off Ambrose Lightship. A similar ramp-type takeoff had been tested earlier off USS* Pennsylvania. *On 12 June, 1929 Adams Air Mail Pickup tried to make one and a drop with* Leviathan *but failed. As had an attempt in August, 1927.*

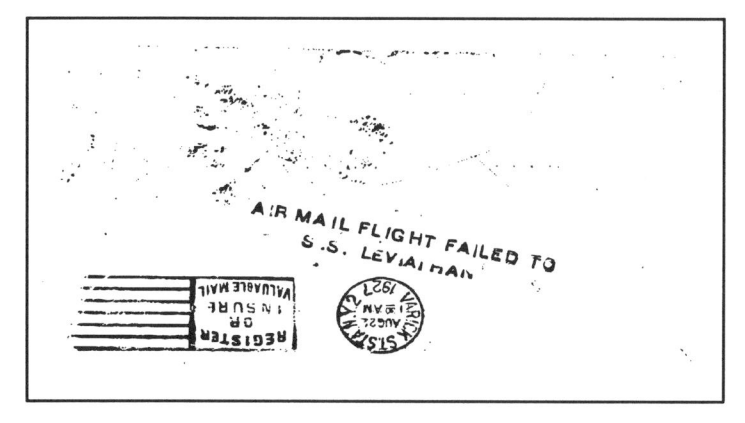

and Coli; Hamilton, Minchin and Princess Löwenstein-Wertheim; Hinchcliffe and Eleanor Mackay." Surely a reminder that on the sea and in the air there is no nationality when heroism ends in disaster.

Secretary of Commerce and the next President, Herbert Hoover at the Civic Dinner said "We owe a debt to the gentlemen we honor today. They have done a brave thing. But more than that, they have given to us in America an occasion to express our admiration for the people who produce such men." Koehl and Fitzmaurice were flyers: von Huenefeld was head of NDL's Literary Department, in effect, Promotion Chief.

In Washington, the flyers visited President Coolidge at the White House and appeared before a joint session of the House and Senate. They then returned to New York where "we had several festive afternoon coffees as a group" said Captain Drechsel. After a U.S.-Canada tour as far as Milwaukee, the flyers and wives sailed for German on *Columbus* on 9 June, 1928. In Plymouth they were met by the Mayor and staff in full regalia, and by Lloyd and other officials who had come to escort them to Germany for events there and in Ireland.

The *Bremen* was brought from its crash site near Murray Bay and taken to Germany for display at an international Air Fair in Berlin. Later, it was presented to the Museum of the City of New York, and finally to the Ford Museum in Dearborn.

Bremen's sister plane *Europa* carried the flyers to Hamburg and Berlin. In September, 1928 Freiherr von Huenefeld and Swedish Pilot K.G. Lindner flew *Europa* with many refuelling stops to Shanghai where they visited Captain H. Hashagen (later head of the Lloyd's Nautical Division) on *Derfflinger*, and on to Tokyo. The planned flight across the Pacific had to be abandoned as it had become the typhoon season. *Europa* was presented to the Japanese Aero Club. Von Huenefeld died in February, 1929 following surgery, never to know of the triumphant record maiden voyage of the airplane's ship namesake *Bremen*, and its catapult flight operations.

In August, 1931, Mayor Walker during a month's vacation in Germany, at Bremen gave to Baroness von Huenefeld,

The Lloyd Flies 205

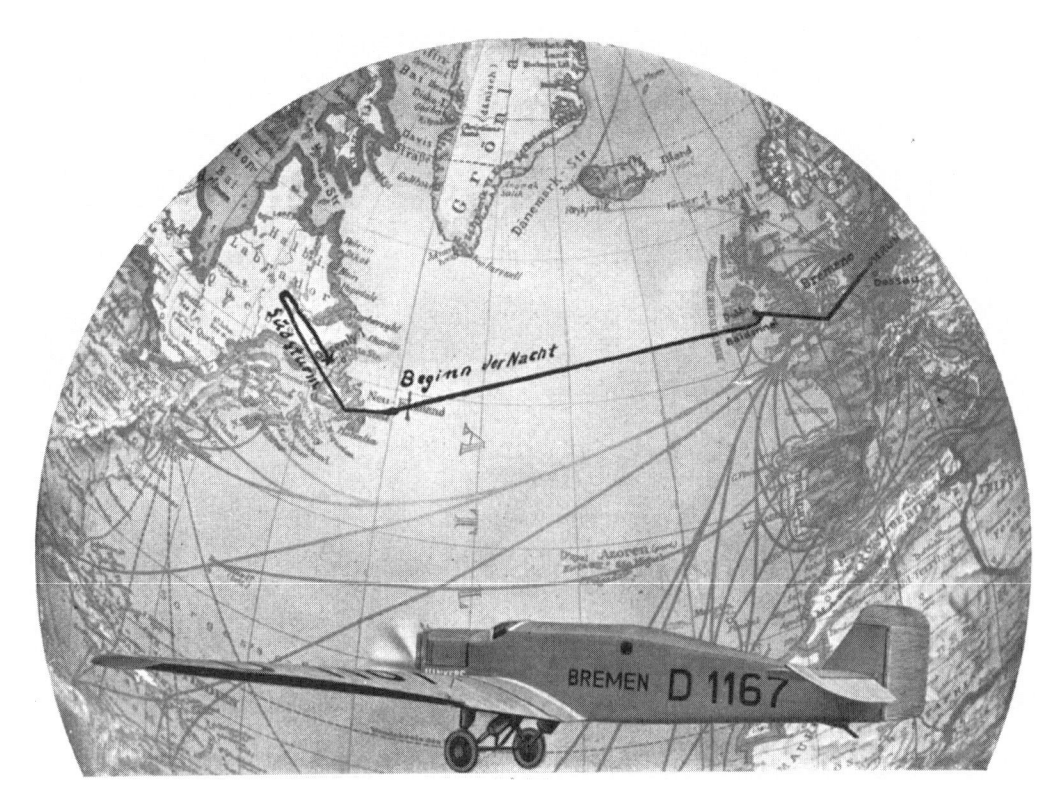

Route of D 1167, Bremen. Actually, the three flyer covered a greater distance, 6,570 kilometers, than the direct route to New York, their target: 6,400 kms. The D-1167 Bremen *aircraft Junkers W33 type hung in the Grand Central Station, New York, into 1930. Later it was moved to the Ford Museum in Dearborn, Mich.* Our Ocean Flight, and Life's Remembrances, Koehl, Fitzmaurice & v. Huenefeld, Union Verlags Gesellschaft, Berlin, 1929.

The three flyers, Koehl, Fitzmaurice and von Huenefeld, at the crash site of Bremen *on Greenly Island,* Acme News Photo, *distribution of actual photo taken by Duke Schiller, of the rescue team.* Seven Seas, May, 1928, *N. German Lloyd magazine.*

THE NEW YORK TIMES, FRIDAY, OCTOBER 19, 1973

Bernt Balchen, Explorer And Pilot in Arctic, Dead

Special to The New York Times

MOUNT KISCO, N.Y., Oct. 18 — Col. Bernt Balchen, U.S.A.F., retired, the aviator and explorer who was chief pilot on Adm. Richard E. Byrd's first flight over the South Pole in 1929, died yesterday in Northern Westchester Hospital. He would have been 74 years old Tuesday. His home was in Chappaqua, N.Y.

Surviving are his widow, the former Audrey C. Schipper and two sons by prior marriages, Bernt Balchen Jr. of Oslo and Lauritz Balchen of McLean, Va.

A military service will be held Monday at noon in the Protestant Chapel of Kennedy International Airport. Burial will be in Arlington National Cementery on Tuesday at 1 P.M.

Many-Faceted Career

Trans-Atlantic Flight

In 1927 he piloted the tri-motor America for Admiral Byrd on his dramatic transatlantic flight. The plane fought its way through fog and a succession of storms to the French coast. Admiral Byrd navigated the plane to a lighthouse at Ver-sur-Mer. With the shore dimly outlined by flares, Mr. Balchen skillfully set the plane down on water and all on board made shore safely.

The following year, Mr. Balchen and Floyd Bennett got up from sick beds to fly a plane to rescue the crew of the German airplane Bremen, which had made a forced landing off the Labrador coast. Mr. Bennett came down with pneumonia en route, was rushed to Quebec and before long was dead. Mr. Balchen pushed on and brought out the Bremen fliers.

Bernt Balchen, who had flown out the three Bremen flyers to New York, died in 1973 near his 74th birthday. In August, 1931 New York Mayor James Walker went on Bremen for a month's vacation in Germany. In Bremen, the Lloyd and the City gave him a festive reception. In Bremen, Mr. Walker visited the Baroness von Huenefeld, the flyer's Mother. He had died early in 1929 from complications under surgery.

Mayor James Walker with the three flyers at the welcoming at City Hall in April, 1929. From: Unser Ozeanflug, Hermann Köhl, Union Deutsche Verlags Gesellschaft. 1929. Mayor Walker was a good friend of the Lloyd, and would visit, especially Captain Johnsen on Columbus. In 1932, Mayor Walker's administration was involved in the pier-lease scandal. See "North Atlantic Community." He did not run for re-election in 1933.

Mrs. Herman Koehl, left, and right Mrs. James Fitzmaurice, came over on the Dresden to New York to join their flyer-husbands for the weeks of celebrations, and return to Europe. Captain R. Wurpts the happy ship commander. He had spent the 1917-19 years in U.S. POW camp, last at Chapel Hill. See "A New Start."

Mayor Walker with Captain Johnsen and NDL President Philipp Heineken at the annual dinner of the Steuben Society held on Columbus.

The Lloyd Flies

The Koehl-Fitzmaurice-von Huenefeld flyers on the boat deck of Columbus, *ready to return to Europe. To the right, facing Herr Heinz Schuengel, NDL director for North America, and Inspector Captain W. Drechsel chief of Port operations. June, 1928 in New York.*

At Shanghai, the Europa *flyers, the Swedish pilot K.G. Lindner, left, Captain H. Hashagen of NDL's* Derfflinger, *and H. von Huenefeld, en route to Tokyo from Germany overland. The return flight via the Pacific Ocean was cancelled because of the Typhoon season. Fall 1928. By naming the trans-Atlantic airplane* Bremen, *and the Asia sister* Europa, *the Lloyd with its financing was preparing for the appearance of its new speedsters in 1929. See color section for a flown cover.*

the memorial coin her son had given to Bernt Balchen in 1928 as a token of thanks for his part in the flyers' rescue.

Also, in 1928 the Lloyd had the "First Air Cruise in History," 10,000 miles by air, sea, river and rail in 52 days. The cruise left New York on *Columbus* on 8 September, and returned to Cologne, fly on to Paris-Berlin-Amsterdam-London to rejoin *Columbus* at Southampton. A second Air Cruise was scheduled for 1929: to leave New York 27 July on *Bremen's* return maiden voyage, and leave Europe on 10 September, again on *Bremen.*

In December, 1927 Lufthansa was flying mail from Munich-Berlin to ships at Bremerhaven and from Prague via Leipzig. On 21 May, 1928 three aircraft awaited *Columbus* at Bremerhaven. Thirty-two passengers filled all seats for Berlin, Frankfurt, Leipzig and Prague. Presumably, mail was also taken. For *Berlin's* Polar Cruise in July the Lloyd offered "Seaplane service throughout the voyage."

A natural development of the ship-to-shore mail experiments of 1926-1928 was the decision to install catapults on *Bremen* and *Europa*. The optimum site was on the roof of the Sun Deck restaurant between the two stacks, with derricks to lift the planes on and off. The Lloyd saw this as an extra service; Lufthansa as valuable experience towards the eventual Europe-South America mail-flying using mid-ocean catapult ships.

This first-ever Air Cruise rated a half-page New York Times story almost forty years later. It helped that the American flyer-writer Mildred Johnson did the "cruise" on her own ahead of the Lloyd's schedule. The cruise was repeated in the following year.

The first catapult shootoff was on the last day of *Bremen's* 16-22nd July, 1929 maiden voyage. Not as air mail histories in print claim from 400 miles out. The Heinkel D-1717 *Bremen* was catapulted off with Pilot Baron von Studnitz and Mechanic Karl Kirchhoff after the ship had passed the trans-Atlantic finish line at Ambrose Lightship with a new time and speed record. The plane landed off Pier 4, Army Base, Brooklyn. The author photographed the arrival. From there, the 300 pounds of mail were sped to the G.P.O. for sorting, onward dispatch and delivery. Future flights did take off usually 600 or more miles from the port of destination on both sides of the Atlantic. On the return voyage, the airplane was shot off five miles outside Cherbourg and flew the 500 miles to Bremerhaven, beating the ship by more than a day. En route to New York, mail was flown to the ships at Cherbourg, saving a day's transit.

Miss Mildred Johnson and Mrs. Esther Wanner, enthusiastic supporters of the international air-mail idea, sailed last month on the Columbus *to tour Europe by air. With them is Lieut. Walter Hagen, pilot of the liner's seaplane. Ex-Seven Seas, June, 1928.*

The first official flight from *Europa* was on 15/9/1930 following test flights westward and eastward. Overall, 212 flights were scheduled 1929-1935. Twelve were cancelled by mechanical problems or weather. One flight ended in tragedy. On 23 July, 1934 *Europa's* aircraft made an emergency landing at Le Croisic, 30 Kms. off St. Nazaire. Pilot Walter Diele had lost his bearings due to wireless trouble. Five *Bremen* flights in 1935 refuelled at Nantucket Island to extend the range and time-saving.

The Heinkel float plane D-1717 *Bremen* made all the ship's flights through the 1931 season. On 5 October, 1931 with Pilot Fritz Simon, 27 years old, and mechanic-wireless operator Rudolf Wagenknecht, 32 years old, an attempt was made to set a new time and distance record from the ship to New York. After refuelling at North Sydney, Nova Scotia, some emergency led Pilot Simon to try to land in Cobequid Bay near Burntcoat Head Light House, not knowing that at low tide there were barely inches covering the

The Lloyd Flies

> **LLOYD** *introduces* **SHIP-TO-PLANE AIR SERVICE** *in Europe*
>
> STEP from your Lloyd Liner and fly (bag and baggage) to any European city! At Bremerhaven, a fleet of de luxe cabin airplanes awaits the COLUMBUS... only a step from gangplank to plane... you re-embark in cushioned luxury... the panorama of Europe drifts beneath... luncheon and refreshments are served... hours are saved.
>
> *Seaplanes are carried on Lloyd Cruises*
>
> ENGLAND **NORTH GERMAN** IRELAND
> FRANCE   **LLOYD**   GERMANY
>
> Broadway, New York City, or your local agent

September, 1928 Lloyd advertisement for its service in Europe: fly from shipside to your destination. And that cruises now carry sight-seeing aircraft. Columbus passengers in May at Bremerhaven were the first to use this service: three aircraft awaited them.

water. This caused the plane to somersault, killing both men. Will Rogers and Wiley Post lost their lives in a similar happening in Alaska: trying to land on water barely covering the tundra. Men's lives pay the price for man's advancement.

The next year, 1932, another *Bremen*, D-1919, a Junkers 46, carried on the memorial tradition. The flights ended in the fall of 1935 when trans-Atlantic air service had become a proven way to travel on *Graf Zeppelin*.

The catapults were removed from the two ships during their Winter 1935-1936 overhaul and replaced with enclosed garage space for fifty automobiles When filled up, the ships were more top-heavy and rolled more, *Bremen* the worse of the two.

In August, 1929, less than a month after *Bremen's* initial catapult shootoff, an airmail experiment-stunt to speed mail from Boston to Britain was made with *Karlsruhe* #149. Mail was picked up from the ship off the Irish coast, flown to Galway, with a quick connection to London. Special envelopes and a sticker AIR MAIL - KARLSRUHE - GALWAY were provided. Mail is known postmarked August 15 in Boston, and from the ship with its BREMEN-NEW YORK Sea Post on the 26th. At Galway, the covers received an oval FIRST AIR MAIL cachet. Envelopes to Birmingham were arrival-stamped the 27th. Pilot Chas. L. Russell autographed some of this ship-pickup mail.

In January, 1931 mail posted too late to catch *City Of Los Angeles*, the former *Grosser Kurfürst* #150, at its pier in San Pedro, was bundled at Grand Central Air Terminal and flown by Curtiss-Wright Flying Services flying boat to the ship. The mail was backstamped "Received 24.Jan.1931, S.S. City of Los Angeles," and with arrival cancel of 30 January in Honolulu. This late mail did not have to wait for the next ship a week later.

In June, 1931 *City Of Los Angeles* was involved in an experiment with Goodyear blimps hooking onto a sack of mail before arrival of the ship at San Francisco or San Pedro. Off New York, a Goodyear blimp once landed on *Bremen* to take off the company's chief.

During these years of experiments and advances in airplanes flying the mails, airships also were being developed for passengers and mails. In 1921, the first postwar new Zeppelin *Bodensee* made various flights from Friedrichshafen before delivery to Italy as war reparations. Similarly, in October, 1924 LZ 126 under Hugo Eckener, flew to the U.S. for delivery. It was taken over by the U.S. Navy, renamed *Los Angeles*. During this flight, the author and family were on Union S.S. Co. of New Zealand's *Makura* en route from Sydney to Vancouver. Reports of the crossing appeared in the ship's bulletin.

In 1929, Deutsche Luftschiffahrt A.G. signed a new agreement with Hapag making it general agent worldwide. Hearst Publications chartered the *Graf Zeppelin LZ 127* for a round-the-world flight. "Charter" in effect meant Hearst guaranteed filling a number of berths, including for its top foreign correspondent Karl von Wiegand. He sent daily radio reports, giving wide publicity to the Hearst papers and the airship. The City of New York gave a festive luncheon on 30 August, 1929 at the Hotel Astor to honor Dr. Eckener, successor to the spirit and drive of Count Zeppelin, and crew. Lady Grace Drummond-Hay, another Hearst correspondent, was one of the speakers. Others were: the Chairman of the Steuben Society of America, Arthur Brisbane (Hearst columnist!), the Chargé of the German Embassy, the Publisher of the New York Staats Zeitung, Rear Admiral William A. Moffitt,

Direct connection from the Lloyd Quay in Bremerhaven to Berlin in less than two hours. This service began in 1928. This Junkers Tri-Motor, preceding that built by Ford Motor Company, sold for the today unbelievable price of $25,000.

U.S.N., later honored with Moffitt Field, the Navy's dirigible base in Sunnyvale, California, Mayor James Walker and in closing, Dr. Eckener.

Europe-South America through passenger and mail service began on 29 August, 1931 with *Graf Zeppelin* from Friedrichshafen to Rio de Janeiro. The air voyage took four days vs twelve days Hamburg-Rio by *Cap Arcona*, the fastest ship to South America. Three round flights were made in 1931, nine in 1932, and nine in 1933.

Also in 1931, *Graf Zeppelin* made a flight to the Antarctic to exchange mail with a German icebreaker. (Bundesmuseum-Frankfurt). When Germany in its drive for self-sufficiency built up a whaling fleet, aircraft into 1939 made occasional mail-exchange flights to the flotillas of mother ships and catchers.

A New York civic luncheon

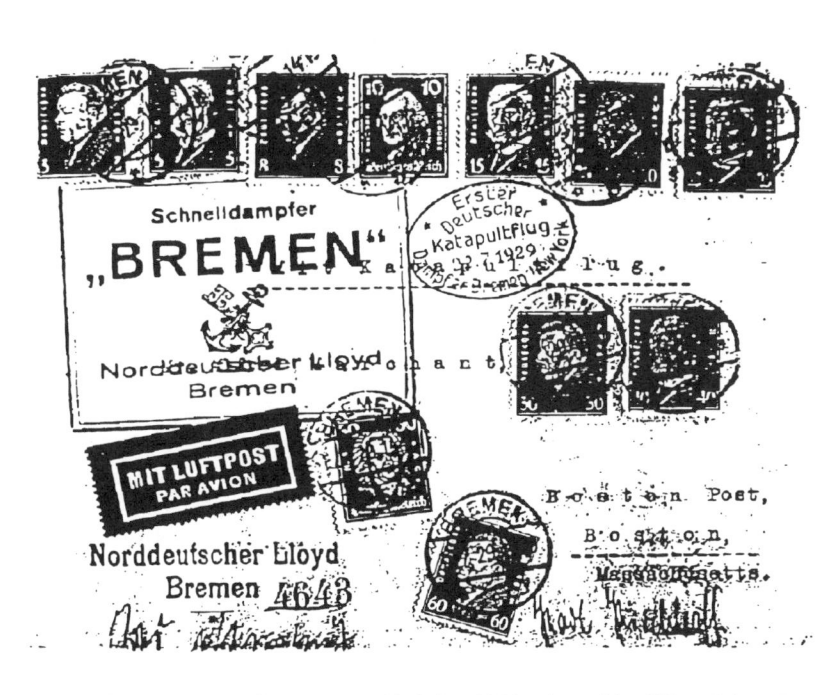

First-flight cover from Bremen on 22 July, 1929, signed by Pilot Jobst, Baron von Studnitz, and mechanic-radio officer Karl Kirchhoff. This first flight was probably the heaviest mail ever so carried. Note number applied to cover.

The Lloyd Flies 211

Daytime shoot-off from Bremen, 1930-31. The ship would turn towards the wind to give more airflow over the wings. The airplane rarely, unlike naval catapult shootoffs, tended to drop very much towards the water before having full-control air speed. Ex Acht Glas, Dr. Becker-Ferber, Kommodore Ziegenbein. Photo - Hanns Tschira.

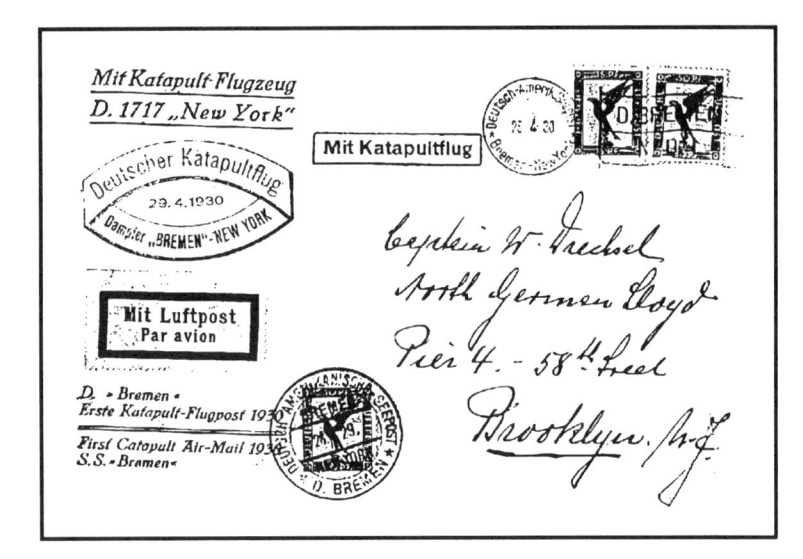

Cover from the first 1930 flight from Bremen, sent by Captain L. Ziegenbein to Captain W. Drechsel. Note double-ring cancel reads 28.4.29, not 30. And message from Capt. Ziegenbein. Hearty Greetings from our first 1930 flight.

was given on 10 May, 1936 at the Waldorf Astoria Hotel for Dr. Eckener, Captain E.A. Lehmann and the crew of the *Hindenburg* on its first arrival. As in 1929, the U.S. Navy was very much involved, seeing in dirigibles an extension of its aircraft carrier strategies. Rear Admiral Ernest J. King, later wartime Chief of Naval Operations, was on the dais, also Commander Charles E. Rosendahl, chief of the Navy's airship operations, the German Ambassador, the editor of the Staats-Zeitung, and Mrs. Amelia Earhart Putnam, soon to leave with Fred Noonan on a planned round-the-world flight that ended in their unsolved disappearance near Howland Island in the Pacific

212   *Norddeutscher Lloyd Bremen*

On the Continent, special mail services flew to Cherbourg to catch Bremen *and* Europa *before they headed across the Atlantic. This envelope is from* Europa's *Captain N. Johnsen while vacationing at Lübeck. Via Cologne, it was flown to Cherbourg and caught the ship. With catapult service at the other end, this cut two days off the normal mail time.*

Ocean. Again, Kurt von Wiegand attended. As did a table of Lloyd officials, including Passenger Director Adolf and Mrs. Stadtländer from Bremen. Dr. Hermann Brückner of the German Seamen's Mission in Hoboken, Ship owners Hugo and Ernst Stinnes, and Father Schulte, the Flying Pastor of Alaska. *Hindenburg* made ten round-trips in 1936.

Arriving at Lakehurst for the first 1937 flight on 7 May, *Hindenburg* caught fire and collapsed to the ground burned out. Captain H. Bockelmann and a crew of twelve from the Hapag-Lloyd piers in Manhattan were there to help with landing and take-off operations. The Captain was talking to Commander Rosendahl when it happened. The H-L crew were able to help some of the passengers and crew.

In 1931, the twelve-engined Dornier flying boat DO-X got to West Africa en route to Brazil. With limited-power engines and the hot tropical thin air it was unable to take off from the River Gambia until given stronger Pratt & Whitney engines. Catapult ships in mid-ocean were seen as an answer to limited range of aircraft until these could fly non-stop across the North and South Atlantic.

NDL's *Westfalen* #218 on 1/7/1932 was chartered, then bought by Lufthansa. In Kiel it was equipped with a catapult forward and huge crane aft. First Experimental flights began in May, 1933, the first service flight on 6/6/1934 under Flight Captain von Studnitz who had flown *Bremen's* first catapult flight in 7/1929. *Westfalen*, like NDL's *Lützow* on cruises, dragged a Kiwull canvas from the stern to smoothen the water for landings by the Dornier WAL aircraft arriving

Baron Jobst von Studnitz (on the right), pilot of Bremen's *first flight, with engineer Karl Kirchhoff, July 1929. Von Studnitz also piloted the first Dornier Wal from The Gambia, West Africa, to the former NDL* Westfalen, *in 1934 a mid South Atlantic catapult "station" for Europe-S. America mails.* Author's Photo. *On both* Bremen *and* Europa, *the catapults were later removed and the area decked over for a garage. This made the ships still more top heavy, so that they rolled a lot.*

The Lloyd Flies 213

The Bremen's *mail plane arrived 22 July, 1929 at Pier 4, Army Basin, Brooklyn.* Author's photos.

Arrival of Bremen's D-1717 mail airplane at Pier 4, Brooklyn 1929.

22 July, 1929. Hoisting the first-flight airplane back into its catapult position. Author's Photo.

from West Africa or Brazil.

Regular service Germany-Bathurst-Brazil, flew twice a month into July, then weekly. Soon another catapult ship, *Schwabenland*, was added, then a third, *Friesenland*. With *Westfalen*, these were managed by the Lloyd for Lufthansa. A fourth, *Ostmark*, was newly built in 1936. There were 47 crossings of the South Atlantic in a1934. By August, 1935, one hundred flights had been made. One Dornier flying boat would be on the catapult ready for launching after taking on the mail from the incoming aircraft. That airplane then would be lifted on board, serviced and ready for catapulting in turn. Until outbreak of the war a total of 328 crossings were made on the North and South Atlantic, according to Captain Detmering.

After the Second War, the Lloyd did not get back into the passenger business until 1954 with the 29 years old *Gripsholm*, renamed *Berlin*, then adding a new *Bremen* and *Europa*. By then, trans-Atlantic liner crossings had declined sharply with the shift to flying. Increasingly, passenger ocean travel became fly-to-or-from-a-ship travel.

In 1957, ten German shipping lines, including Lloyd and Hapag, founded the Deutsches Luftcharterkontor Gmbh, Air Charter Company, to organize charters of aircraft or space aloft for passengers and cargo.

After the Hapag-Lloyd merger in 1970, it was evident that if the new concern were to be a viable worldwide transport enterprise, it had to provide more than sea movement of cargo, mail and passengers. To broaden its base, it formed in 1972 the wholly-owned Hapag-Lloyd Flugzeug (Aviation) Gmbh. It bought three Boeing 727s, later additional aircraft. Control was centered in Bremen, as was the management of the cruise ship *Europa*. In 1994, the chartering of a second vessel, renamed *Bremen*, once again gave the public a *Bremen* and *Europa*.

In its aircraft operations., Hapag-Lloyd is tied closely to the Belgian *Sabena*. The first aircraft with the Cognac and Blue Hapag-Lloyd colors and logo arrived from Boeing's Wichita plant on 3 February, 1973. On 30 March, the first paid-passenger flight, sold out with vacationers, flew from Hamburg to Ibiza. Today, as a continuing worldwide transport enterprise, Hapag-Lloyd can meet its clients' needs "At Sea, on Land and in the Air; Around the Corner, or Around the World."

Junkers D-1717 back on board at Pier 4, Brooklyn after Bremen's *22 July 1929 maiden voyage arrival. When the airplane was shot off in night hours, always a few hardy passengers came topside to watch and be thrilled: this airplane vanishing into the night.*

Catapults speed the mail. First catapult flight from Europa *on 15 September 1930. Two earlier experimental flights were made.*

The Lloyd Flies 215

**Katapultflug ausgefallen
SeepostD. „Bremen"**

**MIT LUFTPOST
ZUM D. „EUROPA"
BEFÖRDERT**

*Nine flights were cancelled due to weather or motor problems. The mail was given appropriate markings: **Schleuderflug Ausgefallen** (Catapult flight cancelled), or "Kein Katapultflug von D. Eupropa nach New York" when mailed was intended for catapulting, but no flight was scheduled. Special markings were applied to mail air-dispatched to the port, Cherbourg or South Hampton at which to catch the ship and subsequent catapulting off.*

Actual flying times and distances of the catapult service show how useful it was to those wanting to speed their trans-Atlantic mails. Europa's first 1932 flight left the ship 9 May at 10:30 a.m., arrived Boston at 4:30 p.m. left at 5:20 p.m., reached New York at 7:10 p.m., a distance of 568 nautical miles to Boston, 200 more to New York, or 768 miles total. The ship reached Quarantine, where mails are normally taken off, at 12:12 p.m. the next day. It was the first flight of the D-2244 aircraft.

The Friesenland rebuilt as a Reefer carrying bananas and other tropical fruit from Italian Somaliland to Genoa, as Castel Nevoso. Ex-Seekiste, 7/1969. It was managed by NDL as a catapult support vessel in the middle of the South Atlantic in the 1930s. See page 228.

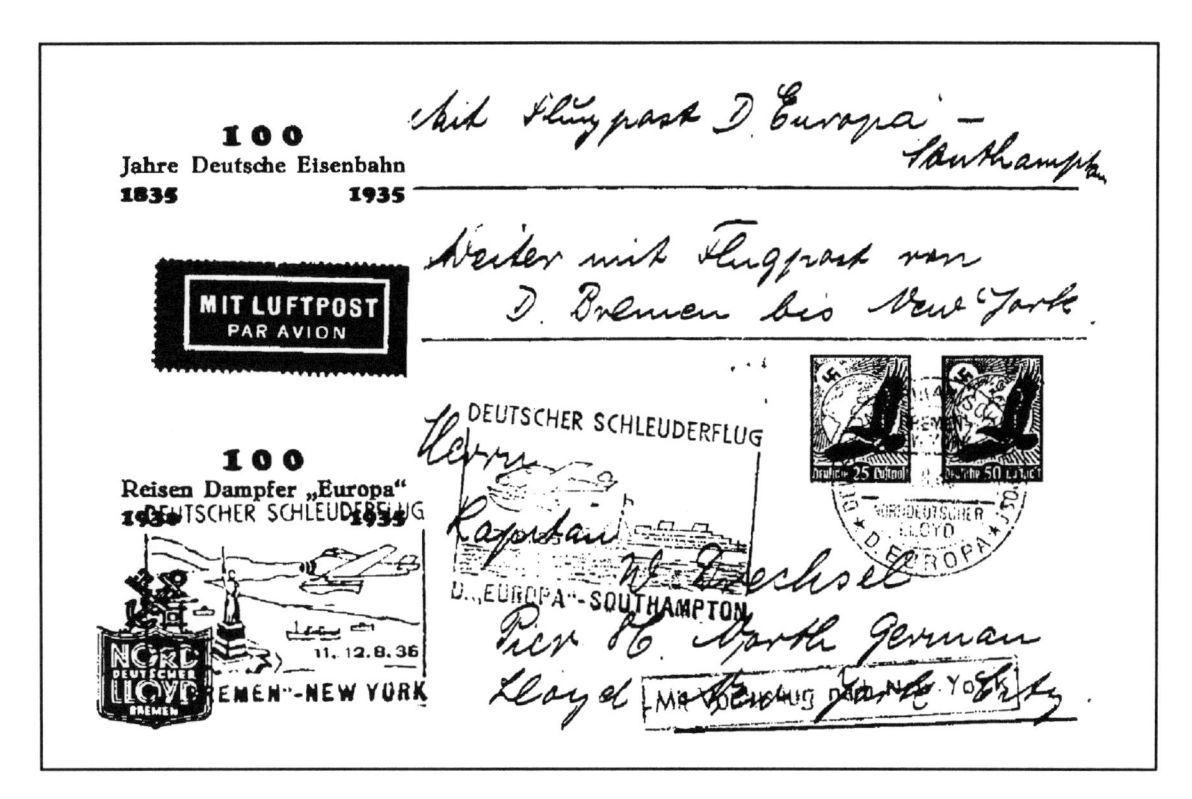

A special flight and a joint Centennial celebration - also German Railways - combination was worked out during Europa's 100th Round Trip in July-August, 1935. This envelope and letter was from Captain Oskar Scharf en route to Bremen. It was shot off at 2 a.m. - one wonders how many passengers after a night following the Captain's dinner were up to see the launching - arrived Southampton at 11 a.m., 6th August. Europa reached Southampton at 11.18 a.m. on the 8th. Bremen left Southampton, with Europa's catapult mailed addressed to the U.S., at noon on the 7th. The mail was shot off at 10 a.m., 664 nautical miles from New York on August 11th, arrived at New York at 4.40 p.m. with 35 Kilos of letter mail. Bremen docked at 2.05 p.m. the next day, 12th. Captain Scharf's letter to Captain Drechsel was delivered at 7:30 that morning.

This cover went from New York to Bremen with the U.S.-German Seapost, then returned cancelled with the Deutsch-Amerikanische Seepost, and catapulted off to New York. Signed by Pilot Fritz Simon, five months before he and Rudolf Wagenknecht crashed. Ex. Covers Magazine June, 1965.

The Lloyd Flies 217

The one aircraft loss of the seven years of catapult service was on 5 October, 1931 after refuelling at North Sydney, Nova Scotia. Needing to make an emergency landing, Pilot Fritz Simon saw the water sheen in Cobequid Bay near Burntcoat Head Light. He did not know the water was very shallow, with mud underneath. The aircraft stuck and tipped over. Simon and Mechanic Rudolf Wagenknecht were killed. Photos by R. Fleischhut, Bremen's Photographer.

First flight of new D-1919 Bremen aircraft from the Europa *on 28 August, 1930, 8:07 a.m. DST, shot off 30 miles from Fire Island Light. Landed at Brooklyn, Pier 4, at 9:23 a.m.*

Card from Bremen's Chief Engineer Julius Hundt to his friend from before 1914 Captain Drechsel in New York, sent ahead from the ship by its catapult mail. Herr Hundt was on the first of the three express steamers for East Asia, Scharnhorst. Julius Hundt was on U-156, photo I-p.452, ordered as a commercial submarine before U.S. entry into the war in 1917.

Every flight received different cachets, so that collectors were driven to try for completeness. This one flown from the ship to Southampton, stresses that Lufthansa also had regular and Zeppelin air mail and passenger services. Mit Vorausflug nach Southampton - With Flight ahead to Southampton.

Julius Hundt, Bremen's Chief Engineer from her entry into service in 1929, and his staff. He and Willy Drechsel were shipmates from the commercial submarine venture, officered by the Lloyd, in the first War. Photo p. 452, Volume I. Hanns Tschira Photo.

The Lloyd Flies

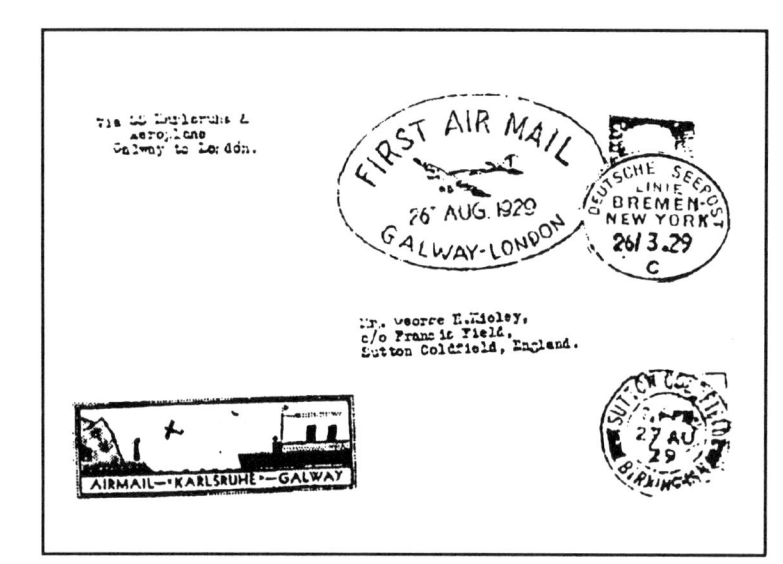

*In August, 1929, less than a month after Bremen's first catapult flight, the Lloyd was involved in another airmail experiment-stunt. This involved mail posted in Boston, loaded onto Karlsruhe. To this was added mail Sea Posted on the ship, hooked into a mail bag suspended overboard and picked up, as the Railway Mail Service used to hook sacks from poles at full speed, and flown to Galway. Special envelopes were printed and an **Airmail - Karlsruhe - Galway** sticker attached. At Galway, the **First Air Mail** cachet was applied. A letter addressed to near Birmingham arrived there the next day. Pilot Chas. L. Russell autographed some of the covers. Sticker from Robert Fernald Collection.*

This was one of five refuelling stops made by Bremen's catapult mail plane in 1935. The last flight of the year and the entire catapult service reached New York pier on 2 October, 3:30 p.m.; it also refuelled at Nantucket. After these flights, Airships Hindenburg *and* Graf Zeppelin *carried the mails until* Hindenburg's *tragic end at Lakehurst.*

The five flights from Bremen *in 1935 that refuelled at Nantucket Island were as much as 901 nautical miles out from New York, the longest of the service, enabled the mail airplane to be catapulted off further at sea. On 3 July, 1935 it was catapuled off at 4:10 a.m. At Nantucket the Coast Guard helped in ferrying the gasoline out to the aircraft. It left Nantucket at 12:15 p.m., reached Pier 84, North River, Manhatten at 2:05 p.m., 901 miles total distance, with 57 kilos mail and 27.5 kilos express items. The Bremen docked 26 hours and 15 minutes after the mail!*

The Nantucket Lightship No. 117 was on station on Tuesday 15 May, 1934 43 miles S.E. of the island at the Nantucket Shoals when at 11 a.m. the White Star Line's Olympic, *the 1911 sister of the 1912* Titanic, *cut her in half, presumably by riding her radio beam too closely. The French Line's* Paris *only a few hours earlier had passed the Lightship only 200' distant. Of the eleven on board, seven lost their lives. The Lightship had been on station, newly built, only eight months. Courtesy Barbara P. Andrews Librarian Emerita, The Nantucket Atheneum, and Joachim Schaper.*

THE INQUIRER AND MIRROR, NANTUCKET ISLAND, MASS., SATURDAY MORNING, J[...]

Bremen's Plane Stopped Here On Flight to New York.

The plane from the steamship Bremen stopped at Nantucket for re-fueling Wednesday morning, on her flight from the big liner to New York with mail. A radio message was received early in the morning that the plane had taken off from the ship 695 miles east of Nantucket lightship and that it would arrive at Nantucket about 11.30 o'clock to re-fuel.

The Island Service Company, which had a supply of the high test gas on hand for airplanes, arranged for prompt service so as not to delay the Bremen's plane any longer than necessary. A barrel of gasoline was run off into five-gallon cans and placed aboard a Coast Guard boat which was at the dock, everything being in readiness long before the plane showed up.

The plane left the Bremen at 4.10 in the morning, conditions being ideal for such a long flight—over 700 miles before reaching Nantucket. The captain of the air-craft estimated his speed about right and was only four minutes later than 11.30 when he brought the plane down onto the surface of the harbor.

Besides the crew of the Coast Guard boat, Walter Huffman, local manager of the Island Airways, William Donnell, Jr., manager of the Island Service Company, and a representative of The Inquirer and Mirror met the Bremen's plane when it alighted on the harbor. A large fleet of pleasure craft was soon circling around, among the boats being Mr. Dealoge's handsome cruiser and the Yacht Club's tender, with Commodore Thebaud, ex-Commodore Satler, and Colonel Praeger on board.

The Bremen's plane remained on the surface of the harbor only long enough to re-fuel, taking off and heading westward for New York at 12.10 o'clock. A crowd of people gathered on the wharves to see the big red ship with the word "Bremen" on each side, as she left the water and circled around over the town before taking her course for New York.

The ship is commanded by Count Schack of Wittenau, flight captain. Paul Dierberg is the radio mechanic and Robert Selchow the catapult pilot.

A letter received from the steamship company at New York expressed appreciation for the service rendered the plane at Nantucket and stated that a new record for a catapult flight had been established—a distance of 901 nautical miles from New York. The letter reads as follows:

Island Airways, Inc.,
Nantucket Island, Mass.
Dear Sir:

We take great pleasure in extending to you our appreciation for the courtesies and cooperation shown when the plane of our S. S. "Bremen" landed at Nantucket, July 3.

Count Schack, the pilot of the plane, spoke very highly of the Nantucket Airport, its facilities for a quick despatch, and last, but not least, the personal courtesies extended by your staff.

Having Nantucket as an intermediate station, made it possible for the plane to take off from the ship as early as 4.00 a. m., July 3. The distance covered from the ship to New York was 901 sea miles and this flight constitutes a new distance record.

With the timely arrival of the plane in New York at 2.05 p. m., all the air mail can still be delivered to the addressees today, July 3. Thus it can still be seen that the possibility and privilege of calling at Nantucket greatly improves the ship-to-shore airplane service.

We are therefore very grateful for the assistance given our plane this morning, and would ask that you replenish your supply with the amount of 87 octave airplane fuel delivered to the plane, sending your bill for the same to this office.

Again thanking you and with kindest regards, we are

Very truly yours,

Captain W. Drechsel
Chief Marine Superintendent,
Hamburg American Line—North German Lloyd.

An experiment was flown by Curtis-Wright Flying Service in Glendale with "Shore to Ship" mail in January, 1931. This was in effect supplemental mail but carried at the 5¢ air mail rate. The flying boat caught up with the City of Los Angeles *and dropped the sack. This was emptied and mail backstamped "received Jan. 24, 1931, S.S. City of Los Angeles." The Honolulu arrival was postmarked on the 30th. This saved days, perhaps a week over having to wait for the next ship. A stunt. But it showed what might happen regularly.*

In June, 1931 the former Lloyd liner *Grosser Kurfürst* was involved in an experimental flight with a Goodyear blimp hooking onto sacks of mail before the ship's arrival from Honolulu in California. The ship was seized in Hoboken in 1917, after the war was rebuilt for Hawaii service by Los Angeles S.S. Co. Bought by Matson Lines in 1931, on its maiden voyage the Curtis-Wright Flying Service of Glendale flew late-posted mail to the ship some hundreds of miles on the way to Honolulu. "It was the first true luxury liner to cruise the South Pacific" *(Larry Benson.)*

In the 1930s Goodyear was using its Blimps, from Type B Dirigible - Limp, for promotion. In New York, one picked up a company official from the deck of Bremen. *In the Pacific, ships from Hawaii nearing San Francisco or Los Angeles, had mail picked up by hook to speed delivery. A stunt but it showed a potential.*

In 1929, Hapag became World Agent for Deutsche Luftschiffahrt A.G., the Zeppelin operating company. The Lloyd through the North Atlantic Community came into this agreement. The German advertisements showed Hindenburg *above New York's skyscrapers and: In Two Days to North America.*

The Lloyd Flies 221

Invitation and program cover of the Civic Luncheon New York gave for Dr. Hugo Eckener and the crew of Graf Zeppelin *on its voyage around the world. The Hearst papers normally covered such German world-renowned activities, widely, as the trips by commercial submarine* Deutschland *in 1916, and* Bremen *and* Europa.

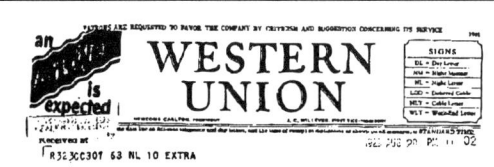

```
WESTERN UNION

R32XCC307 63 NL 10 EXTRA

NEWYORK NY AUG 28 1929

CAPTAIN H DRECHSEL
    CARE NORTH GERMAN LLOYD 57 BROADWAY NEWYORK NY
MAYOR WALKER CORDIALLY INVITES YOU TO BE A GUEST OF THE CITY AT A
LUNCHEON IN HONOR OF DR HUGO ECKENER COMMANDER OF THE GRAF ZEPPELIN
HOTEL ASTOR FRIDAY AUGUST 30 1:00 PM SHORTNESS OF TIME REQUIRES
IMMEDIATE TELEGRAPHIC REPLY IN ACCEPTING GIVE NAME AND ADDRESS
ADMISSION BY TICKET ONLY
                GROVER A WHALEN  CHAIRMAN MAYORS COMMITTEE
                2234 MUNICIPAL BUILDING NEWYORKCITY
```

Mayor's Committee on Reception to Distinguished Guests
LUNCHEON
in Honor of
DR. HUGO ECKENER
COMMANDER
and Crew of
GRAF ZEPPELIN
Friday, August 30th, 1929
HOTEL ASTOR
NEW YORK CITY

SEATING LIST

RECEPTION AND DINNER

in honor of

Dr. Hugo Eckener,
Captain E. A. Lehmann,
and the officers and crew of the LZ-129

on the occasion
of the first arrival in the United States

of the

Airship Hindenburg

given by

THE BOARD OF TRADE
FOR GERMAN - AMERICAN COMMERCE, Inc.

HOTEL WALDORF ASTORIA
NEW YORK CITY
MAY 10th, 1936

GUESTS OF HONOR

Dr. Alberto C. Bonaschi
President, Association of Secretaries of Chambers of Foreign Commerce, in the U. S. A. Inc.

Dr. Hans Borchers
German Consul General

Dr. Walther Becker
Commercial Attache of the German Embassy

Dr. Alexander V. Dye
Director, Bureau of Foreign and Domestic Commerce, Washington

Dr. Luiz de Faro
Consul General of Brazil in New York

Hon. J. M. Johnson
Assistant Secretary, Department of Commerce

Dr. James H. Kimball
Principal Meteorologist, U. S. Weather Bureau

Rear Admiral E. J. King
Chief of Bureau of Aeronautics

Dr. Hans Luther
German Ambassador

Hon. John McKenzie
Commissioner of Docks

Hon. Edward Mulrooney
Commissioner of Correction

Prince Louis Fordinand von Preussen

Amelia Earhart Putnam

Commander Charles E. Rosendahl

John F. Sinnott
Bureau of Foreign and Domestic Commerce, New York City

Col. Ralph C. Tobin

Dr. Conrado Traverso
Consul General of Argentina

Eugene E. Vidal
Director of the Bureau of Air Commerce

Hon. Grover A. Whalen

RECEPTION and ARRANGEMENTS COMMITTEE
John Schroeder, Chairman

F. W. Lafrentz	R. W. Ilgner
Karl Eilers	M. H. Waldhausen
Walther Becker	F. W. von Meister
H. A. Johnson	Theodore Thiesing
E. Schmitz	A. Degener

Hapag-Lloyd Passenger Director John Schroeder headed the organizing committee for the May 10, 1936 Reception and Dinner at the Waldorf-Astoria Hotel tendered to Dr. Hugo Eckener, Capt. E. A. Lehmann, the Officers and Crew of the airship Hindenburg *on its first voyage to New York. Noteworthy among the Guests of Honor were: Rear Admiral E. J. King, in the war Naval Chief of Staff, Prince Louis Ferdinand of Prussia, and Amelia Earhart Putnam. The speakers included Commander C. E. Rosendahl, Lakehurst Naval Air Station and chief of the Navy's Dirigible operation. Dr. Hermann Brückner, Pastor of the Seamen's Mission in Hoboken, gave the invocation.*

Travel by ship or by air: it will be booked for you by Hapag-Lloyd. May 1936.

> ## To Europe
> ### BY AIR
> # Hindenburg
> ### BY SEA
> **Bremen · Europa · Columbus
> New York · Deutschland
> Hamburg · · Hansa
> St. Louis · Berlin**
>
> **Hamburg-American Line · North German Lloyd**
> 57 BROADWAY, NEW YORK, N.Y.   UPTOWN, 609 FIFTH AVENUE
> Tel. BOwling Green 9-4000   Tel. WIckersham 2-4300

Hapag-Lloyd were agents for the German Luftschiff A.G., Air Ship Company. This photo shows Hindenburg *flying ovr Hapag's New York, Commodore F. Kruse, on 11 July, 1936, the Olympic Games period in Germany. Exactly ten months later, after the 7th May, 1937 explosion and burning of* Hindenburg, *26 of the 36 who died went back to Germany on the* New York *now under Capt. T. Koch.*

The Lloyd Flies

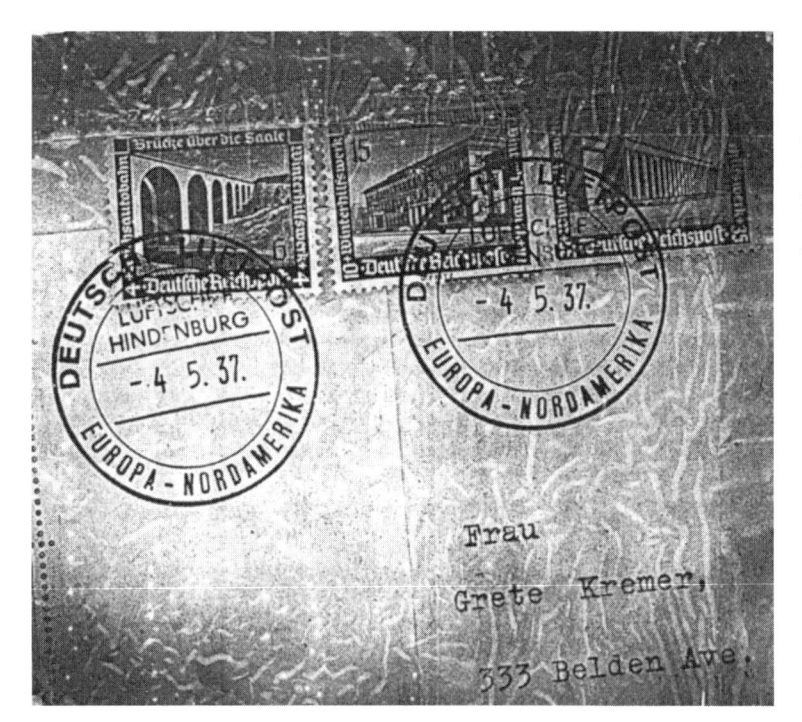

One of the few mail items to survive from Hindenburg's *disaster at Lakehurst in May, 1937.* From Christie's Robson Lowe auction, June, 1987.

The Airship, Zeppelin Hindenburg *in May, 1936 made its first flight to the U.S., followed by nine more. Here following a dinner on Hapag's flagship* New York *on 23 June, 1931, are some closely involved in the New York activities. Most can be identified: Front row: Captain W. Drechsel, Inspector, North Atlantic; Captain Wagner, S.S.* New York*; Consul General Dr. H. Borchers; Dr. Hugo Eckener; J. H. Hoffman; Otto Firle, son of NDL's Director General; Christian F.Beck, Director, North America Hapag-Lloyd Gemeinschaft; John Schröder, Passenger Director, Gemeinschaft; ???. Second Row: Captain Kief; H.H. Holleson; ???; Captain F. Jarka, Jarka Stevedoring Co.; Emil Schmitz, Chief German Railways Agency; F.W. von Meister, Deutsche Luftschiff Gesellschaft; J. Pannes, Hapag-Lloyd, Passenger Manager; E.E. Baron von Aschenberg; ???; Devoe. Third Row: ?, Engelke; Dr. Walter Becker, Embassy Counsellor; ???; H. Mühlenbrock, Passenger Manager; Dr. Crossmann; Edgar Hunt, Hapag-Lloyd, Legal Counsel. Herr and Frau Pannes died in the May, 1937* Hindenburg *fire at Lakehurst, N.J.*

224   *Norddeutscher Lloyd Bremen*

After three years of mostly experimental flights such as the 1929 round-the-world, and one to the Antarctic in 1931 to exchange mail with whalers. In 1932, Graf Zeppelin began regular flights to South America. Hapag was the booking agent for passengers and freight, and with the Lloyd, for Hindenburg *when it entered service in May, 1936, to North America. The time for mail Germany-Brazil was reduced to four days, to Chile to eight days. The* Graf *flights from 1932 on were supplemented by the aircraft services using catapult ships in the mid South Atlantic as refuelling points. NDL's* Westfalen *freighter in July, 1932 was chartered by Lufthansa. It went to Kiel for rebuilding equipped with a large crane aft for lifting aircraft from the water, and a catapult forward to shoot them off. In June, 1933,* Westfalen *was on station halfway between The Gambia and Natal, Brazil. The first flight on 2.6.33 was made by Baron von Studnitz who also made the initial* Bremen *catapult flight in July, 1929.* Westfalen *was managed by NDL, 7.9.1944 was lost in a Swedish minefield off Vinga,* Westfalen *had lost contact with its convoy, some 150 died. All three catapult ships were registered in Bremen,* Westfalen, Friesenland, *and* Schwabenland, *ex* Hansa (of Bremen)*s'* Schwarzfels.

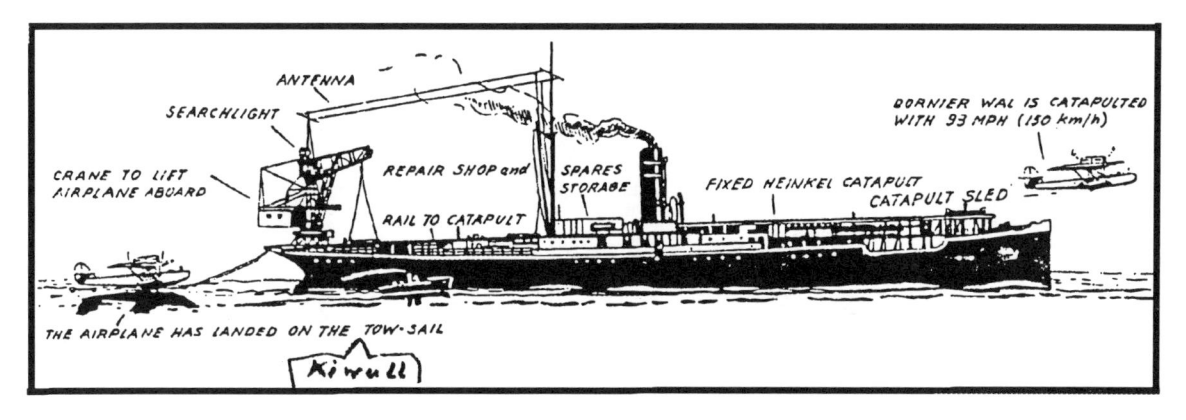

Westfalen *as rebuilt to take on board the seaplanes at the stern and shoot them off over the bow. 1933-1935.* Smithsonian's Air & Space June/July 1992 - Romer. Courtesy Hans H. Amtmann.

The Lloyd Flies

First official flight using the mid-Ocean catapult for the air service Europe-Africa-South America, from Westfalen, *bought from and still managed by NDL.*

Below: One of three stamps issued in 1969 by The Gambia, 35th anniversary of the first catapult flights from Africa to Brazil.

Another stamp, a pair, issued by Brazil shows the passenger aircraft, a Dornier passenger aircraft and the Westfalen, *also shown in The Gambia stamp. Ex American Philatelist.*

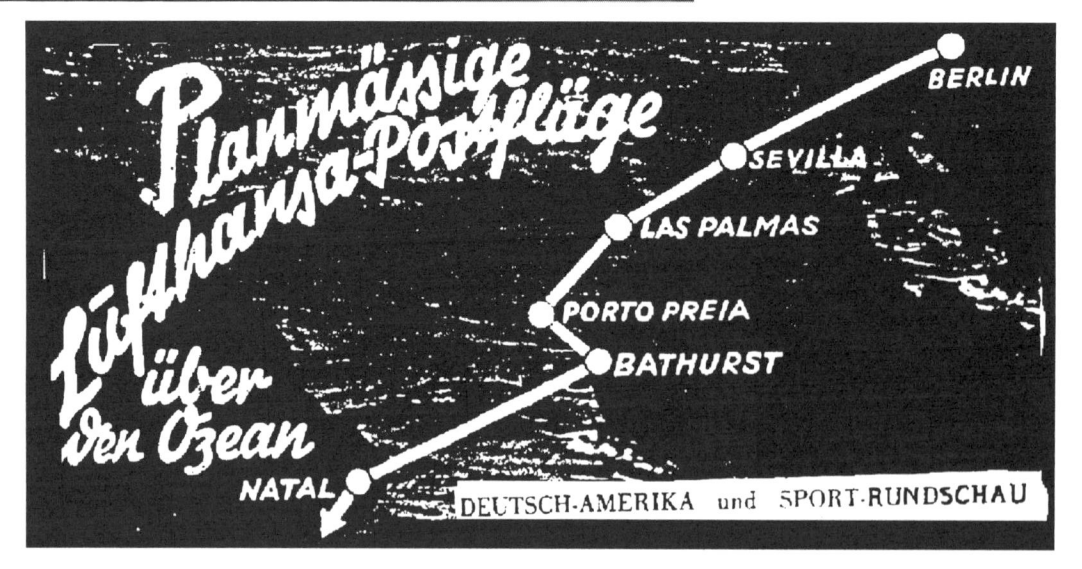

Scheduled Lufthansa Mail Flights Across The Ocean. The catapult ships were stationed midway between Bathurst and Natal, the mail from there distributed by Condor flights around South America.

New York Times, 28 August, 1935

NOTES OF INTEREST IN SHIPPING WORLD

Passenger Bound for Europe Can Send Letters Back in Six Days.

An experiment in the transmission of mail by airplane catapulted from the Hapag-Lloyd liner Bremen while at sea has established the fact that a passenger en route to Europe may be in communication with New York by mail within six days.

The Bremen left New York on July 6 and catapulted her mail plane to Southampton on July 9 at 9:30 P. M., when 340 miles from Southampton. The Europa, sister ship of the Bremen, docked at Southampton July 10, on her way to New York, and picked up a letter carried by the Bremen's plane, which had been sent by Commodore Leopold Ziegenbein of the Bremen to Captain William Drechsel, marine superintendent of the line in New York.

The Europa, en route to New York, also catapulted her mail plane at sea, and it arrived with Ziegenbein's letter and other mail near the line's North River pier Sunday night, July 14.

Extolling the speed of the Catapult services 2½ months before the end of the seven-years operation.

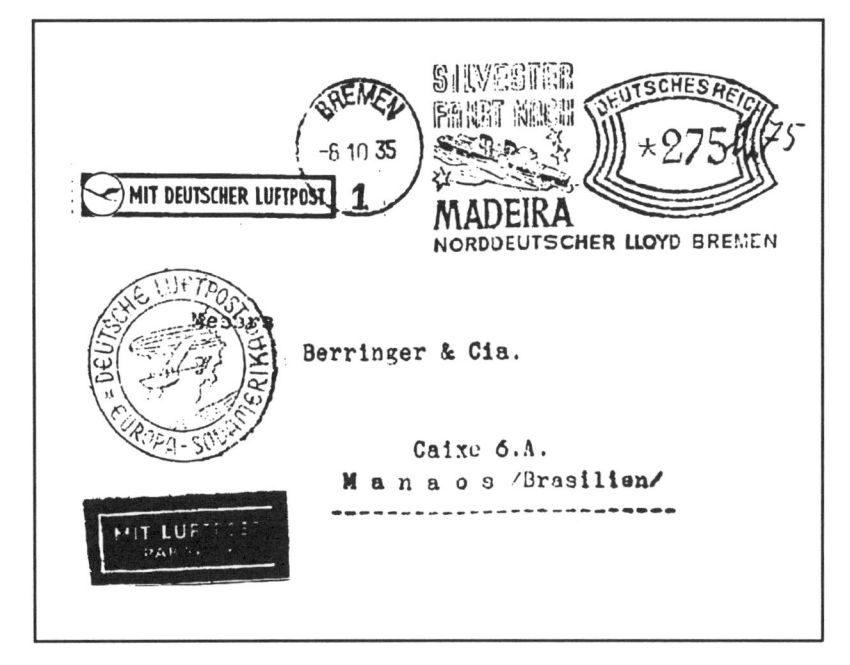

German air mail to South America, Five Days to Manaos. Unheard of speed and regularity of service, combination of land and sea planes and Graf Zeppelin, depending on time of year.

Lützow, evidently along the Norwegian coast, setting out its cruise aircraft. The same airplane had earlier been used by Columbus. ex-Von Segelschiffsjungen zum Lloydkapitän, Captain Adolf Winter, last on Stuttgart in 1929. Koehler, 1929.

The Lloyd Flies

Zur Erinnerung an die **100. Rundreise** des Lloyd-Schnelldampfers »EUROPA« Juli – August 1935 NORDDEUTSCHER LLOYD BREMEN	With the compliments of the NORTH GERMAN LLOYD BREMEN as Souvenir of the **100th Roundtrip** of the Lloyd Express Liner »EUROPA« July – August 1935

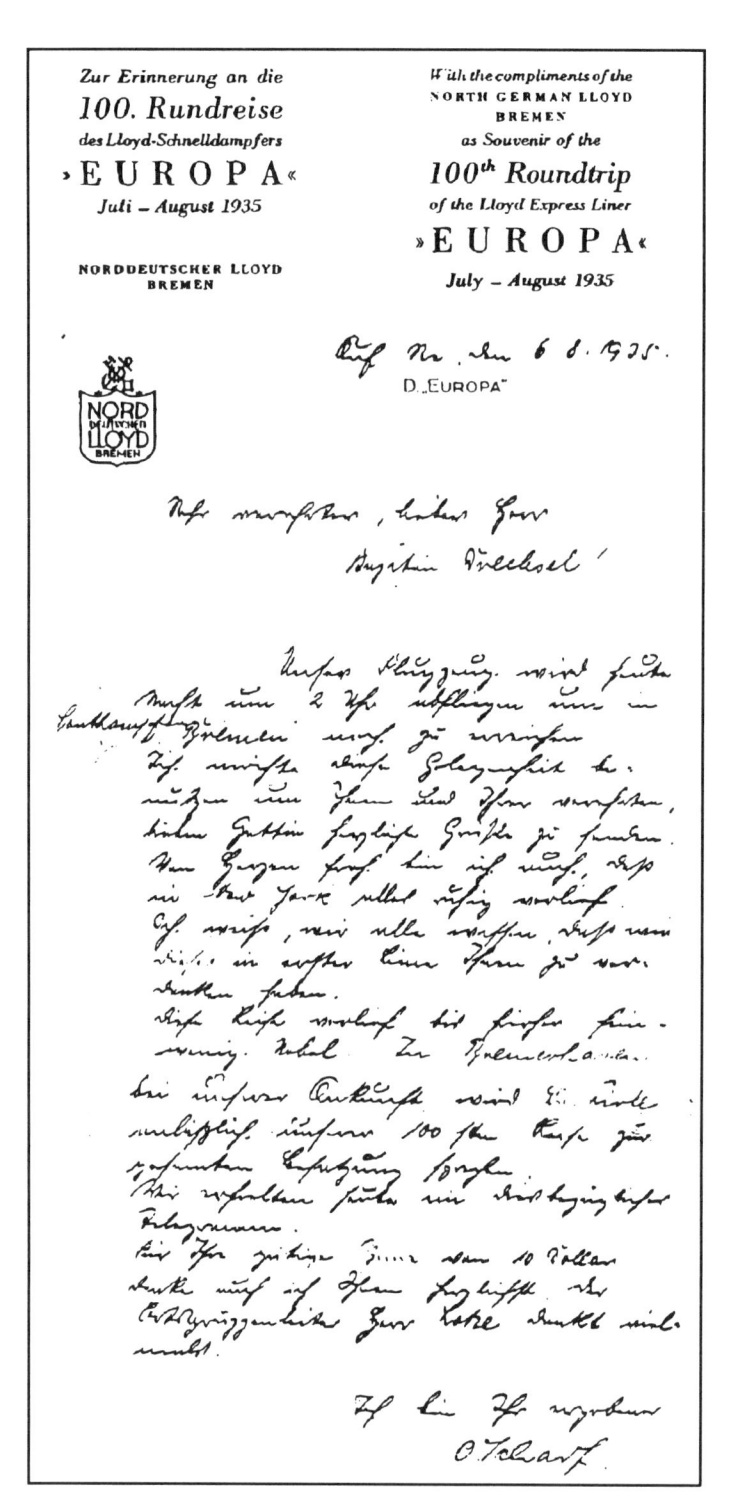

[Handwritten letter from Captain Scharf, dated 6.8.1935, aboard D. "EUROPA", addressed to Kapitän Drechsel.]

Letter enclosed from Captain Scharf to Captain Drechsel in New York.

New York Times, October 14, 1957

ALLIED WAR PRIZE NOW BANANA BOAT

Friesenland Was Used Here in Late 30's as Terminal for Ocean Flights

A pioneer in trans-Atlantic aviation, the former German vessel Friesenland, an Allied war prize, is still enjoying a useful career, although somewhat less exciting than when she served as a catapult ship for the Deutsche Lufthansa in the late Thirties.

Damaged during World War II, she was acquired by the Allies after the war and, after lying idle at Hamburg, Germany, was sold by the British Government to the Alvion Steamship Corporation of Panama. The latter had her repaired in Germany and then taken to Amsterdam for conversion into a refrigerator vessel.

At present the sturdy vessel, once a floating aerodrome and maintenance base for German seaplanes spanning the North and South Atlantic, is engaged in the prosaic calling of a banana boat, plying between Genoa, Italy, and Chisimaio, Italian Somaliland, under her new name, the Fairsky.

The 427-foot, 5,400-ton ship was built especially for the German airlines by Howaldtswercke in Kiel in 1937 and first saw service in the South Atlantic as a floating landing field for the German air service from Dakar in North Africa to Natal, Brazil.

Seaplanes employed in the service used to land near the ship, were taken aboard by means of a huge crane mounted on the vessel's afterdeck, serviced and refueled quickly and then dispatched into the air again by means of a steel-railed catapult that ran along the port side of the vessel's deck.

In the late Thirties, when several nations were vying for the honor of being the first to operate regular air service across the North Atlantic, the Friesenland became a familiar sight in New York harbor. She was anchored off City Island in Long Island Sound to serve as the North American terminal for German ocean flights.

Nothing is known of her career during the last war, and she apparently was not taken over by the Kriegsmarine as a naval auxiliary. According to the Navcot Corporation, 11 Broadway, New York agents for the vessel's owners, she can look forward to a long and useful career as a "reefer."

CHAPTER 7

Passengers: The Heart of the Lloyd's Business

The difficulties and yet some early pluses of the Lloyd's rebuilding are told in "A New Start." It was fortunate for the German shipping enterprises that they could not know what lay ahead. They might never have left port. Perhaps that is the story of life, even for the victors in the war. They got millions of tons of ex-enemy shipping to replace what they lost. This meant largely outdated vessels, while Germany was beginning to build new ships. The surplus of tonnage and the depression of 1920-1921, meant that particularly British shipbuilding was hard hit. The British ended up rejecting some German ships as not worth taking (Hamburg Süd's *Cap Polonio*, Hapag's *Hansa*) or selling back what fitted German needs, particularly to the Lloyd. This was quick help. In the long run, it meant a disparate fleet of ships, primitive enough for even the cruise staff to make wry jokes. Example: Some of the prewar passenger ships still had no running water. Stewards filled the water tank in the top of the washstands in the cabins, then emptied the bottom receptacles of the soiled water dumped there with closing of the basin.

Fortunately for both sides, the U.S. and German postwar shipping needs could be mutually met. The U.S., with no prewar major maritime mission or capability, but with millions of war-ordered tonnage and with several large ex-German ships to be put to work, lacked the expertise. This the Lloyd and Hapag could provide. Hapag had been Number One in world overall in 1914, the Lloyd the largest trans-ocean passenger carrier ever, and Number Two to Hapag. Their know-how led the major trans-Atlantic shipping interests, the Harriman Group to join with Hapag, the new U.S. Mail S.S. Co., with the most U.S. Shipping Board vessels to put to work, with the Lloyd to help open, manage and represent their new trans-Atlantic services.

The agreements gave Hapag and Lloyd the right to insert their own ships as they were able to acquire these. In this way, almost worldwide new services were opened for U.S. shipping, with similar arrangements elsewhere, such as Africa. For Hapag and Lloyd it meant they were back in their old service area, for the time being under the U.S. umbrella, while they worked to rebuilt.

In retrospect, Hapag made a better deal with the Harrimans, covering worldwide services except to the Far East, than the Lloyd with U.S. Mail. That agreement covered only the North Atlantic. For lack of experience on other routes, U.S. Mail went bankrupt in 1921. Fortunately for the Lloyd it was succeeded by the new more capable United States Lines.

Thus there were new players, although many old ships, on the North Atlantic, the main sail, then steam shipping highway of history, coached by the leading old players. It was a different

> ## Good News for Returning Aliens
>
> Whereas heretofore resident aliens returning from a visit abroad and traveling Third Class could not be admitted by the immigration authorities immediately after the steamer's arrival, but had to pass the various immigration stations, in New York for instance Ellis Island, the Commissioner General of Immigration has just now issued instructions to all immigration stations in the various ports that RETURNING ALIENS holding an unexpired Return Permit to reenter the United States and traveling Third Class on a steamer, shall be examined at the same place where Cabin passengers are examined and
>
> **Will Be Admitted Direct from The Steamer If Found Admissable.**
> From: 1926 Passenger List.

Help for immigrants began long before they ever got to the ship at Bremerhaven. Going back to 1885, the Lloyd contracted with, and later absorbed the firm of Misslser & Co. to provide emigrant agencies throughout eastern Europe. There the emigrants would be helped to know what conditions of health, etc. they had to meet, the care and help they would receive along the way to the ship (their passage price always included several days of pre-departure stays in Bremen, if need be.

With the strict control of and sharp reductions in the allowable immigration by the U.S. from 1921, still more severely in 1924, help was needed in meeting the many requirements. Whereas in the past Third-Class arriving immigrants were handled separately, in New York at Ellis Island, from the other classes, as the flow decreased, returning Aliens, those not yet citizens, holding a valid re-entry permit, were examined at the same time and same places as other passengers. And once ashore, a major service in New York by the German newspaper, was a handy booklet on: "How do I become a citizen." The "Golden Door" still held some welcome inside. The immigration restrictions of 1921 and 1924 were not rescinded until 1965, 1986 and 1990.

trade: the U.S. no longer the magnet for mass trans-Atlantic travel. This had peaked in 1913 with 1,714,000 persons arriving in the U.S. by ship. Of these, 1,141,000 were Third Class or Tweendeckers, i.e., mostly immigrants.

That flow ended with the war, and could not resume (see p. 304 ff, Vol. I). The Quota Act of 1921 reduced the permitted landings to a basic three percent of the 1900 Census representation in the migrant nationalities, for a maximum of 375,000.

In 1924, the National Origins Act, reduced the allowable to two percent. Chinese immigration was excluded entirely, preventing even Chinese wives of U.S. citizens from entering the country under a U.S. Supreme Court ruling. No longer did the Statue of Liberty signal the welcome of an Open Door. It required later legislation to rescind the Chinese Exclusion Acts.

With no German passenger ships on the North Atlantic and the U.S. making only a beginning, the British Canadian Pacific and Royal Mail Lines for the first time offered Germany-France-Britain-U.S.-Canada services. The U.S. Lines turned around at Bremerhaven; the British at Hamburg. Royal Mail opened Hamburg-Southampton-Cherbourg-New York sailings in April, 1921; Canadian Pacific in 1922. Both lines gave up these services as ships were needed on their traditional routes, as immigration quotas cut the continental emigration potential, and as the Lloyd and Hapag again provided weekly, then more frequent crossings. The immigration drop off was so much sharper than expected that both the Lloyd's *Columbus* and Hapag's *Deutschland* on their completion in 1923, were laid up for the winter. Not to make their maiden voyages until the Spring of 1924. Two NDL ships redesigned from freighter configuration to carrying Third Class and Tweendeckers to the U.S. on completion in early 1922 were diverted to South America service. Following long-standing Bremen and Lloyd catering services for emigrants, those heading for South America had included in their $102.50 Third Class passage price up to five days stay in Bremen before departure. The emigrant firm of F. Missler, largely NDL-owned, with agencies all over Eastern Europe, from 1885 through 1932 handled some 1,820,000 passengers for the Lloyd (A. Rehm), at a total passage price of 325 million Marks. This service and reputation, confirmed at sea, remembered and handed down to the next generation in nostalgic story-telling, helping bring the Lloyd back to pre-eminence in the 1920s and, after World War II, to a smaller but still world-reputation enterprise.

The Lloyd's rebuilding program ended with *Berlin* #308 in 1925, a "small *Columbus*;" the nostalgia of *Columbus*. Its design was from 1912; construction began in 1914. Now, ten years later, it was touted as Germany's largest vessel. A quiet modernity, a comfortable ship, but technically outmoded. A sister for *Berlin* was cancelled. Instead, in 1927 the prewar *Zeppelin* #269, which had never sailed under the Lloyd flag, was bought back and became popular under Captain F. Rehm. Both these ships were a slow under-16 knots. And *Columbus* at best 19½ knots. Hardly world-beaters.

NORTH GERMAN LLOYD GAZETTE

"Oh! What care I if the waves dash high
And the wind swings by in glee?
A stalwart Captain is standing nigh
He laughs at the gale and the sea.
And what is the steamer our good Captain sails
So steady with scarcely a motion?
The North German Lloyd in its pride gladly hails
The "Berlin" the gem of the ocean.
And who is the Captain so sturdy and bold,
So well deserving of fame?
With an eye of steel and a heart of gold—
Rehm, Captain Rehm is his name.

There are endless snaps of him taken by and with enthusiastic passengers. He is always the same, jovial, kind and jolly. Captain Rehm in his ducks (all ship's officers look nice in their ducks, don't they?) on the sun bridge with summer-clad girls crowding round him. Captain Rehm, earnest and watchful on the bridge. Captain Rehm drinking a toast with celebrities, Captain Rehm fathering the little girls and explaining to the little boys how the ship runs . . . . .

Ah yes! Mustn't it be grand to be a captain? A full life! A man's job, if ever there were one. Work and hardship, sure, but adventure and achievement, respect and honor. Don't such things make life worth living? And when the last trip is over, what memories to enliven the declining years!

Contributed by NDL Passenger Manager E.J. Schroeder, in 1927.

Captain Friedrich Rehm's Autograph Album became a rich record of people who travelled with him, on Seydlitz, Dresden, Berlin, *etc. Some wrote brief verses, which themselves became memorable, such as:*
"A pair in a hammock
Attempted to kiss
And in the Attempt
They ended up like this."

Comments by Oscar Strauss, and Roald Amundsen: "Thank you for the most perfect voyage across the Atlantic. Through Menu and Sea, I relied on Thee."

Passengers: The Heart of the Lloyd's Business

Captain Rehm about 1927 on Dresden *with two ladies who probably just signed the book, got a tour of the Bridge. Note the canvas hung to deflect winds. This wind problem was solved on* Bremen *and* Europa *with built-in funnel deflectors. See #417.*

The famed Austrian orthopaedic surgeon Dr. Adolf and Mrs. Lorenz came to the U.S. on Bremen *in 1924, Captain W. Drechsel. His 1927 trip on* Berlin, *Captain F. Rehm, was his seventh to this country. Dr. Lorenz became famous pre-1914 when he performed the first "bloodless" operation in this country on Lolita Armour of Chicago, daughter of the meat packing industrialist. The Lloyd Gazette of January, 1927, reported "The famous surgeon is advising thin folks to stay thin and plumper people to cease trying to become slender, as otherwise they are going against what nature intended, and are likely to injure themselves in attempting to change. He considers judicious drinking of beer as conducive to good health."*

Dr. Hans Luther and his family and fellow-passengers on Berlin *in August, 1936, with Captain Fritz Krone, and Captain Drechsel, Dr. Luther was Reichs Chancellor 1925-1926, then President of the Reichsbank, and now Ambassador to the U.S.*

The U.S. Ambassador Jacob Gould Schurman on 15 August, 1928 launched the Europa *at the Blohm & Voss Shipyard in Hamburg. The Ambassador made several voyages on the two ships. The Portrait of Mr. Schurmann hung in the lobby of* Europa. *Here are excerpts from his comments in August, 1935 contributory to the celebration of* Europa's *century-voyage arrival in New York:*

On the Europa's *first voyage five years ago, she made without any special effort a new trans-atlantic record for speed, and only a month ago she sailed from New York with less than a dozen short of 2,000 passengers — a new record in passenger traffic since 1932.*

I am not surprised at this manifestation of public favor and unequaled patronage. Who that has traveled on the Europa *can ever forget the beauty and simplicity of the decorations and furnishings, the excellence of the accommodations, the perfection of the appointments, the universal comfort and the luxury for those who want it, the incomparable service, the strict discipline and the sense of security which it creates, and, finally, the unsparing labor and the devotion of the highly trained and long-tested commander himself, the sentinel and guardian of the good ship and all the precious souls she carries?*

The Europa *and the* Bremen *are the jewels of the North German Lloyd. They are a triumph of the German shipyards.*

In this spirit I look forward with confidence to the Europa's *second hundred round-trips across the Atlantic. What the good ship has done so well she can continue to do. I share your pride in her and join you confidently in good wishes for her future. FLOREAT SEMPER! (signed) Jacob Gould Schurman*

Europa *and the Bull in the First Class Stairwell. The legend is that the mythological Princess Europa was carried from her home in Asia to a new domain across the Seas by Zeus disguised as a bull. They were still there when the U.S. in 1945-1946 used the ship as a transport: bringing home thousands, taking over many to be involved in the U.S. occupation of Germany.*

Passengers: The Heart of the Lloyd's Business   233

A rewarding example of a business relationship leading to friendship. Mrs. Blanche and Harry Reese with Commodore Ziegenbein on Bremen *in November, 1929. Mr. Reese's firm supplied engine, deck and steward supplies to the Lloyd, to Hapag-Lloyd Gemeinschaft and other shipping lines. Here as always with a cigar. Photo courtesy Howard Reese.*

A 1937 visit by Mr. Reese to Venezuela led to our meeting in La Guaira and his signing this card to the author's parents. He was en route to Curacao where the Maduro firm acted for him in supplying oil company vessels. Mrs. Madura also signed the card.

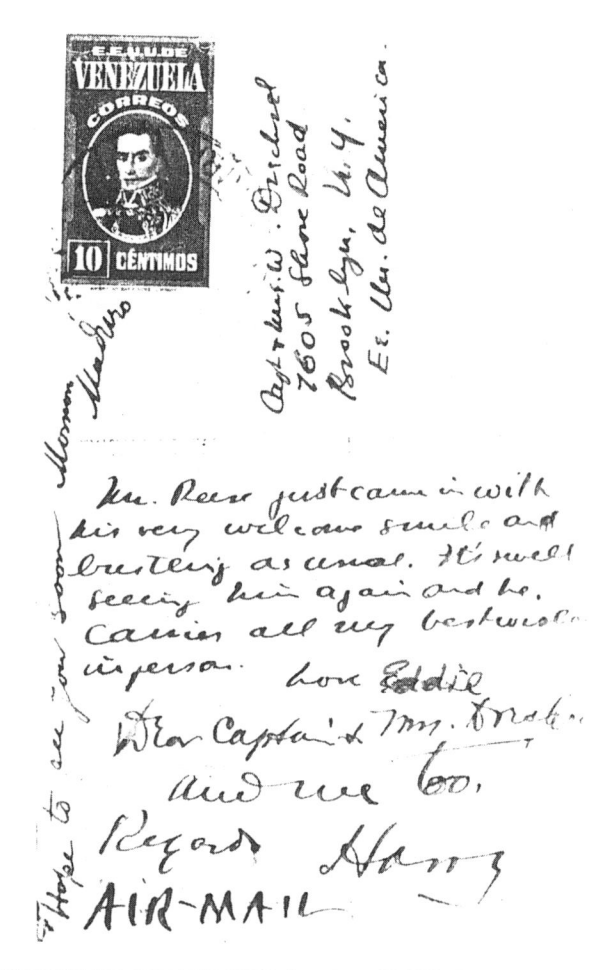

Special Advisory Service for Travelers

A FEATURE OF THE BREMEN · EUROPA

HAMBURG-AMERICAN LINE
NORTH GERMAN LLOYD

A Versatile and Competent Consulting Staff is prepared to give on the Bremen and Europa (the two fastest ways to England, France, Germany) expert, impartial counsel and particular, personal service to passengers in all classes . . . Reliable information on the countries you intend visiting . . . Contacts prearranged and facilitated with institutions, societies and individuals in those countries . . . Meetings arranged on board with passengers of mutual business and professional interests . . . Special attention to passengers traveling alone.

FOR INSTANCE . . .

● An architect traveling to Germany can arrange through the Advisory Service to meet the German architects in whose work he may be particularly interested, or to confer with certain architectural societies, which will enable him to see special types of architecture.

● A buyer of fabrics could learn in advance of his arrival just where to look for the latest designs in materials.

● An electrical engineer or any student traveling on the BREMEN or EUROPA could find out through the Advisory Service whether there were any of his professional colleagues on board, and could arrange to meet them.

● A child or an invalid traveling alone could receive special attention through the Advisory Service which might make the voyage more pleasant or insure particular care on arrival abroad.

Bremen *and* Europa *from 1931 had their Sonderdienste, Special services, a full-time assistant to the Captain for relations with and helping passengers with their problems, if any, or just to do what they most wanted to do. This helped stretch the Captain's ability to supervise running of his ship, and meeting the needs of his, occasionally, 2,000 guests on board, with crew more than 3,000 persons. It could have been a full 24 hours a day job.*

Important guests for the Lloyd, and by choice for them to travel with the Lloyd: Left to right: Gräfin Ingeborg (Countess) von Luckner, ?, ?, Captain Leopold Ziegenbein, Graf Felix von Luckner, Lowell Thomas' "Sea Devil," and Henry Ford on Bremen, late 1929 or 1930. Henry Ford also was a shipping operator: a major Great Lakes fleet to support the automobile enterprise. During WW I, he built 199 wooden tugs and mine sweepers. He showed interest in Diesel propulsion. Paul Cwojdzinski Photo.

Graf von Luckner's inscription in his Seeteufel, Koehler Verlag, Berlin, 1926, to the Author in New York that same year: "Stand Fast like the Oak and look towards the sun. Your Sea Devil." He again signed the book in San Francisco in 1949 to the Author's son: "May Your Lucky Star Always be With you. Never say die, by Joe." His favorite expression.

"Young Henry" continued the Ford Family friendship with the von Luckners. Here he reminds the Count that his Grandfather read to him from Lowell Thomas' "Sea Devil" the Luckner exploits in WWI. The Count then told how he once toasted Henry Sr. with a tribute that was turned into a Model-T slogan in the 1920s: "Ford Made a Lady Out of a Lizzie." Luckner was also known worldwide from his lecture tours to the U.S., in 1926, 1949, from a two-years cruise on the sailing yacht Mopelia around the world, also named Vaterland. American forces in 1945 found him at Halle, he moved to Malmö, where he died in 1966. See "A New Start."

Passengers: The Heart of the Lloyd's Business   235

Three generations of Fords enjoyed travelling on Bremen *and* Europa. *Mr. Henry Ford, founder of the firm, became a friend of the ships' captains. Here son Edsel and family on the Sun Deck of the Bremen, from the* Frank Pichardo Collection, *photo by Hanns Tschira.*

Two "passengers" of note were Captain Frank Hawks and his Texaco No. 13. After a then record trans-continental flight of 12 hours, 23 minutes, 3 seconds in 1931, Captain Hawks took his aircraft to Europe on the Europa, *sailing from New York on 31.III.1931.* Cwojdzinski Photo.

Artists felt at home with the Lloyd. Bremen as a departure port was more personal than bustling Hamburg. Alexander Moissi was one of the great Shakespearean actors of the 1920s, part of the Max Reinhardt Company (Germany issued a stamp in his honor in 1993, fifty years after his death). Here he is between the author's sister Evelyn and his Mother on the Stuttgart *in March, 1929 en route to Germany after his U.S. tour. Captain Adolf Winter, who later wrote of his Lloyd Years, is in white in center. The Author's Father, Captain Drechsel behind and to the right. Author is the Chief Officer in center rear.*

Alexander Moissi with his staff and the Drechsel family on Stuttgart *en route to Europe in March, 1929.*

Passengers: The Heart of the Lloyd's Business 237

Passengers boarding Sierra Cordoba *in Bremerhaven in the 1930s for a Strength through Joy Movement cruise. Clearly a predominantly worker type passenger in contrast to the trans-Atlantic voyagers.* Columbus *lies ahead.*

In November, 1936 Lord Beaverbrook, the Canadian publisher, in the war Munitions Director, was on the Bremen *bound for New York when the King Edward abdication crisis occurred. He returned immediately on* Bremen *to Britain.*

It was the *Bremen* in 1929 that marked a new age on the Atlantic, and a near-return for the Lloyd to its pre-1914 glory. That prior age on the Seven Seas had marked the shift from sail to steam, from wood to iron to steel. And from wanting to get there as speedily as possible because of the acute discomforts at sea, except for the privileged few in First Class, to the pleasure and relaxation, albeit the excitement, of just being at sea.

While the decline of emigration, which made the money so ships could have luxurious First Classes, changed passenger shipping, it was the shift from transportation, getting there, to Tourism, to enjoy each day afloat, that marked the 1920s and the new passenger ships that began to be built.

Bremen's looks alone spelled exciting newness: long, sleek, low in silhouette; severely modern comfort at high speeds, an experience far above the every-day that had not existed before. In contrast, British ships took with them the historic country-mansion fittings, panelled walls, columns, even fireplaces with brick inglenooks.

It was the rich and famous, some from prewar but also newly from the 1920s, who gave an immediate social imprimatur to *Bremen* and *Europa*, and to the French Line's *Ile De France*. Being at sea in comfort, in rich surroundings and with service unaccustomed even at the best hotels. Being courted, cosseted, catered to, made to feel special, gave a feeling of well-being. And when the Captain invited you to tea, or to the Bridge, or you met him and a select few others, at his Dining Table, travellers developed a loyalty to him, to the ship and to the line.

In the first Winter of 1929-1930, *Bremen* carried more passengers round-trip than in-season when traffic was heavily one-way. Some voyages made 50% return over costs. It was on *Bremen's* seventh outward voyage, in December that she carried her 25 thousandths passenger, Swiss Karl Sutter in Third Class. He was given a Gold Watch. See p. 302ff, Volume I. In 1913 it was the ten-millionth passenger, a Hungarian. On the New York

Sports figures travelled on the Bremen *and* Europa *often going on one, returning on the other. They were really quite different in atmosphere. Bobby Jones, arrived on* Europa *in July, 1930 as golf champion to the traditional ticker-tape parade up Broadway. Max Schmeling also travelled to New York on* Europa. *In 1928, he beat John Tunney, then in 1932 lost to Jack Sharkey. He returned home on the* Bremen, *was interviewed for radio at Bremerhaven. Here with Relief Captain Hagemann.*

In January, 1936 members of the U.S. Winter Olympics team travelled to Europe on München. *Then in June, 1936 most of the U.S. Olympians heading for the games in Germany travelled on* Bremen, *including Eleanor Holm, the swimmer. Avery Brundage, perennial head of the U.S. Olympic Committee, barred her from the games when he heard she had "broken training" on the* Bremen *by partying and drinking champagne. A petition signed by 220 fellow-Olympians for her reinstatement was rejected by Brundage.* Author's photo taken on board.

The gaiety of Skiing...

Meets the Leisure of

LLOYD CABIN

on the MUENCHEN, *January 16*

The American skiers set out for the Alps via Bremen, on this favored liner of Lloyd Cabin Quartet—which includes the BERLIN, STUTTGART, *and* DRESDEN. *A special tour has been arranged for skiers by* LLOYD.

NORTH GERMAN LLOYD

service more than 80% of the passengers were non-German.

In 1931 a Client-Service was offered on *Bremen* and *Europa*. Passenger-reservation lists were examined for "Old Friends," people who needed special help or consideration, frequent voyagers, almost looking for excuses to do something special.

Passenger lists were a Who's Who. On that December, 1929 voyage to New York on board were William K. Vanderbilt, Edward Hershey, of chocolate fame, Plutarco Calles, the former President of Mexico, and many more. Sailing for Europe that week were Anton Fokker and Claudius Dornier, the Dutch and German airplane designers-builders.

Thomas Wolfe in 1925 returned on White Star's *Olympic* from Europe, in 1931 went abroad on *Europa*. He wrote a composite journey, but it seems mostly *Europa*. Noel Coward signing autographs before sailing on *Bremen*; Count and Countess von Luckner were arriving, he Lowell Thomas' "Sea Devil."

Artists, scientist, academics, sports figures, politicians, nobility, aviators. Henry Ford sailed to Europe on *Bremen*, returned on *Europa*. He then presented to Captains Ziegenbein and Johnsen four-door Ford sedans. When the captains were unable to pay the high German duty, that was defrayed by Ford. And so long as these

A group of the ship-news reporter at the rail of the revenue cutter on the way to Quarantine. From: Seven Seas, August, 1928.

two captains came to New York, chauffeured Lincolns were put at their disposal for any going out from far-away Brooklyn! they wanted to make.

Movie producers Sam Goldwyn and Louis Schenck. Theodore Steinway. Top Lloyd officials, even from Hapag as the two lines' managements travelled each other for compatibility (See "Bremen and Hamburg"), and to test the other's service reputation. Lord Beaverbrook. The Maharajah of Boroda. Czar Ferdinand of Bulgaria. Harold Nicholson and his wife Vita Sackville-West. William Mowrer. Max Schmeling before and after becoming world champion boxer, briefly. Swimmer Eleanor Holm on *Bremen* in June, 1936, sailing early for the Olympics. She angered U.S. Olympics Chief Avery Brundage for "breaking training". For this he removed her from the team, despite the appeal of 220 other U.S. Olympians. (See photo). William Randolph Hearst was probably the most frequent personality on *Bremen* and *Europa*. It was Hearst's International Library Co. that in 1916 published "The Voyage of the Deutschland," the commercial submarine (See "D.O.R.", Vol. I), by Captain Paul König

For journalists, if one could not be a foreign correspondent, being ship news reporter was the most sought-after job at New York newspapers. It meant meeting and writing about the exciting people in life, and getting to know the captains who had a flair for satisfying the egoes of their passengers, and were able to impart, but discreetly, exciting things that happened on their ships. And through them some of the ships became famous.

One of them reported in 1928 "There was a time when the ship-news reporters went down the (New York) Bay in rowboats to meet incoming vessels. A ship or two, perhaps 100 - 250 passengers; this made the day." In the 1920s, at times a dozen or more passenger ships arrived in one day. Before radio, it was these journalists that first reported important shipboard news. During the Spanish-American War, many of the news-beats were broken by the ship reporters. In World War I, it was they who first reported the off-shore German U-Boats. Their stories were not believed until the sinkings were officially acknowledged. From the New York dailies, and the wire services, the news spread around the world.

Reporters and photographers, in the 1920s and 1930s, boarded liners at Quarantine, off Staten Island, from the Coast Guard cutter that took down also government, customs, immigration and medical officers. The reporters then had an hour or so, until the ship reached her pier, to probe for what and who was newsworthy, and get the stories. With large liners, perhaps 1500 or more passengers, it took knowing the key people on board, up to the Captain-Commodore, to be alerted. And then to tell something different from the competition. ("Passengers," Vol. I)

On 10 August, 1932 George Britt wrote that Captain Johnsen greets the ship reporters with "Good Morning, Gentlemen. Have a cigar. We had a fine crossing." No spinning of tales, rejection of all requests that he tell incidents from his life or that he write his memories. But another reporter chose him as "The Skipper of the Year."

As with *Bremen's* December, 1929 stormy

Seasickness largely has been banished. It was not always so, per this 1935 Sea Posted card from the Europa. The Lloyd Gazette in 1927 had a passenger pleading: "Captain, Captain Stop the Ship. I must get off and end this trip."

The caption on this card, roughly:
A Pleasure of a Special kind,
Is being an ocean passenger, to my mind,
An Experience unique
Is, at sea, not what you seek.

voyage, delayed more than two days, it could be the weather en route that became the story, told my name-people. A 1920s version of "Stop the World, I want to get off", was the verse written in Captain F. Rehm's autograph album during one stormy crossing: "Herr Kapitän, Herr Kapitän. Ich halts nicht aus! Ich will heraus. Ich steige aus." Very loosely: "Captain, Captain, I can't take it any more. Stop the ship so I can swim ashore."

But then the storm subsides, and the sick ones emerge from their cabins. "First a tentative stomach-settling Angostura Bitters, and a very small sandwich and boullion in the deck chair. Gradually, the menu again becomes a challenge, and a champagne dinner finishes the cure." (John Schröder, then NDL's Passenger Manager in New York.)

Seasickness largely has disappeared from ship travel, with liners only occasionally bound to keep a trans-Atlantic schedule regardless of weather. Ships have stabilizers, two sets on some vessels; the ships are wider then ever before, and their size, even going above 90,000 tons on new-orders, is so huge, one hardly knows one is at sea. Mal de mer is hardly something to dread nowadays.

But long-ago, seasickness spoiled ocean crossings for untold thousands, the depth of misery, "I wish I were dead," depending on whether one had servants along in First Class, or one was deep in the hold, the emigrant wretches. Many a card or letter written at sea mentions sickness, even a death in the Red Sea from heat. One traveller en route to South America, wrote "Today our ship is bouncing just terribly. Steward, quick: two glasses of cognac." In 1928, the Lloyd introduced on its trans-Atlantic vessels a new service: inhalation of oxygen which had vaporized two drugs of an undisclosed nature (oxygen and atropine?). On *Columbus* during a Spring westward voyage when "the weather was unusually rough," the ship's physician, treated some fifty patients twice daily with the inhalation. "Every one of the patients responded to it. Many were completely cured of seasickness at once and had no recurrent attacks. Even in the most extreme cases the pas-

Passengers: The Heart of the Lloyd's Business 241

✠ Bunter Abend ✠

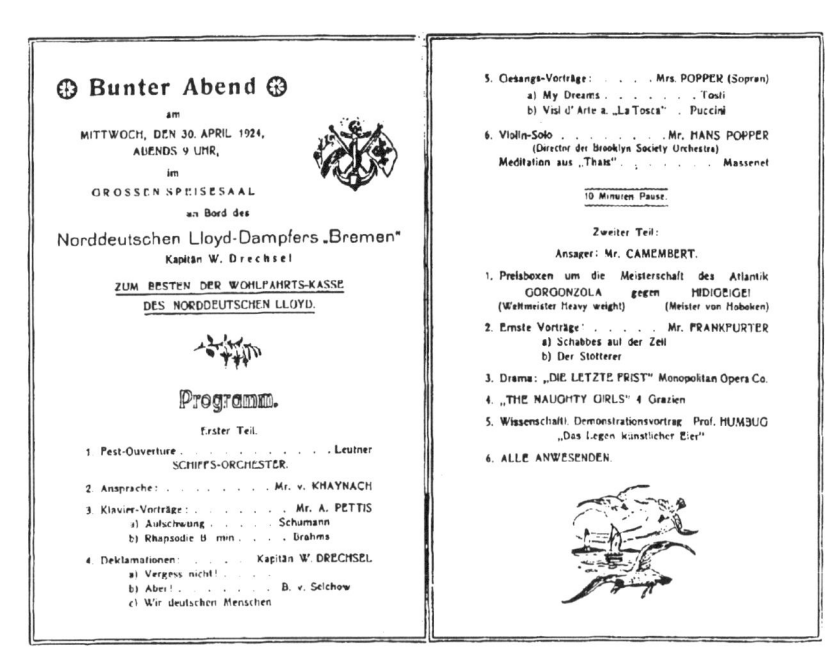

am
MITTWOCH, DEN 30. APRIL 1924,
ABENDS 9 UHR,
im
GROSSEN SPEISESAAL
an Bord des
Norddeutschen Lloyd-Dampfers „Bremen"
Kapitän W. Drechsel

ZUM BESTEN DER WOHLFAHRTS-KASSE
DES NORDDEUTSCHEN LLOYD.

Programm.

Erster Teil.

1. Fest-Ouverture . . . . Leutner
    SCHIFFS-ORCHESTER.
2. Ansprache: . . . . Mr. v. KHAYNACH
3. Klavier-Vorträge: . . . . Mr. A. PETTIS
    a) Aufschwung . . . . . Schumann
    b) Rhapsodie B min. . . . . Brahms
4. Deklamationen . . . . . Kapitän W. DRECHSEL
    a) Vergess nicht!
    b) Aber! . . . . B. v. Selchow
    c) Wir deutschen Menschen

5. Gesangs-Vorträge: . . . . . . Mrs. POPPER (Sopran)
    a) My Dreams . . . . Tosti
    b) Visi d'Arte a. „La Tosca" . . Puccini
6. Violin-Solo . . . . Mr. HANS POPPER
    (Director der Brooklyn Society Orchestra)
    Meditation aus „Thais" . . . . Massenet

10 Minuten Pause.

Zweiter Teil:
Ansager: Mr. CAMEMBERT.

1. Preisboxen um die Meisterschaft des Atlantik
    GORGONZOLA gegen HIDIGEIGEI
    (Weltmeister Heavy weight) (Meister von Hoboken)
2. Ernste Vorträge . . . . . Mr. FRANKFURTER
    a) Schabbes auf der Zeil
    b) Der Stotterer
3. Drama: „DIE LETZTE FRIST" Monopolitan Opera Co.
4. „THE NAUGHTY GIRLS" 4 Grazien
5. Wissenschaftl. Demonstrationsvortrag Prof. HUMBUG
    „Das Legen künstlicher Eier"
6. ALLE ANWESENDEN.

A sort of Amateur Night on board Bremen *in 1924 for the benefit of the Lloyd's Welfare Fund. There probably was a receptacle for contributions at the door. There was story-telling, playing by the ship's orchestra, passengers singing, playing the piano and violin. After an intermission a boxing match between crew-members, "serious lectures," some operatic skits, and a magician: the laying of artificial eggs. With all joining in to close a jolly evening. Daytime there was a Great Sport Fest, with first and second prizes, followed by a (Tea) Concert. The games such as youngsters play at a home-coming or Fourth of July: Three-legged and sack races, rope pulls, relays, threading needles, running holding eggs, quoits, again anybody could join anything. The Lloyd contended at the time that it introduced Tourist Class with* Bremen *3.*

Grosses Sport-Fest

an Bord des
Norddeutschen Lloyd-Dampfers
„BREMEN"
Kapitän: W. Drechsel
am
Sonnabend, den 3. Mai 1924,
Nachmittags 3 Uhr,
mit
=== Konzert. ===

Es werden für jeden Wettkampf ein
Erster und ein *Zweiter Preis* verteilt.

*Preis-Verteilung während des
Abend-Konzertes im
Speisesaal.*

Programm gilt als Eintritts-Karte.

Spielfolge:

1. Ringwerfen.
2. Sackwerfen.
3. Eierlaufen.
4. Tauziehen.
5. Sacklaufen.
6. Staffettenlauf.
7. Dreibeinlaufen.
8. Hahnenkampf.
9. Nadeleinfädeln.
10. Kartoffellegen.
11. Wettmarsch der Dicken.
12. Wettmarsch der Dünnen.

sengers were able to eat their usual meals." The author found no further mention of this seasickness "cure" or about the Johns Hopkins' doctor who participated in the demonstration on *Columbus*.

On board there was hardly anything not available: One could use ship stationery and cards, write one's mail, buy the stamps for dispatch by the Sea Post, send Ocean Letters from one ship to another to be mailed at the next port. Use the library, pool, deck games, smoking room, the shops, Kosher cooking, eat more than one comfortably should, see films, listen, dance, or eat to live music, singalong in "One Hundred Favorite German Songs", a give-away for German-Americans on the way to revisiting family, friends and country; attend church or synagogue services, bet in the pools on the day's mileage, or horse races, many natural and "accidental" occasions to meet people, the luxury of deck chairs, warmly wrapped up, a good book, a chat with new-found friends. The lack of barriers at sea that keep people apart on shore. A doctor if needed, secretarial services, a daily newspaper. An Equator-Crossing certificate.

In dining, the first evening no one would dress. After that, certainly in First Class, dressing up was de rigeur. Many travelled by ship in order again to live, even for a brief week, the old niceties and courtesies. Then there'd be a Get-Together occasion to help break the ice, sit with people one had met on deck, strolling, or at deck games, or at mid-morning boullion and biscuits, at tea, or at the midnight snack after a last turn around the deck. Second and Third Classes had lesser but very adequate versions of these niceties. Finally, the Farewell Dinner. The menu for *Bremen's* on 4 July, 1936 was printed as a letter card, perforated edge, gummed and ready to mail on board. Complete convenience for the passenger. But also subtle promotion for NDL's serv-

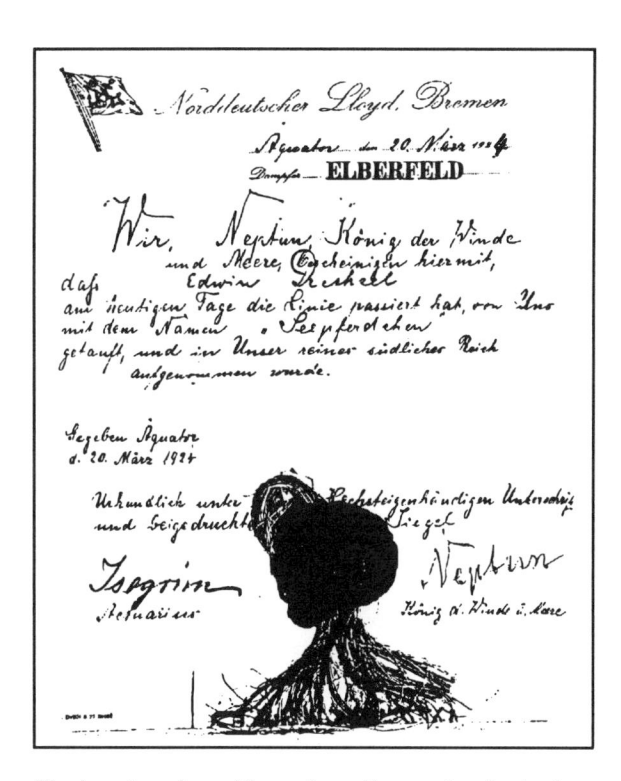

The baptismal certificate from Neptun for the Author, one of his new residents after crossing the equator en route from Europe, around Africa to Australia: "I have named (the nine-years old) Little Sea Horse and received him into my southern domain." 20 March, 1924, signed Neptun, King of the Winds and the Seas. See also p. 307, Vol. I.

ice to its guests. Finally, the voyage log: distances, speed, weather, a record to keep. For many, their voyage was a lifelong memory. The author remembers the night before *Bremen* reached Cherbourg at 6 A.M. in early June, 1936. A group of friends broke up their champagne festivities reluctantly about 3 A.M. in time to pack, dress for shore, a quickie breakfast then, watch the docking. One more hug, or handshake, even some tears.

Whether the crossing was restful, or hectic with activities, it was an experience most never forgot, and always loved to talk about. This, over the years was the Lloyd's strength: Its moment in the lives of millions who crossed the oceans, and the perhaps twenty-five millions (guesstimate from 1990 U.S. Census) who had some one come over on the Lloyd and enter the country via Ellis Island. A part of people's roots.

As the nature of ocean travellers changed in the 1920s, so did the nomenclature of classes. The former First, Second and Third changed in name and meaning. Tweendeck disappeared to be replaced with dormitory quarters on ships carrying emigrants to South America. In 1928 NDL was telling its South America-bound passengers that

Birth, Baptism, and death at Sea: They occur, and ships have to be prepared for all eventualities. Births at sea often mean the new baby is named for the ship. When Captain Harry S. Truman returned from France in 1919 on USS Zeppelin #269 a baby born at sea was named Zeppelina. Baptism is unusual, except on longer voyages for crossing the Equator for the first time. Death is a sadness, with the choice of taking the body "home" or for burial at sea, here with a service, music, a flag as last honor and remembrance. "We commit this body to the deep...."

"Third Class attractions, include comfortable accommodations, the best feeding, and roomy promenade decks."

NDL's first postwar passenger ships carried Cabin and Third. When *München* appeared in 1923 it carried I, II and III Classes. In 1925, I and II were changed to the Cabin designation. In late 1925, NDL announced "A new class of accommodation has been provided known as Tourist Third Cabin. This class is entirely separate and distinct from, and is superior to, regular Third Class." The first approach was to cut Tourist Third out of the old Third. There was not enough distinction. Then, the best of the Third and poorest of Second was combined to make Tourist Cabin. Then Third Class aft was abolished, renamed Tourist Third. On *Bremen* and *Europa* in 1932, Second Class aft was divided into Second Cabin for the best space, Tourist Cabin for the lesser space. Eventually,

Passengers: The Heart of the Lloyd's Business 243

Food was a topic unto itself. Menus ranged from very basic in the lower classes on the less important services, to the ultimate of literally hundreds of items available in small-print menus, with notice that passengers could request what they did not find listed. And, on Bremen *and* Europa, *the Sun Deck Restaurant where one paid, but had an allowance off the passage price. Besides the set meals, there were numerous possibilities for eating and drinking: even pre-breakfast, the eleven o'clock boullion and ... on Deck or inside if weather was inclement, the afternoon tea and coffee, the late evening-midnight snack perhaps after a last turn around the deck. And, depending on one's accommodation with the steward/stewardess, in the cabin.*

If the ship left early in the day, that night there'd be a Get-Together Dinner, sometime a Captain's Dinner, and a Goodbye dinner. On the slower ships one could become acquainted, and these dinners would be that much more sociable.

Dampfer „COLUMBUS" Freitag, 25. April 1924

Fasten-Speisen

Gefüllte Kiebitzeier

Austernsuppe Lady Morgan

Hummer Amerikanische Art

Kriekente, Rahm-Sauce
Chicorée Salat

Frische Artischocken, Sauce Mousseline

Walderdbeer-Rahmeis, Waffeln

Früchte
Mokka   Tee

Steamer „COLUMBUS" Friday, April 25th 1924

Lent Dishes

Plovers Eggs à la Russe

Oyster Soup Lady Morgan

Lobster American Style

Criquet, Cream Sauce
Chicorée Salad

Fresh Artichokes, Sauce Mousseline

German Strawberry Ice Cream, Wafers

Fruits
Mocha   Tea

NORDDEUTSCHER LLOYD BREMEN

SPEISEKARTE

III. KLASSE

Frühstück
Gedünstete Pflaumen
Eiergrütze in Milch
Haferschleim   Krumbles
Pfannkuchen mit Marmelade gefüllt
KALT:
Leber-, Rot- und Plockwurst
Romadour Käse
Frühstücksgebäck   Kaffee   Tee
Butter   Marmelade

Mittagessen
Linsensuppe mit Würstchen
Gebrat. Lammkeule mit Bratensaft
Kartoffelpüree
Wachsbohnen-Salat
Rahmeis, Kokosnußschnitte

15 Uhr
Kaffee, Butterkuchen

Abendessen
Kalbsschulter, Paprika-Sauce
Kartoffeln, Makkaroni
KALT: Deutscher Hering-Salat
Rahm-Käse
Für Kinder:
Milchreis mit Zucker und Zimt

21 Uhr: Tee, Zwieback

D. »COLUMBUS« Sonnabend, den 28. September 1928.

Breakfast
Stewed Prunes
Semolina in Milk
Oatmeal Gruel   Krumbles
Pancake with Marmalade Stuffed
COLD:
Liver, Black and Plock Sausage
Romadour Cheese
Breakfast Pastry   Coffee   Tea
Butter   Jam

Dinner
Lentil Soup with Sausage
Roast Leg of Lamb with Gravy
Mashed Potatoes
Wax-Bean Salad
Ice Cream, Cocoanut Cake

15 o'clock
Coffee, Short Cake

Supper
Shoulder of Veal, Paprika Sauce
Potatoes, Macaroni
COLD: German Herring Salad
Dutch Cheese
For Children:
Milk Rice with Sugar and Cinnamon

21 o'clock: Tea, Zwieback

SPEISEKARTE

Mittagessen
Minestra
Kraftbrühe in Tasse

Gedämpfte Rindshüfte
Perlbohnen in Butter   Speck-Kartoffeln

Himbeer-Rahmeis, Mürbes Gebäck

Auf Wunsch:
Makkaroni mit Schinken

Nachmittags
Kaffee   Tee   Kuchen

Dinner
Minestra
Consommé in Cup

Braised Haunch of Beef
Buttered String Beans   Bacon Potatoes

Raspberry Ice-Cream, Pastry

To Order:
Macaroni with Ham

Afternoon
Coffee   Tea   Cake

Donnerstag, 11. August 1932   D. „Bremen"
3. Klasse

NORDDEUTSCHER LLOYD BREMEN

Dampfer „Madrid"
Sonnabend, den 27. Oktober 1928

Mittag:
Erbsensuppe
Rinderbrust mit Senfsauce
Weißkohl - Brühkartoffeln
Gedünstete Pflaumen

Nachmittag:
Kaffee - Breslauer Gebäck

Abend:
Gebratenes Weißfischfilet
Petersilienbutter - Gekochte Kartoffeln
Tee, Weißbrot, Graubrot, Schwarzbrot

Für Kinder: Haferschleim

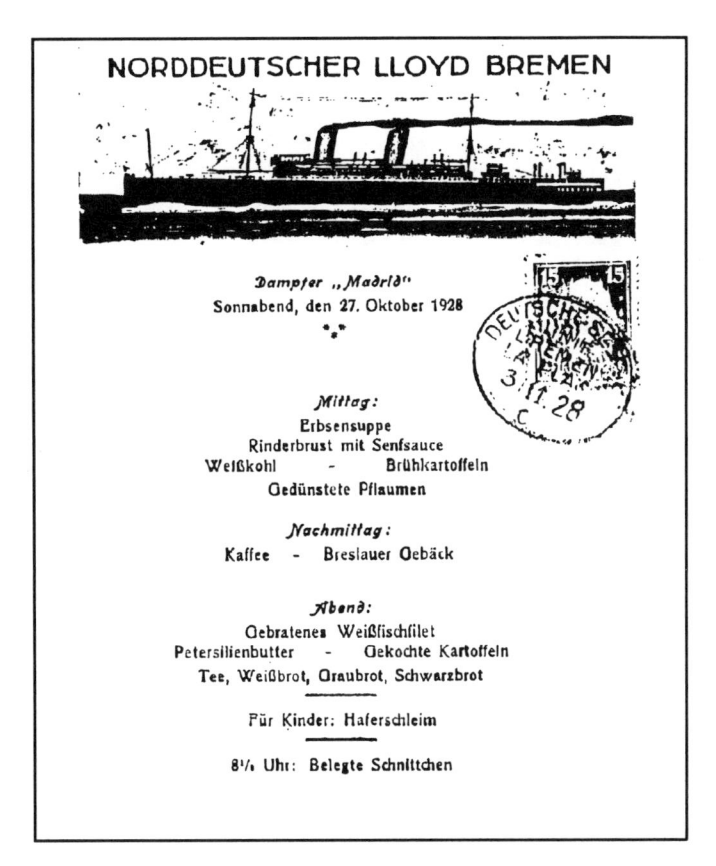

8¾ Uhr: Belegte Schnittchen

Day's menu from the Middle-Class Steamer Madrid *to South America. Breakfast must have been basic and the same each day, from its non-mention on this menu. The menu-card was mailed with the Bremen-La Plata Sea Post on 3.11.28. back to Germany at domestic German postage rate.*

First Class Breakfast menu from the Europa *in 1931. There might be a depression on world-wide. But once on board, one could eat and relax to ones heart's content.*

| Touristen-Klasse. | Dampfer „München" | Sonntag, den 13. Juni 1926 |

Frühstück / *Breakfast*
Grape Fruit
Haferflocken in Milch Maisflocken Haferschleim / Oatmeal in Milk Corn Flakes Oatmeal Gruel
Frische Bratwurst, Bratkartoffeln / Fresh Pork Sausage, Fried Potatoes
Gefüllter Pfannkuchen / Stuffed Pancake
Gekochter Prager Schinken Edamer Käse / Boiled Prague Ham Edam Cheese
Frühstücksgebäck Butter Marmelade / Breakfast Pastry Butter Jam
Kaffee Tee / Coffee Tea

10 Uhr vorm. Bouillon und Brötchen / *10 o'clock a. m.* Bouillon and Rolls

2. Frühstück / *Lunch*
Italienische Minestra / Italian Minestra
Königsberger Klopse, Kapern-Sauce, Salzkartoffeln / Koenigsberg Collops, Caper Sauce, Boiled Potatoes
KALT: Geräuchertes Bücklingsfilet / COLD: Smoked Fillet of Bloater
Amerikanischer Geflügel-Salat / American Chicken Salad
Gemischter Aufschnitt / Cold Cut
Mandelhörnchen / Almond Crescents
Kaffee / Coffee

Nachmittags Schokolade und Butterkuchen / *Afternoon* Chocolate and Short Cake

Hauptmahlzeit / *Dinner*
Kraftbrühe mit Sternnudeln / Consommé aux Pâtes d'Italie
Gebackene Zander, Remoulade-Sauce / Fried Slices of Zander, Remoulade Sauce
Gebratene Ente, Römischer Salat / Roast Duck, Romaine Salad
Himbeer-Rahmeis, Linzer Schnitte / Raspberry Ice Cream, Linz Cakes
Obst Kaffee / Fruit Coffee

Abends 9 Uhr. (Auf Wunsch) Tee und belegte Brote. / *9 o'clock p. m.* (To Order) Tea and Sandwiches

Passengers: The Heart of the Lloyd's Business

Farewell Dinner

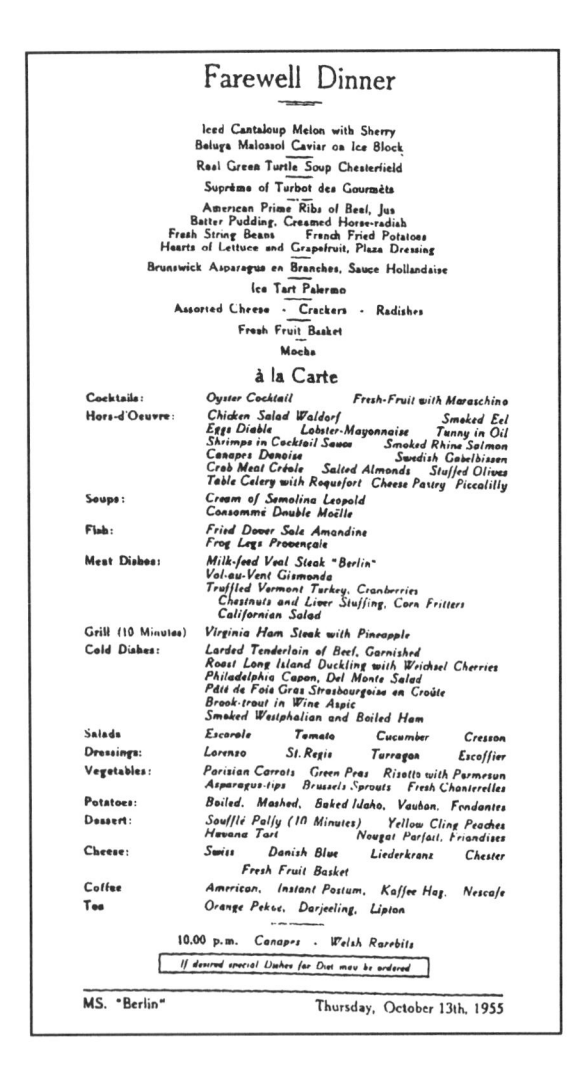

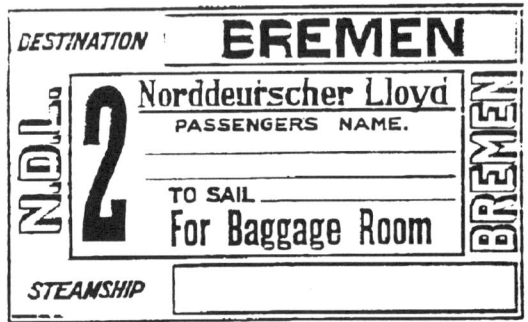

Iced Cantaloup Melon with Sherry
Beluga Malossol Caviar on Ice Block
Real Green Turtle Soup Chesterfield
Suprême of Turbot des Gourmêts
American Prime Ribs of Beef, Jus
Batter Pudding, Creamed Horse-radish
Fresh String Beans   French Fried Potatoes
Hearts of Lettuce and Grapefruit, Plaza Dressing
Brunswick Asparagus en Branches, Sauce Hollandaise
Ice Tart Palermo
Assorted Cheese - Crackers - Radishes
Fresh Fruit Basket
Mocha

à la Carte

Cocktails:	Oyster Cocktail Fresh-Fruit with Maraschino
Hors-d'Oeuvre:	Chicken Salad Waldorf Smoked Eel Eggs Diable Lobster-Mayonnaise Tunny in Oil Shrimps in Cocktail Sauce Smoked Rhine Salmon Canapes Danoise Swedish Gabelbissen Crab Meat Créole Salted Almonds Stuffed Olives Table Celery with Roquefort Cheese Pastry Piccalilly
Soups:	Cream of Semolina Leopold Consommé Double Moëlle
Fish:	Fried Dover Sole Amandine Frog Legs Provençale
Meat Dishes:	Milk-fed Veal Steak "Berlin" Vol-au-Vent Gismonda Truffled Vermont Turkey, Cranberries Chestnuts and Liver Stuffing, Corn Fritters Californian Salad
Grill (10 Minutes)	Virginia Ham Steak with Pineapple
Cold Dishes:	Larded Tenderloin of Beef, Garnished Roast Long Island Duckling with Weichsel Cherries Philadelphia Capon, Del Monte Salad Pâté de Foie Gras Strasbourgeoise en Croûte Brook-trout in Wine Aspic Smoked Westphalian and Boiled Ham
Salads	Escarole Tomato Cucumber Cresson
Dressings:	Lorenzo St. Regis Tarragon Escoffier
Vegetables:	Parisian Carrots Green Peas Risotto with Parmesan Asparagus-tips Brussels Sprouts Fresh Chanterelles
Potatoes:	Boiled, Mashed, Baked Idaho, Vauban, Fondantes
Dessert:	Soufflé Polly (10 Minutes) Yellow Cling Peaches Havana Tart Nougat Parfait, Friandises
Cheese:	Swiss Danish Blue Liederkranz Chester Fresh Fruit Basket
Coffee	American, Instant Postum, Kaffee Hag, Nescafe
Tea	Orange Pekoe, Darjeeling, Lipton

10.00 p.m.   Canapés - Welsh Rarebits

If desired special Dishes for Diet may be ordered

MS. "Berlin"   Thursday, October 13th, 1955

everything aft became Tourist Class. This, as the nature of the clientele changed.

Before the summer of 1926, NDL announced "For certain sailings during the summer vacation period Tourist Third Cabin will be reserved exclusively for college students, teachers, literary people and other engaged in intellectual pursuits." It soon was known as College Class. To encourage this broadly academic audience, the shipping lines provided free passage for college music groups to play their way across the Atlantic. In the Summer of 1926, a joint Dartmouth-Swarthout group went "Student Third Class" with the Lloyd to visit and study at universities in London, Paris and Berlin, and to visit the League of Nations in Geneva. "Our cabins were just over the propellers" (on *Bremen*) said Dartmouth student Don Norstrand, "just large enough to back out the door and turn around. The cost of my three-months trip was just under $1000. To earn our way into First Class areas we put on skits for the entertainment mostly of the College girls who could afford to pay."

By 1928, only *Columbus* for the Lloyd carried First Class on the North Atlantic. *Berlin* and the other ships provided a weekly Cabin - Tourist - Third service. First Class disappeared in 1934, renamed Cabin, even on the top liners, a desperate move to lure passengers during the depression. First, Second and Third classes survived on Italian liners, even after WWII, as Italy was the last continuing source of emigrants, separate from the growing number of political, religious and economic refugees.

In May, 1933 the Lloyd and Hapag jointly advertised they would accept Reichsmark for payment of passages. The lines would continue to get

In olden days the class passengers travelled with steamer trunks stored in the baggage room, and one could at given hours have access. This meant baggage labels, the amount allowed (fifty pounds free on the first Weser River craft). Nowadays, one travels with less, and it fits into the cabin.

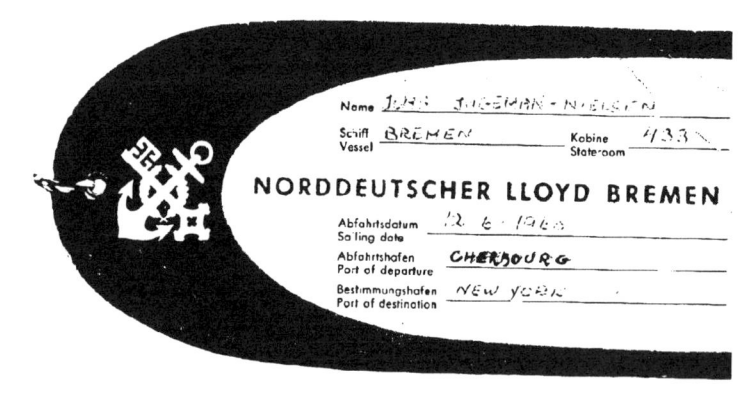

246   *Norddeutscher Lloyd Bremen*

Alternate name for Tourist Class was College Class, an appeal to Academics to travel at a reasonable rate but in immaculately clean and tasty surroundings. Stuttgart was a family-type ship. Its Tourist-College Class made one feel at home, albeit a small step higher: fresh flowers daily in the Ladies Room or the Dining Room, linen serviettes, crystal ware, good food, usually good company, and good Lloyd service.

The Smoking Rooms First Class on Homeric *right (ex-*Columbus I*), and* Columbus II *(below) show that they came from the same design. The fireplace is in the center. What was inside the glassed-in insets on either side?* Columbus II *had pillars, possibly to reduce vibration.* Bremen *in 1930 had pillars added around her circular dance-floor to dampen vibration.*

Passengers: The Heart of the Lloyd's Business 247

Europa was more quietly furnished than Bremen. The Sun Deck Restaurant on Europa. Bremen's was same-sized, and very similar. Note table-partitions for rough weather, more noticeable in this highest part of the ship. The Library has above the door: Inter Libros Requies Inter Filia Fructus.

their full fares in Mark terms. But foreign creditors would be paid a discount, some 20%, the purpose of the move: to repay debt. They would be the losers. And the competition, as this amounted to cutting fares. The North Atlantic (Passenger) Conference on 24/5/1933 telegraphed its protest, including Hapag and Lloyd as members and signers. On 2 June the practice was discontinued. The Lloyd was fined $130,500, Hapag $69,800 to be prorated among the rest of the Conference members. They refused the fines, and the affair ended. There seems to be nothing in the files on this now.

A Dartmouth College group in Summer, 1926 worked its way to Europe and back by playing music and putting on skits. It was a way of emphasizing that the new Tourist Class also was a College Class, to attract more students and academics.

In carrying passengers the emphasis was long-distance: across the North, Central and South Atlantic, to Asia, pre-World War I also to Australia, many routes in the Mediterranean. Since the Lloyd until the 1920s never had much of a cruise program, it customized travel for clients with segments from regular schedules, even overnight coastal voyages such as Genoa to Naples, or between Bremerhaven, Southampton, Cherbourg or Queenstown. The sort of routes now served by hundreds of high-seas ferries all over the world.

In August, 1936 the son of Admiral Earl Jellicoe, of World War I fame, now the second Earl, and President of the Royal Geographic Society, travelled on *Bremen* from Southampton to Bremerhaven with Prinz Friedrich, the youngest son of the former Crown Prince, to stay in Potsdam as guest of "Fritzie" while studying German. "I remember the trip well and with pleasure" he wrote me recently.

This is mentioned in preface to an account of the visit of the Admiral and Lady Jellicoe to the *Bremen* in Southampton on Saturday, 3 November, 1934. *Bremen* was on the start of her 100th round trip (see "Blue Ribbon"). Captain and Mrs. Drechsel were returning to New York from a business visit to Bremen, NDL Head Office. Once tied up, a gentleman and three ladies boarded *Bremen*. The gentleman introduced himself as "Jellicoe" and expressed a desire to see the ship. Captain Drechsel was informed, and joined the Admiral. The ladies were entrusted to Mrs. Drechsel for a tour and tea, while the two Naval men spent 3½ hours in talk and inspecting the more technical aspects of *Bremen*. They ended up in Commodore Ziegenbein's day-cabin, then all had luncheon in the Sun Deck restaurant. Excerpts from Captain Drechsel's report follow:

"His Lordship was interested in everything I was able to show him. Naturally, his conversation turned to the World War, asking about my role as an officer of the Imperial German Navy and about the war at sea on submarines. Lord Jellicoe mentioned that shortly his new book "The Submarine Peril" would be out. "A good many of my countrymen will not like the language. But in the interest of all I have been compelled to tell the truth, whether some like it or not." Lord Jellicoe said that inasmuch as the convoy system was vital to the existence of his country, it had to be perfected in preparation for the next war if England were to survive. He criticized the methods of the convoy system during the last war. Lack of experience on the part of merchant ships and, to some extent, of the navy brought about the main difficulties and 'never enabled us to make the convoy system a full success.' Lord Jellicoe said he was earnestly warning his countrymen in strongest terms to pay more attention to the training of the merchant sailors and the navy in convoy sailing. The only way to perfect the system was to practice in peacetime during the annual fleet maneuvers.

"Having served both on a torpedo boat destroyer and a submarine during the war, Lord Jellicoe asked about my experience on board small craft during the usually prevailing bad weather conditions in home waters with regard to their usefulness in wartime. I frankly stated that in the North Sea, English Channel, etc. small craft in bad weather were of little if any use. The Admiral fully agreed. I recounted an incident which happened while serving on a submarine in bad weather:

"In the late summer of 1917 I served as executive officer on U-156, a submarine cruiser. (See "D.O.R., Vol. I.") Drechsel was awarded the Iron Cross First Class for saving the submarine and crew during a diving malfunction.) Equipped to stay at sea for about 4½ months our orders were to go around the North Coast of Great Britain into the Atlantic. The British had large and small vessels on patrol from the North Coast to the Shetlands, respectively the Faroe Islands to prevent breakthroughs by German naval vessels or the raiders they were sending out. The chances

The cartoonist in a New York City newspaper in 1936 may have inspired John Maxtone-Graham's comment in "The Only Way to Cross," 1978, that "there was no more effective purgatory in the world than a North River pier in early September." Delays sometimes, misplaced baggage, but no "purgatory" in my remembrances.

to pass the closely-watched passages were best in fog when visibility was low and in bad weather when the small craft on patrol had to return to port. Often both fog and storm come up suddenly and craft were caught outside before they could make port. In our case, trying to pass from East to West, we experienced a hurricane with high seas and swells in which we hardly made any progress. Visibility was low because of the dense spray.

"About 7 A.M. on the day we were to run the patrol line we suddenly sighted a dark object through the spray not far off. As visibility got a bit better we saw a British torpedo-boat destroyer, minus his two masts, a play thing for the high waves, more so than we as a submarine. Only one man could be seen on the bridge. In better weather both sides would have been quick with their weapons. But neither side could use anything in this case. All effort was on keeping our vessels afloat. We both drifted to and fro, the nearest to each other was about one hundred feet.

Trans-Atlantic fares were low in the 1933-1934 bottom of the travel depression. Third Class All-Expense tours for $183. Squeezed into a two-weeks vacation, going and coming on Bremen *or* Europa, *thus saving more days for abroad.*

At times waving to each other, we both watched our chances to let loose. None came. With the hurricane still near full force, the last we saw of the "Englishman" was about 4 P.M. when visibility turned to darkness. The next morning with seas and swells still running very high, but visibility fairly good, we saw nothing, least of all our friend the Torpedo-boat destroyer.

"Lord Jellicoe had high praise for the German Navy. He strongly advocated placing young and able officers in higher positions regardless of the traditional system of promotion by the Navy List and Eye. The Admiral mentioned that he had corresponded with the Kaiser after the war. I mentioned I had also, and that I got to know the members of the Kaiser's family, and that he had been my guest on board *SMS Meteor* (the Submarine School's Mother Ship) in Kiel on September 25, 1918, the last naval vessel he had set foot on. I also mentioned I had been on very friendly terms with Prince Heinrich, the Kaiser's younger brother (See Epilogue, Vol. I). We discovered we had mutual friends in these circles. That knowledge brought us closer to each other in a few hours than it takes years in other cases. The Admiral invited the Drechsels to "pay us a visit on your next trip; just send me a wireless three or four days before you reach England." Sadly, this visit never came about. The Admiral became ill, and died a year later. He was buried in Westminster Abbey with National Honours. Not to be forgotten by us in our lifetimes." That November, Admiral Jellicoe's book *The Submarine Peril* arrived from his publishers. The then Kapitän Leutnant, Commander Drechsel, also received the Lifesaving Medal on Ribbon, which means at the risk of his own life, from one of the small German patrol vessels.

On the Atlantic the rest of the 1930s were a time of gradual recovery in passenger numbers, high-lighted by the appearance of *Normandie*, probably the greatest liner ever built, counting the *United States* more as a naval than a merchant vessel, and *Queen Mary*. (See "Inspectorate"). But numbers crossing the Atlantic did not again reach the one million mark until and only briefly long after the Second War.

Even in the depression some could still afford being pampered. *Bremen* and *Europa* perhaps had the extreme: The Sundeck Restaurant on top of which were the mailplane catapults during the May - October good-weather months. Passengers choosing to eat all their meals in that restaurant were allowed $25 off their cabin fare. Not really an inducement, but a bargain for the Lloyd. One British passenger said that on the express liners put into the Far East route in 1935 "the First Class service was unforgettable."

During this time the New York Times editorialized about the Class System on liners: The Captain, Staff and Crew were the Bureaucracy.

During the Jellicoe Family's visit on Bremen, *while the Admiral and Captain Drechsel were inspecting the ship, Staff Captain Otto Prehn showed them the bridge. Lady Jellicoe, left, daughter Prudence, Prince Friedrich Wilhelm, youngest son of the Crown Prince and Crown Princess, and Princess Cecilie, named for her Mother. Photo p.269, Vol. I on board her namesake. During a cruise from Bremerhaven to and around the Isle of Wight.*
R. Fleischhut Photo.

Admiral, The Rt. Hon. the Earl Jellicoe, in November, 1934 on board Bremen *during its call at Southampton. Photo by Wendell McRae. The Jellicoe Family and Captain and Mrs. Drechsel as hosts, and other guests had luncheon in the Sun Deck restaurant. Captain Drechsel ended his report of Lord Jellicoe's visit by recalling, in answer to the Admiral's question, his contacts with the Kaiser and his Brother, Prinz Henry. "We discovered we had mutual friends in these circles, and that knowledge brought us closer to each other in a few hours as it takes years in other cases."*

Passengers: The Heart of the Lloyd's Business   251

In 1928, Prince Louis Ferdinand, older brother of Prince Friedrich Wilhelm, friend of the Second Earl, shown in the photograph with Lord and Lady Jellicoe, returned home from a visit to the States on Columbus. *At Bremerhaven, he was met by his Mother, the former Crown Princess Cecilie, and Lloyd President Philipp Heineken. Prince Louis Ferdinand died at age 86 in September, 1994 at Bremen, his home for many years. He and his wife, the Countess Kira Kirillovna visited the U.S. several times. The Prince in the 1930s worked as a mechanic for the Ford Motor Company to learn about the modern labor world.*

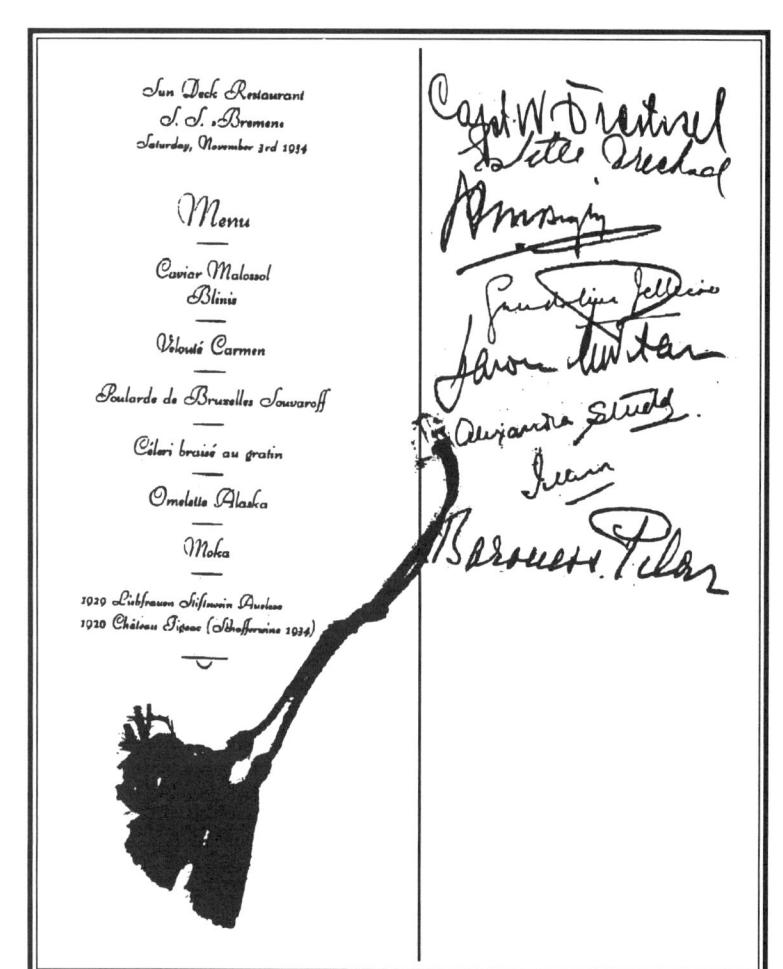

The menu from the luncheon in Bremen's *Sun Deck Restaurant for the visiting Jellicoe family, and signed by them, Captain and Mrs. Drechsel, and Baroness Pilar, wife of a Lloyd official. November, 1934. It was* Bremen's *100th round-voyage, and one on which she set a time record. See caption on page 438.*

252   Norddeutscher Lloyd Bremen

On Bremen's *first call at Southampton in July, 1929, Captain Ziegenbein was made an honorary member of the Master Mariners' Club, the first such case. In November, 1934 when Lord and Lady Jellicoe and daughter Prudence visited the ship, the Harbor Pilot must have been on the Bridge and met the group. This Christmas card to Captain Drechsel that December resulted from that meeting. Captain Percy F. Smith also was a member of the Master Mariners' Club. Almost twenty-five years later, when* Bremen 5 *called at Southampton in July, 1959 on her maiden voyage, thirty years after* Bremen 4's *first call, a journalist making the voyage in his radioed story to his newspaper reported that "At Southampton the pilot had tears in his eyes as he brought in this Bremen. He had piloted* Bremen 4 *before the war." The fellowship of the sea.*

First Class the Aristocracy.
Below that the Bourgeoisie, and
In Third, the Proletariat.

Then and now, freighter travel has an appeal for particular people, satisfied with a slower pace, self-reliant for what they wanted to do. Prewar, pre-container ships, most freighters carried some passengers. Up to twelve under international agreement, without a doctor. The Lloyd's first post-WWI ships *Vegesack* and *Bremerhaven* could take seven, although they must have been housed below the main flush deck. *Porta* and *Eisenach* had twelve berths for their 1923 voyages to the U.S. East Coast. On highly competitive routes, such as Continent to U.S.-Canada West Coasts, freighters had small-scale versions of luxurious liner facilities. *Elbe* #433 and *Weser* #434, the Lloyd's fastest prewar freighters, for that run in their 1933 rebuilding were given 16 berths. *Aller*, the first of the Lloyd's eleven-ships River Class in 1927, had space for twelve. The later ones could take sixteen. Did they often carry more than twelve? If so, with a doctor? The records or memories are inadequate or gone. *Friderun* #325, originally fitted for eight, in 1932 was expanded to twenty Cabin, and 29 Third for the Hong Kong-Australia route.

When in 1934 the Lloyd began building ships for its entry into the South America West Coast service, the first had twenty berths. The others got an awning deck and 28 berths. The last three even got tiled pools, a first on freighters.

For those who truly love the sea the longer the voyage, the better. For them, freighters can be ideal. A 1924 voyage on *Elberfeld* #298 round the

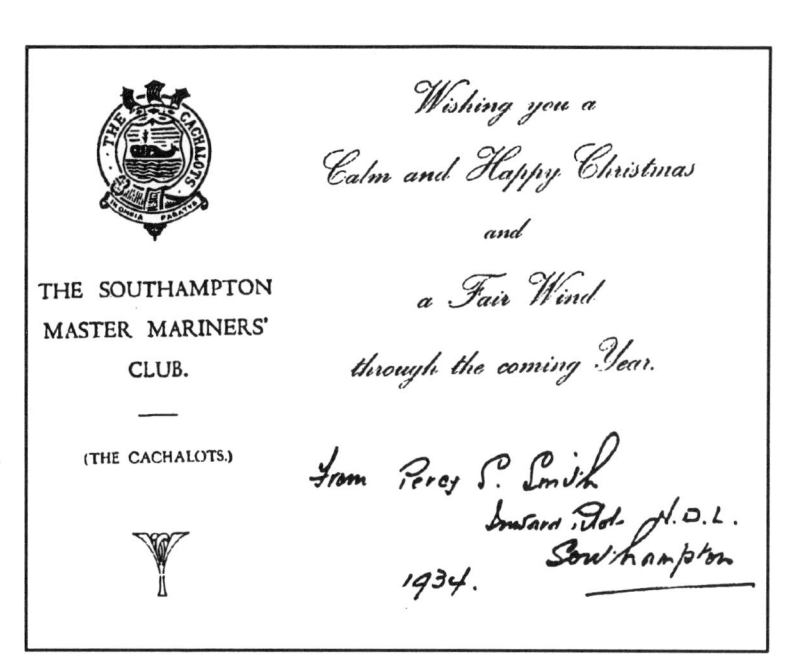

1931 advertisement in "Glimpses of the East." Long voyages, but there were no airplanes for the ordinary passengers. The General Agents for the Far East are Melchers & Co., a Bremen-based firm that represented the Lloyd in China and Hong Kong going back to the Imperial Mail services that began in 1886.

Passengers: The Heart of the Lloyd's Business 253

Cape took 54 days to Adelaide, ten more to Sydney. Occasionally, cabin-mates had too much togetherness. In the jet age, one can get off and fly home. Nowadays, the huge container ships may have an owner's suite. Crew members have all the amenities, even a hot tub, or sauna, and individual cabins. But stays in port are hours, not days. No one has time for passengers. But other freighters cater to passengers. Blue Funnel's *Centaur* in 1965 between Fremantle and Singapore introduced the passengers-aft, freight-forward combination, including pool, followed by Ivaran's *Americana* in the 1990s round South America. So a life at and close to the sea still is possible.

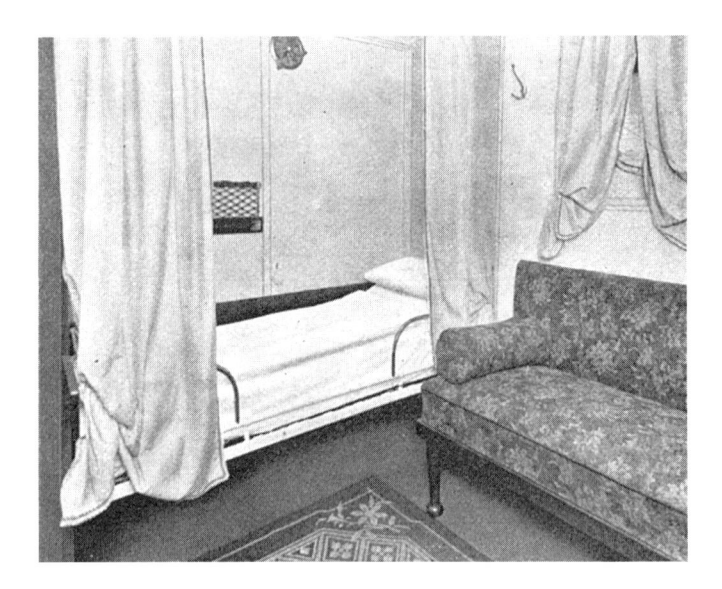

Freighters, too, had their devotees. Normally not more than 12, but on the fastest freighters, to the Far East or Australia, and the U.S.-Canada West Coast, 16 to 18. The later West Coast South America ships could accommodate 28, and provided a tiled pool. Dining Room with the officers, and a cabin on Franken, *built 1926 for the West Coast service. The couch opens into a bed.*

A high-season welcome, Pier 86, N.R., with Bremen *docking with 2,150 passengers, 20 August, 1936.* Author's Photo.

Twelve passengers, the limit, in 1927 to San Francisco on Witram, *in a friendly pose with the ship's officers. Lloyd Gazette of December, 1927, carries the ship as Roland Line. It was absorbed by the Lloyd in late 1925, and became the means for NDL to open new routes.*

At British and Continental ports, passengers reach or depart shipside by trains, as here at Bremerhaven. It was the accepted way of voyaging at sea, unlike New York. But most of those passengers, too, arrived by train. Page 298, Vol. I, for railroads competing for the immigrants' passages. And the 1920's Lloyd shipside air connections in Bremerhaven. NDL Photo Archive.

Passengers: The Heart of the Lloyd's Business 255

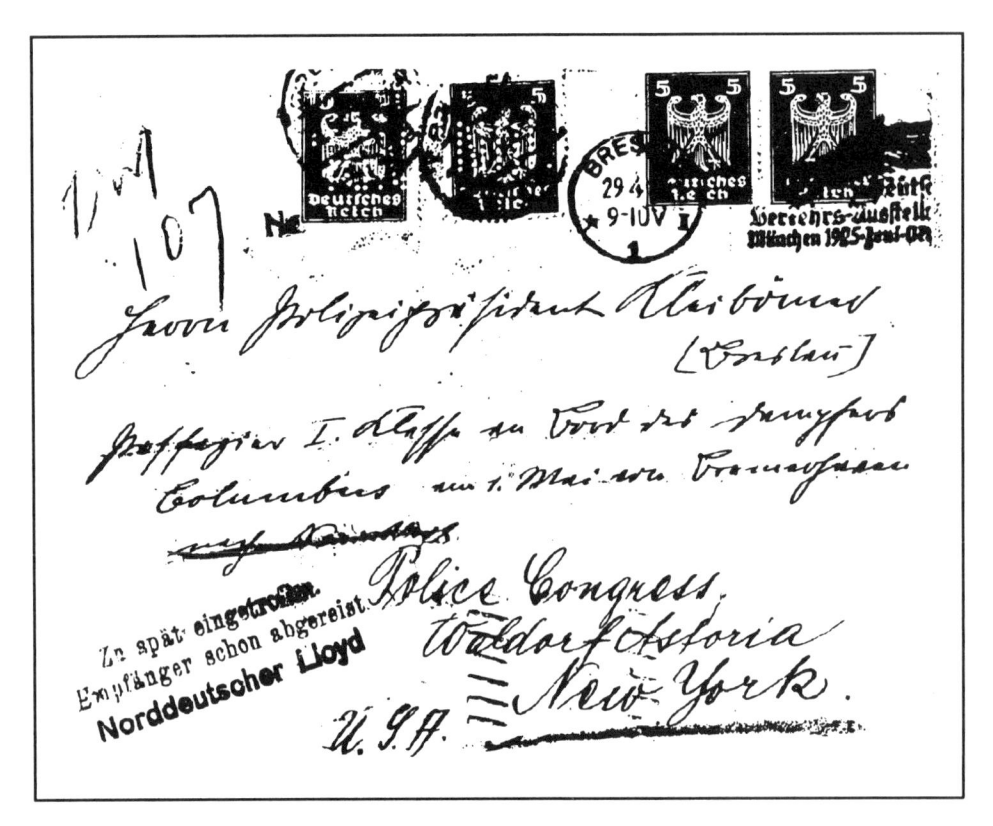

An example of Lloyd service. A letter from the wife of Breslau's Police President addressed to him as Passenger I. Class on Columbus leaving Bremerhaven on 1 May. The blue-stamped NDL notice says: Arrived too late. Addressee already departed. Then the foreign rate postage was affixed with NDL-perforated stamps to Herr Kleibömad at the Police Congress, Waldorf Astoria Hotel, New York. It is backstamped by the Hotel on 14th May, and presumably delivered. The NDL perforations on the 10 pfennig stamp are reversed.

CHAPTER 8

Masters Next To God

It was still in the age of sail that an apprentice youth boarded his first ship. Meeting the Master on deck, he said "Good Morning, Captain." The quick reply: "Young man. On this ship I decide the weather."

The esteem captains were held in is reflected in the advertisement showing a Navy captain on his Sun Deck, his steward beinging him coffee, and the caption: "A title on the door — rates a Bigelow on the floor." And in comments in the albums many captains kept. These became cherished memories in their retirement. Captain Friedrich Rehm kept such an album. There had also been an earlier-generation Rehm captain at the Lloyd. His son Arnold was the knowledgeable lecturer on many Lloyd cruises in the 1920s and 1930s. He perfected his Engish and knowledge of literature as a P.O.W. in the U.S. Postwar, we collaborated on Lloyd research.

The Captain fills many roles: He is manager, mediator, psychiatrist, doctor, the personage important to all on board. He presides over a floating city, large luxurious hotel. The manager of Hamburg's famed Vier Jahreszeiten Hotel, says: "A great hotel is like a ship. I am determined to keep it both classic and up-to-date, like a Rembrandt." Nowadays, with thousands on board cruise vessels, it takes consummate skills to keep them occupied and satisfied. The Captain in effect is God on earth. No one has power over him at sea, not even the owner, only the physical forces and his own body's ailments. As the advertisement

Captains on the bridge of the Bremen: *A photo from 1929, left to right, H. Kempf, later assistant to Inspector Drechsel in New York; then Chief 1.Officer W. Daehne, later Captain of* Columbus, *General Director of the Lloyd Carl Stimming, Captain Leopold Ziegenbein, commander then of* Bremen *and 1.Officer Fritz Leusner, in 1953 captain of freighter,* Werrastein, *and in 1959 of* Berlin, *then the* Bremen.

Obituaries from the New York Times. *How important trans-Atlantic shipping was to New York in olden days. Thursday, December 8, 1932.* The New York Times.

said: "the title ... rates a Bigelow on the floor." Or a prayer rug.

In olden days, men at sea under sail learned to read the weather, and set their course accordingly. But once storm-tossed, they could at best guess their location, unlike skippers on the British Columbia-Alaska Inside Passage who learned to tell from echoes in the fog where they were, sometimes. Celestial navigation was the first tool taught to cadets as they began their training. One recalls those on *Tinto*, heading for home in the Winter of 1916-1917 from Chile around Cape Horn, lined up with their own sextants taking the sights. Or their teacher, Carl Reumer, so good at navigation that he aimed for and got within seven miles of the St. Paul's rocks in the South Atlantic in overcast weather. Captains and crews were close to the sea. ("War"-Volume I)

Nowadays they flash the input from the Global Satellite Positioning System. It literally pin-points a ship's position anywhere. And computers permit the equivalent of a car's cruise control: maintaining a constant speed despite the occasional hills (waves) or winds.

Captains nowadays with multiple technological capabilities at finger tips, can leave running of the ship to staff, and concentrate on passengers: the reason the ship is at sea: how to increase the fun, leisure, recuperation or whatever for so many people that ships ordered at 90,000 tons are enlarged while still in the pre-keel-laying phase. Or advising the home office how things can be done better. He is the senior consultant with overall management control. It is a rare home office that will dispute a senior captain.

On the latest container ships, theoretically one person can control the entire vessel from the bridge. Where even "pint-sized" freighters used to have 30 or more crew, today's giants, as big as the *United States* or *Bremen*, have perhaps fourteen. It is a lonesome profession, on a lonely ocean. One container giant can do what twenty or more ordinary freighters used to do.

The Lloyd's first Commodore, **Captain Nicholas Johnsen** of *Europa*, died peacefully at 2.45 A.M., 7 December, 1932. His last words to his old friend Willy Drechsel, at his side, were "If the end is to come, turn my face to the sea."

Born in 1869, at age fifteen he went to sea, in sail as did all youngsters wanting to see the world. Thirteen times he rounded the Horn. In 1895 he became officer of the Kingsin Line run-

THURSDAY, DECEMBER 8, 1932.
THE NEW YORK TIMES,

1,200 AT FUNERAL OF CAPTAIN JOHNSEN

'If End Comes, Turn My Face to Sea,' Last Words of Europa's Master, Throng Is Told.

SERVICE ON SHIP AT PIER

Eulogies by Two Ministers and North German Lloyd Official— Music by Liner's Orchestra.

A funeral service for Captain Nicolaus Johnsen, who died in the Bay Ridge Sanitarium early yesterday morning of complications that followed an appendicitis operation performed at sea, was held at 4 o'clock yesterday afternoon in the ballroom of his ship, the Europa of the North German Lloyd Line, at Pier 4, Fifty-eighth Street, Brooklyn. More than 1,200 persons attended, including all the officers and crew of the ship, numbering nearly 1,000. The Rev. H. A. Kropp of St. Paul's Evangelical Lutheran Church at 312 West Twenty-second Street, Manhattan, and the Rev. Herman Brueckner of the Seamen's Church, Hoboken, officiated.

"If the end is to come, turn my face to the sea," were the last words uttered by Captain Johnson, said Captain William Drechsel, marine superintendent of the Line, to whom he spoke them. Eulogies were delivered by Captain Drechsel, the two ministers and Heinz Schuengel, resident North German Lloyd director.

The Europa's orchestra of seventeen pieces ,directed by Franz Koennecke, played the Beethoven and Chopin funeral marches and the hymns, "Jesus My Defense" and "Whatever God Ordains." The ship's chorus of forty-three voices, led by Konrad Elfers, sang "Rest in Peace."

Among those at the service were Captains from nearly all the important steamship lines in the city.

All flags on the North German Lloyd and Hamburg-American ships, piers and offices were at half staff yesterday. Many expressions of regret were received, including a telephone message from the German Ambassador at Washington.

The body of Captain Johnson was not placed on the ship until 8 o'clock last night.

Special Cable to THE NEW YORK TIMES.
Whole Fleet in Mourning.
BREMEN, Dec. 7.—Flags on the steamships and buildings of the North German Lloyd Line were flown at half mast today in tribute to Captain Johnsen, commodore of the fleet. In obituaries printed in the German press the days are recalled when he commanded the only passenger vessel of the line after the World War. It was a diminutive craft compared with the big vessels he had commanded before the war. It did not even negotiate the ocean, but ran on the Baltic between Stettin and East Prussia. Captain Johnsen frequently told how little he expected in those days to see himself the commander of the fastest liner afloat.

From the Final Edition of Yesterday's TIMES.
One of Last of Old Seadogs.
Captain Johnsen was one of the last of the old seadog type of mariner who served on sailing vessels round Cape Horn and the Cape of Good Hope and over the seven seas before they joined steamships in the North Atlantic trade. He served thirty-three of his fifty years' sea career with the North German Lloyd.

Above average height, the commodore was heavy in build, but very nimble on his feet, which he ascribed to his early "windjammer" days when he had to clamber barefooted up the rigging to stow sail. He had a powerful, deep voice that had been trained to carry stirring words to men he thought were "soldiering" on topsail yards instead of reefing the sails.

CAPTAIN NICOLAUS JOHNSEN

In his long career he saw the Lloyd fleet grow, ship by ship until the "big four," the Kronprinzessin Cecilie, Kaiser Wilhelm II, Kronprinz Wilhelm and the Kaiser Wilhelm der Grosse, were operating a weekly express service between New York and Channel ports every Tuesday with the regularity of transcontinental trains. After the World War, however, the great Lloyd fleet disappeared and Captain Johnsen found himself, like thousands of other officers and engineers in Germany, without a ship or a job.

Brought Europa Here Amid Cheers.

When North German Lloyd directors decided to build another merchant fleet they commenced with a little old cargo boat, the Gruessgott, of less than 1,000 tons gross, and gave the command to Captain Johnsen. From that small command he was transferred to the Hanover and then to the Karlsruhe and Columbus, from which he was appointed to the Europa in the early Winter of 1930. He brought the liner here in March to the cheers of thousands of spectators along the bay and river shore watching the new Atlantic recordbreaker steaming majestically to her pier.

During the war Captain Johnsen was in command of a 6,500-ton freighter named the Dessau, in which he ran the risk of mines and Allied guns, carrying coal and supplies from Sweden and Denmark for the German battleships. When peace was signed he was ordered to take the Dessau and deliver her to the Allies at Dundee which left him at the age of 50 without a ship and without a job.

Refused to Write Memoirs.

He did not despair, however, but carried on and finally ended his career on board the Europa. He was respected and admired by all who knew him.

Many journalists here and in Europe begged the veteran mariner to write some of his adventures and write his memoirs, but he steadfastly declined. "I have had no adventures," was his invariable reply, "and I am not going to write a book. Too many have been written by shipmasters already."

He always took pride in docking his ship. His stand was amidships just behind the helmsman to whom he issued order and to the officers standing by the telegraphs on the bridge as he "conned" the ship. Captain Leopold Ziegenbein, who commands the Bremen, was a junior officer under Captain Johnsen when he was chief of the Kronprinzessin Cecilie.

Captain Johnsen was born Sept. 19, 1869, in Gross-Steinrede, near Lubeck, Germany, the son of a school teacher. He went to sea at 13 in a 500-ton bark bound round Cape Horn to the west coast of South America. He remained on sailing vessels for five years and then joined a steamship on the China coast before entering the service of the Lloyd Company.

258 *Norddeutscher Lloyd Bremen*

Painting by Claus Bergen during the maiden voyage of Columbus *in April, 1924. From Captain Adolf Winter's "Von Segelschiffjungen zum Lloydkapitän" Koehler, 1929, "From Sailship Boy....". With Captain Nicholas Johnsen is Captain Paul König, then head of the Nautical Department, in 1916 commander of the first merchant submarine, Vol. I-p. 453-456. Painter Felix Schwormstädt also was on board. The two painters did literally thousands of paintings, sketches, etc. for the German shipping lines over decades. British artist Harry Hudson Rodmell also painted* Columbus *and did posters on commission for NDL. See Dust Jacket.*

1st Officer O. Prehn, Staff Captain P. A. Petersen and Commodore N. Johnsen on Europa *in 1932.*

Masters Next to God 259

In 1952, with Mrs. Petersen along, Captain Petersen brought the first German ship postwar into Cairns, Queensland. It was the M.S. Gloria *of Ernst Glässel's Bremer Reederei Merkur. Their Photo is from prewar on* Europa. *See page 121.*

ning to the Far East from Hamburg. When it was taken over by the Hapag and Lloyd in 1898, the ships were divided and Nicholas Johnsen became a Lloyd officer. During the 1914-1918 war he served on transport merchant vessels. After, he became captain of NDL's largest vessel the 781 tons Tender *Grüssgott*, after giving up almost everything else with Germany's defeat. In 1920, it ran to East Prussia when plebiscites were held there, bypassing the Polish Corridor.

In 1924, he was Captain of *Columbus* from its maiden voyage on. In April, 1929 he was named the Lloyd's first Commodore. In May, the Drechsel family celebrated that with him in his Day Cabin during our voyage to New York on *Columbus*. He then led the Lloyd team at the Blohm & Voss shipyard in Hamburg for *Europa's* completion and entry into service in March, 1930. On that voyage, *Europa* beat the record, winning the Blue Ribbon of the Atlantic that *Bremen* had won the preceding July, 1929. At age sixty, Captain Johnsen had reached the seaman's pinnacle: Captain, Commodore, Blue Ribbon holder with his ship, the *Europa*.

Captain Johnsen had become ill before *Europa* sailed on her 53rd voyage from Bremerhaven on Tuesday, 29 November, 1932. He refused the request of Dr. Fritz Lamszies, the ship's Senior Physician, the evening before to remain in bed. Dr. Lamszies left him in care of the 1. Doctor and went on a planned vacation. Johnsen supervised the departure and the first miles as far as Borkum Island. Sudden pains forced his retiring, turning command over to Staff Captain P. Petersen. In Southampton, he seemed better. In Cherbourg, the Lloyd's Paris Agent begged him to come ashore for medical attention. He refused, kept saying "Tomorrow I shall get up." On Friday, 2nd, the ship wirelessed Bremen and New York: "Our Captain is seriously ill with inflamed or ruptured appendix." On Saturday, third, at 11 A.M. in the presence of Captain Petersen and Chief Engineer Schneider, Johnsen radiophoned Captain Ziegenbein on Bremen heading towards Europe. He mentioned he would probably have to miss the next voyage.

That evening fog; Capt. Petersen was tied to the bridge. About eight P.M. the first Doctor told Captain Petersen he had called in the Second Doctor and that an operation was necessary. Captain Johnsen agreed, asked that the auxiliaries under his cabin be turned off. The ship was slowed to half-speed. Second Doctor Bisping operated, the first standing by. Later, in Cabin 243 when Captain Johnsen spoke, he asked "Are the engines running full?" Yes. "Everything going well?" Yes. "Has High Tank 3 been filled?" Yes. "Please save me the appendix; I'd like to see it." Medical staff, officers, his Steward Krueger, remained nearby for his needs.

On Sunday, the 4th, he was fitful, could not sleep. That afternoon he had cold shivers and acute slowing of the heart. At 3.45 A.M. on Monday the 5th, Captain Petersen went to the cabin, hearing the Captain was not sleeping. Petersen told his "We shall pass Nantucket Light Ship about 6 A.M." He asked about everything, stressed the ship should arrive on time and that he expected Captain Drechsel to come on board at Quarantine. At 10 A.M., Petersen wirelessed New

York that he would call by radio at eleven. He asked that a specialist come on board with Captain Drechsel.

Captain Drechsel and Brooklyn Dr. Spiegel boarded Europa with the health and customs staff at Quarantine as soon as the anchor was down at 2 P.M. Dr. Spiegel examined Captain Johnsen, ordered immediate hospitalization. This had been organized for as soon as *Europa* docked, at 4 P.M., at Bay Ridge Sanatorium, nearest to the pier. Johnsen's Steward Krueger stayed with him the entire time, as did two specialty nurses. Two other doctors were called in for consultation. That evening, Captain Johnson became worse, talked a mixture of German and English about his ship.

At 9 A.M. the 6th, Tuesday, the chief surgeon called Captain Drechsel, asked what alcoholic drinks Captain Johnsen enjoyed on board. Drechsel replied: "Whiskey and Champagne." The surgeon said "The only thing that might make a difference in meeting the crisis is an accustomed beverage. Please bring a bottle quickly." This during Prohibition, with customs seals on all supplies on board! I asked: "Would not the hospital more quickly be able to obtain alcohol through the controls?" The reply: "The red tape is such the Captain will die before we can succeed."

"I went on board, but the customs seals spoke a silent but understandable language: do not enter. I entered the wine cellar, found requested bottles and broke the seals. With two bottles each of whiskey and champagne in a briefcase. At 10 A.M. at the pier entrance I entered a Taxi. Nearby as usual stood a Customs inspector. We always had very cordial relations with these officials. So this inspector in a friendly curious way asked: "Where to so early?" I replied: "It is a matter of life and death: some alcohol for our Commodore in the sanatorium." And off we went to the Sanatorium. There the chief surgeon indicated the allowable amount for Commodore Johnsen who enjoyed this unexpected drink. I then sat for four hours at his bedside. He was in good spirits and completely clear in his mind. Whenever I wanted to leave so as not to tire him he begged me to stay. That late P.M. I came again and stayed with him. At 2:45 A.M. on 7 December, the next morning, he died with my arm around his shoulder!

As the news spread, flags around the port were lowered. Radios, telegrams, phone calls came from many who esteemed Captain Johnsen as a sailor and a friend. Crew representatives asked that "Our Commodore come home with us" on the ship.

At 4 P.M., a service was held in Europa's social hall, the entire crew there except those on stations, and hundreds more, some 1,200 total. Dr. Hermann Brückner of the Seamen's Mission in Hoboken and Pastor H.A. Kropp of St. Paul's Evangelical Luthern Church in Manhattan led. The ship's orchestra played Beethoven and hymns. The 46-voices ship's chorus sang in German. Lloyd North American Director Heinz Schuengel and Captain Drechsel gave the eulogies.

At 7.30 P.M. the body of Captain Johnsen came on board. The ship sailed at 12.30 A.M., the 8th, Captain Petersen in command. "The Old Viking's Last Voyage", so per former Director Ernst Glässel.

"Two days later" Captain Drechsel later reported to Bremen, "I received a telephone invitation, not a command for my appearance, from the Collector of Customs, Harry M. Durning. Not only an important political person, but also a Customs specialist. We Marine Superintendents of U.S. and foreign lines having ships to clear, with freight, passengers and mails were occasionally invited to see him when there were seeming irregularities or actions contrary to customs regulations. He gave us lectures, but seldom were any penalties levied. Sans preliminaries he said: "Captain Drechsel. You don't need to defend yourself for what happened at Pier 4. If need be, I shall do the defending. And if ever such a case happens again, don't hesitate to do again 'what you did'." I managed only a very few thank you words. But outside his door I had to stop to get hold of myself. Later I discovered roundabout what had happened. The pier-entrance inspector mentioned to his superior what had happened: I was taking liquor out. He told him verbally. Not written as required. And so it went up the ladder to Mr. Durning. The name and needs of the esteemed Lloyd Captain had broken the seals of customs laws.

In Bremerhaven, the entire top management came from Bremen. The moving part for all was when the hearse was opposite the bridge, the ship's syrens blew three long blasts: Farewell on the journey into history and eternity.

The tragedy is that it need not have happened. If Dr. Fritz Lamszies, *Europa's* Chief Surgeon, had not planned his vacation for that particular voyage. Later he told me "If I had been on board our Commodore would still be alive." Or, if as physician he could have convinced even ordered Captain Johnsen to stay home and go into a hospital. It was evident to all concerned later that the 1. Doctor was afraid to perform the operation, and hoped it could wait until New York.

The Author with Dr. Fritz Lamszies, Europa's Chief Surgeon, and Janet Aitken on 1 April, 1932. Photo by Donald Watt Aitken. Dr. Lamszies told the author, "Had I been on board the Commodore would not have died."

Not until Saturday evening in the fifth day after leaving Bremerhaven did he call in the 2. Doctor. He immediately urged an operation and performed it at 11:30 that evening, the 1. Doctor standing by. Professional incompetence shielded by false professional pride. A roughly similar case occured in 1959. *Liberte*, ex-*Europa*, picked up the sick captain of a French collier some 800 miles off Bishop Rock. "The doctors decided against operating; the ailment was thought to be appendicitis." (New York Times, 2/7/1959.)

The infallibility of superiors seems a professional point of honor that should have no place in society. I was told of a similar case during my time as member of the Aviation Writers Association, in the late 1940s. When one airline's first Lockheed Constellation was delivered, the Senior Pilot and others took the aircraft up for a ride to celebrate. On approaching landing at Burbank, the Senior Pilot failed to put down the landing gear. The other pilots noticed this. Not one said anything. Later I saw the wreck of that aircraft beside the runway.

Richard Hough, in "Admirals in Collision," Ballantine, 1959, recounts how the Senior British Admiral, this in 1893 in the Mediterranean, ordered a turning-a-circle-towards-each-other maneuver. The captains on the ships involved and those with the Admiral saw what would happen. Not one dared to countermand the order. It ended with the fateful ramming by *HMS Camperdown* of *HMS Victoria*, and sinking her

Letter from NDL President Philipp Heineken to Captain Drechsel about the Commodore's death, and immediate appointment of Captain Ziegenbein as successor, "so that there be no break...." Also: "May 1933 be a better year in the economy and politics...."

in peacetime, in broad daylight, on a completely calm sea.

The esteem with which Captain Johnsen was held by every one led Bremen to decide for immediate succession. Captain Leopold Ziegenbein of the *Bremen* at Christmas-time was formally named Commodore and for four years brought honor to that title, as had Captain Johnsen.

Leopold Ziegenbein was born in 1874, at age 16 went to sea in a Bremen sailship. He attended Navigation School in Geestemünde, getting his patent for sailing in all waters, and at the turn of the century joined NDL as 4.Officer. He spent several years as officer, then captain of a number of the East Asia coastal vessels on routes that helped feed into and distribute from the Main lines.

In all, he served on twenty-seven different Lloyd vessels. In 1892, he landed for the first time in New York, with a silver dollar in his pocket. In 1929, at the end of *Bremen 4's* maiden voyage, it was with the Blue Ribbon at the masttop. As a result of that voyage, he became the first foreign member of the Master Mariners Club of Southampton. He was also named an honorary Citizen of the City of New York.

Less austere than Captain Johnsen, he was a loved Father figure for his crew. A story is told that one morning after a foggy night on the bridge two sailors outside his bedroom were polishing the bull's eye one showing the other how, talking a blue streak. Finally the older says "Hol de Muul, Vadder schläft." Shut your trap, Father is sleeping. They could see Captain Ziegenbein napping, but fully dressed.

In November, 1934, at the end of the *Bremen's* 100th round trip, setting a new westward time record, Captain Ziegenbein celebrated his 60th birthday. A festive dinner included as guests his first captain in 1900 at the Lloyd and others he served under. In the Fall of 1936 he retired. After the war, he lived in his own home as guest of the occupying U.S. forces. He died at age 75 in 1950. At the service, Director Johannes Kulenkampff reminded the large personal and Lloyd family

Captain Ziegenbein and Staff Captain Daehne at the A.G. "Weser" shipyard, Bremen, in April, 1929 during the final weeks of completing the Bremen. Author's Photo.

Captain Leopold Ziegenbein in May, 1929 while awaiting taking command of Bremen *for her 16 July Maiden Voyage. Signed "To the Drechsel Family in remembrance of our pleasant chats in Bremen."*

The Lloyd's third and last Commodore, Adolf Ahrens, with the second Mrs. Ahrens (He heard at sea in March, 1937 that his first wife had died), and Renate on 20 November, 1948 taken by a street photographer Am Wall in Bremen. In the background bombed out structures.

present that it was not the technical properties of a ship but the imprimatur that the captain gives to his vessel that becomes its hall-mark. "The Lloyd will survive if the Ziegenbein spirit remains in its people."

One story goes back to 1912 on board the East Asia steamer *Prinz Ludwig* #217. Sudden screams in a First Class corridor. "Help Help." from the wife of the Secretary of the Imperial Embassy in Peking. "A rat in my cabin ...." Stewards, stewardesses hurry up; the Purser is called, 1. Officer Ziegenbein takes over. He knocks at the cabin to which the lady has returned. "Madam, did I hear correctly. You saw our rat? What wonderful news. We have all been so worried because our tame, mascot rat disappeared. And we all, superstitious seamen, were afraid it would mean bad luck. But you saw it. Wonderful. So sorry it frightened you. But it is perfectly harmless. Thank you so much." Blather. But it saved the situation.

Captain Ziegenbein appears in several places in this volume, and in his Commodore's uniform, with me, and Hapag's Commodore in Volume I. A genial man whose retirement left many with a feeling of emptiness.

Adolf Ahrens was named third Commodore of the NDL in thanks for his taking *Bremen* on the eve of World War II from New York to Murmansk, to become one of 22 German ships seeking refuge there, and then in December, bringing the ship safely to Bremerhaven.

Ahrens was born in 1879. He grew up among the steel-girded slipways of the Rickmers shipyard in Geestemünde where his father was gardner for the founder: Rickmers Clasen Rickmers. In later years, the Lloyd chartered, then bought a number of Rickmers ships. It had its training ship built there. After the Hapag-Lloyd merger in 1970 with Rickmers it served the route to China, in the 1990s became part-owner, the Rickmers Linie Gmbh., at the same Freight Office in Bremen.

At 14½ years, young Adolf signed up on *Renee Rickmers*, a sailing ship, going on to Navigation School. In 11/1901 he began at the Lloyd as 4.Officer, serving on East Asia mainliners and coastal vessels. In August, 1914 he was 2.Officer on *Derfflinger* #242 in the Red Sea. The ship sought refuge in the Suez Canal, by international agreement held a neutral area. But the ship was forced out into the Mediterranean, the crew taken prisoners. It spent the war as such on Malta. Ahrens returned home in December, 1919.

With no ships available, Ahrens opened a Greengrocery. In March, 1923 he returned to the Lloyd as 2.Officer on *Bremen 3* #149. He made Captain in 1927 on *Eisenach* #291, then *Werra* #292, it in 1931 "The Ship of Fools," and in December 1929 of *Columbus* after its rebuilding in looks and for higher speed the better to fit in with *Bremen* and *Europa*. He led *Columbus* trans-Atlantic and on its many cruises to the West Indies, around the world, the Atlantic Islands and the Mediterranean until he became *Bremen's* second commander when Commodore Ziegenbein retired in late 1936. Ahrens took *Bremen* on her round-South America cruise in 2-3/1939, he like many passengers expecting they'd go around the world the next year. Then bringing *Bremen* home in wartime. Ahrens retired 1/1/1941, began writing *Männer, Ozeane, Schiffe* "Men, Oceans, Ships", 1949, Adam Reitz Verlag, Worpswede near Bremen. Postwar, he was house father active in rebuilding Haus Seefahrt, the Seamen's Retirement home outside Bremen. He served in the Bundesrat in Bonn 1949-1953. Ahrens died in January, 1957, one month before the Lloyd cele-

Walter Stein on leave in the Harz Mountains in January, 1933.

Walter Stein in his cabin on Scharnhorst, *August, 1936, Author's photo.*

On Berlin *as Chief Officer.*

In 1935 wearing his Iron Cross First Class earned in World War I, the photo signed for the Author's 21st birthday. See also "Ad Astra...." on Berlin *after rescue of* Vestris *survivors, and #438* Scharnhorst.

Masters Next to God 265

Captain Stein's last letter to me from Kobe where he was interned with Scharnhorst, *postmarked 19.3.41, received by me in Venezuela 13, May, 1941, across the Pacific by* Nitta Maru. *He went down with the ship on 17 November, 1944. See 438.*

brated its Centennial, but knowing his shipping company again was an honored name on the oceans.

Walter Stein was born 1885 in East Prussia. He joined the Lloyd on 18/2/1909 after the usual time in sail. He was 3. Officer in 1914. As a submariner, he won the Iron Cross First Class in the War. Like most, he had to wait for a ship after the war. He served as 1. Officer on *Sierra Cordoba* #302, and as relief captain. Then, as 1. Officer on *Berlin* #308 under Captain H. von Thühlen, he was every four weeks in New York, when we became acquainted and went to the movies together: (Jesse Crawford on the organ at the Paramount, also the Roxy and Radio City Music Hall.) In 1934, he was named captain of *Scharnhorst*, then under construction, the first of three NDL express liners to the Far East. I stayed on board in August, 1936 as his guest, in effect, the son he as bachelor would never have. In 1939, *Schanrhorst* was caught by war in Japan. It was taken over by Japan when it entered the war and converted as an auxiliary aircraft carrier. Stein stayed on board, by command. He lost his life when as *Jinyo* the carrier was sunk on 17/11/1944 by the U.S. submarine *Spadefish* some 140 miles N.E. of Shanghai. His last letter reached me in 1941: "via Nitta Maru" across the Pacific to the U.S. and on to Venezuela where I was working.

Wilhelm Daehne was born in 1892, already in 1907 mustered on NDL training sailship *Herzogin Cecilie* #184, then on *Herzogin Sophie Charlotte* #143. He signed on the NDL

Captain Walter Stein of Scharnhorst *#438 and NDL General Director Dr. Rudolf Firle, May 1935 before its maiden voyage. Stein, as Berlin's Chief Officer and Evelyn Drechsel are on p. VII, Volume I. This work is dedicated in part, to my Friend Walter Stein.*

Captain W. Daehne in a photo sent to Captain Drechsel on 6 December, 1939, his last communication before Columbus *set out from Vera Cruz on its fateful journey. Inscribed: "To Captain Drechsel from your faithful W. Daehne, Antonio Lizardo (Lagoon, Vera Cruz)."*

as 4. Officer in 1914 on *Hessen* #308. It and he were seized in August, 1914 by, and became a prisoner of war in Australia. Back home, in the 1920s he served on a succession of Lloyd passenger ships until appointed in 1928 Leitende Erste Offizier, Chief First Officer, i.e., Staff Captain, on *Bremen* while fitting out, under Captain Ziegenbein. It was at the "Weser" shipyard in April, 1929 that I first met Herr Daehne. In 1932, the New York Sun chose him as Number One Chief Officer of the Year. In 1933, with major reshuffling at the Lloyd, he headed the Nautical Department. He became captain of *Potsdam* when it entered service to the Far East in 1935. He was given command of *Columbus* in December, 1936, in time for the winter cruise season, when its commander, Ahrens became captain of *Bremen*. He stayed with her through its tragic sinking on 19/12/1939 off the mid-Atlantic coast. Daehne came

Captain Oskar Scharf. Photo in the Scharf Family's advice to relatives and friends of his death on 24, September, 1953. There are photos of him elsewhere in this volume.

with the crew to Angel Island, San Francisco Bay, in January, 1940, then later at camp in New Mexico, until exchanged in late 1944. Postwar, Captain Daehne's ability was recognized by the U.S. Occupation officials, and he was named head of the Weserhafen Ports Authority. In 1951 he went to BLG, the once huge Bremen Warehouse Company, destroyed like almost everything else in port of Bremen. He rebuilt it to even greater size and importance until his retirement. In July, 1959 he made *Bremen 5's* maiden voyage to New York, his first visit in 20 years. He died in May, 1966 only 74 years old.

Oskar Scharf was born in 1886, the year in which the Lloyd expanded its routes beyond the Atlantic and the Americas, to the Far East and Australasis. At age 15 he went to sea, in sail, of course. He joined the Lloyd in 1907, worked his way up the Officers' ladder. He served in the Imperial Navy during the war, then back to the

Captain Heinrich Lorenz, master of the Lloyd's first passenger ship postwar, out in February, 1954 as Gripsholm, *in partnership with the Swedish-America Line, a year later renamed* Berlin. *She served well, despite her age (built in 1925 for Sweden), into 1966. See also #511.*

Lloyd. In 1930, Scharf became Chief 1.Officer under Captain Johnsen on *Europa*. He stayed on board until named Captain of the ship following Captain Johnsen's death in December, 1932. He remained its commander, bringing the ship home to Bremerhaven on the day Britain entered the war. See "War". He became a British prisoner of war in 1940, was released in 1945. He was on board for *Europa's* first voyage as a U.S. Transport in June, 1945. He died in September 1953, eight days before his 67th birthday.

The first captains after World War II were the old generation, some still with time under sail. **Heinrich Lorenz** was born in 1899 at Bad Kreuznach. Here as a High School student when the teacher asked each one what he wanted to be, young Lorenz replied: "Seaman." And that happened. He joined the Lloyd as 4.Officer on *Hameln* #281 in 1922. Up the ladder until he was 1.Officer on *Bremen*. His first command was the reefer *Orotava* running to the Canaries. During the war, he was *Bremen's* captain, tied up in Bremerhaven. The day of the fire in March, 1941 he was visiting Bremen city.

After the war, he was luckier than most. In 1948, NDL chartered from the U.S. Military Occupation entity OMGUS the ex-Kriegsmarine minesearch boat M 611, and converted it to carry passengers on the Bremerhaven-Wangerooge-Norderney line, Heinrich Lorenz as Captain. It was a traditional Lloyd service going back to its founding in 1857, and the first again in 1919. As newly-built freighters got into service, Lorenz commanded them. Then, in 1954, when the Swedish-America Line and the Lloyd joined to put *Gripsholm* under the German flag and resume passenger service to New York, Lorenz was on the bridge. He married an American woman, a distant cousin of U.S. Ambassador Henry Cabot Lodge to the United Nations, their children U.S. citizens, with a home in Manhattan and Germany. Lorenz had several heart attacks. He died at Bad Kreuznach in 1966, where he was born.

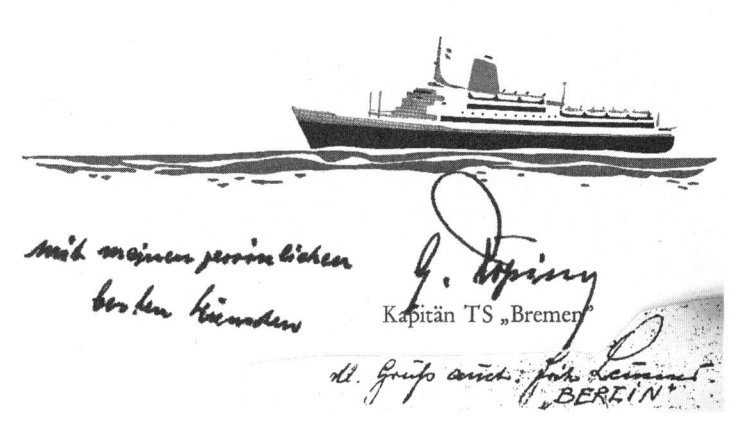

At the change of command in December, 1960, Captain Rössing transferred from Berlin *to* Bremen, *Captain Fritz Leusner replacing him on* Berlin. *Both signed the 1960 Christmas wishes. "And Happy Voyaging into the New Year."*

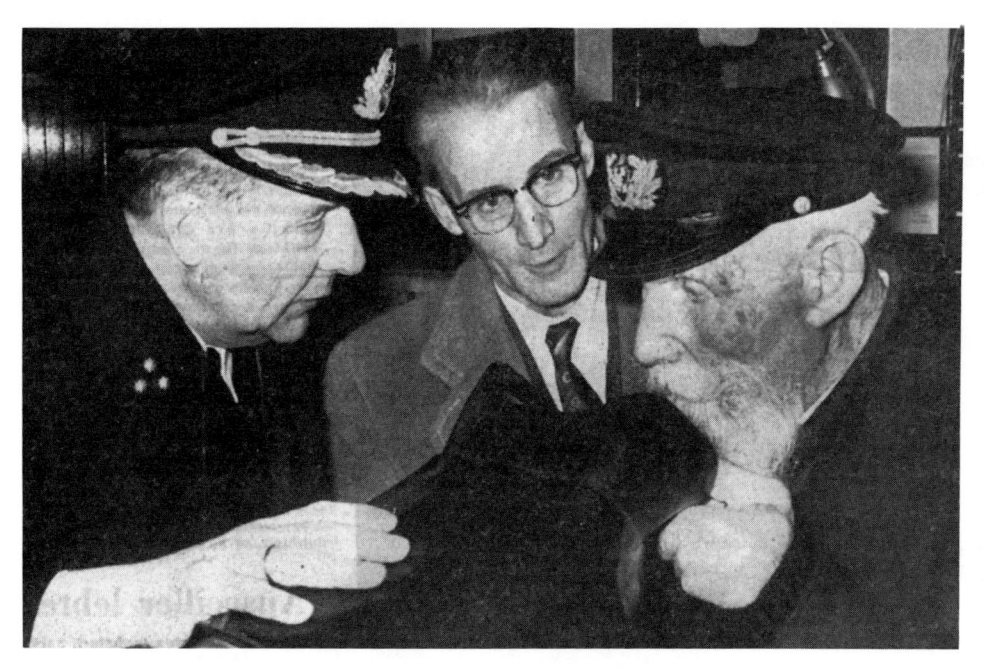

In April 1962 the oldest living Lloyd Captain, Gerhard Bolte, with whom the Author, Mother and Sister travelled to Australia on Elberfeld in 1924, visits Berlin *on arrival in Bremerhaven to meet his son, Hans-Hinrich, arriving from Canada. He and his wife brought along a cake to be cut at the Father's 100th Birthday. Bolte's oldest son fell in World War I. The youngest is a doctor in Minden. With Father and Son is Captain Heinz Vollmers. Ex.-Nordsee Zeitung, Bremerhaven. Captain Gerhard Bolte was historic in the Lloyd. At the centennial celebration of the Lloyd in February, 1957, he was then near 95, he it was who rang again the bell from* Kaiser Wilhelm der Grosse *which had gone under with the ship in September, 1914 when it was sunk off the Rio de Oro West African coast by* HMS Highflyer, *while recoaling for its role as auxiliary raider. The Spanish Government salvaged the bell and returned it to Germany in time for the centennial. Bolte had been First Officer when in 1897 it captured for Germany the Blue Ribbon of the Atlantic. See Lloyd Sails.*

Capt. Guenther Roessing

After a year's work supervising the installation of safety equipment on the North German Lloyd's new Bremen, Capt. Guenther Roessing is returning to sea. He will be on the bridge of the company's liner Berlin when she arrives here on July 14. His sea career spans forty years.

The reconverted Bremen, which was the former French liner Pasteur, is due here July 16 on her initial voyage under the German flag. Near the Statue of Liberty she will exchange salutes with the Berlin heading out for Europe. The Berlin was formerly the Swedish American liner Gripsholm.

Fritz Leusner, like the other postwar passenger-ship captains, served as officer on *Bremen 4* in the 1930s. He commanded NDL freighters in the 1950s as they were built, one the Turbine *Werrastein* #485 to the Far East. He took command of *Berlin* in 1959, then of *Bremen 5* in 1960, until forced to retire in December with illness. He was replaced by

Günther Rössing. Born in 1901, he joined the Lloyd in 1922 as 4. Officer. By 1936 he was Chief Officer on *Potsdam* #439, one of three express liners to the Far East. After naval service in the war, he returned to NDL in 1952 as captain of *Brandenstein* #481, the first of an eventual series of eleven near-sisters. In 1954, he put *Hessenstein* #491 into service, one of six Lloyd and Hapag combi-vessels to the Far East. In 1959, he briefly captained *Berlin*, then at year-end 1960 took command of *Bremen*. He made more than 75 voyages on her. He died at sea at age 63 in 1965 en route to Halifax and New York.

Heinz Vollmers was born in Lehe, near the North Sea, in 1922 came to the Lloyd, serving mostly on passenger ships to the Far East, also the new freighter *Nürnberg* #407 in the late 1930s. In 1950, he captained the former NDL *Porta* #397, after the war given to Holland. It lay severely damaged until in 1950 it was bought by F.A. Vinnen & Co., Bremen, renamed *Adolf Vinnen* and chartered to NDL with Vollmers as captain. In 1953, he took over *Schwabenstein* #488, first German passenger ship after the war, with space for 86 in solid comfort, one of six Lloyd and Hapag sisters. He stayed on for 100 voyages. In December, 1960 he succeeded Captain Rössing on *Berlin* when the latter moved to *Bremen*. He stayed on

Friendship and respect developed among the top commanders of the Lloyd and Hapag where they met occasionally, especially in New York where they used the same piers, 84 and 86, N.R. They worked with the same Inspectorate there in the hustle to get their ships unloaded, cleaned, turned around, loaded, refueled, rewatered, repaired when something needed overhauling. Also, sometimes they travelled on another captain's ship, going home on vacation from a cruise (as did Commodore Kruse, Hapag, after world cruises). Or, as Commodore Kruse and Captain Oskar Scharf of Europa *cooperated in the rescue of the* Sisto *crew. The 5-nations operation was under Captain Kruse's control, as the senior captain on the scene, September, 1934. See "Ad Astra...." and Title page, Volume I, the Author with the two Commodores.*

Dies on Bridge

Capt. Guenther Roessling, 63 year old veteran of 40 years at sea, collapsed and died on the bridge of the German liner Bremen as it neared the Canadian coast Tuesday night. The skipper of the 32,000 ton vessel had just phoned the engine room when he was stricken with a heart attack. The Bremen is due in New York Friday.

At a Maritime Congress in Bremen (early 1960s?) Captain P.A. Petersen with British Captains Murchie and Wiseman from Glasgow.

270 Norddeutscher Lloyd Bremen

her until retirement in 1964.

Paul Vetter was born in 1912. He did get sail training on the cadet ships *Herzogin Elisabeth* and *Deutschland*. In 1936 he obtained his patent for local waters, in 1942 his captain's patent. In 1957, he became Chief Officer on *Berlin*, took the same post on *Bremen* for its July, 1959 maiden voyage at age 47. In fact, most of *Berlin's* crew moved to *Bremen*. In August, 1967 he took command of *Bremen*, his eleventh ship for the Lloyd.

In 1958, **Captain B. Heye** celebrated his forty years with the Lloyd in a function M.C.'d by Director Dr. Johannes Kulenkampff in the Administration building in Bremen. In 1911 he had signed on NDL's sail training ship *Herzogin Sophie Charlotte*. In August, 1914 he was officer candidate on the freighter *Mark*, then at Shanghai. He transferred as a naval reservist onto the Auxiliary Cruiser *Kormoran*, seized by the U.S. in 1917. He returned from P.O.W. camp in 11/1919, and began at the Lloyd as 4. Officer in 1921. In 1924, he became training officer on the sailship *Grossherzogin Elisabeth*, then back to the Lloyd. In 1938, he was captain of *Stuttgart*, then of the new freighter *Lech* #454. He saw naval service in the war. After, like most seaman, he had to take what came, serving as supercargo on several freighters. In February, 1951 he was named captain of *Rheinstein* #472 at its launching. With his cadet-training experience, he was named captain of *Nabob* #480 when it was fitted out for carrying officer aspirants. When *M.S. Rothenstein* was similarly equipped, he took its command.

Perhaps Captain Heye's greatest pleasure in his career was that Mrs. Heye was the Matron of Honor at the launching of *Bodenstein* #505 on 16/10/1956, the first Lloyd ship so honored by a crew-family.

Captain and Mrs. C. J. Gebauhr, Hapag-Captain friends of the Drechsel family. And envelope addressed to him c/o of the Union of German Captains and Ship Officers.

Captain Otto Prehn was seventy when he joined on 13/8/1958 the launch of *M.S. Lech*, a fit occasion for celebration by personal and Lloyd family. Prehn had four decades with the Lloyd, in 1934 was Staff Captain on *Bremen* when Admiral and Lady Jellicoe inspected the ship at Southampton, see "Passengers." He compiled the 350-ships fleet list in the Lloyd's 1957 Centennial history.

Several Hapag Captains became friends during the 1930s when its and the Lloyd's ship had joint schedules, used the same Piers in Manhattan, and their shore operations were headed by my Father. Hapag **Commodore Fritz Kruse**, "Cruise with Kruse" from his days taking *Resolute* or *Reliance* around the world, visited my sister Evelyn Drechsel Aitken and family in Hawaii during those voyages. He was on *Bremen* on the way home on leave from *Reliance's* 1936 voyage in June, 1936. See photograph with him and Commodore Ziegenbein on the bridge, Volume I. Captain Kruse's flagship *New York* and Captain Scharf's *Europa* cooperated in the rescue of the Sisto crew in 1934. See "Ad Astra..." He lived out his days in Pinneberg near the Elbe, close to the ships, if not the sea, he loved.

C.J. Gebauhr was on *Siberia* when in 1900 Albert Ballin, Hapag's Chief, on a trip around the world, took the ship up the Yangtse to Hankow. He then decided Hapag should buy into the China coastal trade, including up the Yangtse in a German Yangtse Service with the Lloyd. "I was just 14 when I left my home in Königsberg and started

A captains' gathering in Bremen in 1954. Of the eleven there each third Friday evening, it's called a Stammtisch in German, regular meeting at the same table, seven are from the Lloyd. Sometimes they play Skat, a game of cards. On 12 May, 1995 the author was guest at the Captain's Table in Bremen. Eleven captains were present. One, Heinrich Behnsen, had served under Captain Walter Stein on Scharnhorst and with Captain Oskar Scharf on Europa. The author also was invited as guest of honor and speaker for the 106th anniversary dinner of the Nautische Kameradschaft Tritonia, Bremen, the Nautical Fraternity. A captain-member since 1924, my father was invited in 1953 to the 409th annual banquet of Haus Seefahrt. It was attended by 195 public figures, shipping and merchant members and guests. Of these, 75 who knew him signed "Hearty Greetings to our longtime always supportive member." Haus Seefahrt was formed in 1545 by eight shipowners and merchants of Bremen to care for Seafarers and their families who might be in need. The festive annual gathering is held in the Ceremonial Hall of Bremen's Rathaus, City Hall. The banquet is the world's longest-existing fraternal gathering. The fare is the same each year. Members and guests financially support the continuing tradition and needs. Guests are invited only once.

roaming over the world from May, 1888 until a few years ago," this written in 1953 to the Australian newspaper that carried an account of the stranding of the British sailship *Fiji*, young Gebauhr on board, and washed ashore on a beach near Moonlight Head, Victoria on a Sunday morning, 6 September, 1891. *"Fiji* had left Hamburg on 22 May with a crew of 25 under Captain Wm. Vickers with general cargo for Melbourne. To help raise money for the survivors' needs, I consented to be exhibited for three days at 'The Waxworks and Museum' in Melbourne." Later, a benefit play was given at the Theater Royal. "During an intermission, I was ushered to the stage. I was presented with a medal for endeavoring to save the life of a shipmate (Katline). One

man recited a poem; its last four lines: 'But so long as ships sail the sea; So long as heave the waves; Forget not Gebauhr and Katline, and the brave.' He was officer on Vaterland when it reached New York in August, 1914 and stayed there. Post-World War II, residing on top of the Palisades, New Jersey, he could see the Hudson and shipping. He became marine consultant for insurance firms and attorneys. I still use the Andrees Handatlas of 1886 he gave me, the most detailed mapping imaginable, and some books and postal items from his time as captain in Hapag's Atlas Service out of New York to the West Indies pre-1914." See also "North Atlantic Community...."

NDL Fleet
Ships 426 — 431

The Lloyd had from 1926 a share holding in **Stettiner Dampfer Co.** and its Orient Linie. This eventually became 100%. In the 12/1930 decision to split up the company effective 1/1/1931, NDL acquired the eight vessels running in the Levant service: *Stettin* ren. *Akka*; *Vaterland* ren. *Alaya*; *Deutschland* ren. *Aquila*; *Oderland* ren. *Avola*; *Marmara* ren. *Albania*; *Ostsee* ren. *Alimnia*; *Galata* ren. *Amantea*, and *Pommern* ren. *Apollonia*. Germanischer Lloyd lists these vessels as NDL. They were included in some schedules and fleet lists. Two ships were sold to the USSR in late 1932. One was broken up in 1933. The rest were managed by Deutsche Levante Linie, from 1/8/1935 were transferred to the Atlas Levante Linie, formed by Herr Richard Adler of Argo, to give Bremen a service to the Near East. NDL maintained ownership in the ships and the operating lines until 1934 the various absorbed companies were released back into their former settings.

The ships expanded the Lloyd's indirect participation in the services to the Levant, already in 1929 strengthened with the new *Agira* and *Abana*.

In 1930, NDL completed acquisition of the Stettiner Dampfer Compagnie. Its eight Near East service vessels went to the Lloyd; the rest were sold off when the enterprise was liquidated. All the NDL-owned vessels were managed in the joint service by the Deutsche Levante Linie. Five in 1935 went to the Lloyd-befriended Atlas Levante Linie, Bremen, two went to the USSR, one was broken up as over-age.

1. Stettin *was renamed Akka, 1935 went to A.L.L.*

2. Vaterland *was renamed* Alaya, *1935 went to A.L.L.*

3. Aquila, *ex-*Deutschland, *1935 went to A.L.L. While all the other ships wear the DLL funnel markings,* Aquila *has the Roland Linie black-topped stack.*

4. Oderland *was renamed* Avola, *here is in Bremen.*

Kythera *previously was* Alimnia, *also 1935 to A.L.L.*

Galata *became* Amantea, *1932 went to the USSR.*

In February, 1931 the burned-out München *#293, returned completely rebuilt as* General von Steuben, *later painted white and used mainly for cruising. Compare with original #293.*

Ships 426 - 431   275

On 27/3/1931 there was an exchange of vessels between NDL and **H. Schuldt & Co.**, including its affiliated **Ozean Dampfer Co.**, Flensburg. The following four ships were acquired in exchange for: *Achaia* #335 ren. *Troyburg*; *Pera* #323 ren. *Norburg*; *Fasan* #314, ren. *Heinrich Schuldt*; *Yalta* #316, ren. *Hansburg*; and three ships from the NDL-owned Hanseatische D.S.Ges., Hamburg: *Oceana* ren. *Hasselburg*; *Olympia* ren. *Breitenburg*; and *Ophelia* ren. *Mildburg*.

426. *Askania*	1931-1937		
Friedrich Krupp A.G., Kiel #443	1922	3367	92.60 x 14.33
Triple Expansion	1450	10	
29	44-41		

426. Askania shown here as Peruvian Marañon after 1937, her fourth name, pre-Lloyd, Lloyd and post-Lloyd. The names record for an NDL ship was Yalta #384, with twelve. William Schell collection.

Launched 24/7/1922 as *Nord Schleswig*, delivery 1/9/1924 to Flensburger D.Co. (H. Schuldt, Manager). 1/1/1931 to NDL, ren. *Askania*. 4/1936 ren. *Schleswig*. 2/5/1937 *Marañon*, Cie. Peruana de Vapores y Diques, Callao, manager for the Government. 1962 RLR.

427. *Münster*	1931-1934		
Furness S.B.Co., Haverton Hill on Tees #22			
	1921	4565	110.76 x 15.91
Triple Expansion	3000	12	
18	44		

Delivery 18/3/1921 as *Louisiana* to A.S. Norge-Mexio Golf Linjen, Tönsberg, W. Wilhelmsen, Mgr., Oslo, 4498 Ts. 7/3/1928 *Nord-Friesland*, Ozean D.Co., 3462 Ts. (H. Schuldt), Flensburg. 1/1/1931 NDL, ren., 4565 Ts. in Havana, "seaworthy for one

427. Münster and Askania were acquired from H. Schuldt in a vessels-exchange in 1931, NDL's way of expanding its Cuba-Gulf-Mexico service.

voyage," 11/1934, with ending of NDL's major services to South America to H. Süd, Hamburg remained reg. in Bremen with Key on stack. 3/12/1937 ren. *Corrientes*. 26/8/1939 LU at Las Palmas. 1/9/1943 forced sale to Spain as *Monte Moncayo*, Naviera Aznar S.A., Bilbao, managers. 1955 *Tajuna*, Cia. Maritima Madrileña S.A., Bilbao. 10/12/1957 broke moorings outside Mazarron en route from Valencia in ballast, and stranded. 1958 towed to Cartagena and BU.

428. Rio Panuco 1931-1934
Friedrich Krupp, A.G., Kiel #459   1924   5945   125.08 x 15.85
2 x Krupp Diesels   2900   12-13   * *
1-82 + 14 Pullmans, II-20   73

Launched 18/6/1924. Delivery 2/10/1924 to Flensburger D.Co. MV to West Indies-Galveston-Mexico. 1/1/1931 to NDL, continued in that service. Evidently LU in Bremen after 19/4/1932 arrival in Hamburg. With sister *Rio Bravo* carried Hamburg/Bremen-Mexiko Ship Posts. 7/1934 Hotel Ship at Kiel Yacht Regatta. With success of New Guinea-Solomons-Hong Kong route by *Bremerhaven* #280 and *Friderun* #325, NDL wanted to renew its pre-WWI Hong Kong-Sydney passenger service. After rebuild, including a tiled pool, ren. *Neptun*, arr. Sydney 6/12/1934 painted white, left 8th for Hong Kong via New Guinea, Borneo, Manila, back to Melbourne-Sydney. There on 7/2/1935 sold to Burns, Philp & Co., to stop the NDL competition. Ship had been examined in 1933 in Germany by B.P. engineers for the Sydney-Singapore route, but was rejected because of machinery defects. These had been corrected by NDL. As *Neptuna* ran to Hong Kong. 11/3/1935 the NDL crew went home on *Alster* #410. 6/7/1940-1/1942 chartered by Ministry of War Transport, London. 19/2/1942 while unloading munitions at Darwin blew up from a Japanese aerial bomb, 45 dead. The attack with 72 high-flying bombers and 18 dive-bombers destroyed the airport, docks, warehouses and eight ships in the harbor. Darwin was set aflame, forcing immediate evacuation; 243 died. Years later Japanese salvagers cleared the harbor of sunken ships.

428. *Rio Panuco* and sister *Rio Bravo* 429 were acquired from H. Schuldt in 1931. They ran with *Sierra Ventana* to Cuba-Gulf-Mexico. In 1934, they were sent to Sydney to re-open an old NDL passenger route to Hong Kong. Overhauled and painted white, they were renamed *Neptun* and *Merkur*. The Australian Burns, Philp, already there, bought them up. In February, 1942, *Neptun* blew up during a Japanese aerial attack on Darwin. *Merkur* survived the war, was a transport for Australia's participation in the Korean war.

Neptuna, *ex* Rio Panuco, *in Burns, Philp colors.* Don Gammon Photo.

Rio Bravo #429 *as the Australian* Merkur, Ian Farquhar Photo. *In Nautical Association of Australia bulletin 1981. Note Name Flag on Foremast.*

DRUNKS LOOTED DARWIN AFTER 1942 AIR RAID

—AUTHOR CLAIMS

The Japanese bombing of Darwin produced looting by drunken soldiers, an "attempted dictatorship" by military police and mass desertion by Servicemen, an author claimed this week.

He said a Supreme Court Judge had been forced to disarm drunken provosts who had been shooting out car headlights with pistols.

So many young men tried to force their way on to an evacuation train reserved for women, children and old people that soldiers with Tommy guns had to stand guard, he said.

The author, Mr Douglas Lockwood, was in Darwin when the first Japanese bombs fell on February 19, 1942.

In the 25 years he has lived in Darwin he has written 10 books and is acknowledged as one of the foremost authorities on the North.

In his new book "Australia's Pearl Harbour" published this week by Cassell Australia ($4) he says a senior member of Federal Parliament referred to the "panic evacuation" as "a day of national shame."

He says a Department of Civil Aviation official wrote in his diary: "The great stampede was on. People of all colours and creeds were fleeing in and on all sorts of vehicles.

"Soldiers, sailors, airmen and civilians were simply 'going through.'

"They were walking, running, riding bikes, driving cars and some were even on horseback."

"Awful panic"

Among the vehicles used for the evacuation were ice-cream carts, road graders, garbage trucks and sanitary carts.

Mr Lockwood quotes Air Chief Marshal Scherger as saying: "There was an awful panic and a lot of men simply went bush. I thought at one stage that they had disappeared to a man. . . . We were in a horrible mess."

Four days after the bombing 278 men were still missing from the Darwin R.A.A.F. base Mr Lockwood says.

During the bombing by 188 Japanese planes, 243 people were killed, more than 300 were wounded and eight ships were sunk in Darwin Harbour.

Much of Darwin was destroyed and commercial life stopped at once.

The death toll made the bombing the worst disaster in Australia's history. But Mr Lockwood claims that comparatively little is known of what really happened on that day.

In an interview years later the Japanese Commander Mitsuo Fuchida told Mr Lockwood that the order to attack Darwin "seemed hardly worthy of us.

Air Chief Marshal Scherger . . . "awful panic."

"It ever a sledgehammer was used to crack an egg, it was then," he said.

After the raids seamen and destitute wharf labourers were so hungry that they took possession of the hospital laboratory and ate 50 guinea pigs and rabbits used for medical experiments.

When a doctor told the men the animals could have had active germs in their bodies one man replied "Well we found 'em first and we cooked 'em well."

The few civilians who remained had to arm themselves to protect their property against looting by Servicemen, Mr Lockwood claims.

"Packs of Servicemen"

Dense smoke pouring from the liner Neptuna, which was hit in the back and caught fire.

stripped unoccupied homes and even took children's toys.

Mr Lockwood says a senior officer was later gaoled for 12 months on two charges of larceny.

"Dictatorship"

He quotes the Administrator, Mr C. L. A. Abbott, as saying: "An instance of the prevalence of looting is that while the Royal Commission was sitting in Darwin from March 5 to 10, soldiers were at that very time taking refrigerators, radios, sewing machines and clothing in Army lorries to the wharf and selling them to sailors for cigarettes and tobacco."

Mr Lockwood says: "There seemed, indeed to be a breakdown of the military control within its own establishment.

"The result was a period of chaos leading to attempted dictatorship by military policemen whose only authority was a uniform and an armband.

"Civilians were given orders in a manner that implied trouble for anyone who disobeyed. A number of men were threatened with revolvers."

But many items had little value in Darwin at that time. Some residents leaving the town gave their motor cars away to friends who were staying, because there was no petrol.

Mr Lockwood also claims:

• Many brave men in Darwin were not decorated by the authorities because of the top-level view, "You don't give medals for a schemozzle."

• Some women deliberately hid themselves to avoid being evacuated.

• Information received by the R.A.A.F. would have given Darwin 24 hours notice of the Japanese attack if it had been acted on.

• Wharf labourers were heroes of the attack but were injustly attacked later.

The famed Australian Journalist Douglas Lockwood told the untellable: that Darwin was looted by drunks after the Japanese attack in February, 1942. In panic, Darwin was ordered evacuated; 188 Japanese aircraft attacked, 243 persons were killed, hundreds wounded, eight ships sank, including Neptuna, #428.

429. Rio Bravo   1931-1934
Friedrich Krupp, A.G., Kiel #458   1924   5946   125.08 x 15.82
2 x Krupp Diesels   2900 (4200?)   12   **
I-82 + 14 Pullmans, II-20   73

> MELBOURNE, Australia, July 21—A Japanese salvage fleet arrived in Darwin today to recover ships sunk there by Japanese planes in 1942. The Japanese expect to salvage within eighteen months about 15,000 tons of scrap from the wrecks Mauna Loa, Meigs, Zealandia, British Motorist and Neptunia.
> **ex NDL's RIO PANUCO.**

Launched 7/1/1924. Delivery 14/8/1924 to Flensburger D.Co., H. Schuldt. Mgr., Flensburg. 9/1926 rescued passengers of Ward Line's *Mexico* stranded on a reef off Yucatan. 1/1931 to NDL, continued Hamburg-now also Bremen-Havana-Vera Cruz-Tempico-Galveston route. Evidently LU after 7 February 1933 return from Middle Americas. Ren. *Merkur* for 8/10/1934 voyage to Sydney to open service via New Guinea to Singapore. Arr. Melbourne 22/2/1935 via Cape of Good Hope. Overhauled, reefer facilities installed. Sailed 26/5/1935, from Sydney 6/6/1935. En route to Singapore bought by Burns, Philp to remove NDL's competition. From there, crew went home on *Saarbrücken* #299. Ship returned to Sydney under an Australian crew. Put into war transport service. Left Darwin 15/1/1940, grounded on East Vernon Island,

Merkur *in 1939 was running between Sydney and Singapore. Mail dropped off on the return voyage at Townsville with Netherlands East Indies postage, and therefore given* **Paquebot** *mail treatment. Ex-Gustav Lund Collection. Ship-Name mark from* Neptun *in 1936. Both ships kept their German names and name-stamps.*

got off at cost of both anchors and chains. 12/12/1941 taken over by Royal Australian Navy as victualling stores ship. From early 1946 ran to Kure supplying the Japan-occupation forces to mid-1948. Then overhauled at Sydney. 22/9/1949 left Sydney for Burns, Philp service to Singapore. Last sailing 27/11/1953 via Brisbane for Penang, Port Swettenham and Singapore. Left for Osaka for BU, arr. 7/1/1954.

From early 1930, NDL held 60% of the shares of the Hamburg-Südamerikanische Dampfschiffs Gesellschaft, in short known as Hamburg-Süd or Hah-Süd. In 1932 the next two ships were chartered and put into NDL's Bremen-LaPlata service. FV. by *Sierra Salvada* on 6/8/1932 Hamburg-Bremerhaven-Amsterdam-River Plate; FV. by *Sierra Nevada* 3/9/1932. NDL withdrew its three *Sierra* steamers from the River Plate service. *Sierra Ventana* and *Cordoba* then ran to Cuba and Mexico. Although they had better passenger space than the Had Sud ships, they were slower than these with rebuilt engines and far greater cargo capacity. When *Cap Norte* appeared in Hamburg as *Sierra Salvada* with Lloyd flag and yellow stack, instead of white with red top it brought angry reactions from the stevedores.

Sierra Nevada *ex* Antonio Delfino *of Hamburg Süd.* Nautical Photo Agency.

Below: Bremen-La Plata Seeposts used 1932-1934 on Sierra Nevada *and* Sierra Salvada. *In 1934, they reverted to the "Hah Süd" from whom they had been bareboat-chartered.*

430. *Sierra Nevada 3*.		1932-1934		
A.G. Vulcan, Hamburg #631		1921	13,502	160.25 x 19.59
2 x Triple Expansion	6000	13.5	* *	
I-184 II-334 Tw-1368	211			

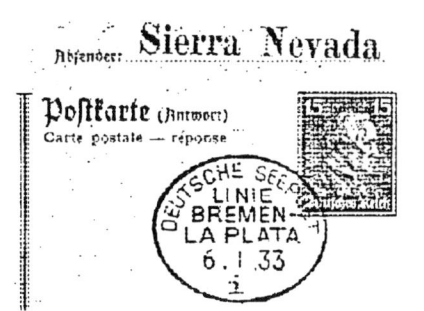

Launched 10/11/1921 as *Antonio Delfino* for H-Süd. MV. 16/3/1922. Summer 1927 given Bauer-Wach Exhaust Turbine, speed raised to 15 kns, 8500 HP. 1932 chartered by NDL, ren., 1934 returned to H.Süd with NDL giving up the La Plata run, given back its old name. 30/9/1939 left Bahia, got safely home. From 17/4/1940 barracks ship in Kiel, 1943 at Gotenhafen (Gdynia). 1/2/1944 command ship for Admiral, Submarines at Gdynia. 1945 evacuated wounded and refugees from East to west Germany, some 20,552 persons in five voyages. 5/1945 taken as prize at Copenhagen, rebuilt for British trooping, Cabin-200, Dormitories-843, 14,056 Ts., ren. *Empire Halladale*, IS 4/10/46 Anchor Line, Glasgow, Manager. The ship transported Australian, British and U.S. naval forces in the Eastern Pacific from Noumea to the Philippines. 30/10/1955 LU. 2/2/1956 arr. at Dalmuir for BU by Arnot Young & Co.

431. *Sierra Salvada 2*		1932-1934		
A.G. Vulcan, Hamburg #632		1922	13,615	160.40 x 19.50
2 x Triple Expansion	6000	13.5	* *	
I-184 II-334 Tw-1368				

Launched 8/5/1922 as *Cap Norte* for Hamburg-Süd. MV. 14/9/1922 Hamburg-LaPlata. Summer 1927 given Bauer-Wach Exhaust Turbines, speed now 15 kns, 8300 HP. 1932 chartered by NDL, ren. until 1934, when returned to H. Süd, back to old name. 9/1939 took refuge at Penambuco. Trying to get home, 9/10/1939 was sighted by *HMS Belfast* N.W. of the Faroes. Owing to stormy weather, to avoid great loss of life, the captain surrendered. Ship taken to Scapa Flow, managed by British India for M.O.W.T., ren. *Empire Trooper*, after repairs, now 14,106 Ts. 4/1955 to Thos. Ward (BISCO), Inverkeithing for BU. 5/1955 caught fire and sank. 19/6/1955 wreck raised and BU resumed. Christmas Day, 1940 hit by torpedo in convoy to Middle East, repaired at Malta.

Sierra Nevada #430 and sister *Sierra Salvada* #431 were chartered from the Hamburg-South American Line, which it owned 60% and replaced the Sierra ships, which went cruising or ran to Cuba-Gulf-Mexico 1932-1934, the same time *Rio Bravo* and *Rio Panuco* were running to there. The ships were more profitable to operate with their huge capacities and knot-more speed than NDL's smaller, slower ships. Both went back to Hah Süd in the 1934 reshuffling of major German shipping routes. NDL lost its South America services except to North Brazil. *Sierra Nevada* ex *Antonio Delfino*, Nautical Photo Agency. *Sierra Salvada* ex *Cap Norte*.

Cap Norte *before being chartered to NDL 1932-1934 as* Sierra Salvada 2.

In 1932, a number of the smaller vessels acquired with Roland, and formerly owned by the "Argo," were under the Hanseatische Dampfschiffahrts Gesellschaft, Hamburg. By decision on 15/11/1932, this name was changed to Argo Reederei A.G., effective from 1/1/1933, with seat in Bremen. "Argo" was back in Argohaus. Taken over were 32 vessels either on charter or as Korrespondent Reeder, managing operator for the actual owner. Most were later acquired by Argo. Herr Richard Adler, who entered the Lloyd with the 12/1925 absorptions, became a Deputy Director and head of the European trades. With the new independence of Argo, Herr Adler acquired a large number of its shares, and in time became the sole owner. In 1935, the Levant Trade was also separated from NDL, and a new Atlas Levante Linie, Bremen organized to manage the vessels acquired from the Lloyd. The Levant Service operated jointly with the Deutsche Levante Linie, Hamburg. Atlas operated with Argo personnel and under the direction of Herr Adler. In 11/1936, for legal reason, Argo's name was changed to Argo Reederei Richard Adler & Söhne. Like the Lloyd, the Argo and the largely owned Atlas Levante Linie, suffered the losses of war, and gradual rebuilding since 1945. The ALL has since disappeared. The Argo, from a peak of nearly fifty ships operated in the mid-1930s, now has only three vessels. The family firm is led by grandson Dieter Richard Adler. In October, 1994 appeared an almost century-history by Reinhold Thiel, whose Father was Engineer with the Lloyd prewar, and after with Argo. The book was published by H.M. Hauschild, Bremen.

CHAPTER 9

The 1930s — Chaos and Confusion

For the Lloyd and German shipping the 1920s and 1930s were like a ride on a roller coaster:- rebuilding from war against the hurdles of the 1920-1921 world depression; - the 1921 and 1924 Quota Immigration Acts, decimating the migrant inflow; - the 1922-1923 inflation that wracked Germany and still controls her banking policies today; then a new upward momentum in late 1925 with absorption of shipping lines NDL already owned or controlled, bringing in as Deputy Director General Ernst Glässel whose drive led to four years of expansion peaking with the Blue Ribbon *Bremen* of 1929 and *Europa*; the Lloyd though smaller than in 1914 again the pace-setter in passenger shipping.

Then, after Black Friday in October, 1929. 1930 spreading worldwide depression.

There followed four years of massive personnel layoffs, ships sold, laid up or scrapped. Into 1934 when some new building and economic activity gave hopes; then again a reclimbing to a lower top of the hill. Until the roller coaster went off the track and crashed with war in 1939.

In more detail: In November 1930 the Reich Government, beset by economic woes, demanded from NDL and Hapag repayment of the 50 million Marks shipbuilding credits extended in 1925 and due in 1935. The two lines could not pay, nor could their banks, in difficulties themselves. The Government became the holder of the majority shares of the Lloyd.

At the same time, foreign creditors demanded repayment of their advances when the U.S. made partial payments of $35 millions in 1930 and 1931 for ship seizures. The $16.9 millions plus interest still due to the Lloyd were never paid. The Reich had to help. It was able through partial payments and moratoria to hold off, if not satisfy, the foreign creditors.

In December, 1930 Bremen wrote NDL's North America director, Heinz Schüngel, that the Government was making public-employee wage cuts from February, 1931 and that private enterprise had to follow. "The shipping situation currently is so chaotic that all measures must be taken to cut costs. In consort with the Hamburg-American Line we are asking employees abroad to take cuts ... up to 7½%."

In March, 1931 the Aufsichtsrat, Board of Directors, authorized a 6% dividend for 1930, made possible by the U.S. restitution payments, and meant to paper over to the world the growing losses and near-insolvency. It was the last dividend for thirty years. Why would any one invest in ships or a shipping enterprise?

In December, 1931 President Philipp Heineken wrote Captain Drechsel in New York "We have had a difficult year behind us and the outlook is

Europa and Bremen continued to sail regularly. But many other Lloyd ships were laid up for various periods of time, here six in Bremerhaven 1931-1932.

The New York Times

NEW YORK, WEDNESDAY, OCTOBER 30, 1929.

STOCKS COLLAPSE IN 16,410,030-SHARE DAY, BUT RALLY AT CLOSE CHEERS BROKERS; BANKERS OPTIMISTIC, TO CONTINUE AID

The Stock Market crashed on Black Friday, 25 October, 1929. Here, as J.P. Morgan did in the 1907 crash - intervened with purchases of securities, etc. - business tried to stem the tide: "U.S. Steel to pay a $1 Extra Dividend." It did not work. Things went downhill, made worse in 1931 by Britain going off Gold, the Kreditanstalt in Austria folding, the U.S. imposing the Smooth-Hawley Tariff that effectively shut off imports, etc.

284 Norddeutscher Lloyd Bremen

Letter from NDL President Philip Heineken to Captain Drechsel. "We have a difficult year behind us and the outlook for the future is anything but bright. But we shall keep our heads up high and not lose courage. The Dear Lord probably will not let us go under, and will bring us better times. For that we all have to strive with our best efforts.
I hope in the New Year to come to New York and look forward to seeing how splendidly you have everything under control and how faultlessly our operations function.
Above all keep healthy and continue your all-out devotion to the Lloyd."
Ever your (signed) Heineken (President).

PH. HEINEKEN
Dr. Ing. h.c.
PRÄSIDENT DES NORDDEUTSCHEN LLOYD

BREMEN

23. December 1931

per S.S. "Europa"

Herrn Capt. V. Drechsel
North German Lloyd
    Pier Nr. 4 Ft of 5d th. Street
    Brooklyn N.Y.   U.S.A.

Mein lieber Herr Kapitän Drechsel!

    Haben Sie recht herzlichen Dank für Ihr freundliches Schreiben vom 11. ds. und die mir damit gesandten liebenswürdigen Glückwünsche.

    Wir haben ein schweres Jahr hinter uns und der Ausblick in die Zukunft ist alles weniger als schön, aber wir wollen den Kopf hoch halten und den Mut nicht sinken lassen, der liebe Herrgott wird uns wohl nicht ganz untergehen lassen und uns einmal wieder bessere Zeiten bringen, daran müssen wir alle mit unseren besten Kräften mitzuwirken versuchen.

    Ich hoffe im nächsten Jahre wieder nach dort zu kommen und freue mich bei meinem Besuch zu sehen, wie glänzend Sie alles dort in der Hand haben und wie tadellos unser Betrieb funktioniert.

    Lassen mich Ihnen ebenfalls alles Gute für das neue Jahr wünschen. Bleiben Sie vor allen Dingen gesund und erhalten Sie dem Lloyd Ihre treue Anhänglichkeit.

    Mit herzlichen Grüssen

    stets Ihr
    Heineken

---

anything but rosy." In July, the J.F. Schröder Bank in Bremen had failed, taking with it millions in NDL deposits. As a Lloyd Director, Schröder had done the juggling that made possible the mergers of the last six years and the building of *Bremen* and *Europa*. Then Austria's Kreditanstalt failed, helping to push Britain off Gold that Fall. And the U.S. imposed the Smooth-Hawley Tariff. This effectively choked off foreign trade and overseas ability to export to the U.S. and thereby pay Dollar debts. The death of General Direktor J.C. Stimming at age 55 in November, 1931 of physical and spiritual exhaustion from the difficult things that had to be done, meant that Herr Ernst Glässel, deputy to Herr Stimming, became operating chief of the Lloyd. It was he who had pushed the expansion of years since his coming to the Lloyd with the mergers of late, 1925. He was "Father of *Bremen* and *Europa*," as Banker Schröder had been the bankroller. Together they brought the Lloyd to its postwar peak of 147 high-seas vessels with 860,324 gross tons.

1931-1932 was the nadir for German shipping, with 36% vessels laid up. On the North Atlantic, the Atlantic Conference reported only 35,577 immigrants, but 103,295 leaving the U.S., the first time in any one's memory that there was a net exodus. In peak year 1907, 1,036,186 Tweendeckers had landed in New York from Europe. In 1933, only 23,068 immigrants arrived from Europe, the smallest number since 1831.

At the March, 1932 annual meetings of Hapag and Lloyd, losses of some M30 millions for the operating year 1931 were forecast. The avoid insolvency, stockholders were asked to infuse immediately M8 millions. The banks, by now themselves as badly off as their clients, asked the Reich for repayment guarantees. They got it. The price: Lloyd and Hapag had to reduce their capitals in the ratio of 3:1. Another reduction was forced in 1934: 4:1. Stockholders in effect had paid their all.

During 1932-1934, the Lloyd: sold fourteen ships for breakup; seventeen were sold off, many to the USSR. It was able to meet its own needs at give-away prices; two were lost; twenty-nine were ceded back to their original owners; nine to "Argo," nine to H-Süd 1934-1937; six to Hamburg-Bremer Afrika-Linie; seven to Atlas Levante Linie at its founding in 1935; eight acquired with the Stettiner D.Co. breakup went; three to the USSR, one was broken up, four continued on the Near East routes; the four acquired from H. Schuldt in 1931 were sold in 1934 and 1937. In 4/1933, Weser #290 was the first postwar ship built to be sold for scrapping.

The 1930s - Chaos and Confusion

Difficult times. In the Fall of 1931 some fifty percent of Bremen-registered shipping tonnage was laid up, sixty percent of the fishing craft. Here in an undated photograph carried by the Weser Kurier *are* General Von Steuben, Sierra Cordoba *and* Dresden *laid up in Bremerhaven.*

Lead story in Bremen's Weekly Revue: 12 January, 1933 - "Thick Air at the Lloyd." Some one at the Lloyd had blown the whistle. "It's an open secret that the very foundation of the Lloyd has become shaky, witnessed by recent massive layoffs. Also, there was intense feuding between General Director Heinrich Albert and his predecessor, still on the Board. Once, when the former Crown Prince visited Bremen, Herr Glässel escorted him to Bremerhaven to see the Europa *without even advising Dr. Albert. In turn, when Herr Glässel was on* Europa *en route to New York, he was delivered a letter addressed 'to the passenger First Class Ernst Glässel.' It demanded his resignation."*

> **To the Holders of**
> ## North German Lloyd
> **Norddeutscher Lloyd (Bremen)**
> **Twenty-Year 6% Sinking Fund Gold Bonds**
>
> North German Lloyd is faced with a critical financial situation, as shown by the letter to Bondholders, dated December 14, 1933, of which this notice is a summary. The Company is reaching the end of its liquid resources wherewith to absorb operating losses and pay interest. Operating expenses have been drastically cut. It is clear that the Company must also substantially reduce its fixed interest charges.
>
> rate of 4%, and, it is hoped, when the Company's business improves, additional contingent interest at the rate of 2%.
>
> Bondholders will, forthwith upon deposit of their Bonds under the Plan, receive in dollars $20 per $1,000 Bond. If the Plan becomes operative, the new fixed and contingent interest rates will be effective from May 1, 1933, said payment of $20 representing the payment of fixed interest at the rate of 4% per annum due November
>
> Messrs. Kuhn, Loeb & Co. and Guaranty Company of New York have advised the Company that, on the basis of the information furnished to them, they believe the Plan of Readjustment is, under all the circumstances, in the interest of the Bondholders.
>
> **NORDDEUTSCHER LLOYD (Bremen)**

On December 15, 1933 the Lloyd advertised in several U.S. newspapers that terms of its twenty-year 6% Sinking Fund Gold Bonds had to be changed, with a reduction from 6% to 4% in interest payments to save Marks 865,000 per annum, inasmuch "as the Company is not in a position to continue such payments even in Reichsmarks." Sharp cutbacks are being made as "the only apparent alternative (in) a forced reorganization." Difficult times worldwide. On January 4, 1995 the Deutsche Bank advised holders of External Debt of the German Reich how to collect interest arrears on Dawes and Young Loans of 1924 and 1930, and Dollar bonds of 1926 and 1927: The past is still with us.

The Reich legislated a M30 per ton scrapping subsidy for which the Lloyd got 2.3 million Marks. A March, 1934 Seaposted card from *Europa*, but photographed earlier, in Bremerhaven shows six NDL ships inside the harbor, all in winter or depression layup.

Another photograph shows NDL's cruise ships: *General von Steuben* #293, *Sierra Cordoba* #302 and *Dresden* #269 tied up in Bremerhaven. Arnold Rehm, perennial cruise lecturer for the Lloyd, wrote in his "Fahrgäste and Fahrensmänner," Cruise Guests and Staffers, "it was during the damned layup times of 1932. Nothing to be earned at sea. Everywhere in the world ships were tied up. It was a boring, a tedious time. *Sierra Cordoba* was tied up in the Kaiserhafen, its normal crew of 235 paid off down to a minimum twenty necessary to keep the ship in shape and safe."

The *Weekly Review*, Bremen, of 12 January, 1933 had a big headline across two-thirds of the front page: "Heavy Going at the Lloyd." Then "Internal strife, massive layoffs, and costly working at cross-purposes." It reported that a few days earlier freighter *Witram* #283 broke its rudder, unable to steer with one screw. *Roland* #372 began to tow her to Southampton, but the hawser broke. A Dutch salvage tug came in response to the SOS, asked in a "No cure, no payment" contract for M400,000, not more since *Roland* had towed the ship part of the way. But a wireless from Bremen ordered *Roland* to "let the Dutchman tow the ship, you continue." The final salvage cost came to M750,000, an unneeded extra payment of M350,000 at the time of ruthless layoffs. Pennywise, Pound foolish.

Savings attempts took various forms. Germans at home were ordered to eat a one-dish meal once a month. On board the ships it was also obligatory for the crew, usually a ragout (of leftovers?), and voluntary for passengers. The lines paid M2.50 into a relief fund for each single-dish meal eaten by passengers. It didn't work, because it brought only resentment.

In March, 1933 when *Columbus* was on a Mediterranean cruise, she was reprovisioned from Germany. There was angry response from the Italians at Naples: "Buy your food here; don't feed passengers refrigerated foods." That was not repeated. In June, NDL bought Hamburg Sued's *Cap Polonio* for breakup at the technical Service, Bremerhaven to keep it going.

1934 turned out to be the bottoming-out year. In May, when *Olympic* ran down and sank the Nantucket Light Ship she had only 158 passengers on board. On 17 March, *Europa* arrived with "159 chests of gold," Europe paying its debts to the U.S. since it could not pay by exports. At month's end, *Europa* arrived with 703 passengers, sailed with 474, a low point for the Lloyd. It marked the end of Second Class. Henceforth everything aft was Tourist.

On 16 November, 1934 at *Bremen's* arrival in Bremerhaven from her 100th round trip, and Commodore Ziegenbein's 60th birthday, General Director Dr. Rudolf Firle commented "German shipping is working with furled sails in stormy weather." By then, most of the 1920s merger absorptions had been sloughed off. In 1935, another seven ships were sold. Salaries still were being cut in 1935 in the U.S. organization. But a new building program was under way. At the end of 1935, NDL had 68 high-seas ships of 562,192 tons.

The economic difficulties for German shipping were compounded when in 1933 the National Socialists took over the government. This led to divided loyalties including among the Lloyd's ship and shore personnel. One official estimated that one-fourth of ship crews were Nazis, one-fourth Communists, the rest neutral, afraid or supportive of whoever scared them more.

The National Socialists did bring Germany relief from the depression at home: subsidized

> HAMBURG-AMERICAN LINE   NORTH GERMAN LLOYD
> New York
>
> December 29th, 1933.
>
> We refer to the North German Lloyd's notice of dismissal dated Nov. 15th, and now take pleasure in advising you that, in the reorganization of the Hapag-Lloyd staff, it has been found desirable to retain your valued services and the aforementioned notice may, therefore, be disregarded.
>
> HAMBURG-AMERICAN LINE
> NORTH GERMAN LLOYD

Happy News for some Lloyd and Hapag employees in New York, after receiving layoff notices: Evidently the new North Atlantic Gemeinschaft, was able to cut costs sizably, which was the purpose for merging the two lines' trans-Atlantic services. For those who did not live through the Depression 1930s the difficulties of the times are hardly believable. The New York Times *cost 2 cents. Even in 1940, The* United States News *weekly cost $2 a year. Unemployed sold apples for 5 cents at street corners.*

> **NORTH GERMAN LLOYD**
> **NEW YORK**
>
> November 15, 1933.
>
> Unfortunately general conditions in the steamship business are such that it is necessary for the two German Lines to effect all possible economies which are afforded by the closer co-operation that has been established between them.
>
> To our sincere regret this imposes upon both companies the necessity of giving notice to all their employes of the termination of their existing employment relations as of December 31st, 1933, and we ask you to kindly accept this as such notice to yourself.
>
> The new management will of course give first consideration to those of the present employes of the two companies who desire to re-enter their services on January 1st next, but as it must be recognized that the purpose of the re-organization is economy and that therefore necessarily not all of the present employes of both companies can be re-employed or all salaries left on the present basis, we earnestly advise any of our employes, who may see an opportunity to make another suitable connection, to take advantage of it.
>
> In view of conditions, the Directors of both Companies have very kindly agreed to pay an additional three months salary on the 1st of January to those employes who unfortunately have to leave us.
>
> NORTH GERMAN LLOYD.

scrapping, selloff and new ship-construction programs, but major problems for shipowners abroad, particularly passenger-carriers. The momentum of high earnings by *Bremen* and *Europa*, as much as three million marks taken in on a trip with two million marks expenses, markedly changed when it became evident that the Nazis were bent on conquest. Boycotts of German ships and goods spread around the world.

National Socialist reaction was to break up both Lloyd and Hapag into their respective services areas, such as New York, East Asia, Cruises, South America; the smaller the units, the easier to control them. Fortunately, the chairman of both companies, Karl Lindemann (of C. Melchers & Co., Lloyd agents in the Far East already in 1886) for the Lloyd, were able to negotiate a way out. The March, 1930's Union Agreement, see "Lloyd and Hapag" was amended to reorganize the various routes, with ships acquired from or passed on to others in the process. NDL got the prestige Far East passenger route, with three fast new ships that set the pace in speed, capacity and service. It had to give up South America except for North Brazil, its first resumed route in 1920.

Dr. Rudolf Firle knew that the Lloyd could not survive without the Government. On 11 May, 1934 at the launch of *Memel* #432, NDL's first new-building since *Este* #424 in 1930, he told the shipyard workers "As the rivets tie the many steel plates of the hull solidly together, so all Germans are insolubly welded together in the belief in the Führer, who forged unity needed by a land that must go out onto the seas." A tip of his Bremen Pilot's cap to the Government. But a mixed metaphor. No longer were ships entirely riveted, nor yet entirely welded.

Reviewing these years in a May, 1946 private letter to Captain Drechsel in New York, Director Hans Karstedt wrote "the protection of our staff from political impact and for the security of our shipping was the reason why it was posed to our officers and captains that becoming National Socialist Party members was to be not for personal gain or preferment, but to preserve discipline on board and to be able to reject any demands or threats by excessively zealful Nazi group leaders on board." These at first were mostly stewards and firemen, the lowest-paid jobs. Here was direct guidance from the Lloyd that being a "PG" (Partei-Genosse, member) could help them to do their duty to the ship. Acting on this, Nautical

Division Chief Captain E. Heims became a PG and thereby was able repeatedly to speak up for those in his the largest single department in the Lloyd at home and on board, who allegedly transgressed Nazi "norms," i.e., were not openly 100% in support. Scharnhorst's Chief Officer in 1936 was hauled before a Nazi "court" for rejecting the Group Leader's demand to dress ship in Manila for Hitler's birthday. When finally he acceded with, "then go ahead with your Christmas tinsel" he was reported. He was allowed to stay with the Lloyd but never made captain.

Several captains were retired early for speaking up for officers, including Captain Fritz Fuhr of Hapag's *Hansa*, Captain Dau of the *Deutschland*, and even Commodore Ziegenbein of the *Bremen*, "retired at age 62 because of too strong an intervention in behalf of one of his officers." Like General Erwin Rommel's funeral, a Nazi propaganda circus following his enforced suicide, Ziegenbein was got rid of "with honors." He actively kept in touch with crew families, particularly their children's activities. *Hansa* forcibly was renamed from *Albert Ballin*, the driving genius who had built Hapag in his thirty years as its chief to the largest shipping enterprise in the world. Because he was a Jew. Captain Fuhr postwar was back at Hapag's Nautical Department in Hamburg.

During this difficult period, the Lloyd captains like Ziegenbein, Scharf, Ahrens, Daehne, Wurpts, Stein carried on the Line's reputation for service, friendly contact with passengers, exceptional thoughtfulnesses at a time when anything German was suspect or to be avoided. The ships largely remained popular with an international clientele despite what was going on in Germany. Captains who sent down to the gangplank for known arriving passengers, inviting them up to the bridge, or their quarters, asking about their families, joining the Captain's Table. Even ship reporters, not used to this, when they travelled with Lloyd captains were treated as personalities as much as the artists, politicians, business people, sport stars, as old friends.

It was the strength of this very personal relationship so many people felt toward the Lloyd that was so helpful after World War I, and was to help again after the Second War to reestablish itself. As one passenger commented "There is another Blue Ribbon: the one the Captain (Ziegenbein) and his Sonderdienst (Special Services) assistant, Dr. Gertrud Becker-Ferber, have earned from their guests at sea." In her book *Acht Glas*, the Biography of Captain Ziegenbein, she writes that the Service "at booking time was informed of special needs or problems; we'd check the lists for any passengers we had before and knew they needed doing things for; or any travelling through tragic circumstances who might require attention or support. In this regard, I think of many Jewish emigrants whom I tried to shield from insults and offenses, each day trying to be a friendly voice." This was written and published in 1940! While Jewish refugees certainly did not prefer travelling on German ships, for many there was no option as everything they had was seized or controlled, with no foreign exchange available to them. *Bremen* and *Europa*, as did other ships, had Kosher kitchens for Jews and Moslems, the former under supervision of the Rabbinate of Bremen.

At sea, the explosive day-to-day frictions between Nazis and Communists led to arson, mutinies, even loss of some ships as Jan Valtin tells in his *Out of the Night*, Alliance Books, New York, 1941.

Ashore, typically in New York, the largest Lloyd and Hapag ship-operations port after Hamburg and Bremen, there were pier demonstrations, shipboard fights, and incidents such as one magnificently told by Irwin Shaw in *The New Yorker* in *Sailor Off The Bremen*. See "The New York Inspectorate."

National Socialist rule of Germany brought crises that kept Europe on edge: Hitler tore up the Treaty of Versailles, especially its military limitations on the Army and Navy; and he created the Luftwaffe; The Rhineland was reoccupied in 1936. The small group of Soldiers, led by an officer were told "if you meet any French forces who block your way, turn around." There were none and "The Rheinland is ours." 1938 marked the Anschluss of Austria and in September, "settlement of Germany's limited demand for the Sudetenland (area of Czechoslovakia)." Not expecting the Anglo-French cave-in, Prime Minister's Neville Chamberlain's return to England with a piece of paper: "Peace in our Time," German ships abroad were ordered to return home quickly.

On 29 September, 1938 the headline in the *New York Staats-Herold* read "War Panic Extends to Shipping." At the Hapag-Lloyd Piers in Manhattan, on Wednesday 28th September, *Hansa* sailed at 9:05 A.M. without passengers - 350 had been booked - and only what little of the 3000 tons of freight for Germany had been loaded.

It did have one passenger: A Pigeon named *Prince*, son of *Kaiser*, the German Passenger pigeon captured by the U.S. Army Signal Corps in 1918, and brought home as "war booty." *Prince* was being sent to Herr Jean Zimmermann in Coblenz; he had trained *Kaiser* during the war, now was being given the offspring as a present.

Bremen sailed at 12:20 A.M. on Thursday the 29th, ten minutes early, with only 272 passengers, 33 in First Cabin! Hapag's *St. Louis* had sailed at 7:05 P.M. the 28th also without passengers and little freight. It was the *St. Louis* that in May-June, 1939 was not allowed to land the 937 Jewish refugees it brought to Cuba, nor in the U.S. or Canada. It ended up taking them back where France, Britain, Belgium and Holland did accept them. Twenty had been allowed into the Dominican Republic. The calling back of ships and sudden departures in September turned out to be a rehearsal for what happened eleven months later when war did come. See "Wars II."

North River Piers in February, 1939, from bottom to top: Hapag's Hamburg, Bremen, Columbus, *French Line's* De Grasse *and* Normandie, *Cunard-White Star's* Britannic *and* Aquitania, *Italia's* Conte Di Savoia, *Furness Line's freighter,* Fort Townsend *and* Monarch of Bermuda, *357 000 Gross tons of shipping.*

CHAPTER 10

Ad Astra per Aspera

It is doubtful that men like H.H. Meier and Eduard Crüsemann, who founded the Lloyd in 1857, would have ventured lives and all could they have foreseen the endless difficulties of running a shipping venture that served and became known and admired around the world. Let alone that just as relentlessly two wars would challenge their successors to bring the Lloyd back to life.

If one could have foretold the problems *Bremen* and *Europa* suffered it is likely they never would have been built. The decision to order two likely Blue Ribbon vessels was made in December, 1926, only eight years after Germany's total defeat in war. Maiden voyages were set for April, 1929. That would have given them six months of total success before Black Friday on 25 October, 1929 catapulted the entire world into the great Depression of the 1930s. Instead:

In 1928, three months were lost with a strike by shipbuilding unions, postponing entry into service into July. Then, in March, 1929, *Europa* burned at the fitting-out quay in Hamburg, delaying her first voyage until March, 1930. Together, these delays cost a total of twentytwo months of high earnings, and with them a start on paying off the huge debts incurred. The final cost of the ships was 28% above the contract price through these delays and design modifications.

Bremen soon was to meet the ultimate test of a ship's design, build and handling in a storm worse than anything Captain Ziegenbein experienced in his seven voyages around Cape Horn under sail. He tells in *Acht Glas*, his biography by his Passenger Services Director Dr. Gertrud Becker-Ferber, 1940 "that voyage was our trial by weather. Hail and rain and snow storms engulfed the vessel. All the paint was scoured off the foremast. The ship was made small by the giant waves and swells and foaming of hurricane winds." Speed was reduced to five knots; then the ship had to heave to for hours, making a delay of two days, six hours in arrival. One unusually high wave buried the entire forepart of the ship up to the superstructure. Captain Ziegenbein later admitted he thought "this is the end." But the ship struggled free. Examination showed that the deck plating had been depressed by several inches. *Leviathan*, ex-*Vaterland*, went through the same storm, but at higher speed. Suddenly, an explosive crack, the deck torn apart across the ship's 100' width, and sixteen feet down the starboard side. Bremen's log tells some of the story: "Rough Seas, high swell; hurricane high wild seas, hove to; mountainous seas; full storm, hail, reduced speed; continuing storm, high wild seas, snow flurries; overcast, driven snow, rough seas, contrary swells." The fog at the end through which the ship had to feel its way to Pier 4 was almost a relief. "We were now under the care of Captain Drechsel and his shore staff." He sent ten tugs out to bring the ship in; at her bows, along the shore, blowing their whistles to give sound if not visual guidance. One passenger who valued the experience was Frederick H. Gibbs, naval architect. Twenty years later he designed the *United States*. The hull was very similar to *Bremen's*.

Bremen *on her seventh voyage in December, 1929 en route to New York. She arrived two days, six hours late. Captain Ziegenbein said later "This storm was worse than any thing I encountered going around Cape Horn seven times under sail." The ship averaged only 17.6 knots vs the normal about 26.5 knots or more. Storm strengths are measured on the Beaufort Scale from one through twelve. It is "hurricane", 70 knots+ wind speeds, waves forty-five high, sea completely white with driving spray; visibility greatly reduced, details from the Defense Mapping Agency, Hydrographic Center, courtesy of The Compass, Mobil Corp. R. Fleischhut Photo.*

Auszug aus dem Schiffstagebuch
Vierschrauben-Turbinen-Schnelldampfer
"BREMEN"
51 656 Brutto-Register-Tons. Länge: 286 Meter Breite: 31 Meter

Kapitän L. Ziegenbein

Abfahrt von Bremerhaven am 4. Dezember 13.18 Uhr (M.E.Z.)
Distanz: 454 Seemeilen
Abfahrt von Southampton am 5. Dezember 13.06 Uhr (M.G.Z.)
Distanz: 82 Seemeilen
Abfahrt von Cherbourg Mole am 5. Dezember 21.30 Uhr (M.G.Z.)

7. Ausreise von Bremerhaven nach New York

Dez.	Breite Nord	Länge West	Sml.	Wind	Bemerkungen
6.	49°59'	9°12'	300	W-SSW 5-10	Bewölkt, stürmisch, grobe See und hohe westliche Dünung.
7.	49°44'	12°00'	120	SW-NW 12	Orkan, hohe wilde See, gewaltig schwere westl. Dünung, lieg. beigedreht.
8.	49°49'	17°54'	225	SW-WNW 12	Anhaltender Orkan, gewaltig schwere See, hohe Wellenberge; liegen beigedreht.
9.	48°34'	28°00'	110	SW-W 10-11	Voller Sturm, sehr hohe See; fuhren reduziert. Hagelböen;
10.	47°02'	38°46'	446	SW-W 10	Anhaltend. Sturm, hohe wilde See, schwere W-Dünung, Schneeböen.
11.	43°05'	51°23'	587	W-WNW 8-6	Bedeckt, Schneetreiben, sehr grobe See u. durcheinander laufende Dün.
12.	41°04'	60°21'	678	NW 5	Bedeckt, mäßig bewegte See und Dünung.
		Rest	341		
		Total	3107		

Passiert Ambrose-Kanal-Feuerschiff 0.24 Uhr (M.75°W.Zt.) 13. Dez. 1929
Totaldistanz: 3 107 Seemeilen
Reisedauer: 7 Tage, 7 Stunden, 54 Minuten
Durchschnittsfahrt pro Stunde: 17,6 Knoten

Voyage log of Bremen's *seventh westward voyage, in December, 1929, the worst storm Captain Ziegenbein ever experienced. For two days the winds were 12 on the Beaufort Scale, as high as it goes. For hours the engines barely kept the bow heading into the waves, except they seemed to come from all directions, the ship in effect hoved to. One wave buried the forepart of the ship, depressing the deck up to seven inches it was discovered later. A test of* Bremen's *strong construction.*

292 Norddeutscher Lloyd Bremen

Fire at Pier 42, Manhattan of NDL'S München, *for hours the streams poured onto and into the ship, clouds of smoke rising above the waterfront.*

München *after the fire at Pier 42, North River.*

Explosion's warning rumble drove crew, officers, firemen, officials and cameramen, scurrying across the liner's decks. They jumped to the pier, to the decks of fire-boats and lighters. Here are some of them being pulled to dock from lighter's deck by the Ship's Captain F. Brünings and others. Daily News Photo.

With *Bremen* to world attention in service in July, 1929; *Columbus* with its new turbines and higher speed expected ready in December, and *Europa* to appear in March, 1930, a parallel weekly Cabin-steamer schedule was offered: *Berlin, Dresden, Stuttgart* and *München*.

München was lying at Pier 42, foot of Morton St., N.R. on 11 February 1930. Stevedores were unloading cargo from Hatch 6. It held 499 sacks Potash, 440 drums shellac, 386 rolls newsprint, 234 bales peatmoss, and aluminum. 204 sacks of Potash had already been put ashore. A sling with another load was in the air when suddenly fire broke out aft, followed by a big explosion. The fire spread forward to hatch six before the fire engines could respond. A second explosion shot deck fixtures and entire sacks of peatmoss into the air. Thick smoke clouds began covering the ship, so that at times only the stacks and masts were visible. The explosion blew out some of the side plating. Water rushed in from the Hudson, and from the streams coming from fireboats and tugs. One fireman was killed when one explosion destroyed the rudderhouse on the tug *Thomas Willet* and threw the man into the river.

One new report bears the captain "Fearless. Captain Drechsel, Chief Marine Superintendent of the Lloyd, risked his life as a ship fire threatened to spread to Pier 42!" The report goes on: "Hero of the shipfire. Captain Drechsel of the North German Lloyd was praised for his courage and quick action at a critical moment during during the *Muenchen* fire. He was running to the middle of the pier's string piece when he saw that fire was about to spread to the lone gangplank to the pier. Standing on it, he chopped with a hatchet at the line holding the gangplank to the pier. When it fell into the water, Drechsel was surrounded by smoke and flames. He hung onto the ship's railing, 40' above the river, until firemen could rescue him." Other photos show him climbing onto a barge to help injured crewmen. The settling of *München* to the bottom of the river threatened the Hudson Tunnel which crossed under the aft portion of the vessel. The tube began to leak and was found to have been bent by 3". After nine hours closure the tube was reopened. NY's fire chief assumes self-ignition, spontaneous combustion, of the chemicals cargo. Some Lloyd officials wondered if it were arson. Why? By whom? Damage overall came to something like $2 millions. The obvious question and lesson: Why were such combustibles ever loaded onto a passenger ship, knowing that back in June, 1900, the Lloyd piers in Hoboken burned up in large part because the thousands of bales of cotton stores there caught fire. One answer: the Lloyd did not have a freighter service to the East Coast as the Passenger ships had adequate cargo capacity to meet the demand.

In the next two months the blown-out port-

FEARLESS!—Captain William Drechsel, marine superintendent of the North German Lloyd, risked life yesterday to save the pier when on the liner Muenchen threatened to spread.

NEW YORK AMERICAN
February 12, 1930

SKIPPER HERO OF SHIP FIRE

Captain William Drechsel, marine superintendent of the North German Lloyd line, was praised last night for his courage and quick action at a critical moment during the S. S. Muenchen fire.

Captain Drechsel rushed to the centre of the ship when he saw smoke and flames threatening the only remaining gangplank. While he was standing on the gangplank chopping at the ropes which held it fast to the pier flames and smoke engulfed him and he was in danger of falling forty feet into the water when the gangplank fell into the water. Captain Drechsel clung to the rails until firemen rescued him.

Ad Astra per Aspera 295

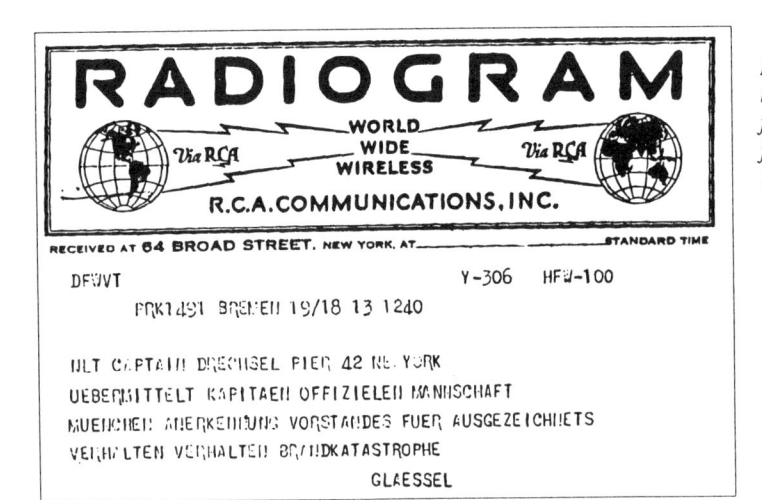

Radiogram from Bremen *expressing thanks to* München's *Captain and Crew for their heroic actions in saving the ship from a worse fate, and that of the New York firefighters.*

holes and plating were sealed off and the hull pumped out until the ship again floated. While being towed to Hoboken for temporary, repairs the outgoing White Star *Baltic* greeted her with three loud blast. The engines were cleaned and *München* returned home under her own power. *Deschimag* in Bremen rebuilt the ship almost entirely: The Promenade deck was extended a foot overboard. Before it had been flush. The deck was windowed in and extended all the way aft. Higher stacks for better draft were added; the boilers converted to oil firing, and Bauer-Wach exhaust turbines were installed. This gave *München* a knot more speed. With all that extra high weight the new-named *General von Steubon* was top-heavy and rolled more than before. It now measured 14,550 gross tons and was painted white for cruising.

Fire, at sea and in port, so often during conversions and rebuilding, is a constant threat. *Europa* burned out just three months before her scheduled maiden voyage. Carelessness? The cause never was definitely determined. Now *München* had cargo that never should have been on a passenger ship. In July, 1930 *Targis* #379 was en route homeward from the West Coast South America. The ship carried saltpeter, cotton, oil cake, zinc, honey, wines and coffee, fully loaded. Days after passing the Panama Canal, the Watch Officer saw thick smoke coming out of the forward ventilators. At the same time a hatch lid flew into the air with a deafening explosion and a sheet of flame shot out of the hatch. It was quickly evident the crew could not extinguish the flames. The boats were set out, first loaded with the ten passengers and some baggage, then the crew of more than 50 men. The smoke cloud was its own call for help. Within hours the *NZ. Rangi-*

Capt. H. von Thülen and officers, 1.Officer W. Stein at right, evidently after the rescue of one boat of survivors from the Vestris *sunk off the Virginia Capes with loss of 110 lives 12 November, 1928. Captain von Thülen's Father was a Lloyd captain. Von Thülen in January, 1955 attended the name-changing ceremony of* Gripsholm *to* Berlin 4. *R. Fleischhut Photo.*

tata arrived and took everyone on board. The thought to send back a few men to try to extinguish the fire was cut short by another explosion, and *Targis* disappearing into more than 4000' of the Atlantic.

Ludwigshafen #297 in the Fall of 1930 was more fortunate. Also laden with saltpeter, nitrates, copper, coffee, etc., the ship was on the Pacific Coast of Colombia bound for the Canal and home. It was the 4th engineer who on his rounds deep in the shaft tunnel noticed smoke. Dashing up to the bridge, he and the captain looked at the ventilators aft. Nothing showed on starboard. They climbed across the after hatch to port. Within seconds flames shot out of the hatch. Burning nitrate flowed across the deck. The crew hurriedly evacuated the ship, and watched as slowly, unbelievably the flames died out. They returned on board, pumped water into the aftermost hatch. Within four hours, the ship could resume getting steam up and continuing the voyage. At Balboa on the Pacific side of the canal a fireboat came along side, found it safe to let *Ludwigshafen* transit the Canal. Ex "Schiffe and Schicksale," Fred Schmidt, 1938.

Saving of life at sea often is an international operation. In October, 1913 ten ships saved 531 people from the burning, then sunk *Volturno* outside New York, including 150 saved by two Lloyd vessels. In November, 1928 it happened likewise. The Lamport & Holt *Vestris* lost its stability in a storm en route New York-South America. Even the battleship *Wyoming* had to turn to and ride out the storm. Near *Vestris* were *Berlin* going to New York, *Ohio Maru, African Shipper, Creole, Santa Barbara* and the tanker *Myriam*. The Bethany Beach, N.J. C.G. station followed *Vestris* signals and knew it had difficulties. It asked forty hours after departure and only 240 miles from New York if help was needed. "Not now" was the reply. But within minutes *Vestris* sent a STANDBY signal. This means "Please keep radio watch in case help is needed." It came at 10 A.M. Monday 12 November in 37É35N, 71É08W. "Require immediate help, HWNK." Boats already were being launched under great difficulties. There were 129 passengers on board. The ship had a 32É list; the starboard promenade deck was under water. Near 4 A.M. Tuesday *Berlin* arrived. *American Shipper* already was there. Others arrived. *Berlin's* searchlights swept the waters looking for boats, floats, and people in the water. At 11:10 *Berlin* radioed: "Have found 23, some more than 20 hours in the water. Continuing search for two boats and rafts, and in the water." No more were found. In total, 159 persons lost their lives. *Vestris* meanwhile had sunk.

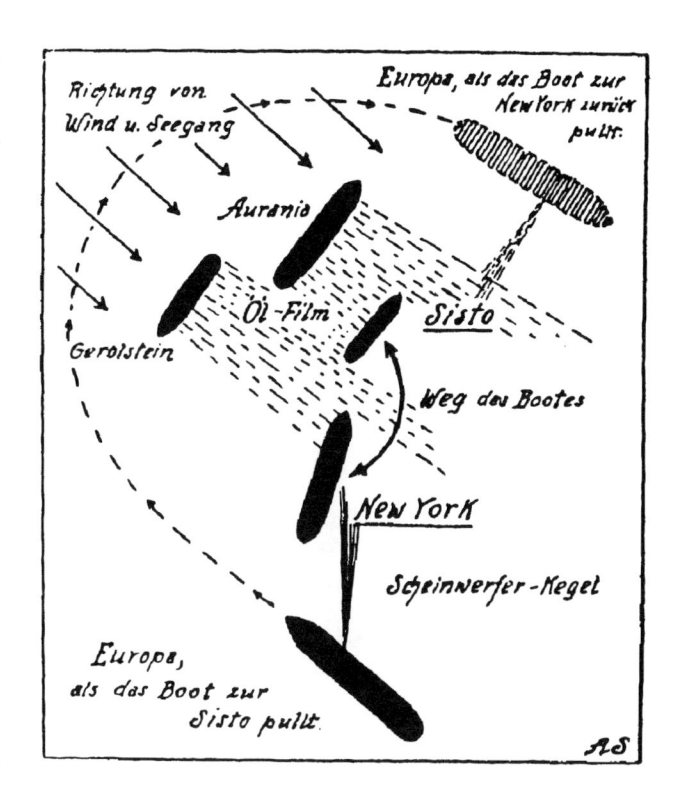

The maneuvering and location of the rescue vessels per New York's *instructions,* Europa *with searchlights moving from one side, to be behind rowers to* Sisto, *and the other side when they are returning with its crew.* Kapitäne Berichten, *Captain F. Schmidt, 1936.*

In December, 1934 another international rescue operation made headlines on both sides of the Atlantic. Hapag's *New York* under Commodore F. Kruse was the Christmas ship to Europe in the joint Hapag-Lloyd schedule. Every Wednesday one minute after midnight one of Hapag's Big Four left New York for Cherbourg, Southampton and Cuxhaven, the passenger ship depot for Hamburg as Bremerhaven is for Bremen. At quarter to Midnight Capt. Kruse bade goodbye to Captain Drechsel. The last line off; three blasts of the whistle reversing from the south side of Pier 86, NR, a slight incoming tide, one tug in attendance. From Saturday 15th the weather was stormy. Monday evening 17th a full hurricane was blowing. At midnight, the Commodore lay down "on the sofa in my living room, dressed as usual in such weather." (Captains Report, Fred Schmidt, 1936.) Minutes later the 3rd Officer entered: "SOS call from the Norwegian *Sisto* located about 49°N, 22°West." On the chart this is ca.220 miles from *New York*. Course is changed. "Tell the engine room to give us the utmost speed," perhaps 22 knts. in smooth weather. *New York*

Photo by Paul Cwojdzinski, *ship's photographer*, Europa *after the* Sisto *rescue. Note airplane stowed on deck below.*

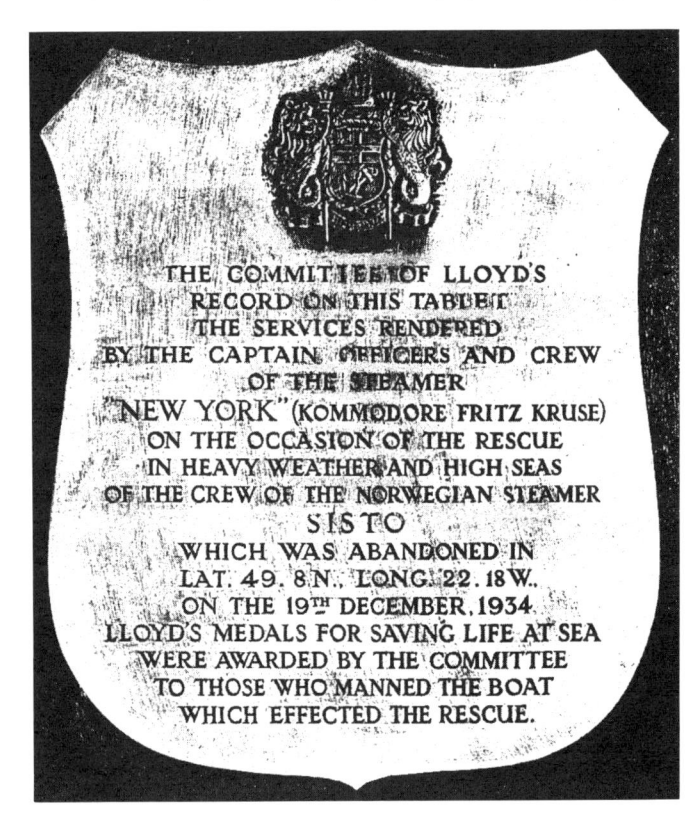

The tablet commemorating the Sisto *rescue by Hapag's* New York, *Kommodore Fritz Kruse. Lloyd's Medal For Saving Life At Sea was bestowed on Second Officer Alfred Wiesen and the ten men chosen from among those of the deck crew who volunteered to man the rescue boat.*
From Hapag-Lloyd's Bridge Across The Atlantic, *Otto Seiler, E.S. Mittler & Sohn Verlag, Herford, 1984.*

radios "Coming" and its position.

Sisto comes back that it is leaking, rudder damaged, drifting helplessly. Besides New York, other ships are on the way. Tanker Mobiloil is already there. It is pumping oil to quiet the waves. Big liners like New York, and Bremen and Europa have small hull openings for pumping out oil. This smoothes the seas and reduces foaming, noticeably eases the motion of ships.

Rain, snow and hail showers reduce visibility as New York approaches. Mobiloil is seen, already 16 hours near Sisto, now also visible, held barely above water by its deck load of lumber, en route from Pugwash, N.S. to Belfast. New York 2.Officer Alfred Wiesen, the only bachelor among the officers, is named as Boat commander. He and the First choose ten men from the deck crew volunteers lined up.

Meanwhile, Cunard's Aurania, Gerolstein of Arnold Bernstein Line, and NDL's Europa under Capt. O. Scharf, arrive. Other vessels reporting by wireless are advised they can proceed. As the sketch by A.S. from "Captains Report" shows. New York organized the rescue. Gerolstein and Aurania take positions upwind and spill oil to reduce wave action for the boat from New York lying below the wind and astern of Sisto to cross toward Sisto, coming as close as safe. Wireless from Sisto: "Can you take us off now?" In answer, Boat 5 is lowered. Europa behind New York turns searchlights towards Sisto, lighting the way for the boat rowers. One can see that a line is thrown from Sisto to Boat 5. Now Sisto's crew jump into the water; one after the other is hauled to the lifeboat, pulled on board. The last the young Captain Reinertsen. Red Light from Wiesen: It means "We have them all." Meanwhile, Europa has moved to the other side of Sisto, to light the way back to New York for the lifeboat. Sisto's crew is taken on board through a side port, then the volunteers, Wiesen the last. The boat is let adrift, New York's whistle announces the successful end of the operation. Others sound their thanks for New York's rescue deed, and "Safe Voyage Home." On Jan. 1st, 1935, Sisto is taken in tow but sinks two days later in 51.25N, and 11.32W.

In Cherbourg and Southampton, New York and the rescue crew are welcomed and feted by port authorities. The festive welcome is at Guxhaven. The rescuers are invited by Hapag and Resort Orb to a long vacation stay. From Norway they are given the Golden Medal for a Heroic Deed. Commodore Kruse is given the Order of St. Olav, granted to only eight Norwegians in the last thirty years and no foreigner. The comradeship of the sea. "When comrades are in danger, no seaman has to be urged to do his best," the Commodore said later. The storm scenes were taken by Paul Cwoidsinski, Europa's Board Photographer the next day. "Kapitäne Berichten" was given to his friend Captain Drechsel by Commodore Kruse.

Ships in the increasingly political twenties and thirties provided an easy target and means for political action in the entire world. Not many questions are asked of prospective crew members if they have a seaman's card and record of having worked for a number of years. In ports, seamen are given almost complete freedom to come and go just by showing their cards. What little is required as ID can easily be falsified. Thus it was that in the twenties the world Communist movement used seamen and ships to spread its propaganda and to take political actions. Jan Valtim in his book Out of the Night, published only in the U.S., tells how he as a dedicated Communist frequently used Lloyd ships to carry out orders of the Party.

One type of "Action" was to buy alcoholic beverages in customs-free countries and smuggle them into controlled markets with their high

Dock strike by the International Longshoremen's Association in New York outside Berlin's *Pier 88 in October, 1959. The ship's crew loaded the baggage left on the pier by the strikers.*

2 BIG SHIPS DOCK AS TUGS ARE IDLE

Europa and Olympia Manage to Come In Safely, but Not Without Rough Moments

UNION TO VOTE ON OFFER

Negotiators Involved Refuse to Comment on Prospects of Ratification of Pact

By WERNER BAMBERGER

The masters of two luxury liners battled wind, time and tide yesterday to bring their ships safely into their berths without the aid of tugs.

The ships, each weighing 30,000 tons, were brought into position through the intricate interplay of powerful twin propellers that were used the way a man might use oars to maneuver a rowboat, delicate rudder movements, the drag of ponderous anchors and gangs of men who tugged at lines both from land and water.

The dockings took place on the sixth day of a port-wide strike of 3,400 towboat workers who are to vote tomorrow on a new employer offer. The offer was announced at 2 A.M. yesterday by the Federal mediator, Robert E. Kennedy.

The masters of the North German Lloyd's Europa and the Greek Line's Olympia, both returning to Upper West Side berths from Caribbean cruises, found the lack of tugs harrowing.

Capt. Carl-Otto Efferoth, master of the 21,164-groos ton Europa, brought his ship into Pier 88, at West 88th Street, on the first try.

Other Ship Made 3 Tries

But, he had a worse time of it than Capt. John Katsikis, master of the 17,269-ton Olympia, who had to make three tries to get his ship safely into Pier 97, at West 57th Street.

Both captains started their docking maneuver at about the same time, shortly after 1 P.M., at the beginning of slack water—that 35-minute period in the Hudson River when no current is running on the surface as the tide turns from ebb to flood.

When forced to dock without the aid of tugs, masters of passenger liners require slack water, a situation that prevails four times a day at six-hour intervals. Under these conditions a master has some assurance that the current is only a minimum concern and that he can maneuver his ship calculating only wind drift and the 35 minutes of slack water.

In bringing the 600-foot Europa in, Captain Efferoth first put the ship parallel to the outshore end of Pier 88. Then running one of his twin propeller forward and the other backward, he angled her bow into the slip without touching the pier.

However, time of slack tide was running low and the tricky forces of an oncoming flood tide and a 20-mile northerly wind caused the vessel to gather too much speed and brought her within four feet of Pier 90—1,000 feet across from Pier 88 quickly the anchor was lowered and the engine reversed to bring the vessel to a halt.

Without Tugs, German Liner Docks the Hard Way

Europa, carried by wind and tide, overshoots pier and drifts near Pier 90 of Italian Line

To correct dangerous situation, hawsers are attached between the liner and her own pier

Then helpless ship is pulled, or winched, back to Pier 88 of the North German Lloyd Line

The New York Times (by Meyer Liebowitz)

By now the ship was too far from Pier 88 for the crew to throw lines to the pier.

A 15-man forward line handling detail ran over to pier 90 to receive the line from the ship looming overhead and then hurried back with the heavy hawser—a manila hawser 12 inches in circumference weighing 436 pounds a 100 feet—to Pier 88.

The line aft was dropped to one of the ship's motor lifeboats and then attached to Pier 88. Then the black-hulled liner was slowly winched across and made fast shortly before 2 P.M.

Captain Katsikis, the Olympia's master, was off Pier 97 at 4 A.M., when the tide was slack, but had to wait with his docking maneuver until the Canadian Pacific liner Empress of Canada, which preceded the Olympia up the river was safely tied up on the south side of the pier at 5:25 A.M.

By the time Captain Katsikis got ready for his first try at about 5:30 A.M., the strong north wind and the by-now running ebb tide forced him to abandon his attempt to try for the north side of the pier.

He backed out into the river, dropped his port anchor and remained at anchor until 1 P.M. when, on the next slack tide, he headed into the pier for the second time but was unable to line up his ship to his liking and backed out once more.

On the third try, he "ferryboated" in — heading his 610-foot ship into the middle of the slip, like a ferryboat coming in for a landing, brought the Olympia to a halt inside the slip sent his mooring lines ashore and ordered power applied to the ship's winches for the slow but steady sideway pull against the pier.

The Empress of Canada docked without incident, but her master, Capt. R. Walgate, used a different method of bringing her in — "bending her around the knuckle."

Worked Ship Up

In this technique, the ship is brought to rest against an outshore corner of the pier, held into place by her engines and rudder, and then worked around the "knuckle" by running lines ashore and "working the ship up" from bollard to bollard with the ship's winches until she is completely alongside.

Capt. Cornelius Rol, master of the Holland-America liner Statendam, had the easiest time of docking his ship. He docked in 15 minutes at the riverside end of Pier 40, at West Houston Street, at 6 A.M. by just lining his ship up parallel to the marginal pier and close enough to get mooring lines ashore without the use of ship's boats and then winched himself in.

It took skilled handling by Europa's *crew on board and ashore, and use of engines, anchor and lines to bring the ship safely alongside Pier 88 during the stevedore's strike. From an article in the New York Times, Saturday February 4, 1967.*

prices, such as Finland. The proceeds went to the Communist party locally, or even to Moscow from where such activities were masterminded. Among the Lloyd ships used for such actions were *Fredenhagen* #312, *Pleskow* #313, and *Amisia* #384+.

In 1926, Valtin was a crew member on *Franken* #385 on its maiden voyage to the Far East. As the Nazis came to power and spread their propaganda and activities, the Communists were the only ones who really took them on, in Berlin, etc., often in bloody battles. Even before the Nazi takeover, activists from both groups sometimes found themselves as fellow-crew members on ships. Communists were adept at proselyting non-German crew such as the Chinese who were hired to reduce crew costs during the depression, and could be scared into action.

Both on *Nienburg* #288 and *Anatolia* #341 Chinese mutinied, under Communist incitement, soon after leaving Buenes Aires for South Africa with cargoes of wheat. *Helgoland* #371 was set aflame by its crew in Puerto Colombia while loading, and then mutinied. All these "accidents" and political actions may well have been behind questions some Lloyd people raised as to the origin of the *München* fire.

Work stoppages are a particular hazard for shipping, always on a tight schedule, that allows little or no waiting. Strikes, among crews, in port the stevedores handling the loading and unloading, and in shipyards, often have their basis in political action more than the immediate economic demands that were given as the reason for striking. Until the demise of the Soviet system, local Communist parties often supported strikes, especially in basic industries, as a way to get support at the next election.

International Longshore men's & Warehousemen's Union on the U.S. Pacific Coast, long was considered Communist-controlled, if not in membership then in its policies, under their leader Harry Bridges. Nothing was ever proven against Mr. Bridges, nor anything else that some unscrupulous and dishonest union leaders were found guilty of. See *Rheinstein* #472 on the first Lloyd voyage to the West coast after the war.

In New York in April, 1960 a nine-hours waterfront strike showed the loyalties of shipping industry unions to each other. Thirty striking office workers at the New York Shipping Association representing 170 shipping operators and stevedoring companies, got near-complete support from a sympathetic walkout by the International Longshoremen's Association. It stopped cargo handling at 65 of the 86 ships actively working in the Port of New York Authority docks. Seventy percent of the port was idle. One solitary picket in Newark effectively halted work on seven ships lying in the basin.

Ships like NDL's *Bremen 5* had to dock without tugs under supervision of Captain H.M. Lampe, shore operations chief. *The New York Times* story shows him and *Bremen,* with ship's engines, and working of lines between ship and pier, gradually bringing the vessel alongside. Crew members helped to tie up the ship.

The passengers on the self-docking ships, aided by shipping companies staffs, had to carry ashore their own baggage. The strike ended after nine hours when the National Labor Relations Board ordered a representation election.

In November, 1956 Ceylon dock workers struck for a Christmas bonus, further contributing to the reputation of Colombo as an unreliable port. Seven of the major shipping companies operating Northern Europe to the Far East, including the NGL, had their ships bypass Colombo; in both directions. This meant offloading cargo bound for there at the next port and shipping it back when the strike ended. In the 1950s at times literally hundreds of ships lay off Lagos, Ghana, waiting to unload. Many had cement cargoes which over time solidified, making the ships further unusable. Some simply were sunk in situ as the cheapest way to get rid of them.

In early February, 1964 the *Bremen* sailed without tug assistance as some 3400 union tug, tanker and barge crewmen struck after their meetings turned down a proposed three years contract. The ship was heading for the Caribbean with 670 passengers. The most recent prior strike in Port of New York was in 1959, it lasted 6½ days. The longest major waterfront strike in the port's history was a thirtysix days tieup in 1957.

Self-docking and undocking by ships usually means delays. Because this can safely be done only at slack water between the tides at most a 35 minutes period when no current runs on the surface in the change from ebb to flood or v.v. Again in February, 1967 the *Europa* returning from a Caribbean cruise had to be docked without tugs during a strike by the same union groups involved three years earlier, with a very short time for turnaround, *Europa* and another vessel had to be brought in against winds and tidal current. This was done with ship engines, hard rudder turns, dropping anchors, shooting lines ashore and gradually winching the ship towards the pier, foot by foot, a nasty and dangerous business for Captain Carl-Otto Efferoth. He and the captain of the Greek Line's *Olympia,* also returning from the

West Indies, "found the lack of tugs harrowing" according to the three-columns, three-photos (of *Europa*) article in the *Times* written by Werner Bamberger.

Failure of a major exporter hurts everyone in the entire chain from suppliers, manufacturers, shippers and distributors. In 1961, the Borgward auto concern, founded in 1905 as Hansa-Lloyd, surely with the interest, possibly support of Dr. H. Wiegand, NDL Director, failed despite attempted bailing out by Bremen City-State. The firm operated three plants, employed nearly a quarter of Bremen's labor force. It was Germany's last privately-owned automobile manufacturer. Its closing meant loss of major export cargoes. See #480, *Nabob* loading.

Wars and revolutions can mean sudden closure of ports, short-term or sometimes permanently. In the 1912-13 Balkan Wars, the Black Sea was closed to Lloyd services from the Mediterranean, including cruises by *Schleswig* #181. In 1913, two of three NDL Caribbean cruises were cancelled because of the Mexican unrest. In late 1959, most lines with West Indies cruises, cancelled calls scheduled for Havana. The unrest there, and the takeover by Fidel Castro, made Havana off limits. It had long been a favorite cruise-port, as for *Columbus* on its last cruise in August, 1939. It was there its passengers were landed when the ship was fleeing prospective outbreak of war. In February, 1959 *Berlin* inside the harbor was surrounded by Cuban naval craft. To avoid any difficulties, Captain Heinrich Lorenz invited Fidel Castro on board for dinner. He there met Captain Lorenz's daughter Marita, on board for the cruise. *Saarstein* #474 was in Havana during the Castro takeover. It arrived 1 January, 1959, the day Fulgencio Batista fled. The news had been followed at sea. The wireless query to the agency brought consent to come in. With a general strike and everything closed, the German Embassy relied on the ship for food supplies. Similarly, the police on the pier were fed from the ship and its phone-lines kept open. All the cargo tackle was prepared for unloading. This began at 13.00 hrs. on the fifth, great excitement among

The highest recorded wave-action took place at the St. George Reef light outside Crescent City, California. At the Astoria, Oregon Maritime Museum is displayed a rock ca 2 x 3" which was found at the Lantern housing, thrown there by the Tsunami that followed the Good Friday, 1962 Alaska earthquake. That stretch of Northern California coast probably is the foggiest section of the U.S. Photo by Inga Spence, Courtesy Crescent City Chamber of Commerce, 1994.

THE NEW YORK TIMES, SATURDAY, FEBRUARY 14, 1959.

In February, 1959 Berlin *arrived late in New York from Bremerhaven having been exposed to forty-foot waves. It is impossible even to guess with any accuracy. Eight weeks later on a subsequent voyage to New York Captain Fritiz Leusner guesstimated two waves sixty to seventy feet from trough to crest hit the ship while barely keeping steerage way hoved to with her stern toward the storm. Four seamen were lost overboard when volunteers rushed to replace a broken hatch cover, the old-fashioned kind with heavy wooden boards with handles at each end fitting onto metal flanges and covered with canvas. The ship was built in 1925, hence still had these old-style hatch covers.*

the workers. On the 8th from 11 a.m. no more work: Fidel Castro was expected. No shore leave. The ninth again normal, and unloading. No cargo was taken on. Before sailing on the 10th a formal written thanks came from the Cia. de Almacenes de Habana, the warehousing (and stevedoring) company, for the ship's helpfulness. Under Castro, the ex-NDL *Berlin* #308, as the Soviet *Admiral Nachimov*, regularly called at Havana, rotating Soviet military personnel and supplies.

Things break, on ships and elsewhere, despite frequent examinations and servicings. On 13 November, 1956 *Berlin* left Pier 97, N.R., for Halifax, Channel ports and Bremerhaven, with 204 passengers. Captain Heinrich Lorenz noticed the rudder responded poorly. He anchored off Quarantine, ordered divers who in four hours could not repair the break. The passengers went to a hotel at Lloyd expense. The ship returned to the Todd Shipyard in Erie Basin, Brooklyn. There repairs were made and *Berlin* sailed at 6 A.M. Thursday. Sixteen passengers who were to have boarded in Halifix were flown to New York. The ship skipped calling there to get back to schedule.

When ships are in port as at Hong Kong, hurricane warnings drive them to sea to avoid piling up on shore. On 30/8/1959, the captain of *MS Rothenstein* #497, NDL's second training ship reported: "We left Hong Kong en route for Yokohama at 13.54 hours the 27th, draft forward 22.1", aft 26.07", so lightly loaded. Typhoon *Joan* had already been reported and its likely course.

Ad Astra per Aspera 303

THE BERLIN DOCKS AFTER ROUGH TRIP

Crew Tells of Pre-Easter Storm as Liner Debarks 535 Passengers Here.

The liner Berlin docked here thirty hours late yesterday after she had lost four seamen during an Atlantic storm a day before Easter.

The 19,100-ton North German Lloyd vessel brought 535 passengers from Bremerhaven, Germany. Her officers said the lost seamen had been swept overboard during the storm while repairing a hatch.

Eleven passengers and twenty-five crew members were treated for cuts and bruises during the rough passage. Two seamen were hospitalized with leg injuries.

At one point, water was three-feet deep in some of the passenger vestibules on the main deck, Chief Officer Ernst Hankewitz said.

2 Huge Waves Hit

Capt. Fritz Leusner said two waves sixty-to-seventy-feet high had hit the ship in an eighteen-minute period as she lay hove to with her stern facing the storm.

He said that the ship was then 1,300 miles out in the North Atlantic from Bremerhaven, and that the time was about 7 P.M. The waves were whipped by hurricane winds of more than seventy-five miles an hour, he said.

"I was barely keeping steerageway, about two and a half knots," he said, "when the sea crashed down on the hatch, bent steel cross-batens on No. two hatch and smashed wooden hatch covers to smithereens. Tons of water began pouring into the hold."

The first wave also knocked down twenty-five feet of portside railing; hurled a one-and-a-half-ton reel of wire rope sixty feet; ripped a seven-foot ventilator pipe from its moorings; mangled a companion ladder, smashed a number of portholes, and tore open a door to the main deck.

20 Seamen Volunteer

Captain Leusner said about twenty seamen rushed voluntarily to the foredeck to batten the hatch and make repairs. The second wave hit about eighteen minutes after the first, he said.

"We didn't konw until later that any of the men had been washed overboard," the skipper related. There was nothing to be done, he said. "It was impossible to put a lifeboat into the sea without sure death to its crew."

THE NEW YORK TIMES
April 6, 1959

Weather deteriorated quickly after passing the south point of Taiwan until the ship could make little headway in Wind Force 9." At midnight the captain changed course from WNW to South to avoid the center of the hurricane. It was too dangerous to head SW because of the many islands in the Strait of Luzon. As the barometer fell winds strengthened to Force #10. Around Noon the 29th the ship was nearest the epicenter, Force #12 and more, blowing a full hurricane. "From Noon we hove to, everybody ordered below deck amidships. Vessel engulfed in foam, windswept wavetops and rain. Ship moving heavily in high seas and westerly swells, listing as much as 40 degrees." This intensity lasted some 19 hours, at midnight was down to Winds #11, barometer climbing slowly from the low of 885 millibars. Winds #9 at 8 A.M. the 30th, resumed slow speed and course for Yokohama. As soon as the deck was safe, all bilges were pumped out. No damage or injuries were reported.

The wind strengths reported are on the Beaufort Scale from 0, the sea calm as a mirror, climbing to 6, strong breeze 22-27 knots, 10 foot waves, 10 = storm 48-55 kns. wind and 29' waves and #12 Hurricane, 66-71 kns., waves to 45'. "Air filled with foam, sea completely white with driving spray, visibility greatly reduced". This from The Mariners Guide Wind Speed and Sea State (courtesy The Compass, Mobil Oil Corp.).

Wave heights are variously reported, always estimates unless there is a specific object, such as a lighthouse, that is damaged. The tsunami following the Alaska Good Friday earthquake of April, 1962 piled onshore and broke windows in the tower of the St. George's reef light off Crescent City, California. A fist-sized stone thrown on to the landing around the light at 133' is displayed in the Astoria, Oregon Maritime Museum.

In July, 1993, experts estimated tsunami waves from a 7.8 Richter quake swept waves as high as 100' onto Okushiri Island in the Sea of Japan.

In October, 1993, 30 foot waves hit the *QE2*. "Looking out the windows we could see nothing but sea" said one crewman. The piano inserted in 4½ metal housings, jumped out of these. All three legs broke.

Guiness credits the highest recorded sea wave as measured from the USS *Ramapo* en route Manila-San Diego in February, 1933 during a 68 knts. hurricane. The wave was computed as 112' from trough to crest.

In April, 1993 a weather satellite measured 40' waves in the Atlantic as the Northeast was swept by blizzards.

The *New York Times*, 6 April 1959 recounts *Berlin's* loss of four seamen to 60-70 foot high waves. Captain Fritz Leusner's estimate, driven by hurricane winds above 75 mph in 49.43N, 23.15W. The first wave smashed two hatch covers so that water poured into the hold, also doing considerable other damage. One estimate is that a fifteen foot wave washes some one thousand tons of water onto a ship. Of the some twenty crewmen who rushed to seal the hole, a second wave swept four overboard. That was not known for several

On her second voyage in September Liberte *encounted such heavy weather that water got into the mail room. Damaged mail received this notice inserted or affixed on the back. The letter had been been mailed in Boston on 2 September for trans-Atlantic air mail. It was back-stamped* **Bahnpostamt 10,** *Railway Mail Office in Cologne on the fourth, then caught* Liberte *at Le Havre the fifth. Note use of Railway Mail Service Postmark at Boston's Air Field.*

minutes, and then nothing could have been done, even had they been visible in the driven seas: August Kammeier 25, Friedel Lüdders 37, Helmuth Engelke 18, Herbert Schmidt 19, he a member of *Berlin's* soccer team. It had won for the second year in a row the Atlantic Trophy. Later, *Berlin* ran that string to four straight victories. The ship cancelled its call at Halifax and reached New York thirty hours late. During that voyage, Dr. Gottfried Wurlitzer, 36, a weather expert, tested a weather-reporting facsimile device: plotting weather maps from radio transmission signals. He considered the test, the first ever from a passenger liner, a success.

In January, 1966 *Berlin's* running mate *Bremen 5*, was hit by waves in two separate gales. One smashed three thick safety-glass windows on the bridge, some 102′ above the water line. Captain Heinz Vollmers spent three nights on the bridge. (See *Weimar* #80 and *Graf Bismarck* #32 Volume I). A similar accident occurred during a West Indies cruise in 1965 (or 66), a bridge window broken, injuring the captain. During *Bremen's* #511 fitting out at the Bremer Vulkan in 1959, two shipyard workers and two from the Lloyd were killed while working inside the funnel shaft, when a pressure valve failed and hot steam exploded.

In 1960, the NDL Agency in Valparaiso reported to Bremen about the coastwide seaquake-earthquake-tsunamis that ravaged all towns from Temuco to Puerto Montt, a major German settlement area. One sees blonde, red-cheeked girls there, my wife Ilona and I did, with long braids, serving in a pastry shop, and a congregation coming out of church speaking nothing but German.

The U.S. Akron *above Brooklyn in the 1930's. One can read U.S. Navy on the lower side.* Author's Photo.

Postwar, a number of old Lloyd tugs were sold to a German-founded port-towing company in Talcahuano, Chile.

Some ships are just plain unlucky, including NDL *Europa 3*: With *Bremen* delayed three months by a shipyard strikes, four months before postponed completion she burned out, delaying entry into service by nine months. After serving briefly as a transport returning U.S. forces from Germany in 1945, she was turned over to the French as compensation for their *Normandie*, burned out in New York in February, 1942 while being converted to a naval transport. On 8 December, 1946 in a storm the ship then without a name broke loose at Le Havre, smashed into the sunken hulk of the prewar burned out *Paris*, and, with holes in her own hull, settled to the bottom. It took four months to raise her. In October, 1949 during reconstruction, she had a major fire in the rebuilt passenger quarters. This further delayed her August, 1950 her maiden voyage as *Liberte*.

In February, 1956 leaving Le Havre for Southampton and New York with 1075 passengers *Liberte* in fog ran onto a sandbank outside the harbor. It took a fleet of tugs six hours to pull her free. Then C.G.T. had to cancel the February 17th and March sailings because of "mechanical difficulties." *Europa's* original wiring was inadequate for her needs, but this deficiency suppos-

Lahnstein #473 with a patch over the hole in the Great Lakes collision. The service area was filled with dangers and uncertainties: would ships get out again before being shut in for the winter? Emsstein #476 in 1966 was a near loss.

306   Norddeutscher Lloyd Bremen

edly had been remedied in the French rebuilding.

In December, 1956 a pounding by three successive waves forced *Liberte's* captain to turn back to Le Havre after picking up passengers at Southampton. The waves crashed over the bow around 6 A.M. Three cargo booms were twisted out of shape. A hatch cover was smashed, and considerable water was taken inboard. There were 533 passengers on board. The captain preferred to return to port to check the ship's seaworthiness, and for repairs.

In August, 1957 *Liberté* lost "many hours" off Southampton when a propeller became ensnarled in a steel cable on a channel buoy.

In New York on 12/12/1959 another small "mechanical difficulty" delayed departure for some six hours, discomfiting the 1275 passengers already on the pier for the Noon sailing. When *Liberte* got to Le Havre, C.G.T. announced that the scheduled annual overhaul from 2 January to February 16, 1960 had to be extended into April, cancelling three sailings.

In September, 1960 an engineers' strike delayed departure from Le Havre for the 1050 passengers already on board. In January, 1961 during the annual overhaul, a strong wind pushed *Liberte* against another C.G.T. vessel docked alongside. With damage to both ships. In May, 1961 heavy fog delayed *Liberte's* docking in New York by an hour, *QE 2's* by 4½ hours. The next month, on 21st June, a dispute with a steward at first delayed, then forced cancellation of the sailing from Le Havre with 1235 passengers. The ship had transferred an unpopular steward table captain from First Class. This led the other stewards to walk out. At 3 P.M., an hour after scheduled departure time, the sailing was cancelled. *Liberte* finally sailed on 7th July.

That was the last straw. On 16/11/1961 *Liberte* was offered for sale, presumably for scrapping. On 30 December an Italian breaking yard bought her. On 25 January, 1962 she left in tow for La Spezia. Almost a thirty-years life, one interrupted by major and minor accidents, by war and by personnel strife. *Life* called it "an embarrassing reputation as a hard-luck ship."

In 1925, the U.S. Navy's *Shenandoah* crashed, Commander C.E. Rosendahl a survivor, he subsequently headed the USN dirigible program. In 1928, the Italian *Italia* was lost in the Arctic, Roald Amundsen losing his life in the attempt to rescue the crew. In the 1930s, the British R100 and R101 were lost. And on 4/4/1933, the U.S. Navy's *Akron* exploded in the air, it the largest in the world with its sister *Macon*. The Danzig-flag tanker *Phoebus* saved the survivors from the Atlantic off New York.

The loss of *Hindenburg* on 7 May, 1937 would not have happened had the U.S. not prohibited export of Helium Gas to National Socialist Germany. Instead, it had to use explosive hydrogen.

On 11 May, 1937 services were held on Hapag-Lloyd Pier 86, Manhattan for thirty of thirty-six victims who died, these to be returned to Germany on the *New York*, Captain T. Koch. Mr. and Mrs. John Pannes, Hapag-Lloyd Passenger Agent in New York, were among the victims.

Captain H. Bockelmann, of Hapag-Lloyd's Pier Crew, afterwards wrote briefly about that day. "It was a beautiful sunny day, perfect for the landing of *Hindenburg* and its 'cargo'. A quick turnaround was scheduled, the airship to leave again the next morning, so our Pier Service was called in. I went to Lakehurst with my Boatswain and a crew of twelve to help with the landing, undocking ropes or anything needed. As *Hindenburg* approached, we could see our Passenger Agent John Pannes and wife waving from a window. Then .... "…. Pastor Brückner of the Seamen's Mission in Hoboken spoke in English and German. The orchestra from the *New York* played the music expressive of such tragic occasions. It was the end of the Dirigible Era. Although periodically ideas are floated to build huge flying "cruise ships." Herr Pannes is in the group photo on *New York* celebrating *Hindenburg's* first arrival in New York: "The Lloyd Flies."

After a Blimp accident in Hayward, California in February, 1995 retired Navy Pilot Ira Rimson, a specialist in reconstructing accidents, said "mooring one of those suckers (Blimps, and worse for Dirigibles) is kind of like threading a tiger's tail through a slot machine. In Lakehurst, the Navy would send a helicopter up and have it sit on top of the Blimp and hold it down until the ground crew could get it moored to the mast."

Ad Astra per Aspera

NDL Fleet:
Ships 432— 443

No new ships were built for NDL after the completion of *Este* in 8/1930 owing to the depression, the sloughing off of most of the smaller firms and share ownerships acquired during the 1920s, and the overall decentralization of German shipping. This included massive layups, scrappings and sell-offs, heavily to the USSR.

The Strength Through Joy Movement was founded in late 1933 as a National Socialist effort to enlist workers after their union groups had been politicized. From 1934 on low-cost cruises offered workers, predominantly from inland, their first opportunity to go to sea. Of the ten ships used, chartered or bought, five were from NDL or ex-NDL. See "Fun and Games at Sea." The others came from the Hamburg-American Line and the Hamburg South-American Line. The largest were two ships built in 1938-1939, designed also for use as Naval Transports or hospital ships. Only two survived the war for further use by the victors.

In 1934-1937, nine ships went to Hamburg-Süd. They remained registered in Bremen with the key on their stacks, just as with the Hamburg-Bremer Afrika Line ships managed from Hamburg.

#251 *Holstein* ren. *Curityba*
#297 *Ludwigshafen* ren. *Tijuca*
#369 *Rapot* ren. *Santos*
#382 *Witell* ren. *Rosario*
#388 *Berengar* ren. *Petropolis*
#289 *Madrid* kept its name
#339 *Alrich* ren. *Sao Paulo*
#374 *Grandon* ren. *Patagonia*
#383 *Witram* ren. *Buenos Aires*
#427 *Münster* ren. *Corrientes*

As in the Hamburg-Westafrika services dozens of ships served routes to South America with a variety of Sea Posts, the most common these oval **Hamburg-Südamerika,** the one with Roman numerals already used pre-1914, the one with letters used from 1923. In 1935, a double-ring Ship Post was issued with single and some double letters.

These latter were almost entirely used on freighters. Only an occasional Sea or Ship Post is known from the nine Lloyd freighters that were transferred to the **Hamburg-Südamerikanische** D.S. Ges. 1934-1937.

432. *Memel*	1934-1940		
Deschimag Weserwerft			
#890, Bremen	1934	3183	118.05 X 15.32
2 x Weser Diesels	3500	14.2	
8	38		

Memel's Maier Bow made her three meters longer, otherwise she was the first of eight almost-sisters built 1934-1939, 115.5 x 15.3 meters, the exact overall dimensions of NDL's six *Minden* #282 class ships 1921-1922. Two *Memel* types started during the war were four meters longer to accommodate the higher speed; as were the six *Rheinsteins* #472 in 1951, allowing a third hatch. Coincidence, or an optimum hull size for various routes? Ordered by Deutsche Levante Linie as *Cairo* and 11/5/1934 so launched; 5/9/1934 as *Memel* to NDL for Cuba-Mexico service. 11/7/1940 sold to USSR, ren. *Viborg* 4/7/1941 sunk in Gulf of Finland by Finnish submarine *Vesikko*.

432. Memel was the lead ship in a series of vessels with gradual changes in cargo-handling arrangements, slight super-structure differences, but overall the same hull dimensions as the seven ships of the Minden #282 *class of 1921-1922, and the* Rheinstein *class of 1951; its projecting cruiser bow the reason for the greater length. Memel and Saar #437 had Maier bows, the later ships did not.*

Saar #437 *H.J. Mayburg,* Bremen Photo. *Leaving Hamburg. It served as barrage clearer in the war, was sunk at Brest by aerial bomb.*

After the chartering of #430-431 during 1932-1934, the first vessels added were #433 and #434, bought in 1934 and completely rebuilt for the prestige service to the West Coast USA-Canada. They were motor ships, as were all freighters from then on, newly built or purchases.

433. *Elbe 2.*	1934-1941		
Deutsche Werft, Kiel #215	1929	6606/9180	140.60x18.47
Diesel Engines	11,000	* *	17
17	59-46		

Launched 26/5/1929 as *Sud Expreso*, 29/7 completed for Linea Sud Americana, Ivar Christensen, Oslo, manager, two stacks. The ship failed to meet contract speed and was returned to the shipyard and LU. 1/1931 to the Deutsche Revisions & Treuhandbank A.G. (trustee for in-debt shipping), named *Holstein*, no owner listed in Lloyd's, on charter to Arnold Bernstein? So listed but crossed out in Lloyd's. 6/1931 - 3/11/1931 ran as *Wenatchee Star* in charter by the Blue Star Line to the Pacific Northwest coast, again LU in Kiel. 1933 entered for Hanseatische Schiffahrt Betreuungs (Trustee) Ges., Bremen. 1934 bought by NDL, rebuilt and reengined by Deutsche Werft, now 148.53 x 18.47 (155.54 O.A.) 9180 Ts., 17 kns, 17 passengers. 15/11/1931 IS as *Elbe*, MV. 22/11/1931 to Vancouver. 3/9/1939 LU in Yokohama 20/4/1941 left Dairen 6/6/1941 during *Bismarck* action sunk ca 900 miles NW off the Cape Verdes by aircraft from *HMS Eagle*. Three lifeboats drifted 12, 14 and 26 days before rescue.

Elbe #433 and Weser #434 were completed in 1929 for a Norwegian service New York-South America. Both failed to meet contract specifications. They were variously used or laid up. Under depression emergency financing they were bought by NDL for use on the very competitive West Coast North America route. Re-engining and the necessary longer forebody made them with 17 knots by far the fastest on that run: carrying valuable refrigerated cargoes.

Above: Elbe *entering Vancouver*, World Ship Society Photo. *The ship was sunk by aircraft from the carrier HMS Eagle during the Bismarck action in June, 1941. Below: And as originally built as* Sud Expreso, *taken by the author at Staten Island, near where New York harbor Quarantine Station is, in 1929.*

German Motorship Sunk by British 1941

NEW YORK, June 25 (AP)—The German motorship passenger liner Elbe, 9179 tons, which slipped out of Kobe, Japan, last February reportedly to raid shipping, has been attacked by a British fleet plane in the North Atlantic and probably sunk, maritime source ssaid today.

They said the attack occurred about 900 miles northwest of the Cape Verde islands and 1300 miles west of Villa Cisneros ,Rio De Oro, West Africa. The powerful and fast Elbe was built in 1929 and was used by the North German Lloyd Line for its pre-war German-Japan service.

Ships 444 - 455a   311

#434 *The North German Lloyd* M.V. Weser *at Ballantyne Pier, loading fruit, lumber and general cargo for United Kingdom and Continental ports.* Ex-Vancouver Shipping Report, 1934.

434. *Weser 4.*	1934-1940		
Deutsche Werke, Kiel #214	1929	6607/9179	140.60x18.47
Two Diesels	11,000	* *	17
17	58-49		

Launched 18/2/1929 as *Sud Americano* for Linea Sud Americana, Ivar Christensen, Oslo, manager. Failed to meet contract speed, hence returned to shipyard, LU as *Schleswig*. Deutsche Revisions & Treuhand (Trustee) Ges., Bremen. 6/1931 to 24/9/1931 chartered to Blue Star Line, ran as *Yakima Star* to Pacific Northwest. Again LU in Kiel. 1934 bought by NDL, rebuilt, re-engined by Deutsche Werft, Kiel. 9179 Ts., 29/9/1934 MV to Vancouver, as *Weser*. 9/1939 took refuge in Puntarenas, with *Eisenach* #337 and Hapag's *Havelland*. 25-26/9/1940 captured by *HMCS Prince George*, ex-Canadian National's British Columbia coastal vessel, off Manzanillo en route to supply Ship 36 (*Orion*, ex-Hapag's *Kurmark*) in the Marshall Islands. Taken To Equimault, B.C., ren. *Vancouver Island*, Canadian Merchant Marine Ministry. Made several trans-Atlantic voyages. 15/10/1941 torpedoed by U-502 in 53.37N, 25.37W, 750 miles SW of Fastnet Light. Lothar-Günther Buchheim in his *The Boat*, has his submarine enter Vigo for reprovisioning, rearming and some R & R for the crew. He says it's the *Weser*. "Unlimited supplies of fruit, fresh bread, showers, clean clothes. *Weser* allowed herself to be interned at the beginning of the war; she's now a floating supply depot restocked from time to time with fuel oil and torpedoes ... also still from peacetime linen table cloths, silverware, thick carpeting." Facts woven into fiction. Actually, it was *Lech* #453 that was laid up by war in Vigo.

#434x was ordered by NDL as Hannover, *first in an improving series of ships. In the 1934-1935 reshuffle of routes and vessels, it was given to Hapag, as* Hermonthis. *It in turn gave up something else,* World Ship Society Photo.

434x ***Hannover 3***		Never		
Bremer Vulkan, Vegesack #708			4833	132.89 x 16.76
M.A.N. Diesel		4800	14.5	
20				53

Launched 7/3/1935 as *Hannover* for Hanseatische Schiffahrt & Betriebs Ges. in behalf of NDL. Before completion it was transferred to Hapag in exchange of several vessels, ren. *Hermonthis*. MV 23/5/1935 to West Coast, South America. 30/6/1936 bought by Hapag. 5/9/1939 took refuge in Callao. 1/4/1941 left to get home or to Japan, was set afire NW of Callao to avoid capture by Canadian auxiliary cruise *Prince Henry*, Ex-Canadian National British Columbia coastal vessel. It sank the wreck with gunfire.

Osnabrück *#435 was the first of NDL's new series for the West Coast South America service. It had a Maier bow, the now-stylish rounded cruiser stern. Here off the western coast, typically cargo-handling to-from lighters.*

435. *Osnabrück*	1935-1945		
Weserweft, Bremen #892	1935	5095	133.31x16.66
M.A.N. Diesel	4400	14	
20	46		

Launched 16/3/1935, Maier Bow. 6/1935 MV Bremen-Valparaiso. 14/10/1939 MRS #11, R-Boat Mother Ship. 11/6/1942 after hitting mine put ashore off Reval, 84 dead. Repaired 12/2/1945 mined and sank off Swinemünde.

Shipping history does sometimes repeat. The seven ships of the *Köln* #112 Class 1899-1902 later had a storm Awning-Boat deck added. The same was done with *Schleswig* #181, in 1904. And 1909-1910, *Prinz Heinrich* #91 and *Prinzregent Luitpold* #90 were given this additional half-deck. This gave the captain his cabin behind the bridge, a wireless room and left more room for passengers on the Main Deck. In 1912, *Gotha* #239, *Gieseen* #240, *Coburg* #249 and *Eisenach* #250 were similarly given an awning deck.

In 1935-1939 this enlarging process was applied to the developing series of ships NDL had built for the West Coast, South America service. The first *Hannover*, ceded to Hapag as *Hermonthis*, *Osnabrück* and *Düsseldorf* had two decks, room for 20 passengers. The later vessels, *Nürnberg, München, Dresden, Leipzig* and *Hannover* received an extra deck, giving room for 28 passengers, and a longer hatch forward. *Dresden, Leipzig* and *Hannover* had a built-in tile pool.

In 1935, from 1 August, the new Atlas Levante Linie was a product of the decentralization of German shipping. It took over from NDL's former Stettiner Dampfer Co.: *Alimnia, Aquila, Alaya, Avola* and *Akka*, from Argo the former NDL *Star* #397 and *Amsel* #393. The ships ran with those of Deutsche Levante Linie, Hamburg, but were managed and owned by Richard Adler's Argo, with mostly Argo personnel.

436. *Düsseldorf*	1935-1939		
Bremer Vulkan, Vegesal #711	1935	4930	131.40 x 16.66
M.A.N. Diesel	4400	14	
20	46		

Launched 4/5/1935. MV 29/6/1935 to Valparaiso. 9/1939 took refuge there. 13/12/1939 left for Montevideo. 15/12/1939 off Caldera near Antofasta captured by *HMS Despatch*. 17th with British prize crew readied at Antofagasta for voyage to Europe. 25/12/ passed the Panama Canal with British flag above the German. 1940 briefly named *Poland*, registered in Kingston, then *Empire Confidence*, 5023 Ts., MOWT, Royal Mail Lines, Manager. 1945 chartered as *Star of El Nil*, Alexandria Nav. Co., Alexandria. 28/6/1950, after refit by Harland & Wolff, Belfast, 4900 HP, 6334 Ts., 6 passengers, ren. *Spenser*, Lamport & Holt, Liverpool. 1955 ren. *Roscoe*. 17/2/1962 arr. Bilbao for B.U.

436. Düsseldorf *was a sister of* Osnabrück *except for the bow. Twenty passengers capacity, which meant a doctor on board.*

437. Saar	1935-1940		
Weserwerft, Bremen #895	1935	3261	115.65 x 15.32
2 x Weser Diesels	3900	14.2	
12	38		

Launched 4/6/1935, Maier Bow. 10/1935 rg. for Hanseatische Schiffahrt & Betriebs Ges., the financing entity for rebuilding Germany's merchant fleet. Like sister *Memel* ran to Cuba-Mexico. 17/9/1939 *Sperrbrecher* (Barrage clearer) 1. 30/3/1944 after mine contact, towed to Brest for repairs. 26/8/1944 sank there two days after a hit by aerial bomb.

Despite the need for new shipping, NDL got rid of the already-outdated-when-built *Weser* #290 class. It was broken up in February, 1933. *Werra* #292, *Saarbrücken* #299, and *Coblenz* #301 were sold to Italy for its War on Abyssinia; *Trier* went in 1936 to Turkey, and only *Fulda,* the lone motorship in the class, was kept, cut down to freighter and ran to East Asia.

The next three ships made NDL the leading service to East Asia, a position it strived for beginning in 1886 with the subsidized Imperial Mail steamers. Financing was through the Hanseatische Betriebs Gesellschaft, Bremen, *Potsdam* was ordered for Hapag, but ceded to NDL. On these 21 knot liners one could get from Genoa, coming from the North by train, to Shanghai in 21 days. *Scharnhorst* and *Potsdam* had turbo-electric drive; *Gneisenau* and *Scharnhorst* had modified Maier bows, the largest ships so built. This design was meant to help ships ride over rather than through the waves. The author travelled with Captain Walter Stein on *Scharnhorst* as his guest in July, 1936. Coming from the Far East, the ship skipped its scheduled stop at Barcelona after Marseilles because of outbreak of the Spanish civil war. *Scharnhorst* and *Gneisenau* had German new-design watertube boilers. They had breaking-in problems. On her maiden voyage, *Scharnhorst* drifted for some hours in the Red Sea during boiler repairs.

The coming into service of the three Express Liners Scharnhorst, Gneisenau *and* Potsdam *in 1935 gave NDL the premier operation to the Far East. The three carried* **Bremen-Ostasien** *Ship Posts, with* **Jungfernreise** *on the Maiden Voyage, at the end removed. Several of the older ships in this service, six of the* Weser #290 *type, continued using the pre-war* **Ost-Asiatische Hauptlinie** *Sea Posts of the former Imperial Mail Service, from February, 1923, into 1935, similar* **Ost-Asiatische Linie**, *also 1922-1935. A new-style oval* **Ost-Asiatische Linie** *cancel was used by* Derfflinger *1928-1931, and by* Stuttgart, *between trans-Atlantic and cruise voyages, 1935-1938. A promotional sticker was available at times.*

M.S. Fulda   **M.S. Trave**

Color promotion sticker available on board.

438. *Scharnhorst 2*   1935-1942
Deschimag Weserwerft,
Bremen #891   1935   18,184   198.73 x 22.66
2 x Turbo Generators   26000, 21 kns, 32400-23 kns   * *
I-149 T-144 + 11 children   277

Launched 14/12/1934. MV. 3/5/1935 to Yokohama. In 1936, steel plates already were on board to cover windows and openings in case of war service. 9/1939 LU in Kobe. 2/7/1942 "sold" to Japan. 9/1942-12/1943 conversion to Escort Carrier *Jinyo* at Kure Naval Yard, 24-40 aircraft capacity. 8-5" guns. Captain Walter Stein remained on board as help in handling German equipment. 17/11/1944 sunk by U.S. submarine *Spadefish* 140 mis. NE of Shanghai in 33.02N, 123.33W. It was under Commander Underwood a unit of Wolf Pack group known as "Underwood's Urchins." The stern sank in 23 fathoms; the bow just protruded from the sea. The aircraft slid into the Yellow Sea. Among a series of stamps commemorating World War II issued in 1993 was one showing an officer at the periscope, and "Submarines shorten war in Pacific, 1944."

Scharnhorst #438 on her maiden voyage in Southampton with Tug Wotan. Nautical Photo Agency. *May, 1935. This and earlier ship photos heading down the Weser to Bremerhaven from the shipyard show the German Red White and Blue flag, not the Swastika.*

The author's photos of Scharnhorst *July, 1936. The Maier bow, with Bremen key insignium; the Olympic flag (the games were being held in Germany July, 1936), and Japan's flag, destination of the voyage; and pulling away from the Columbus Quay in Bremerhaven Captain Stein waving goodbye to the author, last time they saw each other, 8 August, 1936.*

Nightime loading. Hurricane lamps for Tulagi, British Solomon Islands, being loaded onto NDL's Scharnhorst *in Hamburg for transhipment via Hong Kong. Machinery for Shanghai will be delivered by* Scharnhorst. *Author's Photos. August 1936.*

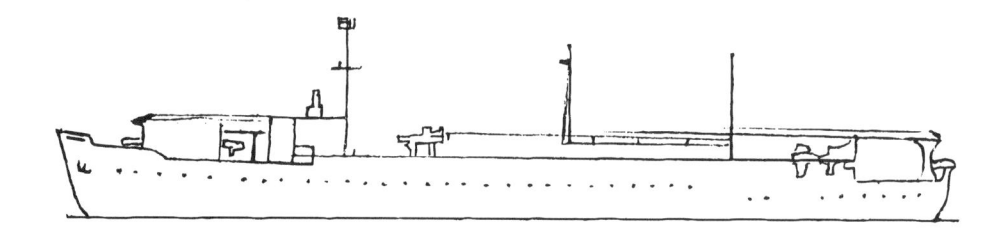

Schanrhorst *as converted to Auxiliary Aircraft Carrier* Jinyo, *by Carnet E. Affleck, Jr., May, 1957.* Intercom, *West Coast Journal of the World Ship Society. The Author was editor in the 1960s.*

318   Norddeutscher Lloyd Bremen

Potsdam *as built in 1935. Postwar, as troop transport* Empire Fowey, *the ten lifeboats were replaced with double mountings, and one double set and two doubles aft were added, for a total of 32 boats vs 10.* V. Seggern Photo.

439. ***Potsdam***	1935-1946		
Blohm & Voss, Hamburg #497	1935	17,528	193.07 x 22.60
2 x Turbo Generators	26,000	21	**
I-134 T-138	277		

1934 ordered by Hanseatische Schiffahrts & Betriebs Ges. for Hapag. Launched 16/1/1935. 28/6/1935 trials assigned to NDL in a reshuffle of ships. MV 5/7/1935 to Yokohama. 25/8/1939 left Southampton for Far East, recalled by wireless order. 22/4/1940 Kriegsmarine dormitory ship at Gdynia. 1942 troop transport. From 12/1942 conversion work as aircraft carrier, not completed, again dormitory ship at Gdynia, Gotenhafen. 1945 carried 53,891 refugees from the East to West Germany, via Hela Peninsula. 20/6/1945 at Flensburg to Britain, reportedly ren. *Empire Jewel*, but not so in register. Arr. Methil 14/7/1945, P. & O. Manager. 20/6/1946 ren. *Empire Fowey*, 19, 047 Ts., 3/1947-4/1950 major rebuild by Alexander Stephens & Sons, Glasgow, given turbines, new boilers, troop accommodations, Orient S.N.Co., Manager. Carried British troops to the Korean War. 19,121 Ts.,, 9/3/1960 LU. 16/5/1960 to Pan Islamic S.S.Co., Karachi, ren *Safinaa-E-Hujjaj*, carried pilgrims to and from Jeddah. 10/1976 arr. Gadani Beach, near Karachi, for BU.

Potsdam *#439 in Jeddah in 1966 as the Pakistani* Safinaa-E-Hujjaj *with the former West Africa Service* Pretoria. *Both ships served the annual Hajj the once-in-a-lifetime obligatory visit to Mecca for Muslims.*

440. **Gneisenau 2.**	1936-1943		
Deschimag Weserwerft,			
Bremen #893	1936	18,160	198.72 x 22.66
Turbine Drive	26,000	21	
I-149 + 15 children = 30 native (servants) T-155			276

Launched 17/5/1935 for Hanseatische Schiffahrts & Betriebs Ges., Bremen, the financing medium 50% Government-owned, 25% each NDL and Hapag. Delivery 28/12/1935. Maier Bow, like *Scharnhorst*. MV. 3/1/1936 to Yokohama. 8/1937 made two Shanghai-Japan voyages with Japanese refugees from the invasion, one evacuation voyage with foreigners to Hong Kong. 1-22 September 1937 one of few ships to survive up to 167 mph typhoon winds; also *Oder* #403. Last ship before war broke to be serviced at the Columbus Quay in Bremerhaven, nearly 400 passengers, some half million eggs from China. 22/4/1940 to Kriegsmarine for troop transports. 22/12/1941 dormitory ship, Hamburg. 1942 intended conversion to aircraft carrier not carried out. 1943 transport and barracks ship in Swinemünde. 2/5/1943 hit mine near Gedser; put ashore on Lolland Island, lay on its side until BU after the war by Danish wreckers. *Scharnhorst* and *Gneisenau* were so lavish with passenger space that it is doubtful they ever earned for NDL.

Gneisenau *#440 was Scharnhorst's sister. These two and* Potsdam *provided the outstanding passenger service to the Far East 1935-1939. The bulk of the passengers were British. In August, 1937* Gneisenau *evacuated foreigners from the Japanese attack on Shanghai, in September survived the hurricane that hit Hong Kong, sinking some twenty other vessels. Photo of* Gneisenau *in Southampton, the 1914 tender* Grüssgott, *NDL's largest vessel left after the war, alongside as now British-flag* Greetings, *bringing and taking passengers and mail when the ships did not go into Southampton docks, to save time.* Nautical Photo Agency.

Nürnberg *#441 was the first of the enlarged* Osnabrück *type, an added awning deck, 28 passengers capacity, and a swimming pool, first such on freighters.* Nautical Photo Agency.

441. *Nürnberg*	1936-1947		
Bremer Vulkan, Vegesack #721	1936	5635	138.00 x 17.16
1 M.A.N. Diesel		4400	14
28		54	

Launched 24/3/1936; 5/1936 MV to West Coast, South America. 14/10/1939 MRS 12, Mineclearing ship. 1945-46 under German Minesweeping Administration, under control of U.S. Navy. 13/12/1947 ceded to Britain. 1948 sold to H.P. Lenahan. Converted by Wm. Gray, Hartlepool, from workshop vessel to carrying passengers. 1948 *Dundalk Bay* for H.P. Lengham & Sons, Belfast, 5579 Ts., 1949 carried displaced persons to New Zealand. 1957 *Westbay* for Duff, Herbert & Mitchell, London. 2/9/1962 arr. Hamburg for BU by Eisen & Metall A.G.

442. *München*	1936-1941		
Bremer Vulkan, Vegesack #720	1936	5619	138.00 x 17.16
M.A.N. Diesel		5200	15
28		53	

Launched 15/5/1936. MV. 11/7/1936 to Valparaiso. 2/9/1939 LU in Callao. 1/4/1941 with sister *Leipzig* #448 and Hapag's *Monserrate* and *Hermonthis* tried to escape, to Japan, to avoid capture by Canadian Auxiliary Cruiser *Prince Henry* (ex-Canadian National's British Columbia Coastal Service, with *Prince David* and *Prince Robert*), scuttled, with Peruvian cruiser *Almirante Grau* adding gunfire. The crew got back to Callao.

#442 München *completing at the Bremer Vulkan shipyard.*

#443 In 1936, NDL again put a sail-training ship into service. Its fleet was being built up, and many of a former generation of sailors had dropped out during the depression. See "The Lloyd Sails and Rows." Here the former Magdalene Vinnen, *as* Kommodore Johnsen *unloading wheat at Cork after The Last Grain Race, in August, 1939. The ship got to Bremerhaven before the war broke, spent that war there, eventually went to the USSR, today still sails for Lithuania as a demonstration ship in OP SAIL and similar gatherings. The nostalgia of being at sea under sail. From* The National Geographic Magazine.

443. *Kommodore Johnsen*   1936-1945
Friedrich Krupp A.G., Kiel #372   1921   3572   117.50 x 14.60
4-Mast Bark, Auxiliary Diesel   500
60 cadets   33

Launched 23/3/1921 as *Magdalene Vinnen* for F.A. Vinnen & Co., Bremen, prewar one of the world's major sailing ship enterprises, with 11 ships in 1914. 26/8/1936 bought by NDL, fitted for cadet training (See #143 and #184), and as freight carrier, ren. In 1939, was one twelve sailships in the last grain race, 107 days from Port Lincoln, South Australia to "Falmouth for Orders." In the Baltic during the war, LU in winter. 5/1945 found at Flensburg. 19/12/1945 to Britain at Hamburg. 1/1946 at Swinemünde to USSR. For years lay almost derelict at Kronstadt, the old Russian naval base. Weyer 1953-1955 incorrectly has K.J. as *Krusenstern*, later correctly as *Sedov*. Training ship, doing oceanographic work, Riga home port. Sea Breezes in 7/1965 reported that "in February, *Krusenstern* and *Sedov* passed down the English Channel and received considerable publicity during a call at Gibraltar." In 1981 "now being refitted for cadets." Participated in various OPSAIL gatherings in the 1980s for the USSR, since its breakup for Esthonia. *N.Y. Times* on 4/7/1986 identified *Krusenstern* as "built 1921." But the same issue reporting on the bicentennial celebration in New York contends "built 1926 as Padua for F. Laeisz." *Seattle Times* for 8/5/1977 shows *Krusenstern* as "built 1933." Typical confusion about anything pertaining to the USSR.

CHAPTER 11

Fun And Games At Sea

The Lloyd's Summer 1914 cruising season was cut short with two ships at sea when the war began: *Schleswig* got home from the third of her four scheduled Norwegian coastal voyages. *Prinz Friedrich Wilhelm* on its Polar Cruise, which included stops at Lloyd-claimed bays on Spitzbergen, escaped to and was interned in Norway until 1916, when it escaped and got home.

German cruising resumed in 1923, the height or bottom of The Inflation, as it is still known in Germany. It was a newcomer, Victor Schuppe, who bought the former Lloyd *Sierra Salvada* #257, had her rebuilt with two stacks after an undocking accident, renamed her *Peer Gynt* for Germany's favored destination: Norway. In 1925, NDL resumed cruising with the prewar *Lützow* #241, repurchased from the British and slightly upgraded. It made three Norwegian coastal voyages. The new *München* #293 made an Atlantic and a Polar cruise. Polar meant that the voyage included Spitzbergen, sometimes also Iceland. Polar voyages had been a Lloyd specialty since in 1910 it laid claim to the shore of three bays on Spitzbergen, then under no international sovereignty. It actually built there a small Lloyd Hotel, the sort of light-eating places on top of ski-lifts or mountain railways in Switzerland. After the war, Spitzbergen was assigned to Norway, extinguishing the Lloyd claims. But the attractions of seeing ice, glaciers, summer flowers was perennial.

In the spring of 1926, four cruises went to the Mediterranean sun, that summer two to Norway, one Polar voyage. This often included the North Cape, the Land of the Midnight Sun. *Columbus* was chartered that early year, the first of many times, by Raymond & Whitcomb, an American travel agency founded in 1879. These charters continued through the thirties, including two around-the-world in 1930 and 1931. *Columbus* was the largest by then to make West Indies voyages a specialty: almost a new port, a new culture every day. *Columbus* during 1931-1939 made forty-seven cruises from New York. It carried a total of 21,368 passengers, from a low of 133 in January, 1939 to a high of 831 in April, 1936, an average of 455. In effect, while the Lloyd as a German concern during the 1933-39 Nazi era suffered from boycotts, angry Communist and other anti-Nazi demonstrations, its ship and shore personnel continued the traditional service to passengers, so that at least the cruises from New York attracted an international clientele in rewarding numbers. *Columbus* on its last cruise in August, 1939 had 725 passengers, more than one would have liked for optimum comfort. On that cruise, when war threatened, they were landed in Havana, taken to Florida and home by trains.

Since cruising was done by liners normally running trans-ocean schedules, they were not equipped with topside pools, only the largest even with inside, deep-down pools. For cruising, the vessels were usually equipped with canvas "pools," hardly larger than the ones traditionally set up for Equator crossings to prepare those who had never crossed for Neptune's Southern Kingdom. Even *Columbus* did not get a topside Lido

NDL's Sierra Salvada *of 1913 in 1924-25 ran as* Peer Gynt *for Victor Schuppe.*

North Cape Fjord Voyages cruise mark for Hapag's Oceana *the former NDL* Sierra Salvada *#257.*

A ship in multiple guises. Volume I shows single-stack Sierra Salvada *#267 being salvaged from its capsizing in Hamburg in June, 1922. It was rebuilt as a two-stacker, renamed* Peer Gynt *by new owner Victor Schuppe. (Marius Bar Photograph, Toulon). A rare Sea Post from the ship in 1925 and cachet: In Memory of the Northlands Voyage with the Steamer* Peer Gynt. *Later, Hapag bought the ship and named it* Oceana *shown in Hamburg Harbor. And a cruise mark it used for North Cape voyages. Later the ship had a Kraft durch Freude (Strength through Joy) cruise cancel.*

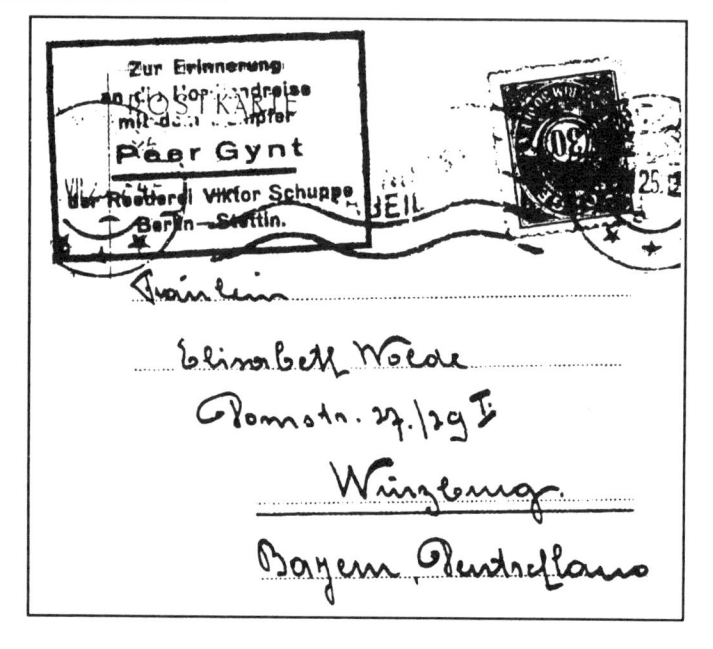

*From NDL's resumption of cruising in 1925; the first **Polarfahrt** since 1914, when* Prinz Friedrich Wilhelm *was on cruise. It was interned in Norway when war broke, got back home in 1916 with this **Seepost**. The use is RRR then, Scarce here. The mark was the last recorded cruise **Seepost** before World War II broke, 26.7.1939 with the Hammerfest Paquebot mark added. The* München *1925 cover has rubber-stamped: "Voyage so far wonderful, Hearty Greetings" and "At the Edge of the Pack Ice, Spitsbergen." NDL had claimed terrain in Spitzbergen and actually put up a small Lloyd Hotel before 1914.*

*Hammerfest's Paquebot applied to the **Norwegenfahrt**/Norddeutscher Lloyd cruise Sea Post introduced in 1913, and very rare in the prewar period. Polar cruises included Spitzbergen and sometimes Iceland and always Norwegian ports going north and returning. The last recorded pre-recorded cruise cancel is **Norwegenfahrt** 17.8.39.*

Not only did ships have Equator-Crossing ceremonies with King Neptun coming on board, but in olden days when crossing the Polar Circle. On the Norwegian coast there is a large steel globe showing only the outlines and the Polar Circle line so travellers know when it actually happens.

In most ports ships on cruises had to anchor, then take their passengers ashore in ship's boats, not an easy method at best. Some modern cruise ships actually have a stern door through which to debark and re-embark on cruises. Here is Stuttgart *off Hammerfest taken from* Lützow, *also on a Norwegian coastal cruise. Photo by L. Hannet, 1926. And the advertisement for the two ships (see following page.)*

Wir veranstalten 3 Nordkapfahrten

15 Tage von RM. 270,— an
Prachtvolle Fahrt in die Fjorde Norwegens
mit D. »Sierra Cordoba« (11 469 Br.-R.-T.)
am 4. Juli, 21. Juli u. 7. August 1933

POLARFAHRT

25 Tage von RM. 520,— an
mit D. »General v. Steuben« (14 690 Br.-R.-T.)
über Schottland, Spitzbergen nach Norwegen
vom 19. Juli bis 13. August 1933
Andere preiswerte Seereisen
Auskunft und Prospekte durch:

Lloydreisebüro G. m. b. H., Leipzig,
Augustusplatz 7, und Verkehrs-
büro d. Leipz. Meßamts, Markt 4.

NORDDEUTSCHER LLOYD BREMEN

1930s advertising to the North Cape and Polar regions. In summers, the Northlands were the favorite cruise destination for Germans, in Winters the Mediterranean, for the sun.

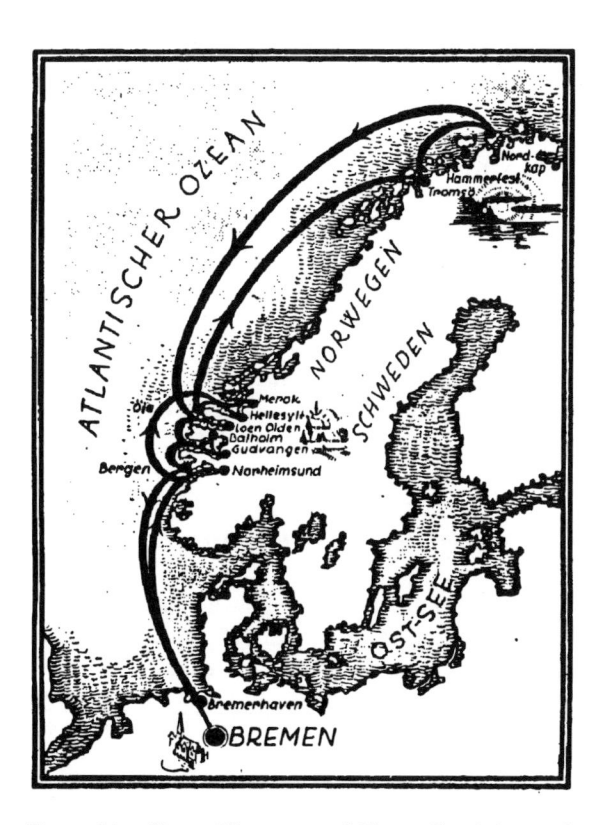

Polarfahrt

über Island nach Spitzbergen
vom 20. Juli bis 15. August 1926
mit dem
Doppelschrauben-Passagierdampfer

„STUTTGART"

am 20. Juli von Bremen über Island nach Spitz-
bergen, dem Nordkap und den norwegischen
Fjorden. Ende der Fahrt am 15. August in
Bremerhaven-Bremen

Zwei beliebte Erholungsreisen zur See

von Bremen nach den schönsten Punkten
Norwegens
mit dem
Doppelschrauben-Passagierdampfer

„LUETZOW"

1. Norwegenfahrt: bis zum Nordkap, 17. Juli
bis 3. August.

2. Norwegenfahrt: 7. bis 21. August.
Gut bürgerliche Verpflegung. Komfort.
Mässige Preise.

Genaue Prospekte durch unsere Vertreter.

Sisterships Sierra Ventana *and* Sierra Cordoba *made three North Cape Cruises in July-August, 1928. Built for the South America run, they offered better cruise facilities than the older North Atlantic steamers,* Lützow *and* Karlsruhe.

---

3. Nordkapfahrt

Dampfer „Sierra Cordoba" / 4. August bis 22. August 1928

Fahrplan und Landausflüge

Abfahrt von	Bremerhaven	4. August mittags
Ankunft in	Norheimsund	6. August vorm.
	Autofahrt nach Tokagjelet	
Abfahrt nach	Merok	6. August nachm.
Ankunft in	Merok	8. August vorm.
	8. August Autofahrt nach Djupvandshütte	
Abfahrt nach	Hellesylt	9. August vorm.
Ankunft in	Hellesylt	9. August vorm.
	Autofahrt durch das Norangtal nach Öie	
Abfahrt nach	Öie	9. August vorm.
Ankunft in	Öie	9. August nachm.
Abfahrt nach	Tromsö	12. August vorm.
Ankunft in	Tromsö	12. August nachm.
Abfahrt nach	Nordkap	12. August nachm.
Ankunft am	Nordkap	13. August vorm.
	Besteigung des Nordkaps	
Abfahrt nach	Loen/Olden	14. August nachts
	via Lyngenfjord	
Ankunft in	Loen/Olden	17. August vorm.
	Ausflug nach dem Kjendal- und Briksdal- Gletscher	
Abfahrt nach	Balholm	17. August nachm.
Ankunft in	Balholm	18. August vorm.
Abfahrt nach	Gudvangen	19. August vorm.
Ankunft in	Gudvangen	19. August nachm.
	Wagenfahrt durch das Naerötal nach Stalheim	
Abfahrt nach	Bergen	19. August nachm.
Ankunft in	Bergen	20. August vorm.
Abfahrt nach	Bremerhaven	20. August nachm.
Ankunft in	Bremerhaven	22. August vorm.

NORDDEUTSCHER LLOYD BREMEN

Fun and Games at Sea

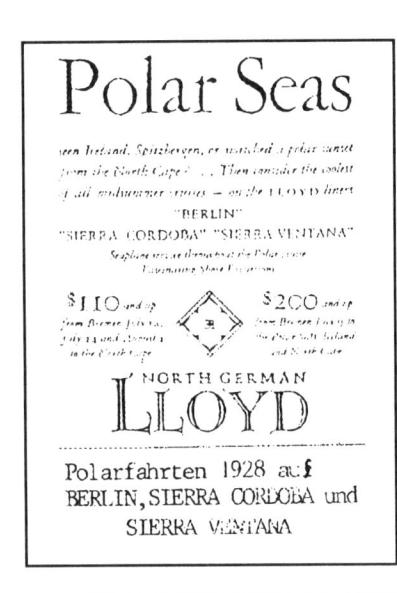

Northlands Cruises 1928.

Deck with pool until late 1937 in time for that Winter's West Indies voyages. Actually, the Lloyd set the pace in the 1930s with tiled pools on several 28-passengers freighters it had built for the West Coast South America route.

In 1927, NDL introduced aerial flightseeing for cruise passengers. *Lützow* on its 13 April departure from Genoa had on board a small float plane. This was lowered into the water and a few passengers got aboard. The flights were limited to near ports or coastal anchorages. *Columbus* in 1928 began carrying a larger aircraft housed on its boat deck and lowered by cargo derricks. See "The Lloyd Flies."

Prohibition, the 18th Amendment ban on alcoholic beverages, lasted from 16, January, 1919 until 5, December, 1933. It was a major problem for U.S.-flag passenger shipping competing against foreign lines, until high-seas exemption was granted. In the 1930s until repeal, a number of lines instituted Cruises to Nowhere and Booze Cruises of two to four days duration, to provide legal drinking. And to keep ships busy between schedules. Some photos seen have inked notations: "No Prohibition here, *S.S. Bremen*" courtesy of Frank Pichardo. But the clientele shown seems to be people on a regular crossing rather than Booze Cruise enjoyers.

KRAFT DURCH FREUDE

Kraft Durch Freude, Strength Through Joy was a division of the National Socialist German Workers Front, the Nazi successor to the destroyed labor unions. KdF organized vacations to build support among its worker members. Cheap voyage at sea had tremendous appeal, especially for Inlanders who had never been on water or at a bathing resort other than a lake; a few perhaps had made a trip to Helgoland, the Friesian Islands or Hörnum. It was the time of worldwide deep depression during which many ships were laid up, scrapped or sold off as superfluous. KdF cruises therefore had a multiple purpose: ships and crews remained occupied, workers got cheap vacations, and the National Socialist Government built support among low-income people, its early support base.

At first, KdF ships were charted from the leading shipping firms: NDL, Hapag and Hamburg-Süd. Later some were bought outright, although still managed by the original owners, and two ships built for KdF, different designs, in wartime to serve as transports or hospital ships. Most of the cruises had special cancels, from 1936 a standard double-ring type. *Dresden* #269 in 1934 had an excised *Nordkapfahrt* Ship Post until she stranded in June, then sank off Norway. It was lost with her.

Sierra Morena #306 was chartered in 1934, then bought and renamed *Der Deutsche*, The German. *Stuttgart* #303 from 1936 made some KdF voyages between trips to the Far East, then in 1938 was rebuilt for those cruises, one-class.

Sierra Cordoba #302 in 1935 was sold to KdF. *Columbus* #300 made 23-29/7/1935 one *Gauturnfahrt*, Sport Group Cruise, with a unique type Ship Post. And from 17/9/1935 one KdF voyage but without a recorded Ship Post. *Berlin* #308 in May, 1939 made two KdF voyages. No Ship Post is known. Hapag's *Oceana*, ex-NDL's *Sierra Salvada* #257 from 1934 also served as KdF charter vessel, then was rebuilt for such cruising. All ships were painted white. In September, 1939 *Oceana*, and *Sierra Cordoba* fetched the *Bremen's* Crew from Leningrad; they had come by rail from Murmansk to which twenty-two German ships fled when the war began.

The KdF cruises carried more than a million people, probably predominantly National Socialist party members or supporters. One card from *Der Deutsche*: "I've just returned to Bremerhaven from a wonderful High Seas trip across the North Sea to the Norwegian fjords. I send hearty greet-

Typical canvas pool rigged on cruise ships. Even Columbus *did not get a Lido deck with tile pool until 12.1937. From 1936 on the new 28-passenger freighters built for NDL's West Coast South America run were given tile pools. Sailors obviously were enjoying the added exposure of passengers. Both sketches by Karl Bedal from Dr. A. Rehm's "Das Fröhliche Logbuch," The Happy Log Book." See p. 311 and p.120.*

Sketch in Seven Seas, *NDL's promotional magazine aimed at the American market in the 1920s.*

Fun and Games at Sea 329

Lützow #241 was repurchased 1924 from England, slightly modified, finally was given a tiled pool on the boat deck, but bathtub-sized to the chagrin of the Cruise Staff. Here it is in the Norangfjord, using a local motorboat to bring voyagers ashore instead of ship's boats. NDL Photo, mid-1920s.

U.S.-flag ships were handicapped during Prohibition in not being able to serve alcoholic beverages, until special legislation was passed. Here a Happy Hour on Bremen during Prohibition, not ended until 1933. Frank Pichardo collection.

Five Lloyd ships were involved in Kraft durch Freude cruises, the former Sierra Salvada *as Hapag's* Oceana, Berlin *in 1939, and the former* Sierra Morena *renamed* Der Deutsche, Stuttgart *and* Sierra Cordoba. *The last three had KdF Ship Posts with their names.*

Card from Der Deutsche, *ex NDL's* Sierra Morena, *sold to the Strength through Joy Movement. With that Ship Post, July, 1936.*

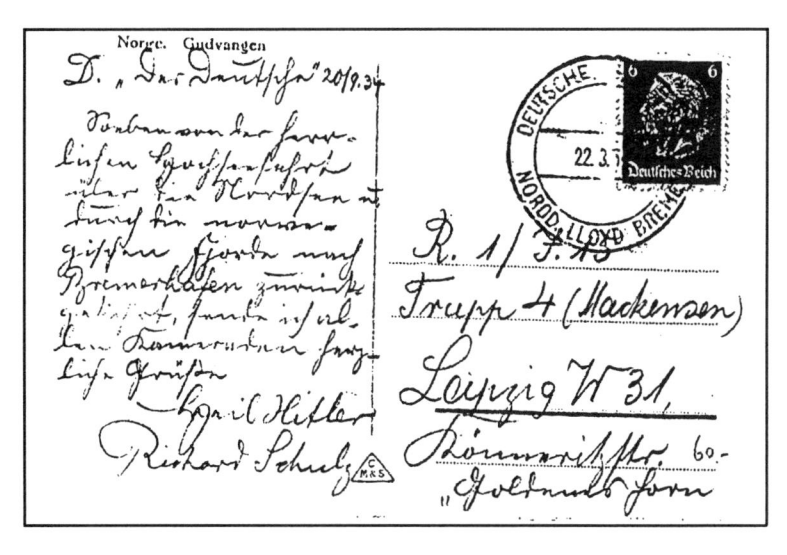

ings greetings to all Comrades" And addressed to a Troop stationed in Leipzig. One wonders whether any of these thousands who visited Norway were shamed when Germany invaded that country in April, 1940?

Another writes to friends: "I send hearty greetings from the lovely fjord country. Last night we travelled out of a most lovely fjord to the melody of Solvig's Lied. It was an unforgettable experience. The only regret: that we already were heading south and homeward." Similar Ship Posts were used on *Stuttgart* and *Der Deutsche*, Ex *Sierra Morena*. Prior to these, NDL ships on KdF charter used **Nordd-Lloyd Bremen** cancel, and *Deutsche Schiffspost*/Kraft durch Freude, this last in Fraktur type. *Oceana* had that mixed-type cancel and one entirely Fraktur.

Stuttgart and *Sierra Cordoba* made cruises in 1928 and following years, usually to the North. *Sierra Cordoba* was known by its repeat passengers as *Sierra Reimers*, for its popular captain. *Berlin* in 1928 made a Polar cruise, its first.

The depression hit shipping hard everywhere: 1934 was the low point in trans-Atlantic travel. An undated photograph shows the Lloyd's *General von Steuben, Sierra Cordoba* and *Dresden* laid up in Bremerhaven, probably the Winter of 1931-1932. *Lützow*, an out-dated vessel even in 1925, no longer went cruising. Passenger Director Adolf Stadtländer hoped with cruising to extend the working life of *Karlsruhe*, ex *Bremen 3*, ex *Prinzessin Irene* of 1900. But the ship was just too old and primitive. After four Spring, 1932 cruises to and in the Mediterranean and summer-season voyages to New York, it was sold off for scrapping. But it was cruises in the depression 1930s, from European ports and New York, not from Florida as predominantly today, that kept ships running when otherwise they might have been laid up. This gave work to crews, to suppliers, earned some foreign exchange and with the traditional Lloyd service, it kept friends. True, some voyages had barely 200 passenger. But there were attractions: several lines had short, squeezed into liner schedules, Booze Cruises, a chance to imbibe beyond the Three Miles Limit, until repeal of Prohibition in December, 1933. And prices were so low: "$65 and up" on *Europa* in December, 1934 for "Four unforgettable days to Nassau."

Europa made only one other cruise, on 26 December, 1938 to Bermuda and Nassau. *Europa* and *Bremen* were the Lloyd's strong pull on the North Atlantic, so kept in service year-round. *Bremen* in early 1939 made a Round-South Amer-

Fun and Games at Sea 331

Dresdens forlis 20 juni 1934 ved, Kopervik.

Dresden *in May 1934 on cruise homeward bound had rescued three French naval aviators off Dunquerque. It landed them in Bremerhaven. From there in June it headed for the North Cape. On the 20th it ran aground below Kopervik and was lost. The Maritime Court's judgment: a loose-drifting buoy misled navigation. No fault for the ship's staff. The Norwegian coastal* Kong Haakon *took on some 535 persons; the rest were put shore and housed nearby. Two women died from heart failure in the process of being boated ashore. At 22.40 the last message: Captain and wireless officer leaving ship.* Stuttgart *had arrived at Bremerhaven the 19th from New York, left at 1 a.m. the 21st to bring passengers and crew home.* Dresden *had a* **Nordkapfahrt Ship Post** *with that wording excised. It was lost with the ship. The ship was sold off for scrapping.*

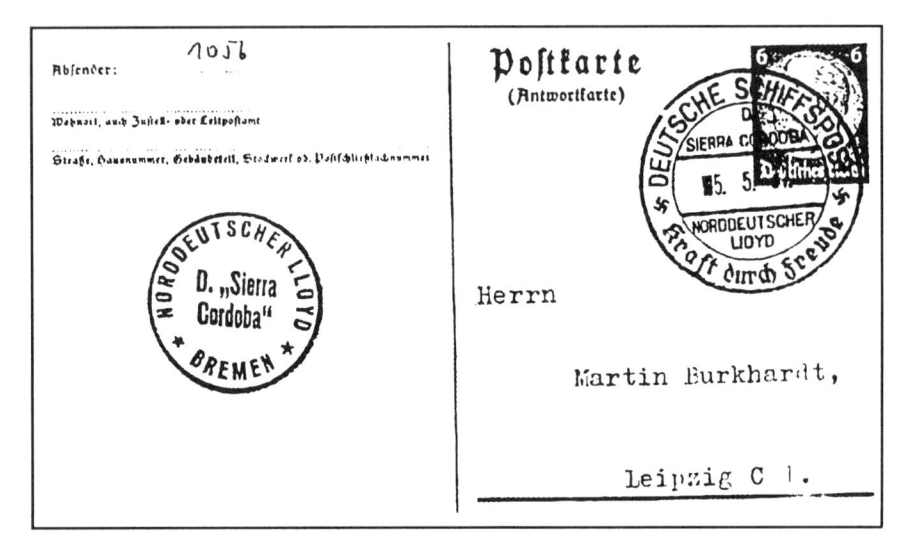

A philatelic card from Sierra Cordoba's KdF cruise in 1937. The ship was chartered to the Kraft durch Freude movement, but remained under NDL operation.

Neujahrs-Gala-Fahrt
— mit der —
Königin der Meere "S. S. EUROPA"
nach NASSAU

Vier unvergessliche Tage $65 aufwärts
auf diesem Prachtdampfer

Unter persönlicher Leitung des deutschen Reisebüros Wm. Becker

Abfahrt Sonnabend, den 29. Dezember, 3 Uhr nachmittags—Rückkehr am 2. Januar morgens

Wenn Sie je eine schöne Reise gemacht haben, so wird es diese sein

Um eingehende Auskunft und gute Kabinen wende man sich an

Wm. Becker
Das beliebte deutsche Reisebüro
145 Vierte Ave., nahe 14. Str. (Central Savings Bank Annex), New York

Telephon: ALgonquin 4-1800

An appeal to New York's German element: Queen of the Seas Europa. Four unforgettable days on this luxurious vessel. If you've ever made a wonderful voyage, it will be this one. December, 1934. Europa made only one other cruise, to the West Indies 29.12.1937 - 4.1.1938. No Sea Posts are recorded.

Bremen *in 1939 was the largest vessel to have transited the Panama Canal, on its round-South America cruise, 14,435 nautical miles in 26 days, 23 knots average at-sea speed. When passengers in New York said Goodbye to Captain Ahrens many hoped "next year around the world." It didn't happen. Cruise Ship Post, given the Cristobal Paquebot datestamp because of the U.S. postage. Note towline at bow for extra guidance. Ship Photograph courtesy William H. Miller.*

Fun and Games at Sea 333

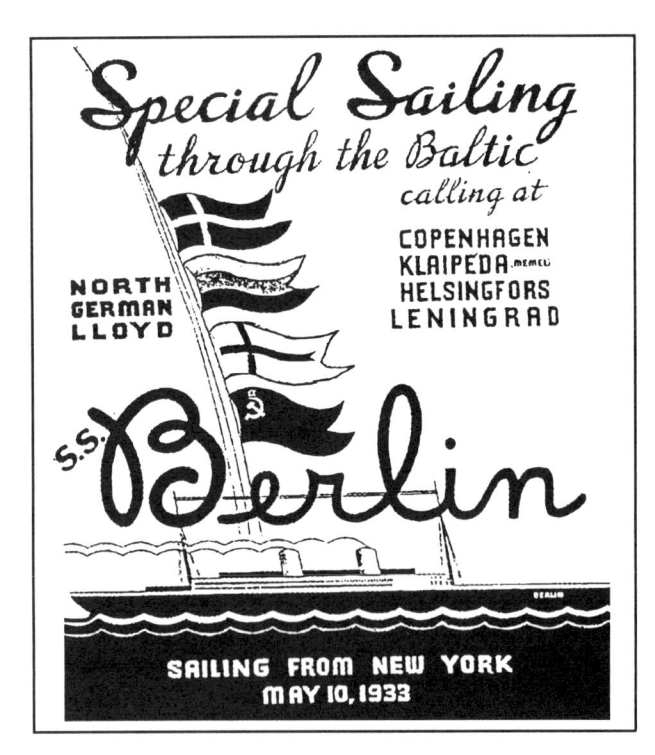

Berlin made the only Lloyd cruise from New York to Northern Europe, in 1933. No Sea Post in known nor from her one voyage to Australia in 1938.

*Berlin made depression-years cruises to the West Indies from New York. Here its cruise Ship Post from 1934 off-stamp because of the Bahamas postage used, and New York's High Seas Mail arrival **Paquebot** cancel.*

ica cruise, the largest vessel up to that time to transit the Panama Canal. Captain Adolf Ahrens in his autobiography relates "on 24 March we re-entered New York. Hundreds at parting asked me 'Where to next Winter?' I replied 'I hope *Bremen* will go Round the World.' Many answered "We'll be there.'" The same happened with Hapag's *Cincinnati* in 1914, for an announced 1915 World Cruise. And its cruises announced for the 1940 Helsinki Olympics, never held. Unfulfilled dreams.

Berlin in May, 1933 made a once-only Lloyd cruise from New York to Northern Europe: Klaipeda, ex-German Memel, Helsingfors and Leningrad. *Columbus* went to the Mediterranean from New York in 1934, from Germany to Madeira, around England and Scotland, to the Mediterranean. Other ships went from Germany to "The Fortunate Islands," a promotional name for the Canaries, even Finland for a one-time cruise with a rare Ship Post, and always to Norwegian waters.

After *München* in February, 1930 burned in New York, it was rebuilt for cruising, the Promenade Deck extended aft, a pool installed in a later rejuvenation, and painted white, coming out as *General von Steuben*, in 1938 shortened to

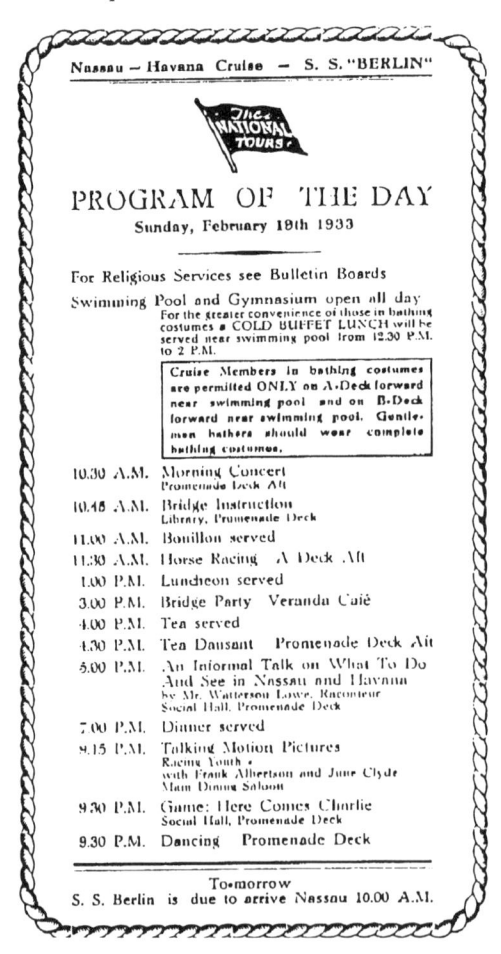

One day's program on Berlin in the West Indies. Note: Bathing costumes allowed only on Deck.

334 Norddeutscher Lloyd Bremen

Columbus Cruise 1935

Hamburg-American Line
North German Lloyd
In cooperation with
Thos. Cook & Son
Wagons-Lits Inc.

RAYMOND-WHITCOMB ANNOUNCE
ROUND THE MEDITERRANEAN WORLD

ROUND THE WORLD » CRUISE «
To sail January 21, 1931

The Cruise Ship will again be the "Columbus" — which is the largest and fastest ship ever to sail round the world. Because of her superior speed, the time spent at sea will be less than on other cruises — and the length of the Cruise will be reduced to 107 days without reducing the number of places visited or the shore programs. With visits to all the usual Round-the-World-Cruise countries and to Penang, Zamboanga, Macassar — and trips to Bali and Angkor Wat. $2000 and up.

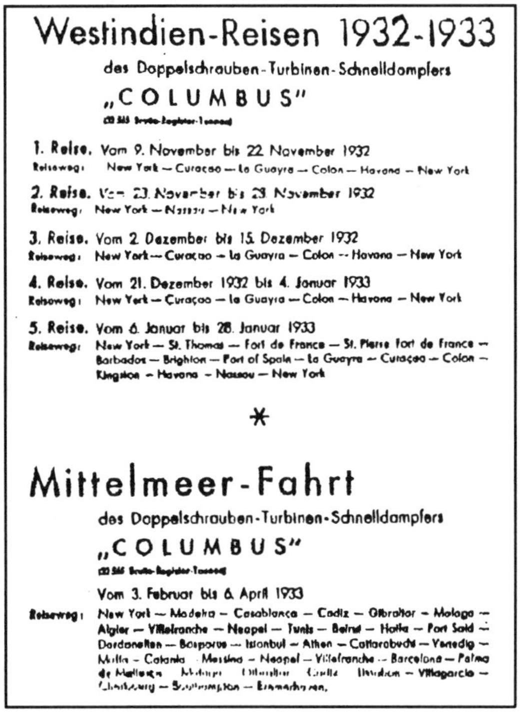

Westindien-Reisen 1932-1933
des Doppelschrauben-Turbinen-Schnelldampfers
„COLUMBUS"

1. **Reise.** Vom 9. November bis 22. November 1932
Reiseweg: New York — Curacao — La Guayra — Colon — Havana — New York

2. **Reise.** Vom 23. November bis 29. November 1932
Reiseweg: New York — Nassau — New York

3. **Reise.** Vom 2. Dezember bis 15. Dezember 1932
Reiseweg: New York — Curacao — La Guayra — Colon — Havana — New York

4. **Reise.** Vom 21. Dezember 1932 bis 4. Januar 1933
Reiseweg: New York — Curacao — La Guayra — Colon — Havana — New York

5. **Reise.** Vom 6. Januar bis 28. Januar 1933
Reiseweg: New York — St. Thomas — Fort de France — St. Pierre Fort de France — Barbados — Brighton — Port of Spain — La Guayra — Colon — Kingston — Havana — Nassau — New York

*

Mittelmeer-Fahrt
des Doppelschrauben-Turbinen-Schnelldampfers
„COLUMBUS"

Vom 3. Februar bis 6. April 1933
Reiseweg: New York — Madeira — Casablanca — Cadiz — Gibraltar — Malaga — Algier — Villefranche — Neapel — Tunis — Beirut — Haifa — Port Said — Dardanellen — Bosporus — Istanbul — Athen — Cattaro bucht — Venedig — Milo — Catania — Messina — Neapel — Villefranche — Barcelona — Palma de Mallorca — Malaga — Gibraltar — Cadiz — Lissabon — Villagarcia — Hamburg — Southampton — Bremerhaven.

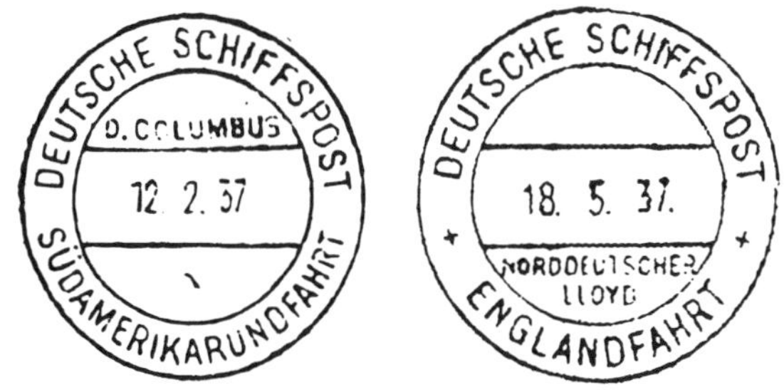

Columbus began cruising in January, 1926 from New York to the West Indies under charter to Raymond & Whitcomb. Some left no record of having provided Sea Post service, as these early cruises, nor the two made round-the-world in 1930 and 1931, nor 1932-1933 Mediterranean cruises, nor the 1935 voyage to the Mediterrean and Indian Ocean. But yes on the Winter 1936-1937 Round South America cruise, the 1939 Around Africa cruise, and Englandfahrt on several cruises to England and Ireland. Stuttgart also went to England. At least one mailed item indicates Schottland, so one or more cruises may actually have been to the British Isles without saying so.

Fun and Games at Sea

Steuben. Ship Post cruise postal cancellers were provided on these vessels for the convenience of passengers and crews, and the advertising they extended to recipients of such "fun at sea" mailings.

Cruises continued from New York in 1939 despite threatening war clouds. *Columbus* went around Africa in the Spring from New York, then back to trans-Atlantic voyages. It arrived from Bremen on 28 June, left for the West Indies the 29th, again on July 8th, 22nd, August 5th, and finally on August 19th, the cruises that ended in Vera Cruz and, in December at the bottom of the Atlantic.

St. Louis, after its failed voyage in May-June to Havana with 937 Jewish refugees, unable to land them even in the U.S. or Canada, returned to Europe. It reached New York 14th July, left the same day on cruise, again on the 24th, again the 31st for Halifax, again on August 5th, the 12th, the 21st. It returned on the 25th and sailed for Europe the 27th, the first of the ships leaving to escape the coming war. Just as they did in September, 1938 in expectation of possible war.

In-port diversion for passengers and crew on a cruise. Hanns Tschira Ship Photographer, Columbus.

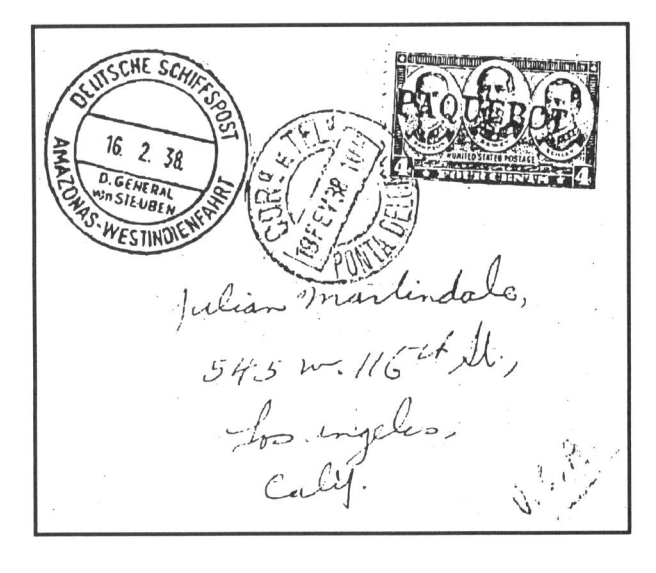

After the February, 1930 Pier Fire in New York, München #293 was rebuilt as one-class for cruising, and painted white. As General Von Steuben, *she cruised to the Mediterranean in 1931, here a card from Lloyd Director Bremermann, details of the four cruises there in 1934, and the special Ship Post from her 1938 Amazonas-Westindien cruise from New York, extending to the Azores, with* **Ponta Delgada's Paquebot** *mark on the U.S. postage.*

336 *Norddeutscher Lloyd Bremen*

1931 Mediterranean Cruise cancel from General von Steuben.

LLOYD • MADEIRA • FAHRT 1936
SCHNELLDAMPFER COLUMBUS
Kapitän Fr. Poser

AUSZUG AUS DEM SCHIFFSTAGEBUCH

Datum	Position Breite	Position Länge	Meilen	Wind	Bemerkungen (Wetter usw.)
7. Juli	—	—	—	OSO/SSO 1–3	Abfahrt von Bremerhaven um 17.06. Passierten 19.12 Weser-Feuerschiff. Wechselnd bewölkt, Gewitterregen.
8. Juli	51° 10' N	1° 36' O	293	SSW/SW 4	Wechselnd bewölkt, leicht bewegte See, zeitweise Regenschauer.
9. Juli	46° 51' N	6° 37' W	432	SSW/W 2–5–4	Meist stark bewölkt, zeitweise Regen, ziemlich grobe See. Schiff stampfte.
10. Juli	40° 01' N	9° 21' W	451	WSW/WNW 4–3	Meist bedeckt, mäßig bis leicht bewegte See.
11. Juli	—	—	381	NNW 3–4	Ankunft in Gibraltar um 12.12.
12. Juli	—	—	11	SO/O 2–3	Abfahrt von Gibraltar um 4.42. Ankunft in Ceuta um 5.42.
12. Juli	—	—	—	ONO 2–4	Abfahrt von Ceuta um 19.00. Wolkenlos, mäßig bewegte See.
13. Juli	34° 12' N	11° 30' W	322	ONO/NO 4–5	Wolkenlos, ziemlich grobe bis mäßig bewegte See.
14. Juli	—	—	283	NO 4–2	Ankunft in Madeira um 5.24. Abfahrt von Madeira um 20.00.
15. Juli	36° 40' N	13° 07' W	262	NO/NNO 2–3	Leicht bewölkt, leicht bewegte See.
16. Juli	—	—	252	NNO/N 3–1	Ankunft in Lissabon um 6.48. Abfahrt von Lissabon um 19.24.
17. Juli	44° 00' N	8° 44' W	333	SSW/WSW 3–7	Bedeckt, ztw. Sprühregen, mäßig bewegte bis grobe See u. Dünung. Schiff rollte.
18. Juli	50° 23' N	0° 26' W	527	WSW/SSW 7–4	Wechselnd bewölkt, grobe See und Dünung, Schiff rollte zeitweise stark.
19. Juli	—	Rest	384	Süd 3	6.00 passierten Weser-Feuerschiff. Ankunft Bremerhaven 17. Juli morgens.
		Total	3831		

Seedistanz: 3831 Seemeilen   Zeit auf See: 8 Tage, 20 Stunden, 54 Minuten   Durchschnittsfahrt: 18,47 Knoten

Columbus *and* Stuttgart *made a number of cruises to Madeira. In October, 1935, NDL was using meter-markings on business mail via Zeppelin and aircraft to South America, to advertise the Silvester (New Year's) cruise in 1935. Here also the voyage log by* Columbus *in July, 1936.*

Fun and Games at Sea

In the 1930s, NDL on its business mail to overseas meter-stamped cruise promotions: Christmas-New Year's voyage to Madeira, Vacations at Sea with the Lloyd, Into the Sunny Mediterranean with the Recuperation Steamer Steuben, Spring Voyages into the Mediterranean, Polar and North Cape Cruises, Lloyd Voyages are always a Lucky Time. This comes from Germans naming the Canaries The Fortunate or Lucky Islands.

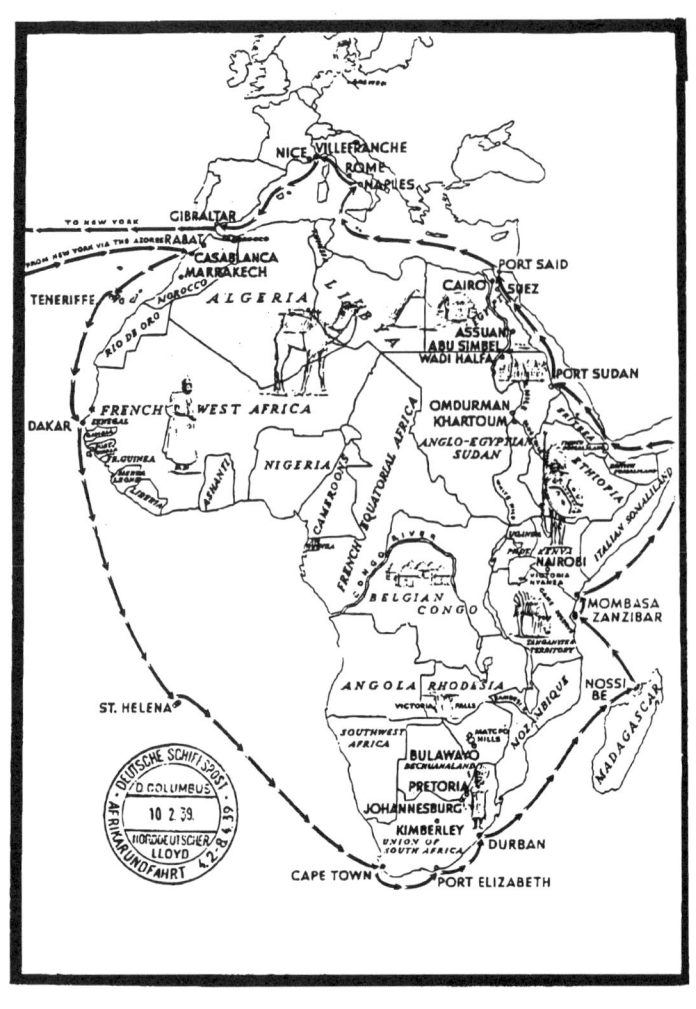

The route of Columbus #300. Round-Africa cruise from 4, February through 8, April, 1939 showing the Ship Post canceller used. Bremen and Europa as recordholders, with their captains, and Columbus as probably the favorite cruise vessel out of New York, were the Lloyd's continued favorable presence with the American public.

338   Norddeutscher Lloyd Bremen

The Columbus's *Ship Post, 1939 with * * removed. As in July/August 1914, when war began in September, 1939, German ships sought refuge in neutral ports. Many were caught in Allied harbors or at sea. A number tried and some succeeded in getting home. The notable exception: NDL's* Columbus. *It had left New York 19.8.1939 with 725 passengers on a West Indies cruise. When war threatened, passengers were landed at Havana. The ship refuged in Vera Cruz. It left 14.12.1939 to try to get home but was scuttled off the U.S. South Atlantic coast when HMS* Hyperion *found her. The crew was taken onto USS* Tuscaloosa. *Crews on refuged ships possibly continued to use their Ship Posts although UPU rules prescribe that a ship in port must use stamps of that nation. Last dates for cancels shown in this record are when the Ship Post equipment was lost or returned. Above, Ship Post used by* Columbus *in 1939 on its West Indies cruises. The photo is from Captain Daehne's last Christmas Greetings in 1938, and "Lucky New Year." The Luck didn't hold. A surprise happening on* Columbus *in December, 1937. The ship had just got back to Pier 84 after installation of the Lido Deck facilities, including a tiled pool ... finally! Captain Daehne was invited to a crew festivity: their presentation to him of a model of* Columbus *including the new topside facilities. It had been built on board.*

Fun and Games at Sea

Rudders on Bremen *and* Europa *differed, as did many other features.* Bremen *had an Oertz Rudder,* Europa *a streamlined but more old-fashioned balance rudder.* Ex. Arnold Kludas' Bremen and Europa, Koehler, Herford, 1993.

CHAPTER 12

The Lloyd Sails and Rows

Following the November, 1918 Armistice, the Allied food blockade continued. Not until 25 March, 1919 did the first aid shipment of foodstuffs arrive: bacon, fats, grains and flour, on the American steamer *West Carnifax*. Everything was scarcer even than during the war. Coal and foodstuffs were the direct necessities.

The same situation existed in Britain after World War II once Lend-lease ended. Conditions were more difficult in many ways than in the war, given there were no more bombs flying. My family and I lived in England for two years from January, 1946.

The Lloyd at the end of the war was left with tender *Grüssgott* of 781 Ts. as the largest vessel, plus an assortment of barges and tugs, and some experienced personnel, that survived the war to begin the rebuilding. An immediate challenge and opportunity was that the Baltic Sea was the only connection to East Prussia, cut off from the rest of Germany by the Polish Corridor mandated by the Treaty of Versailles.

It could be spanned by tenders, tugs and barges. Hans Jürgen Witthöft in his "Norddeutscher Lloyd", Koehler Verlag, shows a Lloyd tug in 1919 towing two lighters. Both have sails set to reduce coal consumption.

In December, 1919 the Deutsche Segelschiff Kontor, Sailship Agency, was founded to supply the German sailing vessels caught by the war in

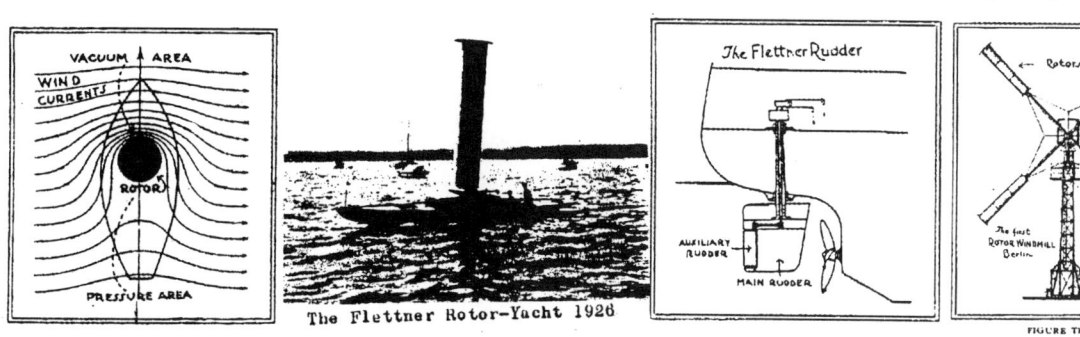

From a 1925 English-language brochure put out by the Flettner Company, Berlin head office, with agents in Holland and the U.S.A. Flettner also developed rudder designs for aircraft besides the ship rudders. By then, some 500 aircraft and one hundred ships had been equipped. His principle also was being tested for windmills.

Rudder of Berlin *#308 in 1925. Despite trying out the Flettner Rudder on* Königsberg *in 1924, the lessons were not applied on later ships.* Bremen *and* Europa *were given stream-lined rudders,* Bremens *a single plane hung vertically from the stern post,* Europa's *L-shaped, suspended at the angle from the bottom of the hull.*

Chile, including NDL's *Herzogin Cecile* #184, and to try to bring them home.

In the 1920s, the Engineer-Inventor Anton Flettner was searching for ways to utilize the wind for ship propulsion in the age of steam. He already had a number of patents to his credit. One was the Flettner stream-lined rudder installed in 1924 on NDL's *Königsberg* #305. The principle: it required less power to turn an auxiliary rudder set into the main rudder, the auxiliary turning it. Lothar-Günther Buchheim in his book "Das Boot" about submarine life in the last war, quotes the Captain of NDL's *Weser* #434: "We have a Flettner Rudder, designed by the same Flettner who invented the Rotor Ship. The rotors were a flop, but the rudder has been a great success. We can turn on a coin. In a narrow harbor that's a big advantage."

After the war, the Germania Shipyard in Kiel was building several three-masted schooners, given the coal shortage. On one two masts were replaced by large steel cylinders 56'1" high, 13'2" diameter resting on roller bearings. These turned with two 35HP electro-motors and the wind, driving the ship forward. This was the experimental *Buckau*, the rotors Flettner's invention. The hybrid was able to reach eight knots solely with the wind-turning of the rotors. They drove the ship through the Magnus Law: i.e., a cylinder rotating in a current of air exercises force at right angles to the direction of the air current. Based on *Buckau's* experience, the Reich Transport Ministry induced the Union of German Shipowners in 1926 to complete the freighter *Barbara* under construction as a three-rotors "sailship." These rotors would be used as auxiliaries to the ship's engine, or could alone provide the power. With its Diesel engines and the three rotors *Barbara* reached a top speed of 13.5 knots. Three knots of this was held due to the rotors. In actual service however due to calms or contrary winds, the rotors were usable only about one-fourth of the time. In principle, this development was a success. It was a way to use wind-power to supplement engine power. Economically, it was a failure as no shipowner was willing to undergo the expense of the installation given the uncertainty of performance.

During the early enthusiasm, the Lloyd, too, showed interest in rotors. In a letter on 19 January, 1925 to Captain Drechsel, Captain Paul König, Director of NDL's Nautical Dept., wrote "the widely discussed Flettner Rotorship - certainly this new way to utilize windpower is an ideal invention - moves with four points to the wind by Windforce 6, almost faster than the same type of vessel with normal sails." A designed tanker of 11,000 tons carrying capacity with three rotors was never built. A meeting of the Shipbuilding Technical Society criticized the unrealistic claims made for the Flettner rotor. The rotor *Barbara* was reconverted to a normal freighter. The rapid improvement in marine Diesel engines and the development of the Bauer-Wach exhaust turbine, using unspent steam from reciprocating engines, made rotors a distant also-ran in improving ship economics.

But the rotor principle remained a challenge. In 1985, Jacques Cousteau during the oil crisis, built the two-rotor 103' long *Alcyone* which achieved a 15-35% fuel saving on its maiden voyage LaRochelle-New York.

The findings: an unreliable system for widespread application. Possibly for bulk-carriers

Ship-picture card mailed on board the Rotor-Buckau on 8.8.1925 by a crew member sent from Swinemünde. See Main *#396 for photo with* Barbara. *Photo right: A third rotor ship* Baden Baden, *visited New York in 1926. Behind one of seven American Merchant Lines combi-vessels serving to the British Isles.*

Buckau *evidently off one of the Friesian Islands in the North Sea. From the number and types of people on board, it looks like a demonstration trip. Provided by a now-unknown member of the Belgian Nautical Research Association, 1960s.*

moving at a slow fifteen knots rotors might be feasible as auxiliaries. Cousteau's rotors were egg-shaped, not round as were Flettners.

Other techniques were tried to use the winds for auxiliary ship propulsion. The Soviet research vessel *Akademik Ioffe* built in 1989 in Finland had a rotor-resembling foldaway "sail". It provided the motive power during research when the main engines would have made interfering noises or vibration. The rotors were ten meters high, made of composite materials.

In 1984, the Japanese steamer *Aqua City*, 31,000 tons, had two computer-controlled sails of 352 square meters surface. On the maiden voyage Yokohama-Vancouver due to unfavorable winds the sails were used only during three days. On the second voyage, the sails operated for eleven days. At 13.5 knots with sails the ship used 13.3 tons of fuel per day, without sails 21 tons.

In 1985, Windstar Sail Cruises sailships *Windstar 1*, appeared, others following. All had 134 meters long sails on four masts, and two jib stay-sails controlled by computers. With no wind, the sails can be rolled up within two minutes; the vessels then run on their Diesels. Part of the attraction on cruising ships is to give passengers

The Lloyd Sails and Rows

Captain König's letter indicating the Lloyd was following the Rotor development. Note "Bremen Piers" in the Hoboken address.

much of the year. These container vessels incorporated two cargo-booms with operator cabins, strong enough to lift twenty-foot containers. Rigged vertically, they became sail-carrying masts. The outgoing voyage saved 12.5% in fuel with periodic use of the sails. All these specialized applications depend on proper wind circumstances to be of any benefit, hence are of limited use or adaptability.

In the 1920s and depression 1930s, a small number of square-riggers still filled a traditional function: long-distance delivery of bulk cargoes, principally grains from Australia, as until 1914 nitrates from Chile, were the main cargo. In 1927, Germany had built the *Deutschland* of 1257 tons as a sail-training ship.

In 1936, it was again time at the Lloyd for a sailship to train a new officers corps as its fleet was being rebuilt from the sell-offs and scrappings of the depression. NDL bought the *Magdalene Vinnen* built in 1921 for the F.A. Vinnen & Co., an old-time Bremen sailship concern. As with the Lloyd's two pre-1914 sailships, the training was provided during cargo-carrying voyages. The ship was renamed *Kommodore Johnsen,* the first NDL Commodore in 1929. See "Captains." In 1937, Hapag, too, bought a sailship for training, the 1908 Rickmers-built *L'Avenir* for Belgium. Its first captain had been NDL's Emil Zanders until Belgium could develop its own staff.

Renamed *Admiral Karpfanger,* it left Port Germain, South Australia, on 5 January, 1938 with a full cargo of wheat. The last wireless contact was on 12 March in the South Atlantic. Nothing was ever more heard. Did the cargo shift in a storm, capsizing the vessel, as happened to *Pamir* in 1957?

In rebuilding *Kommodore Johnsen* for cadets, a 500 HP Diesel was installed, the only remaining sailship with power. It was used only in port or difficult circumstances. Presumably, the propeller was removable as they were in the mid-to-late 1800s on warships still equipped with and using sails on long voyages. A length-wise bulkhead

the actual experience of handling the sails. The Japanese also have developed vessels with hollow rotor-masts from the inside of which the sails are spread by computer. A German version: Dyna-Ship, at one time licensed for U.S. construction, had free-standing masts that could be rotated. Sails stored inside were furled or spread by vertical rollers.

Another application in 1985 was the German-operated 6000 gross tons *Bold Eagle* and *Proud Eagle* for the Europe-Australia service via Cape of Good Hope where uni-directional winds blow

Jacques Cousteau's Rotor experiment used an egg-shaped contour, not Flettner's completely round design. 1986.

The fold-away rotor "sails" on the Soviet research vessel Akademik Ioffe. *Photo by L. van Ginderen, World Ship Society, 1989.*

was installed through the lower and tweendecks to prevent cargo shift. Despite this on one voyage Buenos Aires to Hamburg part of the grain cargo did shift. An *SOS* was sent out, but the crew was able to contain the situation. On *Kommodore Johnsen* as many as sixty cadets per voyage received their nautical training from the Captain and five merchant seamen officers-teachers. On board also were a Doctor, two engineers, a sailmaker, a carpenter, still referred to as Chips, and engine and kitchen staff, a total of seventy-seven.

The still-named *Magdalene Vinnen* in 1936 had won the Australia-Continent grain race described by Alan Villiers, the sailor-author. It was the first to reach the English Channel for orders, in 76 days, twenty days faster than the winner in "The Last Grain Race" of 1938-1939, by Eric Newby, a participant. "Beautiful as these ships were, they bred a tough race of men" wrote Villiers. Newby mentioned that on his ship, the *Moshulu*, there were some sails marked with *Herzogin Cecilie* stencils, it the Lloyd's pre-1914 training ship. Sailmakers usually put their logo and date onto

The Lloyd Sails and Rows   345

A 1980's German experiment with container vessels going around Cape of Good Hope to Australia, a route with long distances with steady winds, and experimental sails worked from and mounted on cargo cranes. Ex. Hamburg Port News.

Magdalene Vinnen, *built in 1921, in 1936 bought by NDL and rebuilt as training ship* Kommodore Johnsen, *taken from* Bremen *by R. Fleischhut. The hull was made from left-over plating intended for warships that were never built. This explains the excellent condition of the hull despite years of neglect by the Soviets.*

Lloyd cadets (training to be deck officers) on Kommodore Johnsen, *with their Bootsmann and officer-teachers, on Sunday Muster 1936.*

Kapitän Fred Schmidt. Presented his book Kapitäne Berichten, Captains Report, for which he had written several stories with this dedication to Captain Drechsel in 1937: As expression of my friendly esteem.

their sails. *Herzogin Cecilie* in 1928 under Finnish flag off the Hebrides Islands in a cross-sea was thrown on her beam end with a 70* list. This put the hatch covers under water. The ship survived but went ashore off the coast of Devon in 1936.

In the 1939 grain race, thirteen sailships participated. On the way out, *Kommodore Johnsen* sailed from the Weser River round Cape Horn for Port Lincoln, South Australia, 13,583 miles. It arrived on 2 March. After loading 5000 tons of grains, it left on the 26th to complete the round-the-world voyage via the Cape of Good Hope. It reached Queenstown "For Orders" on 11 July, then unloaded at Cork. From there, the ship sailed home for Bremerhaven and spent the war years there. One of the racers did not reach the Continent until after the war had begun. Captain Clausen stayed on board until *Kommodore Johnsen* was surrendered to the British in December, 1945. In 1937, at age 35 he was the Lloyd's youngest captain. The British did not put the ship into service. In 1946, it was passed on to the USSR. It vanished from western eyes. Evidently it lay untended for years off Kronstadt, the former Naval Base near Leningrad. In the 1970s, the ship was completely rebuilt, the hull still sound. As *Sedov* it became a training ship for the rapidly-expanding Soviet Navy. Later, in the Gorbachev era, paying passengers were carried to earn foreign exchange. As *Sedov,* the ship participated in New York's bicentennial *Opsail* gathering organized by Frank Braynard, ex-Shipping Reporter, now Curator of the American Merchant Marine Museum at Kings Point, Long Island, and other such gatherings. *Sedov* now is in the Lithuanian Navy.

Pamir was one of four former Flying P Line

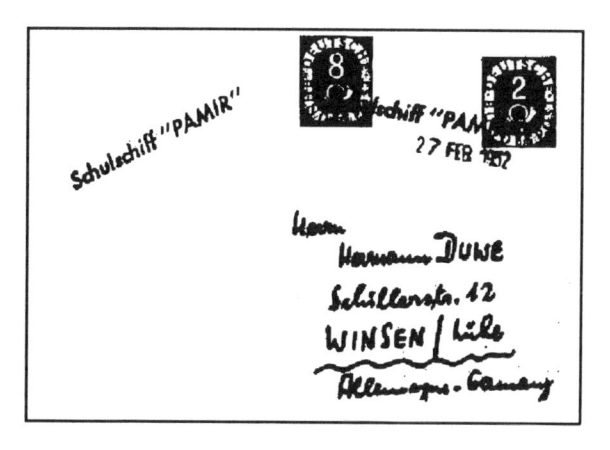

Cover from the Training Ship Pamir *owned by the Schliewen Reederei in 1952, along with sister* Passat.

The Lloyd Sails and Rows

A Dartmouth College student, William F. Stark, 1950, heard in Winter, 1948 that a sailship lay in the Thames. He found it was *Passat* en route to South Australia to pick up a cargo of grain, along with *Pamir*. Stark bought a low-cost ticket on an aircraft ferrying Italian farmers to Australia. When he got to Port Victoria he found work as stevedore until the two ships arrived with full crews. He wrote "unloading *Pamir's* ballast of sand and gravel and then loading 60,000 bags of barley took nearly a month. Three days before the job was finished, a brawl broke out in a waterfront pub. Authorities sentenced three *Pamir* crew members to ninety days each in the Adelaide jail. I was signed on as an able-bodied seaman and joined the thirty-man crew of Australians, New Zealanders and Finns. I was the only American.

We set sail from Port Victoria in May 1949 bound for Falmouth, England, 16,000 nautical miles away. Thus began the world's last commercial Cape Horn voyage under sail, an event that helped mark the end of the sailing era. It was winter in the Southern Hemisphere, and we sailed toward Cape Horn. Soon we were plowing through heavy gray seas less than 600 miles from the Antarctic Circle. We were constantly wet, cold, and exhausted.

The work was unbelievably demanding. We spent much of the time aloft, taking in sail in the heavy winds, then letting it out as the winds diminished, only to take it in again. The tops of three of the *Pamir's* four masts were 168 feet above the deck. To get aloft, we climbed rope ladders made up of heavy vertical lines called shrouds, with smaller horizontal ropes servings as rungs, called ratlines. Upon reaching the yardarm (the horizontal spar to which the sail was fastened), we edged out on a cable foot-rope. With our feet balanced on this single cable, we pulled in the canvas and furled it to the yardarm, with nothing but a void and certain death below for the unwary. We worked for hours in these heights; I was amazed how quickly I had grown used to being aloft.

The *Pamir* was now well south, with raging Antarctic gales the norm. With only six hours of daylight in 24, we worked much of the time in the dark both aloft and on deck. There were many times when I desperately wished I'd never left home and college.

One night, not far off Cape Horn, the wind began to freshen rapidly. The mate blew the whistle and we stumbled onto a dark, heaving deck. He ordered three of us to take in the fore royals, the uppermost sails. With the wind clawing at our clothes, we climbed a rope ladder as high as a 14-story building. Below, the 316-foot ship performed like an acrobat. The three of us spent 15 or 20 minutes on the yardarm, furling canvas. We worked only a few feet apart, but it was so dark that we were barely visible to one another. The shrieking wind made it impossible to hear, and the masts thrashed around violently. It took a real effort to hold on.

Finished, we edged our way along the yardarm to the mast. I saw a line that still needed securing. The other two started climbing down. I followed a minute later. Meanwhile the temperature had plunged and I could feel a light icy glaze on parts of the shrouds. This was a new experience. As I descended I grasped the ropes as tightly as I could.

I was 150 feet above the deck when a terrific sea smashed into the ship. The mast gave a convulsive lurch. My feet were wrenched from the ratlines. I clung desperately to the icy ropes, my feet vainly seeking the ratlines in the black night. I knew it was only a matter of seconds before I would lose my grip and plummet through the dark Antarctic night. I remember exactly what I shouted into the wind: "Dear Lord, please help me get my body back on the ship."

Whether I imagined it or not, the ship seemed to make an unusual motion, almost the reverse of what had created my predicament. My right foot found a ratline. Ten minutes later I had climbed down to the ice-coated deck.

We rounded Cape Horn on July 11 and as we turned north the winds dropped, the seas subsided, and the temperature rose. We crossed the equator on August 5. On October 5, 1949, after almost five months at sea, the *Pamir* dropped anchor in Falmouth, England. Stark concludes "That trip on the Pamir with all its difficulties satisfied my longing to go to sea."

Pamir *in rough weather.* Norman MacNeal Photo *in* National Geographic Magazine.

Greetings to Edwin Drechsel by Captain Richard Sietas, in 1955 at the Schliewen Reederei which in 1952 bought Passat *and* Pamir *to keep them in service and as historical vessels. In 1959, Captain Sietas attended that year's gathering of the Amicale Internationale des Capitaines Au Long-Cours, the Albatrosses, now all gone. Count von Luckner also attended (see below). Sietas was Honorary Chairman of the Amicale's Hamburg chapter. During the period 1908-1927 he went around Cape Horn twenty times under sail. Many an attempted rounding of the Cape ended in the ship turning around and going via Africa. In early 1954 he wrote the author "On 24.4.54, it will be decided if* Pamir *and* Passat *again will be put into service. The best regards, Capt. Sietas."*

Capt. R. Sietas
Schulschiff „PASSAT"
Schliewen - Reederei
Travemünde

The best regards
Capt. Sietas.

Am 24.4.54 wird sich entscheiden, ob die beiden Schiffe "Passat" u "Pamir" wieder in Fahrt kommen.

Alte Cap-Horniers bei dem Treffen in Hamburg (von links nach rechts: Graf Luckner, Kapt. Geissler, Kapt. Grubbe, Kapt. Schütze).

Foto: Conti-Press

The Lloyd Sails and Rows

100 Jahre

Jubiläum unseres Seniors

Foto: Klaus Wolfgang Vogt

Überreichung der Cap-Hornier-Medaille an Kapt. Gerhard Bolte in Elsfleth durch Kapt. Mellert am 6. Juni 1962

(links Kapt. Schönicke, rechts Kapt. Giese, Elsfleth)

A birthday cake came from Canada in 1962 for the Lloyd's oldest captain: Gerhard Bolte. Of his three sons, the oldest fell in World War I, the youngest in 1962 was studying medicine in Minden. The middle son Hans-Hinrich had emigrated to Canada. Now, on Berlin, Captain Vollmers on the bridge, he was bringing a birthday cake for 6.6.1962, his Father's 100th birthday. A Cap Hornier, too. Here the Cap Hornier Medal-Emblem is being given to Captain Bolte on 6.6.1962 by Captains Schönicke and Giese, photo by Klaus Wolfgang Vogt in Der Albatros, *of the German unit of the Amicale Internationale des Capitaines au Long-Cours.*

> WER DES MORGENS DREI MAL SCHMUNZELT
> MITTAG'S NICHT DIE STIRNE RUNZELT
> ABEND'S SINGT "DASS ALLES SCHALLT
> DER WIRD 100 JAHRE ALT! —

At the time, the author's Father sent him this verse, my translation, author unknown:

> *He whose morning smile spreads pleasure*
> *Noontime can enjoy his leisure*
> *Evenings sings "All's well that's told,"*
> *He'll wake up one hundred years old.*

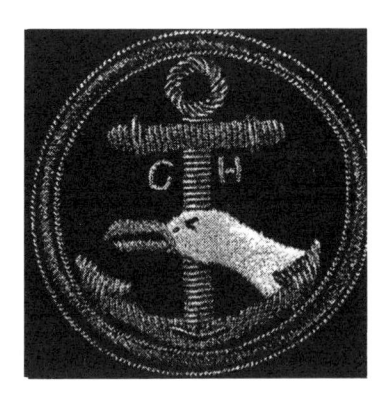

Insignium badge of the Cap Horniers with the "Wandering Albatross." Rounding the Horn under sail marked ships and men as a breed apart. And in 1994, French women.

sailships to participate in the 1930s grain races. *Pamir* was lost on 21 September, 1957 during Hurricane Carrie in 35.57N, 40.20S, some 600 miles WSW of the Azores. Evidently the cargo of barley shifted. *Pamir* capsized with loss of eighty of her 86-man crew. Captain Fred Schmidt was on board as First Officer. He was gathering material for a book on the ship. In the 1930s Captain Drechsel had contributed sea stories to Schmidt's first book *"Kapitäne Berichten"*, Captains Report.

In 1940, members of the crew from the scuttled *Columbus* #300, see "War," then living on Angel Island in San Francisco Bay, made a scale model of *Pamir* and prepresented it, with a whaleboat model and painting of Mount Lassen done by *Columbus'* Purser Hans Thielbaar, to Captain Drechsel in thanks for his work in their behalf and that of other interned or rescued German seamen in North America. The models were presented by me to the Museum on Angel Islands, along with other artifacts from *Columbus*.

On 6 June, 1962 the Cap Hornier Medal was bestowed on Captain Gerhard Bolte on his 100th birthday by a delegation from the Internationale Amicale Internationale des Capitaines au Long-Cours, with seat in St. Malo. Bolte spent ten years under sail. He obtained his Captain's Patent in March, 1897 and came to the Lloyd as 2. Officer on *Friedrich Der Grosse* #96, in 1896, the first German ship of more than 10,000 tons. He then served on *Kaiser Wilhelm der Grosse* #100, the Lloyd's Blue Ribbon holder. He used a trick learned in his sailship days to free The Great Kaiser from its pier in Hoboken during the 30 June, 1900 fire, see "Per Aspera ...
- I: Crossing the docking lines he had the winches pull

Sacked grain stacked in readyness for loading onto the sailships, at a port on the Gulf of Spencer, South Australia. Photo from Captain Robert Clauss of the Flying P, F. Laeisz Line, in Neue Kapitäns-Berichte, Captain Fred Schmidt. Verlag Dietrich Reimer, Berlin 1937.

so that the bow came away from the pier while the stern was pulled in. The current in the Hudson did the rest and *KWDG* got free with minor damage. In February, 1919 Bolte was captain of *Sierra Ventana* returning French prisoners to Brest when the France seized the ship. In 1923, he took over the new freighter *Elberfeld* #298. My Mother, Sister and I travelled on her in March-April to Australia around the Cape. There was a brief mutiny by part of the crew in the South Atlantic. Bolte had a Dobermann Pinscher on board.

All who rounded Cape Horn under sail were known as Cap Horniers. Those who sailed as captains were called Albatrosses. The 1959 annual Amicale meeting was held in Hamburg, Count von Luckner among the Albatrosses. Now they belong to history. The Amicale's Museum in St. Malo has preserved much of the records and artifacts of the Cape Horn sailship era. In 1986, the last German Albatross, Captain Gottfried Clausen, died. He had spent fifty years at sea, thirty-two of them as Lloyd officer and Captain, last on *Ravenstein* #495 and *Regenstein* #516.

The Chinese probably were the first to send sailing ships on many-thousand miles voyages as far as Africa.

The U.S. was the first to require lifeboats on ocean-going vessels beginning in 1852 with the organization of the U.S. Steamboat Inspection Service. First specific regulations were issued in 1875, undoubtedly requiring stowing of sails and masts.

The ability to handle a lifeboat at sea literally can decide for life over death for a ship's crew in trouble. Seamanship is what being on a ship at sea is all about. As should be rowing in close quarters, perhaps taking a line from one vessel to another, the start of rigging a buoy to bring across people, or sailing over vast distances to try to reach land from a lost ship.

During accidents at sea it was found that ship crews rarely had experienced rowing together. And that most lifeboats were too heavy to row. Lifeboat races thus were suggested as helping the Safety-of-Life-at Sea programs.

The first known such race in modern times was held quite incidentally in the Chincha Islands off Peru in the 1860s. A number of sailships lay there loading guano. The American crews were joined by other nationalities in a July Fourth celebration ashore. This ended in some one's challenge and a resulting life-boat race. Who won in unrecorded. Ex "The Lamp," Fall, 1963.

The U.S. Navy, the Coast Guard and even the Army in Hawaii began holding boat races as good for physical development and as safety training. In 1927, in New York Harbor, merchant ship lifeboat racing was begun in modern times with mul-

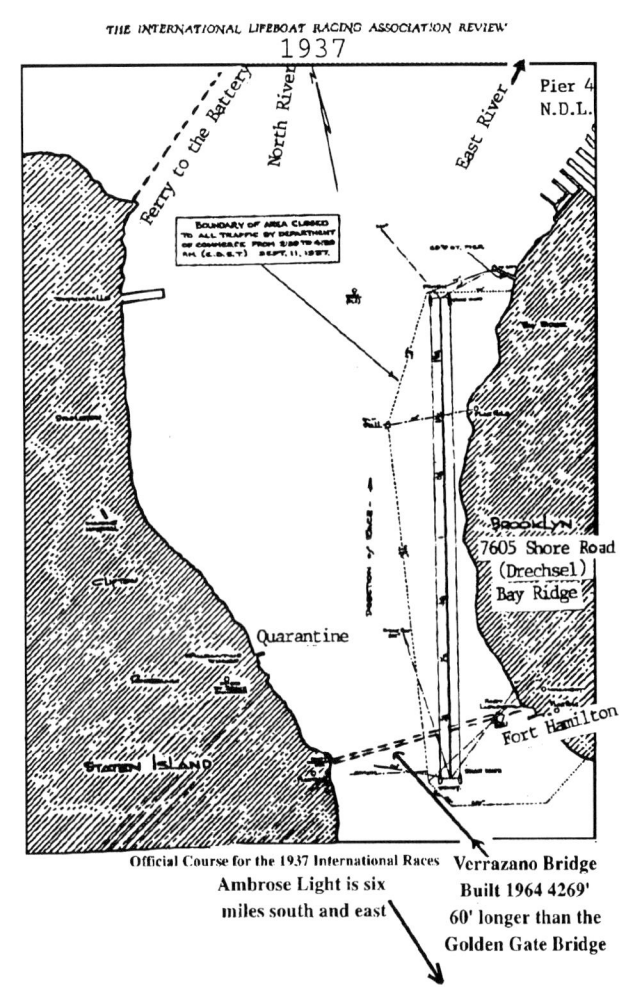

Site of the International Lifeboat races from 1931 on was off Bay Ridge, Brooklyn.

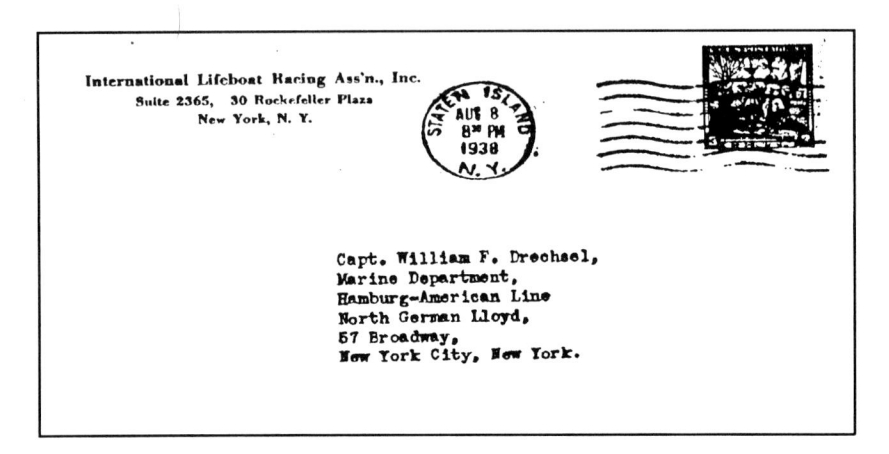

The International Lifeboat Racing Association had its offices on one of the Standard Oil of New Jersey floors, 23-29th, in 30 Rockefeller Plaza, with the Rockefellers themselves on the top floors, beneath the Rainbow Room, the spot to spend an evening when wishing to impress. Captain Robert Hague of ESSO (Standard Oil) donated the new trophy after the Norwegians lifted the original one with five victories.

tiple sponsorship: The Neptune Association of Shipmasters and Officers, The Coast Guard, tugboat concerns, the city's Police Marine Patrol. Besides teaching boat-handling, the aim was to strengthen the bond within New York's foreign and domestic maritime industry and to remind the public of shipping's worldwide role and importance.

Twelve boats from seven nations entered the race. No two boats were alike. A Norwegian crew from the *M.S. Segundo* won, covering the mile course from the Statue of Liberty to the Battery in 15 minutes, 17 seconds. In 1929, it was another Norwegian crew from *Sud Americano*, in 1934 it became NDL's *Weser* #434, that won. The International Lifeboat Racing Trophy was donated by Robert L. Hague, head of Esso's shipping operations. Since then lifeboat races have been held and still are being held in ports around the world. That in New York is considered the equivalent of Churchill Downs. The Norwegians eventually lifted the Trophy with five wins and the best time ever for the mile distance: 9 minutes, 6 seconds. Shipping lines used advanced scheduling to organize crews for practice months ahead of the Labor Day weekend races, held until the war without break. The competitors all had to be working seamen.

The location changed several times: first north from the George Washington Bridge across the Hudson and again in 1935. In 1931, the race was moved to Bay Ridge, Brooklyn: two miles from outside the Narrows, where now the Verrazano Bridge crosses the harbor entrance, to the 69th Street jetty: starting and finishing line between Coast Guard cutters.

The annual events led to redesign of lifeboats for better handling and usability at sea. And alerted ship officers, and owners, to provide training for crews that might have to handle them. The benefit, too, was that the Port of New York's shipping personnel became something of a fraternity tied by common interests. The officers, judges, inspection, rules and ballast committee members, timekeepers, starters, course patrollers, committee directors were an international Who's Who of shipping.

In 1932, the Norwegian *Bergensfjord* set the still-standing

The wreck of Elbe #50 *was found in the 1960s 42 miles offshore by fishermen from Scheveningen. The first dive to what was named The Porthole Wreck was made in 1972. The Diving Club Sirene bought an old Zuider Zee Botter and rebuilt it over two years. They brought up artifacts, including this trim from the Dining Room, the sugarer, and from the cargo these figurines made by the Rudolstadt Pottery.*

The find was announced on 28 January, 1993, and artifacts and history were displayed April-October, 1994 at the Scheveningen Museum. P.P. de Keijzer is writing a book about the Elbe *and Wreck, due out in 1995. He provided the information and photographs.*

From left to right: Cor Wauben, skipper of Pluvier, *Paul de Keyzer, Frans van der Horst, Hans Grootscholte, Arie Visser. Not shown: Jan Dubbelman and Nico van Moerkon*

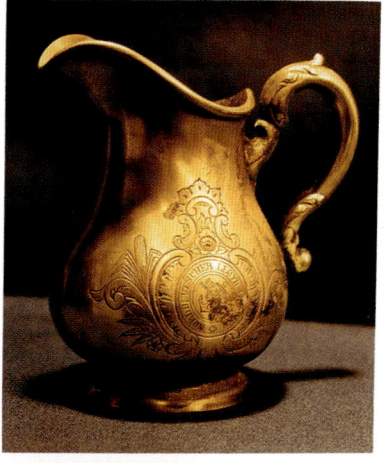

Color Album   353

Examples of trans-Atlantic mail carried on Lloyd steamers and the relevant postal markings. Both are "by Steamer Bremen", NDL's first ocean vessel. The top cover from the David L. Jarrett collection, Courtesy Christie's Robson Lowe auction, in 1859 shows the America über Bremen *marking of the U.S. Postal Agency 1847-1867 in Bremen, also the New York arrival marking* Bremen P(ac)K(et).

Below: From correspondence of Koecher & Co., Manchester via the "St. Main" of NDL's weekly trans-Atlantic service to the Melchers and Schaefer agencies in Honolulu. The Bremen-based Melchers were the Lloyd agents in Hong Kong and China. From the March, 1987 Heinrich Koehler auction in Wiesbaden.

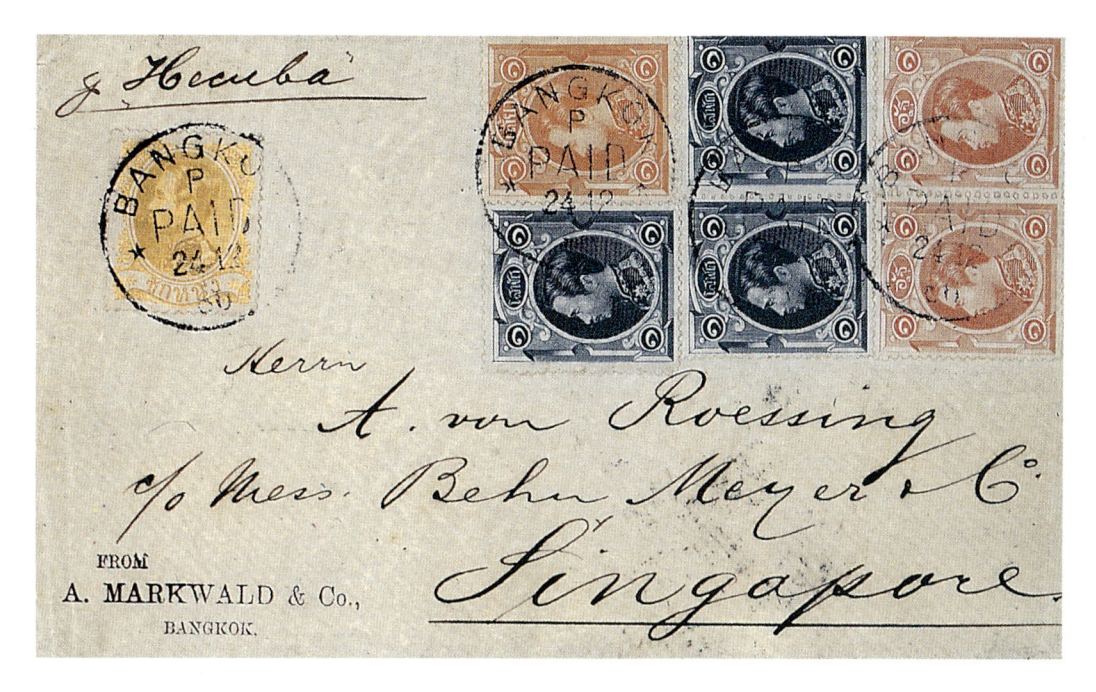

In 1899, NDL bought two British East Asia coastal fleets with twenty-five vessels to expand the distribution from and into the East Asia Imperial Mail Line opened in 1886. This envelope from German shipping agents in Bangkok went to the Lloyd's agents in Singapore via Alfred Holt's Hecuba, *in 1899 among the ships bought by NDL, and renamed* Kudat. *The sender of the letter, Markwald & Co., in 1911 bought NDL's Mekong River rice distributor* Langeoog #197. *Courtesy Christie's March, 1995 auction in Singapore.*

In 1928, as publicity promotion for its express steamers Europa *and* Bremen, *due to make their maiden voyages in April, 1929, the Lloyd financed twin aircraft with the ships' names ("The Lloyd Flies").* Bremen *crossed the Atlantic East to West in April, with Captain Herman Koehl, Major James Fitzmaurice and Freiherr von Huenefeld, NDL's Press-Promotions Chief. In September,* Europa *with von Huenefeld and Swedish K.G. Lindner as Pilot, flew across Asia to Tokyo. This cover is from the flight of the Calcutta-Bangkok-Tokyo segments. Collectors provided 93 items all marked with Huenfeld and Europa rubber stamps. Courtesy Christie's Robson Lowe March, 1995 auction in Singapore. See page 208.*

Color Album 355

Typical Steerage/Tweendeck quarters for emigrants on Lloyd ships pre-1900. The card has the Lloyd's name in Cyrillic characters, so these probably are Russians. The Lloyd, Hapag, and Lloyd emigrant agent Missler, had stations on the eastern borders to eliminate those not likely to gain admittance to the U.S., for health or other reasons.
Frank Pichardo Collection.

In 1898, Hapag bought the Kingsin Line and its Far East freight and passenger service. Seven of the ships were sold to the NDL in the agreement for Hapag to enter the East Asia Imperial Mail Service, for which it then ordered two NDL-type passenger ships.

The Lloydheim, Bremen Senior Retirement Center, at the head of Admiral Strasse. It was torn down in 1988; there now is the Diakon House, a Church Retirement Center. The card was Seaposted **Bremen-La Plata** *in 1925. "From Spain you shall hear again from us."*

Lloyd Guide to its Mediterranean services and 1906 schedules. Although the Lloyd for years offered no pleasure cruises, its various lines especially in the Mediterranean, made "cruises" possible and popular.

Cover of an annual booklet for passengers travelling on the Imperial Mail steamers to East Asia and Australia.

Cap band worn by Deck Personnel with dress uniform. Barbarossa was one of the 10 000 tonners that set the pace to Australia and East Asia. They also ran to the U.S. East Coast in season.

Color Album 357

Top photo: Transfer of mail at Quarantine from the incoming liner to Postmaster General, the Post Office's tender, and below: Sorting the mail at the G.P.O. Painted by Reginald Marsh.

Left: Cover of a booklet prepared in the Red Cross workshop to celebrate the "Glorious America-Voyage of the Merchant Submarine "Deutschland", 1916, actually two voyages. Sistership "Bremen" was lost on her outward voyage in August.

Bottom: Post Card written 21.1.1917 to go via the third sailing of the U-Deutschland. Same-day cancel of T(auch) B(oot) of D(eutsche) O(zean) R(eederei), the name of the shipping company organized largely by NDL personnel to operate the planned eight submarines. The large Zurück mark was applied when the voyage was cancelled due to break of diplomatic relations with the U.S., soon followed by war. I show on the card the Diving Boat Sea Post mark given to Postmaster/Censor Chief Officer W. Drechsel for use at sea.

Bottom right: From the first set of six mail-insurance stamps issued for the commercial submarine service from Bremen to the U.S. in 1916. The stamps bear "delivered" and date when the items were handed in. The second issue lacks the wording "Deutschland-Amerika". It also had M75 and M100 values.

Color Album 359

1924 and 1931 schedules of the Lloyd's North Sea island resorts services. Like NDL's river-towing services, these began in the year of founding, 1857, along with two routes to Britain by bird-named sail-assisted steamers. These three services provided cash flow until trans-Atlantic service began in mid-1858. And, in 1919-1920 after World War I, and after 1945, they were the beginnings of rebuilding from war.

The three were together in service only from Europa's maiden voyage in January, 1966 to Berlin's last cruise arrival in Bremerhaven on 15 October, after which she left for Italy and breakup. From: Bridge Across The Atlantic, Hapag-Lloyd A.G.

Color Album 361

362 *Norddeutscher Lloyd Bremen*

Mosel Express in *1970 loading Hapag-Lloyd containers at Elizabeth, New Jersey, one of four sisters that opened trans-Atlantic service in 1968-69. The ships had high bows to minimize wave impact on deck loads, and self-adjusting fin stabilizers. The four were lengthened with midbody inserts to increase their capacity in 1973. Painted by Albert Brenet for* Tow Line *of the Moran Towing & Transportation Company, active in almost every New York docking by Lloyd vessels.*

Above: Bremen 6, *chartered with option to buy. Built 1990 as* Frontier Spirit, *one-eighth Hapag-Lloyd ownership, for 184 passengers. November, 1993 renamed for first cruise in H-L colors. Note passengers are going exploring in Zodiacs.*

Below: Europa 4 *in the Kiel Canal, mast tops down to pass under bridges, 1960s. Later she was painted all white.*

Right: The initial compromise in the 1970 Lloyd and Hapag merger was for all ships to fly the Lloyd anchor-key-wreath flag and wear the Hapag black-white-red topped stacks. Bremen 5 *and* Europa 4 *kept their golden-yellow stacks into 1972. Then* Bremen *was sold and* Europa *first showed the new cognac stacks and blue HL logo on stack and houseflag. The freight ships kept the old stacks and flag to 1.1.1987 when they, too, switched. Gone were the Lloyd flag and Hapag stack.*

364   *Norddeutscher Lloyd Bremen*

General Von Steuben's *crew as second in 1933 receiving its trophy. Inspector Drechsel at right. 2. Officer Sempt was Coxswain.*

Finish line off the old 69th Street ferry from Bay Ridge to Staten Island. The Coast Guard cutter, right, is the shoreside end of the line. In 1932 and again in 1933, the crew from General Von Steuben *#293, came in second. In 1933, the association did not know what the current German flag was with the National Socialists in power. So a two-sided flag was made: one side the black-white and red, the other the swastika flag.* Photo by W. Kaune, Board Photographer - Stuttgart.

The Lloyd Sails and Rows

1933. The starting scene. General Von Steuben *second from right. And its boat and crew.*

In 1937, Europa's *crew arriving at Bay Ridge led by 3. Officer Heinz-Alwin Wode. At right Captains Drechsel and Oskar Scharf,* Europa's *Commander. The Lloyd flag at left.*

Norddeutscher Lloyd Bremen

THE INTERNATIONAL LIFEBOAT RACING ASSOCIATION PROGRAM

OFFICIALS
INTERNATIONAL LIFEBOAT RACING ASSOCIATION, INCORPORATED

Hon. James A. Farley, *Chairman of 1935 Racing Committee*
John D. Reilly, *President*

J. J. Kelleher, *Vice President*	Captain John F. Milliken, *Secretary*
Fred B. Dalzell, *Vice President*	Robert F. Hand, *Treasurer*
Henry Herbermann, *Vice President*	M. D. Stauffer, *Asst. Treasurer*

Directors

R. J. Baker	Robert L. Hague	Captain John W. McGrath
Ernest M. Bull	E. F. Johnson	Aroldo Palanca
Ira Campbell	Franklin D. Mooney	Joseph W. Powell
Captain Wm. Drechsel	Hon. Edward P. Mulrooney	E. P. Rees
John M. Franklin	A. B. Sharp	

Entertainment Committee
R. L. Hague, *Chairman*

Committee on Arrangements
Captain J. F. Milliken, *Chairman*

Referee
Hon. Edward P. Mulrooney

Judges
Sir Gerald Campbell (*England*)
Hon. J. R. Dahl (*Denmark*)
Hon. H. H. Durning (*U.S.*)
Hon. C. H. Marie de Ferry de Fontnouvelle (*France*)
Hon. E. Hougen (*Norway*)
Dr. Pasquale P. Spinelli (*Italy*)
Dr. Siegfried von Nostiz (*Germany*)

Honorary Judges
James French
Captain J. F. Hottel
J. L. Luckenbach
Captain T. H. Taylor
Hon. Joseph B. Weaver

Judges of the Course
Capt. Thomas M. Molloy, *Chairman*
R. J. Baker
Commander J. S. Baylis
Major D. W. Calhoun
Fred B. Dalzell
P. A. Kjeve

Course Patrol
Captain H. A. Malley (*N.Y.P.D.*)
Lieutenant G. H. Miller (*U.S.C.G.*)
Lieutenant B. E. Moodey (*U.S.C.G.*)
Lieutenant George English (*N.Y.P.D.*)
Commander Chester H. Jones (*U.S.C.G.*)

Starters
Paul Revere Smith, *Official Starter*
G. W. Milliken   Captain T. T. Tonnesen
George Clay   Thomas H. White

Timekeepers
Willard F. Jones, *Official Timekeeper*
Charles S. Hand   James O'Connor
R. K. Kelly   Arthur Tode   James Rundel

International Rules and Regulations Committee

Captain Wm. Drechsel, *Chairman*	H. E. Frick
Captain George Fried, *Vice Chairman*	Captain W. H. Lee
Samuel Aitken	Captain H. N. McDougall
Captain S. Christensen	Joseph Sirignano
H. J. Esselborn	Captain James Thompson

Ballast Committee
Captain Wm. Drechsel, *Chairman*
Captain J. Elligera
Dr. A. Lauria
Captain C. Lindholm
A. Warner Melvin
Captain H. N. McDougall

Inspection Committee
Captain Karl C. Nielsen, *Chairman*
C. S. Durfee
A. D. MacCorkindale

Police Committee
Chief Inspector John J. Seery
Deputy Chief Inspector David J. McAuliffe

The diversity and professionalism of New York's Maritime Community is shown in this 1935 list of Race Officials. A strong phone-call-away Kameraderie developed.

two-miles record: 17 minutes, 27 seconds. NDL's *General von Steuben* crew came in second, again was runner-up in 1933. Not knowing what German flag to fly since the National Socialists only recently had seized power, a flag was made with the Black, White and Red on one side and the Swastika on the other. An estimated 250,000 persons lined the Shore Road and the Brooklyn waterfront to watch the race.

In 1934, Postmaster General James Farley presented the trophy to the winning crew from the Italian *Rex*. In 1935, Hapag-Lloyd's Marine Superintended Drechsel was chairman of the Ballast Committee. Crews from *Hamburg* and *Europa* competed, its boat under 2. Officer Kax Kuhlig as coxswain. The Coast Guard's Commander J.S. Bayles was Judge of the Course. In 1939, when war broke, Captain Drechsel gave his binoculars to Commander Bayles for the duration.

From 1937 on standard Coast Guard boats were used by the competitors. That year also the 11th race of the Apostleship of the Sea and the First International Surfboat races were run. At that year's Maritime Day celebration, presided over by Maritime Commission Chairman Joseph P. Kennedy, waters from the North Sea were mixed with those of other seas and of New York harbor in commemoration of the seamen who lost their lives during the year. Names of the *Hindenburg* dead also were read.

In 1938, Rear Admiral Emory S. Land, USN (ret.), Chairman of the Maritime Commission, was Race Committee Chairman. And the first annual Coast Guard Capsize Race was held, an extension of the need to meet any eventuality.

No races were held in 1939 and into the 1950s because of the war. They then were resumed with a new trophy and new committees. San Francisco, in typical California fashion, widened the whaleboat racing appeal with women's and co-ed crews, including entries by Anchor Steam Beer, a San Francisco specialty. In the 11th annual race, in 1994, there were female bowhooks in the fourteen boats. Over a three-quarters mile course American President Lines won the men's, the Coast Guard the women's, and International Trading Company the mixed division.

World War II had incidents similar to those in the earlier war: Crews trying to reach home or a friendly shore from loss of their ship, or from their interned vessel. Lifeboats in the last war rarely were equipped with sails as in WWI. But

The Lloyd Sails and Rows

> **Waters for Maritime Day**
> For the first time since the observance was instituted, German waters will be included in the annual Maritime Day ceremony at the Battery when waters from all the seas are mingled with that of New York harbor in commemoration of the seamen who lost their lives during the year. Capt. William Drechsel, chief marine superintendent of the Hamburg-American Line-North German Lloyd, has this year arranged for a flask of North Sea water to be brought over especially for the ceremony, which takes place today in accordance with President Roosevelt's proclamation of this date as National Maritime Day in remembrance of the sailing of the steam ship Savannah from Savannah, Ga., May 22, 1819. This year the names of the officers and crew of the Hindenburg who lost their lives in the airship's destruction will also be read.

In May, 1937, with Joseph P. Kennedy as new chairman of the USMC, National Maritime Day was celebrated on 22 May, in commemoration of the sailing of the Savannah, *first ship to use steam as an aid to sails. The tributes included wreaths for the lost crews of the USS Dirigible* Akron *and the* Hindenburg, *with water from the North Sea, and other parts of the world mixed with those of the Hudson River. All Mankind is the same on the seas. A message of Tribute to the* Hindenburg *crew was broadcast by Mrs. Clara Adams, on behalf of the National Maritime Association from the Hapag* Deutschland, *which brought over the water from the North Sea. Captain Drechsel (see below) also spoke over the NBC-disseminated program.* Courtesy of the New York Times.

officers at least knew how to rig makeshift sails and how to navigate to land. Reliance on sail was fairly frequent:

- *Columbus* lay in Antonio Lizardo Lagoon fourteen kms south of Vera Cruz. There it had sheltered when war began, but it was exposed to hurricanes. Weekly, one of her lifeboats sailed from the anchorage to Vera Cruz for mail, news, supplies, etc. The fuel on board for the motor was being saved for possible later use.
- When war broke nine German ships took refuge in Curacao, then neutral waters, including NDL's *Hannover* #452 and *Este* #425. They tied up side by side. The Chief Officer on *Hannover* and several crewmen prepared a lifeboat in the hope of sailing to the Canary Islands, from where getting home might be feasible, some 3,500 miles. The captain refused to let them proceed.
- The *Alster* #410, see Captain Scharf's report in "War", was captured by the Royal Navy in the German seizure of Norway. In British service it was sunk in April, 1941. Twenty-eight survivors sailed for twenty days from 450 miles north of Scotland until they were found and taken aboard a rescue ship.
- At the end of August, 1939 *Erlangen* #419 lay in Dunedin at the end of a long fjord. The next stop was to be Port Kembla, N.S.W., to coal, then to head for home. But at sea the wireless warned "War." On 30 August off Auckland Island south of N.Z.'s South Island, with only 250 tons of coal on board, the ship was run ashore near where trees were seen. The felling of trees and cutting them up provided 250 tons of burnables: All hand-loaded onto the ship. The voyage summary prepared by Captain A. Grams provides details:
  - Left the Auckland Islands on 6 October, 1939.
  - Reached Ancud, Chile on 11 November, or 35 days, 18 hours en route.
  - The ship sailed with makeshift sails made on board for 1,507 nautical miles.
  - It steamed for 3,319 miles, or a total of 4,826 miles.
  - Burned on the voyage were a total of 510 tons: coal - 154 tons, burnables taken from the ship itself - 121 tons, wood from trees cut on Auckland Island - 235 tons.
- *Frankfurt* #416 was trying to get home from where it had taken refuge when war broke. On 4 August, 1941 it was scuttled when a British warship caught up with it. One lifeboat with the captain and twenty-five crewmen was taken by the naval vessel. A second boat with the 1. Officer and several men was not seen and sailed away. The target: the Azores some 540 miles distant. En route they met the *S.S. Pan Norden*. It took on only a sick crewman. Then the boat met the Portuguese *Vouga* which took the remaining twenty to Lisbon.

```
         NATIONAL MARITIME DAY
              MAY 22nd, 1937
           Aerial and Foot Pilgrimage
                Under Auspices of
       NATIONAL MARITIME ASSOCIATION
             LILY W. REED, Founder-Organizer
            2 Broadway, New York, N. Y.
                        ✠
                  ... PROGRAM ...
Dawn till 11:30
National Memorial Wreath on display New York Produce Exchange
11:45
PROCESSION_____Wreath to U. S. Custom House under Color Guard of Honor of
                    U. S. COAST GUARD, U.S.S. WHEELING and U.S.S. ILLINOIS
CALL TO COLORS_____Bugler, Receiving Ship, U. S. Navy Yard
ESCORT OF HONOR_____Retired Master Mariners, Sailor's Snug Harbor
        Mrs. John Franklin McDougall, Chairman, Patriotic Societies of America
                    Mrs. Lily W. Reed, Creator and Designer of Wreath
Flower Girls___Misses Genieve and Martha Huntington, daughters of Capt. Robert Huntington,
                                          Seaman's Church Institute
                             Miss Ruth L. Scarr and Millicent Reed
12:00
PLACING OF WREATH_____Tribute to Heroic Dead of U. S. Merchant Marine
Bouquets by State and Patriotic Societies
PLACING OF PROPELLER_____Tribute to Five American Airships lost at Sea
                                by Clyde Pangborn, Around the World Flyer
Placing of "Akron" Crew Tribute_____by Rear Admiral Yates Stirling, Jr.
Placing of "Hindenburg" Crew Tribute_____Lily W. Reed
PRAYER_____Rev. H. Kelly, Seaman's Church Institute
Placing of NATIONAL FLAG_____U. S. Coast Guard
Presentation of NOLAN-STIRLING American Merchant Marine Achievement Trophy
                   Dedicated by Mrs. James Roosevelt, Mother of the President of the U. S
1937 AWARD to Hon. ROYAL S. COPELAND, U. S. Senator from N. Y.
                         by Hon. HARRY M. DURNING, Collector of Customs
1 till 4:30
Wreath under Color Guard, on View on the steps of the U. S. Custom House
4:30
Procession to Pier "A"_____Reception by the Hon. John McKenzie, Commissioner of Docks
Release at the Change of Tide
INVOCATION_____Rev. George Greene, Sailor's Snug Harbor
Consignment of Wreath to the Waters of the Hudson River_____By Millicent Reed
            In Memory of Capt. Reginald Fay, N. Y. State Merchant Marine Academy
            Ruth L. Scarr, in Memory of Dr. James H. Scarr, U. S. Weather Bureau
BAPTISM OF WREATH with waters from United States for National Heroes
BAPTISM OF WREATH with water from the North Sea for Heroes of "HINDENBURG" Crew
SALUTE TO THEIR DEPARTED MARINER COMRADES
                         By Retired Master Mariners of Sailor's Snug Harbor
Basket of Roses, Gift of SOCIETY OF FOUNDERS & PATRIOTS OF AMERICA
                                       ✠
CAPT. WILLIAM MOORING_____Grand Marshall and Officer in Charge
MRS. LILY REED, New York_____National Chairman
JOSEPHINE PFEIL, Milwaukee, Wis._____Chairman, Great Lakes District
LUCILLE EDMUNDSON, San Diego, Cal._____Chairman, Pacific Coast District
```

National Maritime Day is celebrated on the day the Savannah *sailed on the first trans-Atlantic voyage using steam as auxiliary power. The commemoration included those lost from airships, U.S., British and German. Re Harry M. Durning: See "Masters Next to God", Commodore Johnsen.*

The confusion over ship-to-shore and shore-to-ship wireless transmission was highlighted during the February-March 1902 visit of Prince Heinrich, younger brother of the Kaiser, to New York. The day after his return to Germany, the Kaiser called for an international conference to determine the best methods of wireless communications, and how to assure their efficient use. The ultimate aim: safety of life at sea. The first international wireless convention went into effect five days after the *Titanic* tragedy had confirmed the price paid for communications negligence and misuse.

The short-term reaction was to pile boats on boats, and stacks of rafts topside. Did anyone seriously think all the boats could have been launched safely, or the rafts lowered or float off and save people? Did they all have stowed masts and sails to rig and sail tos safety? This pileup of boats and rafts made many vessels top-heavy. This forced the redesign of ships then building or planned to include more lifeboats and, as on Hapag's *Imperator,* to put some onto lower decks so the boats would be closer to the water, and to give a lower center of gravity. This lower-deck mounting of lifeboats is standard design on cruise ships of the 1990s. All have motors. But motors cannot always be relied upon. On *Cuba* in September, 1923, the former NDL *Coblenz* #101, a motor tested the day before a stranding did not work, and the crew had to row to the mainland. In the 1990's, with even the biggest container vessels with crews of only about fourteen persons, self-righting, non-sinkable escape boats are let down by gravity, the same way rescue boats, such as the Deutsche Gesellschaft zur Rettung Schiffbrüchiger, German Society for the Rescue of Shipwrecked Persons - It's first Director was NDL's founder, H.H. Meier drop daughter boats into the sea to aid vessels or persons in distress.

The question of training the follow-on next generation of seamen became critical for German shipping after WWII. Thousands of seamen had been lost in the conflict. Most of those who survived, were too old to be rehired with any expectation of staying active for long.

In 1949, Captain Otto Prehn, head of NDL's Nautical Department, in Hansa (Shipping) Magazine, raised the question of training the future officers, engineers, and crews. "Only the sailship builds character, steeling of the body, ability and readyness to make and carry out decisions, acceptance of deprivations, moral strength and discipline." In contrast, "steamer crews are workers, not seamen." In the 1950s, the sailships Parmir, Passat and Deutschland met some of this need. (Kapitän Otto Prehn, NDL Nautische Abteilung. In "Hansa," 1949: "Fast alle andere Seemächte halten an der Segelschiffsausbildung. Nur das Segelschiff gewährleistet Charakteraulese, Stählung des Körpers, Förderung von entschlussfreudigkeit und Wendigkeit, Gewöhung an Entbehrung, Härte und Disziplin." Dampferbesatzungen sind zur See fahrende Arbeiter, keine Seeleute. And when Cata storphe occurs, "it's all up. Where would a Steam Sailor have learned to row and sail?")

On 21/5/1959 Director Helms Jr. of the D.D. Ges. "Hansa," Bremen said that "one of the many problems lying on our shoulders is that of the training of the nautical next generation. Of the 245 nautical officers in the Hansa, only fourteen

BROOKLYN DAILY EAGLE
January 17, 1940

LINE ON LINERS
by FRANK REIL

German Steamer Furnishes Another Epic of Sea Lanes

The war, which has produced such sea epics as the secret maiden voyage of the Queen Elizabeth, the Bremen's running of the British blockade and the City of Flint's odyssey under three flags, has furnished another, less well known but in some respects more remarkable than those which captured the front-page headlines.

It is a yarn which would have delighted Joseph Conrad or Herman Melville and today, on the anniversary of the completion of her trip across the vast Pacific, we recount the tale of the German freighter Erlangen. A booklet, "The Adventurous Trip of the North German Lloyd Steamer Erlangen," printed recently by the New York offices of the line, has added greatly to the few details originally known about the unusual 4,826-mile voyage made possible by burning wood and rigging crude sails.

The Erlangen, with her coal supply down to 250 tons, was in New Zealand waters at the outbreak of the war. Her skipper realized that the only safe, neutral port he could make was in distant Chile. But how to get there with such scant fuel was the first of many problems to be overcome. So they decided to go to uninhabited Auckland Island, several hundred miles to the south of New Zealand. There was a good harbor which rendered her invisible from passing ships which might wander to this island far off the beaten track.

Wood Too Hard

The island had plenty of wood and the crew was set to work chopping down trees and hauling the wood aboard the ship, which had been deliberately beached in order to facilitate loading. The ship's engineer, by experiment, found that three tons of wood was the equivalent of one ton of coal. By careful calculation it was figured that 400 tons of wood would be needed for the trip to Chile.

For over a month the men chopped and sawed wood but the timber was so hard that all the axes and saws became blunt, and even the files which had been keeping them sharp were worn out. The supply of wood obtained was only 250 tons, below the estimated minimum.

Meanwhile those sailors who had served on sailing ships had been set to making two square sails and four jibs out of canvas hatch covers and tarpaulins.

Finally, on Oct. 6, after being at the island five weeks, the Erlangen started her voyage—getting off the beach with her engines and then setting sails. They made four and a half knots under canvas until they ran into calms. As the ship kept below 54 degrees latitude most of the time, they encountered much freezing weather.

Chop Up Everything

But the engines were consuming the fuel too rapidly and finally the engineer came to the discovery that if the wood was cut into one-foot lengths the ship could operate on one boiler and save six tons of fuel a day. So the sailors again had to go back to sawing, doing their best with dull, toothless tools.

In addition they cut up doors, paneling, some of the decking and even the beds and chairs aboard the Erlangen in order to feed the engines. It was hard work and eventually the men, weakened by the lack of proper food, could not continue.

Ever since the trip started they had been on rationed food. For days on end they lived on soups made from peas, beans and barley. Milk was so scarce it was saved for the sick, and these included many whose stomachs became affected. They even had to ration the castor oil. They ran out of potatoes and flour. But there was one bright spot—the supply of beer held out to the very end.

Oddly enough Captain Grams found inspiration to carry on by reading a volume of the adventures of Horatio Hornblower, an English sea captain whose fictional exploits have become famous.

By Nov. 1 they were nearing the coast of Chile and they had 100 tons of coal and 130 tons of wood left for the final 500-mile dash. The captain wanted to have some speed available in the event he encountered other ships. But they didn't meet anything until they were inside the three-mile limit, where they were safe.

When the ship arrived at Ancud just a year ago today Chilean port officials could hardly believe their eyes and the captain's story that he had sailed 1,507 miles and steamed 3,319 miles in a 35-day voyage across the south Pacific. The ship is still there and will stay there until Captain Gram and his men can figure some other impossible voyage.

---

have ever sailed in cross-arm sailing ships. And only two among these as steersman, those who most have the feel of their ship in their hands. Many of us consider that the fate of our vessels lies in men with inadequate training at sea." At the Hansa, the then-youngest captain was thirty-one years old, a taking of early responsibility unthinkable a generation earlier. In 1960, Captain Günther Rössing wrote "aside from the 1.Officer, I have only very young people around me. That means having to be constantly 'on the job.'" Yet, ten years later the fifteen ships caught by closing of the Suez Canal, including Hapag's *Münsterland,* evidently all had sails for their lifeboats. Racing them was the prime recreation for the crews.

Other than naval sail training vessels, the experience of sailing rests largely in the enthusiam and skills of uncountable yachtsmen around the world. The quadrennial America's Cup stirs interest less related to sailing skills than the technology incorporated in succeeding series of contenders. The Whitbread round-the-world races do get international attention. The 1994 race was won by New Zealander Grant Dalton. He and fellow yachtsmen follow in the maritime tradition that dates back to the first Maories, who beached their canoes on the "Land of the Long White Cloud" a thousand years ago. Dalton says "we sail for sport. But the sea still dominates our thinking, our imagination, our aspirations."

The singing of sea chanties at Maritime Museums in Vancouver or San Francisco brings back a bit of nostalgia. But how long can memories keep relevant a vanished way of life?

Last Landfall - H.D. Milne

The long haul's done, the anchor's down
And the harbor lights shine clear;
The charts are stowed and I gently ride
on the lift of life's endless swell:

I must stand the watch till the new dawn breaks
and a quiet berth is free -
And the pilot's aboard to guide me in
To secure at the timeless quay.

The Shipping Reporter for the Brooklyn Daily Eagle, *Frank Reil, wrote up the story of* Erlangen's *steaming-sailing voyage from Auckland Island to Chile in 1939. Deeds filled with imagination and daring.*

NDL Fleet
Ships 444 — 455a

In 1936, after splitting off acquired lines and Argo again in business for itself, and the founding of a new (Bremer) Atlas Linie to run to the Near East, some Argo and Roland-named ships were given traditional NDL nomenclature:

Anhalt 2, ex *Ansgir* #343, 1922
Borkum 2, ex *Antares* #361, 1922
Dessau 3, ex *Wido* #380, 1923
Eisenach 3, ex *Alda* #337, 1921
Hameln 2, ex *Roland* #372, 1921
Helgoland 2, ex *Arcturus* #371, 1922
Inn, ex *Abana* #422, 1929
Norderney 2, ex *Altair* #368, 1922
Schleswig 2, ex *Nord-Schleswig* #426, 1922
Spree 2, ex *Agira* #423, 1930

444. *Eider 2*	1937-1945		
Deschimag Weserwerft,			
Bremen #925	1937	3288	115.05 x 15.32
2 x M.A.N. Diesels	3900	14.2	
12	40		

Launched 12/1936, delivery 4/3/1937. 1940 naval transport. 16/2/1941 target ship for Luftwaffe. 9/4/1942 after hitting a mine used as depot ship in Hamburg. 6/1943 to Wilhelmshaven for conversion to *Sperrbrecher* #36, barrage-clearer. 12/4/1945 sunk at Wilhelmshaven in air raid. Refloated. 15/10/1946 towed into North Sea, sunk with gas munitions.

445. *EMS 2*	1937-1942		
Deschimag Weserwerft,			
Bremen #926	1937	3287	115.05 x 15.32
2 x M.A.N. Diesels	3900	14.2-14.5	
12	40		

Launched 16/1/1937. Delivery 15/4/1937. 12/1939 conversion by Howaldt Werft, Hamburg to raider began: 6 x 5.9 guns, 2 x 37mm, 4 x 20MM AckAck, 1 - 60mm, 6 torpedo tubes, 2 Arado seaplanes, 1 speed boat, 4 prize officers, 15 officers, 250 crew, this after the plan to have sister *Iller* #450 at Murmansk, converted there. Left Gdynia 3/7/1940, the first German ship to make the Arctic passage

Eider *#444* and EMS *#445* were basically sisters of the earlier Memel *and* Saar, *but the winches were on raised housings, giving the operator a better view of the hatch and the quay. Unusual to see a freighter dressed with flagging as* Eider *is*. Ems *is entering Hamburg harbor.* Ex-Merchant Ships 1942 Talbot-Booth.

to the Far East disguised as the like-sized Soviet Freighter *Dejnev*, 3578 Ts., during the Nazi-Soviet friendship pact period. USSR supplied its heaviest icebreakers to shepherd *Ems*, now Ship 45 *Komet;* 2960 miles covered in 18 days, 720 of them through ice. *Komet* operated in the Indian, Pacific and Antarctic Oceans, sank 64,500 Ts., of shipping. It shelled the phosphate-loading facilities on Nauru, into 1914 part of Germany's vast islands colonial holdings in the Pacific, set ashore 490 prisoners from Raider *Atlantis*, on Emaru Island, off Kerguelen Island was given mail and munitions from supply vessel *Alstertor. Ems/Komet* returned via Cape Horn to Hamburg on 30/11/1941. On 14/10/1942 on its planned second raiding cruise in English Channel on way from Cape de la Hague it was blown to pieces by British Motoro Torpedo Boat 236. One crew member survived. (Hümmelchen).

Ems as Komet *in camouflage. Photo courtesy* Schiffahrt International.

446. **Dresden** 1937-1944
Bremer Vulkan, Vegesack #735   1937   5567   138.00 x 17.16
M.A.N. Diesel   5200   15
28   53

Launched 26/5/1937 for Hanseatische Schiffahrts & Betriebs Ges., Bremen. MV. 12/7/1937 to Valparaiso. Late 1937 transferred to NDL. 27/9/1939 took refuse in Coquimbo. 19/10/1940 left for Santos, arr. 25/11/1940. Left 28/3/1941 for rendez-vouz with Raider *Atlantis*, on 18/4 took on seventy-seven crew and passengers from sunken Egyptian *Zamzam*, including David Scherman, photographer with *Life* Magazine, my Dartmouth 1936 classmate. He wrote in August, 1994 "we were allowed to use the tiled pool occasionally when the ship was near the Equator." The stupid Kriegsmarine personnel ashore ordered *Dresden* to proceed, dan-

#446 Dresden, #448 Leipzig and #452 Hannover, were the last of the South America combi-vessels built. All were lost through scuttling, fire, or seizure. Dresden, however, was raised postwar, rebuilt in France, re-entered service in 1949, only to be lost again, through stranding near Cape Gardafui in 1950. The dangers at sea take their perennial toll. Photo Ex-Sea Breezes.

Ships 444 - 455a   373

gerously exposed to naval or air attack, to Bordeaux, arriving the next day. The non-Americans were interned there. "The Americans from the ZamZam were put ashore at St. Jean de Luz and transported to nearby Biarritz, a fancy French resort, where they were housed by the Germans in small hotels until officials from the U.S. Embassy in Madrid, together with the Red Cross, arranged their repatriation by train across Spain to Lisbon, from where most were taken back to New York by well-lighted ships of the American Export Line. I (David Scherman) returned by Pan American Clipper from Lisbon." 14/10/1942 left for the Far East, but sunk in mouth of the Gironde by British MTB 236. 251 lost their lives. 2/3/1946 raised, repaired. 6/6/1949 MV as *Doba*, Chargeurs Reunis, Le Havre, 7096 tons. 21/7/1950 stranded near Ras Hafoun by Cape Gardafui in 10.22N, 51.20E, total loss.

Bogota *#447 and* Quito *#449 were built as replacements for the old and slow* Cali *#312 and* Manizales *#313 that connected the ports of Ecuador and Colombia to the Panama Canal and the ships serving the West Coast. They could carry 12 passengers coastally, a good deal for merchants. Attempts to sell them at Coquimbo to Chilean interests during the war failed. Both escaped to Japan.* Bogota *survived the war, in 1950 was returned to the Lloyd, the largest ship left to it by the war. They were registered for the Lloyd Colombiano. Hapag-Lloyd Photo.*

447. **Bogota**   1937-1945/1950-1955
Schiffbau-Ges. Unterweser,
Wesermünde #259
                                    1937   1230   79.90 x 10.57
2 Krupp Diesels   1680
12   28

Launched 15/12/1937. Delivery 18/3/1938 for Lloyd Colombiano in weekly Cristobal-Buenaventura-Tumaco-Esmeraldas-Bahia de Caraquaz-Manta-Guyaquil and return feeder service, with *Quito* #449, replacing *Cali* #312 and *Manizales* #313, sold to Chile. 31/8/1939 at Guyaquil, LU. 1/3/1940 left for Coquimbo, arr. 11th. Attempted sale to local interests failed. 18/5/1940 with *Quito* left for Japan, en route disguised as *Heizan Maru* of K Line, served as supply ship to blockade runners, took Hapag's *Osorno* in tow. It had taken refuge 9/1939 in Talcahuano, was trying to get to Japan, but broke down. All three arr. 12/8/1940 in Yokohama. With *Quito* from Japan served as supply ship to raiders in the Pacific. 6/5/1944 chartered to Japan, ren. *Teishu Maru*, 6/5/1945 taken over with Germany's collapse. After Japan's surrender, under U.S. control served as repatriation transport, mainly Japanese from China, Korea, South East Asia back to home islands, probably also Chinese and Koreans back to their homes. 7/1950 back to NDL, reg. for Roland Line Schiffahrts Gmbh., Bremen, a Lloyd subterfuge to avoid vessel seizures over any unsettled debts. Largest vessel left to NDL after the war. 28/5/1955 *Astrid Sven*, Rederi of 1955, Copenhagen. O. Svendsen, manager, trading between Karachi and Persian Gulf. 12/1957 *Phrygia*, Hellenic Mediterranean Lines, Piraeus. Arr. damaged 1/8/1963, repaired, 13/5/1964 to Cia. Maritima de Transporte y Pesceria, Panama. Ren. *Alcyone*. 9/5/1964 explosion in engine room gutted the ship; 10th abandoned in 16.49N, 162.9W, 200 mis. off Dakar, while serving as reefer-storage ship for trawlers. Sank in 16.47.30N, 16.32W. on 11th.

448. *Leipzig*   1938-1941
Deschimag Weserwerft,
Bremen #931   5898   145.00 x 17.16
M.A.N. Diesel   5200 (or 6000?)   15
28   56

Launched 15/2/1938. 4/1938 MV to Valparaiso. 1/9/1939 at Colon. Instead of turning around, trying to get home, transited the Canal. 8th arr. Guyaquil, left 18th, 21st arr. Callao, LU. 1/4/1941 scuttled in port to avoid capture through Canadian Auxiliary Cruisers *Prince Robert* and *Prince Henry*, offshore, when *München* and Hapag's *Hermonthis* were sunk trying to get to Japan. On 4th burned out.

Leipzig #448, München #442, *with Hapag's* Monserrate *and* Hermonthis *(ordered as NDL's* Hannover *#434x in 1934) at Callao roads. At Berlin's order they all tried to get away on 1 April, 1941 but were caught or scuttled to avoid capture by HMCS* Prince Henry, *ex Canadian National S.S.Co. British Columbia coastal service. The utter destructiveness of war. Lovely ships serving a useful purpose lost to a madman's perversion. And the lives at sea, on land and in the air. Group Photo ex Witthöft's Hapag-Lloyd, Koehler, 1974.*

Peacetime garb of Prince Henry *along the British Columbia coast, one of three sisters built in Britain in 1930. All three did naval service during the war. HMCS* Prince Robert *was waiting off Manzanillo when Weser #434 tried to escape to Japan and seized her. They made good auxiliary cruisers with their 22 knots. The two forward funnels were trunked into one, spoiling the ships' looks. Ex-*Sea Breezes.

Posted on the High Seas Mark *from Canadian National's* Prince Henry *in the West Indies service, 1936. Mail dropped at Kingston, Jamaica, with foreign postage, it received that city's* **Paquebot** *cancel for mail posted at sea but not cancelled.*

Leipzig *loading in Hamburg in 1938 or 1939. The tiled pool was directly behind the stack. Collection of* Frank Pichardo.

Leipzig *burning on 1 April, 1941 is from* Raul Maya's collection courtesy of William Schell.

Bremerhaven #280, ex *Island Trader*, repurchased and put back on the Hong Kong-New Guinea trade.

---

449. Quito   1938-1941
Schiffbau Ges. Unterweser, Wesermünde #260
                              1230   79.90 x 10.57
2 Krupp Diesels   1680   13   * *
12   28

Launched 15/3/1938. Delivery 9/6/1938 for Feeder service Panama Canal-Colombia/Ecuador, reg. for Lloyd Colombiano. Took shelter in Coquimbo. Attempt to sell her with *Bogota* to local interests failed. 18/5/1940 both vessels left for Japan, *Quito* proceeding direct, arr. Yokohama 27/6/1940. Served as supply vessel to raiders in the Pacific. 9/1944 stranded near Penang. Salvaged and repaired by Japan, ren. *Teishu Maru*, operated for Navy. 29/4/1945 sunk by U.S. submarine *Bream* off Balikpapan, Borneo, in 04.11S, 111.17E.

450. Iller   1938-1944
Deschimag Weserwerft, Bremen #927
                              1938   3290   115.05 x 15.32
2 M.A.N. Diesels   3900   14.2
12   40

Launched 7/1938. Delivery 10/1938 for Cuba-Mexico service. 19/8/1939 left Havana with full cargo and 16 passengers. 3/9/1939 arr. Murmansk, first of 22 German ships seeking safety there. Chosen for first wave of raiders as a small motor ship, yet relatively fast: 14.2-15 knots, was held ideal for a raiding-cruiser. But necessary conversion could not be done in a Soviet port. So *Ems* #445 was chosen instead. 31/10/1939 left with crews from other vessels, 12/11/ arr. Hamburg. 9/10/1944 sunk by Soviet aerial bomb off Manut, Oesel island.

Iller #450 was one of seven very similar good-looking Lloyd freighters. In August, 1939 it left Havana with a full cargo and 16 passengers, escaping to Murmansk. Already near the trans-Arctic route to the Pacific, Berlin wanted to convert it to a raider and send it into the Pacific Ocean. But Murmansk was not the port to get that done. Instead, sistership Ems *#445 was so converted.* Hapag-Lloyd photo.

451. **Ulm 2**   1938-1942
Danziger Werft (Int.S.B. & Eng. Co.) #78
                        1938   3071   102.57 x 13.92
M.A.N. Diesel   3950   16
10   38

Ordered by A.S. Görissen, Oslo for Caribbean reefer trade. Launched 11/1937 as *Rapide*. 3/1938 bought by NDL, delivery 20/4/1938 for Canaries-North Brazil service. 30/8/1939 arr. LasPalmas from Brazil. Left at once for Tromsö disguised as Danish, arr. there 12/9/, at Kiel 24th, Hamburg 25th. 18/3/1940 minelayer. 31/7/1940 almost destroyed while fitting out at Stülcken Werft, Hamburg. 25/11/1940 again minelayer after rebuild. 25/8/1942 as such 100 miles off Bear Island, Barents Sea, sunk in 74.45N, 26.5E by British destroyers *Mane, Martin* and *Onslaught*. Lost were 120 officers and crew. In the night 2-3 Sept. a lifeboat reached Vardö after 8 days, some 300 miles, 4 crew alive, 20 dead. Ship was burning from shelling, sank when torpedo blew it up, bow down, stern with torn flag going under last. The builder was the former Kaiserliche Werft, after Versailles and Danzig independent, operated as Danziger Werft. Closed in depression. Poland raised foreign capital which reopened it as International Shipbuilding & Engineering Co., Ltd. (Podolsky).

Ulm *#451 was bought from the Danish firm that ordered it for reefer service. 1938 ran to the Canaries and North Brazil, a service renewed in 1951, also 16 knotters, in the first year of new ships again showing the Lloyd flag. Minelayer during the war, sunk in the process in the Barents Sea in 1942 by British destroyers.* Talbot Booth, Merchant Ships 1942.

1938 - M.S. *Coburg* into service, rebuilt by Deschimag's Weserwerft, Bremen from *Havel* #412.

M.S. *Marburg* into service, rebuilt by Deschimag's Weserwerft, Bremen from *Saale* #411.

M.S. *Regensburg* into service, rebuilt by Stettiner Vulcan from *Trave* #406.

Havel *#412 as rebuilt into* Coburg, *speed increased by three knots. Below:* Saale *#411, with Dutch* Boissevain *at right of her.* Trave *#406, rebuilt into* Regensburg.

Hannover #452 *(top photo) was the last of the West Coast South America combi-vessels. Trying to get home from Willemstad, Curacao it was caught by the British, rebuilt into an escort carrier* Audacity. *(see below) "She had wonderful cabins" her British crewmen reported. Sunk off Cape Finisterre, by torpedo.   Ship photo from Hapag-Lloyd.*

452. *Hannover* 1939-1940
Bremer Vulkan, Vegesack #765   1939   5537   145.00 x 17.16
M.A.N. Diesel   5200   15
28   56

Hannover ready for launching at the Bremer Vulkan, March 1939. Launch photo from Bremer Vulkan.

Launched 29/3/1939. MV. 22/6/1939 to Valparaiso. 9/1939 took refuge in Willemstad, with *Este* #424, among seven German ships to do so. 5/3/1940 left, trying to get home. 9/3/1940 off Mona Passage brought up by HMC destroyer *Assiniboine* before scuttling could succeed. Ship taken to Kingston, briefly named *Sinbad*, Ministry of Shipping, Cunard-White Star manager. 1940 ren. *Empire Audacity*, London. 1/1941 conversion to escort carrier *Audacity* for 6 aircraft began. Night of 21-22/12/1941 en route Gibralter-Britain sunk in 44.N, 20.W by U-751 ca. 400 mis. NW of Cape Finisterre. The crew got to Santo Domingo; 17 flew to Puerto Colombia, got home on *Helgoland* #371. All German notices had been left on her. "She had wonderful passengers cabins" was a crewmember comment. The carrier deck was built above the two-deck superstructure. "She was so manageable." In contrast to so many ugly ships NDL had, the River Class of the 1930s, #432 etc., and the combi-vessels for the West Coast South America route, were a pleasing design, appreciated by crews and passengers alike, even tiled pools on the later 28-passenger ships.

Lech #453 was the last of her class completed before the war; two more went into war service as completed then. Built for the Cuba-Mexico service. Very efficient vessels.

453. *Lech* 1939-1941
Deschimag Weserwerft, Bremen #928
                                    1939   3290   115.05 x 15.30
M.A.N. Diesel   3900   14.2
12   35

Launched 15/2/1939. Delivery 4/4/1939 for Cuba-Mexico route. 9/1939 LU in Vigo. 1940 moved to Bordeaux. 28/5/1941 en route to South Atlantic during the *Bismarck* action, was caught up by *HMS Edinburgh*, scuttled in 45.33N, 23.25W. Lech had two boats on her after housing, the only one of the River Class. Easier escape for the crew, now housed aft instead of in the bow, the old conventional way.

---

454. *Minden* - under war-captured-managed ships

---

455. *Linz* 1943-1945
Danziger Werft #101   1943   3374   102.57 x 13.96
M.A.N. Diesel   4800   16
12   38

Order 12/1938 by NDL. Launched 11/1942. Sister of *Ulm* #451. Was supposed to have a sister *Graz* ordered at the same time, No. #114, but never laid down. Towed to Odense Staal Skibsvaerft (A.P. Möller owned) for completion as minelayer. 27/7/1943 sabotaged, partly flooded, electric equipment ruined. 16/8/1943 towed to Stettin for repairs. Delivery 26/1/1944, Reg. in Bremen. 8/7/1945 turned over to Ministry of Transport, London, ren. *Empire Wansbeck*, Ellerman's Wilson Line, Hull, manager. 1948-1961 shuttled with troops between Harwich and Hoek van Holland. 1/1952 with 900 aboard stood by *Pamir*, ex Flying P.Line (F. Laeisz) in trouble in the English Channel. Late 1961 LU after decision to fly all troops between Britain and Germany. 6/1962 to Kavounides Shipping Co., Piraeus for use as inter-island ferry, ren. *Esperos*. 14/3/1980 left in tow for Spain and BU.

Linz #455 in her hull was a sister of Ulm #451. A third sister, Graz, was to have been built, but the war ended that. Linz went to the British after the war, shuttled troops between Harwich and Hoek van Holland for the British forces in Germany, until this was done by air. Photo Dr. Dieter Jung, BNRA.

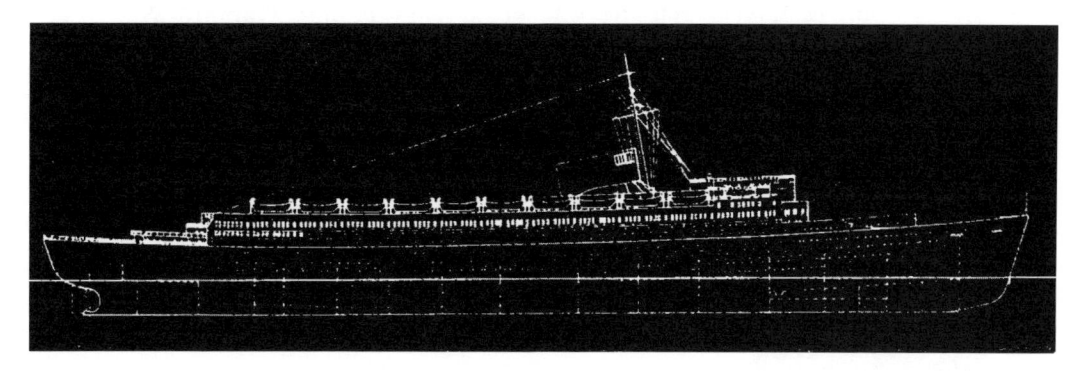

455x Project Amerika-Viktoria*: a design study for the Lloyd by A.G. Weser, Bremen, for a ship to beat* Normandie *and the two* Queens, Queen Elizabeth *still building. Even had no war come and this had eventually been built, the* United States *in 1952 would have been the ultimate record-holder.* Original from L.L. von Münching.

455x *Amerika/Viktoria*   Design Study 1937-1939

An 80,000 tons design study was done by Deschimag (A.G. "Weser"), Bremen for a Blue Ribbon liner to beat *Normandie, Queen Mary* and the *Queen Elizabeth*, under construction: 300,000 HP on five shafts, 35 kns. A model was tested. The keel was to have been laid in Winter 1939-1940 per L.L. von Münching in April, 1963 *Sea Breezes*. Because of the size of the vessel and the over-burdened (with warships) German shipyards, construction would be in the Kaiserdock I, of the Lloyd's Technical Service in Bremerhaven under Deschimag supervision.

The *Amerika* proposal recalls an earlier one from 1902, made for NDL following the *Kaiser Friedrich* #104 fiasco, by Johann Schütte for a 25.5 knots five-stacked, cruiser-stern liner within the then evident maximum horsepower of quadruple-expansion reciprocating engines, some 10,000 HP, to be applied two in tandem per propeller.

Pophanken wrote about this in 1927 after *Bremen* and *Europa* were announced, and Arnold Kludas in Volume II of his *History of German Passenger Shipping*. At the time, NDL already had its third four-stacker, *Kaiser Wilhelm II*, under construction. This project would not have fitted into a weekly schedule which *Kwii's* sister, *Kronprinzessin Cecilie* in 1907 brought about. Some Unorganized thinking lay behind the consideration for a new North Atlantic superliner, less to replace *Bremen* and *Europa*, designed in 1926, than to round out a Lloyd threesome, the *Columbus*, as the most comfortable ship, to be used entirely for cruising, except occasional trans-Atlantic fill-ins.

Due to the 1930s depression, the Lloyd and Hapag perforce had begun serious cooperation, pressured also by the National Socialist Government. Hapag's Big Four went back to 1924-1927. They had been twice rebuilt, but still were rated at the low end by the North Atlantic (Passenger) Conference. So Hapag designed and ordered the first of a three-ships replacement: *Vaterland*, 23.5 knots, like the *Imperator-Vaterland-Bismarck* trio of 1912-1916, to provide a weekly service. *Vaterland* was under construction at

Blohm & Voss when the war began. My Father, Captain W. Drechsel, General Marine Superintendent for the Hapag-Lloyd North Atlantic operation, left New York on 3/3/1939 on *Normandie* at Hapag's request to check *Vaterland's* design for optimum handling in the Port of New York. See "North America Inspectorate." *Vaterland* was launched in 1939. It was heavily damaged during air attacks, and scrapped after the war.

End of vessels ordered before the war.

Linz #451 *in camouflage seen from a Kriegsmarine destroyer?* Photo from Seekiste, now Schiffahrt International.

Gotenland, *NDL managed during the war, in 1942 in Copenhagen.*
Photo from BNRA.

CHAPTER 13

North Atlantic Community New York Inspectorate

Having piers to receive and dispatch its vessels is vital to any shipping enterprise. Piers in the right location can be an advantage over the competition. NDL began its New York Line in 1858 with a pier in Manhattan. It soon leased, then bought and developed with three piers terrain in Hoboken, across the Hudson. Hapag did the same, at first sharing the Lloyd piers. When those piers burnt out in 1900, see I - "Per Aspera ..", cooperation by other lines enabled the Lloyd to continue operating. Kaiser *Wilhelm der Grosse* sailed on schedule a few days later, from the Cunard Pier in Manhattan fully loaded with passengers, and crews from the burned-out ships.

Both Lloyd and Hapag, also Holland-America Line, stayed in Hoboken until World War I. After the War, Hapag made an early coup, signing with the Harrimans' United American Lines, which gave access to its Piers 84 and 86, North River, while the Lloyd returned to Hoboken. It did begin in 1922 pier negotiations with the City of New York. But when *Columbus* arrived on 1 May, 1924 on its maiden voyage it had to use Pier 4, Brooklyn, a primitive facility and a subway or taxi ride from Manhatten.

Berlin *sailing from Pier 42, Christopher Street, N.R., Inspectors Captains Emil Maurer and George Baronsky in front. Unusual in that well-wishers are at the pier-head. Some, at right, must have been late because they are still clutching undelivered flowers. A cat by the white vertical? at right. Pier Mascot? This is the Pier the Royal Mail Steam Packet Company used during its brief service to Germany in the early twenties, before the Lloyd and Hapag again had vessels available.*

385

The realization that neither the Hoboken Piers nor available Pier 42, Manhattan could handle the express liners being built led to negotiations with Department of Docks to build a great new Pier 32 and lease it to NDL. It soon became clear that this project was mired deep in politics and would take years, if ever, to become an actuality. Bremen became desperate: where else to go? Our big ships come out in April, 1929 and no piers?

In desperation, another look at Pier 4, Brooklyn Army Base. The Army had leased it to Tidewater Terminal Company. Tidewater wanted to end its lease on 31/12/1928 as "no longer usable." But when we talked to them (Captain Drechsel's report to Bremen), they saw a future, retracted the giving-up decision. The lower level had been rented out for occasional passenger-ship dockings, the upper deck for storage. We needed mostly the upper deck. But 50,000 sacks of sugar had been stored there. The sugar had melted under the summer heat to a 1½" thick layer. It took 150 men some three weeks to clean it off. The elevators were out of service. Some thousand painted-black windows had to be cleaned or replaced. Some two hundred outer doors and fire exits had to be made operable, cleaned and painted. The toilets were in an unbelievable condition. There were no real waiting areas. But Tidewater knew we were in trouble, so we had to take the pier 'as is'. It cost more than $150 thousand to get the pier ready for passengers, baggage and waiting areas, food service, communications, etc.

"In every way we were at a disadvantage compared to Manhattan or Hoboken. Taxis to Grand Central or Pennsylvania Railway stations were $10 vs $2 from North River piers. Only two trucking companies were interested in serving the pier vs ten available in Manhattan. Also, the tugs had much further to go to work out ships. They had to use the Bay River Channel for two miles rather than the easier Hudson River Channel. Width was only 900′ vs 3000′. Water depth also was a problem. *Bremen* and *Europa* would be down to 36′, plus one to two feet going ahead, as their bows tended to "dig in."

The 1926 charts indicated water depths, but were they still correct? The Corps of Engineers had done no dredging for many years as the small ships using it had adequate depth. Even the Sandy Hook Pilots had no reliable information about depths. So, we took hand-soundings ourselves, thousands of them to get an accurate picture of channel depth. We found the chart indications only partly correct. We entered depths we found, and made the corrected charts available to the Corps and Pilots. That winter, Bremen wrote Captain Drechsel: "what you have organized can be carried out in your absence. We suggest a voyage here, with your family, for relaxation, and for you to see and known everything about our new ships *Bremen* and *Europa*." We sailed 28 February on *Stuttgart,* returned in May on *Columbus.*

On 22 July, 1929 when *Bremen* was due on its maiden voyage, the Sandy Hook pilots suggested waiting until 10 PM for the docking as giving the best water conditions. But "we knew that Deputy Director Ernst Glässel on board had radioed invitations to other shipping concerns and officials to view the arrival. Also, thousands of people had massed by mid-afternoon on the streets, on roofs, everywhere they could see the Bay and across to *Bremen* at Quarantine. She arrived there at 4 PM, got rapid clearance, at 5 resumed her voyage, bedecked with flags, surrounded by untold small craft, to Pier 4. Placement of gangplanks went quickly and smoothly. Herr Glässel greeted the invitees and guests as they came aboard. Not until they and the passengers had left were we, the shore staff, able to talk to him. Glässel told us that the speaker for the guests said 'After all the rumors and reports about pier problems we expected difficulties and some disgruntlement. But nothing happened. It all went so smoothly and quickly. Quite fantastic. Congratulations.' We had made it and met Bremen's orders that this pier, because of its distance from Manhattan's everything, had to provide amenities and service unlike any other in New York or New Jersey. In time, we even had train service into the Pier. Captain MacNeil of Mauritania came out on the subway to congratulate Captain Ziegenbein in July, 1929.

The danger of fire at sea or ashore was a constant concern, fanned anew by recent burning of several big ships at sea. *Bremen* had a kitchen fire on her second voyage which foam quickly was able to extinguish.

Bremen wrote "we plan to supply ships with *Minimax* extinguishers, to put them everywhere." Pier 4 was similarly supplied by the Walter Kidde company. Drechsel advised Bremen "We are working on having a fire-fighting tug constantly near our piers." An expensive proposition. Most tugs were so equipped. When *München* #297 burned at Pier 42 in February, 1930 it took all available tugs and fireboats to contain, then extinguish the fire.

Herr Glässel closed his 21/12/1929 letter with "I express the hope that it may long be granted to you, in your accustomed energy and exemplary judgment, to serve in this position, for which you have our full confidence. Your responsible activ-

DAILY NEWS, WEDNESDAY, DECEMBER 23, 1931

DEMANDS MAYOR TESTIFY IN PIER QUIZ

By DORIS FLEESON.

A DEMAND that Mayor Walker be subpoenaed immediately and "given his day in court" came from the Democratic side of the Hofstadter Committee last night on the heels of testimony that the Mayor personally had promised to help the North German Lloyd obtain a pier lease.

The Walker assurances were testified to by Heinz Schuengel, Resident Director of the German line. Schuengel also identified a letter of thanks he sent the Mayor under the impression that the lease—crown of eight years of tortuous negotiation—had been signed. Actually the Sinking Fund Commission did not approve the lease until a month later, Nov. 12, 1930.

Schuengel revealed that in 1928 he had—such was desperation at the tossing around of his lease application—implored the aid of George W. Olvany, then Tammany leader. In 1929, he said, Philip Heineken, Lloyd's President, received personal assurances of success from James F. Egan, then Secretary of Tammany Hall.

City Quiz Witness Huddle

They used the huddle system in the Hofstadter inquiry yesterday. Here are l. to r. William H. Hickin, who got pier lease after exacting $50,000 fee; Heinz Schuengel, resident director of the North German Lloyd line, and Edgar W. Hunt, General Counsel for the line, all of whom took stand yesterday, discussing developments outside hearing.

Another milestone on the pier trail to Tammany Hall came in Schuengel's testimony that William H. Hickin, the lawyer who got the lease after exacting a $50,000 fee, constantly allayed the firm's anxiety with assurances that "uptown" they said everything was "O. K." Hickin is President of the National Democratic Club.

Demand Mayor Testify.

The demand that Walker be called was then made by minority Senator John J. McNaboe. It conspicuously lacked an echo from his colleagues, Assemblymen Cuvillier and Steingut, who still remained quiet when Chairman Hofstadter said the committee would take the matter under advisement.

Actually, Walker will be summoned in Seabury's own good time.

Schuengel said he met Mayor Walker first at a Steuben Society dinner at which David C. Maier, the ex-brothel keeper who accompanied Mayor Walker on his recent trip abroad, was also present. As in Monday's testimony of Edgar W. Hunt, General Counsel for the Lloyd line, Schuengel's story was spangled with Maier's name, Maier's efforts and Maier's assurances of success.

Got Confidential Report.

Hickin, whose fee the line considered "excessive and exorbitant," slipped them a strictly confidential report of the Dock Department about Pier 32, which they eventually got, Schuengel said. The report came, he said, from Traugott F. Keller, chief engineer, who committed suicide last Summer on his way to a Seabury private hearing.

LEASING A PIER

NEWS ITEM:—"North German Lloyd attorney had to do business through 'intermediaries' to obtain pier lease from city."

As soon as the Lloyd again crossed the Atlantic to New York in 1922 it began looking for a pier in Manhattan in preference to Hoboken. Dealing with the City in those years meant dealing with Tammany Hall, the political focus. In 1931, this cartoon in the New York American *told part of the story. A* New York Daily News *photo the same day shows Lloyd North American Director Heinz Schuengel and company counsel Edgar Hunt, in consultation. NDL had to do with Pier 4 in Brooklyn until the North Atlantic Community, solved the problem by moving to Hapag Piers 84 and 86 from 1.1.1934.*

NORTH GERMAN LLOYD
57 BROADWAY
NEW YORK

Norddeutscher Lloyd.

Albert [signature]

Norddeutscher Lloyd Bremen.

Norddeutscher Lloyd.

Heineken [signature]

(President Philipp Heineken)

ity in the interests of the Lloyd has found in you the right Curator, whose great professional ability and constant dutiful execution is for us of inestimable significance." Herr Glässel was on Europa's March, 1930 maiden voyage, radioed dinner invitations to New York's maritime leaders.

The maneuvering for Piers, Cunard and others also wanted Piers 84/86, of the 1920s became a "scandal that eventually brought the ouster of Mayor James Walker." In December, 1931, big headlines told about alleged bribes to obtain pier leases, the Lloyd having made payments to individuals promising results. These never came. Mayor James Walker resigned in 1932 to be succeeded by Fiorella La Guardia.

For the Lloyd, the pier situation was solved with the Spring, 1933 naming of Captain Drechsel as Chief Inspector, this position remaining his when Hapag and Lloyd later that year formed the North Atlantic Gemeinschaft, Community, com-

Letters poured in on Captain Drechsel. That of 17 January, 1933, signed by new Director Dr. Albert, advised: "It gives us particular pleasure to advise you that the Vorstand (Management Board) has named you as Oberinspektor, Chief Marine Superintendent, in New York. We ask that you understand this naming of you to our most important foreign position of our enterprise as responsive to the valuable services you have rendered and our thanks for the never-tiring devotion to duty and joy in your labors. You have in your years in New York not only our full trust and appreciation, but also with your counsel and knowledgeable working together with the various authorities you have earned their regard and confidence.

Especially valuable was and is your involvement in the important pier situation, and we add to our thanks for what has been done the hope that you will be able in this soon to attain the well-deserved success.

May you have many more years of successful activity in health and joy in the effort in behalf of our firm.

In German usage Inspektor is the head of the Inspektion, the on-shore management of the ships and all their needs. Herr Oberinspektor means being in charge of the largest port operations the Lloyd had. In the 1907 *Fifty Years History* of the Lloyd by Dr. Paul Neubaur, the two Operinspektoren flank the General Direktor Dr. Heinrich Wiegand in the formal protrait of the Direktorium und Inspektoren. Thus there is both esteem and affection in H. A. Seebers letter from Bremen in March, 1933: How pleased I am to be able to address you as Mein lieber Herr Oberinspektor.

The author's father was a hands-on leader and innovator. He gave his all for the Lloyd and so did those under him, for him and the Lloyd. It was what made the Hapag-Lloyd North-Atlantic Community, Gemeinschaft's New York operation such a success, and the ideal of what could be done when, finally in 1970, the two lines, became a single corporate entity. Here at the docking of Europa *(on right) at Pier 4, Brooklyn, March 1933 of* Columbus *(below), and* Dresden *(above) at Pier 42, North River.*

NEW TITLE FOR DRECHSEL.

Now General Marine Superintendent of North German Lloyd Here.

The directors of the North German Lloyd Line have designated Captain William Drechsel as general marine superintendent of its activities in New York, it was announced yesterday. Captain Drechsel is now marine superintendent of the line and the change of title will not entail any change in his duties.

A letter from Adolf Stadtlaender, director of the line, notifying Captain Drechsel of the action, said that it was taken in recognition of his "valued and distinguished services which are reflected in the capable administration" of the marine activities of the line in New York.

Captain Drechsel was appointed marine superintendent in 1924. He was born in the inland city of Dresden and has followed the sea since he was 15 years old.

This "promotion" is preliminary to his getting the same title and responsibilities over the shortly-after merged Lloyd and Hapag North Atlantic services, with NDL ships beginning also to use Piers 84 and 86, North River, and giving up Pier 42, Bremen, Europa and Columbus continued to use Pier 4, Army Basin, in Brooklyn. New York Times, February 3, 1933.

Freundschaftlichst
NORDDEUTSCHER LLOYD
Nautische Abteilung.

When at the end of 1933, Captain Drechsel was made Oberinspektor for the new Hapag-Lloyd North Atlantic Union, Gemeinschaft, Hapag's management in Hamburg advised its captains that in future they would be under Captain Drechsel when in U.S. waters. The first meaningful approach to all-out day-to-day working togetherness of these two enterprises. The advice was signed by Captain W. Dähne, new head of the Nautical Department in Bremen, later Captain of Columbus *#300.*

bining their services to the East and Gulf Coasts. This let the Lloyd give up its leases to Pier 4, Brooklyn, and Pier 42, N.R., and move to the United American Lines piers 84 and 84, now leased to Hapag. In the period 1/1/1929 through 1933, 287 NDL ships were handled at Pier 4, Brooklyn, one every six days, without any inci-

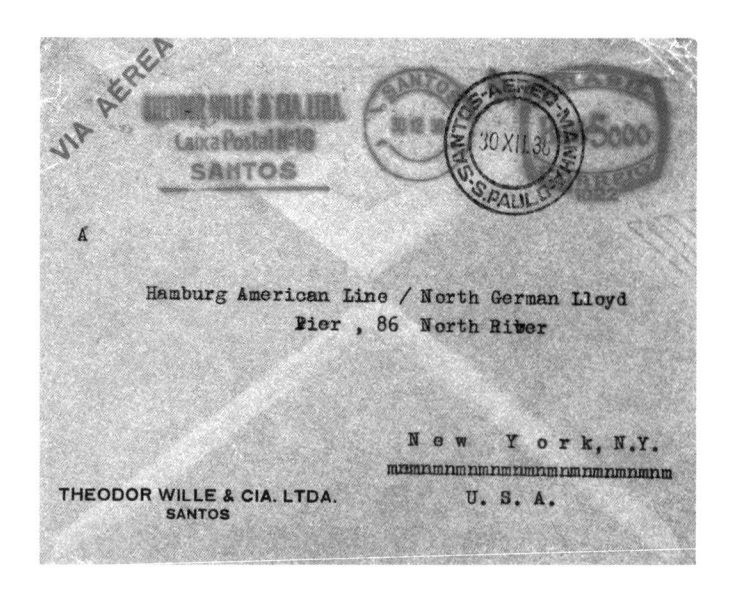

In the 1930s, Hapag-Lloyd Gemeinschaft opened several new routes, trying to find business in the depression, from the U.S. East and Gulf Coasts to the East and West coasts of South America, also to Australia. Agency mail from these routes came to New York. Here from Tampico and Santos. That letter came on NDL's Goslar *#421.*

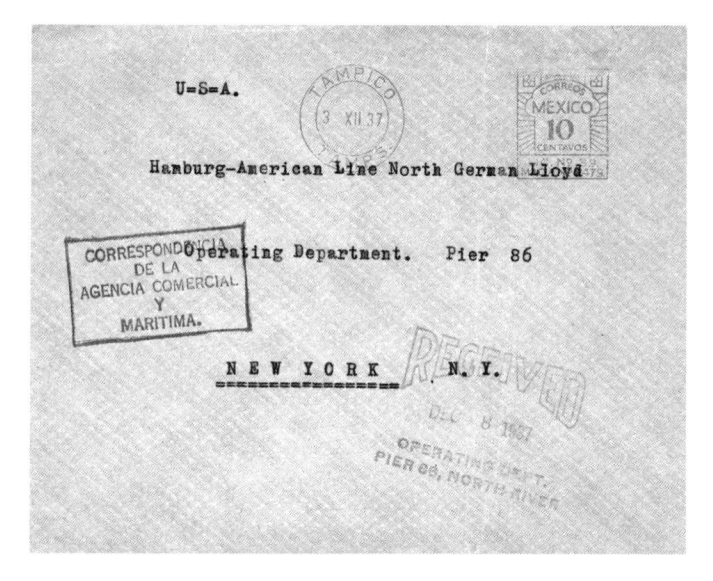

dents under all sorts of conditions and at all hours. In 1931, some dredging was done to keep the channel deep enough.

Congratulations had poured in on Captain Drechsel for his naming as Chief Inspector for the Lloyd and in September, 1933 for the Hapag-Lloyd Gemeinschaft. Director Mück from Bremen wrote: "Now that the entire outports operations of Hapag-Lloyd are in your hands I am pleased that it makes your Father of it All, and wish you much luck and success."

While during 1933 and 1934 all German shipping was reshuffled with the aim of decentralizing operations for maximum efficiency within traditional lines, the Hapag-Lloyd North Atlantic Community of Interests in effect became the proof that joint operations under skilled and dedicated leaders would work, melding the personnel of the two lines into friendly cooperation. In large part, it was this experience that thirty-seven years later brought acceptance of the formal corporate Hapag-Lloyd merger of 1 September, 1970. Bremen and Bremerhaven also benefited because the Hapag sailings from Cuxhaven for New York stopped at Bremerhaven for passengers and last-minute freight.

Europa *approaching Pier 4, Army Base, Brooklyn about 75th Street in Bay Ridge. Staten Island is directly across the Lower Bay. Quarantine is to the left of the trees.*

Christmas Abroad. Rarely did Captains and crews get to spend holidays with their families, especially Christmas. On Bremen-New York ships it was not so bad as most got home every three to four weeks. One could celebrate early: Sixth December is St. Nicholas Day in Germany. Children if they were good got fruits, if not, a piece of coal to find under the bed on getting up. Or until sixth January, the Feast of the Three Kings, the traditional day to take down the tree. In December, 1930 Bremen arrived in New York with lighted Christmas trees on top of both masts. This soon became a tradition on other ships, by yachtsmen, also on some buildings in the city.

For weeks ahead the entire crew was busy making the decorations, rehearsing the musical program, preparing a gift package for every one. Included would be a personal item from Captain Ziegenbein: a photograph of the ship with him at left and his signed, for one thousand people, autograph; another time a small leather notebook, also signed. We Drechsels and the Inspectorate staff were invited to join the festivities in the Promenade Deck Social Hall. Pastor Brückner from the Seamen's Mission in Hoboken read the Christmas story and spoke. The ship's orchestra accompanied the men's chorus and played for the singing of German Christmas carols. Everybody stayed the evening to drink and talk and relax. Those on station were relieved so they too could share. Finally, Captain Ziegenbein spoke: "Unable to be with our families tonight at home, this here now is our family beyond what we already are as shipmates. I thank you all for your dedicated labor together. I know I can rely on you all. That this continues is the best present you can give me tonight. As we return to our work, let us all take some of this Christmas spirit with us."

For those at sea at Christmas there also were gatherings, with presents and Christmas spirits. Volume I tells how the *Tinto* crew in the midst of war sailing for home around Cape Horn celebrated Christmas with gifts from the German colonies in Chile. For many, Christmas without a tree is not a real holiday. Even in Hawaii, with sun and no snow, except on top of Mount Kilauea. Matson ships from Portland bring some 200,000 Christmas trees to the islands for their Mele Kalikimaka.

There were many occasions for the members of the Maritime Community of the Port of New York-New Jersey to get together: sharing a meal on each other's ships, discussing mutual problems, being fellow-committee members or officials for the Annual Maritime Day celebrations in May, or the Labor Day International Lifeboat races. They became close colleagues and friends.

Months ahead of the French Line's *Normandie's* maiden voyage, 29/5/1935, its Marine Superintendent, L. LeFriant, asked for Captain Drechsel's experience in handling his big ships. Growing size meant new problems. *Normandie* was to be the largest vessel ever built. Her bridge would project so far as to touch the girders on top of the pier. To prevent this, Captain Drechsel designed, and Thomas Rinaldi's Hamilton Marine Contracting Co. built on Hapag-Lloyd's pier, a 250 tons fender 65′ x 25′6" to keep this ship from the pier.

The 1930 Christmas celebration in Bremen's Social Hall; Captain Ziegenbein sits at the head of the table in the middle with his guests to right and left.

Christmas on Bremen in New York, 1930. Around Captain L. Ziegenbein's table his guests from the Inspectorate, and Pastor & Mrs. H. Brückner, Seamen's Mission in Hoboken. From front to left and around: Captain Emil Maurer, Evelyn, then Edwin Drechsel, Mrs. Brückner, Pastor Brückner, Captain Ziegenbein, Mrs. Drechsel, Mrs. Maurer, Captain Drechsel, Mrs. Baronsky, Captain G. Baronsky. Behind, the crew at tables, each with a present.
R. Fleischhut Photo.

Christmas in Germany Sailings 1938.

Christmas at Pier 4, Brooklyn, December, 1933. The reception area outside the Inspectorate's office. Note the Bremen *model. R. Fleischhut Photo.*

The Tree at Columbus' *bow, Christmas, 1933, in New York. Hanns Tschira photo.*

Each Christmas abroad, Captain Ziegenbein gave to each crew member a little memento from him. In 1933 it was this photo of their Bremen *with him and each of the some 1,000 cards signed by him, including this one.*

North Atlantic Community 393

Christmas concert on Columbus *in New York. In right center: Captain Drechsel looking out from behind the screen, Captain Ahrens to the left, then Mrs. Drechsel and Mrs. (Captain) E. Maurer, and crew members with guests. 1932.*

The Tree at the mast top continued after the war. Here Christmas Greetings from Captain G. Rössing of the Berlin *to the Drechsels.*

Drechsel found *Normandie's* 3/3/1939 sailing to best fit his timing for a visit to Bremen and Hamburg, the French Line insisted he travel as "Guest of the Company."

In preparation for the first arrival of *Queen Mary* a year later, Captain Drechsel was a member of the Conference on Port Development's Welcome-Organizing Committee. Some time later, Cunard-White Star's Marine Superintendent, Henry McConkey, wrote: "I have no hesitation in calling upon you at any time ... knowing that ... I could always count upon your friendly help."

Relations with the several pilot groups had to be and were mutually supportive. In April, 1933 Bremen accepted Captain Drechsel's suggestion that Captain Herbert Miller, a member of the Sandy Hook Pilots, be named as Company Pilot. He would be assigned to every arrival of *Bremen* and *Europa*. While Captain Johnsen of *Europa* preferred to "con in" his ship, he did want the Port Pilot to be there, ready to answer any questions. Captain Ziegenbein, in contrast, welcomed Captain Miller taking charge of the approach and docking. One less burden for him. Not further explained is an entry in Captain Drechsel's Arrival-Departure Log on *Europa's* 29/12/1934 3.10 PM sailing on a cruise to Nassau: "Miller Overboard." I show a photograph of him later, so presumably he knew how to swim.

Some time later, M. LeFriant questioned Captain Drechsel over the correct signal ships should give on backing into the stream on departure: One whistle as soon as the stern was in the river, and three when the entire ship is out of the slip? Or three when the ship is backing out as soon as the stern protrudes? It was settled, with quoting of the U.S. signal rules: one long blast on backing; the three in effect the Goodbye when the ship began heading downstream. During that first *Normandie* visit, the French line gave an invitational dinner dance. Captain and Mrs. Drechsel attended. When in the Spring of 1939 Captain

In May, 1936 Sandy Hook Pilot Captain William Sullivan sent Captain Drechsel a color postcard of Hapag's *Deutschland,* with the note: "A hobby of mine is to have the Master of each vessel I pilot to autograph a card on the ship-picture side." He had Captain Friedel sign on the front. In April, 1934 President Harrie Arnold of the Sandy Hook Pilots' Benevolent Association wrote Captain Drechsel assuring him that he had acted properly in reporting an unstated incident between Captain and Pilot on Hapag's *Reliance.*

Relations with the towing companies, too, had to be based on trust and reliance, to assure the

Hamilton Marine was founded by Mr. Thomas Rinaldi, typical of smaller firms serving the maritime industry.

Fender for Normandie

A large fender to be used in docking the French liner Normandie was launched Thursday afternoon at the plant of the Hamilton Marine Contracting Co., Brooklyn, under the supervision of Capt. William W. Drechsel, marine superintendent of the North German Lloyd. The fender, which is said to be the largest ever built here, is 65 feet long, 25 feet 6 inches wide and 9 feet 4 inches deep. It weighs 230 tons. The same company built fenders for the Bremen, the Rex and other large vessels.

April 26, 1935. Another one was built at Pier 84, off W. 43rd St., Manhattan.

Both Cunard-White Star for the 1936 Maiden Voyage of *Queen Mary*, and the French Line awaiting May, 1935 arrival of Normandie, were helped by Hapag-Lloyd's Captain Drechsel in preparing for handling these giant liners in New York. The 260-tons pontoons to keep *Normandie's* overhanging bridge from hitting Pier 88 girders were designed by Captain Drechsel and built by Hamilton Marine Corp., Thomas Rinaldi, President. The Drechsels were guests at Normandie's maiden voyage Dinner-Dance. When Captain Drechsel sailed for Europe in March, 1939 he went as guest of the French Line. And on August 30th, when *Bremen* sailed two days after her arrival, and delay because of inspection for arms or any war materials (the same inspection being done on *Normandie*, etc.), she thrice dipped her flag, in tribute to Drechsel and *Bremen* itself on her 6:37 p.m. departure into war, as both groups knew. A last expression of the comradeship of the sea, before a second world war broke. Interestingly, *Normandie's* coming led to clearning up conflicting interpretations of the "rules of the road" as ships backed from their North River piers into the Hudson for sailing. It was NDL's understanding that "as soon as the stern of the ship was in the river, the signal to be given was three short blasts. We have sought the advice from the pilots and from Captain George Fried (ex Captain *George Washington, Amerika*, etc?) Supervisor of Steamboat Inspection, "that the three short blasts should be given only when the ship is already in the river and completely out of her berth. One blast is to be given when the stern begins to protrude from the slip." The three in the stream in effect are a mutual Goodbye, Bon Voyage.

North Atlantic Community

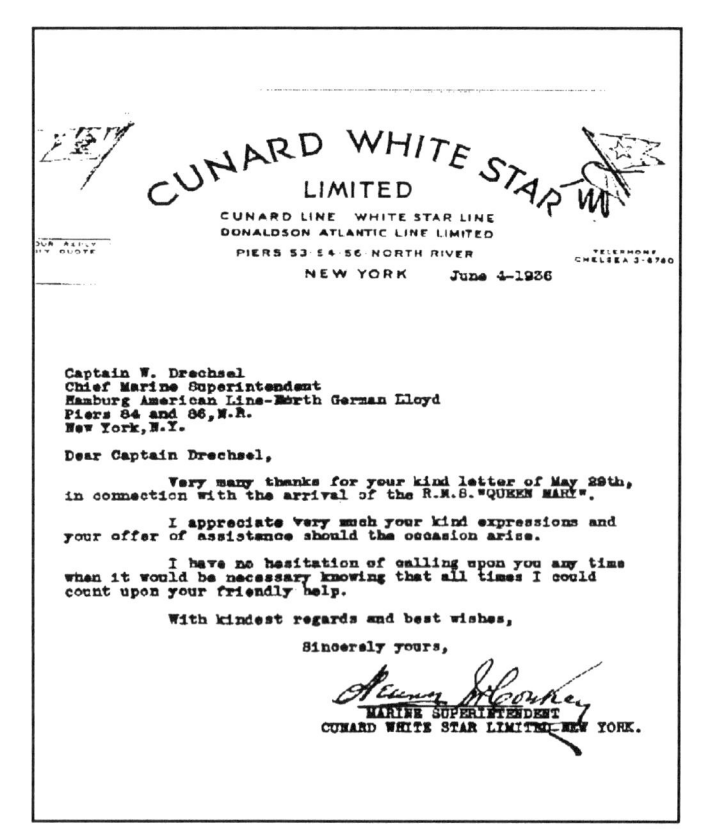

Captain Drechsel was the only seaman-member of the committee appointed by the Conference on Port Development (New York) to handle arrangements for the maiden-voyage arrival of Cunard White' Star Line's Queen Mary *June 1, 1936. The line's Marine Superintendent thanked Drechsel; "I have no hesitation in calling upon you any time ... knowing that ...I could count upon your friendly help."*

The United Sandy Hook Pilots Benevolent Ass. remained the Pilots' group for New York/New Jersey harbor during the changes in speed-run end points from Sandy Hook to Fire Island Light, to Nantucket, to Ambrose Channel light and last to the automated stationary light there. Sandy Hook actually is the N.E. point of New Jersey.

safety of ships in New York and the outports: Boston, Philadelphia, Baltimore, etc. Demands on tug crews and shore staff were high, given occasional extreme conditions, such as fast-flowing masses of ice down the Hudson when a ship had to dock or lose valuable hours. Or when wind and tide combined to make any landing or departure risky. Experiences and lessons were shared. The shipping and towing companies each had competitors. But there was a higher calling: that of a seaman. There was a cordial thank you from Moran Towing Co. President Eugne F. Moran to Captain Drechsel when he commended the Moran tugs for a recent skilled handling of *Normandie* under difficult conditions. Obviously, Drechsel had been watching.

Fast Turnarounds. The needs of normally tight schedules sometimes made impossible demands on the Captain, ship and the Inspectorate. As the Marines like to say: "The difficult we take care of right now. The impossible takes a bit longer." With only two fast ships - *Columbus* at 21½ knots too slow to fit into a three-ships weekly schedule with *Bremen* and *Europa's* 26½ knots, as Cunard and White Star could with three ships each and one less day steaming time, *Bremen* and *Europa* in season sometimes were scheduled for a 17, even 16 days turnaround. Add to that bad weather or some incident or fog at sea which forced taking a more southerly track, as *Bremen* had to do on her maiden voyage, and turning ships to keep their schedules made for hectic hours.

In late 1959, The New York Times reported that the *United States* had made her fastest turnaround in her eight-years career after arriving in New York twenty-eight hours late. She was held in Le Havre for sixteen hours to avoid the passenger-discomfort that the storm then sweeping the North Atlantic would have imposed. That put her so far behind, she slowed another eight hours to avoid a pre-dawn arrival at Quarantine in New York. That forced a twenty-eight hours turn-

Bremen *docking at Pier 86, N.R. Docking Pilot Captain Herbert Miller in center, Commodore Ziegenbein at right, content to have an expert with him on the bridge.*

After the docking, a chance to relax and enjoy each other's company: Three Captains: Hapag-Lloyd Port Pilot Herbert Miller, William Drechsel, Inspector, Leopold Ziegenbein, NDL Commodore. Mid-1930s. On Bremen's bridge. Captain Miller had become the Hapag-Lloyd Port Pilot, handling the big ships each time they came and sailed.

around instead of the normal fifty-two hours. Quite a contrast to the pre-1914 times when NDL's four express liners kept a weekly schedule: one week under way, one week in ports, that mostly occupied with coaling and subsequent cleanup.

Without disparaging *United States'* fastest turnaround, NDL had many that perforce were very much shorter. *Columbus* reached her pier at 0.21 hours on 29 December, 1928, and sailed at 2.15 PM that day for Plymouth. Less than fourteen hours. *Europa* arrived in Brooklyn on 10 January, 1936 seventeen hours late due to weather, 5,000 bags of mail were discharged at Quarantine. She left there at 9.12 AM, arrived at Pier 4 at 10.42 AM. The rest of the mail was unloaded there. Docking with nine tugs in flood-running waters; 600 passengers went ashore and 550 tons of cargo were unloaded. Departure

North Atlantic Community 397

Pilot Captain Joseph Sullivan collected photo postcards of vessels he piloted with the captains' signatures. Here is one he sent to Captain Drechsel from the outgoing Hapag Deutschland *with Captain Friedel's signature next to the ship. May, 1936.*

preparations were going on at the same time: loading 557 tons of cargo, 1,653 bags of mail, 5,412 tons of fuel oil from barges alongside from 11 AM to midnight, 3,396 tons of fresh water taken on also from 11 AM to midnight. The ship sailed at 12.40 AM with 522 passengers. Turn-around time: 13 hours 58 minutes. On 6 December, 1935 *Bremen* arrived at the pier at 8.05 AM; she sailed at 12.30 AM just after midnight, after taking on a record load of 6,900 tons of fuel oil. Time in port 16 hours, 25 minutes.

Rarely was the 12.30 AM departure not met. On 31 January, 1936 *Europa* arrived thirty hours late; there had been Atlantic storms all month. She arrived at Pier 4 at 4.35 PM, sailed a 5 AM the next morning, 4½ hours late. She took on 5,788 tons of fuel oil, 4,039 tons of water, 390 tons of cargo in, 396 tons out, and 1,237 bags of mail, in 12 hours, 25 minutes. It took supreme organization, all-out work afloat and ashore to get this done. What higher demands could *Bremen* make on its staffs? No wonder the Lloyd was happy with its New York operation: it performed the impossible time after time. It made possible squeezing in an extra sailing during the top of the season.

Fog could be the most difficult and time-consuming condition that had to be met. On *Bremen's* December, 1929 stormy voyage she reached Quarantine at 1.30 AM, two days and seven hours late. By 10.30, she and other ships still lay fog-bound. Captain Drechsel sent ten tugs down to bring her in. They surrounded the ship, and stationed themselves along the Bay Ridge shore to whistle their locations. "Two tugs guided her in, one close to her bow to warn the lookout in case of threatening collisions." It worked.

On 1 December, 1936 Hapag's *Hamburg* was similarly brought in with tugs to Pier 84 in thick fog while other ships remained at Quarantine. *Europa* nine days later could not make it even with tugs. She had to wait with other arrivals for the fog to lift.

On 16 March, 1936 *Europa* passed Fire Island

FEBRUARY 4, 1936   NEW YORK AMERICAN

On The GANGPLANK
with John McClain

JOHN McCLAIN.

The night before the Europa was scheduled to arrive last week, Captain William Drechsel, pier superintendent for the Hamburg-Lloyd Line, set his alarm clock for 6 a. m. and went to sleep.

In the night he had a nightmare and kicked the covers off his bed and was awakened by the cold breeze fluttering his curtains. It was then about 2 a. m., but the captain had a strange premonition, an uncanny tingling in his bones such as men who have been to sea experience all their lives and can never explain. He felt the wind was changing.

Reaching under his bed, he pulled out the barometer he always keeps there and noted that it was dropping slightly. Then he got up and looked at the wind indicator just outside his window.

His worst fears were realized. The wind that had been blowing from the southwest was shifting to the north, and the temperature was falling in direct ratio. Sitting there in the cold bedroom, his eyes smarting from the sudden strain put upon them, he thought.

"Ice is coming down the river and filling the Europa's slip. In reasonable weather the ice is loose and a big ship like the Europa can push it aside. But when you get a sudden cold spell, like now, the ice will congeal and pile up, and it may take hours to dock the ship.

"Look what happened to the Ile de France the other afternoon—three hours off the end of the pier. I don't know what I can do about it, but if I go down to the pier maybe I can figure some way out. If I go back to sleep, as I would like to, certainly I will not prove anything."

On the way to the pier Captain Drechsel worked out a tentative plan. Tugs seemed to be the only chance. Tugs stirring up the ice and pushing it out into the river and then, somehow, keeping it out there until the Europa could come along and slide in.

Before daylight, Drechsel arrived at the pier and put in a call to Captain Miller, the Lloyd docking pilot. Together they discussed the problem and then Drechsel called the towboat company and got five tugs sent around. The liner New York was docked on one side of the slip, and he ordered her moved to another pier.

After the New York had left the slip, just after daybreak, the five tugs pushed into the space cleared by the liner and began breaking up the ice on the other side, where the Europa would berth. When it was floating loose, three of the tugs tied up to the pier with their sterns sticking straight out into the slip and went full speed ahead on their engines. The churning of their propellers created a current and gradually forced most of the ice out of the slip. By noon it was clear, but there was still the problem of keeping it clear.

It was then Drechsel had his greatest inspiration. He had two tugs tie up at the pier end, with their sterns standing out across the entrance to the slip at an angle, their engines working.

Ice floes coming down the river, instead of turning into the iceless slip, were deflected by the current set up from the tugs' propellers and shunted out into the middle of the stream. From about noon until 4 o'clock, when the Europa came up the river, those tugs guarded the portals.

Then they cut loose and went about their job of warping the big ship in.

• • •

The Europa left Quarantine shortly after 3 o'clock in the afternoon and was tied up fast, with all lines out, before 4:30. She doesn't do much better than that in midsummer, when there is no ice anywhere around.

I saw Captain Drechsel when I got off the ship that afternoon. He looked tired, and his eyes were red.

But he was smiling.

Getting the ship docked, resupplied, and then out again was the challenge. Reporters found and told the happenings.

at Noon in heavy fog. It anchored at Ambrose Lightship, the entrance channel to Lower Bay, until 11.30 PM. At 12.45 AM she headed for Quarantine under tug escort, docked at Pier 86 at 9.15 AM against strong ebb currents with help of eight tugs. She sailed at 2 AM in fog, two tugs escorting her to Ambrose Lightship.

On 4 March, 1934 "at 12.30 AM departure time No Visibility. *Bremen* remained at the pier until 11.10 AM. We took her out in thick fog with one tug on each side forward, calling megaphoned instructions to the bridge, as far as Ambrose Light Ship. By then the fog was less thick; the ship proceeded. Tugs and Drechsel back to the pier."

New York's shipping fraternity later referred to this as The Big Fog of 1935. It had one humorous happening. One Monday in January, 1935 Captains Drechsel and Miller went down the bay by tug *Richard J. Barrett* looking for Hapag's *New York* with 300 passengers. Finding a large steamer's dark shape, they called by megaphone, got a reply, and turned the tug around: "Follow me," slowly upstream, shouting directions or warnings. Two slow hours of this when the fog lifted and there, on the bow of the ship, was read *Pennsylvania,* of the Panama-Pacific Line, an intercoastal vessel. Mutterings, turning around, hunting some more for the *New York*. She was found at midnight, and eighteen hours late guided to the pier. Pilot Captain Miller's comment "It's like looking for a black cat in a cellar on a dark night." Reminds one of Mr. Churchill's broadcast comment on 1 October, 1939: "Russia is a riddle wrapped in a mystery inside an enigma." Enigma later was a most secret coding system.

Painting up the draught marks on Europa *in New York, feet and meters. From XI up to 40, the medium blackness between above and below is where the white stripe was, some 18" wide. It was given up during the bottom of the depression, so 1931-1933.* Photo from National Geographic Magazine.

There was a song then current about "Like a Ship at Sea I'm just lost in the fog."

Carl Sandburg said it poetically:

The fog comes on little cat feet;
It sits looking over harbor and city
On silent haunches, and then moves on.

Specialty Freight: The big ships had little time or space to carry other than the more valuable or exotic cargoes: things needing to get there almost as fast as passengers. This had been very much the situation with the eleven River Class express liners of the 1880s and 1890s: to meet the competition each one had to be a bit faster than the one before. This meant bigger engines, leaving less room for freight. In 1936, Prime Minister Mackenzie King heeded a call from Germany for some fresh blood for a herd of bison. The twenty bison and seven elk from Canada arrived on a Tuesday. Where to put them? *Bremen* had docked late Monday at 10.30 PM with heavy ice in the river; it took eleven tugs to guide her in. Normally, such animals are not taken on an express liner. But Hapag's *Deutschland,* more suitable, would not sail until the Saturday midnight. When the RR people called: "the animals are here." Drechsel said "send them over." "We have no personnel here." "OK, I'll send ours." So a pier crew went and brought the animals to Pier 86. They were lifted onto the catapult deck, actually the roof over the Sun Deck restaurant. The freight people's fear the animals would feel the cold, was put to rest by the keeper travelling with him. "They like the cold," plus the several tons of oats and hay shipped with them.

When a reporter was called the day of the sailing and told about the animals, his reply in effect was "Pshaw." But when he read from a competitor the next A.M. that Mrs. Calvin Coolidge and Mr. & Mrs. Franklyn Hutton (Woolworth) also had sailed, then he was upset at not having been told that.

Actually, race horses were a fairly frequent cargo on *Bremen* and *Europa*. Nowadays they fly. A five-day ship was the best available then. And, once the catapults were removed permanently in the winter of 1935, that space became a garage, and up to fifty cars could be carried there, usually as baggage, also occasionally race cars, museum pieces, and so on. And sometimes a different deck

Ice in the slip at Pier 84, North River. Conditions somewhat like those described for Europa's *arrival in January, 1936.*

Europa *as the French* Liberte *docking at Pier 88 in February, 1955, in slush ice. See #489 for* Berlin *in similar weather. Liberte's bow shows the weather she went through during the crossing. This angle shows the highest version of* Europa-Liberte's *stacks. Later, CGT cut them down.* Photo by Fred J. Sass for The New York Times.

New York American

A Paper for People Who Think — FRIDAY, FEBRUARY 14, 1936

On The GANGPLANK
with John McClain

The other afternoon I was informed by a voice from the Hamburg-Lloyd line that twenty cow buffalos were sailing that night in the express liner Bremen. The buffalos, according to the voice, were to be placed on deck in crates and cared for during the voyage by loving hands of the ship's able seamen.

This intelligence struck me first as something of more than passing importance—but then, when I awoke the next morning (yes, *morning*), I was alarmed to see in the paper, on page one, that Mrs. Calvin Coolidge and Mr. and Mrs. Franklyn Hutton had sailed in the ship. The press department of the line had taken limitless pains to let us all know that 20 buffalos were sailing in their ship, but had failed to report the three most important humans on the list!

It just happens, in this case, that the story of the buffalos' sailing is probably a better feature than the departure of the more articulate voyagers, but it is a bad precedent.

Some night President Roosevelt is going to sail unexpectedly and the Hamburg - Lloyd line will call to tell us that a one-eyed Manx cat is being sent abroad as a gift to the Sultan of Jodhpur.

Actually, and to get back to the buffalos, the strange shipment that went out aboard the Bremen the other night was composed of 19 cow buffalos, one bull buffalo and 7 moose.

They are the gift of Prime Minister MacKenzie King, of the Dominion of Canada, to Minister Hermann Goering, of Germany — head of aviation, who bears the supplementary title of Jadgmeister, or game to a national park in East Prussia to replenish the diminishing European bison and moose herds.

When the gents in Germany who are interested in such matters learned a few years ago that their own bison and moose were losing their looks there was serious concern about what could be done to build them up. The ravages of the war had depleted the herds and there was no fresh stock available.

As a result a gentleman named Lutz Heck was sent over here by the Reich government to see if he could make a deal to import new blood from American game animals. The best specimens were found in Canada and so, as a sort of good-will gesture, Minister King agreed to send an assortment from his own Canadian Buffalo Park, at Ottawa.

* * *

The shipment arrived by train Tuesday afternoon and was switched into the 34th st. yards. An attendant called up Capt. William Drechsel, marine superintendent of the Hamburg-Lloyd line and said:

"The buffalos are here."

That presented the captain with what is called a "knotty" problem. Large animals are not usually shipped by express liners, and yet the next available smaller ship of the Hamburg-Lloyd line on the schedule was the Deutschland, sailing Saturday.

That would mean that this precious cargo, representing international good-will, would have to cool its heels for three days in an uncomfortable and inclement freight yard.

Drechsel made a quick decision.

"Send them right to pier 86," he said.

The railroad man said there were no laborers around who could be used to load the crates in the trucks and make the delivery. Drechsel thought a minute and then replied:

"Okeh. I'll send my own gang."

The buffalos arrived at the Bremen pier toward nightfall and were put up on the airplane deck, near the spot where the catapult stands. Worry developed at first over the fact that the animals would get cold during the crossing, until the keeper who had been sent along explained:

"That's what these fellas like —cold. They can take 30 degrees below zero and never bat an eye, but the thing that gets 'em down is sudden changes in temperature. They ought to be very happy up here."

Along with the buffalos and moose went several tons of oats and hay, food for the crossing.

* * *

Not to mention, as the Hamburg-Lloyd failed to do, Mrs. Calvin Coolidge and Mr. and Mrs. Franklyn Hutton.

---

cargo as Captain Frank Hawk's airplane with which he flew a trans-continental record.

The pressure to keep schedules came in part from the line's mail obligations, the fact that carrying the mails was a sizeable additional income. At Christmas time, the last vessel to arrive in time for deliveries often brought, or took over, as many as 25,000 sacks. The 33,000 sacks taken out by the *United States* in December, 1959 may well be the record-lifting of all time. Nowadays, surface mail goes in containers. And despite the high speed of these ships, nearly equal to that of the faster passenger liners prewar, it takes weeks longer to get across the oceans than prewar.

Midnight Sailings. These had begun with NDL's pre-1914 express liners as providing optimum arrival times at Plymouth, Southampton or Cherbourg, allowing same-day arrivals by train at London or Paris.

It wasn't only passengers that ship and shore staff tried to keep happy by sailing on time. After all, midnight, actually 12.30 A.M., departures could already be part of the vacation: a going away party in the cabin or sundeck restaurant, champagne-cork popping in high spirits, confetti. That happened still only on longer cruises, like round-the-world, occasionally at overseas ports. But the depression ended that in New York. Captain Drechsel and Passenger Director John Schroeder would bid the captain goodbye, and be the last ones off the ship. Drechsel going to the pierend. As the Bridge passed the end of the Pier there'd be mutual waving from the pierend and the bridge: Goodbye, Auf Wiedersehen, Gute Reise.

With Captain Adolf Ahrens, on *Columbus* and then on *Bremen* after 1936, it was different. He'd come to the pierend after midnight and join Captain Drechsel and Bockelmann - he the Pier Captain; he was at Lakehurst in May, 1937 with a crew of twelve to help dock the *Hindenburg* when she exploded and burned. Ahrens would throw a piece of wood into the water to see how fast the current was flowing. Then he shook

22 ** MARCH 18, 1936 DAILY NEWS, WEDNESDAY,

ONE OF my BEST FRIEND ST...

Tootling Tug Can't Find Europa in Fog

By CARL WARREN

The mighty Europa and the majestic Berengaria arrived yesterday. But this is another story—a tale about one of those tiny black water bugs that haul the sea giants into port.

There's nothing exciting about the tugboat Richard J. Barrett. And a perilous four-hour search for

The gallant tug Richard J. Barrett at its berth, Pier 43.

Capt. Herbert Miller "You just keep blowing your whistle."

the Europa through a fog as murky as mud, to hear Capt. Herbert Miller tell it, is a routine job. You might ram another boat or be rammed and no rescue ship could find you, he admitted, but, well, you've got a whistle.

"It's something like looking for a black cat in a cellar on a dark night out there," the grizzled skipper explained. "You just keep blowing your whistle."

The Europa, 49,000-ton North German Lloyd liner, was due to reach Quarantine at 2 P. M. Monday. She didn't show up. At 4:30 P. M. the tugboat with Capt. William Drechsel aboard was ordered out to look for her somewhere south of Sandy Hook. Meanwhile, James Donahue, cousin of Countess Haugwitz-Reventlow; Michael Farmer, former husband of Gloria Swanson; Miliza Corjus, German opera star, and 776 other passengers fretted at the delay.

All evening the tugboat poked her inquisitive nose through the zero-zero visibility fog. He could no' see men on his own deck, Capt. Drechsel said.

"We kept a sharp lookout but nobody can see in a fog like that," said the tugboat captain. "If we hit anything we counted on our fender to bounce us off. After nearly four hours we gave it up."

A south wind brushed the fog aside later after the Europa was held up fourteen hours. The Richard J. Barrett helped warp her into lock.

Maybe his tug would bring in the Queen Mary when the new British liner arrives, but Capt. Miller had no time to talk about it. Another job was waiting.

"So long, we're going after the Berengaria," he called from the pilot house.

Weather, fast currents downstream, tides incoming, fog, ice, and sometimes winds, caused problems in finding the ships as far out as Ambrose Light Ship and bringing them in, in the docking and undocking of the ships at Piers 84 and 88. Looking for ships in the fog didn't always find the right ship. In January, 1935 Panama Pacific's Pennsylvania was found, at least a big black bow, and invited to follow up the Hudson. When the fog lifted a bit, the tug-guide found it had the wrong ship, not the sought-for New York.

Tug Has Long Search For Big Liner

Like the blizzard of '88 the Big Fog of '35 will be memorialized in anecdotes.

It was Captain William Drechsel who went down the bay in a tugboat Monday looking for the Hamburg-American liner New York, overdue with 300 passengers aboard.

He came under the bow of a giant steamer and, grabbing a megaphone, stepped to the deck and spoke to the big steamer. A halloo from the bridge echoed back so the skipper swung his tug about and started up the channel, shouting warnings from time to time of fogbound craft that lay in the course.

Two hours of this and the fog lifted enough to reveal the name on the prow of the steamer: It was the Panama Pacific Liner Pennsylvania. Captain Drechsel muttered a few expletives as they say in the Navy and turned back for the New York.

He found her at midnight and 18 hours later guided her to her berth in the Hudson River.

Staten Island Advance
January 9, 1935

NEW YORK TIMES, February 3, 1935

NEWS OF INTEREST IN SHIPPING WORLD

Tug Goes Down the Bay in Fog and Brings Up Wrong Liner— But Such Errors Are Few.

CHICAGO AN 'OCEAN' PORT

Captains Report Weather at Sea Is Balmy—Hudson Ice 8 Inches to 2 Feet Thick.

Race horses were a high-value freight that went with the fastest ships, and got the best care. Loading horses at Pier 4, Brooklyn, 1930s. In November, 1936 Captain Victor Lackmann replaced New York's *Captain Theodor Koch, taking a voyage off to supervise construction of his new home at Pinneberg near the Elbe. Hurricane winds during the voyage gusting to Beaufort Scale 10, even 12. The ship docked 6th November with 602 passengers, 5,000 tons of freight including 6,000 canaries.*

Loading car at Pier 84/86 in 1930s.

hands and went on board. Lines off, then one long whistle as the ship pulled astern, usually one to three tugs in attendance, sometimes as many as ten if there was a strong outgoing current or incoming tide and wind. The best sides of Piers 84 and 86 to tie up to on arrival were not always the best side to sail from.

Service with a Capital S: After the ships had cleared the slip while the Lloyd still docked in Brooklyn, it was easy for Drechsel to drive down the Shore Road and flick his lights as the ship passed him near Fort Hamilton, a last All's Well! No wonder these captains were close companions. They shared a love for the sea and their ships: it was their lives, and serving the travelling public.

Occasionally, a little bit of extra service. In May, 1935 when *Stuttgart* was ready to sail at 11 A.M. a Mother and son from Manhattan and Marie Halmen from Winnipeg, Manitoba, had not yet arrived. Captain Hagemann waited ten minutes. At 11.12 his patience ran out, and he signalled for "astern." Just then the three

midnight sailing

The double virtue of Midnight sailings for the express steamers from New York was the celebrations it made possible for passengers and well-wishers. The need was to optimize arrival times at Plymouth-Cherbourg-Southampton, whatever the combination for passengers to the British Isles and the Continent. Richard Pratt in 1929 wrote in The Lloyd's Seven Seas *"You can never know how wide the circle of your friends is until you are about to sail on a liner with a nocturnal departure. A daylight sailing is fun, but not nearly so flattering. The darkness ... calls out the party spirit. It lets fantasy flourish. It makes the city seem to disappear. Though you may only be a visitor on board, you get the fleeting sense of having sailed away..." With her going-astern long whistle, "this visiting city now becomes a ship again....A tug nudges close, perhaps taking off a too-festive goodbye-wisher, "kisses the ship goodbye."*

It was a bit tricky at a midnight sailing of Columbus *in 1928. Two late-arriving passengers were put on a tug lighted up by the ship's search light and ferried out. Presumably their baggage was hauled up by rope; they had to climb a lowered Jacob's ladder to the lowest-opening port.*

Bremen *ready to sail, from New York, with Christmas Greetings from its Captain Adolf Ahrens, 1936-1939.*

August 23, 1937 EVENING JOURNAL AND NEW YORK AMERICAN

On The GANGPLANK
With John McClain

TRANS-ATLANTICA: Captain William Drechsel, chief Marine Superintendent of the Hapag-Lloyd line, has a little game of his own which he plays with the skippers of outbound ships of his company. Just before one of his liners sails he stops by the captain's cabin and says to the old man: "Bet you a stein of beer I can get home before you do." That doesn't seem to make much sense, but the fact is Captain Drechsel lives on the shore road, in Bay Ridge, Brooklyn, at a point where the liners pass within a quarter of a mile of land, as they go out through the Narrows. What Drechsel means is that he can get in his car, drive down the elevated highway, over the bridge, through Brooklyn and out the shore road to his home before the liner whose captain he's betting with passes his house.

Most German ships sail at midnight, which makes it possible for Drechsel to employ a unique method of signaling the ship as she goes past. He backs his car into the driveway, so that the lights point directly toward the Narrows. Then his signals, by Morse code, "Tee-hee, you lose," or words to that effect.

The captain, seeing this, flashes the big electric sign on the side of the ship—the one which says Bremen or Europa, as the case may be. In the smaller ships, like the Hamburg and Berlin, the skippers flash back Morse messages: "Nuts to you," or "Try to collect!"

Thus far Drechsel has had good luck beating the Bremen and most of the smaller ships, but he can't take the Europa. He doesn't know why that should be — probably just bad breaks on the traffic lights go through Brooklyn.

missing ones arrived by taxi. By coincidence, *Deutschland's* crew entering the Labor Day lifeboat race was practicing in the adjacent slip. Captain Drechsel commandeered the boat and crew, put the three with baggage on board, and they had a real rowing practice getting out to the ship before it turned downstream. When the rowers returned, Drechsel stood them each a stein of beer.

A reporter once lucked out the same way. He had missed the Customs cutter with officials, reporters and photographers heading for Quarantine to await *Europa's* clearance by the Health Department. *Columbus* happened to lie at the other side of Pier 4. As the reporter strolled around waiting for *Europa's* arrival, he ran into Captain Drechsel and told him why he wasn't on the Cutter. Drechsel ordered one of *Columbus'* motor boats to be lowered with an officer and crew of three. They took him top-speed across the bay to the ship anchored off Staten Island. As they came alongside the Cutter to the hoots of his colleagues, he climbed up and joined the others in going on board. Small wonder that Drechsel was popular with reporters. "He knows his stuff." He made good copy. He provided service, even a reporters' telephone in his Pier office. He made himself accessible. And he'd come up with surprises that made him and his ships good copy. One innovation he introduced was shooting lines from pier to ship or ship to pier, this then used to pull a bigger line across until the big hawser was in place, and the capstan could help pull the ship in.

Another story concerned an elderly couple who had come from Chicago to see their daughter off on *Europa*. Delayed, they reached the pier after the "no visitors" sign went up. Discouraged, they somehow found their way to the pier-end, closed to the public. Nobody noticed them, being busy with casting off preparations. Then Captain Drechsel did see them, asked what they were doing? Hearing their story, that they at least hoped to write their daughter and tell her from where they had seen it sail, he replied: "Nothing easier; I'll have the ship brought out of the slip so you can see her." As the ship glided by all lit up, the deep bass sounding a long note, they stood transfixed. Never had they seen such a sight. As they shook hands, Captain Drechsel said: "You see it was no problem." The elderly lady raised her finger in admonition: "You shouldn't have done it."

Ship Design for Port Handling: As ship got bigger, and more expanse exposed to the winds and tides and currents, it became more difficult for the line crews on the pier and the tugs to work the ship in or out. Ships had to have appropriate openings forward aft in the hull for lines, and bitts and capstans in the right places on deck and below.

Early in 1939 Hapag asked Captain Drechsel to come to Hamburg to inspect plans for their new 45,000 tonner *Vaterland* then building, first of three larger, faster ships to replace the four units of the *Albert Ballin* class. Drechsel had studied shipbuilding at the behest of the Lloyd before making captain in 1919. After his report, Hamburg-Amerika Line gave a luncheon for him on board its Express Steamer *Hamburg*. He evidently was the only to command both a Lloyd ship, Bremen 3 in 1924, and Hapag's pre-1914 Yacht *Meteor* which he had commanded in 1918 at Kiel as Submarine School Mother Ship. At the luncheon Drechsel was handed a message from Hapag Commodore Kruse at sea on *New York* sending "Best Greetings." Drechsel arrived on *Hamburg* in New York on 31 March. Back to "normal" at the Inspectorate:

- On 14th April, *Bremen* arrived a day late due

The Lloyd and then Hapag-Lloyd piers in Brooklyn and Manhattan. Top Photo has Karlsruhe *behind* Columbus *at Pier 4, Brooklyn, with* Bremen *on the North side on 14 July, 1930. Cargo vessels are at the other piers, and a Dollar round-the-world liner in the floating dock. In the middle photo:* Columbus *and* Bremen *at Pier 86, and* Hamburg *and* Milwaukee *at Pier 84. The French Line's Pier 88 is to right, as is the later Cunard Pier 90. The 1961 photo, (bottom photo) courtesy Moran Towing's Tow Line' shows* Berlin *docking at Pier 88, Pier 86 now used by* United States Lines, *and Pier 84 by* American-Export-Isbrandtsen Lines, *here also by* Vulcania.

North Atlantic Community 407

Dressup of Pier 86, North River for Europa's *100th Voyage, 1935.*
Hapag-Lloyd Photo.

to storms at 9:42 A.M., needing ten tugs for the docking. It sailed on schedule that 12.30 A.M. with an ebbing tide, three tugs.

- In June, *M.S. St. Louis* was expected with more than 900 Jewish refugees who had been denied permission to land in Cuba, and now similarly denied landing by the U.S. and Canada. There was "crisis in the air," as there had been earlier in the decade.

Anti-German Impact: Once the National Socialist seizure of power in Germany was recognized as world-antagonistic, boycotts of anything German spread throughout the world. Most visible targets overseas were German ships.

At Hapag-Lloyd in New York there was extra effort to assure the smooth operation of the ships. On 26 May, 1935, the "Day of German Shipping", counterpart to the U.S. Maritime Day, was celebrated on Pier 86, N.R. In port were *Resolute, Reliance* and *Albert Ballin,* named for the genius who built Hapag into the No. 1. ranking in the world. Due to arrive that day, Captain Ziegenbein from *Bremen* sent his greetings.

Captain Drechsel, with his staff responsible for organizing the celebration, in his remarks said "We all today think of our comrades on the High Seas. It shows the true Seamen's Spirit that for this festivity we are able to welcome the entire crew of the Steamer *Königstein* from the Arnold

NEW YORK POST
October 20, 1933

A CERTAIN ship news reporter has earned the puzzled, half scornful envy of his fellow seascribes by a little incident that occurred the other morning, reports Rayness Copeland, who chases notables up and down gang-planks himself.

The giant Europa of the North German Lloyd was swinging at anchor off Quarantine, while mail boats, the Quarantine doctor's launch and the customs cutter, loaded with Government officials, reporters, photographers and so forth clustered about her, waiting for her to be cleared. Everybody was pretty bored until a smart white motor-sailer, a type of ship's life-boat, was spotted, skipping toward the big liner at a fast clip. Something, the watchers opined, must be up. They soon ascertained that the motor-sailer was from the Columbus, another North German-Lloyder then at her dock in Brooklyn. To the amazement of the reporters they made out the figure of one of their fellows, who had been unaccountably missing when they left the Barge Office in the chill dawn. He was standing erect in the bow of the little craft, like Washington crossing the Delaware. The watchers surmised that the reporter, having missed the regular cutter, had been lucky enough to catch the Columbus's launch as it was about to visit the Europa on company business.

But the launch came to smartly alongside the customs cutter, the reporter scrambled aboard, and the craft which had brought him turned about and sped back across the harbor.

The reporter airily responded to the cries of "Hurrah for the Admiral!" that greeted him and explained that, after missing the cutter, he'd gone to the North German Lloyd pier to await the docking of the Europa. He decided to wait aboard the Columbus, and there encountered that vessel's genial master, Captain Drechsel. He told him of his predicament. The captain, he asserts, promptly ordered out the motor-sailer, carrying a crew of an officer and three men, and had him ferried across the bay in style.

Here a ship news reporter makes an item out of himself - having missed the cutter to Europa at Quarantine.

THE NEW YORK AMERICAN
A Paper for People Who Think—

On the Sun Deck

All-Atlantic Selections for the Year Reveals a Wealth of Good Material.

By JOHN McCLAIN.

With the summer rush definitely past and a tough winter ahead, the time arrives for this department to make its annual all-Atlantic selections for the year.

The Lloyd was well represented when Ship Reporter John McClain in the New York Sun *listed his "All-Atlantic Team for 1932: on 21st November, 1932: Captain - Nicholas Johnsen, of* Europa. *(Tragically, he died in Bay Ridge, Brooklyn in December, following a too-late ruptured appendix operation at sea.) Chief Officer: Staff Captain W. Daehne of* Bremen, *later Captain of* Columbus *(#300). Chief Engineer, Honorable Mention: Julius Hundt of* Bremen. *(See D.O.R., Vol. I). Chief Steward, honorable mention, K. Wieja of* Karlsruhe.

Kreuz und quer...
New Yorker Staats-Zeitung
Von X. Y. Zett

Kapitän William Drechsel, der Marine-Superintendent des Hapag-Lloyd, ist uns schon immer als einer von der Zeitungsgarbe vorgekommen. Nicht nur daß er an Nebel- und anderen Schlechtwettertagen wie die Bordberichterflatter Tag und Nacht ein wenig beneidenswertes Dasein auf Tendern und in zugigen Lagerschuppen führt, sondern seine ganze Art, ein Wetter- oder Landungsvorkommnis zu beurteilen und zu erklären, ist die eines Zeitungsmannes: Ronzis werden von ihm die schwierigsten Dinge mit einer Einfachheit erläutert, daß sie nachher auch der simpelste Zeitungsleser versteht. Kapitän Drechsel ist daher bei allem, was einen Bleistift zum Broterwerb führt, eine hochbeliebte Persönlichkeit von unschätzbarem Werte.

Baronsky Off for New Post.

Captain George Baronsky, assistant to the marine superintendent of the Hapag Lloyd Line, sailed Friday night for Bremen to assume new duties as representative of the line in a foreign port. He will make several trips as master of the line's vessels to ports of Europe and then will be assigned as marine superintendent in a port that has not yet been designated.

Captain Baronsky had been in New York eight years on the staff of Captain William Drechsel, at the German line piers. He has served with the Lloyd line since 1912 except for the war time years he spent in the German navy. He was on the Herzogin Cecelia in a Chilean port at the outbreak of the war and escaped after a period of internment. After a trip of 124 days during which he traveled 12,000 miles he arrived at Drontheim, Norway, and then made his way by land to his home, where he received a naval assignment.

The Inspectorate Staff had people of varied and long experience. Captain Baronsky, in March, 1935 left his work as No. 2 in New York to become Inspector at Rotterdam after serving on various vessels for actual at-sea Captaincy. Vol. I tells of his voyage with 21 other Lloyd people in a crew of 28 that in 120 days sailed from Chile round Cape Horn to Germany in the Winter of 1916-1917, wartime. He is in the Christmas photo on Bremen.

New York Sun, Feb. 19, 1934
NEW LLOYD PIERS.

The most sincere thanks of this department to Capt. William Drechsel, marine superintendent of the Lloyd, and his office staff who have been recently transferred from the Brooklyn piers to their new quarters in Pier 86, North River. It was a very heartening experience the other day, after a long and cold morning, to step from the Europa into the warmth of that new office and be given a phone and a chair.

A pier phone in the winter (or in the heat of summer, for that matter) is a device calculated to weaken the morale of the strongest man. It is so cold, as a rule, that one can barely make his fingers work the dial; if the door is closed the light is too dim to permit reading one's notes, and if it is open the noise of the pier drowns out the voice. Add to that the fact that pier phones are usually busy no matter when you get to them and you will understand why we are so grateful to Capt. Drechsel.

This same courtesy to the press has been a policy of the French Line for several years. If we could only make a similar arrangement with the other lines along the Chelsea piers the time might actually come when we would have very little to say in the way of self-pity.

* * *

Helping reporters do their job was an important part of the Inspectorate's self-assumed tasks. Through the ship-news articles the public was kept aware of the shipping industry in general and Hapag-Lloyd's part in those specifically. Here a reporter's thanks for that telephone when needed. Also another: a special ride to the ship for one who missed the cutter.

The sea mellows men.

It takes them over the hair-narrow boundaries of geography and breeds a brotherhood which is quite beyond ken of men who see no beauty in the North Star or the Southern Cross or the rolling bosoms of waves that crown the crest of a contented sea.

JAMES STREET

Like aged tobacco and old clothes and old shoes, the sea makes men feel close and secure and outside the veil of selfish emotions.

We had dinner with Captain Oskar Scharf of the Europa. He—his eyes as frosty as an Indiana Autumn—sat right over there. Over yonder was Captain Dreschel, marine superintendent of the North German Lloyd. And here at our left sat John Pannes, passenger traffic manager of the line.

The white wine was split in five glasses. Captain drank mineral water and used a butter knife to spread caviar on thin toast. Proper in the evening dress of a seafaring man, the master sat erect in his whites. The third glass of wine, the fish course and the barrier of Captain Scharf's timidity was shattered with this question:

"Captain, tell us a story?"

He gruffed a "grumpf" and began:

"The Europa is on her century voyage. This is her 100th round-trip. We ask you newsmen here to help us celebrate at a quiet little dinner, H-mm!"

We urged:

"Yes, Captain, we know that, but tell us a story."

The red wine was poured. The master likes red wine. The frozen smile on his lips softened and he talked, without stint or reserve:

CAPT. OSKAR SCHARF,
Liner Europa's Skipper.

shoe on a gangplank. I was a cadet. Back in those days—h-mmm — the Japanese defeat of Russia still was news — they called cadets Moses. I was a Moses, a — what do you call them? — agreenhorn? H-mmm.

"It was a square rigger. We went away in her. My mother cried.

"I've followed the sea ever since."

Pannes took up the line:

"My son, captain, is a sailor. He went to sea at 15. Now he's on the Joseph Conrad, a sailing craft. Last we heard, his vessel had cleared Singapore and was squared off for the Straits."

The captain took up there:

"The Far East. H-mmm. I've been there."

The champagne bubbled and flattened. The brandy glowed—so did the cigars. The master arched his Teutonic eyebrows and began weaving all the gentle memories of youth into the happy twilight song of middle age:

"Have you, comrades, ever seen the sea burnished like copper? Well, I have in the Indian Ocean. I've been around the world often—have you ever traveled the North Atlantic in Winter when the winds froze the marrow in your bones? I'll have

Sea. I've taken some beautiful ships over there—Burma, Rangoon, Hong Kong—where seas are smooth and men are gay.

"The Normandie. She must be a wonderful ship. I've never seen her."

A German praising a French rival.

"The Rex? H-mmm, she's trim. I saw her coming in. Records? H-mmm. I have a schedule to keep. So long as I make it, I'm happy. Married? Yes. My wife and son live in Bremen. They've been on vacation. I'll see them this trip. Last month I had a vacation. We took a trip in the Columbus. It was my wife and son's first voyage. We traveled lightly. Some passengers saw me strolling the deck in a coat and said to friends:

"'Ah, see that chap. It's his first trip to sea.'

"The sea? It's all I know. War? I hate wars. It ruins good ships, and friendships."

H-mmm. The sea makes men mellow. For the sea has no borders except the horizon.

Article by The Ship New Reporter of the New York American, *James Street, about* Europa's *100th voyage. How it was sixty years ago. Herr Pannes and his wife died in the* Hindenburg *tragedy in May, 1937.*

In March, 1939 Captain Drechsel went to Hamburg to counsel Hapag on construction details for the new Vaterland *building at Blohm & Voss to make the vessel properly fitted out with capstans, bitts, hull openings and hawse pipes for passing lines to tugs and piers. Story of 3 April, 1939 from* The New York Herald-Tribune, *Photo from Hapag.*

New Hamburg Line Ship To Make 7-Day Crossings

The new 36,000-ton passenger and freight liner now under construction at the Hamburg yards of Blohm & Voss for the Hamburg-American Line's trans-Atlantic service, will make the crossing from Hamburg to New York in seven days and from Southampton and Cherbourg a day under that time, it was disclosed yesterday by Capt. William Drechsel, general marine superintendent of the Hamburg-American-North German Lloyd Lines at New York. Capt. Drechsel returned Friday on the company's liner Hamburg after a conference with company officials abroad on plans for the new ship. The vessel will be propelled by turbo-electric machinery and have a speed of twenty-three knots.

Scheduled to be commissioned in the Hamburg-Lloyd's service in the spring of 1941, the new vessel will be provided with accommodations for 1,300 passengers in cabin, tourist and third classes, Capt. Drechsel said.

Construction has progressed to the extent that the outlines of the lower decks and the hull are taking shape. The ship will have two funnels and two masts.

Bernstein Line." Arnold Bernstein in 1934 had bought the old Red Star Line and this spring converted it into a low-cost carryer of one-class Tourist passengers and of unboxed automobiles. In 1937, the National Socialists seized his shipping firm. He was in concentration camp for 2½ years until American friends bought his release in 1939. He went into shipping in the U.S., became a citizen, and in 1959 formed the A(merican) B(anner) Line, again with the one-class, low-cost principle. He died in 1971 aged 83. He had won the Iron Cross First Class in WWI fighting for his native Germany.

The Curio-Snack-Tuck shops on Piers 84 and 86 were run by the Johnson Family. They were Jewish and had Jewish helpers. They never were molested. They were part of the friendly atmosphere that existed on the piers.

In 1938, one Mr. Kopp complained about the "slovenly appearance" at the shop, and being talked to rudely by some person in Captain Drechsel's Pier Office. Evidently, this Kopp complained to Hamburg, which in turn wrote to Passenger Director John Schroeder in New York who turned that letter over to C.J. Beck, Director of the Hapag-Lloyd North-Atlantic Community.

Mr. Beck wrote to Hamburg, rejecting the Kopp complaint out of hand. "Mr. Kopp's complaint obviously is based on racial prejudice .... The members of our crews trade freely in their small shops and are on good terms with the Johnsons. ... We really consider them an asset to the Lines as it would be difficult to find anyone that gives such close attention to their business and deport themselves so well."

There were very occasional demonstrations at the Hapag-Lloyd piers at West 44th and 46th Streets. In 1936, - the Olympics were being held in Germany and the Spanish Civil War had begun, - there were anti-Nazi demonstrations against German ships. On 22 August, 1936 *Bremen* was due to sail at 12.30 A.M., the 23rd. About 11 P.M. some hundred persons dressed in evening wear, evidently seeing off friends, went on board. Once there, they took off outer things to show white "Hands off Spain" T-shirts. They spread through the ship, passing out anti-Nazi handbills. In groups they yelled "Hitler must be kept out of Spain." A riot call brought some seventy policemen, ten detectives and four radio cars. Some of the demonstrators seized deckchairs and battled with the police. Some cries of "Communists" were heard. Eight women and four men were taken in custody to the W.47th Street station. (Ex-New York Times).

On 29 September, 1936 an estimated 250-300 "Communists" demonstrated before the piers prior to *Europa's* sailing at 12.30 A.M. the 30th. There was no interference with departure activities on the pier or on board.

There were occasional other boardings by activists. These twice were successful in tearing down the Swastika flag. In 1938, the Gestapo took into custody two ship officers accused of having been negligent in not preventing such flag-seizures. *See also* "Chaos and Confusion."

North Atlantic Community 411

NEW YORK HERALD-TRIBUNE
MARCH 7, 1940

Prize Nazis Wouldn't Take

The larger cup, about two and one-half feet in height, is soccer trophy the crew of the Bremen left behind last August. The smaller cup, along with gold medals presented in absentia yesterday, will be sent to Germany
Herald Tribune—Fein

Bremen's Crew Will Get Soccer Prize Won Here

Team Turned Down Big Cup on Eve of Last Voyage; To Receive Medals Instead

The soccer team of the North German Lloyd liner Bremen won the international soccer challenge trophy, a large cup worth $2,500, for the season 1938-'39, but declined the award the day before the Bremen sailed from New York on Aug. 30, on what turned out to be a long and mysterious voyage to Bremerhaven via Murmansk, Russia. The hazards of the impending trip were too great, they felt.

Officials of the Y. M. C. A. Seamen's House, who have sponsored soccer matches between crews of American and foreign ships in New York for the last fifteen years, announced yesterday that gold medals and a smaller silver cup had been made and would be taken from New York next week to the victorious German soccer team by a German official. His name was not divulged, nor was it revealed how he would travel.

In a ceremony yesterday at the Seamen's House, 55 West Twentieth Street, J. C. Clark, executive secretary of Seamen's House, presented the big cup, the smaller cup and the gold medals to Capt. William Drechsel, marine superintendent of the Hapag-Lloyd.

Mr. Clark praised the "true sportsmanship" of the Bremen's team, recalling that a spokesman for the crew had cited the fact that the cup is retained for only one year aboard ship by the winners and explained the team preferred not to risk taking it with them.

Captain Drechsel, replying, said: "The comradeship so prevalent among the teams in the soccer games was ample proof that all the men had learned to understand and respect one another, and our greatest hope is that the whole world may be filled with the same spirit as was displayed by players of all nations."

Because of the few ships able to compete here now the trophy soccer events have been held in abeyance until the termination of the war.

The $2,500 Caroline Delow de Lancey Cowl Trophy, as the large cup is known, will be held at the Seamen's House until after the war. It is about two and a half feet high.

Crew Activities: *Bremen* and *Europa* and most of the other Lloyd and Hapag North Atlantic ships had activities clubs: sports, music, chess, etc., something they enjoyed doing when off duty or even formally to compete ashore as representatives of their ship and line against similar teams from other vessels. *Berlin's* soccer team had won the North Atlantic Cup four times in a row. *Bremen's* team won it in 1938-1939 season. The Trophy has due to be taken on board for display at the end of August. But that was *Bremen's* last departure before the war, into the unknown. The crew preferred to have the trophy kept in New York at the YMCA Seamen's House on 55 W. 20th Street. However, in March, 1940 during the war a small replica cup and the team's gold medals were taken to Germany by an unnamed individual and an unnamed ship. The trophy remained in New York. Captain Ziegenbein took great pride in how *Bremen's* teams and cultural groups did. He donated a Cup which he would present personally. He founded the Speckenbütteler Kinderfest for the children of his crew members. And he would attend.

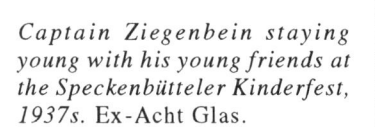

Captain Ziegenbein staying young with his young friends at the Speckenbütteler Kinderfest, 1937s. Ex-Acht Glas.

412 Norddeutscher Lloyd Bremen

A huge job of keeping the ship spick and span, especially during the first year when the low stacks contributed to heavy on-deck pollution: cinders and gases. The stacks were raised by fifteen feet. Giving more area to be painted.

Captain Ziegenbein with one of Bremen's *sport groups, 1931.* Ex-Acht Glas.

Top Deck of Pier 86, Manhattan. The Dora Johnson-Kahn's Tuck-News-Curio Shop was at the far center right. The Inspectorate offices were at the left back.

The staff at the Inspectorate's Pier 86 offices worked long hours with dedication. Ships arrived and sailed at all hours. It was a self-felt duty to meet every need for their turnaround, the handling of passengers with courtesy and dispatch, and the cargo. It was work that required consummate knowledge, skill and patience. With all the difficulties: political, economic and material, the operation was the model for the shipping industry. The author just wished he knew all the names in that staff and outside. 1932-1936 he was away at college and worked or studied summers. From October, 1937 he was in Venezuela with an ESSO affiliate.

CHAPTER 14

Countdown To — And Again War

During the September, 1938 Munich Crisis German shipping at sea or in ports abroad had a foretaste of what would happen if war again threatened. See end of "Chaos and Confusion." In 1938, sealed orders were opened on orders of wireless messages "to run for home or to seek a neutral port."

After Christmas 1938, the Lloyd's Technical Service in Bremerhaven during *Bremen* and *Europa's* annual overhauls, installed air-conditioning in First Class topside public rooms, just in time for *Bremen's* Round-South America cruise from New York on 11th February. Also that month the annual Atlantic (Passenger) Conference was held in Paris, with Waldemar Klose and B. Lampe from the Lloyd and W. Voss, . Neumann, and H. Striddle from Hapag. On 3rd March, his 60th birthday, Captain Drechsel left New York on *Normandie* for consultations in Hamburg about in-port handling for Hapag's *Vaterland* under construction.

Tensions could be felt, a seeming inevitable rushing towards another confrontation, wanted or to be allowed to happen on one side, on the other with seeming disbelief. Ralph Freeman in his "Sea History" reported that in the Spring of 1939 *Queen Mary* and *Bremen* passed in the Atlantic. "The ships came close, their vast wakes a sight to behold. Although passengers on both liners crowded the decks, no one waved, no greetings, no blowing of whistles, no signals were exchanged. A precursor of dark times ahead." This in sharp contrast to when the two ships first met in May, 1936 in the English Channel on the *Queen's* maiden voyage. Commodore Leopold Ziegenbein messaged to Commodore Sir Edgar Britten "Heartiest greetings on the completion of our youngest and largest comrade on the seas. May our first meeting be the beginning of a long and good working togetherness." What binds seamen is first the love of the sea and then their ships on the sea.

Seafarers and the shipping industry more than any other wanted and needed peace. As in the Summer of 1939 the approaching crisis widened, the faint hope was that as in September, 1938 somehow differences could finally be worked out. But Hitler forced the ultimate decision. And for the second time in a generation German shipping, far more even than from World War I, lost almost everything.

In August, 1939 a series of *QWA* wireless warnings were sent out from Germany telling ships to return home or to seek neutral waters. The messages were so unclear, even contradictory, that several ships were captured by the enemy-to-be instead of getting home.

The first *QWA* on 25 August told ships to leave their courses by 30-100 miles. The same day

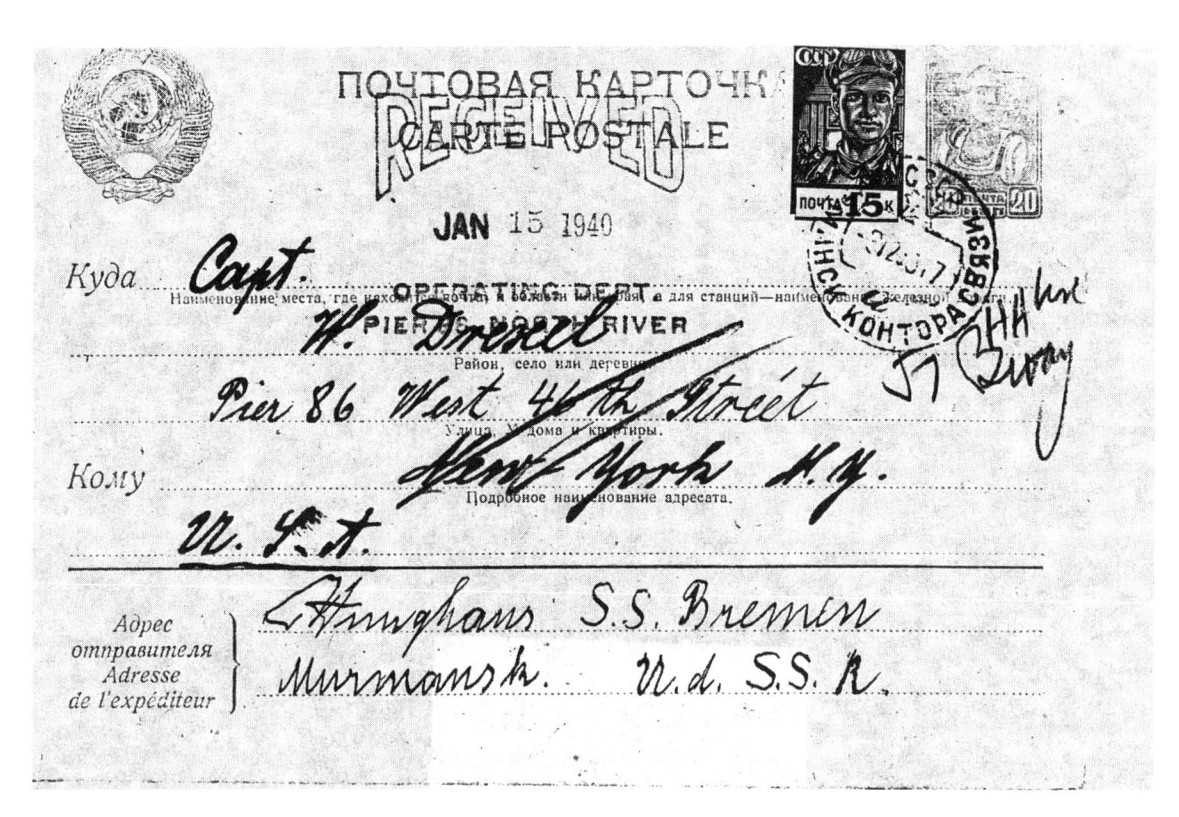

Two mailings from ships that took refuge at Murmansk:
1. Written 8 December, 1940 by B. Junghans, an officer on the Bremen, wishing Captain Drechsel and his family a Merry Christmas and Happy New Year.
2. To Captain Bockelmann, of NDL's Marine Staff in New York, written 18 September, 1939 asking that the sender's (Capt. Gustav Schröder) trunk with his picture and autograph collection, which he had entrusted to Captain. Kempf, Captain Drechsel's assistant, be stored safely somewhere. And that no mail be sent onward to me. Everything is to stay there (in the U.S.). I received Captain Drechsel's telegram re the above. Best wishes and thanks to all.

In 1974, New York Times *correspondent Hedrick Smith was allowed to visit Murmansk. He found it a depressing place. Murmansk's value to the Soviet Union was that the end of the Gulf Stream helps to keep it clear of ice year-round while other northern ports are frozen for long dark winter months. In April, 1994 the* New York Times *again reported "Once among Russia's mightiest and most active ports, Murmansk, the world's largest Arctic city, now sits practically idle, the rusting hulls of a dozen ships rotting in the harbor. A tug boat captain says 'It used to be ... around the clock ... the port was filled with people. Now nobody comes unless they have to....' When the sun sets on November 29, it does not rise again until the middle of January."*

By HEDRICK SMITH
Special to The New York Times

MURMANSK, U.S.S.R., Feb. 21—The kind of Soviet-American maritime traffic that made this port city famous to Americans during World War II as the landing point for lend-lease is now just beginning to revive in the warming climate of relations between the Kremlin and White House.

After a hiatus of more than two decades of cold war, American vessels are once again seen at Murmansk, a port vital to the entire Soviet north because the final fling of the Gulf Stream keeps its harbor open year-round while other northern ports are frozen in for seven months.

The New York Times/Feb. 28, 1974

QWA 8 ordered camouflaging of ships and immediate return home, but not via the Strait of Dover. On the 27th, *QWA* 9 ordered return home in the next four days if possible, or to seek a neutral port. Confusing text led several vessels to enter neutral ports when they could have got home. *QWA* 10 on the 28th was meant to rectify that confusion. It was too late as ships had committed themselves to head for Murmansk or to neutral ports closer in. *Python,* a banana carrier for F. Laeisz, the former sailship "Flying P Line," was already signalling to enter Kristiansand when it got the signal "Go to Murmansk". It turned around, headed north and became one of twenty-two German ships to harbor there. Most eventually got home from Murmansk, including *Bremen* on 3 December, 1939.

A number of ships did get back to Germany at the end of August-early September, 1939, and later in response to specific orders to leave their neutral refuge to get home. But many were lost in the process, either captured or sunk or scuttled to avoid capture, as was *Columbus* #300.

For a seaman to lose his ship to nature's excesses or through accident is traumatic, so much so that many a captain has deliberately gone down with his ship. But to destroy or to scuttle a ship, even in wartime to avoid capture by an enemy, was "the most terrible experience in my life" one captain admitted.

Most dramatic of the prewar happenings was *Bremen's* 187th outward voyage. She left Bremerhaven at 2 P.M. of Tuesday, 22 August with some 1,220 passengers. It passed Dover about 6.30 A.M. the 23rd in heavy traffic, many small craft. To make Cherbourg the same day, *Bremen* anchors for two hours below Southampton instead of docking. Its own *Greetings,* NDL's *Grüssgott* of 1914, brings down the passengers and mail, and takes some of each back to port. Some 500 passengers joined the ship at Southampton and Cherbourg. One Tourist passenger who boarded in Southampton had his train fare back to Boston paid by the Lloyd, just as it had been paid from there to New York when he was coming to Europe. NDL had given up Boston stops early in the depression.

Early Thursday the 24th *Normandie* is visible to the north, en route from Le Havre via Southampton to New York. Current radio news is included in the daily Lloyd Post, so passengers know the war winds are stirring. When *QWA* 7 was received by *Bremen* on the 25th Captain Ahrens turned a bit south and continued towards New York. He felt with some 1,770 passengers it made no sense to turn around, contrary to what *Kronprinzessin Cecilie* #234 did in 1914. One passenger said later "the Farewell Dinner was held as usual on Sunday evening, with a very early dinner Monday before our 6.00 P.M. arrival at Pier 86," Lloyd consideration for its passengers to the end. With a strong flooding tide, it needed ten tugs to put *Bremen* alongside.

Orders from Berlin were for *Bremen* to leave without passengers, cargo or mail as soon as the ship could be got ready the next morning the 29th. Captain Drechsel and Passenger Manager John Schroeder are the first up the gangplank. Drechsel advises Captain Ahrens that "at 7 A.M. is the best water" for sailing. This meant twelve hours to get everything unloaded, refuelled, resupplied with full fuel tanks and off. This the shore staff had repeatedly achieved when ships were late or needed repairs, etc.

British Navy Has Bremen, London Told

(Special Cable to The News)

London, Sept. 21 (Thursday).—Germany's 51,000-ton will-o'-the-wisp liner Bremen has been captured by the British Navy and is now held in British waters, according to

German liner Bremen was captured by British navy and is held in British waters, London Daily Express says today. (NEWS foto)

this morning's Daily Express. Although the paper states that its information is believed reliable, it cautiously adds that "confirmation is lacking in official quarters and on that account the report must be treated with reserve."

The Express report adds that the Bremen's crew, numbering more than 800, including Capt. W. Drechsel, "have left the district where the ship lies to be interned elsewhere."

The Bremen left New York last Aug. 31, the day before Germany invaded Poland. Since then it has been reported in ports from South America to Iceland and Murmansk, Russia, but general opinion has been that it was taken into British hands.

September 1, 1939

Cruiser Prepared to Pounce on Bremen

(Copyright, 1939, United Feat. Synd., Inc.)

Originally it was secretly planned to hold the Bremen, giant German passenger liner, indefinitely. Roosevelt knew that the German army was inching up on Poland and that the question of peace or war was a matter of hours. So it was proposed to hold the Bremen until Hitler had cast the die.

Later a better plan was evolved. The brand new 10,000-ton British cruiser Berwick had been basking in New England waters, where natty English officers beaued wealthy American debutantes. Suddenly the Berwick disappeared — destination unknown.

That destination can now be revealed. At the present writing the Berwick is pacing the Bremen across the Atlantic, ready to pounce on her.

It was decided that there was no use holding the big liner in New York when the British could take her, if war broke, at sea.

Propaganda was part of every war-participating nation, especially with regard to ships, keeping the enemy confused.

"But" Mr. Schroeder intervenes, "President Roosevelt has just today signed an executive Neutrality Order requiring all departing foreign vessels to undergo inspection to assure that they carried no weapons, ammunition or contraband." The examing staff would and did appear at 8 A.M. the 29th. They dispersed around the ship, took their mid-day break, then left the ship at 4 P.M. Captain Drechsel asked the Chief Inspector: "did you find anything?" "Nothing." "I could have told you that." The inspectors returned at 8 A.M. the 30th, presumably they had already searched everywhere. At 9 A.M. two inspectors from the Steamboat Inspection service arrive to check out ship-security equipment. At noon, again the midday break. No instructions yet to their chief to cease the "inspection." *Normandie* at adjacent Pier 88 similarly has inspectors on board.

Inspectors return after lunch, desultorily continue their "Inspection." At four, they leave *Bremen*. Drechsel tells Captain Ahrens "The Collector of Customs says you can sail towards evening." Tugs and Port Pilot Miller are ready for a 5 P.M. departure. Still no clearance. At 6 P.M. a knock at the Captain's office door. "A personal message being delivered by a Customs official to be signed for by Captain Ahrens." The clearance. Quickly Schroeder and Drechsel shake hands with Ahrens, leave the ship and go to the pier end. Whistles to throw off lines or take them on board. At 6.37 *Bremen* starts backing into the Hudson with two tugs helping. The ship's band is playing. At Pier 88, *Normandie* three times lowers her stern flag in salute and thanks to the Lloyd people who have been helpful to the C.G.T. since before the ship came to New York in 1935. See "Inspection." and Farewell. Both knowing what probably lies ahead. As *Bremen* passes Ambrose Lightship where the sea pilot is dropped, twenty-six lookouts are on watch. *Bremen* reached Murmansk in 6 days, 13 hours, 36 minutes, 4,045 nautical miles, at an average speed of 25.65 knots, per A.

A lonely watch in the fog during war heading to what destiny? An Officer on the after side-bridge. Bremen *in September, 1939 approaching the Soviet coast near Murmansk. These photos are from Captain Ahren's book:* Männer, Schiffe, Ozeane, *out in 1941, photos by Hanns Tschira.*

The Vorpostenkette, chain of outward screen vessels, in the North Sea as
Bremen *reaches home waters.*

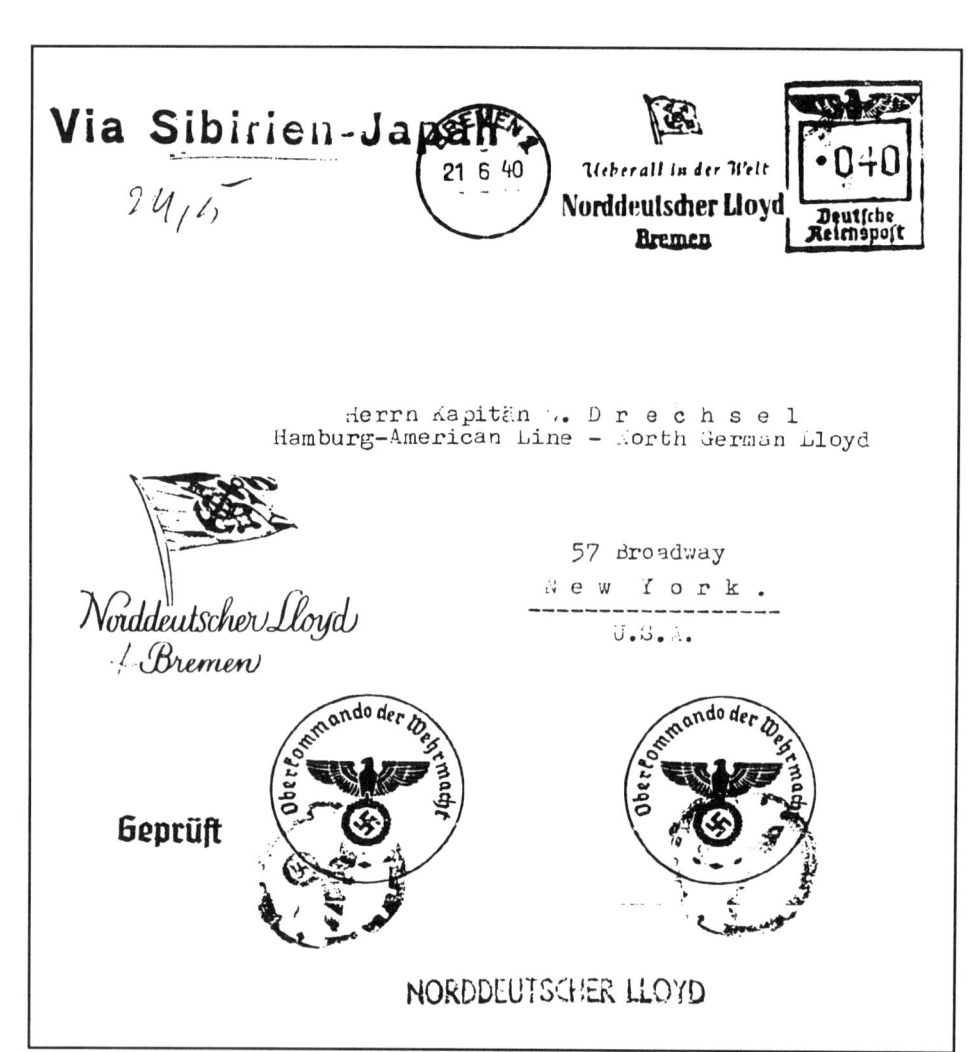

In 1940 and in 1941 until Germany attacked the Soviet Union in June, mail could still get to and come from the U.S. via Japan and across the USSR. Here a letter from Bremen with the prewar slogan: Everywhere in the World, and marked "Via Siberia-Japan." The censor labels were on back. This one concerned the needs for German seamen interned in the U.S. and the rest of the Americas. Hapag-Lloyd officials worked with the American Red Cross, Seamen's Missions and other groups to provide basic necessities. The need remained but with U.S. entry into the war, the internees became prisoners of war. At bottom Censor sticker, High Command of the Wehrmacht, Armed Forces.

Ahrens' *Männer, Schiffe, Ozeane,* 1940. In New York, on 9 September, the French Line's *Champlain* is moved from the south side of Pier 88 to the North side of Hapag-Lloyd's Pier 86. She sails from there the 11th. On 8 September, Managing Director C.J. Beck wrote Captain Drechsel that "Due to the present uncertainty caused by the European War, we must very reluctantly and to our deepest regret ask you to inform all your staff that their services will have to be terminated as of Sept. 30, 1939." On 15 October, the piers are handed over to the New York City Dock Department.

Some of the crew members of Lloyd and other German ships laid up with the war's start in the Far East got home via Siberia, from *Fulda* #307, *Augsburg* #399 and *Bremerhaven* #280 tied up in Dairen. Some from the Hapag-Lloyd staff in New York entrain for San Francisco, Captain C. Kempf and Director Christian Ahrenkiel among them, and take the N.Y.K.'s *Asama Maru* to Japan and then via Siberia for home. Frau Ahrenkiel got home from New York on the Spanish *Magellanes,* and then across occupied France to Germany.

It went otherwise for *Columbus* #300, the Lloyd's popular cruise liner. It had reached New York on 18th August, Friday from the West Indies, sailed again the next day, Saturday, at 11 A.M. with 725 passengers. First stops were in Jamaica, Haiti and Puerto Rico. Captain Daehne received the QWA 7 wireless, decides to skip the next scheduled port, St. George's, Grenada. *Columbus* reached Curacao the 26th and refuels. Passengers are not allowed to land. The ship leaves in the afternoon. On Sunday the 27th a wireless orders: "Land the passengers, proceed to Haugesund, enter a U.S. port only in an extremity" for that was where Daehne was heading, to land his passengers before heading for Norway. He turns the ship around, anchors on Monday the 28th before Aruba. No one may go ashore; the next day 29th that is permitted. The ship refuels, receives another wireless "Land Passengers in New York." Daehne sets course for the Mona Passage between

420 *Norddeutscher Lloyd Bremen*

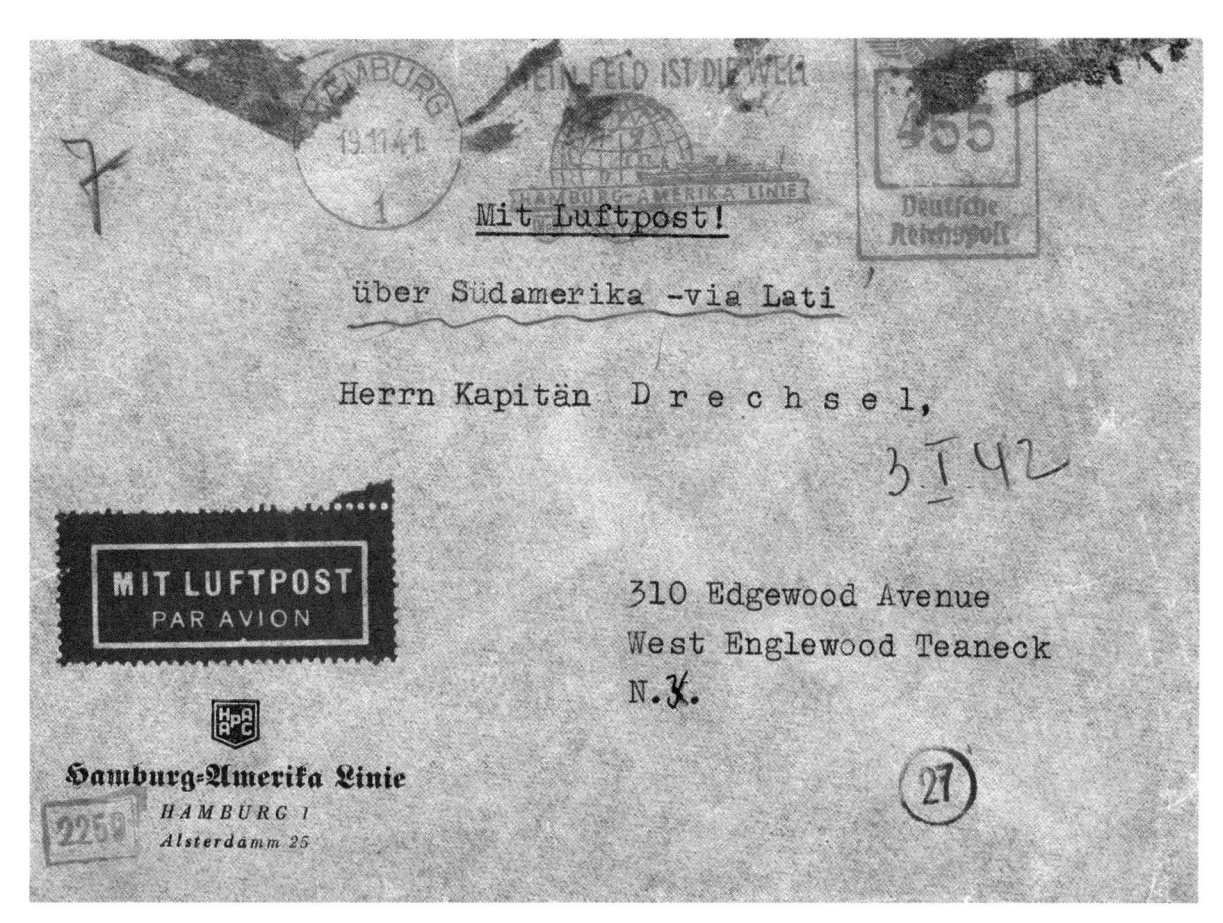

Hapag-Lloyd's Freight Traffic Department Director Christian F. Ahrenkiel in New York got back to Germany via N.Y.K. liner from San Francisco to Japan. On 11 February, 1941 he wrote from the Imperial Hotel, Tokyo to Captain Drechsel about the necessary papers for crossing Siberia by train, etc. This later letter from Herr Ahrenkiel postmarked 19.11.1941 was sent by air mail via South America, reached New Jersey on 3 January, 1942. It never would have arrived had it gone the former route via Siberia and Japan, as that country attacked Pearl Harbor on 7 December, 1941. Censored in Germany and — circled 27 — in the U.S.? It got delivered despite the two cities named, neighbors, and N.Y. instead of N.J. Herr Ahrenkiel wrote that the Lloyd and Hapag had been privatized. Bremen and Hamburg again were making decisions. He now was a Hapag director. "We are facing questions about the new construction of ships and organization for which your experience and knowledge are lacking for us here. We hope ... soon ... we jointly can resume working at peaceful activities." In May, 1941 he had written to thank for safely storing the family's furniture. "We hope that in foreseeable time we can get them out again." Wartime delusions.

Hispaniola and Puerto Rico.

On Thursday the 31st a wireless cancels the "Head for New York" order with "Land passengers in Havana." *Columbus* arrives there Friday, 1st September. Passengers are ferried to Florida on the U.S. - flag *Florida*. From Miami, all but 106 of the original 725 take train to New York, reach Pennsylvania Station on the 4th. *Columbus* heads for Vera Cruz, arrives there the 4th. Hapag's *Arauca* already is there; NDL's *Hameln* arrives soon after.

On the 14th, *Columbus* moves to a more protected anchorage off Green Island, then to a still safer anchorage in Antonio Lizardo Bay, fourteen miles south of Vera Cruz. Some 25,000 barrels of oil are obtained. The ship's white surfaces are painted greyish, also the stacks. These were given black tops, somewhat like White Star liners.

Meanwhile, NDL was trying to negotiate a sale to local Germans in the hope of obtaining Mexican registry and presumably exemption from seizure on the high seas by Allied forces. This never succeeded, strangely enough as German propaganda had made tremendous inroads in Latin America so that the funds for buying *Columbus* and maintaining her until departure should have been available.

Three times Captain W. Daehne through German Consular officials in Vera Cruz or the Mexico City Embassy protested to Berlin that any ordered breakout was futile, so deep within the Caribbean, so easy to follow out into the Atlantic. The

Everybody off the ship, except the three who failed to heed the alarms. Photo by Kurt Hinsch.

Sunday, 27th August, Columbus *was headed north, presumably back to New York, when it received a wireless: enter a U.S. port in an emergency. So Captain Daehne turned around and headed for Aruba. The passengers still did not know what was going on as they were not being given the normal daily Lloyd Post or Cruise News. Despite that, they continued to eat well, as this Sunday luncheon menu indicates.*

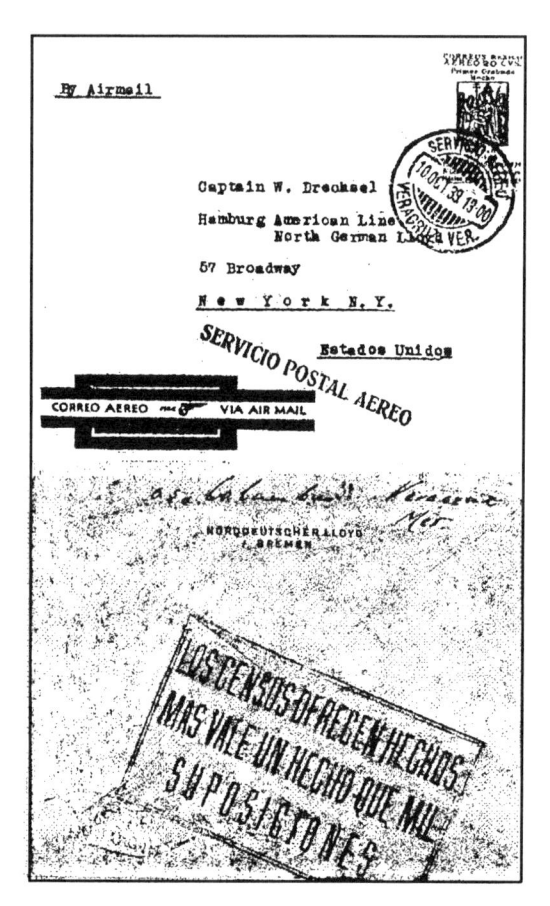

Envelope from the Columbus's *Captain, W. Daehne, to Captain W. Drechsel. The ship lay at Antonio Lizardo Lagoon south of Vera Cruz. It has a large lavendar rubber back stamp: BETTER ONE DEED THAN A THOUSAND SUPPOSITIONS.*

422   Norddeutscher Lloyd Bremen

same applied to the other German ship's at Vera Cruz, Hapag's *Idarwald* and *Orinoco* in addition to its *Arauca* — I had visited her in Caripito, Venezuela where I was working for an ESSO affiliate, on her maiden voyage early in 1939, unloading oil field equipment — and NDL's *Hameln*. A Mexican tanker twice transferred oil to *Columbus* and *Hameln* made three trips from Vera Cruz with water for her boilers.

On 30 October, a High Command wireless advised all ship captains that if they scuttled their vessels to avoid capture, or made it home, they would be given medals. But if they let themselves fall into enemy hands, allowing enemy use of the ship, they faced a disciplinary hearing ... if as and when they eventually got home.

After the Germans overran France, they evidently tried Captain Knübel because he let a French submarine capture *Chemnitz* #418. He had been made prisoner by the French. Outcome of the trial or hearings is unknown.

Meanwhile, non-Germans are sent ashore, including seventeen Chinese launderers, one of whom had been on board since the 1930 World Cruise, leaving 579 Germans on board. All the ship's tableware was landed. It was returned on a Lloyd freighter in 1952.

On Tuesday, 12 December, *Columbus* leaves Antonio Lizardo Bay, anchors off Vera Cruz. Clearance papers arrived the 14th, but weather is so bad, the consul cannot get on board. All the papers Captain Daehne had wanted to entrust to him perforce remain on the ship.

Since mid-November, *USS Dettinger,* had kept watch off Vera Cruz. On the 13th, it noticed return of the tanker that had topped off *Columbus* at its anchorage; then it in turn arrives. By then, *USS Benham, DD397* had arrived. On Thursday, 14 December, with the same orders as *Columbus*, by 8 A.M. *Arauca* gets under way. *Benham* follows her. She had filed for New Orleans with its cargo of sulphur and hides. At 12.40 P.M. *USS Lang, DD399,* sights *Columbus* and so reports to Naval Headquarters. At 19.00 hours, *Columbus* steams into the night, Daehne having filed for Oslo. Lang follows one-half mile behind. *Benham* comes up to follow directly behind *Columbus*. It shows a small stern light for *Benham* to follow. Bedding for the crew has been laid in the Promenade Deck social hall and nearby.

Arauca was left on her own, hugging the Gulf Coast. On the 19th, it entered Port Everglades. It was there interned. On 30 March, 1941, the U.S. seized Arauca, converts her into the naval transport *Sting*.

On 15 December, during *Columbus'* escape attempt, I was on Grace Line's *Santa Rosa* en route from LaGuaira to New York. In the Mona Passage dividing Puerto Rico and Hispaniola, the French training cruiser *Jeanne D'arc* came alongside to inspect the ship. With its two squat stacks from the distance it could have been *Columbus*. The cruiser had waves painted on its bow to simulate running at high speed, to mislead any submarine trying to torpedo the warship.

Columbus' departure on 14th December was the day after the Battle of the River Plate in which the *Graf Spee* was driven into the estuary and subsequently blown up. It took only three British cruisers to overcome Germany's Pocket Battleship contrary to the Kriegsmarine's boast that the three warships "could outrun anything they could not outgun, at 26 knots, and outshoot anything they could not outrun." The fallacy was that the three had only two three-gun turrets. So if two naval vessels fought it out, one each against one turret, then a third naval vessel, outside the range of the ship's other 5.9" guns, could pound away at will until enough damage had been inflicted to force surrender or entry into neutral waters. So there were British naval vessels in the North Atlantic alert to *Columbus* and other German ships trying to get home.

On 15 December, *Jouett DD396* joined *Benham* and *Lang*. Then *Benham* left and rejoined *Arauca*. On the 16th, 0/9/30 hours *Jouett* and *Lang* were relieved by *Schenck* DD159, an old Four-piper, and *Phillip* DD76, off Key West. As *Jouett* left she thanked *Columbus* for her stern light and in German "Gute Reise, Sichere Ankunft and Frohliche Weihnachten." Bon Voyage, Safe Arrival, Merry Christmas. *Columbus* thanked in reply. It passes Key West at fourteen knots. While the ship's turbines installed in 1929 gave her a top speed of 23 knots, this never was used during her service life. Nor was that sufficient to run away from any Allied naval vessels that might accost her. In the event, growth on her bottom gave the ship probably 18 knots at most.

On the 16th, *Columbus* advises *Norddeich*, the North German wireless station, "since Vera Cruz being shadowed by two U.S. destroyers, am at south entrance to Florida Strait, plan to run north near the coast until Hatteras." Captain Daehne expected this to lead to countermanding the "proceed to Haugesund" order, but the wireless received on Sunday, the 17th, orders no change, so Daehne is forced to continue to try to get home. It tells that "Wireless Tables 4 and 7 are lost, so the enemy probably reads your signals. Do not message further."

The two DDs follow *Columbus,* itself blacked

The crew coming off Columbus. *A marvel none died in evacuating into the boats.*
Kurt Hinsch photo.

The Columbus *crew leaving the ship. Most boats are still only for rowing or sailing; only four were motorized for cruise passengers going ashore, mostly at Caribbean ports.* Kurt Hinsch photo.

Columbus *burning on 19 December, 1939, taken from the USS* Tuscaloosea *which took the crew to New York.* Kurt Hinsch photo.

out, fully lit up so that every nearby ship knows something is happening. Below Cape Hatteras two replacement DDs come up, the departing ones signal Goodbye.

On the 17th at Noon the heavy cruiser *Tscaloosa* joins the escort, the destroyers departing. It periodically radios its position in the clear. *Columbus* stays close to the coast as it heads northward. By then, *Columbus* is ca 200 miles East of Norfolk, still inside the 300 miles U.S. Neutrality Zone where no foreign military action is to take place.

On the 19th, at 15.30 hours, smoke and masttops approach from the ocean direction, not coastally. *Tuscaloosa* three times sends it position, 38.02N, 65.35°W. It is recognized as a British Destroyer, later know to be *Hyperion,* approaching. Orders from the Bridge: prepare for scuttling. *Tuscaloosa* changes course away, as if it has nothing to do with what is happening. At 16.06, *Hyperion* messages "I am sending a boat." It approaches to within 100 meters, turns around as *Columbus* starts to burn and sink. A canvas sack with codes, etc. is thrown overboard. Lifeboats with crews are already in the water. Captain Daehne slides down a rope into the last boat. It once goes around *Columbus*, then sets the German flag and follows the others. *Hyperion* has lowered its flag to half mast, "A gracious gesture to a sinking enemy," (Frank O. Braynard). What a contrast, to the Captain on *HMS Dorsetshire* who confined Midshipman Joe Brooks to his cabin for leaving his ship without permission when he climbed overboard to try to get a line around a *Bismarck* survivor so he could be pulled on board. Brooks spent the next three months a prisoner on his own ship. In the end, charges were dropped (Dr. Robert Ballard.)

Of the 579 men left on the ship, only 576 get off. The other three, stokers Carl Glaspa, Heinz Leibsden and Helmut Dien, evidently slept through the alarm (Rehm), in cabin 246, or thought it an exercise, or could not get out in time. *Tuscaloosa* wirelessed to *Hyperion* "We shall take them on board" and did so. Captain Daehne was given the Skipper's day cabin. On Wednesday, 20 December, the entire crew was taken to Ellis Island. Captain Daehne was given the Director's quarters.

On January 14th, 1940, 512 *Columbus* crew members on two extra trains left for San Francisco. On board, in addition making it 514 were NDL Director Christian Ahrenkeel, and Captain W. Drechsel who was working with the Red Cross and other organizations to help care for interned German seamen in North America, see below. One

What can the son whom Reporter Frank Reil was considerate enough to mention in his letter say? I, the son, had just arrived from Venezuela on long leave from my work there with an affiliate of Standard Oil Co. (N.J.), now EXXON. On the way from LaGuayra the Grace Line's Santa Rosa, *while passing the Mona Passage between Puerto Rico and Hispaniola, was examined by the French cruiser* Jeanne d'Arc *on the lookout for* Columbus *#300. It was trying to get home by orders of Berlin and contrary to Captain W. Daehne's warnings that the ship could not possibly make it without being intercepted. I let Mr. Reil's comments about my Father stand as an impartial tribute. He had years of contacts with him as reporter while I was away at school or out of the country.*

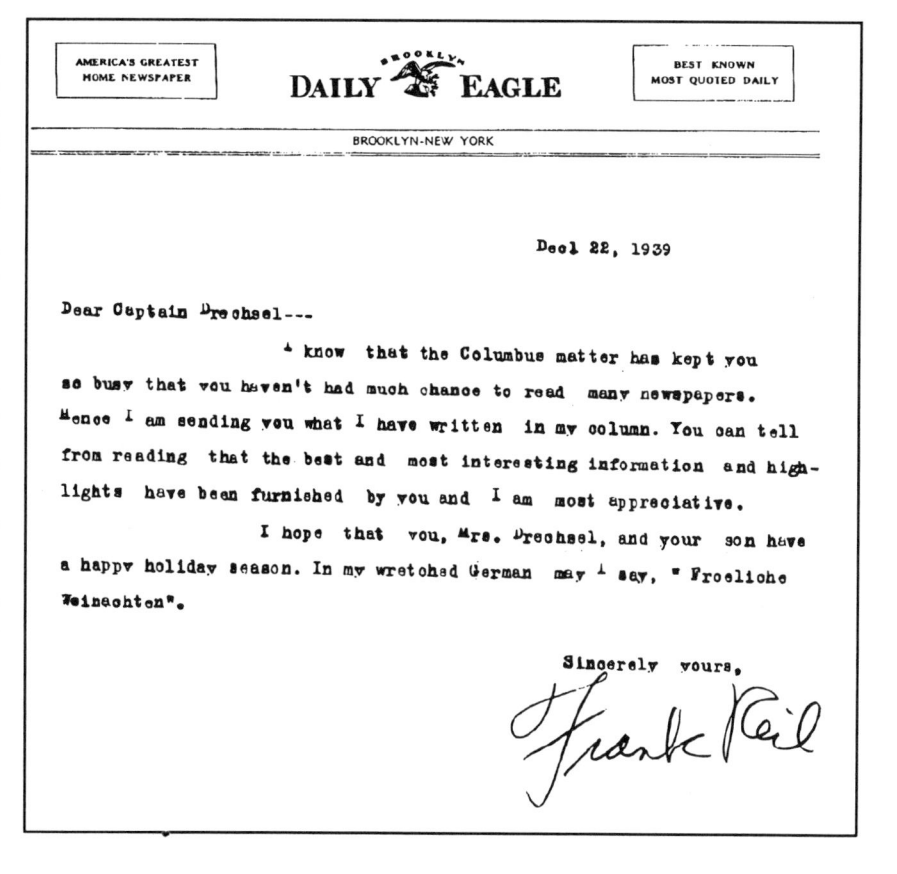

AMERICA'S GREATEST HOME NEWSPAPER	DAILY EAGLE	BEST KNOWN MOST QUOTED DAILY

BROOKLYN-NEW YORK

Dec. 22, 1939

Dear Captain Drechsel---

I know that the Columbus matter has kept you so busy that you haven't had much chance to read many newspapers. Hence I am sending you what I have written in my column. You can tell from reading that the best and most interesting information and highlights have been furnished by you and I am most appreciative.

I hope that you, Mrs. Drechsel, and your son have a happy holiday season. In my wretched German may I say, " Froeliche Weinachten".

Sincerely yours,

Frank Reil

```
                    DEPARTMENT OF STATE
                         WASHINGTON

In reply refer to
FA 740.00115 European War, 1939/196
    Mr. Gustav J. Lund,              January 6, 1940
    924 Court Street,
    Martinez, California.
My dear Mr. Lund:
        Acknowledgment is made of the receipt of your
letter of December 20, 1939, and I regret to advise
you that the Department of State has no information
as to the whereabouts of the Captain and members of
the crew of the German ship Columbus.  It is suggested
that you may desire to communicate with the "German
Consul General, San Francisco, California" who doubt-
less will be able to advise you in the matter.
        Sincerely yours,
                For the Secretary of State:

                        Nathaniel P. Davis
                        Chief, Division of
                        Foreign Service Administration
```

Surprising admission from the U.S. State Department replying to Gustav Lund's query about the whereabouts of the Columbus *crew. At the time they were still on Ellis Island.*

On the train from New Jersey to Oakland with 500 some members of the Columbus *crew for internment on Angel Island. With Captain Drechsel, second from left are Engineers Reichstein, Fortmann and Thode.*

Columbus being scuttled on 19 December, 1939. Kurt Hinsch, 2. Officer, was married to Liselotte Gastmeyer, daugher of the Drechsels' oldest friend, Volume I and II (A New Start). Married to a U.S. citizen, he was able to "immigrate," after the war became manager of Mr. Gastmeyer's food import business.

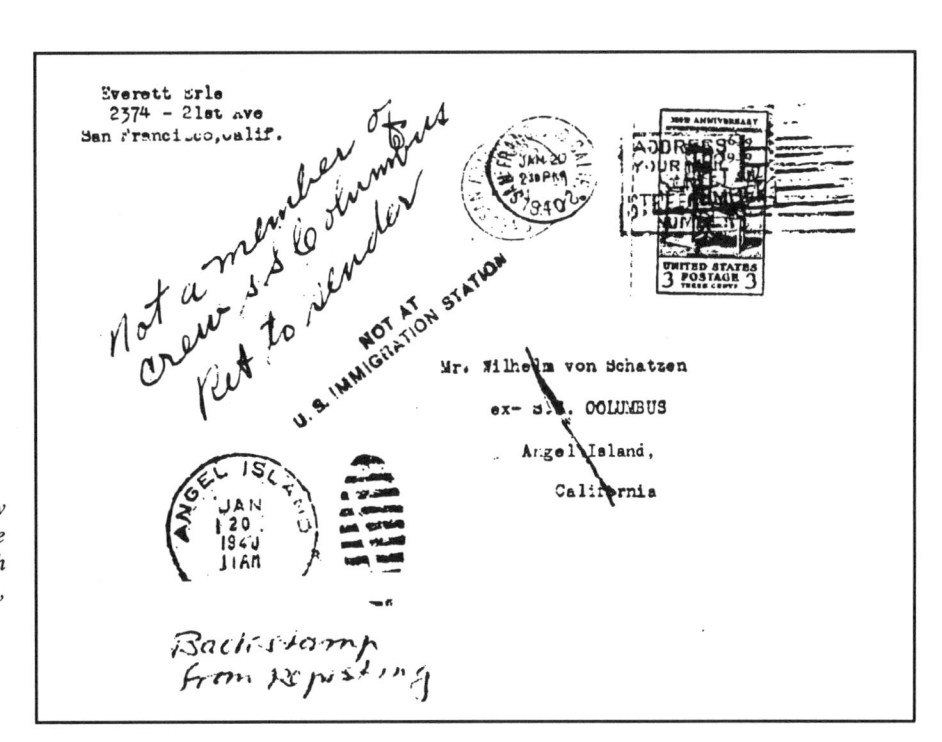

A letter to a member of the crew at Angel Island drew the response: not a member, with the island's Postal backstamp, returned to Everett Erle.

Countdown To - And Again War 427

Angel Island in San Francisco Bay, the former Quarantine Station. There now is preservation of the old buildings and a museum that has a model of Pamir, *see "The Lloyd Sails...", made there by* Columbus *crew-members brought here in January, 1940, and donated by the Author to the Angel Island Museum. Belvedere and the Tiburon (Spanish for shark) Peninsula lie beyond.*

night, while the trains were sidetracked somewhere in the Midwest waiting for a clear track, an Immigration Inspector came on board for a head count. He took a long time, on leaving told Drechsel, Daehne and Ahrenkiel: "Congratulations. I counted twice, not only 514, but 515 each time. Have a good trip on to Oakland." What had happened Drechsel explained is that an old-time *Columbus* steward, who years ago had deserted, married an American woman and settled down, had read about the crew heading for California. He boarded to join old friends in New York and had a wonderful time with them. He disappeared before the trains reached Oakland at 4.30 A.M. on Thursday, 18th of January. On the 17th, 57 mostly officers, presumably all reservists, had sailed from New York on *Rex* for Italy and so home overland. When the U.S. got into the war, the *Columbus* people were moved to New Mexico from where they were repatriated after the war. Captain Drechsel made several more trips to Angel Island, the former Quarantine Station, where the Crew was housed, in S.F. Bay. In thanks for his efforts on their behalf, crew-members built a 3-foot model of the German sailship *Pamir* which went down in the South Atlantic in 1957, of a 20-inch whaleboat model. And Purser H. Thielbaar did a painting of Mount Lassen. All three were given to Drechsel, and passed on to me. The *Pamir* model now is in the Angel Island museum.

The care by the New York Hapag-Lloyd representatives for the interned German seamen of all lines in North America continued actively as the war expanded. Shipping Reported Frank Reil for the Brooklyn Daily Eagle on 9 November, 1939 wrote that Captain W. Drechsel, who before the war was Chief Marine Superintendent for the Hapag-Lloyd North America union, 'now was virtually Marine Superintendent for the fleet of forty-odd ships that the German lines have tied up in Latin America. With the exception of *Columbus,* all the other vessels are freighters."

Captain Drechsel, as the senior representing German shipping firms, worked with the American Red Cross, the Seamen's Church Institute, the Y.M.C.A. and other organizations to provide the crews with material and financial support to ease their life in internment camps. There were so many that envelopes for individual communications were printed.

Those interned in Canada even were able at times to send greetings by short wave to their families in Germany.

A 3 April, 1940 letter from Dr. Otto Dettmers in Bremen to Captain Drechsel details what currently is happening to try to safeguard the NDL. In addition to the Director's position, Dettmers had taken over as chief of the Deutsch-Amerika Linie, the corporate merger of the Lloyd and Hapag north-Atlantic liners, when Herr Heinz Schuengel, who ran this operation from Bremen 1933-1939, died in that year. "Our immediate task here (as CEO in Bremen) is the sound continuance despite the war of our organization's capability (in expectation of an early settlement of the war.) You, Dear Captain Drechsel, are the last support of your, in normal circumstances, so important shore Operating Division. Especially, the tragic affair of *Columbus* means for you on shore, and for Captain Daehne, a major undertaking in caring for the crew. We hope very much that Captain Daehne in the not too distant time will again be available with his usual energy and enthusiasm. (A vain hope, expectation, that the war would soon end.) In hopes we all soon can again unite our efforts in peaceful work, Your (signed) P.S. Please give my regards to Captain Daehne at next opportunity."

Germany's occupation of Norway in April, 1940 was in a race with Britain to seize this ocean-facing indented coast as a base for both naval and air attack on the other. Germany's naval and mer-

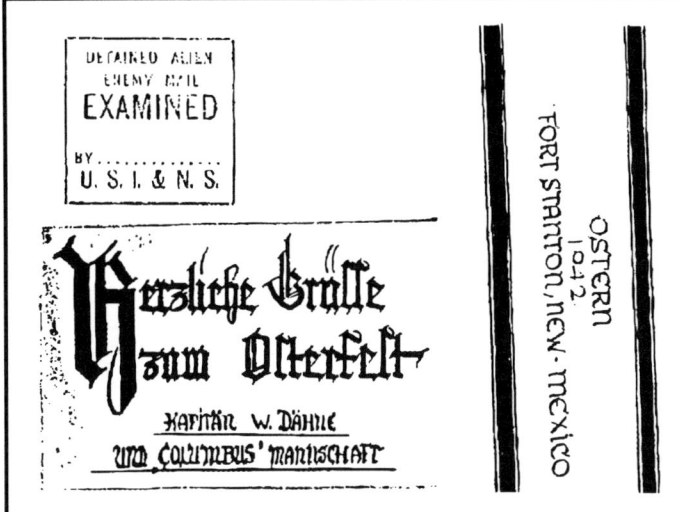

Easter Greetings from Captain Daehne to Captain Drechsel in 1942, from Fort Stanton, New Mexico. The Columbus people had been moved to there from Angel Island after the U.S. got into the war. At Fort Stanton the Columbus people had considerable freedom to move around in the neighborhood. Some just disappeared and presumably in time settled down and became Americans, with new names?

Captain Daehne was exchanged in late 1944 and became quickly involved in working for and with the U.S. Occupation from late Spring, 1945.

Dr. Arnold Rehm, to whom this work in part is dedicated, arrived in the U.S. in 1944 as a POW. "I began my life behind barbed wire, then about every two months was moved, to Mississippi, Oklahoma, Arkansas, Idaho and New Jersey." Some of his fellow prisoners in 1945 were sent home via San Francisco. He had a good time, reading every newspaper he could get, perfecting his English. He returned home, eventually again did some cruise-lectures for the Lloyd. And continued his writings about life of ships and people, and research. The author corresponded, and visited him in Bremen, until his death.

Line on Liners
by Frank Reil

German Marine Superintendent Still a Busy Man

Before the war the two busiest piers along the waterfront were those owned by the Hamburg-American and North German Lloyd Lines. And the busiest man around them was Capt. William Drechsel, the marine superintendent for the German lines.

Almost every day he had to look after the scores of details connected with the arrival or departure of a large liner and as most of the ships sailed at midnight it was nothing for him to work 16 hours a day.

We have written previously how it was Captain Drechsel's custom at night sailings to drive along the West Side Highway in his car and keep pace with his ship as she went down the river. Then he would cross over to Brooklyn and do the same along Shore Road, waiting at the Narrows until the lights of the ship had faded away. He would then go to his Bay Ridge home and get a few hours' sleep before it was time for him to be at the piers to meet a ship arriving.

Well, the German lines no longer have their piers, the Broadway offices of the lines are all but deserted and Captain Drechsel hasn't sent a ship out to sea since the Bremen left here on Aug. 30 on her famous voyage to Murmansk. Incidentally, we have a hunch that the Brooklynite had a lot to do with mapping out the course that enabled the $20,000,000 liner to elude the British fleet.

You would imagine that today Captain Drechsel would be sitting around twiddling his thumbs and waiting for the war to end. But on the contrary, He is just as busy as ever. In fact, he has to face a lot of new problems.

Chinese Problem

He is now virtually marine superintendent for the fleet of 40-odd ships that the German lines have tied up in Latin American waters at such ports as Vera Cruz, Tampico, Aruba, Curacao, Callao, and Valparaiso. With the exception of the Columbus, which rides at anchor at Anton Lizardo, 15 miles south of Vera Cruz, all the vessels are freighters.

These ships communicate with New York in order to obtain advice and information on many matters. For instance, Captain Drechsel's present headache is what to do with the 300 Chinese on eight of the "interned" ships. Their skippers report that the Chinese among the crew members are becoming restless and want to go home.

They signed on for two years and now their time is up. Furthermore, they are worried whether their families are getting their money back in China. By arrangement, an individual in Shanghai looks after the pay due the seamen's kin. But the Chinese think that perhaps their hard-earned money is falling into the hands of the Japanese instead of their families.

The Chinese have been assured that their money is reaching their families but still they want to go home. They can't go ashore at any of the ports where they are now and Captain Drechsel is considering the idea of chartering a ship, rounding up all the Orientals and returning them to China.

Musicians Happy

The Columbus has been in Mexican waters ever since she unloaded her 750 cruise passengers in a hurry at Havana just before the war started. Like all other German ships, she had orders to go to a neutral port and this meant NOT a United States port.

Captain Drechsel gets regular air-mail reports from Capt. W. Daehne, master of the Columbus. According to them, Captain Daehne's hardest job is keeping the 600 members of the crew busy and happy.

Anchored several miles from land, the ship is virtually cut off from the world. Usually you can keep sailors busy from morning to night by having them paint and repaint. But it is an expensive proposition to keep on painting and furthermore the Columbus is running short of paint.

Any one who has been aboard the Columbus knows what a luxurious ship she is but to the seamen aboard her now she is nothing more than a prison. They get occasional shore leave but they haven't any money to spend and time hangs heavy.

Probably the most contented people on the ship are the members of the band. Through the German Ambassador they have been busy giving concerts in Mexico City. They have played for the German Club, the Red Cross, in Mexican penitentiaries, at the Naval Academy and have a date to serenade President Cardenas. Each concert brings them more engagements and they are happy that their success keeps them from returning to their anchored "prison" at Anton Lizardo.

While the war in Europe was nearing the Phony Peace of Winter 1939-1940, Shipping Reporter Frank Reil wrote this report about the activities in North America in behalf of the crew members of some forty interned or laid up vessels, including Columbus.

Countdown To - And Again War 429

chant seamen knew the Norwegian coast well, going back to when the young Kaiser Wilhelm soon after his accession of 1888, made Norway his favorite vacationing area. In fact, early German cruising was literally "in the wake of the Kaiser's yacht Hohenzollern" in Norwegian waters. (Arnold Rehm). There must have been many Germans who hated what was being done to Norway in 1940. See Kommodore Kruse in "Per Aspera .... II."

Germany paid a heavy price for the capture: 13 cruisers and destroyers lost and numerous smaller craft. Included in the invasion or subsequent support were NDL's:

- *Aachen* #295 - sunk on 14 April, 1940 in Narvik Fjord
- *Alster* #410 - captured by the British off Bodö
- *Donau* #409 - sunk 17/1/1945 while evacuating German troops from Oslo
- *Main* #396 - sunk on invasion night by a Norwegian gunboat
- *Lippe* #408 - sunk 13 April in Narvik Fjord
- *Tübingen* #425 - 24 April, 1945 sunk in the Kattegat in last days of the war
- *Wigbert* #330 - 10 April sunk in the Kattegat en route to Norway
- *Wesergau* #456 - torpedoed off Stadtlandet 6/4/1944
- *Wangerooge* #461 - 25/10/1944 mined, sank off Stadtlandet
- *Ilmar* #395 - 4/3/1941 sunk by HMS Offa in Vaagsfjord
- *Greif* #356 - 12/11/1944 sunk by British destroyers off Egernsund
- *Hornsee* #321 - 6/3/1944 mined off Stavanger
- *Schwaben* #386 - 4/10/1944 partly sunk during British air attack on Bergen. Postwar raised, repaired, to Yugoslavia as merchant vessel.

Ironically, the invasion was code-named Weserübung, Weser Exercise. It was a heavy loss for the Weser Shipping Concern, NDL.

Overall, twenty-six merchant ships in the invasion carried 8,105 tons of stores, 2,660 vehicles and 1,641 horses.

The other major operating area, besides the Norwegian campaign, for Lloyd ships was the Mediterranean: supplying General Rommel's Afrika Korps. The British had been able to retain Malta as an unsinkable aircraft carrier. Also, they had broken the German codes, so knew when and where ships would be:

- *Ingo* #387 was lost off Libya in January, 1941
- Atto #347, *Arta* #344, ex *Aegina*, and *Troyburg*, ex *Achaia* #333, were lost on 16 April, 1941 in a convoy.
- *Marburg* #411 sank off Naples, cause unknown, and
- *Norburg,* ex *Hornsund* #323 sank in September off Crete.

Report by Captain Oskar Scharf, pre-War Commander of *Europa,* as Captain of NDL Steamer *Alster,* #410, 1928, 8,514 Ts., en route to Norway for the invasion of that country on 10 April, 1940. Courtesy of his son Wolfgang Scharf now resident in Bremerhaven:

"From 24th March *Alster* was anchored in Brunsbüttel Roads at the Elbe end of the Kiel Canal. On 3 April, a Naval officer at 2 A.M. brought the charts for the voyage to Narvik, we to arrive there on 9th April at 7 A.M. to discharge the cargo loaded in Hamburg. On deck some 500 tons of coke covered the hatches. Weather was foggy.

"At 5 A.M. we headed north, clearing the Skagerrak that night, arriving 4th April, 14.00 hours at Kopervik. The Norwegian authorities checked the ship's papers and examined the vessel, then released it. It had only coke as cargo. Two Norwegian pilots came on board. We left 5th April at 9 A.M. We were again examined off Bergen and off Bodö.

"In order to reach Narvik at the appointed time, we anchored during the nights of the 5th and 6th, again during a heavy N.W. storm on the 6th from 11.30 to 4.20, 7th April. We passed Bodö on 8 April at 13.00. Some eight miles North of Bodö we were stopped by a Norwegian guard vessel and advised orally that British forces that same day at 4.00 hours had laid mines some ten miles north of Bodö from shore into the Westfjord, up which any sea forces attacking Narvik would have to come. Strong British forces were then in the Westfjord, apparently behind the islands some two miles offshore.

"*Alster* that morning received wireless warning that British forces had laid mines at three places along the coast. Weather was clear. We were still some 125 miles from Narvik, and could, even if bad weather came, reach there at the ordered time. I decided to return the few miles to Bodö to await less clear weather. We anchored off Bodö at 15.00.

"On 9 April at 10.00 I sent 1. Officer Tietje to the German consul in Bodö, he to contact the Consul in Narvik. He advised to await further orders in Bodö. He confirmed the presence of strong British forces in the Westfjord. While waiting, the necessary procedures for sinking the ship, if necessary, were gone over with the crew

In accordance with a series of Wirelessed instructions from the German High Command, merchant ships that could not get home sought refuge in neutral ports; but many were seized, and the crews became war prisoners or were interned. Captain Drechsel as the Senior Maritime person representing German shipping firms in North America, worked with the Red Cross, the Seamen's Church Institute and other organization to provide the crews with material and financial resources to ease their lot in prisoner or internee camps. There were so many that envelopes for individual communications were printed.

Here is an example of a home office, the Hamburg-South American Line, trying to keep in touch with, care for its interned crew-members.

This one concerns coal-trimmer Ludwig Muskotel, born 1917, on H.S.'s Parana, *evidently in their Montevideo refuge, transferred to NDL's* Borkum *#361, which on 18 November, 1939 was captured by the British off the Orkneys while trying to get home, the crew imprisoned and evidently sent to Canada, as were many others, including German Jewish refugees (see #191,* Princess Alice*). H.S. sent Muskotel a small package, to Camp R, No. 13652, Canada, which was returned "deceased." "But we have nothing to confirm this and would appreciate your trying to locate Muskotel. With many thanks."*

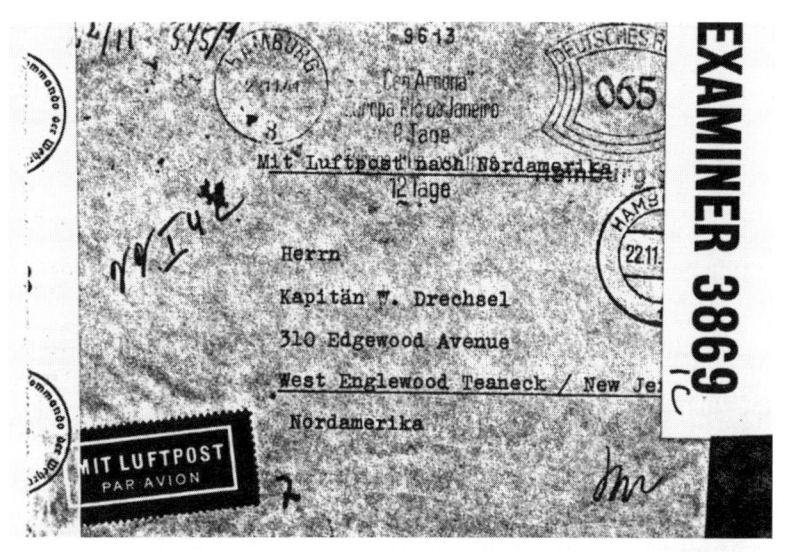

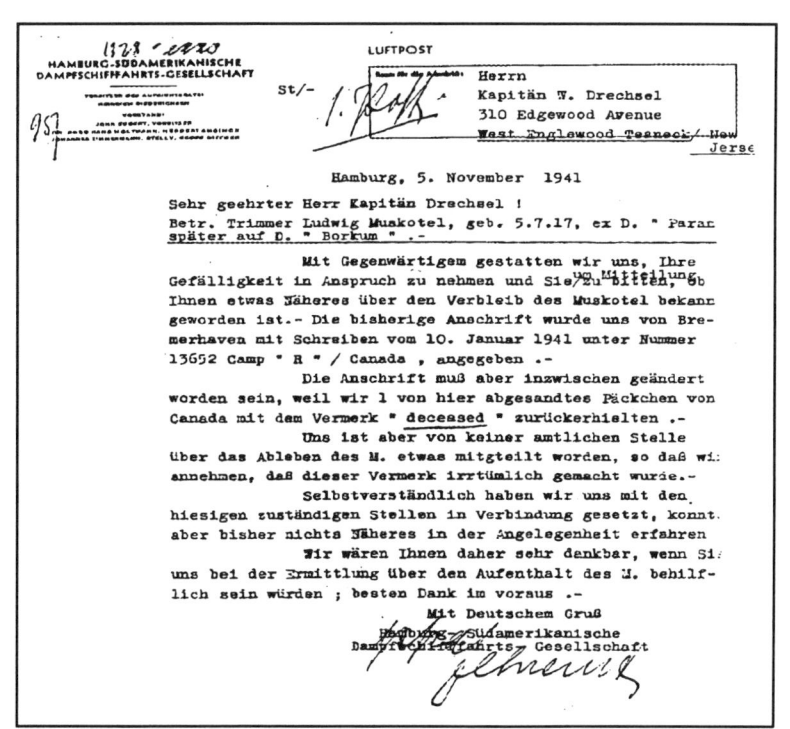

Countdown To - And Again War   431

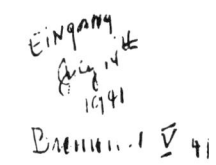

Letter from the Rev. Harold Kelley, superintendent of the Seamen's Church Institute of New York, to Captain Drechsel concerning care of the Columbus and other merchant seamen, written just before the Columbus crewmen left for California. There was so much mail to the internees forwarded that envelopes were preprinted to speed the process.

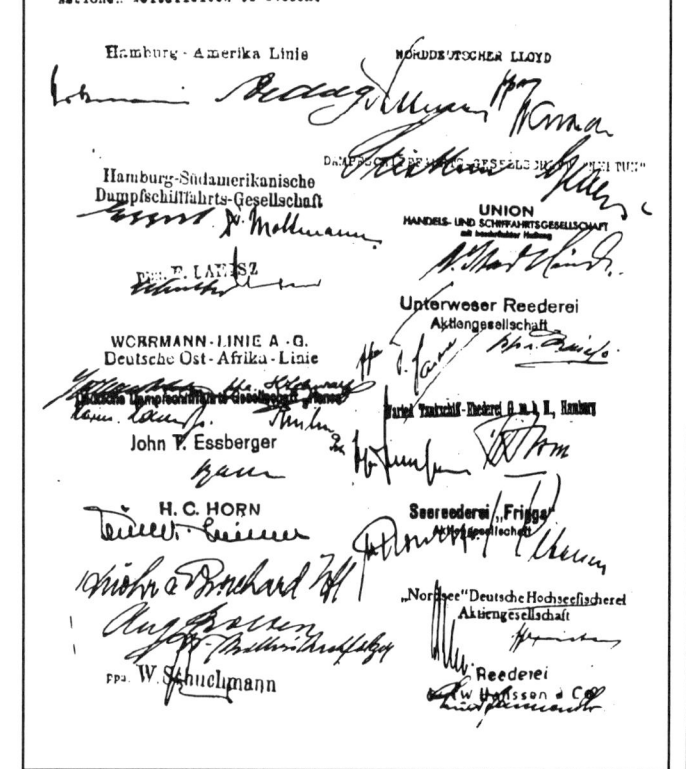

Group letter from fifteen shipping lines with vessels laid up in the Americas thanking Captain Drechsel for his work in behalf of their employees. That they did this in the midst of war reflects their concern for their employees.

Further to Mr. Reil's comment about the some forty German ships tied up throughout Latin America, here is a letter to Captain Kanow of Tacoma *at Buenos Aires, and his reply. Courtesy of Gustav Lund.*

Columbus' *attempt at escape back to Germany occurred at the same time as the Battle of the River Plate in which the German Pocket Battleship* Graf Spee, *after being badly damaged by three British cruisers, was scuttled on the mud banks. Hapag's U.S.-Canada West Coast service's* Tacoma *took the crew to Buenos Aires.*

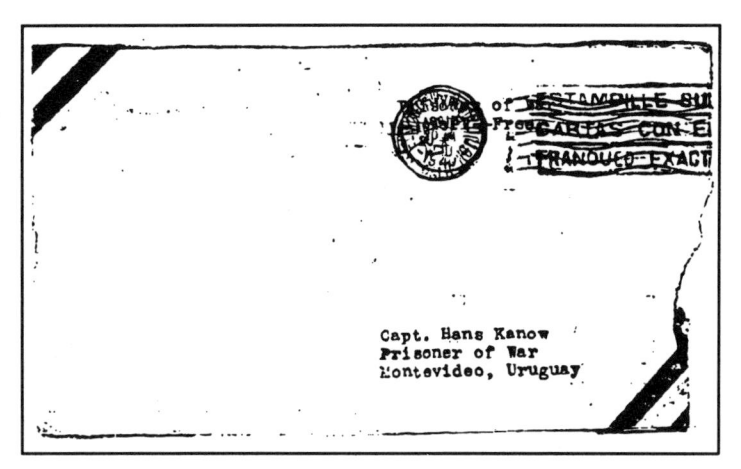

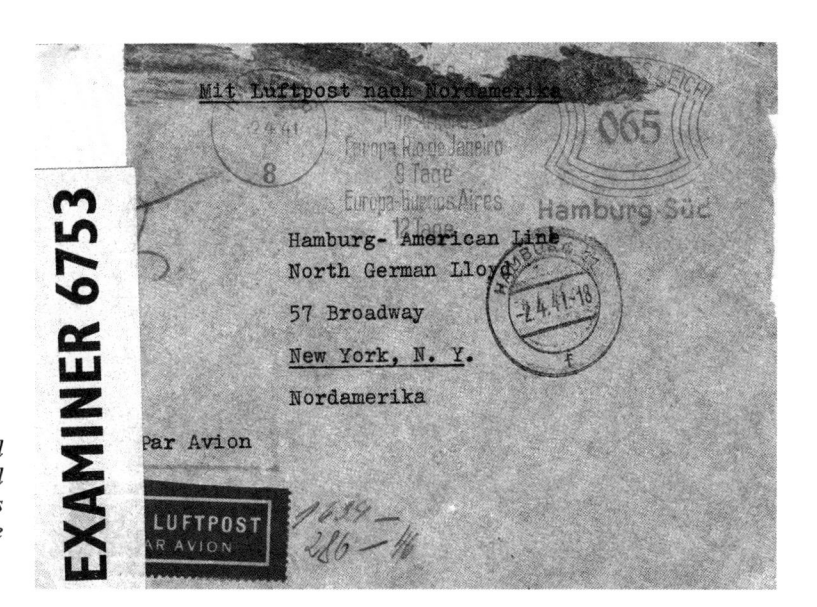

Hah Süd was still cancelling mail with its peacetime promotional meter. With Cap Arcona, *the Line's flagship, nine days into Rio de Janeiro, twelve to Buenos Aires.*

Countdown To - And Again War   433

After the Graf Spee Battle of the River Plate, German war and merchant ship crew members were sent to Argentina's Prison Island of Martin Garcia. Here is an envelope mailed from there on 9 October and received the 16th via Panagra (Pan-American Grace Airways) air mail. Sender was one Peters, Internment Camp "Admiral Graf Spee," Martin Garcia Island. It was Argentina's Devil's Island. In 1987 we saw at Punta del Este, off which the battle took place, the anchor of Ajax (Graf Spee's is at Buenos Aires), and this inscription: "Perduren los Ideales Que Hoy Juntos Defendemos. May the Ideals Survive that Today we Jointly Defend." To the dead on both sides.

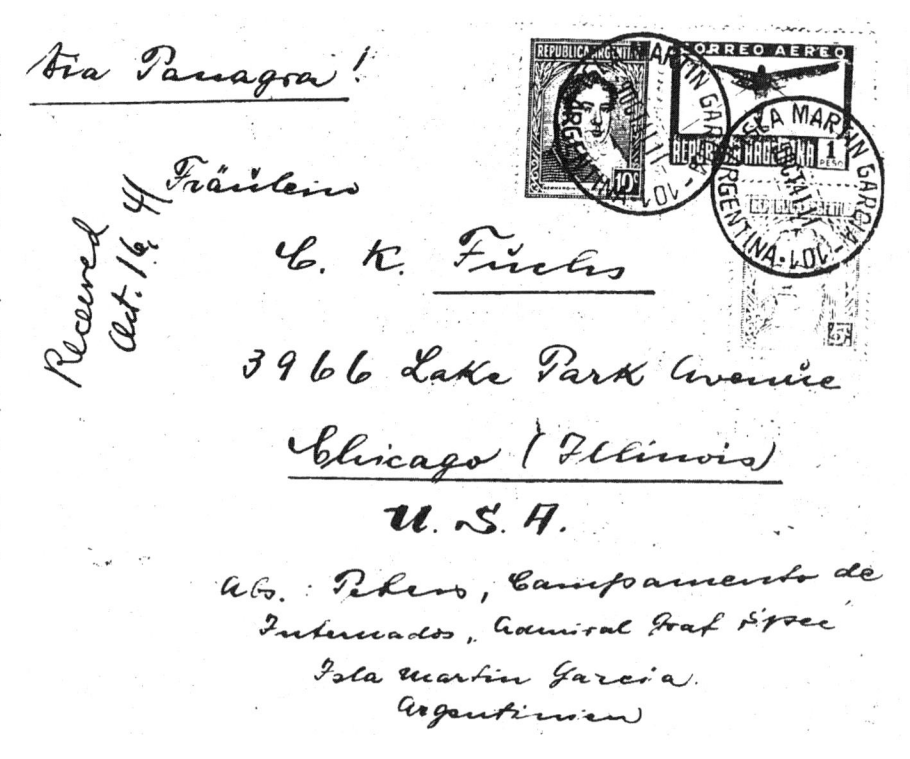

members assigned that job. The 1. Officer was to set light fuses of the explosive charges on the starboard side of Hatch III and 3. Officer von Spreter those at Hatch VI, starboard. Engine staff was to set off the charges clamped on the inside port side of the reserve bunker, and open the sea cock.

The attempt at Noon on 10 April to reach the Consul in Narvik failed. The two pilots meanwhile had left the ship. I decided at dusk to continue towards Narvik. That afternoon we received wireless order to reach Narvik under any circumstances and to proceed northward in Westfjord at high speed. (Normal speed was 14 knots.)

At 19.00 dusk we left Bodö, coursed some fourteen miles to south, then turned northwards. On 11 April, 0.30 hours, some 80 miles from Narvik, to starboard, we sighted at 1000-1500 meters four darkened vessels; impossible to determine if they were German or enemy. The possibility that they were German was not to be rejected, as shortly after leaving Bodö we had wireless contact with German naval forces, that must have been nearby. The watch-officers were of the same opinion. The four were heading northwards abreast. We at once turned three points to port. Engine room was advised of the likelihood of sudden maneuvers. Then the engine was stopped. The crew was alerted, remained midships. No wind or sea motion.

The now-seen destroyers at high speed approached *Alster;* I was certain they were enemy vessels. At this time English-language transmissions occurred; "Do you see him?" I ordered fusing the charges and to sink the ship. I threw the secret papers off the starboard side of the bridge. Very quickly the destroyers were alongside at 20-30 meters distance and opened heavy machine gun firing. One destroyer who tied to our portside called to me: "If you scuttle your ship I will knock the bloody Hell out of you."

From that destroyer some thirty British stormed on board, across deck and into the engine room. The portside boat, not yet in the water, was squeezed, and shot at. It hung at an angle. Eight crewmen fell into the water.

The fuses to the explosive charges in the reserve bunker's portside were set by 1. Engineer Stoecker and 3. Engineer Alpers. One condenser cup was removed and the sea cock was opened; the turning handle for that was removed and thrown into the bilge; it was recovered three weeks later. The attempt to bend the spindle on the sea cock with a hammer failed.

The British seized the engine and boiler rooms. On the ladderway they met Fireman Röhrs and forced him at pistol point to remove the explosive charge on the port side in the bunker room. Röhrs later said they immediately disarmed the charge.

I called to the boat lying off the port side if all men were on board,, and was told 'Yes.' I let myself down into the boat on the tackle. We picked up the men in the water; one was dead. When our boat was some forty meters behind the

American Red Cross letter to Captain Drechsel concerning rejection of an earlier answer to a query from Welfare Director Hans Karsted asking if the Thilomart concern had taken over the supplying of items to the internees or are you still handling this? And Drechsel's new message in reply.

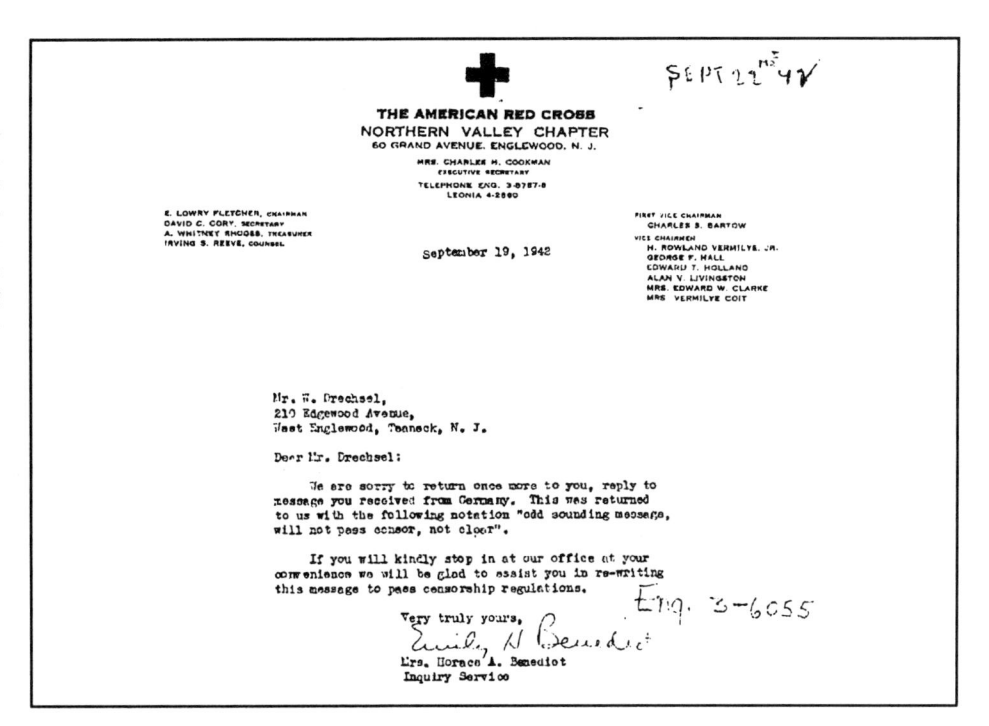

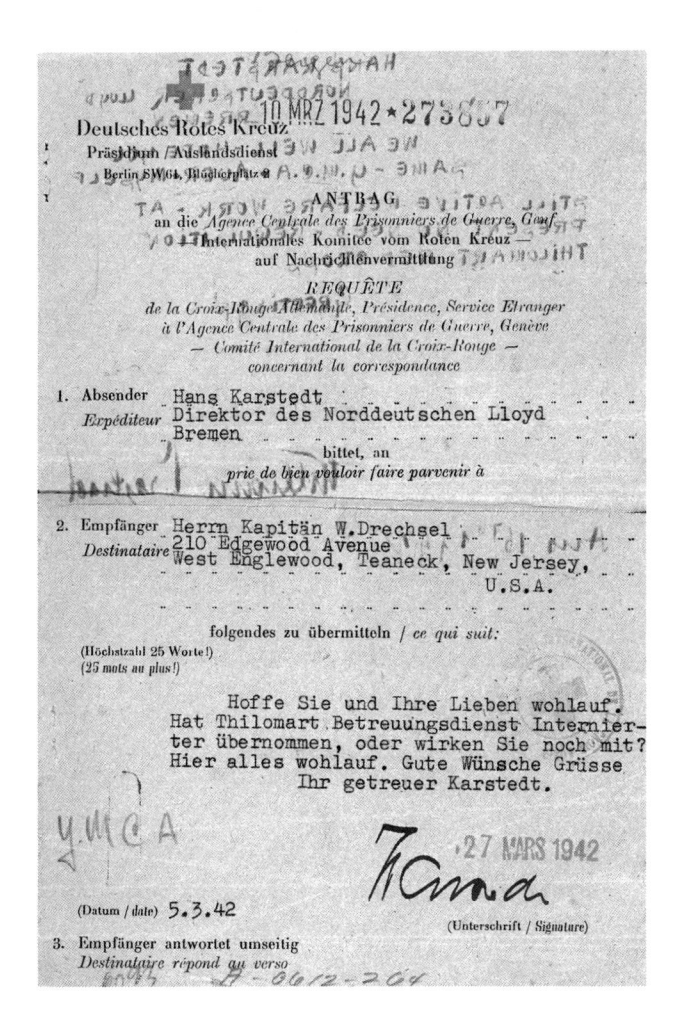

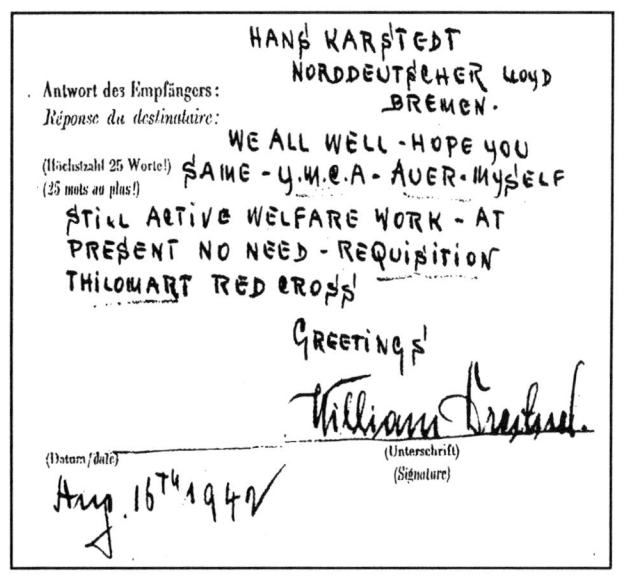

THE AMERICAN RED CROSS
NORTHERN VALLEY CHAPTER
60 GRAND AVENUE, ENGLEWOOD, N. J.

SEPT 22nd 42

September 19, 1942

Mr. W. Drechsel,
210 Edgewood Avenue,
West Englewood, Teaneck, N. J.

Dear Mr. Drechsel:

We are sorry to return once more to you, reply to message you received from Germany. This was returned to us with the following notation "odd sounding message, will not pass censor, not clear".

If you will kindly stop in at our office at your convenience we will be glad to assist you in re-writing this message to pass censorship regulations.

Very truly yours,

Mrs. Horace A. Benedict
Inquiry Service

Deutsches Rotes Kreuz
Präsidium / Auslandsdienst
Berlin SW61, Blücherplatz 2

ANTRAG
an die Agence Centrale des Prisonniers de Guerre, Genf
Internationales Komitee vom Roten Kreuz
auf Nachrichtenvermittlung

REQUÊTE
de la Croix-Rouge Allemande, Présidence, Service Étranger
à l'Agence Centrale des Prisonniers de Guerre, Genève
— Comité International de la Croix-Rouge —
concernant la correspondance

1. Absender / Expéditeur: Hans Karstedt
   Direktor des Norddeutschen Lloyd
   Bremen
   bittet, an / prie de bien vouloir faire parvenir à

2. Empfänger / Destinataire: Herrn Kapitän W. Drechsel
   210 Edgewood Avenue
   West Englewood, Teaneck, New Jersey,
   U.S.A.

folgendes zu übermitteln / ce qui suit:
(Höchstzahl 25 Worte!)
(25 mots au plus!)

Hoffe Sie und Ihre Lieben wohlauf. Hat Thilomart Betreuungsdienst Internierter übernommen, oder wirken Sie noch mit? Hier alles wohlauf. Gute Wünsche Grüsse Ihr getreuer Karstedt.

(Datum/date) 5.3.42

27 MARS 1942

3. Empfänger antwortet umseitig
   Destinataire répond au verso

Antwort des Empfängers:
Réponse du destinataire:

HANS KARSTEDT
NORDDEUTSCHER LLOYD
BREMEN.

WE ALL WELL - HOPE YOU SAME - Y.M.C.A. - AUER - MYSELF STILL ACTIVE WELFARE WORK - AT PRESENT NO NEED - REQUISITION THILOMART RED CROSS

GREETINGS

William Drechsel

(Datum/date) Aug 16th 1942

Countdown To - And Again War

BROOKLYN EAGLE, FRIDAY, JAN. 17, 1941

LINE ON LINERS
by FRANK REIL
Hapag's Famed Captain Drechsel Rounds Out Another Anniversary

If the North German Lloyd and Hamburg-American Lines were not in the "dog house" during these unhappy days of war there would have been some celebration on Wednesday to mark Capt. William Drechsel's 40 years of service with the companies. Only his personal friends in the steamship business observed this milestone in the career of this popular and efficient marine superintendent.

It was on Jan. 15, 1901, that he entered the service of the North German Lloyd as a fourth officer, having spent seven previous years at sea, five of them on sailing ships. He went through all ranks to captain, to which position he was promoted in 1919. But what makes Captain Drechsel such a valuable marine superintendent is that he is a combination of master mariner and shipbuilding engineer.

Supervised Shipbuilding

In 1912 the N. G. L. sent him to a technical college of shipbuilding in order that he might be able to supervise efficiently the construction of new ships and to act as representative of the line in the German shipyards. The World War, during which he served as master of many types of ships, including the Kaiser's flagship, interrupted his studies but he finished them after the war. He was then appointed to supervise the line's building program in the Stetin yards.

He became marine superintendent at New York for the line in 1924 and when the merger between the two German lines went into effect in 1934, he advanced to general marine superintendent for the joint company.

Known for Sage Suggestions

But it was with the commissioning of the Europa and Bremen that the steamship industry really became aware of Captain Drechsel. He proved his talent for organization and careful attention to details when these large and powerful ships arrived and departed on a perfect schedule. As a member of several Maritime Exchange committees interested in port improvements, Captain Drechsel made himself known through his sage observations and suggestions.

Fog is always an enemy to ships wishing to dock and to depart. Captain Drechsel hit upon the scheme of going down the bay on a towboat and leading the fog-bound liner up through the channel. Frequently he did this with great success but the one time he failed is responsible for one of the amusing legends about Captain Drechsel.

Oft-Told Story

In February, 1935, he went down on a tug for the New York. According to the popular story, he came under the bow of a great liner and directed the ship's captain to follow him up the bay. It was not until two hours later when the fog lifted that Captain Drechsel discovered that he had led up the Panama Pacific liner Pennsylvania and not his own ship.

He always laughs heartily when this story is retold but he insists that some of the facts are not quite true. He did go down for the New York but when he couldn't find her, he was on his way back when he sighted this other ship. He didn't know what ship it was but offered to lead her up anyhow. But why spoil a good story with facts?

At Midnight Sailings

However, the German ships always arrived and sailed on schedule, no matter what the conditions. The Europa and Bremen docked out in Bay Ridge when a gale was blowing across the bay. And Captain Drechsel never went to bed nights when he had a midnight sailing until he was sure the ship had passed out of Sandy Hook. He would follow the ship in a car down Shore Road until her lights disappeared. Then he would return to his home at 7605 Shore Road, where he has lived for 13 years, and wait until he felt sure the ship had passed out.

As he looks back at the 40 years, Captain Drechsel finds he has no regrets. He has certainly had his share of the headaches, too. He was the last man to leave the Muenchen when she caught fire at her pier and exploded. He bore the brunt of the F. B. I. investigations regarding spies traveling on German ships and also when the Bremen was held at her pier just before she sailed on her last voyage.

The Bremen was the last ship he sent to sea, but although he has no more ships coming into New York, there is still much for him to do. He looks after the German ships that are tied up in Western Hemisphere ports, and handles the affairs of the 300 seamen from the Columbus and also those German sailors interned in Canada.

On 15 January, 1941 Captain Drechsel completed forty years with the Norddeutscher Lloyd. He began as a 4.Officer on Stuttgart, monthly wage M100, then $25.; of course free room and board while on a ship. His by then close friend, Brooklyn Daily Eagle reporter Frank Reil wrote a thoughtful article. From Bremen came a letter dated 9 December, 1940, allowing time to reach the U.S. in wartime, signed by six Lloyd officials who had close relations with the New York Inspectorate, including Waldemar Klose, Hans Karstedt, Captain E. Heims, Georg Richter, Captain W. Hagemann and E.M. Schmidt. "The Honors which our management had planned for your fortieth anniversary, will have to be postponed until after the war. It is solely your accomplishment to have organized the structure that made possible the handling of our great ships in record times."

ship the charge at Hatch VI detonated between the bow of the destroyer fastened there and the ship's side. It blew open, and Hatch VI filled with water. The charge at Hatch III failed. From the time of sighting the destroyers until this detonation was some 8-10 minutes.

After picking up those in the water, the destroyers helping with their searchlights, we were ordered to come alongside. Men were at the ready with guns as we came on board. Meanwhile, *Alster* developed a strong port list. The engine room was flooded up to the floor plates. The stern was down to about 45'. The crew quarters' port holes remained just above water. Foreward the ship had no draft. *Alster* had become inoperable. During the night the British towed the ship into a protected bay in the Lofoten Islands.

Six men had died in the British random shooting to prevent our vessel being scuttled. The rest of the crew became prisoners.

Bremen, 2 June, 1944. (signed) O. Scharf, Captain.''

Following a hearing before the Admiral's Court against Captain Oskar Scharf and the Supercargo Kaptain Johann Regeser for military insubordination this charge was called off. "No blame can be attached to Captain Scharf, and since none to him neither to the Supercargo" for failure of the preparations for sinkings.

Signed by Vice Admiral Lohmann, 29 November, 1944.

Alster was taken into a fjord and repaired. In May with some of the German crew still on board, it proceeded to Kirkenes and took on a cargo of ore, then went to Harstad, from where in a convoy it went to Kirkwall, and further war duty. The crew was imprisoned in the U.K., then Canada.

Raiders. Direly in need of raw materials to support its ravenous war machine, Germany sent a small fleet of fast motorships to trade with Japan, both across the North of the Soviet Union, and around Africa into the Indian and Pacific Oceans. It also used merchant ships, able to stay out months at a time, as raiders to divert and destroy Allied shipping.

At first, *M.S. Iller* #450, which was at Murmansk, was chosen as raider. But then its sister *EMS* #445 in home waters, was decided on. Conversion to Ship 45, *Komet,* as raider began in 12/1939. Other sisters, *Eider* #444 and *Drau* #459, all with 14.2 knots speed, were converted to blockade breakers.

Komet left on its voyage to the Far east on 3/VII/1940, up the Norwegian coast and across Russia-Siberia's Arctic. Its intended raider area was the Pacific but extending into the south Indian, even Atlantic Oceans if opportunity offered. Especially if there were allied whaling ships in the Antarctic. En route, the ship was disguised as the Soviet *Dejnew,* this with still peace between Germany and USSR. Soviet icebreakers helped open the way. On 5 September, *Komet* passed the Bering Strait into the Pacific. On 27 December, it lay off the phosphate island of Nauru, British held but until WWI part of Germany's vast mid-Pacific colonies. *Komet* returned via Cape Horn, thus having gone around the world, in November, 1941. In 516 days it covered 87,000 nautical miles. It carried an observation airplane to give it eyes in search of the enemy. But it had been able to sink only six vessels with 31,055 tons (Gerhard Hümmelchen.) Other Lloyd vessels served as actual or intended supply vessels to raiders: *Regensburg* #495, *Crefeld* #286, *Oder* #403 and *Weser* #434.

Invasion. After the British evacuation of some 335,000 forces at Dunquerque, and Hitler's envious looking across the Strait of Dover at the coast that looked so near, yet so unattainable, preparations for Operation Seelöwe, Sea Lion, the invasion of England, were stepped up from ongoing to a possible reality. The armistice with France on 21 June, 1940 speeded up thinking and activity: 20 September was held the earliest possible to launch the invasion, with massive air attacks the first phase.

Naval preparations had been minimal. Germany just did not have an effective fleet for the high seas, other than submarines, let alone one for invasion. This would involve an endless variety and number of specialty craft, as the fiftieth anniversary of the Allied invasion on 6/6/1944 reminded us.

The size of the transport requirement was enormous: to transfer and provide for the armed and material needs and support for forty divisions. This was quickly reduced to thirteen, some 260,000 men, as it became evident the original effort could never be mounted.

At first *Europa, Bremen* and *Potsdam,* it serving as dormitory ship, were to be converted to transports. *Bremen* and *Europa* were moved to Hamburg to test their stability. Lloyd officials insisted Reichswehr plans for placing heavy equipment on board were impossible. Some walls were removed so that tanks and armored vehicles could be stored in the social and dance halls on the Promenade Deck. Finally, Blohm & Voss shipyard personnel, where *Europa* had been built, convinced the military such high loadings would

Photo in a New York newspaper of Captain Scharf's landing in a Scottish port with others from Alster, April, 1940. Son Wolfgang Scharf advised that the French report and photograph were the first news the family had of Captain Scharf. "I then was a soldier in North France. A comrade brought me the newspaper. I believe it was in Arras."

(Wide World cable foto)

CAPTURED. The former commander of the Europa, Capt. Oskar Scharf, is shown as he landed at port in Scotland with other Nazi naval officers. British took them off troopship at Narvik.

Postcard from Captain Oskar Scharf, imprisoned in Canada after losing Alster to the British during the German invasion of Norway. The photo side shows twelve men, evidently all German prisoners, including Baron von Pilar, of the Lloyd New York Office, fourth standing from left, and Captain Scharf.

438   Norddeutscher Lloyd Bremen

endanger the invasion: the ships probably would capsize with loss of all their vital cargoes.

Then the three were to be converted to aircraft carriers. But this also came to nothing. Land people running a land war with no knowledge of and feel for the sea and ships. *Bremen* and *Europa* returned to Bremerhaven; *Bremen* there burned out in March, 1941. Freighters *Tübingen* #420 and *Wolfram* #332 were planned to serve as transports.

When in the fall of 1940 massive air attacks against Britain failed to inflict the widespread destruction counted on to minimize resistance to the German invasion, the Target date, already changed from early September, to late September, was shifted to Spring, 1941, again with massive preliminary air attacks to take place. With the last great raid on London on 10 May, 1941, and Britain still as unapproachable as nine months earlier, the dream of invasion was given up. All attention turned to the early invasion of the Soviet Union.

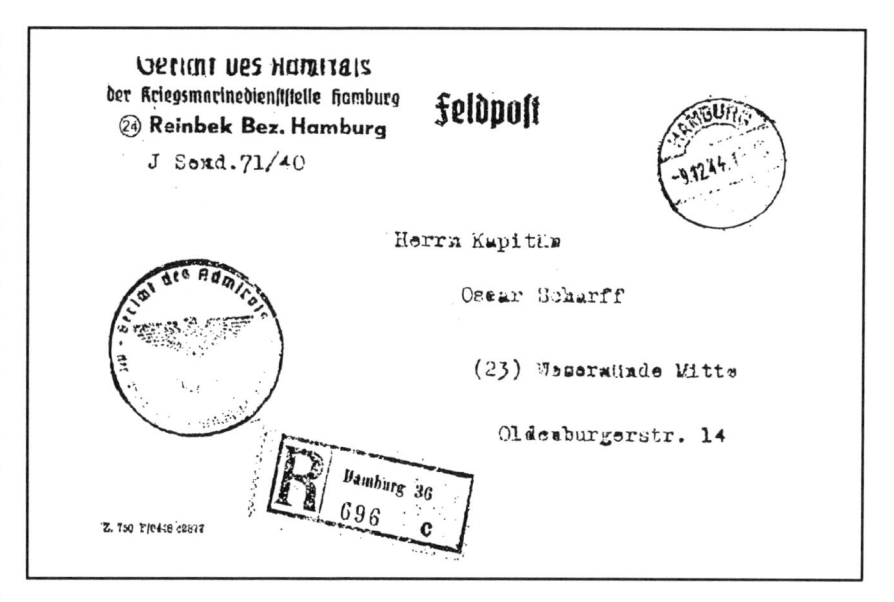

Among the various AWK wireless messages sent to German ships at sea before the war began and for a time after included a warning that those who let their vessels be captured would be punished. British Admiralty orders to merchant vessels were similar. Standard instructions to vessels was, if armed, to open fire, if unarmed, to attempt to ram. Legal action would be taken automatically against any captain who surrendered his ship. (David Butler, Lusitania, Futura Publications.) *Formal advice from the Court of the Admiral advising Captain Oskar Scharf that his actions in the Alster loss were not contributory and all charges and action against him are dropped, and with him the Supercargo, similarly charged, is freed of that action. Courtesy of Wolfgang Scharf.*

In 1942, despite the failure to end the war in the East with a quick victory over the USSR, one still believed a German victory was possible, and a return to peacetime shipping. To facilitate this, and remove the money-losing North Atlantic operation from the rest of the Lloyd and Hapag services, the German-American Line had been formed in April, 1941: ownership 50% the Reich, 25% each Lloyd and Hapag, with seat in Bremen. *Europa* and *Berlin,* and the German travel agencies of NDL and the Hapag were "sold." What remained, was privatized from Reich control, with new managements. The two Hapag directors of DAL remained in Hamburg. In Bremen were Waldemar Klose and other Lloyd people. A letter of 1, May, 1946 from Director Hans Karstedt in Bremen to Captain Drechsel, retired, in New York, says that "the travel bureaus in part are still active. Otherwise DAL as shipping concern without ships has no meaning. Herr Klose now is the Manager. DAL in time will be dissolved. The setup of the travel bureaus hopefully can be preserved. Perhaps, eventually they'll be returned to NDL and Hapag."

As the destruction of inland Germany spread with massive Allied air attacks, and of her armies in the East and the Mediterranean, and as from D-Day on 6 June, 1944 in France and the Low Countries German armies were driven back, the end became inevitable but remained unacceptable to those in command, meaning a capricious and increasingly removed Adolf Hitler.

The former Lloyd headquarters building, in design and decoration a relic of a more opulent age, and finished almost in time for NDL's 50th Anniversary in 1907, was massively bombed in an air attack on Bremen on 1 October, 1944. It burned out down to the cellar. In the process, "almost all our files and current-work and personal papers, as in the Nautical Department, were destroyed. The building itself had been sold earlier to the *Deschimag* shipyard concern. The Lloyd activity moved into a small restaurant on the Osterdeich, Where we stayed until shortly before the siege of Bremen. We then returned to our cellar. The sole structure left to the Lloyd, it actually property of the Deutsche Amerika-Linie, is one on the corner of the Gustav Deetjen Allee

Map of courses and action by various German merchant raiders, including NDL's Ems *#445, going the Arctic route to the Pacific. Note the Arado observation aircraft foreward of the bridge.* Ems *as raider was known as* Komet.

Ex "Hitler's High Seas Fleet", in Ballantine's Illustrated History of the Violent Century, Weapons Book #23, 1971 Richard Humble.

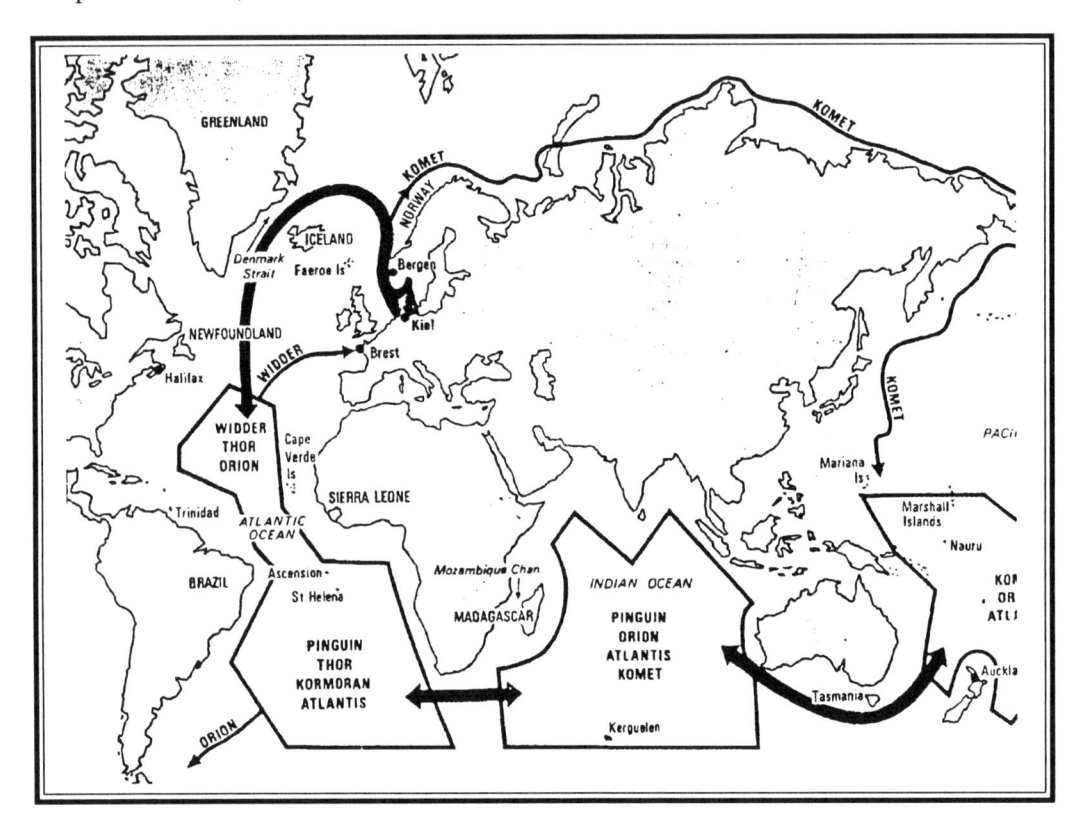

where prewar the baggage activity was centered." Later this building became the new NDL Head Office in 1943, and continued so post-war, rebuilt and expanded. It is all that is physically left of the Lloyd in Bremen, now Hapag-Lloyd in contrast to Hapag's big Hamburg office, which in effect is the Hapag-Lloyd Head Office. War and postwar details from May, 1946 letter from Director Hans Karstedt to Captain Drechsel in New Jersey. (See "A New Start")

An NDL survivor from WWI - it is the ship on the Dustjacket of Volume I - under U.S. ownership was *George Washington* #246, taken over with some thirty-one other Lloyd ships when the U.S. entered the war in April, 1917. In 1919, G.W. became President Wilson's "Peace Ship" to the Versailles Conference. After merchant service in the 1920s and 1930s under the U.S. flag, in 1940 the U.S. Navy took over the ship, had it rebuilt and in 1941 offered it to Britain, named *Catlin*.

440 *Norddeutscher Lloyd Bremen*

The Europa *in Bremerhaven as Barracks Vessel, this after inexpert attempts to convert her to transport configuration for the invasion of Britain.* Dieter Jung Photo, BNRA.

Bremen *and* Europa *were intended as tank and equipment carriers for Operation Sea Lion, the invasion of the British Isles.* Bremen's *port captain, Heinrich Lorenz, told the New Yorker Staats-Zeitung on 17.2.1957 "I was transferred to Norway, took over command of* Bremen. *She was intended for the invasion of Britain and the armored division's tanks and equipment were already on board." That never happened, although it was planned: Operation Autumn Journey, Herbstreise: This was intended both as support for and a diversionary-flanking attack: by* Bremen, Europa, Potsdam *and* Gneisenau *and ten Transports departing from Southern Norway and the Bay of Helgoland for the Scottish East Coast between Aberdeen and Newcastle.*

Here follow exerpts of her British service from *Merchantment Rearmed* by the later Sir David Bone, Captain. He was sent to examine *Catlin* at the Philadelphia Navy Yard and prepare it for transfer in August, 1941. Wrote Bone: "From the dockside I was struck by the patent strength of her construction and the fineness of her lines. (On the) small section (of her hull) that had been scaled for examination, the bright Swedish steel was clean and uncorroded. (This twenty-two years of its construction!) ... The ship's conversion had been decided upon by the British Ministry of War Transport and the U.S. Maritime Commission under Lend-Lease ... Problems ... were aggravated by the absence of many of the original plans, diagrams, blueprints of engines, boilers and internal systems ... some (of which) had been destroyed by German sabotage in 1917. See p. 424, Volume I for a card from an electrician repairing G.W., and 427. "The boilers were the originals of 1909 ... All metal grows old, and boilers perish more quickly than less actively used components in a ship. Gradually, she took on much of the appearance that had once impressed the transatlantic traveller ..." Now again named *George Washington*, the ship remained a coal-burner. Other seized German ships were converted to oil for transport or merchant use. G.W. was not finally made an oil-burner until 1942. "We sailed (from Philadelphia) 10 January, 1942, the Delaware River a grinding mass of ice. Her guns were well-placed and fitted. A gale had arisen ... I had not guessed at her sea kindliness in adverse weather. The ship, if not quite seaworthy, was worthy of the sea again. (In New York, G.W. went to the Bethlehem Steel Shipyard where in peacetime her repairs had been carried out.) "(We made) ... a steady speed of fourteen knots on the passage from New York to Halifax. (There) a total of 4,100 troops, officers, men and nursing staff were embarked and a crew of some 500. We were to proceed in convoy to the Clyde. I had been appointed Commodore." Two boilers developed cracks. There were indications others would not stand up to pressure. I learned that a complete set of water-tube boilers, originally intended for the ship, were stored away in the Boiler Shed in the (Philadelphia) dockyard.... I saw the convoy

> **HITLER ON PARADE**
>
> Hitler prided himself on his "iron nerve," but his temperament was mercurial rather than steadfast. The Norwegian campaign of April, 1940, offers a good example. In the face of overwhelming British naval superiority, the German invasion of Norway was a daring gamble, which Hitler approved with full awareness of the hazards and inevitable losses. The initial landings were almost miraculously successful.
>
> But as soon as Dietl was cut off at Narvik and Pellengahr met opposition on his march from Oslo to Trondheim, Hitler fell into a panic. On one day, Dietl must be evacuated by air or surrender his force to Swedish internment; Jodl has to persuade his Fuehrer not to abandon the venture yet. The next day the liners Bremen and Europa are to be sent with reinforcements to Trondheim, and Admiral Raeder must spend hours convincing Hitler that such an undertaking is sheer folly.
>
> When, by dint of the Wehrmacht's prowess, Hitler emerged as the master of Europe, he had no idea how to exploit his sudden dominance.

Bremen *still smoldering from the arson fire on 18 March, 1941.* Ex Witthöft, p. 115.

weigh anchors without us ... We had two months immobility at Halifax while the boilers were being patched and strengthened. When I reported that the ship was ready for sea, it was only to learn that the voyage would be short ... to New York, where she was to be handed back to the U.S.M.C.... In October, 1943 from my ship, the *Circassia* in Bombay Harbor (among) the other vessels in harbour I recognized the *George Washington*. Except for one funnel having been removed, she was little altered and was wearing the American Ensign. I met the Captain: Water-tube boilers had been fitted and she now burned oil fuel instead of coal. The elimination of coal bunker space had made it possible to enlarge the troop deck and she could now transport 5,000 men in reasonable comfort. A speed of eighteen knots could be made without special effort. She was a grand seaboat and was quick and handy in maneuvers."

Briefly, there was confusion over two U.S. transports named *George Washington*. The other one was the former *G.W.* of the Eastern Steamship (coastal) line. The "Little George" arrived in 1942 at Hamilton, Bermuda to load 1,200 troops and personnel. But the orders to the Army Transport Corps was "7000" persons. Over the resistance of Little George's captain, the boarding process was begun. "Orders are Orders" insisted the Army Colonel. Fortunately, Big George" arrived just then with space for the 7,000. Those already on Little George had to transfer.

Laid up after the war, *George Washington* burned in New York in 1947, was moved to and burned out again in Baltimore in 1951, then was sold for breakup at age forty-two. A ship that carried both name-passengers and thousands of immigrants from Europe seeking a better and different life in America. And served its new country in two wars.

The Soviets had indicated they would not respect the Geneva Convention status of German hospital ships: painted white with large red crosses on the side. The unfit from the Eastern front were therefore evacuated in grey-painted liners classed as Verwundetentransporter, Wounded-Transports. This made them marked targets. Ex-Die deutschen Lazarettschiffe, Motorbuch Verlag, Stuttgart 1978.

The last months of the war brought many more serious losses to the Lloyd.

- *Berlin* on 31/1/1945 in heavy floating ice hit a mine before the entrance into Swinemünde. Hours later, trying to put the ship onto the bottom in flat waters, it impacted a second mine and settled in 13 meters depth. The superstructure remained

S. S. GEORGE WASHINGTON

Prewar mail from George Washington *while in service for the United States Line New York-Bremerhaven with U.S.-German Sea Post service.*

mostly above water. There was only one life lost in the whole incident.

- *Der Deutsche,* the former *Sierra Morena* #306, left Wismar as a Hospital Ship, took on board refugees from East Prussia from rafts and boats in the Baltic. It transferred 34,474 persons to the West. While bunkering off Fehmann Island on 3/5/1945 it was bombed, settling onto the sea bottom. Postwar, the ship was raised, repaired in East Germany for Soviet account, that means, the USSR paid nothing, and ran as *Asia* between Vladivostock and Japan until broken up in 1963.
- *Steuben* #293, left Pillau near Danzig on the evening of 9 February with some 2,500 wounded, around 2,000 refugees, and 450 ship-crew members, among these 15 doctors and 320 nurses. It was hit by two torpedos of the Soviet submarine *S-13,* and within minutes sank in 55.09N, 16.37W. Some 3,000 persons lost their lives.
- *Robert Möhring,* the former reefer *Orotava* #391, also was a transport for wounded. The ship was set aflame on 6/3/1945 in a Soviet air attack off Sassnitz, the trans-Baltic ferry terminal with Sweden, on Rügen Island. High flames devoured the ship; some 350 died.
- *Weserstein* #464, one of the Hansa Program freighters, was sunk off Pillau on 12/4/1945 by air attack.
- *Göttingen,* also a "Hansa" freighter, with some 4,500 refugees on 28/1/1945 left Danzig. It landed all these safely in the western Baltic. On 23 February outside Libau, *Göttingen* was sunk by the Soviet submarine *K-52.* Some 130 died.
- *Potsdam* in seven trips brought out 51,891 persons.

Fritz Brustat-Naval, in his book *Unternehmung Rettung,* Operation Salvage, the history of the refugee fleet in 1945, reports that the Lloyd ships were able to rescue the largest numbers: 234,137 persons of the 1,541,354 individuals carried westward beyond Soviet reach. One wonders who kept these records?

The Soviets had indicated they would not respect the Geneva Convention status of German hospital ships: internationally painted white with large red crosses on the side. The unfit from the Eastern front were therefore evacuated in greypainted liners classed as Verwundetentransporter, Wounded-Transports. This made them marked targets. Ex-Die deutschen Lazarettschiffe Motorbuch Verlag, Stuttgart 1978.

Overall, the Lloyd had seventy-six high-seas vessels of 580,000 gross tons at the beginning of the war. Fourteen new ships came into its control during the war, or a total of eighty-seven. It lost forty-two vessels sunk or scuttled; ten were seized at sea or in enemy ports; eleven were sold off, two stranded or were beyond salvage, and the *Bremen* burned out, a total loss of 455, 787 tons. After the Allies took what was left, including from the Lloyd and others the ships sunk at sea with gas munitions, NDL had left:

- Two resort steamers: *Delphin* built in 1905, and *Glückauf* built in 1913 for the Hapag, bought by NDL in 1930;
- Two Kümos - small freighters shuttling cargo between Bremen-Bremerhaven-Hamburg;
- Some fifty barges and lighters, and - fourteen tugs, the oldest built in 1897, still coal-fired, a total of some 5,500 gross tons, the size of one medium-sized freighter. This compared with just under 58,000 tons left at the end of WWI, after Versailles Treaty deliveries. Added to that were six vessels of 39,505 tons the Lloyd was allowed to keep under the Columbus Agreement. See "A New Start." Left over were 97,156 tons, a significant start on rebuilding. Post WWII was very different. Of Germany's some four million gross tons of shipping in 1939, only 118 000 tons were left, plus a graveyard of sunk, half-sunk, blown up wrecks in ports and along the coasts.

NDL Fleet
Ships 456 - 471x

Given the great number of German ships lost with the start of the war, through remaining in neutral harbors or being captured or scuttled while trying to get home, a standard-type ship construction program was held the quickest way to provide new tonnage. For this purpose a consortium of eight shipping companies on 23/7/1942 formed an entity called Schiffahrts Treuhand Gmbh, Shipping Trustee Corp., Hamburg. Three basic designs were decided upon:

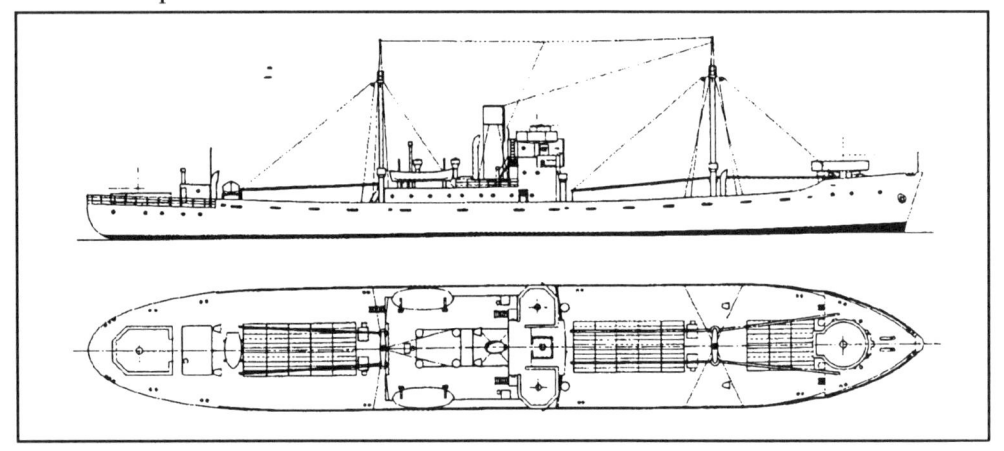

The basic Hansa "A" type, 1923 tons. Nine were assigned to the Lloyd. Much more elaborately built than the U.S. Liberty ship design meant for mass production.

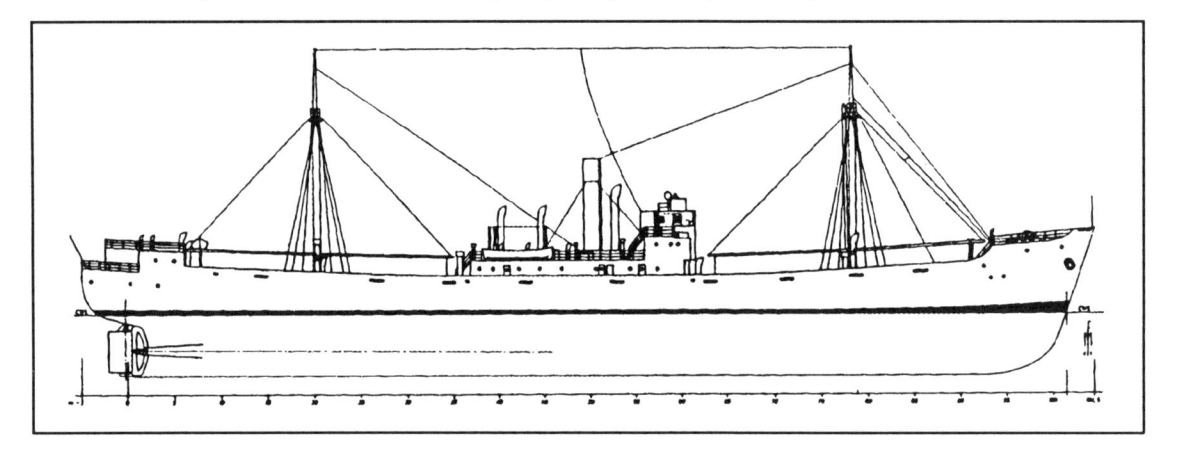

The HANSA "B" type of the Wartime Program, 2,800 tons, ex Hans-Jürgen Witthöft, Das Hansa Bauprogramm, Lehmanns Verlag, 1968. NDL's Wangerooge, Spiekeroog, Langeoog Type.

444 Norddeutscher Lloyd Bremen

- Hansa Type A: Ships with 3,000 tons carrying capacity, ca.1900 gross tons
- Hansa Type B: Ships with 5,000 tons capacity, ca. 2800 tons gross
- Hansa Type C: Ships with 9,000 tons capacity, ca. 6200 tons gross

Of A, 128 were planned, eventually 52 completed and put into service, varying from 1923 Ts. to 1942 Ts.

Five Type B were completed, only one Type C. They were ordered from German and occupied countries shipyards. The Lloyd vessels were all given WESER...names. Several non-Hansa types were finished for NDL as "Hansa Completions." With postwar completions 76 A's, 33 B's, and three C's were built. (Witthöft).

456. *Wesergau* 1945-1944
Deutsche Werft, Hamburg-Reiherstieg #428
　　　　　　　　　　　　1943　　1,923　　91.83 x 13.50
Double compound engines　1,200　　10　　　　　25

Launched 17/5/1943. Trials-Delivery 14/7/1943. 6/41944 torpedoed by Norwegian submarine ULA off Standtlandet. Run aground, but total loss. BU after the war.

#456. The nine Hansa "A2" types assigned to the Lloyd were all the same design, although built at various yards in and outside Germany. Not all are known photographically.
Wesermarsch *#457 shows the type as built with gun platform forward but not yet armed. Several Lloyd and other lines' HANSA wartime program types survived to go into foreign ownership. A few were bought back and put under the flag of their original managers-to-be.* Wesermarsch *went to the USSR, was broken up in Japan in 1973. Hapag-Lloyd A.G.*

457. *Wesermarsch* 1943-1945
Lübecker Maschinenbau
Ges. #401　　　　　　　1943　　1.923　　91.83 x 13.50
Double compound engine　1200　　10　　　　　25

Launched 1/7/1943. Delivery 1/11/1943. 5/1945 at Bergen. 16/11/1945 to Norwegian Govt., ren. *Bragernes*, Bruusgard, Klosterud & Co., Oslo operators. 1946 to USSR, ren. *Dnjepropetrovk*, reg. in Kholmsk. 17/1/1973 arr. Kobe for BU.

458. *Mur*   1943-1945
Deschimag's Weserwerft, Bremen #929   1943
                           3,290   115.10 x 15.30
2x M.A.N. Diesels   3900   14
(designed for 12)   40
Memel-Eider type.

Ordered at Deschimag's Weser Werft, Bremen, but hull subcontracted to sister-yard Seebeck at Wesermünde, #628. Launched 13/9/1939, LU. Completed as Sperrbrecher, mine-clearer, 32, IS 26/10/1943 - 26/8/1944. 13/9/1944 ren. *München* as hospital ship 5, not so put into service. 5/1945 to France at St. Nazaire. 20/8/1945 commissioned as naval transport *Ile D'Oleron*. Later accommodation ship at Brest with cruiser *Tourville*. 1959, after conversion by Chantiers de Provence and Arsenal de Toulon, I.S. as guided-missile experimental launching ship A610. 1/8/1988 fitted for testing MM38 Exocet and Crotale missiles. "There are no plans for decommissioning this vessel as so much has been spent on her conversions" (David Lees, World Ship Society). 1992 SE.

Mur #458 *and* Drau #459 *were the wartime units of the* Eider *class.* Mur *became a French naval transport and finally a guided-missile experimental launching ship, SE 1992, as* Ile d'Oleron. Drau *was part of the 1945-1947 German Minesweeping cleanup operation, as dangerous as wartime service. From 1948 into 1974 it served commercially.*

459. *Drau*   1944-1947
Ordered at Deschimag's Weserwerft, Bremen #930, but hull subcontracted to Sister-yard Seebeck, Wesermünde #627
                         1944   3,290   115.10 x 15.30
2x M.A.N. Diesels   3900   14   40
Memel-Eider type.

Launched 13/11/1940. LU. 26/10/1943 delivery to Kriegsmarine. 14/9/1944 I.S. as *Sperrbrecher 33*, 1944 scuttled in France, raised, repaired. 5/1945 at Copenhagen. 1945-1947 operated by U.S. Navy-supervised German Minesweeping Administration (see "Bremen's Drive to the Sea.") until 30/10/1947. To U.S. on reparations account but not put into service. 5/1948 to Norway, taken to Uddervallavaerft for rebuilding, for Olsen & Ugelstad, Oslo. 3/1939 ren. *Sunny*, then *Tindefjell*. 1950 *Cebu* for Cia. Maritima, Manila, 3,326 Ts. 27/9/1973 stranded near Paganan. Pulled off, LU in Cebu. 8/7/1974 left for BU in Kaohsiung, arr. 2/8/1974 in tow.

William Schell, World Ship Society, explains why different tonnages appear for *Memel* #432, *Mur* and *Drau*:
Memel was built with a tonnage opening in her upper deck. This can be seen clearly from her listing in Lloyd's Register which shows

her as a single deck vessel but with deck erections of a 30 foot poop and a 314 foot combined bridge and forecastle, and a 22' upper forecastle. In fact as laid down *Mur* and *Drau* were to be similar. Schwadtke and Gröner, both list them as 3290 grt. The gross tonnages of 4737 - *Drau*, and 4731 - *Mur* that are listed in Abert are no doubt taken from registration records and reflect the probability that the tonnage openings were plated up when the pair were completed as Sperrbrechers. After the war *Drau* seems to have reverted to an open shelter decker, as the Philippine *Cebu* with some alterations to provide for passenger cabins she had a gross tonnage of 3326.

During the war, NDL managed some captured, taken-over vessels, or seized as prizes. Some were given NDL-type names, not necessarily indicating Lloyd management: *Bonn*. Ordered 1938 by Gdynia-America Line at Danziger Werft. 4/1939 launched as Bielsko. 9/1939 taken over by Germany. 1940 complt., to NDL as manager. Requisitioned for conversion to hospital ship; actually in 1941 built into auxiliary cruiser *Michel*, complt. 17/9/1941. 3/1942 ready for operations. Escorted through the Strait of Dover, 20/3/1942 left the Gironde, arr. Kobe 2/3/1943, having sunk 14 ships of 94,362 Ts. 17/10/1943 sunk off Yokohama in 33.31N, 139.05E by U.S. submarine *Tarpon*.

Darss. Ordered as *Castleville* by A.F. Klaveness at Framnaes Mek. Verks., Sandefjord. Launched 11/1941. 1/1/1945 to NDL management as Versuchsschiff, Experimental vessel. After war back to Klaveness.

Drau. Built in Britain in 1919; 1933 *Marietta Nomikos'* Piraeus. 20/10/1939 seized as prize in Hamburg, to NDL management as *Drau* until its own *Drau* was completed in 1943. 5/5/1945 taken by British at Flensburg. 17/10/1945 scuttled in Skagerrak with munitions.

Elima. Built 1916 as by Henry Koch, Lübeck. Later French owned, seized 13/9/1942, put under NDL management. 20/2/1944 grounded off Trondheim after collision. Sank the 23rd.

Giessen. Built 1921 as *Gouverneur General Chanzy*, Messageries Maritimes. 1943 seized by Italy at Marseilles, renamed *Nicostra*. 6/1943 German hospital ship *Giessen* (NDL manager?) 8/1943 scuttled at La Ciotat drydock; 1/1945 refloated 10/1945 back in French service.

Among wartime German captured vessels managed by NDL were: Minden *#454, ordered at Danziger Werft by Gdynia-America Line as* Lodz, *and sister* Bonn, *ordered as* Bielsko. *Shown is mail from her while in Polish service as* General Walter, *1950s.*

Hoegh Silverbeam, *1941-1945 managed by NDL as* Goslar. *Originally launched for Leif Hoegh & Co. as* Hoegh Silvermann, *and returned to it after the war.*

4/1963 sold for BU at La Spezia.

Goslar. 1941 launched as *Hoegh Silvermann* for Leif Hoegh by Burmeister & Wain, Copenhagen. Completed for Germany, ren. Goslar, NDL manager. 1945 back to Leif Hoegh as *Lappland*, then *Hoegh Silverbeam*, 1958 to Italy, renamed *Zeonobia Martini*.

Gotenland. Brustad, p. 250, has as NDL 20/8/1942. 28/8/1945 to Norway.

Gotha. Launched 1940 as *Merwede* for N.V. Houtvaart, Rotterdam. Seized by Germany after invasion, on completion ren., NDL manager. At Kristiansand after capitulation, back to builders for repair, 1/5/1946 I.S. for A. Vuyck & Zonen.

Kanonier, ordered by Cie. Maritime Belge, at Cockerill, Hoboken, completed 1942. *Seekiste* 7/1971 has as managed by NDL, but actually so by Hapag. 1958 to Yugoslavia, renamed *Bled*. 18/7/1970 arr. La Spezia for BU.

Kapitän Hilgendorf. Groener in 1942 has as "managed by NDL", built 1918 in California, used as Navigation Training ship by Kriegsmarine, later hulk *Cordelia*, BU 1951. Actually never under NDL. (Schell).

Minden. Ordered 1938 at Danziger Werft by Gdynia-America Line (see *Bonn* above), to be named *Lodz*. 1943 completed at Helsingör, to NDL management as *Minden*. 11/7/1945 to M.O.W.T., renamed *Empire Nidd*, 1946 to USSR as *Denis Davydov*. 1947 to Poland as *General Walter*. 1970 BU in Hong Kong.

Putzig. Built in 1924 in UK as *Salmonpool*. 4/1940 seized in Norway, coaling stores ship, NDL managed. 1945 back to Britain, again old name. 1958 BU at Aviles.

Stella Polaris. Built 1927 as cruising yacht for Bergenske D.S.S. by Götaverken. Seized 1940, dormitory ship in Norway for Kriegsmarine. Postwar operated by Sweden's Clipper Line.

A postwar listing by Captain Ewald Püts in NDL's Nautical Department sent to Ernstjosef Weber includes as NDL managed during the war only: *Darss, Elima, Goslar, Gotha, Kurland* (The Fleet of Leif Hoegh & Co., A.S., Oslo 1928-1968, published by World Ship Society, 1968 has "transferred to the Kriegsmarine although in the management of Norddeutscher Lloyd," managed by Hamburg-Süd, actually a Hapag name), *Putzig*, and *Stella Polaris*.

Other NDL-type names used during the war included: *Coburg, Erlangen, Fulda, Göttingen,* and *Tübingen*, but not "managed by NDL" in any records.

Göttingen *#460 had only three months of service ferrying evacuees from the East until torpedoed off Libau. Her sister Hansa's* Argenfels, *survived, in 1950 was chartered by the Lloyd when it resumed trans-Atlantic sailings.* Hapag-Lloyd A.G.

Göttingen *#460 sinking off Libau in February, 1945 while ferrying evacuees.* Ex Hans-Jürgen Witthöft's Norddeutscher Lloyd, Koehler, 1973.

460. **Göttingen**	1944-1945		
Lübecker Flenderwerke #345	1944	6,267	144.50 x 18.41
2 x Double Compounds			
with Exhaust Turbine	4000	12	* *
	ca.50		

Launched 12/4/1944, Sister of Hapag's *Greifswald*. Booked as #261 at Deutsche Werft, Hamburg, then assigned to Penhoët Yard, St. Nazaire. Delivery 11/11/1944. Carried evacuees from the East. 23/2/1945 torpedoed by Soviet submarine K52 off Libau while in convoy. *Göttingen's* sister, "Hansa's" *Argenfels*, survived the war, rebuilt, was chartered by NDL in 1950.

461. **Wangerooge**	1944		
Bremer Vulkan, Vegesack #764	1944	2,819	109.50 x 15.56
Double Compound &			
Exhaust Turbine	1800	10	33

Hansa B Type. Launched 25/3/1944. Delivery 6/5/1944. 25/10/1944 mined, sunk off Stadtlandet.

Wangerooge #461, Langeoog #470 and Spiekeroog #471 were NDL's three Hansa "B" type-assigned vessels. #461 lasted seven months in 1944 before it was mined. #470 became the Soviet Mekhanik Afanasiev, ran until broken up in 1975. Spiekeroog #471, 1947-1963 served under the French flag, finally became the Indian Kr.Avinash, but disappeared from the records. Haussa was built by Bremer Vulkan #763 while sister Wangerooge was Building No. #764. Haussa laid up in the North River, Manhattan. Don Gammon Photo.

462. *Weserwald*	1944-1945		
Deutsche Werft, Hamburg-			
Reiherstieg #430	1944	1925	91.83 x 13.50
Double Compound	1200	10	25

Launched 20/11/1943. Delivery 27/1/1944. Transport to Norway. 5/1945 in Lübeck. 29/10/1945 assigned to Ministry of War Transport, London, ren. *Empire Galveston*, managed by F. Nichols & Son. 1946 to USSR, Sovtorgflot, Tallin, ren. *Volochaevsk*. 1973 BU in USSR.

462 Weserwald as the Soviet Volochaevsk 1946-1973. William Schell Collection.

463. *Weserstrom*   1944-1945
John Cockerill, S.A.,
Hoboken #701   1944   1923   91.83 x 13.50
Double Compound   1200   10   25

    Launched 25/8/1943. Delivery 31/1/1944. Norway Transport. 5/1945 at Kiel. 26/6/1945 to MOWT, London, renamed *Empire Galena*, managed by W. Tulley & Co., 1947 *Albatross*, General S.N.Co., London. 4/1958 Port Capetown, National Shipping Line, Cape Town, 1959 *Frontier*, African Coasters, Durban. 11/1964 unloaded at Durban a record 2,050 tons of sugar. Late 1966 to Summit Nav. Co., Panama, renamed *Fortune*. 11/1969 arr. Hong Kong for BU by Mollers, Ltd.

464. *Weserstein 1*   1944-1945
Nederlandsche Scheepsbouw Maatschapij, Amsterdam #352
                                1923   91.85 x 13.50
Double Compound   1200   10   25

    Launched 30/11/1943. Delivery 1/6/1944. 12/4/1945 sunk by Soviet aircraft off Pillau during evacuation of troops and citizenry to escape Soviet advances.

465. *Weserwehr*   1944-1945
Deutsche Werft, Hamburg #449   1944   1923   91.85 x 13.58
Double Compound   1200   10   25

    Launched 14/11/1944. Delivery 12/2/1945. 5/1945 in Bremerhaven. 24/6/1945 to MOWT, London, renamed *Empire Gangway*, managed by Whitherington & Everett, 1947 transferred to Canada, managed by Clarke S.S. Co., Montreal, for Terra Nova S.S. Co., 2,828 Ts., oil-fired. 1948 it took over management. 1950 renamed *Novaport*. 1964 *Fury*, Trionfo Cia. de Nav., Panama, reg. in Monrovia. 1/12/1964 stranded 1 mile W. of Wedge Island, Nova Scotia due breakdown of steering gear in heavy weather en route Quebec-Halifax in ballast. Crew saved, ship not.

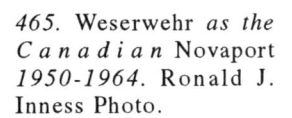

465. Weserwehr *as the* Canadian *Novaport 1950-1964.* Ronald J. Inness Photo.

463. Weserstrom as Albatross 1947 for the General Steam Navigation Co., London, later Frontier, African Coasters, Durban. I show this to portrait the curved bow, so built in wartime, in contrast to the flat-plate Liberty ship bows. Hapag-Lloyd A.G.

466. *Weserberg*	1944-1945		
P. Smit, jr., Rotterdam #585	1944	1923	91.85 x 13.50
Double Compound	1200	10	25

Launched 15/6/1944. 17/10/1944 moved to Bremerhaven for completion in Bremerhaven by NDL's Technical Service. 91/2/1945 delivery. 5/1945 at Kiel. 13/7/1945 to MOWT, London. Wm. Brown, Atkinson & Co., managers. 1947 *Kampar*, Straits S.S. Co., Singapore. 8/1957 *Anglia*, Hellenic Lines, Piraeus. 23/2/1974 arr. Gemlik for BU. Listed in Lloyd's Register as *Weserburg*.

Hunte #467 and Leine 471x were lengthened Eider #444 types, 4.5 meters longer to give a larger hatch. Toronto City, 1956 was the former Leine, Bristol City Lines. Copyright A. Duncan, Gravesend.

467. *Hunte*	Never		
Boele's Schiepswerf & M.N.F. Bolnes #908			
	1940	3350	119.54 x 15.27
M.A.N. Diesel	3950	14.2	36+

Lengthened *Memel* #432/*Eider* type. Launched 15/4/1944. 24/10/1944 in tow for completion in Germany sunk by air attack off Borkum.

468. *Weserstrand*	1945		
Nederlandsche Scheepsbouw Maaj., Amsterdam #354			
	1945	1923	91.83 x 13.50
Double Compound	1200	10	25

Launched 1/7/1944. 10/1944 towed to Bremerhaven, completed by NDL's Technical Service 16/3/1945. 5/1945 at Bremen, Neustadt, 25/6/1945 to MOWT, London, renamed *Empire Gala*, managed by France, Fenwick & Co., London. 1946 to USSR, renamed *Podolsk*, 9/1/1948 grounded on Amherst Rocks, 60 miles off Woosung, on voyage Odessa-Shanghai-Vladivostock. Sank 11th.

469. *Weserbrück*	1945		
P. Smitm jr. Maschinenbouw, Rotterdam #587			
	1945	1923	91.83 x 13.50
Double Compound	1200	10	25

Launched 22/7/1944. 11/1944 towed to Bremerhaven for completion by NDL's Technical Service, Bremerhaven. 2/1945 tsfd. to Deutsche Werft, Hamburg, for completion. Trials 20/3/1945. 5/1945 to Britain there. 6/1945 to M.O.W.T., London, renamed *Empire Fraser*, managed by Indo-China S.N. Co., Hong Kong. 1947 *Chaksang*, reg. Hong Kong. 7/9/1949 due to sabotage of cargo of potassium chlorate and piece goods for North China blew up. Crew lost. Ship sank on 8th, refloated 22/3/1950. BU in situ.

470. *Langeoog 2* 1945-1947
Helsingör Skibsvaerft & Maskinbyggeri #279
                    1945   2818   109.48 x 15.56
Double Compound &
Exhaust Turbine   1800   10   33

Hansa B Type. Launched 9/1/1945 as *Huberfels* for D.D.S.G. "Hansa," Bremen, commissioned for NDL 17/4/1945. Not put into service. 5/1945 seized at Copenhagen. 30/11/1947 to Sovtorgflot, Vladivostock, renamed *Mekhanik Afanasiev*. 12,770 Ts. 20/9/1975 arrived Aioi, Japan for BU.

471. *Spiekeroog 2* 1944-1947
Aalborg Vaerft A. S. #80.   1944   2818   109.48 x 15.56
Double Compound &
Exhaust Turbine   1800   10   33

Hansa B type. Launched 2/9/1944. 5/1945 seized unfinished by Denmark at Aalborg. Completed at 18/4/1947 to French Government, renamed *Jacques Duroux*, managed by Les Cargos Algeriens, Algiers. 1957 *Saint Bertrand*, Societe Navale de l'Ouest, Dunquerque. 1963 *Kr. Avinash*, Rajkumar Lines, Calcutta, arr. Bombay 25/7/1963, reg. in Bureau Veritas. 2,784 Ts. 3/1988 still in Lloyd's. Query to owner's address remained unanswered.

471x. *Leine*   Never
Boele's Scheepswerf, Bolnes #909 1944   3350   119.54 x 15.27
Reciprocating & L.P. Turbine intended for Burmeister & Wain #681
laid down as a Hansa C type
                    3950   14.2   36+

Lengthened *Memel* #432/*Eider* type. Keel laid 1944. 9/1944 seized by Netherlands. Sold to Det Forenede Dampskibs Selskab. 8/7/1947 launched sans name, LU. 1948 sold to Rederi Ocean A.S., Copenhagen, towed to Aalborg Vaerft for completion as a motor vessel. Original engines thus became surplus. Delivery 16/2/1949 to J. Lauritzen as *Leena Dan*, 4,567 Ts., 23/11/1956 to Bristol City Lines as *Toronto City*, 4,730 Ts. 1963 *Olga*, Seaway Co., Piraeus. 1966 *Emmanuel M.*, Cia. de Nav. Astro Naciente, Piraeus. 3/12/1967 stranded on Scharnhörn Bank near Elbe Light Ship en route Rostock-Rotterdam. 1968 wreck bought by Hamburg interests. 7/7/1970 pulled off. 16/7/1970 arr. Hamburg for BU by Eisen & Metall Gmbh.

End of ships owned, ordered or managed into 1945.

CHAPTER 15

A Second New Beginning

As, in early 1945, a demoralized and vastly destroyed Germany saw the inevitable end coming, but still fighting on, the concern of civilians was: what can be saved?

From 3 February, 1942 reorganization of NDL's Board of Directors and Management Team (Vorstand) its interests were under the joint control of Dr. Johannes Kulenkampff, a name going back to the founding of the Lloyd in 1857, and Richard Betram. "At the beginning of 1945" wrote Welfare Director Hans Karstedt to Captain Drechsel in May, 1946 "Dr. Kulenkampff and Herr Bertram went to Bremerhaven to see what could be salvaged and kept from last-minute destruction, ruining what was left so that nothing would be available to the 'enemy', what could be used to make a new start. Several ships were there, most importantly *Europa* entirely undamaged, the Columbus Passenger Quay later so important for the U.S. Navy, and the locks from the Weser River in to the Inner Harbor. Everything was saved by the capitulation. The Americans were able to seize the *Europa* undamaged. The necessary work for putting it back to serviceability was done by the Lloyd's Technical Service at the expense of NDL, although the ship actually belonged to the Deutsche-Amerika Linie."

In the postwar Allied examination of leading Germans into possible National Socialist involvement, the findings about Kulenkampff and Bertram "proved positive". They were confirmed by the U.S. Authorities in their Lloyd positions. But, as they lacked authorizations to sign without confirming Board meetings and supportive legislation, accepted signatures were made by Herr Stünkel of the Finance Department, and by Herr Karstedt, prewar and continuing as Director of the Welfare and Insurance funds. Postwar, as in fourteen-pages typed May, 1946 letter he kept Captain Drechsel informed. He, in turn, began his private welfare help for his old colleagues with food, clothing, even books to the replacement Haus Seefahrt, retirement facility for needy captains and widows, destroyed in the war. In 13 August, and 6 September, 1946 letters to Captain Drechsel Dr. Kulenkampff wrote "Your letter to Herr Karstedt gave everyone here great joy because after such a long time it gave us detailed reports about so many of our people over there. Please remember that we all, especially the former interned seamen, never never will forget your sacrifices and work in their and our behalf. We know that your own claims and needs have suffered. Regretfully, as with everything else, we must wait and see what eventually can be done." In all he had done to help needy, Captain Drechsel had the help of other Lloyd people and the Red Cross, YMCA, Seamen's Missions, etc.

Dr. Johannes Kulenkampff, a Lloyd name going back to the 1850s, and Richard Betram, led the enterprise from the reorganization of the Vorstand, Management Board on 3 February, 1942 into the 1970 merger with the Hapag. Herr Bertram continued with Hapag-Lloyd A.G. as spokesman until his retirement.

On 6 March, 1952 Hapag's G. Thunemann wrote Captain Drechsel enclosing a list of eighty recipients of welfare parcels through U.S.-Europa Corporation, in which former Passenger Director John Schroeder was involved, people who are still very much dependent on such help. "You and Herr Schroeder in the meantime will have received individual thank-you letters, and I am sure will be getting more. Some cannot very well write." The help organized in and from North America continued for years, declining as recipients died, and as Germany slowly rebuilt.

Captain Oskar Scharf, who was imprisoned in Britain following capture of *Alster* during the German invasion of Norway, was repatriated in time to participate in the putting back into service of *Europa*. Excerpts from his report follow:

"*Europa* on 7/2/1945 was taken over by the Kriegsmarine, Bremerhaven. It was used as dormitory ship for persons from the Marine, the Army and shipyard personnel. These latter were mostly refugees from the F.Schichau shipyards in Danzig and Elbing. From the 5 to 9th May, 1945, some 2500-3000 front-line troops were accommodated on board. On 7 May on an interim basis *Europa* was taken under control of a British Commando. Captain Scharf and the skeleton crew of 149 men remained on board.

"On 9 May, *Europa* was taken over by a U.S. Prize Command, and all Germans except for the actual *Europa* crew-members, were put ashore. At 15:00 hours the U.S. flag went up. In the very first days, the U.S. authorities established elaborate safety-watch measures. Extensive fire-protection

THE NEW YORK TIMES
May 10, 1945

475 GERMAN SHIPS SEIZED BY ALLIES

Liner Europa Among Naval and Merchant Craft Found Intact—10 Cargo Ports Workable

By DREW MIDDLETON
By Wireless to THE NEW YORK TIMES.

PARIS, May 15—The American flag or the White Ensign of the Royal Navy has been hoisted over about 475 naval and merchant vessels, including the transatlantic liner Europa, which have been found in north German ports by British-American forces.

Preliminary reports show that ten ports on the North Sea and the Baltic are in better condition than was expected and that berths for twenty-eight Liberty ships already are available in Bremen and Bremerhaven alone.

The Europa was found at Bremerhaven in relatively good condition, although she had been silted in. Recently she had been used as a German naval barracks. The Bremen, which has been hit by Allied bombs, is a total loss.

Cruisers Almost Worthless

The Europa, one of the contestants for the blue ribbon for speed on the North Atlantic run while she was the pride of the Hamburg-American Line, was the most important prize found in the northern ports. Two cruisers, the Hipper and the Emden, have been found, but they are almost worthless. The Allies also have taken three destroyers and twenty-seven submarines.

Kiel, the German naval headquarters in the two World Wars, was in far worse conidtion than had been expected. All its shipyards were devastated. The eight-inch-gun cruiser Hipper was found sabotaged in her dock and the six-inch-gun cruiser Emden was found stranded and burned out. About a dozen U-boats had been scuttled and there are more than eighty wrecks to the south of Tirpitzhaven. Fourteen medium and fifty small merchant ships, with seven large and two medium-size tankers, were found in the harbor.

Bremen and Hamburg, the largest of the North Sea ports, both appear to be in fairly good shape. Both will be used for supplies moving to the American and British zones of occupation from the United States and Britain.

The surprisingly good condition of the northern ports probably will make it possible for the United States and Britain to return some of the Atlantic ports to France and use other northern ports, in addition to Hamburg and Bremen, for bringing in supplies for the armies of occupation.

Reports on Other Harbors

Here are preliminary reports on other ports in addition to Kiel:

Brunsbuettel—The port appears to be undamaged. One destroyer, one submarine escort vessel, four U-boats, two minesweepers, one flak cruiser, seventeen gunboats, fifteen ferry and landing craft and a few small merchant ships were taken over in the port.

Bremen—The harbor works are badly damaged but berths for eight Liberty ships are available. Sixteen prefabricated U-boats were found on stocks. Nine were already completed but had been sabotaged.

Bremerhaven and Wesermuende—Berths for about twenty Liberty ships appear to be available. Dock facilities were not so severely damaged as had been expected. Thirteen medium and large-size cargo ships were found, of which only five are seaworthy. About twenty-five trawlers, twenty-four tugs and 100 barges were found, most of them serviceable. Columbus Quay at Wesermuende is in good condition.

Cuxhaven—All port installations and ships in the harbor were found intact. The German ships in the harbor were two destroyers, six boom breakers, four flak ships, twenty-two minesweepers of which fifteen were M-class, seven U-boats, thirteen R-boats, twenty-nine harbor defense anti-aircraft ships, a depot ship and two medium-size merchantmen.

Hamburg—More than fifty large and medium merchant ships, nineteen floating docks and many small vessels were reported sunk at Hamburg, but a number of deep-water berths are clear and the damage in the dock area is not so severe as was expected.

Helgoland—The town is completely destroyed and there are no accommodations for civilians. Seven U-boats were found in the harbor.

Luebeck—All port facilities at this Baltic port are normal, but their use depends on the working of the power stations, which are out of action. Many wrecks, among which are scuttled U-boats, have been found in the approach to the channel.

Rotterdam—Lack of coal prevents use of the harbor installations, but they are not in as bad condition as has been expected. Entrance to the harbor is impeded by sunken block ships.

Wilhelmshaven—The port installations and dockyard were found in good condition except for bomb damage. One destroyer in a floating dock was found fit for sea, but all U-boats had been scuttled and, although many small craft were available, only one seaworthy merchant ship was found. A dozen minesweepers are ready for service and more than 100 smaller craft used for this purpose are being reconverted for fishing.

Hamburg-Amerika Linie

Nautische Abteilung,

den 16. Jan. 1950.

Herrn
Kapt. W. Drechsel,
150 Kensington Road,
RIVER EDGE, New Jersey,
U.S.A.

Captain Fuhr postwar was in Hapag's Nautical Department, in January 1950 provided the list of recipients of the month-before Christmas sendings which Captain Drechsel had organized which "with the great need has given great joy...." Hapag was forced to retire Captain Fuhr early before the war because of his alleged lack of enthusiasm for National Socialism.

provisions were taken, including replacement of all fire hoses. Fire-watches were set. These measures were a belated recognition of the carelessness that led to the *Normandie* fire in New York in February, 1942 when it was being converted for Navy use as transport. Just like the two *Queens*, each able to take an entire division anywhere, *Normandie*, renamed *Lafayette*, was counted on to do the same for the U.S. war effort. The three ships' high speeds, in excess of thirty knots, made them invulnerable to submarines, except through utter fortuitous circumstances.

From June into 8 September *Europa* was put into shape for transport use by the Lloyd's own Technical Service in Bremerhaven. Thousands of bunks were set up on the Promenade Deck. These later during further work at the Navy Yard in Bayonne, N.J., were removed. Instead, some 4,000 bunks were installed in the First-Class cabins, and more than 700 in the Social Hall, giving a total troop capacity of near 6,000. A, B, and C Decks were left empty. New generators and a fire-quenching system were installed. Of the 26 lifeboats, 22 were removed to reduce topheavyness. In their place sufficient rafts for all were piled up on the Upper Deck. In New York, some 3000 members of the National Maritime Union demonstrated in protest against rumored use of ex-*Europa* crew members to help run her for the Navy. This had been a faint hope with some 50,000 German seamen unemployed, and no ships of their own left to operate.

"A few at a time, U.S. Navy crew members came on board during August and September. On 25 August the entire German crew except for ten men was paid off. On that day the ship formally was taken for the U.S. Navy by Captain B.F. Perry. On 11 September *Europa* left Bremerhaven and headed seawards escorted by two Royal Navy minesearch corvettes. Near Hull these were released and *Europa* steamed northwards along the coast, through the Pentland Firth, and past the West Coast of Ireland southward to Southampton, which it reached on the 15th. On the 17th, *Europa* left Southampton with 4,800 U.S. forces on board under escort of the cruiser *Philadelphia*. Of the former NDL crew left on board were: Captain O. Scharf, 1.Officer J. Weitzel, Chief Engineer Hase, three other engineers and three machinists, plus seven technicians from the Blohm & Voss shipyard which had originally built *Europa*." Cabin doors still had chalk marks on them to indicate how many men would be housed there for the invasion of England, Operation Seelöwe. New York was reached on 24 September.

While *Europa* was put into the Navy's big drydock off Bayonne for further conversion work, on 26 September before a Prize Court with Captain Perry and another Captain, and of Captain Scharf and 1.Officer J. Weitzel, the ship was declared a prize and lawful U.S. property. On the 28th, the Chief Engineer and the six former NDL crew members were sent back to Germany. Captain Scharf and 1.Officer Weitzel remained on board until 25 October when they boarded the Liberty Ship *James W. Wayne*, arriving in Bremerhaven on 11 November.

Captain Scharf had seen Captain Drechsel in New York, they exchanging news of their experiences since they last met in August, 1939. This

```
165 DHq # 0 J ND--NSB--41116--4 Mar 44--200M.

          THIRD NAVAL DISTRICT
         OFFICE OF THE PORT DIRECTOR

    ............11 July, 1945............, 194....

Memorandum for ----------------------------------


       Received from Captain W. A. Drechsel:

       3 Folders

       A number of photographs

       4 lists, containing data pertaining
          to the particulars of construc-
          tion and lay-out of the
          S.S. EUROPA.

       These are for the use of the Bureau of
    Ships, of the Navy Department, in converting
    the EUROPA to a Troop Transport.

                         M. L. WORRELL
                         Captain, USNR.
                         Operations Manager.
```

Captain Drechsel supplied blue-prints and other data on Europa *to the U.S. Navy for aid in rebuilding the ship for transport use.*

enabled Captain Scharf to fill in Bremen on Lloyd interests in the U.S. Captain Daehne, of *Columbus* had seen Captain Drechsel in late 1944 when he was exchanged to Germany, and was able to fill in Bremen on what he, Daehne, Drechsel and relief groups had been able to do for the former German seamen in the U.S. and Canada.

Europa on 29th September sailed for Britain. The expectation was that she would make a round-trip repatriating and exchanging personnel at Southampton about every three weeks. A sprinkler system had been installed at Bayonne, and several new stairways were cut between decks to give readier up and down access. The ship's decorations in First Class remained untouched, including the murals and gold and tile mosaic in the Social Hall. The red-marble Europa and the Bull at its entrance remained in place. Until 2 May, 1946, *Europa* operated in the Navy transport service.

Again from Herr Karstedt's May, 1946 letter: "At the beginning of May, 1946 *Europa* lay at the Columbus Quay in Bremerhaven. Nothing had been decided about her future. The Americans had rejected keeping her because she did not meet U.S. safety requirements, especially fire-security. The French, to whom the ship had been offered as replacement for their *Normandie*, rejected her seemingly for the same reasons. At one time, a far-out idea was that Captain Scharf and some 130 German crewmen would take over *Europa*. But to do what? As Hotel ship as many other German vessels had become? On 2 May, 1946, the U.S. released *Europa*. A month later, in June, the French accepted her and she was transferred to LeHavre. See #423. After Bremerhaven became the U.S. support base for Germany, Captain Daehne was appointed Harbor Director. He capably organized the port operations with the help of Captain H. Kempf, former assistant to Captain Drechsel in New York. He had left New York by train for San Francisco on 3/3/1940; on the 14th sailed on *Asama Maru* for Japan and then across Siberia home. He later was captured and imprisoned. He was released to assist Captain Daehne. Once Bremerhaven was running smoothly for U.S. Navy operations there, Captain Daehne was transferred to Bremen to head the Harbor and Traffic Authority, at first under supervision of U.S. Army Colonel Boyle, then by Spring, 1946 under the direction of Bremen's Senate.

"His right hand is the son of our worthy Schorse Richter who, at age 65, has gone into well-deserved retirement and relieved not to have to struggle with the Lloyd's insurance, retirement and welfare programs. All these I (Karstedt) have had to take over. That after again having to take over the Personnel Division which I had until 1935 when I was forced out as a non-National Socialist Party member. This is what more or less I did in the 1920s under Director Bultmann. But with no future in sight, this division is cut down from some 750 before the war to something like forty. In addition, we have had to let go some 800 seamen. How bitter that is."

What remained at the end of the war was a nearly thoroughly destroyed Bremen-Bremerhaven. To the Lloyd there were left some damaged hotels used for transient personnel, the Hotel ship *Knurrhahn*, see "Small vessels", the travel bureaus, dispersed, hence less or not at all damaged, some warehousing facilities with lighters and barges and 14 tugs, and a resort service that was resumed, as after WWI, with the veterans *Delphin* and *Glückauf*, and an ex-minesearch vessel converted to resort vessel *Wangerooge*. That, and the dedication, skill and determination of the Lloyd people who survived, led by Dr. Johannes Kulenkampff, and Richard Bertram, during the last years of the war and now, the joint management. It took courage and an optimism that some-

Captured Liner Europa To Sail in U. S. Service

By DANIEL DE LUCE,
Associated Press Staff Writer.

1945

ABOARD THE S. S. EUROPA, BREMERHAVEN, Germany, June 6.—Deep within the shabby steel hull of the Europa, once assigned to carry a German invasion army to England in 1940, mighty steam turbines are being overhauled today to power the United States vessel on the Seven Seas.

If present tentative estimates are correct, the 49,700-ton liner which won and lost the Atlantic blue ribbon for speed a little more than a decade ago will be ready for service under the Stars and Stripes within three months.

Crew Volunteers.

Capt. Oskar Scharf, who brought the Europa safely into Bremerhaven after a wide detour around the Royal Navy in the North Sea on the day Great Britain declared war in 1939, is expected to stay aboard when she makes her first voyage in six years. Seventy-nine other members of the German crew have volunteered for sea duty under American supervision.

A 24-man naval prize crew under Lt. Richard O. Read, of Oakland, Calif., and Lt. (JG) Robert M. Bliss, of Cedar Lake Iowa, currently commands this $16,000,000 bit of booty.

It is about the first time Lts. Read and Bliss ever have been in charge of anything afloat. One of their chief motor machinist mates, Theodore Haas, of Maspeth, N. Y., has been on American warships for many years.

Rotund Gustav Pflueger, chief steward of the Europa for nine years, grinned with embarrassment when a visitor inquired about black crayon scrawls on doors of the suites on "A" deck, where one-way passage once cost $3000. One scrawl says "16 mann." Another says "8 mann."

Altered for Troops.

"You'll find such markings on every stateroom," said Pflueger. "You see, back in 1940 after Dunkirk, the military came aboard and started doing things to our ship.

"They noted down the capacity of all accommodations for troops. They had bulkheads removed so the ballroom could be used for storing panzer vehicles. They cut away the kindergarten room to widen the promenade deck. They began installing steel mounts for artillery.

"They didn't tell us officially where we would be sailing the Europa. But we gathered we could only have one destination at that time—England.

"After a while, the preparations stopped. There was no explanation."

THE NEW YORK TIMES June 10, 1945

NMU BANS GERMANS FOR EUROPA'S CREW

A protest against the reported manning of the German liner Europa with the German captain and crew that took the vessel back to Germany at the outbreak of the war was made yesterday in a telegram to President Truman, signed in behalf of 3,000 members of the National Maritime Union, CIO, Mr. Joseph Curran, president.

"The seamen bitterly resent and vigorously oppose this insult to the nation and to the memory of our honored dead in this war," the telegram said. "The seamen warn that to permit Nazis to man the vessel would serve as a green light to Nazi sympathizers and soft-peace proponents to intensify their disruptive efforts.

"The seamen further warn that such permission would pave the way for pro-Nazi elements to return to the American merchant marine and seriously endanger inefficient operation for the nation's security. The seamen therefore urgently demand that official sanction of this move be immediately revoked and that an American crew of merchant seamen, or Army or Navy personnel, sail the Europa to this country."

---

how, as at the start in 1857, the difficult first ten years, from 1919 on after the earlier war, and now again in 1945, saw the remote possibility of a third existence for the Lloyd, that somehow those still there, with limited means, could make a new start. And overseas, there was the Lloyd's reputation for service, for its capability, its name, its history. And that those who were "enemy", realized, as once before, that the enmity of war must be replaced with the hopes of peace. Also, of almost immediate help, were the needs of the U.S., principally the U.S. Navy, that used and needed Bremerhaven and its ship-handling facilities and capabilities, to service American activities. It was the Lloyd's Technical Service that became, in effect, an operation of the U.S.-Bremerhaven and Bremen became an American enclave. They were the staging area for the U.S. presence on the Continent and its occupation zone in Germany.

"Fortunately, in Bremerhaven, the Technical Service is operating all-out under Herr Wille, on orders and work for the Americans, some 1000 workers currently. Also from our Inspection Messrs. Obering and Schneider and Captain Schröder. The Bremen City harbors were severely damaged, and entire sections now are still unusable. The derricks and cranes are only partly operational. Still usable are the Lloyd's former laundry installation, the ice cream factory, and the refrigeration facility.

"All are under American control. Otherwise, the Lloyd's own work places and warehouses are entirely destroyed. We have been able to organize a small repair facility for our lighters. And we have taken over the housing and feeding of some 2500-3000 harbor workers. These people are furnished from American supplies a hot mid-day meal for 50pf. without ration stamps, a blessing

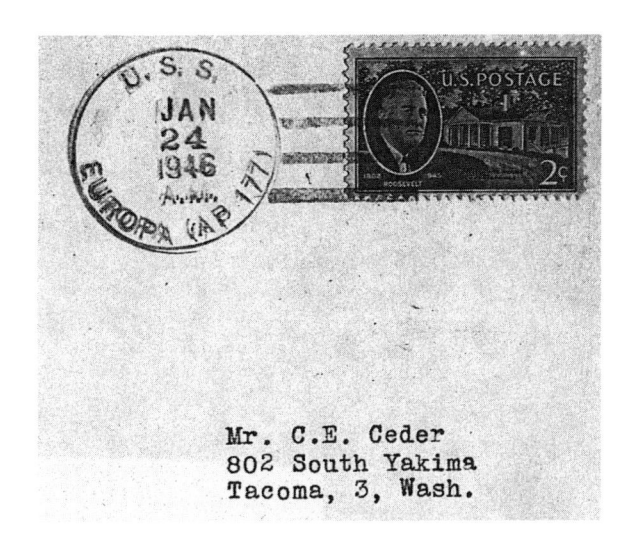

Naval Postmarks from the Europa *during the period 25/8/1945-2/5/1946 she was used as transport bringing home personnel from Europe, and taking to Europe those participating in the U.S. occupation of Germany.* Gustar Lund and Edward Ceder Collections.

for these people. Without that, given the overall food situation, the prompt handling of ships in our harbors would be impossible."

Also fortunately in terms of providing work for ships and seamen, was the German Minesweeping Administration, operating under U.S. Navy controls, from May 1945 through December, 1947. Although this happened postwar, it was as dangerous and costly in lives and vessels lost as anything during the war. In its operations, GMSA with some 400 craft and 15,000 personnel cleared out 3,500 mines and one thousand detonating devices with a loss of seventeen vessels and 277 lives lost. (Seekiste May, 1956). *Drau #459, Puddefjord* and *Wangerooge* were involved in this. See Small Craft fleet list.

To continue Herr Karstedt: "So far as the NDL is concerned, we are 'on the mat,' as Captain Scharf will already have told you. Left to us are two old resort steamers, *Glückauf* and *Delphin*, the coastal motorships used prewar to transfer cargoes between Hamburg and Bremen, 14 tugs and some 50 barges and lighters; a total of about 5,500 tons. Equal to one of our *München* class freighters. Apart from the two *Tills*, 375 tons shuttle freighters we are active only in the towing business. But with little freight to move, everything destroyed, so little being produced unless it comes in from abroad, mainly to and by the U.S. naval authorities using Bremerhaven as their shipping base in Germany. After WWI we could put our then largest vessel, resort Steamer *Grüssgott* of 781 tons, into service under Capt. Johnson. Now, with U.S. permission we are doing the same with *Delphin* between Bremen and Bremerhaven on week days. People who have the time prefer the ship, as in the pre-railway 19th century days, than being inside in heated rooms during the winter is far preferable to using the railway, overfilled, many wagons still without window panes. Captain Terkorn has the ship. Before the war he led *Delphin* on its trips to Wangerooge. Also with him are Herr Viet and Purser Herr Voigt." Individuals still counted at the Lloyd.

The Karstedts had three different homes during the war, "the Contrescarpe Guesthouse of the former (NDL President Carl) Stimming home, the happiest time of my life. I lived there from 1933, after Herr Stimming died, and in 1936 when I married, until 1940. Then near the main Railway Station. And from Fall, 1942 in the Wachmannstrasse home of Martin Schmidt, who was transferred to Dresden as there was nothing left for him to do here. All three homes were destroyed. In the rebuilt Stimming Home the U.S. Military Government is headquartered. In these homes we experienced it all: spread bombs, fire bombs, benzine canisters, pressure and vacuum-working aerial mines. The one roof was blown-sucked away four times, same with doors and windows, even when bricked up. Neighboring streets literally levelled in the repeated bombings. We spent days, weeks in deep bunkers. Gradually over six years one adjusts to the endless dangers. Bremen had some two thousand alarms during the war."

"Structures needed for the occupying forces, now beginning to be joined by their families, of course are being rebuilt. Bremen ended the war with 18% of its prewar housing capacity. And much of that is going to the Americans: Some

A Second New Beginning

New Yorker Zeitung und

n Newspaper Printed in the Germa

MONTAG, den 24. SEPTEMBER 1945

"Europa" trifft heute abend in New York ein

Der 49,746 Tonnen große deutsche Schnelldampfer "Europa" ist wieder nach New York unterwegs. Die wertvollste und größte Prise in der Geschichte des Krieges und Schiffbaus wird heute abend hier eintreffen und soll um 7 Uhr 30 am Pier 88, nahe West 48. Straße, docken. Doch die "Europa" hat nur 4314 heimkehrende amerikanische Soldaten an Bord, was weniger als die Hälfte ist, die sie seit ihrer Umwandlung in ein amerikanisches Truppentransportschiff der Bundesmarine aufnehmen kann.

Jetzt offiziell als "AP 177" bekannt, wird der frühere Dampfer des Norddeutschen Lloyd nicht den Versuch machen, seinem transatlantischen Schnelligkeitsrekord von vier Tagen, siebzehn Stunden und sechs Minuten, den er bei seiner Jungfernfahrt im März 1930 erreichte, auch nur nahezukommen.

Die "Europa" begibt sich nach ihrer Ankunft hier zum Erweiterungsbau in die New Yorker Marinewerft zu Bayonne, N. J., wo auch die Truppen ausgebootet werden. Sie wird etwa 45 Tage lang auf der Werft bleiben, um ihren in Bremerhaven begonnenen Umbau zu vollenden. Bis heute, so wird ausdrücklich betont, konnte nur eine teilweise Umwandlung vorgenommen werden, da das Schiff nach Jahren der Nichtbenutzung zum ersten Male wieder flottgemacht wurde. Sobald der Umbau vollendet ist, wird die "Europa" ihre Fahrten für der Transportdienst der Marine aufnehmen.

Wie die "Europa" in den Besitz der U. S. überging

Die "Europa" wurde ein Kriegsprise am 8. Mai 1945, al Leutnant Richard O. Read vo der USNR aus Oakland, Kalifor

(Fortsetzung auf Seite Drei)

Again a (former) Lloyd ship arriving in New York. Big news for the German-speaking community. The last ship had been Bremen *which sailed on 30 August, 1939. "Europa arrives tonight in New York." Excerpts from the press interview with Captain Oskar Scharf by the New Yorker Staats-Herold the day after* Europa's *arrival. Scharf had made the voyage by request to help the Navy to learn how to run the ship. The interview was held in the former Sun Deck Ritz Restaurant. He told that when the ship docked at Cherbourg through his glasses he recognized a former passenger, and sent down for him to come up onto the bridge. Now 59 years old, after six years of war, four in POW camp, he still had his old uniform, the gold braid paled. A reporter commented: "We never saw you so,..." Scharf looked at his cap. "Yes, it is the old one." From early 1933 into 1939 he had made one hundred forty roundtrips on* Europa. *"At least I still have four wonderful children and my beloved wife. The oldest was in the war, Dr. of Physics and Mathematics. Another son is only fifteen. Two daughters are studying medicine. Of his brothers and sisters in Schlesien he has heard nothing. His house? "Not totally destroyed. All my old officers are gone, all of them". Winston Churchill's "...the havoc of war...."*

Tho' "Peace on Earth" is not yet near.
This world a stay of tears and fear

On Western skies we see appear
A gentle glare like daybreak clear!

Far over see their helpful hand
In Sympathy good mates extend:

"You're deep in woe and sorrow, Friend.
"Cheer up! We aid. You can depend!"

The pace of history is slow
And streams of tears will further flow.

It's more than food and clothing, tho'
What ye good Friends on us bestow.

It's hoping for another start
That once through clouds the sun will part.
That now we hear the heavenly art:
"Good Will" henceforth from heart to

For Christmas, 1947 "The American Enclave (Bremen)," i.e. the Lloyd Contingent formerly involved in the Bremen services to North America, sent Greetings, to the Lloyd people in New York and this poem in English by E. N. Oltenius, an honored Bremer name. This bespeaks the closeness the Lloyd people felt towards each other across the oceans, and the faith that help will come, and that there is a future ... for the Lloyd and its family.

entire city sections, such as the Schwachhauser Heerstrasse vicinity in the Neu Stadt." Here the Drechsels lived 1913-1921.

"We transferred the Lloyd management to the Weser Terrasse Restaurant on the Osterdeich late in the war after the near-destruction of most of the Alt Stadt. Then we were able to return to our cellars where we now have been more than a year, with artificial light, no fresh air as all the blown-out windows have been bricked shut, or otherwise everything would be stolen. The only structure left to the Lloyd is the old Baggage Department; actually it belongs to the Deutsche Amerika Linie, to where we shall move as soon as the ruin has been rebuilt, at least to be above surface." This still today is the Passenger department head office and Hapag-Lloyd's Bremen Office, supposedly equal to Hamburg, but as La Vegas is bigger than Reno, L.A. bigger than S.F., so Hamburg is bigger than Bremen, and runs the show. Its weight was overwhelming. At one count it had more foreign consulates, 90, than New York with 87.

The Lloyd and Bremen reached out toward

Lloyd Headquarters after the war, in the former Baggage Department building, with dome, and the Lloyd Hotel, both directly behind the main railway station. After the 1970 merger, this structure became Hapag-Lloyd's supposedly coequal Bremen office. Compare with the old ornate 1907 structure, Volume I, p. 405, 411, Volume II, p. 590.

former and present employees. "Because most are gone or no longer working, there's little coming in from security co-payments. Investments no longer are paying dividends or interest, to the extent they still exist. The Lloyd still is paying 100% of due pension amounts, compared with the Hamburg firms which have cut theirs to 15%. Hapag has almost wholly ended its volunteer welfare program. It wants to save money now to survive over an indefinite period, then be more ready to resume. We are using any available resources to continue for now, to minimize need and suffering. We have no foreign exchange. We even during the war kept paying our Dollar debt, but it was returned because of Trading with the Enemy Laws forbade accepting payments." One of the ironies of war.

Continuing Herr Karstedt's letter: "Immediately postwar, some of the prewar top officers were let go because they had Nazi Party memberships, disregarding the fact that in this way they had been able to protect the normal functioning of the Lloyd. **Captain E. Heims** frequently intervened in the personnel affairs of the Nautical

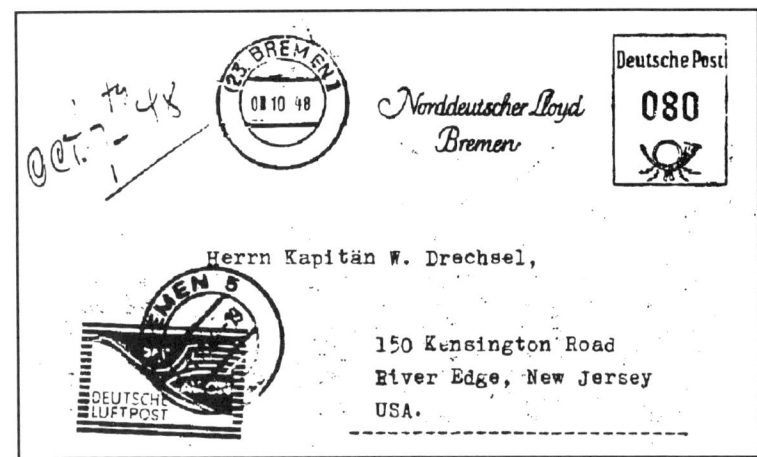

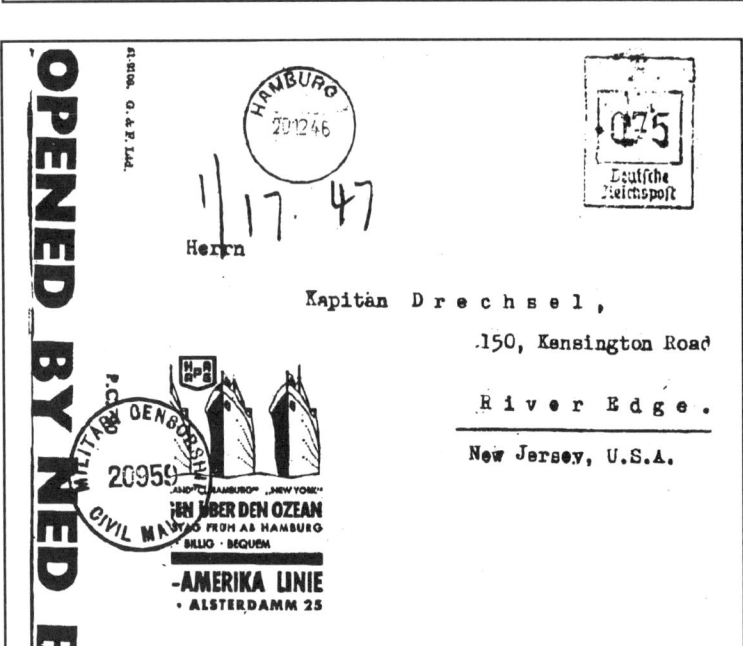

Not until January, 1950 was Germany allowed to handle overseas mails. This Air Mail authorization sticker was required by the Occupation for business letters from 1 May to 19 October, 1948.

Mail into and out of Germany remained subject to censorship by allied authorities into 1948. Hapag was still using prewar envelopes: Every Thursday Early from Hamburg to New York: Cheap-Comfortable. Its Big Four steamers.

Department, protecting and gentlemen in his care from political encroachments.

"Captain Heims 'went out the door' although all he did was to try to protect those in the Nautical Department from Nazi excesses. For health reasons he is retired and lives quite happily on the Island of Föhr.

Prokurist, empowered to sign, **Ernst Path** also is out the door, a member of the NSDAP from 1933, although we know he and Captain Heims never were Nazis. There he fishes for plaice and is his old comfortable philosopher. His forced departure from the Lloyd so soon after his fortieth anniversary was sad for him and for us all who so much wished him a happy departure. But the orders of the U.S. Military are not to be denied. The question remains whether these ex-party members are entitled to their pensions and other benefits. They are allowed to draw a maximum of 300 Marks a month. But who can live on that if he does not have a considerable saved-up substance? We and they all need replacements for lost clothing; there is no leather to resole shoes, materials for the repair of repairable buildings. Later Herr Path was back as the third member of the Vorstand, as deputy for Herr Bertram and Dr. Kulenkampff.

"**Dr. Rudolf Firle** was an experienced high-seas officer. After WWI he went into shipping management. In 1933, he came to the Lloyd as Freight Director, then General Direktor. He was a member of the Armistice Group in Paris and Wiesbaden, and last in charge of the Reichkommissariat for Shipping in Paris. Since 4 May, 1945 he is in prison but where we do not know. We assume he will soon be released. From Paris, he got excellent references. Inside he was a decent character. He always wanted to do the right thing." In 1955, he made a five-months survey trip to the Far East for the Lloyd, and in 1955-1956, a seven months Australia trip. He went out, surely as guest of the Lloyd, on Freighter *Havelstein* #492 in November, 1955, returned on *Reifenstein* #496 in June, 1956.

"**Herr Ernst Glässel** is very active. (He was Deputy General Director 1925-1931, the one year had the top job.) He is persona grata with the Americans, and was installed at the Lloyd as their Trustee. He belongs to the Zonal Commercial Council. He is concerned with shipping questions overall, and owns a fishing steamer which has had good catches. With British encouragement he expanded that fleet to provide needed food. He is busy in all sorts of activities. His son, who later ran the Glässel Shipping Co., works with him. We get together when he visits us in our catacombs checking out for the Allied Property Control." Herr Glässel was instrumental in finding and having built housing for retired captains and their widows, until a new Haus Seefahrt could be built in the 1950s.

"**Adolf Stadtländer**, formerly passenger chief, at the end of the war was Vorstand, Operating Chief, of the Union Reederei, in peacetime a reefer specialist firm. He worked there with other former Lloyd people. He is living on his property at Lübbestadt, en route to Bremerhaven. I doubt he'll ever again be involved as he is in his mid-sixties.

"**Geheimrat** (Privy Councillor) **H.F. Albert**, Finance Minister under Chancellor Cuno during Germany's 1920's inflation, into 1933 was General Director of NDL. He was pushed out by and suffered heavily under the National Socialists. He again became private attorney. He survived the war. We are still in touch. His son of whom he was so proud died in the last days in the Berlin fighting. He is too old to start fighting again. In an August, 1946 letter Dr. Kulenkamff wrote:

"With Dr. Albert I am constantly in touch. He is all alone in Berlin, the son-in-law in POW camp, the daughter with grandchildren somewhere in S.W. Germany. He himself is now in his 11th living place, one room. He is trying to resume his law practice, but is disappointed that among his former American contacts he's not heard from one. His imprisonment from the 20 July, 1944, the Count von Stauffenberg group's attempted coup d'etat against Hitler, into March, 1945 was a personal and morale-destroying experience. **Dr. Dettmers** gave up his General Director post during the war and again has become an attorney. He still lives in Bremen. His houses repeatedly were plundered. He was able to save only what he wore. His parents lost their lives despite being in a deep bunker during one of the bombings. He again was a member of the Aufsichtsrat, Board 1951-1953, then continuing as emeritus with his law firm. He died in 1986.

Captain H. Hashagen was head of the Nautical Department in the latter 1930s; he was a party member, and was fired soon after the capitulation. As his health is poor, he was not forced into doing something else.

Herr Kessemeier had fabulous success with Fortra, a trading firm. When, with few goods available, it declined, he moved with family to Ammersee. He was strong there for the Nazis, and tried to teach the Bavarians to say 'Heil Hitler' without success. The Bavarians, of course, were the first ones to start that, and the first one to quit that.

Herr Gerhardi, partner with Kessemeier held directly opposite views, and saw things clearly. He was arrested after the British had made him Buergermeister in his town Vechta. Evidently over there (US?) his activities were examined as he had been active for the Nazis. But when he got back here, he saw the truth and changed his outlook. He then fought the Nazis in any way he could, and therefore was constantly opposing Kessemeier, with whom he was often eyeball to eyeball.

Herr Ewig, whom you knew from before, and who after his Paris activity had to go into the war again as ordinary soldier, but only got as far as Norway. He now is Harbor Director as he was not a PG (Party Member). He is a director of Bremer Lagerhaus Gesellschaft, which Captain Daehne later rebuilt and headed for years. He has a very responsible position as he handles the steamers reaching Bremen.

Director **Carl Stapelfeldt**, Freight Manager at the Lloyd pre-war. He was imprisoned by the Nazis for about a year until the capitulation. Then the Americans imprisoned him again. He was released only in recent weeks. He has just been installed as head of the Bremen Chamber of Commerce. I doubt he'll again be involved. See end of "1957 Centennial".

Director Christian Ahrenkiel was a Vorstands member and part of the Hapag-Lloyd North-Atlantic Community management team in the U.S. He got back to Germany via Japan. Postwar, he became a member of Hapag's Vorstand but had policy differences with the top people and left. With lifting of restrictions on German shipping, he formed his own concern, and later built and chartered several vessels to Hapag-Lloyd, including *Main Express and Rhein Express* in 1972.

Dr. Arnold Rehm, prewar Social Director on many Lloyd cruises, in the war last was Naval Commander at Brest. With the American break-

Having suffered little in the war, in sharp contrast to the British, U.S. policy was more lenient than could be expected from the victor. In 6 September, 1946 in Stuttgart, U.S. Secretary of State James Byrnes enunciated U.S. policy towards Germany. To reflect the unanimous views, Senator James Connolly, Democrat of Texas, and Arthur Vandenberg of Ohio, Republican, sat behind Mr. Byrnes during the speech. Germans later called this the beginning of "Our Way Back to Freedom." With Konrad Adenauer becoming Chancellor in 15 September, 1949, and his subsequent close relations with General Charles DeGaulle, Germany's return to the comity of nations was under way.

through, he was imprisoned. He spent 15 months in the U.S., basically had a good time as he spoke excellent English, was a very likeable person. Although behind barbed wire, he was in touch with the world through the U.S. and British press. He was released in early 1946, and wrote a number of books about shipping people, and organized an extensive archive on the NDL, finally giving his photo collection to it. We corresponded until his illness and death.

Staatsrat Karl Lindemann is still in confinement. However, he is well. He lost his son Peter in the last days of the war. The family had to evacuate the house on the Wachmannstrasse. From 1933 into 1945 he was Chairman of NDL's Aufsichtsrat, Board. Also, from 1943, head of Melchers & Co., the Bremen firm that was NDL agents in the Far East.

Dr. Kulenkampff lives outside Bremen in Lesum. His house was saved. He himself lives in the gatekeepers home of the estate. **Herr Bertram** also had to leave his home. He lives near me on the Schwachhauser Ringstrasse 51. His wife and three children stayed in Bavaria during the war, returned after the debacle. Health wise both families are well, subject to the 1000 calories a day maximum here, in contrast to the 1250 allowed in the U.S. zone in South Germany. The nourishment question is the problem of the future for all Europe, not only Germany. And that of coal. If the forests continue to be cut and nature to be over-exploited, our entire climate will change. Then Germany will slowly turn into steppes. Recent British papers spelled it out: what Germany lacks is twofold: Nourishment and Hope. Both until now denied to us. But we hope when the determination to punish has somewhat subsided, we will be allowed some reason for hope and endeavor. The industrial policy is directed (Morgenthau Plan) to bring and keep Germany primitive. But we are supposed to pay our debts and the cost of the war and that of the occupation. Yet the means by which we could earn enough to repay are being denied with the willful destruction, or by the Russians of the removal, of our productive means. Everyone's standard of living will be even lower than now. It will take at least two generations to rebuild our cities. The benefits of those no longer able to work will have to be cut because the rest of us cannot produce enough to continue them at needed levels. The only thing flourishing in Germany is the black market and denunciation. Everyone who had a responsible position is suspect and attempts are being made to shoot him down.

"We have more than enough from the war and the Nazis in our generation. The western powers for us came as deliverers, so now they mean to let us simply verrecken, slang for "die like a dog." If so, the danger of Bolschewismus will become acute for Germany and therefore for all Europe." This parallels what happened after WWI in Germany with the Inflation. This still starkly determines Bundesbank financial policy and therefor, in effect, that of the entire European Union as the Mark is the strongest currency in that union. - See report of the Stettin and other shipyard Communist uprisings in March, 1921, "Especially England will suffer if this happens."

After every war the pressure among the victors is maximum punitive exactions of the defeated and hated enemy after twelve years of National Socialist rule and mass-murder, this was permanently kept an agricultural state. In Britain, the attitude based on its shipping industry, was that Germany must not again become an all out competitor just across the North Sea. Buildup to and two wars brought that lesson home. "Now, in May, 1946, a whole year after the war ended", continues Herr Karstedt "in Bremen we have a few bunker hotels and some four rooms in the former Hotel Columbus. Our largest shipyard, the Deschimag, is in large part already gone to Russia by ship; the rest will follow.

"Hapag has substantially more personnel than the Lloyd. The Hamburgers seem to have better connections to British and American shipping circles than the undemanding Bremers. We are less interested in being talked about than in trading." This paralleled 1920-1921, when Hapag got the jump on the Lloyd with its deal with the Harriman interests. This gave it immediate support for using its expertise to support U.S. shipping's entry into the North Atlantic. Hapag thus had a prime pier position in Manhattan when it again could send out ships."

Herr Karstedt, a truly caring individual for the personnel whose welfare he had in his charge, ends this fourteen-pages, single-spaced letter in May, 1946 to Captain Drechsel:

"Now that we are again permitted to have mail contact with overseas, I want to send you a sign of life and report concerning what will be most important to you:

"Our first word from you was the letter you sent with Captain Scharf on his return from the *Europa's* voyage to New York. I have passed along your comments and messages to the various people. Also, through Martin Schmidt to pass along to, and bring back information from your sister in Dresden. Presumably you are now in direct contact. In that Russian-occupied area the situation is very difficult: food, heating, and the removal of entire factories, rails, etc." Almost a repetition in 1993-94 when the Russian forces departing from the former DLR, East Germany, stripped their barracks of anything that might be usable at home: doors, windows, plumbing, electric cable, gutters. At one air base, even the concrete runway was cut up and shipped home. Nearly fifty years after the end of the war, the deprivation the Germans faced at home, the occupation Russians are struggling with, by bringing what they needed ... from Germany. The irony of history.

"So my Dear Captain Drechsel: I have spilled out what I have so much to heart. I trust this letter will find its way to you, and that it finds you and your dear ones in good health! Please give our greetings to all the old Lloyd friends and acquaintances, and to inform them of things that may of concern to them. My wife, too, send her regards. For her the voyage to the U.S. in the Spring of 1937 (after the Karstedt's wedding), remains unforgettable." Your devoted, (signature) Hans Karstedt. Herr Karstedt enclosed a photo of his wife Ilse, "with the smile she shows when there is Post from Amerika."

The gradual comeback of the Lloyd's and German shipping played out against these world events, and gradual easing of Allied controls and restrictions:

- In July, 1945 German coastal shipping was allowed between Emden and Lübeck, to support the gradual rebuilding of the railways. Individual-voyage approval was required!
- In Spring, 1946, traffic on the Rhine was released, and coal transport Emden-Hamburg-Schleswig.
- - In Mid-1946, per-voyage approval could be granted to the East, and from the North and Baltic Seas to adjacent foreign lands. Freight rates are quoted in $. Thus 1946 saw the beginning of relaxations that the Germans called "Der Weg In Die Freiheit," The road to Freedom. On 6 September, 1946 U.S. Secretary of State James Byrnes, with Senators Tom Connally, D., Texas, and Arthur Vandenberg, R., Illinois, sitting with him, enunciated U.S. policy toward a defeated Germany.
- 26 September, 1946 the Potsdam Declaration allowed the use of ships available if coal-fired, with not more than 12 knots speed, 2,000 miles range, and derricks not larger than three tons. "We can neither build, charter nor manage ships" a Lloyd official pointed out. Every German ship had to show an Allied Control Number beneath its name.
- Into 1947, mail coming into or leaving Germany still underwent censorship by the Occupying powers.
- The Marshall Plan, proposed by the General on 5 June, 1947, eventually poured $12 billions into Europe, including some help for German shipping.
- From 1 April, 1948 German shipping concerns again could deal directly in handling any foreign business. Allowed Voyages now could include Northern Europe. On 20, June, 1948 a Sunday the D Mark was issued, trucks spreading throughout West Germany to deliver the money to distributing banks. Every citizen was entitled for 60 Reichsmark

In June, 1948 nineteen former Lloyd Captains and former and still active, Lloyd officials met in Bremen. The Senior Captains are further described in the "Masters Next to God" chapter.

Front Row: **Waldemar Klose**, Director of the Deutsche-Amerika Linie which took over the money-losing part of the Hapag-Lloyd North Atlantic operation. He succeeded Heinz Schuengel who died in Bremen just before the war. In December, 1970 at age ninety he lived in the Verdener Strasse, per Captain G. Lomnitz, head of NDL's postwar Nautical Department, where on the same Street the author had last visited Dr. Arnold Rehm in 1985.

Captain **H. Kempff**. 1939 Chief Assistant to Captain Drechsel in New York. He got home via NYK's Asama Maru across the Pacific and by rail across Siberia. In 1945-1946 by OMGUS (U.S. Occupation forces) selection he assisted Captain Daehne in the reorganization of Bremerhaven, then Bremen's harbor facilities for U.S. use.

Captain **Oskar Scharf**. There is much of him elsewhere in this work. His son Wolfgang lives, 1994, in Bremerhaven. He died, fittingly fate would have it, on 24 September, 1953. It was 24 September, 1945 that he as advisory captain to the U.S. Navy again arrived in New York on the USS *Europa*.

Captain. **Adolf Ahrens**. Named third Commodore after bringing *Bremen* safely home from Murmansk in December, 1939.

Captain **Leopold Ziegenbein**, of *Bremen*, 1929, named Commodore after Captain Johnsen died in December, 1932.

John Schroeder. NDL, then Hapag-Lloyd North Atlantic Gemeinschaft General Passenger Manager, New York. He was active in the support organized in the States for the former shipping colleagues in Germany. Probably visiting for that reason.

Captain **H. von Thülen**, last of Berlin, son of a Lloyd captain, and still able to see *Gripsholm* come into service in 1954, and be named Berlin in January, 1955.

Roland Soltmann. Successor to Waldemar Klose as head of Deutsche-Amerika Linie. He lived in Oslo and Stockholm during the war.

Captain **Otto Prehn**. In a 1929 group photo on *Bremen's* bridge. 1934 Staff Captain when the Admiral Jellicoe Family visited the ship in Southampton. He organized the 350-ships fleet list in the NDL Centennial History, 1957.

Dr. Johannes Kulenkampff, from February, 1943 with Richard Betram co-director of the Lloyd into the 1970 merger with Hapag into Hapag-Lloyd A.G. His son is an attorney in Bremen, 1994. The Kulenkampffs go back to Lloyd founding in 1957.

Herr Meyer - part of the Deutsche-Amerika Linie.

> **G. Lange** - Also part of the Deutsche-Amerika Linie.
> Back row: **Herr Fuhrmann**.
> **Herr Stuenkel**. In 1946, as Finance Chief he signed documents until Messrs. Kulenkampff and Bertam could be legally confirmed in their co-director posts.
> **Schorse Richter**. Succeeded by Hans Karstedt as head of the Social Welfare Programs. His son worked with Captain Daehne in the port-rebuilding.
> **Hans Karstedt**. In 1925 already Prokurist (empowered to sign), longtime Social Welfare director. His fourteen single-spaced typed pages letter of May, 1946 to the author's father gave me much of the during the war and early postwar conditions. He died of sudden illness in his 72nd year in April, 1961.
> **Captain W. Daehne**. After return from U.S. POW camp he in 1945-1946 was chosen by OMGUS, the U.S. Occupation authority, to organize Bremerhaven, then Bremen port facilities for U.S. Occupatin forces use. He subsequently rebuilt the destroyed Bremer Lagerhaus (Warehouse) Gesellschaft.
> **Captain F. Krone**. Captain of *Berlin* after Herr von Thülen, also at the *Gripsholm* 1954 reopening of passenger service celebration.
> **Captain P.A. Petersen**. Former Staff Captain on *Bremen*, in 1952 Captain of *M.S. Gloria*, Glaessel Shipping's first vessel to Australia after the war, with Mrs. Petersen on board.
> **Missing: Richard Betram**, with **Dr. Kulenkampff** co-director of the Lloyd's fate 1943-1970. He began at the Lloyd in 1930; in 1936 became Prokurist, in 1937 joined the Vorstand, in 1943 became co-director. He stayed on through the 1970 Hapag-Lloyd merger as Vorstand spokesman until his retirement in July, 1972. He died in May, 1979. He had been born in Chile, part of that major German involvement in that nation which the author and wife Ilona visited and saw still active, German spoken in so many places, in 1987. Photo by **Leo Hannel**,

to receive 60 D Marks, forty at once, twenty after two months. Rents, salaries were to be continued on a Mark for Mark basis. Savers would get for every 10 Reichsmark 1 D-Mark as credit. Half could be paid at once; the rest was blocked. Of that blocked amount, later 70% was cancelled. In effect, the saver finally received for every 100 Reichsmark 6.00 D-Marks. Including the Drechsel savings deposited in Germany to help relatives and friends.
- In mid-1948 permission was granted to lift and rebuild sunken German ships not larger than 1,500 tons.
- End, 1948 permission to build new ships up to 1,500 tons.
- January, 1949 - The Mediterranean now could be travelled by German shipping.
- On 23 May, 1949 the Federal Republic of Germany was proclaimed. Germany again had a government, its authority prescribed, the three occupation powers dominant.
- Mid-1949: approval to raise and rebuild ships up to 2,700 tons.
- July, 1949: the last voyage restrictions were lifted. But ship-building controls remained very specific.
- On 15 September, 1949 Konrad Adenauer

Chancellor Konrad Adenauer at the White House, with former U.S. High Commissioner for Germany John McCloy, President Eisenhower, and Henry Kissinger. In Time Magazine, *20 April, 1953.*

became Bundeskanzler, Chancellor. That he was a staunch Roman Catholic, as was General Charles De Gaulle, made Franco-German Rapprochement easier. During a twelve-days visit to the U.S. in 1953 and talks with President Eisenhower they had "a full and frank exchange ... in a spirit of friendship and cooperation ..., a far-reaching identity of views and objectives." The Chancellor held that office into October, 1969, the key German to help bring his country a renewed measure of acceptance in the world.

- On 21 September, 1949 the three occupying powers restored German Civil Rights.
- 21 November, 1949: the building ceiling was raised by the Petersberg Agreement to 7,200 tons, 12 knots maximum speed. Germany could import up to 400,000 tons within those restrictions.
- In April-June, 1950 Bremen's Mayor Kaisen, with the city's representative in Bonn, Karl Carstens, later President of Germany, visited the U.S. to explain Germany's need for lifting of trade and other restrictions.
- Start of the Korean War in June, 1950 immediately changed U.S. outlook on the world. Japan was needed as a base and supply source for that war effort. In Europe, it speeded Germany's re-acceptance into the Western Alliance, and in 1955 membership in NATO, and as a counter-weight to the pressures of the USSR on Europe.
- On 23, February, 1951, Allied control Flag "C" was replaced with the new Bundes Flag: Black, Red and Gold.
- On 3 April, 1951 the Second Petersberg Agreement lifted all restrictions in shipping except some aimed at meeting the three Occupying Powers' own needs.
- On 2 July, 1951, the Occupying Powers and Germany resumed diplomatic relations.

Also in 1955, The Bundesrepublic joined NATO, becoming its largest member in number of military personnel available or committed. External circumstances thus brought Germany's rehabilitation within the Western Alliance.

On 4 May, 1955, the day the Lloyd flag and golden yellow smokestack again were worn by all vessels, at the dinner following the launch of *Tannstein* 498 Dr. Kulenkampff said "today we feel ourselves standing on the summit of a foothill" in our recovery from the devastation of war.

In the Lloyd's first post-war business report issued in July, 1955, covering the period from 21 June, 1948 through December, 1954, the Aufsichtsrat, Board of Directors, reported loss of 99.5% "of our actual resources to the war, the postwar cession of ships, and the Currency revaluation of 1948." There were few material things left to start with anew. But the spirit and determination of its people made Norddeutscher Lloyd Bremen a continuing enterprise. "Their (former crew members) sense of duty, experience, reliability and eager taking of responsibility is a considerable plus in the constant service readiness of our ships, in the careful handling of cargo and exact maintenance of schedules."

1950 word from prewar Hapag captain Thormöhlen on the New York run. In 1950, he was lucky to get a place as supercargo on one of the first German ships again to cross the Atlantic. He advised when the ship would be in New York so that the author's Father could come down to see him. The first time since pre-1939. Supercargo meant the Captain-ranked seaman was given a chance to get back to sea for his keep and probably a very nominal wage. But it kept him and other captains going until they, too, could get a ship.

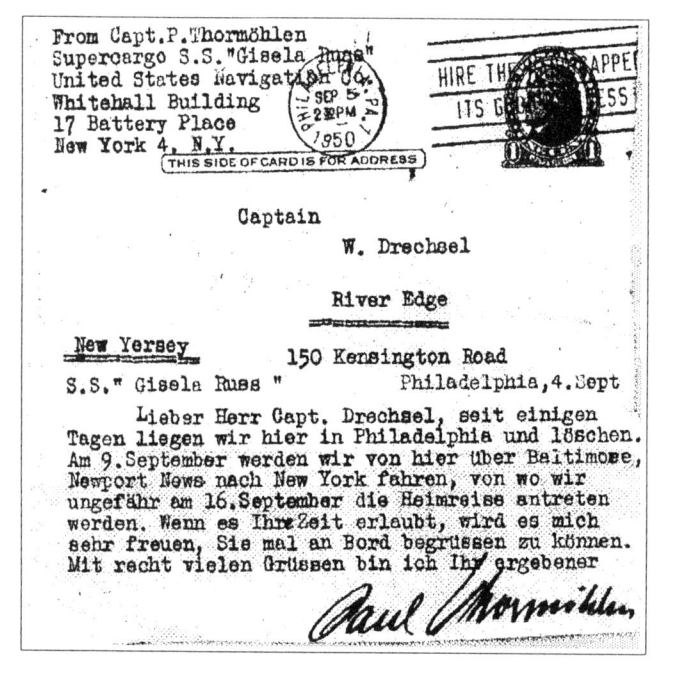

470 Norddeutscher Lloyd Bremen

NDL Fleet
Ships 472 — 489

The earliest postwar service for the Lloyd was, as in 1857 and again after World War I, a passenger service to the Friesian islands, this time to the island of Wangerooge, four hours from Bremerhaven, an always-popular resort, an escape. Into 1949 any overseas service or building of new vessels was forbidden to the Lloyd and all German shipping.

The first postwar venture abroad was with the *S.S. Hermod* chartered from the Frigga Seerederei. It was the former *Essex Envoy*, before that *Therese Horn* built in 1922. *Hermod* left Bremen on 22/2/1950 in ballast, reached Baltimore thirty days later. Then on to Norfolk and New York, leaving there on 30 March with 1,600 tons lard, 860 tons tobacco and 2,550 tons of grains. The biggest shortage foodwise in Germany was fats. Bremen was reached on 17 April. The later Captain G. Clausen of *M.S. Ravenstein* #495 was supercargo on this voyage, as other captains and officers had to be for lack of ships to let them keep their ranks. Ten years later he wrote a memorial poem which I have translated and put to verse:

>   It's only ten short years since the day
>   that we in *Hermod* got under way
>   I dare to take a backward look
>   To that great day we undertook
>   To once again build up a fleet
>   With which in time we would repeat
>   To serve the world for years ahead
>   And that allowing us to spread
>   Abroad the Lloyd's ships great and small.
>   Thus sends your *Ravenstein* Captain salutes to all.
>
>   Nachdem 10 Jahre heut' vergangen,
>   seit wir mit *Hermod* Angefangen, erlaub ich mir zu diesem Tag,
>   an dem man wohl mal rückschaun mag,
>   zu Ihres Werkes gut Gelingen
>   der Flotte Glückwunsch darzubringen,
>   erhoffend, dass noch lange Zeit
>   Ihr Können uns erhalten bleibt.
>   Für alle Schiffe gross and klein
>   spricht der Kapitaen der *Ravenstein*
>
>   - Captain G. Clausen 1950 Supercargo on *Hermod*
>   on the 10th anniversary of that voyage.

NDL's first post-war voyage was the charter of Frigga Seerederei's Hermod, *bought from Britain named* Essex Envoy. *She was built as* Therese Horn *in 1922. The voyage lasted fifty-five days, from Bremen in ballast to Baltimore, Norfolk and New York, back with 4800 tons of precious cargo: grains, fats, even tobacco.*

Below: Then the Hansa's Argenfels, *sister of NDL's* Göttingen *#460, was chartered after complete rebuilding. In the meantime, six basic-type 2700 tons freighters were ordered, fortunately not so soon that they could not be completed as 14.5 knotters rather than 12 knotters, the then-Allied-allowed limit.*

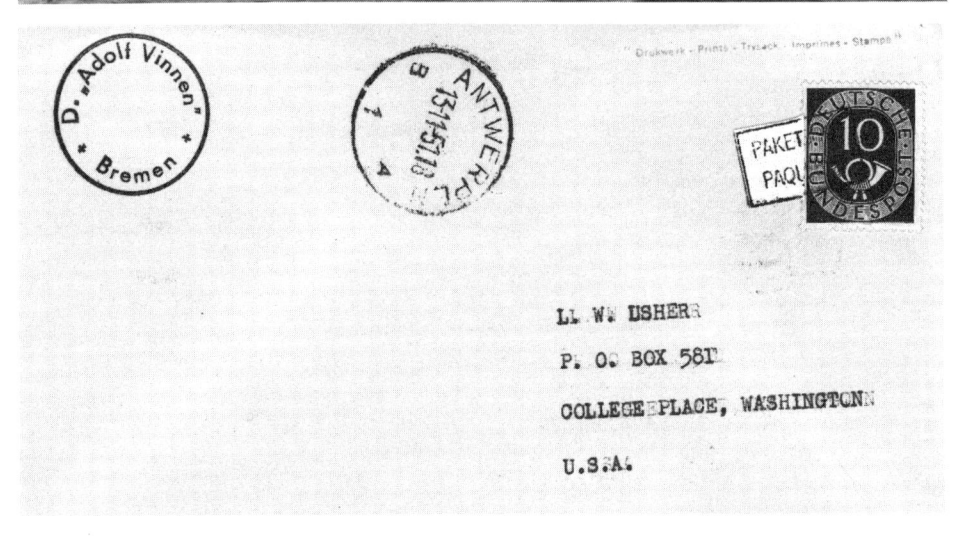

Mail posted on the Adolf Vinnen, *chartered from the F. Vinnen & Co., Bremen concern. This was NDL's* Porta *#287 of 1922, postwar the Dutch* Walcheren, *bought back and rebuilt, in 1955 bought by the Lloyd and renamed* Trierstein. *The* **Paketboot/Paquebot** *explains acceptance of German-stamped mail being handled at Antwerp for onward dispatch under Universal Postal Union rules for Mail Posted on the High Seas.*

Other charter ships followed: *Adolf Vinnen*, ex NDL's *Porta* of 1922, which was bought back as *Trierstein* in 1955, and *Argenfels* a sister of NDL's *Wangerooge* #461 of the Deutsche Dampfschiffharts Ges. Hansa of Bremen, after the Lloyd Bremen's biggest shipping concern, a subsequent victim of the 1970s "oil schock" as its main trading field was the Persian Gulf. Only with the Petersberg Agreement in 1949 under Chancellor Konrad Adenauer was a resumption of overseas shipping and shipbuilding allowed under strict limitations. Freighters, e.g., could as after World War I not exceed 12 knots. The first new group of ships, the *Rheinstein* class, was designed and ordered as 2400 Hp, 12 knot vessels with the same hull form as *Hunte* #467, the lengthened *Eider* #444 type.

Fortunately, restrictions were lifted just in time so the ships could be built with 3900 Hp Diesels for 14.5 knots. Very handy small vessels for a startup on several routes. Hapag ordered earlier than the Lloyd; its first two new ships were limited to 12 knots. In 1951 when these ships entered service it was a new world for the Lloyd. When Captain W. Schott in *Rheinstein* in July, 1954 for the first time again came to the West Coast, he ordered his crew to prepare the cargo tackle for unloading, as was customary prewar, including opening the hatches. On arrival in Los Angeles the representative of the stevedoring firm told him the ship would not be unloaded unless all these preparations were undone. The stevedores discussed walking off the dock. It was agreed that the crew would again prepare the ship for sea, cover the hatches, stow and fasten the derricks and tackle. This took 2½ hours. Then the stevedores came on board and prepared the ship for unloading. Later, when some crew members were overboard knocking rust, one stevedore said they would all leave the ship unless this infernal noise ceased immediately. So the rust scraping had to stop.

With the exception of *Nabob* #480 and passenger vessels, all ships were given ....*Stein* Names, names of castles, such as *Bartenstein* in East Prussia and *Ravenstein* in Holland. The joke was that one of the ships mistakenly might be named *Gallenstein*.

For legal reasons and fears that ships might be attached or laid up over unresolved claims in Germany or abroad, the Lloyd used the colors and flags of the Roland Linie, acquired by NDL in 1926, and the *Orlanda* Reederei, a telegraph address of the former Rhederei A.G. von *1896*, #401, once owned by NDL, and to charter them. They all carried the ochre stacks with black tops. In 1955, the Bank Deutscher Länder assumed the surety for any residual obligations, and on 4/5/1955 the Roland and Orlanda flags were replaced with the Lloyd's crossed-anchor-and-key flag. The stacks were again painted a dark yellow as prewar. The Roland Linie remained as a paper entity, in 1970 again became active 50-50 with Unterweser Reederei as bulk carriers. See "Marriage..." A later Orlanda Reederei had no Lloyd or Hapag-Lloyd connection.

In 1955, the Lloyd reappeared legally as the sole owner of its fleet. But already on some routes joint services were being offered with the Hamburg-Amerika Linie, Hapag, as had been done on the North Atlantic during the 1930s. These joint services were formalized when from 1/9/1970 the two companies merged as Hapag-Lloyd A.G.

All the following vessels were Diesel-driven unless marked otherwise. Most were built at the Bremer Vulkan, Vegesack below Bremen, which became the Lloyd's House Yard. The six *Rheinstein* vessels had spaces enclosed that raised their tonnages later by some 100 tons.

Rheinstein #472 *gave her name to the class of six ships ordered in 1950 while Allied restrictions still limited new vessels to 12 knots. The limit was lifted in time to change to bigger Diesels for 14.5 knots. General-purpose vessels well adapted to reopening prewar routes.* Rheinstein *was the first German ship to reach Los Angeles harbor on 1 July, 1954. It had one two-bed cabin for passengers. All postwar NDL ships received names of castles ending in ...*Stein, *except ex-Escort Carrier* Nabob *and the three passenger ships:* Berlin, Bremen *and* Europa.

#472. Rheinstein   1951-1971
Bremen Vulkan #809, Vegesack 1951   2693   119.60x15.30
M.A.N. Diesel   4200   14.5
3   31

Launched 3/2/1951. Delivery 15/3/1951 to Roland Linie Schiffahrts Ges. First new-built Lloyd ship postwar. Eighty percent welded, as was the entire class. 1/9/1970 to Hapag-Lloyd A.G., 2790 tons, Burghard Heye, NDL's first postwar high-seas captain. 5/8/1971 LU in Hamburg. 9/1971 to Mayo Shipping Co., Monrovia, 12/1971 resold to Nelson Seeschiffahrtsagentur & Reederei Ges., Vienna, renamed *Donautal,* along with *Saarstein* #474 and *Emsstein* #476. 1974 to Friedrich Glatz, Vienna as owner, D. Wardel & Co., Singapore, managers. 1980 to Laurgain Towage Co., Panama, renamed *Laurgain Express.* 14/10/1980 arrived Kaohsiung for BU.

473. Lahnstein   1951-1972
Bremer Vulkan, Vegesack #810   1951   2693   119.60x15.30
M.A.N. Diesel   4200   14.5
2   31

Launched 3/3/1951. Delivery 17/4/1951. 4/1959 in Hapag-Lloyd-Ernst Russ service to the Great Lakes along with *Rheinstein.* 1/9/1970 to Hapag-Lloyd A.G. Left Hamburg 1/4/1959, heavy fog from Borkum to The Lizard, avoided ice en route, got into thick ice near Cape Ray. Changed pilots at Trois Rivieres and Quebec, tied up at Trois Rivieres; no stevedores so tourists fastened the lines. Next day continued upstream through heavy ice. Due to crowding all ships awaiting opening of the St. Lawrence Seaway ordered to anchor 30 miles above Montreal. *Lahnstein* with needed

Lahnstein #473 is shown with the Black-topped Roland Linie stacks. NDL avoided the possibility of seizure of its ships because of uncertainties re prewar or wartime liabilities by registering them under Roland Linie or Orlanda Schiffahrts Gesellschaft, and chartering the ships from them, into 1955 when the Lloyd flag and smokestacks returned. Lahnstein here in Hamburg. The burned-out warehouses behind can be seen, so probably 1951-1952.

Before vehicle-carrier "garages" were built, freighters carried cars inside, some times on deck. Lahnstein brought to a Great Lakes port a cargo of Opel cars made by General Motors' German subsidiary.

engine repairs was allowed to tie up. Of 13 ocean ships arriving Montreal by 16-17 April, only *Lahnstein* arrived without ice damage. In July, 1960 *Lahnstein* and *Rheinstein* were detained by U.S. Customs at Cleveland during smuggling attempts. 1/9/1970 to Hapag-Lloyd A.G. 9/1971 to Konrad Shipping Co., Panama, renamed *Konrad*. 1973 *Clarkia*. 1974 *Victoria*, One-Star Shipping Co., S.A., Panama. 7/7/1977 *Victoria S.*, Cia. Nav. Transvictor S.A., Panama, Mediterranean Shipping Co., Panama, Swiss owners. 14/4/1980 *BU* began at La Spezia.

474. *Saarstein*	1951-1971		
Bremer Vulkan, Vegesack #811	1951	2693	119.60x15.30
M.A.N. Diesel	4200	14.5	
2	31		

Launched 31/3/1951. Delivery 17/5/1951. On 4/5/1955 first ship to arrive from the high seas at Bremen with the yellow instead of ochre and black stack of the Roland Linie, and under the Anchor and Key Lloyd flag. See #498. 1/9/1970 to *Hapag-Lloyd A.G.* 4/8/1971 *LU* in Hamburg. 9/1971 to Mayo Shipping Co., Monrovia. 12/1971 resold to Nelson's Seeschiffahrts Agentur, Vienna, renamed *Drautal*. 28/2/1972 due to rudder failure stranded off St. Malo en route from Sfax, towed in. 10/5/1972 arrived Hamburg for *BU* by Eisen & Metall.

Saarstein #474 ready for launching on 31.3.1951 at the Bremen Vulkan yard. The air view shows the attraction of this small-size freighter: five hatches, not four.

Innstein #475. *The six ships of the class were built almost at assembly-line speed. The first launch was March 15, 1951, the sixth July 14th.* Innstein *served for 29 years sans major mishap.*

475. ***Innstein***		1951-1971		
Bremer Vulkan, Vegesack #812	1951		2693	119.60x15.30
M.A.N. Diesel		4200	14.5	
2		31		

Launched 8/5/1951. Delivery 16/6/1951. 13/10/1959 on leaving Hamburg for Guatemala collided with oil barge *Opeter* which sank while being beached. 1/9/1970 to Hapag-Lloyd A.G. 6/1971 to Ship Investment Co., Panama, ren. *Siccarabic*. 3/1973 with bankruptcy of its owner, tied up in Bordeaux in 3/1973. 1974 to Cominco S.A., Panama, ren. *Mato*. 1975 Libertas, Xeriantes Shipping Co., Panama. 1977 *Cloud,* Innstein Shipping Co., Panama. 1978 *Shenton*, Holstein Shipping Co., Singapore. 1979 *St. Anna,* 4,953 Ts., Skorpios Maritime, S.A., Singapore. 22/5/1980 *BU* began at Kaohsiung.

476. ***Emsstein***		1951-1971		
Bremer Vulkan, Vegesack #813	1951		2699	119.60x15.30
M.A.N. Diesel		4200	14.5	
2		31		

Launched 16/61951. Delivery 15/7/1951. 6/10/1966 beached in St. Clair River, Detroit after collision with Liberian *Olympic Pearl* en route Antwerp-Chicago. Heeled over onto side with 27° list in shallow water. 28/10/1966 refloated, locally, then at Lauzon repaired for return to Bremen for major repairs. 1/9/1970 to Hapag-Lloyd A.G. 9/1971 to Mayo Shipping Co., Monrovia. 12/1971 to Nelson's Seechiffahrts Agentur, Vienna, renamed *Murtal*. 1972 *Murjo*, Imperatur Enterprises, Mogadisciu. 1976 *Violetta,* Bayswater Shipping Co., Monrovia. 7/1978 to Universal Trades & Carriers, Singapore, resold to Alyas Investment Co. for *BU* at Gadani Beach, 66 kms W. of Karachi. Work began 19.4.1980.

Gadani Beach is typical of the low-labor-cost breakup operations that in the 1970s ended Japan's near-monopoly in scrapping. The cut-up steel is hauled to Karachi's steel mills by trucks. The ships are run up onto the beach at high tide, so sizes tend to be smaller. Each ship usually is broken up by a separate "company" formed for that work. Hulls are acetyline-torched down to the waterline over a period of months. Also *BU* at Gadani Beach were *Ravenstein* #495, *Bischofstein* #502, *Breitenstein* #501 and *Lechstein* #508.

```
           (FREIGHTERS)
     ST. CLAIR, MICH.--COAST GUARD BOATS TODAY PUMPED WATER ON THE
SMOULDERING HULK OF A GERMAN FREIGHTER, VICTIM OF AN ODD MID-RIVER
COLLISION WHICH THREATENED THE LIVES OF 19 MEN.
     THE 392-FOOT EMSSTEIN, ITS PORT SIDE SHEARED AWAY FROM THE BOW
TO MIDSHIPS, LISTED ON THE MUDDY BOTTOM OF THE ST. CLAIR RIVER.  ONLY
THE RIVER BOTTOM KEPT IT FROM CAPSIZING AS FLAMES AND SMOKE BILLOWED
FROM ITS HOLD AND STARBOARD SIDE.
     ITS 19 CREWMEN, PLUCKED FROM THE FLAMING DECK IN A RAPID U.S-
CANADIAN RESCUE OPERATION, RESTED AT SARNIA, ONT., ACROSS THE RIVER
FROM ST. CLAIR.  THERE WERE NO INJURIES.
     THE OLYMPIC PEARL, A LIBERIAN BULK CARRIER, MEANTIME STEAMED
FOR MONTREAL WITH A LOAD OF GRAIN.  THE 576-FOOT PEARL COLLIDED
HEAD-ON WITH THE EMSSTEIN LAST NIGHT BUT THE LIBERIAN VESSEL SUFFERED
ONLY SLIGHT BOW DAMAGE AND THE COAST GUARD GAVE IT CLEARANCE TO
CONTINUE ITS VOYAGE.
     THE COAST GUARD SAID THERE WAS NO APPARENT EXPLANATION FOR THE
COLLISION.
      10/7--3F38  1966
```

A near thing with Emsstein *off Detroit. The* United Press *report as it went out over the wire and carried by the* San Francisco Examiner.

Below: Emsstein *#476 with NDL tug* Sirius, *one of six leased, then bought from OMGUS, the U.S. umbrella for government activities in Germany. See Small-craft fleet list.* Emsstein *was a major casualty outside Detroit in October, 1966. "Only (settling on) the river bottom kept it from capsizing."* United Press *reported.*

Page 2—S.F.Examiner ★★★ Fri., Oct. 7, 1966

St. Lawrence Seaway Ships Crash, 19 Safe

ST. CLAIR (Mich.) — (AP) —. Nineteen crewmen were rescued from a burning West German freighter last night after it collided with a Panamanian ship in the St. Clair River near Lake Huron.

The Coast Guard plucked the men from the 393-foot Emsstein as flames spread over a fifth of the vessel and it listed sharply to port. Nobody was injured.

The Emsstein, out of Bremen, collided nearly head-on with the 576-foot Olympic Pearl owned by Falmouth Marine of Panama.

A 100-foot gash was ripped along the port side of the Emsstein, just offshore from St. Clair in southeastern Michigan.

The Emsstein's port bow was ripped "all the way back. It was cut wide open," said State Police Trooper Jack V. Trombly.

Coast Guard fireboats controlled the fire hours later.

The Olympic Pearl suffered a gash more than 25 feet along her port bow, but the damage was high above the water line.

The ship proceeded downriver, en route to Montreal.

478 *Norddeutscher Lloyd Bremen*

Ruhrstein #477 in San Francisco ca 1955. Traded to the U.S.-Canada West Coast, up the Amazon, to the Gulf states. In October, 1966 incoming from Philadelphia in fog it collided with a Greek ship off Texel Light Ship. Ruhrstein *burned out, was later put ashore, and sold off for scrap.* Author's Photo.

477. *Ruhrstein* 1951-1970
Bremer Vulkan, Vegesack #814 1951 2697 119.60x15.30
M.A.N. Diesel 4200 14.5
2 31

Launched 14/7/1951. Delivery 16/8/1951. 1960 traded up the Amazon. 5/10/1969 en route Philadelphia-Hamburg after collision in fog near the Texel Lightship with the Greek *Martha*. The crew left; the ship burned out, later was put ashore off Den Helder. 7/10/1969 towed to Bremerhaven. 11/1969 sold to Eisen & Metall, Hamburg for *BU*.

478. *Lichtenstein* 1951-1968
Bremen Vulkan, Vegesack #806 1951 2353 105.10x14.23
M.A.N. Diesel 3900 16
12 36

Launched 28/8/1951. Delivery 6/10/1951. 15/11/1951 chartered to Yeoward Line for its Liverpool-Canaries Islands. Built for NDL's reefer service with the Canaries and North Brazil, with sister *Liebenstein*. 22/3/1928 *Don Camilo,* Universal Shipping Lines, Carlos A. G. Thong & Co., Cebu. 1973 to Sulpicio Lines, Managers. 25/11/1975 stranded at entrance to Cebu. 1/12/1975 refloated. 1977 sold by insurers to Universal Shipping Lines, evidently for rebuilding. Never carried out. 1988 BU in Manila.

Lichtenstein *#478 and* Liebenstein *#479 were 16-knots reefers, right after the six* Rheinstein-*class ships. The Atlantic Islands route for fruits and vegetables were a long-standing Lloyd service;* Orotava *and* Arucas *in 1927 were earlier specialty ships for this trade. Also, ideal vacation cruise vessels. Both ships later went to the Philippines where the ship stranded in 1973. Never rebuilt.* Lichtenstein *unloading bananas at Bremen.*

Liebenstein *#479 en route to the Amazon. Two large dump trucks on deck forward.* Hapag-Lloyd A.G.

479. **Liebenstein** 1951-1968
Bremer Vulkan, Vegesack #807   1951   2353   105.10x14.23
M.A.N. Diesel   3900   16
12   33

Launched 27/9/1951 for Canaries-North Brazil reefer trades. Delivery 13/11/1951. 16/12/1951 left Nordenham in ballast for Gandia, Spain to load 30,000 boxes of oranges. Due to the storm that sank the *Flying Enterprise* it did not arrive until 1/1/1951. 1968 *Don Lorenzo,* Go Thong Lines, Cebu. 1977 *Doña Julieta,* Universal Shipping Lines, Cebu. 30/6/1977 burned out in Manila, settled on bottom. *LU* "as is" at Cebu. 1978 repurchased from insurers by Sulpicio Lines (Go Thong) for planned rebuilding, not carried out. Sulpicio Lines had a disastrous record with inter-island ship accidents, in 1987-1988 lost more than 1000 persons on two accidents. It carried 20% of the inter-island traffic. 6/1984 sold to L.Acuario Marketing Co., Caloocan for *BU*.

The combination of treacherous waters, heavy inter-island traffic, inadequate navigation lights, buoys, etc., poorly-trained personnel and poor maintenance of vessels has made Philippine waters the most dangerous in terms of lost lives. The sinking of *Doña Paz* in 1987 with the loss of 3,132 persons was the worst peacetime shipping disaster.

480. *Nabob* 1951-1967
Seattle-Tacoma S. Bldg. Co., Tacoma #36
                          1943   7907   152.19x21.22
Turbine   6800   16
8   62

Launched 27/9/1943 as U.S. Navy Escort Carrier *Edisto*, CVE-41. 1/11/1943 Lend-leased to Britain, converted to Royal Navy needs at Esquimalt, British Columbia, Jan. 1944 commissioned as *Nabob* with a Canadian crew. In August, 1944 escort-carrier *HMS Nabob* and other British war ships lay off the Altenfjord. They sent out aircraft to bombard and hopefully sink the *Bismarck*. After *Nabob* was torpedoed by *U-354* (and also an aerial torpedo?) 130 m. W. of Tromsö, the escort-carrier group withdrew. The torpedo exploded aft, shot one man from the engine room through a ventilation shaft and out the smokestack. He survived this incredible experience. When *Nabob* began slowly to sink, one of its aircraft, still loaded with its magnetic torpedo, returned. For fear of dropping the torpedo and possibly having it sink one of his own ships, the pilot managed to land on *Nabob's* sloping deck; the after part already partly under water. The crew managed to keep *Nabob* afloat and bring it into Scapa Flow in the Orkneys. Nabob was so heavily damaged that it was not considered worth trying to repair so late in the war. It lay there until 17/9/1947 when it was towed for BU by Justen & Skein at Hendrik Ibo-Ambacht. Instead, the flight deck was stripped off, the ship offered "as is." In 1951, bought by Roland Linie. 10/1951 towed to A.G. Weser, Bremen for rebuilding and re-engining. 15/6/1952 del. to NDL, FV. to Canada with 18 cadets. On return voyage stranded 4-8/7/1952 near Montreal. Also ran in East and West Coast services under Captain "Kax" Kuhlig. 9/11/1967 to Chi Shihi Nav. Corp., Panama as *Glory*. 6/12/1977 arr. Kaohsiung for *BU*.

Loading BMW Isettas at Bremen on Nabob *for the U.S.* Hapag-Lloyd Photo.

Old, New Crews of Multi-Lived Ship Meet

VANCOUVER, B. C. — When the North German Lloyd cargo vessel Nabob called at Vancouver B.C. recently, a pact of comradeship of the sea was sealed between old and new crew members of the ship. The Nabob was formerly the HMS Nabob, a baby flat-top, which was torpedoed by a German submarine in European waters during the war. Miraculously surviving the vessel was so badly damaged that she was condemned. She was later sold for scrap and then in a last minute decision it was decided to completely rebuild her. The Germans, contrary to custom, have maintained the original name, perhaps because she is such a stout-hearted ship. (See story Nov. 17 issue.) From left to right: Capt. Glen McDonald, Vancouver B.C., navigation officer on the wartime Nabob, Capt. Carl Kuhlig, master of the present Nabob, NLG cadet Tammo Logemann and Rev. William Hill, from Victoria who was chaplain aboard the ship during the war years.

Nabob #480 was NDL's only non-Stein-named freighter to honor its past. Built as Escort Carrier on a C-3 hull in Tacoma in 1943, it went Canadian. In August, 1944 without Royal Navy vessels it was near the Altenfjord where Bismarck was hidden. Hit by a torpedo, its crew managed to keep it afloat and get it to Scapa Flow. So heavily damaged, it was not worth repairing. Postwar it was towed to Holland for scrapping, but lay there into 1951 when NDL bought it for rebuilding at Bremen. The first voyage was to Canada, with cadets, future officers, on board, also back to the West Coast under Captain Kax Kuhlig. See "A Young Again Centenarian." Below - Nabob as Escort Carrier and Above: Captain Kuhlig, a Cadet and Welcomers at Vancouver.

Norddeutscher Lloyd Bremen

In September, 1951 an old ship in new guise came back into Lloyd service: Alda *#337, later* Eisenach, *during the war damaged at Puntarenas, Costa Rica, rebuilt as* Ultramarino, *towed to Germany, and rebuilt again as* Traunstein. *As so many other times: reliance on an old German-built ship to rebuild and start anew with.*

Traunstein, ex-*Eisenach* #291, in 9/1951 back into the Lloyd fleet, as rebuilt prewar with bigger engines, higher speed, cruiser bow and stern, which was used for crews instead of forward housing (dangerous in collisions), gave more cargo space and better riding for the ship in a following sea.

481. *Brandenstein*	1952-1972		
Bremer Vulkan, Vegesack #822	1952	5567	151.80x18.04
M.A.N. Diesel	7800	16.5	
5	40		

Launched 20/10/1952. Delivery 29/11/1952 for Central and West Coast South America routes. MV. 27/11/1952 to U.S. East Coast. 3/1963 re-engined to 18 knots. 1/9/1970 to Hapag-Lloyd A.G. 6/6/1972 to Ignazio Messina & Co., Genoa, with *Bieberstein,* ren. *Fernandaemme,* 5,723 tons. 13/1/1981 BU began at La Spezia by C.N. Santa Maria.

Brandenstein *#481 was the first of three new and eventual nine "B" named ships, each building group providing for heavier lift gear. Two others became sisters when their initial engines were upgraded. Eleven like ships, usable basically trans-Atlantic, and to the West Coast. In 1962-1963 their engines were upgraded from 16.5 knots to 18. Room for five passengers in three cabins plus, later a "hospital cabin" for two. Was it ever sold? What happened if it was needed as "hospital?"* Brandenstein *#481 in the Howaldtswerke floating dock at Hamburg in 1959. To the left the bow of the white Hamburg-Süd's* Cap Roca.

Biebertein in San Francisco in October, 1955. Note the clutter on the deck which made it difficult to carry even a few containers when the transition to that system began. The "B" ships had the new MacGregor accordion-type hatch covers. Author's photo.

Below:Biebersten #482 under the Lion's Gate Bridge, leaving Vancouver for Puget Sound, down to the Canal and home, a long schedule. Some of the ships took on a deck cargo of lumber at Coos Bay.

482. ***Bieberstein***　　　　　　　1953-1972
Bremer Vulkan, Vegesack #824　1953　　5,546　　152.14x18.04
M.A.N. Diesel　　　　　　　　7800　　16.5
5　　　　　　　　　　　　　41

    Launched 15/1/1953. Delivery 19/2/1953 to Orlanda Reederei. 11/1962 engine rebuilt to 18 knots. 1/9/1970 to Hapag-Lloyd A.G. 31/5/1972 to Ignazio Messina & Co., Genoa, renamed *Robertoemme*. 5/3/1980 arrived La Spezia for *BU*.

483. *Bärenstein*	1953-1971		
	5547		152.14x18.04
M.A.N. Diesel	7800	16.5	
5	42		

Launched 15/4/1953. Delivery 27/6/1953 to Orlanda Reederei for West Coast Central-South America routes. Jan. 1959 on voyage Cristobal-Rotterdam fish meal in Hatch 4 burned. In Rotterdam the hatch was flooded to extinguish the flames. 12/1962 engine rebuilt to 18 knots. 1/9/1970 to Hapag-Lloyd A.G. 23/8/1971 - 22/1/1972 ran as *Pratita* for P.T. Perusahaan Pelajaran Samudera but under Hapag-Lloyd management and German flag. 7/1972 to Ignazio Messina & Co., Genoa, ren. *Ignazioemme,* 5,665 tons. 24/7/1980 *BU* began at C.N. Santa Maria, La Spezia.

Bärenstein *#483, registered for Orlanda Reederei into 1955 when the Lloyd flag and stack appeared on all ships again.*

For their joint Express Freighter service to the Far East, occasionally on other routes, the Lloyd and Hapag ordered 17 knots turbine vessels: NDL seven, Hapag nine. The seven Lloyd ships 1963-1964 were re-engined to Diesel with 14 400 HP, 6-7 meters longer with bow bulbs, now 19.5 knots. On 9/7/1953 *Weserstein* reopened this service after 14 years out of this trade: Hamburg-Bremen-Continent to Colombo-Penang-Port Swettenham-Singapore, Hong Kong, Manila, Kobe and Yokohama. The round voyage took almost four months, hence the need for so many vessels to keep a weekly service.

Ships of one class, like the *Weserstein* seven, built by different shipyards, usually are distinguishable: *Werrastein* #485, *Havelstein* #492 and *Isarstein* #493 had two high King Posts in front of the Bridge structure very near the windows. *Neckarstein* #486 and *Moselstein* #487 had low King Posts built into the bridge structure. *Weserstein* #484 and *Travestein* #490 had the king posts built half into the front of the bridge structure.

Weserstein was the first of an eventual eleven NDL ships the Chinese People's Republic bought, also #485 - 486 - 490 - 492 - 498 - 499 - 506 - 507 - 512 and 513, part of a large fleet bought as shift to containers made old tonnage cheap. Ownership was disguised through registration in friendly countries: Cyprus, Somaliland, Panama, Hong Kong, Macao. The ships at times for long did not appear on shipping lanes, hence were not reported in Lloyd's Shipping Indexes or lists. They were difficult to keep track of.

AG 'WESER'

modernisierte die NDL-Frachter „Werrastein", „Havelstein" und „Isarstein"

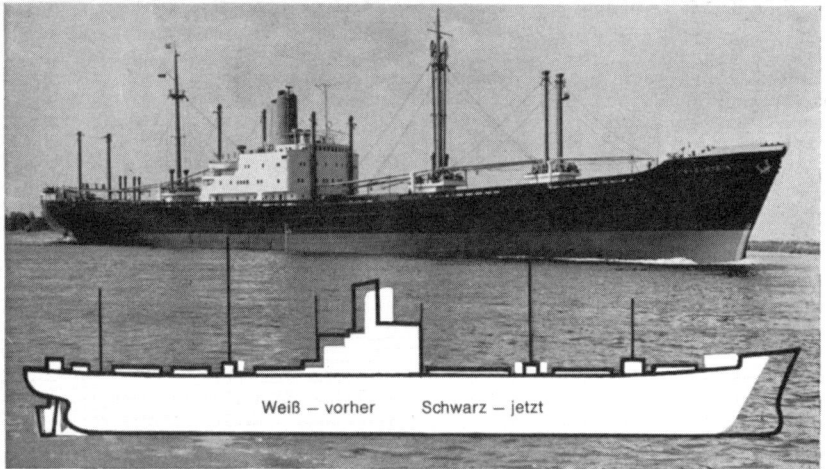

Die Linienfrachter wurden von Dampfturbinenbetrieb auf Dieselbetrieb umgestellt. Durch Verlängerung des Vorschiffs und Einbau eines Wulstbugs, Veränderung des Hintersteven bei Einbau eines zum Patent angemeldeten AG 'Weser'-Heckwulstes und Wahl des passenden Dieselmotors konnte die von der Reederei gestellte Forderung nach der optimalen Lösung erfüllt werden.

Aus ehemaligen 17-Knoten-Schiffen sind moderne Schnellfrachter mit 20 Knoten Dienstgeschwindigkeit geworden.

AG 'WESER'   WERFT BREMEN | SEEBECKWERFT BREMERHAVEN

Sixteen turbine 17.5 knots freighters were built for the Lloyd and Hapag for their return to the East Asia route. They are distinguishable according to who built them. NDL's Weserstein #484 was the first to sail in July, 1953. Shown is the A.G. Weser advertisement for rebuilding three of the vessels: in 1964. Photo of Weserstein 484 and the after silhouette -black- imposed on the before -white. The ships were given both a bulbous bow, proved out originally on American vessels and a stern bulb to smooth the flow around the propeller and rudder. These had been built into the last of NDL's pre-1914 Express Liners. From Seekiste, December, 1964.

Right: *The important telephone connections in October, 1953. On the reverse seven different freight groups plus "Towing". Note Wine Cellar under "night Numbers," Stauerei-Stevedoring. Hafen-Harbor. Reise-Travel and Remner Bierstuben, Beer Parlor, after-hours talk-time?*

Die Lloyd-Zentrale ist zu erreichen über	**0**
Fernschreiber	293
Direkte Anschl. Lloyd Hotel	
Büro	397
Empfang	391
Enchelmaier	395
Grögor, Frl.	390
Hofferberth, Frau	396
Handwerker	382
Restaurant	394
Direkte Anschl. fremd. Firmen	
Gebr. Specht	370
Herm. Dauelsberg	371
Direkte Leitung Bremerhaven	
zu erreichen über	0
Stauerei (Überseehafen) Geschirrlager (Tag u. Nacht besetzt)	258
Nachtschaltungen	
Dir. Dr. Kulenkampff	8 20 07
Dir. Bertram	8 23 36
Dir. Karstedt	8 31 37
Dir. Path	8 33 06
Prok. Wefing	8 22 92
Prok. v. Uslar	8 07 50
Hafen-Inspektion	8 21 86
Hafen-Werkstatt	8 34 01
Weinkeller	8 32 10
Hauptanschlüsse	
Hapag-Lloyd Reisebüro Zentrale	8 30 09
Hapag-Lloyd Reisebüro Verkehrspavillon	2 24 28
	2 65 85
Staackmann	2 69 06
Hapag-Lloyd Reisebüro Hauptbahnhof	2 69 12
Café Hillmann	2 39 16 / 17
Lloyd-Hotel	8 41 91
Remmer Bierstuben	2 78 25
NDL-Stauerei	8 50 82
O. C. C., Überseehafen	8 32 97
Überseeheim	
Schwarzer Weg	7 04 22
Flughafen	5 04 09
Camp Lesum	7 57 28
	7 56 58
Vahr	4 23 15
	4 79 24

484. *Weserstein 2*	1953-1973		
Lübecker Flenderwerke #433	1953	6795	160.15x19.27
Siemens Turbine	17.5		
9	45		

Launched 31/3/1953. Delivery 1/7/1953 to Orlanda Reederei. *MV.* to Far East. In January, 1959 *Weserstein* and tanker *Fina America* ran onto a sandbank in the Schelde River trying to avoid an outgoing French freighter. *Weserstein* got stuck in the middle, the hull bent, forcing major repairs once the for and aft hatches had been lightened and the ship got off. 27/6/1964 arrived Bremer Vulkan, Vegesack for conversion to Diesels: 14,400 HP, 19.5 kns., 167.42 m. with bulbous bow, 6,903 Ts. 1/9/1970 to Hapag-Lloyd A.G. 13/2/1973 to Ocean Tramping Co., Beijing owned, reg. in Mogadisciu, ren. *Nantao*. 30/5/1975 Nan Yang Shipping Co., Macao. 1977 to Golden City Maritime Co., Panama, 6,660 Ts. 3/2/1985 to China National Minerals & Metals Import & Export Co., 15/2/1985 arr. at Whangpoa, Shanghai for *BU*. Of the seven ships in this class, five were bought by China on the second-hand market. Many did not remain in Lloyd's Register although still in service, or LU awaiting service or BU.

Weserstein after her conversion, with her six sisters, from turbine to Diesel drive, with a bulbous bow extension, and speed increased to 19.5 knots from 17.5 knots. The quick way to remain competitive to East Asia.

485. **Werrastein**	1953-1973		
Deutsche Werft,			
Hamburg-Finkenwerder #651	1953	6737	159.15x19.16
AEG Turbine	9000	17.5	
9	45		

Launched 29/4/1953. Delivery 16/7/1953 to Orlanda Reederei. 1/8/1953 arr. in New York on M.V. 28/11/1963 arr. A.G. Weser, Bremen for re-engining with M.A.N. Diesel, 14 400 HP, 19.5 kns, 166.26 m with bulbous bow, 6,905 ts., given heavier-lift derricks, superstructure enlarged. 1/9/1970 to Hapag-Lloyd A.G. 19/3/1973 to Nan Yang Shipping Co., Macao, Operator High Seas Nav. Co., Panama, ren. *Nancheng,* 6,880 Ts. 1984 ran Hong Kong-Shanghai-Korea. 20/1/1985 L.Kokura, arr. Xingang ca. 1. February for BU.

Werrastein #485 was given heavier-lift derricks in the 1964 re-engining. "The rebuilding did not succeed" in providing the additional performance, according to the experts, the work of the subsequent four ships would not have been done except the competition on the route required like-performance vessels.

486. *Neckarstein*	1953-1973		
Howaldtswerke, Hamburg #878	1953	6969	161.50x19.24
Brown Boveri Turbine	9000	17.5	
9	45		

Launched 15/7/1953. Delivery 26/9/1953. 15/3/1955 propeller problems en route to New York. 3-8/1964 re-engined with M.A.N. Diesel, 14 400 HP, 19.5 kns., bulbous bow, 167.3 m., at Bremen Vulkan, Vegesack, 6,993 Ts. 1/9/1970 to Hapag-Lloyd A.G. 5/1/1973 to Beijing-controlled Ocean Tramping Co., reg. in Mogadisciu, ren. *Nanwu*, 6,688 Ts. 1975 reg. to N an Yang Shipping Co., Macao. 1985 sold by High Seas Nav. Co., Panama to China National Metals & Minerals Import & Export Co. 14/2/1985 delivery at Shanghai for *BU*.

Neckarstein #486 after the rebuilding in 1964. It took almost five months. Like many out-dated NDL freighters, she went to China-controlled operators and final breakup there. BNRA photo.

New York Times, *December 30, 1966.* Associated Press Cablephoto.

Below: Moselstein #487 had two major mishaps, one a collision, the other cargo explosions and burnout of the foreship. She was towed to Hamburg for repairs. Here she is in Puget Sound after the lengthening re-engining of 1964. BNRA Photo.

GERMAN FREIGHTER WRACKED BY BLASTS: Huge fireball erupts from the 7,000-ton Moselstein, docked in Antwerp, Belgium. Ship, loaded with chemical products, was considered a total loss after two explosions ripped her apart. Three men were injured but none was killed.

Ships 472 - 489   489

487. *Moselstein*   1954-1977
Howaldtswerke, Hamburg #879 1954   6968   161.47x19.24
Brown Boveri Turbine   9000   17.5
9   44

> Launched 31/10/1953. Delivery 4/1/1954, MV to East Coast, then to Far East. 15/11/1957 collides on the Elbe near Glückstadt with the British freighter *Martagon* which sinks. *Moselstein* is put aground forward, is towed to Hamburg for repairs. 2/6/1964 re-engined to M.A.N. Diesel and lengthened by Bremer Vulkan, 14,400 HP, 19.5 knots, 167.30 meters, 6,994 Ts. 28/12/1966 in Antwerp shaken by two explosions, foreship burned out. Towed to Hamburg for repairs. 1/9/1970 to *Hapag-Lloyd A.G.* 11/1974 to Hapag-Lloyd International, Panama. 21/10/1977 to Healthy Star Nav. Co., Panama, kept name, 9,438 Ts. 2/2/1982 arr. Madras on last voyage ex Hsinkang. 20/2/1982 arr. Calcutta for BU by S.S. Jain Co.

As with the sixteen express freighters for the Far East, the Lloyd and Hapag jointly ordered six Combi-Ships for a three-weekly passenger service. With 17 knots and 86 berths the ships were comfortable and held in high esteem by travellers. The six were sold for delivery in 1967 to C.Y. Tung, Hong Kong. They came under the Liberian flag for Orient Overseas Lines, Monrovia, ran from the Far East to USA Gulf Coast, until jets and the container revolution made them uncompetitive. The three Lloyd ships had an East Asia Ship Post 1954-1966 for passenger and crew convenience.

On 25 June, 1957, the Day of German Shipping, a special stamp showing the six Far East sisterships was issued.

Following up the sixteen express freighters built for the Far East run, Lloyd and Hapag 1954-1955 put six combi-vessels with the same 17.5 knots speed onto this route. Schwabenstein #488 was the first. They had space for 86 passengers, a pool topside. They were "the preferred way to go" until the jet age forced their sell-off to the C.Y. Tung interests which ran them trans-Pacific to the U.S. Gulf Coast and Europe. A different trade. They are the six M.V., Motor Vessels in the following advertisement.

```
          ORIENT OVERSEAS LINES
          INAUGURATION OF THEIR
          FAR EAST/EUROPE SERVICE
                in 1967
  S.S.  ORIENTAL JADE
  S.S.  ORIENTAL PEARL
  M.V.  ORIENTAL LADY
  M.V.  ORIENTAL MUSICIAN
  M.V.  ORIENTAL RULER
  M.V.  ORIENTAL WARRIOR
  M.V.  ORIENTAL INVENTOR
  M.V.  ORIENTAL HERO
```

488. *Schwabenstein 1*.	1954-1967		
Bremer Vulkan, Vegesack #829	1954	8955	164.15 x 19.40
M.A.N. Diesel	10,560	17.5	* *
86	91		

Launched 24/10/1953. 24/1/1954 delivery, first German postwar new passenger ship. First of six sisters, all built by Bremer Vulkan. 28/1/1954 MV for Orlanda Reederei to Far East. In July, 1955 seriously damaged en route Hong Kong-Manila, required several weeks for repairs in Hong Kong. The local German community looked after the skeleton crew (Otto Seiler), helped organize parties on board. To many the name of Peggy, the barkeeper was more familiar than Captain Heinz Vollmers. The crew formed a choir and sang over Hong Kong Radio. Soloist was Head Chef Schaumlöffel. 13/10/1966 all six sisters were sold to C.Y. Tung. Delivery 3/5/1967, ren. *Oriental Ruler*. Reg. Monrovia. To mid-1976 in passenger service Far East-U.S. Gulf and Atlantic coasts, first arrival in New York 3/9/1967. Then as freighter with containers carried on deck. 25/5/1978-10/1/1979 LU in Hong Kong. 1/1979 to Han Tain Iron & Steel Co., Kaohsiung. Arr. 4/2/1979 for BU.

Resumption of various routes from 1951 with freighters in most cases were joint Lloyd and Hapag. With *Gripsholm* Bremen was determined that the passenger operation be solely Lloyd.

Gripsholm, soon renamed Berlin, during her 12 years with the Lloyd, 1954-66, used ten different types of **SCHIFFSPOST** cancels, starting with her Maiden Voyage to New York as Gripsholm a **NORDA-MERIKA-DIENST/a** mark. This was replaced with one including her name Berlin. The "a" mark was used on several West Indies cruises before a cancel reading **WESTINDIENREISEN** was put into use in 1958 and into 1961. The "a" cancel was used only 1954-55, the successor 1955-1966. Briefly, a **POSTALIA** meter cancel was used on Gripsholm. A proof impression with Berlin but without the word Schiffspost is known. It was never used on board. In addition to West Indies cruises, Berlin made Norway cruises with **NORWEGEN-FAHRT**, 1-7, from 1961-66. **BERMUDAS** was used 1965-66, **LLOYD HERBSTREISE** 1963-66, **WEIHNACHTSREISE** 1963-65, **OSTSEE-FAHRT** in 1966 and **IRLANDFAHRT** also only 1966. The cancels are know largely from collector sendings to the ship.

The details and history of the following Ship Posts are from the author's "*1886-1986, A Century Of German Ship Posts*" published in 1987 by Christie's Robson Lowe, Ltd., London.

M.S. „Bayernstein"

In 1954-1955, the Lloyd and Hapag renewed the passenger service to the Far East with six sister-ships. NDL's Bayernstein opened the service in January, 1954; its Ship Post was not supplied until the second voyage. It reads **OSTASIEN-DIENST** with the name of the ship. Hessenstein and Bayerstein followed. The three Hapag sisters had a Hapag generic Ship Post, with names at bottom and identifying letters a - c. The cancels were used into December, 1966 - early 1967 when the ships were delivered to their new owner. In 1957, the Bundespost issued a stamp showing the Far East liners. The **POSTALIA BREMEN-YOKOHAMA** meter was to have been issued to Hessenstein on its second voyage to begin 1 November, 1954, instead was put onto Schwabenstein from 2 October. It and the other Meter Schiffsposten are rare genuinely used. The ships also had Registry service, but mostly collector mail is so known. Business mail envelopes tend to be discarded by recipients, or the stamps torn off.

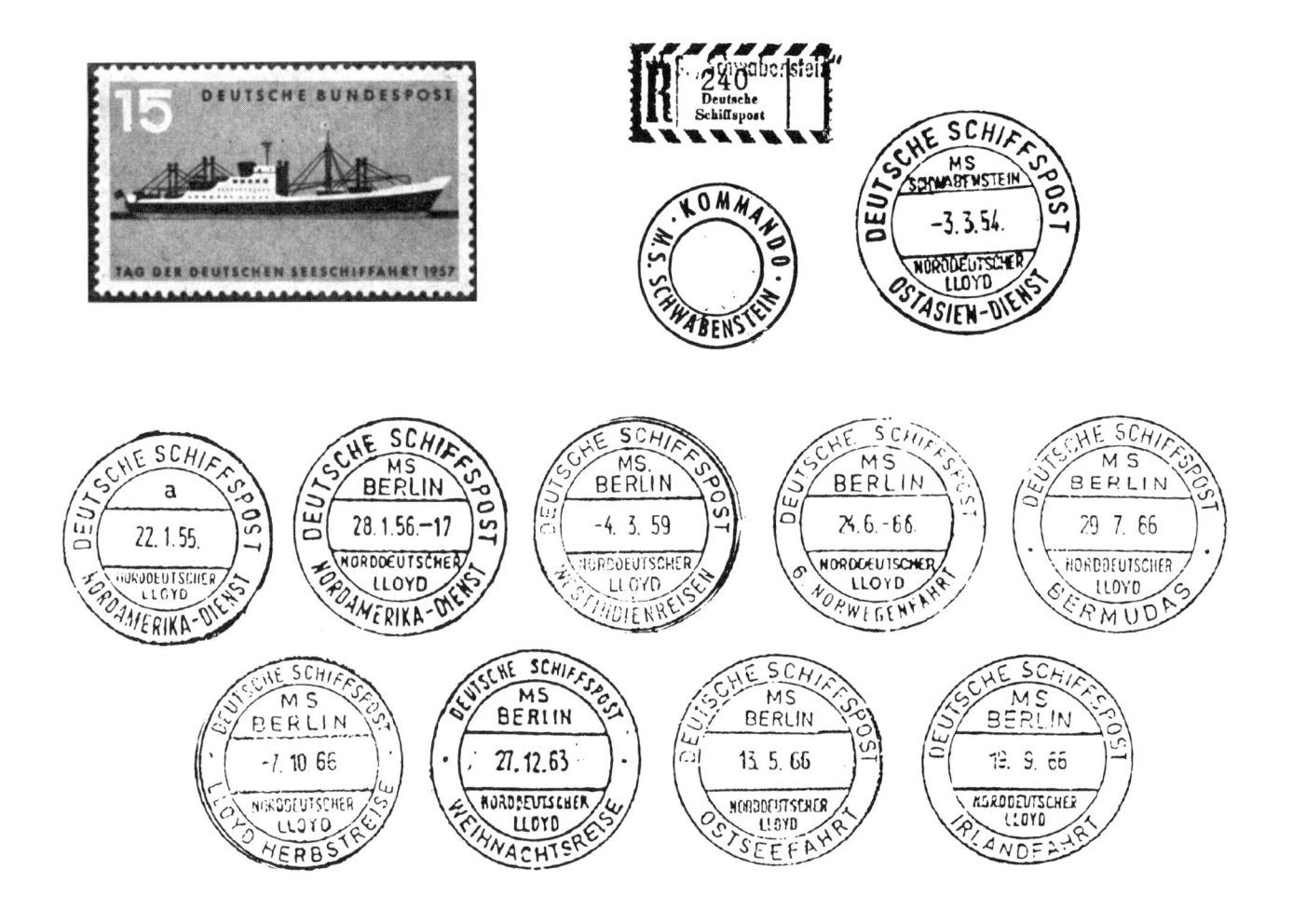

492   *Norddeutscher Lloyd Bremen*

489. *Gripsholm/Berlin*   1954-1966
Sir Wm. G. Armstrong-Whitworth & Co.,
Newcastle #999   1925   18,600   179.83 x 22.65
Burmeister & Wain Diesel   13,500   16   * *
I-127 II-482 III-948   340

Launched 26/11/1924, the break-through for the double-acting Burmeister & Wain Diesel engines. MV. 21/11/1925 Göteborg-New York. 2/1932 painted white for S.A.L. cruising. 4/1940 - 3/1946 Exchange Ship for the International Red Cross, operated by American Export Lines 1942-1945. In Winter 1949-1950 modernized in Kiel for Swedish-America Line, passenger capacity reduced from 1557 to 976, new bow installed. 1/1954 to Bremen-Amerika Linie, Bremen, owned 50-50 by Swedish-America Line and NDL under German flag, NDL as operator, 19,105 Ts. "One of the reasons for taking over *Gripsholm* was to bring the Lloyd name again to public notice as passenger-ship operator" (Waldemar Klose to Captain Drechsel) 14/12/1953 *MV* 1/2/1954 Bremerhaven-Göteborg-Halifax-New York with 704 passengers. When *Gripsholm* reached Halifax on 11 February, 1954 a Canadian Press reporter noted that "half the lifeboats bore the name *Bremen,* the others were lettered *Gripsholm.*" The Lloyd officials wanted to name the ship *Bremen,* but deferred to the Swedish-America Line's management to keep the ship's Swedish name for the first year. The name-changing of lifeboats was halted when half-done. See #571. 7/1/1955 ren. *Berlin 4,* 18,600 Ts. I-133, T-843, *Crew*-354. 22/1/1955 first cruise from New York to the West Indies. On 28/3/1959 en route to New York during a hurricane four crew members were washed overboard trying to secure a leaking hatch. 4/1959 NDL bought S.A.L.'s 50% ownership. 13/6/1962 arr. in

Gripsholm's *first arrival in New York in February, 1954, in the ice, so often a problem on the Hudson, with a Moran tug at the bow. Working with Swedish-America Line meant the Lloyd had a pier available in Manhattan.* Photo by U.S. Coast Guard Warrant Officer James E. Watson. Ex-Tow Line.

New York on her 100th crossing from Bremerhaven. In that time she carried 138,000 persons or 685 per crossing and covered 711,000 statute miles. In her old age she could manage only a steady 15.5 knots. 15/10/1966 arr. in Bremerhaven from last cruise. Sold for £220,000 to shipbreakers, arr. La Spezia 26/11/1966.

Germany made her re-entry into the trans-Atlantic passenger business with Gripsholm, *a year later renamed* Berlin, *in February, 1954. To get back into the passenger business, NDL with Swedish America Line formed a joint-ownership, it to be the operator. In Germany, and in New York for the thousands of ethnic Germans there, it was front-page news. On all her voyages* Gripsholm-Berlin *provided* **Ship Post** *service to her passengers and crew, an NDL service going back to 1886.*

Sometimes there had to be adjustments for emergencies. *Berlin's* scheduled 30 January, 1958 departure from Bremerhaven to Halifax and New York, there to leave for the West Indies on 13 February, was delayed by fog for 56 hours. The stop at Halifax was skipped, the 239 passengers for there sent by train from New York. "All shipboard preparations for the cruise were carried out as planned, such as setting in the swimming basin ..." It probably meant a canvas pool, as was done on all cruises until *Columbus* was given a Lido deck with tiled pool in December, 1937. The cruise date was kept: to San Juan, Bridgetown, Port of Spain, Port-au-Prince, Havana and return to New York.

Gripsholm *over six years sailed some 150,000 miles on eleven voyages. Photo is from* Newsweek *Magazine.*

The celebration on board as Gripsholm *in January, 1955 was renamed* Berlin. *Captain Heinrich Lorenz at right, talking to Captain H. von Thülen,* Berlin *3's captain prewar, Captain Krone his successor, and the Mayor of Berlin toasting with champagne. An important milestone on the road to recovery.*

Bremen 5 and Berlin *meet off lower Manhattan. ex Hans Jürgen Witthöft's Hapag-Lloyd, Koehler Verlag, Herford, 1974.*

Registry service was available on Berlin, *with Board Post Office mark imposed.*

Logs from Berlin's *September and October, 1955 voyages, East and West. Unusual in that the average speed is not given. The reason: In her old age the ship could manage at best 15.5 knots, not her original 16.5. The passengers travelled on her despite her age, so the speed was immaterial.*

Abstract of Log
M.S. "BERLIN"

19100 Gross-Register-Tons   Length: 598 feet   Beam: 74 feet

Captain Heinrich Lorenz

11th Voyage - Eastbound
September 22nd, 1955 from New York to Bremerhaven

1955 Sept./Oct.	Noon-Position Latitude North	Noon-Position Long. West	Miles	Wind	Remarks
22	New York		—	West 2	03.18 p.m. Departure, fine and clear, smooth sea
23	41° 04'	67° 37'	316	NxE 2/3	fine and clear, slight sea
24	43° 25'	60° 10'	360	ESE 3	fine and clear, slight sea
25	46° 28'	53° 16'	355	SSE 2	mostly overcast, slight sea
26	50° 17'	45° 51'	374	SSE 6	mostly overcast rather rough sea
27	53° 42'	37° 25'	373	WxS 7	cloudy, rough sea
28	56° 10'	27° 52'	361	West 3	overcast, rain, moderate sea
29	57° 45'	17° 02'	367	SWxS 6	overcast, rain, rather rough sea
30	58° 42'	6° 05'	351	WSW 7	cloudy, rough sea 18.10 passed Pentland Firth
1	58° 57'	3° 28'E	363	NWxW 4/5	fine and clear, moderate sea
			236 Rest		Total Distance to Bremerhaven
			3456		

October 2nd, 1955, 01.23 a.m., passed Weser Lightvessel
Total Distance: 3456 Nautical Miles

Abstract of Log
M.S. "BERLIN"

19100 Gross-Register-Tons   Length: 598 feet   Beam: 74 feet

Captain Heinrich Lorenz

12th Voyage - Westbound
October 5th, 1955 from Bremerhaven to New York

1955 Oct.	Noon-Position Latitude North	Noon-Position Long. West	Miles	Wind	Remarks
5	Bremerhaven		—	SSE 3	12.30 p.m. Departure, mostly overcast, moderate sea
6	51° 03'	01° 19'E	344	SWxW 7/8	cloudy, rough sea
7	49° 54'	06° 58'	334	WSW 5	overcast, rain, rather rough sea
8	50° 26'	15° 42'	337	SSW 5	cloudy, rather rough sea, WSW-ly swell
9	50° 12'	24° 08'	323	West 5	some clouds, rather rough sea
10	49° 00'	33° 23'	367	WxS 3/4	fine and clear, moderate sea
11	47° 15'	41° 22'	337	WSW 5	fine and clear, moderate sea
12	45° 12'	49° 32'	360	West 4	fine and clear, moderate sea
13	43° 56'	58° 01'	371	North 3/4	cloudy, rainshowers, slight sea
14	41° 19'	66° 27'	407	SSE 7	fine and clear, rough sea
			364 Rest		Total Distance to New York
			3544		

October 15th, 1955, 09.05 a.m., passed Ambrose Lightvessel
Total Distance: 3544 Nautical Miles

496 *Norddeutscher Lloyd Bremen*

CHAPTER 16

From Crossing to Cruising

The target at the Lloyd from the very beginning, its raison d'etre, was to carry passengers in comfort, with style and service that nobody else offered. It was the regard for the Lloyd that this brought which after both wars gave it the chance to confirm its reputation.

In 1954, Dr. Kulenkampff commented that although the Lloyd had again been operating freight services for four years, "Passenger Shipping Is The Heart of Our Business."

After World War II it took longer than in the early 1920s. A modest beginning was made with the first six new freighters of the *Rheinstein* #472 class appearing from March, 1951 with space for just two passengers: It meant they ate with the Captain, officers and engineers. Following new ships offered more space, up to the traditional freighter limit of twelve without carrying a doctor. Such as the reefers *Liebenstein* #479 and *Lichtenstein* #478 running to the Canaries and North Brazil. A very pleasant voyage; almost as if one owned the ship.

From 1953, Express Freighter Service operated from New York in 8-9 days to Antwerp, 9-10 to Rotterdam, 10-12 to Bremen and Hamburg. Fares were about mid-way between those for First and Tourist classes. In 1953, the Lloyd and Hapag ordered six combi-ships with very comfortable amenities for 86 passengers, including pools, for

Before the Lloyd and Hapag could again provide passenger service, their jointly-owned Travel Bureau was selling passages on the foreign-flag steamers serving German ports to the U.S. and Canada; mostly under the Italian flag. "Whether you want to go to the Vahr (district of Bremen) or out into the Big World, we can help you." Later the slogan was: "Around the Corner, Around the World."

HOME LINES

DIREKTER Deutschland DIENST

mit deutscher Besatzung

der **HOME LINES**
auf dem luxuriösen 22,000 Tonnen Motorschiff **ITALIA**
nach **HAMBURG** (CUXHAVEN)

Abfahrten von NEW YORK
23. September — 19. Oktober — 16. November

Spezial WEIHNACHTSREISE mit S.S. ATLANTIC
am 12. Dezember 1953

Mindest-Fahrpreise:
TOURISTENKLASSE **$170** Erste Klasse $280

Das grosse Motorschiff der HOME LINES, "Italia", das New York mit Hamburg (Cuxhaven) verbindet, hat schon viele tausende unserer deutschen Passagiere zufriedengestellt. Die so beliebte "ITALIA" hat moderne Kabinen, grosse Sport- und Promenaden-Decks, ausgezeichnete deutsche Küche, "Air-Conditioned" Speisesaal und Aufenthalt-räume, gedecktes, gekacheltes Schwimmbad, türkische Bäder und Turnsaal. Und die ganze Besatzung der "ITALIA" Kapitän, Offiziere und Stewards geben in der hundert-jährigen Tradition der Hapag-Lloyd umsichtige und höfliche Bedienung.

Besuchen Sie Ihren Reiseagenten

HOME LINES
42 BROADWAY, NEW YORK 4, N. Y.
HAPAG-LLOYD-REISEBÜRO
GENERAL-VERTRETER FÜR DEUTSCHLAND

Italia *was crewed by Hapag almost entirely with its old personnel.*

the long voyage to the Far East, the prestige route for both lines after that to New York.

In the absence of a German passenger service across the North Atlantic, outside lines came in. The Greek Line opened a Bremen-Southampton-Cherbourg-Cobh-Montreal service, then in 1951 also Bremen-Southampton-Cherbourg-Cobh-New York. In 1951, the new Home Lines' *Homeland,* the former *Bergensfjord,* operated from Hamburg to New York with Hapag as German agent. Then the Swedish *Kungsholm* was bought and, renamed *Italia,* was staffed with a Hapag crew. The Hapag-Lloyd Travel Bureaus did the bookings in Germany and Europe.

In late 1953, the Greek Line with its new *Olympia* due in service, wanted to staff its hotel department with 258 ex-NDL stewards, a way to assure good service and a sympathetic market for its Bremen-New York route. Greek law required Greek crews. So these stewards ended up on NDL's *Gripsholm* in January, 1954.

The United States Lines, which prewar operated to Hamburg and carried U.S.-German Sea Posts, with its refurbished *Washington* made occasional turnarounds at Hamburg. The prewar *America,* until then the largest and fastest U.S.-built vessel, extended its trans-Atlantic runs to Bremerhaven, docking at the rebuilt Columbus Quay. This again was offering shipside railway service. In January, 1953, the new record-breaking *United States* made its first turnaround at Bremerhaven. A glorious day for Bremen and Bremerhaven: to have the world's fastest ship offering Bremen-New York service.

Meanwhile, in August, 1952 there was mention in the Bundestag that the Lloyd and Hapag were considering ordering three or four 20,000 tonners, 23-24 knots, for a seven-days joint service. This new-building dream extended into September, 1955 when Transport Minister Christian Seebohm announced that five shipyards were designing vessels of 28,000 tons to carry 1450 passengers, at 22-23 knots, thus still seven-day ships. 23 November the New York Times had a Hamburg-datelined story that Hapag and the Lloyd "had placed tentative orders for one each such ships. They would run in a joint schedule."

The reality was different. In August, 1953 Mr. Seebohm announced that discussions were active for a resumption of German Trans-Atlantic passenger service, Hapag negotiating for use, if not purchase, of Home Lines' *Italia,* and NDL with Swedish-America Line for its *Gripsholm.* S.A.L. was taking delivery of a new *Kungsholm* in November, hence was willing to let its *Gripsholm,* built in 1925, go to a joint SAL-NDL operation. NDL's negotiation worked out, Hapag's with Home Lines did not.

In late January, 1954, *Gripsholm* #489 was transferred to the new Bremen-Amerika Linie, owned 50-50 SAL and NDL. On 1 February, *Gripsholm* left Bremerhaven under the German flag, made a courtesy call at Göteborg and on to Halifax and New York. A Lloyd ship again was crossing to New York with a Lloyd crew, management, flag and stack, and registered in Bremen. A glorious day for all: from Dr. Kulenkampff and Herr Bertram on down the line. In 1959, NDL bought out SAL's 50% share. In January, 1955 the

Ship Mail markings from Gripsholm, *its second voyage from Bremerhaven to Gothenborg, Halifax and New York. The* **Paquebot** *mark was applied at Gothenborg on Mail Posted on the High Seas and deposited in a post office foreign to the ship and the postage. A year later, the ship was renamed Berlin. The envelope was signed for Ship Mails collector Gustav Lund by Captain H. Lorenz.*

Fittingly, the stamp commemorates Carl Schurz, probably the most famous German emigré ever on the American scene. Born in 1823, he was a major participant in the 1848-1849 people uprisings for Democracy in Europe. He came to the U.S. in 1852. During the Civil War he was a Brigadier General, and in 1877-1881 under President Rutherford B. Hayes Secretary of the Interior. He later was Hapag's Chief Representative in the U.S. It named a ship for him.

When Gripsholm *came into service in February, 1954, the emphasis was on liner-crossings of the North Atlantic. "1955 the entire year Direct to Germany." Although in January-February the ship, now renamed Berlin, made the first cruises — to the West Indies.*

Berlin's Farewell Dinner on Thursday, October 13th, 1955 was also a Farewell to the Lloyd's way of caring for its passengers, until the next voyage? Between the wars one Missouri Congressman of German extraction made 85 Lloyd voyages.

From Crossing to Cruising 499

NORTH GERMAN LLOYD joint schedule with SWEDISH AMERICAN LINE
PROPOSED SAILINGS 1954 (SUBJECT TO CHANGE)
NEW YORK—BREMERHAVEN—GOTHENBURG—COPENHAGEN

EASTBOUND					WESTBOUND			
From New York	Due Gothenburg	Due Bremerhaven	SHIP		From Bremerhaven	From Gothenburg	From Copenhagen	Due New York
Eastern Standard Time A.M.								
			GRIPSHOLM		Feb. 1*	Feb. 2		Feb. 13
			STOCKHOLM		Feb. 13*	Feb. 12	Feb. 12	Feb. 22
Tue. Feb. 16 10:00	Feb. 26	Feb. 27	GRIPSHOLM		Mar. 3*	Mar. 4		Mar. 15
			STOCKHOLM	THRIFT SEASON	Mar. 13*	Mar. 12	Mar. 12	Mar. 22
Wed. Mar. 17† 10:00	Mar. 28	Mar. 29	GRIPSHOLM		Apr. 2*			Apr. 13
			STOCKHOLM		Apr. 8*	Apr. 7	Apr. 7	Apr. 17
Thur. Apr. 15 10:00	Apr. 25	Apr. 26	GRIPSHOLM		Apr. 29*			May 10
Wed. May 12 10:30	May 22	May 23	GRIPSHOLM		May 27*			June 7
			STOCKHOLM		June 3*	June 2	June 2	June 12
Wed. June 9 10:30	June 19	June 20	GRIPSHOLM		June 29*			July 10
Tue. July 13 9:00		July 23	GRIPSHOLM		July 28			Aug. 7
Tue. Aug. 10 9:00		Aug. 20	GRIPSHOLM		Aug. 24	Aug. 25		Sept. 4
Tue. Sept. 7 9:00		Sept. 17	GRIPSHOLM		Sept. 22	Sept. 23		Oct. 4
Wed. Oct. 6 10:00		Oct. 16	GRIPSHOLM		Oct. 26			Nov. 5
			STOCKHOLM	THRIFT SEASON	Nov. 20	Nov. 19	Nov. 19	Nov. 29
Tue. Nov. 9 10:00		Nov. 19	GRIPSHOLM		Nov. 24			Dec. 4
Tue. Dec. 7† 10:00	Dec. 18	Dec. 19	GRIPSHOLM					

†Calls at Halifax, Canada, two days later.
Gripsholm sails from Pier 97, North River, Foot of West 57th Street, New York.
*Via Halifax, Canada.

Expected arrival dates shown herein are calculated on average of past performance but are subject to change.
M.S. Gripsholm is operated by North German Lloyd, M.S. Stockholm is operated by Swedish American Line.

---

ship was renamed *Berlin,* and made its first cruises from New York to the West Indies, a gamble for NDL because this was its only passenger ship, but it lacked air-conditioning. Many cruised and crossed as repeat passengers on *Berlin* because it was a Lloyd ship and offered the traditional Lloyd service, not because of the quality of the ship. It had been thoroughly rebuilt in Kiel in 1948-1949 for resumed S.A.L. service, her passenger capacity cut from 1557 to 976, essentially one-class, with a small segment of First Class cabins. Third Class was eliminated. Cabins aft were refurbished, with fewer four-berths.

In 1956, *Berlin* averaged 852 passengers westward, 751 eastward, indicating a continuing emigration from Europe. In December that year, and January, 1957 *Berlin* brought 202, respectively 155 Hungarian refugees. They had assembled in Austria, were taken by trains directly shipside at the Columbus Quay in Bremerhaven. On its 7/9/1959 departure from New York, *Berlin* carried its 100,000ths passenger. The Swedish-America Line continued acting as passenger agent in the U.S. and Canada. This made unnecessary a costly NDL agency effort, with only one ship in service.

In February, 1957 at the Lloyd's centennial celebration, Director Waldemar Klose had said "Unfortunately the construction of a profitable and competitive ship for the Lloyd and the Hamburg-Amerika Linie still lies in the distant future. A modern *Columbus* would cost 200-220 million Marks. Technical advances are so rapid one hesitates to freeze a design. Then, too, shipyards are committed for years ahead. The Government has promised help, but the Transport Minister is more concerned with re-election of the Adenauer Government in September."

It turned out that 1957 was the postwar peak in Trans-Atlantic ship passenger traffic: 1,036,000 persons with some seventy vessels in service. This compared with 1,427,000 passengers carried in 1913.

With *Berlin* doing well, and NDL's hopes for Trans-Atlantic and cruise travel on the positive side, the Lloyd in September 1957 bought the laid up French *Pasteur*. It had been completed in 1939 for the Bordeaux-South America service, but start of the war prevented sailing. Then it was a transport in the war, after for the French campaigns in Indo-China, and in 1956 during the Anglo-French invasion of the Suez Canal.

It took twenty months to rebuild her from top to bottom for some $25 millions, a third to one-half the time and money needed for a new ship. The City-State of Bremen guaranteed DM 27 millions in rebuilding funds for *Bremen*.

On 12 February, 1959 co-Director Richard Bretram faced 150 invited journalists from around the world at the Park Hotel in Bremen to ... present the fifth *Bremen*. With lights out a spotlight pinpoints the bow of a ten-foot model of the new ship gliding down the aisle. The first concrete idea outsiders had of what the new ship would look like. First question: "How can you Lloyd people sleep nights when you know it'll

Director Richard Betram provides the first look at the New Bremen. *It was a huge gamble for the Lloyd rebuilding for the second time, over almost the same time span: In 1920 services resumed: 1929 the record-breaking* Bremen *4. In 1950 the first charter services. Now, 1959 -* Bremen *5. See #511. Photo by L. Kull.*

have cost nearly $25,000,000 to rebuilt the ship, but you are facing a declining liner-traffic market, with the jets "flying high." "Truly" Herr Bertram said, "I sleep well. While travelling by ship may be a lesser percentage of total travel, the travel volume is increasing rapidly. We are so certain of that that we even insisted in naming the ship *Bremen* for all that that implied: Why? It is an obligation, the fifth *Bremen*."

"The first, a propeller ship when most new vessels still were sidewheelers, set the pace in 1858:

"*Bremen 2* in 1897 set a new standard for size and appointments to Australia and the Far East; in fact the Suez Canal Company was forced to enlarge the canal and put its operations on round-the-clock; our schedule was so tight we couldn't have made it without ability to transit the canal at any hour. No holdups. Models of two of our ships were shown by the Suez Canal Co. at the 1900 Paris Fair: 'This is what we're doing: expanding our potential and service.'

"*Bremen 3* in 1923 was the first, really, to offer Tourist class on the North Atlantic, *Bremen 4*, well you know about her: in 1929 regained the Blue Ribbon for Germany. A new standard, including with her sister *Europa*, offering catapult airmail service at both ends of their route:

"So here is *Bremen 5*. As before, we shall offer travellers the ultimate service. Able completely to relax, or to be as busy as he wishes, with fun-things to do or business. 'R and R' in effect as the military call it. *Bremen* will be transportation par excellence. And a vacation and restorative facility. All things the airplane cannot offer, except speed in getting there. And often one is glad to get the flight behind one. With a ship, with a *Bremen* you'll arrive refreshed in body and mind. With a worthwhile and rewarding experiences. We think we can make it all come off for the Lloyd and for the travelling public. I'd say 90% plus of the medical treatments or cures available on shore you can get on board."

In 1994, the cruise lines were promoting their Spa facilities as the extra dimension in services for their clients. *Bremen* in 1959 was 35 years ahead of this.

Herr Bertram's hopes turned out to be well-justified: On 9 July, 1964 *Bremen* left New York on the return leg of her centennial voyage, exactly five years after starting her maiden voyage from Bremerhaven. She sailed with 1,116 passengers of her capacity of 1,122. Captain Günther Rössing commander for 75 of those voyages. On eighty trans-Atlantic round trips: In 1994 the

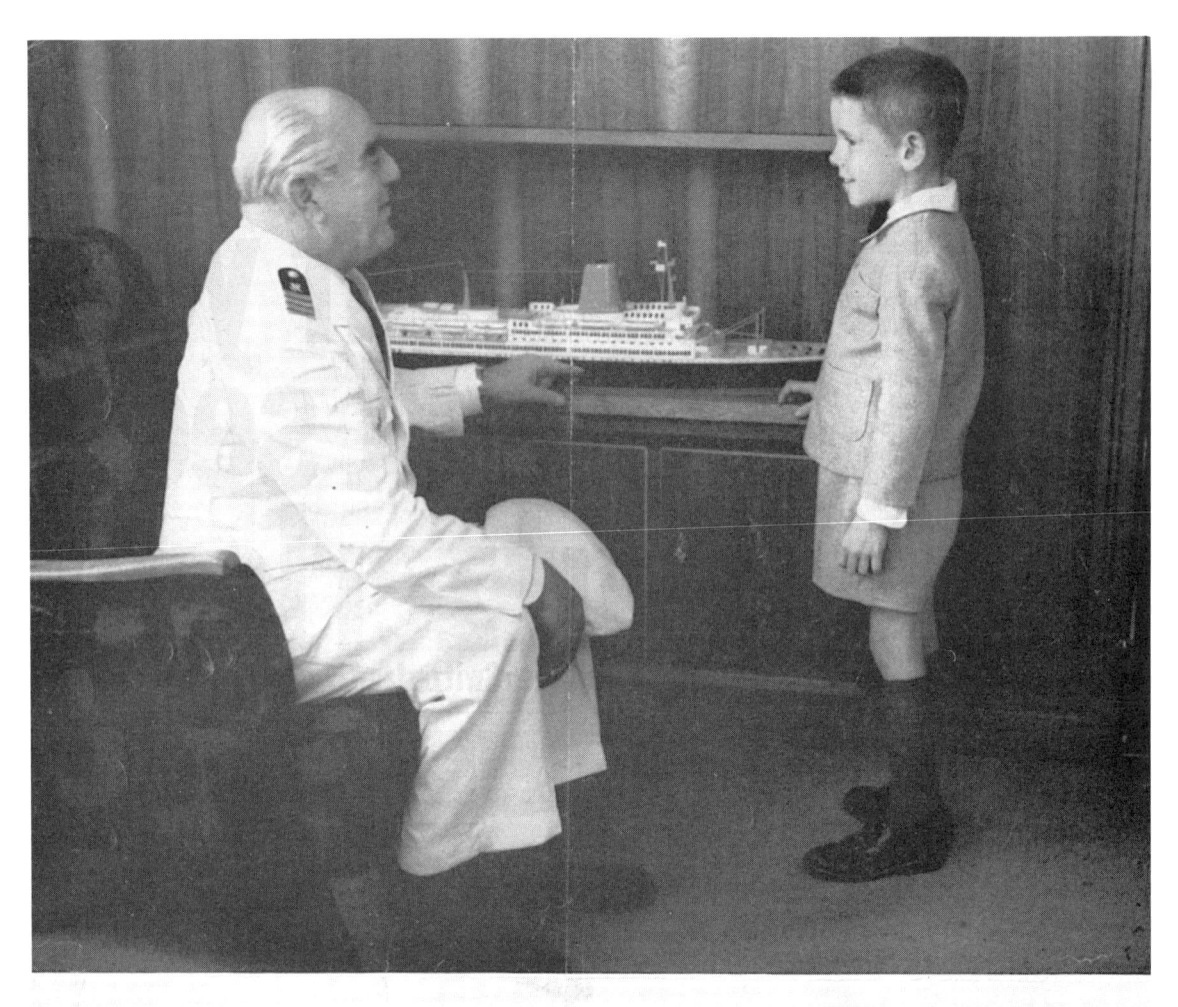

Why Captain Lorenz is so proud of the new BREMEN

Captain Lorenz has commanded many a fine ship in his 39 years of distinguished service with the North German Lloyd.

When he talks about the new Bremen his eyes light up and there is pride in his voice. Not only because she is the largest and fastest of all German ships. Not only because her 22 splendid public rooms are beautiful, her spacious, air-conditioned cabins equipped with the most modern refinements of comfort...her great silent engines and highly effective stabilizers provide the smoothest possible ocean ride.

What fills Captain Lorenz with particular pride is the pleasantly glowing atmosphere aboard this magnificent ship and the tremendous enjoyment passengers derive from their trips. It goes without saying that the unsurpassed food and wines and the world-renowned Lloyd service contribute much to the captain's pride and the passengers' pleasure.

Ask your travel agent to book your next trans-Atlantic passage or Caribbean cruise on the new Bremen or her sleek fleet mate, the popular Berlin.

T. S. BREMEN
New York to Cherbourg
Southampton • Bremerhaven
Mar. 15, Apr. 5, Apr. 23, May 12

3 Gala Inaugural Cruises
To the West Indies and South America
on the T. S. BREMEN ★ Jan. 15 • 15 Days • 10 Ports
Feb. 1 • 24 Days • 18 Ports ★ Feb. 27 • 14 Days • 8 Ports

M. S. BERLIN
New York to Bremerhaven
Jan. 5, Feb. 1, Mar. 2;
Mar. 29 (via Southampton)

NORTH GERMAN LLOYD
PASSENGER AGENCY, INC.

666 Fifth Avenue, New York 19, New York • BOwling Green 9-6050 / CHICAGO • LOS ANGELES • TORONTO

Sailing the Seven Seas Since 1857
1960

Above: Greetings from Captain Günther Rössing, TS Bremen, *at St. Pierre, February, 1961, in a rainbow. O.C.C. - Ocean Comfort Company, NDL's Century + affiliate for handling Passenger amenities: Deck Chairs, Postcards, etc. Photo by Ship's Photographer.*

In May, 1959 Cadets from the U.S. Military Academy at West Point came with their instructor to spend the day on Berlin, *later on* Bremen, *by when it had become an annual affair, and speak nothing but German.*

THE NEW YORK TIMES

Class for Cadets

Twenty cadets from the Military Academy at West Point will be learning German nautical expressions aboard the North German Lloyd liner Berlin in New York Harbor today.

The class is part of the curriculum for advanced German-language students. It will be conducted at Pier 88 and the ship's master, Capt. Fritz Leusner, will act as host and professor.

SATURDAY, MAY 14,

34 CADETS TOUR A GERMAN LINER

West Point Class Forbidden to Speak English on Visit

By WERNER BAMBERGER

A platoon of future Army second lieutenants established a linguistic beachhead aboard the West German liner Bremen here yesterday.

The platoon of 34 West Point cadets, led by their German language instructor, Lt. Col. Howard Reiner, boarded the North German Lloyd liner shortly after 10 A. M. at West 48th Street for their annual visit to German-speaking territory, during which English is strictly verboten.

The cadets went through the 32,335-ton liner, from engine room to bridge, speaking nothing but German during the two-hour tour. According to Second Officer Helmut Janssen, their guide, "They asked some pretty technical questions in excellent German."

On the bridge the cadets were welcomed by Capt. Heinz Vollmers, master of the liner, who noted that these annual visits of West Point cadets to North German Lloyd liners had become almost a tradition.

Captain Receives Gift

After the welcome, the cadets broke into two groups for "eine kleine Brueckenfuehrung" (a short tour of the bridge) during which they saw such nautical gear as gyrocompass, automatic steering gear and true motion radar, the names of which sound entirely different in German.

Following a presentation to Captain Vollmers of a color photograph of the West Point color guard on parade, as a momento of their visit, the platoon went below for refreshments and lunch. Cadet Craig S. Carson of Aurora, Illinois, snapped the gift photograph.

Colonel Reiner, who is an assistant professor of German at the United States Military Academy, explained that once a cadet gets beyond a 25-mile radius from West Point he is allowed to partake of anything as long as he remains a gentleman.

A Hearty Meal

Not a single bottle of Coca-Cola was in evidence during the refreshment period nor during luncheon in the ship's first-class dining room. Much in evidence, however, were tall glasses of Beck's beer, a German export.

Glancing down the menu, which featured tiny shrimp and caviar and, as the main course, sauerbraten with dumplings and red cabbage. Colonel Reiner expressed doubt that the cadets would have done as well at the West Point Mess Hall yesterday.

The showing of a German mystery movie, entitled "Ein Schuss im Dunkeln" ("A Shot in the Dark") concluded the cadets' foray into foreign territory.

Yesterday's annual visit to a German vessel was the sixth to be made by the Academy's German language class.

From Crossing to Cruising

Promotional Meter Postmarks on Lloyd business mail: **Herbst** *(Autumn) Voyage to the South, 1963 and the first Norway Cruise in 1961. In 1957, NDL's promotion Office had Herr Windels and an aide vs seventy prewar.*

cruise lines were promoting their Spa facilities as the extra dimension in services offered to their clientel. It was the latest availability that all were rushing to equip new vessels with or retrofit not-so-old older ones. *Bremen* in 1959 was 35 years ahead of this.

She carried 143,422 passengers, plus 16,618 on nineteen Caribbean cruises and one in Europe, for a total 160,040 passengers, overall 85% sold out. She covered 654,827 nautical miles, burning some 400,000 tons of oil, consuming some 1.3 million bottles of wine, the crew is counted in on this! and some two million liters of beer. Captain Rossing told a visiting reporter: "Americans make the best travellers. They are the best sports. They accept a reasonable explanation more readily than others." But, they are just as ready as anyone else to be spoiled.

In January 1961, Herr Bertram noted that in *Bremen's* fifteen months in service some 150,000 persons had visited her at its various ports, a tremendous exposure for the Lloyd, for Germany and for travel by ship. In June, 1962 *Berlin* left New York on her two-hundredth Atlantic crossing; she had carried some 138,000 passengers, an average 685 per voyage. Her capacity was 975. "Her Gemütlichkeit is largely responsible for this success," an American travel agent commented. In Spring, 1962 a 6% dividend, the first in thirty years, was authorized for the year 1961.

In 1962, the Trans-Atlantic Passenger Conference still had twenty-five members. In a questionnaire, responders, giving more than one answer, 46% chose having a good time afloat as their

One-time Transatlantik Ship Post for what used to be the main operation.

prime reason for going by sea, 32% to get away from routine, 25% each exciting experiences and good shopping, 20% entertainment. Not mentioned, but more than a fringe benefit, were the health cure and treatments available on *Bremen*.

With the inevitable retirement of the aged *Berlin* near, in the Fall of 1965 NDL bought Swedish-America Line's *Kungsholm,* one of the loveliest looking vessels ever built. In January, 1966 she began fifteen years of rewarding service under the Lloyd flag. In October, 1966 *Berlin* was "paid off" with honors. Once again the Lloyd had a *Bremen* and *Europa;* this was repeated in 1993 when a small cruise liner was chartered, renamed *Bremen* as running mate to *Europa 5* of 1982.

From mid-1967 through 1968 the Lloyd tried out something that did not work out, as had the Hapag-Lloyd North Atlantic Community of the 1930s, and the 1970 full corporate merger: a joint schedule for Atlantic crossings and for cruises with the Hamburg-Atlantic Line. Both lines had two vessels. The joint schedule and promotion ended when H.A.L. decided to drop out of liner sailings to concentrate on cruises. While NDL continued to offer both, plus what others rarely had been able to match: serving the passenger even above his or her expectations.

In the transition from liner traffic, ships shuttling back and forth across the ocean: Bremen-New York; San Francisco-Hawaii-Japan-China; Sydney-Wellington, a few Lloyd captains made two-hundred crossings on one ship! one even three hundred, this in the 1890s-1914 era; even into the 1970s most cruise vessels were liners, some several times rebuilt and refurbished to cruise format. At Hapag-Lloyd the Trans-Atlantic voyage was so rare that in 1988 a special *Ship Post* was issued for what used to be the norm: *Transatlantic* by *Europa 5*.

QE2 still does liner crossings, but promoted mostly as "*QE2* one way, *Concorde* return." Several liner shipping enterprises were driven out of the passenger business by the jets taking over, before cruising in sufficient volume could catch on. This happened to Matson Lines, its own lovely white ships sold off in 1952, and in 1963, their replacements, converted freighters, in 1970-1971 sold to the Pacific Far East Line. The Pacific Ocean is not exactly cruising waters, except in the South Seas, or up to British Columbia and Alaska. In contrast, Florida is the world's top cruise

Everyone is a First Class Passenger on our Cruises
TS BREMEN MS EUROPA

Sail in grand style to the West Indies and South America

When you cruise on the TS Bremen or the MS Europa, there is no class distinction. You have full run of the ship. The number of passengers is limited. There is no crowding. First class travel on our famous trans-Atlantic liners has always been the height of luxury. This same luxury is now yours on our cruises: elegant accommodations, gourmet food, deft, attentive service...a glittering social life. There are no second class citizens on our cruises.

Ports of Call: Bermuda • Nassau • San Juan • St. Thomas • St. Croix • Martinique • Guadeloupe • St. Maarten • St. Vincent • Barbados • Antigua • St. Lucia • Grenada • Trinidad • La Guaira • Curacao • Cartagena • Canal Zone • San Blas • Kingston • Montego Bay • Port-au-Prince • Cap Haitien

From New York: Nov. 21; Dec. 2, 18; Jan. 4, 24; Feb. 1, 7, 23, 28; March 11, 15, 26; April 9; May 1, 11   **1969**
6 to 27 Days — 2 to 15 Ports — From $185.00

Also cruises from Port Everglades to the West Indies and South America aboard the ultra modern Hanseatic. Jan. 28; Feb. 9, 23; March 8, 21; April 4, 11. Seven to 14 Days. From $215.00

Ask for illustrated brochure. Book through your Travel Agent

NORTH GERMAN LLOYD
GERMAN ATLANTIC LINE

Dept. NW, 666 Fifth Avenue, New York, N.Y. 10019. Tel. (212) 757-9300
Chicago • Los Angeles • Miami • Toronto

SAFETY INFORMATION: The Bremen*, Hanseatic** and Europa* registered in West Germany meet International Safety Standards for new ships developed in 1948* or 1960**.

Invoking the old names Bremen *and* Europa, *so famous 1929-1939, again 1956-1972, and again from 1993: a part-owned chartered* Bremen *to join* Europa 5.

HOUSE PARTY ON THE HIGH SEAS

If you like parties, you'll love NGL ships. From the get-acquainted cocktail party to the Captain's farewell dinner, every social function sparkles with gaiety. And there are social functions every day.

Life aboard Lloyd steamers is attuned to the young at heart. Dances, games, sports, first-run movies—and lots of music. Keen appetites, thanks to the bracing sea air, are delectably appeased by five gourmet meals a day. The gym, the sauna and the Bremen's unique under-water massage help you keep in trim.

And what can be more relaxing than stretching out in a comfortable deck chair...? Perhaps sipping a drink, or—if you must work—dictating to a multilingual secretary?

Service on NGL ships is legendary. Attentive stewards anticipate your every wish and skilled, tactful hostesses help you enjoy your journey.

GO BY SHIP—GO NGL

ᵀˢBREMEN ᴹˢEUROPA ᴹˢBERLIN

From New York to England, France and Germany
See Your Travel Agent

NORTH GERMAN LLOYD

666 Fifth Ave., New York, N.Y. 10019, PL 7-9300
Chicago—Los Angeles—Toronto

NGL Ships are of West German registry

Your suitcases can be any size and you may take as many as you like

Suitcases, trunks, lockers and all personal effects travel free on North German Lloyd ships. In fact, aboard the Lloyd's luxurious steamers almost everything is on the house—parties, gourmet food, entertainment, first-run movies, deck sports, dances, games ...to say nothing of your spacious, comfortable stateroom with the equivalent of a valet and maid. Drinks cost a song, 30 cents for a *real* dry martini, not the factory-made, pre-mixed variety. Your low fare on NGL ships includes so many extras that the transportation seems merely a fringe benefit.

GO BY SHIP—GO NGL

ᵀˢBREMEN ᴹˢEUROPA ᴹˢBERLIN

From New York to England, France and Germany
See Your Travel Agent

NORTH GERMAN LLOYD

In 1966, the High point of the Lloyd's Post-war passenger service: three ships. Each with its own personality, yet all three Lloyd Service, "The staff pampers you as if you owned the ship."

---

origination: It has the American clientele and The West Indies and Central America where one can see and leave an island by dinner time, have a wonderful evening on board, sleep the night, and the next day a new island, a new culture. And on board, each day a flight from reality. No wonder that as ships were designed for cruising that the demand fed on itself. Ship after ship was lengthened to increase capacity, a cheaper and quicker way than building a new vessel. And even after a contract for the largest-ever ship was signed by P. & O., the size was increased, to close to 100,000 tons! as the market potential kept expanding.

Being a ship news reporter used to be, after Foreign Correspondent, the most sought-after job on newspapers. Today's ship news, if it is carried at all, lists only a few arrivals and departures. No longer does one read as a matter of course who came, who departed:

- In October, 1959 Thornton Wilder sailed on the *Bremen* to Bremen.
- In mid-1958, President Theodor Heuss travelled on *Berlin* for a state visit to the United States and to Canada.

Today it's all different. But one knows travelling by ship will survive; one couldn't be sure even into the 1960s. It no longer is going by sea to get there, but to be at sea on a floating resort. And the shipping companies that survive, and the new ones that have come in as a business, are adjusting, as did the Norddeutscher Lloyd and, as Hapag-Lloyd, since 1970.

no rock and roll

You'll have smooth sailing on the "Bremen" and the "Europa". Both are equipped with the most up-to-date motion stabilizers. The service is smooth, too—the food superb. But if you like rock and roll, there is always the dance floor. Take the fun-route to Europe.

TS BREMEN MS EUROPA
FROM NEW YORK TO
ENGLAND · FRANCE · GERMANY
August 8, 17, 26; Sept. 8, 13; Oct. 1, 19

Fall and Winter Cruises to the West Indies and South America.

Coming Soon

TS HANSEATIC
For The Young At Heart

The ultra-modern successor of the immensely popular "Hanseatic" will enter trans-Atlantic service next spring. Prior to that she will make 7 Caribbean cruises from Port Everglades, Florida starting January 28, 1968.

Write for sailing schedules—book through your travel agent.

NORTH GERMAN LLOYD
GERMAN ATLANTIC LINE
510 West Sixth Street, Los Angeles, Cal. 90014/627-8753
New York • Chicago • Miami • Toronto

SAFETY INFORMATION: The Bremen*, Hanseatic** and Europa* registered in West Germany meet International Safety Standards for new ships developed in 1948* or 1960**.

The Lloyd and German-Atlantic Line in 1967-1968 merged their cruise and trans-Atlantic schedules. When G.A.L. dropped the liner voyages in favor of cruising only, it was good news for NDL; it found it preferred to go it alone — with its standards.

LLOYD NORWEGENFAHRT
MIT MS -BERLIN- 19100 BRT
ÜBER DEN POLARKREIS
Reisedauer: 11 Tage vom 3.-14. Juli 1963   1963
Fahrtstrecke 2646 sm = 4901 Kilometer

POLARTAUFE · INTERESSANTE LANDAUSFLÜGE
Mindestfahrpreis DM 880.-

NORDDEUTSCHER LLOYD BREMEN

KRÖNUNG DER LLOYD SEEREISEN

BREMEN
KREUZFAHRT

SCHOTTLAND · ISLAND · NORWEGEN

Reisedauer: 8 Tage vom 20.-28. Juli 1963   1963
Fahrtstrecke: 2901 sm = 5373 Kilometer

EDINBURGH · REYKJAVIK · BERGEN

Stadtrundfahrten · Überlandfahrten
Mindestfahrpreis DM 1080.-

When cruising, just being, not just going, is the joy and relaxation. "One feels so comfortable, that German word Gemütlich, on Lloyd ships," from a non-German passenger.

NORDDEUTSCHER LLOYD BREMEN
LLOYD
HERBSTREISE
IN DEN SÜDEN
mit MS."BERLIN" 29. Sept.-16. Okt. 64   1964
ab DM 1170.-

LISSABON · FUNCHAL · TENERIFE · CASABLANCA · LA CORUÑA

From Crossing to Cruising

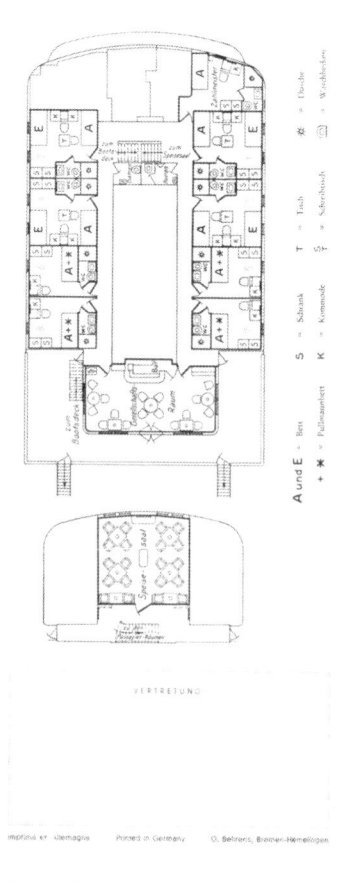

On the reefers Lichtenstein *and* Liebenstein *to the Atlantic islands and North Brazil twelve passengers could be carried in eight cabins. The Dining Room and Social Hall had sixteen places, and a Bar.*

From a January, 1962 folder: Cargo Ship Travel. 20,000 copies printed, so widely distributed. Service to West Coast Central-North America.

The unusual still does make the news: Like Edward Everett Hale's "The Man Without a Country," condemned to remain at sea on U.S. Naval vessels until his death, an immigrant whose re-entry permit had run out, shuttled back and forth on *Gripsholm* in 1954, told to leave by Germany, his temporary residence where he had become destitute, and refused by the U.S. Captain Lorenz commented "He stalks the ship day and night like a ghost." I do not know the end of this story.

- In October, an 18-years old German stowaway on the freighter *Bärenstein* #483, went for eleven days without food or water to reach the land of his dreams. At the Brooklyn pier, the ship's cargo

They train them young on NGL ships

Most stewards who serve you aboard North German Lloyd ships started going to sea in their early youth. They were carefully selected from among hundreds of eager youngsters and painstakingly trained for their responsible jobs. Mind-reading is part of the job. So is an unobtrusive presence whenever you want something.

Your Lloyd steward is likely to know your name before you embark and when you order steak the second time you need not tell him how you want it done. The way he serves your gourmet foods and vintage wines does full justice to their superb taste and quality.

NGL ships carry more personnel than staterooms and every crew member represents the century-old tradition of gracious hospitality which has made the Lloyd the by-word among sophisticated travelers.

Your travel agent will be proud to book your next trip on the magnificent flagship Bremen or her fleetmate, the ever-popular Berlin. See him soon.

Send for free dining guide, "Famous Restaurants of Europe," Dept. K-2

TS BREMEN
New York—Cherbourg—Southampton—Bremerhaven
Apr. 1, Apr. 27, May 15, June 2
and regularly thereafter

MS BERLIN
New York—Southampton—Bremerhaven
Apr. 29, May 27, June 21, July 29
and regularly thereafter

NORTH GERMAN LLOYD
666 Fifth Avenue, New York 19, N.Y. PL 7-9300/CHICAGO • LOS ANGELES • TORONTO

1957, Centennial Year, Promotion for NDL's freight ship passenger services. Some routes were served jointly with other lines, German and/or non-German.

remained enclosed due to the longshoremen's strike. When the crew opened a hatch to get out a rope, sixty feet down a man was seen crawling towards the ladder. He was brought out, temporarily blinded from the sudden light. He had had no water, and had lost sixty pounds. He revived after he was fed warm milk, cereal, crackers, orange juice and a soft-boiled egg. When told by immigration officials he would be deported - the rule is you return on the ship you arrived on - he replied "I am going to work and save up money, get a visa and come to America the legal way."
- And often babies are born at sea, sometimes twins, on *Berlin* in July, 1960 by a mother-to-be who thought she could reach Germany and relatives in time. On another crossing of *Berlin* the son born at sea was named Lloyd. When working in Venezuela in the 1930s I knew a family who had been evacuated from Mexico during the U.S. invasion of 1916-1917 on the *U.S.S. Dixie*. Their daughter born on board was so named.

Cruising has become a huge business, where profits are the attraction, until financiers and operators learn the lesson that to keep this wheel going they also have to offer every imaginable kind of service, meet every whim of the guest on board. It is a different clientele: no longer the arrival or departure of headline and news-making noteworthy people; rather what is available on the ships: name bands, performers, lecturers. While people no longer travel with steamer trunks and servants, it is the suites built onto the tops of several liners, *Norway,* the former *France,* and *QE2,* that sell out first.

From Crossing to Cruising 509

The Statue of Liberty-Ellis Island Foundation, Inc.

proudly presents this

Official Certificate of Registration

in

THE AMERICAN IMMIGRANT WALL OF HONOR

to officially certify that

Theodor Archie Drechsel

came to the United States of America from

Germany

joining those courageous men and women who came to this country in search of personal freedom, economic opportunity and a future of hope for their families.

Lee A. Iacocca
The Statue of Liberty-Ellis Island
Foundation, Inc.

LIBERTY
1886-1986

A New York Times survey in the Fall of 1994 found that twenty-eight cruise vessels were under construction or planned by the year 2000, averaging some 70,000 tons, with capacities for more than two thousand passengers each.

In 1980, there were some 1.4 millions who went on cruises. It was expected to reach five millions in 1994 and perhaps eight millions in 2000: A huge but competitive market and potential, but requiring extensive promotion. A very different, but who is to say a less enjoyable, way of life at sea than in olden days?

What there is of immigrant inflow comes by air. But the history of Ellis Island remains a strong attraction. Millions visit the museum there, following its centennial-restoration in 1992.

In October, 1994, The American Immigrant Wall of Honor had 480,000 names on it, with the remaining space for 20,000 expected to be filled by year end. The author has had his older brother Theodor Archie Drechsel's name put there; he left no children. See Immigrant coverage in Vol. I, p. 293-304.

Lloyd ships carry the mails and the cruise ships provide SHIP POST service to passenger and crew.

As contractual partner of the German Bundespost and foreign postal authorities, Hapag-Lloyd ships transport Letter and Package Posts from and to overseas destinations in accordance with rules of the Universal Postal Union. The ships carry the German mail flag.

Volumes of mail carried could be substantial. But with the rarity of trans-Atlantic liner sailings, the freighters did the mail-hauling.

At Christmas time 1960, 34,629 sacks of package mail went to New York:
- 12,000 on *Göttingen*
- 12,229 on *Bischofstein,*
- 10,400 on *Breitenstein*, plus sacks of letter mail.

In its schedule Hapag-Lloyd shows this German Mail Flag and stresses "regular carriage of mails."

The Lloyd's return to passenger shipping in 1954 was recorded postally with the issuance of Ship Posts Appropriate to the event:

For *Gripsholm*:- in March, 1954 **Nord/-Amerika-Dienst/a** from its second voyage Bremen/New York. The Ship Post remained in service into May, 1955 after the ship had been renamed *Berlin* in January. It also was used during *Berlin's* first West Indies cruises in January-February, 1955 from New York although some items mailed on board bore a so-identifying rubber-stamp marking. The combination is rare, as German ship mail collectors were not yet able extensively to follow their hobby.

From May 1955 through *Berlin's* last trans-Atlantic crossing in September, 1966 the same type Ship Post was used but with BERLIN in the top segment instead of "a."

Three Postalia Meter cancels also were intended for *Gripsholm-Berlin*. Trial impressions exist of the first: **Bremen-New York An Bord M.S.Gripsholm** from 1954. The cancel never was used. It lacked the words *Schiffspost*.

The second is *RRR: Bremen-New York/Schiffspost/ An Bord M.S. Gripsholm*. The third type *Bremen-New York/An Bord M.S. Berlin* was issued in 1955. An envelope to me from Purser H. Müller dated 1/3/1957 is the last sending known.

Registry service also was available on *Berlin* with R labels.

Cruise Ship Posts issued for *Berlin* included:
- *Westindienreisen/M.S. Berlin* from 1958 into 1961.
- *1.Norwegenfahrt/MS Berlin*, then with numbers through 7, from 1961 into 1966.
- *Bermudas* during 1965 and 1966.
- *Lloyd Herbstreise*, Autumn Cruise, 1963 - 1966.
- *Weihnachtsreise*, Christmas Cruise, 1963 - 1965.
- *Ostseefahrt*, Baltic Sea Cruise, 1966.
- *Irlandfahrt*, 1966.

The Postal Administration of West Berlin in March, 1955 issued a 10Pf. and a 25Pf. Stamp showing the *Berlin*. A commemorative postmark was used on the day of issue: 12/3/1955.

The details and history of these Ship Posts are from my "1886-1986, A Century of German Ship Posts" published in 1987 by Christie's Robson Lowe, Ltd., London.

Sometimes there had to be adjustments for emergencies. The scheduled 30 January, 1958 departure from Bremerhaven to Halifax and New York, there to leave for the West Indies on 13 February, was delayed by fog for 56 hours, most unusual. The stop at Halifax was skipped, the 239 passengers for there sent by train from New York. "All shipboard preparations for the cruise were carried out as planned, such as setting in the swimming basin..." It probably means a canvas pool, as was done on all cruises pre-1939 until *Columbus* was given a Lido deck with tiled pool in December, 1937. The cruise date was kept: to San Juan, Bridgetown, Port of Spain, Port-au-Prince, Havana and return to New York.

SHIP POSTS issued for *Bremen's* use on the North Atlantic and for cruising: Two *Jungfernreise: Bremen* (Maiden Voyage) were issued. The first shows only the starting date: 9/7/1959. It is RRR. The second bears the round-trip dates: 9-28/7/1959. It also received a *Nordamerika-Dienst/TS Bremen* used from the Maiden Voyage into 1971, except that after the Hapag-Lloyd merger of 1970, the cancel had that wording at the bottom instead of *Norddeutscher Lloyd*. Registry service also was available. Cruise Ship Posts issued for *Bremen* included:

- *Westindienreisen/TS Bremen* -1960 - 1970.
- *Bermudas* - 1966 - 1968. In 1971, the lower segment read: *Hapag-Lloyd A.G.*
- *Schottland - Island - Norwegen* - 1963.
- *Nordsee-Ostseefahrt* - 1964.
- *Island - Norwegen* - 1965-1966.
- *Nordkapfahrt* - 1967 - 1968.
- *Silvesterfahrt* (New Year's) - 1967 - 1970. Free champagne New Year's Eve!
- *Kreuzfahrten - Nordatlantikreisen*, combing Cruising and Atlantic Crossing in one Ship Post - 1971 - 1972.
- *Mittelmeerfahrt* (Mediterranean)

Some cruise route designations were used on more than one vessel:
- *Westindienreisen*: *Berlin* and *Bremen*
- *Norwegenfahrt*: *Berlin* and *Europa*
- *Bermudas*: *Berlin* and *Bremen*
- *Lloyd Herbstreise*: *Berlin* and *Europa*
- *Ostseefahrt*: *Berlin* and *Europa*

Eventually, specific cruise indications were replaced by a generic cancel reading **Kreuzfahrten-Nordatlantikdienst** under Hapag-Lloyd ownership from 1970.

Although built for North Atlantic service, *Europa* had all-outside cabins, and was easily configured for cruising, the more so when painted white.

Europa had SHIP POSTS on all her voyages from January, 1966 to Halifax and New York into October, 1981, the return from her last cruise. From then into January, 1982 there was no Lloyd passenger service until *Europa 5* began her Gala Maiden Voyage-Cruise to Africa from Genoa.

SHIP POSTS for *Europa*: One *Jungfernreise* 9-18/1/1966. It also received a *Nordamerika-Dienst/MS Europa* used from April, 1966 into 1971. Registry Service also was available. Cruise Ship Posts issued for *Europa* included:

- *Westindienreisen/MS Europa* -1966 - 1971.
- *Norwegenfahrt* - 1968 - 1970. The . from the excised numbers shows.
- *Lloyd Herbstreise* - 1967 - 1969.
- *Ostseefahrt* - 1968 - 1970.
- *Spitzbergenfahrt* - 1966 - 1970.
- *Frohlingsfahrt*, Spring Cruise - 1969 1970.
- *Mittelmeerfahrt*, Mediterranean Cruise - 1969 - 1970.
- *Schwarzmeerfahrt*, Black Sea Cruise 1969 - 1970.
- *Kreuzfahrten,* Cruising - 1975, with Hapag-Lloyd A.G. in lower segment.

This Ship Post was used on *Europa's* last voyage, a cruise to West Africa, returning to Bremerhaven on 4/10/1981. She then was sold off to Italy. A fifth *Europa* entered service, a new-building from the Bremen Vulkan shipyard, began its GALA-JUNGFERNREISE AFRICA on 8/1/1982. It remains in service at this writing in 1994, now with a chartered cruise-liner renamed *Bremen* as running mate. The use of Ship Posts continues on both vessels as a service to passengers and crews. Rubber stamp markings are laid out beside the Purser's Office indicating segments of cruises undertaken. I have seen passengers apply these extensively to their correspondence, then throwing it into the Mail slot for postmarking with the appropriate cruise Ship Post and onward dispatch. It reminds recipients that the name and spirit of the Lloyd remain active.

Bremerhaven's postmark for Bremen's maiden voyage.

Postalia meter Ship Post used on Berlin, ex Gripsholm.

A Sampler of Norddeutscher Lloyd liner and cruise promotions, from one-ship service with Berlin, *then two, also a* Bremen, *and briefly three in 1966, with an* Europa. *All stress that every facet of life can be enjoyed: relaxing, playing, recuperating, exercising, working, eating. "Lloyd service and care is something you, the traveller, have a right to expect."*

Fabulous West Indies Cruises aboard NGL's newest ship
the Trans-Atlantic liner
MS EUROPA
COMPLETELY AIR-CONDITIONED
Feb. 25 1966

NEW YORK—SAN JUAN—ST. CROIX—GUADELOUPE—BARBADOS—TRINIDAD—ST. VINCENT—ST. THOMAS—NEW YORK. • 14 delightful days—from $425.00. Ten other winter cruises with similar itineraries. Better hurry, all NGL cruises were sold out in the past three years.

Send for lavishly illustrated brochures.
Book through your travel agent.

NORTH GERMAN LLOYD

IDEAL MID-WINTER
Cruise TO THE WEST INDIES AND SOUTH AMERICA
on the Famous Ocean Favorite
M. S. BERLIN
(formerly the "Gripsholm")

17 GLORIOUS DAYS
LEAVING NEW YORK
FEBRUARY 17
1956

Kingston, Jamaica; Cartagena, Colombia; San Blas, Panama; Cristobal, Canal Zone; Havana, Cuba. The BERLIN is your "hotel" throughout, offering all the splendid cuisine and service for which NORTH GERMAN LLOYD is famous. Wide choice of optional shore trips.

SEE YOUR TRAVEL AGENT OR
Swedish American Line Agency, Inc.
General Passenger Agents
636 FIFTH AVENUE, NEW YORK 20, N. Y.

CRUISE FARES AS LOW AS **$20.00** per day

NORTH GERMAN LLOYD

DELUXE SUMMER CRUISE
aboard the popular
Trans-Atlantic Liner
M.S. BERLIN
TO GASPE—HALIFAX—BERMUDA
from New York

July 26 1966

return to New York August 6. Rates from $260.00.

GOURMET FOOD
TOP RATE ENTERTAINMENT
SERVICE IN THE GRAND MANNER

Send for illustrated folder
Book through your travel agent

NORTH GERMAN LLOYD
Dept. A 666 Fifth Ave., New York, N.Y. 10019 PL 7-9300/Chicago—Los Angeles—Toronto
NGL ships are of West German registry

CONNOISSEURS Cruise
to the West Indies and South America
aboard the
new luxurious 32,335-ton flagship T.S. **BREMEN**
completely air-conditioned

1961

Leave New York Mar. 2, 14 Days, 9 Ports, From $395. Visit the glamorous ports of St. Thomas, St. Pierre, Fort-de-France, Barbados, Grenada, Port of Spain, La Guaira, Curacao, Port-au-Prince.

Sail aboard the sleek new Bremen to the sun-drenched playground of the Caribbean. Ports carefully selected for their beauty, variety, gaiety and unusual shopping bargains. Food prepared by renowned master chefs... entertainment planned by experts... service in the century-old Lloyd tradition. Perfect itinerary... perfect ship... perfect time to sail to the West Indies and South America. Only one sitting at meals.

Other Bremen Cruise: Feb. 14
See Your Travel Agent
NORTH GERMAN LLOYD
666 Fifth Avenue, New York 19, N. Y. • PL 7-9300 / CHICAGO • LOS ANGELES • TORONTO

Great Vacation Idea
Cruising the St. Lawrence, the Saguenay, the Scenic Canadian Islands and Charming Bermuda
ABOARD THE
TS **BREMEN**
July 19 • August 18 1970
11 and 13 Days—From $350.00

THE FASCINATING ITINERARIES INCLUDE:
NEW YORK • ST. LAWRENCE RIVER • TADOUSSAC • THE SAGUENAY • CAPE TRINITY • ST. CATHERINE • MURRAY BAY • MONTREAL • QUEBEC • CAPE BRETON ISLAND • CAPE NORTH • NORTH SYDNEY • INGONISH HARBOUR • BERMUDA • NEW YORK.

Ask for Illustrated brochures—book through your travel agent

NORTH GERMAN LLOYD

CRUISE OF THE YEAR
From Port Everglades, Florida
FEB. 9 • 21 DAYS • 12 PORTS
MS **EUROPA**
THE SHIP BUILT FOR CRUISING

PORT EVERGLADES • HAITI • SANTO DOMINGO JAMAICA • PANAMA CANAL • SAN BLAS CARTAGENA • ARUBA • VENEZUELA ISLA MARGARITA • TRINIDAD • MARTINIQUE ST. MAARTEN • ST. THOMAS • PORT EVERGLADES

Fully air-conditioned. Motion stabilizers. Outdoor and indoor swimming pools. All outside staterooms—all with private bath or shower. Night Clubs. Haute Cuisine. Service in the grand manner. Distinguished entertainment from two continents. Highly experienced cruise staffs—superbly organized shore excursions. 1970

NUMBER OF PASSENGERS LIMITED TO ASSURE LUXURIOUS DINING... ONLY ONE SITTING AT MEALS

RATES FROM $710.00

Other Winter & Spring Cruises from Port Everglades and New York from $175.00
NORTH GERMAN LLOYD

From Crossing to Cruising

DOLCE FAR NIENTE

Sweet doing nothing—what a beautiful phrase! And what better place for it than a deck chair aboard a Lloyd ship. To relax after a night of dancing...a swim in the pool...a brisk walk on deck...a stint in the gym. On NGL ships you also have a beautiful stateroom, five gourmet meals a day, first-run movies, gay parties, exciting games—all in an atmosphere of old world graciousness and luxury.

GO BY SHIP—GO NGL

ᵀˢBREMEN ᵀˢEUROPA ᴹˢBERLIN

From New York to England—France—Germany

Apr. 26, 28; May 14, 24; June 2, 9, 15   1966
and regularly thereafter.

See Your Travel Agent

NORTH GERMAN LLOYD

Dept. A, 666 Fifth Ave., New York, N.Y. 10019 PL 7-9300/Chicago • Los Angeles • Toronto

NGL ships are of West German registry

NGL Business Office Afloat

Aboard the NGL flagship Bremen you can dictate your letters lolling in a deck chair to a multi-lingual Lloyd secretary. If you must work en route, this is a wonderful way to do it.

ENGLAND • FRANCE • GERMANY

The Flagship **BREMEN**   The Popular **BERLIN**

FROM NEW YORK Feb. 28; Mar. 18, 28; April 8, 26, 27;
May 14 and regularly thereafter.   1964

SEE YOUR TRAVEL AGENT

NORTH GERMAN LLOYD

510 W. 6th St., Los Angeles 14, Calif. • MA 7-8753/NEW YORK • CHICAGO • TORONTO

YOU TRAVEL WELL WITH NGL

Tourist Class is Great aboard the friendly

ᴹˢBERLIN

Tourist class passengers on the popular "Berlin" enjoy virtual run of the ship. Of 975 beds only 48 are used for First Class. The food is fit for kings—the service unsurpassed afloat or ashore. You get all this and much more for $23 a day.

From NEW YORK to ENGLAND and GERMANY

JULY 28   1965

also May 26, June 21, August 21, Sept. 15 and regularly thereafter.

SEE YOUR TRAVEL AGENT

NORTH GERMAN LLOYD

666 Fifth Ave., New York 19, N.Y. PL 7-9300 / CHICAGO—LOS ANGELES—TORONTO

NGL Ships are of West German Registry

TRANSPORTATION
is merely a fringe benefit

when you travel NGL to Europe

Aboard North German Lloyd's floating vacation resorts almost everything you do and enjoy is on the house. Five gourmet meals a day, first-run movies, gay parties, exciting games, swimming pools, deck sports, gyms, libraries, plus a beautiful stateroom with the equivalent of a valet and maid. Your low fare includes all this and many other luxuries. Lloyd ships are superbly comfortable—Lloyd service is legendary.

GO BY SHIP—GO NGL

ᵀˢBREMEN ᵀˢEUROPA ᴹˢBERLIN

From New York to England-France-Germany

May 14, 24; June 2, 9, 15, 19 and regularly thereafter.

See Your Travel Agent   1966

NORTH GERMAN LLOYD

666 Fifth Ave., New York, N.Y. 10019 PL 7-9300/Chicago • Los Angeles • Toronto

---

FLOATING SPA

On your way to Europe or cruising the Caribbean the TS Bremen and MS Europa offer you the extra benefit of extensive health facilities including the unique underwater massage. Plus luxurious accommodations, superb food and service in the grand manner. Enjoy your trip, go by ship—go Hapag-Lloyd.

ᵀˢBREMEN ᴹˢEUROPA

From New York to England, France and Germany

June 13; July 1; Aug. 1, 30; Sept. 16; Dec. 14

Frequent cruise departures to the Caribbean, South America, the Bahamas and Bermuda.

1971

Write for illustrated brochure—book through your Travel Agent

Hapag-Lloyd

North German Lloyd Passenger Agency Inc., Gen. Agt.

New York • Chicago • Toronto
Dept. A-81, 510 West Sixth St., Los Angeles, Cal. 90014. Tel. (213) 627-8753

Bremen and Europa are of West German Registry.

SERVICE WITH A SMILE

Yes, it still exists. North German Lloyd service standards are as high today as they were a century ago. Stewards virtually read your mind. All hands on board bend every effort to make your trip a memorable experience. And memorable it will be! Luxurious surroundings, five gourmet meals, first-run movies, music, dancing, entertainment, parties, games, swimming pools, gyms—and many other things just for the low price of your ticket.

GO BY SHIP—GO NGL

ᵀˢBREMEN ᵀˢEUROPA ᴹˢBERLIN

From New York to England—France—Germany
Feb. 18, Mar. 18, Apr. 2, Apr. 18, Apr. 26,
Apr. 28 and regularly thereafter   1966

See Your Travel Agent

NORTH GERMAN LLOYD

Dept. A, 666 Fifth Ave., New York, N.Y. 10019 PL 7-9300/Chicago • Los Angeles • Toronto

NGL ships are of West German registry

NDL Fleet
Ships 490 — 506

490. *Travestein*	1954-1973		
Lübecker Flenderwerke #441	1954	6752	160.15 x 19.27
Siemens Turbine	9000	17.5	
9	45		

Launched 2/2/1954. Delivery 29/4/1954 to Orlanda Reederei. Left Hamburg 9/7/1957, had a collision on 16th, arrived La Union 14 August after repairs, for Seattle. Left Hamburg 5/8/1964 for conversion at Bremer Vulkan, Vegesack: re-engined with Diesels, 14 400 HP, 19.5 kns, lengthened to 167.43 m., bulbous bow, 7008 Ts. 1/9/1970 to Hapag-Lloyd A.G. 17/3/1973 to Ocean Tramping Co., Hong Kong, renamed *Nanhua*, Nan Yang Shipping Co., Macao, operator. 1977 Golden City Maritime Corp., Panama, 6,646 Ts. On 5/2/1985 delivery at Shanghai to National Metals Import & Export Co. for BU.

Travestein #490 had a serene life other than one minor collision en route to Seattle in 1957. In contrast to the other turbine freighters, the king posts for hatch III before the superstructure are built into that structure, not before it. Photo Collection of Y. Bertrand, Lyon.

Hessenstein #491, second of the combi-ships, some passengers watching the Lloyd ship from which this photo was taken in 1955 or later; the stack is Lloyd gold-yellow, no longer the black-topped Roland color.

491. *Hessenstein 1*	1954-1973		
Bremer Vulkan, Vegesack #833	1954	8929	163.90 x 19.44
M.A.N. Diesel	10,560	17.25	* *
86	90		

Launched 22/3/1954. Delivery 17/6/1954 to Orlanda Reederei. MV 20/6/1954 to Far East. Ret. 20 Oct., 15 days late. 6/6/1960 arrived Hong Kong during Typhoon Mary with *Ravenstein* #495. Both tied up to typhoon buoys. Five-days delay; neither suffered damage. 12/2/1967 delivery to Malaysia Overseas Lines, Monrovia, renamed *Oriental Musician*, Far East-U.S. Gulf Coast passenger service. 17/2/1978 delivery to Shun Fun Shipbreakers, Hong Kong.

Lloyd's daily List over the years records many accidents. *Havelstein* had its share. On 1/12/1956 ran aground, sld. from Las Palmas the 9th after repairs. On 29/3/1961 she had a collision on the West Coast-South America. On 8 January, 1962 she left Hamburg, the 10th had a collision, arrived Seattle 21 February. On 9/8/1962 collision at Antwerp en route Hamburg-Valparaiso. Other ships had fires in engine rooms or holds, or propeller problems, etc. 7/2/1962 *Ravenstein* grounded after leaving Seattle for the Continent. One wonders if such happenings resulted from pushing to keep tight schedules. Or from crew reductions to cut costs?

492. *Havelstein*	1954-1973		
Deutsche Werft, Hamburg #669	1954	6734	159.06 x 19.16
A.E.G. Turbine	9000	17.5	
9	46		

Launched 21/5/1954. 26/7/1954 delivery to Orlanda Reederei. 1964 re-engined to Diesel and lengthened, 14 400 HP, 19.5 kns.,

168.00 meters, 6,903 Ts. 1/9/1970 to Hapag-Lloyd A.G. 30/1/1973 to Ocean Tramping Co., Hong Kong managers, reg. in Mogadisciu, renamed *Nankuo*. 1975 Nan Yang Shipping Co., Macao, operator. 1977 to Brilliance S.S. Corp., Panama, 6,899 Ts. 25/8/1984 arr. Xingang for BU by China Metals & Minerals Import & Export Co.

Havelstein *#492 in San Francisco in the 1950s.* Dudley Thickens, World Ship Society Director, Photo.

Havelstein *#492 had her share of accidents, this a deep gash forward when in February, 1958, a Soviet freighter hit her in the fog. Here in the Weser-Kurier, Bremen, photo, the damage areas are painted. A worker can be seen in the gash. One of the stevedores is quoted in Plattdeutsch, Low German: "That's big enough for a lot of fresh air" to get inside.*

Isarstein #493 in Hong Kong in 1976 loading and unloading at the same time. Author's Photo.

493. Isarstein   1954-1973
Deutsche Werft, Hamburg #673 1954   6717   159.10 x 19.16
A.E.G. Turbine   9000   17.5
9   46

Launched 2/8/1954. Delivery 1/11/1954 to Orlanda Reederei. 6-9/1964 re-engined to Diesel, 14 400 HP, and lengthened to 166.27 meters by Bremer Vulkan, 6,900 Ts., 19.5 kns. 1/9/1970 to Hapag-Lloyd A.G. 25/1/1973 to P.Z. Perusahaan Pelajaran Samudera, Djakarta, ren. Pratita, 6,900 Ts. same name used by *Barenstein* #483 while under Indonesian charter 1971-1972. 15/6/1983 sold to Bangladeshi breakers, arr. Chittagoing from Surabaja on 10/7/1983.

494. Bayernstein 1   1955-1967
Bremer Vulkan, Vegesack #839   1955   8999   163.90 x 19.44
M.A.N. Diesel   10,560   17.25   * *
86   91

Launched 12/10/1954. MV. 8/1/1955 to Far East. 10/1966 sold to C.Y. Tung interests, Hong Kong, Orient Overseas Lines. Delivery 12/1/1967, renamed *Oriental Lady*. 1/1979 sold by United Overseas Export Lines to Kaohsiung for BU, arr. 25/1/1979. The six sisters were sold for $7.5 millions.

Bayernstein #494, last of NDL's three combi-vessels. The ships were sold for $1,250,000 each, in 1966, delivered in 1967. Here in Lloyd stack. Hapag-Lloyd A.G.

495. *Ravenstein*	1941-1944/1955-1971	
J. Cockerill, Hoboken #697		
1947	7822/8065	166.50 x 19.66
Cockrill Diesels	12,000 17.5	* * *
4	56	

Ordered 1941 by NDL as *Regensburg* in name-replacement for #406. Designed for triple screws as bigger engines were unavailable. 4/8/1943 construction stopped, 9/1944 seized by Belgium. Launched 14/2/1946 sans name for Regie de la Marine, Bruxelles. 27/7/1947 completed, mngd. by Cie. Maritime Belge as *Bastogne*. 14/3/1955 arr. Antwerp with two sisters bought by NDL, ren. *Ravenstein*, Is 18/4/1955. 8-11/1961 installation of 3 new M.A.N. Diesels at Bremer Vulkan, 12,000 HP, 17.5 kns. 1/9/1970 to Hapag-Lloyd A.G. 11/8/1971 to Costoula Shipping Corp., Cyprus, renamed *Ravens*. 10/6/1978 left Basrah, arr. Gadani Beach for BU by Capricorn Enterprises on 21/6/1978.

496. *Reifenstein*	1941-1944/1955-1971	
J. Cockerill, Hoboken #696		
1946	7859/8065	166.50 x 19.60
3 x Cockrill Diesels	12,000 17.5	* * *
5	53	

Ordered 1941, intended name *Marburg 3* after *Marburg 2* lost. Launched 17/5/1944 for NDL. 4/9/1944 sunk by Germans in retreat. Raised, work resumed for Belgian Govt. Delivery 13/7/1946 to Regie de la Marine, Bruxelles, mgd. by Cie. Maritime Belge as *Houffalize*. 7/1955 bought by NDL. IS. 17/8/1955 as *Reifenstein*. 6-8/1961 given new M.A.N. Diesels at Bremer Vulkan. 1/9/1970 to Hapag-Lloyd A.G. 11/8/1971 to Costoula Shipping Co., Famagusta, renamed *Reifens*. 8/1972 to Elektra Shipping Co., Famagusta. 1978 sold through Marubeni Co. to Kaohsiung for BU, arr. 22/2/1978.

Three unusual ships, Ravenstein #495, Reifenstein #496 and Rothenstein #497, reflect the fortunes of war. Ordered in Belgium in 1941 as replacement for war losses, construction stopped, then resumed under Belgian control. Postwar, they served into 1955 on the Belgium-Belgian Congo-U.S. East Coast routes. NDL bought them in 1955 to expand and upgrade its Australia services. The vessels had triple screws because only small Diesel engines were available during the war. The only such freighters ever built. When the container revolution hit, they were too old to rebuild, in 1971 were sold off ... to Cyprus. An unusual flag for a shipowner.

Ravenstein *#495 in Bremen.* Photo by Karl-Heinz Böttcher, Bremen-Kattenesch.

Reifenstein *#496 and its official NDL Photo Archive picture. The three sisters had the wind-up sweeping vents before the bridge, as did* Bremen *and* Europa.

Rothenstein *#497, still as the Belgian* Stavelot *in Weehawken directly across the Hudson from the former Hapag-Lloyd Piers 84 and 86. 1949 or earlier as the* Aquitania, *four stacks, is in port. The Van Cortlandt Street Ferry is just reaching Weehawken. The author rode it in the 1920s for six cents, across the Hudson to 42nd Street for four cents, when he lived in Weehawken 1924-1929.* Rothenstein *is 4-masted ship at left.*

497. *Rothenstein*	1941-1944/1955-1971	
J. Cockrill, Hoboken #695		
1946	7834/8065	166.50 x 19.66
3 x Cockrill Diesels	12,000 17.5	* * *
5	54	

Ordered 1941 as *Coburg 3* to replace lost *Coburg 2* namewise. Launched 8/12/1943. 4/9/1944 sunk by retreating Germans. 27/12/1944 raised, worked resumed for Regie de la Marine. Delivery 23/4/1946 as *Stavelot*, 7,834 Ts. Cie. Maritime Belge, Antwerp, operator. 15/3/1955 left Boma for New York on last voyage, then to Antwerp and 11/5/1955 purchase by NDL. IS. 18/6/1955 as *Rothenstein*. 9-12/1961 given three new MAN Diesels by Bremen Vulkan. 1/9/1970 to Hapag-Lloyd A.G. 11/8/1971 to Costoula Shipping Co., Famagusta, renamed *Rothens*. 2/1972 to Tatiana Shipping Co., Famagusta. 16/3/1979 arrived Kaohsiung for BU.

Trierstein into service 2/1955 bought as *Adolf Vinnen*, ex *Porta #287*.

Trierstein *put under the Lloyd flag in Spring, 1955. It was built as* Porta #287 *in Stettin in 1922, in 1939-1940 rebuilt as were several sisters, for the South Africa-South America route (and by demand of the Kriegsmarine to have fast freighters far away from home to use as raiders in case of war?) Assigned to Holland postwar, not put into service. 1950 bought by an old Bremen firm, F.A. Vinnen, rebuilt as* Adolf Vinnen, *chartered by NDL until bought in 1955 and named* Trierstein. *It served into 1964, 32 years old. Hapag-Lloyd A.G. Sister originally and as rebuilt* Traunstein *was the former* Alda #337.

Until 4/5/1955 all Lloyd ships had been ordered and operated by Roland Linie Aktiengesellschaft or Orlanda Reederei because of unresolved legal claims. With a Bremen bank assuming residual liability, the crossed Key and Anchor flag was raised on that day on all ships: 36 ocean vessels of which 28 were new construction, 21 of those built by the Bremer Vulkan, NDL's House Yard. *Tannstein* was the first postwar launch under the Lloyd flag; *Blankenstein* was the first ship ordered direct for NDL rather than Roland or Orlanda.

Kabine

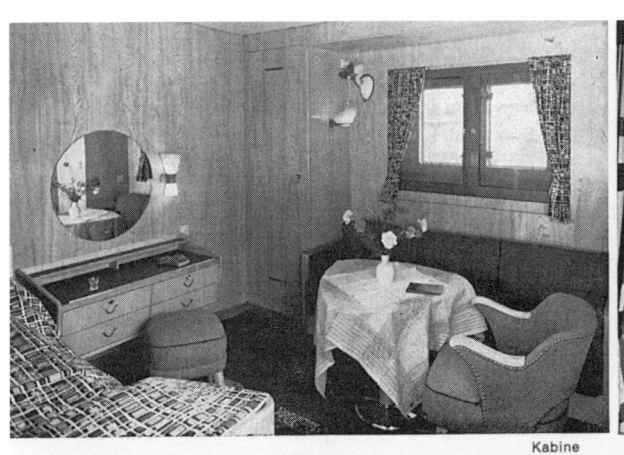

Speisesaal

M.S. Birkenstein *and its eight sisters can accommodate five passengers in three cabins; two have an additional sofabed. On the boatdeck there is a two-bedded "Hospital Cabin." See page 508.*

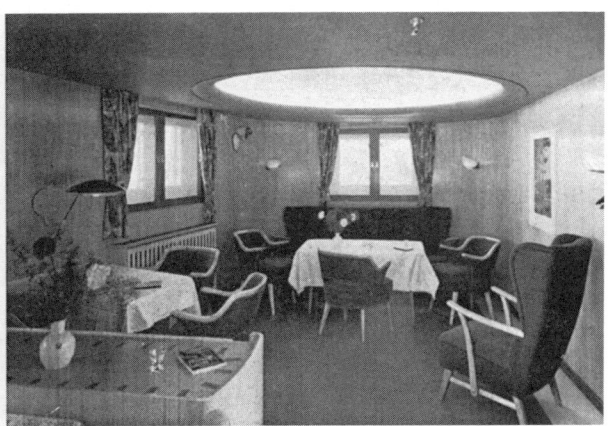

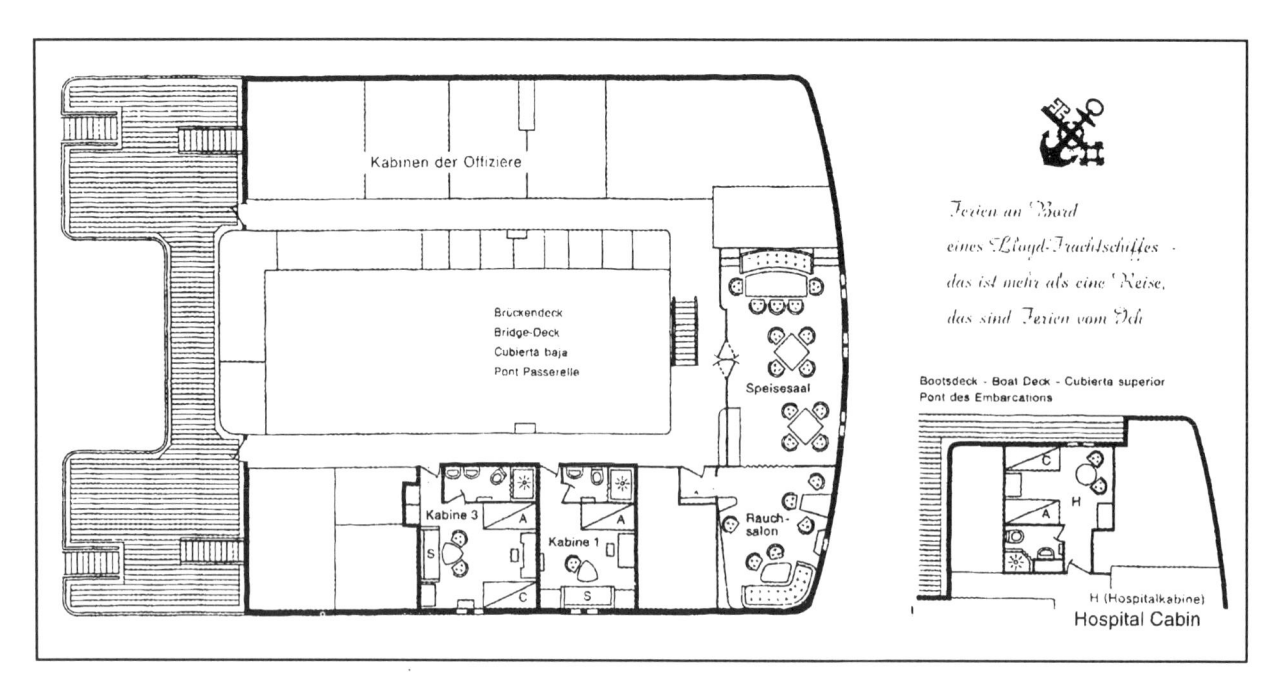

"Vacation on a Lloyd Freighter; It is more than a voyage; it's a vacation from one's self" (one's normal life). Officers' cabins to port, passengers to starboard, and on the Boat Deck a Hospital Cabin.

The Passenger Deck on the Rheinstein *class, the Lloyd's first postwar and smallest freighters.*

498. *Tannstein*	1955-1972		
Bremer Vulkan, Vegesack #843	1955	5572	151.82 x 18.44
1 Danziger Werft, 1 M.A.N. Diesel		4,700	14.3
4		41	

Launched 4/5/1955. MV 29/5/1955 with "Horse" and "Donkey" engines. The "Donkey" was the old Diesel taken out of *Erfurt* #296 when it was re-engined and rebuilt in 1939. 11/1962 new Diesels installed by Howaldtswerke, Hamburg, 8,480 HP, 17.5 knots. 1/9/1970 to Hapag-Lloyd A.G. 18/12/1972 to Ocean Tramping Co., Hong Kong, reg. in Mogadisciu, with *Torstein* and four Hapag ships, renamed *Meiru*. 1975 Nan Yang Shipping Co., Macao, manager. 1977 to High Seas Nav. Co., Panama, 5,180 Ts. 12/1985 delivery at Shanghai to China National Metals & Minerals Co., BU at Nantong. But there were memories of *Tannstein*, e.g. In March, 1959 *Tannstein* was headed south from Seattle, Portland, Oakland, Richmond, Los Angeles and San Diego. Captain Karl Hillmann's wife was on board and three passengers. Easter Sunday the ship called at San Juan del Sur in Nicaragua, then Colon, Cristobal, the Azores, Antwerp, Amsterdam, Bremen and end of voyage at Hamburg. *Tannstein* barely escaped the trap of the Great Bitter Lake imprisonment of ships during the closure of the Suez Canal. On 4 June, 1967 instead of anchoring outside Port Said the order was to enter the harbor sans pilot. That evening, the Canal pilot came on board; *Tannstein* became 10th in a convoy of 21 vessels. 5.25 a.m. on the 5th, change of pilot at Ismailia. Convoy now only 13 ships, continued at 7.30; the other 8 were tied up earlier as one evidently tried to block the canal. Late a.m. the convoy of 21 ships from Suez reached the Great Bitter Lake and anchored. Aerial fighting already was going on. Ismailia radio shut down with a "Red" signal: Canal closed. Late p.m., the radio reopened; our orders to continue towards Suez. Further ships had come from the north, anchored in Great Bitter Lake, also then headed south, *Tannstein*, again 10th now among 28 vessels. Hapag's *Münsterland*, in Great Bitter Lake, called, asked *Tannstein*

Tannstein *in San Francisco 16 May, 1958, just arrived from San Pedro.* Author's Photo.

to advise Hamburg where it was. Suez was passed at 14.30 hours on the 6th; the Canal pilot was relieved by the Sea pilot; The Agency representative advised the canal would shortly be closed. Short of Newport Rocks Lighthouse the Pilot was picked up and at 15.00 hours *Tannstein* proceeded for Penang. Captain Scheding sent a long wireless to Bremen via the Norddeich Station. Not until 7 May, 1975 was *Münsterland* with the other 12 vessels caught by the Arab-Israeli War released from Great Bitter Lake.

Tannstein #498 *and* Torstein #499 *were sisters of the* Brandenstein #481 *design except they each got prewar Diesel left over when* Trierstein, Traunstein *and sisters were rebuilt, and a new M.A.N. engine. This gave them 14.3 knots, not the original 16.5 of the "B" class, later raised to 18 knots. Similarly, these two were given new Diesels in 1962 for 16.5 knots.* Tannstein *escaped from the Suez Canal the day of its closing, in June, 1967 which left thirteen ships locked up for the duration - into 1975.*

Torstein #499 heading downstream at the Weser Elbow near Vegesack where she was built at the Bremer Vulkan. H. Saebens Photo.

499. **Torstein** 1955-1972
Bremer Vulkan, Vegesack #848 1955 5572 151.80 x 18.44
1 Danziger Werft, 1 M.A.N. Diesel   4700   14.3
4   40

> Launched 7/6/1955. MV. 25/8/1955 to U.S. East Coast, with "Horse" and "Donkey" engines, a new M.A.N., an old one from a prewar conversion. 12/1962 replacement of the prewar and 1955 engines with new M.A.N.s by Howaldtswerke, Hamburg, 8,480 HP, 17.5 knots.

In 1963, *Tannstein* and *Nabstein* #515 were accused of breaking the U.S. trade embargo with Cuba, *Tannstein* having sailed from Corpus Christi on 12/3/1963 with a cargo of cotton linters, usable for making explosives, and *Nabstein* on 4 May. 1/9/1970 to Hapag-Lloyd A.G. 11/12/1972 to Ocean Tramping Co., Hong Kong management for Beijing ownership, reg. in Mogadisciu, renamed *Meiki*, 5,139 Ts. 1975 under Nan Yang Shipping Co., Macao. 1980 for High Seas Nav. Co., Manama. 2/1986 sold to Chinese breakers.

In October, 1974 Hapag-Lloyd transferred nine freighters that ran through the Panama Canal to the U.S.-Canada and South America West Coasts to Hapag-Lloyd International, S.A., Panama. A paper move as the ships remained under the German flag, with their German crews and kept their Bremen registrations. The idea: A Panamanian ownership might ease access to the international capital markets. No proof that it ever did: #487, 500-502, 505, 506, 509, 510, 514.

500. *Birkenstein* 1956-1976
Bremer Vulkan, Vegesack #844 1956 5798 151.80 x 18.44
M.A.N. Diesel 9000 17.5
5 41

Launched 6/9/1955. Delivery 8/12/1955. 1/9/1970 to Hapag-Lloyd A.G. 10/1974 to Hapag-Lloyd International, S.A., Panama, reg. in Bremen. 27/8/1977 with *Blankenstein* and *Bartenstein* sold to Pacific International Lines, Singapore, renamed *Kota Berani*, 5,854 Ts. 20/11/1980 - 9/1981 converted to offshore oilfield pipe and maintenance vessel with helicopter platform. 10/6/1986 arr. Kaohsiung for BU by San To Steel Co. Birkenstein and her later sisters had a two-bed "hospital" although no doctor was carried. Just in case.

The Launching Party for Birkenstein *#500 at the Bremer Vulkan on 6 September, 1955. Third from left Dr. Johannes Kulenkampf, with Herr Richard Betram co-General Director of NDL. Fourth - Herr Brand, operations chief of NDL's Technical Service in Bremerhaven. Fifth - Director Ernst Path. 6th - 1. Officer Schmidt. 7th - co-General Director Richard Bertram. 8th - Frau J. Kulenkampff. 9th - Dr. Hermann Richter, member of Aufsichtsrat, Board. 10th - Director Hans Karstedt. 11th - Mrs. H. Karstedt. 12th - Consul Nebelthau, Board member, Bremer Vulkan Shipyard. 13th - Mrs. Nebelthau. 14th - Director Muller, Bremer Vulkan. 15th - Frau Dr. Boden, Launch Patron. 16th - General Director Dr. Boden, Bremer Vulkan. 17th - Frau Richter. 18th - Fräulein Richter. 19th - Director Schilling, Bremer Vulkan Aufsichtsrat. 20th - Frau Wimmer. 21st - Frau Richard Bertram. 22nd - Fräulein Dr. Roester. 23rd - Dr. Roester, Bremer Vulkan. 24th - Frau Schneider. 25th - Director Wimmer, Bremer Vulkan.*

Usually there was a festive dinner afterwards.

The six-units second group from 1956 of the "B" named freighters, see #481, four years later had much heavier lifting gear: two King Posts remained for and aft of the superstructure. The two forward and two aft King Posts on the earlier ships were replaced with free-standing single masts, the foremast could take thirty tons. Birkenstein #500 ended her days in Indonesia as an offshore oilfield pipe and maintenance vessel, with helipad. Michale Pryce Photo ex Marine News, W.S.S.

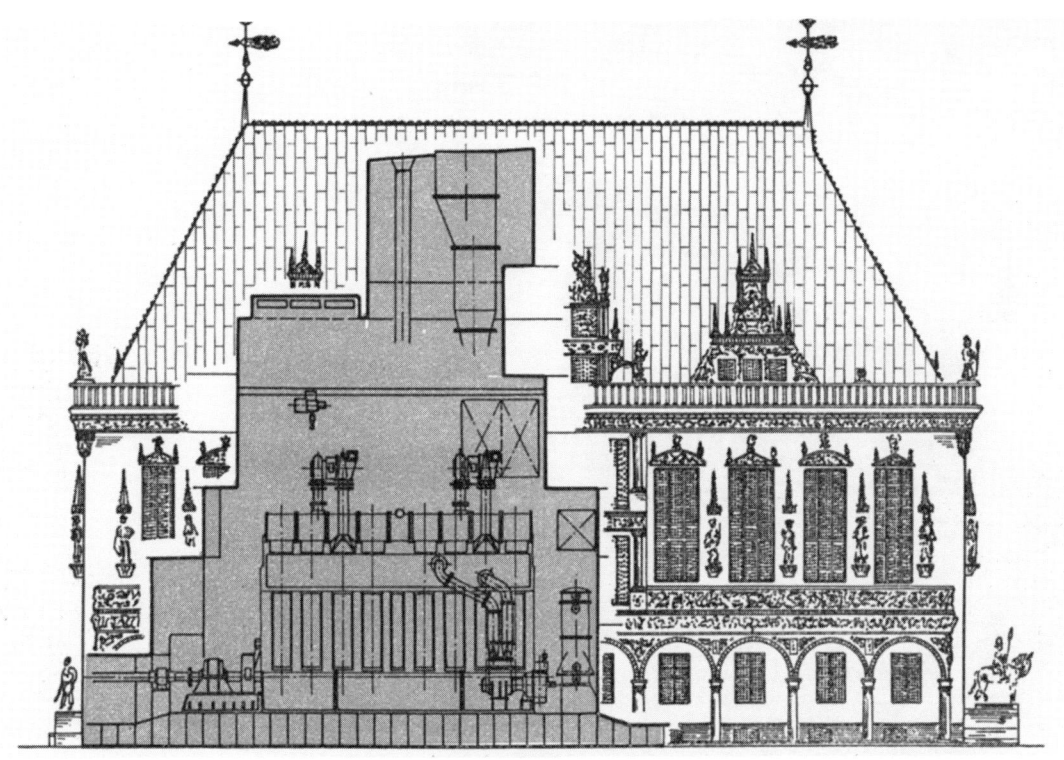

Shipping Lines used to display the size of their vessels in comparison with tall structures, like Queen Mary stood on its stern, or wedged into a street between tall buildings, like Kaiser Wilhelm II. Here the comparison is of the size of the Diesel Engine in the Birkenstein #500 class, and Torstein #499 and Tannstein #498 after re-engining with the Rathaus in Bremen. Almost to the roof line. Weight of the engine is 545 tons, of each piston 2.7 tons, metric.

501. **Breitenstein**	1956-1976		
Bremer Vulkan, Vegesack #846	1956	5794	151.80 x 18.44
M.A.N. Diesel	9000	17.5	
5	41		

Launched 1/11/1955. Delivery 7/1/1956. 24/1/1956 MV arr. in New York, Captain H. Wachtel. 12/1960 brought 10,400 sacks of Christmas mail from the Continent to New York. 1/9/1970 to Hapag-Lloyd A.G. 10/1974 to Hapag-Lloyd International S.A., Panama, reg. Bremen. 22/9/1976 sold to Soc. Armadora Diego,

Panama, an affiliate of Mediterranean Shipping Co., Monrovia. Arr. Bremerhaven 24/9/1976 from Far East on last NDL voyage, renamed *Diego*. 5,318 Ts., MV. Bremen-Hamburg-Rotterdam-Antwerp-Aquaba-Port Sudan. Last voyage left LeHavre 5 November, 1982. 16th lost part of cargo in the Mediterranean. 25th passed Suez, 26 December arr. Djibouti. 30/12/1982 arr. Gadani Beach for scrapping by Pakistani breakers.

Breitenstein *#501, in San Francisco, the single-standing masts fore and aft, instead of twin King Posts, are evident. Lloyd ships almost always looked immaculate, even* Lahnstein *#473 after being holed on the Great Lakes.* Andrew Kilk, World Ship Society Director, Photo.

502. *Bischofstein*	1956-1976		
Bremer Vulkan, Vegesack #850	1956	5794	151.80 x 18.44
M.A.N. Diesel	9000	17.5	
5	44		

Launched 28/11/1955. IS 4/2/1956. 22/3/1959 at night collided with and sank Soviet *Kholmogory* in Weser Estuary off Wangerooge. 12/1960 carried 12,229 bags of mail to the U.S., probably a postwar record and unusual for a freighter. Prewar, *Bremen* and *Europa* sometimes had 25,000 sacks of Christmas mails to the U.S. 1/9/1970 to Hapag-Lloyd A.G. 13/12/1976 to Cia. Nav. Pantera, Panama, renamed *Pantera*, 5,318 Ts., part of Mediterranean Shipping Co. group, Monrovia. Later 7,848 Ts. Left Durban 4/3/1983 for Karachi; sold to Pakistani breakers, 19/3 arrived Gadani Beach for BU.

Bischofstein #502 arriving in New York, Moran tug turning her into the basin, 1950s.

Starting with *Blankenstein* through *Bayernstein* #526 all freighters except the purchased *Lindenstein* #519 and the Full-Container ships, were built for conversion from Shelter-deckers (formerly also Spar or Stormdeckers) to Fulldecker configuration. By these, the free-board is figured from the Upper Deck, by Shelterdeckers from the second deck, so these have less draft, hence less carrying capacity. Since Harbor, canal and other charges are levied per ton, the owner can configure his ship optimally according to route being served and freight volumes available. For lesser and lighter cargoes the Shelterdeck configuration is optimal, for heavy or full cargoes as Fulldeckers. *Burgenstein* #509 could carry 10,850 tons as Fulldecker, 8,500 tons as Shelterdecker. Ships can cube out, the extreme example woodchip carriers, before they weight out, reach the weight limit and load line. Others can weight out, and have sizable unused space for cargo but not usable. The ship has reached its load line.

Blankenstein *in the Euro-Pacific Service with the French Line Continent-West Coast North America in the 1950s. Note containers on deck.* Dudley Thickens Photo, Director World Ship Society.

503. **Blankenstein**	1956-1977	
Bremer Vulkan, Vegesack #857		
1956	5827/8053	151.80 x 18.44
M.A.N. Diesel	9000 17.5	
5	44	

Launched 20/6/1956. Delivery 30/8/1956. 1/9/1970 to Hapag-Lloyd A.G. 10/1974 to Hapag-Lloyd International, S.A., Panama, reg. in Bremen. 28/9/1977 to Pacific International Lines, Singapore, along with *Bartenstein* and *Birkenstein* for $2.75 millions, renamed *Kota Bakti*, 8,034 Ts. 8/4/1983 arrived Kaohsiung, 21/4/1983 BU began at Li Chong Steel & Iron Co.

504. **Bartenstein**	1956-1977	
Bremer Vulkan, Vegesack #861	5827/8053	151.80 x 18.44
M.A.N. Diesel	9000 17.5	
5	33 + up to 22 cadets	

Launched 2/8/1956; original launch set for 23/7 but postponed due to high river runoff. Launches at Bremer Vulkan require static water conditions. Delivery 4/10/1956. 1/9/1970 to Hapag-Lloyd A.G. 10/1974 to Hapag-Lloyd International S.A., Panama, reg. in Bremen. 30/4/1975 arrived Balboa from Hamburg in tow of salvage tug *Doña Maria*. She had been aground on 4/4/1975. 17/9/1977 to Pacific International Lines, Singapore, with *Birkenstein* and *Blankenstein*, renamed *Kota Benar*, 8,001 Ts. 3/7/1983 arrived Bangkok for BU.

Postmark shows that there really is a Bartenstein *in prewar Prussia, 1884.*

Shipping Industry promotion with an excuse: the maiden arrival of a new vessel Bartenstein #504, *at Port of Long Beach, with the Mayor, left, Miss Port of Long Beach, the chairman of NDL agents Balfour-Guthrie, and president of the Port Commission.*

505. ***Bodenstein***		1956-1977		
Bremer Vulkan, Vegesack #862		1956	5827/8034	151.80 x 18.44
M.A.N. Diesel		9000	17.5	
5		44		

Launched 16/10/1956, patron was Mrs. (Captain) Burghard Heye, he the first postwar captain on *Rheinstein*; the first time the wife of a seaman had this honor. Also invited by Director Dr. Johannes Kulenkampf were crew-comrades of Heye and their wives, to the launching and the following dinner. Delivery 29/12/1956. 1/9/1970 to Hapag-Lloyd A.G. 10/1974 to Hapag-Lloyd International, S.A., Panama, reg. in Bremen, 5,911 Ts. 13/4/1977 to Chong Chiao Shipping Co., Singapore, renamed *New Panther*, 8,034 Ts. 15/6/1979 arrived Hsinkiang for BU by China Metals & Minerals Import & Export Co.

Bodenstein backing out of her San Francisco pier, 1950s, Andrew Kilk, World Ship Society director, photo.

Spreestein and *Siegstein* were improved and enlarged Rheinstein types, with *Illstein* #512 and *Wiedstein* #513 with additional improvements on these two.

---

506. *Spreestein*	1957-1972		
Bremer Vulkan, Vegesack #855	2998/4913		126.02 x 16.04
M.A.N. Diesel	4000	15	
2	33		

Launched 12/3/1957. 20/5/1957 delivery voyage in ballast to Safi, Marocco for a cargo of phosphate. 1/9/1970 to Hapag-Lloyd A.G. Early 1972 with *Siegstein* LU in Bremerhaven. 1/2/1972 to Nan Yang Shipping Co., Macao, Ocean Tramping Co., Mogadisciu, operator, renamed *Minhao*. Delivery 1/5/1972. 1976 to China Ocean Shipping Co., Guandong, renamed *Lei Shan*, 4,875 Ts. 1981 *Ocean Jupiter*, Shipping Co., Panama. 1983 *Wan Ping*, China Ocean Shipping Co., Wuhu. Then to Guangzhou Ocean Shipping Co. 1994 still in Lloyd's Register. The ship had a 60 tons lift derrick.

Spreestein #506 and Siegstein *were improved versions of* Rheinstein #472, *6.5 meters longer and with heavy-lift gear. Now sixty-tons. Both were sold in 1972 to a China-controlled shipping operator in Macao.* Eric Steinfeldt Photo.

CHAPTER 17

A Young Again Centenarian - 1957

Planning for the Norddeutscher Lloyd's centennial on 20 February, 1957 was a time for somber reflection, unlike in 1907. Then there was a torchlight parade through old-town Bremen to the Rathaus and a city-sponsored festive dinner. NDL's huge new headquarters building was almost ready; it reflected the grandeur of a peaceful age. A commemorative gold metal was issued. Bremerhaven, too, celebrated. The Lloyd was its life.

In 1907, the Lloyd was near its peak: the greatest trans-ocean passenger carrier of all times. With a following from the top of the Social Scale to the unnamed thousands, albeit millions, seeking a way to the new world, so many going with the Lloyd. In 1913, it was the ten-millionth.

But between 1907 and 1957 lay two World Wars, two near-destructions that left only the heart of the enterprise: its dedicated and capable personnel. In a September, 1956 letter Hans Karstedt wrote that artisans were working sixty hours a week, although the unions forced the shipyards to reduce the workweek from 48 to 45 hours. Re-building Germany from the destruc-

The Lloyd's invitation to the Centennial Celebrations was included in the presentation copies of its History written by Dr. Georg Bessell. In the Upper Hall of the Rathaus a reception; in the lower Hall a display of ship models, artifacts, documents, etc. which portray the Lloyd's 100 years.

Zum hundertjährigen Bestehen in freundschaftlicher Verbundenheit überreicht vom

NORDDEUTSCHEN LLOYD

Am Jubiläumstage, dem 20. Februar 1957, findet von 11 bis 14 Uhr in der oberen Halle des alten Rathauses in Bremen ein offener Empfang statt. In der unteren Halle des alten Rathauses wird eine Ausstellung von Schiffsmodellen, Bildern usw. die 100jährige Lloyd-Entwicklung zeigen.

Bremen, im Januar 1957

An Stelle etwa zugedachter Aufmerksamkeiten bitten wir, der Elisabeth-Wiegand-Präsident-Achelis-Stiftung, Konto: Norddeutsche Kreditbank, Bremen, die satzungsmäßig Unterstützungen in Notfällen an Betriebsangehörige des Norddeutschen Lloyd leistet, oder der Deutschen Gesellschaft zur Rettung Schiffbrüchiger, Bremen, Konto: Bremer Bank Kto.Nr. 2334, eine Zuwendung zu machen.

535

tions of war, and building for the future: ships, industries, housing, roads, everything, still demanded all-out effort. It was most unusual as the 20th, *the* day neared: not one Lloyd ship in port after *Bischofstein* sailed on the 18th. Nor on the 19th. Then on Wednesday three arrived to share in the festivities: *Ravenstein, Isarstein* and the coaster *Norder Till.* It shuttled cargo between Bremen-Bremerhaven-Hamburg. So three ships in port.

The celebration was limited to a reception at the Rathaus for some 1,500 guests, and an Exhibition of Lloyd history: after shaking every hand, Herr Bertram's needed medical treatment. For the third time the Lloyd had found its role, its niche among shipping enterprises, and much again to be proud of: - thirty-six highseas ships under the Lloyd flag and eight more building; for a total of 330,000 tons. They covered NDL's traditional routes: to New York and the Atlantic and Gulf Coasts; the West Indies and Central America; to the North and South American west coasts; to South America's East Coast, out to Australia, and the prestige route to East Asia. There was looking back, and looking forward.

One of the Lloyd's sons attending, Captain Gerhard Bolte, at 95 was almost as old as the Lloyd. See "Sails." And, a 25 January, 1957 letter from Director Dr. Johannes Kulenkampff to Captain Drechsel, with a copy of the Lloyd's new Centennial History, mentions the hope that you will see that our *Berlin* will appear in another and younger guise with a name still closer to our tradition. This the first word of what in July, 1959 came to be the fifth Bremen #511.

Original planning for the Centennial was mentioned by Director Hans Karstedt to Captain Drechsel in a letter of 20/9/1955: A brochure of some 50 - 70 pages, and an Exhibition of Lloyd documents, schedules, passenger lists, promotional materials, posters, photos and ship models, the few that remained from the many that had been on display in the stately old home office building. Drechsel offered his help in producing artifacts for display, etc. He had earlier sent the *Bremen's* Gyro Compass and other items from the ship, also books to start a new library at the new Haus Seefahrt for retired captains and widows.

In December, 1955 Herr Karstedt sent Drechsel Volume I of Dr. Carl Thalenhorst's *Bremen Binnen un Buten*, Bremen Inside and Out, a collection of stories by Bremers about Bremen and its happenings. Thalenhorst was the son of the Lloyd captain who commanded the first of the Imperial Mail Steamers, *Oder* #45, when it sailed on 30 June, 1886 for the Far East. Drechsel enjoyed the book, wrote to that effect to Herr Karstedt. He passed the letter on to Dr. Thalenhorst. He at once wrote to Captain Drechsel: "I am planning a follow-up volume. Will you write one or more articles or experiences for that?"

Drechsel wrote fourteen articles, 150 handwritten pages about pre-1914 and later happenings, about captains who had done so much to give the Lloyd its world renown, and who had become living models for the Nachwuchs, the follow-on growth. Drechsel sent the articles to Herr Karstedt to read and pass on if they pleased him and seemed appropriate. A hand-written note from my Father to me at that time says: the stories show that his life's work was dedicated to the blooming and thriving of the Norddeutscher Lloyd.

Herr Karstedt liked the articles so much that

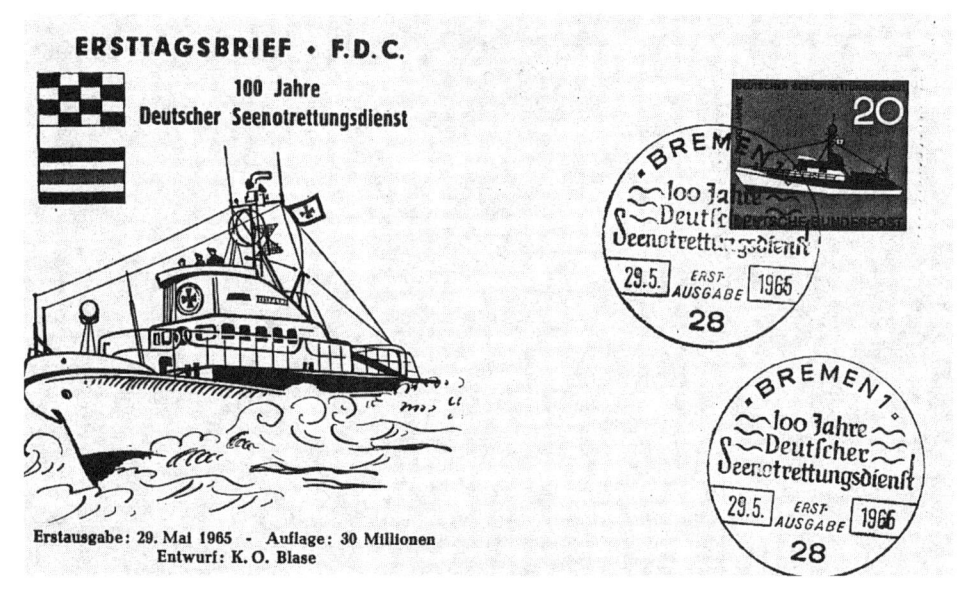

The Lloyd invitation to the Centennial celebration mentions the Elisabeth Wiegand-Präsident Achelis Foundation, she wife of the former General Direktor, he former NDL President, and the Society for the Rescue of Shipwrecked Persons. NDL's founder was its founding chairman. In 1966 a commemorative stamp was issued, this a First Day Cover: 100 Years of Sea-Need Rescue Services.

Letter from NDL's, then Hapag-Lloyd's North Atlantic Passenger Director John Schröder: quoting the cable he was sending for the Lloyd Centennial Celebration in Bremen from: Somia, joined 1896, Drechsel, Gericke, 1901, Stude 1903, Schröder 1906, Becker 1909, Froehlich 1910. Oldtimers all. Herr Schröder sketched the table with Lloyd flag at the concurrent New York gathering. He is among the group in the June, 1948 photo in "A Second New Start." Herr Schröder was active in the U.S.-Europa Corp. which for years following the war handled the organizing and sending of thousands of parcels with food, clothing and other necessities to the needy in Germany.

he passed them on to Co-Director Dr. Johannes Kulenkampff, who shared them with others in top management, and on to Dr. Thalenhorst. On 1 June, 1956 Dr. Kulenkampff wrote Captain Drechsel "There are hardly any of the old co-workers who have so many memories of the time before 1914, especially one to whom it is given to bring it all in such fluent form onto paper."

As Dr. Thalenhorst received the articles, he writes again: "It is such good material. I shall be using much of it in Volume II." A 15 September, 1956 letter from Herr Karstedt advised that Dr. Kulenkampff has agreed that "one or more articles you submitted will be used in our Jubilee Brochure. I had returned it all to Dr. Thalenhorst, but on Dr. Kulenkampff's request asked for its return to allow us to make selections." Dr. Thalenhorst points out that you wrote these articles for *his* use, not for ours. However, we feel that the Lloyd, of whom you still are a part, has precedence for any publication. The upshot was that the availability of the stories sparked a complete change in plans. Historian Dr. Georg Bessell was instructed to write a full history, with illustrations, and a high-seas fleet list to be compiled by Captain Otto Prehn. On 1 November, 1956 Herr Karstedt advised "your experiences will appear as 'Stories of an old Lloyd Captain.'"

On 11 November, Dr. Bessell wrote Captain Drechsel "for the fourth or fifth time I am reading proofs. You cannot believe what a stroke of luck it was for me when I received your articles from Herr Karstedt. Suddenly in the best imaginable manner a problem was solved: How can a Lloyd book turn out right if it is only about business reports, balances, schedules and the like? I was certain that I could never tell a living story in that way. Suddenly it was clear: here are the stories that I have wanted; I couldn't ask for better mate-

Decorations in front of Bremen's Main Railway Station for the Lloyd's Centennial Celebration. February 20, 1957.

rial. And from a Captain who writes so well that one can simply turn it over to the printer. You have earned my thanks and those of all future readers."

The Book was entitled Norddeutscher Lloyd, 1857-1957, Geschichte einer bremischen Reederei, The History of a Bremen Shipping Enterprise. 235 pages, some 35 photos, a list of 350 high-seas vessels, and an index of people and ships. Captain Drechsel's thirteen pages are the only personal experiences. The dust jacket has a dark blue Mercator-projection world on Lloyd

A Young Again Centenarian 537

FEBRUARY 20, 1957
THE NEW YORK TIMES, WEDNESDAY,

North German Lloyd to Mark 100 Years of Atlantic Service

In April, 1964, the New York Times in effect added a postscript to this article on the Lloyd's Centenary: headlining Bremen as a "Distant Suburb of U.S. Busy Bremen Never Forgets Historic Links with Major East Coast Ports." See "Bremen...."

Ship Line to Celebrate Its Anniversary Today--The Bremen Made First Run to New York in Sixteen Days

The North German Lloyd, one of the oldest lines active in North Atlantic steam navigation will celebrate its 100th anniversary today.

Since its founding on Feb. 20, 1857, the company has been making notable contributions to shipping. Its passenger lines have held the mythical emblem of Atlantic speed supremacy five times.

Actually the company's association with passenger shipping on the Bremen-New York run goes back at least ten more years through its founder, F. H. Meyer. In the early Eighteen Forties, he invested in the Ocean Steam Navigation Company here. That company's first vessel, the 236-foot paddlewheeler Washington, made her maiden voyage under the American flag to Bremen in June, 1847.

First Crossing in 1858

The company's houseflag, the blue key of the city of Bremen crossed with a blue anchor on white ground, was seen here first on July 4, 1858, when the passenger-mail steamer Bremen made her maiden arrival.

The Bremen, Captain Johann Wessels commanding, was the first of four sisterships, built in Scotland. The vessels measured 318 feet, averaged 2,700 gross tons, made 11.5 knots and had accommodations for 1,000 passengers, predominantly in steerage. She docked at Chambers Street on her maiden voyage.

The first voyage took sixteen days. Another and more modern North German Lloyd liner, the Europa, in 1930 captured the Atlantic speed record with a crossing of 4 days, 17 hours 6 minutes. Other Atlantic speed queens belonging to the line were the Bremen, Kaiser Wilhelm II, Kronprinz Wilhelm and the Kaiser Wilhelm der Grosse.

The history of the company can perhaps be characterized as a living parallel to the course of Germany throughout the last 100 years. Reflecting the political changes in that nation, North German Lloyd ships have served under five different national flags.

They have flown the ensigns of the Bremen Free State, the North German Federation, Imperial Germany, Nazi Germany and the black, red and gold standard of the Weimar Republic and of the present German Federal Republic.

Twice within this century, at the end of World War I and again at the end of World War II, the attrition of war and peace treaties have practically wiped out the fleet of passenger and cargo liners.

However, on both occasions rebuilding efforts have enabled the company to stage a comeback and to reappear on the world's shipping lanes.

However, in contrast to the post-World War I era, the emphasis on fleet rebuilding in the years following 1945 has been on cargo and cargo-passenger tonnage. The company now owns and operates a total of thirty-six vessels. Only one passenger ship, the Berlin, the former Swedish American liner Gripsholm, is among them.

Tonnage Total Listed

The thirty-five cargo liners, active in service to North and South America, the Far East and Australia, include vessels with first-class passenger accommodations for eighty-six passengers. The company fleet now totals 217,388 gross tons, smaller when compared to the 494 ships of 983,000 tons before 1914 and the eighty-six-vessel, 614,000-ton fleet of the late 1930's.

In view of German plans for the construction of two modern Atlantic passenger liners, it is not inconceivable that the North German Lloyd will have again a modern liner on the New York run.

The anniversary will be observed on this side of the Atlantic on Wednesday with an anniversary dinner aboard the liner Berlin en route on a Caribbean cruise between Trujillo City, Dominican Republic, and Havana, Cuba.

blue, gold-yellow stacked ships spread around the oceans.

Copies sent to former employees enclosed a formal invitation to the Rathaus reception and displays on the lower level.

In Bremen, the evening before the City Reception at a gathering of leading Lloyd personages Captain Prehn read some of the experiences submitted by retired captains and chief engineers. Later, Dr. Kulenkampff wrote Captain Drechsel "So the time before 1914 again came to life before our eyes. At the gathering, several mentioned enjoying your articles in our book. With them Haben Sie sich eine bleibende Erinnerung geschaffen, with them you have made for yourself a lasting remembrance."

In his talk to the reception in the Rathaus, Dr. Kulenkampf stressed that at the Lloyd's founding by H.H Meieir in 1857, his brother was Bremen's Bürgermeister. So right from the beginning the Lloyd and Bremen belonged together. "We shall continue to carry the Bremen Key in our flag and on the bows of our ships." Sadly, the flag no longer flies over any of what today is the Hapag-Lloyd fleet: "The Bremen key does still grace both sides of the bows of Hapag-Lloyd ships registered in Bremen, as they alternate with Hamburg. "We thank you for your friendship and trust in us in the past. Our priority is to continue to earn this trust. Our greatest joy at this Jubilee is that we were able to care for the material well-being of our pensioners. The Lloyd never would have become and remained what it was and is had not all its people strived for it with love in their work. For the second time we have not been repaid for our wartime losses. We have been granted credits for rebuilding. Since our renewal we have been working in closest understanding with our friends in the Hamburg-Amerika Linie. We believe that a shipping enterprise like the Lloyd never must submit to an impersonal automation, rather it must ever retain its individual stamp and character if it is to meet its obligations. That depends on the crews of our

Lloyd stationary used during 1957 had this logo, and company-mail used this postage meter. New York used the same design for its invitation to the 100 Anniversary dinner on Berlin *for old Lloyd and Hapag employees and travel and transport agents. In 1959, with purchase of Swedish-America Line's half-interest in* Berlin, *and* Bremen *5 coming into service, NDL again established its own passenger agencies in the U.S. and Canada.*

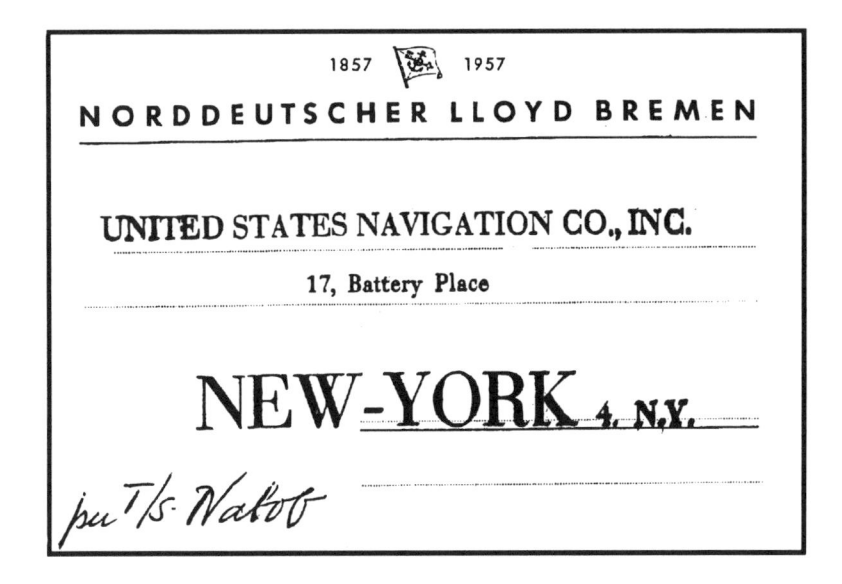

United States Navigation was the Lloyd Agency in the U.S. after the war. The Consulate General and other German activities were in this same building, the last before the Battery. From there one could see the ships passing in or outgoing. This label with the Dr. Georg Bessell Centennial Work on the Norddeutscher Lloyd. Fittingly was shipped on Nabob #480, U.S.-built, later Canadian, then British operated, and finally to the Lloyd.

ships rather than their technical facilities, as much as on the concern with which we care for and foster the ties to our business friends around the world. We have kept the most important capacity, which earlier made us great: The Unbending determination to carry out our self-imposed tasks in step with the changing times. And to do so with complete independence and self-responsibility. Today we feel ourselves standing on the summit of a foothill in our recovery effort." Federal Transport Secretary Seebohm sounded the end of the first century and the start of the second on the bell of *Kaiser Wilhelm Der Grosse,* lost in 1914, given back to the Lloyd by Spain in 1952.

In New York, G. Hilmer Lundbeck, President of the Swedish-America Line agency for the Lloyd, issued invitations to a black-tie dinner on *Berlin* on 27 March, 1957. John Schroeder, prewar the Passenger Manager, for the North America Hapag-Lloyd Community, drew the sketch of the Lloyd flag on the table. The Lloyd was not forgotten overseas, nor did it forgets its own.

Most of the Drechsel stories in the Bessell Centennial work or the Thalenhorst *Bremen Binnen Un Buten* are touched on in various connections in Volume I or in this Volume. Two are timeless:

"We were on the voyage to New York on *Kaiser Wilhelm der Grosse.* I was 2.Officer and had the evening watch: 8 p.m.-Midnight. Around 10 p.m. the Chief Boatswain came onto the bridge and said he could not sleep. His cabin on the starboard of the foc'sle. The Chief Carpenter's cabin was exactly opposite. He also noticed, and this is what's keeping me awake, something rubbing up and down up and down outside the hall. I sent an assistant into the Provision Room foreward of our cabins. It was even more noticeable there. We thought it might be a large fishing net snagged onto the bow.

A Young Again Centenarian 539

Anything pertaining to the Norddeutscher Lloyd in olden times, in Bremen, Bremerhaven, and in the German community in New York, was front-page news. New Flagships, a Centennial, a Blue Ribbon crossing. A matter of pride. With the demise of liner passenger traffic, this immediacy has been lost. With today's cruise ships, short voyages, crowded programs, 2000+ passengers, there no longer can be the one-on-one relationships that carries over to the next looked-forward-to voyage. A way of ocean travelling for a century or more that this book and others try to preserve for the record.

ruar 1959

Weser-Zeitung / Bremer Börsen-Zeitung
Wirtschafts-, Handels- und Schiffahrtsblatt der Bremer Nachrichten

Nordd. Lloyd schwamm 1957 auf Konjunkturwogen
Über 56 Mill. DM Abschreibungen eingefahren — Volle Laderäume bei hohen Frachten

In this report in February, 1959, for the operating centennial year of 1957, the headline in Bremen's Weser Zeitung tells the good news: "NDL floated in 1957 on the economic boom. More than 56 million marks depreciation covered. Full hatches at high freight rates." The article also looks into the future: The overall cost of getting Bremen 5 *(bought from the French as* Pasteur *and completely rebuilt) into service will come to DM104.5 millions of long-term debt. The optimistic side: buying and rebuilding a ship at a time of heavy shipyard order books, saves three years time and at one-third the new-building's final cost of perhpas DM300 million.*

"Around 4.30 a.m. it was light enough to see ... there was a large dark mass draped around the bow. We immediately thought: a whale's carcass, or a prehistoric sea serpent! The Watch Officer ordered hard rudder starboard, port changes, but they did not dislodge the mass. We did not want to stop the engines as passengers might become concerned, and certainly Captain Polack would immediately in his sleep sense the change. I reported the happening and our conclusion to Captain Polack. He replied: 'you must have had one too many last night.' But he got dressed and we all went to the bow. Now it was completely light. Captain Polack called to the Bridge: 'Stop Engines.' Then 'Full-speed reverse'. Then again 'Stop,' as the object separated from the hull. It was a dead whale, perhaps 70' long. We went forward slowly to look at it, passengers coming onto deck and wondering what was happening. Captain Polack: 'If I had not seen it I would not have believed it.' Evidently the whale was asleep on the surface and we hit it exactly in the middle so that the head on one side and the flukes on the other were rubbing, making the noises the Bosun and Carpenter heard. When, after arrival in Bremerhaven I routinely made a report to the Nordwestdeutsche Zeitung, describing the whale incident, the paper returned the article with: "we can run it only when Captain Polack signs it."

Another story concerned a pig, two pigs. "On 8 February, 1908 I signed onto *Seydlitz* #188, Captain A. Ahlborn for the voyage to New York and return. We had a heavy cargo of piecegoods, and the Cabin Class and Tweendecks were mostly full. Interesting for us was a group of twenty German artists, clowns and jugglers en route to New York to perform in Madison Square Garden with the Ringling Brothers and Barnum and Bailey Circus. Weather was good so they did their acts and tricks topside where everybody could watch. Obviously, they were skilled. One particular Artist Braun impressed all who saw him exercising the pig he had been training for years to do all sorts of tricks. This was in the baggage room, near Hatch Four, where the Carpenter had built a wooden cage for the pig. Herr Braun spent most of his daytime there putting the pig through its routines.

"When we arrived in Hoboken, clearing of the ship and passengers went smoothly. Our by now famous pig was listed in the cargo manifest. The Customs examination of this quickly discovered the pig. 'The pig may not be landed! Quarantine rules.' Herr Braun was aghast. After New York, he had counted on his own tour of major U.S. cities with rich rewards. Since I as Cargo Officer was responsible for 'Cargo Not Landed,' he handed me the key to the cage so he could go ashore to argue his case. The news reporters wrote many column inches about him and his pig.

"This was Herr Braun's first visit to the U.S. but he must have found some good counsel, perhaps from Barnum's attorney? The next day he came to my cabin near the down entrance to the baggage room, and asked for the key to the cage. 'Please don't see or say anything about what I shall be doing.' I did follow quietly, and saw that two men were putting into a large elongated basket a pig with a cloth around its muzzle and the legs tied. In the cage was another pig. Which pig was the original, which the replacement? They left and went onto the Pier over the lower-level gangway. It was still lunch time, so no stevedores were on board, nor visible on the pier. How the three men with their basket got past the Customs at the pier entrance I do not know. The following morning news stories told that Herr Braun had found on a pig farm an animal that was highly intelligent and, he felt certain, could perform the tricks he had taught his German pig. (The follow-

A Young Again Centenarian 541

Commemorative postmark for the Lloyd's 100 Years used in 1957 in Bremen. The envelope shows H.H. Meier, founder of NDL, and mentions the Exhibition in the Overseas Museum adjacent to the Main Railway Station. Another was mounted in the lower hall of the Rathaus during the formal reception upstairs on 20 February. The stamp shows the six-ship Schwabenstein class of 1954-1955, on the Far East route, the first passenger ships built after the war.

ing is an embellishment not in the printed story but told me by my Father: Herr Braun, on the basis of the news story, was allowed by Customs to bring the American pig on board so, as he said, he could have it learn the tricks more quickly by watching the German pig perform. He came on board each day until our departure with his American pig 'for training.' The afternoon before our departure, Herr Braun came on board, still with his new pig, When ready to leave he gave me the key: 'I make you a present of my pig!'

"We sailed on schedule before the circus performance took place, so we never knew how well the new pig had performed. On sailing morning Customs officials came to assure themselves that the pig still was on board. One raised his stick and said in German 'Spring, Spring.' But the pig did not respond.

"Four days later at sea our Chief Engineer had his birthday so I had the pig butchered by our Chief Butcher. The next morning in the Officers Mess we had the Birthday Surprise: Boiled Pork, Fresh Warm Sausage, and Beer. Captain Ahlborn came by during his daily round of the ship and spent a pleasant hour, leaving with praise for the delicacies served to him.

"We reached Bremerhaven in mid March after not a bad Winter voyage. The next day Captain Ahlborn went to Bremen to make his voyage reports. As he was leaving Freight Director Carl Stapelfeld's office, Herr Stapelfeld said 'I heard that you had an artist on board with a trained pig. The manifest reads 'Short Landed.' Where is the pig now, Captain?' Ahlborn was embarrassed, finally said that Cargo Officer Drechsel knew all about it. The next morning the North America Freight Division called me in Bremerhaven, asked what happened to the 'Short Landed' pig? Oh, that went overboard. Overboard? Why what happened to the pig? Hard to say what was wrong. The Ship's Doctor refused to treat it. Bremen: Oh. Well, if you have nothing to do tomorrow please come by and see us."

"The next morning I reported to the North America Division, and was immediately led to the all-holy precincts of Director Stapelfeld. He shook hands, then offered me a cigar. We chatted idly, then 'I hear you had a 'short landed' pig on board. Do you remember what happened?' I sat there inhaling the cigar and watching my smoke. Suddenly, laughing, Herr Stapelfeld said 'It's my turn tonight to talk to our regular Stammtisch gathering (the same table, the same friends), and I need a good story. Please help me, Herr Drechsel.' I poured out my heart to his hearty laughter. I then remarked that by eating the pig in our Officers Mess we had saved the Lloyd quite a bit of money. As we parted, Herr Stapelfeld handed me an unopened box of cigars, as a memento. I took the train back to Bremerhaven. I didn't get back to New York for another year. There I found out that Herr Braun had done well at Madison Square Garden and on his U.S. tour. 'All's Well that ends well.' Or, as O. Henry wrote 'Pigs is Pigs.'"

CHAPTER 18

From Little Boxes To Big Boxes

As "A New Start" details, not until 1950 could the Lloyd again venture out to sea. As with the founding in 1857, so NDL's towing, lightering, river and North Sea passengers were the start-up operations in 1919, and after 1945. When one could again operate ships in 1950 it was from Bremen to the U.S. East Coast, the Lloyd's historic purpose.

Re-establishing old routes and some new ones went slowly. The first new-buildings came out in Spring, 1951. Better to have a number of small ships on several lines than a few bigger high-volume routes of which there weren't any for German shipping.

Looking back to the success of the Lloyd's and Hapag's joint North Atlantic services in the 1930s made it easier to work together right from the start: Shippers want frequent and regular service. Two can provide this better than one; sometimes three, as with the Great Lakes, or even more: the eventual consortium to the Far East. Competing lines sometimes built sister or near-sisterships to make the marketing of joint services easier: every ship provides the same speed, the same capacity. These same pressures: to meet changing needs while providing regular, fast, frequent service, were the ones that finally pushed the Lloyd and Hapag into corporate merger in 1970.

For the new German Government constituted in 1948, the immediate priority was rebuilding the country from the massive destruction of war. There was little help available for the shipping industry: some modest low-interest loans, minor tax exemptions. The cargo volume from the U.S. to a largely destroyed Europe was helped by the Marshall Plan. It was American generosity to include the former enemy Germany in that help, as the U.S. had used the Boxer indemnity funds from 1901 to improve relations with China. The Soviet Union's great mistake was to reject this aid, and force its satellites - Czechoslovakia had actually accepted, also to reject it. They could have been rebuilt with U.S. Dollars.

An important postwar development were the MacGregor Hatch Covers. These operate like an accordion from flat extension through V-shape to flat stowing open. NDL's first corporate report after the war covering 21 June, 1948 - 31 through December, 1954 says "most new buildings were given MacGregor hatch covers which have proven themselves remarkably well with their easier and quick action, absolutely waterproof, safe against seawater action, and minimal upkeep costs." See *Berlin* #489 for problems with the old woodenboards method of hatch covering.

After the East Coast, the next line was jointly to Cuba-Mexico-Gulf ports, then to the West Coasts of South and North America, to the Far

> **HAMBURG-AMERIKA LINIE**
> HAMBURG
> Ballindamm 25
>
> **NORDDEUTSCHER LLOYD**
> BREMEN
> Gustav-Deetjen-Allee 2-6
>
> ROB. M. SLOMAN JR. HAMBURG
>
> Hamburg/Bremen, im Mai 1953
>
> Betrifft: **Wiederaufnahme des Ostasien-Dienstes der Hamburg-Amerika Linie und des Norddeutschen Lloyd**
>
> An die Herren Verlader!
>
> Wir freuen uns, Ihnen mitteilen zu können, daß wir, wie in der Presse bereits bekanntgegeben, unseren Dienst nach Ostasien in Kürze wieder aufnehmen werden. Ab Mitte dieses Jahres kommen die speziell für diesen Dienst gebauten Turbinen-Schiffe laufend von den Werften zur Ablieferung. Es sind Schiffe mit einer Tragfähigkeit von 10 000 t und einer Geschwindigkeit von 17,5 sm, die, mit allen Neuerungen der Technik versehen, Ihnen die beste Gewähr für eine gute Unterbringung Ihrer Güter bei schneller Beförderung bieten.
>
> Als erstes Schiff wird TS. „WESERSTEIN" (N.D.L.) Anfang Juli in Hamburg, Bremen, Rotterdam und Antwerpen mit dem Laden beginnen.
> Bestimmungshäfen:
> Colombo, Penang, Belawan, Singapore, Hongkong, Manila, Kobe, Yokohama, außerdem Bangkok mit Umladung in Singapore.
>
> Diesem Schiff folgt TS. „BRAUNSCHWEIG" (H.A.L.) Ende Juli/Anfang August ab Hamburg, Bremen, Rotterdam und Antwerpen.
> Bestimmungshäfen:
> Colombo, Penang, Singapore, Hongkong, Manila, Kobe, Yokohama, außerdem Bangkok mit Umladung in Singapore.
>
> Anlaufen von Nebenhäfen nach Bedarf.
>
> Die genauen Abfahrtsdaten werden wir durch Segelkarten und Pressenotizen noch bekanntgeben. Weitere Abfahrten in dreiwöchentlichen Abständen.
>
> Die Hamburg-Amerika Linie und der Norddeutsche Lloyd sind Mitglieder der Ostasien-Konferenz.
>
> Unsere Vertretungen in den Hafenplätzen wie im Inland geben über Frachtraten usw. bereitwilligst Auskunft. Namen und Adressen sind auf der Rückseite dieses Schreibens angegeben.
>
> Wenn wir uns trotz der unsicheren Zeiten zu der Wiederaufnahme unseres Ostasien-Dienstes entschlossen haben, so geschieht dieses in der Gewißheit, daß wir damit zum Ausbau des Handels mit dem Fernen Osten beitragen. Wir bitten daher die Herren Verlader, diesem Dienst, den beide Gesellschaften als Gemeinschaftsdienst betreiben, durch tatkräftige Unterstützung zu einem Erfolg zu verhelfen.
>
> Wir geben die Versicherung, daß wir unserer Tradition getreu die Interessen unserer Verladerschaft, soweit es in unseren Kräften liegt, wahren werden.
>
> Mit dieser Versicherung empfehlen wir uns Ihnen
> mit vorzüglicher Hochachtung
>
> HAMBURG-AMERIKA LINIE   NORDDEUTSCHER LLOYD

Joint announcement of the resumption of service to the Far East, with seven Lloyd, and nine Hapag identical turbine freighters. The Lloyd's later were rebuilt for two knots more speed while Hapag built an entire new series, reflecting the importance of this route to the two lines and German foreign trade. We do this "despite the uncertain times..."
Rob. M. Sloman Jr. is a famous Hamburg Freight broker-expediter. In the 19th century the firm had its own shipping, and into this century.

East, to Australia. Only NDL's long-time route to North Brazil, the first opened in 1920, and kept in the 1930s when other South America routes were given up, did it serve alone, as Hapag alone renewed its traditional strong interest in the West Indies. At first the 2700 tons *Rheinstein* class, and the smaller but faster *Liebenstein,* 2,400 tons, 16 knots ships ran only to Belem and other Northern Brazil ports. Calling at the Canary Islands, sometimes Madeira, en route, for fruits, vegetables, woods, tropical nuts, and passengers where they were willing to stay long on board, as these ships later went up the Amazon, to Manaos, and even further to Leticia, Colombia, and Iquitos, Peru. In 1956, *Saarstein* took 3,000 tons of cement direct from Gdynia to Manaos; it has become a million-inhabitants city.

Effective from 1/1/1957, four lines: the Lloyd, Booth S.S., Liner Holdings, and Det Norske Syd-Amerika Linje formed the U.K.-Continent-North Brazil-Amazonia Freight Conference, a protective move against intrusion by outsiders. Conferences regularize competition, prevent rate-cutting, act jointly to provide shippers with optimum services. Conferences engaged in trade with the U.S. run into American anti-trust legislation as, allegedly, in restraint of trade.

In May 1961, *Ruhrstein* left on its 45th voyage up the Amazon to load 500 tons of Para nuts. It took four days from Belem to Manaos against the 3½ knots current; that is regained coming down. In April, 1972, *Lechstein* was the 400th voyage up the Amazon.

Serving the Far East had been a prestige route for the Lloyd back to the 1886 opening as an Imperial Mail line. In 1953, Hapag and Lloyd reopened this route with identical 17.5 knot express freighters: seven from NDL, nine from Hapag. The next year, they added the first postwar German passenger ships, six vessels, three each run by the Lloyd and Hapag with 86 berths, swimming pools, quiet luxury, also 17.5 knots, a good speed for those times. Over the years seventy percent of the passengers were British. The minus for this service were the long voyage times, 110 days round-trip with the many ports called at for cargo. Conference rules made it difficult to call at non-conference ports, although in June, 1960 *Schwabenstein* called at Miri, Sarawak. The conference system was no protection when the USSR cut rates and offered both ship and trans-Siberia railroad service Europe-Far East. In September, 1956 the Japanese members of the Far Eastern Freight Conference settled their inter-lines dispute. Hapag-Lloyd were conceded a higher quota of traffic, up from 9% to 18%, and from 26 voyages a year to 36.

Another problem for the conference was new nations wanting to have their own shipping lines and preferring them for cargoes.

The intense competition among conference members and from outsiders, pushed the Lloyd into rebuilding its seven freighters to 19.5 knots, while Hapag built an entire new series of express freighters for this route. This meant, the freighters were faster than the passenger ships. With that, and the growing reliance by passengers on the jets, the six combi-vessels were sold off in 1967.

Actually, in the 1930s, NDL's Far East route ran at higher speeds and, with fewer ports called at, had shorter roundtrip times, *Scharnhorst* #438, *Gneisenau* #440 and *Potsdam* #439 at 21

On the six combi-liners to the Far East, the entire ship belonged to the passengers, up to 86, including the bridge at almost any time. Most of the German passengers were from inland, so they had many questions about ships and the sea. The contacts made were cherished and continued by many. They had a pool on the sun deck. What else can one do on a forty-days or so voyage? The Lloyd and Hapag also promoted them for Mediterranean vacations and honeymoons (see Volume I) Ship to or from there, the other way by train. In 1965, with jets taking the long-distance passengers, the Lloyd promoted its Far East combi-ships: one way by ship, the other by Lufthansa. It wasn't enough. Two years later they, with their three Hagap sisters, went to the Tung interests of Taiwan.

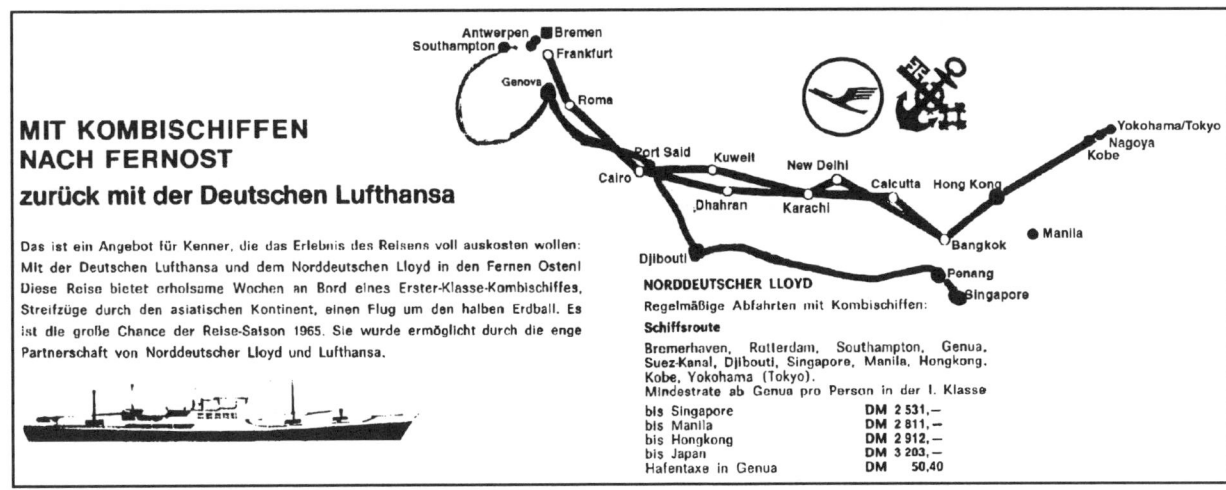

HAMBURG-AMERIKA LINIE
NORDDEUTSCHER LLOYD
Ostasien-Dienst

NORDDEUTSCHER LLOYD - LUFTHANSA

MIT KOMBISCHIFFEN

1965

MIT KOMBISCHIFFEN NACH FERNOST
zurück mit der Deutschen Lufthansa

Das ist ein Angebot für Kenner, die das Erlebnis des Reisens voll auskosten wollen: Mit der Deutschen Lufthansa und dem Norddeutscher Lloyd in den Fernen Osten! Diese Reise bietet erholsame Wochen an Bord eines Erster-Klasse-Kombischiffes, Streifzüge durch den asiatischen Kontinent, einen Flug um den halben Erdball. Es ist die große Chance der Reise-Saison 1965. Sie wurde ermöglicht durch die enge Partnerschaft von Norddeutscher Lloyd und Lufthansa.

NORDDEUTSCHER LLOYD
Regelmäßige Abfahrten mit Kombischiffen:
Schiffsroute
Bremerhaven, Rotterdam, Southampton, Genua, Suez-Kanal, Djibouti, Singapore, Manila, Hongkong, Kobe, Yokohama (Tokyo).
Mindestrate ab Genua pro Person in der I. Klasse

bis Singapore	DM 2 531,—
bis Manila	DM 2 811,—
bis Hongkong	DM 2 912,—
bis Japan	DM 3 203,—
Hafentaxe in Genua	DM 50,40

From Little Boxes to Big Boxes 545

HAMBURG-AMERIKA LINIE HAMBURG

Ferienreisen ins *Mittelmeer* mit den OSTASIEN-KOMBISCHIFFEN

NORDDEUTSCHER LLOYD BREMEN

---

on Board M.V. "Hessenstein"
February 20th, 1953.

F A R E W E L L - D I N N E R

Beluga Malossol Caviar in Ice Block

Real Turtle Soup with Sherry
Cream of Peas St. Germain

Fried Scallops with Bacon
Sauce Remoulade

Roast Bölts Turkey with Stuffing
Cranberries, Asparagus, Lima Beans
Corn Fritter, Mashed Potatoes
Salad Florida

Sizzling Steak with Onions
Haricots Verts, Pont Neuf Potatoes

Cucumber, Tomato, Lettuce,
Cream Dressing

Asparagus, Lima Beans, Haricots Verts,
Carrots, Spaghetti Plain

Mashed, Baked Sweet, Boiled, Pont Neuf,

Eis Bombe "Hessenstein"
Katzenzungen

Cheese – Fruits in Season

Mocha in the Hall

Children: Pineapple Pancake

22.00 hrs: Sandwiches

knots spent 46 days at sea, and 36 days in some twenty ports, or 84 days for the round voyage. The 14 knot River-Class freighters spent 60 days at sea, 44 days in up to 25 ports, or 104 days roundtrip. In 1994, with 23 knots container ships, it takes 31 days from Hamburg-Bremen to Yokohama. See below.

Service to Australia was reopened in 1954, but at two-monthly intervals, only gradually expanded. Fast ships were bought, the *Ravenstein* #495 class, and built, the *Regensteins* #516-517. These vessels had short-period use and profitability in the wool auction season, so had to operate elsewhere much of the year, with slower-speed replacements for non-wool cargoes. Australia is a difficult route to serve, with notoriously sporadic stoppages for spurious union or capricious reasons. Often, captains do not know if there'd be a tug to help landings. Australia was proof that it doesn't pay to have better ships than your competition because conference rules won't let you lift additional cargoes offered or only at a penalty. One has to wonder why anyone would invest in shipping with so many uncertainties.

Chartered Ships:

Chartering ships is a way to extend one's activities without the cost in time and money to build or buy vessels. Just as one leases a car or an airplane. As NDL expanded its cargo services pre World War I, a number of freighters entered service in 1913-1914, with more on order, most completed during the war and surrendered in 1919 to the Allies. The 1913/14 Yearbook in "Voyages of Lloyd Steamers in 1913" lists fifteen vessels chartered for cargo voyages:

Altair, D.S. Ges. Argo, Bremen via Brazil to LaPlata, picking up a return cargo at Rosario. Two voyages.

Alster, Syndikats Reederei, Hamburg, to Cuba, returning via Galveston, probably a load of cotton.

Alrich, Roland Linie, Bremen (largely controlled by NDL) to Australia. Also from Roland Linie:

Durendart, once for an outward voyage to Brazil only, twice more to Brazil.

Ganelon, two voyages to Australia.

Olivant, to Brazil, return via Galveston. To New Orleans, via Cuba.

Ascot, Britain S.S. Co., London, Bremen-Cuba, return via Baltimore.

Craigvar, Craig Line S.S. Co., Leith, to Galveston via Cuba.

Erhard, Halifax-Baltimore-Galveston.

Hermiston, Borderdale Shipping Co., Glasgow, Outward only to La Plata.

Ingbert, Hamburg-Bremer Afrika-Linie (NDL controlled), outward only to La Plata.

Javorina, Rhederei Vereinigung, Hamburg, outward only to Australia.

Strathalbyn, Burrell & Son, Glasgow, to La Plata.

Strathcarron, Burrell & Son, Glasgow, outward only to Baltimore.

Wyneric, homeward only from Baltimore.

No Year Books since have detailed the report year's voyages. In October, 1920, NDL chartered *Rapot*, 1913 Ts., and six other ships from the Roland Linie for voyages to Brasil, the first service resumed postwar. All were in the ten small vessels acquired by Roland Linie from Holland in exchange for two large new freighters ordered but not begun during the war, which it could not use.

In 1931-1933, NDL chartered Hamburg South American Line's *Antonio Delfino* and *Cap Verde* under pressures of owning 60% of the line's shares.

In 1950, NDL resumed the freight business with the chartered *Hermod*, from Frigga Seerederei, Hamburg, also *Argenfels* of the D.S. Ges. "Hansa," and *Adolf Vinnen*, from F.A. Vinnen & Co., Bremen, actually the formed NDL *Porta* #287.

In the 1950s and 1960s, as the Lloyd, and Hapag expanded their lines to something resembling prewar, and entering new trades, as to the Great Lakes, a number of chartered ships were in almost continuing service for NDL. In January, 1960, for example, *Clivia*, "Triton" Schiffahrts Geselschaft, Bremen, also *Silvia* was making its sixteenth charter voyage to Miami and the Gulf.

Here is a sample of 1950s and 1960s chartered vessels taken from NDL schedules, in many cases including "A Ship" where no vessel at printing time had been signed up:

- U.S. Gulf - Cuba - Mexico: Not all ships covered all the ports - *Adolf Vinnen* 1954, F.A. Vinnen & Co., Bremen; *Clivia* 1955-1955; *Johanna* 1955 "Alferra" Schiffahrts Ges., Hamburg; *Mary Nübel* 1959, Emder Dampferko; *Wihinapa* 1959; *Silvia* 1955.
- Central America West Coast: *Aquila* 1960, Richard Adler Söhne, Bremen; *Edwin Reith* "Orion" Schiffahrts Ges., Hamburg and *Luise Bornhofen* 1959, Robert Bornhofen, Hamburg; *St. Michael* 1967; *Tarpenbek* 1961.
- Miami - Gulf: *Amazonas* 1961, F.A. Detjen, Hamburg; *Clivia* 1960-1961; *Dora Oldendorff*, E.L. Oldendorff, Lübeck; *Luise Bornhofen* and *Magdalena Vinnen* 1964; *Wihinapa* 1959, De Vries & Co., Hamburg.

Chicago Tribune JAN. 12, 1969

Caribbean Cruising in the Grand Old Way

By H. P. Koenig

AT SEA IN THE CARIBBEAN — Only travelers who remember what cruising was like in the great, pre-war days of shipping [circa 1935 or so] will get the full impact of what the North German Lloyd has set out to create on its liners Europa and Bremen.

North German Lloyd's cruise liner Europa makes an off-shore stop at the port of Kingstown, St. Vincent Island in the Caribbean. A cruise on the Europa, writes H. P. Koenig in accompanying article, is a return to cruising in the grand tradition.
[Geo. Koenig Photo]

Here, suddenly, is a return to cruising in the grand tradition. Ships are run with a finicky attention to the smallest detail that belongs to a far less frantic age than our own. Consider this cruising for connoisseurs—those who appreciate the difference between a merely satisfactory passage and the truly extraordinary sea-going experience.

This season's North German Lloyd Caribbean cruises are designed according to the high standards set down in the "good old days" when only the really rich were passengers.

Now, at similar prices to what other lines are charging, the traveler can return to an opulent era of impeccable service, the best of food and wine served in luxurious surroundings, along with tastefully furnished accommodations likely to appeal to Old World types for whom First Class on the high seas was synonymous with a splendor hardly to be duplicated ashore.

To board the Europa or Bremen in New York or Port Everglades, Fla., is like sailing into a world of a generation or more ago.

The reader may wonder how much this correspondent knows about ship travel in that distant time. Coming from a traveling family, I made my first Atlantic crossing by ocean liner at the ripe old age of nine months [service was satisfactory, accommodations proved somewhat cramped] and by the time the war in Europe put a stop to such frivolity I had chalked up quite a few trips—eight in all.

While this may not qualify me as an expert, it does on occasion fill me with nostalgia for the way travel was achieved in a more leisurely age.

As we mounted the gangway of the Europa and started down the red-carpeted hallway to our stateroom there was the warm, comfortable feeling of returning to a place of one's fondest memories.

Suddenly there was *deja vu*. The feeling *I had been here before*.

Of course I hadn't. The original Europa I had sailed on—back in 1936 was it!—had long since gone to its just reward. This was merely a namesake. But there was the same quiet elegance. The white-haired steward who greeted us with, "Good evening, my name is Hans," might have spoken the identical words more than 30 years ago.

From the start there was a sense of well-being I hadn't experienced on the half-dozen ships I had sailed on in the past seasons. Here was the real thing at last: total commitment to the good life at sea. The passenger could relax. He was in good hands. He knew everything was going to be all right. And it was.

Somehow the North German Lloyd has been able to maintain a standard of excellence at a time when a general falling off of service and a stinting on the amenities has become the rule both ashore and afloat, at home and abroad. Only in the handful of the top European hotels is it possible to live as well as one can on the Europa.

And here are the small, important touches that made shipboard travel so great in another age, from morning bouillion followed by an oom-pah-pah brass band concert to the midnight snack and final nightcap. And without a doubt this must be the cleanest ship on the seas. There is a constant shining of brass. Vacuum cleaners are going all the time. I never saw so much *putz-putzing* in my life. And it is a *friendly* ship.

The French used word *ambiance*. The German term is *stimmung*. It means the mood or atmosphere projected in any given situation or set of circumstances. In terms of ship travel it implies an intangible sense of well-being.

Since all cruises cost about the same price, stop at virtually identical ports, and feature roughly equivalent rounds of activity, it is the ship itself and how it is run [the mood, atmosphere, sense of well-being] that can, over a two-week period, make the difference between a highly successful voyage and a merely satisfactory one.

Not to labor this theme unduly, let me just mention the matter of food. All Caribbean cruise ships try to come up with classic continental cuisine. As a rule, caviar finds its way onto the menu one or two times on the cruise, usually at the first or last gala dinners. On the Europa caviar is available every second or third night, along with *pate de foie gras*, smoked salmon, and a host of other delicacies.

Each day [usually at noon] the menu features one dish native to northern Germany, a fish or meat course one would not be likely to order anywhere except in the cities of Bremen, Hamburg, or along the Baltic sea. It's doubtful whether more than a dozen passengers appreciate how special these chef's creations are; yet this, too, is part of the tradition [and *pride*] manifested aboard the German ships.

For me the crucial test of cruise cuisine is how well it stands up after a week or 10 days. Some ships come on with all sorts of razzle-dazzle the first night or two at sea, then slowly the whole thing falls apart. Either the kitchen staff is incapable of maintaining high standards or the menu is simply not sufficiently varied to keep one's interest aroused for the long haul. Here, after 12 days there is the same sense of anticipation as one sits down to table as on the first night. Which should say it all.

On a purely personal basis, what impresses me most is that, for those who want it that way, this can become a cruise for people who don't really like cruises. There are travelers who can do without all the hoopla attending these southern voyages, the same round of activities: filmed horse races, sessions of bingo and bridge, pirates night, grand costume ball, elaborate variety shows, and so on. Ad infinitum.

Sophisticated souls might prefer to skip most of the la-di-da and concentrate on a more basic cruise program limited to sun, sea and sociability. On the Europa the schedule can be as crowded as one wants it to be—trap-shooting at 11, dance lessons a half hour later, bingo, ping pong, dress up nights—the whole bit. But no one pressures the passenger into joining. One can remain aloof, should such be the inclination.

On the Europa a group of us have taken this route. We spend mornings at pool-side, make use of the sauna in the afternoon, give ourselves up to the luxury of underwater massages. Evenings we indulge in cocktail parties and wine-tastings, gourmet meals.

Later, while everyone else whoops it up en masse, we repair to a discreet lounge, drink cognac or champagne [or both] and trip the light fantastic to the strains of Waldemar Prukner and his magic violin. For this small society of sybarites the trip is like a stay in a European hotel *de grand luxe*, with occasional fascinating ports tossed in for good measure. Such elegance hasn't existed since the '30s.

Reprinted with permission of the Chicago Tribune.

What more could any shipping line expect in the way of praise and a passenger in expectations?
See page 505.

SAFETY INFORMATION: The Bremen and Europa, registered in West Germany, meet International Safety Standards for new ships developed in 1948 and meet the 1966 Fire Safety Requirements.

Europa 5 *is operated by Hapag-Lloyd under long-term charter from its subsidiary Bremer Schiffvercharterungs A.G. The vessel has had major internal rebuildings, the last costing ten million Marks in Singapore in early 1995. All to maintain Europa's Five Star rating for cruising.*

**THE NEW YORK TIMES
June 21, 1954**

RED LANDS CUT IN ON LATIN MARKET

Fast-Growing Field Is Object of Much Wooing From All Parts of the World

By SAM POPE BREWER
Special to The New York Times.

RIO DE JANEIRO, June 20—Latin America's fast-growing markets are the object of covetous attention from all parts of the world. Even Iron Curtain countries have been cutting in recently.

An agreement between Brazil and Hungary was negotiated a few months ago. The North German Lloyd freighter Silvia is reported by the Brazilian Communist press to have arrived at Fortaleza and begun to load cotton for Hungary, which had been sold by the Bank of Brazil through local merchants.

An official Mixed German-Brazilian Commission is functioning here to promote further trade with West Germany. Walder Sarmanho, head of the Brazilian section, is due to visit Bonn, West German capital, early next month to negotiate new agreements. As of April 30, West Germany had a sizable credit balance of $57,400,000 with Brazil.

Flavia *in Lloyd charter and colors, standing by the burnt-out cable ship* Ocean Layer *in June, 1959 in mid-Atlantic.*
Flavia *was built in 1959 by the Rickmers Werft, Bremerhaven, 5,326 tons, sister of* Clivia, *also chartered by NDL, owned by "Triton" Schiffahrts Ges., Bremen, managed by Herman Dauelsberg.*

From Little Boxes to Big Boxes 549

- North Brazil: *Ernst Schröder* 1963, Reederei Richard Schröder, Hamburg; *Gerda Schnell* 1967; *Lasbek* 1959, Knöhr & Burchard, Hamburg, *Silvia* 1957.
- North America West Coast: *Silvia* 1957, Bernhard Howaldt 1963, Bernard Howaldt, Hamburg; *Hannoverland* 1966, *Neuharlingersiel*, 1967, Bugsier Reederei, Hamburg.
- South America West Coast: *Bellavia* 1963, Hermann Dauelsberg, Bremen.
- The St. Lawrence and Great Lakes: *Johanna* 1954-1955; *Monsun* 1955, *Adolf Vinnen*, 1954, *Sabine Howaldt* 1961, *Wiedenborstel*, January, 1959 barely escaped being frozen in, as were other ships, by a sudden freeze.

In 1972, Hapag-Lloyd charted *Main Express* and *Rhein Express* from C.F. Ahrenkiel, almost-sisters of the four container ships put onto the North Atlantic run in 1968-1969. Herr Ahrenkiel had been Freight Director, New York for the Hapag-Lloyd Gemeinschaft 1933-1939. He got home during the war, after joined Hapag's Executive Board until he formed his own concern.

In 1982, *Europa 5* entered service, owned by the Bremer Schiffsvercharterungs A.G., but managed by Hapag-Lloyd. In 1993, *Bremen 6* appeared in Hapag-Lloyd colors, owned by Frontier Cruises (Japan), Ltd. of which one-eighth is held by Hapag-Lloyd, but managed by Hanseatic Cruises GmbH, Hamburg. Convoluted ways of getting ships. The public considers them Hapag-Lloyd.

In the 1980s and 1990s, Hapag-Lloyd occasionally chartered in, even out, vessels needed to fill out a route, or superfluous, or while selling off older tonnage and awaiting new ships.

The new route opened by Hapag-Lloyd in 1954 was to the Great Lakes in partnership with Ahrenkiel & Bene and the Hamburg-Chicago Line. This was in anticipation of the opening of the St. Lawrence Seaway in 1959 in order to establish a clientele base before that led to a sudden big increase in lines wanting to enter this trade. Until 1959, given the shallow depth of the Welland Canal lock and some ports, the Great Lakes were served by the small *Rheinstein* class of freighters, and Hapag's counterparts. Not having that many small vessels, both lines chartered other German ships, an occasional practice where a route offers more potential than can be met with one's own vessels. In winters until the Seaway ships served only the St. Lawrence river ports. On 31/12/1958, Hapag and Lloyd ended their partnership with Ahrenkiel & Bene and the Hamburg-Chicago Line. They resumed the Lakes season on 1 May, 1959 with Ernst Russ & Co. of Hamburg, in time for the opening of the Seaway.

Lahnstein arrived at Montreal on 13 April, 1959, having fought ice on the St. Lawrence up to nine feet thick. The harbor of Montreal was still filled with ice. By the 17th, fourteen ships had reached Montreal, *Lahnstein* the only one not damaged. Before the Canal locks could be used, more than sixty vessels were waiting at the time of *Lahnstein* captain's report, thirty alone for

Christian Ahrenkiel had been the Hapag-Lloyd's North Atlantic Community Freight Transport Director in New York in the 1930s. After a period at Hapag after the war, he opened this line and others, but continuing to work closely with the Lloyd and Hapag.

Here 1962 Christmas greetings from Herrn Ahrenkiel to Captain Drechsel. The line's flag bears the Hamburg coat of arms, and three fish inside two oak branches.

Seaway Ships Race Winter Freeze

December 4, 1971

By ROBERT LINDSEY
Special to The New York Times

MONTREAL, Dec. 3—The skipper of the Greek freighter Monsun stood on deck today as his rusty ship glided out of the St. Lawrence Seaway, looked back briefly, and raised his right arm in a farewell salute as the craft headed for home under a sky filled with wind-driven snowflakes.

The Monsun was out. But Seaway officials said today scores of other ships, which are racing toward Montreal from as far away as Chicago and Duluth, Minn., may not get out of the 1,300-mile waterway before it freezes and bottles them up for winter.

"If you ask me, there'll be at least 50 or 60 left in there," said Maurice Patenaude, a Montreal harbor pilot, as he glanced up at a cold, gray sky that seemed to be closing in over the St. Lambert Locks, the eastern terminus of the Seaway.

The Seaway, a system of canals, lakes, rivers, locks and man-made waterways that permits deep-draft oceangoing vessels to sail from Atlantic ports into the Great Lakes heartland of the United States, is scheduled to close on Sunday Dec. 12. This is because freezing temperatures are expected to congeal the water about that time.

More than 135 ocean-going ships are still in the Seaway, almost twice the usual number at this time. This is a record high for this date, largely because hundreds of ships were diverted to Great Lakes ports because of the East and Gulf Coast dock strike.

Although longshoremen went back to work on Monday under a court order sought by the Nixon Adminministration, there is still a large backlog of ships in Great Lakes ports waiting to be unloaded. Snow and rain are delaying the operations.

There are 23 ocean-going vessels in Detroit, 20 in Milwaukee and 18 in Chicago. Often, cargo is being dumped any place the captains can find a berth, and being left for trucks or trains to carry to the final destination.

J. F. Pilon, assistant regional director of the St. Lawrence Seaway Authority, said in his office overlooking the St. Lambert Locks this morning, "It all depends on the weather."

He said the authority would keep the waterway open beyond Dec. 12 if possible—usually there are two or three days when the Seaway is passable beyond the official deadline—and added that it was too soon to project how many ships, if any might get trapped.

But, noting that there are still more than 100 ships backed up at the far end of the system, below the Welland Canal near Buffalo, he said: "Time is running out."

He said water temperatures this year were below normal, and this would mean trouble if the trend continued. "A year ago today," he said, "the water temperature here was 36 degrees Fahrenheit. Today, it's 34.5 and dropping."

He said the waterway could be made somewhat passable after temperatures hit the freezing level of 32 degrees by the use of icebreakers, but added that even then, cracked ice soon clogs up the channels.

"And it's not just the temperature," he said. "If we get repeated snowstorms, or high winds or fog, we lose the use of the system. In the summer, it takes six days to go from Chicago to Montreal, but in this time of the year it takes 12."

The Seaway Authority has been warning shippers by radio since Nov. 9 of the possibility of large numbers of ships being stuck in the ice. Yet since then, more than 90 ships have entered the Seaway on the condition that they would be last in line to get out if there were a jam-up.

These ships traveled west despite a warning from the Seaway—four vessels had to owners of any vessel that "insisted" upon entering the system after Nov. 12 would "accept the possibility and the responsibility for being trapped."

Ships have been trapped by winter ice just once before in the 22-year history of the seaway—four vessels had to spend the winter in Great Lakes ports in 1964.

Technical Experiments

technical teams have been experimenting with ways to keep the seaway open—including generation of air bubbles to prevent the formation of ice in locks, and the "anchoring" of shore ice so it is not torn loose by winds and then blocks channels.

But so far the goal of opening the seaway the year around has been elusive, technically and economically, as one seaway official said yesterday, half-seriously:

"In the future it may be possible to get ships out when they get trapped in the winter, but it might cost as much as it takes to get a man to the moon."

Although ocean-going ships are threatened with being bottled up in the seaway, fresh-water vessels such as the giant 700-foot-long iron ore craft that ply the Great Lakes will still be able to operate in the Sault Ste. Marie Locks of the seaway until next month.

nI the St. Lawrence Canal system near here, ice forms sooner because the frigid Ottawa River flows into the St. Lawrence and accelerates the formation of ice.

The International Association of Great Lakes Ports sent a message to ships yesterday saying that if they all did not get under way within three days, "some ships are going to spend winter in the system, and this could include up to 30 vessels.

"Presently, there is no lineup at the Welland Canal, and there must be a queue of 25 to 35 ocean-going vessels waiting to exit the Weland on Frdiay or they will not all meet the established deadltse."

Some of the backlogged ships may not get out of the Seaway before it freezes in winter

The New York Times/Dec. 4, 1971

First Day Cover for the twin Canada and United States stamps commemorating the opening of the St. Lawrence Seaway, 26 June, 1959.

Toronto where only eight ships at a time can tie up. In the previous winter of 1958-1959, thirteen vessels ended up stuck in the ice in Montreal: three each German and Swedish, two each British and Norwegian, and one each Liberian, Italian and Dutch. Initial cargo tonnages on the Seaway proved to be disappointing. During another early-ice winter, on 3 December, 1971 more than 135 ships still were in the lakes inside the locks ten days before closure. Not all made it out.

The Cuba-Gulf ports-Mexico service was resumed in 1950 with chartered tonnage, the next year with the first new vessels. In 1954, a service was every four weeks. Entry into the route was eased by joining the conference. It has power to accept or reject. Rejection means the applicant either stays out or cuts prices and operates independently, something major carriers like Hapag and Lloyd with long-term commitments are reluctant to do. In 1954, service was every four weeks.

In June, 1956 the above service was divided: one line serving Cuba-Mexico with calls at Gulf ports when needed. The other was a new line Continent-London-Miami-Gulf. *Emstein* #476, 14.5 knots, was the first ship, roundtrip sixty days. London and Miami were entirely new ports for Lloyd and Hapag. Contacts had to be made, attitudes to be learned. In London, stevedores are very capable but very methodical; read slow. They smoke despite No Smoking signs. As in Australia, agents and crews are reluctant to test the men. Tea pauses are religiously observed. Later Felixstowe was added. London's major export then was whisky and uncrated autos, before the time of floating garages pioneered by Wallenius and the Japanese.

With larger cargoes, metal products from the Continent, more vehicles from London, *Travestein* was put onto the run with nearly double *Emstein's* capacity and three more knots. It had a full cargo going out, including 310 autos and 12,006 cases of whisky. Homecoming from Houston and New Orleans it brought a record 16,550 bales of cotton, 12,795 for Bremen, Germany's main cotton, tobacco and coffee import city.

The South America West Coast service began in early 1953 with the *Brandenstein* #481 class: 16.5 knot ships, also used for the U.S.-Canada west coast as cargoes there increased. Handy ships. Eventually nine were built, then two others converted to the same standard. Ships every four weeks; in 1955 already every three, then three ships a month, from April, 1956 a weekly vessel scheduled at each port for the same day. That impresses and attracts shippers: reliable regularity. In December, 1957 *Rheinstein* sailed direct to Puntarenas, unloaded 3000 tons in eight days. Normally cargo for there is unloaded in Val-

HAMBURG-AMERIKA LINIE
NORDDEUTSCHER LLOYD

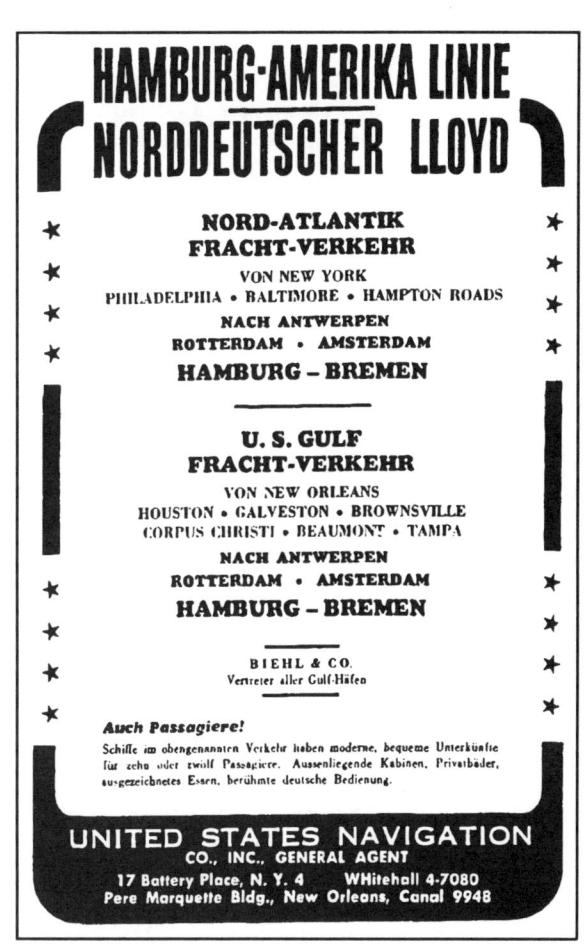

NORD-ATLANTIK
FRACHT-VERKEHR

VON NEW YORK
PHILADELPHIA • BALTIMORE • HAMPTON ROADS

NACH ANTWERPEN
ROTTERDAM • AMSTERDAM
HAMBURG – BREMEN

U. S. GULF
FRACHT-VERKEHR

VON NEW ORLEANS
HOUSTON • GALVESTON • BROWNSVILLE
CORPUS CHRISTI • BEAUMONT • TAMPA

NACH ANTWERPEN
ROTTERDAM • AMSTERDAM
HAMBURG – BREMEN

BIEHL & CO.
Vertreter aller Gulf-Häfen

Auch Passagiere!
Schiffe im obengenannten Verkehr haben moderne, bequeme Unterkünfte für zehn oder zwölf Passagiere. Aussenliegende Kabinen, Privatbäder, ausgezeichnetes Essen, berühmte deutsche Bedienung.

UNITED STATES NAVIGATION
CO., INC., GENERAL AGENT
17 Battery Place, N. Y. 4   WHitehall 4-7080
Pere Marquette Bldg., New Orleans, Canal 9948

Joint Hamburg-Amerika Linie and Norddeutscher Lloyd cargo services across the North Atlantic. "Also Passengers" in modern comfortable accommodations for ten-twelve persons, exceptional food.

Shipping Magazine advertisement of routes served by Norddeutscher Lloyd and Hamburg-Amerika Linie in 1957. Interesting that the names are switched so that one month one heads the advertisement, the other the partner.

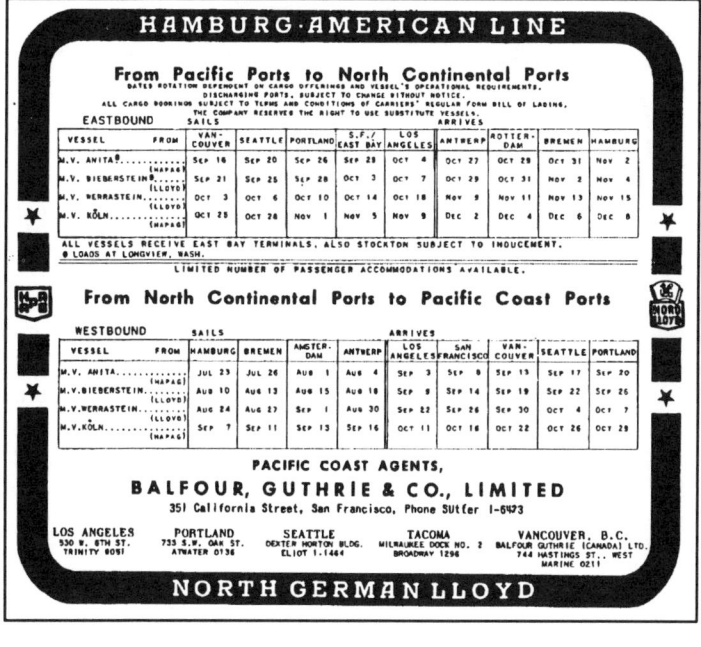

SERVING AMERICA'S
FOUR COASTS
HAPAG LLOYD

Hallmark of dependable service

EXPRESS
CARGO AND PASSENGER SAILINGS
TO AND FROM
ANTWERP, ROTTERDAM, AMSTERDAM
HAMBURG, BREMEN

HAMBURG AMERICAN LINE
NORTH GERMAN LLOYD

Contact:
UNITED STATES NAVIGATION CO., INC
17 Battery Place, N. Y. 4 (Head Office) BOwling Green 9-6000

Hapag joined the West Coast route in August, using sisterships of NDL's Lahnstein. *The first* Weissenburg *was in San Francisco on 4 September when the author visited her.*

From Little Boxes to Big Boxes 553

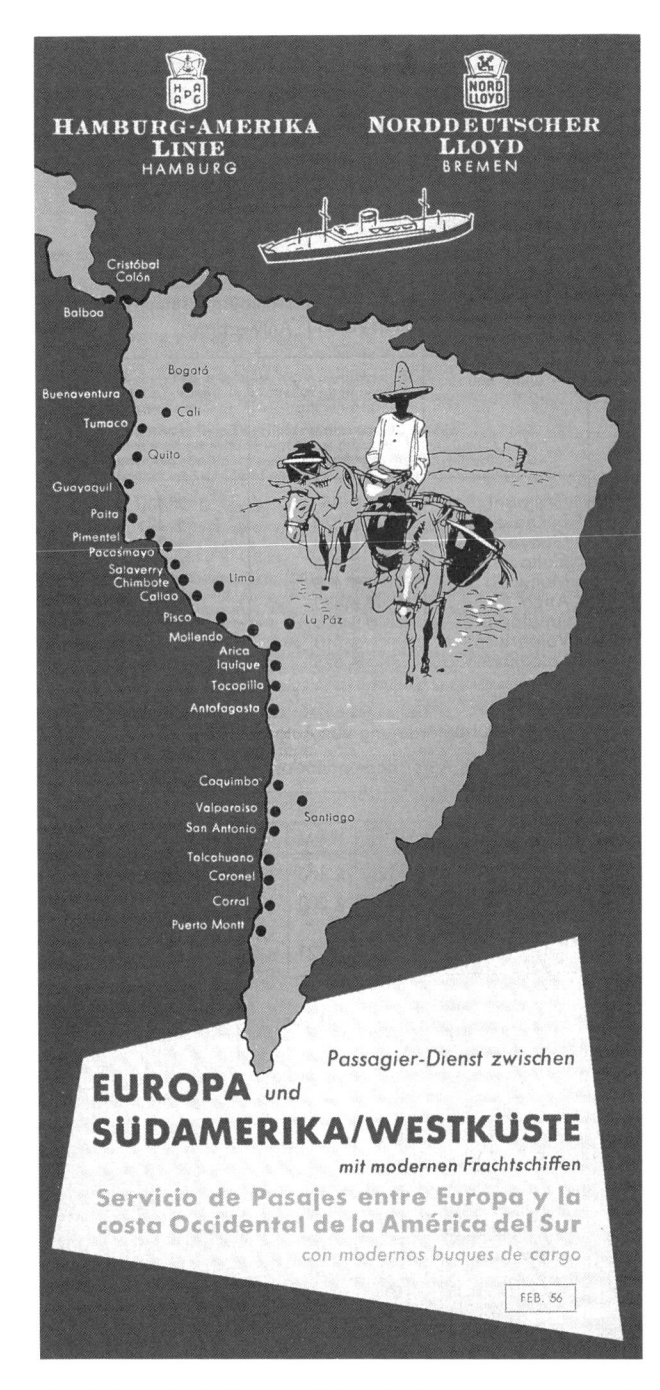

South America's long and largely barren west coast. At several ports cargo still has to be lightered to and from the ships. The postwar resumption of this route from 1953 used freighters with space for up to twelve passengers; Prewar it had been 20-28.

paraiso, then transloaded on coastal ships that operate uncertainly and in difficult islands terrain. The ship returned via Brazilian ports. In January, 1958 *Saarstein* followed, a boon for Magellan-area Chile: quicker deliveries of imports at considerably lower freight rates.

The U.S.-Canada West Coast line was resumed in June, 1954. See *Lahnstein* #473 for the Captain's account of unexpected difficulties at first arrival in Los Angeles. This line requires high-class, fast, reefer-space vessels for food exports to Europe, and lumber. It is a very competitive route.

Contract, in effect, private charter voyages were an important part of NDL's cargo carryings. Some ships made their maiden voyages, or between scheduled trips went in ballast to pick up entire cargoes at one port. *Spreestein* #506 made its trial-delivery-maiden voyage from the shipyard, briefly via Bremerhaven, to Safi, Marocco in May, 1957, for a full cargo of phosphate.

Lahnstein had left Santa Cruz de Teneriffe in December, 1956 for Northern Brazil. One day out the ship was ordered by radio to turn around, unload the Brazil cargo and proceed to Safi for a load of phosphate. In Santa Cruz the port captain had a Marocco coastal-area chart; the captain found it unusable. But he could not supply a Maroccan flag. The captain headed for a known light south of Safi, then worked his way up the coast. The ship had to wait 1.5 miles outside for the pilot and agent. He did bring out a Maroccan flag to come in with. The captain made a map of the entry and harbor from his radar screen, and followed this in, with the pilot. The ship loaded 4,250 tons in eight hours, returned to Bremen where it had left two weeks before.

The last line in the Bremen report of this voyage reads: "In the Freight Department lies a large stone that fell from some one's heart after this delicate operation." A sense of humor and of pride.

Another time it was *Reifenstein* #496. It left Bremerhaven on 30 January, 1956 at Noon with a small group from Bremen's management group as passengers. The ship arrived at Safi at 18.00 hours four days later. *Reifenstein* anchored outside, a long mole protecting the harbor from the normal western swells. At 6 a.m., the pilot came out and with help of a tug the ship entered, 166.5 meters long, the largest vessel until then to come into Safi. At 8 a.m. the ship was tied up. Phosphate, called Wüstensand, Desert Sand, by the crews, comes in open railcars, is conveyored to shipside and from there through large piping, as with grain, is pumped into the holds. Day and a half loading time. Safi also has a grain silo, modern storage sheds, a fishing port, but no industry. On 5 January, 13.30 hours, *Reifenstein* left, completely covered with Wüstensand. A thorough clean-ship at sea. On 10 January, arrival at

To attract attention there always has to be a Young Lady, here a Miss Weser-Ems, the ports on the estuaries of these two rivers, see Chapter 20... This is the first cargo of Pacific Northwest fruits and vegetables, Libby, McNeill & Libby's, at the port of Emden on the M.S. Blankenstein #503. Captain G. Clausen in 1966. Emden again was trying to tie into the world shipping network, just as had happened in 1914 when the Lloyd and Hapag agreed with the Kingdom of Prussia to open lines from Emden. From Seekiste *December, 1966.*

Brunsbüttelkoog, the Elba River end of the Kiel Canal. The report by Captain Krause was carried in NDL's monthly information bulletin.

In 1956, fifteen such special voyages were made against thirteen in 1955. Tonnages carried were 90,100 tons of phosphates, 87,696 tons of grains, 9,901 tons of sugar, 3,060 tons of cement, and 2,338 automobiles. The freight charges paid for wages afloat and ashore, for paying off ship mortgages, and perhaps even something for the stockholders.

As the 1950s progressed, the nature of cargoes changed, requiring different methods to handle them. Increasingly, raw products from overseas arrived in specialty vessels, bulk carriers, some OBO's, Oil - Bulk - Ore. Outgoing cargoes began to include heavy individual loads: machinery, boilers, refinery towers, locomotives, steamrollers. Many of these as deck cargoes requiring heavy-lift equipment, on board or dockside.

In 1957, two steel rolling mills weighing 157 tons each were to be taken by *Nabob* #508 to the U.S. East Coast. The only crane big enough in Bremerhaven was a 250 tonner owned by the Army, actually ex-German from the war. Delicate negotiations with Washington got approval for it to provide the lift. The bottoms of two hatches had to be shored crossways with heavy wooden beams so as to distribute the loads evenly. It took five hours for the two Walzenstände to be lifted off the rail cars, floated to, and then lifted into *Nabob*. The job was finished at 2 a.m.

In most ports heavy lift equipment is not available, so vessels had to provide this. Beyond the initial six *Rheinstein*-class ships, successors were given thirty-tons, then eventually sixty-tons lifting capacity, finally with a free-standing mast. This required a tremendous strengthening of the hull. Another innovation was to make the freighters convertible from open to closed shelter-deckers. As the latter, they could go to a deeper draught, hence carry more inside. The decks could be cleared by reducing the number of king posts for on-deck cargoes, including the beginning of carrying containers.

Breakthrough!

The only containerships with adjustable fin type stabilizers for "passenger ship" smoothness

The sailing of the "Weser Express" from New York on November 8 marks the start of a new era in transatlantic shipping. At last, a cargo vessel can promise the same smooth ocean crossing once expected only aboard fine luxury liners. Our adjustable fin type stabilizers make the difference, and only Hapag-Lloyd containerships have them.

And this is just the beginning. The "Weser Express" will be followed into service by three sister ships, the "Elbe Express," the "Alster Express," and the "Mosel Express" (each with a capacity of up to 736 containers and a speed in excess of 20 knots), to provide regular weekly service between U. S. Atlantic ports and Northern Europe.

The finest in modern equipment, the latest techniques in cargo handling, the "know-how" gained in transporting over 80,000 containers to date, and over 100 years of transatlantic shipping experience make Hapag-Lloyd your best choice for shipments to or from the Continent.

We treat your container like a passenger.

HAMBURG-AMERICAN LINE—NORTH GERMAN LLOYD
General Agent
UNITED STATES NAVIGATION CO., INC.
Head Office: 17 Battery Place, New York, N.Y. 10004 269-6000
Chicago · Cleveland · Milwaukee

One of the early lessons of the container age was that in bad weather they would break their couplings and go overboard or waves would wash them off. Hence this BREAKTHROUGH: Container ships with stabilizers. One unexpected benefit of a container ripped open en route Hong Kong to Tacoma in 1992 with 29,000 bath-tub toys that spilled. As the plastic toys began washing ashore, scientist realized by charting the site of the spill and the routes the toys took, they could learn much about the currents and the winds.

A summing up in 1959 showed that the forty-two freighters built and bought through *Wiedstein* #513 had cost DM425 millions. Of this 39% or DM165 millions came from depreciation, 21% or DM88 millions from (Government) rebuilding loans, and 40% or DM172 millions from long-term credits, average time eleven years. Four freighters came out in 1960, then no new construction until 1967, the *Friesenstein* #520 class. The passenger ships *Berlin*, *Bremen* and *Europa* involved separate financing.

The gradual containerization of cargoes began to be felt in the late 1950s. The U.S. military had shipped personnel gear and light-weight commodities in vans during and after the war. In 1941, Matson Lines had 6 x 6 x 4 lock boxes for cargo vulnerable to pilferage. In 1957, White Pass & Yukon Railroad shifted to containers on its vessels serving Skagway. From there they went inland on flat cars. In 1958, the first of six Matson freighters with decks cleared for carriage of containers went into service as lift-on, lift-off vessels. The holds continued to take piece goods. Matson's first full container ship sailed on 19 May, 1960 from San Francisco. From then on, the system began to spread worldwide. (Fred Stindt, Matson's Century of Ships, Modesto, California.)

In its report for 1965, the Lloyd Board commented about the coming containerization "It would be welcomed as a way to avoid major losses if an evolutionary development were to take place rather than the revolutionary one that currently seems to be happening."

In 1963-1964, NDL had re-engined the seven turbine-driven ships of the *Weserstein* class to Diesel drive, and with a new fore-body with bulbous bows, upped their speed by two knots to remain competitive on the Far East route. Seven 21-knot freighters, again for the East Asia route, came out in 1967, the *Friesenstein* class #520. Each got a two-armed Stülcken heavy-lift mast serving hatches IV and V, two cranes with cabs serving hatches I and VI, and one free-standing heavy-lift mast for 60 tons serving hatches II and

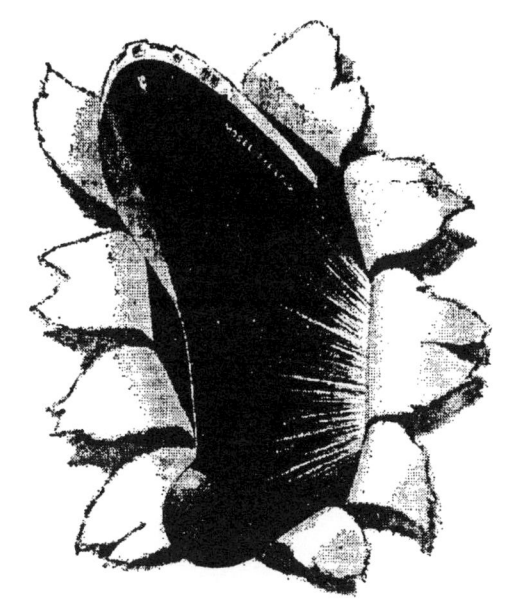

III. This gave Hapag and Lloyd together fourteen comparable freighters. But their decks were so cluttered that they could carry few containers.

Also in 1967, Lloyd and Hapag announced orders for four container ships to cost M35 millions each, to carry 616TEU's and at twenty knots provide a weekly trans-Atlantic service. They entered service in October, 1968-January, 1969. Meanwhile, ten freighters running between Hamburg-Bremen-Continent to the U.S. East Coast had decks cleared so they could carry containers and conventional cargo on two weekly services. Earlier, in 1968, the two lines had formed the Deutsche Containerdienst Gmbh. to buy, lease, organize containers and traffic ashore and afloat. In October, 1969 the four container ships ran Hamburg-Bremen-Felixstowe-New York-Baltimore-Norfolk. In 1970, LeHavre was added as experience showed how more ports could be served within the weekly schedule. With the most important route for both Lloyd and Hapag a pace-setting weekly container service, the road to merger in 1 September, 1970 was made easier.

Experience with running the four container ships allowed extra ports to be added to the schedule and still provide weekly service. Here the announcement that Philadelphia would be added and spelling out the benefits of containerization, the computer-recording of cargoes, and fins to stabilize the ships and cargoes.

From Little Boxes to Big Boxes 557

NDL Fleet
Ships 507 — 531

507. *Siegstein*
Bremer Vulkan, Vegesack #856   1957   2998/4913   126.02x16.04
M.A.N. Diesel   4000   14.5
2   33

Launched 11/4/1957. Delivery 29/6/1957 as closed shelter-decker. 1/9/1970 to Hapag-Lloyd A.G. 25/2/1972 with *Spreestein* sold to Nan Yang Shipping Co., Macao, Ocean Tramping Co., Mogadisciu operator, renamed *Minai*. 1976 *Xiang Shan* China Ocean Shipping Co., Beijing, 4,875 Ts. 1981 *Ocean Mercury*, Ocean Mercury Shipping Co., S.A., Panama, 4,829 Ts. 4/4/1986 at Hwa Ta Steel & Iron Co., Kaohsiung, for BU.

Siegstein *#507 shown at a grain installation, with her heavy-lift main mast and forward post, in consort able to lift sixty tons. Eric Steinfeldt Photo.*

508. *Lechstein*   1958-1972
Atlas Werke, A.G. Bremen #397 1958   3660/5430   130.60x16.26
M.A.N. Vulkan Diesel   4000   14.5
2   33

Launched 13/8/1958. Delivery 12/12/1958. Heavy-lift 60 tons heavy-lift derrick on free-standing mast to leave more room for deckloads. MV. was the 100th postwar to Cuba and U.S. Gulf ports, arr. Brownsville 6/2/1959 in the Hapag-Lloyd joint service, predating their formal merger in 1970. 1/9/1970 to Hapag-Lloyd A.G. 5/4/1972 left on 400th H-L sailing to North Brazil postwar, the first in 2/1951. 8/1972 to Reederei Klaus-Peter Offen, Hamburg, Liberia flag, renamed *Holstendeich*. 8/9/1977 total loss after fire in the Bay of Biscay. 1/1978 wreck sold to Greece, arr. Piraeus 13/Nov/1977 in tow of salvage tug Jaki, repair made there. Renamed *Amalinda*, 5,214 Ts., Amalinda Shipping Co., Piraeus. 1984 Zacharion, Thomas Shipping Co., Piraeus. 1986 renamed *Shahinda*, 5,164 Ts. 12/5/1986 arr. Gadani Beach for BU.

Lechstein *#508 arriving, sister of* Nabstein *#515, while* Brandenstein *or a sister is just leaving. Three NDL tugs helping, one just visible at the bow,* Widder *in front, another at the stern.* Copyright Laurence Dunn.

509. *Burgenstein*   1958-1982
Bremer Vulkan, Vegesack #880 1958   6215/8495   146.85x19.84
M.A.N. Diesel   9000   17.5
8   47

Launched 12/8/1958. Delivery 15/10/1958, MV 21/10 to West Coast, South America. 1968 with its two sisters fitted to carry containers astride the hatches. 1/9/1970 to Hapag-Lloyd A.G. 29/10/1974 to Hapag-Lloyd International S.A., Panama, reg. Bremen. 10/1/1977 huge explosion of lethal cargo in Bremerhaven. Three Turkish crewmen missing. Rebuilt. 7/1981 to Saudi Palm Nav. Co., Jeddah, renamed *Saudi Palm*, 8,281 Ts. 6/1984 arr. Lianyungang for BU.

Burgenstein was the 75th vessel built by Bremer Vulkan and its predecessor shipyards for the Lloyd, and the 25th since the war. The first was the sidewheeler *Forelle* in 1880 built for the passenger trade on the Lower Weser, but also used between Bremerhaven and Wangerooge Island. The years since have shown major changes in ships: Before 1914, average speed of ships built for NDL was 12.35 knots, 3,513 HP, 6,290 tons. Between the wars, average speed was 13.28 knots, 5,075 HP, 7,052 tons. The postwar averages to 1958 were: 16.31 knots, 6,715 HP, and 5,365 tons.

Burgenstein *arriving empty at San Francisco in the 1950s. En route to Vancouver and way ports. There is an old-style Jacob's ladder hanging midship.* Author's Photo.

Burgenstein *#509 and sisters* Buchenstein *#510 and* Buntenstein *#514, were designed for the West Coast South America trade with greater hatch sizes and lift-capacity to fifty tons and engines aft making it easier to have below-deck hatch openings for large cargo items and use of fork lifts. In was the 75th vessel built by Bremer Vulkan and its predecessors for the Lloyd, and the 25th postwar unit.*

The cover of the launch program on 12 August, 1958, signed by Dr. Arnold Rehm.

STAPELLAUF

des Frachtmotorschiffes

»*Burgenstein*«

des 75. Schiffes und gleichzeitig des 25. Nachkriegsschiffes, das vom

Schiffbau und Maschinenfabrik, Bremen-Vegesack
für den
NORDDEUTSCHEN LLOYD
erbaut wurde
BREMER VULKAN

Dienstag, 12. August 1958

560   *Norddeutscher Lloyd Bremen*

Buchenstein *#510 and its two sisters of 1958 ten years later were fitted to carry containers on deck, the year NDL and Hapag with four new vessels opened their trans-Atlantic container service. The ships had reefer rooms, and tanks for vegetable oils and for wine. Coals to Newcastle. Chilean wines to Germany.* Photo by Karl-Heinz Schwadke, B.N.R.A.

510. **Buchenstein** 1958-1982
Bremer Vulkan, Vegesack #881
1958   6223/8519   146.97x19.84
M.A.N. Diesel   9000   17.5
7   47

Launched 30/9/1958. MV. 23/12/1958 to West Coast, South America. 1968 rebuilt to carry deck containers. 1/19/1970 to Hapag-Lloyd International S.A., Panama, reg. in Bremen. 14/7/1977 rescued 19 from burning *Anco Glory*, landed them at Penang. 9/1980 put into "Hansa Service," routes taken over from the failed Deutsche D.S. Ges. "Hansa," of Bremen, a victim of the Arab oil boycott. 7/1981 to Saudi Rose Maritime Co., Jeddah, renamed *Saudi Rose*, 8,269 Ts., reg. at Jedda. 7/7/1984 arr. Qingdao for BU by China Minerals & Metals Co.; it had been sold to India for BU, evidently resold.

511. **Bremen 5** 1959-1972
Chantiers et Ateleiers de St. Nazaire #94
1939   32336   212.40x27.49
4 x Turbines   53,500   23   * * * *
I-216 T-906   544

Launched 15/2/1938 as *Pasteur*. Delivery 8/1939, 29,253 Ts., 26 kns. to Cie de Nav. Sudatlantique, Bordeaux. I-297, II-126, III-338. MV. due 10/9/1939, cancelled by war. 2/6/1940 actual first voyage Brest-Halifax with French Bullion. There taken over by British. France had fallen during the voyage. Ran as troop transport under Cunard-White Star management. 11/4/1946 ret. to France and owner. Transport to French Indo China, 30,477 Ts. Nov/1956 transport in Suez Canal Invasion by British and French. 25/1/1957 LU at Brest. 18/9/1957 bought by NDL, departure delayed by French protests. 26/9/1957 left Brest in tow for Bremerhaven. Preliminary work done by NDL's Technical Service. 8/1/1958 arr. at Bremer Vulkan for rebuilding with new bulbous bow, superstructure, stabilizers, "from the bottom up" (Dr. R. Bertram) rebuilding inside and out. 23/5/1959 renamed *Bremen 5*. Eight of ten boilers replaced by four high-pressure new ones. Medium-pressure stage of four turbines replaced, stabilizers in-

Before and After
Pasteur *of 1939 after 18 years of various war services, bought by NDL, arriving in Bremerhaven in September, 1957.*
Below: Bremen *of 1959 with thirteen years under the Lloyd flag ahead of her.*

Promotion for BREMEN'S *maiden departure, probably done by an outside firm, as NDL's in-house promotion department was two persons in 1955, against as many as seventy pre-war.*

There she is!
The New BREMEN. The Flag ship of the Norddeutscher Lloyd.
The roominess and the comfort of the cabins,
The Social Halls and Activity Rooms,
The best technical installations,
The Lloyd Kitchen and the Lloyd Service in the Old Tradition.
And the unique Lloyd care that means:
The BREMEN. The ship that leaves no wishes unfulfilled.

But instead of the new BREMEN the cleaning woman comes sailing over the horizon, and reports "All clear. Maiden Voyage on 9th July!"

Ah. But that's really overdoing it. The obligation to use knife and forks belongs to the daily duties even on the New BREMEN:
8 Kitchens
10 Pastry Konditoren
28 Chefs turn Duty into Pleasure
242 Men on Deck and with the Engine
All bring you a crossing without daily chores
That is the Course for the new BREMEN.

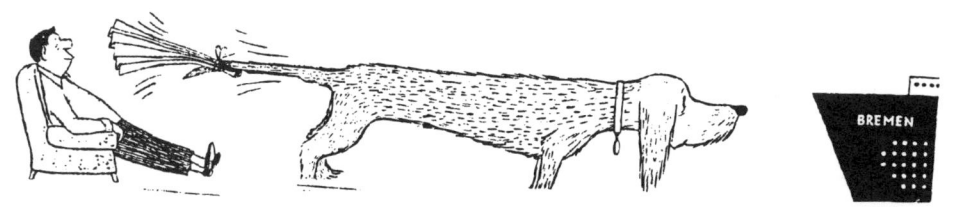

Should one bring one's dog to fan the air? But if you have no dog, the new BREMEN
From the De Luxe Cabins to the Tavern
Of course provides a thoroughly adequate air conditioning
On July ninth you can convince yourself.

stalled. In June, 1959, so the story goes, two men came before a judge in Bremen, one very bloodied, struck by the other. Judge: "You hit the defendant?" "Yes, Your Honor." "How can you possibly hit a peaceful person who did not even resist?" "Well, Sir. I am the ship painter. I painted forward right, forward left, aft right, aft left, Bremen, Bremen, Bremen, Bremen. When I had finished and walking along the quay, this man asks me: 'What is the name of that ship?' Sir, Your Honor. I could not contain myself and hit him." (See #489). MV. 9/7/1959 to, 21/7 from New York, owned by Bremer Nordatlantikdienst GmbI. 15/1/1960 first cruises to the West Indies. 1965 reg. for NDL. Winter 1965-1966 given a new bulbous bow for cruising with less power and vibration, 32,316 Ts. 1/9/1970 to Hapag-Lloyd A.G. 10/7/1971 sold to the Chandris Group, Piraeus. 12.1.1972 arr. from last cruise. 19.1.1972 del. to Chandris. Ship overhauled. MV. 25/5/1972 from Tilbury as *Regina Magna*. 17/10/1974 LU at Piraeus. 6/10/1977 left Piraeus in tow after sale to Saudi-Philippine Hotel group, arr. Jeddah 1/11/1977 for use as dormitory ship by Filipino construction workers, renamed *Saudi-Phil I*. Mid-1980 sold by Philippine-Singapore Port Corp. to Taiwan breakers, renamed *Filipinas-Saudi I*. Towed from Jeddah bound for Kaohsiung, 9/6/1980 foundered in 07.35N, 60.12E, southeast of Socotra evidently from leaking valves.

Bremen *provided Registry, and a gamut of business services.*

Bremen 5's *maiden departure from the Columbus Quay in Bremerhaven on 9 July, 1959 was indeed a festive event. Again a* Bremen, *not so big nor so fast as* Bremen 4 *in 1929, but a day for national pride and rejoicing. In what she offered to her passengers she was ahead of the times, as Herr Bertram told the world press in February, 1959 when a three-meters model was displayed. The new* Bremen *began life as the French* Pasteur *in 1939, taken over for war before she could voyage for peace.* Bremen *in 1959 was a sea-going spa. A 25 September, 1994 headline in the* San Francisco Examiner's *Sunday Travel section: "Seagoing Spa: The New Wave in Fitness Centers."* Bremen *had it thirty-five years earlier.* Photo Peter and Monica Plesch.

Bremen *sailing from the Columbus kaje, Bremerhaven, evidently on her maiden voyage in July, 1959. Thousands to see her off, as they did thirty years earlier with* Bremen 4.

Just as Bremen's *maiden voyage in July, 1929 was a national event, so was the resumption of German passenger service to New York in February, 1954, and now in July, 1959* Bremen 5's *maiden voyage, almost twenty years since the war ended all German shipping services.*

The New York Times.

37,064. © 1959, by The New York Times Company. Times Square, New York 36, N.Y. NEW YORK, FRIDAY, JULY 17, 1959.

Port Welcomes Germany's Fifth Liner Bremen

The North German Lloyd liner moving past the lower Manhattan skyline on arrival here

Capt. Heinrich Lorenz with Miss Marita Lorenz, daughter

By EDWARD A. MORROW

West Germany's first postwar entry into the North Atlantic luxury passenger trade, the Bremen, slipped into New York Harbor yesterday with all the grace her namesakes had shown in the past. The fifth North German Lloyd liner to bear the name of the German port in a century made her maiden voyage here in poor visibility. Nevertheless, her 780 passengers were thrilled by the salutes of tugs, freighters, fireboats and helicopters. The 32,336-gross-ton liner was known as the Pasteur when she sailed under the French flag; she was formerly a troop ship. Bought for about $7,500,000 from the

Continued on Page 4, Column 4

Continued From Page 1, Col. 4

French and reconditioned at a cost of almost $17,000,000, the Bremen is now the largest and most luxurious ship in West Germany's merchant marine. Her twenty-three-knot cruising speed does not compare with her immediate namesake, which twenty years ago was capable of thirty-two knots.

Several members of the crew sailing under Capt. Heinrich Lorenz described their liner as a "legend-encrusted ship." They recalled that the last Bremen had inched out of New York Harbor in August, 1939, after being delayed by the United States for thirty-six hours. Only her running lights were aglow because it was believed a British fleet was ready to capture her on the high seas.

The liner managed to reach Murmanski in the Soviet Union, and later reached the port of Bremen, where she was destroyed by fire in March, 1941. Captain Lorenz yesterday rejected the generally accepted version that she had been set afire by the Royal Air Force. He attributed the ship's end to the carelessness of a German seaman who had set a mattress afire.

Capt. Lorenz was welcomed yesterday by Commissioner Vincent A. G. O'Connor of the Department of Marine and Aviation and James J. O'Brien, deputy commissioner of commerce and public events. They boarded the ship from a tugboat in the lower bay.

Richard Bertram, managing director of North German Lloyd, said that the line had bought the ship from the French because "it was and is one of the finest hulls afloat."

A new ship, he explained, would have cost about $44,000,000 and "we wouldn't get delivery before 1963." He said the German line would use French Line passenger piers in New York because both companies had found it mutually profitable.

Mr. Bertram was the chief speaker last night at a dinner aboard the Bremen sponsored by Dr. Wilhelm Grewe, Ambassador of the Federal Republic of Germany.

The liner is scheduled to depart July 21 with nearly 1,100 passengers. Her capacity is 1,200.

Bremen *began service with a* **Nordamerika-Dienst Schiffpost** *and also a* **Jungfernreise** *cancel with one having only the dates for the outward voyage, immediately replaced with one with the roundtrip dates. The former is very rare. Some of* Bremen's *cruise cancels are the same as* Berlin's: **Bermudas** *used 1966-68,* **Westindienreisen** *used 1960-70,* **Island-Norwegen** *used 1965 only;* **Nordkapfahrt** *1967-68;* **Nordsee-Ostsee** *1964 only;* **Schottland-Island-Norwegen** *1963 only, and* **Silvesterfahrt** *(New Year's Cruise) 1967-70. Eventually, specific cruise indications were replaced by a generic cancel reading* **Kreuzfahrten-Nordatlantikdiest** *under Hapag-Lloyd ownership from 1970.*

How technology improves. As with the rebuilding of the Weserstein #484 class of freighters, the addition of a bulbous bow and a stern bulb to smoothen water flow, so Bremen-Pasteur's bow of 1939, right, was replaced in Winter 1965-1966 by 165 tons of larger bulb. From Tow Line, *Moran Towing Co. Work performed by NDL's Technical Service, the Lloydwerft, in Bremerhaven.*

Abstract of Log
T.S. »BREMEN«

32335 GRT · Length: 696,88 feet · Beam: 87,93 feet
Captain Heinrich Lorenz

Maiden Trip - Eastbound - July 21st, 1959
from New York to Bremerhaven

July	Noon-Position Latitude North	Noon-Position Longitude West	Miles	Wind	Remarks
21	New York		25		Departure 00.18 a.m., 02.18 p.m. passed Ambrose Light Vessel
	40° 14'	69° 00'	217	SSW 2/3	Slightly cloudy, fog, slight sea
22	41° 24'	56° 51'	556	SW 2	Mostly cloudy, slight sea
23	43° 54'	45° 05'	553	SSW 4	Mostly cloudy, slight sea
24	47° 18'	33° 10'	540	WNW 4/5	Overcast, hazy, moderate sea
25	49° 12'	20° 32'	517	NNW 4/5	Overcast, moderate sea
26	49° 39'	07° 53'	495	NW 4	Fine and clear, slight sea, passed Bishop Rock 02.41 p.m.
27	Cherbourg		250		Arrival 06.42 a.m., Departure 09.00 a.m.
	Southampton		96		Arrival 02.30 p.m., Departure 04.42 p.m.
28	Bremerhaven		529		
	Total		3778		

July 28th, 1959, 2.06 p.m., passed Weser Lightvessel
Total Distance from New York to Bremerhaven: 3778 Nautical Miles
Average speed: 22.22 kn

Moran Towing in the 1920s and in the 1930s and again postwar, did much of the Lloyd and Hapag-Lloyd tugging in New York.

Bremen's return log of her maiden Voyage in July, 1959. A respectable 22.22 knots average, what the pre-1914 four-stacker express liners did on their good voyages.

512. **Illstein**   1959-1972
Bremer Vulkan, Vegesack #872
1959   3049/4952   125.06x16.04
M.A.N. Diesel   3900   14.5
2   32

Further slight improvements to original *Rheinstein* class, and *Siegstein* and *Spreestein* changes. Launched 25/5/1959. MV. 26/8/1959 to C. America & Gulf ports. 1/9/1970 to Hapag-Lloyd A.G. 3/5/1972 at Bremerhaven to Nayang Shipping Co., Hong Kong, owners, managers Ocean Tramping Co., Mogadisciu, renamed *Minshan*, one of five ships sold at the same time: *Spreestein, Wiedstein, Siegstein*, and Hapag's *Rendsburg*. 1978 to People's Republic of China, Guandong, renamed *Long Shan*, 4,891 Ts. 1985 on Hong Kong-Shanghai-Japan run. 3/1986 still afloat, no action report in Lloyd's Shipping Index. 1993 RLR.

513. *Wiedstein* 1959-1972
Bremer Vulkan, Vegesack #873
1959   3049/4952   126.06x16.04
M.A.N. Diesel   3900   14.5
2   33

Keel laid 5/1/1959. Launched 23/6/1959. MV. 17/9/1959 to Central America West Coast and U.S.A.-Canada. 1/9/1970 to Hapag-Lloyd A.G. 1/5/1972 to Ocean Tramping Co., Hong Kong, reg. Mogadisciu, renamed *Mintsung*. 1977 sold by Nan Yang Shipping Co. to Fortune Sea Transport Corp., Panama, kept name. 20/2/1986 arr. Xingang for BU.

Illstein #512 and Wiedstein #513 were a still further improvement, beyond #507 and #508, of the original Rheinstein class #572. All freighters now were being built for ready conversion from open to closed shelter deckers. That meant, openings could be closed to allow greater cargo weight and deeper draught, a way to get more out of the same ship. And no king posts ahead of the superstructure. Both photos NDL Fotoarchiv.

514. *Buntenstein*   1960-1980
Bremer Vulkan, Vegesack #882 1960   6233/8520   146.95x19.84
M.A.N. Diesel   9000   17.5
10   47

Launched 16/11/1959. MV. 6/1/1960 to West Coast, South America. 1968 rebuilt to carry deck containers. 1/9/1970 to Hapag-Lloyd A.G. 19/12/1974 to Hapag-Lloyd International, S.A., Panama, reg. in Bremen. 18/4/1980 to Cia. Transvictor, Panama, renamed *Sandra S.*, ran to Mogadisciu, Mombasa and Tanga. 1984 sold through Exkhardt Marine Gmbh. to Pakistan. 25/8/1984 left Durban, arr. 14/9/1984 at Chittagong for BU.

Buntenstein's *launching on a rainy day by Frau Dr. Kulenkampff, wife of NDL's co-General Director, on 16 November, 1959.* Weser Kurier Photo.

*Below:*Buntenstein *#514, third and last of the special-design ships for the West Coast South America. Under tow for a paint job and repairs, probably in Bremerhaven.* B.N.R.A. Photo.

Nabstein *#515, sister of Lechstein #508, lasted twelve years with the Lloyd, in 1972 went to a Hamburg owner operating under the Liberian flag. In 1985, under the Saudi flag. She was abandoned in heavy weather in the Adriatic when cargo shifted. Evidently never again in service after cargo was discharged. Here at Brindisi to where she was towed.* A. Scrimali photo in Marine News, World Ship Society.

515. *Nabstein*	1960-1972	
Atlas Werke, Bremen #399		
1960	3660/5347	130.60x16.26
M.A.N. Diesel	4000	14.5
2	33	

Launched 18/9/1959. MV. 11/1/1960 to U.S.-Canada West Coast. 1/9/1970 to Hapag-Lloyd A.G. 15/6/1972 to Claus-Peter Offen, Hamburg, Monrovia registry, renamed *Holstenfleet*. 30/10/1978 to Syros Nav. Co., Piraeus, renamed *Syros*. 1980 to Sea Giant Nav. Co., Piraeus, renamed *Christoforos T.*, 5,202 Ts. 11/1982 to Samur Abdil Kader, Jeddah, renamed *Sheikh Ali*, Amal Line. In 1985, left Koper for Jeddah on 18 Feb. On 25th in the Southern Adriatic abandoned after cargo shifted in heavy weather. Later that day towed to ca. 2 m. S.E. of Brindisi and beached. In December, still reported "discharging." 30.8.1985 refloated and towed to Brindisi where the ship was arrested on behalf of the salvors. 9.1990 reported to be lying at the Confier shipbreaking yard awaiting sale for BU. 14.4.1991 arr. Aliaga in tow for BU.

Regenstein *#516 and* Riederstein *#517 were designed for the Australia service, convertible from open to closed shelter deckers to carry maximum cargoes of baled wool. In 1968, both were fitted for carrying containers on deck. In 1976, both were sold to Singapore owners but continued on Hapag-Lloyd routes under charter. It was cheaper to charter a foreign-flag ship than man it under the German flag.* Regenstein *in 1960,*
Gustav Bödecker Photo, Hamburg.

570 Norddeutscher Lloyd Bremen

516. *Regenstein*   1960-1978
Howaldtswerke, Hamburg #953
1960   7375/10091   106.67x19.97
M.A.N. Howaldt Diesel   9000   17.5
6   44

Launched 25/6/1960. MV. 28/9/1960. With sister built for Australia service. 6-8/1968 given flush-deck container capacity. 1/9/1970 to Hapag-Lloyd A.G. 12/11/1976 to Avalon Bay Shipping Co., Singapore, Monrovia registry, kept name. 9,736 Ts. 22/5/1984 arr. Qinhuangdo for BU.

Riederstein #517 shows how the winches are mounted on a raised platform around the four masts, allowing more clear area on deck. NDL Fotoarchive.

517. *Riederstein*   1960-1978
Howaldtswerke, Hamburg #954
1960   7357/10092   106.67x19.97
Howaldt M.A.N. Diesel   9000   17.5
9   44

Launched 20/8/1960. MV. 21/11/1960 to Australia. 3-5/1968 fitted with flush-deck carriage of containers. 1/9/1970 to Hapag-Lloyd A.G. 3/12/1976 to Cape Sable Shipping Co., Monrovia, but Singapore registry, kept name. 9,736 Ts. In 1977, passed Suez from Hull en route to Shanghai on 20 May, no owner listed in Lloyd's Index. 22/2/1984 left Hamburg, arr. Xingang 6 June, Qinhuangdo the 15th for BU by China Resources Co.

518. *Europa 4*   1965-1980
N.V. Koninklijke Maats. de Schelde, Vlissingen #273
                             1953   21514   182.87x23.47
2 x Burmeister & Wain Diesels 18,300   * *   19-21
I-122 T-721   418

Launched 18/10/1952 as *Kungsholm* for Swedish-America Line. MV. 24/11/1953 Göteborg-New York. At Noon 15/10/1965 at Göteborg delivery to NDL, refurbished at Bremerhaven, all outside cabins, even a crew pool, 21,164 Ts., renamed *Europa*. MV. 9/1/1966 Bremerhaven-Halifax-New York. 22/1/1966 first cruise, to the West Indies. 1/9/1970 to Hapag-Lloyd A.G. From 1972 only cruising: I-176, II-546, 80 interchangeable. 11/5/1972 painted all-white, with broad blue and cognac stripes on side and new HL logo

Europa *nearing Pier 88, on her maiden voyage in January, 1966. The two piers behind her are the former Hapag-Lloyd Piers 86, left - now with the* United States *tied up, and 84, right, with American Export-Isbrandtsen's* Independence. Moran Towing Company Photo.

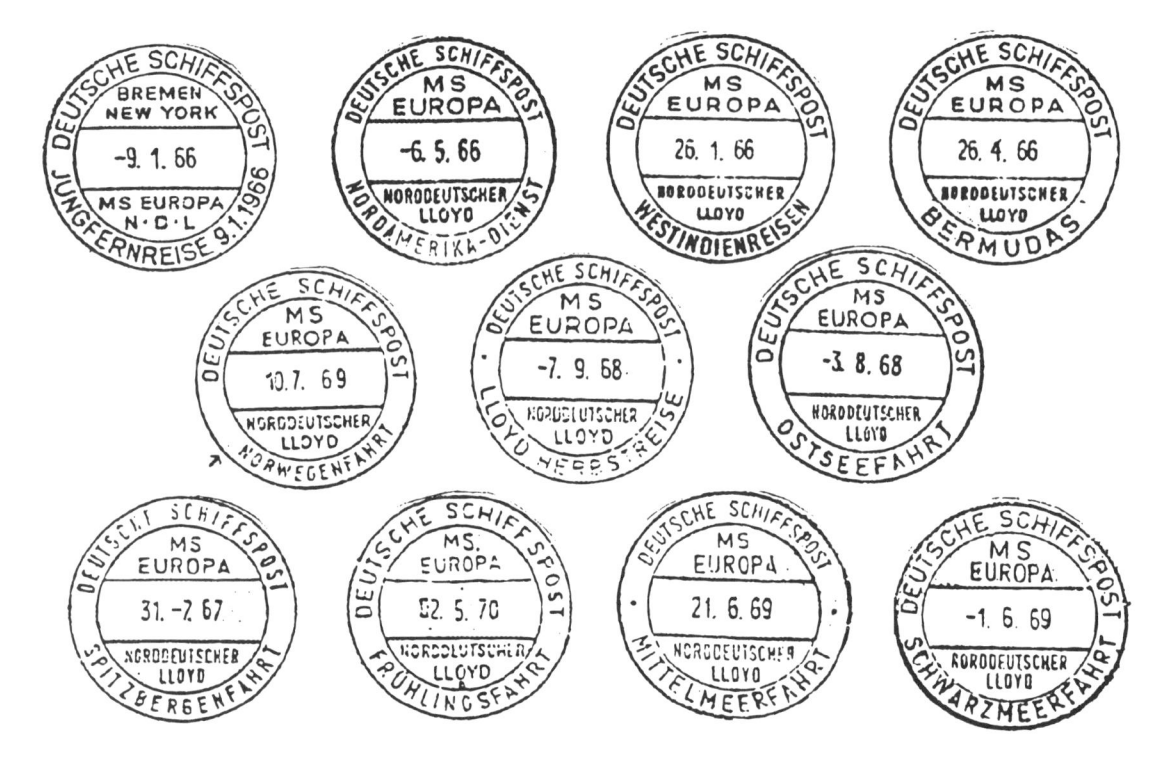

Europa *had* **Schiffspost** *service during her entire life with the Lloyd. She began with* **Jungfernreise** *1966, and* **Nordamerikadienst** *1966-71. Then* **Westindienreisen** *1966-71,* **Bermudas** *1966-69;* **Norwegenfahrt** *1968-70;* **Lloyd Herbstreise** *(Autumn Cruise) 1967-69;* **Ostseefahrt** *1968-70;* **Spitzbergenfahrt** *1966-70;* **Frühlingsfahrt** *(Spring Cruise) 1969-70;* **Mittelmeerfahrt** *(Mediterranean Cruise) 1969-70, and* **Schwarzmeerfahrt** *(Black Sea Cruise) 1969-70. Berlin's Norway Cruise cancel with the number removed but the period remaining is the first stamp in the second row down.*

572   *Norddeutscher Lloyd Bremen*

on the cognac stacks. 7/1981 sold, delivery to Costa Armatori Spa, Panama. 12/9-4/10/1981 last NDL cruise, to West Africa. 12/1981 delivery to Costa: Independent Continental Lines, managers Transoceanic Armec Spa, Panama, renamed *Columbus C.*, 16,317 Ts. 29/7/1984 struck breakwater on entering Cadiz. Settled to bottom with engine room flooded. 2/11/1984 refloated. Sold to Mirak S.A. for ca $850,000 for BU at Barcelona, arr. ca. 6/4/1985. One of the loveliest looking ships ever.

Lindenstein *#519 was bought in Denmark in 1966 to expand the reefer capacity on the Canaries-North Brazil route, to supplement* Lichtenstein *and* Liebenstein *which were sold off in 1968.* Lindenstein *was converted by the Technischer Betrieb so all holds became accessible to forklifts. Bananas instead of coming on board each stem on a conveyor, could be palletized. Sold in 1971 but chartered back to Hapag-Lloyd, with two other charters. Again, cheaper to charter than to run under the German flag. Hapag-Lloyd A.G.*

519. **Lindenstein**	1966-1971		
Uddevallavarvet A.B.,			
Uddevalla #138	1954	4785	132.60x17.25
Götaverken Diesel	7500	18	
12	40		

Launched 9/10/1954 as *Clary Thorden*. Delivery 19/12/1954 to Thorden Lines A.B., Uddevalla, 4,848 Ts. 10/3/1966 bought by NDL for DM5.5 millions, renamed after conversion by NDL's Technischer Betrieb in Bremerhaven making all holds accessible to fork lifts. MV. to Mexico, then on the reefer trade to the Canaries and North Brazil. 1/9/1970 to Hapag-Lloyd A.G. 10/1971 to Neptunea Panoceanica S.A. Piraeus, kept name, chartered to NDL. 5/1975 ran for Hapag-Lloyd between Peru-Colombia to Amsterdam while chartered *Boma* and *Bogota* ran to Northern Brazil. In 1976, all three did the route to North Brazil-up the Amazon, under H-L charter. 1976 renamed *Navikapol*, 4,214 Ts., Cia. Navikapol, Panama. 1983 on Hong Kong-Shanghai run. 1984 to Gizo Feng Steel Enterprises, Kaohsiung. Demolition began 26/10/1984. One-of-a-kind ship for NDL, then Hapag-Lloyd.

Friesenstein *and six sisters were the first newly-built vessels in seven years. Twenty-one knotters, they equalled in performance seven Hapag ships for the Far East route built three years earlier. Each had a Stülcken heavy-lift mast with eighty tons capacity. The introduction of third-generation container ships to the Far East outmoded this class of vessels, and they were shifted to other routes. Three were rebuilt in 1980 for container carrying and speed upped to 22.5 knots. The others were sold off.* Hapag-Lloyd A.G.

```
520. Friesenstein              1967-1984
Lübecker Flender Werke #567    1967    7485/10481    161.80x22.56
M.A.N. Vulkan Diesel           18,400    21 - 22.5
12                             48
```

First of seven new-building sisters in seven years, with 80 tons heavy-lift derricks. For the most competitive freighter run: to the Far East. NDL lagged the Hapag by three years. In 1972, the route shifted to container vessels, so these soon were outmoded. Three were lengthened for higher speeds, their decks cleared for container carriage. They went to other trades. Launched 26.5.1967. MV. 4/10/1967 via Cape of Good Hope because of closure of the Suez Canal, arr. Yokohama 11. Nov. under Captain Gottfried Clausen, Cape Hornier, 1937 captain of NDL's sail training ship *Kommodore Johnsen* #443. 9/1970 Hapag-Lloyd A.G. In May, 1980 NDL announced *Friesenstein, Holstenstein* a n d *Schwabenstein* would be lengthened by Thyseen Nordseewerke, Emden 15 ms. to 176.54 m., for containers on deck. In 2/1984 the three were sold to Societé de Gestion EVGE, Piraeus, renamed *Kinaros*, 9,443 Ts., for Tilsamar, S.A., Panama. 1988 renamed *Athinai*. Sold by Greek South America Lines Shipping Co. to Indian breakers, arr. Alang 12/1/1994.

Holstenstein #521, sister of Friesenstein. *Visible on the side are the Plimsoll marks for when running as open or as closed shelter decker. There is a round 3000 tons difference.* Copyright Hans-Joachim Reinecke.

521. ***Holstenstein***	1967-1984	
Lübecker Flender Werke #568	1967	7485/10481
		161.80x22.56
M.A.N. Vulkan Diesel	18,400	21 - 22.5
12	48	

Launched 13/7/1967. Delivery 28/11/1967. 1/9/1970 to Hapag-Lloyd A.G. 1980 lengthened by Nordseewerke, Emden to 176.54 m., 12,700 Ts., for container carriage. 4/1/1984 to Societé de Gestion EVGE, Piraeus, renamed *Karos*, 12,702 Ts., for Tilsamar S.A., Panama. 1987 to Greek Regular Lines Special Shipping Co. Sold to Indian shipbreakers and anchored off Alang on 31.5.1994.

Hessenstein #522. *With their 21+ knots, the seven ships cut the Continent-Japan round trip by up to fifteen days In 1974, sold to an Ecuadorian operator as part of an agreement to operate jointly and supportively, a foot in the Ecuador door.* Florent Van Otterdijk Photo.

Ships 507 - 531   575

522. *Hessenstein 2*   1967-1974
Bremer Vulkan, Vegesack #931
1967   7485/10,481   161.80x22.56
Vulkan M.A.N. Diesel   18,400   21 - 22.5
12   47

Launched 1/9/1967. MV. 25/11/1967 to Penang, Port Swettenham, Singapore, Manila, Hong Kong, Keelung and Kaohsiung. The high speed cut the Continent-Japan round trip by up to 15 days. 14/6/1974 as part of a cooperative operating agreement sold to Transportes Navieras Ecuatorianos, delivery in Guyaquil, renamed *Isla Puna*. 10,481 Ts. 25/9/1987 arr. Kaohsiung for BU.

Badenstein #523 *also went to South America in 1978, to improve relations with coastal companies.* Badenstein *found one of the three empty liferafts from the Lash* München *which disappeared in December, 1978.*

523. *Badenstein*   1968-1978
Lübecker Flenderwerke #569
1968   7474/10481   161.72x22.56
Vulkan M.A.N. Diesel   18,400   21 - 22.5
12   47 + 18 cadets

Launched 5/10/1967. Delivery 18/1/1968. 1/9/1970 to Hapag-Lloyd A.G. 12/1978 to Cia. Sudamericana de Vapores, Valparaiso, along with *Sachsenstein*, renamed *Rapel*. 29/4/1984 arr. Kaohsiung for BU by An Tien Steel & Iron Co. *Badenstein* found one of the three empty liferafts from the December, 1978 disappearance of the LASH ship *Münchehn*.

Schwabenstein #524 sailing from Hong Kong. All the cargo tackle is stowed. A Star Ferry is just by the forward crane. It and the other two units, #520 and #521 that were lengthened in 1980 for on-deck containers, were sold in 1984 to Greece. Their rebuilding still left them uncompetitive with original-build container vessels. Wm. A. Schell Photo.

524. *Schwabenstein 2*	1968-1984	
Bremer Vulkan, Vegesack #932		
1968	7485/10481	161.72x22.56
Vulkan M.A.N. Diesel	18,400 21 - 22.5	
12	46	

Launched 18/10/1967. Delivery 8/1/1968. 1/9/1970 to Hapag-Lloyd A.G. 1980 lengthened by 14.5 meters at Nordseewerke, Emden for carriage of containers, 12,701 Ts. 2/1984 to Societé de Gestion EVGE, Piraeus, renamed *Karpathos* by operator Tilsamar S.A., Panama. 1994 SE.

Sachsenstein #525 *went to* Linea Sudamericana de Vapores, Chile, in 1979, along with Badenstein. *All the ships had a small lifeboat aft on a raised housing. Subsequent development went to single-unit sealed, self-righting lifeboats dropped astern by gravity. Shown in the 1970 merger compromise: Hapag stack and* Lloyd *flag*. Hapag-Lloyd A.G.

Ships 507 - 531   577

525. *Sachsenstein*   1968-1979
Lübecker Flender Werke #570
1968   7485/10481   161.72x22.56
Vulkan M.A.N. Diesel   18,400   21 - 22.5
12   48

Launched 13/12/1967. Delivery 14/3/1968. 1/9/1970 to Hapag-Lloyd A.G. 80 tons heavy-lift gear. 3/1979 to Cia. Sudamericana de Vapores, Valparaiso, renamed *Renaico*. 26 February 1983 had a collision, major repairs at Newport News. 21/1/1984 left Inchon for Kaohsiung for BU.

Bayernstein #526 in 1979 was chartered to the Bolivian Shipping line, operating without a national harbor, which it lost in 19th century wars, but using the La Paz-Arica railway as its contact to the seas. As South Star, Singapore by J.M. Kakebeeke, World Ship Photo Society. *Sold for scrapping in 1993, only 15½ years old, but technologically out of date.*

526. *Bayernstein*   1968-1979
Bremer Vulkan, Vegesack #933 1968   7485/10481
                                                       161.80x22.56
Vulkan M.A.N. Diesel   18,400   21 - 22.5
12   43

Launched 15/12/1967. Delivery 7/3/1968. 1/9/1970 to Hapag-Lloyd A.G. 1979 chartered to Linea de Navigacion Boliviana. 1/8/1980 to South Star Shipping Co., Singapore, renamed *South Star*, made two more voyages to South America for H-L. 24/10/1983 arr. Kaohsiung for BU.

In 1976, Weser Express brought to Baltimore the 1000th Volkswagen container; in white Captain Dietrich Huster, and local port and shipping agency people. How many Beetles fit into one container?

Weser Express #527 *was the first of four sisters with which the Lloyd and Hapag in 1968-1969 began trans-Atlantic container service. A revolution in cargo handling. The ships had stabilizers to prevent early container-ship problems: losing containers overboard in bad weather.*

Weser Express *ready for launching at the Bremer Vulkan, Vegesack, 28 June, 1968, with three sisters for the start of the Joint Lloyd-Hapag North Atlantic container service. Cover Photo from "Von der Dampfbarkasse zum Containerschiff" by Peter Kuckuck and Hartmut Roder, Steintor Verlag, Bremen, 1988.*

527. *Weser Express*   1968-1985
Bremer Vulkan, Vegesack #944   1968   13,382   170.87x24.56
Vulkan M.A.N. Diesel   15,750   20.6   34

Launched 28/6/1968. Trials 10/10/1968. MV. 25/10/1968 to U.S. East Coast, 736 TEUs-20′ containers capacity. Given stabilizers to reduce strain on above-deck containers. 1/9/1970 to Hapag-Lloyd A.G. 5/9/1973 arr. Rheinstahlwerke, Emden for insertion of a 29.5 m. midbody to increase capacity to 1114 containers. 17,088 Ts. The same was done with *Mosel Express, Alster Express* and *Elbe Express* which had given the Lloyd and Hapag in 1968 their entry into trans-Atlantic containerization. All four were lengthened. Beginning January, 1978 all four were put on Hapag-Lloyd's trans-Pacific service in effect giving it round-the-world connecting schedules. Two more planned ships never entered that service. It was a heavy-losses operation. 9/1985 all four were sold to Lykes Bros. S.S. Co., New Orleans, for their trans-Pac route. Renamed *Charlotte Lykes*. 16,891 Ts. When Lykes, in turn, gave up the route, the four were put on its Gulf Coast-Continent service. SE 1994.

528. *Mosel Express*   1969-1985
Bremer Vulkan, Vegesack #945   1969   13,396   170.90x24.56
Vulkan M.A.N. Diesel   15,750   20.6   33

Keel laid 2/7/1968. Launched 16/11/1968. Trials 31/12/1968. Delivery 9/1/1969 for joint Lloyd and Hapag U.S. East Coast container route. 738 TEUs. 1/9/1970 to Hapag-Lloyd A.G. 1973 insertion of 29.5 m. midbody to up capacity from 736 to 1114 containers, 17,108 Ts. 9/9/1983 driven aground by Typhoon Ellen in Hong Kong. Left Seattle 2/6/1985 on last trans-Pacific voyage. 9/1985 all four vessels in that service sold to Lykes Bros. S.S. Co., New Orleans, renamed *Adabelle Lykes*, put into Lykes' trans-Pac route, 16,891 Ts. 1994 in Lykes' Gulf Coast-Continent service.

Mosel Express #528 *ran to the Pacific Northwest coast and trans-Pacific. Here at the Seattle container terminal, ca. 1979. Sister of* Weser Express. *In 1985, these two and their Hapag sisters, when Hapag-Lloyd gave up the trans-Pacific service (only to re-enter it in 1993), were sold to Lykes Brothers S.S.Co.*

Melbourne Express #529 *and Hapag's near-sister* Sydney Express *were ordered for the Australia trade before the 1 September, 1970 merger and delivered in that month. Maiden voyage roundtrip took 65 days, via Cape of Good Hope as the Suez Canal was closed. Lloyd tug* Triton *at bow.* Hapag-Lloyd A.G.

529. *Melbourne Express*	1970		
Bremer Vulkan, Vegesack #956	1970	25,558	217.90 x 29.02
Vulkan Stal Laval Turbine	32,450	21.5	40

Launched 25/4/1970. Trials, 3/9/1970 and delivery 5/9/1970 postponed to make it the first ship under the 1 September Hapag-Lloyd A.G. merger. Built for Australia route, 1526 TEUs, to cut round trip to 68 days; the maiden voyage took only 65. 8/11/1982 LU in Bremen as conversion to Diesel drive not held cost-effective. 1/12/1984 arr. Hamburg for repairs from Bremen in tow, LU. 1/1986 renamed *Melbourne* for Projex Ges., Hamburg. 7/1/1986 arr. Lübeck in tow, LU. 10/1987 sold to a St. Vincent-flag owner, renamed *Melbourne Range*. 10/1987 to Dalmeijer, Rotterdam. 1988 resold to Kuo Dau Steel Enterprise Co. 25/2/1988 arr. Kaohsiung for BU, work began 10/3/1988.

530. *Bremen Express*	Never		
Bremer Vulkan, Vegesack #977	1972	57,535	287.60x32.24
2 x Stal Laval Turbines 2 x	40,550	26	* * 40+

1969 ordered by NDL along with *Hong Kong Express*, while Hapag ordered *Tokio Express* and *Hamburg Express*, basically sisters, for their joint Continent-Far East express service. 1/9/1970 orders shifted to merged Hapag-Lloyd A.G. Launched 1/3/1972. Trials 4/8, delivery 9/8/1972. MV. 21/8/1972 via Cape of Good Hope due to closed Suez Canal. 11/11/1981 arr. Bremen for conversion to single-screw motor ship by A.G. Weser, 23 kns. 9/11/1982 LU in Bremerhaven. 1/12/1982 back in service. 12/8/1985 now 57,495 Ts. 1989 in Far East service. 12/1991 to Orient Overseas Container Line, ren. *Oocl Fame*. SE 1994. In 1993, *Hamburg Express* was renamed *Bremen Express*, 7/1994 in Oakland on trans-Pacific route.

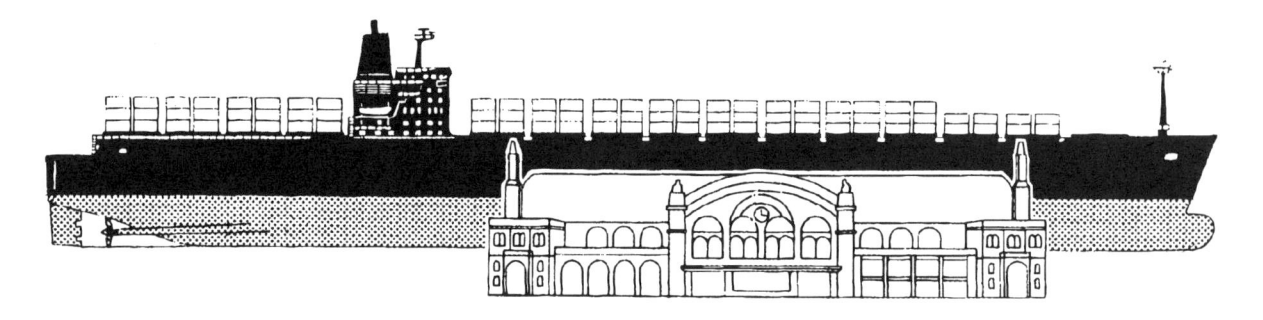

Bremen Express *compared with Bremen's Main Railway Station.*

2. Stapellauf* zur 3. Containergeneration

TS Bremen Express

Bremen Express #530 with sister Hong Kong Express #531 and two Hapag near-sisters were the third-generation giants, bigger than Bremen and Europa, and as fast in normal operating speed, near 27 knots. Both were ordered in 1969, before the merger, but not completed until 1972. Both were built by Bremer Vulkan, NDL's postwar House Yard. The ships no longer were "stick built" as still is most housing. Rather, bridge structure, the bulbous bow, here being installed, are assembled ashore and then installed. The Launching Patron was Mrs. Agnes Ponto, wife of a Management member of the Dresdner Bank, major holder of Hapag-Lloyd shares. With their 27 knots, the ships reduced the roundtrip Hamburg-Bremen-Japan from 100 days to sixty-three.

Es ist soweit. 1. März 1972. Stapellauf des TS „Bremen Express". Das zweite von vier Vollcontainerschiffen. Für den Ostasiendienst. Schnell, modern, rationell. 52.000 BRT, 42.400 t Tragfähigkeit. Länge 287 m, Breite 32,24 m, Tiefgang 12,04 m. Insgesamt 2972 Containerstellplätze (20'). Jeder Container ist erreichbar. Noch mehr Sicherheit für Ihre Ladung.
Außerdem: 63 Tage Rundreisedauer anstatt 100 Tage. Weniger Seetage. Verkürzte Liegezeiten. Ihre Ladung: Noch schneller zum Empfänger. Alles spricht für das TS „Bremen Express".

✱ Frau Ignes Ponto, die Gattin des Vorstandsmitgliedes der Dresdner Bank Jürgen Ponto, wird am 1. März 1972 gegen 16.00 Uhr den Neubau Nr. 977 des Bremer Vulkan auf den Namen „Bremen Express" taufen.

Hong Kong Express *#531 in Hong Kong with its Hamburg-registered counterpart* Hamburg Express. *These two and their sisters were ordered before the September, 1970 merger. After the oil shock of 1975, the operating speeds were sharply reduced. Later, the ships were rebuilt from turbine twin-screw drive to single-screw Diesel drive, to operate at 21 knots. Everybody did it so it worked out well.* Hamburg Express *in 1993 was renamed* Bremen Express 2, *after 1 was sold to Taiwan, to clear the name for a new* Hamburg Express *completed in December, 1994.* Hapag-Lloyd Photo.

531. *Hong Kong Express*   Never
Bremer Vulkan, Vegesack #978   1972   57,525   287.03x32.26
2x Stal Daval Turbines   2x   40,500   26   * *

1969 ordered NDL. 1/9/1970 order taken over by Hapag-Lloyd A.G. Launched 27/7/1972; trials 30/11/1972, 2972 TEUs. Reg. in Bremen. All newly-added Hapag-Lloyd ships were registered alternately Hamburg and Bremen. The 111 vessels brought into the

Hong Kong Express *loading for its maiden voyage in December, 1972. Not everything goes into containers. Some equipment or units such as these trash truck bodies, are too big.*

Hong Kong Express *on the return portion of its maiden voyage came home via the Panama Canal. The last of the container ship size progression to be able to transit; here in the Miraflores Lock. American President Lines' C-10 vessels serve trans-Pacific but are too big to go through the Canal should their routing ever be changed.*

merger continued with the Black-White-Red-topped yellow Hapag stacks and flew the blue crossed-anchor-and-key with oak-wreath-on-white Lloyd flag. In 1987, all ships were given "cognac yellow" stacks and a stylized HL new house flag. Putting into the record as history the Norddeutscher Lloyd, of Bremen and the Hamburg-America Line, continuing in their joined Hapag-Lloyd A.G. names. 27/7/1992 arr. A.G. Weser, Bremen for rebuilding as single-screw motor ship, 40,000 HP, 23 kns., 20/11/1982 redelivered, 5/1992 to Orient Overseas Container Lines, ren. *Oocl Frontier*. SE 1994.

Lloyd Frachtdienste
Regelmäßige Abfahrten mit 46 schnellen Frachtschiffen nach Nordamerika, Ost-u. Westküste, Kanada/Große Seen, Golfhäfen, Golf v. Mexico, Zentralamerika Westküste, Südamerika Westküste, Nord-Brasilien, Ostasien, Australien und Neuseeland. Fruchtdienst nach den Kanarischen Inseln. 2 Vollcontainerschiffe von u. nach den USA.

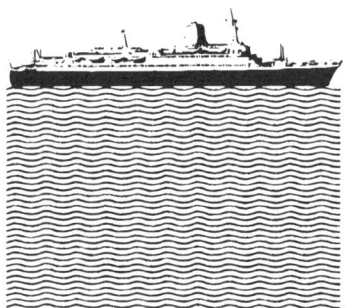

Lloyd Passagierdienste
Liniendienste mit TS »Bremen« und MS »Europa« nach den USA und nach Kanada.
Kreuzfahrten in der Caribic,
in europäischen und afrikanischen Gewässern.
Fahrgasteinrichtungen bis zu
12 Personen auf 46 Frachtschiffen.

Norddeutscher Lloyd Bremen

The Lloyd services in mid-1969 before the merger: 46 fast freighters to all the Americas, East Asia, Australia-New Zealand, Fruit service from the Canaries; two Container Ships to the U.S. Up to twelve passengers can be carried. Liner services with Bremen *and* Europa *to the U.S. and Canada, cruising in the Caribbean, European and African waters.*

CHAPTER 19

Marriage At Age 123 And 113

The pressures pushing the Lloyd and Hapag into corporate merger were not sudden events. As "Bremen and Hamburg, Hapag and Lloyd" relates, they had fought each other, cooperated, and everything in between almost continuously in this century. The Kaiser allegedly bought shares in both companies to give him a basis for urging an end to enmity. Fact or rumor; nothing changed.

The near-destruction that World War I brought and the starting anew led to some cooperation. But soon the Grössenwahn, the compulsion to grow, resumed, with mergers, acquisitions, take-overs, competitive building that made for continual friction between Bremen and Hamburg. Even in 1933, when they formed their North Atlantic Gemeinschaft, which showed that doing it together could work, in fact, helped Bremen to accept the merger, Hapag Chairman Marius Böger remained critical that *Bremen* and *Europa* had given NDL too much weight in the Community; they were built for pride, not for economic reasons.

The rationale for merger was that one can perform better than two: older ships can be sold off without reducing capacity or frequency of service; agencies can be combined or closed, with big cuts in staffs; the same in home offices; financing jointly alone 1.1 billion Marks for container ships for the North Atlantic, Australia. the Far East is cheaper than competing for scarce funds one can bargain more effectively against others for strength in conference quotas. Finally, this is Hamburg thinking: merger will allow new ways of doing things where tradition and habits had restricted innovation.

Whatever one can say against the Merger of 1970, that:
- it was less than welcomed by some in Bremen;
- Herr Glässel in 1933 (see his letter in "Bremen and Hamburg; Hapag and Lloyd") was not that far wrong when he predicted that in a full fusion the Lloyd in three years, at most five, would be a nonentity;
- Bremen lost to Hamburg in relative importance; The agreement makes Hamburg the seat of the new firm, with management centers in Hamburg and Bremen, and "The founding of a seat also in Bremen is to be sought."
- Most of the post-merger acquisitions and expansions were Hamburg determinations. Some subsequently had to be undone;

The basic question remains: could either Hapag or Lloyd separately have survived the post-1970 years given the wrong business decisions made either jointly or separately, plus the outside events that neither could control: devaluation of the Dollar; the runaway increases in all costs; the

Die größten Reedereien der Welt sind nach ihrer Linien-Tonnage gerechnet:		
Stand Mitte 1969		
Reederei	Schiffe	BRT
Mitsui-OSK-Lines, Japan	94	776 904
Hapag-Lloyd AG, Hamburg/Bremen	118	754 141
Nippon Yusen Kaisha, Japan	90	729 780
Ocean Steamship Co., Ltd., London	105	698 795
Irvine Cayzer & Co., London	56	506 843
Kawasaki Kisen KK., Japan	58	486 837
Peninsular & Orient, Steam Nav. Co., London	27	456 461
Cunard Brocklebank Ltd., London	35	418 806
Lykes Bros., USA	60	414 040
United States Lines, USA	39	384 211
Royal Interocean Lines, Holland	56	375 446
Shaw, Savill & Albion Co., Ltd., London	32	365 738
Shipping Corp. of India, Ltd., Indien	56	365 738
Andrew Weir & Co., Ltd., London	56	358 240
American Export Isbrandtsen Lines, USA	39	350 569
Brit. India Steam Nav. Co., Ltd., London	45	339 784
Messag. Maritimes, Paris	42	336 745
Japan Line, Ltd., Japan	43	326 574
Cie. Générale Transatlantique, Paris	43	325 924
Wilh. Wilhelmsen, Oslo	51	313 930
Ellerman Lines Ltd., London	47	311 255
Axel Johnson, Stockholm	42	309 978
Moore McCormack, USA	39	309 479
"Italia" S. A., Rom	17	308 576
American President Lines, USA	27	302 593

Die größten Reedereien der Bundesrepublik
Nach dem Stand vom 31. März 1970 betreiben 180 deutsche Reedereien Hochseeschiffahrt. Davon verfügen 29 über 55 % der Gesamttonnage. Die Größengliederung nach Bruttoregistertonnen zeigt die Reedereien mit einer Tonnagezahl von über 100 000 BRT wie folgt:

Reederei	Anzahl der Schiffe	BRT
Hamburg-Amerika Linie	62	464 815
Egon Oldendorff	35	434 355
Norddeutscher Lloyd	67	395 702
Deutsche Shell Tanker GmbH	10	379 751
Hamburg-Süd-Gruppe	35	358 765
Esso Tankschiff Reederei	13	335 384
Schulte & Bruns	21	280 397
DDG "Hansa"	42	271 439
Seereederei "Frigge"	9	241 180
John T. Essberger	16	238 960
Ernst Russ	20	182 491
DAL Deutsche Afrika-Linien	12	131 271
Alfred C. Töpfer	8	129 153
Leonhardt & Blumberg	12	128 685
Unterweser Reederei GmbH	40	120 377
Schlüssel Reederei KG	8	104 141

In 1969, pre-merger, counting Hapag and Lloyd together, they ranked second only to Mitsui-OSK lines of Japan in total tonnage and led at that time in the number of vessels: 118. This was down to 110 at merger time, 1 September, 1970, plus four small coasters, and nine container ships under construction. Ex-Lloyd's Register of Shipping's List of Shipowners, 1969-1970.

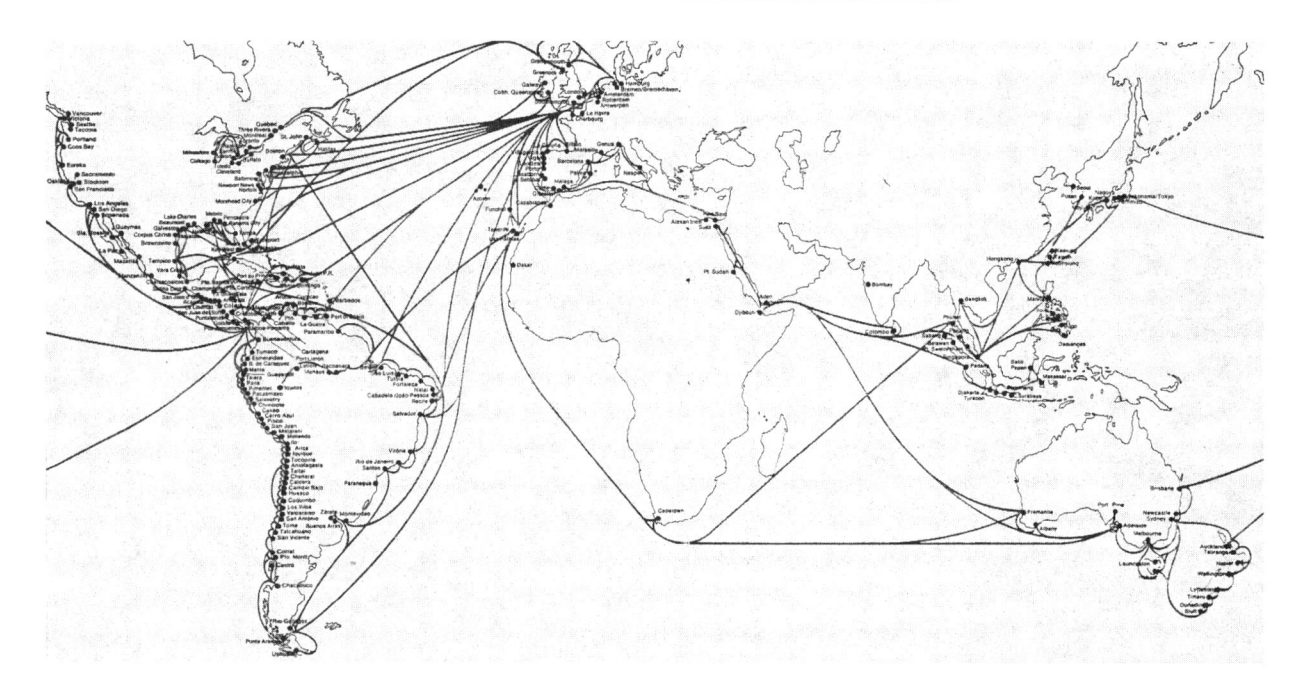

Hapag-Lloyd's freight services, including every actual and sometime route served, e.g. both through the Suez Canal and around Africa during its closing; ports called on inducement; Hong Kong Express *going around the world on its maiden voyage to the Far East and home via the Panama Canal.*

oil embargo; the closing of the Suez Canal, the conflict with U.S. shipping policy.

Possibly yes, probably not, certainly not survive and build to the major role in world transportation that Hapag-Lloyd eventually achieved.

And so it happened: On 9 April, 1970 Hamburg-Amerikanische Paketfahrt Aktien Gesellschaft, Hapag, and Norddeutscher Lloyd Bremen, the words run together in Bremen thinking, voted to merge as Hapag-Lloyd A.G. Aktien Gesellschaft, Share Company, on 1 September, but uniting all accounts back to 1/1/1970. The entry into service of the last ship for either company before 1 September, the Lloyd's *Melbourne Express*, was delayed by a week to make it a celebratory start for the new enterprise. The tea leaves didn't show that it would be a bad-luck vessel.

Brought as dowry: by NDL - 45 break-bulk freighters; two container ships, the passenger liners *Bremen* and *Europa*, four coastal freight-distributers, 13 port and sea tugs, 6 river tugs, and barges and lighters; and 50% ownerships in the Horn Linie, Übersee Hotel, Bremen and Roland Linie Schiffahrts Ges.; by Hapag - 52 Diesel and 6 turbine freighters, two container ships, one - *Münsterland*, caught in Great Bitter Lake by the closure of the Suez Canal and already written off, and nine ships building: two NDL, seven Hapag. The combined freighter fleet could accommodate 697 passengers. The two jointly owned the extensive Hapag-Lloyd Reisebüro travel network. Hapag had a major towing subsidiary. And the Lloyd had its Technical Service a world-rank facility with 2000 workers. Originally only servicing Lloyd ships, then other repairs, conversions, later building four NDL tugs to keep the work force busy.

With the merger, Dr. Johannes Kulenkampf stepped down as co-General Director of the Lloyd. Herr Richard Bertram became spokesman for the new Vorstand, Executive Board until he retired in 1972. To support continuity, the Black-White-Red topped Hapag stacks remained, going onto the former NDL vessels. And all ships flew the old Lloyd Crossed Anchor and Key with Oak wreath flag. I recall my surprise on seeing this combination for the first time in San Francisco Bay on, I believe, *Blankenstein* in September, 1970. The compromise lasted only until late 1972 when *Bremen* was sold off, leaving *Europa* the sole passenger vessel. It was painted white, given broad "Cognac" and Blue striping, the stacks cognac and a blue logo HL. The freighters followed from 1.1.1987.

The compromise in the 1970 Lloyd and Hapag merger was that all ships wore the Lloyd flag and carried the Hapag stack and continued until 1986 when they were given a cognac colored stack with a blue HL insignium which also became the new HL flag.

The size of the difficulties the merger had to surmount were evident:
- Revaluation of the Deutschmark vs the Dollar cost M56.5 millions in 1970. Income to shipping firms is paid predominantly in Dollars. As these lost value against the Mark, the proceeds dropped.
- Costs were escalating. There had been a general 20% rise in wages for the two firms in January, 1970; another of 30% came in January, 1971. More than one hundred captains, officers and engineers were let go in 1971 as ships were sold.
- By summer, 1971 the basic freight rate of 275 for Fall, 1970 fell to 70 in Summer, 1971.
- While the technology of ships continued its rapid and costly development, world trade failed to match the increased capacity. Shipping firms were forced to construct new tonnage to stay competitive before the trade justified this, and/or brought the cash flow to finance it.
- In June, 1970 the Lloyd had begun one of the new businesses that Hapag-Lloyd then expanded into, and years later dropped as a consistent money-loser: bulk cargoes. NDL's Roland Line Schiffahrt Gesellschaft, acquired in full fusion although already

Europa in 1972 was painted white as most of her voyaging was on cruises, and was given the new Hapag-Lloyd colors: a cognac stack with a light-blue HL logo. She resembled an over-sized yacht.

share-owned in December, 1925, was reconstituted into a bulk-carrier specialist. Half interest was taken by Bremen's URAG, Unterweser Reederei A.G., largely a towing specialist. Together, the two partners ordered thirteen multi-purpose carrier: *Roland Bremen* and *Kelkheim*. The stack was Lloyd yellow. The flag the old Roland Linie's. What looked like a sure-growth segment in shipping was overtaken by outside events and possibly reaching too far, too fast for sound judgment. Merger by itself solved little. It had to be forged by people sometimes with conflicting viewpoints trying to adjust to and shape events for survival of Germany's largest shipping enterprise, through the large participation of major banks, close to a national instrument.

Growing world demand led to orders for ever larger crude carriers, including by Kosmos. In June, 1967 the Six Days War closed the Suez Canal until 1975. This led to higher prices (the longer round-the-cape shipments), reduced oil use, hence less need for tankers. Millions of tons of crude carriers were laid up.

Flag and smokestack insignium of the Kosmos Bulkschiffahrt Gesellschaft, the out-growth of the Roland Linie — U.R.A.G. joint operation. The last use of the Lloyd flag into 1983. The Kosmos slogan was "Young in Years, Rich in Experience."

Kosmos
Jung an Jahren, reich an Erfahrung.

Jung und erfahren zu sein; das schließt einander nicht aus. Wir sind jung, weil wir noch im Wachstum sind. Als Trampreederei mit Bulkcarriern, Mehrzweckschiffen und Supertankern. Mit einer Mannschaft, die es versteht, aus guten Ideen ein vernünftiges Konzept zu machen.
Wir sind erfahren, weil wir uns das Wissen und den Weitblick eines weltweit operierenden Dienstleistungsunternehmens zunutze machen können.
Denn wir gehören zur Hapag-Lloyd AG.
Kosmos: das ist ein solides, starkes Fundament für die Zukunft. Mit Sicherheit.

Kosmos Bulkschiffahrt
ein Unternehmen der Hapag-Lloyd Gruppe

The gradual shift from little boxes to big boxes: coffee bagged individually and loaded and unloaded by sling.

A load of heavy equipment in a transition vessel with heavy lift gear and bigger hatches, eventually opened for fork lift usability.

From the merger date to the end of 1970 only two ships were sold off. By the end of 1971, it was thirty, and by Spring, 1973 some fifty of the 108 conventional break-bulk vessels that were got rid of. To maintain capacity until its own new ships could get into service, newer ones than those sold were chartered. At the same time, Hapag-Lloyd units were being fitted to carry some containers by removing loading masts, upgrading those kept to heavier-lift capacities. In time, even these were sold off or converted to multi-purpose or to container ships. The cargo-handling revolution was accelerating.

Late in 1971 Hapag-Lloyd wrote shareholders that these were difficult times to remain solvent: The U.S. had twice revalued the Dollar. "We are paying Deutsch Mark costs but as conference members have to stick to Dollar cargo rates." Dock strikes hurt. The cost of switching to containers was enormous: DM 1.1 Billion for the ships, the containers, the new methods along the entire transportation chain: Just the first phase!

On the Atlantic, one container vessel with 1,200 TEUs capacity replaced seven old conventional, break-bulk but in effect, piece-goods freighters. Nine such container voyages could handle 220,000 tons of cargo, the same as twenty-one conventional voyages. On the Far East run, one of the new 50,000 tonners through speed and huge capacity replaced ten conventional freighters. So why would any one buy the older ships? - They were available at bargain prices. New owners had a much lower break-even point; - Much of the world would take years to change from individual cargo item packing to containers: - The new age required not piers but miles of quays with vast container-marshalling yards behind. There were not that many ports around the world that could make this shift: San Francisco was one. In 1950, the San Francisco Bay ports had some 5000 longshoremen. Now it's 900, while cargo tonnage has more than quadrupled. "What automation means is that for fifteen years I haven't used my old longshore hook ... except to occasionally scratch my back" Reg Theriault commented in 1994. "It does not mean the hard work has been eliminated from the docks. There are still 85-pound turnbuckles to heave around and ocean-going containers to be secured against heavy seas. It does mean that not one of my three sons has been able to follow me into my industry." Ports with room to adjust like Oakland, California, or Bremerhaven with its Container Kreuz, survived and grew. Overall, containers reduce congestion

The initial measures to confirm equality eventually disappeared, certainly as seen from the outside. In part for both partners. The compromise of continuing the Hapag stack colors yellow with black white and red stripes at top, and the Lloyd flag: crossed anchor and key with oak wreath on white for all ships got lost in the "redesign." Now the stacks are "cognac" with a stylized blue HL symbol, difficult to decipher from any distance.

There were supposedly two equal office centers. The passenger business (there now is also a chartered small Bremen *to again give Hapag-Lloyd a Bremen and Europa) is run in Bremen, as is the air operation. But decisions are made in Hamburg. Basic Bremen files have been packed up and are in storage in Hamburg, available only for corporate purposes, not for outsiders to research and/or use the shipping and photo files.*

Ships are still registered alternately in Bremen and Hamburg, and bear these cities' emblem on their bows. But overall, Hamburg runs the show. Just as Los Angeles predominates over San Francisco in California, or Las Vegas over Reno in Nevada. The disparity in mass continues to grow.

as do Airbuses replacing 737s. Handling costs were reduced drastically as port times were cut from days to hours. That was also the rationale, although costly and not widely adopted, of the few LASH ships, Lighters Aboard Ship, that were built. Like the ill-fated *München* able to take 83 barges, these could be floated out and the ship load new ones and leave, within hours.

Bremen-Bremerhaven became headquarters for several Hapag-Lloyd operations under direction of Dr. Horst Willner, Bremen's voice, along with Richard Bertram and Karl-Heinz Sager on the Vorstand, Management team. Willner felt that the two ports are "the place of the future" as shipping became more and more containerized.

Passenger shipping - In January, 1972 *Bremen 5* made its last cruise. It had served for thirteen successful years. But the North-Atlantic liner run for which it basically was rebuilt, no longer was the backbone of business. For cruising it now was felt she had limited adaptability. It would cost just too much to rebuild her once again. Fortunately, the *Europa*, bought in 1968, was a highly-successful cruise vessel, helping Hapag-Lloyd to expand its tourist-oriented activities. In good years it earned as much as DM 5 millions.

Although a small part of the total Hapag-Lloyd activity, the cruise ship is profitable and helps in the rapidly expanding tourist portion of the firm's total business. Willner said "when a favorable opportunity occurs the intention is to buy another passenger liner," *Europa* dating from 1953. She ended her service for Hapag-Lloyd in October, 1981, but by then a fifth *Europa* was nearly ready for its maiden voyage, in January, 1982 from Bremerhaven to Genoa for its Gala Maiden cruise.

Europa has had major but hardly visible overhauls and rebuildings. The major benefit is that no longer need guests choose a first or second sitting for dinner. There now is space for everybody. So passengers are free to eat when they want, within limits. The ship has an indoor pool for the crew, one for passengers and two outside, one under a sliding roof which *QE2* only recently added at a cost of $1.5 millions. Adjacent is a fitness center with gymnasium, massage facilities and a sauna. As *Bremen 5* before her, *Europa 5* is a floating hotel, resort and spa. The big news is that again there is a *Bremen*, the 164 passenger former *Frontier Spirit* built in 1991 for a syndicate that included Hapag-Lloyd. The expectation, both ships will continue *Europa's* historic 80-85% occupancy during cruises and occasional trans-Atlantic voyages.

The two ships' passengers are so predominantly German that there is no real competition with the huge cruise ships coming into service largely geared to the American market. The growing volume of the Tourism sector helped maintain profits when the liner operation had difficulties.

On all her voyages *Europa* provides SHIP POST service to passengers and crew. I have watched passengers come to the Purser's office with a dozen or more postcards or letters, apply

Checking a container before loading. The Lloyd part of the Line's name often was not visible. Years later the container had the names side by side. Lloyd's Daily Shipping Index listed Hapag as owner, no room for Lloyd.

the rectangular cruise mark set out for self-help on a shelf, and then drop them into the mail box for application of the cruise Ship Post, and onward dispatch.

Through 1994, eleven different Ship Posts were issued for *Europa*, including one in 1990 for the centennial of the Lloyd's first cruise in the modern sense: 201 gentlemen and fourteen ladies on *Kaiser Wilhelm II*, #79, painted white, to the Norwegian coast.

Also in Bremen: the entire Tourism Operation: chiefly the Hapag-Lloyd Reise (travel) Büro, the outgrowth and combination of the two lines' former passenger bureaus, organizing tours to "around the corner, or around the world."

In 1993, the tourism part of Hapag-Lloyd provided 42% of revenues, shipping 44%. It had been 70%+ in the 1970s.

In 1992, Hapag-Lloyd formed the **Hapag-Lloyd Flugzeug GmbH.** Three Boeings were bought from other carriers and refurbished by Boeing's Wichita plant. Technical guidance was obtained from SABENA, the Belgian national carrier. The first 727 arrived from Wichita on 3 February, 1973. On 30 March the first flight fully loaded, left Hamburg for Ibiza. It was a difficult time to start. Four air carriers had shut down in a year. But tourism was becoming more a ship and air combination. Bremen was management and operations center for Hapag-Lloyd's air tourism until a move to Hannover for a new and larger operations-service facility. In 1976, the air operation already had more than one thousand employees.

In 1977, Hapag-Lloyd Flugzeug took over Bavaria German Air of Munich including its two A300 Airbuses, and British BAC 1-11s. Along with Hapag-Lloyd's eight 727s this gave it about 25% of the German flying market. In 1978, Hapag-Lloyd ordered its first new 727s. By April, 1994 it got rid of all the 727s and operated 7 Airbuses and fourteen Boeing 737s-400s and 500s. The Tourism part of the firm's business had reached the size of the shipping involvement: The bulk of the flight destinations were to Spain, its Atlantic islands, and around the Mediterranean. The Germans' search for the sun.

The Lloydwerft in Bremerhaven, outgrowth of the 1862 founded Technischer Betrieb, is a world-renown all-purpose shipyard. It even built four tugs for the Lloyd when business was slow. It was founded in 1862 as the repair facility for the Lloyd's own ships; Over the years it expanded, making components and equipment to store at important pexus ports like Singapore and Hong Kong for servicing Lloyd ships. In the 1930s, it scrapped ships, anything to keep going. In 1938, it was bought by the Kriegsmarine to improve its ability to handle repairs and conversions of merchant ships, if as and when war came. It was privatized during the war, as were the Lloyd and Hapag. After the war, along with the Lloyd's left-over collection of two resort steamers, some tugs and barges, it was given priority in

Europa 5's delivery-trial in January, 1982 voyage was from Bremerhaven to Genoa where it began its first passenger voyage around Africa back to Genoa for the next series of cruises. The cruise Ship Post reads "The New Europa."

*New cruise designations Ship Posts were issued as Europa covered much of the world. She called at San Francisco on her first World cruise with an **Erste Weltreise Ship Post**. For later cruises, the **Erste** was removed. On another visit, en route to Alaska, she carried **Alaska-Kreuzfahrten**, in 1986, also **Pazifik Kreuzfahrten**, and a generic **Kreuzfahrten**, and **Grosse Polar Kreuzfahrt** and many more and continuing, including the **Transatlantik**. Longer cruises also are sold in segments, including flying to or from that location. This leads to different cachets. So passengers can this way easily tell the recipients of their en-route mailings where they are or were. While thousands of such sendings go out, very little non-philatelic mail is ever seen.*

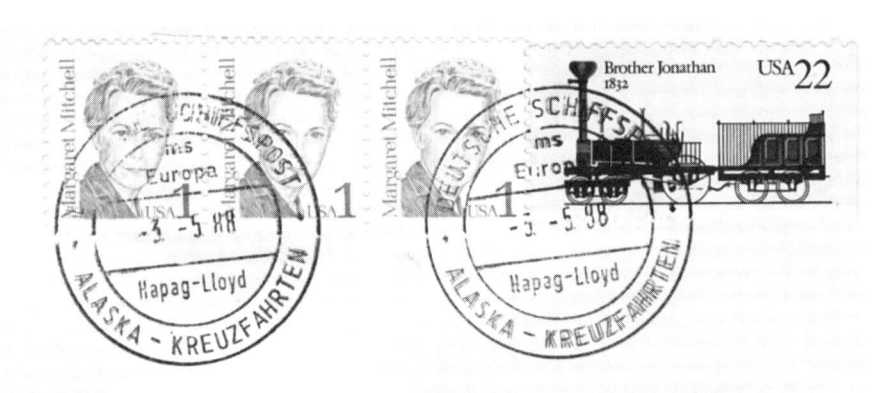

Alaska-Cruises Ship Post with one of a variety of segment cachets available during the voyage.

592   Norddeutscher Lloyd Bremen

The Lloyd introduced cruising in the modern concept in 1890 with its white-painted Australia-route flagship Kaiser Wilhelm II *#70 with 201 Gentlemen and 14 Ladies to the Northlands, always Germany's favorite cruise destination. In commemoration, Europa 5 went to the Caribbean with this centennial Ship Post.*

A Hapag-Lloyd Airbus 310 at Fuerteventura Island, another in the maintenance shops, and the welcome on coming On Board. From 1993 Annual Report.

Marriage at Age 123 and 113   593

The Lloyd Werft in 1970 with NDL's Europa *in dock for annual overhaul. Several other vessels also being worked on: Nuclear Vessel Otto Hahn, managed by Hapag-Lloyd in forefront, behind* Europa *a United Fruit Co. reefer with* Chiquita, *its brand, painted on the side.*

repairing wartime destruction so as to serve the U.S. occupying forces, in Bremerhaven, their funnel into Germany. By the time of the 1970 merger, some 2000 workers were active at the Lloydwerft.

Under Hapag-Lloyd, the Werft diversified into conversions, such as a bulk-carrier into a floating drilling rig. Big contracts were for updating and repairs on *Queen Elizabeth 2*. The first was a $6.8 millions overhaul in 1983 while the work-numbers were down to 1200 in Bremerhaven. Its largest-ever contract was the $115 millions conversion of *QE2* from turbine to Diesel-Electric propulsions and related mechanical and amenities improvements from November 1986 to May, 1987. According to 100A1 "Lloyd Werft won this huge contract basically because they are reliable, could deliver on time and their price was right." Lloydwerft chairman Eckart Knoth said that since *QE2* was on an absolute liner and cruise schedule, "The most critical point was that we could deliver on time. We have a worldwide reputation for this kind of word, having done about forty major passenger ship conversions in the last twelve years. And because *QE2* had been here twice before for refits. It would be a disaster if the ship were not ready for her voyage on April 29, 1987 because she is already fully-booked."

It turned out to be a near-thing. *The New York Times* on 5 May, 1987 headlined "Problems Tarnish *QE2's* Arrival in New York. It was to have been a triumphant return of a grand trans-Atlantic liner ... But the refitted *Queen Elizabeth 2* arrived ... to a more modest welcome after a crossing blemished by flooded cabins, cold meals, empty swimming pools ... that prompted her master to offer refunds that could total more than $1 million."

On board were some 1,300 passengers, nearly 1,000 crew, and 200 West German workers who spent the five-day voyage from Southampton working feverishly to finish the renovations. Explanations:

- It is normal rather than not for a new ships, and *QE2* essentially came out as that, to have workers on board on the delivery trip and even on the first voyage.
- During the actual work, to avoid some spending Cunard supplied old or inadequate items to be installed that slowed the work,

ended up having to be replaced.
- Some were service problems on board. Seventy crew had walked off in Southampton, so the ship had many new, non-union attendants. "We had yet to receive a second bedspread and we had no blankets" said one couple. Another: "I had no wardrobe. I had a rail for my clothing - in First Class." Somebody's design goof that was built in as specified.

Overall, the problems were soon remedied, *QE2* as befitting an old-timer was brought into and ahead of her times in 179 days of work. This included $20 millions for television and computerized telephones in every cabin, new furnishings and decorations in public rooms, etc.

The work to be done "is very extensive" a Cunard official said. "Totally refurbishing (four) restaurants and 1033 cabins." Capacity of the main show room was expanded from 250 to 500 seats. A new sports bar and teenage centre. And eight additional penthouse suite. (On *QE2* as on *Norway*, ex-*France*, essentially an extra deck was added on top.) And a business center, with telex, facsimile and dictating machines, and secretarial services. A board room for 26 persons and a private dining facility. Providing facilities for passengers to work and vacation at sea. For the crew a new servery, dining room, club room, bar, shop and quiet room for their off-duty hours.

Cunard had begun the rebuilding proposal in 1983 when it invited engine manufacturers what was to be done needed to be discussed and shipbuilders from Germany, Britain, Japan, Holland, Denmark and France. These worked together to make overall decisions; specifications were sent to shipyards wanting them. It ended up with only three German yards in the running. One backed out as they were working on the conversion of the *United States*. The other lacked the recent experience of Lloydwerft. The first work was dismantling: taking off the funnel, opening up the ship to remove old or redundant machinery and equipment: some 4,700 tons of ... scrap metal. The new propulsion system was contracted for 32.2 knots, service speed to be 28 knots. With that, the new machinery would save 200 tons of fuel a day. Part of this saving results from five-bladed, convertible pitch propellers. Mounted aft of these a new technology: six-bladed Grim wheels, the vanes resemble whale fins, which turn in the ship's slipstream, adding thrust to the propeller shaft.

In 1983, as part of Hapag-Lloyd's reorganization to concentrate on shipping and tourist-related activities, the Lloydwerft was taken over by a holding company that rescued Bremer Vulkan Shipyard from bankruptcy and several other Bremerhaven and Weser River shipyards. This gave Hapag-Lloyd a one-eight share in the new concern. This was later sold off.

But the name and reputation of the Lloyd Werft remains. **New ventures** don't always turn out as successful as old ones. Also centered in Bremen-Bremerhaven was the carrying out of NDL's move into the bulk-cargoes and tramping business. It began modestly in June, 1970, a partnership with URAG, Unterweser Reederei A.G., of Bremen, to convert NDL's **Roland Linie Schiffahrts Gmbh.** Two multi-purpose bulkers were ordered, *Roland Bremen* for the Lloyd, *Kelkheim* for URAG. In 1973, Hapag-Lloyd took URAG, Unterweser, over entirely, including seven bulkers built in the 1960s. From 1/1/1976, the expanding operation became the Kosmos Bulkschiffahrts Gmbh. In time, it was bigger than its parent, in the process becoming the worst of several continuous-loss operations.

In 1973, it was decided to add tankers: orders were placed for two *Europa*-design 386,000 ton vessels.

By then, two 150,000-tons tankers were under long-term charter and a German OBO, Oil-Bulk-Ore carrier. In October, 1975, one of the tanker orders was changed to six multi-purpose freighters, a lucky decision. On 1/1/1977, *Kosmos* took over four Greek Colotronis interests' tankers on long-term charter. From June, 1977 into 1978 the omni freighters were delivered. Three others were ordered in Brazil. Later, the third was cancelled.

In late 1978, when the 386,000 tons tanker *Bonn* was completed, it was laid up for five months before a charter was found. In 1980, Texaco chartered it long-term, but later backed out when the oil crisis deepened.

At the end of this hurried expansion, Kosmos had twenty vessels, mostly chartered non German ships, of 1.9 million dead-weight tons capacity, sizably more than parent Hapag-Lloyd had, including five tankers of 1,458,000 tons. In 1980, Hapag-Lloyd lost DM 31.5 millions. No dividends were paid 1979-1985.

In late 1982, it was fully evident that expansion had brought major difficulties. There had been a forty percent drop in North Atlantic cargo tonnage. 1981 net income had been only DM 13.2 millions on revenues of DM 4.4 billions.

In November, 1982 the Board of Directors approved "Management's plans for restructuring the Company" for survival and restoration to a healthy enterprise. A hasty retreat from a grandiose but disastrously costly diversification and expansion. Each management seems to have to learn that fixed costs allowed to run rampant on the upturn are destructive on the downturn. By December, 1982 drastic moves were being made to cut costs. Layoffs and a hiring freeze. Reorganization began. The U.S. representation at 17 Battery Place, Manhattan, was moved to lower-rent Staten Island, and staff cut. In March, 1983 Hans Jakob Kruse took over as Vorstand chief. Later he admitted "We will no longer be so wild on wages as we were in the 1960s and 1970s." The concern's head office on Ballinndamm, Hamburg was sold to raise cash. It was decided to shut down the Kosmos bulk-carrying operation by 1 October, 1983. The outlook was that would lose some DM 110 millions in 1983 and 1984. All the bulkers were sold off except two on long-term charter. The two 150,000 tons tanker were unsellable except as scrap. So was the 392,580 tons *Bonn*. It was laid up in Brunei Bay in hope of some recovery in the market. It did not come. *Bonn* was sold off for some $10 millions for breakup against its cost of DM 173 millions.

The Pracht Spedition (Forwarding) Company bought in 1979, in four years had cost Hapag-Lloyd DM 70 millions in losses and would continue in red ink for another two years. It was up for sale, Herr Kruse said. "Pracht does not fit into our business philosophy." Pracht in German means Splendour, but it was not glittering for Hapag-Lloyd. It remained as a subsidiary into 1994 with admitted uncertain prospects.

A continuing operation, also run from Bremen-Bremerhaven, that, too, has had its ups and downs is **Hapag-Lloyd Transport & Services Co.** It was formed to take over all of the Lloyd and Hapag Tug operations except the separately owned Lutgers & Reimers tug operation in Hamburg acquired by Hapag and kept separate from its own harbor operations. T & S basically operates in the estuary of the Jade - Wilhelmshaven - a major oil terminal, Bremerhaven and Hamburg.

In 1975 the first offshore tug-supply vessel was built: *TS 41 Rough*, a 198' sister delivered in 1976. Mainly these and other vessels operated in the North Sea and immz adjacent areas. The report for 1993 states in April, 1994: "The supplying and managing of offshore platforms, until now handled by us with our two special vessels, was given up because of declining and unfavorable prospects." Offshore joint operations, as in Brazil or Spain, were given up. T & S also had built lighters and pontoons for lifting and delivering heavy equipment trans-ocean, even entire vessels up to 25,000 tons.

Apart from the separate tug subsidiary in Hamburg of Lütgers & Reimers, all the tug and towing offshore activities of Hapag-Lloyd Transport & Service Co. are managed from Bremen-Bremerhaven, in 1976, 32 towing-related craft. One is the pollution-cleanup *MS Rose Mary*. This reminds of the New Yorker Carton 26/8/1972, his wife waving Goodbye to the tanker Captain: "Bye, dear. Try not to spill anything."

Germany's counterpart to the U.S.'s nuclear vessel *Savannah* was built in 1964 for the Gesellschaft für Kernergieverwertung in Schiffbau und Schiffahrt, Corporation for Nuclear Evaluation in Shipbuilding and Operating. The ship was designed to serve as ore carrier, to provide normal operating parameters. Hapag managed the ship, from 1 April, 1977 it was time-chartered by Hapag-Lloyd to operate as freighter but also to learn about nuclear power for ships. In February, 1979 *Otto Hahn* made its last voyage, up the Elbe to Hamburg. In 1981, it was sold for breakup. At Hapag-Lloyd it was its Transport & Services Gmbh that operated *Otto Hahn*.

It also has managed and crewed under contract with the Ministry of Research and Technology, Bundesministerium für Forschung und Technologie, the Polar Research vessel *Polarstern*; The actual research is under the Alfred-Wegener Institut for Polar Research at Bremerhaven. The ship has a SHIP POST for the convenience of crew and research staff. This periodically is lifted by air, mail and light-weight equipment, etc. arriving that way. Non-German scientists normally also are on board. In 1979, former Bundes Chancellor Helmut Schmidt and wife were on board as guests for the last leg of a voyage to the Barents Sea and Spitzbergen. The entire tug and offshore activity was sold off in early 1994.

The liner operation for all the years since the merger remained the largest component of Hapag-Lloyd's business, although a gradually declining one as diversification took hold. As it was for Lloyd and Hapag pre-1970, only a continuing building and rebuilding, chartering in and chartering out, a changing mix of the type and capabilities of vessels in service, kept Hapag-Lloyd a pace-setter in world shipping.

In 1972, Hapag-Lloyd chartered two new ships, essentially sisters of its own four that were the first all-container service on the North Atlantic in 1969, from C.F. Ahrenkiel. Mr. Ahrenkiel had been a director in New York in the prewar Hapag-Lloyd North Atlantic Gemeinschaft, then with the merger became a Hapag-Lloyd director before going off on his own. These ships allowed a weekly service with a larger number of ports served. In 1973, the original four were jumboized

*The first of four TS, Transport Service, offshore oilwork support vessels: TS 41-*Rough, *the others* Tough, Force *and* Power.

to increase capacity from 736 to 1114 TEUs.

When they, in turn, proved to be too small and too slow for the North Atlantic, they were shifted to the Euro-Pacific U.S.-Canada West Coast route, served with the French Line and Holland America Line. Then in January, 1978 the four opened Hapag-Lloyd's trans-Pacific service California-Japan-Hong Kong-Taiwan, making it now a round-the-world, via connecting schedules, operator. This proved to be an earnings drain. In Fall, 1985 the four were sold to Lykes Brothers S.S. Co., who continued them in their trans-Pacific service until it, too, withdrew after consistent losses.

The rebuilding into omni and container vessels of the more recent ships Hapag-Lloyd took over in 1970, as well as the continuing series of improved performance all-container ships, was one way of fighting the growing flag discrimination practiced by newly-emerging nations that wanted to have their own flag lines. Deputy Vorstand Karl-Heinz Sager commented that "the freedom of the seas is dead." It was the old free-trading idea, every one open to compete, although preferably within conference rules.

Two second-generation container ships were built for the Lloyd and Hapag. Both went into service to Australia soon after the 9/1970 Hapag-Lloyd merger. They were almost double the size of the four 1968-1969 Atlantic vessels. They operated at 21.5 knots. The competitiveness of the fourteen 21 knot freighters of 1964 and 1967 as the Far-East run proved short-lived. They were shifted to alternate routes when the third-generation container giants, two each for Lloyd and Hapag ordered before the merger, but delivered in 1972, entered service. Bigger then *Bremen* and *Europa*, and with a 26+ knots service speed, they were in the pre-oil crisis era a profligate expression of high speeds at high costs. When the Oil Shock hit, they were converted to run economically at 23 knots, that in following years became the top speed that various competitors held to. A commonsense ceiling. All the later container ships had bow-thrusters for easier docking and undocking, usually sans tugs, and stabilizers to prevent the occasional early container-ship losses of containers in rough weather.

The LASH technology, Lighter Aboard Ship, was part of the rapidly-developing container revolution. The difference: these were floating Boxes, with special vessels to float-guide them into the open-ended hull. Lykes Brother S.S. Co. and Holland America Line invested in this new approach. HAL ordered two LASH vessels. One order was taken over by Hapag-Lloyd soon after the merger, to provide the joint Combi-Line service between the Continent-U.K.-Miami-Gulf ports. The ship was named *München*, to be registered in Bremen, this part of the merger philosophy: ships added to the fleet would be alternately registered in Bremen and Hamburg.

München was launched 12/5/1972 at Cockerill's Shipyard in Hoboken. Capacity to be 83 floating lighters with lift up to 376 tons. First route: Bremerhaven-Rotterdam-Sheerness to Savannah, New Orleans and Houston. Later Miami was added. H.A.L.'s sister was *Bilderdyjk*. The two would provide a departure every 17-18 days. Each ship has a 510 tons Gantry Crane to lift the barges for stacking as is done with containers on a solid-deck vessel.

Everything went well until December, 1978. *München* was en route for the U.S. The ship last

Mail from two specialty vessels managed by Hapag-Lloyd:
1. The Nuclear Otto Hahn, *entirely experimental but operated as a freighter to expose it to actual service needs. Special postmark for entry into service.*
2. The Arctic-Antarctic research Polarstern *with cachet from its seventh Antarctic Voyage on a European Union project. And its Ship Post.*

was heard from 46.27N, 27.30W. It was heading into a heavy storm north of the Azores. Nothing further ever was heard. Three empty liferafts, two empty lifebelts were found, plus two LASH barges seen by search aircraft, one by Hapag-Lloyd's *Erlangen*. Missing with the ship, 81 lighters, "with very sophisticated gear" in the cargo per a Lloyd's insurance spokesman. It was the largest marine loss to that time: $80 millions for the ship and content. All 28 on board, 27 crew and the wife of one of the men. Extensive surface and aerial search continued for ten days before it was called off.

As Michael Grey, managing editor of Fairplay International Shipping Weekly wrote for the *Financial Times* of London in February, 1979: "München ... on the face of it, a vessel of such phenomenal structural strength that even the worst possible weather should have had little effect on her ... North of the Azores the vessel met with a storm of such exceptional violence that other large ships were forced to heave to and were unable to turn around in the heavy swells ... An interrupted SOS, a second-hand report of a list (in April Hapag-Lloyd still was trying to find the source of the report heard by a Soviet ship in the area) and then complete silence was the end of the *München* ... a most unlikely candidate for disaster ... One can only speculate on whether her unconventional design ... contributed to the loss."

In 1974, Hapag-Lloyd bought the Rickmers Line of Bremerhaven, a condition-precedent imposed by China before it would grant Hapag-Lloyd the freedom to serve Chinese ports. Rickmers had had China coastal routes since before 1900. Also in 1974, Hapag-Lloyd committed itself to its second major-investment program, this to cost DM 1.3 billions. It involved building

**Hapag-Lloyd:
Nordatlantik
wöchentlich direkt**

Vier neue Containerschiffe Stuttgart Express Düsseldorf Express · Nürnberg Express · Köln Express ersetzen gegenwärtige Flotte, beginnend mit der Stuttgart Express Anfang Oktober · Hamburg, Bremerhaven, Rotterdam, Antwerpen nach/von New York · Philadelphia Baltimore · Norfolk.

Pünktlich, regelmäßig und zuverlässig

Hapag-Lloyd in 1977 introduced four new 22 knots container ships for weekly "punctual, regular, reliable" trans-Atlantic service. The older vessels from 1968-1969 were put onto the West Coast U.S.A.-Canada route, and then ran trans-Pacific for several years until continuing losses led to their being sold off to Lykes Brothers S.S. Company.

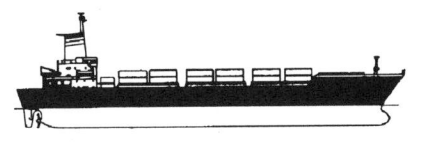

Nordatlantik 1968/69.

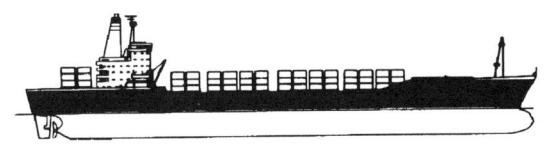

Australien 1970.

The three container generations of Lloyd and Hapag and Hapag-Lloyd: North Atlantic 1968 - Australia 1970 - East Asia 1972.

eight new container ships, including becoming members in a three-lines joint West Indies operation. And going to semi-container ships, then full-container ships on the Euro-Pacific service to the U.S.-Canada West Coast, and with Holland America Line in the Combi-Line to the Gulf of Mexico ports. In 1978, Hapag-Lloyd put the four new *Köln* class container ships of 28,000 tons, 22 knots, and 1380 TEUs on the North Atlantic, the third generation. With them Hapag-Lloyd had the second largest container fleet in the world - 22 ships with some 37,000 TEUs, including the four Omni-class vessels being jumboized. Deputy Vorstand Herr Sager labelled the *Köln* class as "ideal vessels of a size and speed widely usable. Their technical parameters are such that later versions would remain basically the same." The crystal ball was cloudy. In 1985, the ships were jumboized to carry 2594 TEUs. It was a quicker and cheaper way to expand capacity, the speed of the longer ships only barely slower than before.

With the four *Kölns* providing the service on the Atlantic, in January, 1978 Hapag-Lloyd shifted its original four North-Atlantic container ships onto a new, independent, trans-Pacific line. In time, *Mosel Express* was added to provide a weekly service. This gave Hapag-Lloyd a round-the-world network. This trans-Pacific service lasted into the Fall of 1985, when Hapag-Lloyd gave it up because of continuing losses. In 1993, in effect, a new round-the-world connection was threaded with connecting container-transfer from Portland, Maine and Boston to New York, then inter-coastal as through-cargo and again a trans-Pacific service. The Jones Act forbids coastal-intercoastal carriage to foreign flags. And U.S. shipping concerns, the old Panama Pacific Line, the American Hawaiian and others long ago gave up this traffic. American President Lines meets the problem with its fast and huge (they cannot transit the Panama Canal) C-10 container vessels, with cross-country by rail.

In 1983, Hapag-Lloyd had connected New England with a weekly feeder: Halifax-Boston-Portsmouth, N.H., to its express trans-Atlantic service with our chartered and renamed "new containership *Yankee Clipper*". Nine days to the Continent, eight days return. Good service.

In 1986, total revenues were DM 4.5 billions, 70+ from shipping activities.

In 1986, Hapag-Lloyd sold off ten ships, including three from the money-losing Indonesia line, two former "Hansa" ships bought when that Bre-

COMBI LASH

COMBI LINE... A COMBINED SERVICE OF HAPAG-LLOYD A. G. AND HOLLAND AMERICA LINE

• From coastal and inland ports to barges • To speedy oceangoing carriers • Across the ocean • To deep water and inland foreign ports

FOREST INDUSTRIES/January 1973

An example of the advantage of the LASH system: A 26 December, 1972 news report showed a photograph of a lighter in Bremerhaven. A 255 tons transformer is being loaded, made by the Elin A.G. in Austria. It was transported to Bremerhaven on a heavy-lift 20-axles railway flatcar. It arrived at New Orleans on München. *The lighter was towed to Memphis. Not quite the door-to-door possible with containers, but close to it.*

In 1988, Hapag-Lloyd committed DM 2.1 billions for additional improved vessels - two of 2300 TEUs were delivered in 1989 and enlarged to 2800 TEUs in 1992, and the first of eight 4400 TEUs, 23 knot vessels in service in 1991-1994. Containerships are written off over twelve years, aircraft over ten, containers over five years. Even these 48,58,000 tons vessels were manned by no more than 13-14 crew.

Crew-size has been a controlling ship-design and economic consideration since the first craft went to sea. When ships were still coal-fired, the largest had hundreds of stokers and firemen, the Black Gang that rarely got topside; they never were really clean. Ships needed days extra in port for coaling and cleaning ship. On *Kaiser Wilhelm der Grosse* #100, the Black Gang was some 250 of the 450+ member crew.

Conversion to oil-firing in the 1920s drastically cut crew size. But freighters continued to need 35-40 alone for the engine room. Diesel engined vessels reduced crew size still more.

NDL's River Class in from 1927 into 1930 had 70-72 in the crew, the three motor ships in the class some twenty less. *Donau* #425 had experimental powdered-coal firing, but she is listed with the same number as sister *Isar.*

Post-war the turbine freighters from 1953 had a basic 44-man crew. NDL's first over-10,000 tons freighter *Riederstein* also had 44, as did the *Friesenstein* of 1967, 44-46.

Hapag's Omni vessels of 1970-1971 were planned for 38 men. They entered service with 35: Captain, three nautical officers, four engine-tech-

men firm went bankrupt as a result of the Mid-East oil crisis and boycott, and the four Omni ships built in 1970-71, partly rebuilt in 1974 to carry 425 containers, then in 1979 completely rebuilt as container vessels.

Also sold off were Hapag-Lloyd's one-eight share in the Bremer Vulkan Shipyard. This had come about in its 1983 recapitalization and merger of several Weser River shipbuilding operations. The Lloyd Werft in Bremerhaven became part of the new combine.

The next year, 1987, was the worst since the merger. Revenues declined to DM 3.5 billions. Number of employees was off 2000 in five years. Cash flow was taken up with necessary investment for new equipment, including nine Boeing long range 737s, and three Airbuses.

LASH München *in Bremerhaven with a deck cargo of barges and a Hapag-Lloyd tug. Ship and cargo were insured for $80 millions. The loss was the largest maritime casualty ever; most was carried by Lloyd's insurance underwriters.* Hapag-Lloyd A.G. Photo.

*Envelope posted on board the maiden voyage of Hapag-Lloyd's LASH ship, Lighter Aboard Ship. "83 lighters on board: the most modern way to transport and deliver cargoes, even up rivers!" With no Ship Post on board, the stamps were left uncancelled when handed in at the Houston Post Office under rules of the Universal Postal Union. A **Paquebot** postmark, as here, on its first day of use is used to prevent the mail being postage-dued en route to the addressee. Courtesy Gustav Lund. In December, 1978* München *disappeared in mid-Atlantic, faint signals heard, three empty life rafts found one by* Badenstein *#521, two containers seen from the air, nothing else ever.*

nical officers, four engineering assistants, one electrician, a bosun, chips-general handyman, radio man, one supply attendant, six sailors and two assistants, three machine attendants, a cook and assistant, four steward/esses, one washer-cleaner.

In 1972, *Erlangen* made two voyages with 25 crew experimentally: Captain, three nautical officers, three technical officers, radio-man, electrician, bosun, five sailors, four engine room attendants and one assistant, cook, three stewardesses, one each laundry and cleaner.

By the early 1980s, the basic crew was down to fourteen: Captain, two nautical officers, two engineering officers, electrician, steward, radio-man, four general crew, cook and cleaner. In a September, 1983 press conference in London, Hapag-Lloyd chief, Hans Jakob Kruse, said "Economies in crew manning have been a success."

Unions accepted these drastic reductions recognizing that German wages and benefits were out of line with other shipping nations. If continued, they could force drastic reduction of the shipping industry, and fewer jobs, less even than in the integrated crews. When *Frankfurt Express*, then the largest container ship in the world, came out in 1981, technically one person per watch

December 15, 1978
CLUES TO MISSING FREIGHTER

HAMBURG (West Germany), Thurs. — An aircraft today sighted two containers in the Atlantic which may be from the missing West German freighter Muenchen, the navy search and rescue service said.

The crew of the reconnaissance plane reported seeing two large grey containers floating about 70km south of the area in which the ship is being sought.

The 37,135-tonne Muenchen was carrying a crew of 27 and the wife of one of the officers.

Similar in size to a cruise liner, the modern vessel carries its cargo in container-barges hoisted over the stern for unloading.

The ship has not been seen since it sent distress calls during severe storms early on Monday, reporting its position as about 700km north of the Azores.

Its owners, Hapag-Lloyd, said today that the United States Air Force base at Rota, Spain, picked up 15 very weak distress calls from the ship last night.

Hapag-Lloyd said it was not certain the containers seen today were off the Muenchen. But if they were it was probable that they were torn loose from the ship rather than an indication that it had sunk.

Hapag-Lloyd said the weakness of the Muenchen's distress calls could mean that its radio aerial had been damaged by the storms, which reached hurricane strength at times.

The ship has gone through similar storms without damage during its six years in service and its master, Captain Hans Daenekamp, is an experienced seaman, Hapag-Lloyd added.

NZPA-Reuter—Copyright

Mystery of 'München' — Hapag-Lloyd appeal

HAPAG-LLOYD is still trying to solve one of the mysteries concerning the loss of the barge carrier *Munchen*.

The West German shipping company is searching for a vessel which relayed a message received from the 45,000-ton dw *München*.

The relayed message — "SOS SOS de DEAT DEAT position 46 degrees 15 minutes north, 27 degrees 30 minutes west, 50 degrees starboard articas" — was picked up by a Russian ship in the area but the source was never traced.

DEAT was the *Munchen*'s call sign.

Hapag-Lloyd's investigation into the loss of the *Munchen*, her cargo and crew of 28 last December, continues and the company would like to contact any vessel that communicated with her

The tragedy will come before the West German Court of Marine Inquiry later this year.

A spokesman for Hapag-Lloyd said that there are indications of what could have happened to the ship but none that are totally convincing.   **9 APRIL, 1979**

December 21, 1978
Freighter Is Still Missing

Hamburg, West Germany

Hoping to hear a distress call, searchers called a two-hour radio silence yesterday in the Atlantic ocean — a final effort to locate a missing West German freighter with 28 persons aboard, the German navy said.

Associated Press

Four months after the disappearance of the LASH vessel München, *Hapag-Lloyd and the shipping world still had no definite clues or conclusions as to what happened. Here is an analysis made by Surveyor William Schell of Holbrook, Massachusetts:*

I have been involved with the Trans-Atlantic westbound steel trade first in agency, then in general agency, and finally as a surveyor, since 1977. I should say that the consensus among my colleagues, particularly those who work for the cargo underwriters involved with exports from the major German mills, is that the München *was probably sunk by her own cargo. The premier port for European steel exports is Antwerp — the loading stevedores there have long experience with properly loading and securing a cargo of steel products. It is very rare that we ever see any shifting in cargo loaded from there. However, the* München *was loaded with barges which had been loaded not on the coast but at mills and docks up the Rhine where the cargoes need only normally be secured enough to get them down the Rhine to the export ports. Much of European steel exports to the U.S. are in the form of large coils of steel sheets - those for the U.S. auto industry often go up above a 20 ton pieceweight. These coils are always stowed, stacked on the round. If you have any sense of the forces involved, it is easy to visualize the havoc a row of three or four of these coils would cause if they parted their lashings. Very soon the barge in which they were stowed would itself no longer be lashed down. In a LASH carrier the barge deck runs over the engine room and structural damage from a loose barge or several loose barges could quickly cause machinery damage and leave the vessel disabled.*

Crew quarters on Hamburg Express, *one of four basically sister container ships ordered by the Lloyd and Hapag before the merger but not completed until 1972:*
  The Social Hall with bar - Chief Officer's office
  Dining Room for Officers - Dining Room for Crew
  Living-Work Room of 1. Steward
  Bosun's day-room.
Two of these four ships were still in Hapag-Lloyd routes in 1994; twenty-two years old but converted and modernized in 1981-1982.

could run it from the bridge. Crew reductions were made feasible by containerization: fewer things to do on a ship; shifting some operations to shore, such as container fastening, repairs and maintenance, and by mechanization.

Mechanization has made jobs easier, eliminated others. The McGregor accordion-type hatch covers of the 1950s replaced the old boards with recessed handles, two men at a time placing them on metal flanges. It was the replacement of such boards on a leaking hatch that on *Berlin* in March, 1959 lost four men overboard. See "Ad Aspera."

The bridge has become a remote-control station, now superimposed on the deck structure with 360° visibility as with airport control towers. There is a bridge computer set with the voyage and engine parameters controls course, steers, a cruise-control adjusts speed to the waves, gives position reports from satellite positioning, warns of approaching other vessels or shore lines, etc. Also: remote control of the gangway that each vessel has on both sides for lowering, davit-like, to the quay or pier string-piece. The Jacob's ladder is lowered and raised hydraulically for taking on-dropping off the pilot. Even the anchors can be dropped and retrieved with bridge-control.

The entire life-style of the crew has changed. Everybody has his own cabin. Some ships have a double for any member who has his wife along. This was restricted to the Captain (or officers) until 1968 legislation made all eligible for stated periods. An added appeal; seamen were exempt from compulsory military service. There is a hobby room, a lounge fitted out like a good-income family's room. Some ships even have a sauna or a hot tub, plus an examination-hospital room. Space is not really a problem on these huge vessels. In return, crews work hard, intensely so; their payscales are higher, they need more specific training. They have more time off so that they could do part-time other work, or family, hobbies. In case of accident or "abandon ship" all can fit into the stern-gravity mounted sealed, self-righting motor life boat. In September, 1956 for *Blankenstein's* trial voyage out to Helgoland, some seventy retired captains and chief engineers were invited, pleased again to smell the sea air and be on board a Lloyd ship. The oldest: Captain G. Bolte, 95 "A bit deaf but otherwise in good health and mood" per Hans Karstedt. For these oldtimers the crew quarters were of special interest. Some felt that if one were allowed to serve on such a ship one should really pay for the privilege, not ask an exorbitant wage. Even "Fritzie", the traditional name for the Chinese laundryman on board many German freighters, had a private cabin. His workroom was the laundry. Some of the seagoing Chinese came from a Chinese colony in Bremerhaven. Others were furnished by a contractor in Hong Kong. They would serve two years on a ship, then would be flown to Hong Kong for a three-months vacation before joining another ship. One *Columbus* Chinese laundryman was on board from 1930 until put ashore in Mexico in December, 1939. Autres temps, autres moeurs. By the 1970s and 1980s the expectations were several factors higher. And many jobs were eliminated.

Gone altogether in this is what used to pull youth to the sea: a life completely different from that ashore.

The revolutionary changes in the shipping industry are evidenced by these figures:
- on 1/1/1914 NDL had 116 high-seas ships of 707,000 gross tons with nineteen of 201,000 tons under construction.
- In 1931, at its between-the-wars peak, the Lloyd had 147 high-seas vessels of 860,324 gross tons.
- In 1994, Hapag-Lloyd had 17 owned vessels of 806, 798 gross tons, or an average 47,458 tons. The largest were *Bremen* and *Tokio Express*, the two remaining of the four third-generation ships, 57,800 tons each, completed in 1972. With container ships of this size doing the work of 30-40 older conventional vessels, "this (the Atlantic) is today an empty ocean," said Captain John Burton-Hall on *QE2*. The same applies to the other oceans. The TRIO Far East route was being operated by nineteen of these huge vessels in 1986 with five partners. Hapag-Lloyd one of them and serving only nine major ports. None of these vessels carry passengers. The ships do not stay long enough in ports to justify visiting. And with small crews, some fourteen to sixteen, nobody has time to fuss with paying guests. The ships just provide the transportation. The tracking of containers, placing them in the holding areas at ports, the sequence of loading and unloading nowadays is all computerised. There no longer is the individual care of the ship's crew and of stevedores with cargoes, care in stowing for non-breakage or pilferage when everything was break-bulk. With door-to-door service provided by what now are world-transportation companies rather than mere shipping enterprises, the whole operation is like a conveyor built from inland source to inland customer. Crossing the ocean just means moving the cargo from one mode to another.

In December, 1994 with delivery of a new *Hamburg Express* Hapag-Lloyd had eighteen Container ships of 810,392 Gross tons, and 910,850 Deadweight tons. Plus *Europa* and *Bremen* of 40,571 tons for a total of 850,963 tons. Not far off what the Lloyd had at its post World War I Peak; 147 high-seas ships of 860,324 gross tons.

While the fleet had shrunk from more than 110 vessels in 1970 to twenty owned ships in 1994 plus chartered vessels, the average size and speed enabled serving the world's heavy-traffic routes with mileage equal to "Every Thirty Days to the Moon."

CHAPTER 20

Bremen, the Weser and the Lloyd's Port, River and Coastal Operations

Passenger, freight and towing services on the Weser were the basis on which the Norddeutscher Lloyd was founded. For centuries, Europe's streams had been its highways. Roads, going back to Roman times, were important for people, locally mostly for the exchange of goods. Of Germany's port cities, Bremen had the smallest hinterland. The Weser was the smallest of the river systems. These natural handicaps were overcome with imagination, drive, energy and resourcefulness. And constant work to keep the Weser from silting up and cutting Bremen's access to the sea. Should that happen, Bremen's participation in world trade would disappear.

For a while, it almost happened. At times only flat-bottomed boats able to cross the Watt, the sand and mud-flats along the edge of the North Sea, could reach Bremen city. Increasingly, sea vessels even with the highest tides and runoffs could get only as far as Vegesack. There, in 1619 a port was built for that reason. Goods for or from Bremen had to be transloaded to and from barges and lighters. Bremen's fortunes ebbed and flowed with the state of the Weser, and how deep a channel could be kept for high-seas shipping.

Early in the 19th century Bremers like Senator Duckwitz and Bürgermeister Smidt saw the dangers of a disappearing future. Into 1817, the mail from Bremen to the coast was carried by coaches. This meant driving through the Kingdom of Hannover, part of the British royal house, although the King since 1714 resided in London.

Steam passenger shipping on the Weser began on 20 May, 1817 with *Die Weser*, built by Johann Lange in Grohn, the forerunner of what today is the Bremer Vulkan shipyard. From 1818, *Telegraph* built in that year by Captain Johannes Wendt, provided passenger service from Bremen to Vegesack, later as far as Brake. After the founding of Bremerhaven in 1827 as Bremen's outer part should the city permanently be cut off from deep-sea shipping, both steamers continued that far.

It was prophetic that the American sailship *Draper* under Captain Hellert on arrival on 11 September, 1830 in effect christened the still unfinished port of Bremerhaven. The vessel belonged to emigrant relatives of Bremen's Eltermann Rodewald. It was a time of flourishing trade, a come-back from the sharp decline at the end of Napoleon's control of Europe. From 1830 on Bremen developed into the largest emigrant port in Europe. In 1847, the young Bavarian Levi

605

Bremerhaven about 1840, Real Photographs, Liverpool.

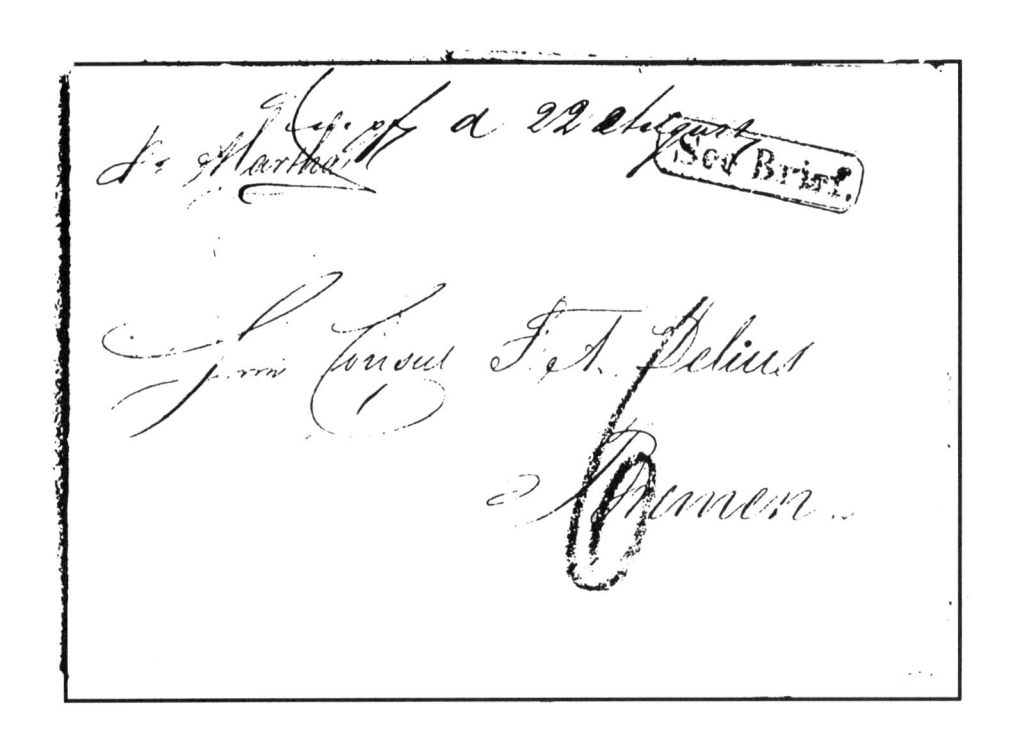

A Sea Letter marking of Bremerhaven of August 16, 1850 on a letter written in Baltimore the 16th July, concerning a consignment of goods to Schumacher & Co. They were the firm that handled the goods shipped by commercial submarine U-Deutschland *to Baltimore in 1916. See Vol. I, p. 443-456. Per Martha, undoubtedly a sailing vessel.*

Helgoland is the preferred offshore visiting place for Germans in the North Sea. From 1714 into 1807 it was under Danish control. The British then took it in a brief war, and held it into 1890, although the predominant population was German. In 1890 Germany got possession in return for giving up claims against British interests in East Africa. After World War II, the British wanted to deny further use of the island and tried blowing up certain features. Nothing much happened. On 7 September, 1952 the island was returned to German control. Helgoland draws more visitors than even "the Isle of Capri."

Strauss and his Mother emigrated to America. Relatives already had made the voyage across the Atlantic. And millions were to follow them, with names like Spreckels, Stroh, Pabst, Busch, the entire alphabet.

Also in 1847, the new U.S. trans-Atlantic service of the Ocean Steam Navigation Company reached Bremerhaven in July. Germans were the largest group of emigrants into America after the Irish, driven out by famines. In 1854, 76,000 persons passed through Bremen's emigrant halls. By the 1860s and into the 1880s Germans were the largest ethnic group, before Scandinavians and Chinese; these latter and their sons built much of the infrastructure: railroads, bridges, contour walls, etc., in the West. In 1854, there already was a German Hospital in San Francisco. There, in the 1870s, German was the second language.

The NDL Yearbook of 1920/21, with little Lloyd activity to report so soon after World War I, describes the development of the North Sea resort of Norderney. In the 1850s, the second *Telegraph* was not commercially successful. Few dared to entrust themselves to it for the North Sea voyage. A news account says: "*Telegraph* was built so weakly that in rough weather it was not taken out from the Watten, the flat coastal sea-edge. Also, no channel buoys were laid out, so that even in calm seas the high tide had to be awaited. With that, the voyage as far as Bremen could be accomplished only in two days. Or, the departure was set so early that the passengers had to board the night before, something that involved dangers for all." *Telegraph* soon was laid up until sold for scrapping. See the following small-ships list.

In 1844, the Weser and Hunte Steam Shipping Co. was founded, one of three Weser concerns that in 1857 were merged, along with an insurance company, to form the Norddeutscher Lloyd, a daring claim in its name with a very small base. In November, 1844 several Bremen ship operators merged as the United Steam Shipping Company on the Lower Weser. Daily service from Bremen began with sidewheeler *Roland* in April, 1845. It had been built of wood in 1838, and survived into 1847. In 1848, *Roland 2* was built by Carsten Waltjen on the terrain where later the A.G. Weser shipyard was founded. Its most famous ship the *Bremen* of 1929. The new *Roland* used the rebuilt engine of the old one.

In the month of its founding, February, 1857, NDL bought *Roland*. On the 24th appeared the

Bremen, the Weser 607

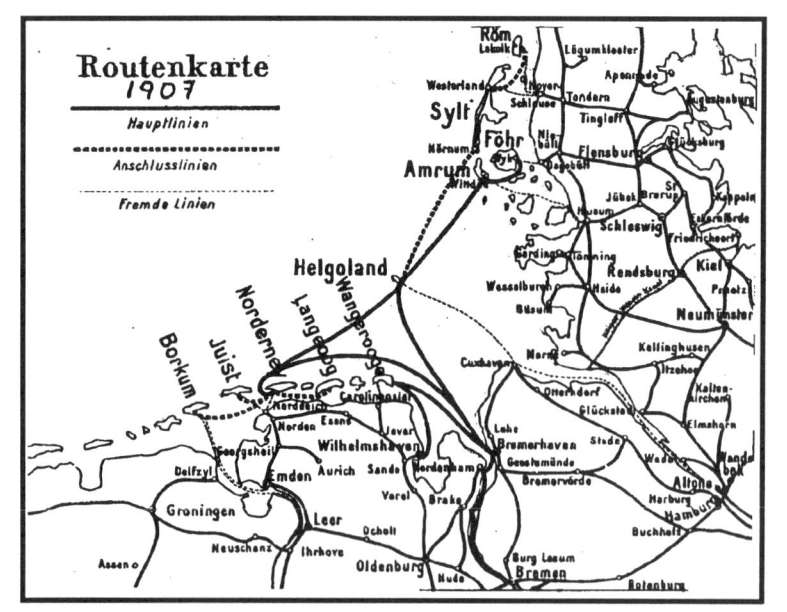

From NDL's 1907 Sea Resort services schedule, the routes to the various islands: Heavy are NDL's, medium are connecting lines and thin are other services. Also, front of 1904 and 1924 Resort Services schedules. And 1931 Season notice of the many islands served by the Lloyd's North Seas Resort Service. "For Club and Group Voyages special fare reductions."

The island with the Lange Anna red cliff at left.

*Green is the Land,
Red is the Rand,
White is the Sand,
Those are the colours of Helgoland.*

608   *Norddeutscher Lloyd Bremen*

first announcement of the new Norddeutscher Lloyd: "A steam shipping service between Bremen and the North Sea resort of Norderney on the iron vessel *Roland* under Captain M. Meyer. This lovely steam ship, especially furnished for this route for all comforts of the passengers ... Passengers were dropped or picked up at Wangerooge and Spiekeroog at the same price, including boat transfer." This started the Lloyd serving the North Sea resort islands, an operation that it continued into 1960.

The opening of the Bremen-Geestemünde railway line in 1862 marked the decline of passenger transport on the Lower Weser. For postal traffic between Geestemünde and Nordenham, Oldenburg and Hannover, the Lloyd-founded ferry at Nordenham was used. In 1862, the passenger service on the Hunte ended. Some of the Lloyd's river vessels were sold off. In 1866, the former Kingdom of Hannover, along with the Frisian Islands were incorporated into the Kingdom of Prussia. The Norderney service was extended to Helgoland. *Nordsee*, built in 1865, on 16/6/1866 for the first time showed the Lloyd flag at that island. It still was British controlled although residents were German. In 1890, Germany took over Helgoland from Britain in return for giving up claims to Zanzibar and other East African areas. Passengers got onto and off the ferrying vessels in huge-wheeled wagons driven into the water. In 1873, a 1200 meters long jetty was built at Norderney - the shallow water reached so far out! - providing a more convenient way to get ashore. In 1872, water conditions on the Upper Weser were so difficult that the Lloyd gave up its passenger and towing operations. Even in a good-water year, "barge-trains got stuck only 31 times because of low water."

On the Lower Weser up to its mouth, too, conditions got worse. In 1874, by resolution of the Bundesrat, a Weser Commission was set up with representatives from Oldenburg, Prussia and Bremen. Planning began in 1878 when Bremen's construction expert Ludwig Franzius joined the Commission.

In 1881, he made specific proposals: a channel five meters deep from the North Sea to Bremen at any tide. A minimal starting target which meant ocean vessels had to come upriver or go down only partly loaded. The "correction" as it still is called took from 1887 into 1894. But earlier, on 21 September, 1892 NDL's *Hannover* #114 reached Bremen's port as the first trans-Atlantic vessel. In October, 1893, the first direct Bremen-South America service was opened with NDL's *Pfalz* #83. At the same time, the Outer Weser was deepened because, just as the smallness of the Locks into Bremerhaven's harbor restricted the size ships NDL could build, so the channel depths at the mouth of the Weser restricted entry of larger ships.

Dr. Paul Neubaur in his 1907 fiftieth anniversary history of the Lloyd reports that "during 1877-1884 the resort lines disappeared almost entirely; at least they had no importance."

Actually, in 1881 the *Forelle* joined the resort services and, when the Weser was deepened, ran between Bremerhaven and Bremen. In 1885, *Libelle* and *Hecht* followed, and in 1889 *Lachs*, all sidewheelers except the little *Libelle*. The locals called them Schlickrutscher, Ooze Sliders.

The resort traffic did grow. From only 832 persons reaching Norderney by sea in 1820, it was 4,040 in 1868, 18,763 in 1892 and well above 38,000 in 1905. In Summer, 1907 there was a daily vessel to Norderney, Wangerooge and Helgoland. The schedule booklet has 64 pages. It includes high-water times at Bremen, Bremerhaven, Wilhelmshaven, Wangerooge, Norderney and Helgoland for the four summer months. A photograph shows the Lloyd Hall in Bremerhaven, a just-arrived train from Bremen on the quay and passengers boarding the "to Norderney voyaging express steamer *Nixe*."

The Lloyd had become the leading trans-ocean passenger carrier in the 1890s, — in 1891 for a time it had three sailings a week Bremen-New York. But a sudden depression in 1893 made the lesson that the attraction for the unskilled immigrants, jobs for the asking, could overnight disappear. The Lloyd's new General Director from 1892, Dr. Heinrich Wiegand, began to expand freight operations to help cushion sharp swings in the passenger traffic. This also meant building up the tug and towing services as Bremerhaven became the nexus for cargo transfers to and from Bremen and Hamburg, so that vessels need not call at both ports. There were some twenty high-seas and port tugs in Bremerhaven, for warping vessels through the locks into the inner harbor, shifting barges to load-unload the freighters, the Weser-Elbe transfers, and some salvage vessels to bring in the ships in trouble on the high seas. In stormy weather, the large-sided express steamers might need ten tugs or more to turn them around for departure. It once took *George Washington* thirty-six hours to leave Bremerhaven in stormy weather.

In the summer of 1910 the following resort and river lines operated:
- 1 Linie von Bremen/Bremerhaven nach Wangeroog und Wilhelmshaven

Proof that without Bremerhaven Bremen never would have become and remained a leading passenger transit port. Here three of NDL's four four-stacker express steamers in winter layup and two other passenger vessels, George Washington *at right. 1910. NDL photo.*

- 1 Linie Bremerhaven-Norderney
- 1 Linie Bremerhaven-Helgoland-Norderney
- 1 Linie Bremerhaven-Amrum-Wyk auf Föhr
- 1 Passagierdampferlinie Bremen-Bremerhaven
- 1 Passagierdampferlinie Bremen-Vegesack sowie:
- 1 Schleppdampferlinie auf der Unterweser und
- 1 Schleppdampferlinie von der Unterweser nach Hamburg

A towing line on the Lower Weser, and One from there to Hamburg

The annual reports during World War I make no mention of the resort steamers or services. The 1917/18 report mentions the growing traffic on rivers and canals, and tugs and barges because of the shortage of coal for the railroads. Several resort steamers were sold off: *Hecht* in 1913, *Libelle* and *Gazelle* in 1915, and in 1919 *Forelle* built in 1881. Only *Grüssgott* was added during the war, ordered as tender for *Columbus* #300 and its sister. At 781 tons, it was the largest vessel left to the Lloyd by a lost war.

At Whitsuntide in 1919, *Delphin* re-opened the line Bremen-Bremerhaven-Wangerooge. On board was a Purser and a letter-box. Normally, mail posted on board was put ashore and handled there. None of the resort steams had Ship Posts. But one usage on 26, June, 1919 had *Delphin's* name-stamp as a postmark. I also have an example from 1939, a new rubber stamp by then.

The 1919/20 NDL report states "this service suffered the entire summer (of 1919) from a lack and uncertainty of coal supplies. This also forced cancellation of the Sunday trips to Helgoland in July. The Sunday trips to Wangerooge had to be given up in August under order of the Reich Coal Commissioner, leaving only the regular connection via Bremerhaven and Wilhelmshaven. Train connections were organized for the Wangerooge steamers. In this way, some 23,000 persons were transported, and 5,200 on the Helgoland line."

In 1919, the Lloyd had opened a towing service connecting the North and Baltic Seas through the Kiel Canal.

To provide work for its kitchen and service personnel, with few ships yet in operation, in Spring 1920 NDL founded the Norderney Kurbetrieb GmbH, the Health Resort Company. It leased the Kurhaus. Captain Charles Polack, in 1914 commander of *Kronprinzessin Cecilie* #234, largest of the Lloyd's four express liners, became manager after he returned from P.O.W. camp in the U.S. The new service was postponed until after completion of the plebiscite shuttles in East Prussia. During this period NDL bought two wartime mine-search boats and had them converted to the resort steamers *Nymphe* and *Grille* for the new passenger service Stettin-Libau-Riga. They were

Despite loss of her colonies, nearly all her merchant marine, and much of Germany itself, in January, 1919 emergency ferry service began to East Prussia, newly cut off from the Fatherland by the Polish Corridor. The North Sea resort services are shown at left.

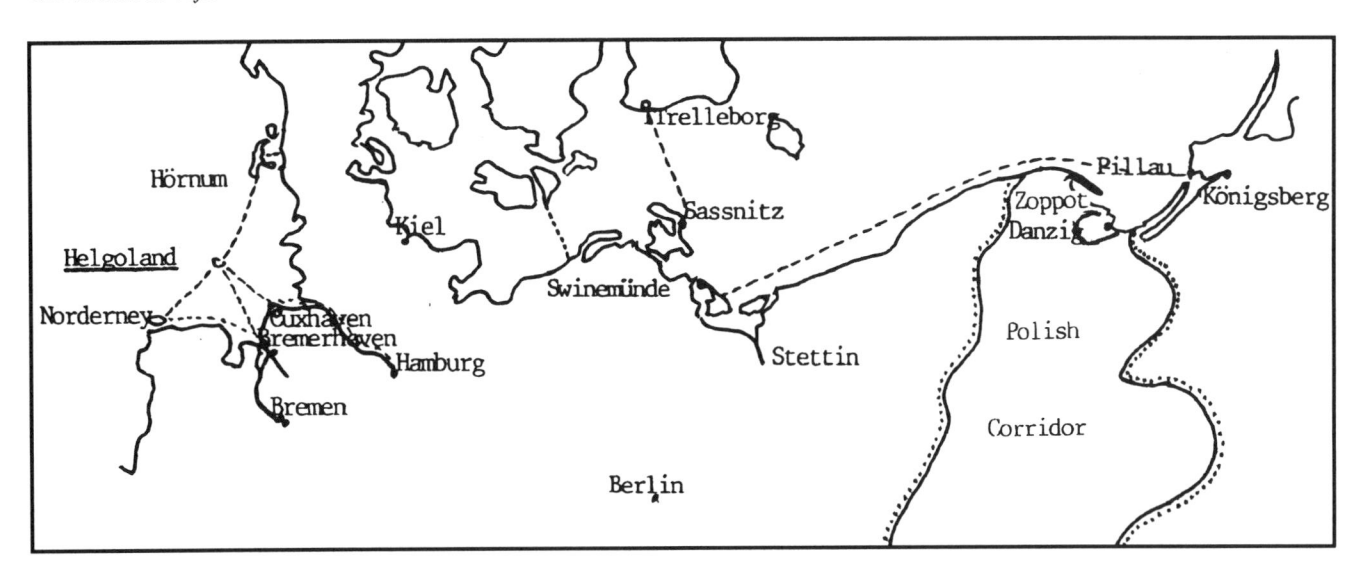

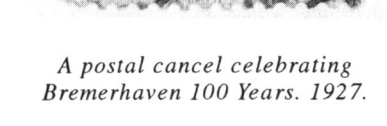

Under the Versailles Treaty, Germany gave up all ships over 1,600 tons, half those 1000-1600 tons. This left resort steamers as the largest passenger ships. Here the former Hamburg-Helgoland steamer Prinzessin Heinrich, *still with its prewar Hohenzollern name, on the run from Swinemünde to Pillau, for Danzig and Königsberg travellers and mails.*

A postal cancel celebrating Bremerhaven 100 Years. 1927.

sold off in late 1922 when this route was given up. Not every venture is successful.

The Treaty of Versailles cut off East Prussia from the rest of Germany by giving Poland a Corridor as access to the Baltic Sea. There was no way to reach East Prussia overland without crossing borders and going through customs. The sea route was the only alternative A hastily-organized fleet, including from the Lloyd *Grüssgott, Najade, Nixe* and *Vorwärts*, carried some 160,000 persons elibible to vote in the Versailles-mandated plebiscites at Allenstein and Marienwerder: to remain German or become part of Poland or Lithuania. (There was plebiscites also in Holstein and the Saar.) German stamps were overprinted in French for use in these disputed areas. All chose to remain German.

In this plebiscite shuttle service *Grüssgott*, Captain Nicholas Johnsen, later captain of *Europa* and NDL's first Commodore in 1929, left Swinemünde the first time at 4 a.m. on 2 July, 1920 with 120 passengers. At 6 p.m. the ship reached Zoppot, then continued through the night to Danzig, now a city-state separate from Germany under the treaty.

During this time, the resort steamer *Glückauf* of 1901 was converted into a combination freighter and tug, and opened a wood-transport line from Finland to Holland, a new venture for the Lloyd. "*Glückauf* is able to take some 400 tons of cargo without being hampered thereby in concurrent towing of barges." NDL Yearbook of 1919/20. Until the entry of the first post-war newbuilding of *Vegesack* #279 in September, 1920, *Glückauf* was NDL's only freighter. A current photo shows such a towing train, with sails set on the lighters, to ease the tug's burden and to save coals. See "The Lloyd Sails."

The Sea Service to East Prussia in 1926 became a key operation for the Weimar republic. Four ships provided the service, two by Hapag, one by the Lloyd, each managing one ship for the Reich Transport Ministry. NDL's was the *Hansestadt Danzig*, built in 1926 and with her sister *Preussen* operated by Hapag, lengthened by ten meters in 1933. The four vessels provided onboard Ship Posts, even into the war. In season, occasional cruises were made to ports in the Baltic and planned to Helsinki during the scheduled 1940 Olympics there. The three largest of these vessels were lost on 9/7/1941 in the Swedish minefield off Öland despite strenuous warnings by a Swedish naval vessel. Its signals either were misunderstood or just ignored. *Hansestadt* was behind the other two transports. It reversed full-out but was unable to avoid also hitting a mine. NDL's former reefer *Orotava* #391, as *Robert Möhring*, was put in as replacement, including painting "Seedienst Ostpreussen" in huge letters on the side of the ship, this in wartime! Some mail is known with the ship-name mark off the postage.

As "A Second New Beginning" tells, getting back after the war to doing what the Lloyd knew best: running ships, was delayed for years. For some five years, all shipping was strictly regulated by the Allies; only allowed were services they needed, albeit including not letting the German population starve to death. Allowed were mine-clearing, towing, repairs at the Lloyd's Technical Service in Bremerhaven, and as Dr. Georg Bessel wrote in the 1957 Centennial History "a bit of resort service."

Again in 1946, as in 1919, *Delphin* was the first Lloyd vessel back into a pre-war service. The Technical Service refurbished the ship for trips from Bremerhaven to Wangerooge. These required staying on the island overnight, so accommodations for a crew of thirty were built in. Inside, there were 105 seats. The first departure was on Monday, 28 January, 1946. Besides Captain Terkorn, there was Purser Voigt and Engineer Viet, just like in 1919. On Monday, 29 August, 1949 with some 600 school children on board bound for Wangerooge, *Delphin* ran aground, began to leak, but was brought back safely. The captain was found at fault, albeit with recognition that these waters are difficult at best: constantly shifting sandbanks and channels. A very similar incident occurred in 1950, involving some 120 children and teachers. They were bound from Langeoog to the port of Bensersiel near the German-Dutch border when their vessel ran aground in heavy fog and developed a sharp list. The captain ordered "abandon ship" and all were taken into lifeboats. The boats were unable to row because of the low state of the tide: The Wattenmeer! They found shelter on a stone breakwater and a rocky island until rescued. The Wattennmeer coast with the Friesian Islands gained fame abroad with publication in 1903 of Erskine Childrens' *The Riddle of the Sands*, "a novel of mystery and adventure" per Smithsonian reviewer Timothy Foote, November 1994. It remains in print.

During 1948-1949, Hapag chartered *Glückauf*, its own former *Bubendey*, for resumption of its resort services. In 1950, it was laid up until the 1954 season. NDL then again ran *Glückauf*, along with the chartered *M.S. Süllberg* into 1955. Then *Glückauf* was sold, and the resort services taken over by the new Bremer Seebäderdienst Gmbh, Resort Services Company, co-founded and funded by NDL. The Lloyd pulled out in 1960, ending a century plus of River and North Sea passenger services.

Meanwhile, the tug, towing, warping, and cargo-transfer activities, also going back to 1857, continued as an operating basis for the Lloyd, ordering the first new tugs in 1954, with them setting the pace with the Voith-Schneider, turn-on-a-dime, applications.

These operations after the Hapag-Lloyd merger of 1970 were put under the new Transport & Service Company, managed from Bremerhaven.

For Bremen-Bremerhaven, the container revolution proved to be the assurance the twin ports needed for building new quays, vast marshalling yards, and the huge cranes, that go with container operations. Into 1971, Bremen had more container turnover than Bremerhaven. Then, when Sea-Land came with its 33-knotters, fastest cargo vessels ever built, Bremerhaven with its deeper water, ability to tie up at any state of the tide, close to the North Sea, not several hours of a tortuous river and then have to turn around in narrow confines, became the new container crossroads. The foresight of 1827, from the lessons of the past, and during the following still-difficult years, have made Bremen today in terms of freight what it earned before as a passenger port: calling itself "A Suburb of the U.S."

Distant Suburb of U.S.

Busy Bremen Never Forgets Historic Links With Major East Coast Ports

By GERD WILCKE
Special to The New York Times

April 16, 1964

BREMEN, Germany, April 16 —The people in this bustling port and in Bremerhaven to the north proudly call themselves "suburbanites" of New York.

Though the River Weser is more than 3,000 miles from the Hudson, active trade links have existed for hundreds of years.

The Talk of Bremen Bremen historians point with particular satisfaction to the fact that President Washington picked their city as the site for the first United States consulate to be established after the United States gained independence.

That was 170 years ago. The consulate was headed by local merchants until President Jackson appointed an American in 1831. For many ensuing decades about 30 per cent of the trading vessels leaving Bremen or Bremerhaven headed for United States ports. Millions of emigrants came through here to seek a new life across the Atlantic.

World War II left the port facilities in ruins. With destruction reckoned at 80 per cent, it was difficult to navigate a kayak, let alone a seagoing vessel, through the debris of sunken ships and smashed warehouses.

Wilhelm Kaisen, the 78-year-old head of the city-state, insists that without American help, often given against the wishes or without the knowledge of the other occupation powers, Bremen would not have revived as quickly as it did.

Though the United States Army needed a usable port of embarkation from the start of the occupation, Mr. Kaisen suspects that much was done by the Americans because they wanted to restore Bremen as a pylon for the trans-Atlantic bridge that existed before.

●

BREMEN is not all harbor and ships. As the smallest of the 11 West German states, the members of its Senate (government) have fought tenaciously to build a university. They have won. Though Bremen normally holds fast to tradition, its university will be a far cry from what a visitor expects to see in a German city.

Tentative plans call for a self-contained campus on a 700-acre plot north of town. Fifteen dormitories will take up about a third of the available space.

A design for the university complex has the appearance of a big wheel with the academic buildings looking like spokes. In the center quadrangle will rise a library, an auditorium and administration buildings. The university, with a student body of 8,000, will teach philosophy, theology, medicine, law, economics, the fine arts, the humanities and the sciences.

The Government is bickering with a landowner over the price of the property needed. Conservative estimates, and Bremen folk are known to be a conservative breed, are that construction can start in about two years.

●

AS their forebears have done for hundreds of years, Bremen folk still like to meet at their Rathaus cellar to taste some of the best wines that any restaurant has to offer.

Bremen is hundreds of miles from the wine country, but with people coming here from all over the world, the burghers learned long ago that the quickest way to conclude a deal was to smooth a palate. Records in Latin from medieval times show that even the Burgher Assembly preferred the Rathaus cellar to discuss town business.

Today's customers can choose from a list of 500 wines, the most expensive being a Niersteiner selling for $50 a bottle.

Another wine, a rosé from Rüdesheim, was bottled in 1653 and is not for sale.

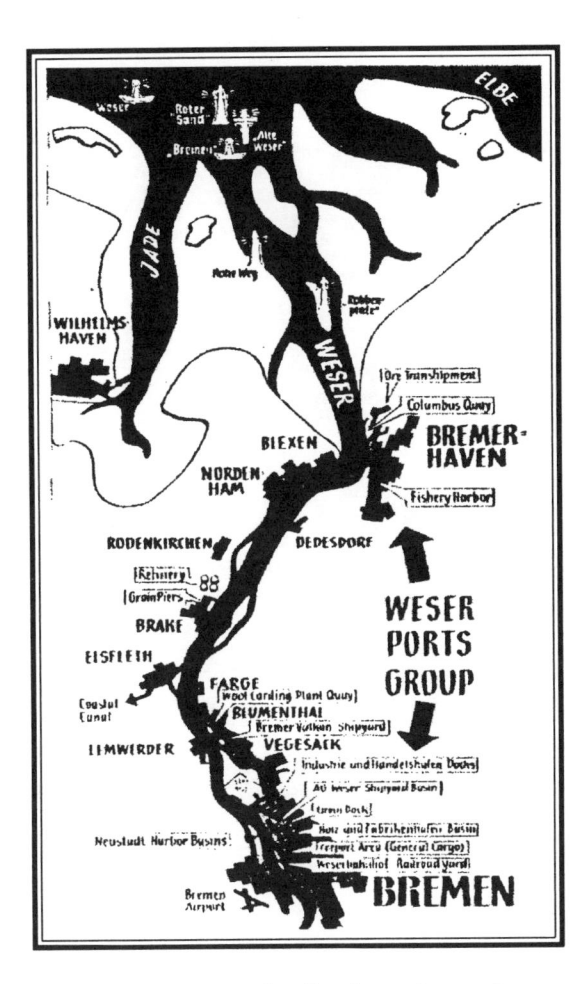

For the U.S. presence on the Continent Bremerhaven was "The Gateway to Europe." Thousands of U.S. service personnel and their families catch their first glimpse of the Old World at Bremerhaven. And it is the last place they see before leaving. This funnel for the U.S. to/from Europe escalated in importance right from the very first arrivals in 1945. This was the "shove" that pushed the reconstruction of Bremen-Bremerhaven and gave the Lloyd its first renewed opportunities and responsibilities. In 1951, the Military Sea Transportation Service set up its continental HQ in Bremerhaven covering all the German ports, Benelux and Scandinavia. In the 1951-1963 period, more than 1½ million passengers were processed through Bremerhaven by MSTS. Reported Sealift Magazine in 1963, "So many of these (MST controlled) ships make regular runs to New York that people here like to think of this as a "suburb of New York."

The first organized emigration of Germans to the U.S. took place in 1683. The tricentennial was celebrated in both countries by the issuance of twin stamps showing the sailship Concord. *Since then Bremen was an active port in trade with the Americas, the surge coming after the Revolutionary War when continental nations were free to trade where the British had before shut them out.*

When in 1846 the Ocean Steam Navigation Co. was formed as the first U.S. passenger-ship venture on the North Atlantic, Bremen already was the leading continental port for trade from/with the U.S. Bremen handled about one-third of tobacco, and a fourth of the rice, whaling oil and cotton imports. When Bremers, there and in the U.S., helped raise funds for building two Ocean Steam vessels, Bremen was chosen as the end-port, actually Bremen's port on the North Sea, Bremerhaven, as the Weser River no longer was deep enough for ocean ships to go up that far. This finally was remedied with the Weser "Correction" forty years later. Eventually, as the map from Fairplay *shows, the entire river as far as Bremen became shipping-active. With Bremen, the Lloyd became the largest trans-ocean passenger carrier of all time. So that the term "suburb" seems very fitting. After WWII, the U.S. Navy used Bremen State, including Bremerhaven, as its base for operations with and in Germany.*

The post-war resumed U.S. trans-Atlantic passenger service, with Washington, America, *and from 1952, the all-time record holder* United States, *used Bremerhaven as their continental turn-around port.*

Bremerhaven's pride in the 1950s, now that there were no longer Bremen *and* Europa *to bring it fame and activity, was that the Blue-Ribbon holder* United States, *for some ten years made its turnaround here. Behind the U.S. is the* Berlin, *put into Lloyd passenger service as* Gripsholm *in February, 1954. In the center top is NDL's Technical Service, later called Lloyd Werft (shipyard), then after the 1970 merger, Hapag-Lloyd Werft.*
The ships are at the rebuilt and enlarged Columbus Quay, with direct rail transport, also behind for the inside port. Before so much development, from 1928 one could fly from almost shipside to major German cities.

Typical scene at Bremerhaven. Troops prepare to embark in USNS Gordon. They arrive early the morning of the sailing. After processing in the Army's Staging Area, they are shuttled to shipside by bus and train. Any ship servicing and repairs needed by the USN and MSTS vessels at Bremerhaven was handled by the Lloyd's Technical Service.Ex-Sealift Magazine, February 1963.

Register of River and Sea Tugs, Tenders, Resort Vessels and Other Craft.

The Lloyd 1913/14 Yearbook names 74 of the 358 tugs, tenders, resort vessels, launches and barges in the fleet: 47 of these, some overseas, are under 100 Ts. The smallest launch is *Wittekind* of 5 tons.

Barges and lighters, numbered from 1857, are not included in this listing. Since all records have been destroyed, and some never appeared in print, what is known is incomplete.

Very helpful sources include: Dr. Ernst Schmidt, "Jubiläum auf der Weser," Hans Szymansky "Der Anfang der Dampfschiffahrt in Niedersachsen 1817-1867," sent me by Hans-Heinz Kuhlmann, "Die Werftchronik des Bremer Vulkans," die "Bremer Boote" by Herbert Kuke in Nautilus, 9/1973," Die bremischen Dampfschiffsposten auf der Unterweser und im Nordseeküstenraum 1817-1867" by Wolfgang Diesner, Lloyd Yearbooks and Ship Registers. Also Helmut Stegemann's listing of German tugs in Schiffahrt International and Jan Mordhorst's "Schlepper," the history of towing in the Bundes Republic, 1988. Some records are contradictory. Often it is difficult to know fact from fiction. Even NDL misstated: "1913 NDL sold besides *Forelle* also *Hecht, Gazelie* and *Forelle*." The fact is *Hecht* was sold in 1913, *Gazelle* and *Libelle* in 1915, and *Forelle* not until 1919.

Weser shipping was the foundation of the Lloyd in February, 1857. Three towing companies were acquired with the new NDL shares and merged, with a fourth, an insurance company, included in the fusion.

Name Year Built	Builder	Lloyd. Years	Tons	H.P.	Speed	Pass/ Crew	L x W.

As prior history:

1. *Telegrapf*
| 1840 | Millwall, London | | 45 | 9.1 | | | 30.00 x 6.65 |

This preceded the Lloyd services. It had an eating facility, small cargo room, ran Bremen-Brake-Bremerhaven, also into the North Sea to Norderney, Wangerooge, Greetsiel, Leer and Emden. Later NDL reported wrongly that "*Telegraph* seems to have disappeared in 1857." Kuke has it "1872 sold to State for BU." Certainly, through the 1856 season *Telegraph* ran to the North Sea islands.

Taken over from the Weser and Hunte Dampfschiffahrts Gesellschaft: It was founded in 1842. Its three vessels were entered for 61, 200 Thaler. NDL paid 82,080 Thaler in shares for these low-pressure iron vessels. Their registration was forgotten in the hurry of merger, was not made until 1874. Fifty pounds of baggage was carried free. With *Roland* these three served 1857-1863 on the Lower Weser.

2. *Hanseat*
| 1845 | Gâche Freres, Paris | 1857-1884 | 83 | 48 | 9 | 243/324 | 10.40 x 4.52 |

From 17/11/1845 ran Bremen-Elsfleth-Brake, on 1/3/1957 opened NDL's Bremerhaven route, from the Grosse Fischerstrasse. 1884 sold for M4,500.

Norderney *with the first vessel to provide regular service to the Friesian Islands into 1857. From 1920, NDL leased the Kurhaus here.*

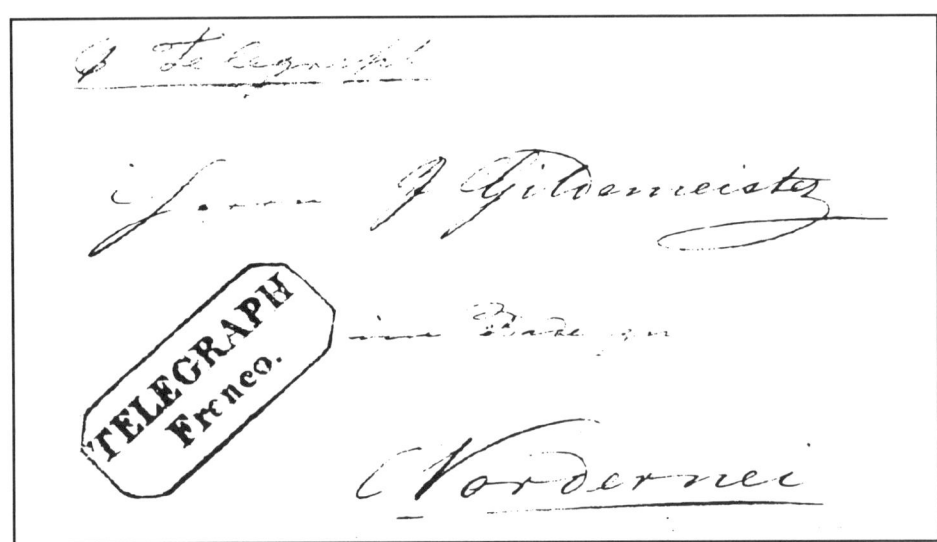

Envelope in the form of a folded letter written and posted on board Telegraph *to Herrn J. Gildermeister in the Resort at Nordernei. Some six of these are known.*

Hanseat *was one of three Weser and Hunte River steamers taken over by NDL in 1857 from the Weser and Hunte S.S. Company, one of three River shipping units merged to form the new Lloyd.*
Photo: Landes (Focke) Museum, Bremen.

Simson, taken over by the Lloyd in 1857. It was the longest in service of any vessel ever under the crossed key and anchor flag. Into 1933!

3. Oldenburg
1845   Gâche Freres, Paris   1857-1873   83   48   9   243/324   10.40 x 4.52
Sold 1873, ending NDL's passenger service on the Hunte River.

4. Paul Friedrich August
1846   Gâche Freres, Paris   1857-1873   104   48   9   243/324   40.60 x 4.52
From 1858 also ran in the North Sea, there could carry only 243 vs 324 on the river. 1874 entered as Seeschiff. 1888 sold for BU. These three supplied cash flow for the Lloyd right from the beginning. Sometimes replaced *Roland II*. 1873 briefly ran on the Ems River.

Taken over from the Schleppschiffahrt Gesellschaft auf der Unterweser were 12 iron barges and three sidewheel steamers:

5. Simson
Joh. Lange, Vegesack #207   1857-1933   187   145   8.5   333/250   38.07 x 6.72
Launched 14/6/1854. *Simson* was the longest in Lloyd service, as tug, tender, icebreaker and salvage vessel. It was built for Captain Schwarz. It had more horsepower than the first "Birds" NDL sent to England. Repeatedly rebuilt. 1875 lost its aft deck in the *Mosel* #34 explosion. 1884 got new engines of 200 HP. With *Pilot* and *Comet* ran between the Weser and the Elbe. In the 1893 examination by Germanischer Lloyd it was evident *Simson* was not worth the needed repair costs. The engine was taken out; the hull first used as lighter then as coal hulk. As the *Nordsee*, *Simson* kept its name instead of a number. BU in 1933.

6. Vorwärts
1856   Maschinenfabrick Buckau   1857-1877   148   8   79   260/195   36.56 x 6.65
Built as *Marschall Vorwärts* for the Ges. für Dampfschiffahrt mit England, mostly ran as tug, sometimes with deck structure added for passengers. 1853 to Schleppschiffahrts Ges. auf der Unterweser. 1877 sold.

7. Vulkan
1857   Carsten J. Waltjen #4   1857-1896   148   8   260   36.56 x 6.65
Building at time of NDL's founding. 1858 towing on the Lower Weser. 1891 listed by Lindemann as 200 tons, 300 HP. 1896 sold.

Gesellschaft für eine Dampfschiffahrt auf der Weser was bought with Th 36,820 NDL shares. The firm contracted on 12/12/1856 with the future NDL to join the fusion.

8. Werra
7/1855   C. J. Waltjen #2   1857-1873   114   7   284   45.72 x 5.30
Werra ran on 15 February, 1857 as first NDL tug on the Upper Weser from Bremen to Preuss. From 1/4/1858 also carried passengers. When at end of 1859 *Hameln*, *Münden* and *Carlshafen* were laid up because of low water in the Upper Weser, *Werra* and *Fulda* were the only Lloyd tugs on that stretch. Also ran to Hameln. From 1/4/1863 carried passengers downstream from Minden when the freight load allowed this. 4/1873 with *Wittekind*, *Armin* and *Germania* sold to the Weser Dampfschiffahrts Gesellschaft in Preuss.

9. *Fulda*
1856   C. J. Waltjen #3   1857-1895   114   7   284   45.72 x 5.30

Began NDL service on 15/2/1857 as tug. From 1/4/1858 carried passengers between Bremen and Preuss. Carried passengers downstream when traffic allowed. 4/1873 transferred to Lower Weser when NDL gave up service on the upper stretch. From 1883 *Fulda II*. 31/12/1891 listed by Lindemann as 153 tons, 240 HP. Sold 1895.

After the fusion of the above three enterprises in Spring 1857 NDL bought the Gesellschaft zur Betreibung einer Dampfschiffahrt auf der Weser with one vessel:

10. *Roland*
1848   C. J. Waltjen #1   1857-1898   187   80   9.5   425   49.36 x 6.37

Roland was given the reworked engines of *Roland* 1839-1847. Iron hull. On 28/6/1857 per NDL's first advertisement *Roland* would make the first NDL resort voyage to Norderney across the Wattenmeer (almost mud flats) by Wangerooge. It made 21 such trips. The judgment of the Resort commissioners was that "*Roland* is well

Above: Roland *became NDL's first vessel to go out into the North Sea across the Watten Meer, the coastal flats that at low tides extend miles out; the incoming tide racing across the sands and mud, often catching daring persons unawares.* Ex Arnold Kludas Collection.

Left: An early advertisement for the Roland's *five-hour trip to Norderney. The service was for residents mostly as often the ship had to spend the night there.*

equipped." It was urged that the channel be buoyed because "His Majesty, the King frequently used it." On 12/6/1858 *Roland* took 170 guests from Bremen to Bremerhaven for the trials of *Bremen* #7, NDL's first vessel to New York. *Pilot* brought them back. In 1872 *Roland* ran the first steamer connection Norddeich-Norderney after the coastal railway from Emden was extended to Norddeich, site in later years of Germany's main radio station to keep contact with ships overseas. 1882 rebuilt with new engines, 450 HP, 12 knots. Through the 1884 season served the various resorts, including Helgoland. 1885 served Lower Weser cities as far as Bremerhaven. 13/4/1895 listed as inland waters vessel. 1897 sold for BU.

Shortly after the founding 12 additional tow-lighters, Nr.12-23 were ordered from James Watt, the inventor of the Steam Engine, for £15 500, and the following three sidewheelers. Their cost Th 36,582. They were to serve on the Lower Weser, but could not as water levels were too low.

11. *Hameln*
1857   James Watt, London   1857-1919   46.20 x 5.08
Ordered for Lower Weser towing. From 1/10/1858 ran Minden-Hameln. From 1860 the low water made all three unusable. 1864 cut in two and rebuilt as lighters, Nr.27 and Nr.28. Engines later built into *Nordsee*. In Spring, 1919 sold to J. H. Schupp, Hamburg, renamed *Hertha* and *Annemarie*.

12. *Carlshafen*
1857   James Watt, London   1857-   46.20 x 5.08
1861 cut in two, rebuilt as lighters Nr.25 and Nr.26. 1867 one of the engines was built into *Cyklops*.

13. *Münden*
1857   James Watt, London   1857-1919   46.20 x 5.08
On 12/2/1859 pushed-towed, like on the Mississippi, the first towing train to *Münden* in Hannover, still then under the British Crown, under an agreement between NDL and several shippers that they would allow their cargoes to be towed only by the Lloyd's tugs. 1864 cut in two, lighters Nr.29 and Nr.30, engine put into *Nordsee*. In 1919 sold to J. H. Schupp, Hamburg, renamed *Luise* and *Ilse*.

During 1857-1858 the C. & W. Earle, shipyard in Hull built six 125' lighters.

In the Fall of 1857 NDL bought the Vereinigte Weser Dampfschiffahrts Gesellschaft, Hameln, founded 1847, the following five sidewheelers, some lighters, a building slipway, some working sheds and the landing pier in Hameln for 30,700 Thaler in Lloyd shares.

14. *Blücher*
1844   In Prussia   1857-1865
1858 ran on the Upper Weser, carrying passengers, and as tug with *Wittekind* and *Aller*. 1865 BU as repairs not held worthwhile.

15. *Wittekind*
1844   Buckauer Maschinenfabrik 1857-1873
4/1848 ran on Upper Weser, later also on the Middle Weser with *Blücher* and *Aller*. At low-water times ran as "the rapid steamer *Wittekind*" between Bremen and Brake, also did towing. 1863-1874 only carried passengers, did some towing on the Middle Weser. 4/1873 with *Werra*, *Armin* and *Germania* sold to the Weser Dampfschiffahrt Gesellschaft in Preuss when Upper Weser towing was given up.

16. *Germania*
1844   Gâche Freres, Paris   1857-1873   38   43.59 x 5.18
1873 sold to W. Langer, Hameln for the Oberweser Dampfschiffart Gesellschaft. 1876 ceded to the Neue Oberweser Dampfschiffart. 1881 out of service.

17. *Hermann*
1843   Gâche Freres, Paris   1857-1873   38   43.59 x 5.18
Sister of *Germania*. 1869 renamed *Armin*. 4/1873 sold to W. Lang with *Germania*. 1881 out of service.

18. *Aller*
1845   Gâche Freres, Paris   1857-1860   38   43.59 x 5.18
Built as *Weser*. 1860 put out of service as held too weakly built for the demanding needs of passenger and towing operation. Also had engine difficulties.

19. *Comet.*
1857   Palmer Brothers, Yarrow   1857-1897   107   73   9.5   100/7   34.29 x
Iron sidewheeler. I.S. 1/10/1857. With sister *Pilot* handled the towing on the Lower Weser. From 1863 did the towing between the Weser and Elbe. 1891 carried by Lindemann as 180 HP. Sold 1897. Into 1908 still in Lloyd's Register.

20. *Pilot*
1858   Palmer Brothers, Yarrow   1858-1879   107   73   9.5   100/7   34.30 x
I.S. on 15/2/1858, towing on the Lower Weser and from 1863 to Hamburg. Nineteen such trips. Certificate for 100 passengers on the Weser. 1879 sold to the Bugsier Gesellschaft "Union", Bremen.

21. *Nordsee*
1865   C. J. Waltjen #6   1865-1933   153   * *   9.5   46.88 x 6.61
Was to have been named *Pionier*. Stuck during launch; took days to work it loose. Given the engines from *Hameln* and *Münden* when coverted to lighters. First twin-screw vessel on the Weser. 16/6/1866 for the first time showed the Lloyd flag in Helgoland. From 18/7/1866 sailed from Geestemünde, closer to the railway station. Through 1885 in resort service, also to Wyk. After the season, the saloon was dismantled. Then served as high-seas tug. 12/10/1870 saved the crews of three foreign vessels stranded in the Jade River: USS *Merrimack*, *Morning Glory* and the British *Gloucestershire*. 1/1887 rebuilt to towing barge and coal hulk, kept its name. 20/1/1933 BU, second-longest for NDL after *Simson*. It carried the Silver Emblem for Service in the Lloyd Register.

22. *Cyklop*
1867   C. J. Waltjen #8   1867-1895   129   200   9.5   252/8   35.02 x
I.S. 1/10/1867 with engine from *Carlshafen*. 1891 in Weser-Elbe towing connection. Sold 1895.

In 1870, NDL had 20 high-seas vessels, 8 Birds running to Britain, 16 small tugs, tenders and resort vessels.

23. *Lloyd I*
1870   C. J. Waltjen #12   1870-1914   390   350   9   297   50.29 x 6.61
Ordered for 61,000 Thaler. Ran as Bremen Boat on the Lower Weser, in the 1880s as tender between the Lloyd Hall and the Steamers lying out in the roads. This eased the transfer of passengers to and from the ships as often they lay in the stream because of tidal circumstances. 1899 to E. Lepont, NDL agent in Cherbourg to serve as Tender for the steamers on the New York line. 1910 registered for Agence Maritime, Cherbourg, 321 tons. Evidently transferred to Bremerhaven. Ran excursions. 1914 BU. Neubaur in 1907 listed as 450 HP. There were several vessels named *Lloyd* at home and overseas. They are impossible to know which was where, or their size. Few ever saw print.

In July, 1872 NDL bought two steamer from Frau Anna Lange, the widow of Shipbuilder Johann Lange. His yard was the forerunner of the Bremer Vulkan, Vegesack-Lobbendorf just below Bremen.

24. *Bremerhaven*
1847   Joh. Lange #176   1872-1893   117   150   9   394/296   52.42 x 4.89
Launched 29/6/1847 as *Bremen*. These two vessels were sharp competition for the Lloyd as Frau Lange offered low fares. 1872 with sale to NDL renamed. Ran Bremen-Bremerhaven. 1893 sold for BU.

This notice from Lloyd's Register advises the Lloyd in Bremen that it's tender Lloyd *has been transferred to E. Lepont in Cherbourg. Lepont was the Lloyd agent in Cherbourg. Below: Willkommen #29 and Lloyd #23 were NDL's tenders in Cherbourg. Both sidewheelers.*

Card written on a Lloyd ship to a friend back in San Francisco: "Tomorrow we intend to celebrate my birthday in Paris." The card bears the Bremen-New York Sea Post of 14.5.09. Willkommen #29 and Lloyd #23 were NDL's tenders in Cherbourg. Both sidewheelers.

Gutenberg *and its running-mate on the Weser* Bremerhaven *were bought by NDL from a competitor, the Widow Lange, who was charging lower fares.* Gutenberg *was immediately resold; the other ran for NDL for another twenty years.* Gutenberg *took off the passengers from* Washington *on its first arrival in Bremerhaven in June, 1947, the first U.S. trans-Atlantic steamer line. Bremen became the U.S. outpost, even with a branch U.S. postal agency, into the 1930s, apart from the intervening war.*

25. *Gutenberg.*
1845   Joh. Lange, Lobbendorf #164

Launched 11/10/1845. His first ship built entirely from iron, for his own account. Proved difficult competition for the Lloyd on the Lower Weser. 19/6/1847 carried the passengers of the just-arrived in Bremerhaven U.S. Steamer *Washington* of the Ocean Steam Navigation Co. to Bremen. This was the first trans-Atlantic steamer to reach Bremerhaven, built from 1827 as Bremen's outer port. 1858 lengthened by 20' by Lange. 7/1872 bought by NDL for 14,000 Thaler to remove the competition, immediately resold and "disappeared from Lower Saxony river traffic activities."

Register 621

A schedule of 18 May, 1872 in the Landes (Focke) Museum in Bremen indicates:
Passenger traffic on the Weser and Hunte: Bremen-Bremerhaven 2 times a day
Bremen-Vegesack - 1 trip
Bremen-Bremerhaven-Oldenburg - 1 daily round trip
Upper Weser: Münden-Minden 2x the week
Münden-Hameln 4x in the week
Carlshafen-Minden - 4x in the week
Bremen-Stolzenau - 2x the week
Stolzenau-Hameln - 2x in the week.

26. *Triton*
| 1874 | J. L. Meyer & Barth, Papenburg | 1874-1896 | 133 | 200 at sea 9.5 | 9 | 34.99 x 5.62 |

Delivery 3/1875. Sidewheeler. Ran as tug, tender and resort steamer. 22/1/1896 sold to G. Seebeck, Geestemünde, served as tug for the shipyard.

Sidewheelers were built until well into the Twentieth Century because they could navigate waters too shallow for propeller craft. Triton *served the Lloyd for 22 years.*

27. *Vorwärts*
| 1879 | C. J. Waltjen #39 | 1879-1897 | 148 | | 275 | 32.98 x 5.52 |

Iron sidewheeler, built as tug. 12/1890 rescued with *Reiher #27* 16 shipwrecked in the North Sea. 1/1891 went to Norderney to help the ferries *Katherine Elisabeth* and Steamer *Norden*, both caught in the ice, and to take off their passengers. 1894 still in register.

In 1880 during high floods on the Weser NDL charted a steamer *Hermann*.

28. *Forelle*
| | H. F. Ulrichs | 1881-1919 | 298, also 442/576 | 540 | 14 | 560- 600 | 61.26 x 6.16 |

Launched 11/11/1880. Sidewheeler. Was to have run on the Lower Weser, but due to low water ran as resort steamer Bremerhaven-Norderney. First vessel built specifically for resort service. This ended the use of the convertible resort steamers-tugs, like *Nordsee*. 1891 ran Bremen-Bremerhaven, 1909 Bremen-Vegesack-Brake. 1919 sold to B. W. Riedemann, remained on the Weser for various owners and several names: *Strandlust, Weserland* into 1932, 1933 BU.

There are four Lloyd river vessels, with the two sidewheelers Lachs *#36, in the foreground, and* Forelle *#28 in the middle. There are enough top hats in the audience to indicate the special affair it was: the festive dedication of Bremen's Free Port on 21 October, 1888.*

29. *Willkommen*
1884   J. C. Tecklenborg, Geestemünde
                                              1884-1907   500   207   10   500/875   54.01 x 7.8

Iron sidewheeler. Built as Tender and Tug. 19/3/1884 took out passengers to *Eider* #55 for its maiden departure. Account from *Zur See*, 1890s: "The express steamer *Eider* lies in the Great Basin (inside Bremerhaven's harbor), then anchors out in the river to receive the last passengers and mail so it can depart at any tide. Two trains come from Bemen, one with some 600 Tweendeckers, the other with the Class passengers and mail, which is heaped up on the foredeck. Just before *Eider* reaches *Rothesand* Lighthouse Willkommen takes on board those going back ashore. Sold 1907 to E. Lepont, Lloyd Agent in Cherbourg, 580 HP, was stationed there with *Lloyd* of 1870, tendered for the New York Line vessels. 1921 named *Castor*, 1922 *L'Avenir*, 1935 BU in Inverkeithing.

30. *Retter*
    J. C. Tecklenborg, Geestemunde
    1885-1924   * *   392   740   13   12   46.12 x 7.50

Delivery 3/1885. Two stacks, build as salvage steamer, carried vacationers out into the North Sea. 1893 361 tons. 1914-1918 served in the Kaiserliche Marine. LU in 1924. 29/4/1925 sold for BU. A humourous incident in *Retter's* varied service as tender, tug and salvage vessel:

In November, 1923 *Retter* had a contract job towing the Russian-owned *Yaroslav*, sequestered by the British during the war and now being returned, from Milford Haven to Einswarden for scrapping. The tow headed up the English Channel, through the Strait of Dover into the

Retter *is the black-hulled vessel among the white ones in the Helgoland roads. The people are awaiting visitors from the ships. Helgoland has more visitors annually than even Capri and other island destinations.*

Register 623

North Sea and worsening weather. The tow passed Haaks Fireship off the Holland coast, then headed N.E. towards Terschelling Island. On the 20th, the tow line breaks, anchors are dropped by *Yaroslav* by the small crew on board. The anchor chain breaks. *Yaroslav* is washed over a sand bank and settles onto the bottom. Nothing *Retter* could do; it headed home. The local Doeksen salvage Company floated the ship in July, 1924. It was towed to Genoa for breakup.

The following happened near the end of the Christmas mail voyage made by *Kaiser Wilhelm der Grosse* after it lost a propeller en route to New York in December, 1910: P.330-332 Volume I. Told by 2. Officer W. Drechsel:

"It was about 8 a.m. on 24 December. We were running along the North Sea coast with following current when we saw near Borkum to starboard a small vessel. Soon we recognized it as our own *Retter*, stopped waiting for us. With no wind, we could not read his hoisted signal. *Retter* turned to come closer to us on starboard. Captain Polack, who had had little sleep since leaving Cherbourg, told me:'ask him what he wants.' As we came closer to *Retter* we could see our Navigation Inspector Captain W. Meissel (former Inspector in Hong Kong who brought the shipwrecked *München* #72 from Yap to the colony for repairs). Through a megaphone he shouted: 'Stop at once; I am coming on board.' Captain Polack told us officers:'anybody who touches that telegraph is a dead man.' By then we were far past him, tooting away.

As was customary, we had taken the Weser Pilot on board at Cherbourg. He and Captain Polack brought us quickly alongside the Lloyd Hall in Bremerhaven so passengers and mail could get off rapidly, most still to keep Christmas Eve. Captain Polack went ashore to catch some sleep. It was my port-watch turn into Christmas Day morning. About 5 p.m. *Retter* arrived. Captain Meissel came on board to see Captain Polack. I excused him, said we dared not lose the tide, already being late because of steaming with only one propeller. So Captain Polack had given up serving him a hot Grog. But the 'Thunder and Lightning' did land on me from Captain Meissel, less hard because it was Christmas. After the holidays, I told Captain Polack what had happened. As consolation for the Donnerwetter he presented me with a box of 25 John Jacob Astor cigars. Mr. Astor had been on board for our New York bound voyage, and he and our Captain were good friends. That was my second present of a box of cigars. See "A Young Again Centenarian."

31. *Hecht*
    A. G. Weser   1885-1913   249   650   13   510/13   54.86 x 6.10
Launched 6/1885. Steel sidewheeler. Tender and substitute resort steamer. Mostly ran Bremen-Vegesack-Brake with *Forelle*. 1913 sold to C. H. Boer, continued running on the Weser. 1920 to H. W. Ritscher for continued river service. 1926 BU in Hamburg.

32. *Libelle*
1885   C. J. Waltjen #78   1885-1915   * *   133   260   12/5   26.36 x 4.60
Mostly ran Bremen-Vegesack-Brake-Blumenthal on the Weser, sometimes with *Gazelle*. 1915 sold, renamed *Anna Luise*. 1920 again *Libelle* for Bernard Riedemann. 1938 still in Germanischer Lloyd register. Evidently BU before the war.

33. *Spica* 1885   FFW

Hecht of 1885 before the Old Lloyd Hall. One of the sidewheelers built for shallow waters.

Mark applied to a card written on KaiserFriedrich and posted on Hecht as it took passengers to the Lloyd Hall in August, 1899.

Herkules #34, and its sister Centaur #37, were iron-hulled. They both served as tugs, even as icebreakers in the very cold winters on the Weser and in Bremerhaven. For use as tenders, as here alongside Rhein *of 1901, they in the season had removable "Promenade Deck." Shelter and eating facilities for passengers. The photo is from an old glassplate.*

34. *Herkules*
C. J. Tecklenborg, Geestemünde   1887-1912   177   380   11   38.86 x

Launched 9/1887. Iron sidewheeler. Served as tug and icebreaker. As resort steamer had a removable "Promenade Deck" housing, taken off after the season. Sister *Centaur*. 2/1909 to N/V Scheepsw. & Koophandel, Slidderveer for BU.

35. *Quelle*
J. C. Tecklenborg, Geestemünde   1888-ca. 1927   350   2   28.99 x 6.80

Launched 7/1888. Tank boat, engine aft. Also river tug? Still 1/1/1926 in fleet list, not 1928 in Germanischer Lloyd but 1932 still in Lloyd's Register. *Quelle* means Source, Spring.

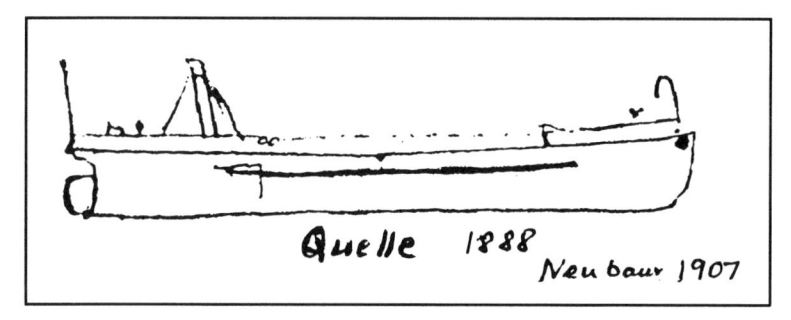

Quelle *was a harbor tanker, taking water out to ships that lay in the river if the tide was not right for landing, or getting ready to sail. Sketch from Neubaur, 1907.*

Puck *and* Neck *evidently were harbor craft, possibly to transfer personnel, take out passengers who missed the sailing. The sketch is from Neubaur, 1907. Without his detailed fiftieth anniversary three-volume history, much of NDL's pictorial past would have been lost.*

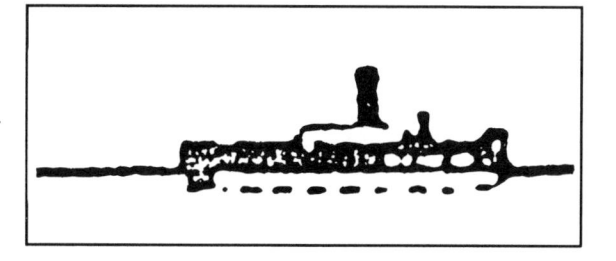

36. *Puck*
1888   A. G. Weser, Bremen   1888-ca. 1923   17   34

37. *Centaur*
1889   A. G. Weser, Bremen #96   1889-pre-1922   177   350   11   38.86 x

Sidwheeler. Towing in the Weser estuary and to Hamburg with *Herkules*. 1913 - 189 tons, 520 HP.

Lachs in typical resort steamer fashion: white-painted sidewheeler, leaving Bremerhaven in the 1920s. It made the first post World War I trip Wilhelmshaven-Wangerooge. It was sold off in 1929 at age forty.

38. Lachs
J. C. Tecklenborg,
   Geestemunde   1889-1929   256   550   13.5   54.86 x 6.10

Launched 5/1889. Sidewheeler for the Lower Weser and Resort service: Bremerhaven-Wangerooge-Norderney. Ascension Day 1919 made the first trip since the war Wilhelmshaven-Wangerooge. 1920 with *Delphin* Bremen-Bremerhaven-Wangerooge. 28/1/1928 sold to B. W. Riedemann. 6/2/1930 renamed *Weserlust*. Riedemann ended its services, sold *Weserland* ex-*Forelle* and *Weserlust* ex *Lachs* for BU. Instead both went to the Navy for target practice. 1933 both sunk in that use.

39. Kehrewieder
J. C. Tecklenborg,
   Geestemünde   1890-1912   477   12   11.7   56.45 x 7.92

Launched 5/1890. Kehrewieder means Come Back Again. Steel sidewheeler. Tender. 1893 reopened NDL's service to Helgoland. 6/1914 brought guests to the launching of *Zeppelin* at the Bremen Vulkan. During the war as auxiliary hospital ship 495 tons. 4/7/1919 ret. to NDL. 1920 to E. A. H. Bouer, Bremen, resold 5/1920 to H. Peters. 12/1933 to Altenwerden, Hamburg for BU.

In September, 1904 the Social Democratic Party met in Bremen. For an outing it chartered *Kehrewieder* for a voyage to Helgoland. Since Captain Paul Vöge had only a Rivers Patent it was illegal for him to command the North Sea voyage. 2. Officer Drechsel from *Kaiser Wilhelm der Grosse* then in port, was asked to be on the bridge with his High-Seas patent. (As told in *Bremen Binnen un Buten*, Dr. Carl Thalenhorst, see "Centenarian").

"In September, 1904 some 300 Social Democratic and families arrived from Bremen for a trip to Helgoland, four hours there, and back. Tall, bearded and very stately, Captain Vöge met them at the gangplank. His mere appearance inspired confidence. He had the years of experience on the river to confirm this. We both understood matters. Under way, we steamed out the river, he, I and the steersman alone on the open bridge. Some of the travellers were so close that soon they dared to ask questions as Captain Vöge told about life on the River and North Sea. Then he touched his cap and said to me in Plattdeutsch, Low German, 'Koptein, wi möt nu erst mal in de Kort kieken.' And proceeded me down the stairs to the canteen on deck. There he told to a strongly built woman 'Mudding, lat us mal in de Kort kieken' Presenting me to his wife, she put two large glasses of cognac before us. They weren't the last, as people came up and asked: 'Is everything all right?' since we weren't on the bridge. It went smoothly until heading into the North Sea *Kehrewieder* began to roll. The liveliness on deck quieted. The musicians who had been playing put their instruments away. Many felt if we could they too could ease their stomachs with 'in de Kort kieken,' looking into the bottle.

In Helgoland few went ashore, not wanting to enter the pitching small-boats used for that purpose. After two hours, we up-anchored and headed south. The sea remained quiet; the music played and all had a good time.

Tender Kehrewieder *alongside the Australia-liner Bremen, painted white for her visit to the Kiel Yachting week and cruise into the Baltic. Hapag-Lloyd Photo. See p.246, Vol. I. Right: Drawing by Herbert Wellmann for the story of the Socialists' outing to Helgoland in 1904.*

About 9 p.m. we tied up alongside. A mass of several thousand with four bands and flaming torches met their fellow Social Democrats. Their leader thanked us heartily in the name of his colleagues, and invited us to be the Party's guest in Bremen. Returning command to Captain Vöge was easy. Mudding (Mother) said to Vadding (Dad): 'We've had a good day.' Vadding replied with a satisfied smile. 'We too, Mudding. Pour us another, but of the best brand.' It was the tail of the evening before I said my goodbyes and headed home."

40. **Vulcan**   200   300
31/12/1891 listed by Lindemann, also in 1893.

41. **Pollux**
1893   Philadelphia   86   24.08 x 5.94
Wooden tug owned by NDL, Captain M. Möller, Inspector in Hoboken, 5 Broadway, New York. So in Eads-Johnson Register.

42. **Roland**
                                  197   450
31/12/1891 and in 1893 listed by Lindemann. Later in NDL fleet lists into 1908. Bremen-Bremerhaven route. A *Roland* shipwrecked 1912 in service from Rabaul around Blanche Bay to plantations.

43. **Saturn**
    G. Seebeck A. G.,
    Geestemünde   120   240   29.43 x
Launched 6/1893. First of a series of almost-sisters tugs. Not listed 1/1/1922.

44. **Najade**
    F. Schichau, Elbing #544
    1894-1929   570/724   1800   16   30   71.21 x 9.28
Launched 4/1894. Resort sidewheeler to Norderney and Borkum. From 1898 ran with *Nixe* Naples-Capri-Ischia. 1914-1918 in naval service. 3/4/1919 back to NDL. April, 1920 one of four Resort steamers- Tenders who brought East Prussians to their plebiscite voting sites. Later ran Bremerhaven-Helgoland-Norderney. 1929 with *Bügermeister Smidt* sold to Rotterdam for BU.

Silhouette from Neubaur, 1907, of eight almost-sisters tugs built for the Lloyd by G. Seebeck A.G., in Geestemünde: Saturn, Neptun, Merkur, Vulcan, Comet, Cyklop, Triton, Arion.

Najade *was the largest of the resort sidewheelers built so far, in 1894. She used a lovely On The Seas mark in 1903.*

45. Neptun
    G. Seebeck A. G.,
    Geestemünde   1895-1930   78   200   23.72 x
Launched 3/1895

46. Merkur
    G. Seebeck A. G.,
    Geestemünde   1895-1930   124   360   29.16 x

Launched 12/1895. In October, 1919 the Allies blockaded the Baltic Sea which "for three weeks prevented any traffic in the Sea." *Merkur* was in the Baltic when the blockade was imposed with two lighters en route to Königsberg. A French torpedoboat forced the train to proceed to Libau where it lay in the roads until released. (NDL 1919/20). Out of service 1926.

47. Comet
1895   G. Seebeck A.G.
    Geestemünde   1896-1933   78   220   23.62

Sister of *Neptun*. I.S. as *Peter Friedrich*. 1896 bought by NDL. By 1938 with Bugsier Reederei und Bergungs A. G., Hamburg, after rebuild as salvage vessel. 1952 BU.

48. Cyclop
    G. Seebeck A. G.,
    Geestemünde   1896-1927   73   220   23.62

Launched 10/1896. Sister of *Neptun* and *Comet* 4/3/1914 with Nr.12 and Nr.19 in tow with tobacco and other freight from *Prinz Friedrich Wilhelm* in from New York in the night en route Bremerhaven to Bremen was cut in two by the British *S. S. Apollo*, 3,774 Ts., Century Shipping Co., departing for Australia.

Unusual but lovely ship-board mark from Seeadler, *built in 1897: "On Board the Twin-Screw, Mail Express steamer." The message reads: Today heavy storm and thunder. North Sea 23.7.11. Evidently the writer was on board* Seeadler, *to where?*

49. *Vulcan*
G. Seebeck A. G.,
Geestemünde   1896-1930   124   360   29.16
Launched 10/1896. Sister of *Merkur* #46. Lloyd records show both with "c". They inter-change.

50. *Vulkan*
Shanghai Shipbldg.
& Dock Co.   1896-1917   * *   28.96 x 6.34
Launched 9/1896. 1917 seized by China with its entry into the war, assigned to Shanghai Tug & Lighter Co., renamed *Vulcan*. 1929 to Taku Tug & Lighter Co., but 1931 still in Register under Shanghai Tug. From Advertisement in N.Y.K. 1931 Yearbook. Served with *Scott* ex-*Bremen* of 1899.

51. *Seeadler*
G. Seebeck A. G. Geestemünde #121
1897-1924   * *   532   950   13.5   600/14   49.98 x 7.99
Launched 1/1897. Two stacks. 1898 briefly under French flag for NDL in Cherbourg. 1906 left Bremerhaven to tow *Hohenzollern* #70 from Crete to Genoa with broken propeller shaft. 1909 ran Helgoland-Amrun-Wyk. 1913-1914 Wilhelmshaven-Helgoland, Mondays direct Wilhelmshaven-Bremerhaven and return. The on-deck passenger structure was dismantled after the season. Also served as tug or salvage vessel. 1914-1919 barrage clearing ship. 1924 to W. Schuchmann, Bremen for salvage work, renamed *Seewolf*. 1926 to Portuguese Government, Colonial Dept. 1934 renamed *Infante dom Enrique*. 1939 BU.

52. *Planet*
A. G. Weser, Bremen #117 1897-9/1954   44   120   20.00 x 4.20
Launched 3/1897. At selloff oldest tug in NDL service.

Planet *and* Oldenburg *built ten years apart were near-sisters.* Planet *was the first tug still in Lloyd service when finally sold in 1954. Ex. Neubaur - 1907.*

Undine *was built as tender for the occasional stops made at Gibraltar, by the Italy-New York line and some of the Far East Line vessels.* Hapag-Lloyd Photo.

53. Undine
R. Holtz, Hamburg   1899-1917   76   130
Launched 6/1899. Tender in Gibraltar. On 26/3/1902 sent to Bangkok to carry passengers to-from Kohsichang. 22/7/1917 seized by Siam. FFW. Replaced by *Grille*.

54. Bremen
1899   S. C. Farnham & Co.,
       Shanghai   1899-1905   211   385   35.05 x 6.43
Tug and tender for NDL in Shanghai. 1905 to Shanghai Tug & Lighter Co., renamed *Scott*. Salvage Steamer? 193? to Taku Tug & Lighter Co., renamed *Yungting*. 1942 war loss in Singapore.

55. Nixe
1899   G. Seebeck A. G.,
       Geestemünde #134   1899-1924   843   2180   16.5   573/32   75.47 x 9.92
Launched 5/1899 Sidewheeler. Summers in resort service, winters in Bay of Naples. Two stacks. Prewar given wireless. 1914-1918 Tender in Kaiserliche Marine. 1920 in Sea Service to East Prussia. 1921 - 728 Ts. After the 1924 season sold to Nord-Ostsee Handels Transport Ges., Alwyn Meyer, Altona. 1927 with Reederei "Frisia," Altona for service to Helgoland. 1928 to Victor Schuppe, Berlin for Stettin-Swinemünde-Bornholm-Sassnitz route. 1930 sold to Holland for BU but sank in storm 2/1/1930 on delivery voyage. Variously measured: 1908-2000 HP. 1925 - 802 tons, 1900 HP.

In 1898, NDL organized a winter service in the Bay of Naples to Sorrento, Capri, Ischia and Procida. Until

Nixe *of 1899 served summers in the resort service to the Friesian Islands, winters in the Bay of Naples.*

then, only small local craft were available, not up to standards expected by foreign visitors. In some weeks, two to four Lloyd ships called at Naples.

At the end of 1901, Captain Walter Freye returned from voyages to Australia and Baltimore. When he reported to Captain Friedrich (made voyage reports in Bremen), he was told: "You are to take *Nixe* to Naples to take up her new service there." Captain Freye's report: "We left Bremerhaven on 9 January, 1902 and crossed the North Sea and the English Channel in tourist weather. *Nixe* with her sharp bow cut through the roughest seas as we crossed the Bay of Biscay.

Being a broad sidewheeler prevented her from rolling. Not a drop came onto the deck altho the entire ship vibrated with the crush of the waves when the shovel casing hit. A sudden gust of air from there blew off Captain Freye's cap. At that moment the speaking tube from the engine room announced that one of the stokers had gone mad. Captain and boatsmans' mate jumped down from the bridge just in time to see some one climbing the railing. He was taken to one of the rooms with bunk, chair and table just aft of the shovel housing. When the ship was running this room could not be used because of the noise of rushing water. Only in port was it usable. The stoker was laid there.

He seemed to be allright when the weather cleared the next day. For two days dense fog kept us from taking observations to determine our exact location. Then suddenly a clear moment gave us one line, the crosspoint in the sextant. We knew we were on the line from Cape Trafalgar to Gib but how far along? Then the fog cleared and we saw the Cape Trafalgar light house 3 miles ahead. On the 29th we reached Naples and turned *Nixe* over to Captain de Vries." Freye returned to Bremerhaven on *Prinzess Irene* on 4 February. He reported to Captain Traue on *Willehad* #89, but was given a few days leave before the ship left for Baltimore.

56. *Triton*
G. Seebeck A. G.,
Bremerhaven   1900-1954   123   340   29.14 x 5.88

Launched 9/1900. Sister of *Arion*, and *Saturn*, 1893 1907 - 270 HP. 9/1954 one of nine over-age tugs sold, still coal-burners.

57. *Arion*
G. Seebeck A. G.,
Bremerhaven   1899-1944   500   123   340   29.14 x 5.88

Launched 9/1990. Sister of *Triton*. 1927 - 270 HP. 23/8/1944 scuttled in Bordeaux when Germans evacuated.

Below: Arion *and* Triton *are enlarged versions of the eight earlier near-sisters G. Seebeck A.G. built.* Triton *lasted into 1954, still a coalburner. Arnold Kludas Collection.* Grille *(right), built in Genoa, succeeded* Undine *as tender in Gibraltar.* Hapag-Lloyd Photo.

58. *Gazelle*
    G. Seebeck A. G.,
    Geestemünde   1901-1915   * *   121   270   32.22 x

Launched 5/1901. Resort steamer. 1904 ran Bremen-Vegesack-Brake, later also to Farge with *Libelle*. 1915 sold. In World War II sent to Antwerp. FFW.

59. *Grille*
    N. Odero & Co., Genoa   1901-1915   112   150   10   24.32

Delivery 10/1901. Replaced *Undine* as tender in Gibraltar. Winters ran in Gulf of Naples to Sorrento-Capri-Ischia. 1914 LU in Algeciras. 6/1920 bought by M. H. Bland, Gibraltar, renamed *Zweena*. 1948 to H. L. Barton, Gibraltar for BU.

60. *Glückauf*
1901 A. G. Weser,   736
      Bremen #129   1901-1927   * *   950   12   850/17   62.80 x 12.72

Launched 4/1901. IS 1/6/1901 for Helgoland route. Used also as tender and tug. 1916 in Kaiserliche Marine. 31/12/1918 back to NDL. 1919 rebuilt as coastal freighter with 400 tons capacity and tug for the wood-import trade from Finland-Sweden-Holland. Until completion of *Vegesack* #279 in 9/1920 was NDL's only freighter. 3/7/1927 to Cie. Francaise de Navigation for use as tender in Cherbourg, renamed *Atlas*. 6/1935 BU by Van Heyghen Freres, Ghent.

61. *Mars*
    G. Seebeck A. G.,
    Bremerhaven   1902-1938?   74   250   23.99

Launched 11/1902. River tug. 1939 still in Germanischer Lloyd register.

I. O. G. T.
Alkoholfreie Helgoland-Fahrt

Donnerstag, 21. Mai (Himmelfahrt)
morgens 5 Uhr, vom Anleger im Freihafen I
mit dem
Salon-Dampfer des Nordd. Lloyd „Glückauf", Kpt. de Vries.
Vorzügliche Küche. — Auf der Rückfahrt **Ball** an Bord.

Preis der Karte im Vorverkauf 5 M. an Bord 6 M. Karten sind in den Logenhäusern Georgstr. 37, Süderstr. 22a, Vegesackerstraße 43/45 und da, wo unsere Plakate aushängen, zu haben.

Advertisement for an Alcohol-Free cruise to Helgoland on Ascension Day, 1925? departure 5 a.m. Outstanding Kitchen on board. On the return trip a Ball on Board. Price 5 Marks, 6 if bought on board. "Saloon-Steamer of the Nordd.Lloyd Glückauf." Below Vorwärts *66 and* Glückauf *60, both built as tenders and for resort services, here are in a montage showing the Lloyd's Express steamer* Kronprinzessin Cecilie *arriving. The fact the two tenders waited at the Old Lloyd Hall in Bremerhaven indicates the ship probably had to anchor in the stream to await the right tide to enter the harbor. The card bears the U.S.-German Sea P.O. #13 of Dec. 20, 1912. The message mentions "beastly weather" and having "passed the* George Washington *yesterday." It was en route to New York, had Christmas at sea.*

Capella. *An eighty tons vessel, no record of where and how it was used. Built in 1903.*

62. Capella
    J. L. Meyer, Papenburg   1903-1920   80   1250   220   20.24 x 6.00
Launched 2/1903.

63. Meteor
    H. Fack, Itzehoe   1904-1921   57   220   21.83
Launched 9/1904. River tug. 1921 to Reederei Niederelbe, Hamburg. 1928 out of service.

64. Pollux
1905   J. Drewes, Groningen   1905-1933   63   250
River Tug. 1933 still in Germanischer Lloyd register, not 1934. Also listed as 71 tons, 280 HP.

65. Delphin
1905   A. G. Weser, Bremen #147   1905-1951   381   1050   14   19   57.97 x 7.22
Delivery 3/1905. Sidewheeler for Bremerhaven-Wangerooge route, very shallow waters in which sidewheelers with their lesser draft can operate. Later closed saloon added. 1905 opened the Wilhelmshaven-Wangerooge-Spiekeroog-Bremen route. 1909 ran daily with *Lachs* Bremen-Bremerhaven-Wangerooge. 6/1914 brought guests from Bremen to Vegesack for launch of *Zeppelin*. 1935 - 404 tons. 1946-1950 ran to Wangerooge and Norderney. 1951 after she had stranded off Wangerooge and heavily damaged sold off.

Delphin *still was in service in 1939 on the route to Wangerooge, still with ship-name mark, and the Purser's signature.* Delphin *was built in 1905 with an open bridge and no saloon on the main deck. This was added later and some cabins as the ships running to Wangerooge could not always return the same day. Photo by C. Joske, Hamburg.*

Register   633

This card was written on Delphin, *and its name-stamp used as canceller, very unusual and rare. This was in July, 1919, when postwar activities were just being allowed by the Allies to Germany. The writer is addressing her husband evidently still in an Army Railway building company.*

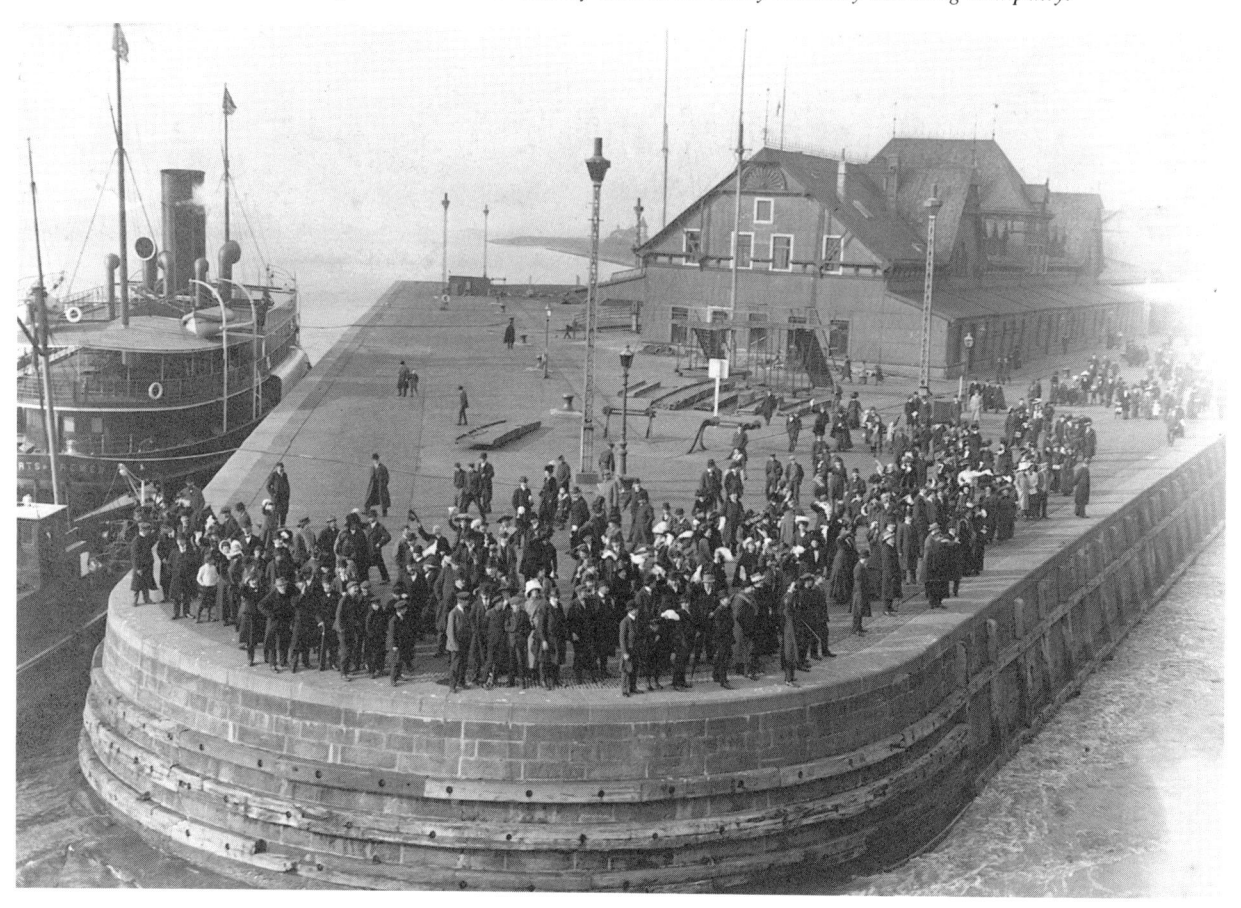

Steamer Vorwärts *at the Old Lloyd Hall in Bremerhaven, ready to take out to the departing steamer anchored in the stream, the last passengers and mail. Photo from 1906.*

Vorwärts, *built in 1906 for use as a resort steamer and tender, with twin screws. The card was written on board "On the High Seas," postmarked at Brunsbüttelkoog, the Elbe River end of the Kiel Canal.*

66. *Vorwärts*
1906	Bremer Vulkan,	1906-		758			
	Vegesack #494	1938	* *	960	12.5	1040/17	62.79 x 9.50

Launched 19/5/1906. Designed as resort steamer and tender. 7/1912 was tender for *Bremen* #99 during its 17-days based in Kiel for excursions during the 25th anniversary celebrations of the Kiel Yacht Club. 1918 with the Finland Expedition with *Grüssgott* and five Lloyd transports. 7/1920 with Sea Service-East Prussia, brought 250 Polish emigrants to Bremerhaven, then train to Rotterdam and U.S.-flag steamer to America. 1921 - 726 tons. 10/1926 used for harbor tour for President von Hindenburg during a visit to *M.S. Fulda* #307 in Bremen. 3/5/1938 to Leth & Co., Hamburg, resold to Kriegsmarine as U-Boat tender, renamed *Warnow*. 1945 taken over by Britain as prisoner vessel. 1948 bought by Hapag, rebuilt, again named *Vorwärts*. 9/9/1951 with 400 Helgolanders voyaged there but not allowed to land. Not until 1/3/1952 was the island returned to German control. 15/11/1952 sold to Eisen & Metall, Hamburg-Altenwarder for BU, not worth rebuilding to register requirements.

67. *Castor*
	Th. Wilminck, Groningen	1906-1954	65	220

Launched 10/1906. Sister of *Jupiter*. 1/1/1922 - 250 HP. 9/1954 sold for BU in Bremerhaven.

68. *Bremen*
1906	Shanghai Dock & Eng. Co.	1906-1917	* *	209	276		42.67 x 7.62

Seized 1917 by China with its entry into the war, to Shanghai Tug & Lighter Co., renamed *Scott*, Salvage steamer. 8/12/1941 seized by Japan, renamed *Koho Maru*. FFW.

Tender Bremen *built in Shanghai for local use after the tug-tender* Bremen *of 1899 was sold to the Shanghai Tug & Salvage Co.*

Tug Sirius *built in 1907 for the Weser-Elbe cargo interchange service. Here shown in the Kaiser-Wilhelm (Kiel) Canal. From NDL Yearbook 1920/21.*

In 1907, Dr. Paul Neubaur in his 50th Anniversary NDL history lists some craft that don't appear otherwise until a 1914 Fleet List:

69. **Bismarck** - 6 tons, 13 HP, "Steamer in European services." Probably river vessel. Still 1/1/1922.

70. **Wittekind** - 5 tons, 14 HP. Still 1/1/1922.

71. **Neck** - 25 tons displacement, 18 HP. Not 1/1/1922.

72. **Oldenburg** - River tug. 28 tons, 70 HP. Already so 1901; 1925 - 29 tons, 120 HP.

73. **Oelboot** already 1901, still 1925, 33 tons, 30 HP.

74. **Apollo**
1907   1907-1919   73 or 189?   220
River tug. 1920 for A. Blume, Rendsburg, 1936 BU. Like *Cyclop* 1906?

75. **Bremerhaven**
1907   50   100
River tug. Still 1/1/1922

76. **Sirius**
1907   J. Frerichs, Einswarden   1907-1952   196   550   32.89 x 7.01
Launched 2/1907. In Weser-Elbe towing service, Captain A. A. August, "who knew the waters of the two rivers like the inside of his vest pocket." Dr. Arnold Rehm.

77. **Vesta**
1907   J. Drewes, Groningen   1907-1954   77   250   24.17
River Tug. Sold 9/1954 among nine tugs far over-age.

78. **Lloyd**
1908   Hong Kong &
       Whampoa Dock Co. #435   1908-19??   105   150   22.86 x 4.57
Built for Hapag as tender *Hapag*. By 1/1/1909 in NDL service as tender in Yap for the Austral-Japan Line: Sydney-German New Guinea-Island colonies-Hong Kong-Japan. With war in 1914, the Australians destroyed Yap's radio station and cut the cable. See "The Lloyd in the South Seas", Volume I. 23/8/1914 *Lloyd* was at

Angaur assisting raider *Prinz Eitel Friedridh* #203. Towed by Raider *Kormoran*, ex-Russian *Rjasan* captured by *SMS Emden*, to Maron in the Hermit Islands where employees of the Heinrich Wahlen Ges. still were working although the Australians had captured the rest of German New Guinea. The Australians got rumors that *Lloyd* was at Maron, sent *Madang*, 194 tons, taken over from the Neu Guinea Co., formerly managed by NDL, to capture *Lloyd*. The Australians first were invited to drinks ashore. During that, *Lloyd* raised anchor and in the dark escaped to Humboldt Bay in nearby Dutch part of New Guinea under Captain Gevers. The crew remained there, hunted birds of paradise for their feathers.

Wega, *built in 1908 as port and river tug, here in Bremen's Free Port zone, still active into the 1950s, as a coal-burner!*

79. Wega
1908   J. Drewes, Groningen   1908-1954   84   300
River Tug. 9/1954 sold for BU.

80. Cyklop
Hong Kong &
Whampoa Dock Co.   1908-1917   151   210   29.26 x 6.10
Launched 1/1908. Stationed in Siam, 22/7/1917 seized there. FFW.

81. Jupiter
John Berg, Delfzyl   1908-1954   66   220
Launched 4/1908. River Tug. Built as *Robert*. By 2/1908 in NDL service. Sister of *Castor*, 9/1954 BU.

82. Stauerei
Bremer Vulkan,
Vegesack #526   1909-1930s   36   55   6.5   14.25 x 4.75
Launched 5/1909. Harbor Ferry, capacity 3 tons, 100 passengers. 1936 still in Germanischer Lloyd register.

83. Nordstern
1911   Atlas Werke, Bremen   1911-1953   170   450   29.96 x 6.64
High-seas tug. 12/4/1955 to J. Johannsen, renamed *Claus*, Lübeck. 157 Ts., 700 HP.

84. Centaur
1913   Atlas Werke, Bremen #100 1913-1953   189   450   31.09 x 6.74
Launched 25/2/1913. Tug. 28/12/1915 - 3/2/1919 in Kaiserliche Marine. Again naval service 8-12/1940. 1942 used as icebreaker. 10/1953 to Cerett & Accinelli, La Spezia, renamed *Centauro*. 1963 - *Chirone*. 1972 reg. in Ancona: Impresa Ing. Spartaco Construzioni. 10/1992 to P. Salvatore, Naples for BU.

Cyclop *was built in Hong Kong in 1908, as were all the Lloyd's steam lighters that transloaded cargo to and from the larger vessels, at the Menam and other rivers. There were many* Cyclops *in NDL's history, some spelled with C, some with K. The same with* Merkur. *Alongside* Petchaburi, *one of the sometimes fifty Far East coastal vessels the Lloyd operated. This between Bangkok-Hong Kong and Swatow.*

Lloyd harbor tug Jupiter *#81 - 1906 and Weser-Elbe cargo-transfer tug* Centaur *#84, of 1908 in Bremen port. In the 1920s.*

638 *Norddeutscher Lloyd Bremen*

NDL's second Lloyd, *replacing #23 built in 1870, also for Cherbourg arrivals and departures. As* Guepe, *used by the French in both wars. Arnold Kludas collection.*

85. *Bremen*
       Tender in Singapore   1913-1914   23   35

86. *Stella*
1913   J. Drewes, Groningen   1914-1954   86   300   24.90
Tug. 1945 sank in Gdynia, raised.

Twelve NDL lighters were delivered during the war for Kriegsmarine use.

87. *Spica*
J. Drewes, Groningen   1914-1939?   86   300   24.90
Launched 2/1914. Sister of *Stella*. 1938 still in Germanischer Lloyd register. FFW.

88. *Lloyd*
1914   Nüscke & Co., Stettin   * *   637   60.47 x 7.53
Tender in Cherbourg under French flag. Seized in war, renamed *Guepé*. 1916 in in Register as bought by the Mission Dahl Belgique. 1919 no owner. Used by the French Navy. 11/1942 scuttled in a Mediterranean port. 1943 raised by Germans, used as tug *Guepé*, then Minesweeper M6061. 1944 sunk..

89. *Grüssgott*
       Nüscke & Co., Stettin   1915-
                                        1939   * *   781   130   11   725   62.60 x 12.60
Launched 12/9/1914, reg. 5/1915. Ordered as tender for *Columbus* and sistership. Spring, 1918 in the Finland Expedition. In April, Hangö was captured. "The merchant ships tied up to the quay after an opening was broken for them through the ice. The Red Guard had left Hango, and the expedition could proceed against Helsingfors. It was attacked on 12 April from land and the sea. Here the Lloyd Tender *Grüssgott* excelled. During the street fighting it entered the inner harbor and with grenades and machine-gun fire cleared the roofs of nearby houses where Red Guards were hidden." (Captain Carl Herbert). Lloyd steamers *Cassel* #174, *Frankfurt* #113, *Schleswig*

Grüssgott, *God's Greetings*, the usual salutation in Southern Germany, was ordered to serve NDL's largest vessels to enter service in late 1914 and 1916. It was the largest vessel left to the Lloyd by the war. It was several times rebuilt, as the photos show. Right: the original version, with lifeboats carried forward and aft.

Below: Unrecognizeable as the French La Bretonniere, now a motor ship. Karl-Heinz Schwadke Photo.

Above: Etiquette sticker supplied to travellers when Grüssgott was on the Sea Service to East Prussia into 1922. Right: The two rubber-stamp marks were used during the annual outing of the German Singing Clubs Association, founded in Hanover in 1804. In the 1920s. And "On the High Seas; voyage to Helgoland." The postcard was printed for the Ocean Comfort Company, NDL's way of handling rental of deck chairs, the curio shop on board, etc.

640   Norddeutscher Lloyd Bremen

#181, *Chemnitz* #176 and *Hannover* #114 were involved. After the war, *Grüssgott* was NDL's largest vessel. 1919 ran to Helgoland as coal supplies allowed. In the new East Prussia Sea Service it first left Swinemünde 2 June, 1920 at 4 A.M., at 6 P.M. was in Zoppot, in the night continued to Danzig, under the Versailles Treaty made a Free City-State. With *Nixe, Najade* and *Vorwarts* carried Plebiscite voters for Allenstein and Marienwerder to remain German. During 1-22 July some 20,000 persons were carried. 1930 sent to Southampton, managed by Alexandra Towing Co., renamed *Greetings*, as tender for *Bremen, Europa* and other Lloyd ships when they anchored down the Nore from Southampton to save time. On 23/8/1939 on *Bremen*'s last voyage it brought down the departing passengers and mail. In Royal Navy services during the war at Gourock, outside Greenock where in 1858 NDL's first *Bremen* was built. 1949 to Societé Cherbourgeoise de Remorquage at Sauvetage, renamed *La Bretonniere*. 5/1969 delivery to Le Havre for BU.

90. *Nymphe*

| 1916 | Bremer Vulkan, Vegesack #604 | 1920-1922 | * * | 385 | 16 | 500/15 | 58.41 x 7.33 |

Built as Mine search boat *M42*, until 17/3/1920. Sold to NDL, with Mine search *M158* for conversion as resort vessels by G. Seebeck A.G., Bremerhaven. Ran Stettin-Libau-Riga with *Grille* into late 1922. Then this service was given up. Sold to Nice, resold to Monaco, renamed *La Nymphe* for Camille Blanc. 1924 owner is *Le Comphe de Guales de Mezaubran*, 452 tons. 1939 Minesweeper for French Navy, AD204. 1944 seized by Germany, renamed *Nymphe*. 19/4/1945 sunk at La Spezia.

Before and After: M-39, sister of M-42 which the Lloyd bought, along with M-158, and rebuilt into the resort vessel Nymphe *and* Grille. *M-39 Bremer Vulkan Photo.*

Below and following page: Nymphe *and* Grille *- Arnold Kludas Collection. The two vessels ran from Stettin to Libau and Riga 1920-1922, while populations in the Eastern Baltic still were adjusting to border changes under the Treaty of Versailles.*

Nymphe.

Grille.

91. Grille
1919   Nordseewerke, Emden   1921-1922   401   500   59.63 x 7.33
Built as minesearch boat *M158*, completed 4/1919. Bought by NDL, rebuilt by Nordsewerke, Emden. Given stronger engines, ran Stettin-Libau-Riga with *Nympee* until that service given up late 1922. Sold to France, renamed *Dinard*, later registered for Le Vicomte de Guales Mezaubran, 437 tons. 1933 bought by the Colombia Navy with *Partenope*, ex-Hapag's resort steamer *Hörnum*, ex *M140*, renamed *Cordoba* for the Coast Guard at Barranquilla. 1946 sold off.

1920 - 1921 mistakenly registered by Germanischer Lloyd as NDL:

92. Franz
1913   G. Seebeck A. G., Geestemünde   247
Built as fishing vessel for the Norddeutsche Hochseefischerei. Only 1922 entered as NDL, obvious error. 10/1954 to W. Ritscher, Hamburg for BU.

93. Donar
       Bremer Vulkan, Vegesack #201   522   42.00 x 10.50
Launched 28/7/1892. Built as icebreaker for Bremen State. 1914-1918 in naval service. 1921 entered as NDL, possibly crewed by NDL? Was allowed to be kept in 1945. 1964 BU in Bremerhaven.

94. Voslapp
1912   Atlas Werke, Bremen
1921 Germanischer Lloyd entry as NDL tug. 1925 Lloyd's Register lists as NDL, copying Germanischer Lloyd? 1928-1938 with Reichsmarine. Not mentioned by Groener in his various naval registers.

---

95. Widder
1921   A. G. Weser, Bremen #399 1922-1959   270   1070   11   36.42 x 7.62
Sister of *Stier* Is 1/1922. At capitulation time was Nr.WT-168. Back to NDL, still 1953.

96. Stier
1921   A. G. Weser, Bremen #388 1921-1944   270   1070   11   36.42 x 7.62
Launched 7/1921. Sea tug. Sister of *Widder*. 15/9/1944 sunk at Brest through aerial bombs.

The icebreaker Donar *was built for the State of Bremen; it served into the 1950s, although built in 1912. Germanischer Lloyd wrongly attributes it and* Franz *and* Voslapp *as "NDL" in 1920 and 1921. NDL may have crewed* Donar. *There are no records current to inform. Built by a predecessor of the Bremer Vulkan.*

97. *Lehe*   34   150
River tug. 1/1/1922 so registered as NDL. 9/1954 sold for BU.

98. *Hector*   28   83
Ferryboat. 1925 listed as river tug.

99. *Herkules*
    Atlas Werke, Bremen   1923-1944   181   27.74
Launched 10/1923. Sea tug. 15/9/1944 scuttled at Bordeaux.

100. *Saturn*   36
Not in 1/1/1922 fleet list, yes on 31/12/1925.

101. *Argo*
    Bremer Vulkan,
    Vegesack #532   1925   65   230   10.5   21.50 x 5.32
Launched 10/1909. In 1922 fused with Argo into Roland Linie. 12/1925 both merged into NDL. Effective 1/1/1933 when Argo again became independent went back with it. 1955 SE.

102. *Nawitka*
Wooden steamer, built 1918, 3349 tons, at National S.B. Co., Orange, Texas, one of a series for the U.S. Shipping Board. 12/1918 completed, reg. at Port Arthur, Texas. 20/8/1920 en route Hamburg-London struck a wreck at the mouth of the Elbe, towed in leaking condition to Cuxhaven, sold there for BU as constructive total loss. Nothing done, stayed there until towed 1923 to Bremerhaven. 1925 bought by Bremer Reedereigemeinschaft, with NDL as leading member. 1925 converted for stationary vessel for training seamen. 1938 renamed *Admiral Bromny*, first German fleet admiral. Bombed during the war, burned out completely.

103. *M.S. Hansestadt Danzig*
1926   Vulcan A.G., Stettin   1926-1941 * *   2431   4500   20   1100/68   90.47 x 11.65
Launched 3/1926. I.S. 17/7/1926 under contract with Reichsverkehrs Ministerium. Sister *Preussen* managed by Hapag. In Sea Service East Prussia: Swinemünde-Zoppot-Pillau-Memel. Both lengthened by 10 meters at Oderwerke, Stettin., H. D. from 6/1933, P. in 1934. Also sailed from Travemünde for occasional cruises. 9/7/1941 with *Preussen* and Hapag's *D. Tannenberg* ran into a Swedish minefield near the island of Oland; all sunk. As replacement, *Robert Möhring*, ex-*Orotava* #391, was put into the service along with Argo's *Adler* and *Brake*.

On High Seas mark from Hansestadt Danzig. *"We are on our way on this beautiful Boat to Berlin," addressed to Cape Town. In German "The steamer is beautiful, much nicer than ours." Who is ours? Scandinavian?*

Built in 1909, Tug Argo *had changing masters. After "Argo" the Roland Line, then the Lloyd and in 1933 again "Argo". Here it is working an Argo steamer in port of Bremen.*

Nawitka *was part of the U.S.'s World War I experiment with wooden and cement steamers. It ended up on the Weser as a training center for future deck officers, including for the Lloyd. It was part-owner from 1925 when it was acquired by a group of Bremen shipowners.* Hapag-Lloyd Photo.

Below:The Lloyd-managed Hansestadt Danzig *ran to East Prussia past the Polish Corridor from 1926 until sunk, with two of its running-mates in 1941. Another Lloyd ship,* Robert Möhring, *ex* Orotava, *replaced it.*

644   Norddeutscher Lloyd Bremen

Bürgermeister Smidt. *The message on back is: "From my voyage to Helgoland with the Youth Gathering."* When built in 1895, Prinz Waldemar and two sisters served this Danish Korsor-Kiel Steamship Post. In 1926, it came to the Weser, NDL bought half a share, then renamed Bürgermeister Smidt, *the man who organized the building of Bremerhaven from 1827. Below: Kaiserliche Marine "Mail canceller" on the Auxiliary Warship* Prinz Adalbert. *"Baltic Sea, 26. Okt. 1915. There won't be further mail until we are relieved." P.A. was part of the Vorpostenkette, outer warning ring against enemy sea intrusions.*

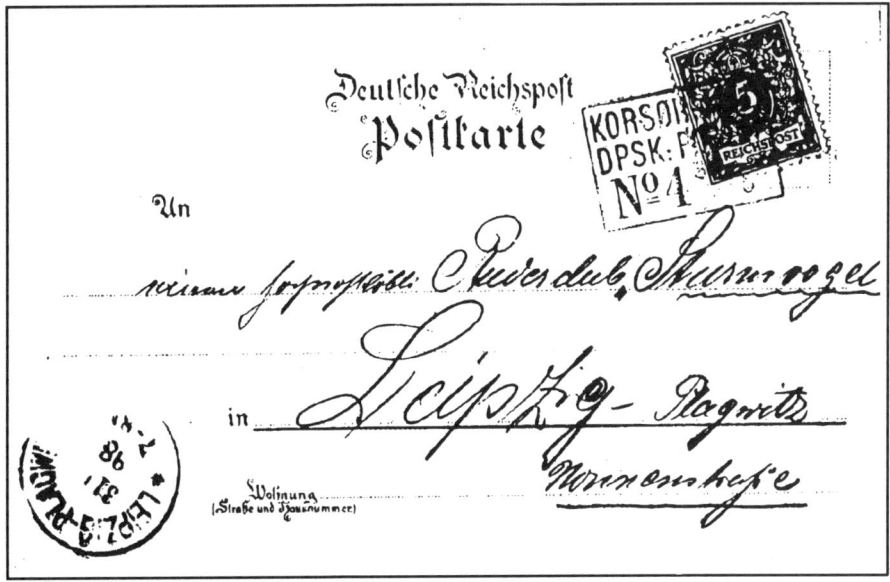

104. *Bürgermeister Smidt*
1895   G. Howaldt Werke, Kiel   1927-1929   * *   699   1200   62.71 x 8.79

One of three sisters built for Sartori & Berger for their Kiel-Korsör service, as *Prinz Adalbert*. 1926 sold to B. Riedemann, Bremen for Weser river service. 26/2/1927 renamed. The same day NDL bought a 50% share, on 28/1/1928 the other half. 658 tons. Ran to Wangerooge. 13/5/1929 with *Najade* sold to Holland for BU. *Nixe* in 1930 was also sold there.

105. *Merkur*
1913   J. L. Meyer, Papenburg   1927-1934   394   42.28 x 8.50

Built as *Loewer* for Hapag as Elbe River Tug and salvage steamer. 1926 to Bugsier Reederei and Bergungs A. G., Hamburg. Late 1927 to NDL, meant for *Bremen* and *Europa* warping duties. 12/5/1934 in releasing from *Albert Ballin* in Bremerhaven was rammed, run over and sunk. Seven dead. Raised and BU.

106. *Vulkan*
1913   J. L. Meyer, Papenburg   1928-1944   395   42.26 x 8.51

Built as *Wendemuth* for Hapag for Elbe River towing and salvage work. 1925 to Lütgers & Reimers, Hamburg. 1927 with *Loewer* bought by NDL, looking ahead to *Bremen* and *Europa* coming into service. 10/5/1944 ran onto a mine in the English Channel.

Bremen *making its first voyage, down the Weser River from the A.G. Weser shipyard to Bremerhaven, on 24.6.1929. Tugs Merkur (105) and Vulkan (106) sisters built precisely for* Bremen *and* Europa *coming into service, are front left. Some tugs also from Urag, see #1970-1994, in the fleet. There are also tugs astern to help control the ship at the curves in the river. A memorable day. Much of the Office staff from* Bremen *were on* Chemnitz *#416, and* Frankfurt *#416, fitting out at the Bremer Vulkan, Vegesack, to watch* Bremen *head to her future on the sea.*

Lloyd's 1914 register shows in the NDL fleet list "No. 164-167, built 1914, 410 tons." These units are not in the register itself. Numbers shown precede and follow these, not these four. Germanischer Lloyd in 1928 shows these under "other towing vessels with 438 tons."

107. **Roland**
1927   J. C. Tecklenborg,
       Geestemünde   1929-1944   * *   2463   18   240   90.82 x 13.00
Launched 12/3/1927. Turbine steamer for the Helgoland-Wangerooge-Norderney-Service. *MV.24*. 5/1927. 1934 modernized, with one stack a more open Boat Deck. 28/8/1939 to Kriegsmarine as auxiliary mining vessel. Supports for 8.8 cm guns installed. 22/3/1944 ran onto mine barrier off Narwa, Esthonia, in 59.42.3N, 27.30.E, sank within two minutes through a double explosion. 130 dead.

108. **Steinbock**   1929 in Germanischer Lloyd as NDL.

109. **Pelikan**   1929 in Germanischer Lloyd as NDL. It is not a Lloyd name.

110. **Glückauf.**
1913   Stettiner Oderwerke #646   1930-1955   * *   849   11   965/16   68.10 x 12.20
Launched 9/10/1913. Built as *Bubendey* for Hapag to serve as tender for the new *Imperator* class. 1914-1914 in Kaiserliche Marine. 1919 back to Hapag, put into resort service. 13/12/1930 bought by NDL as replacement tender in Bremerhaven for *Grüssgott*, sent to Southampton, and as resort vessel. 20/9/1939 as Hospital Ship, Kriegsmarine. 1945 back to NDL. In a 13/8/1946 letter from Director Dr. Johannes Kulenkampff to Captain Drechsel in New York "Of all our sea ships only *Glückauf* is left serving between Norway and Germany as Hospital vessel." 1948 in Hapag's resort service under charter. LU after the 1949 season. NDL then founded with Bremen banks the Bremen Seebäderdienst Gmbh. The Lloyd Technical Service installed two Diesels, one stack, two dining rooms and a Verandah, Cafe, even a Dance Floor. 15 kns, now 1062 tons, 750 passengers, 3½ hours Bremerhaven-Helgoland three times a week into 1960 with chartered *M.S. Süllberg*. Also to Wangerooge. 1960 with entry into service of the new *Bremerhaven* sold to Hadag, Hamburg, renamed *Kehrewieder*. After modernization at the Hanseatic Werft, 1172 tons. 1961 to Jade Schiffahrts Ges., Wilhelmshaven. 1963 *Isola Del Sole*, Soc. Traghetti del Lazio, Gaeta for DM266,000. 1965 *Anna Maria Lauro*, A. Lauro, converted to Ro-Ro.

*Helgoland in Sight by Roland, NDL's ocean-liner resort motor ship of 1927. Later it was rebuilt to one stack. It used a **D.Roland On the High Seas mark**. The postmark reads: Most Effective German North Sea Spa-Resort: Helgoland.*

"On High Seas" mark used on Glückauf during the 1950s while under the Lloyd flag. The mark used as Bubendey in 1920 when it ran to Helgoland for Hapag.

Built in 1913 for Hapag as Bubendey *for its resort routes, the vessel in 1930 went to the Lloyd. After World War II it was rebuilt and given Diesel engines. Here it is in the 1950s at the Columbus Quay in Bremerhaven with NDL's* Berlin *ready to sail. The gangway reads:* United States Lines. *From 1953 until it went out of service in 1963, the* United States *made Bremerhaven its turnaround port. It is the liner Blue Ribbon trans-Atlantic champion of all time.*

111. *Tac*
1929   Schiffswerft Unterelbe,
         Wewelsfleth   1933-1955   307   240   40.03 x 7.51

Launched 11/1929. Delivery for NDL use under Argentine flag as trans-loader with Montevideo and other La Plata ports. 12/1930 registered to Enrique Arnold. 9/1932 with sister *Tic* sent to Bremen and reg. for NDL, as transloader of cargoes between the *Weser* and *Elbe*. 22/12/1936 sank off Cuxhaven after collision with *Anna Rehder*. Raised and repaired. 17/1/1939 renamed *Wester Till*. 3/1955 to Joh. Pahl as *Anke Pahl* for London-Denmark service, 328 tons. 1961 given new Diesel engine. 1964 *Bergland* for Karl Heinrich, Hamburg. 1966 to Rudolf Nicolaus, Hamburg. 1967 again *Anke Pahl*, Johannes Pahl, Hamburg. 19/12/1971 stranded near Raven Point, Wexford, Ireland after the mooring lines broke, en route Belfast-Par, Cornwall. Sold to J. Doyle Co., Wexford "as lies". Got off and sold to Haulbowline Industries, Cork. 5/1973 BU there.

112. *Tic*
1929   Schiffswerft Unterelbe,
         Wewelsfleth   1933-1944   300   240   40.03 x 7.51

1929 delivery for NDL use under Argentine flag in La Plata delta cargo transfers. 12/1930 reg. to Enrique Arnold. 9/1932 sent to Bremen for NDL Weser-Elbe cargo transfers. 22/12/1936 sank off Cuxhaven after collision with *Anna Rehder*. Raised, repaired. 17/1/1939 renamed *Oster Till*. 1940 in Kriegsmarine service as *Lat 3*. 30/3/1944 mined off Wilhelmshaven. Repaired. 29/4/1945 sunk by aerial bomb.

113. **Norder Till**
1924   J. Frerichs & Co.,
         Einswarden   1938-1964   475   350   8.5   50.23 x 8.05

Built as *Mangan* for Ernst Komrowski, delivery 19/1/1924. 12/1938 bought by NDL for Weser-Elbe freight connection, renamed. 4/1954 in Bremerhaven given MAK 350 HP Diesel. 1956 in North-Baltic seas service, coke and wood cargoes. 1964 to Theodor Vavatsoulias, Saloniki, renamed *Memi I*. 31/1/1967 sunk in the Mediterranean S.E. of Gelidonya Burnu in 36.13N, 30.25E.

Tic *and* Tac *(below) were sister ships. But* Tic *was rebuilt with the added-on after housing after her collision and sinking in 1936. Built for NDL's cargo trans-loading in the La Plata delta, then to Bremerhaven for the same Weser-Elbe transfers. Wolfgang Fuchs Photo.*

Norder Till *like* Tic *and* Tac *transferred cargoes between Bremen-Bremerhaven and Hamburg so ships could call at any of these ports without going to the other(s). This speeded turnaround of vessels and made transportation efficiency a common aim for otherwise embattled Bremen and Hamburg. Of 475 tons,* Norder Till *was the largest ship left to the Lloyd by the war.* William Schell Collection.

Register 649

Löwe of 1939 in June, 1959 was the lead tug in towing the rebuilt Bremen from the Bremer Vulkan shipyard to Bremerhaven. In 1960, warping a vessel through the Kaiser Lock with two other tugs, one NDL's Stur, pushed under water. Two of the crew drowned.

Below: the account in the Wessr Nachrichten.

Schwerster See-Unfall in Bremerhaven seit sechs Jahren

Schlepper „Löwe" sank vor der Nordschleuse
Von der „Pegasus" unter Wasser gedrückt / Zwei Besatzungsmitglieder vermißt / Sechs Gerettete

114. *Hengst*
| 1939 | Howaldtswerke, Kiel | 1939-1963 | 146 | 450 | | 27.71 x 7.12 |

Sea tug. 1955 - 126 tons. With *Aade* delivery 19/5/1963 to Societé de Remorquage de l'Escaut, Antwerpe, renamed *Schelde VIII*. 1973 - *Afon Goch*, 123 tons, Holyhead Salvage Co., 1978 - *Sorte Encel*, 121 tons.

115. *Aade*
| 1939 | Howaldtswerke, Kiel | 1939-1963 | 146 | 450 | | 27.71 x 7.12 |

Sea tug. 1951 NDL as operator. 1958 - 126 tons. 1963 with *Hengst* to Societé de Remorquage de l'Escaut, Antwerp, renamed *Schelde VII*.SE 1978.

116. *Löwe*
| 9/1939 | Schiffsbau Ges. Unterweser, Wesermünde | 1939-1961 | 213 | 11 | 1200 | 33.40 x 7.80 |

Sea tug. 1955 converted to oil, 1400 HP. 23/5/1959 with other NDL tugs towed the converted *Bremen 5* from Bremer Vulkan, Vegesack to Bremerhaven. 1960 in taking the Greek *Pegasus* through the Kaiser Lock with *Stur* and *Nordenham 9*, pushed under water, two dead. Raised. 29/10/1961 sold to Achille Lauro, Naples, renamed *Portonevere*.

Hunte *later* Harle *under NDL management, and sister* Puddefjord *were part of the U.S. Navy's Labor Service, Unit Baker in Bremerhaven. They served variously as tenders and tugs.* Puddefjord *and* Wangerooge *were the only Lloyd vessels involved in the 1945-1947 German Minesweeping Administration, the postwar clearing of some 4500 mines and other detonating devices. It proved to be just as dangerous duty as the war itself: seventeen vessels and 277 persons were lost in the clearing. See picture of* Wangerooge, *also a sister of* Hunte *(Harle) and* Puddefjord.

117. *Hunte*
1940   D. W. Kremer & Sohn,
        Elmshorn   1940-1945   * *   667   1000   12   67.75 x 9.02
Sister of *Puddefjord*. 1940-1945 Minesearch boat. 27/2/1946 taken over by Omgus, Office of the Military Government U.S., trustee of all shipping ceded to the U.S., served as *USN-104* in the Weser Estuary. Managed by NDL, renamed *Harle*, still under U.S. flag, Labor Service Battalion of the U.S. Navy. 1950 towed the Hansa Line's *Axenfels*-to-be, with Hansa crew on board, from New Orleans to Bremen for rebuildting, ex *Heimvard*, 1930. 1951 towed two surplus U.S. frigates from Baltimore to Kiel, the start of Germany's new navy. 11/12/1956 to Bundesmarine, renamed *Ems*, A-53 Auxiliary Minesearch tender, and crew-training vessel. SE 1962.

118. *Puddefjord*
1943   D. W. Kremer & Sohn,
        Elmshorn   1943-1945   * *   667   1000   12   67.75 x 9.02
Sister of *Hunte*, sea tug for Mine search craft. 1943-1945 managed by NDL? 1945 to Omgus, renamed *USN-101*, NDL as operator? In U.S. Navy's Labor Service Battalion, Bremerhaven. 1956 again under German flag. 21/1/1957 to Bundesmarine as *Oste*, A-52, mine search tender, with *Harle*. SE 1967.

13/8/1946 letter from Dr. Joh. Kulenkampff to Captain Drechsel in New York: "Our entire activity is concentrated on the 14 tugs and some 50 lighters, most are organized in the pools formed by the Americans in Bremen and Bremerhaven,"

118x. *Kolibri*
1943   Werft Gebr. Wiemann, Brandenburg   72.5   350
So carried by Helmut Stegemann as NDL. Not a Lloyd name. 1963 to Captain Johann Schumacher, Borkum. 1964 rebuilt, 900 HP Diesel, 12.5 kns, 82 Ts., Kort Düse. 1988 SE.

Wangerooge, Harle *and* Puddingfjord *were sister minesearch craft in the war. Postwar* Puddefjord *and* Wangerooge *were part of the minesearch and clearing operation, then under charter from OMGUS were used as tugs, tenders, etc.* Wangerooge *was in 1948 rebuilt for resort service 1948-1950.* Hapag-Lloyd Photo.

119. *Wangerooge*
1944   A. G. Neptun, Rostock   1947-1952   * *   667   1000   12   67.75 x 9.02

Sister of *Harle* and *Puddefjord*. Mine search boat *M611* in the war. 1945 used as tug by OMGUS in the Weser Estuary and participated in mine-clearing. 1948 chartered by NDL, converted at the Technical Service for passengers in resort service. 26/5/1948 under Captain Heinrich Lorenz ran to Norderney, renamed *Wangerooge*. Helgoland still was forbidden territory for Germans. The British tried to prevent its reuse with some 8,000 tons of explosives, but little happened. 1950 LU. 8/10/1951 to U.S. Navy's Labor Service Unit Baker as *M 206*. 15/8/1956 to Bundesmarine, renamed *Seeschlange*. 1957 renamed *M191*. 13/2/1960 paid off. Served as dormitory ship *WBM IV* in Emden and Flensburg. 29/5/1967 struck from Bundesmarine list. Sold for BU.

120. *Knurrhahn*
1916   J. Frerichs, Einswarden   1945-1950   1408   8.94 x 10.42

Built as lighter. 1/7/1939 rebuilt as dormitory vessel, 300 beds for the Kriegsmarine in Wilhelmshaven and Pillau. 1945 seized by U.S. 2/3/1948 opened in Bremen as hotel ship, managed by NDL. It had some 80 beds, a restaurant, bar, barber for visitors as Bremen was practically destroyed. The Maitre d'Hotel was the former Chief Steward of the *Europa*. 21/3/1950 towed to Bonn for the same use as that city built up as the West German capital. 6/3/1953 back to Bremerhaven. 1955 used as dormitory ship by the Bundesmarine. 2/1987 closed down.

121. *Gulosenfjord*
1943   Moss Vaerft &
       Dokk Ko. #106   1949-1959   299   800   39.93 x 7.50

1945 to OMGUS. 12/1946 NDL as operator. 1949 towed two cement barges from Liverpool to Haugesund. 8/1954 bought by NDL. 1959 to N. V. Scheepvaart & Bergingsmij G. Doeksen, Terschelling. It in 1924 salvaged the steamer *Retter* was towing to Holland for scrapping, see *Retter*. 1985, renamed *Doggersbank*. 1964 for L47,500 to Mediterranean Salvage & Towing Co., Malta, renamed *Maltese Terrier*, 321 tons. 1972 renamed *Maltese Samson* of Universal Investment Co. 1988 to K & M, Ltd., Malta, renamed *Atlantic Ocean*. SE.

The following tugs bought from OMGUS 1949-1951 were the backbone of NDL's towing activities until it could built anew.

122. *Stur*.
1943   Consolidated Shipbldg. Co.
       City Island, N.Y.   1949-1961   132   700   26.85 x 7.36

Built as *ST 771* for the U.S. Navy, one of many for the invasion of France. 1945-1946 *Lucien Samure*. 1946 in OMGUS service, Bremerhaven. 22/10/1949 first of six of these tugs chartered, then bought by NDL. 25/1/1954

652   *Norddeutscher Lloyd Bremen*

sank after collision with sunken U-boat wreck off Bremerhaven. Repaired by S. B. Ges. Unterweser. 9/7/1959 was Press Boat for the maiden voyage departure of *Bremen 5*. 11/1961 saved the crew of the *M.S. Martha Friesecke* after its collision in the Weser estuary with *American Merchant*. All six ex-OMGUS tugs were sold in 1968 to Brodospas, in Split. Renamed *Altair*. SE 1978.

Gulosenjford *was taken over from Germany by the U.S. in 1945. Under OMGUS in 1946 managed by NDL in extensive towing operations. Bought in 1954, sold off in 1959.* William Schell Collection.

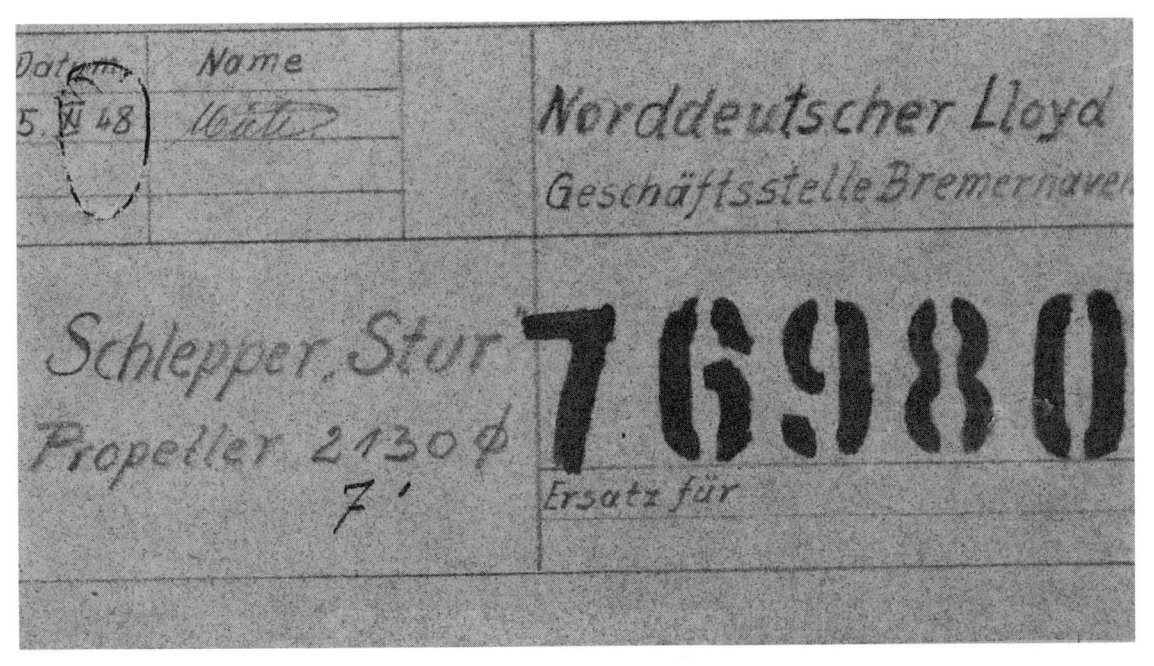

Stur *was the first of six sister-tugs eventually bought by NDL after years of chartered operations in behalf of OMGUS. This Propeller diameter inventory entry at NDL's Business center in Bremerhaven indicates that the name-change to Stur had been made by 5.XI.48, date of the entry. The Lloyd actually bought a seventh of these tugs, but wooden-hulled, it proved unserviceable and was sold off after one year.*

#122 Stur. Pasteur arriving in September, 1958 from France for rebuilding into Bremen, in care of six NDL's tugs.

Arion, *another of the six ex-Army tugs built for the invasion of France the Lloyd managed, then owned. Here in Bremen in the 1950s.*

123. Vulcan
1943   Decatur Iron & Steel Co.,
        Decatur, Alabama   1950-1959   129   700   26.85 x 7.36

Built for U.S. Navy as *DPC*, then *ST776*. 1945 in OMGUS service in Bremerhaven. 19/3/1951 bought by NDL. 1968 sold to Brodospas, Split., renamed *Vega*.

124. Arion
1943   Consolidated S.B. Corp.
        City Islands, N.Y.   1950-1968   129   700   26.85 x 7.36

Built for the U.S. Navy as *ST763*. 19/3/1951 delivery to NDL as purchase, rebuilt into its tug needs. Delivery 16/1/1968 to Brodospas, Split, renamed *Jupiter*.

125. Steinbock
1944   Decatur Iron & Steel Co.,
        Decatur, Alabama   1950-1968   129   700   26.85 x 7.36

Built as *ST779* for the U.S. Navy, ex *DPC-49*. Postwar ran for OMGUS in Bremerhaven, crewed by NDL? Bought by and delivery to NDL 19/3/1951, renamed 16/1/1968 sold to Brodospas, Split, renamed *Argus*.

126. Herkules
1944   Continential S.B.Co.,
        Brooklyn   1949-1950   130   700   26.85 x 7.36

Built as *ST757* but with wooden hull. 11/1949 bought by NDL but proved unusable. 11/1950 sold to Spain, FFW.

127. Herkules
1944   G. Lawley & So. Corp.,
        Neponset, Mass.   1951-1968   130   700   26.85 x 7.36

Built as *DPC-27* for Defense Plant Corp, then *ST782* for U.S. Navy. Postwar ran for OMGUS in Bremerhaven, crewed by NDL? Delivery 19/3/1951 to NDL, renamed 16/1/1968 sold to Brodospas, Split, renamed *Saturn*.

128. Kurefjord
1943   Nylands Mek. Verksted,
        Oslo #364   1952-1962   178   800   30.75 x 6.74

1945 ran for OMGUS in Bremerhaven. From 2/1947 crewed by NDL. In 1948, towed the former NDL *Eisenach* #337, ex *Alda,* from Lisbon to Bremerhaven, for eventual repair and purchase by the Lloyd as *Traunstein*. 1954 bought, renamed. 28/4/1959 to Bundesmarine, renamed *Friedrich Vöge*, Y888.

High-seas tug Kurefjord *built under Germany's wartime ship replacement programs in Norway. 1945 came under OMGUS in Bremerhaven, the U.S.-control for ex-enemy property. From 1947 crewed by NDL under contract, then bought and kept for ten years. William Schell collection.*

Süllberg *at anchor off Wangerooge. Originally built in 1928 for service in the Baltic, it survived the war, in 1950 was rebuilt, and given Diesel drive. NDL chartered it 1954-1955 to run with its own* Glückauf *to Wangerooge. Below: Envelope posted on board has the same type of* On the High Seas *shipmark as* Roland *of 1927. Ship photo by Foto-Haus Becker, Wangerooge.*

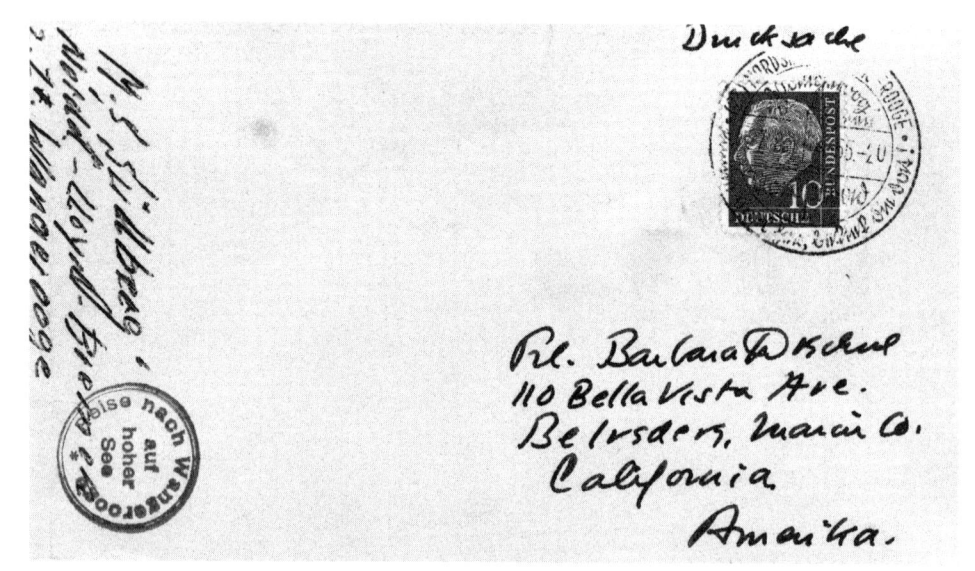

129. *Sirius*
1943   Ira S. Bushey & Sons,
       Brooklyn   1952-1968   130   700   26.85 x 7.36
Built as ST781 for U.S. Navy. Postwar ran for OMGUS, Bremerhaven, NDL crewed? 9/7/1959 one of tugs helping *Bremen 5* for its maiden voyage departure. 1968 sold to Brodospas, Split, renamed *Regulus*. See #476 for photo.

130. *Habicht*
1916   Atlas Werke, Bremen   1954 bought by NDL   84   360   21.76 x 5.84
Delivery 21/1/1955. 1967 sold to Georg Dietrich Fehner, Lemwerder, delivery 2/6/1967.

131. *Süllberg*
1928   Paul Lindenau, Memel   1954-1955   12.5   362   540 HP   50.43 x 7.18
Built as *Kurischeshaff* for the Bäderverkehr der Memeler D.S. Ges. 1945 brought Holstein. 1946 chartered to Hadag, Hamburg's harbor and resort vessels operator, 1948 sold to Hadag. 1950 modernized, rebuilt as motorship. 1954-1955 chartered by NDL for the service to Wangerooge, ran with *Glückauf*. 1955 to the A. G. Ems, Wilhelmshaven for its Borkum service, renamed *Hannover*. 1962 *Faraglione*, rebuilt in Italy for Bay of Naples services where NDL until 1913 sent one or more of its resort steamers in the winter.

During 1948-1954 NDL sold off as over-aged and no longer fitting into current port and cargo methods: 16 sea lighters, six river lighters, 17 harbor lighters. In September, 1954 nine tugs, one going back to 1897, all coal-fired were sold off. The six ex-OMGUS, ex-U.S. Navy tugs NDL had managed, then bought as the backbone of its towing and warping activity, until in 1954 the first of the new-design Voith-Schneider propeller tugs came into service.

All are Diesel-driven: All in service in 1970 went over to Hapag-Lloyd A. G. They are all equipped with fire-fighting equipment. This design is also known as Trekker or Trecker Tugs. This allows the tug and tow to be in the same line, i.e., the tug can run parallel to the vessel being warped, against the old design where the tug would pull at right or lesser angle, often got into a wrong position and turned over, or was run over. See *Löwe*. These tugs had a four-man crew. In the 1980s, tugs worked with three men. Mechanization of some functions permitted this.

132. *Stier*
1954 Jade Werft,
     Wilhelmshaven   1954-1970+   76   700   12.7   * *   19.90 x 6.20

Launched 18/1/1954, delivery 28/4/1954. First tug with Voith-Schneider propeller which lets tugs literally turn on a dime. NDL pioneered their use. Ideal for in-harbor Bugsier, warping, work. Experience with *Stier* led to the later versions being enlarged. 20/2/1978 put on display permanently at Deutsches Schiffahrt Museum, Bremerhaven.

Stier was the prototype for introduction of the Voith-Schneider propeller which made possible tugs literally turning in place. NDL pioneered this use. Five bigger versions were built later. With the six ex-U.S. Army harbor tugs, they were the nucleus of NDL's towing and warping capacity for more than ten years.

133. *Mars*
1955 Jadewerft,
     Wilhelmshaven #14   1955-1970+   95   840   11   22.80 x 6.23

Launched 12/1954. Voith-Schneider equipped warping tug. Two Klockner-Humboldt-Deutz Diesels. 1977 to Ocean Shipping, Bunker & Barges SpA, Trieste, renamed *Tak*, delivered by Enship B.V., Scheveningen.

134. *Bär*
1955 Jadewerft, Wilhelmshaven 1955-1970+   95   840   11   * *   22.80 x 6.23

1978 sold to Ocean Shipping SpA, Trieste, renamed *Bat*.

Mars - Bär - Wolf - Luchs - Wal *were the enlarged Stier-type Voith-Schneider propellered tugs. Four-man crew into the 1980s on the typical harbor tugs. Luchs is shown with* Buntenstein #520.

Wal *operating in port of Bremen. The coming of the container revolution in the latter 1960s ended the need for towed-barges to transfer cargo from the port of unloading.* Photo by Karl-Heinz Schwadke.

135. *Wolf*
1957   Jadewerft,
        Wilhelmshaven #58   1957-1970+   95   840   11   * *   22.80 x 6.24
1978 to Bugsier Reederei & Bergungs A. G., Hamburg. Renamed *Bugsier 18*/1986 to Heinz Schumacher Schleppschiffahrt, Elsfleth, renamed Wesertug. SE 1988.

136. *Luchs*
1958   Jadewerft, Wilhelmshaven   1958-1970+   95   840   11   * *   22.80 x 6.24
Launched 11/12/1957, delivery 30/7/1958. 1981 chartered to along with *Centaur* and *Löwe* to Underwater Services, London, all three with options to buy. These were not taken up, all returned December, 1981. Renamed *West Reef*. 1982 to Busumer Werft, renamed *Max*. After bankruptcy of yard, owner Harmstorf Group auctioned 25/11/1986 to Schleppbetrieb Unterweser, Bremen, renamed *Greif*. 1988 SE.

137. *Wal*
1958   Jadewerft,
        Wilhelmshaven #59   1958-1970+   95   840   11   * *   22.80 x 6.23
Launched 7/1958. Trials-Delivery 29/7/1958. 1975 listed as 1010 HP, re-engined? 10/3/1983 delivery to Husumer Schiffswerft, renamed *Süderoog*.

138. *Centaur*
1958   Jadewerft, Wilhelmshaven   1958-1970+   159   1060   11   29.56 x 7.92
This design tug was called *Düsenjäger*, Jet Hunters, for their tremendous power. Built to handle supertankers at Wilhelmshaven. Trials 25/9/1958. 12/1975 listed as 1400 HP. 12/8/1981 to Hapag-Lloyd (U.K.), renamed *Daunt Reef*. 1982 to Busumer Werft. 1983-1986 the firm failed, the tug auctioned off to Ems Offshore Service, renamed *Ems*. With *Centaur* in service, NDL's tug fleet had 23 units.

139. *Hein Mück*
1943   Stockton Construction Co. 1956-1960   308   760   11   * *   400/16   45.48 x 6.72
1944 built as Landing Craft *LCG 181* for Royal Navy. 1948 rebuilt by J. Bolson & Sons, Poole, into Resort Vessel, renamed *Rochester Queen*, Medway Steam Packet Co., Rochester. 4/1956 bought by Seebäderdienst Gmbh, NDL part-owner, renamed for service to Wangerooge by Wangerooge Dienst Gmbh. On 30 May, 1958 *Hein Mück* and NDL's former *Glückauf* were chartered to take Lloyd workers on their annual outing to Wangerooge, and again on 30 June to Helgoland. On 23/6/1959 chartered by NDL with guests to lead the "Parade" downriver of Bremen from the Bremer Vulkan shipyard to Bremerhaven. Again carried the guests who watched from the stream *Bremen's* maiden voyage departure on 9/7/1959. 1/1961 *Commodore Queen*, Commodore Shipping Co., Guernsey. 1962 - Lion Shipping Co., 1972 to D.I.H. Clark. 1973 *Jersey Queen*, Jersey Car Ferries, Guernsey. 1976 rebuilt as Research Vessel for KG (Specialist Ships), Ltd. 1991 still in Lloyd's Register.

140. *Rose Mary*
1944   Odenbach S. B. Corp.,
        Rochester, N.Y.   1960-1976   632   700   * *   54.65 x 9.14
Built as Harbor tanker for the U.S. Army, engine aft. 1948 to Rosa Maria Corp., Puerto Cortes, Honduras. 1949 to Cia. de Nav. Teresita. 1954 reg. in Puerto Limon, Costa Rica. 1960 bought by NDL as harbor-cleaning vessel. Took waste, especially from tankers, that before was just dumped at sea or in port, to the incinerator. In 1962 a harbor official could say of Bremerhaven: "Today the harbor is clean again." Named for the warship that before the eyes of *Henry VIII* capsized. 6/1976 sold to Brake for BU.

Hein Mück *ran 1956 through the 1960 season to Wangerooge for a resort-shipping firm partly owned by NDL. The Lloyd separately chartered* Hein Mück *for several employee-outings.*

**NEW YORK TIMES
August 18, 1962**

TANKER REMOVES WASTE IN HARBOR

German Ship Is Equipped to Treat Oil and Sludge

BREMEN, German, Aug. 17 — The ports of Bremen and Bremerhaven are experimenting with a new approach to the control of harbor oil waste — the floating disposal plant.

Port authorities have remodeled the tanker Rose Mary to function as a general harbor waste-disposal vessel. The Rose Mary has been fitted with special equipment for treating oil waste and sludge.

The vessel moves about the two ports on the Weser River, collecting in its tanks oil waste from ships in port, primarily tankers.

After tankers discharge cargoes, their tanks are cleaned and the waste is normally pumped into the harbor. Under the sludge-control plan being tested here, all vessels using Weser ports are required to discharge oil waste into the Rose Mary's tanks. The Rose Mary's equipment then separates the waste from water, which is pumped back into the harbor.

The equipment has a capacity of 600 tons of oil-contaminated water an hour. The Rose Mary also is fitted with fire-prevention safeguards. Gas accumulating in oil tanks is a special fire hazard in oil-waste disposal.

Port officials report that the plan has been a success. Compliance is nearly perfect and the Weser ports for the first time are free from oil waste.

"Bye, dear. Try not to spill anything."

Rose Mary *was bought to clean up and keep clean the harbor of Bremerhaven and the adjacent Weser. From* The New Yorker, *26 August, 1972.*

Karl-Heinz Schwadke

Jupiter *and* Sirius *#129 or one of its sisters maneuvering* Europa *in 1966*. Arnold Kludas photo.

141. *Jupiter*
1961   Lloyd Werft, Bremerhaven   1961-1970+   161   1060   11   27.07 x 7.52
Kort Düse tug. Delivery in Bremerhaven on 21/2/1981 to Empresa Portuaria Talcahuana, Ltda, renamed *Caciane*. Left 23rd for Chile under own power. *Löwe*, *Widder* and *Nordstern* were sold to the same firm, founded decades before by German interests. Sister of *Jupiter*. 12/1975 listed as 1540 HP. SE 1981.

142. *Löwe*
1962   Lloyd Werft, Bremerhaven   1962-1970+   161   1060   11   29.60 x 7.59
Sister of *Jupiter*. 1981 chartered to Unterwater Services, London *Luchs* and *Centaur*, renamed *Carric Reef*. 12/1981 again *Löwe*. 1984 to Cia. Portuaria Talcahuano, Ltda, renamed *Pehuen*.

143. *Wester Till*
1962   S. B. Fes. Unterweser,
    Bremerhaven #433   1962-1973   470   350   9   7   49.56 x 8.82
Launched 2/10/1962, trials-delivery 15/11/1962 for Weser-Elbe cargo transfer. 9/1972 LU in Bremerhaven. 1973 to A. J. Broekmeulen, Woerden, Holland, ran under Panama flag as *Rosa B*. 1974 *Inter Voltzee* I, Panama. 1975 - *Eben Haezer*, Peter Cornelius Leem van Weenen, Panama. 1982 to H & M Marine Services, Ltd. Panama, renamed *Ruth G*. 1989 *Askham*, Askham Shipping Co., Panama, 1991 *Ad Tempus*, Streamforce Cia. Ltda. Panama. SE 1994.

144. *Oster Till*
1962   S. B. Ges. Unterweser,
    Bremerhaven   1962-1970+   470   350   9   7   49.56 x 8.82
Launched 30/8/1962, delivery 27/9/1962 for Weser-Elbe cargo transfers. 1973 to J. H. Havemann, Joost, renamed *Harma*. 1977 to H. W. van Weeldon, Panama, renamed 1978 *Pax I*. 1980 to T. K. Kroezen, Panama. 1990 renamed *Gannet*, Medtrans Ltd., Kingstown, St. Vincent. SE 1994.

M/S OSTER TILL

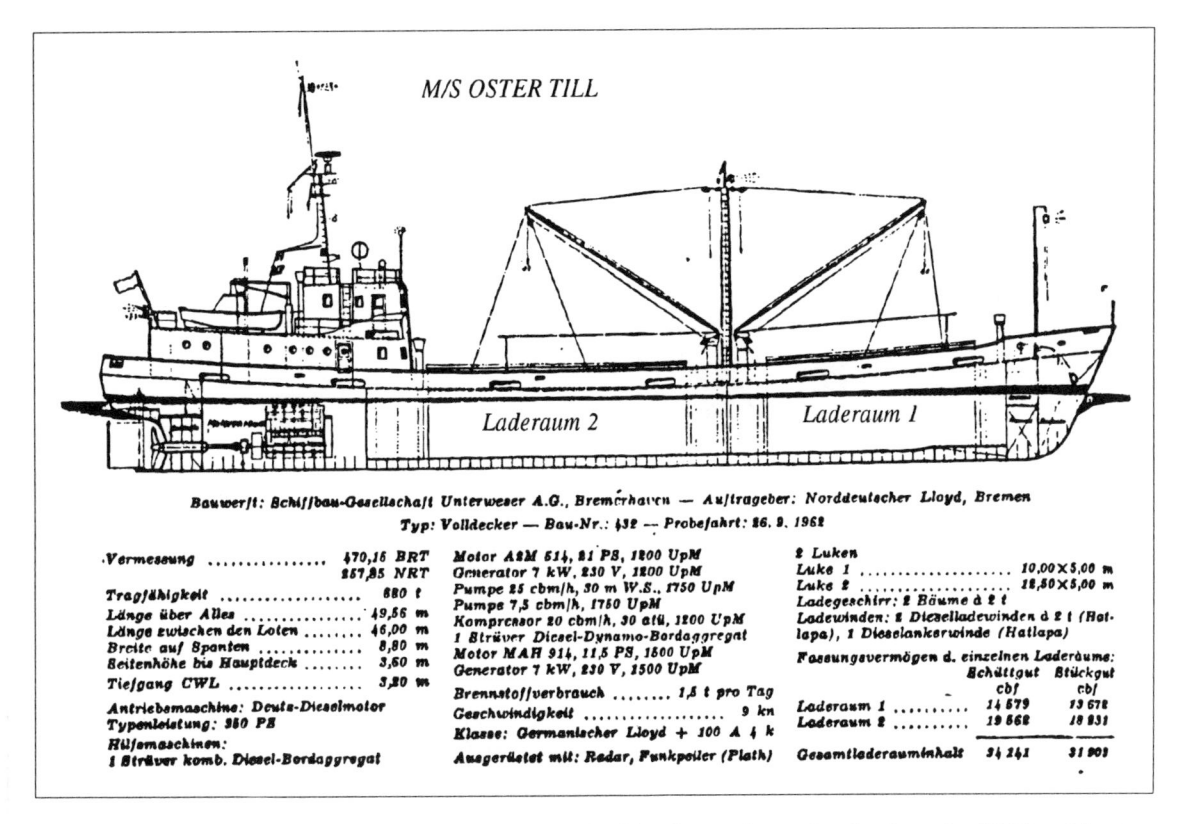

Bauwerft: Schiffbau-Gesellschaft Unterweser A.G., Bremerhaven — **Auftraggeber:** Norddeutscher Lloyd, Bremen
Typ: Volldecker — **Bau-Nr.:** 432 — **Probefahrt:** 26.9.1962

Vermessung .... 470,15 BRT / 257,85 NRT	Motor A2M 514, 21 PS, 1200 UpM	2 Luken
Tragfähigkeit .... 680 t	Generator 7 kW, 230 V, 1200 UpM	Luke 1 .... 10,00×5,00 m
Länge über Alles .... 49,56 m	Pumpe 25 cbm/h, 30 m W.S., 1750 UpM	Luke 2 .... 12,50×5,00 m
Länge zwischen den Loten .... 46,00 m	Pumpe 7,5 cbm/h, 1750 UpM	Ladegeschirr: 2 Bäume à 2 t
Breite auf Spanten .... 8,80 m	Kompressor 20 cbm/h, 30 atü, 1200 UpM	Ladewinden: 2 Dieselladewinden à 2 t (Hatlapa), 1 Dieselankerwinde (Hatlapa)
Seitenhöhe bis Hauptdeck .... 3,60 m	1 Strüver Diesel-Dynamo-Bordaggregat	
Tiefgang CWL .... 3,20 m	Motor MAH 914, 11,5 PS, 1500 UpM	Fassungsvermögen d. einzelnen Laderäume:
Antriebsmaschine: Deutz-Dieselmotor	Generator 7 kW, 230 V, 1500 UpM	Schüttgut cbf / Stückgut cbf
Typenleistung: 380 PS	Brennstoffverbrauch .... 1,5 t pro Tag	Laderaum 1 .... 14 579 / 13 672
Hilfsmaschinen: 1 Strüver komb. Diesel-Bordaggregat	Geschwindigkeit .... 9 kn	Laderaum 2 .... 19 562 / 18 231
	Klasse: Germanischer Lloyd + 100 A 4 k	Gesamtladerauminhalt 34 141 / 31 903
	Ausgerüstet mit: Radar, Funkpeiler (Plath)	

Sister-ships Wester Till *and* Oster Till *continued the Lloyd practice going back to the 1930s of having small cargo-carriers for shifting freight between Bremen, Bremerhaven and Hamburg so the high-seas ships could drop cargo at any one.*

Widder, *also built by the Lloydwerft, in 1963 with the Kort Jet powered by Diesel-electric drive. Four such sisters. Photo Richard Marder for Verlag Grusskarten GmbH., Bremen. With sister* Hektor *towing the reefer* Bremerhaven *of Scipio & Co., Bremen, partly owned by the United Fruit Company. Former NDL Passenger Director Adolf Stadtländer postwar was a member of Scopio's Board.*

145. *Widder*
1963   Lloydwerft,
         Bremerhaven #6   1963-1970+   161   1060   11   29.60 x 7.59
Diesel-Electric Drive, Kort-Düse propeller tug. 12/1975 listed as 1540 HP. Delivery 6/1/1984 in Bremerhaven to Cia. Portuaria Talcahuano, renamed *Antuo*.

146. *Hektor*
1963   Lloydwerft, Bremerhaven   1963-1970+   161   1200   12.5   29.60 x 7.59
Sold before 1970 Hapag-Lloyd merger. Why?

Register

Castor *and* Pollux *were enlarged-*Mars *type Voith-Schneider powered tugs. Here* Pollux *(see below) is bringing barges to Hapag-Lloyd's* München *of 1972, its only-ever LASH-principle freighter. It disappeared at sea in December, 1978.* Hapag-Lloyd Photo.

147. *Castor*
1963   F. Schichau,
        Bremerhaven #1721   1963-1970+   170   1350   12.3   28.80 x 8.00
Voith Schneider Propeller. Delivery 27/9/1963. 12/1975 - 1625 HP. 1987 to Rimorchi Salvataggi, Trieste, renamed *Cala Azzura*.

148. *Pollux*
1963   F. Schichau,
        Bremerhaven #1722   1963-1970+   170   1320   12.3   28.80 x 8.37
Delivery 12/10/1963. 12/1975 - 1625 HP. SE 1988.

149. *Norder Piep*
1963   S. B. Ges. Unterweser,
        Bremerhaven #440   1963-1970+   452   350   9   49.60 x 8.80
Delivery 23/11/1963 for Weser-Elbe cargo transfers. 1973 to S. Bergsma, Panama, renamed *Griend*. 1977 to Union Transport (London), Ltda. Panama, renamed *Union Mercury*. 1986 to Ritmar Nav. Co., Kingstown, St. Vincent. 1990 to Moby Dick Shipping Ltd., Kingstown, renamed *Cormorant*. 1994 S.E.

150. *Süder Piep*
1963   S. B. Ges. Unterweser,
        Bremerhaven   1963-1970+   452   350   9   49.65 x 8.82
Launched 28/11/1963 for Weser-Elbe cargo transfers. 1973 to E. Slobben, Panama, renamed *Albert S*. 1974 to Union S. C., Panama, renamed *Kai I*. 1980 to Overseas Shipping Agencies, Chittagoing, renamed *Karma L*.1994 S.E.

151. *Nordstern*
1964   Lloydwerft, Bremerhaven   1965-1970+   161   1200   12   29.84 x 7.56
Kort Düse drive. Sister of *Jupiter* and *Löwe*. 12/1975 - 1540 HP. Delivery 25/8/1988 in Bremerhaven to Cia. Portuaria Talcahuana, renamed *Antilen*.

23 June, 1966 the bark *Seute Deern*, 1919 built at Gulfport, Mississippi, arrives from Emden to the Old Harbor, Bremerhaven, for use as a hostelry and museum. Hans Jürgen Witthöft in his Norddeutscher Lloyd, Koehler, 1973 lists *Seute Deern* as NDL (managed?).

KORT-DÜSENRUDER

bietet

höchste Leistung und ideale Manövrierfähigkeit

für

**SCHLEPPER
FISCHEREIFAHRZEUGE
FRACHTSCHIFFE**

Ingenieur-Büro KORT
Hamburg 13, Hallerstraße 76, Ruf 44 68 11

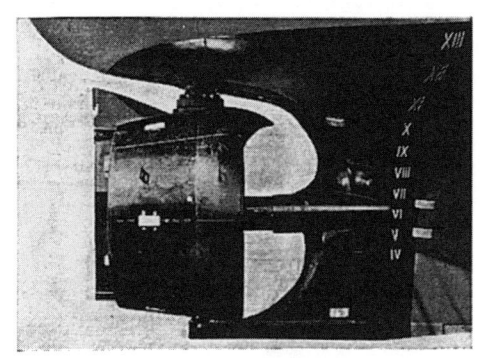

Kort-Düsenruder für einen 2 000 PS See- und Hafenschlepper

The Kort Düse, Jet Rudder worked like the jet-water drive invented in New Zealand. The propeller has a funnelled housing which turns like a rudder, driving the water in the direction the tug should go. This system and the Voith-Schneider propeller revolutioned the use of tugs in ship-warping. Advertisement in 12.1967 See Kiste. Stella, Triton, Vesta and Vega all had Kort-Düsenrudder installations.

In November, 1965 to replace sold-off older tugs and have twenty units in service, NDL ordered six tugs for 1967-1968 deliveries: Four with 1200 HP Deutz Diesels and Kort Düse from the Jadewerft, and two with 1600 HP and Voith-Schneider propellers from F. Schichau. The four tugs built at the Lloydwerft for NDL were done during a slowness in orders.

152. *Stella*
1967   Jadewerft,
        Wilhelmshaven #109   1967-1970+   158   1200   12.5   29.29 x 7.50
Built with room for eight crewmen. 12/1975 - 1540 HP.

153. *Triton*
1967   Jadewerft,
        Wilhelmshaven #110   1967-1970+   158   1200   12.5   29.29 x 7.50
12/1975 listed as 1540 HP by Hapag-Lloyd.

154. *Vesta*
1967   Jadewerft,
        Wilhelmshaven #111   1967-1970+   158   1200   12.5   29.29 x 7.50
Delivery 11/1967. 1992 to Esaro Sv I, Italy, renamed *Esa Ro*.

155. *Wega*
1967   Jadewerft,
        Wilhelmshaven #112   1967-1970+   158   1200   12.5   29.29 x 7.50
12/1975 listed as 1540 by Hapag-Lloyd. 1993 still in Hapag-Lloyd service. Now 1320 HP.

156. *Comet*
1967   F. Schichau,
Bremerhaven #1742   1967-1970+   170   1600   12   27.90 x 8.37
Voith-Schneider propeller. 12/1975 - 1930 HP.

157. *Cyclop*
1968   F. Schichau,
        Bremerhaven #1743   1968-1970+   170   1600   12   27.90 x 8.37
Voith-Schneider propeller. 12/1975 - 1930 HP for Hapag-Lloyd. 1993 to Wundermeer Reederei, S.A., Slovenia, renamed *Kyklop*.

The Lloyd tug fleet in 1968 had: *Mars - Bär - Luchs - Wolf - Wal - Centaur - Jupiter - Löwe - Widder - Hektor - Castor - Pollux - Nordstern - Stella - Triton - Vesta - Wega - Comet - Cyclop - Stier*.
Before the 1/9/1970 merger with Hapag into Hapag-Lloyd A. G. *Hektor* was sold, leaving: 13 Sea tugs: *Centaur - Castor - Comet - Cyclop - Jupiter - Löwe - Nordstern - Pollux - Stella - Triton - Vesta - Wega - Widder*.

6 River tugs: *Bär - Luchs - Mars - Wal - Wolf - Stier*. 4 Kümos, Coastal transloaders: *Wester Till - Oster Till - Süder Piep - Norder Piep*.

The high-seas tug *Planet* of 2,000 HP built in 1973 was the last to carry the traditional Lloyd colors: a black hull, white superstructure and a yellow stack and signal mast. After that the hull and signal mast-stack were the new cognac color, with the H-L logo in blue.

The last generation of Lloyd tugs built just before the 1970 merger.

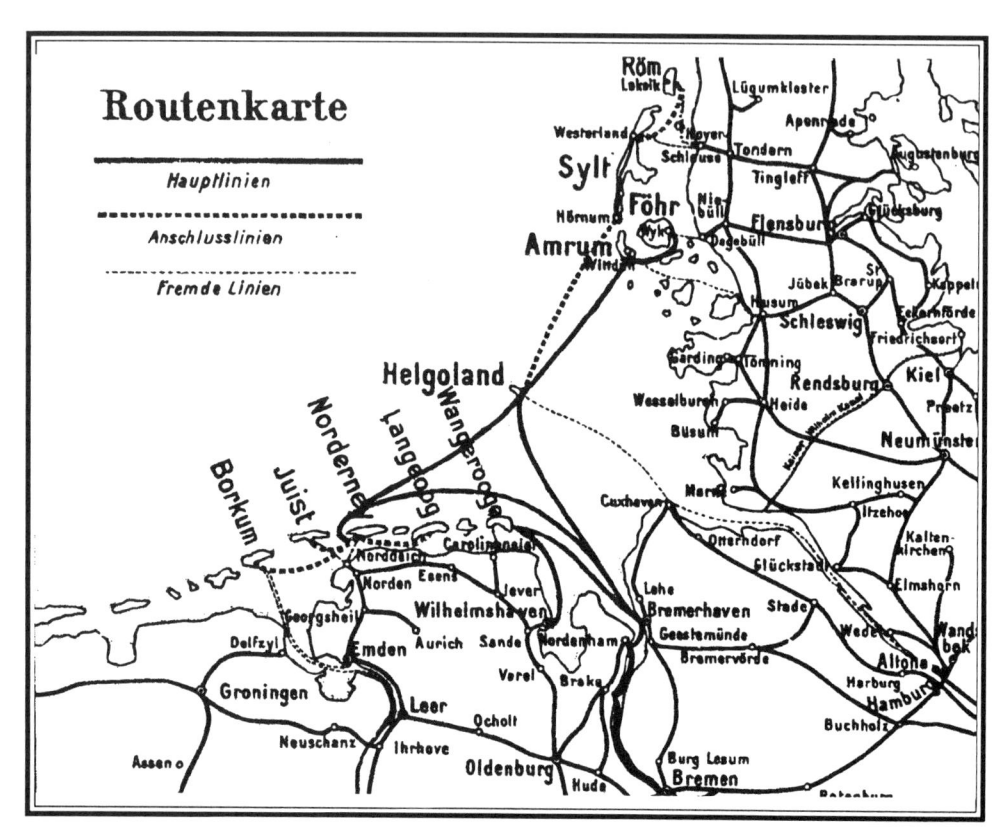

From the Lloyd's 1907 Resort Steamer Schedule. The heavy lines are Lloyd routes, the dotted lines connecting services. Served, and this continued into the 1950s with war interruptions, were the islands of Wangerooge, Langeoog, Norderney, Helgoland, Amrum and Föhr, from Bremerhaven and Wilhelmshaven.

Epilogue

The lifering I had painted for the front door of their new home in California. Artist-friend Robert Canfield inserted the Lloyd coat of arms.

The Drechsel Family at Bredow near the Vulcan Shipyard, 1923. My brother Theodor just 18, my sister Evelyn 13. I have forgotten my dog's name. When we were to move into Stettin, we gave the dog to friends in the country, taken there in his house on a truck. Days later he was back, broken chain at his neck. See "A New Start."

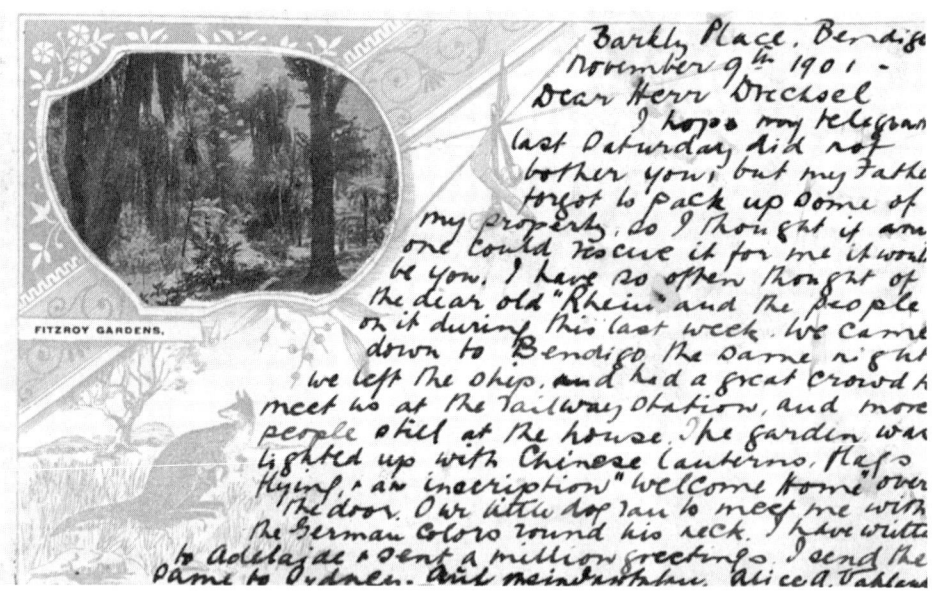

At the end of Rhein's voyage from Bremerhaven in September-October, 1901, the one on which my parents met, at Sydney my Father received this postcard from a passenger who had landed at Melbourne. Her Father forgot to "pack up some of my property, so I thought if any one could rescue it for me it would be you..." As Fourth Officer, Herr Drechsel had time for other passengers besides the Smiths and his future bride. Lloyd service at its best.

After the war, for the first time the Drechsels had leisure to make day-trips and began what became annual summer drives to Bonny Oaks on Lake Morey with their German shepherd Dulo. He lay quietly on the back seat until, nearing the lake, he'd sit up, recognizing the country from the year before. On one return, the New Yorker Staats-Zeitung called. They quoted my Father: "Here we've been for years without being aware of the beauties of this blessed part of this earth." They would drive into Vermont and New Hampshire, always to Hanover where Dartmouth is located. One rainy day, their Buick skidded into a ditch. Nearby farmers spent an hour getting them out, absolutely refused any compensation. The supposed crusty Vermonters!

The last exchange of letters between Bremen and my Father was in February and March, 1963. In January, I had moved my parents from wintry New Jersey to warmer Marin County, California. On 3 March, my Father reached his 84th birthday. On March 23rd my parents had their sixtieth wedding anniversary.

On 25 February, Richard Bertram, co-director with Dr. Johannes Kulenkampff in running the Lloyd since 1942, wrote: "I especially regret that I could not arrange to be in the U.S. for your birthday and to personally press your hand. And to tell you how much all of us here thank you, especially since shortly you and Mrs. Drechsel will celebrate your sixtieth anniversary. With heartfelt thoughts and greetings."

On 26 February, Dr. Kulenkampff wrote. "I send heartiest birthday greetings with remembrance of the long, long years we together went the same path for the Lloyd. I recall as if it happened yesterday your presentation in the breakfast room of our management, Dr. Albert had just become chairman, on the pier situation in New York, so vital to us (Summer, 1932).

"Much has happened since. But the decisive fact is that the spirit, dedication and tradition has not changed at the Lloyd. With that, we hope we have successfully built the continuity to prewar. I need not tell you what the training and example of our older captains, officers and engineers means to the new generation. For us in management the challenge is to pass on this people-based asset — one cannot value it in money terms — on which the merit and success of the enterprise rests. With heartiest remembrances, yours sincerely devoted."

He wrote again on March 18th for the anniversary: "For us, almost a quarter-century younger, a lifetime such as yours is scarcely imaginable. We surely will not attain the same, given the extreme stresses of the last twentyfive years.

"That you in your relocation still feel close to the Lloyd and can see (in Angel Island) a visual expression of that closeness, gives us great joy. (In replying to the earlier letter, my Father had mentioned that he could see, when it was not foggy, Angel Island from Belvedere. He had brought to there in January, 1940 the *Columbus* crew after they lost their ship (See *Columbus* in "Countdown ...") and made later visits.") We assure you that your decades-long example and training for our successors was not in vain and has been taken up and will be passed on in turn by the younger generation. We all here wish for you and Mrs. Drechsel health and happyness in the circle of your family on your Day of Honor. Ever yours ..."

My Father died peacefully on April 23rd. I was with him when his time came.

Addendum

I want to record some persons not otherwise mentioned whom I knew personally, albeit some as a child, but whose names I often heard:

- Erich Blew. On my Fathers staff at the Vulcan Shipyard in Stettin, 1921-1924. I recall with my sister Evelyn going to visit, standing before the sign: Blew, wondering how that spelling come to be pronounced Blu. We knew no English then.

- Thilo Sachse. Close family friends in Bremerhaven and Bremen, fellow-officer. After the Second War he was shipbuilding consulting engineer in Bremen. In 1962, the Sachses lived on Klugkist Strasse, Bremen, named for the two Captains Klugkist, Volume I, p. 132. In June, 1995, his son, also Thilo, my father's Godson, wrote to me after seeing the May 31st news-report in the Weser Kurier, Bremen, about me and the Lloyd volumes. Our Fathers attended the Bremen Technikum together to learn shipbuilding. Their last contact was in 1963.

- F. Brünings. First captain of *Stuttgart* #303 in 1924. He was captain of München #293 in February, 1930 when it burned at Pier 42, North River.

- Edmond von Reeken. Second Officer on *Eisenach* #291 at Stettin 1922, later captain of *Cavalla* #350.

- Adolf Winter. Captain of *Stuttgart* in February, 1929 when we travelled on her to Bremerhaven. He later wrote about his experiences "Vom Segelschiffsjungen zum Lloyd Käpitän," From Sailship boy to Lloyd Captain.

- Rudolf Wurpts. Fellow-officer pre-1914, in the 1920s captain of *Dresden* #269, etc. He is the First Officer standing behind Kronprinzessin Cecilie on her name-ship, Volume I, page 269.

- Heinrich Zuppe. Fellow-officer pre-1914, in the 1920s captain of *Lützow* #241, etc. He is with my Uncle Archibald Smith on page 332, Volume I.

- G. Goy. Captain of *Gerwin* #398x in 1928. Before 1912, young Mrs. Goy at timess stayed with my family on the Bürgermeister Smidt Strasse in Bremerhaven, in the same corner apartment house lived Lloyd Engineer Schriever, Uncle and Aunt of the later U.S. Air Force General Bernard O. Schriever, like I born in Bremen. In the 1950s he headed the Research and Development Command.

- Hinrich Hashagen. He went into sail at age 15, rounded the Horn ten times, in 1907 became 4.Officer. He was on the training ship *Herzogin Cecilie* #184 in Chile in 1914, was among the 28, 22 from the Lloyd. who rounded the Horn in the winter of 1916-1917 to reach Germany in 120 days. See "The Lloyd Sails", Volume I. In 1928, captain of *Derfflinger* #242, in the 1930s in management, then head of the Nautical Division until the war.

- H. Gössling. He joined the Lloyd in 1907, in the 1920s commanded freighters. He was uncle of Dr. Arnold Rehm, cruise lecturer, himself son of a Lloyd Captain and grand-nephew of Captain Gerhard Bruns of *Weser 2* #17.

- Captain H. Kempf. My Father's assistant in New York. He got home in 1940 via San Francisco, *Asama Maru* to Japan and across Siberia. Postwar he worked under Captain Daehne in restoring ports operations in the U.S. enclave.

- Captain F. Jarka. Owned the stevedoring firm that handled Lloyd ships on the East Coast. He helped care for the interned German seamen 1939 - 1941. Sadly, at his death his office files, Lloyds Registers, etc. were inadevertently discarded.

- Captain Frederick Stannard. With Shipping agents Funch, Edye. He provided the car and chauffeur when we arrived from Australia in 1924 from Hoboken to Weehawken, N.J. That is when I saw five huge factory smokestacks in line, was jokingly told that was the largest U.S. liner. He was typical of the many who were helpful to my Father with Rat und Tat, Word and Deed, as he learned the ship-operations ropes.

- Hans Müller. In the 1930s Chief Purser on *Europa*. Postwar he served on the Greek *Olympia* to the U.S.-Canada until 1954 he could come back to the Lloyd as Purser on *Hessenstein* #491. "Two years to the Far East I wont mind, those 105+ days round trips, but then I hope to get back to the New York." Which he did on *Berlin* #489, then on *Bremen* #511. His father was Purser on *Rhein* in 1901 when the Smith family returned to Adelaide from Britain and my future parents met. They lived for three years in the Müller house in Lehe before moving to Bremerhaven. Herr Müller's letter to me from *Hessenstein*, one of the six Lloyd and Hapag new Far East liners of 22 October, 1954, tells "we arrived with 15 days delay as we went to several remote Philippine harbors to load copra (this for a passenger ship!) . Today we go into drydock in Bremerhaven, then to Vegesack where the Vulkan Shipyard has to do guarantee-work. On 1 November we are due in Hamburg to start loading. It goes so day and night." And he sent some Ship Posts from the vessel.

- Theodor Dellith. In July, 1959 Chief Purser on *Bremen 5's* maiden voyage. It was his 200th trans-Atlantic round trip. Dellith joined NDL in 1923, served on *Bremen, Europa*, was on *Columbus* when it was scuttled in December, 1939. In 1955, he was Chief Purser on the new *Bayernstein* to East Asia, then that on *Berlin*. He was helpful to me in providing examples of his vessel's Ship Posts.

- Arnold Petzet. Lloyd Director from 1906, in 1925 on the Management Board. He authored the 1932-issued Life of Heinrich Wiegand who in 1892 at age 37 became General Direktor until his early death in 1909. I have the book with his inscription to my Father, and correspondence.

- Henry and Frances Greenebaum. He was purveyor of comestibles to the Lloyd in New York.

- Kurt Hinsch. Second Officer on *Columbus'* last voyage in 1939, then U.S. internee and P.O.W. He married Liselotte Gastmeyer, daughter of Carl Gastmeyer, my Father's lifelong closest friend, Volume I, page 214, etc. He then managed Herr Gastmeyer's food import firm until his death in 1961. The Gastmeyers lived two blocks from us in Weehawken from their 1927 immigration.

- F. Baum. In the 1930s on *Bremen's* Purser Staff. He sent Sea Posts to my Father. Fellow collectors.

- Dr. Freiherr von Geyr. I have postcards from him from various parts of the world. He joined the Lloyd in 1925. Postwar he was Chief Doctor on *Berlin*, then on *Bremen* with its entry into Service in 1959.

- Carl Zeumer, Grabley A. Sagemühl and August and Lena Schmiege, helpful in many ways.

Many of these, also the Böhme and Brake fellow-officer families, Volume I, kept in touch through correspondence and during my parents visits to Germany. It was a close-knit family.

The photo bears the notation: In remembrance of our evening of 23 August, 1934, on Hapag's Flagship New York, *signed: Lohmann, and pencil note: Dr. Hoffmann, Bremen and Hamburg officials in New York.*
Left to right: Captain F. Mensing, No Name, C.J. Beck, North Atlantic Community (Lloyd and Hapag) Director New York. Mrs. Drechsel, No Name, Irene Muehlenbrock, No Name, No Name, Mr. Muehlenbrock, No Name, No Name, Commodore Fritz Kruse, Mrs. Muehlenbrock, Captain Drechsel, Mrs. Mensing, No Name. This evening was four months before Commodore Kruse led the rescue team effort in saving the Sisto crew in *mid-Atlantic*. See "Ad Astra...."

Not long after this evening together on the New York *Thank You letters to the New York Operating (Inspectorate) Department came from Commodore Ziegenbein at the end of* Bremen's *record-breaking 100th voyage. "We value your cooperation to the fullest and know we could never manage without it." And from Hapag's Commodore Kruse just after he directed the Sisto crew rescue ("Ad Astra ....") "For my (rescue) boat's crew and all of us our thanks on your congratulations and your ever-ready shoreside support for our ship, for understanding our needs, and for the comradeship. Your very fitting verses I shall enjoy on the cruise ... (by Resolute around the world.)" The photo shows the Drechsels with Commodore Ziegenbein at the end of that 100th voyage. Also, Captain Drechsel at his Pier 86 desk on March 28, 1938.*

Part of the New York-New Jersey Lloyd Family, about 1928: Irmgard Schroeder, Mrs. Schroeder, John Schroeder, Passenger Manager, Mrs. Muehlenbrock, (wife of H. Muehlenbrock, Asst. Passenger Manager), Captain Kurt Grahn, Rose Muehlenbrock, Mrs. Drechsel, Evelyn Drechsel, Irene Muehlenbrock. Some months later, Captain Grahn died on the bridge as the ship was pulling out from the pier. Writing this in early 1995 it is sad that one cannot trace people one knew intimately. Then lives separated by war, and marriage. Women disappear through name changes. I traced Irmgard Schroeder, after losing her husband, into a second marriage to Karlsruhe. But by then she had left that city. Even a computer search of family counsellors failed to find her.

ABSTRACT OF LOG

Twinscrew Express Steamship »Kronprinzessin Cecilie«, Captain Ch. Polack.

July 1914.	Miles	Lat. N.	Long. W.	Remarks
28.				Ambrose Channel lightvessel at 3.00 a. m. Standard time.
28.	196	40°10'	69°35'	Overcast; rainy; light sea.
29.	535	40°10'	57°55'	Cloudy; moderate sea.
30.	534	40°45'	46°22'	Cloudy; hazy; moderate sea.
31.	549	45°25'	35°36'	Cloudy; moderate sea.
31.		46°46'	30°21'	10.09 p. m.
1. Aug.	539	46°09'	37°42'	Clear weather; moderate sea.
2.	523	44°56'	50°02'	Cloudy; 7 hours fog; reduced speed; light sea.
3.	501	42°58'	61°18'	Overcast; 10 hours fog; reduced speed; light sea.
4.	350	Rest		Overcast; fogshowers; reduced speed; light sea.
				Great Duke Island (Bar Harbour) at 4.54 a. m. Standard time.

Total distance: 3727 Miles.   Passage: 7 Days, 1 hour, 54 minutes.
Average speed: 21,94 knots.

Log of Kronprinzessin Cecilie's #234 last voyage under the Lloyd flag in July-August 1914, where she turned back in mid-ocean en route New York -Bremen, and sought refuge in Bar Harbor, Maine. Frank Pichardo Collection.

Historical Note: The *Alta California* of 20 October, 1868 citing an item in the 6 October *Baltimore American* reported that Mary Todd Lincoln, widow of the President, with son Tad had driven on 1 October to Locust Point, Baltimore and boarded the (North German Lloyd) steamer *Baltimore*. At her request, their names were not put on the passenger list. The purpose of the voyage was to place Tad in a school in Germany. (Robert Parkinson, S.S.H.S.A.) *Baltimore's* first arrival from Bremen in March, 1868 was celebrated as of state importance. Schools, markets, the Customs House all were closed. A procession headed by the governor, and members of business and labor groups paraded through the city, followed by a civic banquet. See Volume I - The Baltimore Line.

Corrections from Volume I:
- Ship 184, *Herzogin Cecilie*: Sven Eriksson was the captain with his wife on board, not Edgar Erikson, son of owner Gustav Erikson.

-**In Index of Ship Names:** *Cöln*-316; *Heidelberg* 1928-375; *Patagonia*-394; *Mercury*-97; *Teiho Maru*-447; *Wiegand*-381.

Above: Postalia meter Ship Post authorized for M.S. but not used as it lacked the word "Schiffspost" above the "An Bord."

Left: Postmark used on the day of issue for the 10 and 25 Pfennig stamps by the City of Berlin for its name-ship.

While the Lloyd's ships are "Finished With Engines," its role 1857-1970 is integral to the history of shipping and people movement. Today, it goes "Full Ahead" as Hapag Lloyd A.G., Germany's largest sea, air and land transportation enterprise.

Sources

There are so many I must thank who through correspondence, discussions, photos, documents, etc. were of immense help, sadly many no longer alive. But I wish to record their names. They are witness to the brotherhood of shiplovers. Many sources I can no longer document as not until some eight years ago did I consider doing more than a complete NDL ship list. Without the decades and memories of those many contacts this Lloyd history would not be so diverse and detailed.

Photos: The majority of photos are from my NDL collection, a sizeable part of which is in the Deutsches Schiffahrts Museum, along with books, the coffee service from the *U-Deutschland*, etc. that I gave to it. And from: NDL and HAPAG-LLOYD photo archives, Nautical Photo Agency, Real Photographs, Alan B. Deitsch, Robert Potts, Frank Pichardo, Eric Johnson, Deutsches Schiffahrt Musem, Arnold Kludas, Karl-Heinz Schwadke, Dahl & Rohweder. Donald Schroth, William Schell, Robert Canfield, Ian Farquhar, Don Gammon. And painters like Willy Stoewer, C. Fedeler and O. Bollhagen. Many illustrations now on record are reproduced photographs of originals long since lost.

Periodicals: I recall vividly the News Shop beside the stairs into the subway under the New York Times building where in the 1930s I found *Motor Ship* and *Fairplay* etc., *Seekiste* later combined into *Schiffahrt International, Towline* of Moran Towing co., the magazine racks at the San Francisco Marine Exchange, New York Times and The World, papers which in the 1920s and 1930s reported daily arrivals with passenger numbers, for years carefully noted in a notebook now lost.

Reports: The Atlantic (Passenger) Conference, 1921-1930, by W.H. Roper, Secretary, London, unpublished. New York Maritime Register, 16 September, 1914. Marine Engineer & Naval Architect, February, 1921 listing the former German ships and their USA record. Official Lists of West German Shipping, 1955 ff. Die Bremischen Dampfschiffsposten, 1817-1867, Wolfgang Diesner in Nordsee-Posta III, 4/1974. Herbert Kuke — "Die Bremer Boote" in Nautilus I, Nr. 5, 9/1973. Christian Piefke — "Die Geschichte der Bremischen Landespost." Hans Szymanski — "Die Anfänge der Dampfschiffahrt in Niedersachsen, 1817-1867," Hannover, 1958. "A Third Class Traveller on NDL to Australia" in 1900, republished 1990 by Charles Ira Sachs.

Hobby Groups of which I am or was a member or have reports: Log of the Nautical Assn. of Australia (B.A. Wilkinson). ARGE Deutsche Schiffspost and Friedrich Steinmeyer, Heinz Evers, Wolfgang Richter, and reports of many members. Maritime Postmark Society and its Seaposter which for seven years I edited. World Ship Society and its Marine News. I am a life member, for seven years edited its USA bulletin "Intercom." Steamboat Bill of the Steamship Historical Society of America. The former Belgian Nautical Research Assn. and its "Belgian Shiplover," founded by Paul Scarceriaux and continued by Yvonne Scarceriaux until her death.

Libraries: Deutsches Schiffahrtsmuseum, Bremerhaven; J. Porter Shaw Library of the National Maritime Museum, San Francisco; Bremer Landes (Focke) Museum, Bremer State Archives; San Francisco Public Library.

Shipping Lines & Shipyards: Argo Reederei, Alfred Holt & Co., Indo-China S.N. Co., Lloyd Brasileiro, Det Forenede D.S. — Photos of the four NDL Birds they bought. A.G. Weser & Diplom Ingenierr Aloyis Somer. Bremer Vulkan & Robert Kabelac. Hong Kong United Dockyards.

Correspondence: With BNRA members G. Andrade, Chr. Dekker, Theodor Dorgeist, F.J. Hermans, F. van Otterdijk, J.P. Visser, Alan Deitsch, Theodor Tedsen, L.L. von Münching, Theodor Siersdorfer, Roberto Andres Delu, Dieter Jung, Ricardo Siepmann, Arman Blancquaert, J.O. Ramos, Ronald Innes, Werner Tobergte, William Muller.

Articles and Lists by Uwe Kinder, Hans-Jürgen Witthöfft, Helmut Stegemann — Die Deutschen Schlepper.

Also: Robert Langner, Manager San Francisco Marine Exchange, Frank O. Braynard — always ready to share his font of information, William Schell and his extensive reasearch on my behalf, J. Bastock, Wolfgang Scharf, Ernst Stoffers, J.R. Maddocks, William Lyons, Diplom Volkswirt Paul Lebach, Peter Tamm, Dr. Karl Schubert, Kaptain Karl Ehlerding, Kammergerichtsrat Josef Dahmann, Captain C.J. Gebauhr.

At the Lloyd: Dr. Johannes Kulenkampff and his Son Stephan, Hans Karstedt, Waldemar Klose, John Schroeder, Captain Emil Maurer and many others over the years.

Bibliography

Abert, Hans Jürgen. Schifflisten (Horn, Globus) in "Seekiste-Seefahrt International, Die Deutsche Handelsmarine 1870-1970."

Ahrens, Komm. Adolf. "Männer, Schiffe, Ozeane," Adam Reitze, Worpswede.

Alfabetisches Verzeichnis der d. Kauffahrteischiffe nach den Beständen von 1.1.1873 und Folge

Angas, W. Mack. "Rivalry on the Atlantic." Lee Furman, New York, 1959.

Barbance, Marthe. "Histoire de la C.G.T." Arts et Metiers Graphiques, Paris, 1955.

Becker-Ferber, Dr. G. "Fünf Dampfer Bremen." D. Reimers Verlag, Berlin, 1959.

    "Acht Glas" (Kommodore Ziegenbein), Dietrich Reimer, Berlin, 1940.

Benja, Günter. "150 Jahre Bremer Seebädertörns 1837-1987." Verlag H.M. Hauschild, Bremen, 1989.

Bessell, Dr. Georg. "Geschichte Bremerhavens." F. Morisse, Bremerhaven, 1927.

    "Norddeutscher Lloyd 1857-1957," NDL 1957.

Blumenschein, Ulrich. "Luxus Liner." Gerhard Stalling Verlag, Oldenburg, 1975.

Bonsor, N.R.P. "North Atlantic Seaway." L.T. Stephenson & Son, Prescott, Lancs., 1955 usw.

    "North Atlantic Seaway No. 2." Brookside Publications, Jersey, CI, 1978.

    "South Atlantic Seaway." Brookside Publications, Jersey, CI, 1983.

Brackmann, Dr. Carl. "50 Jahre Deutsche Afrikaschiffahrt." D. Reimer Verlag, Berlin, 1935.

Bremer Landes (Focke) Museum. Abteilung Schiffahrt

Bremer Vulkan. "Werftgeschichte/Schiffschronik." Carl Schünemann, Bremen, 1955.

Brinnin, S.M. "Sway of the Grand Saloon." Delacorte Press, New York, 1971.

Brustat-Naval, Fritz. "Unternehmung Rettung." Köhler, Herford, 1970.

Bureau Veritas Registers

Crüsemann, Korv. Kapitän Fr. "Deutsche Marine Schiffspost, Poststempelgilde Rhein-Donau." Düsseldorf, 1959-72.

Detlefsen, Gert Uwe. "Ship Lists: Horn, Argo." Schiffahrt International, 1978, 1980.

Dinklage, Ludwig. "Die Deutsche Handelsflotte" 1939-1945. I: Muster-Schmidt Göttingen 1971; II: Hans Jürgen Witthoft.

Drechsel, Edwin. "Belgian Shiplover 1961-1963." Shiplists: NDL, Argo, Horn, Roland, H.B.A.L., Rickmers.

    "Seeposter," Journal der Maritime Postmark Society, von 1951.

    "1886-1986, A Century of German Ship Posts." Christie's London, 1986.

Drechsel, Willy. "NDL 1857-1957." (Bessell), C. Schünemann, 1957. Stories.

    "Ship Movements, New York 1924-37," Private Log Book.

    Stories told in: "Bremen: Binnen un Buten" I & II, Dr. Carl Thalenhorst, H.M. Hauschild, Bremen, 1953, 1958.

    "Sklavenfahrer & Kuliklipper." (Kapt. Fred Schmidt).

    "Neue Kapitäns Berichte." Kapt. Fred Schmidt, Dietrich Reimer, Berlin, 1937.

    "Norddeutscher Lloyd 1857-1957," (Bessell).

Eckhardt & Messtorff German Shiplists, 1972 & ff.
Eckstein Biographischer Verlag: "Historisch-biographische Blätter, Berlin 1906-1911."
Ehlers, Wilhelm, Chief, Literary Division of NDL. "U-Deutschland" aus "Was Wir Vom Krieg Nicht Wissen," Editor Walter Jost, Leipzig, 1938.
Evers, Heinz & Friedrich Steinmeyer. "Deutsche Schiffspost nach 1945," Arge Schiffspost, 1986.

Friedemann. Wittmann. "Die Postgeschichte und Entwertungen der deutschen Postanstalten in den Schutzgebieten und im Ausland," München, 1971.
Fleischer, F.W. "Sturmfahrt der *Tinto*," Gerhard Stalling, Oldenburg (undated).
Franck, Harry A. "A Vagabond Journey Around the World." The Century Co., New York, 1910.

Gerard, James W. "My Four Years in Germany, 1914-1917." Doran, New York, 1917.
Germanischer Lloyd Registers.
Gibbs, C.R. Vernon. "Passenger Liners of the Western Ocean". John de Graff, New York, 1954.
Groener, Erich. "Handelsflotten der Welt, 1942 und Nachschlag," 1944
    "Die Schiffe der deutschen Kriegsmarine und Luftwaffe, 1949-1945 und ihr Verbleib." J.F. Lehmanns Verlag, München, 1972.

Haack, R. & C. Busley. "Die Technische Entwicklung des NDL und der HAPAG. Sonderdrücke aus den Zeitschriften des VDI, 1889-1892." Julius Springe Verlag, Berlin 1893.
HAPAG-LLOYD A.G. "A Century of Liner Shipping to Australia; and to the Far East," 1986.
    "Bridge Across the Atlantic," 1983. Photo Archive.
    "Informationen," Annual Reports.
Hardegen, Friedrich. "H.H. Meier, Der Gründer des NDL". Vereinte Wissenschaftliche Verlag, Berlin 1922.
Haws, Duncan. "Merchant Fleets in Profile" No. 4. Patrick Stephen, Cambridge, 1980.
Hennig, Bernard A. "German Submarine Mail of World War I." Germany Philatelic Soc. No. 10, 1991.
Herbert, Kapt. Carl. "Kriegsfahrten deutscher Handelsschiffe 1914-1918." Broschek & Co., Hamburg, 1934.
Hill, Max. "Exchange Ship." Farrar, Rinehart, New York, 1942.
Hubbard & Winter. "North Atlantic Mail Sailings 1840-1875." U.S. Philatelic Classics Society, Canton, OH, 1988.
Huldemann, Bernard. "Albert Ballin." Gerhard Stalling Verlag, Oldenburg, 1922.
Hümmelchen, Gerhard. "Handelsstörer,."R. Lehmanns Verlag, München, 1962.

"Jane's All the World's Warships"
Jose, A.W. "The Royal Australian Navy 1914-1918." Juddock Farquhar, 1928.

Karig, Capt. Walter. "Battle Report." Farrar, Rinehart, New York, 1944.
Kippenberg, Anton. "Geschichten aus einer alten Hansestadt." Insel Verlag, Bremen, 1949.
Kludas, Arnold. "Die Geschichte der deutschen Passagierschiffahrt" I-V, Ernst Kabel Verlag, Hamburg, 1986-1989.
    "Rickmers, 150 Jahre Schiffbau und Schiffahrt." Köhler, Herford, 1984.
    "Die Hamburg-Amerika Linie, 1847-1970." With Dr. Herbert Bischoff, Koehler, Herford, 1984.
    "Deutsche Ozean Passagierschiffe, 1850-1895." Steiger, Moers, 1983.
    "Die Schiffe der deutschen Afrika-Linien, 1880-1945." G. Stalling, Oldenburg, 1975.
    "Die Deutschen Schnelldampfer." G. Stalling Verlag, Oldenburg.
    "Die Grossen Passagierschiffe der Welt." G. Stalling Verlag, Oldenburg

Koch, Alfred. "Deutsche Schiff- und Seeposten." Archiv für deutsche Postgeschichte, 1964-65.
Kraus, Michael. "Immigration: The American Mosaic." D. Van Nostrand Co., Princeton, NJ, 1966.
Kuckuk, Peter und Hartmut Roder. "Von der Dampfbarkasse zum Container Schiff." Steintor, Bremen, 1988.
Kuckuk, Peter. "Die A.G. Weser." Steintor, Bremen, 1987.

Le Fleming, H.H. "Ships of the Blue Funnel Line." Adlard Coles, Southampton, 1965.
Lindemann, Friedrich. "Sohn seiner Firma." Heinrich Döld, Bremen, 1960.
"Literary Digest History of the World War," Vols IX and X, Funk & Wagnalls, New York, 1921.
Lindemann, Dr. Moritz. "Geschichte und Handbuch des NDL." Bremen, 1892.
Lloyd's Registers of Shipping, 1858 to the present.
Lloyd's Shipping Index, Lloyd's List, Annals of Lloyd's History, 1934.

Maack, Hans. "Reeder, Schiffe und ein Verband" (1907-1957), Hamburg, 1958.
Marx, Hans. "The U.S. Merchant Marine, 1789-1963."U.S. Naval Institute Press, 1963.
Mason, Kenneth. "Soviet Merchant Ships, 1945-1968." World Ship Society.
Mathies, Otto. "Hamburgs Reederei, 1814-1914". L. Friederichsen & Co., Hamburg, 1924.
Mitchell, W.H. & L.A. Sawyer. "Empire Ships of World War II."
    "Sea Breezes," 1965.
Morton, Allan. "Directory of European Passenger Steamship Arrivals, 1890-1930 at New York." Genealogical Publishing Co., Inc., Baltimore, 1987.
Musk, George. "History & Fleet List of Canadian Pacific, 1891-1961." World Ship Society, 1962.

Nauer, Karl. "Anker Auf." Drei Quellen Verlag, Königsbruck (Dresden), 1934.
Neubaur, Dr. Paul. "NDL: 50 Jahre der Entwicklung," 3 Bänder, 1857-1907, Verlag von F.W. Grunow, Leipzig.
Norddeutscher Lloyd: Annual Reports, Schedules, Passenger Lists, Prospecti, Seven Seas, Lloyd Gazette, Handbooks, Monthly Information & Year Books, Fleet Lists, Photo Archive.
    "Lloyd Zeitung," 1909.
    "Die Entwicklung des NDL 1910."

Petzet, Arnold. "Heinrich Wiegand, Ein Lebensbild". C.A. von Haley Verlag, Bremen, 1932.
Plagemann, Volker und 49 Autoren: "Übersee: Seefahrt und Seemacht im Deutschen Kaiserreich." Verlag C.H. Beck, München, 1988.
Prager, Hans Jürgen. "Blohm & Voss". Koehler, 1975.
Precht, Hans Hermann. Atlaswerke 1945-1965.

Rehm, Dr. Arnold. "Fahrgäste und Fahrmänner." Walter Dorn Verlag, Bremen, 1947.
    "Das Fröhliche Logbuch." Dietzen & Co., Bremerhaven, 1958.
    "Alles über Schiffe und See." Kabel, 1985.
    Access to his archives
"Rickmers, 1834-1959." Nordwestdeutscher Verlag, Bremerhaven, 1959.
Roder, Hartmut. "Der Bremer Vulkan." Steintor, Bremen, 1988.
Rohbrecht, Gerhard. "Die deutschen Fahrgastschiffe"
Rothke, Claus. "Deutsche Passagierschiffe 1896-1918." Transpress Berlin, 1986.

Schmalenbach, Paul. "Die Deutschen Hilfskreuzer 1895-1914." Stalling Verlag
Smelzkopf, Reinhart. "Die Deutsche Levante Linie, 1890-1967." Karl-Heinz Butziger, Hamburg, 1964.

"Die deutsche Handelsschiffahrt, 1914-1919." Schmelzkopf.

"Die deutsche Handelsschiffahrt, 1888-1918." Schmelzkopf.

"Die deutsche Handelsschiffahrt, 1919-1939." Schmelzkopf.

"Die Deutsch-Australische Dampfschiffs Ges., 1888-1926." Strandgut, Cuxhaven.

Schmidt, Kapt. Fred. "Neue Kapitänsberichte." D.Reimer Verlag, Berlin, 1937.

"Sklavenfahrer und Kuliklipper." D. Reimer Verlag, Berlin, 1938.

Schmidt, W. Hans Werner. "Geschichte der deutschen Post in den Kolonien und im Ausland." R. Rudolph, Leipzig, 1939.

Schwadte, Karl-Heinz. "Deutschlands Handelsschiffe 1939-1945; 1952, 1958, 1964, 1972." Stalling, Oldenburg

"Die neue deutsche Handelsflotte im Bild." Stalling, Oldenburg, 1966.

Siedler, Ernst; Sims, Paul und Fuchs, Klaus. "Da Lacht der Hafen." Verlag Bremer Nachrichten, 1954.

Smith, Eugene W. "Passenger Ships of the World." George H. Dean Co., Boston, 1963.

Spindler, Karl. "The Mystery of the Casement Ship." Kribe-Verlag, Berlin, 1931.

Staff, Frank Bowen. "The Transatlantic Mail." Adlard Coles Ltd., London, 1976.

Stegemenn, Helmut. "Die deutschen Schlepper." Schiffahrt International, 1988, and following.

Steinweg, Günther. "Die deutsche Handelsflotte im Zweiten Weltkrieg." Otto Schwarz & Co., Göttingen, 1954.

Stindt, Fred A. "Matson's Century of Ships." Stindt, 1982.

Strohbusch, Erwin. "Deutsche Seeschiffe im 19. & 20. Jahrhundert," Führer 2 des deutschen Schiffahrtsmusum, 1975.

Talbot-Booth, E.C. "What Ship Is That?" Ca. 1940. Sampson Lowe, London.

"Merchant Ships." Sampson Lowe, London, 1942.

"Merchant Ships." 1949-1950, McGraw-Hill Co., New York, 1950.

"Merchant Ships." 1963, Journal of Commerce, Liverpool

Talbot, Frederick A.. "Steamship Conquest of the World." J.B. Lippincott, New York, 1950.

Thalenhorst, Dr. Carl. "Bremen: Binnen un Buten" I & II. H.M. Hauschild, Bremen, 1953-1957.

Tyler, David Budlong. "Steam Conquers The Atlantic." D. Appleton-Century Co., New York-London, 1959.

Valtin, Jan. "Out of the Night." Alliance Book Co., New York, 1944.

Wall, Robert. "Oceans Liners." Chartwell Books, Secaucus, NJ, 1977.

Weyers Taschenbücher der Kriegsflotten

Winter, Adolf. "Vom Segelschiffsjungen zum Lloydkapitän." Köhler, Minden, 1929.

Witthöft, Hans-Jürgen. "HAPAG-LLOYD." Köhler Verlag, Herford, 1979.

"Norddeutscher Lloyd." Köhler Verlag, Herford, 1973.

"Die deutsche Handelsflotte, Studien & Dokumente zur Geschichte des Zweiten Weltkrieges." Band II: 1939-1945, Arbeitskreis für Wehrforschung, Stuttgart.

"Das Hansa Bauprogramm." J.F. Lehmanns Verlag, München, 1968.

Wulle, Armin. "Stettiner Vulcan." Koehler, 1989.

Glossary

German	English
AB, Able-bodied Seaman	Vollmatrose
Abbruch	Scrapped, Broken Up
Abdampf Turbine	Exhaust Turbine
(Abg)eliefert	Delivered
Abgemacht	Agreed
An(ge)kauft	Purchase(d)
Aufgelaufen	Grounded
(Aufg)elegt	Laid Up
Aufsichtsrat	Board of Directors
AD, Ausser Dienst	Out of Service
Back	Forepeak
Bau Nr.	Construction Number
Bergung, Geborgen	Salvage(d)\
Besatzung	Crew
Beschädigt	Damaged
Beschlagnahmt	Seized
Besegelung	Sails
Bestellt	Ordered
BU, Broken Up	Abgewrackt
BRT	Gross Tons
Bugspriet	Bowsprit
Dampf(er)	Steam(er)
Deutsche Levante Linie	DLL
Eingestellt	Into Service
FR, Frste Reise	First Voyage
Fahrt	Voyage, Trip, Cruise
Fertig	Completed
FD, Freidecker	Open Shelter Decker
Fusion	Merger
Galion (Figur)	Cutwater, Figurehead
Gefrieranlage	Reefer
Gekapert	Captured
Gmbh, Gesellschaft	Company
Gesunken	Sunk
HAPAG	Hamburg-Amerikanische Paketfahrt A.G. Hamburg-American Line
Havariert	Damaged
Heck	Stern
HSDG, H-Süd-Hamburg	South American Line
ID, In Dienst	Into Service
JR, Jungfernreise	Maiden voyage, MV
Kessel	Boiler
Kiel Gestreckt	Keel Laid
Kn(oten)	Knots
Korrespondentreeder	Operator, Partner
Küstendampfer	Coastal Feeder Vessel
LÜA	Overall Length
LZL/S	Length Between Perpendiculars
LR, Letzte Reise	Last Voyage
Luke	Hatch
Mittelmeer	Mediterranean
MS	Motor Ship
Passagiere	Passengers
PS, Pferdestärke	Horsepower
Poopdeck	Achterdeck
Raddampfer	Side/Sternwheeler
Raaen/Rahen	Square Yardarms
Reise	Trip, Voyage
Ren(amed)	Umgenannt
Rhederei/Reederei	Shipping Company
Reichspostdampfer/ Dienst/Linien	Imperial Mail-Steamer, Service, Lines
Reparatur, Repariert	Repair(ed)
Schaufelrad	Side/Sternwheeler
Scheitern, Gescheitert	Founder, Wrecked
Schiffbruch	Shipwreck
Shpbldfg & Eng., S. & E. Co.	Schiffs- & Machinenbau Gesellschaft
Schnelligkeit, Geschwindigkeit	Speed
Schraube	Screw, Propeller
SD, Schutzdecker	Shelterdecker
Segel	Sails
Spardecker/Sturmdecker	Awning Deck
Sperrbrecher	Barrage/Mine clearer
Stagsegel	Stay Sail
SL, Stapellauf	Launch(ed)
SS	Dampfer
Stempel	Postmark
Takelage	Rigging
Totalverlust	Total Loss
Track	Festgelegter Reiseweg
TS	Turbinenschiff
Übernommen	Taken Over
Umb(enannt)	Renamed
Umg(ebaut)	Rebuilt, Converted
Verkauf(t)	Sale, Sold
Verlängert	Lengthened
Verlust	Loss
Verschrottet	Scrapped
Versenkt, Versunken	Sunk
Versorger/Vertreiber	Feeder Ship
Verwalt(et, ung)	Managed, Manager
VD, Volldecker	Full Scantlings Ship
Vom Register Gestrichen	RLR, Removed From Register
Vorstand	Management Board
Weiteres Unbekannt	Further Data Unknown/Needed
Welle	Propeller Shaft
Werft	Shipyard
z.B(eispiel)	For Example
Zuflucht	Refuge
Zw	Tweendeck
****	Zahl der Schrauben — Number of Screws
86.5 x 17.9	Länge x Breite — Length x Width
I, II, III	Klasse — Class

Index of Small-Craft Names

Name	Page	Name	Page	Name	Page	Name	Page
Aade	115	Friedrich Vöge	128	Luise	13	Seeschlange	119
Admiral Bromny	102	Fulda	9			Simson	5
Ad Tempus	143			M 42	90	Sirius 1907	76
Afon Goch	114	Gannet	144	M 158	91	Sirius 1952	129
Albert S.	150	Gazelle	58	M 206	119	Sorte Encel	114
Aller	18	Germania	16	M 611	119	Spica 1885	33
Altair	122	Glückauf 1901	60	Maltese Samson	121	Spica 1914	87
Anke Paht	111	Glückauf 1913	110	Maltese Terrier	121	ST 757	126
Anna Luise	32	Greetings	89	Mangan	113	ST 771	122
Anna Maria Lauro	110	Greif	136	Mars 1902	61	ST 776	123
Annemarie	11	Grille 1904	59	Mars 1955	133	ST 779	125
Antilen	151	Grille 1919	91	Max	136	ST 781	129
Apollo	74	Grüssgott	89	Memi I	113	ST 782	127
Argo	101	Guepé	88	Merkur 1895	46	Stauerei	82
Arion 1899	57	Gulosenfjord	121	Merkur 1913	105	Steinbock 1929	108
Arion 1943	124	Gutenberg	25	Meteor	63	Steinbock 1944	125
Armin	17			Münden	13	Stella 1914	86
Asklam	143	Habicht	130			Stella 1967	152
Atlas	60	Hameln	11	Najade	44	Stier 1971	96
Atlantic Ocean	121	Hannover	131	Nawitka	102	Stier 1954	132
		Hanseat	2	Neck	71	Strandlust	28
Bär	134	Hansestadt Danzig	103	Neptun	45	Stur	122
Bat	134	Hapag	78	Nixe	55	Süderoog	137
Bergland	111	Harle	117	Norder Piep	149	Süder Piep	150
Bismarck	69	Harma	144	Norder Till	113	Süllberg	131
Blücher	14	Hecht	31	Nordsee	21		
Bremen	24	Hector	98	Nordstern 1911	83	Tac	111
Bremen 1899	54	Hein Mück	139	Nordstern 1965	151	Tak	133
Bremen 1906	68	Hektor	146	Nymphe	90	Telegrapf	1
Bremen 1913	85	Hengst	114			Tic	112
Bremerhaven 1872	24	Herkules 1887	34	Oelboot	73	Triton 1874	26
Bremerhaven 1907	75	Herkules 1923	99	Oldenburg 1845	3	Triton 1900	56
Bugsier	135	Herkules 1949	126	Oldenburg 1907	72	Triton 1967	153
Bürgermeister Smidt	104	Herkules 1967	127	Oste	118		
		Hermann	17	Oster Till 1	112	Undine	53
Caciane	141	Hertha	11	Oster Till 2	144	Union Mercury	149
Cala Azzura	147	Hunte	117				
Capella	62			Paul Friedrich August	4	Vesta 1907	77
Carlshafen	12	Ilse	13	Pax I	144	Vesta 1967	154
Carric Reef	142	Inter Voltzee	143	Pehuen	142	Vorwärts 1856	6
Castor 1906	67	Isola del Sole	110	Pelikan	109	Vorwärts 1879	27
Castor 1963	147			Peter Friedrich	47	Vorwärts 1906	66
Centaur 1889	37	Jersey Queen	139	Pilot	20	Voslapp	94
Centaur 1913	84	Jupiter 1908	81	Planet	52	Vulkan 1857	7
Centaur 1958	138	Jupiter 1961	141	Pollux	41	Vulkan 1891	40
Centauro	84			Pollux 1905	64	Vulkan 1896	49
Claus	83	Kai I	150	Pollux 1963	148	Vulkan 1896	50
Comet 1857	19	Karma	150	Portonevere	116	Vulkan 1913	106
Comet 1895	47	Kehrewieder	39	Prinz Adalbert	104	Vulkan 1943	123
Comet 1967	156	Knurrhahn	120	Puck	36		
Commodore	139	Koho Maru	68	Puddefjord	118	Wal	137
Cormorant	149	Kolibri	118x			WBM IV	119
Cyclop 1867	22	Kurefjord	128	Quelle	35	Wangerooge	119
Cyclop 1896	48	Kurischeshaff	131			Wega 1908	79
Cyclop 1908	80	Kyhlop	137	Retter	30	Wega 1967	155
Cyclop 1968	157			Robert	81	Wendemuth	106
		La Bretonniere	89	Rochester Queen	139	Werra	8
Daunt Reef	138	Lachs	38	Roland 1848	10	Weserland	28
Delphin	65	La Nymphe	90	Roland 1891	42	Wester Till 1	111
Dinard	91	L'Arenir	29	Roland 1927	107	Wester Till 2	143
Donar	93	LCG 181	139	Rosa B.	143	West Reef	136
		Lehe	97	Rose Mary	140	Widder 1921	95
Eben Haezer	143	Libelle	32	Ruth G.	143	Widder 1963	145
Ems	117	Lloyd 1	23			Willkommen	29
Ems	138	Lloyd 1908	78	Saturn 1893	43	Wittekind 1844	15
Esa Ro	154	Lloyd 1914	88	Saturn 1925	100	Wittekind 1907	70
		Loewe 1939	116	Schelde VII	115	Wolf	135
Faraglione	131	Loewe 1962	142	Schelde VIII	114		
Forelle	28	Loewer	105	Scott	68	Yungting	54
Franz	92	Luchs	136	Seeadler	51		